NEW TOURISTS' FAVORITE DESTINATION

**The Beautiful Philippines
and Its
Known and Little Known Facts
Plus
Conversational English,
Tagalog, Ilocano, Bicolano, Cebuano,
Ybanag and Gaddang Dictionary**

by

Gertrudes Bandong Dy-Liacco

Library of Congress Control Number: 2019900082
ISBN: Hardcover   978-1-9845-7207-3
          Softcover   978-1-9845-7206-6
          eBook   978-1-9845-7205-9

Print information available on the last page.

Rev. date: 09/06/2019

To order additional copies of this book, contact:
Xlibris
1-888-795-4274
www.Xlibris.com
Orders@Xlibris.com
783015

CONTENTS

WHY THIS BOOK IS UNIQUE

This book, **"New Tourists' Favorite Destination: the Beautiful Philippines and its Known and Little Known Facts plus Conversational English, Tagalog, Ilocano, Bicolano, Cebuano, Ybanag and Gaddang Dictionary,"** makes known the amazingly beautiful landscapes and seascapes in the Philippines, and about the ethnicity, nature, mores, practices, culture and a few native tongues of the Filipinos.

It is also the **first book to make use of the new and complete 28-letter Tagalog alphabet.** In 1987 which is thirty-two long years ago, the Philippine Department of Education, Culture and Sports amended the old Tagalog abakada from its original 20 letters which were 14 consonants B-D-G-H-K-L-M-N-P-R-S-T-W-Y plus the Filipino digraph NG, and 5 vowels A-E-I-O-U into a more complete 28-letter alphabet **by adding** into the existing alphabets the letters C-F-J-Q-V-X-Z, plus the Spanish alphabet Ñ. And in 2001, the Komisyon Sa Wikang Filipino renamed this new abakada into a more appropriate name, which is **Alfabeto**. Inexplicably however, those added alphabets have been minimally used in most Tagalog writings up to this day. Hence, **for the very first time, the complete Tagalog Alfabeto is brought to the fore and given importance in this book.** Correspondingly, with the use of the new alphabets, **this book introduces new spellings never before used in Tagalog lexicons.** It is important to emphasize that fortunately, there are no strict rules on how Filipino words are spelled as long as such words are understandable, and the reason for this is explained and illustrated in the upcoming topics titled "Why There Are No Strict Rules On Spellings of Filipino Words" and "Spellings and Pronunciations".

This book is also the first of its kind to outline an uncomplicated but in-depth exploration of the Filipino grammar to make it easier and simpler for the learner to form word and sentence constructions. This book provides clear and simple guidelines on spellings and pronunciations of Filipino words, as well as configurations of verbs, nouns, adjectives and adverbs through affixes (prefix, infix and suffix). This book also imparts the elements of a syntax such as articles or nominative adjectives, linking verbs, prepositions, gender forms, pluralizing methods, postpositive words, past, present and future tense-formations, command/request configurations, side-by-side illustrations between the standard sentence construction that the world use, specifically English, in comparison to the unique sentence structure that Filipinos use, and pronunciations of unique words like kvetch, mnemonic, carte du jour, cache, and many more. Previously and currently, most of the explanations and illustrations presented here have hardly been covered in other Filipino dictionaries written by other authors.

The lexicon section of this book is more comprehensive and multi-faceted than the other Filipino dictionaries that are in the market today. It provides a richer and more detailed definition of words by expounding on diverse meanings and interpretations, besides the addition of synonyms, correlated words and antonyms. Also added into this book are root words, commonly-used expressions, and current hi-tech terminologies owing to the continuous upgrading of technology.

Also added in the dictionary section of this book, <u>defined mostly in English (written in italics),</u> are **motivational tips** like -

Ability, Abilities *(English)*
Above and beyond the call of duty *(English)*
Above board; Transparency *(English)*
Activities that are healthy, lawful, and enjoyable that promote advancements and
    success *(English)*
Be smart and live the dream
Best foot forward *(English)*
Best interest *(English)*
Better late than never *(English)*
Calm *(worth looking into)*
Careful *(worth looking into)*
Caring *(worth looking into)*
Character, improving one's *(English)*
Charitable *(English)*
Common sense *(English)*

Happiness-triggers to use or think anytime *(English)*
High-minded *(English)*
High road, take the *(English)*
Honest, Honesty *(English)*
Humanitarian *(English)*
Improve oneself *(worth looking into)*
Incentives *(English)*
Informed decision *(English)*
Kindness - Spreading kindness has its blessings *(English)*
Leave no stone unturned *(English)*
Live and let live *(English)*
Live within your means *(English)*
Love *(worth looking into)*
Loyal, Loywalty *(English)*
Magnanimous *(English)*
Make both ends meet *(English)*
Make hay while the sun is shining *(English)*
Moral and ethical values *(English)*
Morality *(English)*
More than one way to skin a cat *(English)*
Multi-tasking, Kill two birds with one stone *(mostly English)*
No pain, no gain *(English)*
Objective viewpoint vs. Subjective viewpoint *(English)*
Own and admit a wrongdoing or a shortcoming *(English)*
Pacify, Pacifism *(worth looking into)*
Parental management *(lots of English)*
Pat on the back *(worth looking into)*
Perseverance, Persevere *(English)*
Poor (very) but realize that you have opportunities in life *(worth reading)*
Practice what you preach; Walk the talk *(English)*
Proactive *(English)*
Productive *(English)*
Proficient, Proficiency *(English)*
Prolific *(English)*
Provident, Providence *(English)*
Prudent, Prudence *(English)*
Put oneself on someone else's shoes *(English)*
Quintessence, Quintessential *(worth looking into)*
Resilience *(English)*

Resolute *(English)*

Resourceful *(English)*

Responsibility; 1] You are the cause of everything that happens to you. Be careful what you cause. 2] Avoiding one's responsibility never brings good result, rather it brings problems *(worth looking into)*

Responsible *(English)*

Rise to the occasion *(English)*

Save for a rainy day *(English)*

Seize the opportunity *(English)*

Self-control *(English)*

Self-reliance *(English)*

Sensitive to people's needs and feelings; With empathy *(worth reading)*

Strive *(English)*

Succeed; Success *(worth looking into)*

Sympathize *(worth looking into)*

Tact *(English)*

Think outside the box *(English)*

Time; Any time is the right time to do what is right; Don't waste time, invest it with beneficial and productive deeds; Strike while you can and while there is an opportunity *(worth looking into)*

Trust - Being trusted is not developed overnight - trust is built and established many years, then maintained every day *(worth looking into)*

Trustworthiness, Trustworthy *(worth looking into)*

Understanding *(worth looking into)*

Untapped abilities; You lose what you don't use *(worth looking into)*

Work ethic *(English)*

Worship *(worth looking into)*

Additionally, there are **cautionary alerts** in the dictionary section like –

Addictions-illegal drugs, alcohol, sex, tobacco/cigarette, phone use *(English)*

Blame-dodging of one's own mistakes and wrongdoings *(English)*

Bully *(English)*

Careless

Crime *(English)*

Criminals: How Society Regard Them *(worth reading)*

Drug addiction *(English)*

Emergency phone numbers in the Philippines and in a few more countries

It takes only seconds to hurt someone but it can take years for them to heal from it

Juul, Juuling, or Vape, Vaping *(English)*
Phone: Obsessive Focus and Dependence On It (and its possible harms)
Play it safe *(English)*
Rape offender *(English)*
Rape prevention *(English)*
Safety; Be certain that you are safe *(English)*
Separate the men from the boys
Spoil a child 1. Results of spoiling a child; 2. Smart, safe and responsible alternative than spoiling a child *(worth reading)*
Untapped abilities; You lose what you don't use *(worth reading)*

The dictionary section is geared towards effective communications and clear understanding among all Filipinos whatever island, region, province or town they are situated in the Philippines, whatever regional dialects they speak, and wherever foreign countries they have migrated to. **Conversational words or commonly spoken Filipino words that are predominantly used throughout the Philippines are presented here, and less on deep, uncommon indigenous words.** Consequently, deep Tagalog and deep Ilocano terms that are recondite and scarcely used among most Filipinos, are minimal in this book.

Filipino dialects have evolved from the blending of vernaculars among their various Malay and Polynesian lineages, as well as impacts from the Spanish and American eras. This book specifically identifies **lingua franca** words that are derived from the Spanish language, which have long been established as Filipino lexis. Filipinos also resort to English words quite so often to make communications more comprehensible and emphatic that such language has become a standard usage in everyday Filipino conversations.

The highlighting of the supplemental Spanish and English words in this dictionary can help increase proficiency, or at the least, familiarity with several languages: Tagalog, Ilocano, Spanish and English, let alone the Bicolano, Cebuano, Ybanag and Gaddang vocabularies that are added into this book.

This book is an essential language reference book for all the libraries in the world. It also serves as a handy translation aid for foreigners doing business in the Philippines, and for the foreign embassies that are based in the Philippines, as well as religious and medical missionaries, charitable institutions, language translators, tourists, foreign students enrolled in the Philippines, expatriates that settled in the Philippines, and for just anyone who is interested in learning about the Philippines and the Filipino languages.

PHILIPPINES: ITS BRIEF HISTORY
AND THE MÉLANGE OF LANGUAGES

The **Asian Continent**, in which the Philippines is a part of, is the largest continent in the world since it covers North Asia, Central Asia, East Asia, South Asia, Northeast Asia, Southwest Asia, and Southeast Asia.

North Asia is Siberia, while South Asia has Afghanistan, Bangladesh, India, Maldives, Nepal, Pakistan, and Sri Lanka. East Asia is composed of China, Japan, Korea and Taiwan. Northeast Asia is Mongolia. Central Asia is Kazakhstan, Kyrgyzstan, Tajikistan, Turkmenistan and Uzbekistan. Southwest Asia are Armenia, Azerbaijan, Bahrain, Cyprus, Georgia, Iraq, Israel, Jordan, Kuwait, Lebanon, Oman, Qatar, Saudi Arabia, Syria, Turkey, United Arab Emirates and Yemen. And the countries of **Southeast Asia** are the **Philippines**, Brunei, East Timor, Indonesia, Burma (Myanmar), Cambodia, Laos, Malaysia, Singapore, Thailand and Vietnam.

The Philippines is also a part of the **Austronesian family** which is also-called Malayo-Polynesians. Austronesians are the **Philippines**, Malaysia, Indonesia, Brunei, Singapore, Myanmar, East Timor, Madagascar, Micronesia, Cambodia, Hainan, Polynesia, the non-Papuan people of Melanesia, the Pattanis of Thailand, the Chads of Vietnam, parts of Sri Lanka, and the original Taiwanese people.

The **Malay Archipelago** extends over 25,000 islands and is the world's largest archipelago by area, and also fourth in the world's most numerous islands. The **Malay Archipelago** embodies the **Philippines**, Brunei, East Timor, Indonesia, Malaysia, and Singapore.

The Philippines, being fragmented by 7,107 islands, is called **the Philippine Archipelago** and is also identified as **Pearl of the Orient**. The Philippines has a total land area of 116,518 square miles. Recent archeological findings like the Angono Petroglyph rock carvings discovered in 1973, and the Palawan Tabon Caves' bones and tools discovered in 1962, and the Cagayan Valley Callao Man's bones discovered in 2010, indicate that the first indigenous inhabitants in the Philippines were cavemen that resembled the Java man, the Peking man and some other Asian tribes.

Early migrants to the Philippines were tribes from Australia, Melanesia and Micronesia that trekked to the Philippines on land bridges during the pleistocene period. The Spaniards called those aborigines as Negritos because they had kinky hair, dark brown skin and short in stature, while the Filipinos call them Agtas or Itas, and the Americans dubbed them as Aetas. The Aetas have been typically reclusive up to this day since they prefer to live in very remote villages, mountains and forests despite recurrent calamities and deforestations. To date, they comprise merely 0.03% of the total Philippine population.

Other Philippine tribes that settled in the Philippines were the Igorots (Ifugaos, Kalingas, Bontocs, Ibalols and Isnegs) whose ancestors were believed to be proto-Austronesians or first Austronesians. These tribes are less introverted than the Aetas, but they preferred living in the Mountain Province of Luzon where they **cultivated rice terraces 2,000 years ago, making these as one of the oldest rice terraces in the world, besides one of the world's most beautiful rice terraces.**

The most extroverted among the Filipinos are the lowlanders who came to the islands through sailing on boats. These groups came from Borneo, which comprises Indonesia, Malaysia and Brunei. They are the early settlers that encompass the majority of the entire Filipino population, and true to form, the various Filipino dialects have similarities to the languages spoken in the Malayan motherland.

Spanish Era

The Philippines was discovered in **1521** by Ferdinand Magellan who was a Portuguese explorer commissioned by Spain to explore and conquer new territories. Not long after Magellan set foot on Philippine soil, he was killed by Lapulapu, a local chieftain who became known as the first Filipino hero for having had the courage to face a strong foreign invader and defeated him. The death of Magellan delayed the Spanish settlement in the Philippines by forty years, but it did not deter them from their goal - instead it drove them to move forward to resolutely colonize the Philippine archipelago. This was effectively carried out by the arrival of Miguel Lopez de Legazpi on February 13, **1565**. Legazpi established the first unified political structure in the archipelago that eventually launched them to be in power for 333 long years. The Spanish reigning monarch, Charles V, had the cluster of islands named **Las Islas Filipinas** in honor of his young son who later became King Phillip II (El Rey Felipe II) of Spain.

In 1571, Legazpi designated the Philippines as part of the Spanish East Indies with Manila as its capital. He also established trade for the Philippine gold, silver, silk and spice products that were marketed across Europe. The sailing route from Manila was through Mexico, and from Mexico to Spain, and this was called the Manila-Acapulco Galleons. Filipino slaves worked in those ships, but many Filipinos jumped ship in California, which was also a Spanish colony at that time. From 1400 to 1898, the Spanish Empire enjoyed a global dominance. Spain established the **New Spain** viceroyalty, which was an administrative unit of the Spanish colonial empire. **New Spain** was comprised of Spain's entire territorial conquests, which were the southwestern United States, the **Philippines**, Mexico, South and Central America, and many islands in the Caribbean.

The Spaniards, as a matter-of-course, called the natives of the lands they conquered as **Indios** particularly in Mexico, the USA, the Philippines, and other subjugated lands. They also called the Filipino Muslims as **Moros**, a similar name for the Moors who once enjoyed opulence in Andalucia province of Spain, notably in Granada, Sevilla and Cordoba.

The Spaniards, in their earlier conquests, compelled the natives to speak Spanish. In the Philippines, due to the fact that the Philippine archipelago is composed of more than 7,000 islands with the natives speaking more than 100 various dialects, it was impossible to make the locals speak Spanish. However, many Spanish words still got integrated into the various Filipino dialects as a result of the Filipinos' exposure to the

Spanish language for 3-1/2 centuries. Currently, however, many Filipinos think those are indigenous Filipino words, not Spanish words, since those words are spelled using the Filipino grammar, **not** Spanish conjugation nor Spanish spellings, and <u>even spoken using the unique Filipino syntax configuration</u> (see Sentence Formation under the Filipino Grammar section). Most Filipino dialects use comosta, corte, husticia, hues, municipio, alcalde, senador, consehal, tesorero, calle, pasahero, maneho, freno, bosina, coche, barco, eroplano, carretela, viahe, maleta, bagahe, escuela, estudiante, leksion, libro, lapis, papel, letra, sobre, sello, plancha, tualya, tela, pantalon, camiseta, blusa, falda, bolsa, corbata, cinturon, cintas, medias, sapatos, chinelas, suelas, siempre, tiempo, semana, fecha, oras, relo, alahas, liave, sala, cosina, cuarto, cama, cubrecama, suelo, tocador, aparador, silla, mesa, lamesa, plato, cuchara, tenedor, cuchillo, tasa, vaso, botella, lata, delata, cepillo, banyo, lavabo, lava, Dios, san, santo, santa, virhen, imahen, misa, campana, mundo, fiesta, trabaho, sueldo, empleyado, bombilla, guapo/pa, vanidoso/sa, carinyosa/so, bigote, trato, maltrato, pacencia, suerte, malas, pobre, venggativo, traydor, infierno, demonio, basura, trapo, bola, bala, bomba, martillo, agraviado, atrasado, atras, avante, antes, antemano, caha, pakete, sustento, garantisado, segurado, derecho, pareho, mismo, mas, pero, para, cine, pelicula, zarzuela, entablado, canta, voces, carne, ensalada, leche flan, caldero, comunidad, moralidad, integridad, prayoridad, responsab-le, imposib-le, sua-ve, gra-ve, and many, many more. Other dialects like Chavacano, Ilocano, Bicolano and Visayan dialects speak other Spanish words besides those mentioned above.

Since Filipinos were separated by islands, regions, and provinces, dialects differed from one area to another, which contributed to their lack of accessibility to each other and to even understand each other. This complexity made it difficult for them to unite and jointly defend themselves from foreign invaders.

The Spaniards governed the Philippines by having both the government and the Catholic friars take charge. Conversion to Catholicism followed, making the **Philippines the only country in Asia where majority of the population are Catholics**. Only two provinces, Lanao and Sulu in

Mindano, remained Muslim. Eventually change occurred when Catholic Filipinos from the islands of Luzon and Visayas, and the Catholic Filipinos from other Mindanao provinces came to settle there making Lanao and Sulu less of a Muslim territory. Recent world survey and the Vatican findings indicate that the **Philippines** is in the **Third Top Country In The World with the Biggest Catholic Population,** even exceeding Spain, Italy, France and the USA.

The basic impacts of Spain in the Philippines were Catholicism and education. Spain established the **oldest university in all of Asia,** which is the **University of Santo Tomas founded in 1611,** and **the oldest colleges in Asia,** which are the **Colegio de San Juan de Letran founded in 1620** and the **Santa Isabel College founded in 1632**, all of which have been thriving outstandingly throughout several centuries of educational undertakings from their naissance to the present. **These three Philippine institutions are even older than the oldest university in the United States, which is the Harvard University that was founded in 1636** and older than the next oldest university in Asia which is **Japan's Keio University founded in 1858**.

The University of San Carlos of Cebu has disputed the title of the **University of Santo Tomas** as the **oldest university in the Philippines and in Asia**. The University of Santo Tomas was a university at its inception that remained intact and thriving without gap, and carried its same name from its founding up to the present. Whereas the University of San Carlos was originally called Colegio de San Ildefonso founded in 1595 by the Spanish Jesuits; but was closed in 1769 when the Jesuits were forced out. In 1783, it opened under the name of Colegio-Seminario de San Carlos and was managed by the Dominican priests. In 1948, it became a university and this time, was named as the University of San Carlos.

Other long-lasting influences of Spain were Catholic practices and celebrations (i.e., *cuaresma* or lent, *semana santa* or Holy Week, Easter Sunday or *Domingo Santo* or *Domingo de Resureccion*, Christmas that ends on Three Kings Day-January 6, *todos los santos* or All Saints Day, religious processions, *fiestas* or town celebrations, *zarzuelas* or stage performances,

18

and the *Flores de Mayo,* which is a tribute to the Blessed Mother Mary, the virgin mother of Jesus Christ, throughout the whole month of May); monikers (names and surnames of Filipinos are predominantly Spanish), the arts (graceful dances like the *jotas and fandangos* and Spanish music that inspired the romantic Filipino *kundimans* and *haranas*), and cuisine (such as *estofado, relleno, morcon, embutido, escabeche, lechon which in Spain, is called by two names: lechon and cochinillo, caldereta, lengua estofada, paella, arroz Valenciana, arroz caldo, bistec, callos, mechado, asado, picadillo, pochero, cocido, torta, ensalada, chorizo* or *longaniza, tocino, tapa, chicharon, maja blanca, empanada* and *leche flan,* which are some of the Spanish bill of fare handed down to Filipinos).

Chinese Traders

Chinese and Indian traders came **earlier** than the Spaniards to ply their trades, but the Filipinos did not embrace their Hindu and Buddhist tenets. Chinese merchants continually came to ply their wares in the Philippines and some eventually settled in the country. Their numbers progressively rose and eventually, they outnumbered the Spanish colonizers. This compelled a Chinese leader to try to gain a position in the Castilian regime, but the Spaniards thwarted his moves. This infuriated the Chinese community that a revolt against the Spaniards was attempted. However, the skilled conquerors crushed and massacred a significant number of them, particularly the non-Catholic Chinese.

The **Chinatown in Binondo, Manila** was established in **1594** making it the **oldest Chinatown outside China**. Since the Chinese are skilled entrepreneurs, their impact in the Philippines have been trade and commerce which in due time, made them succeed in gaining a strong grip on the Philippine economy.

Currently, when Filipino-Chinese people migrate to other countries, they still seem to find it more comfortable associating with the innately pleasant Filipinos, who are likewise immigrants, and Filipinos equally consider them as compatriots since affinity and bonding had been fostered for having had associations with the Chinese settlers longer than the foreign colonizers.

British Invasion

The Seven Years War had been raging between Spain and Great Britain at the seaside of France and somehow, the Philippines got into the mix. In October 1762, the British forces captured and occupied the province of Cavite and the city of **Manila, which was considered the greatest Spanish fortress in the western Pacific area at that time**. Less than two years later, in May 1764, the Spanish-British war ended, and Manila was returned to the Spaniards in compliance with the Treaty of Paris. Spanish rule was restored and advancements were implemented like the cultivation of abaca, corn, cocoa, pineapple, sugar, and **tobacco, a product that made the Philippines the world leader in tobacco production at that time**.

A Few of the Numerous Filipino Heroes

By mid-1700, the peaceful and docile Filipinos were now starting to stand up for their rights. In December 1762, the Ilocano hero, Diego Silang, expelled the Spaniards from Vigan in order to establish an autonomous government in that area. Diego Silang's success was short-lived, however, since the Spaniards were able to slay him despite his triumph. His wife Josefa Gabriela Silang took over her husband's undertakings, similarly leading the Filipino revolutionaries to fight the Spaniards. Unfortunately, she was also killed in the process.

In time, other Filipino heroes emerged to show their courageous allegiance to their country. One of them was Jose Rizal who started school at the Ateneo de Manila, then enrolled at the University of Santo Tomas to take up Philosophy and Letters. Rizal then went to finish his degree at the Universidad Central de Madrid. His medical studies and ophthalmology specialization were from the University of Paris in France, and University of Heidelberg in Germany. He formed the La Liga Filipina, a cooperative society among Filipinos without aggression towards the Spaniards. He wrote books titled Noli Me Tangere and El Filibusterismo, which made the Spaniards uncomfortable and prompted them to put Rizal into exile in Dapitan, Zamboanga. Sympathizers persuaded Jose Rizal to escape from his seclusion as it would have been easy for him to do so, but Rizal, being the gentleman that he was, downright stood for his honor to defend himself against the false accusations imputed on him. Nonetheless, he was still executed by firing squad on December 30, 1896. Shortly before Jose Rizal's execution at Luneta, he wrote a poem titled Mi Ultimo Adios (My Last Farewell) expressing his love for his country and for his countrymen.

> **Note**: The Philippines put up memorials such as a monument, statue, shrine or a bust of Jose Rizal in several places like at Luneta Park and Fort Santiago in Manila, in Dapitan (Zamboanga), in Calamba, Santa Cruz, and Biñan (Laguna), in Daet (Camarines Norte), in Daraga, Camalig, Tabaco, and Oas (Albay), in Angono, San Juan, and Cainta (Rizal), in Candon (Ilocos Sur), in Sorsogon (Sorsogon), in Iloilo City, Passi, and Zaragoza (Iloilo), in Tarlac (Tarlac), in Tacloban (Leyte), in Catbalogan (Samar), in Cagayan de Oro (Ozamis), and in Calapan (Mindoro), to name only a few. In the USA, Jose Rizal's sculptures are in San Diego and Carson City (California), in Maui and Kauai (Hawaii), in Seattle (Washington), in Chicago (Illinois), and in Jersey City (New Jersey). There are also statues and busts of Jose Rizal in Heidelberg and Wilhelmsfeld (Germany), in Geneva and Schaffhausen (Switzerland), in Litomerice (Czech Republic), in Paris (France), in Tokyo (Japan), in Jinjiang and Fujan (China), in Sydney, Ballarat, and Campelltown (Australia), in Cavenagh (Singapore), in Lima (Peru), and in Mexico City. In Madrid, Spain is where the Spaniards erected an almost replica of Jose Rizal's monument at Luneta Park in Manila, Philippines with Rizal's Mi Ultimo Adios poem engraved on its pedestal, and this monument is located at the Avenida de Filipinas near the Islas de Filipinas subway station in downtown Madrid.

Another hero was Andres Bonifacio who founded the Kataastaasan, Kagalang-galangan, Katipunan ng mga Anak ng Bayan (Supreme and Venerable Society of the Children of the Nation, and in Spanish: Suprema y Venerable Asociacion de los Hijos del Pueblo); or Katipunan for short, or simply KKK. The Katipunan was a secret nationalistic society that called for the ouster of Spain from the Philippines. Emilio Aguinaldo, a capitan municipal in Cavite, became the Katipunan's most effective member when he overpowered the Spanish Guardia Civil in Cavite, making Cavite the center of the revolution. Consequently, Aguinaldo had himself elected as the president of the Katipunan, much to the consternation of the Katipunan founder, Andres Bonifacio. As a result, Emilio Aguinaldo formed his own KKK group which Bonifacio refused to recognize. As a result, this led to their troops fighting against each other and on Aguinaldo's orders, Andres Bonifacio and his brother were killed in May 1897.

Emilio Aguinaldo's troops continued to fight the Spaniards after Bonifacio's death, but he now suffered a number of setbacks. The Spanish government put intense pressure on Aguinaldo that he eventually agreed to negotiate for a surrender and go into exile in Hong Kong. It was there in Hong Kong where the Americans met with Aguinaldo to obtain information about the fleets and artilleries of the Spaniards in the Philippines because at that time, the USA and Spain were already having a dispute over Cuba.

American Regime

For some years, Cuban revolutionaries had been opposing and clashing with the Spanish colonizers in order to gain independence from them. Cuba's close proximity to the United States was a matter of concern and the USA believed that Cuba's independence from Spain would bring peace and tranquility in that region. When the USA's battleship Maine sank in Cuba under mysterious circumstances, USA went to war against Spain and defeated them on July 3, 1898.

In reality, on May 1, 1898 which was two months **prior** to the USA's defeating Spain in Cuba, American Commodore George Dewey sank the Spanish naval armada at Manila Bay and decisively defeated the Spanish dominion in the Philippines. Consequently, Spain ceded the Philippines to the Americans in accordance with the Treaty of Paris. The USA's victories over Spain in the battle at Manila Bay and in Cuba were a **turning point** for the USA. It definitively vanquished the world supremacy of the Spanish Empire and empowered the USA with a reinforcing and fortifying strength that embarked them to rise up into becoming a world power.

Then on May 19, 1898, eighteen days after Spain's defeat in Manila Bay, the Americans brought Emilio Aguinaldo back on Philippine soil from his exile in Hong Kong. On June 12, 1898, Emilio Aguinaldo declared the independence of the Philippines from Spain with himself as the president. Six months later in January 1899, Emilio Aguinaldo was sworn in as the first president of the Philippine Republic. However, the USA did not give recognition to the new independent government of Emilio Aguinaldo. Aguinaldo was outraged and went to war against the Americans, but his troops' weapons were no match to the more superior American armaments. Aguinaldo fled to the mountains but was eventually captured in Palanan, Isabela. On April 1, 1901, Aguinaldo pledged his allegiance to the United States of America and that ended the Philippine Republic.

The Americans first took over the Philippines in 1898 and named the entire Philippine archipelago as **The Philippine Islands** which is the English facsimile for **Las Islas Filipinas**. America's major contributions to the Philippines were the English language, a democratic form of government, public health (with the introduction of artesian wells, sanitation, and hospitals like PGH that opened its doors in 1910), commute (construction of roads and bridges), sports (basketball, baseball, volleyball) and through missionaries, the Protestant religion which did not gain much following because the Philippines at that time was devotedly Catholic. However decades later, by 1960 to the present, the efforts of Protestant Christian missionaries and Christian televangelists were finally remunerated when a significant number of Catholic Filipinos became saved-by-God's-grace-born-again Christians.

Americans made education a core contribution in the Philippines with English as the standard language for academic instructions. Major establishments like the government, trade and commerce, and the media also began their transition to English in every scope of their management and operations. **The English language promptly took roots and became the Philippines' second language,** next to Tagalog. In fact, based on international surveys, **the Philippines is in the Top 5 English-speaking countries in the world.**

The Americans developed, paved and opened Kennon Road to make Baguio City accessible to everyone. The old route, Naguilian Road, was merely a horse trail at that time. The Americans designated Baguio City as the Summer Capital of the Philippines to escape the hot weather in Manila. They built The Mansion House in Baguio to make it the official residence of the American Governor-General of the Philippines at summertime.

In 1935, the American regime in the Philippines held its **election for the first Filipino president**. Emilio Aguinaldo ran against Manuel L. Quezon during that election, but Aguinaldo lost. **Manuel L. Quezon became the first Filipino President of the Philippine Commonwealth**. As a president, Manuel L. Quezon turned out to be an exceptional executive who worked commendably with the American officials. **President Manuel L. Quezon proved to be an excellent precedent for succeeding presidents to emulate** as he loved his country and was an altruist with a heart for both the poor and the aggrieved (read the upcoming multi-topics article in this book titled "The Philippines Has Been a Safe Haven and Sanctuary for Refugees from Several Other Countries" under "Spanish Republicans", "Jewish Refugees Who Fled the Holocaust" and "Residents of the British colony of Hong Kong"). As for Emilio Aguinaldo, he is remembered in history as the most enduring and most determined revolutionary, and is given credit for his lengthy and persistent struggle for Philippine independence during the Spanish and American regimes.

Pacific War (World War II)

On December 7, 1941, **just nine hours after Japan launched a surprise attack at Pearl Harbor, Hawaii**, Japan bombed the Philippines since they believed that the American occupation in the Philippines hindered Japan's plan for a forceful and vigorous territorial expansion in Southeast Asia.

Consequently, Japan's aggressive bombardments started the Pacific War. Japan tried to persuade the Filipinos to support the Japanese by taking the Japanese's side as both are Asians, but the Filipinos having had congenial relationship with the Americans for over 40 years put their trust on the Americans. The attack on the Philippines by Japan and the Japanese invasion in the Philippines was considered the worst USA defeat due to the fact that 23,000 American military personnel and 100,000 Filipino soldiers were either killed or captured by the Japanese army. An estimated 10,000 Filipino and American soldiers also died at the Japanese-compelled Death March of Bataan.

On June 19, 1944, the Japanese attempted to make a decisive defeat on the US fleet, but it ended up with the Japanese themselves sustaining the decisive defeat. Finally, General Douglas MacArthur returned to the Philippines to fulfill his "I shall return" promise. On October 23-26, 1944, another battle occurred at the Battle of Leyte, Samar and Luzon which was also referred to as the second battle on Philippine seas, but more recognized as **the largest naval and aerial battle in World War II** or **the largest naval and aerial battle in history**. In this battle, the Japanese fleets were virtually destroyed with 12,000 Japanese fighters dead. The US army and Filipino allies had 2,500 human casualties, but they finally triumphed over the Japanese army once and for all.

The Spanish and American colonizers left valuable impacts in the Philippines, but the Japanese left only death and devastation. Yet the Philippines regard Japan as another fellow Asian country, not as an enemy, leaving the atrocities of the war forgiven and buried in the past. **Why? Because Filipinos do not let negative things get the better of them owing to the Filipino's calm and stress-free disposition, let alone their cheerful leanings**.

Philippine Independence

The United States of America granted the Philippines its Independence on July 4, 1946 and the **Republic of the Philippines** was born after 333 years of Spanish rule and 48 years of American regime. After almost 4 centuries of being under foreign powers, **the Philippines became free and independent from foreign controls from July 4, 1946, that it started to be self-governing and finally, became empowered with jurisdiction, dominion, and control over its own territory.** The Philippines, therefore, can be considered as a young nation because this year, 2019, it has only been 73 years since it gained its independence.

Filipino Dialects

Filipino dialects have similarities with the languages of their Malayan ancestors. Owing to the fact that the Philippine archipelago is separated by various islands, **dialects are diversified**. In the islands, regions, provinces, cities, towns and barrios where the Filipinos live, they spoke the native tongue congruent to their area. These numerous and varied dialects were barely comprehensible from one regional dialect to another that a search for a Filipino mother tongue was necessitated.

Since the Philippines was previously under foreign powers, Filipino dialects had been infused with the Spanish and English languages, besides a few business and food terminologies in Chinese due to their lengthy association with the Chinese settlers in the Philippines. The Spanish lexis that have been incorporated into the Filipino vocabulary for more than three centuries remained intact and authenticated as real Filipino language.

In December 31, 1937 while the Philippines was still an American territory, President Manuel L. Quezon proclaimed Tagalog as the Filipino national language. And even in 1946, when the Philippines already became self-governing and now free from foreign powers, advocates for the nationwide usage of Tagalog increased. However, government sectors, schools, books and periodicals were still using English as the medium for communications, except for weekly magazines written in regional tongues like Liwayway (its first publication was in 1922), Bisaya (1932), Hiligaynon (1934), Bikolano (1935) and Bannawag (1940).

26

Evolution of the Filipino Alphabet

The first known alphabet in the Philippines was brought in by the Malay ancestors of the Filipinos, which was a Malayan-Sanskrit writing called **baybayin** or **abugida**.

Upon the arrival of the Spanish colonists, the Spaniards introduced the Spanish alphabets written in Roman script, which was called **abecederia** – an alphabet still being used in Mexico, and in South and Central America. The abecederia in the Philippines evolved in numbers, sequentially from 28, 29, 31 and 32 letters just because Spanish alphabets have their own unique national consonants.

Later, the **abakada** took the place of the abecederia to indigenize the Tagalog alphabet, but still retained the Roman script. The Tagalog abakada had merely 20 letters composed of A-B-D-E-G-H-I-K-L-M-N-O-P-R-S-T-U-W-Y plus the Filipino digraph NG. However, the Tagalog abakada, with its 20 letter-alphabet, also underwent changes. **In 1976**, the Department of Education, Culture and Sports (**DECS**) revised the 20-letter abakada into a 30-letter alphabet by adding C-F-J-Q-V-X-Z and the Spanish Ñ plus the Spanish digraphs CH, LL and RR; but immediately after, went back to the 20-letter abakada.

In 1987, with the help of **DECS**, President Corazon Aquino had the 20-letter abakada increased into 28 letters by adding the C-F-J-Q-V-X-Z again and this time, with the Spanish consonant Ñ, and she had this enacted as the Makabagong Alpabeto. **In 2001**, the Komisyon Sa Wikang Filipino renamed the 28-letter Makabagong Alpabeto into a more appropriate name, the **Alfabeto**.

The retaining of the Spanish consonant Ñ to the new Filipino **Alfabeto** is quite relevant because the new Filipino alphabet is no longer indigenized. Besides that, Filipino names are predominantly Spanish, far outnumbering the enduring native names, the Malay names, the Moslem names, the Chinese names, and the Filipinized-Chinese names. Examples of Filipino names with the Ñ consonant are Ibañez, Zuñiga, Villaseñor, Acuña,

Castañeda and Saldaña. Besides people's names, the Ñ is also used in other local names like Bulakeña, Caviteño, Pampangueño, Zamboangueña, and of course, the renowned **Malacañan Palace** or **Malacañang Palace**, which is the residence and office of the President of the Philippines.

Alphabets of The Non-Tagalog Filipinos

Many people presume there is only one Filipino alphabet, the Tagalog abakada, so it may surprise them that the **non**-Tagalog Filipinos (i.e. Ilocanos, Cebuanos, Pangasinenses, Bicolanos, Ybanags, Maranaws, Pampangueños, Warays, et al) **have their very own regional alphabets which were more replete and more stocked** because their alphabets had **one to six more letters than the old 20-letter Tagalog abakada**. For those that have no set-up alphabets, their dialects are proof enough to substantiate that they have more letters in their dialects than the old Tagalog abakada. The dialect that had the most number of letters was Ybanag, which always had C, F, J, Q, V, and Z in its alphabet. Examples of alphabets that are **not found** in the old Tagalog abakada are the following: in Ybanag, words like bathe is *mazzigo,* open is *vuca,* residence is *padjanan,* wipe is *funat,* tongue is *zila* and heart is futó; in Ilocano, words like offer is *ofrecer,* confess is *confesar,* rescue is *salvar,* shoo is *fuera,* and value is *valor*; in Bicol, words like great or strong is *fuerte*, young is *joven* (*hoven*), easy is *facil,* and hard is *dificil*; in Cebuano, words like family is *familia*, elephant is *elefante* and small quantity is *jutay;* and in Gaddang, words like lips is *bifig,* accompany is *vulon* and white is *furaw.*

With the ratification and designation of the new and more advanced 28-letter Alfabeto as the Philippine National Alphabet, the Alfabeto has now superseded **all the alphabets of the various Filipino dialects that the non-Tagalogs and some Tagalogs accepted and embraced the new Alfabeto**.

The Puzzle of The "F" Consonant

The most intellectually perplexing and disconcerting among the once omitted letters in the **old** Tagalog abakada was the missing letter **F** since the country's name, **Filipinas or Philippines have always been pronounced with an "F" both worldwide and by all the non-Tagalog Filipinos** (Ilocanos, Cebuanos, Bicolanos, Pampangueños, Pangasinenses, Ilonggos, Igorots, Warays, Ybanags, Maranaws, Gaddangs, Itawis, Chavacanos, et al) and by some Tagalog Filipinos **who have always enunciated the "F" consonant correctly and appropriately.**

With the evolution of the Filipino alphabet from the Malayan-Sanskrit script named **Baybayin/Abugida** to the Spanish **Abecederia** to the indigenized **Abakada** and to the present-day **Alfabeto**, the letter **F** has passed through a number of stages. And with the Filipinos' exposure to foreign languages, Filipinos can pronounce all the letters of the alphabets effortlessly, **unlike** two or more foreign races where some consonants are uncommon to them that it takes efforts for them to articulate such unique letters, therefore they pronounce the "problematic" consonants either phonetically imperfect or with inflections. Fortunately, Filipinos do not have that problem since they have the familiarity and capability to pronounce all existing alphabets accurately and without difficulty because of the mélange and fusion of Spanish, English and Chinese languages into the indigenous Filipino dialects.

Hence, puzzled **non-Tagalog Filipinos** try hard to explore the reason why many Tagalogs continue to replace the **F** with a **P** even though the **F** is the right letter to the word, and such practice is evident in the verbal and written vernacular communications of most Tagalogs. Should the Tagalogs who ignore the **F** continue to do so despite the fact that the old Tagalog abakada is quite deficient? Or should they now use the new more stocked and replete Alfabeto as it is warranted and justified since the complete, full-packed Alfabeto was ratified in 1987 in order for Filipinos to categorically use it for verbal and written communications, and especially because the name Philippines and Filipinas are pronounced with an "**F**" worldwide and by most Filipinos. It is definitely the choice of the

Tagalogs to do whatever they want as the Philippines is a free country. But it cannot be denied that the new complete, all-encompassing **Alfabeto** is definitely more proficient, more ingenious, and a more precise alphabet, while the old deficient abakada has expired and gone. Fortunately, some Tagalogs, especially those in the higher hierarchy, shun substituting the **F** with the **P** in their Tagalog communications and whenever they speak foreign languages.

Tagalog, the Mother Tongue of Filipinos

Originally, Manila was a fort and a walled city, which was the seat of the Spanish rule for over 300 years. Its first name was Intramuros until it was renamed into its current one - Manila. Manila is also the Philippine center of authority and distinction since it situates Malacañan Palace, the residence and office of the President of the Philippines.

Manila is in the center of the Tagalog region with all its provinces having joined borders around Manila. It was for this reason that Tagalog was chosen as the national language of the Philippines. In the early 1900s, Tagalog already had an upper hand among all the Filipino dialects due to the popularity and dominance of Manila. Metropolitan Manila has been the center of the Philippine government, and the hub of activities for arts, for the information industry, and for business and trade, besides being the capital of the Philippines that the world recognizes (there was an attempt to make Quezon City as the capital of the Philippines but the effort fell short). For several years, majority of Filipinos have been seeking the best employments found mainly in Metropolitan Manila where all the big businesses thrive, while many youths likewise have been pursuing their college education in Metropolitan Manila, where all the finest universities and the elite colleges have been based since the Spanish era. Nowadays, Cebu, Davao, Dumaguete, Naga, Baguio, and other big cities and big towns throughout the archipelago have competitive big businesses and elite educational institutions established in their areas.

In the mid-1930s, both the Filipino movie and radio industries used Tagalog as the medium for entertainment and information. And with the advent of television in the 1950s, this TV industry likewise chose Tagalog as the dialect for communications. From their inceptions, each of these media agencies were based in Metropolitan Manila and have been extensively airing, broadcasting and spreading out all over the entire Philippine archipelago. As a result, they helped tremendously in the propagation of Tagalog as the Filipino's major and principal tongue for communications, transactions, and interactions all over the Philippines.

Such end result replicates the worldwide effect of books, music, cinema and television shows from both the United States of America and the United Kingdom which made English become the major language for communications globally. Chances are, all of these may have been unplanned and unintended yet it produced a surprisingly worthwhile result and worldwide acceptance.

In 1990, Philippine President Corazon Aquino officially mandated the use of Tagalog as the language for communications in all departments and operations of the government, and also in schools all over the entire Philippine archipelago for the very first time after 333 years of Spanish colonization when the Spanish language prevailed, followed by 48 years of American regime when the English language was forefront in communications in all government, business, media and educational entities in the Philippines.

The government decree to use Tagalog as the communications tool for overall administrations and interactions was long overdue yet warmly welcomed. **Finally, Tagalog has become the unifying language for all Filipinos all over the entire Philippine archipelago and even among Filipinos who have migrated abroad.**

KNOWN & LITTLE KNOWN FACTS
ABOUT THE PHILIPPINES

Beautiful Philippines With Its UNESCO Protected Sites

The Philippines has a paradise-like beauty and is known as the **Pearl of the Orient.** The Philippines stands unique and out-of-place in Asia since there are **neither** oriental temples **nor** apparent Buddhist and Hindu practices that are common sights and practices in other Asian countries. Instead, the Philippines manifests the Spanish-colonization in the country through centuries-old Spanish baroque Catholic churches that are found everywhere in the Philippines, and crosses and large statues of Jesus Christ that tower over at public centers and hills, while Catholic practices are evident during town fiestas and Christian holidays (Lent, Holy Week, Easter, Christmas, etc.), and Spanish names and surnames are widely dispersed. The American influence is also overflowingly evident among books, periodicals, business names, public notifications and directions, advertisements, media communications, the Filipinos' proficiency in English, and the Filipino way of writing which is the Roman script that is used globally for international communications and interactions. Letterings or alphabet scripts in China, Japan, Indonesia, Malaysia, Korea, Russia, Arab countries and other not globally-utilized writings are **not used** in the Philippines.

The Philippines is blessed with rich natural resources, which are evident through mesmerizingly beautiful panoramas that are either developed or undeveloped. The marvelously ravishing milieus in the Philippines are rarely exposed and only very few of these natural attractions are publicized or consigned to business. So one can still enjoy the gorgeous blessings of nature as freely and peacefully as much as one can without a horde of tourists roaming around. The explored sites maintain their enchanting features while the untouched and unspoiled spots usually emerge as hidden gems.

Despite **not** being widely known and commercialized, the Philippines' natural vistas caught the attention and admiration of a number of international travel publications, like the Travel + Leisure Magazine, Conde Nast, and the National Geographic Traveler, that rated the Philippines as having the world's most beautiful islands and the most beautiful beaches. As a matter of fact, **for two years in a row** (2016 and 2017), **Palawan Island** has been voted as the **Best Island In The World**, and because in 2013, it also won that distinction, it is now the **third time** that it has been designated as such. **Boracay Island** was also voted both as 2017's **third best island in the world** and as 2017's **third most beautiful beach globally**, according to 2017 world travel surveys. **Cebu Island** is 2016's **second best island in the world**, whereas it was the **sixth** in 2017. The catchphrase "**It's more fun in the Philippines**" was actually labeled by tourists who have been enjoying their travel to the Philippines, and this "trademark" stuck until today and deservingly so. It is therefore no surprise that the Forbes magazine cited the Philippines as one of the **Top Five Asian International Tourist Destinations of 2018**. As of 2018, plans were being launched to have cruise ships from Hongkong sail to beautiful Philippines.

The Philippine archipelago is composed of 7,107 islands, hence there are at least as many beaches to explore. The Philippines has three main divisions namely Luzon, Visayas and Mindanao, bynamed Luzviminda. These three main divisions are comprised of several provinces and thousands of smaller islands around them. Todate, there are 81 provinces in the Philippines and each province has its own interesting sites and beautiful sceneries. Foreigners have noted that **the blessings and assets of the Philippines are its amiable people, its beautiful vistas, and its rich natural resources**.

The wonders of nature in the Philippines through its numerous panoramic views, are captivatingly beautiful which are pristine, unspoiled and secluded for not having been exploited yet, except for just a few that have already been explored and developed. There are numerous panoramic sceneries which are terrestrial and aquatic wildlife, idyllic hinterlands, virgin forests, invigorating waterfalls, relaxing white beaches which a few of these have soft-powdery sands, while some beaches extend with sandbars where one can playfully race or run around on a long stretch. There are also mesmerizing caves and caverns that invite fun-filled spelunking, also soothing tranquil coves, subterranean rivers, intriguing deep craters, fascinating rock formations, majestic mountains, idyllic rolling hills, enchanting mangroves, secret tarns, rejuvenating natural springs, exotic coral reefs replete with colorful marine life under crystal clear see-through blueish waters with calm currents that's great for swimming or gigantic sea waves that's ideal for surfing, and shimmering waters in the midst of verdant foliage of lush tropical jungles or serene rustic countrysides, and gorgeous sunrise or sunset.

As expected, noteworthy and significant sites in the Philippines have been designated under the **World Heritage Sites** in the Philippines and protected by the United Nations Educational, Scientific and Cultural Organization or **UNESCO** for short. UNESCO designated six World Heritage Sites in the Philippines, while more Philippine sites are in its "Tentative List." The six designated sites are 1. **Baroque churches** that were built in the 16th century which are the San Agustin Church of Manila, the Santa Maria Church, and the Paoay Church both in the Ilocos Region, and the Miaogao Church in the Visayas; 2. **Tubbataha Reefs Natural Park** in Palawan which is from the pleistocene period, and this Tubbataha Marine Park that covers the north and south reefs, has a high density of marine life, pristine coral reef, large lagoons and two coral islands; 3. **Rice Terraces of the Cordilleras** which date back to 100 BC as their origins. These rice terraces are the Batad and Bangaan that are both in Banawe, Mayoyao in Mayoyao, Hungduan in Hungduan, and Nagacadan in Kiangan. Such rice terraces exhibit the harmony of man's diligence and resourcefulness and the use of ecological potentials; 4. the **Vigan Historic City** in Ilocos Sur that was built in the 16th century and still retains its typical Spanish colonial town appearance, is unusual and peculiar in Asia; 5. **Puerto Princesa Subterranean River National Park** in Palawan which dates back in the pleistocene epoch. It is a mountain covered with the most valuable trees in Asia and underneath it is an underground river; 6. **Mount Hamiguitan Range Wildlife Sanctuary** in Davao Oriental also dates back in the pleistocene period. This is a mountain that provides essentially needed habitat for a wide variety of endangered flora and fauna - plants and animals - that include the Philippine eagle and the Philippine cockatoo.

UNESCO has more tentative lists of Philippine sites that are being considered as World Heritage Sites and for UNESCO protection, but this usually take years for such to be finalized. These Philippine sites are the **Apo Reef Natural Park**; **Baroque Churches** which are the Laboc Church in Bohol, Boljoon Church in Cebu, Guluan Church in Samar, Tumauini Church in Isabela, and Lazi Church in Siquijor; the **Batanes Protected Landscapes and Seascapes**, the **Butuan Archeological Sites**, **Chocolate Hills Natural Monument**, **Coron Island Natural Biotic Area**, **El Nido-Taytay Managed Resource Protected Area**, **Kabayan Mummy Burial Caves**, **Mayon Volcano Natural Park**, **Mt. Malindang Range Natural Park**, **Mt. Matalngajan Protected Landscape**, **Mt. Pulag Natural Park**, **Neolithic Shell Midden Sites** in Lallo and Gattaran towns, **Northern Sierra Madre Natural Park**, two **Paleolithic Archeological Sites**, five **Petroglyphs and Petrographs of the Philippines**, **The Tabon Cave Complex**, and the **Turtle Islands Wildlife Sanctuary**.

Paradise-like Philippines

The Philippines is rich with beautiful landscapes and seascapes but only a few will be named here. The first one is **Palawan** which is viewed as a paradise attributing to its exotic islands with geographic regions of cliffs, rock formations, caves, caverns, waterfalls, big lagoons, small lagoons, a secret lagoon, see-through crystal clear waters in blue or turquoise color, white beaches, beige beaches, a hidden beach, and many more. Palawan's underground river is known as St. Paul Underground River and has famous thalassic features in its subterranean river that extends to a five-mile course from the mountain's entry opening to its exit egress, making it the second longest subterranean river in the world.

Furthermore, Palawan's subterranean river is also the third deepest cave in the world. The cave has breathtaking views of stalactites, stalagmites, caves and waterfalls. Palawan also has rare and endangered creatures like the bearded pig, the calamian deer, the pangolin ant-termite eater, and the purple crab. Enjoyable and exciting activities in Palawan are beach sunbathing, swimming, wading, scuba diving, surfing, snorkeling, exploring the Tubbataha Reef Marine Park, hiking, biking, tricycle hopping, motor biking, firefly-watching at night, and sightseeing through overhead zip-lines or by bus tours, boat tours, night tours, nature and wildlife tours, and underground river tours.

Boracay Island is popular for its environmental attractions of lush tropical forests, volcanic rock formations, white beaches and captivating sunset. Activities in Boracay are motor biking, swimming, surfing, scuba diving, snorkeling, diving to view the colorful marine life, island-hopping, parasailing, cliff diving, kayaking, banca cruising, sunbathing, wading or soaking in sea waters, relaxing at nearby spas, and many more.

The six **Rice Terraces** of Mountain Province namely Banaue, Batad, Bangaan, Mayoyao, Nagacadan and Hungduan rice terraces are rice plantations on the sides and slopes of mountains that were carved out about 2,000 years ago by the Igorots, making those farmlands **one of the oldest and most beautiful rice terraces in the world**. There are also furrowed rice terraces on mountains in Negros Oriental and Antique, and on the hills in Bohol.

Pangasinan's **Hundred Islands** have various natural attractions and offer exciting activities such as overhead zip-lining on which one is harnessed on a protective gear and hovered over an island or over several islands to get a bird's eye view of the sea and the islands below, and other enjoyable activities like jumping from water caves or cliffs, swimming, wading, relaxing at peaceful beaches, bird and bat watching, parasailing, island hopping on a motorboat, on a kayak or on a banana boat, or snorkeling on a helmet to view the Coral Garden's beautiful underwater marine life such as the giant clams.

Siargao are 48 beautiful islands in the province of Surigao del Norte that boast of white beaches, sandbars, coastal reefs, waterfalls, incredible rock formations, coconut trees, and is delightfully considered as the **surfing capital of the Philippines**.

Bohol's **Chocolate Hills** has a total of 1,268 hills that are green during the rainy season but turn chocolate-brown during the dry season. It is in Bohol where one can find the endangered tarsiers, the smallest primates that have large goggle eyes and live in trees. Tarsiers are nocturnal as they are active at night, and not vegetarians since they eat insects, lizards, snakes and birds. Bohol has other attractions such as white beaches, cold spring, waterfalls, and rice terraces on a hill.

Waterfalls

The waterfalls in the Philippines may reach up to a thousand since the 81 provinces in the Philippines evidently possess several known waterfalls, even though other waterfalls may have yet to be discovered. For example, in just one city, Iligan City, there are 23 waterfalls in its suburbs; in Cebu province, there are at least 20 waterfalls; and in Cotabato province, there are 27 known waterfalls. The two recent waterfall discoveries in Cotabato are the **Asik-asik Falls** (*asik-asik* is sprinkling in Hiligaynon dialect) that was discovered only in 2010 which has about 40 sprinkling waterfalls in just **this one place** and all these waterfalls spring out from rocks at a beautiful verdant mountainside but the source of the flowing waters is a mystery since neither a lake nor a river are found above it; and the **Daday Falls** in which no one knows how to get to it yet because it has **not** been developed and it can only be seen from a hard-to-reach mountaintop. There is also another unique waterfall, the **Villa Escudero Waterfall**, which is just one of at least ten known waterfalls in the province of Quezon. Unbelievably, the Villa Escudero Waterfall serves as a backdrop for a restaurant, where live performances are presented.

There are various types and visages of waterfalls and to name a few, these are the plunge, horsetail, multi-step, segmented, tiered, fan, cascade, bridal veil, slide, and punchbowl. The *horsetail* waterfall that descends vertically is exemplified by the **Pagsanjan Falls** in Laguna, the **Kabigan Waterfalls** in Ilocos Norte and the twin **Maria Cristina Falls** in Lanao. The Pagsanjan Falls and the Kabigan Waterfalls also exemplify the *bridal veil* falls. The **Alalum Falls** in Bukidnon and the **Tinuy-an Waterfalls** in Surigao are *cascade* waterfalls that descend on a series of rock steps. The **Mimbalot Waterfalls** in Lanao represent the *segmented* waterfalls because it has parts of waterfalls that are separate from each other, and also as a *slide* waterfalls because it surges on slanted rocks. The **Tamaraw Waterfalls** in Mindoro is also an example of the *segmented* waterfalls and the *tiered* waterfalls. The **Limusudan Falls** in Lanao and the **Seven Falls at Lake Sebu** in Cotabato represent the *plunge* waterfalls because these are fast moving waterfalls, and also as a *punchbowl* waterfall for having a pool on the base drop where people can swim. The **Kawasan Falls** in Cebu and the **Tinago Falls** in Lanao are also both *punchbowl* waterfalls for having pools for swimming. Punchbowls or no punchbowls, one can always have fun with the showers and torrents that downpours from these exhilarating waterfalls. The rivers that flow from these waterfalls are both crystal clear blue in color and mirror-like in transparency, and in some of these places, bamboo-raftings are available.

Coral Reefs

The Philippines has 9,600 square miles of coral reef area and **ranks third in the world's total coral reef expanse**. The Philippine coral reefs boast of several species of beautiful and colorful marine life and are protected by the United Nations World Heritage Convention, and the Ramsar Convention on Wetlands of International Importance. To name a **few** of the numerous coral reefs in the Philippines, these are the **Apo Reef National Park, Batanes Protected Landscape/Seascape, Fugo Island Marine Reserve/Tourist Zone, Tubbataha Reefs Marine Park** and **the Initao National Park** which is a land and sea resort that offers caves, rain forest and **pure, unsullied coral reefs**.

Volcanoes

The Philippines is situated in the Pacific Ring of Fire, therefore it is filled with volcanoes, 60 in all, with 20 active volcanoes while the rest are dormant or inactive. In alphabetical order, these are Ambatungan, Amorong, Apo, Arayat, Babuyan Claro, Balatukan, Balut, Banahaw, Biliran, Binuluan, Bulusan, Cabalian, Cagua, Calayo, Camiguin de Babuyanes, Cancanajag, Canlaon, Cuernos de Negros, Dalupri, Didicas, Hibok-Hibok, Ibugos, Iraya, Iriga, Isarog, Jolo, Kalatungan, Labo, Laguna Caldera, Latukan, Leonard Range, Magaso a.k.a. Cuernos de Negros, Mahagnoa, Makaturing, Malabsing, Malinao, Malindang, Malindig, Mambajao, Mandalagan, Mariveles, Masaraga, Matutum, **Mayon which is the most beautiful in its perfect cone shape and also the most active volcano in the Philippines**, Musuan, Natib, Paco, Panay, Paniutan (Cagayan), Parker, Patoc, Pinatubo, Pocdol, Ragang, San Cristobal, San Pablo, Santo Tomas, Silay, Smith, Taal, and Talinis (Negros Oriental).

Philippines Caves and Caverns

Caves and caverns usually have hanging rock stalactites and stalagmites, but the difference between a cave and a cavern is that a **cave** has an opening to a single tunnel that may go straight or upward or downward; whereas a **cavern** is usually a steep underground tunnel that contains caves or cave chambers. Named here are just a **few** of the numerous caves and caverns in the Philippines. The **Sumaging-Latipan-Lomyang Crystal Cavern** in Sagada, Mountain Province is the deepest cave and the fifth longest cave in the Philippines with six entrances to natural streams, beautiful stone walls and amazing limestone formations. During World War II, Filipino soldiers used this cave as one of their fortresses. On the cliffs of this mountain are **hanging burial sites** of the Mountain Province people (discussed in a subsequent topic in this book). The **Mummy Caves** or **Cavern** of Benguet, Mountain Province contains 200 years old mummies of the ancient wealthy tribal people. The cool temperature in the cave prevents decomposition of the mummies, as well as these mummies were preserved with tobacco smoke, herbs and saltwater, washed and dried over a low fire besides having been dried under the heat of the sun. The **Callao Cavern** in Cagayan province is a huge seven-chambered cave with gigantic limestone and rock structures. The Callao Caverns has an interior chapel and skylights with chambers that have natural crevices that allow the light to come in. This cavern is categorized as a cathedral cave because some of the rock and limestone formations resemble identifiable forms of a chapel, a skeleton, a praying angel, a rocket, and heads of an elephant, of a lion and of a dog. The **Tabon Cave** in Quezon province is famous for the discovery of a 22,000 years old skull that is called the Tabon Man. This cave is believed to be half a million years old. Both the Tabon Cave and the Callao Cavern are discussed previously under the Brief History of the Philippines in this book. The charm and allure of the **Biak-na-Bato Cavern** in Bulacan are hanging bridges and staircases that connects rivers and caves for enjoyable exploration, but it is more significant for being the hideout of the revolutionary soldiers during the Spanish regime. The **Langun-Gobingob Cavern** of Samar is the biggest cave in Southeast Asia, and the 2ⁿᵈ largest cathedral cave in the world with an area of 2,968 hectares. It has 23 caves that include underground spaces adorned with stalactites and stalagmites, and streams. The **Odloman Cavern** in Negros Oriental has galleries, streams, and various crystalline formations of stalactites and stalagmites with five unique entrances that are connected to each other. This Odloman Cavern is considered as the 2ⁿᵈ longest and 6ᵗʰ deepest cave in the Philippines. The **Odessa Tumbali Cavern** in Cagayan province, also called **Abenditan Cavern,** has a canal, lagoon and diving spots.

Natural Springs

There are numerous natural springs in the Philippines which are hot springs, cold springs, hot and cold springs, saltwater spring and mud spring. To name a **few** of these springs, these are the **Malumpati Cold Spring** in Antique, the **Timoga Cold Spring** in Lanao, the **Macao Cold Spring** in Camiguin, the **Danicop Cold Spring and Waterfall** in Bohol, the **Mainit Hot Springs** in Compostela, Mindanao, the **Mado Hot Spring National Park** in Maguindanao in which both Mado and Mainit come from waterfalls; the **Balite Hot Spring** in Davao, the **Hidden Valley Hot Spring** in Laguna, the **Tiwi Hot Springs** in Albay, the **San Benon Hot Spring Resort** in Sorsogon, the **Puning Hot Spring** in Pampanga, the **Manleluag Hot Spring** in Pangasinan, the **Tangka Saltwater Lagoon** in Iloilo, and the **Langco Agco Mud Spring** in Cotabato, which is believed to be good for one's complexion; while both the cold and hot springs are the **Marawer Hot and Cold Springs** in Davao, the **Mabugnao Mainit Hot Spring National Park** in Cebu, and the **Marquez Hot and Cold Springs** in Sultan Kudarat.

Geothermal Power

The worldwide organization, International Geothermal Association **considers the Philippines as <u>second</u> to the United States in geothermal energy production**. The Philippines' geothermal fields are located in Makiling-Banahaw, in the Bicol region, in Leyte, in Negros, and in Mindanao. Philippine exploration of geothermal energy started in the 1950s under the leadership of Professor Arturo Alcaraz who was the head of the Commission of Volcanology. They surveyed and made mappings for possible sources of geothermal energy. And as of 2010, the USA had a capacity of 3093 megawatts of geothermal power, while the Philippines had 1904 megawatts, and Mexico that followed in rank, had 958 megawatts.

Philippines: Rich in Precious Metals

The volcanic activity of the Circum-Pacific Belt or Pacific Ring of Fire has an abundance of the world's gold and copper deposits. The Philippines has the greatest number of proven deposits of metallic and non-metallic minerals in the world. It also has the world's biggest unexplored and untapped copper and gold deposits (not gold <u>reserves</u> as the advanced countries have). **The Philippines ranks <u>second</u> in the world among countries having the <u>largest gold deposits</u> at present**, but with the increase of mining sectors in the Philippines, it is evident that its **global ranking will rise because the country has the richest untapped gold**

deposits on earth. Previously, **the Philippines ranked the fourth largest in excavated copper in the world, and fifth largest in excavated nickel**, but that can change because the country is **rich and prolific in precious mineral resources**.

Philippine Natural Gas and Oil Resources

Natural gas is the cleanest and safest source of energy from fossil fuels that are mostly methane. The Philippines has a substantial **natural gas deposit** but it still needs to be exhumed in a large scale. Currently, the production of natural gas does not even meet the local demand. In 2002, the Philippines set up a natural gas industry through the Malampaya gas field which is a gas reserve situated in the West Philippine Sea. It is expected to power the entire country with natural gas for the next two decades.

Shell Philippines also discovered **oil deposits** in the Malampaya field in 1990, and this oil-rich deposit lies under the field's natural gas deposits. The Malampaya oil rim is believed to have the Philippines' largest oil reserve. There are also several oil and gas deposits in various parts of the Philippines, but only a few have been explored. New discoveries of vast oil and gas deposits in Isabela, Cebu, Palawan and Mindanao are potentials to look forward to. As a matter of fact, the Philippine government is now taking steps to drill the oil desposits in Liguasan Marsh, Mindanao which is believed to bring $1-trillion (yes, in US dollars) to the country, and oil and gas deposits in Cebu which are believed to also raise as much or even much more wealth to the Philippine economy. Both Liguasan and Cebu natural gas drillings were being launched in May 2018.

The Philippine National Motto and the Philippine Flag

The Philippine national motto is "**Maka-Dios, Maka-Tao, Maka-Kalikasan at Maka-Bansa**" meaning to be godly, to be considerate of others, to preserve our natural resources and to be patriotic to the

Philippines, or in short "For God, For the people, For nature, and For the country".

The Philippine national flag has a unique feature that other flags in the world do not have. It is the only flag in the world that denotes the status of the country on the way it is flown when raised on a flagpole. When the flag is flown with the **blue** section of the flag on top, the Philippines is **at peace**; when the **red** section is on top, the Philippines is **at war**.

The three stars on the Philippine national flag represent the three major sectors: Luzon, Visayas and Mindanao, and the sun represents liberty, equality and brotherhood.

The Philippine National Anthem and a few Other Filipino Songs

The melody of the Philippine National Anthem was composed during the Spanish regime by Julian Felipe so as to be played during Emilio Aguinaldo's proclamation of Philippine Independence on June 12, 1898, distinguishing Emilio Aguinaldo as the president. After a year, Jose Palma wrote a Spanish poem titled "Filipinas" which became the original lyrics of the anthem. In 1919 during the American regime, English lyrics of the anthem titled "The Philippine Hymn" were written by both the Filipino writer Camilo Osias and an American named A. L. Lane. During Ramon Magsaysay's presidency in 1956, the lyrics were translated into Tagalog by Juan Cruz Balmaceda and Ildefonso Santos, and titled it "Lupang Hinirang" meaning "selected land," with another title called Bayang Magiliw meaning "beloved country".

Other patriotic songs for the country are Ang Bayan Ko (or Ang Bayan Kong Filipinas), Filipinas Kong Mahal, Philippines My Philippines, Sa Sariling Bayan, Ang Bayan Ko't Lahi, Perlas ng Silanganan, Mutya ng Silangan, Ang Aking Bandila, Pagpupugay sa Republica, Handog ng Filipino sa Mundo, and the We Say Mabuhay music which is played when the president of the Philippines makes a formal appearance in ceremonial events.

Filipino classical kundimans were composed in the early and mid-1900s. These songs are considered classical because they are sang in a way that adhere to the established artistic standards of music in operatic fashion and in classical presentations (i.e., renditions by Sylvia la Torre). The Filipino classical songs are Lambingan, Bituing Marikit, Sa Sariling Bayan, Dinggin ang Awit sa Kamorohan, Sa Kabukiran, Madaling Araw, Maligayang Araw, Nasaan Ka Irog, Pakiusap, Mutya ng Pasig, Anak ng Dalita, Ilang-ilang, Ibong Sawi, Ang Maya, Ako'y Kampupot, and Kulasisi.

Older Filipino musics are usually considered *kundimans* like the Halina't Magsaya, Sa Libis ng Nayon, Sampaguita, Cariñosa, Fiesta, Pandanggohan, Ang Tangi Kong Pag-ibig, Dahil Sa Iyo, Maalaala Mo Kaya, Barong Tagalog, Ang Dalagang Filipina, Bella Filipina, Gintong Silahis, Gintong Araw, Lawiswis Cawayan, Huling Awit, Matud Nila, Usahay, Pobring Alindahaw, Dandansoy, Rosas Pandan, Ang Bol-anon, Waray-waray, Manang Biday, Pamulinawen, Ti Ayat ti Maysa Nga Ubing, Dungdungwen Canto, Atin Cu Pong Singsing, Sarumbanggi, Malinac Lay Labi, and Lappaw nga Mangayayá. This also includes the *haranas* like the Ibig Kong Magtapat and Dungawin Mo Sana.

More recent Filipino songs are no longer considered *kundimans* but are classified as love songs, popular songs, easy listening songs, jazz, hip hop and many more like Maging Sino Ka Man, Doon Lang, Ngayon at Kailanman, Paano, Pitong Gatang, Kahit Maputi Na Ang Buhok Ko, Manila by the Hotdogs, Mahal by Pabs Dadivas, Kabilogan ng Buwan by the Apo Hiking Society, Anak, Ugoy ng Duyan, Paano Pa Kita Malilimutan, Bakas ng Lumipas, Salamat sa Alaala, Sa Aking Pag-iisa, Kung Ikaw Ay Isang Panaginip, and many more.

Philippine National Costumes That Use Indigenous Materials

The finest traditional Filipino costumes are made with exclusive Filipino materials derived from indigenous products that are woven into fabrics. Such native products that are woven into textiles are the **Piña fabric** that comes from pineapple leaves, the **Jusi fabric** that comes from abaca, and the **Banana fabric** that comes from banana leaves. **All traditional Filipino costumes have been made from such natural products since the Spanish era**. However, for some time now, there has been a decline of hand-loom weavers of such products that it has become harder to find such fabrics. If such fabrics are available, those are more expensive. So most Filipino costumes these days are made from ordinary textiles, but from fine and transparent fabrics like the organza fabric, which are comparable to the indigenous fabrics used for Filipino costumes.

The following are two Philippine National Costumes for Women which are traditional Filipina attires that use the *piña, jusi* or *banana* fabrics. The **Maria Clara terna** has four separate pieces namely the *camisa* (collarless waist-length blouse that has medium-low neckline and loose long-sleeves), the *panuelo* (transparent and stiff scarf because this is the part where either the *piña* or *jusi* or *abaca* fabric is *used* and is square but is folded to a triangular shape to wrap around one's back and towards the front where it is pinned with a brooch), the **floor**-length *saya* (long skirt) that is wide and billowy, and the *tapis* which is a hip-hugging **knee**-length skirt that wraps around the *saya*. Although the Maria Clara terna was popular during the Spanish era and even in the early part of the American era, the *Maria Clara terna* is now used merely on ceremonial community events, or for Filipino folk dances, or theatrical performances where Filipino culture or history is presented, or worn by the bride on her wedding day. The other traditional Filipina attire that use the mentioned *piña or jusi or abaca fabric* is the **Balintawak dress**, which is either **floor**-length for formal wear or **knee**-length for casual wear, with a medium-low neckline with transparent butterfly sleeves where either the *piña* or *jusi* or *abaca* fabric is used.

The attire for man that uses the *piña* or *jusi* is the **Barong Tagalog** which is the Philippine National Costume for Men. The *Barong Tagalog* is a man's shirt that is totally made of the transparent *piña or jusi fabric*, so it needs to be worn with a *camisa de chino* underwear and formal pants. The *Barong Tagalog is* collared with embroidered shirt-frontage and is a formal wear worn for ceremonial events like VIP events, and weddings, and for folk dances if it is warranted.

Philippine National Bird

Previously, the Philippine national bird was **Maya**, a peaceful-looking, pleasant but seemingly unexciting bird that was a common sight in Philippine countrysides. A Filipino composer loved the Maya so much that he even composed a song for it. However, in 1995, Philippine President Fidel Ramos opted for the Philippine eagle called **Agila** to now become the Philippine national bird because it is native and endemic to the country since it is found only in the Philippines. The Agila exemplifies the Filipino nature of being resilient, strong, free, and unfettered. The Agila is a raptor or bird of prey and its scientific name is *pithecophaga jefferyi.* Its habitat is the forest and volcanic slopes. Since there is a problem of deforestation in the country, President Ramos had a law enacted to safeguard all endangered species because the Agila is in danger of extinction. Currently, there are only about 200-500 surviving Agilas. Moreover, Filipinos need to be eco-friendly - not environmentally harmful - in preserving the habitats of all creatures because the Philippines is home to 1,100 species of land vertebrates (mammals, birds, reptiles, amphibians and fishes) and out of these, 170 species of birds and 100 species of mammals are native and endemic to the Philippines. The Agila is now a protected bird under the Wildlife Resources Conservation and Protection Act of 2001, and **killing the Philippine eagle is punishable by up to 12 years imprisonment**. The Agila is one of the largest eagle in the world, besides being one of the most powerful birds. A sketch of the Agila now appears in a Philippine 50-cent coin that was issued by the Bangko Central ng Filipinas and in several Filipino items.

Other Philippine Symbols

The Philippine national personification or the symbol of the Filipino people is **Juan de la Cruz** or simply **Juan** (John in English). Juan de la Cruz's humble replica wears a *camisa de chino,* native trousers, *chinelas* (slippers) and a *salakot* hat, while its formal replica wears a barong tagalog, formal pants, *sapatos* (shoes) and a *salakot.* The **salakot** is also a symbolic Filipino hat ever since the Spaniards were in the Philippines.

The *salakot* has a variety of forms and materials. It is wide brimmed and may be shaped as conical or carved or pointed at its top. It may be woven or non-woven and may be made of rattan, *buri*, nipa, *upo* (gourd fruit), bamboo or *pandan*.

The Philippine national flower is **Sampaguita** with a scientific name of *jasminum sambac*. This national flower is comprised of two sampaguita species: one is clustered with several petals on its bud, and one with just single petals around a row on its bud. The sampaguita is a white fragrant flower with its oil extracted for perfume. The sampaguita is also used as a lei, as a headwear, garland and corsage for one's own adornment, or used to welcome arriving VIPs or to honor dignitaries.

The national gem is the **pearl** or **perlas** with a scientific name of *pinctada maxima*, and is very appropriate for the country because the Philippines, since time immemorial, has been known as Pearl of the Orient. It is also in the Philippines where the largest pearls were found. As for athletics, the National Sport and Martial Art is **Arnis** or **Escrima** (fencing).

The national tree is the durable **Narra** with the scientific name of *pterocarpus indicus*. It is durable and termite-resistant that it is used to make houses, furnitures, cabinets, canoes, paddles and musical instruments. It is colored red with a sweet rosey odor. The resin from the narra is used to heal sores and mouth tumors.

Recently, there have been some deliberations to make changes or lengthen the list of the Philippine National Symbols. The proposed subjects are carabao as the Philippine National Animal; mango as the National Fruit; *sinigang* or *adobo* as the National Food; *tinikling* as the National Dance; and *sipa* as the National Sport.

Agriculture

Farmlands in the Philippines like the rice terraces on mountains and hills, and the crop plantations on plain fields all over the Philippine archipelago are a beauty to behold. Such are the evidence of the **diligence and hard work of Filipino farmers**.

The Philippines is the top coconut producer in the world. Coconut is a delightful and healthful drink and its meat is made into pastries or ice creams and Bicol dishes in which coconut is a common ingredient. Besides food and drink, there are other uses of the coconut. Locals halve the shell with its husk still on but its meat scooped out, to be used as floor polisher called *lampaso*. The coconut is also used as a dance enhancement - locales halve it, remove the entire husk covering, and scoop out its meat to transform these as coconut shells, then used as hand props to make rhythmic knocking sounds, as well as body accessories on the chest and the knees of male dancers to cavort and whirl with the *Maglalatik*, a popular Filipino cultural dance.

The Philippine national tree is the narra tree which is described in a previous topic under "Other Philippine National Symbols". A few other popular Philippine trees are the *acacia* tree, bamboo tree, *achuete* tree with fruits that are used for food coloring, *cacao* tree with fruits that are used for cocoa and chocolate, and hundreds more. Sturdy forest woods for housing, and nipa and bamboo materials for huts (*bahy kubo*) are easily obtainable. There are orchards of fruits in provincial towns and barrios, and there are distinct "forests" that can be seen on roadways or while paddling by the river, lake or ocean like sylvan clusters of coconuts, bananas, guavas, mangoes, papayas, and bamboos.

Philippine fruits are *atis, aratiles, avocado, balimbing* (star fruit), *bayabas* (guava), *camachile, camias, casoy* (cashew), *calamansi, chesa* (canistel), *camote* (sweet potato), *camoteng kahoy* (cassava), *cundol, dalandan, dalanghita, dayap, duhat, durian, granada, guyabano* (soursop), *kamias, kaong* (arenga pinnata), *langka* (jackfruit), *lanzones, lukban, mabolo, macopa, manau* (rattan fruit), two kinds of *mangga* (Manila mango and Indian mango), *mangosteen*, papaya, *mani* (peanuts), *manzanita, maiz* (corn), *niyog* (coconut), *pakwan* (watermelon), *piña* (pineapple), *pili* nuts, *rambutan, rimas* (breadfruit), *saging* (bananas in various sizes and thickness), *sampaloc* (tamarind), *santol* (sandor/cotton fruit), *singkamas* (jicama), *suha* (pomelo), *tubo* (sugarcane), lychee and strawberry both grown in the Mountain Province, and the Spanish-introduced fruits like the *caymito* (star apple), *chico* (sapodilla) and the *siniguelas* (Spanish plum).

Poultries, piggeries and ranches are usually found in the provinces, but in the barrios, free-range chickens, ducks, dogs, cats and goats may roam around, attracting curiosity among non-locals.

Religious Traditions

During the Spanish era, Filipinos converted to Catholicism, a Christian denomination. However, before the turn of the 21st century (2000), a significant number of Catholic Filipinos embraced the Protestant Christian religion through the discipleship and diligence of Protestant Christian missionaries and Christian televangelists (television preachers).

Whether Catholics or converted Protestants who are mostly saved-by-God's-grace-born-again Christians, Filipino's devotion to God is quite evident in their customs and values. They go to church on Sundays and Christian holidays. Catholic Filipinos have an altar in their homes where the entire family would kneel before it and pray the rosary followed by the litany with usually the mother or the eldest child leading the entire prayers. While alone commuting in a public transportation, a Filipino usually pray the rosary silently. A rosary also hangs by the driver's rearview mirror in front of the driver's seat of a family car. When bogged down with a problem, Filipino Catholics, with the entire family or solely by oneself, pray a 9-day novena.

Filipino Protestants or more known as "saved-by-God's-grace-born-again Christians" likewise pray a great deal and read the Bible often, alone or with the family. Besides a church service that is held every Sunday in a Protestant church, there are also prayer meetings and Bible studies (separate from each other) that are held either once-a-week or once or twice a month either in the church, or at the pastor's house, or at a congregation member's house.

Christmas ambiance in the Philippines is the longest in the world commencing from the month of September to January 6th, which is Three Kings Day. At the start of this 4-month-period, shopping malls begin to display Christmas decorations with music to entice customers to keep on coming. In due time, the air all over town carries Christmas ditties bringing to life the exhilarating Christmas atmosphere, while residential houses start to display the colorful and beautifully decorated star-shaped *parol* or *farol-Sp*, an emblematic Filipino Christmas lantern. Filipino groups, which are mostly youths and little kids, do Christmas caroling house-to-house throughout the month of December - from the 1st to the 31st. Filipino Catholics attend the pre-dawn nine-day church mass from December 16th to the 24th. This 5:00 a.m. pre-dawn mass/ *misa* is called *Simbang Gabi* or *Misa de Gallo* meaning when the rooster starts to crow. The *Simbang Gabi* or *Misa de Gallo* was put into practice to allow farmers to hear mass before going to work on the fields. Currently, this Christmas 9-day mass before daylight is convenient for employees and school children to comply with this Catholic practice and still allows them to have time to eat breakfast and do the usual routinary preparations before going to their jobs or to school. On Dec. 24th midnight, the Christmas midnight mass for Catholics and Christmas church service for Protestants are held in their individual churches, and after that, both Catholic and Protestant churchgoers go home to enjoy the Christmas *Noche Buena* feast that has the traditional *queso de bola* and *hamon*, besides the usual party foods prepared by Filipinos. Both Filipino Catholics and saved-by-God's-grace born-again Christians show so much adoration and reverence in commemorating the Birth or the Nativity of God the Son, Jesus Christ. On November 1st which is All Saints Day or *Todos Los Santos* (also called All Souls Day), Filipinos go to the cemetery to visit a deceased relative.

Lent or *Cuaresma* starts with Ash Wednesday, when the Catholic priest gently scrawl the sign of the cross using ash on the foreheads of churchgoers. Throughout Lent from Ash Wednesday to Holy Saturday or *Sabado Santo*, every Friday until the Holy Week's Good Friday or *Viernes Santo*, Filipino Catholics observe fasting by abstaining from eating meat, let alone desist from celebrations and jubilations in reflection and empathy on the sufferings and death of God the Son Jesus Christ on the cross. When Palm Sunday or *Domingo de Ramos* comes around which is the start of Lent's Holy Week or *Semana Santa*, Filipino Catholics bring palm leaves to church. On any day throughout the Holy Week, they do a *Visita Iglesia* by praying at every Station of the Cross spot inside the Catholic Church to commemorate the sufferings of Jesus Christ. They also either join the *Viernes Santo* (Good Friday) procession of the *Santo Entierro* (Holy Interment) or stand in reverence as the religious procession passes by their house. In Pampanga and Bataan, some Catholic men flog themselves with thorns (called flagellations) and some even allow their hands to be nailed on a cross. Easter Sunday or *Domingo de Resureccion* brings back rejoicing with a Catholic sunrise service at the frontage of the church where a child performing as an angel is lowered by a lever to take off the black veil and exchange it with a white veil from a lady who is performing as the Blessed Mother Mary, the virgin mother of Jesus Christ. Both Catholics and saved-by-God's-grace born-again Christians commemorate with joy the Risen Christ on Easter Sunday when Jesus Christ resurrected from His death on the cross and then appeared to His disciples again, dined with them, and instructed them to spread His teachings. The disciples' took a look at Jesus Christ's pierced palms where the nails penetrated through on the cross, and His side where a spear punctured it, and then they witnessed Him ascend back to heaven.

Family Values, Courtship and Weddings in the Philippines

Filipinos are education-oriented that parents sacrifice a lot just to be able to send their children to college to obtain a professional degree. It is not unusual to find children having careers that cover all the major professions like being a physician, dentist, engineer, lawyer, nurse, teacher, accountant and even a Catholic priest or a Protestant pastor in one family. One Filipino profession that is making a big recognition around the world is nursing – global surveys indicate that **the Philippines has the highest number of licensed nurses working in medical facilities all over the world**. And this is after their compliance to the Philippines' requirements that they first work in the Philippines for at least two years after their graduation from a nursing institution before they can leave the country to work abroad.

Even the lowly farmers work hard to be able to send their children to college, or at least to graduate from high school. Those who finished merely high school are contented getting a job as a worker in a restaurant or a store, most especially in shopping malls, whereas the determined and ambitious ones advance their education by continuing to pursue college while working.

The only two countries in the world that do not allow divorce are the Philippines and the Vatican City. So it's not surprising that Filipino marriages last a lifetime until death do them part. Filipinos are family-oriented and closely-knit, and Filipina wives value fidelity and faithfulness as a spouse. The Philippines has the highest number of mothers breastfeeding their babies. Parents inculcate moral and ethical values on their children and instill *delicadeza* (being modest, tactful and prudent) on their daughters. Flirting and sex-before-marriage is a big No-No. Outside the big cities, *harana,* which is serenading a lady with a guitar accompaniment, is either a courtship practice or a preliminary "may-I-personally-meet-you" encounter. Courting a girl entails visiting the lady at her house, love letters are welcomed, and conservative families necessitate chaperons. When a couple fall in love and decide to get married, the beau has to go ask the Filipino parents for the lady's hand. The dowry from either the groom-to-be or the bride-to-be that was practiced a century ago is no longer in effect.

When a Filipino starts working, he/she also starts helping his/her family financially, or may even have extended family like siblings or parents or grandparents live with him/her. For the welfare of the family or for one's own ambitious motivations, it is **not** unusual for a Filipino to try to migrate to the more advanced countries for greener pastures, for a more promising career or for a better life. They write or go to the foreign embassies set up in Manila to apply for immigration to these embassies' country. Filipinos have been able to migrate with their impressive professions or even with simply a satisfactory educational attainment. Some have also been able to migrate through an immigrant relative petitioning and endorsing support for them. At this age of advanced technology, however, some have used social networking to find a marital partner from progressive countries, as a means for them to migrate to a highly developed country. <u>Long distance relationships, however, are not a reliable means to learn the character of a person, which is essential and crucial for a successful marriage</u> – but sometimes with some determined efforts on inquiries and investigation using the internet (read Counseling and background checks before pre-engagement/premarital decisions in the <u>dictionary section of this book</u>), one may find online the informations needed, and from that point, **one can make a wise decision that is for this person's very best interest**.

Filipino weddings, both in church and at the reception, are patterned after Spanish and American weddings. However, in the provinces, some Filipino weddings conduct a money dance during the wedding reception when the groom and the bride perform their first dance as a married couple. Male guests go and stand in line to take turns pinning money on the bride's gown before they take their turn to dance with her, and likewise, the female guests stand in line to pin money on the groom's attire before they also take their turn to dance with him.

Fiestas

Fiestas are annual festivals in the provinces to honor God the Son Jesus Christ or the Blessed Virgin Mother Mary or the town's patron saint. Fiestas start with a morning Holy Mass at the Catholic Church. The day may start with either a Catholic procession or a town parade. On the Catholic processions, religious statues saunter around town, then return to the church. On the town parades, school children and adults in colorful costumes march and dance during the parade and behind them are decorated floats that motorcade around town carrying the town dignitaries, or a pretty muse and her lady entourage, then end at the community center or community park where festive presentations subsequently follow. Processions and parades have different themes like honoring the *Santo Niño* (Baby Jesus) as in the Ati-Atihan cortege, or the Obando fertility rites where childless couples do a petitioning dance throughout the procession. After a town parade, school children present dances and dramatic performances at the community center during the day, while in the evening, ballroom dances for adults are held at the community center before and after the coronation of a chosen town queen for the occasion. Ferries wheel or circus acrobats may come to town to offer more fiesta fun, and exhibits and food fairs may be set up on the grounds of the community center. A beauty pageant or a dance contest or *sabungan* (cockfighting) may also be held. At home, a family serve their guests with fiesta carte du jour, while at the backyard, the men and their buddies may have a drinking spree with the centuries-old Philippine brewed cerveza San Miguel or with another centuries-old Philippine rum, the Tanduay Rum, or simply with the family-concocted tuba or basi with *pulotan* or *kilawen* tidbits that go with any of these drinks.

Filipino Dances

Whatever American dances are in vogue, it is likewise popular in the Philippines. Spain, however, left a strong influence on Filipino cultural dances like the fandangos, habaneras, mazurkas and jotas and these are the Filipino *curacha, rigodon de honor, cariñosa,* the various regional *jotas,* the *abanico* or fan dance, *pantomina, pandanggo sa ilaw, pandanggo rinconada,* and many more. Filipino native dances are the *bulaklakan, sayaw con payong, alay,* and many more. Attires for the Spanish-influenced dances and the Filipino native dances are elegant gowns like the Maria Clara *ternas* and the floor-length butterfly-sleeved *balintawaks* for the ladies, while men's attires are the ceremonial *barong-tagalogs.* Attires for the rustic Filipino dances like the *tinikling, itik-itik, maglalalatik, bakya, salacot, sayaw sa banko, magtanim ay di* *biro, lulay a*nd *binasoan* are, for the men, the Filipino *camisa de chino* with a neck scarf; and for the ladies, usually the Filipino *kimona* top with *tapis* or *saya*, or sometimes the *balintawaks*. Popular Mindanao dances like the *singkil, dayang-dayang* and *sagayan* are worn with elaborate Filipino muslim attires like *malongs* and *sarongs*. Mountain tribal dances like *uyaoy, banga, palayok* and *salidumay* are worn with their tribal garbs like colorful Igorot costumes for women and the primitive G-strings for men.

Filipino Native Cuisine

Filipino cuisine is comprised of various Spanish-influenced dishes (see Spanish era), but authentic Filipino cooking are likewise as common, popular, and well-loved. To name a few of the native gastronomy are *adobo, sinigang, paksiw, kare-kare, dinuguan, pinakbet, dinengdeng, inabraw, bagnet, tinola, bulalo, batchoy,* crispy *pata, sarciado, sisig, laing, ukoy, kandingga, Bicol* express, *bayabas sa gata, palabok, pansit, sopas,* fried *lumpia,* fresh *lumpia, achara, balut, penoy, itlog-maalat, tapa, tinapa, tuyo* and many more. Filipino desserts and snacks are *suman, puto, cuchinta, guinatan, banana-Q, palitaw, bibingka, turon, polvoron, brazo ni Mercedes, sapin-sapin, pandan or ube* cake, *pastillas de leche, yema* candies, *halo-halo, taho, mamon, pili marsapan, pacencia, broas and many more.* Drinks like coffee, cocoa, tea, soda or simply water are perfect with these desserts.

There seems to be a populat **trend** in the provinces lately to eat on a long table fully covered with banana leaves, instead of a tablecloth, where banquet foods are arrayed at the <u>middle</u> throughout the length of the table, where guests help themselves by putting their food on the <u>side</u> of the table over banana leaves, then eat the *kamayan* way (hand-use). The reason for this newly popularized practice may be to solve the scarcity of plates and silverwares when they anticipate more guests are coming.

Filipinos use spoon and fork, **not** chopsticks like other Asians, and for crabs, *kamayan* or hand-use. Contrary to rumors, majority of Filipinos do **not** eat dog, and those who eat dogs are usually men who dauntlessly ingest the food with their buddies during beer or wine-drinking sprees, and such dog-eating gatherings are neither frequent nor held on a regular basis. And Filipinos definitely do **not** eat cats, rats, insects and worms.

Locales In The Old Manila And The Current Manila

Old Manila had streets bearing the names of the provinces in Spain like Andalucia, Asturias, Extremadura, Cataluña, Galicia and Dos Castilas, but were changed and named after Filipino leaders at the end of the century between the 1960s and 2000. Currently, the areas that kept their Spanish names to this day are España Boulevard and Magallanes Village named after Ferdinand Magellan who discovered the Philippines, and whose name in Spanish is Fernando de Magallanes, while in Portuguese, it is Fernão de Magalhães.

During the American regime and soon after, Manila streets bore the names of American officials like Harrison Boulevard that later became Dewey Boulevard, but now renamed Roxas Boulevard as a tribute to the former Philippine president, Manuel Acuña Roxas. The American names that still exist to this day are the MacArthur Highway as a recognition to General Douglas MacArthur who returned to the Philippines to help the Filipinos defeat the Japanese army during the Pacific War; Taft Avenue named after William Howard Taft who was the first American Governor-General of the Philippines and later became the 27th President of the United States; and Forbes Park which was and still is a Metropolitan Manila's upscale area where millionaires reside and which was named after William Cameron Forbes, a Governor-General of the Philippines during the American regime.

Distinct Filipino Qualities, Customs and Mores

Since this contains several topics, it is sorted out in numerals.

1. The ancestors of Filipinos are a mixture of Malays (who are primarily Asians) and Polynesians (because Filipinos are also Austronesians or Malayo-Polynesians). However, some Filipinos have been infused, through inter-racial marriages, with the DNA of the Spanish and American colonizers, and the Chinese traders who settled in the Philippines. Hence, Filipinos have varied looks – some are fair, some are *morena* or *kayumanggi*, some have chinky eyes, some have almond eyes. One reliable way of telling if somebody is a Filipino is: if he/she looks like an Asian or a Polynesian or an Oriental-looking *mestizo/mestiza* and his/her last name or middle surname is Spanish, most likely this person is a Filipino.

2. **Filipinos are the assets of the Philippines because they are polite, congenial, peaceful, hardworking and cheerful people.** Filipinos are unquestionably resilient, persevering and can endure a lot of difficulties despite the Philippines being constantly deluged with natural calamities (volcanic eruptions, earthquakes, landslides, typhoons, floods, etc.), and in the past, four centuries of takeover by Spanish and American invaders, then vanquished during World War II by the Japanese army, and both currently and in the past, being disappointed by the lack of sustainable jobs, or weighed down by grafts and corruptions in the government and private firms, or besieged by threats of communist guerillas and rebels, and stressed by discriminations, unfair treatments and bullying. One clear proof of the Filipinos' tranquil demeanor was the People Power Revolution, which was a non-violent revolution that started in 1983 and culminated in February 1986 when former President Ferdinand Marcos was peacefully banished from his rule.

3. **The happiness of Filipinos do not depend on wealth, health or fame – they are simply a cheerful race that smile and laugh often, and possess a penchant for jokes.**

4. Filipinos love music and singing that the guitar, karaoke, videoke, or cocolele (Philippine-made coconut ukulele) fulfill their fondness for chanting.

5. **Filipinos are respectful.** Filipino youths greet older adults or grandparents with *"Mano po"* as they gently take the adult's hand to dab it on their forehead as a polite salutation for older family members. Besides that, Filipinos address elders with respect by saying *Po* (sir/ma'am) like *Opo* (yes, sir/ma'am) or *Hindi po* (no, sir/ma'am). They also address older siblings or friends with respectful names like *Kuya* for an older guy, and *Ate* for an older girl. They also identify a middle-aged man as *Tito, Tiyo* or Uncle; a middle-aged woman as *Tita, Tiya* or Auntie; an elderly man as *Tatay* or *Lolo*; an elderly lady as *Nanay* or *Lola*. Adults also call younger kids with endearing names like *Iho* or *Totoy, Iha* or *Nene,* or *Anak* meaning "my child" whether they are relatives or not.

6. **Filipinos are self-reliant and diligent**. They take a *"Bahala na"* attitude ("I'll leave the outcome to God") when embarking on efficacious steps to carry out inevitable or necessary undertakings.

7. **Filipinos know the value of education**. Rich, middle-class, and poor families see to it that their children achieve academic learning or college degrees for the sake of their children's best interest (read the preceding topic in this book titled Family Values, Courtship, and Weddings in the Philippines).

8. There are so much room for potentials and growth in the Philippines, but most Filipinos are laid-back and not into entrepreneurship, probably because for four centuries, they have been under Spanish and American subjugators, as well as Chinese settlers who have always been inherently business-minded, that Filipinos have become *campante* or carefree and blithe that they leave the opportunities for progress and success for foreigners to explore and exploit (like the Philippines' abundant cache deposits of gold, nickel, and copper, geothermal energy, oil and gas deposits, and mesmerizingly beautiful landscapes and seascapes, the Filipino's proficiency in English in which schools for teaching English to other Asians who come to the Philippines to learn how to speak English are even under Foreign entrepreneurs), and many more.

9. **Yet Filipinos are amazingly hardworking for their love of their families.** They even have fortitude and resilience when facing difficulties - their sunny disposition keeps them going despite hardship, like farmers endure the heat and the rain while tilling the land or harvesting the crops, yet they feel fulfilled; OFWs keep looking overseas for better opportunities to earn more, which are beneficial to their families despite being away from loved ones for a length of time.

10. **Filipinos are hospitable and open-handed.** When friends ride together in a jeepney or a tricycle or a horse-drawn *calesa*, sometimes they try to outbeat each other in paying for the fare that includes their friends' fare.

11. Filipino hosts urge or even insist that guests go for second helpings for the food during parties in their homes. When anyone, be it a friend or a utility meter-reader, arrives at a house during mealtime, the family invites the drop-by caller to dine with them.

12. Filipinos are hesitant to take the last piece or the last portion of food on the table in case somebody else wants it.

13. The Filipino Balikbayan Boxes that are in business abroad are booming because Filipinos who are immigrants in foreign countries and the OFWs working abroad, love to send goodies and gifts in large jam-packed filled boxes to their loved ones in the Philippines on a regular basis.

14. Filipinos love to entertain people while entertaining themselves as evident on their sense of humor and penchant for glee, and one very public evidence of this is a traffic enforcer who does his work in the middle of a two-way street - this traffic enforcer directs traffic for both directions with dance movements at his restricted and confined post to entertain pedestrians, passersby, and himself.

15. Filipinos are hygienic - they take a bath daily, and do a cleansing *pawpaw* after using the toilet. In their bathrooms, there are always soap and *tabo* (large mug to fill water with) for the *pawpaw*.

16. Nicknames are BIG with Filipinos but usually the nicknames do not sound like their real names at all, and since nicknames are **always** used by pals and kins in addressing each other, **the real name sometimes**

is unknown to friends because <u>real names</u> are used only for ID cards in schools, employments, driver's licenses, bank accounts, passports, and other legal documents.

17. Filipinos wedge their way between two people or between a group putting both palms together like praying but forwardly pointing out to show they are passing by, while stooping and uttering "Excuse me." They consider it rude to pass through without apology just because they are blocking the group's view or interrupting the conversation.

18. When dropping by a house, whether they knock on the door or not, they politely call out "*Tao po*" ("Person here to see you, sir/ma'am").

19. When being asked for directions, or asked where a certain thing is kept, or where a person is at the house or at the office, the responding Filipino would **point the location with his/her lips and eyes looking at the direction**.

20. Some Filipinos swiftly move their eyebrows up and down to say "Yes" to a question.

21. When passengers of a jeepney, taxi, bus, tricycle or *calesa* reach their destination, they make the driver stop by audibly saying "*Para-Sp.*" In a jeepney, before a passenger gets off the vehicle, he/she hands out the fare payment which goes from one passenger's hand to another until it reaches the driver.

22. When trying to catch an elusive word, or they simply forgot a word, they would say "*Cuan*" (Whatchamacallit);

23. For congratulatory clap of upraised palms with another person, they exclaim "Appear!" instead of "High five!"

24. Filipinos use their fingers to determine the rice and water measurement so as to get the right amount of quantity before cooking it.

25. **Like other fellow-Asians, rice is a staple in every meal**.

26. Like a lot of Asians, Malays and Polynesians, Filipinos use the umbrella, not just for rain-cover but most especially when the sun is out and sweltering, so as not to get tanned.

27. Queer Filipino beliefs: 1-Superstitions vary in each region, but one superstition that subsists in most regions is the *kapre* monster dwelling in *balete* trees found in remote areas. This *kapre*, according to beliefs, has hypnotic goggle eyes that can make a passersby lose his/her way,

but if one takes off his/her clothes, the *kapre* would laugh that his large thick lips would cover his hypnotic eyes and the straying person finally finds his/her way. 2-When a baby smiles or giggle in his/her sleep, an angel is playing with this baby. 3-Gulp down large amounts of **unchewed** cooked rice whenever one accidentally swallows a fish thorn so that the rice masses swathe around the thorn which Filipinos believe would prevent the digestive tube from being pierced. 4-The *salabat* drink which is boiled water seasoned with sliced gingers and sugar prevents sore throats and/or starting coughs from persisting or getting worse. 5-Filipino parents encourage their children to jump as high as they can at the stroke of twelve during New Year's celebration so as to make the children grow taller.

28. Filipinos love to watch basketball competitions like the Philippine NCAA (National Collegiate Athletic Association), and the PBA or PBL (Philippine Basketball Association or League) on TV or at the stadium; and Filipinos also love USA's NBA (National Basketball Association) competitions which have been telecasting on Philippine TV for at least half a century now.

29. There is always a basketball court or simply a basketball stand in any city, town or barrio since **basketball is the Filipino's favorite sport**. Tall or short Filipinos play it, even grade school boys and little kids love to play it.

30. Filipinos wear *chinelas-Sp* (slippers) inside the house and *bakya* (wooden clogs) around the yard.

31. They sleep under a *mosquitero-Sp* (mosquito net) to prevent being bitten by mosquitoes.

32. In the provinces, some locals who encounter Caucasian tourists, label them as "Americano" or "Joe" taken after their great grandfather who regard all whites as Americans because early in his life, he used to see American soldiers around, and would hear locals greet them with "Hey Joe!".

33. Filipinos celebrate the New Year with joyful noises like blowing on the colorfully decorated cardboard trumpets *(torotot),* and banging on pots and pans; while others usher in the New Year with **banned** fireworks and firecrackers (*paputok*) just because it is a source for noise on New

Year's Day, despite the risk of losing their own life and limbs. They also use the bamboo cannon (*canyong cawayan* or *bugá*) which is a noise-making device.

34. Many older Filipinos call a pen, ballpen.

35. Some Filipinos in the provinces who are tired of the boring life in rural areas relocate to the big cities anticipating a more exciting life and better conditions. Such resettlements make the cities increasingly overpopulated. Those who lack proficiency and/or college degrees find themselves getting poorer because of their settling for lower earnings in exchange for city life. They are even over-burdened by the higher cost of city-living, but once they are there, they can no longer afford to return to their previous milieu.

36. In the city, the poorest Filipinos live in slums or squatter shanties in cemeteries, or beside train tracks, under a bridge or at riverbanks, in order to provide shelter for their families. They work hard to support themselves with all of them, parents and children alike, putting in their share of the work - they are proactive and resourceful despite not having adequate education or not educated at all; they use whatever strength and capabilities they have like gathering bottles, metals and whatever else they find at the dump to sell to recycling centers, or they sew clothes or go into buy-and-sell goods, or clean buildings or houses, and many other earnable or gainful livelihood.

PAL, Jeepney and Other Filipino Public Transportations

PAL or the **Philippine Airlines is the oldest airline in Asia** that is still in operation under the same name today. It was founded in 1941 by a group of businessman led by Andres Soriano. It was **also the first Asian airline to traverse over the Pacific Ocean en route to the USA** in 1946.

Right after the Pacific War of World War II, the leftover US military jeeps were transformed into inexpensive public transportations for commuters in the Philippines and they called it **jeepney**, which is a portmanteau word for jeep and jitney. These vehicles turned out to be exclusively Filipino and the one and only type of public transportation in the world, which was born out of both the country's necessity and Filipinos' ingenuity. Now the current jeepneys are made by local jeepney manufacturers and adorned with showy, colorful and ornate images and writings. Besides the jeepney, one can also take the city train, or hail a taxi or take the Uber, or ride in a bus to reach other parts of the city.

Public conveyances in provincial towns and barrios are motorcycles, tricycles and the diminishing horse-drawn *calesas* or *carretelas*. To travel from one town to another, one has to catch the bus. Families that own a vehicle, use this to commute anywhere. Farmers transport their crops on a carabao-drawn *carreton*.

To travel to the three major Luzviminda islands, one can board a plane or a ship. There are also ocean ferries that navigate back and forth to the islands of Luzon, Visayas and Mindanao which are even capable of accommodating private-owned vehicles. To hop from one island to another, the conveyances are the ferries, kayaks, native *bancas*, outrigger *bancas*, and pump boats which are outrigger canoes powered by a small gasoline or diesel engine.

Largest Pearl in the World

Besides **Palawan Island** being voted by world travel publications as the **Best Island In The World**, it is also in Palawan where **most discovered giant pearls came from**, like the Lao Tzu pearl, which was considered the largest pearl for sometime. And then, ten years ago, a fisherman found inside a giant clam a gargantuan pearl that was 30 cm. wide (1 feet), 67 cm. long (2.2 feet) and weighs 34 kg. (75 lb.) which is way larger than the Lao Tzu pearl. Its worth may be 130-million in US dollars. However the fisherman was unaware of its value so he kept it for good luck. When he had to relocate to another town, he remembered the pearl under his bed but because it was too heavy, he handed it to a Puerto Princesa City Tourism Officer. Since 2016, the pearl has been available for public viewing at the Puerto Princesa City Hall in Palawan.

Capiz Shells and the Philippine Capiz Shell Windows

The capiz shell marine mollusk or mother of pearl shell is scientifically called *placuna placenta* oyster and found on Philippine coastal waters. Secondarily, it is a well-loved seafood, but first and foremost, it aroused the Filipinos' creative skills that throughout the centuries, they made various products out of it. During the Spanish regime, Filipinos took the pearly white part of these shells, then flattened these and installed them on window panes, a <u>unique decoration that can only be found in the Philippines</u>. Currently, the capiz shell has been created into several more products like a floor lamp, a table lamp, chandelier, jewelry, picture frame, plate, bowl, cup, star-shaped Christmas *farol* (lantern), curtain, windchime, tile, wall panel, box, chips, and other adornment accessories.

The Sagada Mountain's Hanging Coffins and The Blue Soil Hill

In the past, Mountain Province people used to place the corpse of their deceased relative in hanging coffins secured on the mountainside of the Sagada mountain. Three reasons for hanging the coffins were due to their belief that raising corpses higher bring them closer to their ancestral spirits, and during the headhunting days, the higher the coffin, the harder for their tribal foes to get the heads of the deceased so as to be displayed as their trophies.

After a relative dies, the deceased was placed on a death chair because the vigil took days. The cadaver was smoked to prevent fast decomposition and also to conceal its putrefying smell. Pigs and chickens were butchered for the traditional wake for the deceased. During the wake, a group of men fastened and secured the coffin on the mountainside. Before bringing the corpse to the coffin at the mountainside, the dead body was positioned into a fetal position tying it with rattan vines because they believe that a person should depart the same way that this person entered this world. This is why the coffin is only about a meter long. As they carried the corpse to the coffin at the Sagada Mountain, mourners would try to touch or rub the body of the deceased so as to be smeared with the dead body's blood or fluid because of their belief that whatever respectable character and valuable skills the deceased had while alive will pass on to them. Currently, these primitive ancient rituals are observed only by Sagada elders, as it is now a dying custom. With Christian conversion among the majority of Filipinos including the Mountain Province people, they now bury their dead in the cemetery. However, the centuries-old coffins are still hanging at the Sagada Mountains, undisturbed and intact.

The Kamanbaneng Peak, near the Sagada Mountain, is where the **Blue Soil Hill** is found. It was reported that researchers tested the blue soil and found it to be heavy with copper. There are also caves near the Sagada Mountain, and these are the Kaipitan and Balangagan Caves.

Philippines: Surveyed as In the TOP 5 English-Speaking Countries in the World

During the American Regime, the English language implanted its roots deeply in the Philippines. Even after the USA granted the Philippines its independence, English retained its existence and could not be dismissed because of the lack of Filipino words for a number of terminologies in commerce, in science, in medicine, in business and trade, and many more. The government, business firms, schools, periodicals and books in the Philippines were and still are using English as the medium for communications. Filipinos have also been used to speaking English for quite sometime now that it has become a common language communications for them.

Hence, it is no surprise that the Philippines is in the **Top Five English-Speaking Countries in the World**. Filipinos learn to speak English from the time they start schooling, and some even from toddlerhood when they start to talk, as parents speak mainly English to them. For sometime now, 92% of the entire Filipino population speaks English, and whether Filipinos realize it or not, **English is the Filipino's second language**, next to Tagalog. With the diversity of Filipino dialects, most non-Tagalog Filipinos would speak either Tagalog or English to other Filipinos who are from other regions in the Philippines so as to understand and be understood, making communications

65

quite easy and effective. **Most** Filipinos pray to God in English rather than in their own dialect and likewise do so when they write letters to their families, relatives, friends and aquaintances. Verbal Filipino communications are never without an English word intermixed into their everyday conversations, even among similar regional dialect speakers speaking to each other – that's because Filipinos just cannot speak pure, straight Filipino without even realizing it or simply due to force of habit. Hence, some English words have become Filipino lexis. Thus the word **Taglish** was coined to mean Tagalog-English or Filipino-English. Besides that, public messages in shopping malls, street-roadside-and-traffic signs, and public advertisements are written in English or mostly English. Filipinos do **not** write in Asian scripts (i.e., Chinese writing) nor in other unique scripts like Arab or Russian writings. Filipinos' proficiency in English and the <u>Roman scripts writing</u> that Filipinos use make finding locations and directions quite easy, and communications with the locals trouble-free.

The Philippines has also become the destination of other Asians who want to learn to speak English, instead of going to more expensive schools and dwellings in the USA or the UK. Additionally, **outsourcing functions of companies** all over the world find satisfaction in using the Call Centers in the Philippines where the universal language of **English is spoken clearly and proficiently, along with the pleasant demeanor of Filipinos**.

Philippines: the Texting Capital of the World

The Philippines was named as the **Texting Capital of the World** because as early as 2013, it was reported that 400 million text messages have been transmitted by Filipinos daily. The reason for this must have been the Filipino's social nature that drives them to stay connected with family and friends, let alone the affordability of text messaging in the Philippines. Such has created the Filipino subculture group dubbed as the Generation Text. However, with the spawned frenzied focus on cell phones and smart phones throughout the world, the Philippines may now have **lost** its label as the Texting Capital of the World (please read Phone Dependence/ Obsessive Focus and Harms in this book).

The Philippines Has Shopping Malls that are considered as one of the Top Ten Largest in the World

Shopping malls in the Philippine are in the **Top Ten Largest Shopping Malls in the World** and such malls keep cropping out almost in every big town in the archipelago. Some of the famous malls that are in the world survey are the SM City North EDSA which ranks as #4, SM Megamall as #5, SM Seaside City Cebu as #6 and SM Mall of Asia as #10.

Philippine Alcoholic Drinks

San Miguel Brewery in the Philippines, also known as San Miguel Pale Pilsen, opened its doors in 1890. Because it retained its name from its founding, it is claimed that the San Miguel Brewery was the **first brewery founded in Southeast Asia** and its Spanish name was La Fabrica de Cerveza San Miguel. The San Miguel beer is also popular in Spain. Another popular Filipino drink is Tanduay rum, which is a product of the Tanduay Distillers, Inc., a diversified beverage company, which was originally named Ynchausti y Compaña, and was founded in 1854, also during the Spanish regime. Some native wines are the *tuba* and the Ilocano *basi* that are either made from coconuts or bananas.

The Philippines Has Been a Safe Haven and Sanctuary for Defenseless Refugees Escaping Conflict, Persecution and Violence

Despite the Philippines being a young nation, having gained its independence and sovereignty merely on July 4, 1946, which has not reached a century yet after four long continuous centuries of being under foreign rules, the Philippines opened its doors to refugees to give them a safe haven and sanctuary. Among several times that the Philippines was able to help and give accommodations to refugees from different countries in the world, two times, it was the only country that opened its doors to refugees to provide sanctuary for them. Filipinos are sympathetic to refugees since these refugees were helpless as they felt threatened and had fears of possible conflicts, persecution and violence against them. Although the Philippines is a developing country thus its economy is modest, and despite being overwhelmed constantly with natural calamities (typhoons, floods, earthquakes, volcano eruptions, fires caused by thunder and lightning), compounded by insurgencies and political problems, these struggles do not even hinder the Philippines from welcoming displaced refugees into the country. Some tourists are taken aback when they ask Filipinos for directions with the Filipino bringing them to places of interest, or to teach them how native things are done, and the Filipinos go all the way to help them, yet when they are offered money for their assistance, most of the time, the Filipinos refuse the payment despite being poor and needy. Foreigners who have come to the Philippines to migrate, or simply as tourists, or have associations with Filipino immigrants living abroad, have discovered the hospitality and amiable manners of Filipinos. Filipinos, whether in the Philippines or abroad, <u>invite any caller,</u> be it a utility meter-reader or an acquaintance that shows up <u>at mealtime, to jointly dine with them</u>. Filipinos take their big-heartedness and open-handedness in a humble way, as if it is immaterial, yet they are naturally and intuitively hooked into their hospitable ways and goodwill assistance to others. Filipinos take the high road with resilience and fortitude, and **not** go down to the level of weakness and wickedness when they are targeted for racial discrimination and bigotry abroad. The following enumerated topics are the humanitarian deeds that the Philippines have been extending to helpless refugees.

Spanish Republicans: During the Spanish Civil War that began in 1936, General Francisco Franco, the head of the Nationalist movement, cracked down on the Republicans forcing the Spanish Republicans to flee to avoid incarceration and death. The first Filipino president during the American regime, President Manuel L. Quezon, provided asylum in the Philippines to the Spanish Republicans with his November 10, 1937 declaration that stated, "<u>The Philippines has no reason to take sides, and our interest must be limited only to see peace be reestablished in Spain</u>". The Americans, Filipinos, loyalists to the Spanish Republic, the Catholic Church, and the Spanish community in the Philippines supported his statement.

Jewish Refugees Who Fled the Holocaust: This was a time when other countries refused admission to the Jewish refugees, and the only country that opened its door to them was the Philippines. President Manuel L. Quezon had compassion for the Jews who were being persecuted by the Nazis in Europe, that he opened his welcoming arms to the first 1,200 Jews who came to seek refuge in the Philippines in September 8, 1937. President Quezon even had his 7-½ hectares Marikina property donated as a dwelling place and working farms for the Jewish refugees to avail themselves of. President Quezon stated that "It is my hope and indeed my expectation that the people of the Philippines will have in the future every reason to be glad that when the time of need came, their country was willing to extend a hand of welcome." He also offered to welcome as many as 30,000 Jews to come and take refuge in the Philippines. However, only an estimated 10,000 Jewish refugees were expected to arrive. Unfortunately, with the outbreak of the Pacific War in December 1941, this prevented those 10,000 to make the voyage to the Philippines. The Jewish refugees who were already in the Philippines discovered that the Philippines was a safe haven for them because of the graciousness and unconditional comradeship that they received from the Filipinos. They were also able to freely practice their Jewish religion sans fear and restraints. The Jew's heartfelt gratitude to the Filipinos are illustrated in the film documentary "An Open Door: Jewish Rescue in the Philippines" by Noel Izon, "Rescue in the Philippines" by Ross Hodge, and in Frank Ephraim's biography titled "Escape to Manila: From Nazi Tyranny to Japanese Terror." In 2009, the Jewish people put up a monument at the Holocaust Park in Rishon Lezion, Israel to give tribute to their one-time shelter and refuge, the Philippines.

Residents of the British Colony of Hongkong were given a benevolent reception by President Manuel L. Quezon when they fled to the Philippines due to the invasion of the Imperial Japanese. President Quezon had a heart for the oppressed and valued human life, prompting him to sign the Commonwealth Act 613 titled The Philippine Immigration Act of 1940 that stated "For humanitarian reasons, and when not opposed to the public interest, the President has the power to admit aliens who are refugees for religious, political, or racial reasons, in such classes of cases and under such conditions as he may prescribe."

Kuomintang Refugees: After the Chinese Civil War, the Kuomintang members or Nationalist Party of China who opposed the communist People's Republic of China, sought refuge in other countries. The Kuomintangs or KMT (also called Guomindang/GMD) was founded by Sun Yat-sen and after his death, was controlled by Chiang Kai-shek. The KMT refugees fled from China in 1949 and the Philippines welcomed them purposefully "for religious, political or racial reasons." Since in that year 1949, the Philippines already gained its full sovereignty and independence, its constitution allowed naturalization of Chinese immigrants, and the Philippine-born children of these naturalized immigrants were now considered Filipino citizens. Being innately business-minded, the Kuomintang members found prosperity in the Philippines.

White Russian Refugees: The White Russians did not only consist of ethnic Russians but also other ethnic groups, yet they were culturally Russian and Russian-speaking people. They were anti-Soviet and anti-Bolshevik forces. When the Bolshevik Red Army was launched, the White Russians, being opposed to communism, feared persecution so they fled to China in 1922. However in 1948, the communist party under Mao Tse Tung took control of China, that it made the White Russians fear that they would be returned to Russia by force similar to the case of 40,000 White Russian Cossacks who were repatriated to Russia only to be killed or sent to work at labor camps. So the leader of the White Russians launched an appeal to the United Nations and to the International Refugees Organization (IRO), even to all the countries in the free world to provide international accommodation and protection to the White Russians. However, the only country that responded and accepted the refugees was the Philippines under President Elpidio Quirino, a humanitarian act that was not made known and kept from the knowledge of the world because the Philippines was considered a very poor country – something that the peaceful and charitable Filipinos do not mind at all after learning currently that the Philippine kindly act was ignored and disregarded, because Filipinos came to know the experiences that the White Russians underwent like being considered social outcasts in some European countries despite some of these refugees were wealthy, professionals, and a few even came from aristocratic families; and Filipinos also learned that the White Russians also underwent severe problems that brought them to poverty in China and Hong Kong due to the White Russians' not being able to find jobs because they could not speak Chinese.

President Quirino offered Tubabao Island as the White Russians' place of refuge. Tubabao was an almost uninhabited island in Samar except for a few Filipino fishermen living by the shores. This island was a former US naval base that was connected to Guiuan by a 515 feet-long bridge. However, when the first batch of these refugees arrived in Tubabao, the old facilities used by the US navy were now dilapidated and the mechanical domestic equipments were no longer functioning due to exposure to the elements and due to rains and typhoons that beset the island. As the White Russians continued to arrive totaling to almost 6,000, the skilled and the professionals among them embarked on shift-by-shift work schedules in putting up tents for their dwellings, a water system, electricity, schools, a hospital, a cemetery, and many more since the UN High Commissioner for Refugees (UNHCR) were also providing help to them. When President Quirino visited them, he noticed the barbed wire fence that surrounded the refugees' community, so Quirino had those removed at once, bringing a sigh of relief to the refugees. President Quirino's statement of "We believe that freedom engenders responsibility, and this responsibility involves a solemn obligation to humanity" was much appreciated by the UN and the refugees.

For the White Russians' fun and pleasure, they paid attention to the beautiful surroundings of land, sea, fragrant flowers and coconut trees in their surroundings; went for swimming daily; enjoyed the sunrise, sunset, and moonlight; held parties, staged entertainment shows, art exhibits and poetry-reading. Besides the professionals and manual laborers among them, there were also painters, musicians, and ballet dancers. They befriended the family of a Filipino doctor who would invite them to parties in this doctor's home in Guiuan. Because the White Russians sang as a choir in a Catholic church in Guiuan, they were allowed to hold their

Russian Orthodox religious services in that church. The refugees then taught the Filipinos in Guiuan to play the piano and danced the ballet. The kids of the refugees enjoyed their stay in Tubabao, but the climate was unbearable for the adults. Besides the very hot weather, the typhoons that occasionally beset the island was tough and challenging to the refugees because one strong typhoon was able to destroy their dwellings including the comfortable amenities that they created. Through the efforts of US Senator William Knowland and Bishop Vladyka John Maximovitch, the Displaced Persons Act was amended, so half of the White Russian refugees were admitted to the USA, 1,500 went to Australia and hundreds went to different countries in South America. By the end of 1951, 210 remained in the camp as they were elderly and TB patients, and by 1953, the rest of the White Russians left Tubabao. The White Russians lived in the Philippines for four years, which was labeled as "Tiempo Ruso."

Vietnamese "Boat People": The Vietnamese who supported the South Vietnam government and the American allies had apprehensions that there would be counterattacks against them. So they fled by boarding boats that were drifting aimlessly at sea until some of these boats were washed on Philippine shores. The Filipinos rescued and welcomed them into their country. From the Filipinos' goodness of their hearts and their caring attitude towards fellow Asians, the Philippine government provided shelters to these thousands of Vietnamese "boat people." While some other Asian countries resolutely refused permanent settlement for these Vietnamese "boat people" for fear that it would result into more and continuous arrival of these refugees into their country, the Philippines on the other hand, took the humanitarian consideration towards them. Despite the Philippines being a young country and still developing after World War II and after just having been liberated from 400 years of foreign rules, it allowed the Vietnamese asylum seekers to settle in the country. In 1975 to 1995, the UN High Commissioner for Refugees (UNHCR) helped the Philippines since the Philippine economy could not afford to care for all the Vietnamese refugees for such a long time. Besides the United Nations' aid, the Catholic Bishop Conference of the Philippines also provided benevolent and compassionate assistance to them. The Vietnamese "boat people" were given accommodations in Ulugan Bay and Tara Island in Palawan where restaurants, Christian chapels, Buddhist/Hindu temples, children's playgrounds were put up for the refugees' religious and daily needs. The fully equipped centers were used to prepare them to get to their ultimate destinations such as the USA. Even at the end of 1996, some 3,000 refugees were still allowed settlements in the Philippines.

Iranians Refugees: The 1979 Iranian Revolution also known as Islamic Revolution overthrew Mohammad Reza Shah Pahlavi (who had the USA support) and was replaced by the Islamic republic under Grand Ayatollah Khomeini. The thousands of Iranians studying and working in Manila were advised by people in Iran to remain in the Philippines since a new administration was now governing Iran. However, tensions broke out because the students held, among themselves, differences of loyalty and alliance to the different blocs of the revolution. The Philippine government then warned the Iranian students of deportation if they commit any criminal act, so fighting was fended off and quashed. Some of these Iranians chose to stay in the Philippines by either assimilating with the local Muslim community, or seek Philippine citizenship, or get married to Filipinos.

Indo-Chinese: During the early part of the Vietnam War, the Philippines sent 50 volunteer doctors, agriculturist and nutritionists to Laos and Vietnam. But from 1980 to 1994, refugees from Laos, Cambodia and Vietnam escaped from their countries due to changes in their governments. The UN High Commissioner for Refugees (UNHCR) worked with the Philippine government to accommodate and prepare these refugees for their future relocations, like learning the English language and other educational curriculums. The Philippine Refugee Processing Center was opened in Morong, Bataan to provide housing to 400,000 Indo-Chinese refugees while they were awaiting to get into the US, Canada, and Australia.

East Timorese: In 2000, 600 East Timor refugees took temporary protection in the Philippines as they struggled for independence from Indonesia. The Philippine government and the Catholic Church raised

$200,000 when they launched a fundraising program for the support of the East Timorese refugees. After 2001 when peace was restored, the refugees were returned back to East Timor.

The Philippines Provided Assistance during the Korean War, the Vietnam War, the Persian Gulf War, and the Iraq War

Despite the Philippines having become an independent and self-governing country, it still maintained a strong alliance with their one time ruler, the USA. And this is evident on the Philippines' support of the USA's military missions in other countries.

Korean War: the Philippines sent expeditionary forces of 7,500 combat troops to Korea, to defend, along with the USA, South Korea from the communist invasion by the North Korean army. The Philippine troops were in the war front fighting for South Korea from 1950 to 1953 that consequently, a number of Filipino lives were lost.

Vietnam War: In 1964 to 1969, Filipino soldiers served in the Vietnam War with 182 officers and 1,882 enlisted troops, and unfortunately, some Filipino lives were likewise lost.

Persian Gulf War: In 1990 to 1991, the Philippines' 200 medical personnel were in the Middle East to help the coalition forces.

Iraq War: In 2003 to 2004, the Philippines sent 60 medical workers, engineers and troops to assist during the Iraq War. However a Filipino was kidnapped and after the demands of the insurgents were met to free the Filipino hostage, the Filipino troops had to withdraw from the Iraq war.

Several Filipino Winners in International Beauty Pageants

Filipinos have frequently won the crowns or the coveted titles in several International Beauty Pageant as far back as the inception of these contests. Filipinos do have the unique Asian, Malayan and Polynesian beauty, but also take into consideration the fact that more than half of the Filipino population had their genealogy intermixed with other races such as the foreign invaders that colonized the Philippines, not to mention other Asians that settled in the Philippines. The ethnicities that merged into the Filipino DNA were the Spanish, Chinese, Indian, American, and a few European genes. Filipino ladies do not put on heavy make-up and they are not into botox and cosmetic surgeries, unlike several other races. Filipinas are beautiful inside and out that this could be one reason why they keep winning in international beauty contests.

In 2018, the Miss Philippines contestant, Catriona Gray, won the Miss Universe crown. The year 2017 was a significant year because a number of Filipino contestants garnered the coveted crowns of international beauty contests. These were Karen Ibasco who won the 2017 Miss Earth crown, Sarah Christine Bona won the 2017 Miss Nature Intercontinental, Mary Grace Jedaver Pancho Opingo won the 2017 Miss Progress Internatonal, Beatrice Andrada won the 2017 Miss Pacific World, Teresita "Winwyn" Marquez won the 2017 Reina Hispano-Americana, Diosem Lleyd Budios won the 2017 Teen World Tourism, Kathleen Patton won the 2017 Miss Teen International, Shirleen Espinosa won 2017 Princess of the World, and Agnes Jakosalem won the 2017 Mrs. Grandma Universe. As for **2016**, Filipino winners were Kylie Verzosa who won the 2016 Miss International crown, Trixia Marie Maraña won the 2016 Miss Asia Beauty Contest, Christine Picardal won the 2016 Miss Diamond in the World, Jeslyn Santos won the Miss United Continents, Andrea Biondo won the 2016 Mr. Southeast Asia International crown and 2nd runner-up on the 2016 Mr. Universal Ambassador, Karan Singhdole won the 2016 Man of the Year title, and Hidilyn Diaz was the first female athlete to win the 2016 Olympic Weighlifting Contest.

Several Filipinas have won the coveted beauty crowns throughout the years, but other Filipinas also placed in the top 3 runner-ups, or the top 5 finalists, or the top 10 semi-finalists. There are many world beauty pageants - well-known and not too well-publicized world beauty contests, and Filipinas won in several of those beauty contests. **I will name only the Filipinas who won the coveted crown or title in chronological order, and only on the more well-known and more recognized world beauty pageants**

in the following listings. They are Catriona Gray-Miss Universe Beauty Pageant 2018, Pia Wurtzbach-Miss Universe 2015, Angela Ong-Miss Earth 2015, Ludwina Nacionales-Miss Asia International 2015, Ann Colis-Miss Globe 2015, Jamie Herrel-Miss Earth-2014, Megan Young-Miss World 2013, Bea Santiago-Miss International-2013, Christine Kan-Miss Asia USA 2012, Carl Crystie de los Reyes-Miss Southeast Asia 2010, Ariana Manibog-Miss Asia USA 2010, April Love Jordan-Beauty of the World 2009, Geramie Dizon-Miss Asia USA 2009, Karla Henry-Miss Earth 2008, Lara Quigaman-Miss International 2005, Jhezarie Javier-Miss Asean 2005, Joanna Paula Abinuman-Miss Global Queen 2005, Ronalyn Ancheta-Miss Young International 2002, Maricar Balagtas-Miss Globe International 2001, Feilani Bennet-Miss Asia USA 2001, Angelina Macaulay-Miss Asia USA 2000, Maria Asuncion Lopez-Miss Southeast Asia 1998, Karen Borja-Miss Asia USA 1998, Jamie Santiago-Miss Asia USA 1996, Cheryl Nuñez-Miss Asia USA 1995, Amelia Joy dela Cruz-Miss Southeast Asia 1993, Michelle Aldana-Miss Asia Pacific-1993, Gemma Hipolito-Miss Asia USA 1992, Lorna Santos-Miss Globe International 1992, Marianne Anicoche-Miss Asean 1990, Lorna Legaspi-Miss Asia Pacific 1989, Katrina Barrientos-Miss Globe International 1989, Gloria Dimayacyac-Miss Asia Pacific 1983, Maria Zaragoza-Miss Asia Pacific 1982, Melanie Marquez-Miss International 1979, Margarita Moran-Miss Universe 1973, Nelia Sancho-Queen of the Pacific 1971, Aurora Pijuan-Miss International 1970, Gloria Diaz-Miss Universe 1969, Pita Santiago-Queen of the Pacific 1968.

The Designated Government Executives and Elected Political Leaders Can Be the Living Heroes and Role Models That The Philippines Is Looking For

The Philippines had heroes in the past - let there be heroes in this present age. Anyone who clings to moral and ethical values and consistently and resolutely carries these out in his/her life is a hero and a great role model. The Philippines is looking for **someone serving the country** and doing the work with dignity, integrity, noble values, indisputable honesty and credibility who brings assistance, succor, accomplishments, developments, growth, and progress to his area of responsibility (town, city, province, region, or the entire Philippine archipelago), rendering and presenting such deeds and attributes that exemplify both as a hero and a great role model.

Fundamentally, it is an injunction that government and political leaders are obligated, duty-bound, responsible and accountable to serve their designated territory, bringing widespread assistance, subsidy, service, peace, knowledge, and success in the entire Philippines or in their area of responsibility. Filipino citizens expect senators, congressmen, governors, mayors, vice mayors, councilors, and their office staff to work diligently, exigently, efficiently, productively and patriotically, which the job absolutely requires and calls for. There is a need for government and political leaders to prove their allegiance to their country and to their countrymen whose taxes pay the wages of government and political leaders. These leaders need to render and present **real** evidence of constructive and useful accomplishments that they **truly had accomplished** as these are what they are paid for during their entire term in office.

There are numerous hard-working and upright government and political leaders that the country is proud of and grateful for, on account of their honest efforts to provide, first and foremost, for the best interest and the greatest benefits for the Philippines and its citizens. However, a great number of the country's leaders representing their towns, cities, provinces and regions all over the Philippines, not to mention leaders for the entire Philippine archipelago, do not seem to commensurate an equal, or proportionate, or corresponding input, results, and accomplishments from them. The country's leaders and even any Filipino citizen can do much, much better than that if they require more of themselves and raise the standards on themselves to the highest scale and give proof of the highly valuable and profitable fruits of their labors. So there is a call for leaders to avoid using their government positions for fame and vainglory mainly for themselves, let alone sense of entitlements that are merely self-serving. Government work was never meant to be *campante, mañana* habit or for *pasikat* or *pakitang tao lamang*.

It is hoped that leaders choose to get into government careers with the full knowledge that the job has an obligation to serve the country in the best and greatest way that they can, and **are truly determined** to do so. It is crucial to enforce **work ethic** from government executives and elected politicians, while selfish goals and unlawful deeds should be totally crushed and abolished. There is also a need for leaders to think outside the box to become constructively creative and able to establish lofty perspectives, dignified principles, and dynamic aspects, instead of relying on customary ways and old habits.

To be a hero and role model, a government and political leader has to be open-and-above-board honest to possess a beyond doubt credibility so that the citizens can trust this leader. Being a hero is working hard perseveringly for the best interest of the country and the countrymen. Being a role model is taking the high road with moral and ethical values and not go down to the level of unproductive ways, self-serving goals, corruption, and unlawful deeds.

Government leaders and elected politicians must resolve the country's problems and contribute gainful and beneficial accomplishments and rewarding impacts for the Philippines. On the Filipino citizens, these leaders must awaken a deep *bayanihan*-community feelings, support and work participations for the benefit and safety of the community. Government leaders and elected politicians must encourage communications - talks and written messages to get information from the town folks because they can be the eyes and ears of the assets, potentials, and needs of the locality. Hold meetings with the town folks that may be scheduled annually, or semi-annually, or quarterly to inform them of the needs of the country or the community, to announce policies, requirements and proposals, or even to get feedbacks from them. Ask local businesses to provide light snacks during those meetings as an advertisement of their business' products. Make community cleanliness a *bayanihan* duty with everyone doing their share of the work, like disposing their trash mainly in garbage containers, while never throwing their refuse and scraps anywhere else, but picking up thrash that are littered anywhere whether it is their own trash or somebody else's. Make them pick up the junk with gloves or with a piece of paper or plastic for sanitary and health purposes. Encourage schools, associations and churches to inspire this *bayanihan* cooperation among all citizens, young and old, among the association members and among churchgoers. Any good deed that people do would definitely make them happy for being a helpful member to their community. This would also make the country much more appealing where pleasant Filipinos live, and where clean, beautiful sceneries can be enjoyed.

Let government and political leaders educate adults and children about the dangers of drugs, alcohol, and tobacco addictions so that they avoid getting trapped throughout their lifetime into these damaging dilemmas. Encourage the folks to use their time productively and rewardingly, **not idling** where they can be persuaded to get into harmful and unlawful deeds like addictions, misdemeanors and felonies. Let the citizens 1] enhance their talents like singing, composing songs, sketching, drawing, painting, playing musical instruments, dancing, and cooking; or 2] utilize earnable skills that they may have like mending, darning, shortening or lengthening skirts and pants, cleaning houses or buildings, gardening, watering or mowing lawns, washing clothes, sewing clothes and even formal wears, carpentry, buying-and-selling goods, newspaper routes, hair cutting or curling, doing make-ups and hairdos for formal events, and cooking, by advertising these skills in simple printed or handwritten leaflets to hand out in public or stuck on walls or blackboards in community centers, schools, churches, agencies, clubs, etc.; or 3] get into health and safety activities like exercises, swimming, jogging, self-defense; and 4] human kindness acts like opening doors for seniors, the handicapped and tots, or carrying things for them, helping them cross the street safely; and many more. For those who **need the knowledge** of the mentioned talents, earnable skills, health and safety activities and human kindness acts, it would be very helpful for these citizens if political leaders can 4] set up **training sessions** for them to attend classes. Politicians and government leaders may ask schools, churches, local entrepreneurs and organizations to sponsor these training classes or even be the trainers or teachers themselves for these classes. Make training classes and meetings free for attendees, besides ensuring safety, peace and much learning for all.

There is also a need for leaders to make auspicious resolutions on jobs and wages in all government and private firms including foreign firms holding businesses in the Philippines, like raise the minimum wage in addition to other valuable decrees and proposals, so that Filipinos have no need to become OFWs (Overseas Filipino Workers) seeking jobs abroad. It is also necessary to totally wipe out graft and corruption within the government and in all private firms, including the foreign companies operating in the Philippines. Filipino leaders should also be wary of foreign companies that take advantage of the natural wealth and opportunities in the Philippines, then leave when the going gets rough abandoning Filipino employees empty-handed. Statutes and controls should be established to prevent such exploitation and unfairness.

The Filipino's strength, motivations and determination may have slumped when the Philippines was under foreign powers for almost 400 years, transforming them into becoming reticent, restrained, laid-back or *campante*. But it has **not** been 100 years yet since July 4, 1946 when the Philippines gained its sovereignty and became self-governing and independent from foreign powers. Thus, it is not yet too late to recover and revive the Filipino's strong willpower, aspirations, creativity, innovation, abilities, skills and talents in order to become one of the most productive and ingenious people in Asia (Please read #8 on page 57 under the Distinct Filipino Qualities, Customs and Mores topic.). 1] However, do not blame the foreign rulers for the Filipinos' losing their dynamism, passion, determination, backbone and productivity because that would only harden a citizen's proclivity to be unproductive and would make them repeat the same inclination again and again, impelling them to disregard their strongest and best capabilities and efforts. Let us always bear in mind that **our deeds and attitudes are our own responsibilities and we are accountable for them**. Instruct people to have responsibility, liability and the guts to accept their shortcomings in order to make great transformations in themselves. 2] **Awaken the Filipino's latent and untapped creativities, innovativeness, capabilities, abilities, skills, and talents** to use these in attaining great accomplishments. 3] **Encourage Filipinos to use their capital, their expertise and intelligence to explore and exploit the Philippines' rich natural resources and opportunities**, rather than leave those for foreigners to be the ones to take advantage of such Philippine assets and opportunities.

1] There is also a need to awaken **human kindness**. The Philippine Age of Consent Law was enacted with an established minimum age of merely 12 years old. It is shocking to know that such law was passed, allowing consensual sex on innocent and immature children when they are still too young, too childish, and too naïve to know what is good or bad for them. Passing this law seems to show lack of human kindness, insight and good judgment, besides being heartless, callous, and uncaring towards youngsters. Other countries in the world endorsed much older ages for this law, yet the Philippines is the **only country where the Age of Consent is in this bottom level - merely 12 years old - despite the Philippines' being a Catholic country**. So there is an urgent and justifiable **need to raise** the Age of Consent **to a much older age like 21** to turn this decree into a legitimate, responsible, considerate, ethical, moral, decent and judicious law. 2] Another case that has puzzled people is the adding of the word "State" on some educational institutions. 3] However, one thing that is disconcerting is the celebration of the Philippine Independence Day. **The true and accurate date is July 4, 1946 when the USA granted the Philippines its independence, which released the Philippines from foreign controls after almost 4 centuries of being ruled by foreign powers. From that date, July 4, 1946, the Philippines finally started to be independent and self-governing, and had sovereignty and supreme power over the entire Philippine archipelago.** Independence was not gained on June 12, 1898 when Emilio Aguinaldo declared it with him as the president because the USA was still legitimately authorized to oversee and govern the Philippines since Spain, after having been defeated by the USA, ceded the Philippines to the USA. Owing to the fact that the real and true Philippine Independence Day in 1946 has not yet reached a century, the Philippines can be considered as a very young nation. Therefore, so much can be implemented to make the Philippines develop as the advanced and productive Asian neighbors like China, Japan and Korea. Yet even for such a short time, the Philippines is now taking steps in pursuit of this goal.

When problems arise, those should be nipped in the bud, not ignored and allowed to continue without restraints and consequences, because such wrongdoings are repeated, prolonged and intensified at the expense of the country and its citizens. When there are no severe ramifications, such problems usually produce copycats that emulate lawbreakers, wrongdoers and criminals.

Filipinos are already being admired for their pleasant demeanors, so encourage them to maintain such pleasantness. Pat their backs for their big and small fine, favorable and helpful contributions - such admiration would make them maintain their good nature and good deeds.

Government executives and politicians would do themselves a great service if, for the sake of the country they serve, they would consider implementing beneficial proposals and useful projects and undertakings that would be a boon for the country. The world and the country need heroes and role models – may these be our Filipino leaders first and foremost.

Responsibilities of the Filipino Citizens

A citizen has a moral obligation to be a good citizen and live as a law-abiding person throughout his/her life. Another obligation which is quite easy and simple, without requiring too much effort but the payoff is immense since it is for everybody's best interest, is voting with their conscience. **They should cast their votes on the truthfully and reliably honest, trustworthy people who are morally, ethically and intellectually fit to make the right decisions, who work diligently and patriotically for the good of the country and their countrymen.** Filipino citizens should **not** blindly cast their votes on those who are simply their *kababayans* (of the same regions and same dialects as theirs), despite those *kababayans* having issues of dishonesty, graft and corruption, abuse of power, and other wrongdoings which obviously indicate the politicians' having **no** compassion, **no** remorse, **no** sense of guilt, **no** personal responsibility

82

and **no** self-accountability on their own misdeeds or their family/political clan's misdeeds.

It is hoped that Filipino citizens shed off their tolerance for politician's questionable activities, and instead **raise their expectations to a higher standard** - not and never accept nor get used to a politician's unproductive, negligent, or corrupt, opportunistic ways. Filipinos who are known in the world as amiable people, **must in the most peaceful way**, voice out and demand politicians to work harder and function with principles, with moral and ethical values, because that is what every human being ought to be and ought to do, and that is what politicians are paid for.

If candidates or their political clans have committed errors, they need to apologize and ask for forgiveness to prove and assure Filipino citizens and voters that they have realized their wrongdoings, and are now full of remorse and conscience-compunction - they should not abstain from this just because of their pride. They should convince voters that they **now truly** take full responsibility and self-accountability for all their guilts, and that they are now on the road to recompense for their past wrongdoings and even pledge sincerely to **now** perform mainly ethical, moral and patriotic deeds for the good of the country and the citizens, then truly and continuously **prove it**. Citizens should pray that they are now voting for the right candidate who would truly be an asset and a role model and a hero for the country.

HELPING YOU USE WHAT
THIS BOOK OFFERS

The previous pages of this book detailed the known and little known facts about the Philippines, its origins, its history, its people, and its assets. Now the grammar section is presented next and is simplified for easy learning using the root words section in this book. The dictionary section (that comes after the grammar section), has three divisions: the first one is English translated into two major Filipino dialects which are Tagalog and Ilocano; and then following that is another dictionary which is for the the root words of Tagalog and Ilocano, needed to configure nouns, verbs, adverbs, adjectives and past- present-future tenses through prefixes, infixes and suffixes (as exemplified in the grammar section); and the last dictionary is for the four additional Filipino dialects namely Bicolano, Cebuano, Ybanag and Gaddang dialects with their regional translations from English. In the first two dictionary divisions that translate English to Tagalog and Ilocano, the first dialect after English is Tagalog although it is not indicated since it is the Filipino national language, whereas the Ilocano dialect that follows Tagalog is indicated with an "Iloc:" abbreviation.

English in this book is the main language used for interpreting the six Filipino dialects. There are also English-derived Filipino words labeled as Taglish (Tagalog-English or Filipino-English) because these words have become parts of the Filipino language for the reason that they **either** supply the semantics that are missing in the Filipino vocabulary, **or** they have become part of the Filipino dialects that make communications clearer and more comprehensible among Filipinos who speak varied dialects. For emphasis, these Taglish words or English-derived Filipino words are written in *italics*.

English words in this dictionary are spelled correctly the English way, unlike the <u>Filipino Spanish-derived words which are spelled the Filipino way</u>. The reason for correct English spellings are 1) **to veer away from regression and retrogression**, as well as 2) to adhere to spellings that are acceptable to both the global community and to worldwide communications, interrelations and interconnection among countries, governments, businesses, commerce, education, science, and many more.

Filipino-Spanish words are indicated as *–Sp* to denote that these words are derived from Spanish. However, Spanish-derived Filipino words are spelled the Filipino way, except for proper nouns like Calle Real, Gigantes Sur or Norte, Joaquin Roxas, Zacarias Quezon, et al. Examples of **Filipinized spellings of Spanish words** are Filipino *embes* or *imbes* for the Spanish word en vez *(pronounced em vez),* Filipino *delata* for the Spanish de lata, *sige* for the Spanish sigue, *espongha* for Spanish esponja, *senyal* for Spanish señal, *viahe* for viaje, *pilyo* for pillo, *cuchilyo* for cuchillo, *engrande* for en grande, and many more. To be in sync with Filipino grammar, the English and Spanish words integrated into the Filipino language are used as root words whether the words are nouns, verbs, adjectives or adverbs and combined with either a prefix or a suffix (refer to succeeding topics titled Filipino-Spanish Words and Filipino-English Words in this book).

There are a few Filipino-Spanish words that are indicated in this dictionary as *–aSp* for **altered Spanish** due to the fact that such words 1) do not use all the Spanish meanings like *derecho* in Spanish is either "the right side" or "straight" or "straight ahead," but in Filipino it is merely "straight" and "straight ahead;" 2) or have a different meaning from Spanish like *engaño* meaning "to deceive" in Spanish, but in Filipino, it means "to encourage" or "to inspire;" and *seguro* meaning "sure" and "certain" in Spanish, but in Filipino, it means "probably"; or 3) have a different word construction like for "too much," it is *demasiado* in Spanish but simply *masiado* in Filipino; *cerrado* and *cerra* in Spanish and Ilocano, but in Tagalog, these are *sarado* and *sara* despite having similar meanings ("close" and "closed") in all three tongues - Spanish, Ilocano and Tagalog.

To make learning easy, here is a helpful guide for abbreviations and style formats in this book.

Meanings of Book Abbreviations

Abbreviations	Meanings
Iloc:	Ilocano word meaning
(Tag. & Iloc.)	Tagalog & Ilocano use the same words
Bic:	Bicolano
Ceb:	Cebuano
Ybg:	Ybanag
Gdg :	Gaddang
Italic words	English-derived Filipino words
-Sp	Spanish-derived Filipino words
-aSp	Altered Spanish-Filipino words
v.	verb
n.	noun
adj.	adjective
adv.	adverb
prep.	preposition

FILIPINO GRAMMAR

WHY THERE ARE NO STRICT RULES IN SPELLINGS OF FILIPINO WORDS

It is important to emphasize that Filipino writing has no restrictions on how a Filipino word is spelled as long as it is clear and understandable. There are two reasons for this: 1) the old deficient abakada which contained merely 20 alphabets had been amended into a fully complete alfabeto which now contains all the English alphabets plus the Spanish Ñ that necessitates the use of the entire alphabet consonants and vowels; and 2) there is a diversity of dialects spoken all over in the Philippines that regional pronunciations, inflections, intonations and accents are in variance from one dialect to another.

Therefore, the letter O can be interchanged with U,

→ the letter E can be interchanged with I,
→ the letter A can be interchanged with E,
→ the letter F can be interchanged with P,
→ C or Qu- can be interchanged with K,
→ B can be interchanged with V,
→ Z or C can be interchanged with S,
→ the letters Ja, Je, Ji, Jo, Ju can be interchanged with Dia, Die, Ji, Dio, Diu,
→ and the letters Tia, Tie, Tsi, Tio, Tiu can be interchanged with Cha, Che, Chi, Cho, Chu.

SPELLINGS and PRONUNCIATIONS

To reiterate the above paragraph, it is important to point out that **in** Filipino writings and texts, SPELLINGS VARY AND NOT STRICTLY FOLLOWED as long as these are clearly understood.

However, the Tagalog dialect has two very common words, **Ng** and **Mga**, that are intact and have been permanently spelled the same way from time immemorial to the present. It is therefore puzzling for non-Filipinos as far as pronouncing it or reading it. **Ng** and **Mga** are articles of a sentence or nominative adjectives that come before a noun, and the pronunciations for these are:

	Pronunciations	Translations
NG	Nang	The, A, An (singular)
Ng MGA or **Ang MGA**	**Nang Ma-nga** or **Ang Ma-nga**	The (plural)

When a <u>Filipino word</u> has the same spelling in English and Spanish (examples are chocolate, natural, debate, popular, tumor, etc.), **the pronunciation must be based on Spanish pronunciation** for the reason that Filipino and Spanish pronunciations are both pronounced and uttered in syllables.

Other Filipino words that have the same or almost the same spellings in English and Spanish that end with "**ble**" and **"ve"** are written **in this dictionary** as **"b–le"** and **"–ve"** since they are pronounced the Spanish way. Examples are comfortab-le, sua-ve, presentab-le, miserab-le, terib-le, posib-le, dob-le and responsab-le. However, please be informed that <u>these hyphenated spellings are</u> **<u>for this dictionary only and exclusively</u>** – *please do not put hyphenations on* FORMAL TEXTS/WRITINGS. **The hyphenations in this book are merely to stress the right pronunciation** which is Filipino-Spanish pronunciations.

All Filipino dialects are uttered in syllables like Spanish words, and they are **pronounced as they are written** or what you see is what you pronounce. **No syllable must be missed but must be pronounced individually**.

It is important to note that **every letter of the alphabet**, not just syllables, **must also be pronounced**. If there are double vowels like "aa", "oo", "ii", "ee" or "uu," **all these vowels must be pronounced individually**.

Pronunciations of such double vowels like "aa" are pronounced **a-a,** "ee" are pronounced **e-e,** and so on and so forth. Examples of such repeated vowels are b**ii**k, **oo,** tut**oo, aa**lis and so on (bi-ik, o-o, tu-to-o, a-a-lis).

The same is true with consonants – **if there are two similar consonants side-by-side, these are both pronounced emphatically** like "rr,' "gg," "tt," "nn," "bb," "dd," and so on. Words in Ilocano, Ybanag and Gaddang have a lot of these double consonants, while Tagalog words barely have them.

Pronunciations of such double consonants are the following:

Bb as in abbong is pronounced   = ab-bong
Nn as in bennek is pronounced   = ben-nek
Dd as in adda is pronounced   = ad-da
Pp as in uppat is pronounced   = up-pat
Ff as in affu is pronounced   = af-fu
Rr as in cerra is pronounced   = cer-ra
Gg as in inggagara is pronounced   = ing-gagara
Ss as in bassit is pronounced   = bas-sit
Kk as in dakkel is pronounced   = dak-kel
Tt as in itatta is pronounced   = itat-ta
Ll as in belleng is pronounced   = bel-leng
Ww as in towwato is pronounced   = tow-wato
Mm as in ummong is pronounced   = um-mong
Yy as in gayyem is pronounced   = gay-yem

The Filipino Spanish-derived digraph of a double L consonant has several pronunciations that in Argentina it is pronounced as SH, in Mexico, it is pronounced as Y, and in Spain, it is pronounced in two ways, as Y and ELYE. ELYE is how Filipinos pronounce the double L Spanish digraph, like calle (street) is pronounced and spelled calye by Filipinos, llave (key) is pronounced and spelled by Filipinos as liave, ballena (whale) is balyena, sello (stamp) is selyo, cuello (collar) is cuelyo, and tortilla is tortilya, which is scrambled eggs with diced potatoes and onions in both Spain and the Philippines, but is a different recipe in Hispanic countries. For names

89

with the Spanish double L digraph, Filipinos use the **correct spellings** like Villegas, Estrella, Bello, Agoncillo, etc., and similarly pronounced those with ELYE, (i.e., Villegas is pronounced as Vilyegas, Estrella is pronounced as Estrelya, Bello is pronounced as Belyo, Agoncillo is pronounced as Agoncilyo).

As in the Spanish language, the letter **V** in any Filipino dialect can either be pronounced as **v or b**. However, when pronouncing proper nouns like Violeta or Vivencio (people's names) or Vallle Vista (city name) or when uttering English words containing the consonant **V**, Filipinos pronounce the **V** correctly like the English **V** for "**victory**".

Filipino-Spanish Words

As I mentioned earlier, Spanish words incorporated into the Filipino language are used as root words combined with either a prefix or a suffix in congruity with the Filipino grammar (examples are *[Tag.]* mag-**viahe,** i-**despacha** or **despacha**hin, and *[Iloc.]* ag-**imbitar** or **imbitar**en, i-**correhir** or **correhir**en), and Filipino-Spanish words are spelled the way Filipinos spell them, not the way Spaniards grammatically spell them. Examples of these are -

> "H" in Filipino is pronounced the way <u>English pronounced "H"</u> like hello, happy and home, *not as a silent "H" as the Spaniards enunciate it.* Hence, the Spanish words "hijo" and "hija" are spelled as "iho" and "iha" in Filipino. However, names like Hernandez or Hermoso are pronounced with an "H" by Filipinos as the way they are spelled, not the way Spaniards pronounced it as "ernandez" or "ermoso".
>
> While "H" is silent or not uttered at all in Spanish, the Spaniards use "**G**" and "**J**" to take the place of "**H**". Examples of these are the following: Spanish spellings of "**g**eneral" and "**g**igante," are spelled in Filipino as

90

"heneral" and "higante." The same is true with Spanish spellings of "junio," "julio" and "caja" whereby Filipinos spell these as "Hunyo," "Hulyo" (both capitalized first letters for names of the months as in English) and "caha."

However, proper names particularly **people's names** with the letter "**G**" and "**J**" in them are pronounced by Filipinos **also as "H" similar to the Spanish pronunciations, and spell them similar to the Spanish spellings**. Examples are Gervacio, Gertrudis, Juan, Jovita, Evangelista, Jorge, Virgilio and Sergio (pronounced hervacio, hertrudis, huan, hovita, evanghelista, horhe, virhilio and serhio).

Since the Spanish-derived Filipino alphabet Ñ has been newly added into the Filipino alfabeto, most Filipinos may not know how to phonetically enunciate it, so when one writes ordinary words like piña (Spanish and Filipino word for pineapple) or muñeca (Spanish and Ilocano word for doll), it is spelled *pinya* or *munyeca* in Filipino. However, first names and last names abide by the Spanish spellings like Ibañez, Saldaña and Acuña.

The Spanish words that have "que-" and "qui-" are not used in Filipino words most of the time. The equivalence of the "-que-" and "-qui-" in Filipino are "**ke**" and "**ki**" both in enunciating and scripting (i.e., the Spanish "para **que**" is "para **ke**" in Filipino). However, if these are people's names, Filipinos both pronounce and write the "Qu-'s" **the way the Spaniards pronounce and spell them** like Quintana, Quezon, Quirino and Enrique (pronounced by Filipinos as kintana kezon, kirino and enrike just like the Spanish pronounciation).

Filipino-English Words

English is widely spoken in the Philippines and it is the Filipino's second language, next to Tagalog. The reason for this is 1) because with the diversity of Filipino dialects, either Tagalog or English is used as a means to communicate effectively that is understandable to all Filipinos, whatever regional dialects they speak; and 2) because there is a lack of word-equivalence in Filipino for some English words especially in the fields of commerce, medicine, and transnational terms. Besides that, some English words necessitate lengthy translations in Filipino to clearly interpret it, therefore it is easier to simply retain and use the single English word. However, in this dictionary, such Filipino lengthy translation is used to make the translation, interpretation and explanation clearer and more understandable.

As mentioned earlier, English words that are integrated into the Filipino dialects are used as root words combined with prefixes and suffixes (examples are mag-**type** *[Tag.]*, ag-**travel** *[Iloc.]*) as illustrated in the Tagalog and Ilocano grammar sections in this book. It is important to note that in this dictionary, the **English words** used in Filipino communications **are spelled correctly the way English words are accurately spelled,** unlike the Filipino-Spanish words in this book where Filipino spellings prevail. The reasons for firmly adhering to the correct English spellings are 1) **not to degenerate or fall backward into retrogression, regression and deterioration by misspelling the English words**, but to move forward into intellectual acceleration most especially when children are around who would benefit now and in the future from correct, true and right ways; and 2) to use English spellings that are recognizable and acceptable worldwide.

ARTICLES

"Ang" *(Tagalog)* or **"Ti"** *(Ilocano)* are Filipino nominative articles for the word **"THE"** *(singular)*.

In both Tagalog and Ilocano, **a person's name need a nominative article** unlike in English and Spanish where Peter or Jane would suffice. Below are examples of such format:

> – **"Si"** + name *(Tagalog)* and **"Ni"** + name *(Ilocano)* are nominative articles placed before the name of a <u>**Singular**</u> person being talked about, like **Si** Pedro *(Tagalog)* or **Ni** Juan *(Ilocano)*.

> – **"Sina"** + names of people *(Tagalog)* and **"Da"** + names of people *(Ilocano)* are <u>**Plural**</u> nominative articles, i.e., "<u>**Sina**</u> Gloria at Josefina" *(Tagalog)* and "**Da** Mariano ken Daniel" *(Ilocano)*.

LINKING VERBS

The linking verbs "Am", "Is" and "Are" are <u>**Ay**</u> in Tagalog and <u>**Ket**</u> or **Ti** or <u>**Ni**</u> in Ilocano. These linking verbs are **for both singular and plural** forms.

PREPOSITIONS

"Sa" *(Tagalog)* and **"Idiay"** *(Ilocano)* are used for prepositions "At", "In", "To", "Into," "From", "On", "Over", or "Through" which are used to indicate either position, location or time.

GENDER

The nominative article **"Siya"** *(Tagalog)* and **"Isu"** or **"Isuna"** *(Ilocano)* are the translations for **He** or **She** which are **for both masculine and feminine genders in Filipino**.

For the word male or masculine or boy, the Tagalog equivalence is "**lalake**" while in Ilocano, it is "**lalaki**." For the word female or feminine or girl, the Tagalog equivalence is "**babae**" while Ilocano is "**babai**."

PLURALIZE

Unlike in English and Spanish, **plural** words in Tagalog and Ilocano **stay in singular forms** without an "s" added at the end of the word. The articles or nominative adjectives "**Mga**", "**Ng mga**" or "**Ang mga**" are the ones used to pluralize Tagalog words (Mga, Ng Mga and Ang Mga are discussed earlier in this book to indicate how these words are pronounced and their meanings).

The pluralizing articles for Ilocano are "**Dagiti**" (the *[plural]*), "**Dagitoy**" (these), "**Dagita**" (those), "**Dagidiay**" (those *[further]*), "**Dagidi**" (those *[in the past]*) and "**Dagitay**" (those *[unseen]*).

POSSESSIVE PRONOUNS

Akin or Ko *(Tagalog)* or Cuac or Kucuak *(Ilocano)* means **My or Mine**

Niya or Canya *(Tagalog)* or Cuana or Kucuana or Canyana *(Ilocano)* means **His or Her**

Iyo or Mo *(Tagalog)* or Cuam or Mo *(Ilocano)* means **Your or Yours** (both *singular*)

Inyo or Ninyo *(Tagalog)* or Cuayo or Kucuayo *(Ilocano)* means **Your or Yours** *(plural forms)*

Atin or Natin *(Tagalog)* or Cuatayo or Kucuatayo *(Ilocano)* means **Our or Ours**

Nila or Kanila *(Tagalog)* or Cuada or Kucuada *(Ilocano)* means **Their or Theirs**

Ni *(Tagalog)* or Kenni *(Ilocano)* means **"owned by" or "the possession of"**

Nito *(Tagalog)* or Cuadaytoy *(Ilocano)* means "**of this**" [thing]

Niyan or Niyon *(Tagalog)* or Cuadayta or Cuadaydiay *(Ilocano)* means "**of that**" [thing]

NUMBERS: Counting and Telling the Time

All Filipino dialects have their own numbers or numerical terms, but because such terminologies are lengthy phrases, they are hardly used at all, so Filipino numbers higher than ten or twenty are ignored. As substitutes, the **English and Spanish numbers are commonly used in conversations and in writing**, like twelve, forty one, one hundred twenty, one thousand, or *kinse, veinte singko, treinta, singkuenta,* and so on. The same is true in **telling the time** of the day – the **English and Spanish time terminologies are also used**, like one o'clock, twelve noon, 6:00 a.m., or *ala una, alas dos, alas tres y media, menos dies para alas doce,* et al.

SENTENCE FORMATION

The standard sentence formation is Subject + Predicate. This is also used in Filipino grammars, but typically and customarily, Filipinos use the Predicate + Subject formation which is a REVERSION of the standard sentence formation and in which the linking verbs "Ay", "Ket", "Ti" and "Ni" (Am, Is and Are) are omitted. The following examples show the differences between the two sentence formations although they have the same meanings

Subject + Predicate	Predicate + Subject (*Commonly used by Filipinos*)

Tag.: Si Devon *ay* mabait   Mabait si Devon.
             Devon is good.

Iloc.: Da Boy ken Totoy *ket* ubbing.   Ubbing da Boy ken Totoy.
             Boy and Totoy are kids.

Iloc.: Ni Daniel *ket* intelihente.   Intelihente ni Daniel.
             Daniel is intelligent.

Tag.: Si Chelsea *ay* mahusay.   Mahusay si Chelsea.
             Chelsea is competent.

Iloc.: Ni Haley *ket* nadalimanek.   Nadalimanek ni Haley.
             Haley is neat and tidy.

Tag.: Ako *ay* si Donovan.   Si Donovan ako.
             I am Donovan.

Iloc.: Siac *ni* Dante.   Ni Dante-ac.
             I am Dante.

Tag.: Si Aubrie *ay* masipag.   Masipag si Aubrie
             Aubrie is diligent.

Iloc.: Da Ray ken Chino *ket* guapo.   Guapo da Ray ken Chino
             Ray and Chino are handsome.

Tag.: Si Claire *ay* namamahala.   Namamahala si Claire
             Claire is managing.

Iloc.: Ni Lauren *ket* nasingpet.   Nasingpet ni Lauren.
             Lauren is well-behaved.

TAGALOG GRAMMAR

TAGALOG AFFIXES

(Use the Root Words section in this book in addition to the affixes specified here to configure nouns, adjectitves, adverbs, verbs, and past, present, and future tenses)

FORMING NOUNS

Sometimes the root word is the NOUN itself
Ganda (beauty)
Bait (goodness)
Isip (thought)
Wika (language)
Samà (badness)
Tindig (posture, bearing)

Prefix KA- + root word + suffix –AN or -HAN to form a NOUN
Ka + ganda + han	=	kagandahan (beauty)
Ka + payapa + an	=	kapayapaan (peace)
Ka + rapat + an	=	karapatan (legal right)
Ka + sundo + an	=	kasundoan (agreement)
Ka + pangyari+ han	=	kapangyarihan (authority)
Ka + lagay + an	=	kalagayan (condition)
Ka + lugod + an	=	kalugudan (appreciation)

FORMING NOUNS THAT CAN ALSO BE ADJECTIVES

Prefix KA- + root word to denote SAME BOND OR FELLOWSHIP
Ka + bayan	=	kabayan (townsman or countryman)
Ka + trabaho	=	katrabaho (co-worker)
Ka + clase	=	kaclase (classmate)
Ka + sama	=	kasama (companion)

Prefix MAG- + root word to denote RELATIONSHIP

Mag + asawa	=	mag-asawa (married couple)
Mag + kapatid	=	magkapatid (siblings)
Mag + ama	=	mag-ama (father and child)
Mag + ina	=	mag-ina (mother and child)
Mag + kaibigan	=	magkaibigan (are friends)

Prefix MAG- + first syllable of the root word + root word to denote RELATIONSHIPS (more than two)

Mag + a + ama	=	mag-aama (father & children)
Mag + i + ina	=	mag-iina (mother & children)
Mag + ka + kaibigan	=	magkakaibigan (3 or more friends)

Prefixes MA- or MAN- or MANG- + the first syllable of the root word + root word to indicate OCCUPATION OR LIVELIHOOD

Mag + sa + saka	=	magsasaka (farmer)
Mang-ga + gamut	=	manggagamot (physician)
Man + du + rucot	=	mandurocot (thief, pickpocket)
Man + lo + loco	=	manloloco (con man, swindler)

Prefixes PAG- + root word + AN or NAN or HAN to denote a place or location

Pag + tulog + an	=	sleeping place
Pag + daan + an	=	place to walk
Pag + pasial + an	=	a place to take a stroll
Pag + kuha + nan	=	a place to get something
Pag + bili + han	=	a place to buy things
Pag + trabaho + an	=	a workplace

Prefixes PAG- + root word + AN to denote a function or use

Pag + luto + an	=	something to cook on
Pag + batay + an	=	something to stand on
Pag + sulat + an	=	something to write on

Prefixes TAGA- or TAGAPAG- + root word or location to denote ASSIGNED WORK

Taga + luto	=	tagaluto (cook, chef)
Taga + alaga	=	tagaalaga (caregiver, babysitter)

FORMING ADJECTIVES

Prefix MA- + root word to denote an ASPECT

Ma + ganda	=	maganda (beautiful)
Ma + saya	=	masaya (happy)
Ma + lakas	=	malakas (strong)
Ma + bunga	=	mabunga (fruitful)
Ma + bunganga	=	mabunganga (talkative)

Prefix NAKA- + root word to indicate an APPEARANCE

Naka + upo	=	nakaupo (sitting, seated)
Naka + bigote	=	nakabigote (bearded)
Naka + alahas	=	nakaalahas (wearing jewelry)
Naka + tirintas	=	nakatirintas (has braided hair)
Naka + hilera	=	nakahilera (in a row)

Prefix NAPAKA- + root word to mean "VERY"

Napaka + ganda	=	napakaganda (very beautiful)
Napaka + bilis	=	napakabilis (very fast)
Napaka + bagal	=	napakabagal (very slow)

Prefix PINAKA- + formed word to denote a SUPERLATIVE DEGREE

Pinaka + mabuti	=	pinakamabuti (the best)
Pinaka + mahusay	=	pinakamahusay (best)
Pinaka + masama	=	pinakamasama (the worst)
Pinaka + Masaya	=	pinakamasaya (happiest)
Pinaka + intelihente	=	pinakaintelihente (most intelligent)

Prefixes TAGA- or TAGAPAG- + root word or location to either denote ASSIGNED WORK OR PLACE OF ORIGIN

Taga + luto	=	tagaluto (cook, chef)
Taga + alaga	=	tagaalaga (caregiver, babysitter)
Tagapag + alaga	=	tagapag-alaga (caregiver, babysitter)
Taga + Filipinas	=	taga-Filipinas (from the Phil.)
Taga + rito	=	tagarito (from here)

The words ANG or KAY + root word to denote an ATTRIBUTE of a HIGH DEGREE

Ang + buti	=	Ang buti (How good)
Kay + buti	=	Kay buti (How good)
Ang + laki	=	Ang laki (How big)
Kay + laki	=	Kay laki (How big)
Ang + liit	=	Ang liit (How small)
Kay + lamig	=	Kay lamig (How cold)

Prefixes PANG- or PAN- (+ consonants except G, B and P) and PAM- (before B or P) to denote a PURPOSE

Pang + umaga	=	pang-umaga (for morning use or breakfast)
Pang + gabi	=	panggabi (supper or for night use)
Pang + oficina	=	pang-oficina (for office use or office wear)
Pan + tasa	=	pantasa (sharpener)
Pam + **B**alot	=	pambalot (for wrapping)
Pam + **P**alambot	=	pampalambot (for making something soft)

Prefix MAKA- + root word to denote a LEANING

Maka + Dios	=	maka-Dios (godly person)
Maka + baya	=	makabayan (patriotic)
Maka + UP	=	maka-UP (root for the Univ. of the Phil. Team)

Prefix MAKA- or MAKAPA + root word to denote CAPABILITY

Maka + tulong	=	makatulong (can help)
Makapa + tulog	=	makapatulog (can make one sleep)
Maka + buti	=	makabuti (beneficial)
Maka + lakad	=	makalakad (can walk)

Prefix NAKAKA- + root word to denote CAPABILITY

Nakaka + tayo	=	nakakatayo (can stand)
Nakaka + sira	=	nakakasira (destructive)
Nakaka + sugat	=	nakakasugat (injurious)
Nakaka + intindi	=	nakakaintindi (can understand)

Prefix NAKAKA- + root word to generate a REACTION or EFFECT

Nakaka + tawa	=	nakakatawa (laughable)
Nakaka + tuwa	=	nakakatuwa (amusing)
Nakaka + consuelo	=	nakakaconsuelo (soothing)

Prefixes MAPAG- or PALA- + root word to indicate a HABITUAL INCLINATION

Pala + simba	=	palasimba (constant churchgoer)
Pala + biro	=	palabiro (constant joker)
Pala + tawa	=	palatawa (laughs quite often)
Mapag + mahal	=	mapagmahal (affectionate)
Mapag + inom	=	mapag-inom (drinks often)
Mapag + kunwari	=	mapagkunwari (pretentious)
Mapag + linlang	=	mapaglinlang (con man, swindler)

Prefix PA- + root word or location to denote SHAPE, DIRECTION, DESTINATION or an ACTION

Pa + bilog	=	pabilog (round)
Pa + canan	=	pacanan (towards the right)
Pa + hintulot	=	pahintulot (give permission)
Pa + America	=	pa-America (bound for the USA)
Pa + baba	=	pababa (downward)

Prefix PA- + root word + *Suffix* -IN or -HIN to mean TO MAKE

Pa + bilog + in	=	pabilogin (to make it round)
Pa + ganda + hin	=	pagandahin (to make it beautiful)
Pa + aral + in	=	paaralin (to make one learn in school)
Pa + lago + hin	=	palagohin (to make it flourishing)

Prefix MAG- + root word + *suffix* -AN to mean DO SOME- THING TOGETHER or DO TO EACH OTHER

Mag + tulong + an	=	magtulongan (help together/each other)
Mag + paumanhin + an	=	magpaumanhinan (excuse each other)
Mag + sulat + an	=	magsulatan (write each other)

Prefix IPA- + root word to mean HAVE IT DONE

Ipa + linis	=	ipalinis (have it cleaned)
Ipa + ayos	=	ipaayos (have it fixed or repaired)
Ipa + gamit	=	ipagamit (let it be used)
Ipa + laki	=	ipalaki (enlarge it, have it enlarged)
Ipa + ubos	=	ipaubos (have it all consumed)
Ipa + alam	=	ipaalam (make it known)
Ipa + alaala	=	ipaalaala (make one remember)

Prefix I- + root word to INITIATE AN ACTION

I + tago	=	itago (keep)
I + tabi	=	itabi (put it aside)
I + bilad	=	ibilad (dry it under the sun)
I + turo	=	ituro (teach it or point it out)

FORMING ADVERBS

Time Adverbs

Ngayong araw na ito	=	today
Bukas	=	tomorrow
Kahapon	=	yesterday
Ngayong umaga	=	this morning
Ngayong hapon	=	this afternoon
Ngayong gabi	=	tonight, this evening
Kagabi	=	last night
Nakaraang lingo	=	last week
Nakaraang buwan	=	last month

Nakaraang taon	=	last year
Sa susunod na lingo	=	next week
Noong nakaraan	=	in the past
Ngayon	=	now
Mamaya	=	later
Kamakailan lamang	=	recently
Kani-kanina lamang	=	just a while ago
Itong nakaraan	=	lately
Sa madaling panahon	=	soon
Kaagad-agad	=	immediately
Ngayon-ngayon na	=	right now

Location Adverbs

Dito, Rito	=	here
Doon, Roon	=	there
Diyan	=	at that place
Sa tabi	=	beside the
Sa lahat ng lugar	=	everywhere
Kahit saang lugar	=	anywhere

Frequency Adverbs

Minsan, Isang beses	=	once
Dalawang beses	=	twice
Tuwina, Firmi	=	always
Palagi, Parati, Malimit	=	often
Kung minsan	=	sometimes
Caraniwan	=	usually
Bihira, Paminsan-minsan	=	seldom
Madalang	=	rarely
Hindi man lang	=	not at all
Hindi kahit kelan	=	never
Pabugso-bugso	=	sporadic
Sunod-sunod	=	successive

Prefix NA- or NAN + root word to denote LOCATION

Na + rito	=	narito (here, in here)
Nan + dito	=	nandito (here, in here)
Na + riyan	=	nariyan (over there)
Nan + diyan	=	nandiyan (over there)

Prefix PAGKA- + root word to indicate TIME of an action

Pagka + kain	=	pagkakain (after eating)
Pagka + tapos	=	pagkatapos (after finishing)
Pagka + basa	=	pagkabasa (after reading)

Prefix KA- + the first syllable of the root word + root word + lamang to denote RECENT TIME of activity

Ka + ra + rating + lamang	=	kararating lamang (just arrived)
Ka + tu + tulog + lamang	=	katutulog lamang (just slept)
Ka + la + lagay + lamang	=	kalalagay lamang (just placed it)

FORMING VERBS TO FORM FUTURE, PRESENT, AND PAST TENSES

Tagalog Tenses

1. **Future** tense uses the *prefix* **MAG-**; while **Present** tense & **Past** tense use the *prefix* **NAG-**; but in both the Future and Present Tenses, the first syllable of the root word is ALWAYS REPEATED

Root	Future	Present	Past
Salita	*mag*sasalita	*nag*sasalita	*nag*salita
Bigay	*mag*bibigay	*nag*bibigay	*nag*bigay
Aral	*mag*-aaral	*nag*-aaral	*nag*-aral

(Salita-speak, say; Bigay-give; Aral-study)

2. **Future** tense and **Present** tense have the following two ways of communications:

Root	Future	Present	Past
Basa	magbabasa	*nagbabasa*	nagbasa
		bumabasa	
Gawa	gagawin	*ginagawa*	ginawa
		gumagawa	
Tapos	*tataposin*	tinatapos	tinapos
		magtatapos	
Ayos	*aayosin*	*nag-aayos*	inayos
		mag-aayos	
		inaayos	

(Basa-read; Gawa-do, make; Tapos-end/finish; Ayos-repair, fix/tidy)

3. **FUTURE TENSE:** *Prefix* **MAG- + 1ˢᵗ syllable of the root word + root word**

Mag + sa + sayaw   =   magsasayaw (to dance)
Mag + la + lakbay   =   maglalakbay (to travel)

4. **PRESENT TENSE AND PAST TENSE use the** *affix* **-IN- within the root word while the** *suffix* **–AN or -HAN is used at the end of all tenses:**

Root	Future	Present	Past
Bukas	bubuks**an**	b**in**ubuks**an**	b**in**uks**an**
Sara	sasar**han**	s**in**asar**han**	s**in**ar**han**
Sama	sasama**han**	s**in**asama**han**	s**in**ama**han**

(Bukas-open; Sara-close; Sama-accompany, go with)

5. **PRESENT TENSE:** *Prefix* **NAG- + 1ˢᵗ syllable of the root word + root word**

Nag + i + isip   =   nag-iisip (thinking)
Nag + pa + pahinga   =   nagpapahinga (resting)

6. **PRESENT** TENSE AND **PAST** TENSE using the *infix* -UM- within the word:

Root	Future	Present	Past
Kain	kakain	k*um*akain	k*um*ain
Pasok	papasok	p*um*apasok	p*um*asok
Kuha	kukuha	k*um*ukuha	k*um*uha
Punta	pupunta	p*um*upunta	p*um*unta
Hingi	hihingi	h*um*ihingi	h*um*ingi
Tulong	tutulong	t*um*utulong	t*um*ulong
Sacay	sasacay	s*um*asacay	s*um*acay
Tawag	tatawag	t*um*atawag	t*um*awag
Tingin	titingin	t*um*itingin	t*um*ingin
Sulat	susulat	s*um*usulat	s*um*ulat
Galaw	gagalaw	g*um*agalaw	g*um*alaw

(Kain-eat; Pasok-enter; Kuha-get; Punta-go, Hingi-ask for; Tulong-help; Sacay-ride; Tawag-call; Tingin-see; Sulat-write; Galaw-move, act)

7. **PRESENT TENSE:** *Affix* -UM- + **1ˢᵗ syllable of the root word + root word, or** *Infix* -UM- or -IN- **within the root word + root word**

Um + a (1ˢᵗ syllable of root word) + awit	=	umaawit (singing)
Um + u + upo	=	umuupo (sitting)
D + um + a + dating	=	dumadating (arriving)
B + um + u + buti	=	bumubuti (improving)
B + in + i + bigay	=	binibigay (giving)
S + in + a + samba	=	sinasamba (worshipping)

8. **PAST TENSE:** *Infix* -IN- or -UM- **within the root word + root word, and** *Prefix* NAG- + root word

Kasal (marry) K + **in** + asal	=	kinasal (got married)
Tindi (intense) T + **um** + indi	=	tumindi (got more intense)
Bagyo (storm) B + **um** + agyo	=	bumagyo (stormed)

9. <u>**PAST TENSE:** *Prefix* **NA- + root word**</u>

Na + wala	=	nawala (lost)
Na + tapos	=	natapos (finished)
Na + ligo	=	naligo (bathed)
Na + tulog	=	natulog (slept)

10. <u>**More on Tenses**</u>

Maging	=	become, becoming
Naging	=	became
Magiging	=	will become

TAGALOG POSTPOSITIVES

<u>Note</u>: The following sentences use the usual <u>Filipino</u> <u>sentence-formation</u> which is Predicate + Subject.

Postpositive AKO or KO for "I"

Nagbabasa *ako*	=	I am reading
Ilalagay *ko*	=	I will put it
Ipapaalam *ko*	=	I will inform
Mag-aral *ako*	=	I study
Ayaw *ko*	=	I don't like

Postpositives MO or KA for you-*singular* and NIYA or SIYA (*singular*) for he/she, and NIYO or KAYO for you-*plural* and NILA or SILA for they

Makinig *ka*	=	You (singular) listen
Makinig *kayo*	=	You (plural) listen
Gusto *mo*?	=	You (singular) like it?
Alagaan *mo*	=	You (singular) take care of it
Itaas-taas *niyo* pa	=	You (plural) raise it
Ibaba *niyo*	=	You (plural) lower it/bring it down
Tumahimik *kayo*	=	You (plural) keep quiet
Inumin *niyo*	=	You (plural) drink it

Nag-*jogging* **sila**	=	They went jogging
Nag-*exercise* **siya**	=	He/She exercised
Itatanong **niya**	=	He/She will ask
Binibigay **niya**	=	He/She is giving it
Nagtrabaho **siya**	=	He/She worked/went to work
Nanood **sila**	=	They watched it
Pinapaliwanag **nila**	=	They are explaining it

TAGALOG COMMAND-REQUEST FORMS

To make the following command-requests forms as more polite and courteous, add a "PO" (SIR/MA'AM or SIRS/ MA'AMS) either BETWEEN or AFTER the formed word and postpositive word KA/KAYO or the MO/ NINYO.

Also be aware that using Kayo or Ninyo (both plural forms) to an older person (singular), instead of Ka or Mo, is also giving respect to that person.

Prefix PAKI- (Please) + root word to ASK A FAVOR IN A POLITE WAY with Ninyo (*plural or to one older person for respect*)

Paki + soli	=	pakisoli (please return)	=	pakisoli po *ninyo*
Paki + bigay	=	pakibigay (please hand out)	=	pakibigay po
Paki + ayos	=	paki-ayos (please put in order)	=	paki-ayos po *ninyo*
Paki + sama	=	pakisama (please include)	=	pakisama po

Prefix MAKI- (May I/May we) + root word is to ASK PERMISSION IN A POLITE WAY

Maki + raan/daan	=	makiraan (may I/we pass)	=	makiraan **po**
Maki + sucob	=	makisucob (may I/we take shelter or take shade under your umbrella)	=	makisucob **po**
Maki + suyo	=	makisuyo (may I/we ask a favor)	=	makisuyo **po**

Prefix I- + root word + postpositive MO (*singular*) or NIYO (*plural or to one older person for respect*) to INITIATE AN ACTION

I + lagay + mo	=	ilagay mo (you put it)	=	ilagay mo **po**
I + tabi + mo	=	itabi mo (you put it aside)	=	itabi mo **po**
I + bigay + niyo	=	ibigay niyo (you give it)	=	ibigay **niyo po**
I + latag + niyo	=	ilatag niyo (you spread it)	=	ilatag **niyo po**

Prefix MAG- + root word + postpositive KA (*singular*) or KAYO (*plural or to one older person for respect*) to GIVE AN ORDER

Mag + salita	=	magsalita ka/kayo (you speak)	=	magsalita kayo **po**
Mag + bigay	=	magbigay ka/kayo (you give)	=	magbigay ka **po**
Mag + aral	=	mag-aral ka/kayo (you study)	=	mag-aral ka

Use formed words with *suffixes* –UM- within the word + postpositive KA (*singular*) or KAYO (*plural or to one older person for respect*) to GIVE AN ORDER

K + um +ain	=	kumain ka/kayo (you eat)	=	kumain kayo **po**
T + um + ingin	=	tumingin ka/kayo (you look)	=	tumingin ka
K + um+ uha	=	kumukuha ka/kayo (you get/take)	=	kumuha kayo **po**

Prefix PAG- + root word + *suffixes* –AN/HAN or –IN/HIN + postpositive MO (*singular*) or NINYO (*plural or to one older person for respect*) to GIVE AN ORDER OR MAKE A REQUEST

Pag + buti + hin	=	pagbutihin mo/ninyo (do your best) pagbutihin mo
Pag + aral + an	=	pag-aralan mo/ninyo (do study) pag-aralan niyo **po**
Pag + bawal + an	=	pagbawalan mo/ninyo (do prohibit) pagbawalan mo

Root word + *suffixes* –HAN or –HIN or –IN + postpositive MO (*singular*) or NINYO (*plural or to one older person for respect*) to GIVE AN ORDER OR MAKE A REQUEST

Sama + han	=	samahan mo/ninyo (accompany him/her)	= samahan mo
Sara + han	=	sarahan/sarhan mo/ninyo (close it)	= sarhan niyo **po**
Gawa + in	=	gawain/gawin mo/ninyo (do it)	= gawin niyo **po**
Basa + hin	=	basahin mo/ninyo (read it)	= basahin ninyo **po**
Tapos + in	=	taposin mo/ninyo (finish it)	= taposin mo

ILOCANO GRAMMAR

ILOCANO AFFIXES

(Use the Root Words section in this book in addition to the affixes
specified here to configure nouns, adjectitves, adverbs, verbs,
and past, present, and future tenses)

FORMING NOUNS

Sometimes the root word is the NOUN itself

Anos (patience)
Dungngo (affection)
Talna (peace, calmness)
Bisin (hunger)
Ayat (love)
Salun-at (health)
Bilang (count)
Isem (smile)
Pintas (beauty)
Kararag (prayer)
Liwliwa (solace)
Banglo (nice scent, perfume)

Prefix PAG- + root word to form a NOUN

Pag + surat	=	pagsurat (handwriting)
Pag + dengngeg	=	pagdengngeg (hearing)
Pag + pangan	=	pagpangan (way of eating)
Pag + kita	=	pagkita (sight)
Pag + anges	=	paganges (breath)

Prefix PAGKA- + root word to form a NOUN

Pagka + dakes	=	pagkadakes (wickedness)
Pagka + ulpit	=	pagka-ulpit (cruelty)
Pagka + linis	=	pagkalinis (cleanliness)
Pagka + luto	=	pagkaluto (the way it is cooked)

FORMING NOUNS THAT CAN ALSO BE ADJECTIVES

Prefix AG- + root word to denote a RELATIONSHIP

Ag + ama	=	agama (father and child)
Ag + ina	=	agina (mother and child)
Ag + gayyem	=	aggayyem (are friends)
Ag + kabagyan	=	agkabagyan (are relatives)

Prefix AG- + first syllable of the root word + the root word to denote RELATIONSHIPS (more than two)

Ag + a + ama	=	agaama (father & children)
Ag + i + ina	=	agiina (mother & children)
Ag + ga + gayyem	=	aggagayyem (friends, 2 or more)

Prefix KA- + root word and with or without a *suffix* –AN to denote SAME BOND OR FELLOWHIP

Ka + bagi + an	=	kabagyan (relative)
Ka + ili + an	=	kailian (townmate)
Ka + bayan	=	kabayan (compatriot, fellow citizen)
Ka + clase	=	kaclase (classmate)

Prefixes PAG- + root word + AN to denote a place or location

Pag + turog + an	=	pagturogan (sleeping place)
Pag + na + an	=	pagnaan (place to walk)
Pag + pasiar + an	=	pagpasiaran (site to take a walk)
Pag + gatang + an	=	paggatangan (site to buy things)
Pag + trabaho + an	=	pagtrabahoan (a workplace)

Prefixes PAG- + root word + AN to denote a function or use

Pag + luto + an	=	paglutoan (cookware)
Pag + batay + an	=	pagbatayan (a thing to stand on)
Pag + surat + an	=	pagsuratan (a thing to write on)

Prefix TAGA- + root word or place to either denote ASSIGNED WORK OR PLACE OF ORIGIN

Taga + maneho	=	tagamaneho (the designated driver)
Taga + tocar	=	tagatocar (the musical accompanist)
Taga + Visayas	=	tagaVisayas (from the Visayas)

FORMING ADJECTIVES

Prefix NA- + root word to form an ADJECTIVE

Na + pintas	=	napintas (beautiful)
Na + imas	=	naimas (delicious)
Na + sakit	=	nasakit (painful, sore)
Na + singpet	=	nasingpet (virtuous)
Na + laeng	=	nalaeng (good or healthy or smart)

Prefix NAG- + root word to denote HIGH DEGREE OF A FEATURE

Nag + pintas	=	nagpintas (very beautiful)
Nag + sayaat	=	nagsayaat (very good)
Nag + laeng	=	naglaeng (very efficient)
Nag + bassit	=	nagbassit (very small)
Nag + lamiis	=	naglamiis(very cold)

Prefix NAKA- + 1st syllable of root word + root word to denote a FEATURE IN A VERY HIGH DEGREE

Naka + pin + pintas	=	nakapinpintas (very beautiful)
Naka + em + emma	=	nakaem-emma (very modest)
Naka + rung + rungsot	=	nakarungrungsot (very cruel)
Naka + kat + katawa	=	nakakatkatawa (very funny)

Prefix PINAKA- + formed word to denote a SUPERLATIVE DEGREE

Pinaka + napintas	=	pinakanapintas (most beautiful)
Pinaka + nasayaat	=	pinakanasayaat (the best)
Pinaka + dakes	=	pinakadakes (the worst)

Pinaka + naragsak	=	pinakanaragsak (happiest)
Pinaka + intelihente	=	pinakaintelihente (most intelligent)
Pinaka + nalaeng	=	pinakanalaeng (most efficient)

Prefix MAKA- + root word to denote CAPABILITY or CONDITION

Maka + tulong	=	makatulong (can be of help)
Maka + turog	=	makaturog (sleepy)
Maka + pagna	=	makapagna (can walk)
Maka + dadael	=	makadadael (harmful, can destroy)
Maka + ventahe	=	makaventahe (advantageous)

Prefix NAKA- + root word to denote a FINISHED DEED or CAPABILITY

Naka + turpos	=	nakaturpos (finished, graduated)
Naka + aramid	=	nakaaramid (did, made)
Naka + pammigat	=	nakapammigat (had breakfast)
Naka + bangon	=	nakabangon (was able to rise)
Naka + libre	=	nakalibre (got it free)

Prefix NAKA + root word to indicate an APPEARANCE

Naka + tugaw	=	nakatugaw (seated or sitting)
Naka + turog	=	nakaturog (asleep)
Naka + mulagat	=	nakamulagat (eyes wide open)

Prefix MAKIN- + root word to denote OWNERSHIP

Makin + kucua	=	makinkucua (owner)
Makin + lugan	=	makinlugan (his/her vehicle)
Makin + anak	=	makin-anak (his/her child)

Prefixes PAM- (before a that starts with B) or PANG- to denote a PURPOSE

Pam + bigat	=	pammigat (breakfast, for a.m. use)
Pang + turog	=	pangturog (for bedwear)
Pang + oficina	=	pang-oficina (for office use or wear)
Pang + simbaan	=	pangsimbaan (for church use/wear)

Prefix TAGA- + root word or place to either denote ASSIGNED WORK OR PLACE OF ORIGIN

Taga + maneho	=	tagamaneho (the designated driver)
Taga + tocar	=	tagatocar (the musical accompanist)
Taga + Ilocos	=	taga-Ilocos (from the Ilocos Region)

Prefix AGKARA- + root word to indicate a CONSTANT OCCURRENCE

Agkara + sakit	=	agkarasakit (always getting sick)
Agkara + pasiar	=	agkarapasiar (always out for a stroll)
Agkara + _shopping_	=	agkara-_shopping_ (love shopping)
Agkara + bulod	=	agkarabulod (always borrowing)
Agkara + ited	=	agkaraited (always giving)
Agkara + tinnag	=	agkaratinnag (always falling)

Prefix AGIN- + first syllable of root word + the root word to denote PRETENSE

Agin + si + singpet	=	aginsisingpet (pretend to be good)
Agin + sa + sakit	=	aginsasakit (pretend to be ill)
Agin + sa + sangit	=	aginsasangit (pretend to cry)
Agin + ku + kuna	=	aginkukuna (pretend)

FORMING ADVERBS

Time Adverbs

Itatta nga aldaw (today)

Nu bigat (tomorrow)

Idi calman (yesterday)

Itatta a bigat (this morning)

Itatta a malem (this afternoon)

Itatta rabii (tonight, this evening)

Idi rabii (last night)

Idi maysa a lawas/domingo (last week)

Idi maysa a bulan (last month)

Idi maysa a tawen (last year)

Idi napalabas (in the past)
Daytoy sumaruno a domingo (next week)
Itatta (now)
Intonucua (later)
Nabiit la a napalabas (recently)
Itattay laeng (just a while ago)
Daytoy napalabas (lately)
Sumarsaruno a nabiit a panawen (soon)
Dagdagos (immediately)
Mismo itattan (right now)

Location Adverbs

Ditoy (here)
Idiay (there)
Dita (at that place)
Dita abay (beside the)
Amin a lugar (everywhere)
Uray inchenna a lugar (anywhere)

Frequency Adverbs

Maminsan, maysa a beses (once)
Dua beses (twice)
Agnanayon, Firmi (always)
Canayon (often)
Pasaray (sometimes)
Kadawyan, Sigud (usually)
Sagpaminsan (occasionally)
Haan man laeng (not at all)
Haan uray man caano (never)
Agsasaruno (successive)

Prefix MAKA- + root word to denote an ENTIRE DURATION

Maka + domingo	=	makadomingo (entire week, all week long)
Maka + bulan	=	makabulan (entire month, all month long)
Maka + tawen	=	makatawen (entire year, all year round)

Prefix **KA- + first syllable of root word + root word to indicate a**
RECENT ACTIVITY

Ka + pam + panaw	=	kapampanaw (just left)
Ka + tur + turog	=	katurturog (just fell asleep)
Ka + pang + pangan	=	kapangpangan (just eaten)

FORMING VERBS TO FORM FUTURE, PRESENT, AND PAST TENSES

ILOCANO TENSES (The **TU** added to the Future Tense means "later" or "these coming times")

1. The **FUTURE tense** has the word "TU" (meaning "later" or "these coming times") and can be *With or Without the **prefix** AG-*, and *With or Without* the **suffix** -N or -EN or -AN

Root	Future	Root	Future
Umay	umay tu	Adal	agadal tu
Aramid	aramid*en* tu	Sacay	agsacay tu
Serrek	sumrek tu	Basa	agbasa*n* tu
Cadwa	cadwa*en* tu	Buya	agbuya*n* tu
Linis	aglinis tu	Rugi	agrugi*n* tu
Obra a	gobra*n* tu	Ipon	agipo*n* tu

    (Umay-come; Aramid-make; Serrek-enter; Obra-work; Cadwa-accompany)

Important: Remember that in the PRESENT TENSE, the FIRST SYLLABLE of the root word is ALWAYS REPEATED

2. **Two ways to form PRESENT tense with *prefix* MA- and *infix* -UM- and PAST tense with *infix* -IM- or -IN**

Future	Present: -UM-	Past:-IM-
Sumrek tu	s*um*sumrek	s*im*rek
Umay tu	*um*-umay	*im*may
Gumatang tu	g*um*atgatang	g*im*matang
Tumangken tu	t*um*angtangken	t*im*mangken
Awaten tu	*um*aw-awat	*in*awat

118

(Sumrek-enter; Umay-come; Gumatang-buy; Tumangken-harden; Awaten-receive)

3. The **FUTURE tense formed here with the** *infix* **-UM-** and **PAST tense formed with** *infix* **-IM-**

Present	Future	Past
Bussog	B*um*sog tu	B*im*sog
Bettak	B*um*tak tu	B*im*tak
Sangpet	S*um*angpet tu	S*im*mangpet

(Bussog-stomach full; Bettak-burst; Sangpet-arrive)

4. *Prefix* **I- + root word for PRESENT and FUTURE Tenses and** *prefixes* **IN- or IM- for PAST Tense**

Root	Future	Present	Past
Cabil	*i*cabil tu	*i*cabcabil	*in*cabil
Tulod	*i*tulod tu	*i*tultulod	*in*tulod
Yeg, Iyeg	*i*yeg tu	*i*y-iyeg	*in*yeg
Ipan	*i*pan tu	*i*p-ipan	*im*pan
Belleng	*i*belleng tu	*i*belbelleng	*im*belleng
Ited	*i*ted tu	*i*t-ited	*in*ted

(Cabil-place; Tulod-bring; Iyeg-Bring; Ipan-bring; Belleng-Throw; Ited-give)

5. **Two ways to form PRESENT Tense with** *prefixes* **AG-** and **MANG-**

Root	Present: AG-	Present: MANG-
Aramid	*ag*ar-aramid	*mang*ar-aramid (making)
Obra	*ag*ob-obra	*mang*ob-obra (working)
Sarita	*ag*sarsarita	*mang*sarsarita (talking)
Baliw	*ag*balbaliw	*mang*balbaliw (changing)
Basa	*ag*basbasa	*mang*basbasa (reading)
Ala	*ag*al-ala	*mang*al-ala (getting)

6. **PRESENT tense: 1st syllable of root word + root word +** *With or Without* **suffix –EN or –AN, and PAST tense with** *prefix/suffix* **IN-/-IN- and** *prefix* **NAG-**

Root	Present	Past: IN-/-IN-	Past: NAG-
Aramid	*ar-ar*amiden	*in*aramid	*nag*aramid
Obra	*ob-ob*raen	*in*obra	*nag*obra
Trabaho	*trabtrab*ahoen	tr*in*abaho	*nag*trabaho
Sarita	s*arsa*ritaen	s*in*arita	*nag*sarita
Basa	*basba*saen	b*in*asa	*nag*basa
Ipon	*ip-ip*onen	*in*ipon	*nag*ipon
Adal	*ad-ad*alen	*in*adal	*nag*adal
Awag	*aw-aw*agan	*in*awag	*nag*awag
Sacay	*sacsa*cayan	s*in*acayan	*nag*sacay
Rugi	*rugrug*yan	r*in*ugyan	*nag*rugi
Linis	*linlin*isan	nilinisan	*nag*linis
Cadwa	*cadcad*waen	k*in*adwa	*nag*cadwa
Malpas	*palpal*pasen	*in*palpas	*nag*palpas
Serrek	*serser*reken	s*in*errek	*nag*serrek

(Aramid-make, Obra-work; Trabaho-work; Sarita-speak; Basa-read; Ipon-save/collect; Adal-study; Sacay-ride; Linis-clean; Cadwa-accompany; Malpas-end/finish; Serrek-enter)

Important: One way to indicate done (PAST TENSE) in Ilocano is adding <u>N</u> at the end of words ending in vowels like a, e, i, o, u, (i.e., magna would be magnan, ammo would be ammon); and adding <u>EN</u> at the end of words ending in consonants like b, c, d, f, g, etc., (i.e., dakkel would be dakkelen)

7. **Two ways to form PAST Tense with *prefixes* NA- and NANG-**

Root	Past: NA-	Past: NANG-
Ala	*na*ala**n**	*nang*ala**n**
Mangan	*na*ngan**en**	
Awag		*nang*awag**en**
Mapan	*na*pan**en**	
Malpas	*na*lpas**en**	*nang*palpas**en**
Tinnag	*na*tinnag**en**	*nang*tinnag**en**
Turog	*na*turog**en**	

(Ala-get; Mangan-eat; Awag-call; Mapan-go; Malpas-end/finish; Tinnag-fall; Turog-sleep)

Prefix PA- + root word + *suffix* –EN to mean TO MAKE

Pa + pintas + en	=	papintasen (to make it beautiful)
Pa + imas + en	=	paimasen (to make it delicious)

Prefix AG- + root word to HAVE IT DONE

Ag + pakawan	=	agpakawan (to forgive)
Ag + pakada	=	agpakada (to bid good-bye)

Prefix AGPA- + root word to HAVE IT DONE or GO TOWARDS A DIRECTION

Agpa + luto	=	agpaluto (to have someone cook)
Agpa + burek	=	agpaburek (to have it boiled)
Agpa + turong	=	agpaturong (go towards)
Agpa + abagat	=	agpaabagat (towards the south)

Prefix IPA- + root word to HAVE IT DONE

Ipa + urnos	=	ipaurnos (put in order or tidy it)
Ipa + ayos	=	ipaayos (have it fixed or repaired)
Ipa + lubos	=	ipalubos (give permission, tolerate)
Ipa + dakkel	=	ipadakkel (have it enlarged)
Ipa + ammo	=	ipaammo (let it be known)
Ipa + lagip	=	ipalagip (let it be remembered)

Prefix I- + root word to INITIATE AN ACTION + postpositive word

I + dulin + ko (postpositive) =		idulin ko (I keep it)
I + subli + c (postpositive) =		isublic (I return it)
I + dulin + na (postpositive) =		idulin na (he/she keeps it)
I + dulin + da (postpositive) =		idulin da (they keep it)

Prefix AG- + first letter of root word + *affix* -INN- + the rest of the root word to mean DO SOMETHING TOGETHER or DO TO EACH OTHER

Ag + t-inn-ulong	=	agtinnulong (help together/each other)
Ag + p-inn-akawan	=	agpinnakawan (forgive each other)
Ag + s-inn-urat	=	agsinnurat (write each other)

ILOCANO POSTPOSITIVES

Note: The following sentences use the usual Filipino sentence-formation which is Predicate + Subject.

Postpositive words –AC, -C or KO for Siac (I or Me)

Agbasa + **_ac_**	=	agbasa**_ac_** (I read)
Nag-email + **_ac_**	=	nag-email**_ac_** (I emailed)
Mapan + **_ac_**	=	mapan**_ac_** (I go)
Immay + **_ac_**	=	immay**_ac_** (I went)
Mangan + **_ac_**	=	mangan**_ac_** (I eat)
Agdigos + **_ac_**	=	agdigos**_ac_** **_tu_** (I'll take a bath)
Idulin + **_ko_**	=	idulin **_ko_** (I'll safekeep it)
Ipan + **_ko_**	=	ipan **_ko_** (I'll bring it)
Kua + **_c_**	=	kua**_c_** (mine)
Isubli + **_c_**	=	isubli**_c_** (I'll return it)

Postpositives –M, KA, -YO, -DA, ISU, KAYO for Sica _(You-singular)_, Isuda (They) and Dacayo _(You-plural)_

Kucua + **_m_**	=	Kucua**_m_** (yours-singular)
Kucua + **_yo_**	=	Kucua**_yo_** (yours-plural)
Kucua + **_da_**	=	Kucua**_da_** (theirs)
Simmangpet + **_da_**	=	Simmangpet **_da_** (they arrived)
Gumatang + **_isu_**	=	Gumatang **_isu_** (he/she buys)
Um-umay + **_kayo_**	=	Umay **_kayo_** (you [plural] come)
Mangmangan + **_ka_**	=	Mangmangan **_ka_** (you're eating)
Agdigdigos + **_da_**	=	Agdigdigos **_da_** (they're taking a bath)

ILOCANO COMMAND-REQUEST FORMS

To make the following command/requests forms more polite and courteous, add a "<u>MAN</u>" (meaning "if you please") BETWEEN or AFTER the formed word + postpositive <u>KA</u> or <u>KAYO</u>.

Be aware that <u>using Kayo or the suffixes -anyo or -enyo</u> (all plural forms) to an older person (singular), <u>instead of Ka or suffixes -m, -am or -em,</u> is also giving respect to that person.

Prefixes PAKI- (Please) to ASK A FAVOR in a POLITE WAY

Paki + duron	= pakiduron (please push)	= pakiduron *man*
Paki + dulin	= pakidulin (please keep in a safe place)	= pakidulin *man*
Paki + awat	= pakiyawat (please pass the..)	= pakiyawat *man*

Prefix I- + root word + postpositive MO or -M (singular) or YO (*plural or to one older person as a means of respect*) to INITIATE AN ACTION

I + dulin + mo	= idulin mo (you safekeep it)	= idulin mo *man*
I + respeto + m	= irespetom (you respect it)	= irespetom *man*
I + pateg + mo	= ipateg mo (you value it)	= ipateg mo *man*
I + subli + m	= isublim (you return it)	= isublim *man*

Prefixes MAKI- (May I) + root word + postpositive –AC (me) to ASK A FAVOR in a POLITE WAY

Maki + favor + ac	= makifavorac (may I ask a favor)	= makfavorac *man*
Maki + lasat + ac	= makilasatac (may I pass)	= makilasatac *man*
Maki + lugan + ac	= makiluganac(may I ride with you)	= makiluganac *man*
Aramid + enyo	= aramidenyo (you [plural] do)	= aramidenyo *man*
Tulong + am	= tulongam (you help him/her)	= tulongam *man*
Awag + am	= awagam (you call him/her)	= awagam *man*
Surat + anyo	= suratanyo (you [plural] write)	= suratam *man*

Prefixes AG- or MA- + root word + *postpositive* KA (singular) or KAYO (*plural or to one older person as a means of respect*) to form a REQUEST /COMMAND

Ag + obra	= agobra ka/kayo (do work)	= agobra kayo *man*
Ma + ala	= mangala ka/kayo (do get)	= mangala kayo *man*
Ag + sagana	= agsagana ka/kayo (be ready)	= agsagana kayo *man*
Ma + apan	= mapan ka/kayo (do go)	= mapan kayo *man*

Root word + *postpositive* -M or -AM or -EM (singular) or -ANYO or -ENYO (*plural or to one older person as a means of respect*) to form a REQUEST/COMMAND

Ikkan + m	= ikkam (you give)	= ikkam *man*
Ikkan + yo	= ikkanyo (you [plural] give)	= ikkanyo *man*
Aramid + em	= aramidem (you do)	= aramidem *man*
I + subli + yo	= isubliyo (you return it)	= isubliyo *man*

CONVERSATIONAL ENGLISH, TAGALOG AND ILOCANO DICTIONARY

MEANINGS OF BOOK ABBREVIATIONS

Abbreviations	Meanings
Iloc:	Ilocano word meaning
(Tag. & Iloc.)	Tagalog & Ilocano use same words/translations
Italic words	English-derived Filipino words
-Sp	Spanish-derived Filipino words
-aSp	Altered Spanish-Filipino words
v.	verb
n.	noun
adj.	adjective
adv.	adverb
prep.	preposition

A

A ang, **ng** *("ng" is pronounced "nang")*; Iloc: ti, iti, ket
Synonyms
   The *(singular)* ang, ng-*pronounced "nang,"* iyong; Iloc: ti, iti, daytay
   The *(plural)* ang mga-*pronounced "ma-nga,"* ng mga-*prounounced "nang ma-nga;"* Iloc: dagiti
A while ago kanina lamang; Iloc: itay laeng, itattay
Abaca punong halaman na mala-saging na tumutubo sa Filipinas at ang hibla o *strand* nito ay nahahabing maging tela-*Sp*/*woven into a cloth*
Aback 1] mapa-atras-*Sp* sa gulat; 2] hanging itulak ang bapor o bangka paatras; Iloc: 1] mapaatras ti kigtot; 2] angin a mangduron iti bapor o bangka a paatras
Abandon iwanan, lisanan, layasan; Iloc: baybay-an, panawan, talawan
Abash mapahiya, hindi mapakali at nalilito; Iloc: mabainan, haan makatalna
Abate *v.,* **Abatement** *n.* 1] bawasan ang dami o tindi; 2] wakasan o pigilin gaya ng pambubwisit; 3] ipawalang-bisa; sugpoin o patayin
Abbreviate paiklihin ang salita at isulat lang ang pinaikling salita gaya halimbawa ng *"abbrev."* sa *abbreviation* para lantad kung ano iyong pinaikli at maintindihan pa rin
Correlated words
   Initial *n.,* **Initialize** *v.* maikling firma na isulat lang ang mga 3 unang letra ng pangalan at dalawang apelyido, halimbawa ang initial ni John Fitzgerald Kennedy ay JFK
   Acronym *initial* (mga unang letra ng salita) lamang gaya ng OPEC para sa Organization of Petroleum Exporting Countries dahil naibibigkas natin ang pamagat nitong OPEC at nakikilala na
Abdicate magtiwalag, magbitiw, talikoran, isuko; Iloc: agikkat iti puesto-*Sp*, panawan, ibbatan, isuko
Abdomen tiyan; Iloc: chan
Synonyms
   Stomach tiyan, sikmura; Iloc: chan, buksit
   Belly, Tummy puson, bilbil; Iloc: pus-ong, buksit
Abduct dukotin, i-*kidnap;* Iloc: agcumaw, i-*kidnap*
Aberrant *adj.,* **Aberration** *n.* lumilihis sa caraniwan at tamang gawa; Iloc: aglislisi iti cadawyan, sigud ken usto-*Sp* nga aramid

Abet sang-ayonan o suportahan ang tao o ang plano o pagpalakad na kadalasan ay masama; Iloc: aprovaran o suportaran ti pagpapagna o tao o plano canayon ket dakes (aprova/aprovar-*Sp*, suporta/suportar-*Sp*, plano-*Sp*)

Abeyance pagpapaliban, pagpaibang-araw; Iloc: itantan para iti sabali nga aldaw, iladladaw

Abhor *v.*, **Abhorrence** *n.*, **Abhorrent** *adj.* poot, muhi, hindi gusto-*Sp*; Iloc: uyong, luksaw, rurod, makaunget

ABIDE magtiis, mapacensiang naghihintay; Iloc: aganos, napacensia-*Sp* nga agur-uray

ABIDE by tuparin, tumutupad sa utos, sumusunod sa utos; Iloc: agtungtungpal ti bilin, sumursurot ti bilin

Ability, Abilities *The following are all abilities, and a person with abilities may have more than one of these: capability, skill, intelligence, understanding, communications, comprehension, ingenuity, cleverness, creativity, inventiveness, strength, might, physical fitness and health, potentials, planning, problem solving, talent, competence, proficiency, expertise, knowledge of operating machines, of facts or playing musical instruments, and many more.*
Correlated words
Untapped ability *abilities that are taken for granted and ignored - **not** taken advantage of at all that such abilities just go to waste.* Nasasayang na abilidad, talento at iba pa dahil hindi ginagamit; Iloc: masaysayang nga abilidad, talento ken sabali pay ta haan nga iyus-usar
Latent ability *abilities that the one who has them, does not know he/ she has them until he/she discovers it by chance, or he/she may never find it out at all that those abilities remain latent for life.* Cacayahan na tago at natutulog at lingid sa mismong taong may angkin nito hanggat madiscobre niya ang mga iyan.

Abject *(Tag. & Iloc.)* pinaka-miserab-le-*Sp*, pinakanakaka-disgusto-*Sp*

Able caya, nakacayanan; Iloc: caya, mabalinan, cabaelan

Abnegate 1] isuko ang *claim* o ang karapatan, 2] di pagbigyan ang sarili, pinagkakaitan ang sarili, *self-denial*

Abnormal *abnormal*, hindi *normal*, tiwali, hindi caraniwan; Iloc: *abnormal*, haan a *normal*, haan a cadawyan

Aboard 1] nakalulan, maglulan, magsacay, 2] kasama sa grupo-*Sp*, organisasyon-*Sp* o negosio-*Sp*; Iloc: 1] nakasacay, aglugan, 2] cadwa iti grupo-*Sp*, organisasyon-*Sp* o negosio-*Sp*

Abode tinitirhan, bahay; Iloc: pagyanan, balay

Abolish *v.*, **Abolition** *n.* tanggalin, puksahin, lipolin; Iloc: ikkaten

Abominable *adj.*, **Abominate** *v.* nakakagalit, nakakainis, nakakadisgusto, galit, inis, disgusto-*Sp*; Iloc: nakakapapungtot, nakakaparurod

Aborigine pinakaunang tao sa isang lugar-*Sp* o nasyon-*Sp*; Iloc: pinakaimmuna a tao iti maysa a lugar o nasyon

Abort *v.*, **Abortion** *n.* ipalaglag ang buntis; Iloc: ipaalis ti sicog

Abound marami, masagana; Iloc: adu, nawadwad, naruay

ABOUT tungkol sa.., hinggil sa..; Iloc: maypanggep iti.., maypapan iti.., maygapu iti

ABOUT-face 1] magtalicod; 2] nagbago ang isip; Iloc: 1] agtallicod; 2] agbalbaliw ti nakem

ABOVE sa itaas ng, sa ibabaw ng; Iloc: idiay ngato iti, diay rabaw ti

ABOVE and beyond the call of duty *Exceed in complying with the expectations, the work, efficiency and effectiveness that are required.* Ginagawa ang katungkulan, kagalingan, kahusayan at pagkabuo na lampas pa sa kinakailangan.

ABOVE board *legal and legitimate, honest, without secret because he/she practices transparency.*
Correlated word
Transparency *The quality of being seen through like a glass; do things in an open way without secrets;* Bukas na libro ang canyang buhay at sa pagpapahayag niya ng canyang buhay-buhay, lantad ang katatao niya kaya mapagkatiwalaan siya

Abrade *v.*, **Abrasion** *n.* *(Tag. & Iloc.)* gasgas

Abrasive *(Tag. & Iloc.)* nakakagasgas

Abreast 1] magkatabi, 2] hindi huli sa balita dahil nagsusubaybay siya parati

Abridge *v.*, **Abridgement** *n.* paiksihin ang kasulatan; Iloc: ipaababa iti kasuratan

Abroad nasa ibang bansa; Iloc: adda diay dayo, adda diay sabali a nasyon

Abrupt bigla, golpe-*Sp*; Iloc: dagdagos, golpe

Abscess pamamaga; Iloc: letteg, bumsog

Abscond biglaang umalis na palihim at caraniwan ay para makalihis sa reglamento-*Sp* ng batas; Iloc: ensigida-*Sp* a pumanaw a palimed para makalisi ti reglamento ti linteg

Absence *n.,* **Absent** *v.* hindi pagsipot, hindi pagdalo, hindi pumasok; Iloc: haan nga agatender, haan simrec, haan a napan, haan a nag-atender-*Sp*

Absenteeism madalas mag-*absent*; nakagawiang pag-a-*absent*

Absolute 1] puro-*Sp* at walang halo, 2] perfecto-*Sp* at completo-*Sp;* Iloc; 1] puro ken awan laok, 2] perfecto ken completo

Absolutely Tama, Siempre-*Sp*, Husto-*Sp*; Iloc: Usto-*Sp*, Siempre

Absolve *v.,* **Absolution** *n.* ipawalang-sala; Iloc: ipaawanan ti basol
Synonyms
Vindicate ipawalang-sala dahil sa pangsuportang prueba; Iloc: naawanan iti basol gapu ti pangpaneknek nga prueba
Exculpate ipawalang-sala; Iloc: ikkaten ti basol
Exonerate i-absuelto, ipawalang sala; Iloc: i-absuelto, paawanen ti basol

Absorb *v.,* **Absorption** *n.* nababad at tumagos; Iloc: sagepsepen na ti basa

Absorbed subsob ang isip at pansin sa ginagawa niya; Iloc: nakaperreng nga usto-*Sp* iti es-estimaren na (estimar-*Sp*)
Synonym
Rapt abala, subsob, buhos na buhos sa ginagawa; Iloc: nakasubsob ti ar-aramiden

Abstain *v.,* **Abstinence** & **Abstention** *n.* mag-abstinencia-*Sp*, ipagkait sa sarili ang kinagigiliwang bagay alang-alang sa isang layonin; Iloc: ag-abstinencia, ipaidam ti bagi iti pagramrambakan na para iti maysa a rangta
Synonym
Ascetic diciplina sa sarili at ipagkait sa sarili ang mga capricho ng mundo; Iloc: diciplina ti bagi ken ipaidam iti bagi dagiti capricho ti mundo

Abstruse mahirap intindihin; Iloc: narigat maawatan

Abdulia or Abouilla sintoma-*Sp* na may diferencia-*Sp* ang utak na may kinalaman sa pagkapinsala o pagkawala na ng pagpayag, pagpili o pagpasya

Abundance *n.,* **Abundant** *adj.* abundancia-*Sp*, sagana, dami; Iloc: abundancia, adu, wadwad, ruay

Abuse *v.,* **Abusive** *adj.* abuso-*Sp*, abusohin, maltratohin, apihin, abusado-*Sp*; Iloc: agabuso, i-maltrato-*Sp*, agmaltrato, abusado

Abut magkadikit, magkatabi, magka-conecta-*Sp*

Abyss *n.,* **Abysmal, Abyssal** *adj.* bangin na napakalalim at hindi masukat ang lalim

Academics tungkol sa academia-*Sp* ng educasyon-*Sp*, escuela-*Sp*, co-lehio-*Sp* o universidad-*Sp*

Academy *(Tag. & Iloc.)* academy, academia-*Sp*, pag-aaral

Acapella *(Tag. & Iloc.)* wala o ni saliw o acompañar-*Sp* na instrumento-*Sp*

Accede magsang-ayon, pumayag; Iloc: umayon, umannugot, agtunos, agmayat

Accelerate *v.,* **Acceleration** *n.* bilisan, padaliin, paspasan; Iloc: pardasan, partakan, agpaspas, darasen

Accent punto; Iloc: ayug

Accept tanggapin; Iloc: akceptaren (akceptar-*Sp*)

Acceptable pupuedeng tanggapin dahil may katangian o uri na mabuti o kinakailangan

Access ang paraan para makalapit, makapasok, makalabas; makapag-balitaan at makagamit; Iloc: pagserkan, pagruaran; makitungtong, mayyusar (usar-*Sp*)

Accessible madaling makuha o magamit o mapuntahan; Iloc: nalaca nga maala o maaramat o papanan

Accessory *n.,* **Accessorize** *v.* accessory, akcesoria-*Sp*, dagdag na gamit o kasangkapan kung gusto lamang na gamitin; Iloc: *accessory,* mang-panayon iti maysa nga aramaten wenno aparato-*Sp*

Accident sacuna *(Tag. & Iloc.)* accidente-*Sp*, disgrasia-*Sp*
Synonym
    Mishap disgracia, accidente, sacuna; Iloc: disgracia, accidente

Accidental, Acidentally hindi sinasadya; Iloc: haan nga inggagara

Acclaim masigasig na pumupuri o nagbubunyi gaya ng pagbulalas ng paghanga o pag-aprova o pagsang-ayon na puedeng kasama ang palakpakan; Iloc: mangngeg o makitkita a pangdaydayaw

Acclimatize, Acclimate *v.* masanay o mabihasa sa clima-*Sp* o kapaligiran; Iloc: mayruam iti clima ken ti lugar

Accolade pagpapahayag sa salita o pagtatalumpati na spesyal na pagbigay ng paghanga at pagbunyi; Iloc: agsarita o agdiscurso a mangdayaw

ACCOMMODATE pagbigyan, paunlakan; Iloc: pagustoan (gusto-*Sp*)

ACCOMMODATE with lodging patirahin, paunlakan ng matutuloyan; Iloc: mangisaad ti pagdagusan

Accommodation matutuloyan, acomodasyon-*Sp*; Iloc: pagdagusan, acomodasyon-*Sp*

Accompaniment 1] canta o instrumento na sumasaliw sa iba, na karaniwan ay *solo*; 2] ang nakakapaggayak o nakakapagpaganda o nakakapagcompleto o nakakapag-alalay

Accompanist tagasaliw; Iloc: mang-acompanyar-*Sp*, taga-tocar-*Sp*

Accompany samahan, ihatid; Iloc: cadwaen, cuyogen, itulod, itulnog

Accomplice kasangkot, kasabuat, kasapakat; Iloc: timpuyog, kasabwat

Accomplish isagawa; Iloc: aramiden, iturpos

Accomplished 1] naisakatuparan, natupad, naisagawa, nayari, nacompleto, 2] may talento at abilidad, experto; Iloc: 1] naicompleto, nayleppas, naytungpal, naaramid, nayturpos, 2] adda talento ken abilidad isu, experto-*Sp*

Accomplishment nabuong bunga ng pinagsikapan; Iloc: nayturpos nga bunga iti pinagpakpakatan

Correlated words

Fruition tagumpay, pagtatamo ng bunga sa mga pinagsikapan; Iloc: balligi, nakagun-od iti bunga gapu iti pinagpakpakatan na

Materialize maisakatuparan, magkatutuo, magbunga; Iloc: napagbalin, nagbunga, nayturpos

Accord, in, In accordance, Accordant umakma, umayon, alinsunod, magkaangkop; Iloc: makibagay, maki-umno

According to batay sa/kay; Iloc: batay iti/ken, segun-*Sp* ti/ken

Accost matapang na harapin; lapitan para batiin o tanungin o mangusap

ACCOUNT *account* sa banco *(i.e., savings o checking), account* sa *insurance (medical, life, accident, fire, car)*

ACCOUNT for, give an magbigay-ulat; Iloc: ipaammo, agcontador

Accountable mananagot, responsab-le; Iloc: mangsungbat, responsab-le-*Sp*

Accountant *(Tag. & Iloc.) accountant*

Accredit ibigay ang saysay o i-ukol ang gawa sa taong gumawa ng mabuti o trabaho-*Sp*

Accrual *n.,* **Accrue** *v.* padagdag ng padagdag; Iloc: agkaranayon

Accumulate *v.,* **Accumulation** *n.* mag-imbak, mag-ipon, mag-impok; Iloc: agurnong

Accuracy kawastohan, katumpakan; Iloc: kaustoan, kapudnoan

Accurate tumpak, husto-*Sp*, wasto, tunay, tama; Iloc: pudno, usto-*Sp*, agpayso

Accursed sinumpa, napailalim sa sumpa; Iloc: indadanes

Accusation *n.*, **Accuse** *v.*, **Accusatory** *adj.* acusasyon-*Sp*, paratang, bintang, acusahin; Iloc: acusasyon, pangpabasol, pabasolen, acusaren (acusa/acusar-*Sp*), irurumen

Accustomed nakaugalihan, nakagawian, bihasa, sanay, costumbre Iloc: nakayruaman, nayruam, nakaugalyan, cadawyan, costumbre

Ache *n.*, **Achy** *adj.* sakit, hapdi, kirot; Iloc: sakit, ut-ot

Achieve *v.*, **Achievement** *n.* tamohin, matamo, makamit; Iloc: magun-od, maala

Acid *(Tag. & Iloc.)* acido-*Sp*

Acknowledge *v.*, **Acknowledgment** *n.* kilalanin, aminin; Iloc: bigbigen
Correlated word
Regard ituring, ibilang; Iloc: bigbigen, ibilang

Acme tugatog, pinakamataas na parte-*Sp* ng bundok; Iloc: tuktok ti bantay

Acoustics tungkol sa tunog, ang pagkagawa ng cuarto-*Sp* kung saan mahirap o madaling marinig ang usapan; Iloc: maygapu iti uni, iti pagkaaramid iti cuarto nu narigat wenno nalaca a mangngeg ti pagsasaritaan

Acquaint makipagkilala, alamin; Iloc: makiam-ammo, amwen

Acquaintance kakilala; Iloc: am-ammo

Acquainted with each other magkakilala; Iloc: aginnam-ammo, agam-ammo

Acquiesce *v.*, **Acquiescent** *n.* tanggapin, sundin o magpapasailalim na walang tutol; Iloc: akceptaren, tungpalen o agpacumbaba nga awan iti pagsupyat

Acquire magkaroon, mag-angkin, matamo, macamit; Iloc: makaala, magun-od

Acquired taste bagong lasang hindi nakagawian, pero kapag nasusundang kainin ng madalas ay nasasanay na rin; Iloc: mayruam a kanen iti dati haan na kanen ni gusto

Acquisition natamong ari-arian; Iloc: nagun-od a sanicua

Acquit *v.,* **Acquittal** *n.* i-absuelto-*Sp,* ipawalang sala; Iloc: i-absuelto, paawanen ti basol
Correlated word
Exonerate i-absuelto, ipawalang sala; Iloc: i-absuelto, ipaawan ti basol
Acrimonious *adj.,* **Acrimony** *n.* masakit at puno ng suklam na pananalita at asal; Iloc: nasakit ken napunno ti gura nga pagsarita ken tignay
Acronym *initial* (unang letra ng salita) lamang gaya ng OPEC sa Organization of Petroleum Exporting Countries dahil nabibigkas natin ang pamagat nitong OPEC at nakikilala na
ACROSS sa kabila ng daan o lugar-*Sp* na kaharap; Iloc: kabatog, lugar nga kasango
ACROSS each other kaharap, magkaharap; Iloc: agkabatog, agbinnatog, agsinnango
Correlated words
Face-to-face magkaharap, *personal* na magkaharapan; Iloc: agsinnango a *personal*, agkasango
Front harap, sa harapan; Iloc: sango, sangwanan
ACT *v.,* **Action** *n.* galaw, kilos, arte; Iloc: garaw, tignay, gunay, cuti, arte
ACT as if nagpapanggap; Iloc: agingkukuna
Activate umpisahang pagalawin para magamit o mapaandar; Iloc: rugyan a pagarawen para may-usar-*Sp* o mapa-andar-*Sp*
Synonyms
Actuate umpisahang pagalawin para magamit; Iloc: rugyan a pagarawen tapno maiyusar
Trigger pukawin para magsimula ng pagkilos; Iloc: rugyan a pagarawen tapno maiyusar
Active malikot, masigla, maliksi, activo-*Sp*; Iloc: nasiglat, activo, alisto-*aSp*
Activist *(Tag. & Iloc.)* activista-*Sp*
Activities that are healthy, lawful, enjoyable and promoting advancements and success. *You and everyone in this world count and matter as an individual – yes it is true, you are important that's why God created you - so be sure that <u>how you spend your time</u> and <u>anything that you do, render, and depict in life</u> is for the very best benefit on your wellbeing, on your safety and your character. Adopt into your life moral and ethical values - retain and maintain these values throughout your life, since what is worth doing is worth*

doing right. 1. Have a pet, enjoy its company, teach tricks and take
care of this pet. 2. Learn to play a musical instrument (guitar, piano,
violin, drums, harp, accordion, flute, clarinet, saxophone, xylophone,
etc.) or join a band. 3. Learn a craft (sewing, darning, crocheting,
quilting, embroidery, decorating). 4. Join summer and winter camps
set up by a church or a legal organization. 5. Healthy exercises
(swimming, hiking, jogging, biking, yoga, dancing, household chores,
roller skating in summer and ice skating in winter). 6. Get into arts
and develop your creativity (write stories or a book, sketch, draw,
paint, sculpt, ceramics, sing, dance, i.e., ballet, ballroom, cultural or
national dances). 7. Start an enjoyable and productive hobby (reading:
borrow free books from libraries, start photography, cooking, baking,
do coloring books, solve crossword puzzles). 8. Plant flowers or
vegetables or herbs or trees in your backyard and cultivate these. 9.
Backyard camping: picnics, sleepovers, karaoke singing outside or
inside the house, watch funny shows, a parade or a movie in the house.
10. Help the Boy or Girl Scouts by selling lemonade drinks on stands
beside streets and give earnings to the scout organization. 11. Youth
games (chess, free computer games, solitaire, hide and seek, name
that tune, jeopardy game, yoyo, limbo stick game, musical chairs,
give a word/topic and find it in the Bible, etc.). 12. Do your share on
household chores to be a great help to your parents (cleaning your
room or the entire house including bathroom – tidying your stuffs,
*wash dishes, laundry, cleaning up after yourself and **not** leave it for*
others to clean up after you-consideration for others). 13. Go to the
gym for exercises, go on outings or visit museums, zoos, libraries,
watch a movie or an opera, picnic at the park. 14. Learn another
language (English, Spanish, French, German, etc.) from tutors, from
books, Internets or CDs. 15. Be a contributing member to society
by volunteering to work for free in school, in church, at the library,
hospitals or charitable institutions (where you may learn new skills
that may be useful for future jobs or necessities), and/or you can also
bring cheer and present musicals, skits or magic tricks at senior
homes, foster homes, etc. - all of these efforts of yours would award
you with self-esteem while people who learn about those would surely

admire you and even consider you as a hero. 16. <u>Play or learn a sport</u>
(basketball, volleyball, swimming). 17. <u>Enjoy chatting with friends,</u>
classmates, family and relatives (face-to-face or via texting, emails,
phones). 18. <u>Focus on your studies,</u> do your homework, aspire to
excel in school. 19. <u>Hold yourself to a higher standard for a better</u>
<u>and rewarding tomorrow</u> by holding on to dignity and integrity,
while raising your intelligence much more with schooling, finishing
a career, reading beneficial and edifying informations, etc. 20. <u>Use</u>
<u>your strength, knowledge, intelligence, abilities, skills, talents and</u>
<u>other assets so that these won't be forgotten and vanished by non-</u>
<u>usage.</u> 21. <u>Use time productively</u> for your very best interest (for your
health, advancements in life like career, knowledge, abilities, skills,
talents), and doing help for family, other people, and organizations.
22. <u>Give time for God</u> by thanking Him for His big and small blessings,
for Him to help you and lead you in whatever endeavors you are
into, by standing on and claiming His promises in the Bible for those
promises to come true in your life, etc. 23. <u>You matter, so please</u>
*<u>be the solution, never the problem</u>. 24. **Never, never go into drug***
addiction, never even try it no matter how persistent the persuasions
***are because it only brings terrible problems and failures in life**, and*
loss of good sense-good judgment-and-intelligence, loss of hygiene
habits that one smells disgustingly, even generates ugly and unkempt
looks, old-age looks, weakness and frailty, illness, and early death.
25. Overcome bad influences, temptations, evil deeds, offenses and
resentments by avoiding them and clearing and cleaning your mind
*of them; and using **to the utmost** your intelligence, good judgments,*
common sense, strength and determination.

Activity, Activities 1] panay-panay na paggamit ng cacayahan at pagkilos at ng lakas at lusog ng katawan; 2] gawain, trabaho-*Sp*, tungkulin, maliksi na galaw

Actor, Actress *(Tag. & Iloc.)* artista-*Sp*, *actor, actress*

Actually sa katunayan; Iloc: ti kaagpaysoan na

Actuate umpisahang pagalawin para magamit; Iloc: rugyan a pagarawen tapno may-usar

Acuity matalas na paningin at pakiramdam; Iloc: nasirib a panangbigbig ken ricna

Acumen katalasan ng isip, intelihensia-*Sp*; Iloc: pagkasirib, intelihensia

Acute malala, malubha, matindi; Iloc: napalalo, grabe-*Sp*

Adage kasabihan, kawikaan, salawikain; Iloc: pagsasarita a makapabang-ar wenno mangpaleksion, popular-*Sp* a kungkuna

Adamant napakatigas na hindi pumapayag at di mapagbigay sa hiling; Iloc: natangken nga agsupiat ken haan a mangipalubos iti pagas-asug wenno kiddaw a favor-*Sp*

Adapt ibagay, makibagay, maki-ayon, iakma; Iloc: ibagay, makibagay, i-umno

Adaptable puedeng bagayan o angkopin; Iloc: mabalin a bagayan o i-*adapt* iti biag

Adaptation pag-angkop at pagbabagay; paraan na ginawa para maka-akma sa bagong kapaligiran; Iloc: pamay-an a makapayruam iti baro a lugar o aramid

ADD magdagdag, dagdagan; Iloc: nayonan

ADD fuel to the fire ginagatongan ang masamang situasyon-*Sp*; salita o gawain na nakakalala sa dati nang mahirap o masamang situasyon

ADD insult to injury saktan ang kalooban ng tao na dati nang nasaktan o nahihirapan sa buhay o namimighati na kaya mas lumala ang dati nang hirap

Addict sugapa, pusakal, *addict,* nalulong sa masamang vicio-*Sp* at hirap nang makawala; Iloc: *addict,* naygalut iti dakes a vicio ken marigatanen a makatammeng
Correlated word
Habit-forming ang nakakagumon o nakakapapusakal sa alak, droga, cigarilyo o sugal na napakahirap kumalag sa mga ito

Addictions *Many problems in the world today like **crimes, failures in life, homelessness, accidents, and serious diseases are sometimes due to addictions. 1] If you are addicted to <u>illegal drugs or alcohol</u>, <u>it seems impossible for you to function as a normal human being</u>. Alcohol and illegal drugs** alter your brain and muddle your intelligence, your thinking, and judgment; alcohol and illegal drugs also **wipe out** your principles (like good aspirations, moral and ethical values), **destroy** your youthful good looks, your hygiene and sanitation practices,* *your good health, and most likely, you **lose** all your opportunities to succeed to achieve your dreams, like **not finish your studies** or you may **be fired from your job for being a drug addict, since many big, able-bodied man have become good-for-nothing or inutile in supporting just themselves that this is a very shameful failure in life; 2] committing sexual assault** due to being a **sex addict and a drug-addict are both criminal acts that would definitely lock you up in jail. 3] If you have **tobacco or cigarette addiction**, these would ruin your respiratory organs, you would lose your youthful good looks **much earlier** than you should and you may **die** at an **early** age. 4] If you have **obsessive phone use or addiction**, you may be vulnerable to criminals who prey on **easy-targets** or you may be **accident-prone** since you are not aware of your surroundings due to your focus on your cell phone while walking and driving.*

Addition, Additional karagdagan, dagdag; Iloc: nayon

Addle litohin, manligalig, balisahin, itaranta; Iloc: rirwen, itaranta, allilawen, itorete

Address *address*, tirahang lugar; Iloc: *address*, lugar-*Sp* a pagyanan

Adept experto-*Sp*, dalubhasa; Iloc: experto

Adequate bastante-*Sp*, casya, sapat na katamtaman lamang; Iloc: bastante, usto-*Sp*, makaanay nga kalkalaengan na
Synonym
Sufficient sapat, casya; Iloc: umanay, bastante

Adhere *v.* dumidikit o cumacapit ng husto; Iloc: agdikkit o agcapet ti usto

Adherence *n.*, **Adherent** *adj.* sumosoporta at sumusunod ng husto; Iloc: mangsupsuportar ken agtungtungpal iti usto (suporta/suportar-*Sp*)

Adhesion *n.*, **Adhesive** *adj.* pandikit, cola-*Sp*; Iloc: pangpigket, pang-dekket, cola

Adjacent katabi, karatig; Iloc: kaabay, kadinna

Adjoin *v.*, **Adjoining** *adj.* icabit, idugtong, pangcabit; Iloc: iconecta, isilpo, pangsilpo

Adjourn ipagpaliban ang pulong sa tinakdang dadating na fecha-*Sp*; paglipat ng lugar sa ibang lugar-*Sp*

Adjudge, Adjudicate atasan o hatolan ng batas gaya ng corte ng husticia-*Sp*

Adjunct 1] bagay na isama o idugtong pero hindi naman talagang kailangang-kailangan; 2] taong kaanib na mas mababa ang estado-*Sp* o ranko-*Sp* o otoridad-*Sp*; 3] taong nagtatrabaho sa escuelahan, colehio-*Sp* o universidad-*Sp* pero hindi permanente ang estado-*Sp*

Adjust *adjust,* ayosin para bumuti o umandar o umangkop; Iloc: *adjust,* urnosen para mas nasayaat o para umandar o ag-umno

Administer, Administrate 1] mangulo o mamahala, 2] sa *Medicine,* magsagawa ng panggamot; Iloc: 1] mangulwan ken mangigaway, 2] sa *Medicine,* mangaramid ti pangpaagas

Administration *(Tag. & Iloc.)* administrasyon-*Sp*

Administrator *(Tag. & Iloc.)* administrador-*Sp*

Admirable kahanga-hanga; Iloc: nakadaydayaw

Admire humanga, kaloguran; Iloc: dayawen, apreciaren (apreciar-*Sp*)

Admission 1] payagang pumasok, 2] pagtanggap ng katotohanan; Iloc: 1] palubosan a sumrek, 2] mang-akceptar-*Sp* iti kaagpaysuan

ADMIT, Let enter papasokin; Iloc: pastreken, paserreken

ADMIT a wrongdoing *You are commendable and dignified because you are conscientious to listen to your conscience and admit your wrongdoing. You have conscience-compunction that you discern your own fault and you take responsibility and self- accountability of the hurt and damage that your wrongdoing has caused. You are conscionable that you accept the ensuing chastisement, and you neither validate your wrongdoing nor justify it, neither lay the blame on other people nor on circumstances. You apologize and ask for forgiveness. All in all, this is an <u>admirable character demonstrating transparency and credibility</u>. This beautiful trait is usually evaded because of pride, lack of empathy, and lack of good sense; but you are much better than that, being honest, fair and compassionate, so please retain your admirable character throughout your life.*

Admittance pahintulot o karapatan para pumasok

Admonish *v.,* **Admonition** *n.* pagpapayo ng marahan o maamo para ipatuwid o itama ang maling asal o gawa, ipaalaala ang obligasyon-*Sp*

Ado kuskos-balungos, ligalig pati sa maliliit na bagay na wala masiadong kabulohan; Iloc: kuskos-balungos, agriro uray iti babassit a banag nga awan unay valor-*Sp* na

Adolescent boy binatilyo; Iloc: bumarito

Adolescent girl dalaginding, dalagita; Iloc: balasitang

Adopt *v.,* **Adoption** *n.* kupkopin, amponin, angkinin at tanggapin sa sarili at sa familia-*Sp*

Adorable nakakahalina at kaibig-ibig; Iloc: nakaay-ayat

Adore ginigiliw, minamahal, sinisinta, iniibig; Iloc: ay-ayaten, dungdungwen

Adorn *v.,* **Adornment** *n.* magdecorasyon, gayakan, gayak, dcorasyon-*Sp;* Iloc: arcosan, arcos, decorasyon

Adroit may *skills,* may galing at dalubhasa sa pag-obra-*Sp* dahil sa kasanayan o sa *training* o sa pinag-aralan

Adulate *v.,* **Adulation** *n.* magpakita ng labis na paghanga o devosyon-*Sp;* pagpuri ng alipin

Adult nasa mayor-*Sp* de-*Sp* edad-*Sp* na; Iloc: nataenganen, nakadanonen ti mayor de edad

Adulterate *v.,* **Adulteration** *n.* adulterasyon-*Sp*, nahaloan ng ibang bagay, hindi na puro-*Sp;* Iloc: adulterasyon, nalaokan ti sabali a banag, haanen a puro

Adultery pagtataksil, nangangaliwa, casal pero-*Sp* nambabae o nanla-lalake; Iloc: adda asawa na ngem adda pay babae na o lalake na, abig.

Advance sumugod, mag-avante-*Sp;* Iloc: ag-avante

ADVANCED mas may kaliwanagang kaalaman sa mga *ideas* o pag-wawari, kagawian at pagsasagawa, pakikisama at pag-aasal kaysa sa caraniwang tao; malayo na nangunguna sa progreso-*Sp*, kaalaman, abilidad-*Sp* o sa pagka-complicado-*Sp*

ADVANCED (Medical) Directive see Living Will

ADVANTAGE ventahe-*Sp*, pakinabang; Iloc: ventahe, gundaway

ADVANTAGE, Leverage lamang; Iloc: gundaway

ADVANTAGE of, take samantalahin, pakinabangan, makinabang, manlamang; Iloc: aggundaway, ag-oportunista-*Sp*

Advantageous kapakipakinabang, mapakinabangan, maka-ventahe-*Sp;* Iloc: makasayaat, makapanam-ay, maventahe, nagundaway

Adventure pakikipagsapalaran; Iloc: makigasang-gasat

Adversary kalaban, kaaway, kagalit; Iloc: kalaban
Antonym

Advocate, Backer mangsuporta, tagapagtaguyod; Iloc: mangsuportar

Adverse nakakabigay-sama, contra sa nakakabuti at nakakatulong; *(Tag. & Iloc.)* contra-*Sp*, antipatico-*Sp*

Adversity kasawiang-palad, kahirapan, kagipitan

Advertise *v.,* **Advertisement** *n.* panghalina at pangpa-engganyo-*aSp* ng cliente-*Sp* na patalastas o pahayag sa TV o *internet* o sa periodico-*Sp* at iba pa

Advice *advice,* payo, balacad, mungkahi; Iloc: *advice,* bagbaga, balacad, singasing

Advise payohan, magmungkahi, *advise*-an; Iloc: *advise*-an, bagbagaan, agsingasing
Synonym
Chide pagsabihan ng marahan para sa pagpapakabuti niya; Iloc: bagbagaan iti nainnayad tapno agpakaimbag isu

Advocate *v.,* **Advocacy** *n.* tao o sangay na nagfa-favor-*Sp*, nagsusuporta o nagde-defensa-*Sp* sa tao o layonin; tagataguyod; mangrecomenda

Affable *adj.,* **Affability** *n.* katangiang nakakapalagayang-loob ma-kipag-usap sa canya; Iloc: custombre-*Sp* nga napintas iti ricricnaen a makisarita canyana

Affair 1] *event* o pangyayari o *performance* o paggaganap 2] *party* o pagdiriwang, *gathering* o pagtitipon-tipon o iba pang tinatag na kasayahang ocasyon-*Sp*; 3] matindi at pag-iibigang pagtatalik na caraniwan ay maiklihang panahon lamang; pangyayari na naglilikha ng salungatan o pagkasirang-puri o scandalo-*Sp*

Affect nakaka-afecto-*Sp*, maafectohan; Iloc: nakakaafecto, maafectaran (afectar-*Sp*)

Affected *adj.,* **Affectation** *n.* asal o salitang pampakitang-tao lamang para makatamo ng favor-*Sp* sa canyang sarili; Iloc: tignay o sarita nga pakitang-tao laeng para makagun-od iti favor para iti bagbagi na

AFFECTION lambing, carinyo-*Sp*; Iloc: dungngo, lailo carinyo

AFFECTION, show carinyohin, naglalambing; Iloc: agcarcarinyo, agdungdungngo, aglalailo, cumarayo

Affectionate malambing, ma-carinyo-*Sp*, carinyoso/sa-*Sp*; Iloc: carinyoso/ sa, mapagcarayo, nadungngo, nalailo,

Affidavit *(Tag. & Iloc.)* *affidavit*

Affiliate *v.,* **Affiliation** *n.* 1] makipisan para bumuo ng asosasyon-*Sp* o pakikipag-ugnayan; 2] bakasin ang pinagbuhatan o canyang angkan

Affinity 1] pagkakaugnayan dahil sa pagkapareho ng pinagmulan nila, 2] natural-*Sp* na hilig na pagka-gusto-*Sp* o pagkaakit sa tao o bagay o pag-iisip; Iloc: 1] adda pagka-coneksion-*Sp* da gapu iti pagkapareho ti pinagtaudan da, 2] natural nga pagkagusto o pagkaay-ayo iti tao, banag o panagpampanunot

Affix 1] idikit, 2] lumagda; Iloc: idikkit, 2] ag-firma-*Sp*

Affliction *n.,* **Afflict** *v.* sakit o hirap o bigat ng katawan at pag-iisip; Iloc: sakit o rigat o dagsen ti bagi ken nakem
   Correlated words
   Agony paghihirap sa katawan o isip; Iloc: rigat iti bagi wenno nakem
   Anguish hapis sa kalooban at isip; Iloc: apgis ti ricna ken nakem, sennaay

Affluence *n.,* **Affluent** *adj.* abundancia-*Sp,* sagana, dami; Iloc: abundancia, adu, wadwad, ruay

Afford abut-caya, cayang bilhin o gawin; Iloc: cabaelan a gatangen o aramiden

Aforementioned, Aforesaid iyong naunang nabanggit o nasabi; Iloc: daytay naybagan

Affront kilos o salita na harap-harapang pagsumbat o mang-insulto-*Sp*; Iloc: tignay o sarita nga makisango nga maki-apa o mang-insulto

Afraid takot; Iloc: mabuteng

AFTER, Afterwards pagkatapos, pagkaraan; Iloc: calpasan na, idi nalpas

AFTER all *(Tag. & Iloc.)* total-*Sp*
   Anyway *(Tag. & Iloc.)* total

AFTER-hours nangyyayari pagkatapos ng trabaho-*Sp* sa oficina-*Sp*; Iloc: aramid palpas ti trabaho diay oficina

Aftereffect *(Tag. & Iloc.)* efecto-*Sp* ng gamot, medicina-*Sp*

Aftermath resulta-*Sp* o kasunod ng pangyayari lalo na ang nakakahamak o mapinsala

AFTERNOON hapon; Iloc: malem

AFTERNOON, this ngayong hapon; Iloc: daytoy malem, nu malem

Aftershock mga yanig pagkatapos ng malakas na lindol; Iloc: dagiti tagtag palpas ti napigsa a ginggined

Afterwards pagkatapos; Iloc: pagkapalpas

Again na naman, muli, uli; Iloc: manen

Against contra-*Sp,* laban sa, labag sa; Iloc: contra, agsalangad, agsuppiat

AGAPE *[uh-geyp]* napanganga sa gulat; Iloc: napanganga ti kigtot

AGÁPÊ *[ä'gä͵pä]* ang pag-ibig at pagmamahal na pinamalas ng Panginoong Dios sa pamamagitan ng Dios Anak na si Hesu Cristo na nagsacrificio para sa ating lahat para mapunta tayo sa langit; pagmamahal ng mga Cristiano sa kapwa-tao dahil sa pagpapatnubay ng Panginoong Dios

AGE edad-*Sp,* taon, gulang; Iloc: edad, tawen

AGE, same magkaedad; Iloc: agkaedad (edad-*Sp*)

Agency *(Tag. & Iloc.)* ahensia-*Sp*

Agenda plano-*Sp;* lista-*Sp* ng mga dapat pag-uusapan, gagawin, aasecasohin, tataposin, pipiliin o ano pa man

Agent *(Tag. & Iloc.)* ahente-*Sp*

Aggrandize palakihin ang kapangyarihan, kayamanan, rangko at dangal; palakihin ang laki, lawak at tindi

Aggravate palubhain, palalain, ipagrabe; Iloc: aramiden a grabe-*Sp,* aramiden a problema
Antonym
   Pacify pacalmahin, ipahinahon, papayapain, awatin; Iloc: pacalmaen, patalnaen, aganawa, ay-aywen, anawaen, paulimeken

Aggress mag-umpisa ng away; unang mang-atake-*Sp* o mangpagalit; Iloc: mangsuron, mang-atake

Aggressive *adj.,* **Aggression** *n.* agresivo-*Sp,* marahas, mapusok, pagkaagresivo; Iloc: agresivo, naranggas ken naulpit pagkaagresivo

Aggrieved *(Tag. & Iloc.)* na-maltrato-*Sp,* na-agraviado-*Sp*

Aghast nanaig ang takot o pagtataka o paghanga; Iloc: napabuteng o siddaaw o dayaw

Agile listo-*Sp,* malikot, masigla, maliksi, activo-*Sp;* Iloc: nasiglat, activo, alisto-*aSp*

Agitate galitin, inisin; Iloc: ruroden, paguraen

Agitated *(Tag. & Iloc.)* aburrido-*aSp*

Agitator nang-u-uumpisa-*aSp* ng away o gulo; Iloc: agparugi ti apa wenno gulo

Ago noon, noong nakalipas, noong araw; Iloc: idi, idi napalabas, idi nabayagen

Agog pinananabikan, ninanasa, inaasam-asam; Iloc: agaggagar, agag-agum, agpappapaos

Agonize *v.,* **Agony** *n.* paghihirap sa katawan o isip; Iloc: rigat iti bagi wenno nakem

Agree magsang-ayon, payag, magkasundo; Iloc: umayon, agmayat, umannugot, agtunos

Agreeable *(Tag. & Iloc.)* amenado, payag/mayat

Agreement kasundoan; Iloc: katulagan

Agriculture agricultura-*Sp*, pagsasaka, pagtanim; Iloc: agricultura, panagmulmula, pagtaltalon, pagtantanem

AHEAD una, nauna; Iloc: umuna, immuna

AHEAD of the game para may ventahe-*Sp* o lamang sa situasyon, nag-preparado-*Sp* nang maaga para mas lalong handa sa mga kinakailangang gawain

AHEAD of time maaga pa ay naghanda na bago dumating ang tinakdang oras-*Sp*; Iloc: nasapa pay ket nakasaganan baro sumangpet ti oras a nay-designar-*Sp*

AID ayuda-*Sp*, tulong; Iloc: tulong

AID and abet tumutulong sa iba; tumutulong o hinihikayat ang iba para gumawa ng masama

Ail may sakit; Iloc: agsakit

Ailment karamdaman, sakit; Iloc: sakit

AIM, Purpose balak, tangka, layonin, sanhi, adhika, pakay, intension; Iloc: pakay, rangta, panggep, intension

AIM weapon at itutok ang baril, i-puntirya-*Sp*; Iloc: ipuntirya ti paltoog

Air *n.,* **Airy** *adj.* hangin, mahangin; Iloc: angin, naangin

Airborne dala ng hangin o himpapawid; Iloc: awiten ti angin o tangatang

Airplane *(Tag. & Iloc.) airplane,* eroplano-*Sp*

Airport *airport*, paliparan at palapagan ng eroplano-*Sp*; Iloc: *airport*, pag-dissaagan dagiti eroplano

Airsickness nalulula't hilo lala na sa eroplano; Iloc: maulaw ken agvakcuar diay eroplano

Airy, Well-ventilated mahangin, maginhawang hangin; Iloc: napariir

Aisle *(Tag. & Iloc.)* pasilyo-*Sp*

Ajar nakabukas ng kaunti; Iloc: nakalucat ti bassit

Akimbo, hands nakapamewang; Iloc: nakabanyikis

Akin 1] magkamag-anak, 2] may pagkaparehoang katangian o clase-*Sp*; Iloc: 1] agkabagyan, 2] adda pagka-pareho-*Sp* iti tipo-*Sp* ken clase

Alarm takotin, balisahin; Iloc: padanagen, butngen

Alarming nakakakilabot, nakakabalisa; Iloc: makapadanag, makapabuteng

Albatross 1] malaking ibon na ang mga daliri ng paa ay magkakadugtong o magkakabit gaya ng *web-feet*; 2] parating pasanin at nakakahadlang sa pag-unlad o tagumpay

Albino tao o hayup na maputla ang balat at may diferencia-*Sp* ang paningin; Iloc: tao o animal-*Sp* a bessag ti cudil ken adda diferencia ti panagkita na

Album *(Tag. & Iloc.) album*

Albumen puti ng itlog; Iloc: puraw ti itlog
> *Correlated words*
> **Glair** puting parte ng itlog; Iloc: puraw a parte ti itlog
> **Yolk** pulang parte ng itlog; Iloc: nalabbaga a parte ti itlog

Alcohol *alcohol,* alak; Iloc: *alcohol,* arak

Alert alerto-*Sp,* handa sa puedeng mangyari; Iloc: alerto, nakasagana iti mabalin a mapasamak

Alfresco sa labas kung saan fresco-*Sp* ang hangin; Iloc: diay ruar nu inchenna ti fresco nga angin

Alias *alias,* falsong pangalan para itago ang canyang pagkakakilanlan o *identity*; Iloc: *alias,* falso-*Sp* a nagan para ilemmeng nu sinno isu

Alibi pagdahilan, palusot; Iloc: pambar, palusot

Alien dayuhan, tagaibang bansa, banyaga; Iloc: tagasabali a dayo, estranhero-*Sp*

Alienate lumalayo o magpakita ng galit o pag-contra-*Sp*

Alight umibis, bumaba; Iloc: agdissaag, bumaba

Align 1] areglohing palinya, 2] makisabwat sa isang partido-*Sp*; Iloc: 1] i-areglo-*Sp* ti linya, 2] makisabwat ti maysa a partido

Alike pareho-*Sp,* magkatulad; Iloc: pareho, agpada

Alive buhay; Iloc: sibibiag

ALL lahat, pulos, panay; Iloc: amin, pulos, panay, pasig

ALL-around maraming alam at nakakasagawa ng maraming bagay at mahusay pa ang gawa; Iloc: maka-obra-*Sp* iti adu nga agsasabali ken nakalalaeng pay

144

ALL day maghapon; Iloc: entero-*Sp* aldaw

ALL ears todo-todong makinig; Iloc: agdengngeg unay

ALL in one piece ligtas, hindi nasaktan, walang pinsala o sira, Iloc: salvar-*Sp*, haan nasaktan, awan peggad ken awan dadael

ALL-inclusive sacop lahat-lahat; Iloc: sacop am-amin

ALL month buong buan; Iloc: makabulan

ALL night magdamag; Iloc: agpatnag

ALL right, Alright *all right* ay ginagamit sa *formal* na panunulat at ang ibig sabihin nito ay "oo", "ligtas", "malayo sa panganib", "mapag-kakatiwalaan", "maaasahan", "mabuti", "nagbibigay-tuwa"; at ang *alright* ay pareho sa *all right* kaya lang ginagamit lamang ito sa basta-bastang panunulat

ALL set handa na; Iloc: nakarubwaten, nakasaganan

All together sabay-sabay, magkakasama; Iloc: aggigiddan, agrarana, agkacadwa
Same sound, different meanings
Altogether lahat-lahat, completo, kasama lahat; Iloc: am-amin

ALL week buong lingo; Iloc: entero-*Sp* dominggo-*Sp*

ALL year buong taon; Iloc: makatawen, entero-*Sp* tawen

Allege *v.*, **Allegation** *n.* magpahayag kahit walang prueba-*Sp* o pangpa-tutoo; Iloc: isawang uray no awan pay prueba wenno pangpaneknek

Allergy ang sintoma-*Sp* ng *allergy* ay pagbabahin, kati, pamumula sa balat o mas grabe-*Sp* na efecto-*Sp* ay hindi hiyang sa gamot o pabango, *pollens* o pagkain; Iloc: ti sintoma ti *allergy* ket paghatsing, paggatel, paglabbaga iti cudil o mas grabe pay nga efecto contra ti agas, bang-banglo, *pollens* o kanen

Alleviate hangoin sa hirap o pighati o sakit, bigyan ng consuelo-*Sp*; paginhawain, magpalubag-loob; Iloc: ikkan ti bang-ar o inana ti nakem o bagi, mangconsuelo, ag-simpatiya-*Sp*, ay-aywen
Correlated words
Ease, Soothe paginhawain; Iloc: pabang-aran
Mitigate pagaanin ang kahirapan o kabigatan; Iloc: palag-anen iti rigat o dagsen

Alley *(Tag. & Iloc.)* pasilyo-*Sp*

Alligator *(Tag. & Iloc.)* buwayang mas maliit ng kaunti pero wala sa Filipinas itong clase-*Sp* ng *reptile* na ito

Allocate maglaan, mambahagi; Iloc: manglasin, manglak-am, mangibingay
Correlated words
Apportion paghati-hatiin, maglaan; Iloc: pagbingay-bingayen, manglak-am
Share magpamudmod, bahaginan, nagpapamahagi, damayan; Iloc: pagbibingayan, mangbingay, mangiramay, mangilak-am
Allot *v.,* **Allotment** *n.* nilaang pera o fondong panggugol para sa tinakdang layonin; Iloc: inlasin a cuarta o fondo-*Sp* nga naysaad para iti maysa a rangta
ALLOW pahintulotan, payagan, itulot; Iloc: palubosan, ipalubos
ALLOW to enter papasokin, bigyang-daan; Iloc: paserken, palasaten
Allowance perang pambili ng pagkain sa paaralan o pang-gastos-*Sp* sa kailangan; Iloc: cuarta para iti kanen diay escuela-*Sp* o panggastos iti kasapulan
Allude *v.,* **Allusion** *v.* hindi derechohan na salita kundi pahiwatig lamang; Iloc: haan a derechoan a sarita nu di pangpasagid laeng
Allure akitin, magkiri, mag-alembong; Iloc: i-tentar-*Sp*, uyotan, sulisogen
Allluring kaakit-akit, kaibig-ibig, kagiliw-giliw; Iloc: nakaay-ayat
Allusion *n.,* **Allusive** *adj.* hindi derechohan na salita kundi pahiwatig lamang; Iloc: haan a derechoan a sarita nu di pangpasagid laeng
Ally *n.,* **Allied** *adj.* magkakaanib at nagkakaisa; Iloc: gayyem, katimpuyog
Almighty Panginoong Dios sa langit na pinakamakapangyarihan sa lahat at Siya ang lumikha ng buong universo at lahat ng nasa universo; Iloc: Apo Dios iti langit nga pinakamannacabalin iti amin ken Isu ti nagparsua iti entero nga universo ken amin nga adda iti universo *(read God in this book for more information)*
Almost halos, halos lahat, muntik na; Iloc: ngangngani, dandani, nagistayan
Alms limos-a*Sp*, abuloy; Iloc: limos
Alone mag-isa, solo-*Sp*; Iloc: agmaymaysa, solo
Aloof matamlay makisama, ilag, mailap; Iloc: natamnay a makicadwa, naatap
Aloud malakas na tinig o boses-*Sp;* Iloc: napigsa nga timec o boses
Alphabet *(Tag. & Iloc.) alphabet*, alfabeto
Already na; Iloc: *ilocano word* + **en**
Alright *(see All right)*
Also din, rin, at, saka, pa, pati, naman; Iloc: met, pay, pati, ken
Altar *altar*, dambana; Iloc: *altar*

ALTER bagohin, ibahin; Iloc: balbaliwan, baliwan

ALTER ego 1] isang kabila ng pagkatao; 2] matalik at madalas na kasamang kaibigan na kaparehong-kapareho niya

Alternate relyevo-*Sp*, kahalili, halinhan; Iloc: relyevo, mangsublat

Alternating torno-torno-*Sp*, naghahali-halili, naghahalinhan; Iloc: agsisin-nublatan, torno-torno, agsinnalisi-an

Alternative, Alternatives mga puedeng pagpipilian, mga alternatiba-*Sp* o opciones-*Sp*; Iloc: dagiti mabalin a pagpilyan, dagiti alternatiba o opsiones
Synonyms
Choices, Options pagpipiliang mga paraan o bagay; Iloc: dagiti pagpilyan a pamay-an o banag

Although bagamat, maski na, kahit na; Iloc: uray nu, uray pay

Altitude sukat ng pagkataas sa himpapawid; Iloc: rukod ti kangato diay tangatang

Altogether lahat-lahat, completo, kasama lahat; Iloc: am-amin

Altruist *adj.*, **Altruism** *n.* nagmamalasakit sa kapwa at hindi siya ma-kasarili; Iloc: mangisaksakit iti dadduma ken haan man laeng a bagbagi na ti pampanunoten na

Aluminum *(Tag. & Iloc.) aluminum*

Alumna-babae, **Alumnus**-lalake: dating estudiante-*Sp* o nag*graduate* sa colehio-*Sp* o universidad-*Sp* na pinasukan niya; Iloc: dati nga estudiante o nag-*graduate* iti colehio o universidad a sinerkan na

Always tuwina, tuwing beses-*Sp*, firmi-*Sp*, panay-panay, parati, palagi; Iloc: cada-*Sp* beses, firmi, agnanayon, pasig
Correlated words
Often palagi, madalas, malimit; Iloc: canayon
Sometimes kung minsan; Iloc: nu dadduma, pasaray
Sporadic pabugso-bugso; Iloc: sagpaminsan
Once in a while paminsan-minsan; Iloc: sagpaminsan
Successive sunod-sunod; Iloc: agsasaruno

Am, I ako ay, ako ang, ako si; Iloc: siac ni, siac ti

Amass mag-imbak, mag-ipon, mag-impok; Iloc: agurnong

Amateur bagohan; Iloc: agdamdamo

Amaze mamangha; Iloc: masdaaw

Amazing kamangha-mangha; Iloc: nakaskasdaaw

Ambassador *(Tag. & Iloc.)* embahador-*Sp*

Ambiance modo-*Sp* o ang nangingibabaw na kalagayan o nararamdaman sa isang paligid o lugar-*Sp*

Ambiguous meron o nakabukas sa maraming kahulogan o iba't iba na interpretasyon-*Sp*, malabo at mahirap intindihin at walang kasigurohan ang uri

Ambition ambisyon-*Sp*, pangarap, adhika, hangarin niyang maging; Iloc: ambisyon, tarigagay, cayat na a pagbalinan
Synonyms
Aspiration, Dream mithi, aspirasyon; Iloc: aspirasyon, essem

Ambitious *(Tag. & Iloc.)* ambicioso/sa-*Sp*

Ambivalent damdaming nasa pagitan ng positivo-*Sp* at negativo-*Sp* kaya hindi malaman kung ano ang kilos o pagturing o paniwala na susundin

Ambulance *(Tag. & Iloc.)* ambulancia-*Sp*

Ambulant cayang lumakad; Iloc: caya na ti magna

Ambulatory tungkol sa o cacayahan ng paglakad; Iloc: maygapu iti o cabaelan a magna

Ambush *ambush*, harang; Iloc: *ambush*, agabang a mangdunor o mangpatay

Amend itama o bagohin para bumuti ang pagkagawa o asal; Iloc: i-usto o pabarwen tapno mas nasayaat ti tignay wenno ti pagkaaramid

Amenities mga calidad-*Sp* o beneficio-*Sp* na makakapaginhawa o nakakapanghikayat sa kalinisan, pagkamaaliwalas, ganda, comfortable-*Sp*, kasiya-siya; Iloc: dagiti *quality* o calidad o *benefits* o beneficio a makabang-ar o makaaw-awis ti linis ken iti nakaay-ayo, napariir, napintas, comfortab-le, nakaay-ayo

American *(Tag. & Iloc.)* Americano/na-*Sp*

Amiable mainam na makipagkaibigan at kaaya-aya; Iloc: naimbag a makigayyem ken nacaay-ayo

Amicable mabuting makipagkaibigan, mabuti ang balak, mapayapang makipag-ugnay; Iloc: nasingpet makigayyem, nasayaat a panggep, napia o natalna nga makicadcadwa

Amid, Amidst nandodoon sa gitna ng kapaligiran; Iloc: adda iti tengnga ti lawlaw

Amiss mali o defectong gawa; Iloc: defecto nga aramid

Amnesia *(Tag. & Iloc)* *amnesia*

Amok, Amuck huramentado, mamamatay tao sa sino man na masalubong o matagpuan niya; Iloc: huramentado a mangpatay iti sinno man a makita na

Among nandodoon na kasama o sa gitna ng kapaligiran ito ng maraming mga tao o bagay; Iloc: adda isu a cadwa wenno tengnga ti lawlaw nga adda tattao ida wenno bambanag

AMOUNT precio-*Sp*, cuenta-*Sp*, halaga; Iloc: precio, cuenta, valor-*Sp*

AMOUNT, total, Total count suma-*Sp*, buong bilang; Iloc: sumar-*Sp* ti entero-*Sp*, bilang

Amphibian hayop na puedeng matira sa tubig at lupa; Iloc: animal-*Sp* nga aggigian ti danum wenno iti daga

Amplify palakasin ang tunog; Iloc: papigsaen ti uni

Amputate putolin; Iloc: putden

Amulet anting-anting, agimat; Iloc: anting-anting

Amuse aliwin, libangin; Iloc: parambaken, liwliwaen, linglingayen

Amusement libangan, aliwan; Iloc: paglinglingayan, pagliwliwaan
   Correlated words
   Hobby *hobby*, kinahihiligan, libangan, dibersion; Iloc: paglinglingayan, dibersion, *hobby*
   Pastime kinahihiligan, libangan, dibersion; Iloc: paglinglingayan, pasa-tiempo, dibersion

Amusing nakakalibang, nakakaaliw; Iloc: nakalinglingay, makaliwliwa

AN ang, ang isa; Iloc: ti, ti maysa

AN arm and a leg gastos na napakamahal, halimbawa ay "Kung bibili ka ng bahay sa San Francisco, ang bayad mo ay abutin ng *an arm and a leg*"

Anal puit, tumbong; Iloc: ubet, kimmut

Analgesic gamot na nakakatanggal ng sakit sa katawan; Iloc: agas a makaikkat iti sakit ti bagi

Analogous *(Tag. & Iloc.)* pareho-*Sp*

Analyze *v.*, **Analysis** *n.* **Analytic** *adj.* suriin, pag-aralan, usisahin, usigin, siyasatin; Iloc: sukisoken, sukimaten, adalen, usigen, usisaen

Anarchy kagulohang hindi mapigil ng govierno-*Sp*, kawalan ng pagsunod sa otoridad-*Sp*

Anathema excomunicadong tao o bagay, kinamumuhian at minumura at sinusumpa; Iloc: excomunicado a tao o banag, kagurgura, ilalais ken idadanes

Anatomy *n.* katawan ng hayop o halaman at mga parte-*Sp* nito o siencia-*Sp* o pag-aaral nito

Ancestors ninuno; Iloc: pupoon

Ancestry lipi, kanuno-nunohan; Iloc: pupoon, kaputotan, nagtaudan

Anchor a boat idaong; Iloc: isanglad

And at, atchaka; Iloc: ken, chaka

Anecdote maikling cuento ng pangyayari; Iloc: storia-*Sp* a ababa maygapu iti naypasamak

Anemia *n.,* **Anemic** *adj. anemia, anemic,* kulang sa dugo; Iloc: *anemia, anemic,* kurang ti dara

Anesthesia *n.,* **Anesthetic** *adj. anesthesia,* pampamanhid; Iloc: *anesthesia,* pangbibineg para haan makaricna

Angel *(Tag. & Iloc.)* anghel-*Sp*

Angelus pagdasal sa Dios bago dumilim, orasyon-*Sp*
Correlated word
Evening prayers *(Tag. & Iloc.) angelus,* orasyon

ANGER *n. & v.* galit, poot, pagalitin; Iloc: pungtot, rungsot, papungtoten

ANGER, suppressed kinikimkim na galit at ngitngit; Iloc: pagsushudot, agngarngaryet iti uneg

Angle *(Tag. & Iloc.) angle,* anggulo-*Sp*

Angry galit, nagagalit, napupuot; Iloc: makapungtot, makaunget

Angst kaba at pangamba na may kalungkotan; Iloc: agkebba-kebba ken maam-amak nga makaladladingit

Anguish hapis o sakit ng kalooban at isip; Iloc: sakit o sennaay ti ricna ken nakem

Animal hayop, *animal*; Iloc: *animal*

Animate gawin o bigyan ng buhay at magpakita ng sigla

Animated *adj.,* **Animation** *n.* vivo-*Sp*, viva-*Sp*, palabas na nagpapakita na ang kalagayan ng buhay ay masigla at masaya

Ankle buol, bukong-bukong; Iloc: lansalansa, lipaylipay

Annal, Annals mga kasulatan mula sa umpisa na nagsasaysay ng mga nangyari ng isang tanging taon o taon-taon sa mga nakaraan

150

Annex 1] gusaling ikinabit sa una o nakatayo nang gusali, 2] dagdag sa nakasulat sa documento-*Sp*; Iloc: 1] gusali nga naydekket iti sigud a nakatacderen a *building*, 2] nayon iti nakasurat iti documento

Annihilate 1] sirain ng husto para mawala na ang lahat; 2] talohin at lupigin; 3] ipawalang bisa

Anniversary *(Tag. & Iloc.) anniversary,* aniversario-*Sp*

Announce i-anuncio-*Sp*; Iloc: i-anuncio, ipablaac

Announcement pahayag, patalastas, anuncio-*Sp*; Iloc: warnac, pablaac, anuncio

Annoy nambwibwisit; Iloc: mangbwisbwisit

Annual minsan isang taon; Iloc: maminsan ti makatawen
   Correlated words
   Yearly taon-taon nagaganap, taonan, tuwing taon; Iloc: tinawen a mapaspasamak, cada tawen
   Perennial patuloy sa buong taon o patuloy na walang hangganan; Iloc: agtultuloy iti entero tawen wenno agtultuloy nga awan patinggana na
   All year buong taon; Iloc: makatawen, entero ti maysa tawen

Annul ipawalang bisa, ipawalang saysay; Iloc: ikkaten ti turay o bisa

Anoint mag-bendisyon-*Sp*, pahiran ng langis; Iloc: bendisyonan, sapsapoan o aprosan ti lana

Anomaly anomalya-*Sp*, lumihis o umiwas sa caraniwang paraan o kalagayan; Iloc: anomalya, aglisi iti sigud a pagpadalan o kasasaad

Anonymous *anonymous*, nililihim ang pangalan; Iloc: *anonymous*, ilimlimed iti nagan na

Another iba; Iloc: sabali

Answer sagot, tugon; Iloc: sungbat, subalit
   Antonym
   Ask tanong; Iloc: saludsod, damagen

ANT langgam; Iloc: cuton

ANT hill punso; Iloc: bunton ti cuton

Antagonist *adj.,* **Antagonism** *n.* pangongontra na may kasungitan; Iloc: pag-contra-*Sp* con-*Sp* todo-*Sp* saur

Antagonize contrahin, galitin, inisin; Iloc: contraen, ruroden, paguraen

Antecede *v.,* **Antecedent** *adv.* nauna sa kasunod

Anthem awit na pagpupuri o pagkamakabayan

Antibiotic gamot gaya ng *penicillin* para pahintoin ang pagdami at pagpagrabe ng microbio o patayin ang mga ito

Anticipate inaabangan, inaasahan; Iloc: ur-urayen, sirsirpaten, segseggaan, namnamaen

Antipathetic *adj.,* **Antipathy** *n.* antipatico/ca-*Sp,* masama ang ugali, masungit, mahilig mangontra; Iloc: antipatico/ca, dakes ti ugali, natangsit, nasaur, makarurrurod, managsupyat

Antiquated wala na sa moda-*Sp* at napakaluma na; Iloc: nakadadaanen, awanen ti moda

Antiseptic malinis at walang microbio-*Sp*

Antler sungay; Iloc: sara

Antonym *opposite,* saliwa o kasalungat sa kahulugan, kabaligtaran; Iloc: *opposite,* balictad a patarus
Synonyms
Opposite, Contrast kabaligtaran, kasalungat; Iloc: balictad
Antonym
Synonym magkasinghulogan; Iloc: agkapareho ti cayat da a sawen

Antsy nababagabag, balisa, nagugusot ang isip, hindi mapakali; Iloc: haan nga makatalna, madanagan, maringgoran

Anus puit, tumbong; Iloc: ubet, kimmut

Anxiety pagkabahala, pag-aalala; Iloc: danag ken riro

Anxious nababagabag, balisa, nagugusot ang isip, hindi mapakali; Iloc: maringgoran, haan nga makatalna, madanagan,

Any kahit ano; Iloc: uray ania

Anybody, Anyone sinoman, kahit sino; Iloc: sinno man, uray sinno

Anyhow 1] kahit pa, 2] kahit anomang paggawa; Iloc: 1] uray pay, 2] uray aniaman ti pagaramid

Anymore hindi na muli; Iloc: haan a mauliten

Anything kahit ano; Iloc: uray ania

Anytime kahit kelan; Iloc: uray caano

Anyway *(Tag. & Iloc.)* total-*Sp*

Anywhere saanman, kahit saan, saan mang lupalop; Iloc: sadino man, sadino man a lugar-*Sp,* uray inchenna
Correlated word
Everywhere nasa lahat ng lugar; Iloc: adda iti amin a lugar

Apart hiwalay, magkalayo, Iloc: naysina, agsina da

Apathetic *adj.,* **Apathy** *n.* walang pakialam, ni pagmamalasakit, ni pakiramdam at hindi man lamang mangonsuelo, ni interes; Iloc: awan biang na, haan mangisaksakit

Ape unggoy; Iloc: chonggo

Apex pinakamataas na lugar-*Sp,* patulis na forma sa ulo ng bundok; Iloc: kangatuan a lugar, natirad a forma diay ulo ti bantay

Apologize, Apologetic humingi ng patawad o paumanhin dahil sa ginawang kasalanan; Iloc: dumawat ti dispensar wenno pakawan gapu iti inaramid na basol

Apology paumanhin; Iloc: dispensar-*Sp*
   Correlated word
   Forgiveness patawad; Iloc: pakawan

Apostasy *n.,* **Apostate** *adj.* talikuran at lisanan ang relihion-*Sp* at paniniwala dito, o sa partido-*Sp,* talikuran ang principio-*Sp* ng buhay o sa layonin; Iloc: tallikudan ti relihion ken ti pammati ditoy o ti partido, tallikudan ti principio ti biag o ti pakay

Apostle *(Tag. & Iloc.)* apostol-*Sp,* dicipulo-*Sp*

App *app,* mga aplikasyon-*Sp* ng *computer* na puedeng i-*download* sa *mobile device* gaya ng *email,* mga libro-*Sp,* proteksion-*Sp* sa *virus,* pagmasdan o suriin ang mundo, pagsasalin ng ibang lengguahe-*Sp,* libangan gaya ng competensiahang-laro, musica-*Sp,* cine-*Sp* at *tourist attractions,* mapa-*Sp* at clima-*Sp,* GPS at pinakamalapit na kainan, tindahan, stasyon-*Sp* ng *gas,* kung saan nakaparada ang coche-*Sp* at iba pa; Iloc: *app,* dagiti aplikasyon ti *computer* nga mabalin i-*download* iti *mobile device* casla *email,* libro, proteksion contra-*Sp* ti *virus,* pagmingmingan ti entero-*Sp* mundo-*Sp,* pagpatarus ti sabali a lengguahe, paglinglingayan casla ti ay-ayam a competensia-*Sp,* musica, cine ken *tourist attraction* ida, mapa ken clima, GPS ken ti pinakaasideg nga panganan, tienda-*Sp,* stasyon ti gasolina-*Sp,* nu inchenna nakaparada iti coche ken sabali pay

Appall *v.,* **Appalling** *adj.* takot na naliito; Iloc: buteng nga adda pagkariro

Apparatus *apparatus,* aparato-*Sp,* kagamitan, kasangkapan, instrumento-*Sp;* Iloc: *apparatus,* aparato, instrumento

Apparel damit, pangsuot; Iloc: cawes, bado

Apparent lantad, halata, kitang-kita, litaw; Iloc: makitkita, nakaparang

APPEAL 1] pagsasamo, pakikiusap, 2] paglipat ng caso sa mas mataas na corte-*Sp* ng husticia-*Sp* para masuri ang decisyon-*Sp* ng mas mababang corte; Iloc: 1] makicacaasi, agkiddaw, 2] pag-acar ti caso-*Sp* idiay mas nangato a corte ti husticia para masukimat iti decisyon iti nababbaba a corte

APPEAL for public help panawagan ng tulong, manawagan; Iloc: mangpablaac para iti pagkiddaw ti tulong

Appealing kaakit-akit; Iloc: nakaay-ayat

Appear lumitaw, magpakita; Iloc: agparang, agpakita
Synonyms
Emerge, Bob up sumipot, umahon, sumulpot, lumitaw; Iloc: sumanglad, agparang, agpakita, lumtaw
Emanate lumabas buhat sa pinanggalingan; Iloc: rumuar nga naggapu idiay pinagtaudan na
Arise bumangon, umangat, umahon; Iloc: bumangon, ngumato, tumpaw

Appears like parang, tila, wari, mistulang...; Iloc: casla

Appearance ichura-*Sp*, anyo; Iloc: ichura, langa
Synonym
Countenance anyo ng mukha o galaw; Iloc: ichura ti rupa ken tignay

Appease pacalmahin, ipahinahon, papayapain, awatin, palubagin ang loob, magpalubag-loob na makipagkasundoan para bumuti ang kanilang pagsasamahan; Iloc: mangpatalna nga makitinnulag tapno agsayaat iti pagkacadwaan da, pacalmaen, atalnaen, aganawa, ay-aywen, anawaen, paulimeken, pabang-aran

Append *v.*, **Appendage** *n.* idagdag o icabit

Appendicitis *(Tag. & Iloc.) appendicitis,* apendicitis

Appetite gana-*Sp*; Iloc: ganas-*Sp*

Appetizer pampagana; Iloc: pangpaganas

Applaud *(Tag. & Iloc.)* palakpakan

Applause *(Tag. & Iloc.)* palakpak
Synonym
Ovation tumayo at magpalakpak; Iloc: tumacder ken agpalakpak

Apple *(Tag. & Iloc.)* mansanas-*Sp*

Appliance kagamitang-bahay na kailangang i-conecta-*Sp* sa electricidad-*Sp*; Iloc: aramat ti balay nga masapul nga iconecta ti electricidad

Applicable aplicado-*Sp*, may tugma o gamit sa paksa o bagay; Iloc: aplicado, naytutop ken maiyusar

Applicant *(Tag. & Iloc.)* aplicante-*Sp*

Application *(Tag. & Iloc.)* aplicasyon-*Sp*

APPLY for a job mag-*apply*; Iloc: ag-*apply*

APPLY lotion or ointment on skin pahiran ng *lotion* o cremang gamot; Iloc: sapsapwan o aprosan ti *lotion* wenno agas-crema

Appoint hirangin, ihirang, itatag o itakda sa isang trabaho-*Sp*; Iloc: i-designar-*Sp* o ipuesto-*Sp* iti maysa a trabaho

Appointment *appointment*, tipanan, tinakdang tipanan; Iloc: *appointment*, pinagtulagan nga agpatang wenno agkinnita

Apportion paghati-hatiin, pagbukod-bukorin; Iloc: bingay-bingayen, paglalak-amen

Appraise suriin o sukatan para malaman ang halaga; Iloc: usigen o rukoden para maamwan ti valor-*Sp*

Appreciate lugod; Iloc: apreciaren (apreciar-*Sp*)
   Correlated word
   Commend kinaluluguran ang mabuting gawain; Iloc: apreciaren ti nasayaat nga aramid

Appreciation pagkalugod, kaluguran; Iloc: pag-apreciar-*Sp*

Apprehend 1] arestohin, dakpin, huliin, 2] maintindihan; Iloc: 1] tiliwen, i-aresto-*Sp*, 2] maawatan

Apprehensive 1] kinakabahan, nangangamba, nag-aalangan, nag-aalinlangan, nag-aatubili, hindi mapakali, 2] nakakaintindi; Iloc: 1] agkebba-kebba, agtibtibbayo, casla maam-amak, agdudua, 2] makaawat

Apprehension 1] naiintindihan ang ibig sabihin; pananaw o pagturing sa mga bagay-bagay; 2] takot o pag-suspecha ng problema o kasamaan sa hinaharap; 3] pag-aresto

Approach lapitan, dumarating; Iloc: asitgan, sumungad
   Synonym
   Come near lumapit; Iloc: umasideg
   Antonym
   Go far lumayo; Iloc: umadayo

Appropriate akma, angkop, bagay; Iloc: umno, naytutop, us-usto-*Sp* para idiay

155

Appropriation nilaang pera o fondong panggugol para sa tinakdang layonin; Iloc: inlasin a cuarta-*aSp* o fondo-*Sp* nga naysaad para iti maysa a rangta

Approve aprovahan; Iloc: aprovaran (aprova/aprovar-*Sp*)

Approved *(Tag. & Iloc.)* aprobado-*Sp*

Approximate *v.,* **Approximately** *adj.* humigit-kumulang; Iloc: agsurok-agkurang

Approximation *(Tag. & Iloc.)* tancha

April *(Tag. & Iloc.) April,* Abril-*Sp*

Apron *(Tag. & Iloc.) apron*

Apt 1] posib-leng mangyari, 2] akma, bagay; Iloc: 1] posib-le-*Sp* a mapasamak, 2] naytutop, bagay

Aptitude kabilisan ng pag-aaral; Iloc: pardas ti pagadal

Aquatic nabubuhay at tumitira sa tubig; Iloc: agbibiag ken agyan iti danum

Arab *(Tag. & Iloc.) Arab,* Arabo

Arbitrate *(Tag. & Iloc.)* maghatol, mag-husgar-*Sp*

Arbitration pag-usig, paglitis at paghatol sa corte-*Sp* ng husticia-*Sp*; Iloc: pag-husgar-*Sp*, pag-usig ken pag-sentencia-*Sp* iti corte ti husticia
Synonym
Litigate maglitis, magsakdal; Iloc: magdemanda, maghusgar

Archaic *(Tag. & Iloc.)* 1] *ancient* at laos na, 2] salita na **di** na ginagamit; Iloc: 1] nagpasaren, 2] sarita nga haanen nga iyus-usar-*Sp, obsolete*

Arche, Arch *(Tag. & Iloc.)* arco-*Sp*

Archetype ang pinaka-orihinal-*Sp* na modelo-*Sp* o tipo-*Sp* kung saan gumaya ang iba; Iloc: ti pinakaimmuna a modelo o tipo nga tinuladan dagiti sumaruno

Archery libangang pana at palaso; Iloc: aglinglingay nga agpana ken sikkubeng

Archipelago grupo-*Sp* ng mga islas-*Sp*; Iloc: grupo ti islas ida

Architect *(Tag. & Iloc.) architect,* arkitecto-*Sp*

Archives paglagyan ng mga importanteng bagay ng *history*; Iloc: pagyanan dagiti importante-*Sp* a banag ti *history*

Arctic sobrang lamig na galing sa North Pole; Iloc: sobra a lamiis a naggapu diay norte-*Sp*

Ardent marubdob; Iloc: nasged, napasnek

Ardous gamitin ang lahat ng lakas at tibay at tiis; Iloc: iyusar iti amin a pigsa ken pakat ken anos

Are ay; Iloc: ti, iti, ket

Area lugar-*Sp*, pook; Iloc: lugar, purok, solar-*Sp*, minoyongan

Arena lugar na pinagcocompetensiahan ng larong *sports*; Iloc: pagco-competensiaan a lugar paraa iti ay-ayam nga *sports*
Correlated word
Theater cine, lugar na pagtanghalan ng pelicula o opera o *symphony orchestra* at iba pang palabas; Iloc: cine, lugar a pagbuyaan ti pelicula wenno opera wenno *symphony orchestra* ken sabali pay a pabuya

Argue magkasagutan, magdiscusyonan; Iloc: agdiscusyonan, agsinnungbatan,

Argument *(Tag. & Iloc.)* argumento-*Sp*, discusyon-*Sp*

Argumentative mahilig maki-argumento-*Sp*; Iloc: mapag-argumento

Argyle nagansilyo na may mga kulay at hugis diamante-*Sp* o manipis na cuadrado-*Sp* na nakatayong patulis na paa gaya ng *diamond-shaped*

Arid tuyo at tigang, mala-deserto-*Sp*; Iloc: namaga ken nabarang, maladeserto

Arise bumangon, umangat, umahon; Iloc: bumangon, ngumato, tumpaw

ARM 1] bisig, baraso, 2] armas-*Sp*; Iloc: 1] takkiag, 2] armas
Correlated word
Hand, Hands kamay; Iloc: ima

ARM, bent or twisted due to an old injury kimaw; Iloc: singkol

ARM-on-arm over their shoulders magkaakbay Iloc: agsallabay
Correlated word
Hold hands magkahawak; Iloc: agkibin

Armament kasangkapang pandigmaan sa lupa, sa dagat at sa him-papawid; Iloc: dagiti aramat nga panggerra ti daga, iti baybay ken iti tangatang (gerra-*Sp*)

Armchair silyon-*Sp*; Iloc: butaca-*Sp*

Armed *(Tag. & Iloc.)* armado-*Sp*

Armistice pinagkasunduang pansamantalang paghinto ng labanan o giyera; Iloc: pinagtulagan a temporaryo-*Sp* nga pagsardeng ti laban o gerra-*Sp*

Armory tagoan ng mga sandata; Iloc: pagidulinan cadagiti armas-*Sp*

ARMPIT *(Tag. & Iloc.)* kili-kili

ARMPIT odor anghit; Iloc: anglit

ARMS armas-*Sp*, sandata; Iloc: armas

ARMS-length dapal; Iloc: deppa

Army *army*, militante-*Sp*, hukbo, mga sundalo; Iloc: *army*, militante, dagiti soldado-*Sp*
  Correlated words
  Troops hukbo, mga sundalo, tropa; Iloc: buyot, dagiti soldado
  Soldiers mga sundalo, militante; Iloc: dagiti soldado
  Navy hukbong pandagat; Iloc: soldado ti taaw
  Airforce hukbong panghimpapawid; Iloc: soldado ti tangatang

Aroma magandang amoy; Iloc: nasayaat nga angot

Around palibot; Iloc: aglawlaw

Arouse 1] gisingin, mangpukaw, 2] bigyang-buhay, pakilosin; Iloc: 1] riingen, parugsuen, 2] biagen, pagarawen

Arraign patawag sa idinimandang tao na humarap sa husticia-*Sp* para sagutin ang paratang sa canya, hinabla; Iloc: pagawag iti indemanda-*Sp* a tao nga sumango diay corte-*Sp* tapno sungbatan na dagiti impabasol da canyana

Arrange areglohin, ayosin; Iloc: i-areglo-*Sp*, tarimanen

Arrangement ang pagkaayos, pagka-areglo-*Sp*; Iloc: ti pagka-urnos, pagka-areglo

Array mga bagay o makain na naka-hilera-*Sp* at naayos para lantad sa mga tao; Iloc: dagiti banag o makmakan a nakahilera ken inurnos tapno nakaparang cadagiti tattao

Arrears utang na hindi pa nababayaran at atrasado-*Sp* na, ano mang atrasado na; Iloc: utang nga atrasadon ti pagbayad, ania man nga atrasadon

Arrest arestohin, dakpin, huliin; Iloc: tiliwen, i-aresto-*Sp*

Arrival pagdating, pagsapit; Iloc: pagsangpet

Arrive dumating, sumipot; Iloc: sumangpet, makadanon,
  Correlated word
  Event arrival sumapit; Iloc: pagsangpet

Arrogant mapagmalaki, mapagmataas, matapobre, hambog, suplado/suplada-*Sp*; Iloc: napangas, mapagpannakkel, suplado/da
  Antonym

Humble mapagpacumbaba, mababang-loob, maamo; Iloc: napacumbaba, umilde, naamo

Arrogate ipasacanya o inaangkin kahit wala siyang karapatan; Iloc: isanicua uray no awan turay na

Arrow palaso; Iloc: sikkubeng

Arsenal bodega-*Sp* ng govierno-*Sp* kung saan nakaimbak at nakatago ang mg armas-*Sp* at iba pang gamit pang-*military* para sa panglupang servicio-*Sp* at pangdaragatang servicio ng *military*

Arson crimen-*Sp* ng pagsunog; Iloc: crimen ti pagpuor

Art sining, arte-*Sp*; Iloc: arte

Artery ugat na nagdadala ng dugo buhat sa puso papunta sa lahat-lahat ng parte ng katawan; Iloc: urat nga mangipan ti dara ti amin -amin a parte ti bagi

Artesian well *(Tag. & Iloc.)* pozo-*Sp* artesiano-*Sp* kung saan nakakakuha ng fresco-*Sp* at malamig na tubig pang-inumin o pampaligo
Correlated word
Water well n., balon, hinukay na malaking butas sa lupa na cinementohan na pagsasalokan ng tubig; Iloc: bubon

Arthritis *arthritis*, sakit sa *body joints* o pagkabitan ng dalawang buto sa katawan; Iloc: *arthritis*, sakit ti *body joints* wenno pagsilpuan ti dua a tulang iti bagi

Article 1] isang bagay, 2] articulo-*Sp* na pinahayag sa periodico-*Sp* o diaryo-*Sp* tungkol sa tutoong pangyayari; Iloc: 1] maysa a banag, 2] articulo nga impadamag ti periodico maygapu iti agpayso a napasamak

Articulate magsalitang claro-*Sp* o maliwanag at madaling maintindihan; Iloc: agsarita nga claro ken nalaca a maawatan

Artifact bagay na gawa ng kamay na nagmula sa nakalipas na panahon o sa ibang cultura-*Sp* at lahi; Iloc: banag nga aramid ti ima a naggapu iti napalabas a tiempo-*Sp* wenno iti sabali a cultura ken lahi

Artifice panlilinlang; Iloc: panggulgulib

Artificial *artificial*, hindi natural-*Sp*; Iloc: *artificial*, haan nga natural
Correlated word
Superficial *(Tag. & Iloc,)* pakitang-tao lang

Artisan experto-*Sp* na trabahador-*Sp* sa paggamit kadalasan ng canyang camay; Iloc: experto a trabahador ti pagiyusar (usar-*Sp*) na canayon iti ima na *(not to be mistaken for artesian well)*

Artist *(Tag. & Iloc.)* artista-*Sp*, taong ang obra-*Sp* ay sa arte-*Sp* gaya ng pintor-*Sp*, palabas sa entablado-*Sp*, pelicula-*Sp* at iba pa

AS gaya ng, gaya ni, kasing...; Iloc: casla ti, casla ni, kapada...

AS far as hanggang sa...; Iloc: inggana ti...

AS if kunwari; Iloc: sinsinan

AS in gaya halimbawa ng; Iloc: casla iti, por-*Sp* ehemplo-*Sp* ti

AS is iyon na rin kung anomang kasalukuyang kalagayan ng isang bagay o tao

AS long as *(Tag. & Iloc.)* 1] puede basta gagawin niya ang.., basta lamang...; 2] tatagal ng..; Iloc: 1] basta laeng.., mabalin basta laeng aramiden na iti..., 2] agbayag ti

AS mentioned umano, ang tinukoy, ang nasabi, daw; Iloc: tay naybaga, tay nasao, canu

AS soon as agad pagkatapos, agad-agad; Iloc: ensigida-*Sp*, dagdagos, apaman

AS soon as possible, ASAP sa posibleng pinakamadaling panahon; Iloc: iti posib-le-*Sp* a pinakanabiit a tiempo-*Sp*

Ascend aakyat, umakyat; Iloc: ngumato, agsang-at, umuli
Antonym
Descend bumaba, manaog; Iloc: bumaba, umulog, sumalog

Ascendant *adj.*, **Ascendancy** *n.* mas dominante-*Sp* o superyor-*Sp*; pataas

Ascending *adj.*, **Ascent** *n.*, paakyat, pataas; Iloc: agpangato, agpasang-at

Ascension 1] pag-akyat; 2] pagbabalik sa langit ng Dios Anak na si Hesu Cristo pagkatapos Siyang pinako sa cruz kung saan Siya namatay, pero pagkatapos ng tatlong araw ay nabuhay Siya muli, nakisalamuha Siya sa Canyang mga dicipulo bago bumalik Siya sa langit

Ascertain segurohin, maniguro; Iloc: seguradwen

Ascetic taong may diciplina-*Sp* sa sarili at ipagkait sa sarili ang mga capricho-*Sp* ng mundo-*Sp*; Iloc: tao nga adda diciplina na nga ipaidam iti bagi na dagiti capricho ti mundo

Ascribe iukol o igawad at turingan ng dangal o pasasalamat sa taong nakakarapat; Iloc: ipaay o isaad iti dayaw wenno pagyaman iti tao nga nayrebbengan o *worthy*

Ash abo; Iloc: dapo, apug

Ashame nahihiya; Iloc: mabain

Ashore sa dalampasigan; Iloc: diay igid ti taaw

ASIDE sa tabi; Iloc: diay igid

ASIDE from maliban sa, bukod sa; Iloc: malaksid iti

Asinine napakatanga, napakapulpul; Iloc: torpe-*Sp*, dagmel

ASK magtanong; Iloc: agsaludsod, agdamag

> *Synonyms*
> **Inquire** magtanong, mag-usisa; Iloc: agsaludsod, agusisa, agdamag
> **Interrogate** usisahin, kilatisin, usigin; Iloc: usisaen, usigin
> **Question someone about a possible infraction** sitahin; Iloc: sitaen
> *Antonyms*
> **Answer** sagutin, tugonin; Iloc: sungbatan
> **Respond** sumagot, tumugon; Iloc: agsubalit, agsungbat

ASK for a favor pakiusapan, makisuyo, humiling ng fabor-*Sp*; Iloc: makicacaasi, makifavor, agdawat, dumawat, agkiddaw

ASK for trouble asal o salita o gawain na nakakabunga ng gulo o sama

Askance 1] may suspecha-*Sp*, duda-*Sp* o pagtutol; 2] tumingin ng patagilid

Askew 1] tagilid, hindi tuwid; 2] inis

Asleep natutulog, tulog; Iloc: nakaturog

Aspect 1] ichura-*Sp* ng mukha; 2] pagturing o kung anong paningin ng isip sa isang bagay; 3] sa puesto-*Sp* na nakaharap sa isang direksion-*Sp*

Asphalt *(Tag. & Iloc.)* asfalto-*Sp*

Asphyxiate hindi makahinga o mawalan ng malay dahil sa *gas* o ibang usok na nakakapinsala sa buhay; Iloc: haan a makaanges wenno umawan iti puot gapu iti *gas* wenno sabali nga asok nga makadakes iti biag

Aspiration mithi, aspirasyon-*Sp*, ambisyon-*Sp*; Iloc: essem, calicagum, aspirasyon, ambisyon

Aspire magpursigi para sa canyang minimithi; Iloc: agpakat tapno maala ti calicagum na

Aspirin *(Tag. & Iloc.)* *aspirin,* aspirina-*Sp*

Assail saktan ang kapwa o pang-atake-*Sp* sa pananalita; Iloc: saktan ti tao wenno mang-atake iti sarita

Assassin mamamatay-tao, pumapaslang; Iloc: agpatay ti tao

Assassinate paslangin ng palihim; Iloc: patayen a palimed

ASSAULT saktan ang kapwa o pang-atake-*Sp* sa pananalita; Iloc: saktan ti tao wenno mang-atake iti sarita

ASSAULT and battery babala ng pananakit sa isang tao na sinundan ng tinutuong pananakit, kahit nasalat lang basta may hangaring maminsala

ASSEMBLE itipon-tipon, pagsama-samahin; Iloc: tipon-tiponen, pagkacadwaen

ASSEMBLE, Get together magpulong-pulong, magtipon-tipon; Iloc: ago-ummong, agtitipon
Correlated words
Meeting pulong-pulong, pagtipon-tipon, *meeting*; Iloc: pagtitipon, *meeting*
Gather or meet together magkita-kita, magsama-sama; Iloc: agtipon-tipon, agsasarak
Conference conferencia, pulong; Iloc: conferencia
Caucus *meeting* ng tanging mga miembro ng partido politico para pag-usapan ang mga importanteng bagay gaya ng paksa o layonin ng *convention* at iba pa
Congregate *v.,* **Congregation** *n.* pagtitipon ng nanalig o congregasyon sa simbahan o relihion para magsamba
Swarm pagsugod, sugoran, pagdagsa, dumogin; Iloc: agaribongbong, agcarambola

Assent magsang-ayon, pumayag; Iloc: agmayat, umannugot, agcanunong

Assert *v.,* **Assertive** *adj.* tumitindig para sa sariling kapapakanan at para sa canyang karapatan, makiharap na may lakas ng loob, katiyakan at tiwala; Iloc: maypannacder na iti bagi ken turay na, makisango nga adda tured, kasegoradwan, confiansa-*Sp* ken tured

Assess suriin para malaman ang halaga o kalagayan; Iloc: sukisoken para maamoan iti valor-*Sp* o kasasaad

Asset katangian ng tao na nakaka-ventahe-*Sp*, nakakatulong at mahalaga; Iloc: calidad-*Sp* nga naventahe, makatulong ken navalor-*Sp*

Assets ari-arian na may halaga at ventahe-*Sp* gaya ng bahay, lupa, pera sa banko-*Sp*, at iba pa; Iloc: sanicua nga addaan ti valor ken ventahe casla balay, daga, cuarta diay banko ken dadduma pay
Correlated words
Possessions ari-arian, pagaaring kagamitan at kasangkapan; Iloc: sanicua, cukcukua nga alicamen ken muebles ken dagiti maaramat
Property ari-arian, aring bahay at lote; Iloc: sanikua, cukua a balay ken lote
Belongings ari-arian, pag-aaring kagamitan at kasangkapan; Iloc: sanicua, cukcukua nga alicamen ken muebles ken dagiti maaramat

Asseverate ipahayag at igiit ng masigasig at serioso-*Sp*

Assidous panay at walang paghihinang magpatuloy; 2] panay ang pagsikap at pagsagawa, masipag, maasecaso

Assign hirangin, ihirang, italaga, itakda, i-puesto-*Sp*; Iloc: i-designar-*Sp* a trabahoen, i-puesto

Assigned as itakda na tagapag-; Iloc: in-designar-*Sp* nga tagapag-

ASSIGNMENT takdang gawain, takdang aralin; Iloc: i-designar-*Sp* a trabaho-*Sp* wenno adalen

ASSIGNMENT, place of naka-destino-*Sp* sa; Iloc: nakadestino idiay

Assimilate 1] bumagay at pumareho, 2] caraniwan ang minoria-*Sp* o imigrante-*Sp* ay nakikiisa sa kaugalian o kagawian ng pinasu-kang bayan o ng mayoria-*Sp* na karamihang mamamayan; Iloc: 1] bumagay ken pumareho, 2] canayon ket iti minoria o imigrante ket makipagkaykaysa iti costumbre-*Sp* ken aramid ti simrekan na a nasyon-*Sp* wenno iti mayoria nga dagiti *citizens* ti nasyon

Assist *(Tag. & Iloc.)* tumulong

Assistant katulong sa oficina-*Sp* o trabaho-*Sp*; Iloc: katulong diay oficina o trabaho

ASSOCIATE *n.* katipon, kasama; Iloc: katimpuyog
Synonym
Ally kaalyado, kaanib, kasapi, kacampi; Iloc: kaalyado, kabuyot, kacadwa, katimpuyog

ASSOCIATE *v.* makitipon, makipagkaibigan; Iloc: makitimpuyog, maki-gayyem, makicadwa

Association kapisanan, asosasyon-*Sp*, samahan, katipunan; Iloc: asosas-yon, timpuyog
Correlated words
Coalition pagsasama, pag-aanib at pagkakaisa ng mga tao, grupo, o ng mga provincia o mga bayan na puedeng hindi permanente
Organization organisasyon; Iloc: organisasyon
Group grupo; Iloc: grupo
Team pangkat; Iloc: timpuyog
Gang barcada o grupo ng mga bata na marami sa kanila ay delinquente

Assorted marami pero sari-sari; Iloc: adu ngem naduma-duma
Synonyms
Variety, Various, Varied, Vary iba't iba, sari-sari, marami; Iloc: agsasabali, naduma-duma, adu

Assuage paginhawain; Iloc: pabang-aran

Assume *v.,* **Assumption** *n.* 1] wari, palagay, kuro-kuro, haka-haka, 2] siya ang magbalikat ng trabaho-*Sp* o responsibilidad-*Sp* ng iba gaya ng umalis; 3] angkinin ang isang bagay; Iloc: 1] patta-patta, pagarup; 2] isu iti mangbagkat iti obra-*Sp* wenno responsibilidad ti sabali casla ti pimmanaw, 3] alaen wenno ipabagi na iti maysa a banag

Assurance *(Tag. & Iloc.)* pangsegurado

Assure *v.,* **Assurance** *n.* bigyang kasegurohan, isegurado; Iloc: ikkan ti kaseguroan, mang-seguro-*Sp*
Synonym
Reassure bigyang kasiguradohan o pangseguridad o prueba; Iloc: ikkan ti kasiguradoan o pangseguridad o prueba

Asthma *asthma,* hika; Iloc: *asthma,* angkit

Astonish mapamangha sa gulat, manggilalas; Iloc: mapanganga iti kigtot, masdaaw

Astound *same as Astonish above*

Astray naligaw, nalihis sa tamang daan, napalayo sa asal at pag-iisip na tama at matuwid; Iloc: naywawa, naylisi o napaadayo idiay usto-*Sp* a dalan, napukaw tay custombre-*Sp* ken pagpanunot na nga usto ken nalinteg

Astride nakabukangkang ang paa; Iloc: nakakayang

Astronomy *(Tag. & Iloc.)* astronomia-*Sp, science* tungkol sa himpapawid lampas o sa labas ng *atmosphere* ng ating mundo

Astute matalinong pagtuturing, matalas na pag-iisip; Iloc: intelihente a mangbigbig, nasirib iti pagpampanunot

Asunder *(Tag. & Iloc.)* hiwalay/agsina, separado-*Sp*

Asylum institusyon-*Sp* na nag-aalaga sa mga tao na nangangailangan ng pag-asecaso-*Sp* at tulong; lugar-*Sp* na nag-aalok ng pagtanggol at kaligtasan.

AT sa, nasa; Iloc: idiay, diay, ti

AT hand napakalapit sa tinakdang oras-*Sp* o distancia-*Sp*

AT once kaagad, ensigida-*Sp*; Iloc: dagdagos, ensigida-*Sp*

AT the expense of sa pagkaagraviado-*Sp* ni/ng...; Iloc: ti pagkaagraviado ni/iti...

AT the place of kina, sa; Iloc: diay lugar ni/da. Idiay.

AT the wink of an eye pagkisap-mata kung gaano kadali; Iloc: pagkirem ti mata nu kasano kadaras na.

Atavism ang ugali ng ninuno sa nakaraan ay bumabalik sa canya.

Atheism doctrina ng **Atheist** na walang paniwala sa Dios

ATHLETE *athlete*, manlalaro; Iloc: *athlete*

ATHLETE's foot *(Tag. & Iloc.)* alipunga

Atmosphere 1] ang hangin o clima-*Sp* o ang kapaligiran ng isang lugar, 2] ang nakakahawang modo-*Sp* o pag-iisip ng kapaligiran; Iloc: 1] ti angin o clima o arrubayan ti maysa a lugar, 2] ti maka-influwensia-*Sp* a modo o pagpampanunot iti lawlawan

Atone gumawa ng mabuti para ipatuwid ang sariling kamaliang nagawa niya; Iloc: mangaramid iti nasayaat tapno maypa-urnos na ti mismo-*Sp* a naaramid na a basbasol

Atop sa itaas ng, sa ibabaw ng; Iloc: rabaw ti, ngato ti
Antonym
Beneath or Under sa ilalim, sa babana ng; Iloc: idiay sirok, idiay baba

Atrocious nakakapatayong-balahibong masamang gawain o ugali; Iloc: makasidsiddaaw a dakes nga aramid o ugali

Attach icabit, idugtong, i-conecta-*Sp*; Iloc: pagcapeten, isilpo, iconecta
Correlated word
Connect iconecta, icabit, pagconectahin, pagcabitin; Iloc: pagconectaen, pagsilpuen, isilpo, iconecta, pagcapeten
Antonyms
Detach bakbakin, tuklapin; Iloc: lekkaben, latlaten
Disconnect tanggalin, putolin; Iloc: putden ti conecta o silpo
Separate hiwalayin; Iloc: pagsinaen
Apart hiwalay, hindi magkasama, nakatanggal, naibukod; Iloc: naysina, agsina

Attaché 1] taong tinakda o nahirang sa *diplomatic mission*; 2] cuadrado-*Sp* at *flat* na *bag* para sa mga papeles-*Sp*

Attached with a letter lakipan; Iloc: ipastrek diay surat
Correlated word
Enclosure nakasilid o nakalakip sa sulat; Iloc: naypastrek a cadwa ti surat

Attachment *(Tag. & Iloc.)* pagcabitan

ATTACK, Beat hampasin, pukpokin, golpehin, saktan; Iloc: malwen, golpien, saktan

ATTACK, heart *(Tag. & Iloc.)* atake-*Sp* sa/ti puso

ATTACK, trigger an sumompong; Iloc: agsumro

Attain tamohin, matamo, makamit; Iloc: magun-od, maala

Attainment nakatapos, natamo, nacamit; Iloc: nakaturpos, nakagun-od

Attempt tangkahin, purbahan; Iloc: padasen, purbaran

ATTEND dumalo, sumipot; Iloc: ag-atender-*Sp*

ATTEND to acecasohin, estimahin; Iloc: acecasoen, estimaren, taripatuen (estima/estimar-*Sp*)

ATTEND to continuously pag-aatupag; Iloc: icascaso ti pag-acecaso-*Sp*

Attendant tagapag-alaga, tagapaglingkod, kasama-sama; Iloc: tagataripato, mangtaraken

ATTENTION *attention*, pansin, asicaso; Iloc: *attention*, estimar-*Sp*, asecaso-*Sp*, cascaso

ATTENTION-calling sound *(Tag. & Iloc.)* sitsit, hoy, psst!

ATTENTION, give bigyang-pansin, pansinin, balingan o gugolan ng oras-*Sp*, patolan; Iloc: talyawen, asecaswen, estimaren, icascaso, ibiang (asecaso-*Sp*, estimar-*Sp*)

ATTENTIVE masinsinang pag-asecaso-*Sp*, pag-alaga at pag-estima-*Sp*; Iloc: firme-*Sp* a pag-asecaso, pagtaraken ken pag-estimar-*Sp*, pagicascaso

ATTENTIVE to details masinsinang pagsunod sa detalye-*Sp*; Iloc: natibker a pagsurot iti detalye-*Sp*

Attest ipagpatutoo o magbigay ng evidensia-*Sp* para-*Sp* patunayan ang katotohanan ng isang caso-*Sp*; Iloc: mangsaksi, mangpaneknek wenno mangited iti evidensia-*Sp* para i-prueba-*Sp* iti kaustoan ken kaagpaysuan iti maysa a caso
Synonym
Testify magpatunay, magtestigo, magsaksi; Iloc: agtestigo, agsaksi, ipaammo ti usto ken agpayso

ATTIRE damit, kasuotan, bestido-*Sp*, baro; Iloc: cawes, bestido, bado

ATTIRE, Filipino *(men)* barong tagalog, *(women)* terna na maria clara, balintawak na may *butterfly-sleeves* na gawa sa husi *(pineapple fibers)*, blusang kimona at tapis o saya, malong at sarong para sa *men and women* bilang *Filipino muslim wear*

ATTIRE, matching damit na magka-terno-*Sp*; Iloc: bado nga agka-terno

ATTITUDE asta, kilos o modo sa pakikitungo sa tao na namamalas ang kalooban nito gaya ng pagkagiliw o pagkainis sa tao; Iloc: garaw ken *disposition* nga ricna na iti tao

ATTITUDE, with an may *attitude* na malamig na makibagay dahil galit o inggit o may hinanakit; ayaw kumibo o umaasta o sumasagot na wari mo'y may utang ka sa canya kahit wala

Attorney *(Tag. & Iloc.)* abogado/da-*Sp*

Attract *v.,* **Attraction** *n.* manghalina, mang-akit, pantawag-pansin; Iloc: mang-awis, mangrayo, pang-awis
Synonym
Gravitate *v.,* **Gravitation** *n.* nahahalina o naa-*attract* kaya napapalapit

Attractive kahali-halina, kaakit-akit, kabigha-bighani, kagiliw-giliw; Iloc: nakaaw-awis, nakarayrayo ti pintas ken libnos na
Synonym
Gorgeous lantad ang kagandahan; Iloc: nakaparang unay ti pintas na

Attribute v. iukol o igawad at turingan ng dangal o pasasalamt sa ta-ong nakakarapat; Iloc: ipaay o isaad ti dayaw o pagyaman ti tao nga nayrebbengan o *worthy*

Attributes *n.* katangian, ugali, ari-arian, simbolo-*Sp* ng katungkulan, estado-*Sp*

Attrition 1] pagsisisi sa kasalanan; 2] unti-unting kumakaunti o humihina dahil sa madalas na *stress*; 3] kumakaunti ang mga miembro-*Sp* o empleyado-*Sp* dahil sa pag-retiro-*Sp* o paglipat-trabaho-*Sp* o kamatayan

Auction *(Tag. & Iloc.)* subasta-*Sp* na pagventa sa publico-*Sp*

Audacious *adj.,* **Audacity** *n.* pagkamatapang at pagkapangahas na may kayabangan at walang pagpansin sa sariling kaligtasan

Audible nadidinig; Iloc: mangngeg

Audience ang madla, mga nakikinig o nanonood; Iloc: dagiti agdeng-dengngeg wenno agbuybuya

Audit *audit,* suriin ang paggamit ng pera; Iloc: *audit,* sukisoken ti pagiyusar ti cuarta

Audition pangsubok ng kacayahang musical-*Sp* o arte-*Sp* para sa pagpili ng gaganap sa entablado-*Sp* o sa pelicula-*Sp*; Iloc: pangpadas ti cabaelan ti musical o arte tapno mapili nu sinno ti umno nga musikero-*Sp* o artista-*Sp*

Auditor tagasuri ng pera ng companya-*Sp*; Iloc: taga-usig ti cuarta-a*Sp* ti companya

Auditorium *(Tag. & Iloc.) auditorium*

Augment dagdagan; Iloc: nayonan

August *(Tag. & Iloc.) August,* Agosto-*Sp*

Aunt *auntie,* tita-*Sp,* tia-*Sp,* tiya-*Sp;* Iloc: *auntie,* tita, tia, tiya, ikit, nana

Auspice, Auspices 1] *patronage* o tagatangkilik; suporta, *sponsor* o panukala; 2] tanda ng nakakabuting bagay o anoman

Auspicious *Good sign or a promising indication of success or something coming that is special or memorable.*
Correlated word
Propitious *Presents favorable conditions that may rise to success.*

Authentic *genuine,* tunay, tutoo, dalisay, lantay, hindi artifisyal-*Sp,* hindi falsificado-*Sp,* hindi imitasyon-*Sp;* Iloc: *genuine,* pudno, puro

Authenticate itatag ang pagka-*genuine* o pagkatutuoo ng isang bagay; ipagpatunay ng naglikha nito, kung saang nanggaling ang mga parte-*Sp* at iba pa

Author tagasalaysay sa pagsusulat ng libro-*Sp,* manunulat; Iloc: tay nagsurat ti libro, mannurat

Authority otoridad-*Sp,* kapangyarihan; Iloc: otoridad, turay, linteg

Authorize tatagan o tulotan ng otoridad-*Sp* o kapangyarihang ofisyal-*Sp;* may *formal* na pahintulot sa paggamit; bigyang-karapatan, bigyan ng permiso-*Sp;* Iloc: ikkan ti otoridad-*Sp,* ikkan ti turay, ikkan ti permiso

Autobiography storia-*Sp* ng sariling talambuhay ng manunulat; Iloc: storia ti biag ti mismo-*Sp* a mannurat

Autocrat *n.,* **Autocratic** *adj.* pinuno o hari na nagpapalakad ng kapangyarihan sa govierno-*Sp* bilang tanging karapatan niya at wala siyang pagsasailalim sa mga bawal gaya ng *restriction* o limitasyon-*Sp;* taong nagsasaad na mayroon siyang buo at ganap na otorisasyon-*Sp;* taong dominante-*Sp* at dictador-*Sp* at mapag-asal na ma-otoridad-*Sp* o makapanyarihan

Autograph *(Tag. & Iloc.)* firma-*Sp,* signatura-*Sp*

AUTOMATIC *automatic,* kusang umoobra kahit walang magpalakad o magpa-andar-*Sp;* Iloc: *automatic,* agobra latta uray nu awan ti mangipaturong o mangpaandar

AUTOMATIC, Mechanical ginagawa ang katungkulan na parang makina-*Sp* at wala ang pagkataos-puso o katapatan; Iloc: agob-obra-*Sp* nga casla makina nga awan ti kapudnoan ti puso
Correlated word
Perfunctory dahil sa patuloy-tuloy na paggawa o bihasang ginagawa o bihasang pamaraan, parang makina na tuloy na magsagawa na walang gana o pagkataos-puso; Iloc: gapu ta patuloy-tuloy ken sigud a cadawyan ti pagaramid o pagpadalan, immawan langaruden iti ganas iti pagobra
Autonomous *adj.*, **Autonomy** *n.* independente-*Sp* at hindi contrôlado-*Sp* ng tagalabas; Iloc: independente ken haan a controlado ti tagaruar
Autopsy *autopsy*, pagkuha ng maliit na parte sa katawan kung saan man may diferencia-*Sp* para malaman ang sakit o condisyon-*Sp*; Iloc: *autopsy*, pangala ti bassit a parte ti bagi nga adda diférencia na para maamwan ti sakit wenno condisyon
Auxiliary *(Tag. & Iloc.)* suplemento-*Sp* o naka-reserva-*Sp* na tulong
AVAIL gamitin, magsilbi, makatulong, pakikinabangan, nakaka-efecto-*Sp*, mahalaga, makatubo ng gana,
AVAIL oneself gamitin para sa sariling pakinabang
Available nagawa na o nakalabas na para magamit o maangkin o mabili; Iloc: naaramiden o nakaruaren para may-usar-*Sp* o masanicua o magatang
Correlated word
Accessible *accessible*, puedeng makuha o magamit o mapuntahan; Iloc: *accessible*, mabalin nga maala o maaramat omaserkan
Avalanche *avalanche*, pagguho ng lupa sa bundok; Iloc: daga iti bantay nga agrumek, agrebba ken agregreg
Avaricious swapang sa pera; Iloc: sarabusab iti cuarta
Avenue avenida-*Sp*, maluwang na calsada-*Sp* sa loob ng ciudad-*Sp*; Iloc: avenida, nalawa a calsada
Avenge maghiganti; Iloc: mangibales
Aver nagpapahayag o nagpapatibay sa caso-*Sp* o paksa na segurado-*Sp* at may confiansang naninindigan
Average caraniwan, regular-*Sp*, ordinario-*Sp*; Iloc: cadawyan, regular, ordinario
Averse tutol, pag-ayaw; Iloc: agsupyat, pagmadi
Avert lumayo, iwasan, hadlangan, pigilan; Iloc: lisyan

Aviator *(Tag. & Iloc.)* aviador-*Sp*, piloto-*Sp*

Avid masugid; Iloc: aggaggagar

Avocado *(Tag. & Iloc.)* avocado

Avocation ang isa pang inaatupag ng tao maliban sa canyang trabaho-*Sp*, caraniwan ay para sa canyang kasiyahan o *hobby* o dibersion-*Sp*

Avoid iwasan, layoan; Iloc: lisyan, aglisi, adaywan
   Synonyms
   Keep one's distance from someone or something layoan; Iloc: adaywan
   Detour lumihis; Iloc: aglisi, likawan
   Dodge ilagan, lihisan, iwasan; Iloc: liklikan, aglisi, lisyan, aglinged
   Parry, Duck ilagan, umilag, lumihis; Iloc: aglisi, lisyan, liklikan

Avoidable puedeng maiwasan at malihisan; Iloc: mabalin a malisyan

Avow ma-confiansa-*Sp* na isabi o aminin sa harap ng mga tao; Iloc: natured a isawang o akceptaren iti sango ti tattao

Await hintayin, hinihintay, inaabangan, mag-aabang; Iloc: segseggaan, agab-abang, ur-urayen

AWAKE gising; Iloc: nakariing

AWAKE all night gising magdamag, puyat; Iloc: agpatnag nga haan makaturog, puyat

Award gantimpala, premyo-*Sp*; Iloc: premyo

Aware may alintana o *awareness*, alam, batid; Iloc: ammo na, adda siput na, sisisiput
   Antonym
   Unaware walang alintana, walang kamuang-muang, walang kamalay-malay; Iloc: haan na pulos ammo

Away malayo, wala dito; Iloc: adayo, awan ditoy

Awe, in namamalikmata sa paghanga; Iloc: nadayaw a siddaaw

Awesome nakakahangang tunay; Iloc: makaasiddaaw a pagdayaw

Awful masama; Iloc: naalas, madi

Awkward mali-mali, asiwa o saliwa ang galaw; Iloc: agkarabiddut, makaam-amak wenno naalas ti tignay

Awning *(Tag. & Iloc.)* tolda-*Sp*

Awry 1] taliwas o mapunta sa maling daan, 2] masirang plano; Iloc: 1] taliwas o mapan iti haan husto a dalan, 2] madadael a plano

AXE *n.* palacol; Iloc: balsig, wasay

AXE *v.* sibakin; Iloc: balsigen

Axiom nakalantad o kinikilala sa buong mundo-*Sp* na katotohanan; *ideology* na tinanggap na katotohanan kahit walang prueba-*Sp*

B

BABY, Babe, Infant sanggol, musmos; Iloc: tagibi

BABY boomers mga napanganak noong 1946 hanggang 1965 sa USA; Iloc: dagiti nayyanak idi 1946 inggana 1965 idiay USA

BABY games 1] *Close-open hand-game:* kemmakem; 2] *Beautiful eyes (close the eyes, then open);* pikit-dilat; 3] *Hand dance:* kumintang, arimunding-munding; 3] *Flying kiss*

BABY, newly born bagong panganak; Iloc: kayyan-anak

BABY's pacifier *(Tag. & Iloc.)* bibiron-*Sp*, chupon

BABY's milk bottle *(Tag. & Iloc.)* dede

BABY's walker *(Tag. & Iloc.)* andador-*Sp*

Babysitter *(Tag. & Iloc.)* yaya, *babysitter*
  Correlated word
  Caregiver tagaalaga ng bata o ng matandang may sakit o baldadong tao; Iloc: tagaawir ti ubing wenno ti baldado a tao o baket wenno lakay nga agsakit

BACHELOR binata; Iloc: baro

BACHELOR's degree pagcompleto ng *undergraduate curriculum* o apat na taong tinapos sa pag-aaral sa universidad-*Sp* o colehio-*Sp*

BACK likod; Iloc: likod, bukot

BACK, turn one's tumalikod; Iloc: agtallikod

BACK off umatras, umurong: Iloc: agsanud, ag-atras-*Sp*

BACK out siya ngayon ay umurong o umalis sa dating pinagkasundoan o sinang-ayonan niya sa kapwa

BACK to basics, Back-to-basics pagbabalik sa tinuro o inutasan o principio na pinagbabatayan gaya ng *arithmetic, grammar* o balarila, *history* o tradisyon

BACK to the drawing board kailangan magplano o gumawa ng panibagong paraan

BACK up 1] reserva-*Sp*, manghalinhan, suporta-*Sp*, 2] tagasaliw sa canta-*Sp*, 3] pag-atras ng sasakyan; Iloc: 1] reserva, mangsublat, suporta, 2] taga-acompanyar-*Sp* o taga-tocar-*Sp* ti ag-cancion-*Sp*, 3] pag-atras-*Sp* ti lugan

Backbite manirang-puri; Iloc: mang-perdi-*aSp* iti reputasyon-*Sp*

Backbone 1] *spine* o gulugod, 2] lakas ng pagkatao at pagpupunyagi o determinasyon; Iloc: 1] dori; 2] pigsa ti pagkatao ken pamuspusan nga agtalinaed o agpatuloy

Backdrop 1] ang tanawin. 2] curtina sa entablado

Backer mangsuporta, tagapagtaguyod; Iloc: mangsuportar (suporta/ suportar-*Sp*)

Backfire 1] nakapagdala ng resultang kabaligtaran at contra-*Sp* sa inaasahan; 2] malakas na pagsabog na pumutok bago sa tinakdang tiempo-*Sp*

Background 1] tanawin sa likod; 2] tungkol sa *history* kung bakit nagkaganoon; ano mang nakapag-usbong sa pagkatao niya ngayon gaya ng educasyon, expiryensa, at iba pa

Backlash 1] malakas at marahas na efecto-*Sp* at *reaction* sa pagbabago ng palakad o sa bagong plano; 2] bigla at mafuersang pabalik na talbog; 3] galaw ng makina dahil sa parte na pudpod na o mali ang pagkakabit

Backslide bumalik sa dating masamang kagawian-makasalanang asal at mahahalay na gawain; Iloc: pagsubli iti haan usto o iti dakes nga aramid manen

Backtrack 1] bumalik sa dating paraan o daanan o pinanggalingan; 2] mag-*reverse* o manauli o sumaliwa o bumaligtad sa *policy*; umurong o nag-*withdraw* sa dating gawain o puesto-*Sp* o kuro-kuro o pangako, at iba pa

Backward pa-atras-*Sp*, paurong; Iloc: pa-atras, pasanud
Antonym
Onward paavante, pagsulong; Iloc: paavante

Backyard likoran; Iloc: likodan
Antonym
Front yard harapan, harap; Iloc: sangwanan, sango

Bacon, Filipino *(Tag. & Iloc.)* tocino-*Sp*, tapa-*Sp*, pindang

Bacteria *(Tag. & Iloc.) bacteria, germs,* microbio-*Sp*

BAD masama, masagwa, malaswa; Iloc: dakes, namadi

BAD attitude *(Tag. & Iloc.)* suplado/da-a*Sp*
Antonym

172

Pleasant mapagmagandang-loob, kaaya-aya; Iloc: nasayaat a makibagay, nakaay-ayo

BAD-intention masamang balak; Iloc: dakes nga panggep o rangta

BAD luck malas-*Sp*; Iloc: daksang-gasat, malas

BAD odor mabaho, mabantot; Iloc: nabangsit, naangdud

BAD taste, Poor taste *(Tag. & Iloc.)* vulgar-*Sp*, bastos-*Sp*

BAD-tempered magalitin, mainitin ang ulo, bugnotin, sumpongin, yamotin, madaling maconsomisyon kahit sa maliliit na bagay; Iloc: alipunget, napudot ti ulo, nalaca nga makapungtot, masursuron, maconconsumisyon-*Sp* uray babassit laeng a banag

Badass 1] mahirap pakisamahan, basag-ulero, maramdamin, 2] mabagsik, agresivo-*Sp*

Badge *(Tag. & Iloc.)* chapa-*Sp*

Badger 1] inisin, suyain, 2] isang hayop na nakatira sa binutasan niyang cueva-*Sp* sa ilalim ng lupa; Iloc: 1] ruroden, paguraen 2] animal-*Sp* nga agigian iti inabutan na a cueva iti uneg ti daga

Badmouth magsabi ng masama tungkol sa ibang tao o bagay; Iloc: mangdadael iti reputasyon-*Sp* iti dadduma

Baffle litohin, balisahin, i-taranta-*Sp*, mang-torete-*Sp*; Iloc: mangtorete, rirwen, itaranta, allilawen,

Baffling katakataka; Iloc: nakasidsiddaaw

BAG, pouch lalagyan na *bag*, supot; Iloc: pangikabilan nga *bag*, supot,

BAG, sacklike (made of nipa leaves with a handle) bayong; Iloc: bay-ong

Baggage *(Tag. & Iloc.)* bagahe-*Sp*, maleta-*Sp*

BAIL *(Tag. & Iloc.)* fianza-*Sp*

BAIL out or **Bailout** 1] pabayaan o lisanan o layasan ang isang si-tuasyon-*Sp* para makalaya dito; sagipin o iligtas lalo na sa problema-*Sp* sa pera o sa situasyong *emergency*; 2] pagtalon sa eroplano-*Sp* para makaligtas bago bumagsak o mag-*crash* iyon

Bait 1] pamingwit o pain sa isda, 2] pang-akit; Iloc: 1] banniit ti ikan, 2] pang-tentar-*Sp*

Bake mag-*bake,* magluto sa horno-*Sp*; Iloc: ag-*bake,* luto diay orno-*Sp*

BALANCE *(Tag. & Iloc.)* balanse

BALANCE sheet *statement* na nagbibigay sulit ng kalagayang *financial* ng negosyo-*Sp* at ang *accounts* nito na nakalista ang mga balanse-*Sp* ng mga *debit* at *credit*

Balanced *(Tag. & Iloc.)* balansiado

Balcony *(Tag. & Iloc.)* balcony
  Correlated word
  Porch *(Tag. & Iloc.)* balconahe

Bald calvo-*Sp*, panot; Iloc: calvo

Balderdash pagka-stupido at walang kabulohan, sobrang malabis na salita o sulat

Bale 1] napakalaking cumpol, 2] demonyo-*Sp*, 3] dusa sa isip; Iloc: 1] nakadakdakkel a cumpol, 2] demonyo, 3] dusa ti panunot

Balk or Baulk maghadlang; huminto bago matapos at ayaw magpatuloy na

Ball *(Tag. & Iloc.)* bola-*Sp*

Ballad romanticong canta-*Sp*; Iloc: cancion-*Sp* nga romantico-*Sp*

Ballerina baylerina-*Sp*, mananayaw; Iloc: baylerina, mannala

Ballet *(Tag. & Iloc.)* bayleng clasico-*Sp*

Ballistic hindi controladong poot dahil bara-bara lamang at hindi ginagamit ang utak; Iloc: haan controlado nga pungtot ken uyong gapu ta haan na iyusar ti utek na

Ballot *(Tag. & Iloc.)* balota-*Sp*

Balloon *(Tag. & Iloc.)* lobo, *balloon*

Balmy maginhawa at mabangong amoy na *herb* o *mint*; Iloc: nabang-ar ken nabanglo nga angot ti *herb* o *mint*

BAMBOO cawayan; Iloc: cawayan, bulo

BAMBOO bench or bed *(Tag. & Iloc.)* papag

BAMBOO shoots labong; Iloc: rabong

BAMBOO split stick patpat; Iloc: bislak

Ban pagbawalan; Iloc: ipagel, iparit

Banal ordinaryo-*Sp*, caraniwan; Iloc: ordinaryo

Banana saging; Iloc: saba

Band banda-*Sp*, grupo-*Sp* na tumutugtog ng musica-*Sp*; Iloc: banda; grupo nga agtoc-tocar-*Sp* ti musica

Bandana *bandana*, talukbong; Iloc: *bandana*, dalungdong

Bandage benda-*Sp*, bendahe-*Sp*; Iloc: bendahe, bedbed

Bandit *(Tag. & Iloc.)* tulisan, bandido-*Sp*

Bane nakakasugat o nakakasira o nakakapatay o nakakaproblema o nakakagambala; Iloc: awan servi-*Sp* na

Banish ifuersang paalisin sa lugar-*Sp* o bayan; Iloc: ag-fuersa-*Sp* nga papanawen iti lugar

    Not to be mistaken with Vanish

    Vanish maglaho, nagpawi, maparam; Iloc: agpukaw, agawan

Banister *(Tag. & Iloc.)* pasamano-*Sp*

BANK *(Tag. & Iloc.)* banko-*Sp*

BANK on umaasa sa isang tao o pangyayari o bagay

Bankrupt *(Tag. & Iloc.) bankrupt*

    Correlated words

    Insolvent *adj.,* **Insolvency** *n.* hindi makabayad ng utang, *bankrupt*

    Lose money in business *(Tag. & Iloc.)* malugi

    Broke *broke*, walang pera; Iloc: *broke,* naawanan ti cuarta

    Financial loss *(Tag. & Iloc.)* lugi

Banner maliit na bandila o watawat; Iloc: bassit a bandera-*Sp*

Banquet bankete-*Sp*, piging, marangyang pulong; Iloc: bankete, ponsion, padaya, dakkel a *party*

Banter cuentohang masaya na nagkakatuwaan at may kasamang mga biro; Iloc: storiaan a naragsak nga addaan ti pagkakatawaan ken aginnangawan

Baptism bautismo-*Sp*, binyag; Iloc: bautismo, bunyag

BAR pagbawalan, sanggahin, ipagbawal na gawin o na pumasok; Iloc: barraen, sanggaen, iparit nga aramiden o sumrek

    Synonym

    Prohibit pagbawalan; Iloc: ipagel, iparit

BAR, iron bareta; Iloc: barreta-*Sp*

Barbed wire alambre-*Sp* na may tinik; Iloc: barut o alambre nga sisiitan

Barber barbero-*Sp*; Iloc: barbero, tagapukis

BARE hubad, walang damit; Iloc: lubos, awan ti bado

BARE from waist down hubad buhat sa bewang pababa; Iloc: nakalucais

Barefoot nakapaa, nakayapak; Iloc: saka-saka

BARGAIN baratilyo; Iloc: laco nga nalaca ken mabalin ti agtawar

BARGAIN, got a nakamura, nakatawad; Iloc: nakatawar

Bark 1] tahol ng aso; 2] marahas na utos o sagot; 3] tao sa harap ng *carnival show* na maingay na nanghihikayat sa mga dumadaan para manood sila dito

Barn *(Tag. & Iloc.)* camalig, camarin

Barometer pangsukat ng kalagayan ng clima-*Sp*

Baroque 1] arkitectura-*Sp* ng gusali na gawa sa Europa sa taong 1700 hanggang 1850, 2] cantang gawa sa Europa noong taong 1600 hanggang 1750; Iloc: 1] arkitectura nga facilidad-*Sp* nga aramid diay Europa iti tawen 1700 inggana 1850, 2] cancion-*Sp* nga aramid diay Europa iti tawen 1600 inggana 1750

Barracks cuartel-*Sp*, tirahan ng mga sundalo; Iloc: cuartel, pagyanan dagiti soldado-*Sp*

Barrel *(Tag. & Iloc.)* bariles-*Sp*

Barren *(Tag. & Iloc.)* baog

Barrier hadlang, sagabal, pangsangga; Iloc: pangbarra, pangsangga

BASE *(Tag. & Iloc.)* base-*Sp*, batayan, saligan

BASE pay or Base wage iyong nakatakdang sueldo-*Sp* at hindi kasama ang mga bayad sa *overtime*

Based on base sa, ayon sa, batay sa, nakasalalay sa; Iloc: base ti, agbatay iti/idiay

Baseless walang batayan, walang pinagbasehan; Iloc: awan pagbatayan, awan pagbasean

Basement silid sa silong; Iloc: cuarto-*Sp* ti sirok ti balay

Bash hambalosin; Iloc: pang-oren

Bashful mahiyain; Iloc: managbabain, kimmi, mikki

Basic unang-una o primerong gawain o aralin; Iloc: umun-una o pri-mero-*Sp* nga aramiden wenno adalen

BASIN for washing laundry *(Tag. & Iloc.)* bacha-*Sp*

BASIN to wash dishes on *(Tag. & Iloc.)* palanggana-*Sp*

Basis batayan, saligan; Iloc: pagbatayan

Bask in the sun magbabad sa araw, magpabilad; Iloc: agpainit, agpabilag

BASKET (flat, round, wide and without a handle) for winnowing off chaff/husk from rice bilao; Iloc: bigao

BASKET made of buri *basket,* buslo; Iloc: *basket,* labba

Bass *(Tag. & Iloc.)* 1] tonong musica-*Sp* na baho-*Sp*, 2] isda/ikan

Bastard bastardo-*Sp*, pinanganak na hindi casal ang magulang; Iloc: bastardo-*Sp*, nayyanak nga haan a nagcasar ti nagannak canyana

Baste 1] temporaryong itahing magkakalayong *stitches* para lamang makuha ang tamang haba o pagkagawa; 2] pahiran ng *marinade* habang iniihaw ang carne-*Sp* o isda; Iloc: 1] temporaryong pagdait; 2] papaidan ti *marinade* mientras-*Sp* nga tuntonwen ti carne wenno ikan

Bastion matibay na mala-campo-*Sp* na pantanggol sa comunidad-*Sp* na iyon

Bat 1] paniki; (Iloc: panniki, curaratnit) 2] ikindat ang mata; 3] pamalo ng bola-*Sp* sa *baseball*

Batch isa sa maraming grupo-*Sp* na magkaka-categorya-*Sp*

BATH *n.*, pagpaligo; Iloc: pagdigos

BATH scrub or face towel *(Tag. & Iloc.)* labacara-*Sp*, dimpo

Bathe *v.* maligo; Iloc: agdigos

Bathrobe *(Tag. & Iloc.)* bata, bata de banyo-*Sp*

Bathroom banyo-*Sp*, paliguan; Iloc: banyo, pagdigusan

Bathtub *(Tag. & Iloc.)* *bathtub*, banyera-*Sp*

Baton *(Tag. & Iloc.)* batuta-*Sp*

Battalion *battalion* ng mga hukbo o *military*

Batter 1] saktan o sirain ng panay-panay na pukpok gaya ng nagbabayo; 2] pinaghalong arina, gatas, tubig at itlog para iluto; 3] *baseball player* na torno-*Sp* na niyang magtira/hampas ng bola

Battery *(Tag. & Iloc.)* bateria-*Sp*

Battle labanan, sagupaan, giyera, digmaan; Iloc: gerra-*Sp*

Bay look na napaligiran ng lupa at may labasan at pasukan ng tubig (ilog) na galing sa dagat; Iloc: danaw a nalawlawan ti daga nga adda pagserkan ken pagruaran ti danum (carayan) a naggapu diay taaw

BE 1] mag..., may buhay, 2] nasa lugar-*Sp*; Iloc: 1] ag..., adda biag na, 2] adda ti lugar

"BE careful," "Beware" "Mag-ingat ka/kayo"; Iloc: "Agan-annad ka/kayo," "Agalwad ka/kayo"

BE like kumuha sa/kay; Iloc: immala ti/kenni

BE smart and live the dream gamitin mo ang matinong isip mo at tamohin ang matuwid at mataas mong hangarin, ano man ang edad mo, ano man ang nakaraan mo

Beach *beach, shore,* tabing-dagat, baybay, dalampasigan; Iloc: *beach, shore,* igid ti baybay
  Correlated word
  River bank pampang, tabing ilog; Iloc: dammang
Beacon 1] pangpatnubay ng daan o pangbabala ng panganib gaya ng *lighthouse* at *buoy* sa lawa; 2] tao o bagay na nagbabala at nagpapatnubay, na nagpapaliwanag at nagbibigay ng inspirasyon-*Sp*
Beak tuka ng ibon; Iloc: sippit ti billit
Beam 1] poste-*Sp*, 2] magliwanag, 3] ngiti; Iloc: 1] poste, 2] agranyag, 3] isem
BEAN butil; Iloc: bukel
BEAN, kidney *(Tag. & Iloc.)* bichuelas-*aSp*
BEAN, lima *(Tag. & Iloc.)* patani
BEAN, mongo *(Tag. & Iloc.)* monggo/balatong
BEAR, Carry buhatin; Iloc: bagkaten
BEAR, Endure tiisin; Iloc: anosan
BEAR fruit magbunga; Iloc: agbunga
BEAR in mind alalahanin; Iloc: laglagipen
Beard balbas; Iloc: barbas-*Sp*, iming
  Correlated word
  Moustache *(Tag. & Iloc.)* bigote-*Sp*
Bearing, Deportment postura-*Sp*, tindig; Iloc: postura, tacder
  Correlated word
  Poise kung paano magdala ng sarili; Iloc: nu casano na awiten ti bagi na
BEAT, Attack hampasin, pukpokin, golpehin; Iloc: malwen, golpien (golpe-*Sp*)
BEAT, Defeat talonin; Iloc: atiwen
BEAT eggs batihin; Iloc: agbatil, batilen
BEAT, musical *(Tag. & Iloc.)* cumpas-*Sp*
BEAT or pummel to a pulp dikdikin, bugbogin; Iloc: taltalen, bugbogen
BEAT or whack with a bat or club hambalosin; Iloc: pang-oren
BEAT someone by inning or being ahead, Outdo naunang nakapag-sagawa o nakapag-umpisa bago ang iba; Iloc: immuna nga nakaleppas ngem dagiti dadduma

Beatitude pinakadakila at pinakamahalagang pagkasagrado at pagka-banal; mga pahayag ng Dios Anak na si Hesu Cristo sa *Sermon on the Mount* tungkol sa ma-sagrado-*Sp na* buhay

Beau *(Tag. & Iloc.)* novio-*Sp, boy friend*

Beautiful maganda, marikit, marilag, guapa-*Sp,* maalindog; Iloc: napintas, nalibnos, guapa

Synonyms

Lovely kaakit-akit, kanais-nais, kabigha-bighani, kagiliw-giliw; Iloc: nakaliwliwa, napintas, nakaay-ayat, guapa

Desirable kanais-nais; Iloc: nakaay-ayat

Attractive, Captivating kahali-halina, kaakit-akit, kabigha-bighani, kagiliw-giliw; Iloc: makaaw-awis, nakarayrayo, napintas, guapa

Gorgeous lantad ang kagandahan; Iloc: nakaparang unay ti pintas na

Antonym

Ugly pangit; Iloc: nalaad, naalas

Beautify pagandahin; Iloc: papintasen

Beauty kagandahan, karilagan, kariktan; Iloc: pintas, libnos

BECAUSE sapagkat, porke-*Sp,* casi, dahil sa; Iloc: gapu ta, gapu ngamin, porque

BECAUSE, just dahil lamang sa; palibhasa; Iloc: gapu laeng iti

Became naging; Iloc: nagbalin

BECK, Beckon hudyat para lumapit, pagtawag na senyas-*Sp* gaya ng pagtango ng ulo o pagkaway; Iloc: senyas a pag-ayab casla pagli-ngaling ti ulo wenno payapayan

BECK and call, at someone's handa parating magsilbi sa isang si-nisilbihang tao; Iloc: alisto-*Sp* nga ag-servi-*Sp* iti sigud a serservian na a tao

Beckon *see BECK, Beckon above*

Become magiging, maging; Iloc: agbalin

Becoming 1] nagiging, 2] akma, bagay; nakakacomplimentong bagay sa ichura ng isang tao; o bagay na bagay sa isang tao; Iloc: 1] agbalbalin, 2] rumbeng, umno, mangcomplimento iti ichura iti tao; bagay para iti tao

BED cama-*Sp,* catre-*Sp,* pagtulogan, higaan; Iloc: catre, cama, pagiddaan, pagturogan

BED of roses kalagayang maluho, maginhawa at kasiyasiya.

Bedbug surot; Iloc: kiteb

Bedding 1] mga gamit sa cama-*Sp*; 2] fundasyon-*Sp*

Bedlam pinangyayarihan ng sigawan, hiyawan, pagkataranta at pagkalito; tirhan ng mga baliw o sira-ulo

Bedridden nakaratay sa cama-*Sp* dahil mahina at may sakit; Iloc: agid-idda iti cama ta nakapsoten ken agsak-sakit

Bedroom silid-tulogan; Iloc: cuarto-*Sp* nga pagturogan

Bedspread mga cumot, cobrecama-*Sp*; Iloc: ul-ules

Bee bubuyog; Iloc: alimbubuyog

Beehive himbubuyog; Iloc: uyukan

Beef carne-*Sp* ng vaca-*Sp*; Iloc: carne ti vaca

Beefsteak *(Tag. & Iloc.)* bistek-*Sp*

Beer *(Tag. & Iloc.)* beer, cerveza-*Sp*

Beetle salagubang; Iloc: abal-abal

Befall mangyari; Iloc: maaramid, mapasamak

Befit akma, bagay; Iloc: rumbeng, umno, bagay

Before 1] bago, antes-*Sp*; 2] noon; Iloc: 1] antes, baro nga.., sakbay, kasakbayan; 2] idi

Beforehand *(Tag. & Iloc.)* antemano-*Sp*

Befriend kaibiganin; Iloc: gayyemen

Befuddle litohin, manligalig, balisahin, itaranta, mangtorete; Iloc: allilawen, rirwen, itaranta, itorete

Beg humingi, humiling, magpalimos; Iloc: agkiddaw, agasug, agpalama, agpalimos
Synonyms
Ask for manghingi, humiling; Iloc: agdawat, dumawat
Plead magsumamo; Iloc: makicacaasi, agkiddaw

Beget lalaking nagkakaroon ng anak; magsanhi ng resulta o mamunga

Beggar pulubi, nagpapa-limos-*aSp*; Iloc: agpalpalimos, agpalpalama
Synonyms
Mendicant nagpapalimos; Iloc: agpalpalama
Vagrant, Bum palaboy-laboy, hampaslupa, *homeless*; Iloc: agwalwalang, *homeless*

BEGIN umpisahan, magsimula; Iloc: rugyan, irugi
Antonym
Finish taposin; Iloc: leppasen, palpasen

BEGIN to see the light nauunawaan na dahil naliwanagan na ang canyang isip; Iloc: naawatan nan ta nalawaganen iti nakem nan

Beginner nag-uumpisa, bagohan; Iloc: mangrugrugi, agdamdamo
Synonym
Newcomer bagito, baguhan; Iloc: kaserserrek, kabarbaro, agdamdamo

Beginning sa simula; Iloc: idiay rugi, idi immun-una

Behalf of, on gumanap para sa/kay; Iloc: mang-representar-*Sp* kenni

Behave mag-asal, kumilos; Iloc: aggaraw, agtignay

Behaved, well- mag-wastong asal; Iloc: agtignay nga usto-*Sp* ken nasayaat

Behavior asal, ugali, galaw, kilos; Iloc: tignay, ugali, garaw, gunay
Synonym
Manner asal at kilos at salita at isip at damdamin; Iloc: garaw ken sarita ken rikna ken nakem

Behead pugotan ng ulo; Iloc: putden ti ulo

Behest pakiusap na hiling pero seriosong pananalita na galing sa otoridad; utos, tagubilin, kautosan

BEHIND, Overdue *(Tag. & Iloc.)* atrasado-*Sp*

BEHIND, Rear sa likod; Iloc: diay likod

Behold tingnan, pagmasdan; Iloc: kitaen

Beholden tinitingala dahil mataas ang katangian o mayaman o dahil may utang siya sa canya; Iloc: tangtangaden na gapu ta nangato ti puesto-*Sp* na o nabaknang o gapu ta nakautang isu canyana

Behoove kinakailangan at naangkop na gawin; Iloc: kasapulan ken masapul nga aramiden ta rebbeng

Being buhay na nilalang; Iloc: sibibiag a parsua

BELCH dighay; Iloc: tig-ab

BELCH out something forcefully from throat ibuga; Iloc: ibel-a, ipugso

Beleaguer 1] yamotin, ligaligin; 2] palibutan; Iloc: 1] ruroden, suronen; 2] lawlawan

Belief paniwala; Iloc: pammati

Believe maniwala; Iloc: mamati

Belittle minamata at minemenos ang pagkatao; Iloc: menmenosen ken bigbigen na a nababa ti pagkatao na

Bell *(Tag. & Iloc.)* campana-*Sp*
Correlated words

Ring or peal the belfry ibatingaw ang campana; Iloc: ipatit o ikililing ti campana

Steeple tore na may campana, campanaryo ng simbahan; Iloc: torre nga adda campana, campanaryo ti simbaan

Belle of the party or of a team paraluman, lakambini, mutya; Iloc: *muse, musa-Sp*

Belligerent *adj.,* **Belligerence** *n.* mapaglaban; parating handang makipag-away at makipag-giyera

BELLY puson, bilbil; Iloc: buksit, pus-ong

BELLY button, Navel pusod; Iloc: puseg

BELLY, large malaking chan; Iloc: butchog

Belong may-ari, kay; Iloc: cukua ni/ti, kua ni

Belongings ari-arian, pagaaring kagamitan at kasangkapan; Iloc: sanicua, cukcukua nga alicamen ken muebles-*Sp* ken dagiti maaramat

Beloved sinta, irog, mahal, giliw, novia-*Sp*, novio-*Sp*; Iloc: ay-ayaten, novia, novio

Below sa baba, sa ilalim, sa silong; Iloc: diay baba o sirok

Belt *(Tag. & Iloc.)* cinturon-*Sp*
Correlated word
Sash bigkis; Iloc: barikes

Bemoan dumadaing, tumataghoy, naghihimutok, tumatangis; Iloc: agsensennaay, umas-asog, agun-unnoy,

Bench *(Tag. & Iloc.)* banco-*Sp*, bangketa-*Sp*

Benchmark or Bench mark pamantayan para ang bagay ay masukat o mahatol

BEND baluktotin, i-curva-*Sp*; Iloc: ikillo, icurva

BEND backward with waist and tummy protruding out magliyad, magtuwad; Iloc: agkiad

BEND downward with back protruding out magyuko Iloc: agcubbo, agsucog

BEND or lower head itungo ang ulo; Iloc: agdumog

Beneath sa baba, sa ilalim, sa silong; Iloc: diay baba, diay sirok

Benediction pagpahayag ng *good wishes*; pagbebendisyon, pagbabasbas

Benefactor nagbibigay ng pera bilang tulong; Iloc: mangit-ited ti cuarta bilang tulong
Synonym

Donor nagbibigay ng donasyon; Iloc: mangidon-donasyon

Beneficent *adj.,* **Beneficence** *n.* magandang loob at maawain at naka-kawanggawa ng kabutihan at pamimigay o pagtutulong sa kapwa; Iloc: naimbag ti puspuso na ken mannangaasi ken mapag-ited ti tulong

Beneficial kapakipakinabang, makakabuti, makabigay ng beneficio-*Sp* o ventahe-*Sp*; Iloc: makasayaat, makapaimbag, makaited ti beneficio o ventahe

Correlated words

Advantageous kapakipakinabang, mapakinabangan, maventahe; Iloc: makasaya-at, makapanam-ay, maventahe

Useful may silbi, napapakinabangan, magagamit; Iloc: adda servi na, mayyusar, adda pagtungpalan na

Helpful *(Tag. & Iloc.)* makakatulong

Expedience *n.,* **Expedient** *adj.* 1] akma sa kinakailangan ng kasalukuyan; nakakatulong na makamit ang sagot ng agad-agad na kinakailangan; 2] nakakatulong sa sariling interes higit sa principio

Asset katangiang ng tao nakakaventahe, nakakatulong at mahalaga; Iloc: custombre ti tao nga naventahe, makatulong ken navalor

Sustainable anomang nakakapanatili ng pagpatuloy na bisa at tagumpay sa tulong ng isang paraan na mangpaefecto nito kahit na sa kaunting fondo pero sapat sa paggamit o pagsuporta ng pinakamadaling makuhang *supply* o gamit sa natural na katutubo (*natural resources*) na hindi nakakasira o nakakabigay ng masamang efecto sa kapaligiran

Favorable nakakabigay ng kabutihan; Iloc: makaited ti pagimbagan

Beneficiary naipangalang makatanggap ng beneficio-*Sp*; Iloc: indesignar nga mangawat iti beneficio

Benefit *(Tag. & Iloc.)* beneficio-*Sp*

Benevolent *adj.,* **Benevolence** *n.* mabait at mapagmalasakit; mapagbigay at gustong makatulong sa kapwa; Iloc: iti pagit-ited iti tulong ken caasi ken kaimbagan

Benign 1] mapagmalasakit, maamo at gracioso/sa-*Sp*; 2] *Medical* – hindi maligno-*Sp*

Bent curva-*Sp*, nakayuco; Iloc: curva, nakasucog

Synonym

Curved curva; Iloc: curva, killo

Bequeath, Bequest ipamana; Iloc: ipatawid

Berate pagsabihan o pagalitan ng matagalan; Iloc: bagbagaan o ungtan ti nabayag

Bereave pangungulila sa pagkamatay ng canyang mahal sa buhay; Iloc: agdungdung-aw gapu ti pagkapatay ti nadungngo canyana a tao o *pet*

Bereft wala sa canya ang kinakailangan niya o inaasahan niya; Iloc: awanan isu ti masapul na o namnamaen na

Beriberi *beri-beri*, manas; Iloc: *beri-beri*

Berserk marahas na nanakit na parang nasiraang-ulo; Iloc: naghuhuramentado

Beseech magmakaawa at humingi ng tulong ng puspusan; Iloc: agpacaasi ken dumawat ti tulong a pamuspusan

Beset, Besiege 1] binabagabag at liniligalig parati, 2] makipaglabanan sa pumalibot na hukbong mang-atake sa canila; Iloc: 1] maringgoran ken torete canayon, 2] makilaban iti nanglalwlaw a tropa-*Sp* a mang-atake canyada

Beside katabi, sa tabi; Iloc: kadinna, kaabay, sikigan

Besides it/that maliban sa, bukod sa; Iloc: malaksid iti

Besiege *see Beset, Besiege above*

BEST pinakaexcelente, pinakamahusay, pinakamagaling, pinaka-mabuti; Iloc: pinaka-excelente-*Sp*, pinakanaimbag, pinakanasayaat, pinakanalaeng

Synonyms

Classic pinakamataas na clase; Iloc: pinakanangato a clase

Perfect *(Tag. & Iloc.)* perfecto

Impeccable *perfect*, walang defecto

Excellent excelente, napakabuti at napakahusay ang pagkagawa at ka-tangian; Iloc: excelente, napakasaysayaat ken nakalalaeng nga aramid ken katatao

Top-notch, Top-flight *(Tag. & Iloc.)* excelente, *first-rate*

Superior 1] napakaexcelente at napakalaki ang halaga, 2] mas mataas ang ranko kaysa iba; Iloc: 1] nakaek-excelente ken nakadakdakkel ti valor, 2] mas nangato ti ranko ngem ti dadduma

Supreme pinakamataas ang kapangyarihan at importancia, pinakama-galing sa gawa at kabutihan; Iloc: pinakanangato ti kababalin ken bileg ken importancia, pinakanasayaat iti aramid ken kaimbagan

Optimal pinakamaventahe, nakakasiya ng husto; Iloc: pinakanaventahe, nakaay-ayat unay

Doozie, Doozy tao o bagay na mahalaga, napakainam at *superior* pa

BEST case ang pinakamahusay na resultang inaasahan

BEST foot forward *To behave, act and appear at one's best in order to make a good impression or gain people's approval or make a good start at a job. So be your very <u>best self</u> in character, mood, attitude, conduct, ettiquette, speech, looks, in showing respect, and in conveying your intelligence and knowledge (needed during job interviews). Of course, manifest these also in school, in church, and with friends and family.* Ipakita ang pinakamahusay na pagkatao, kilos, dunong at iba pa para matanggap siya sa trabaho o maganda ang pagtingin sa canya ng mga tao.

Correlated words

Give one's best shot gamitin ang pinakamahusay at pinakamatalinong sikap at kacayahan

BEST interest *Best interest is any or all of these: benefit, sustenance, moral support, welfare, peace, safety, development, advancement, success, empowerment (in intelligence, skills, abilities, knowledge, expertise), health-maintenance, happiness, comfort, and other things for the well-being of a race, a group, a person or a family.*

BEST man (wedding) *(Tag. & Iloc.)* abay

Bestial *adj.,* **Bestiality** *n.* katangian ng hayop

Bestow ipagkaloob, ibigay; Iloc: ipaay, iparangkap, ited

Bet mag-pusta-*aSp*, tumaya; Iloc: agpusta, agtaya

Betel nut for chewing nganga, hitso; Iloc: mama, bua

Bethlehem *(Tag. & Iloc.)* Belen-*Sp*

Betrayer traidor-*Sp*, taksil; Iloc: traidor

BETTER mas mahusay, mas magaling, mas mabuti; Iloc: mas nasayaat, mas naimbag, mas nalaeng

BETTER half kabiyak, asawa; Iloc: asawa

BETTER late then never *It is alright if one is late if there is a pressing or unavoidable reason for it, as long as one can execute and fulfill it, and succeed in completing it into fruition, most especially if it done quite excellently.*

Between sa pagitan, sa gitna; Iloc: nagbaetan, nagtengngaan

Beware mag-ingat; Iloc: agalwad, agannad

Bewilder litohin, manligalig, balisahin, itaranta, mangtorete; Iloc: rirwen, itaranta, allilawen, itorete

Bewitch *(Tag. & Iloc.)* igayuma, i-engcanto

Beyond lampas; Iloc: labes

Bias pagtuturing na mababa o masama ang tao o grupo o lahi at ipawalang-pansin ang pagkahalaga nila; Iloc: bigbigen a nababa wenno dakes ti tao wenno grupo wenno lahi ken haan nga bigbigen ti valor da

Bib *(Tag. & Iloc.)* bibero-a*Sp*

Bible *God's holy words, the Bible, was written by the prophets and disciples through the inspiration of the Holy Spirit. In the Bible, we learn that God created the universe and everything that is in the universe. It also reveals God's divine love for all mankind, and through God's love, how mankind can go to heaven despite our sins (read about **God** in this book – under letter **G** - to know how we can get to heaven). It also reveals blessings that we can get from God by our obedience to Him and living for Him, and standing on and claiming His promises in the Bible so that those would come true in our life. In the Bible, God said in Matthew 4:4, "Man shall not live by bread alone, but by every word that proceedeth out of the mouth of God."* **(KJV)** *We need to read the Bible because it is God's words where we can find God's loving directions for us.*

Biceps ang laman sa harap ng baraso at ang laman sa likod ng hita; Iloc: lasag ti sango ti baraso ken ti lasag ti likod ti luppo

Bicker pag-aaway tungkol sa wala man lamang kabulohan; Iloc: apa maygapu ti awan kavalor-valor na

Bicycle *(Tag. & Iloc.)* *bicycle,* bisicleta-*Sp*

Bidding *(Tag. & Iloc.)* subasta-*Sp*

Bide mamalagi, manatili para dito maghintay; Iloc: agtalinaed, agfirmi ti sigud a lugar para ditoy aguray

Bifocal eyeglass *(Tag. & Iloc.)* antiparra-*Sp* na doble-vista-*Sp*

Big malaki; Iloc: dakkel
Correlated words
Huge malaki, napakalaki, malaking-malaki; Iloc: nakadak-dakkel, dakkel unay
Humongous sobrang-sobrang malaki; Iloc: sobra a kadakkel
Antonym

Small maliit, munti; Iloc: bassit

Bigamy crimen ng pagkakaroon ng dalawang asawa; Iloc: crimen iti addaan ti dua nga asawa

Bigger mas malaki; Iloc: dakdakkel, mas dakkel

Biggest pinakamalaki; Iloc: pinakadakkel, kadakkelan

Bigot, Bigotry nakapako siya sa canyang paniwala at panata at walang pagsasaalang-alang sa ibang paniwala o panata; Iloc: nakafirmi iti pammati ken sapata nga awan ti pangawat o pangbigbig na cadagiti sabali

Bile pali, limpa; Iloc: apro, papait

Bilingual nakakapagsalita ng dalawang lengguahe-*Sp*; Iloc: makasarita iti dua a lengguahe

BILL singil sa binili, o kinain, o inutang; Iloc: singir ti ginatang, o kinnan, o inutang

BILL of fare listahan ng mga ulam; Iloc: lista cadagiti sidsida
    Correlated word
    Menu, Food course potahe, ulam; Iloc: potahe, sida

BILL of rights listahan ng mga karapatan ng mga mamayan batay sa batas; Iloc: listaan cadagiti katurayan dagiti tattao ida batay iti linteg

Billet patirahin at paunlakan ng tutuloyan lalo na sa mga sundalo; Iloc: mangisaad ti pagdagusan lallalo cadagiti soldado-*Sp*

Billion *(Tag. & Iloc.) billion*

Bimbo babaeng ang inaatupag lamang ay ang pampabighaning *sexual* niya; Iloc: babai nga as-asecasoen na laeng ket ti *sexual* a pang-aw-awis na

Bin lagayan na gawa sa cahon-*Sp* o *plastic* o kahoy; Iloc: pagikabilan nga aramid ti cahon o *plastic* o kayo

Bind itali, igapos; Iloc: igalot, siglotan, isiglot

Binding 1] tinatali, 2] obligadong sundin ang kasundoan o katungkulan; Iloc: 1] sigsigloten, 2] obligado-*Sp* nga tungpalen ti napagtulagan a contrata-*Sp* wenno ti obligasyon-*Sp*

Binge pagbibibigay-hilig sa sarili sa alak o pagkain; Iloc: pangpaganas iti bagi iti arak wenno makmakan

Binoculars *(Tag. & Iloc.)* largavista-*Sp*, *binocular*, telescopio-*Sp*

Biography talambuhay ng isang tao na sinulat ng ibang tao o manunulat; Iloc: storya ti biag ti maysa a tao nga sinurat ti sabali a tao o mannurat

Bipolar 1] dalawang *poles* sa mundo ay ang *South* at *North Poles*; 2] sa *Psychiatry*, ito ay sakit sa utak na tinatawag na *bipolar disorder* o *manic-depressive disorder* na may tiempo-*Sp* ng *mania* o lubos na ligaya at may tiempo rin ng *depression* o lubos na kalungkotan; 3] sa *Electronics*, ito ay gumagamit ng pareho-*Sp* na positivo-*Sp* at negativo-*Sp* na *charge carriers*

BIRD ibon; Iloc: billit

BIRD or chicken flapping their wings nagpapagaspas; Iloc: agpaypayakpak

BIRDS and the bees kung paano nagkakaroon ng anak

BIRDS of the same feather flock together nagkakatipon-tipon ang mga taong may pagakapareho-*Sp* gaya ng libangan, paniwala, ugali, lengguahe-*Sp*, culay ng balat at iba pa

Birth pagsilang, pagpanganak, pagluwal; Iloc: pannacayanak, aganak
Synonym
Natal tungkol sa pagsilang o panganganak

Birthday kaarawan, cumpleanyo-*Sp*; Iloc: pannacayanak, cumpleanyo-*Sp*, kasangay

Biscuit *(Tag. & Iloc.) biscuit*

Bishop *(Tag. & Iloc.)* obispo-*Sp*

Bit katiting, malinggit, kapiraso lamang; Iloc: balabattit

Bitch 1] babaeng aso, 2] babaeng dominante-*Sp* at malaswa o mahirap pakisamahan; Iloc: 1] babai nga aso, 2] dominante a babai ken *sexual* o narigat a pakicadwaan

BITE cagatin; Iloc: cagaten, kittaben

BITE (small) magcagat ng maliit; Iloc: agkitteb, agkinnet, agcurib

Bitter mapait; Iloc: napait

Bittermelon ampalaya; Iloc: parya

Bizarre kakaiba sa caraniwan ang ichura at asal o pangyayari na puedeng nakakadiri o nakakatakot o nakakapatayo ng balahibo; Iloc: sabsabali ngem iti sigud nga garaw ken ichura o mapaspasamak nga makaaryek wenno nakabutbuteng wenno makapasumgar ti dutdot

Blabber *(Tag. & Iloc.)* magyakyakan, magsatsatan, magdaldalan

BLACK itim, negro-*Sp*, *black*; Iloc: nangisit, pugot, *black*, negro

BLACK gold *(Tag. & Iloc.) petroleum*

BLACK ice *(Tag. & Iloc.)* yelo o *snow* sa calsada-*Sp*

BLACK out himatayin, mawalan ng malay; Iloc: matalimudaw, maawanan iti poot

BLACK sheep of the family ang pinakamasamang miembro-*Sp* ng familya-*Sp*

Blackboard *(Tag. & Iloc.)* pisarra-*Sp*

Blacklist listahan ng mga tao o organisasyon na minultahan o nawalan ng favor dahil sa maling gawain kaya pinagpoprotestahan ang mga ito at hindi binibigyan ng pagtaguyod o pagtangkilik (lista-*Sp*, organisasyon-*Sp*, multa-*Sp*, favor-*Sp*, protesta-*Sp*)
Correlated word

   Boycott samahang nagpapakita ng pagprotesta sa pamamagitan ng hindi pagtatangkilik o hindi pagsuporta; Iloc: agkaykaysa nga mangipakita ti protesta tapno ipaammo da iti haan da mangtaguyod o mangsuporta

Blackout pansamantalang walang electricidad sa sangkabayanan o parte ng bayan; Iloc: temporario-*Sp* nga awan electricidad-*Sp* iti entero-*Sp* nga ili o parte-*Sp* ti ili

Bladder pantog; Iloc: basisaw

Blade *blade,* talim; Iloc: tadem, *blade*

Blame pagbintangan, sisihin, paratangan; Iloc: pabasolen, babalawen

Blame-dodging of one's own mistakes and wrongdoings *Don't justify your mistakes and failures, nor put the blame on others because that <u>would only harden your proclivity to do the wrongdoings again and again</u>. The practice of putting the blame on other people or things or incidents <u>as an excuse because of pride and to hide from the embarrassment of having been caught in your misdeeds</u>, also proves there is no conscience-compunction nor responsibility and accountability on your transgressions. It will only lead you to **<u>not use</u>** your strongest and best efforts to be a competent and efficient person, even in being a trustworthy and credible person. You matter as a person, so take the noble path and transform into being a righteous person.*

Bland taste matabang; Iloc: nalab-ay

Blank *(Tag. & Iloc.)* blanko-*Sp*

Blanket cumot; Iloc: ules

Blasé nasuya na at nawalan na ng gana dahil sa pagpapalugod sa canyang mga gusto o capricho; Iloc: nasuyan ken naawananen ti ganas gapu ti canayon a pangpaganas canyana cadagiti capricho na

Blasphemy pagsusulat o pagsasalita contra-*Sp* sa Panginoong Dios

Blast ugong, sabog; Iloc: uni ti pagbettak o pagputok

Blaze alab, liyab, siklab, ningas, apoy; Iloc: apoy, gillayab

Blazing sumisiklab, nag-aapoy, nasusunog; Iloc: umap-apoy, mapupuor, agur-uram, gumilgillayab, agdardarang, sumsumged

Bleach pangpaputi; Iloc: pangpapuraw

Bleed magdugo; Iloc: agdara

Blemish mancha-*Sp*, bahid, batik; Iloc: mancha

Blend pagsama-samahin at haloin; Iloc: paglaok-laoken ken kiwaren, kiburen

Bless pagpalain, basbasan, biyayaan, consagrahin; Iloc: iconsagrar, bendisyonan, maikkan ti gracia-*Sp* (consagra/consagrar-*Sp*, bendisyon-*Sp*)
Correlated word
Anoint bendisyonan, pahiran ng langis; Iloc: agbendisyon, sapsappoan o aprosan ti lana

Blessed pinagpala, sagrado, banal, maluwalhati, binendito, nabendisyonan; Iloc: nabendito, nabendisyonan, naisagrado, naigracia, nasantoan (sagrado-*Sp*, bendito-*Sp*, bendisyon-*Sp*, gracia-*Sp*, santo-*Sp*)

Blessings mga pagpapala at biyaya ng Panginoong Dios, biyayang hulog ng langit; Iloc: dagiti bendisyon-*Sp* ken gracia-*Sp* ni Apo Dios
Correlated words
Boon biyaya na sagot sa hiniling; Iloc: gracia nga sungbat iti kiddaw
Godsend ang biglang pagkakatutuo o pagdating o pagbubunga ng minimithi o kinakailangang bagay
Windfall tiba-tiba dahil nagkaroon ng bigla at hindi inaasahang suerte o dating ng maraming pera; Iloc: tiba-tiba gapu ta naaddaan iti golpe ken haan nga inek-expectar nga suerte ken pagsangpet iti adu a cuarta
Blight nakakadismaya at nakakahadlang ng progreso-*Sp*; Iloc: nakakadismaya ken makalapped ti progreso

BLIND in one eye bulag sa isang mata; Iloc: bulding

BLIND, totally bulag; Iloc: bulag, bulsek

Blindfold *(Tag. & Iloc.)* piring

Blindside 1] walang kamalay-malay na may plano o may mangyayaring bagay na hindi mabuti, 2] manggolpe sa taong walang kamalay-malay at nasa puestong madaling matablan ng masama; Iloc: 1] awan pulos ti ammo na nga adda plano wenno adda mapasamak nga haan a naimbag; 2] manggolpe iti tao nga awan ammo na a magolpe isu ken adda isu iti puesto nga nalaka a macabil

Blinking kukurap-kurap; Iloc: agkirem-kirem
   Correlated word
   Wink kindatan; Iloc: kiddayan

Bliss malaking kaligayahan, kaligayahang *spiritual*; Iloc: dakkel a ragsak, ragsak nga espiritual-*Sp*

Blithe masaya, campante-*Sp* at hindi nag-aalala; Iloc: narambak, campante ken awan ti pagkadanag

Bloat hindi comfortableng ramdam na parang pagkabusog sa chan; Iloc: haan a comfortab-le-*Sp* a casla bussog ti chan

BLOCK *(Tag. & Iloc.) block,* bloke-*Sp*

BLOCK, Obstruct harangin, magsagabal, sanggahin; Iloc: barraen, sanggaen

Blocked *(Tag. & Iloc.)* barado

Blog sa *website* ng *internet*, ang manunulat ay isulat ang canyang ka-ranasan, naobserva, kuro-kuro o anomang gusto niyang isulat na puedeng may kasamang retrato o *link* sa ibang *website*

BLOOD dugo; Iloc: dara

BLOOD pressure presyon-*Sp* ng dugo; Iloc: presyon ti dara

BLOOD pressure, high *(Tag. & Iloc.)* alta presyon-*Sp*

BLOOD vessel mga ugat, *capillary* at *artery* na pinag-aagosan ng dugo; Iloc: dagiti urat, *capillary* ken *artery* a pagayosan ti dara

Bloom, Blossom mamulaklak, mamukadkad; Iloc: agsabong, panagukrad ti sabong

Blot 1] mancha-*Sp*, libag, bahid, batik, 2] punasan ang basa; Iloc: 1] mancha, rugit, pilkat, 2] punasan ti basa

Blotch manchang itim o pula o puti sa cutis o balat ng tao Iloc: mancha a nangisit o labbaga wenno puraw iti cutis o cudil ti tao

Blouse *(Tag. & Iloc.) blouse,* blusa-*Sp*

BLOW hampasin, pukpokin, golpehin; Iloc: malwen, golpien

BLOW, Puff hipan; Iloc: puyotan

BLOW off mucus isinga; Iloc: ipangres

Blue *blue,* bughaw; Iloc: *blue,* azul-*Sp*

Blunder magkamali; Iloc: agbiddut, makaaramid ti haan a nasayaat

Blunt mapurol; Iloc: namudil
> *Antonym*
> **Sharp** matalas, matalim; Iloc: natadem

Blurred malabo, hindi maliwanag; Iloc: nacudrep, nacusnaw, haan a nalawag

Blurt ibulalas, magbulalas, mamutawi sa bibig; Iloc: maysawang

Blush mamula ang mukha; Iloc: aglablabbasit o aglabbaga ti rupa

BOARD, Lodge magcasera, matira; Iloc: ag-casera-*aSp*, agyan
> *Correlated word*
> **Lodging** tuloyan; Iloc: pagdagusan

BOARD, Plank *(Tag. & Iloc.)* tabla-*Sp*

Boast magyabang, magpasikat, maghambog; Iloc: agparayag, agpasikat, aglangsut

Boastful mapagmalaki, mayabang, hambog, pasikat; Iloc: napangas, parayag, langsut

Boat *(Tag. & Iloc.)* banca
> *Correlated words*
> **Native canoe** banca; Iloc: banca, barangay
> **Ship** *(Tag. & Iloc.)* bapor, barco
> **Raft** *(Tag. & Iloc.)* balsa

BOB lilitaw-lulubog, tataas-bababa; Iloc: lumtaw-lumned, ngumato-bumaba

BOB up umahon; Iloc: lumtaw

Bode, Presage nagpapahiwatig o naghuhudyat o nakakapagparamdam o nakikinita ang mangyayari sa hinaharap

BODY katawan; Iloc: bagi
> *Synonym*
> **Physical** *physical,* tungkol sa katawan; Iloc: *physical,* maypapan ti bagi

BODY dirt libag; Iloc: kabkab

BODY joints gota, paghugpongan o cabitan ng dalawang buto gaya ng tuhod, sico, balakang, balikat; Iloc: pagsilpoan ti dua a tulang casla ti tumeng, sico, patong, abaga

Body sides (from shoulders to feet) tagiliran; Iloc: bakrang, sikigan

Bogus *(Tag. & Iloc.)* peke, *bogus*

BOIL kulo; Iloc: burek
>*Correlated word*
>**Parboil** ipakulo ng sandali lamang; Iloc: ipaburek ti nabiit laeng

BOIL food maglaga; Iloc: aglingta

BOIL, Lump in the body bukol, pigsa; Iloc: bukol, busali
>*Correlated word*
>**Swelling in the body** manas, maga; Iloc: manas, letteg

Boiler pot *(Tag. & Iloc.)* caldero-*Sp*

Boisterous barumbado at nag-iingay; Iloc: barumbado ken nakarir-riri

Bold matapang; Iloc: natured

Bolster palakasin ang loob; Iloc: patibkeren ti nakem para agtured

BOLT *(Tag. & Iloc.)* candado-*Sp*

BOLT out sumibad; Iloc: agtalaw a dagdagus
>*Correlated word*
>**Scoot out** biglang pagtakbo; Iloc: golpe a pagtaray

Bomb *(Tag. & Iloc.)* bomba-*Sp*

Bombard bombahin ng bombahin, tirahin ng tirahin; Iloc: bombaen nga panay-panay, tira-tiraen (bomba-*Sp*, tira-*Sp*)

Bona fide tunay, *genuine*; Iloc: usto-*Sp*, *genuine*

Bon mot intelihenteng kasabihan; Iloc: nasirib a bagbaga

BOND *(Tag. & Iloc.)* fianza-*Sp*

BOND together as a group magsama-sama, barcadahan; Iloc: ag-timpuyog, agkacadwa

BONE buto; Iloc: tulang
>*Correlated words*
>**Fish bone** tinik; Iloc: siit
>**Skeleton** calansay; Iloc: tulang ti bagi ti natay

BONE of contention ang sanhi ng pagkakaalitan, disgustohan o argumento-*Sp*

Bonus *(Tag. & Iloc.)* *bonus*

"Boo!" *(Tag. & Iloc.)* "Bulaga!"

Booger kulangot; Iloc: duggong

Book libro-*Sp*, aklat; Iloc: libro

Bookcase estante-*Sp*, aklatang aparador-*Sp*; Iloc: estante, aparador ti libro-*Sp*

Boom 1] malakas na tunog; 2] lumaki, lumago at umunlad/magprogreso gaya ng negocio

Boomerang *flat* o patag na aparato-*Sp* na bilog na kapag hinahagis ito, bumabalik sa nanghagis; Iloc: *flat* wenno patag nga aparato-*Sp* nga agtimbukel nga nu ipalladaw ket agsubli idiay nangpalladaw
Correlated words
Frisbee itcha-salo na laruan; Iloc: ibato-sippaw nga ay-ayam
Bounce, Ricochet talbog, itira pero bumabalik; Iloc: talbog, itira ngem agsubli

Boon biyaya na sagot sa hiniling; Iloc: gracia-*Sp* nga sungbat iti kiddaw

Boondocks makapal na kakahuyan o kagubatan, gubat; Iloc: napuskol a kabakiran o kakaywan, bakir

Boondoggle hindi kailangan at hindi nakakabigay ng bunga kaya nasasayang lamang ang pagod at pera na ginugugol dito; Iloc: haan a masapul ken haan makaited ti bunga isu a masaysayang laeng ti ling-et ken cuarta nga isaad ditoy

Boots *(Tag. & Iloc.)* botas-*Sp*

Border gilid; Iloc: igid

Bore butasan; Iloc: abutan

Bored naiinip; Iloc: matektekan

Boring nakakaantok o nakakainip dahil hindi nakakalibang; Iloc: makapaturog o mangpatektek gapu ta haan a makalinglingay
Antonym
Amusing nakakalibang; Iloc: nakalinglingay

BORN ipinanganak, isinilang, niluwal; Iloc: naypasngay, nayyanak

BORN, newly kapapanganak; Iloc: kayyan-anak

Borrow manghiram, humiram; Iloc: bumulod, buloden

Boss tagapamahala, amo-*Sp*, pinuno, pangulo; Iloc: pangulo, amo, apo

Bosom dibdib; Iloc: barukong

Botch, Botched sira ang ginawa dahil sa hindi pag-iingat o barabara lamang ang paggawa o kaya wala o kaunti lamang ang kaalaman sa ginagawa; Iloc: nadadael ti inaramid gapu ti kaawanan ti pagannad o bara-bara laeng ti pagaramid wenno awan wenno bassit laeng iti pagkaammo na iti ar-aramiden na
Synonym

Muff sira ang ginawa dahil sa hindi pag-iingat o bara-bara lang ang paggawa o kaya wala o kaunti lamang ang kaalaman sa ginagawa; Iloc: nadadael ti inaramid gapu ti kaawanan ti pagannad o bara-bara laeng ti pagaramid o awan wenno bassit laeng iti pagkaammo na iti ar-aramiden na

BOTH persons kapwa sila, silang dalawa; Iloc: isuda a dua, dua da,

BOTH sides magkabilaan; Iloc: agsinnumbangir

Bother gambalain, abalahin, mag-estorbo-*Sp*, mag-molescha-*Sp*; Iloc: agestorbo, ag-molescha

Bottle botelya-*Sp*, bote-*Sp*; Iloc: botelya

Bottled up kinikimkim na sama o sakit ng loob; Iloc: napempen a rungsot o sakit ti puso

BOTTOM kailaliman; Iloc: kababaan, kasirok-sirokan

BOTTOM line 1] ang kahuli-hilihang resulta, 2] ang pinakaimportanteng diwa, 3] ang pinakamababang linya kung saan pinapakita ang lubos na gana/kinita o pagkalugi ng companya

Bounce talbog, itira pero bumabalik; Iloc: talbog, itira ngem agsubli

BOUNDARY gilid ng teritoryo-*Sp* o lugar-*Sp*, hangganan; Iloc: igid ti solar-*Sp* o teritoryo, patinggana

BOUNDARY landmark *(Tag. & Iloc.)* mohon-*Sp*
Correlated word
Demarcate markahan ang hangganan ng pag-aaring lupa; Iloc: markaan ti patinggana ti minoyongan o solar

Bouillabaisse pagkaing pinagsama-sama ang mga nahuli sa tubig gaya ng isda, talaba, tulya, halaan, alimango, pugita at hipon; Iloc: kanen a pinaglalaok dagiti natiliw diay taaw casla ti ikan, talaba, cabibi, bennek, curita, alimango ken pasayan

Bounty abundanciang pamigay na caraniwan ay buhat sa govierno-*Sp*; Iloc: abundancia-*Sp* nga ited ti govierno

Bouquet pumpon o cumpol ng bulaklak; Iloc: nakareppet o cumpol a sabsabong

BOW magyuko, magtungo, mag-saludo-*Sp*; Iloc: agdumog, ag-saludo

BOW and arrow pana at palaso; Iloc: pana ken sikkubeng

BOW-legged sakang; Iloc: pakkang

BOW out magbitiw at lumisan; Iloc: umikkat ken agtalaw

BOWEL *(Tag. & Iloc.)* bituka

BOWEL movement pagtae; Iloc: pagtakki

195

BOWEL leak wisik na tae; Iloc: pugtit

Bowl mangkok; Iloc: malucong, sucong

BOX *(Tag. & Iloc.)* cahon-*Sp*, caha-*Sp*, carton-*Sp*

BOX, Punch suntokin, buntalin; Iloc: danogen, disnogen, sulongen

BOX, small *(Tag. & Iloc.)* cahita-*Sp*

Boxer *(Tag. & Iloc.)* boksingero

Boxing *(Tag. & Iloc.)* boksing

BOY batang lalake, totoy; Iloc: ubing nga lalaki, barok

BOY friend, Beau kasintahan, novio-*Sp*; Iloc: kaayan-ayat, novio

Boycott samahang nagpapakita ng pagprotesta sa pamamagitan ng hindi pagtatangkilik o hindi pagsuporta; Iloc: pagcacadwaan nga mangipakita ti protesta ken iti haan da pagtaguyod o pagsuporta

Bra *bra*; Iloc: *bra*

Brace 1] buhayin, palakasin ang loob at ipaghanda, 2] *noun*: capitan o suporta, *verb*: idugtong, icabit at icapit para tumibay at pumirmi ng husto; Iloc: 1] biagen, patibkeren ti nakem para agtured, papigsaen ken ipapreparar o ipasagana, 2] *noun*: pagcapetan o suporta, *verb*: isilpo, iconectar ken icapet para agfirmi ti napigsa ken nalagda

Bracelet *(Tag. & Iloc.)* pulseras-*Sp*

Braces pangpaayos sa hindi pantay na ngipin; Iloc: pangpausto iti awan ti usto a forma a ngipen

Brag magyabang; Iloc: agparayag, aglastog

Braid tirintas; Iloc: sallapid

Brain utak; Iloc: utek

> *Correlated words*
>
> **Mind** isip; Iloc: nakem
>
> **Thought** isip; Iloc: panunot
>
> **Memory** memoria, ang parte ng utak na nagpapaala-ala ng mga nakalipas at mga kasalukuyan; Iloc: memoria, parte ti utek a mangpalagip iti napalabas ida ken itatta
>
> **Cognitiveness, Cognition** obra ng utak gaya ng pag-isip, pag-alam, pag-ulirat, memoria, pagrason, paghusga, pagkilala o pagturing; Iloc: obra ti utek casla ti pagpanunot, pag-ammo, pagkapoot, memoria, pagrason ken paghusgar ken pagbigbig
>
> **Mentality** kung ano ang cacayahan ng utak at isip, kung paano kumilos o magturing ang utak o isip

Psyche ang utak na nagpapalakad ng isip, emosyon at asal na dito nakikita ang kaluluwa o spiritu ng tao

Brainstorm biglang silakbo o pagbulalas dahil sa pagkabagabag ng utak; biglang bugso at udyok na kilos na hindi normal-*Sp*

Brainstorming malalim at masuring pag-uusap ng dalawa o mahigit sa dalawang tao para lutasin ang problema o mga maraming infor-masyon-*Sp*, o maglikha o magyabong ng bagong matalinong isip/*idea* o pagturing/*perspective* o pagpalakad o plano-*Sp*

Brainwash parati o fuersahang pangsulsol para pumareho ang paniwala at costumbre-*Sp* sa hinihimok niya; Iloc: canacanayon nga uyotan o sulisogen a fuersa-*Sp* tapno pumada ti pammati ken costumbre na a casla iti isulsulisog na

Braise i-gisa-*Sp* ang carne-*Sp* o gulay sa mantica pagkatapos lagyan ng konting tubig; Iloc: i-gisar-*Sp* ti carne o nateng iti manteca-*Sp*, palpas na ket ikkan ti bassit a danum

Brake of a vehicle *(Tag. & Iloc.)* freno-*Sp*

BRANCH of a tree *(Tag. & Iloc.)* sanga

BRANCH of an office *(Tag. & Iloc.)* sangay

BRANCH out ipalaganap sa iba pang lugar-*Sp*

BRAND 1] marka-*Sp*, tanda, 2] para malaman kung canino ang nag-memay-ari ng vaca o calabaw, minamarkahan ang balat ng mga ito sa pamamagitan ng mainit na bakal; Iloc: 1] marka-*Sp*, 2] para maammuan iti akincucua ti vaca ken nuang, mangmarka iti cudil dagitoy animales nga mangiyusar iti napudot a landok

BRAND name medicine ginawa itong *brand name medicine* para madaling maalaala at ibigkas at ibaybay o i-*spell*. Ang *brand name medicine* ay, kung minsan, may combinasyon na ibang medicina at mga ito'y nakasulat sa cahon o botelya nito

Brandish *(Tag. & Iloc.)* iwasiwas

Brat batang matigas ang ulo at makasarili; Iloc: ubing a natangken ti ulo ken bagbagi laeng ti pampanunoten na

Bravado arogante-*Sp* at mapagsuway o mapagtutol, peke sa pagtatapang-tapangan

BRAVE *Brave, courageous, intrepid, heroic.* Bravo-*Sp*, matapang, magiting, bayani; Iloc: bravo, natured, bayani
Synonyms

197

Bold matapang, hindi duwag o mahiyain; Iloc: natured, haan a cobarde o mabain

Courageous matapang, malakas ang loob; Iloc: natured

Dauntless *Courageous, brave, daring, unflinching even when threatened, intrepid, resolute in purpose.* Matapang, walang takot, malakas ang loob, hindi umourong kahit tinatakot, matibay kung magpasia
Antonym
Coward cobarde, duwag; Iloc: cobarde, takrot, tarkuk

BRAVE front magpakita ng kalakasan ng loob kahit na siya'y may pangangamba sa puso niya

Brawn, Brawny laman ng katawan na kung saan masculado-*Sp*, matipuno; Iloc: lasag ti bagi nu inchenna iti masculado, napuner
Synonym
Biceps ang laman sa harap ng baraso at ang laman sa likod ng hita; Iloc: ti lasag ti sango ti baraso ken ti lasag ti likod ti luppo

Breach paglabag sa kasundoan; Iloc: haan a pagtungpal ti tulag

BREAD and butter ang pagkakakitaan o kung saan sumusweldo ang tao (suweldo-*Sp*)

BREAD, Filipino *(Tag. & Iloc.)* tinapay, pan, pan de sal-*Sp*, pan de leche-*Sp*, *tasty bread*

Breadth, Width kalaparan, kaluwangan, lawak; Iloc: kaacaba, lawa
Correlated word
Vastness lawak at laki at haba at luwang at lalim; Iloc: lawa ken acaba ken pagkadakkel ken pagkaadalem

BREAK, Smash mabasag; Iloc: mabuong

BREAK, Snap off baliin, putolin, bakliin, lagutin, patirin; Iloc: pugsaten, pugsoten, tukkolen

BREAK a record makatamo ng pinakamagaling na resulta-*Sp* sa anumang larangan na ninuman ay wala pang nakapagkamit; Iloc: makaturpos iti pinakanalaeng nga resulta iti aniaman a larangan nga awan pay pulos ti nakagun-od

BREAK down (<u>not</u> *same as Breakdown below*) makina o *appliance* na biglang nasira

BREAK even gastos-*Sp* at kinita ay pareho lamang dahil walang ti-nubo, puhunan at kinita ay pareho lamang, venta-*Sp* o servicio-*Sp* ay pareho-*Sp* lamang sa kinita; Iloc: puonan ken ganancia-*Sp* ket agpada laeng, laco o servicio ket pareho laeng ti kinita, awan tubo, amanos

BREAK free, Cut loose kumacalas, kumacalag, magpumiglas para makatakas; Iloc: mangwarwar ti galot o ikkaten na ti rehas-*Sp* ti bagi na para makatammeng o makabulos o makalibas ken makawaya

BREAK, get a magkaroon ng mabuting pagkakataon o oportunidad-*Sp*, suwerte-*Sp* o kaginhawaan

BREAK-in, Breaking and entering, Home Invasion fuersang pagpasok sa silid o bahay o gusali na ang tangka ay masama; Iloc: fuersa-*Sp* a pagserrek ti cuarto o balay o gusali nga ti rangta ket dakes

BREAK somene's fall saluhin ang nahuhulog o natotomba na tao para hindi masaktan at mapinsala

BREAK the glass basagin, biyakin; Iloc: buongen

BREAK the ice para mabuksan ang pakikipagkaibigan at hindi nagka-katungahan lamang, kausapin ang katabi o malapitang tao

BREAK the shell pisain; Iloc: ipis-ak

BREAK up taposin na ang pag-uugnayan at makipaghiwalay sa novio/novia-*Sp*

Breakable babasagin; Iloc: nalaca a mabuong

Breakdown 1] magkaroon ng nervios o hindi macontrolado ang emosyon kaya nag-iiiyak na lang, 2] bigla at grabeng panghina ng katawan o kaisipan, 3] sumaria ng mga importanteng bagay; Iloc: 1] agnervios ken haan na macontrolado iti emosyon na, 2] golpe ken grabe a pagcapsut ti bagi wenno nakem, 3] sumaria cadagiti importante a banag

Breakfast almusal-a*Sp*; Iloc: almusar-*Sp*, pammigat
Correlated words
Lunch pananghalian; Iloc: pangngaldaw
Dinner or Supper hapunan; Iloc: pang-rabii

Breakthrough *(Tag. & Iloc.)* makalusot sa/diay problema

Breast suso, dibdib; Iloc: suso, barukong

BREATH *n.*, hinga; Iloc: anges

BREATH, bad mabahong hininga; Iloc: nabangsit a sang-aw

BREATH, gasp for humihingal; Iloc: agas-asog

BREATH of fresh air habang sa kalagitnaan o pagkatapos ng *stress* o problema-*Sp*, may sumipot na napakainam na lunas o tao o palabas o pamamaraan na nakakabigay ng ginhawa o buntong-hininga

BREATHE *v.*, huminga; Iloc: aganges
Synonym

Inhale and exhale huminga; Iloc: aganges

BREATHE heavily, Pant humahangos, sumasagap ng hininga; Iloc: agasasog, agal-al-al

Breathing space 1] cuarto na makabuntong-hininga ang tao; 2] sa kalagitnaan ng maraming trabaho o problema, ito ay panahon o chansa na makapagpahinga

Breed magpalaki at mag-alaga ng hayup; Iloc: mangpadakkel ken mangtaraken ti *animal*

Breeze simoy ng hangin; Iloc: pul-oy ti angin

BRIBE with money suhol, huthot, lagay; Iloc: pasuksok

BRIBE by flattery magsipsip, mambola; Iloc: agsipsip, bola-bolaen

Bride babaeng ikakasal; Iloc: babai nga ag-casar-*Sp*

Bridegroom lalaking ikacasal; Iloc: lalaki nga agcasar

Bridge tulay; Iloc: rangtay

BRIEF, Concise maikli; Iloc: ababa

BRIEF, man's calsonsilyo-*Sp*; Iloc: carsonsilyo

Briefing pagpapahayag ng kinakailangang malaman

Bright maliwanag, masinag; Iloc: nalawag, nasillag, naranyag
  Correlated words
  Brilliant maningning, masinag, makintab; Iloc: nasillag, nasilap, nasileng
  Radiant sumisikat, kumikislap, sumisinag, nagniningning; Iloc: sumilsilap, agranranyag, sumilsileng, agkirkirap
  Resplendent masikat, makislap, masinag, maningning, maluningning; Iloc: nasilap, nasillag, naranyag
  Antonym
  Dim kulimlim, madilim; Iloc: nasipnget, nacudrep, nalidem

Brilliance sikat, kislap, sinag, ningning, luningning, kintab, kinang; Iloc: silap, sileng, sillag, ranyag

Brim gilid o bibig ng *canyon* na bundok; bibig ng platong mangkok; Iloc: igid o bibig ti *canyon* nga bantay; bibig ti plato a sucong

Brine *n.*, **Briny** *adj.* maasin na tubig o lawa; Iloc: naasin a danum o danaw

BRING dalhin, magdala; Iloc: mangiyeg, mangipan, mangikuyog, mangitugot
  Correlated word
  Take kunin; Iloc: alaen, awaten

BRING above dalhin sa taas; Iloc: ipan diay ngato, ingato

BRING-along-provision baon; Iloc: balon

BRING as company isama; Iloc: ikuyog

BRING down *(Tag. & Iloc.)* ibaba

BRING home iyuwi; Iloc: iyawid

BRING out ilabas, iluwal; Iloc: iruar

BRING someone to a destination (i.e., home) ihatid, dalhin patungo sa..; Iloc: itulnog, itulod idiay.., ipan idiay

BRING up pagpalaki ng anak; Iloc: pagpadakkel ti anak

Brink bingit, gilid; Iloc: igid

Bristle matigas na buhok ng aparato-*Sp* na parang escoba-*Sp*; Iloc: natangken a buok ti aparato a casla escoba

British *(Tag. & Iloc.) British*

Brittle malutong, madaling maputol o madurog; Iloc: narasi, nakersang, nalaca a matukkol wenno maburak

Broach ilabas na paksa para pag-usapan; Iloc: iruar a paksa tapno pagsaritaan

BROAD malapad, malawak; Iloc: nalawa, naacaba

BROAD-minded nakakaintindi, maunawain, malawak ang pang-unawa; Iloc: makaawat cadagiti kasasaad, nalawa ti pagawat na

Broadcast *broadcast,* ipasahimpapawid, magpahayag; Iloc: *broadcast,* ipablaak, iwarnak

Broaden palaparin, palawakin; Iloc: palawaen, i-acaba

Broil mag-ihaw, ihawin; Iloc: agtuno, ituno

Broke 1] *broke,* walang pera, 2] basag; Iloc: 1] *broke,* naawanan ti cuarta, 2] nabuong

Broken nabasag; Iloc: nabuong

Bronchitis *(Tag. & Iloc.)* bronkitis-*Sp*

Brood malungkot o pagtampo sa pag-iisip; Iloc: naliday o maluksaw nga agpampanunot

Brook batis; Iloc: waig

Broom walis; Iloc: sagad

Broth sabaw, caldo-*Sp*; Iloc: caldo, digo, labay
   Correlated word
   Soup *(Tag. & Iloc.)* sopas, caldo

BROTHER, Bro kapatid na lalake; Iloc: kabsat nga lalaki, kabagis

BROTHER-in-law bayaw; Iloc: kayong, bayaw

BROTHER, older kuya; Iloc: manong

BROTHER, younger mas batang kapatid na lalake; Iloc: ading a lalaki, adi

Brotherhood kapatiran; Iloc: panagkakabsat

Brotherly parang kapatid; Iloc: caslala kabsat

Brow noo; Iloc: muging

BROWN *brown,* culay cafe-*Sp*; Iloc: *brown,* color-*Sp* ti cafe

BROWN-skinned *(Tag. & Iloc.)* morena/no, kayumanggi

Brownout, Outage pansamantalang walang electricidad-*Sp* sa sangkabayanan o parte-*Sp* lamang ng bayan; Iloc: temporario-*Sp* nga awan electricidad iti entero-*Sp* o parte ti ili

Browse 1] marahang nagpipili o nagtitingin-tingin o nagbabasabasa ng informasyon, 2] naghahanap ng informasyon sa *internet*; Iloc: 1] nainnayad nga agpilpili wenno mangkitakita o agbasabasa laeng, 2] agsapsapul ti informasyon diay *internet*

Bruise sugat, galos; Iloc: dunor, sugat

Brunch kainan sa kalagitnaan ng umaga bago magtanghali na combinasyon-*Sp* ng almusal-*aSp* at tanghalian; Iloc: pannangan iti katengngaan ti bigat baro ag-alas doce-*Sp* nga combinasyon-*Sp* ti almusar-*Sp* ken pangngaldaw

Brunt malaking problemang pasanin; Iloc: dakkel a problema nga ibaklay

Brush *(Tag. & Iloc.)* escoba-*Sp*

Brusque *(Tag. & Iloc.)* brusco-*Sp*

Brutal makahayop, salbahe-*Sp*; Iloc: kaugali ti narungsot nga *animal*

Bubble bula; Iloc: labutab

    Correlated word

    Sud, Suds bula ng sabon; Iloc: labutab ti sabon

Bubbly masigla at nakasisiya; Iloc: ganado-*Sp* ken nakaliwliwa

Buck 1] peso, dollar; 2] lalaking hayop gaya ng *deer*

BUCKET *(Tag. & Iloc.)* balde-*Sp*, timba-*Sp*

BUCKET, drop in the kaunti lang at hindi man lamang sapat sa kinakailangan; Iloc: bassit laeng nga haan man laeng umanay iti kasapulan

BUCKET list mga gustong gagawin bago makarating sa tinakdang edad-*Sp* o bago mamatay; Iloc: dagiti cayat nga aramiden baro nga makadanon ti inkeddeng nga edad wenno baro a matay isu

BUCKET, kick the *(Tag. & Iloc.)* pagkapatay

BUCKLE cinturong kabitan sa pag-upo sa coche-*Sp*; Iloc: cinturon-*Sp* a pagkawitan ti tao idiay tugaw ti coche

BUCKLE up gamitin ang *seatbelt*, mag-*seatbelt* habang nakasakay sa coche-*Sp* para mas ligtas sa accidente-*Sp*

Bud usbong; Iloc: saringit, rusing

Buddy kaibigan; Iloc: gayyem

Budge gumalaw ng konti, ibahin ang canyang *position*; Iloc: aggaraw ti bassit, balbaliwan ti puesto-*Sp* na

Budget *budget*, binukod para sa panggugol; Iloc: *budget*, naylasin a panggastos
> *Correlated word*
> **Appropriation, Allotment** nilaang pera o fondong panggugol sa tinakdang bagay; Iloc: inlasin a cuarta nga iyusar iti indesignar o inkeddeng a banag

Buffer anoman o sinomang nakakapahina ng sakit o nakakaprotecta o nakakahadlang sa masamang efecto-*Sp*; Iloc: daytoy ket ania man o sinno man a makapangpacapsut iti sakit o makaprotecta o makalapped iti dakes nga efecto

Buffet *restaurant* na isang tinakdang precio lamang pero kumain ka ng kumain hanggang caya mo; Iloc: *restaurant* a maysa a precio laeng ti bayad ngem kaan ka nga kaan ingganat macayam

Buffoon *clown*, mahilig magpatawa sa mga tao

Bug 1] anomang insecto-*Sp*, 2] sakit gaya ng *flu*, 3] defecto-*Sp* ng *computer*, 4] estorbo-*Sp* o gumagambala sa tao, 5] aparato-*Sp* na palihim na makinig o manubok o mangsubaybay ng tao; Iloc: 1] aniaman nga insecto, 2] sakit a casla *flu*, 3] defecto ti *computer*, 4] mangtantan; mang-estorbo; 5] aparato a palimed nga agdengngeg o mangtectec ken mang-espia-*Sp* ti tao

BUILD magpatayo ng bahay o gusali, magpuesto, magtatag; Iloc: ag-patacder ti balay o facilidad-*Sp*, mangsimpa, mang-plastar-*Sp*, mangbangon, mang-puesto-*Sp*

BUILD-up 1] paglago o pagdami; 2] *publicity* na nakakaventahe; 3] dumadaming dumi

BUILDING *(Tag. & Iloc.)* *building*, gusali, stractura-*Sp*, facilidad-*Sp*
> *Synonyms*
> **Facility** facilidad, gusali, *building*

Edifice *(Tag. & Iloc.)* gusali, *building*

BUILDING floor *(Tag. & Iloc.)* palapag, *floor*

Bulb, electric *(Tag. & Iloc.)* bombilya-*Sp*

Bulge tambok; Iloc: butchog, baskag

Bulk *(Tag. & Iloc.)* bulto-*Sp*

Bulkhead pader o partisyon-*Sp* sa sasakyang barco-*Sp*, eroplano-*Sp*, coche-*Sp*, *RV* o *bus* na nakakahadlang ng sunog, tubig at iba pa

Bulky *adj.* matambok, bumukol; Iloc: nagbukol, bumsog, bimsog

Bullet *(Tag. & Iloc.)* bala-*Sp*

Bully *Please don't be a bully. Be kind to others because that is being kind to yourself as well, valuing yourself with self-respect for being permissive, tolerant and lenient with people. Having that attitude will bring you peace and opportunities. People will like you for **not** being judgmental and critical on them. Being a bully only brings problems and failures to you because you attain a bad reputation, or a police record, or even jail time. Because you have fears of being trounced, you do not bully bigger-built people or people your own size; but you bully only smaller-built men and the weaker gender, women. Do not think that just because you are taller, or have a bigger built, or you are armed with a weapon, or in a gang, that supposedly you have leverage over others. **Not true** because irrationally inflicting cruelty on others is considered a cover-up of **cowardice** and **self-condemnation**. The truth is, **a real man or a real macho** is nice and considerate to others while he lives a humble, peaceful life and strives to attain higher beneficial achievements. **A remarkable real man or a remarkable macho** is nice and considerate to others and possess all these qualities: peace, humility, kindness, intelligence, good judgments, righteous deeds, noble principles, self-confidence, persevering endeavors, productive activities, useful accomplishments and successful results. **A man is admired and respected when he uses his strength for purposes** that are valuable and peaceful for himself and for others. If bullies just like you oppress and maltreat **your own** brother, sister, mother and father, or **your own** son, daughter and spouse, would you be pleased with that? Of course not, so please don't be cruel to others. And please **do yourself a great service by***

being a righteous contributing member to society and be part of the solution, not the problem. Ang *bully* ay nanakit sa tao pero iniiwasan ang kasinlaki niya o mas malaki sa canya para hindi siya maagraviado. Kaya sa mga babae at lalaki na mahihina siya nanlalait at nang-aabuso, nambubogbog at nanghahampas; sumasali siya sa barcada ng kapwang nagbalatkayong mga maton kahit takot silang mag-isa kaya akala nila may lamang sila dahil sa "lakas ng barcada" para ipamalas ang "pagkalalake naman daw nila" kahit alam ng lahat na pakitang-tao lamang iyan dahil takot silang mag-isa. Sa katunayan ang nambu-*bully* ay gawain ng taong walang talino at wala ring kabutihang puso at gawa kaya namvivictima sa mas mahina at hindi kasing laki o dami nila. Huwag laitin o saktan ang mas mahinang lalake o mga babae dahil ang gumagawa niyan ay **duwag** o **cobarde** lamang at galit sa sarili niyang pagkatao. **Gamitin mo ang tunay na pagkalalake mo sa marangal na gawain at sa pagiging mabuting katatao** para marespeto mo ang mismo mong sarili at para ang ligaya at unlad ay lalapit sa iyo.

Bum *homeless,* nakatira sa calsada, palaboy-laboy, hampaslupa; Iloc: *homeless,* aggigian idiay calsada, agwalwalang

Bumble nauutal, nabubulol; Iloc: agum-umel

Bummer 1] salita na ginagamit kung nadisgusto o nabigo siya; 2] isang pangyayari na nagbibigay ng kasamaan, lungkot, kabigoan o disgusto; 3] taong ayaw magtrabaho, taong pagala-gala lang, tao na inutil o walang kacayahan; 4] ang uri o pagkagawa ay napakasama o napakawalang cuenta; 5] ang masamang kahihinatnan sa pagkakaroon sa katawan ng alak o narcotico na nakakapagguni-guni sa canya ng nakakatakot o nakakapagparamdam sa canya ng sakit sa katawan.

BUMP mabundol, mabunggo; Iloc: madalapus, madungpar

BUMP into someone, Run across someone nagkataong nagkita sa isang lugar na hindi sinasadya o inaasahan.

BUMP one's head maumpog, mauntog; Iloc: maytim-og

Bumped under the chin, be nabunggo ang baba; Iloc: naytibab

Bumpy ride *(Tag. & Iloc.)* matagtag

Bunch *(Tag. & Iloc.)* cumpol

BUNDLE balutan, supot, *bag*; Iloc: balkot, bungon, *bag*

BUNDLE up magsuot ng makapal para hindi ginawin sa lamig; Iloc: agcawes iti napuskol para haan nga malammin

Bungle mali-maling gumawa; Iloc: mali-mali nga agaramid

Buoy lumolutang sa lawa na palatandaan kung saan may panganib; Iloc: agtumtumpaw ti taaw a pangmarka nga addaan peggad diay a lugar

Buoyant *adj.*, **Buoyancy** *n.* 1] capabilidad-*Sp* na tumaas at lumotang; 2] magaan ang loob, masayang makihalobilo

Burden kabigatan, pasanin; Iloc: dagsen wenno bantut a baklay a bakbaklayen

Bureaucracy *(government)*, **Bureaucrat** *(official)* administrasyon-*Sp* ng govierno-*Sp* na may mga sangay na mga *bureau* o departamento-*Sp* na minamahala ng mga ofisyal-*Sp* na hindi dumaan sa pagboboto; sistema ng administrasyon-*Sp* na kinakailangan na sumunod sa mga complicadong paraan na nakakahadlang na ma-efectivong paggawa.

Burglar *n.*, **Burglarize** *v.* panloloob at pagnanakaw na crimen-*Sp*; pag-pasok sa bahay o gusali para magnakaw.

Burial libing, burol; Iloc: pamumpon, tabun

BURN sunogin; Iloc: uramen, puoran

Antonym

Douse buhosan ng tubig; Iloc: sebseban

Burning sumisiklab, nag-aapoy, nasusunog; Iloc: gumilgillayab, umap-apoy, mapupuor, agbarbarang, agdardarang, sumsumged, agur-uram

Burnout 1] sunog na natupok ang buong bahay; 2] **Burn-out** *(with hyphen)*: pagod na pagod dahil sa kadamihan ng trabaho, siphayo o pakiramdam ng kabigoan, at pagkalatoy dahil sa katagalan at kabigatan ng trabaho; 3] pagkasira ng lampara o makina-*Sp* o anong aparatong electricidad-*Sp* dahil sa init ng coryente-*Sp* na umaagos dito

BURNT food sunog, tutong; Iloc: nakset

BURNT out bulb *(Tag. & Iloc.)* bombilya-*Sp* na pundido o napundi

BURP dighay; Iloc: tig-ab, bel-a

BURP a baby after feeding tapikin ang likod ng sanggol para padighayin pagkatapos siyang nagdede; Iloc: pikpiken ti likod ti tagibi tapno agtig-ab

Burst sumabog; Iloc: bumtak, agbettak

Bury ilibing, ibaon; Iloc: icali, itabon, ipumpon

BUS *(Tag. & Iloc.) bus*

BUS stop lugar kung saan maghintay ng *bus*, sakayan at babahan ng *bus*

Bush pandak na punong-kahoy para pang-hardin-*Sp* o bakuran; Iloc: pandak a cayo a panghardin wenno pang-alad

Correlated word

Hedge nakahilera na mga palumpong o pandak na halaman na ginawa na bakuran

BUSINESS *(Tag. & Iloc.) business,* negosio-*Sp*

BUSINESS office *office,* tanggapan; Iloc: oficina-*Sp*

BUSINESS Office Information Center, or Customer Service or Member Services sanggunian, pagtatanongan; Iloc: departamento-*Sp* ti informasyon-*Sp* a pagsaludsodan.

BUSINESS partners magkasocio-*Sp*; Iloc: agkasocio

Businessman *(Tag. & Iloc.)* negosiante-*Sp*

Buss halikan; Iloc: angwen

Bust 1] dibdib o suso ng babae; 2] ulo na estatua-*Sp* at walang katawan; 3] pumutok; 4] lusobin, saliksikin o arestohin ng mga *police;* 5] **Go bust** – ma-*bankrupt,* malugi

Busted nahuling gumagawa ng masama kaya ngayon ay nasasailalim siya ng problema-*Sp* o gusot o bilanggoan

Bustle kumilos na punong-puno ng sigla; pagkapuno ng enerhia-*Sp, activity* o gawain o ang mga tao at iba pa

Busy *busy,* ocupado, abala, nagtatrabaho, may inaatupag; Iloc: *busy,* ocupado-*Sp*, agob-obra-*Sp*

Busybody taong nag-uusyoso at nakikialam sa kabuhayan ng kapwa, pagkatapos ay ichi-chismis-*Sp* ang mga ito

But ngunit, pero-*Sp*; Iloc: ngem, pero

Butcher or Slaughter an animal magkatay ng baboy o vaca o cordero-*Sp*; Iloc: agparti ti baboy o vaca-*Sp*, agpugpogan ti carnero-*Sp*

BUTT 1] itulak sa pamamagitan ng sungay, 2] ginawa na *target* ng biro o tuya, 3] puit, 4] hindi sunog na parte ng cigarilyo; Iloc: 1] iduron nga iyusar ti sara, 2] aramiden a *target* ti angaw o paglais, 3] ubet, 4] haan a nauram a parte ti cigarilyo-*Sp*

BUTT in nanghihimasok o nakikialam o nang-iistorbo

Butte ang nahiwalay na bundok o mga bundok na nakatindig sa pantay lamang na lupa sa kapaligiran na mag-isang bundok lang o mag-isa-isa sila at magkakalayo

Butter *(Tag. & Iloc.)* mantekilya-*Sp*

Butterfly paroparo; Iloc: culibangbang

BUTTOCKS pigi; Iloc: ubet

BUTTOCKS, protruding matambok na puwit; Iloc: kiad, duriri

Button *(Tag. & Iloc.)* butones-*Sp*

Buttress anomang pangsuporta o pangpatibay ng *structure* o stractura; Iloc: aniaman nga pangsuporta o pangpapigsa ti stractura
> *Correlated word*
> **Bulkhead** pader o partisyon sa sasakyang barco, eroplano, coche, *RV* o *bus* na nakakahadlang ng sunog, tubig at iba pa

Buy bibili; Iloc: gumatang

Buzz 1] tinig bubuyog; 2] tawag sa telefono-*Sp*; 3] chismis-*Sp* o *report*; Iloc: uni ti alimbubuyog; chismis

BY (location) sa; Iloc: idiay

BY (person) siya ang taga-, siya ang mag-, siya ang nag-; Iloc: isu ti taga-, isu ti ag-, isu ti nag-

BY and by mamaya, maya-maya; Iloc: madamdama, itat-tanto, intonukua

BY force sapilitan, fuersahin; Iloc: ag-fuersa-*Sp*, fuersaen

BY means of sa pamamagitan ng, sa paggamit ng; Iloc: iti pangiyusar iti

BY-product *(Tag. & Iloc.)* producto-*Sp*, bunga

Bye, Bye-bye paalam na; Iloc: pumanawacon

Bygone ang mga nakalipas na; Iloc: dagiti napalabasen

Bypass, By-pass 1] daanan para mga sasakyan ay makaiwas sa siksik na *traffic*; 2] hindi pansinin, ipawalang-bahala o magpabaya sa payo o decisyon-*Sp* o tinakdang paraan; 3] *bypass* ay isang paggagamot sa pamamagitan ng operasyon-*Sp* sa ospital-*Sp*

Bystander *(Tag. & Iloc.)* taong stambay *(stand-by)*

C

Cab *(Tag. & Iloc.)* *taxi*

Cabbage *(Tag. & Iloc.)* repolyo-*Sp*

CABINET *(Tag. & Iloc.)* aparador-*Sp*, tocador-*Sp*

CABINET drawer *(Tag. & Iloc.)* lacasa

CABINET for displaying collections *(Tag. & Iloc.)* escaparate-*Sp*, estante-*Sp*

Cable *(Tag. & Iloc.) cable*

Cacao buto ng cacaw-*Sp*; Iloc: bukel ti cacaw
Synonym
   Cocoa *(Tag. & Iloc.)* cacaw na giniling o pulbos

Cache *[kash]* pagtagohan ng anoman - ng mga armas na panlaban sa giyera, ng mga pagkain at mga kayamanan at mahahalagang bagay

Caddy, Caddie 1] *rack* at iba pang kasangkapan na lagayan o tagoan para sa kaayosan o pagka-areglo-*Sp* ng mga gamit; 2] taong binayaran para magbuhat ng *player's clubs* at tagakuha ng lumihis na *golf ball* sa *golf club*; 3] ang *cart* na paglagyan ng mga mabibigat na bagay para ilipat sa ibang lugar

Cadet *(Tag. & Iloc.)* cadete-*Sp*

Cadre *[kad-ree, kah-drey]* grupo-*Sp* ng matataas na ranko-*Sp* at mga *enlisted personnel* sa *military* na kinakailangang magtatag at mag-*train* ng mga buong *army units*; grupo ng *trained* at qualificadong empleyado na cayang magtatag, mag-*train* at mangpatnubay sa lumaking organisasyon-*Sp* gaya sa *skilled work force* o sa partido-*Sp* ng politico-*Sp* o sa relihion-*Sp*

Cafeteria *restaurant* sa loob ng escuela-*Sp* o sa oficina-*Sp* na sa *counter* mag-*order* at maghintay ng in*order* at daladala ang *tray* para sa *order* niyang pagkain; Iloc: *restaurant* diay uneg ti escuela o oficina nga idiay *counter* ag-*order* ken aguray ti in*order* na nga awiten na ti *tray* nga pagikabilan iti inuray na a kanen.

Cage *(Tag. & Iloc.)* haula-*Sp*

Cahoots lihim na samahan na nakakasuspecha; Iloc: limed a pagcadwaan nga nakakasuspecha

Cajole sulsolan; Iloc: isungsong

Cake *(Tag. & Iloc.) cake*

Calaboose preso-*aSp*, bilangguan, carcel-*Sp* o calaboso-*Sp*

Calamity *(Tag. & Iloc.)* calamidad-*Sp*

Calculate mag-calcula-*Sp*, sumahin, mag-cuenta-*Sp;* Iloc: ag-calcular-*Sp*, ag-sumar-*Sp*, agcuenta
Synonyms
Count bilangin, cuentahin; Iloc: bilangen, icuenta
Sum up sumahin, magsuma, cuentahin; Iloc: agsumar, icuenta

Calculation *(Tag. & Iloc.)* calculasyon-*Sp*, calculo

Calendar *(Tag. & Iloc.)* calendario-*Sp*

CALF batang vaca-*Sp* o batang toro-*Sp*; Iloc: ubing a vaca o toro

CALF of leg (back, fleshy part) binti; Iloc: gurong

Caliber *(Tag. & Iloc.)* calib-re-*Sp*

Caliph, Kaliph, Khalif pinunong espiritual ng Moslem na kasunod ni Muhammad; sino man sa mga dating *ruler* sa Bagdhad (hanggang 1258) at sa Ottoman Empire (buhat sa 1571 hanggang 1924)

Caliphate sa *jurisdiction* o kapangyarihan ng Caliph, ito ay mga ranko-*Sp*, gobierno-*Sp*, paghahari, o teritoryo-*Sp* nila

CALL tawagin; Iloc: ayaban
Synonyms
Beck, Beckon hudyat para lumapit, pagtawag na senyas gaya ng sa pagtango ng ulo o pagkaway; Iloc: senyas a pagayab casla ilingaling ti ulo wenno payapayan
Summon tawagin, palapitin; Iloc: ayaban, awagan, paasitgen
Antonym
Drive away, Shoo bugawin, itaboy; Iloc: bugawen

CALL back tumawag din o tumawag ulit; Iloc: umawag met wenno umawag manen

CALL by phone tawagan sa telefono-*Sp*; Iloc: umawag iti telefono

CALL-in mga nanonood o nakikinig ay puedeng tumawag sa TV o radio para magtanong o magcomentario

CALL it a day ang trabaho sa isang araw ay tapos na at puede nang umuwi; Iloc: nalpasen ti trabaho it maysa nga aldaw ken makaawiden

CALL it quits magbitiw na sa anomang pinagkakaabalahan o pinag-tatrabahoan o sa relasyong pagmamahalan; Iloc: umikkat ken sumina

CALL, on- magtrabaho kung kailan siya tawagin; Iloc: agtrabaho nu caano isu nga awagan

CALL the shots siya ang namumuno, tagagawa ng decisyon-*Sp* o tagaplano kung ano ang dapat gagawin; Iloc: isu ti mangigaway

Calling 1] tumatawag; 2] vocasyon, profesyon o negosyo; 3] malakas na tulak ng *impulse* o bugso, udyok, simbuyo

Callous matigas ang loob at walang malasakit o pakialam sa iba, at walang pagsisisi sa mga ginawang kasalanan o pananakit sa iba; Iloc: natangken ti puso ken awan asi o pakibiang iti dadduma ken awan ti pagbabawi na iti basbasol na ken iti inted na a sakit ken liday iti tattao

CALM calma-*Sp*, calmado-*Sp*, mahinahon, mapayapa, mapanatag, matiwasay; Iloc: calmado, calma, natalna, naulimek

Synonyms

Gentle disposition mahinahon Iloc: naemma

Peaceful mapayapa, tahimik; Iloc: natalna, naulimek, napia

Tranquil *(Tag. & Iloc.)* calmado

Composed mahinahon; Iloc: natalna

Placid calmado lamang kahit sa kalagitnaan ng gulo at kapahamakan; Iloc: calmado laeng uray iti tengnga ti gulo ken riro

Mellow mahinahon; Iloc: natalna

Serene mapayapa, tahimik; Iloc: natalna, nalinnaay, naulimek

Blithe masaya, campante at hindi nag-aalala; Iloc: narambak, campante ken awan ti pagkadanag

Relaxed maluwag ang loob at pakiramdam, nagpapahinga; Iloc: nabangaran, agin-inana

CALM, cool and collected mahinahon, matatag, mapanatag, matiwasay; Iloc: nanam-ay, natalna, naulimek

CALM down pacalmahin, mag-calma-*Sp*, ipahinahon, papayapain, pumayapa, awatin; Iloc: pacalmaen, patalnaen, agcalma, agtalna, aganawa, ay-aywen, anawaen, paulimeken

Calumniate *v.,* **Calumny** *n.* salita na kasinungalingan at malisyoso-*Sp* para makapanglait; Iloc: sarita a kaulbodan ken malisyoso tapno makapanglais

Calvary *(Tag. & Iloc.)* calvario-*Sp*

Camaraderie samahang may pagdamdam na pagkakaibigan sa isa't isa; Iloc: pagcadcadwa nga aggagayyem ti panagricricna da maysa ken maysa

Cameo 1] alahas-*Sp* na may inukit; 2] maikling parte-*Sp* na ginanap ng bantog na artista-*Sp* sa isang tagpo sa pelicula-*Sp* o sa TV

Camera *(Tag. & Iloc.)* camera, pang-retrato-*Sp*

Camisole *(Tag. & Iloc.)* camison ng babae

Camouflage paraan o bagay para maitago o hindi makilala o mahalata para malinlang ang victima o kalaban; kasuotang khaki o kulay-lupa at kulay-dahon o verde na caraniwan ay sinusuot ng mga sundalo

Camp *(Tag. & Iloc.)* campo-*Sp*

Campaign *(Tag. & Iloc.)* campanya-*Sp*

Campus *(Tag. & Iloc.)* bakuran/solar-*Sp* ng escuela-*Sp* o ng colehio-*Sp* o universidad-*Sp*

CAN maari, puede-*Sp*, posib-le-*Sp*; Iloc: mabalin, posib-le

CAN opener *(Tag. & Iloc.)* abrelata-*Sp*

CAN, tin *(Tag. & Iloc.)* lata-*Sp*

Canal *(Tag. & Iloc.)* canal-*Eng/Sp*, imbornal-*Sp*

Canapé *cracker* o maliit na hiwa ng tinapay na pinatungan ng iba't ibang pampasarap; Iloc: *cracker* o bassit nga iwa ti tinapay a pinatungan ti agsaba-sabali a pangpaimas

Cancel i*cancel*, ipa*cancel*, ipahinto, ipawalang bisa; Iloc: ipa*cancel*, ipa-awan ti bileg

Candid tunay na asal na hindi pinaghandaan at hindi kaartehan; Iloc: usto a tignay nga haan pinagsaganaan ken haan a kaarteaan

Candidate *(Tag. & Iloc.)* candidato-*Sp*

Candle candila-*Sp*; Iloc: candela-*Sp*

Candor, have may katapatan at mapagkakatiwalaan ang canyang si-nasabi, makatarungan at walang tinatago, franka at tapat, *sincere*; walang kinacampihan o pinapanigan *(impartialility)*

CANDY *candy*, matamis; Iloc: *candy*, dulce-*Sp*

CANDY, suck or munch in mouth sinisimsim at tinatakam-takam; Iloc: mulmulmolen, ammolen

Cane 1] baston-*Sp* o tungkod na pantulong sa paglakad; 2] tangkay ng kahoy na cawayan at iba pang kahoy na kapareho-*Sp*; 3] ini-*split* o biniyak na *rattan* para maging lubid at ipulopot sa upuan at ano mang gawa sa sulihiya o *wickerwork*; 4] *sugarcane*; Iloc: baston-*Sp*, sarrukod.

Canned good *(Tag. & Iloc.)* delata-*Sp*

Cannery fabrica-*Sp* para i-delata ang isda o carne o gulay

Cannibal tao na kumakain ng ibang tao, hayop na kumakain ng ibang hayop

Cannot hindi puede; Iloc: haan a mabalin

Canoe, native banca-*Sp*; Iloc: banca-*Sp*, barangay

Cantaloupe *(Tag. & Iloc.)* melon-*Sp*
   Correlated words
   Watermelon pakwan; Iloc: sandia-*Sp*
   Honeydew *(Tag. & Iloc.)* honeydew

Cantankerous mapusok, mainisin, mainitin ang ulo, yamotin, walang pasencia pero pikon; Iloc: alipunget, nalaca a makapungtot, napudot ti ulo, naunget, awan iti pasencia-*Sp* na ngem pikon isu

Canvas 1] obra-*Sp* na arte-*Sp* *(arts)* gaya ng pinta-*Sp* o *watercolor* o *oil*, retrato-*Sp*, printa o imahen-*Sp*, 2] tolda-*Sp*

Canvass 1] magtanong-tanong o makipagdiscusyon o maki-debate-*Sp* para malaman ang pagturing o pagtanggap ng publico-*Sp*, 2] mag-campanya para sa voto-*Sp* o para sa mga pamili o producto na ibenta
   Correlated word
   Survey 1] mangolecta ng mga importanteng detalye, 2] magmasid, mag-*inspect* at mag-imbestiga ng husto para malaman ang condisyon at halaga at kung saan ang mga gilid, posisyon, lawak at kung aplicado ang principio sa *geometry* at *trigonometry*

CAP for the head *(Tag. & Iloc.)* cap

CAP, soda *(Tag. & Iloc.)* tansan

Capability mga kacayahan at mga talento-*Sp* at mga kaalaman; Iloc: dagiti cabaelan ken dagiti talento ken sirib

Capable caya, cayang-caya; Iloc: caya, cabaelan

Capacitate gumawa ng paraan para macayanan; Iloc: agaramid ken agpurbar amin tapno macabaelan

Capacity capacidad-*Sp*, dami ng macarga; Iloc: capacidad, kaado ti ma-carga-*Sp*

Cape 1] capa-*Sp* para takpan ang balikat o para pangpaakit ng toro, 2] patulis na lupa sa tabing dagat na nakaturo sa dagat; Iloc: 1] capa-*Sp* para pangbalabal iti abaga o para pang-awis iti toro-*Sp*, 2] natirad a daga iti igid ti baybay a nakatudo iti taaw

CAPITAL city/town cabecera-*Sp*, capital-*Sp* ng provincia-*Sp* o *state* kung saan nandodoon ang capitolyo ng provincia; Iloc: cabecera, *capital* ti provincia o *state* nga adda idiay iti capitolyo ti provincia

CAPITAL for business *capital*, puhonan para makapagnegosyo-*Sp*; Iloc: *capital*, puonan para makapagnegosio

Capitalism sistema-*Sp* ng *economics* tungkol sa pag-aari, puhunan at *investment*, paglikha ng mga producto-*Sp*, pangangalakal at pagbeventa at iba pa ay nanatili sa camay ng mga privadong nagmemayari o ng corporasyon

Capitol capitolyo-*Sp*, oficina-*Sp* ng gobernador-*Sp*; Iloc: capitolyo, oficina ti gobernador

Capitulate ibawi ang pagtutol at sumuko ng kusa o sumuko kapalit ng tinakdang condisyon-*Sp*

Caprice *(Tag. & Iloc.)* capricho-*Sp*

Capricious pagpapalugod sa sariling kagustuhan o capricho-*Sp*; Iloc: pagustoan iti bagi cadagiti capricho na
Antonym
Ascetic diciplina sa sarili na ipagkait sa sarili ang mga capricho ng mundo; Iloc: diciplina ti bagi nga ipaidam iti bagi na dagiti capricho ti mundo

Capsize tumaob, bumaligtad, tumiwarik; Iloc: agbalintuag, agbalinsuek, agbalictad

Captain *(Tag. & Iloc.)* capitan-*Sp*

Caption pamagat o maikling pagpaliwanag sa nakalarawan; Iloc: titulo o pang-explica iti nakaretrato

Captivating kahali-halina, kaakit-akit, kabigha-bighani, kagiliw-giliw; Iloc: nakaaw-awis, nakarayrayo, nakapimpintas, nalibnos

Captive bihag, bilanggo; Iloc: balud

Captor ang dumakip at nambihag

Capture hulihin, dakpin, arestohin; Iloc: tiliwen, iyaresto

CAR, Auto *(Tag. & Iloc.)* coche-*Sp*

CAR horn *(Tag. & Iloc.)* bocina-*Sp*

Carabao, Water buffalo calabaw; Iloc: nuang

Carbide *(Tag. & Iloc.)* carburo-*Sp*

Carbonated *(Tag. & Iloc.)* *carbonated*, carbonada-*Sp*

Carcinogen nakakabigay ng *cancer*; Iloc: makaited iti *cancer*

CARD *(Tag. & Iloc.)* *card*

CARD, calling *(Tag. & Iloc.)* *calling card*, tarheta-*Sp*

CARD, greeting *(Tag. & Iloc.)* *greeting card*

CARD, ID *(Tag. & Iloc.)* *ID card*

CARD, playing *(Tag. & Iloc.)* baraha-*Sp*

CARD with religious images *(Tag. & Iloc.)* estampita-*Sp*

Cardboard box *(Tag. & Iloc.)* carton-*Sp*, cahon-*Sp*

Cardiac tungkol sa puso; Iloc: maypanggep ti puso

Cardiogram pang-*record* ng galaw ng puso para masuri ang condisyon-*Sp* ng puso; Iloc: pang-*record* ti gunay ti puso para mausig ti condisyon-*Sp* ti puso

Cardiovascular tungkol sa puso at ang tubong ugat na nakacabit sa puso na kung saan dumadaloy ang dugo; Iloc: maypanggep ti puso ken tay tubo nga urat a nakaconecta iti puso nga isu ti pagayosan ti dara

CARE nagmamalasakit; Iloc: mangisaksakit

CARE for, Tend kupkopin, alagaan, arugahin, asecasohin; Iloc: taraknen, asecasuen, aywanan, awiren

Correlated words

Foster arugain, pasiglahin, palagoin; Iloc: taraknen, papigsaen, palapsaten

Nourish, Nurture buhaying, arugain, palusogin, pasiglain; Iloc: biagen, taraknen, pasalun-aten, papigsaen

Guardian tagapag-alaga, tagasustento; Iloc: mangaw-awir, mangay-aywan, tagasustento

Career *(Tag. & Iloc.)* carrera-*Sp*, ocupasyon-*Sp*, *career, profession*

CAREFUL maingat; Iloc: naannad, naalwad

Correlated words

Prudent maingat; Iloc: naannad, naalwad

Precaution pag-iingat; Iloc: pag-annad, pagal-alwad

When doing something, it is wothwhile doing it with care and efficiency than fouling it up and going into a complex problem if things go wrong, mas simp-le at mas madali ang pag-iingat at pag-iiwas sa nakakasama kaysa maospital sa sakit o matagalang paghihirapang ayosin at pagkakagastosan ng malaki kung magsasagawa ng bara-bara lamang

CAREFUL, be Mag-ingat ka; Iloc: Agan-annad ka, Agalwad ka

Caregiver tagapag-alaga ng bata o ng matandang may sakit o ng may kapansanang tao; Iloc: tagataraken ti ubing wenno baket o lakay nga agsakit wenno baldado a tao

Careless hindi maingat, busalsal, pabaya, walang pakialam, pabara-bara lamang; Iloc: agliwliway, haan nga naannad, awan ti pangicascaso na, awan ti biang na, mangbara-bara laeng

Caress yacap na ma-carinyo-*Sp* at ma-consuelo-*Sp*; Iloc: aracop a ma-carinyo ken ma-consuelo

Caretaker tagapagbantay ng bahay habang wala ang may-ari; Iloc: tagabantay ti balay mientras nga awan tay makinbalay

Cargo *(Tag. & Iloc.)* cargamento-*Sp*, cargada-*Sp*

Caricature *(Tag. & Iloc.)* caricatura-*Sp*

Caring nagmamalasakit, nagkakalinga, may considerasyon-*Sp*; Iloc: mannangaasi, nadungngo, adda considerasyon-*Sp* na
Synonyms
Altruist *adj.*, **Altruism** *n.* nagmamalasakit sa kapwa at hindi siya makasarili; Iloc: mangisaksakit iti dadduma ken haan man laeng a bagbagi ti panunoten na
Sympathetic simpatico/ca, mapagsimpatiya, maawain, kalinga; Iloc: simpatico/ca, mapagsimpatiya, mannangaasi
Empathy *n.*, **Empathic** *adj.*, **Empathize** *v.* makilala niya at maintindihan niya ang katayoan, ang dinaranas, damdamin o layonin ng kasama; Iloc: mabigbig ken maawatan na iti kasasaad o ricna o rangta iti cadwa na
Considerate pagtuturing at pag-uunawa sa kalagayan ng iba at sinisikap niyang makatulong kung caya niya at sinisikap niyang hindi siya makakabigat o makahadlang sa canila; Iloc: makabigbig ken makaawat ti kasasasad ti dadduma ken ipakat na a makatulong nu cabaelan na ken isegurado na nga haan a makapadagsen o makapalapped canyada
Beneficent magandang loob at maawain at mapagbigay ng tulong; Iloc: naimbag ti puspuso na ken mannangaasi ken mapag-ited ti tulong
Kind maawain, mahabagin, may malasakit; Iloc: mannangaasi, nasingpet, nalukneng ti puso
Compassionate may malasakit, mahabagin, maawain, nagbibigay ng linga; Iloc: nalukneng ti puso, mannangaasi, mangisaksakit
Merciful mahabagin, mapang-awa; Iloc: mannangaasi
Clemency *n.*, **Clement** *adj.* nakakapagpakita ng kaluwagan o awa o pagpapatawad sa kapwa kahit sa kalaban o masama na tao; Iloc: makapagpakita ti pagliway o asi o pagpakawan iti sabali uray iti kalaban wenno dakes a tao
Insight *n.*, **Insightful** *adj.* intelihenteng pagkaalam, paningin at panturing at pangdamdam ng kalooban ng iba, matalas na pagpapalugod at pagpapahalaga ng nararapat, at matinik na pagkakakilala ng mabuti at masama

Supportive nakikiramay at nagbibigay ng pampalubag-loob at consuelo; Iloc: makiramramay ken mangted ti liwliwa ken consuelo

Solicitous masinsinang pag-asecaso, pag-alaga at pag-estima; Iloc: firme a pag-asicaso, pagtaraken ken pag-estimar

Carjack mafuersa at mabagsik na kunin at nakawin ang sasakyan ng iba; Iloc: naranggas ken naulpit nga agawen a fuersa-*Sp* o takawen ti lugan ti sabali

Carnage pagpatay ng maraming tao gaya sa giyera; Iloc: pagpatay iti nakaad-adu a tao casla ti gerra-*Sp*

Carnal *(Tag. & Iloc.)* makamundo o *sexual*

Carnival *(Tag. & Iloc.)* carnabal-*Sp*

Carnivorous kumakain ng carne o laman; Iloc: mangmangan ti carne o lasag

Carol, Caroling masayang awit ng Pasko, *Filipino Christmas-season custom* na kumacanta sa mga bahay-bahay sa buong buwan ng Diciembre para mabigyan ng aginaldo-*Sp*

Carom tirahin pero tumalbog pabalik, sa *billiard* naman ay tirahin ang bola at tagumpay na matira ang dalawang bola; Iloc: tiraen ngem agtalsik

Carp pintasan, laitin; Iloc: agdillaw, aguyaw, laisen

Carpal tunnel syndrome pananakit sa mga ugat sa *wrist* o galang-galangan; Iloc: saksakit iti urat ti *wrist* o pungo-pungwan

Carpenter *(Tag. & Iloc.)* carpintero-*Sp*

Carpet *(Tag. & Iloc.)* *carpet*

Carve *(Tag. & Iloc.)* ukit

CARRIAGE, carabao-drawn roofless 2-wheeled *(Tag. & Iloc.)* carreton-*Sp*

CARRIAGE, horse-drawn 2-wheeled *(Tag. & Iloc.)* carretela-*Sp*, calesa-*Sp*, caruahe-*Sp*, caromata

CARRIED AWAY by the wind ilipad o ipadpad o tangayin ng hangin; Iloc: itayab ti angin

CARRIED AWAY by water currents maanud o tangayin ng agos ng ilog o ng baha; Iloc: mayyanud o mayyayos ti agos ti carayan o ti layos

CARRY cargahin, buhatin; Iloc: cargaen, bagkaten, awiten (carga-*Sp*)

CARRY a baby pangkohin; Iloc: ubbaen

CARRY-on baggage bagahe-*Sp* na puedeng sariling buhatin ng pasahero-*Sp* at ipasok sa *passenger compartment* sa taas ng upuan niya sa eroplano-*Sp*

CARRY on one's back or shoulders i-*piggy-back* o buhatin ang anak sa balikat o likod

CARRY on one's hand magbibit, bitbitin; Iloc: agbitbit, bitbiten

CARRY on one's head magsunong, sunongin; Iloc: susuonen

CARRY on one's lap candungin, calongin; Iloc: sakluten

CARRY on one's back or shoulders, Piggyback pasanin; Iloc: baklayen

CARRY some woods mangahoy; Iloc: agbulig

CARRY with both arms on the chest kipkipan; Iloc: kepkepan

Carte du jour *[kart dy zhoor]* lista ng mga makakain (*menu*) sa araw na iyan o sa tinaglay na araw

Carton *(Tag. & Iloc.)* *carton*

Cartoon *(Tag. & Iloc.)* mga *cartoon* sa babasahin o TV o cine at hindi retrato

Carve, Etch ukitin; Iloc: ukiten

CASE *(Tag. & Iloc.)* caso-*Sp*

CASE (box and wooden) *(Tag. & Iloc.)* caha-*Sp*, cahita-*Sp*

Cash cuarta, pera; Iloc: cuarta, pirak

Cashew nut *(Tag. & Iloc.)* casoy

Cashier *(Tag. & Iloc.)* *cashier*, cahero/ra-*Sp*

Casket cabaong, ataul; Iloc: lungon

Cassava *(Tag. & Iloc.)* kamoteng-kahoy, *cassava*

Casserole *(Tag. & Iloc.)* caserola-*Sp*

Cast 1] ihagis, 2] mga artistang gumaganap sa pelicula-*Sp* o *television* o sa entablado-*Sp*; Iloc: 1] ipallato, 2] dagiti artista-*Sp* nga agparparang iti pelicula o TV o entablado

Castigate matinding pamimintas, pagbaticos; Iloc: castigaren, grabe a pag-uyaw, ag-castigar-*Sp*

Castle *(Tag. & Iloc.)* palacio-*Sp*, castilyo-*Sp*

Castrate *(Tag. & Iloc.)* capon-*Sp*

Casual hindi formal kundi ordinaryo-*Sp* lamang, magaan ang pag-uugnayan; Iloc: haan a formal nu di ordinaryo laeng; nalag-an a pakicadwa

Casualty mga taong nasaktan o namatay o nahuli ng kalaban o hindi mahanap sa labanan o sa accidente; Iloc: tao a nasaktan wenno natay wenno natiliw ti kalaban wenno haan a masapulan gapu iti gerra o accidente.

Cat *(Tag. & Iloc.)* pusa
  Correlated word
  Kitten kuting, Iloc: muning

Catalog *(Tag. & Iloc.)* *catalog,* catalogo-*Sp*

Catalyst tao o bagay na nakakalikha ng pagbabago
  Correlated word
  Dynamo 1] *generator,* 2] taong napakasigasig at puno ng fuersa sa paglikha at pagsagawa; Iloc: 1] *generator,* 2] tao nga nasagiksik ken napunno ti fuersa nga agparnuay ken ag-trabaho

Cataract *(Tag. & Iloc.)* catarata-*Sp*

Catastrophe kapahamakan; disgracia-*Sp*, calamidad-*Sp*; Iloc: disgracia, calamidad

CATCH hulihin, dakpin, arestohin; Iloc: tiliwen, aresto-*Sp*

CATCH a thrown or falling object salohin, hagipin; Iloc: sippawen

CATCH red-handed nabulilyaso at nabuco dahil huling-huli siya habang siya ay gumagawa ng hindi mabuti; Iloc: mabuco gapu ta matukmaan isu mientras-*Sp* nga agar-aramid iti dakes.

CATCH up mahabol, maabutan; Iloc: macamacam, macamatan, maabutan

Catcher tagasalo; Iloc: tagasippaw

Category *(Tag. & Iloc.)* uri, categoria-*Sp*, clase-*Sp*, tipo-*Sp*

Caterpillar (hairy insect) uod; Iloc: sambrid, budo-budo, igges

CATFISH hito, isda na walang kaliskis pero may dalawa na mahabang balbas gaya ng pusa; Iloc: paltat, ikan nga awan ti siksik na ngem addaan ti dua nga atiddog a barbas a casla pusa.

CATFISH, Person with false identity taong nagpapanggap sa *online/ internet* para makipagkasintahan pero siya ay *impostor* lang at tangka ay makakikil ng pera; Iloc: tao nga peke o *impostor* a makiayan-ayat sa *online* para makakikil ti cuarta

Catheter maliit na tubo na nababaluktot na pinapasok sa butas o sa ugat ng katawan para kumuha ng dugo upang ma-examen ito, o mag-tanggal ng *fluid* o tubig sa katawan gaya ng ihi.

Catholic *(Tag. & Iloc.)* *Catholic,* Catolico-*Sp*

Catnap umidlip, mag-siesta-*Sp*; Iloc: rumidep, agridep, agsiesta

CATTLE *(Tag. & Iloc.)* mga vaca at toro

CATTLE ranch ranchong vacahan; Iloc: vacaan a rancho (vaca-*Sp*, rancho-*Sp*)

Caucus *meeting* ng tanging mga miembro-*Sp* ng partido-*Sp* politico-*Sp* para pag-usapan ang mga importanteng bagay gaya ng paksa o layonin ng *convention* at iba pa

Cause dahilan, sanhi, rason-*Sp*; Iloc: maygapu, rason, gapu, poon

Caustic makagawa ng sunog, agnas, paglusaw o kalawang; Iloc: makapuor, makarumek, makarunaw o agkalawang.

Caution ingat; Iloc: annad, alwad

Cave cueva-*Sp*, yungib; Iloc: cueva, rukib
Synonym
Subterranean sa baba ng lupa gaya ng cueva, yungib/*cavern* o minahan

CAVEAT babala; Iloc: pangpaalwad

CAVEAT emptor, Buyer beware mag-ingat ang bumibili para usigin muna ang uri ng producto bago bilhin ito; Iloc: agalwad iti gumat-gatang nga usigin umuna ti pagkaaramid ti producto-*Sp* baro gatangen daytoy

Caviar itlog ng isdang *sturgeon*; Iloc: bugi ti ican nga *sturgeon*

Cavity maliit na butas; Iloc: bassit a lubbot

Cavort magsaya; Iloc: agragsak

Cease maghinto, tumigil; Iloc: agsardeng

Ceasefire pinagkasunduang pansamantalang paghinto ng labanan o giyera; Iloc: pinagtulagan a temporaryo-*Sp* nga pagsardeng iti laban o gerra-*Sp*

Cede isuko, magbitiw, iwanan, ipaubaya; Iloc: isuko, ibbatan, panawan

Ceiling *(Tag. & Iloc.)* kisame

Celebrate magdiwang, magdaraos, mag-*party*; Iloc: agrambak, agpadaya, ag-celebrar-*Sp*

Celebration celebrasyon-*Sp*, pagdaraos, pagdiriwang; Iloc: celebrasyon, padaya, pagragragsakan
Synonym
Festival pista, pistahan; Iloc: fiesta

Celebrity kilalang tao sa larangan ng arte o musica o sa kagalingan sa *sports*

Celibate hindi nakikipagtalik ng *sexual* kahit kanino man gaya ng mongha o madre.

Cell *(Tag. & Iloc.)* celda-*Sp*

Cement *(Tag. & Iloc.)* cemento-*Sp*

Cemetery cementerio-*Sp*, libingan; Iloc: cementerio, camposanto-*Sp*

Census *(Tag. & Iloc.) census*

Cent *(Tag. & Iloc.)* centavo-*Sp*, centimo-*Sp*

Center centro-*Sp*, kalagitnaan, gitna; Iloc: centro, akintengnga, tengnga

Centipede alupihan; Iloc: gayaman

Central centro-*Sp*, kalagitnaan, gitna; Iloc: katengngaan, centro, akintengnga

Century siglo-*Sp*, isang daang taon; Iloc: siglo, sangagasut a tawen

Ceremony *(Tag. & Iloc.)* ceremonia-*Sp*

Certain, Certainty *(Tag. & Iloc.)* segurado, tiyak na tiyak; Iloc: segurado

"Certainly" *(Tag. & Iloc.)* "Siempre", "Segurado"

Certainty katiyakan; Iloc: kaseguradwan

Certificate *(Tag. & Iloc.) certificate*, certifico-*Sp*

Certified *(Tag. & Iloc.)* certificado-*Sp*

Certify ipa-certifica-*Sp*, certificahan, ipagpatunay; Iloc: ipa-certificar-*Sp*, certificaran, paneknekan

Cessation paghinto, pagtigil; Iloc: pagsardeng

Chafe hilod o kayod na makagasgas o galos; Iloc: radrad o gusogos a makagasgas o makadunor

Chaff labas o balat ng palay; Iloc: ruar o ukis ti pagay

CHAIN cadena-*Sp*, posas-*aSp*; Iloc: cadena, kawar

CHAIN reaction pangyayari na may kasunod at sunod-sunod pa; Iloc: pasamak nga adda kasaruno na ken agsasaruno pay

CHAIN-smoke paninigarilyo na sigue-sigue-*Sp* at paraparati; Iloc: pag-cigarilyo-*Sp* nga sigue- sigue ken cana-canayon

Chair silya-*Sp*, upuan; Iloc: silya, tugaw
  Correlated words
  Armchair silyon-*Sp*; Iloc: butaca-*Sp*
  Bench *(Tag. & Iloc.)* banco-*Sp*

Chalk tisa-*Sp*; Iloc: *chalk*

Challenge hamunin, kanchawan, udyokan, utoin; Iloc: kanchawan

221

Champetry ang napagkasundoang pagbahagi-bahaginan ng nacolectang pera o *proceeds* sa litigasyon-*Sp*

Champion *(Tag. & Iloc.)* campion-*Sp*

CHANCE pagkakataon, chansa; Iloc: paggasatan, chansa, waya

CHANCE to, have a... magkapanahon na..; Iloc: makalugar o maka-waya nga...

CHANGE palitan, bagohin, ibahin; Iloc: sukatan, baliwan, pabarwen, sabalian

CHANGE one's mind magbagong isip; Iloc: agbaliw ti nakem

CHANGE, loose (coins) barya, sukli, sencilyo-*Sp*; Iloc: supli, sencilyo

Changeable pabago-bago, salawahan; Iloc: agsaba-sabali, agsukat-sukat, agbaliw-baliw

Synonyms

Turncoat taong nagpalit ng lapi at umanib sa karival; Iloc: tao nga agbaliw ti katimpuyog na ken kimmadwa ti karival

Flip-flop 1] paatras na balintong, 2] pabago-bago, salawahan; Iloc:1] paatras a balintuag, 2] agsukat-sukat, agbaliw-baliw

Fickle pabago-bago, salawahan; Iloc: agsaba-sabali, agsukat-sukat, agbaliw-baliw

Antonyms

Stable mapagpanatili at naasahan siya; matatag at hindi basta-basta la-mang na magturing sa mga pagbabago; mapamalagi; malinaw mag-isip at hindi sumasanding sa hindi relevante at sa mga kalocohan, hindi madaling mahikayat o maestorbo

Unchanging walang pagmamaliw; Iloc: awan ti pagbalbaliw

Channel *(Tag. & Iloc.)* *channel*, canal-*Sp*

Chaos malaking gulo; Iloc: dakkel a gulo

Chap *(Tag. & Iloc.)* lalake

Chapel *(Tag. & Iloc.)* capilya-*Sp*

Chaperon *(Tag. & Iloc.)* *chaperon*, kasamang tagabantay sa dalagang makipagdate sa nobyo o manliligaw

Chapter *(Tag. & Iloc.)* capitolo-*Sp*, cabanata

Char masunog, mapaso; Iloc: mauram, masinit

CHARACTER ugali, costumbre-*Sp*, pagkatao; Iloc: ugali, costumbre-*Sp*, katatao, kababalin

CHARACTER, improving one's *When the media (publications, internet, TV, films, videos, etc.) are presenting crimes, deplorable activities of*

*criminals and wicked people, and new fads and ideas that may carry some risks, do not be swayed nor be drawn into those influences, and never blend with anyone practicing and supporting those. Let us seek information that is for our very best interest, **not** something that will bring us problems and downfall. We must raise ourselves to a higher standard for self-improvement, energy-enhancement, and over-all success. Let us utilize our intelligence, abilities, skills and talents. Let us study hard and work hard to merit triumph and acclamation; and instill and retain the following qualities in us: integrity, honesty, trustworthiness, reliability, kindness, compassion, and conscience-compunction, which is having remorse and taking responsibility and self-accountability of our deeds – good or bad. Let us face our wrongdoings and resolve to get rid of them. Let us not make excuses or validate or justify our transgressions because those would only get hardened on us, impelling us to continue doing those offenses. Monitor ourselves, self-examine and self-judge. Let us take the high road with God and not go down to the level of wickedness. Crimes and wickedness **merely** bring terrible, destructive, and painful consequences, then regret comes at the end. So let us not consort with the bad elements of society like criminals, embezzlers, drug dealers, drug addicts, robbers, lewd, indecent and corrupt people, murderers, and no conscience-compunction people. Let us resolutely choose to be good individuals by maintaining moral and ethical values throughout our lives. **Let's rely on God always** and thank Him often for His big and small blessings on us. God is waiting for us to ask Him for His help because His holy words, the Bible, imparts "Create in me a clean heart, o God, and renew a right spirit within me" **(NIV)** (Psalm 51:10), and "My help comes from the Lord, the Maker of heaven and earth" **(NIV)** (Psalm 121:2). God is more than willing and happy to guide and help us, even make us maintain a respectable, happy and rewarding life by our asking God to purify our thoughts, words, deeds, emotions, attitudes, intentions, decisions, desires, aspirations, in our dealings with people, in our reactions towards them, in our work, in our daily life, in the use of our intelligence, knowledge, expertise, abilities, skills, and talents. God heals, transforms and purifies our whole being*

and nature, and all aspects of our life if we depend and rely for His
help and guidance, then we work on, applying those in our lives. <u>God</u>
<u>*wants us to have a close relationship with Him*</u> *by our communicating*
with Him in worship, praises and gratitude, and communicating our
petitions to Him, and reading His words, the Bible. Everyone matters
to God because He truly loves us. Let us be used for God's glory so
that we bear fruit in every good deed, and so that we have peace and
contentment, so that we become part of the solution, not the problem,
and become a valuable contributing member to society. The world, the
*country, the community, a group, even the family needs a hero and **a***
***role model**, so let us become such. We will be pleased with ourselves,*
and even by God and our family that love us and want the best for us,
will be pleased.

Charcoal uling; Iloc: uring, uging

CHARGE by an animal with its horns masuwag; Iloc: masangdo

CHARGE for payment singilin; Iloc: singiren

CHARGE, in- pinuno, pangulo, hefe-*Sp*, cabesa-*Sp*; Iloc: cabesa, hefe

Charitable *This person may or may not be rich, but loves to give help and*
donations to those who need assistance, goods and reliefs who are the
poor, the sick or handicapped, the weak, helpless and hopeless. This
*person is **not** quick to judge people, but is kind, caring, understand-*
ing, compassionate and considerate of others and even to animals.

Charity *This is a charitable act or an institution that bestows gene-*
rous donations to help the poor, sick, handicapped, weak, helpless
and hopeless. Mga gawain na mapagbigay ng donasyon at tulong sa
mga may sakit at sa mga walang pag-asa/*hopeless*; mga institusyon,
fundasiyon at fundo para sa mga sawing-palad; pagbigay ng limos-a*Sp*
at pag-aalay ng kawanggawa para-*Sp* sa kapakanan ng mga nangangailangan; Iloc: pangited ti limos ken servicio-*Sp* para iti pagimbagan
cadagiti makasapul

Charlatan taong nagpapanggap na madunong o marami ang cacayahan o
mayaman; Iloc: tao nga agincucuna nga adu ammo na o adu ti macaya
na o nabaknang

Charm mambighani, mang-akit; Iloc: libnos a pangaw-awis, mangrayo

Charming kabigha-bighani, kaakit-akit; Iloc: nakaaw-awis, nakarayrayo

Chart *(Tag. & Iloc.) chart*

Chase habulin; Iloc: camaten, camacamen, tiliwen
> *Correlated word*
>
> **Catch up** mahabol, maabutan; Iloc: macamacam, macamatan, maabutan

Chaste *This person is a virgin and does not have sexual relations before marriage. He/she is pure, decent, refined and free from obscenity.* Virhen-*Sp* at may moralidad-*Sp*, busilak, puro-*Sp* at fino-*Sp* sa isip at asal at hindi nakikipagtalik sa lalake sa catre bago icasal; Iloc: virhen ken adda moralidad na, puro ken fino iti nakem ken aramid, ken haan maki-idda ti lalake baro agcasar da

Chastise dusahin; Iloc: dusaen

Chat masayahang cuentohan; Iloc: nakaliwliwa nga pagtungtongtongan

Chatter *(Tag. & Iloc.)* yakyakan, satsatan, daldalan

Chatty madaldal, daldalera, daldal ng daldal; Iloc: tarabitab, daldalera

Chauffeur *(Tag. & Iloc.)* privadong chofer/*driver*

Chauvinism *n.,* **Chauvinist** *adj.* paniniwalang siya'y nasa grupo-*Sp* na mas *superior* o mas mataas na katatao kaysa sa iba gaya ng pagiging lalake o pagiging taga isang bayan na mataas ang economia-*Sp*

CHEAP mura, barato-*Sp*; Iloc: nalaca
> *Antonym*
>
> **Costly, Expensive** mahal; Iloc: nangina

CHEAP shot asal o salitang mabagsik at hindi karapat-dapat na inuukol sa mahina o walang kalaban-laban na tao, nambabastos, nambabaticos

CHEAT dayahin, locohin; Iloc: guliben, switiken, agdarogas, agcusit, lokwen (loco-*Sp*)

CHEAT on one's spouse or on one's girl/boy friend mangaliwa, magtaksil, mambabae, manlalake; Iloc: agkaliwa, agkerida, agbabai, aglalaki uray no adda asawa nan o kaayan-ayat nan

CHECK, bank *(Tag. & Iloc.)* cheke-*Sp*

CHECK mark, Mark with a check i-*check* o humugis ng "X" o "√" sa tamang sagut sa mga tanong, markaan ng *check*; Iloc: i-*check* o i-ukit ti "X" wenno "√" ti usto a sungbat iti saludsod, markaan ti *check*

CHECK on someone, Check something out siyasatin kung tama o tunay o tutoo, suriin ang kalagayan; Iloc: sukimaten ti kasasaad tapno masiguro nga usto-*Sp*

CHECK up (medical) magpaexamen o magpaconsulta sa doctor, magpatingin; Iloc: agpaexamen ti doctor, agpaconsulta-*Sp*

Checker game, Filipino *(Tag. & Iloc.)* dama-*Sp*

Cheek pisngi; Iloc: pingping

CHEER, Root for hangaan, purihin, palakpakan; Iloc: dayawen, apreciaren, palakpakan

CHEER someone up aliwin, libangin, pagalakin, patawanin; Iloc: linglingayen, liwliwaen, pakatawaen
Synonym
Enliven pagalakin; Iloc: paragsaken

Cheerful masaya, maaliw, parating nagpapatawa o nagpapasaya; Iloc: nakalinglingay, naragsak, nalaeng nga agpakatawa o agparagsak

Cheerless matamlay; Iloc: natamnay, awanan ti ganas-*Sp*

Cheese *(Tag. & Iloc.)* keso-*Sp*

Chef *(Tag. & Iloc.)* cusinero-*Sp* pero siya ang *boss* o pinuno ng mga cusinero/ra-*Sp*
Synonym
Cook *(Tag. & Iloc.)* cusinero/ra

Chemical *(Tag. & Iloc.)* *chemical*

Chemise *(Tag. & Iloc.)* camison-*Sp*

Chemistry mga elemento na nakapagbubuo; mapag-ugnayang damdam o galaw sa iba't ibang personalidad o katauhan; masimpatiyang pag-intindi, kapalagayang-loob gaya ng "Magkaibigan sila dahil may *chemistry* sila sa isa't isa"

Cherish estimahan; Iloc: estimaren (estima/estimar-*Sp*)

Cherub batang anghel-*Sp*; Iloc: ubing nga anghel

CHEST dibdib; Iloc: barucong

CHEST, Trunk *(Tag. & Iloc.)* lacasa, baol-*Sp*

CHEST pain pananakip ng dibdib; Iloc: sakit ti barucong

Chestnut *(Tag. & Iloc.)* castanyas-*Sp*

Chew nguyain; Iloc: ngalngalen

Chick sisiw; Iloc: piyek

CHICKEN *(Tag. & Iloc.)* manok
Correlated words
Hen inahing manok; Iloc: dumalaga
Rooster tandang; Iloc: cawitan

CHICKEN pox bulutong-tubig; Iloc: burtong, tuko

Chickpea *(Tag. & Iloc.)* garbansos-*Sp*

Chide pagsabihan ng marahan para sa pagpapakabuti niya; Iloc: bagbagaan iti nainnayad tapno agpakaimbag isu

Chief hefe-*Sp*, pinuno; Iloc: hefe

Chieftain *(Tag. & Iloc.)* pangulo ng grupo-*Sp* o ng tribo-*Sp*, datu, sultan

CHILD bata; Iloc: ubing

CHILD, One's offspring anak, supling; Iloc: anak

CHILD, unclean batang madungis; Iloc: cochino/na-*aSp*

CHILDBIRTH isilang, ipanganak, iluwal; Iloc: ipasngay, iyanak

CHILDBIRTH pains or delivery pains dag-is; Iloc: pasical

Childhood kabataan; Iloc: pagkaubing

Children mga anak, mga bata; Iloc: annak, ubbing

Chili *(Tag. & Iloc.)* sili

CHILL 1] ipalamig sa yelo-*Sp* o sa *freezer*; 2] nanginginig dahil sa lamig; Iloc: 1] ipalamiis ti yelo wenno idiay *freezer;* 2] agtigerger gapu iti lamiis

CHILL due to cold exposure *(Tag. & Iloc.)* pasma

CHILL out huminahon at mag-calma-*Sp*; Iloc: agtalna ken agcalma

Chilly napakaginaw, nakakangaligkig sa ginaw; Iloc: nakalamlamiis, nakalamlam-ek, makatigerger ti lam-ek

CHIN baba; Iloc: timid

Correlated word

Jaw panga, Iloc: sangi

CHINNED, double- cabil; Iloc: tammi, akak

CHINNED, long- *(Tag. & Iloc.)* babalu

Chinese inchik; Iloc: inchik, sanglay

Chinky-eyed *(Tag. & Iloc.)* singkit, chinito-*Sp*

CHIP lamat, bitak, nabungihan; Iloc: birri, tipping

CHIP in 1] magbigay ng canyang parte sa pagtulong sa trabaho o ng canyang bahagi sa bayaran, 2] sumabad para magbigay ng canyang paniwala o kuro-kuro, 3] maglagay ng canyang taya sa sugalan

CHIP off the old block anak na kamukhang-kamukha ng tatay o nanay o kumikilos na gaya nila; Iloc: anak nga karuprupa na ti tatang wenno nanang na wenno aggunay nga casla canyada

CHIP on one's shoulder parating nakikipagtalunan o labanan dahil sa puot sa puso niya; Iloc: canayon a makipagdiscusyonan wenno makilaban gapu ti pagpungpungtot na

Chirp, Bird tweet huni ng ibon; Iloc: uni ti billit

Chit *bill,* pirasong papel na nakasulat ang dapat bayaran sa kinain o ininom sa *restaurant* o *bar*

Chivvy galitin o inisin ng madalas Iloc: ruroden o paguraen a canayon

Chocolate *(Tag. & Iloc.) chocolate,* chocolate-*Sp*

Choice *(Tag. & Iloc.)* napili, pinili

Choir grupong kumacanta sa simbahan; Iloc: grupo nga agcanta diay simbaan

CHOKE sakal; Iloc; bekkel

CHOKE on food or liquid masamid, mahirinan, mabulonan, mabila-okan; Iloc: maltutan

Choler galit, poot; Iloc: pungtot, rungsot, uyong

Cholera grabeng *diarrhea* o pagtatae; Iloc: buris

Chomp nguya-nguyain, ngalotin; Iloc: caremkemen

Choose magpili; Iloc: agpili

Choosy pihikan; Iloc: napili

CHOP tadtarin; Iloc: tadtaden

CHOP for firewood magsibak ng panggatong; Iloc: agbalsig ti pangsungrod

CHOP shop lugar na pinagtatagoan ng ninakaw na sasakyan na tinatanggal-tanggal para ibenta ang mga parte nito

Chopping board sangkalan; Iloc: langdet

Chore trabaho-*Sp* na caraniwang ginagawa araw-araw; Iloc: cada-*Sp* aldaw nga trabaho nga ordinaryo-*Sp*

Chorus *(Tag. & Iloc.)* grupong kumacanta o canta ng grupo

Christ Jesus – *Jesus Christ is God the Son who love all His creations, most especially mankind. Jesus Christ is divine, holy, sacred, pure and perfect without sin, but He took the punishments of our sins upon Himself, instead of us-mankind being punished in hell for our sins. He endured despite suffering being hit, beaten, slapped, lashed, flogged, mocked, shamed, spitted on, and was made to carry a heavy cross to Mount Calvary where His hands were nailed to crucify Him on that very cross He carried, then He died and was speared on His chest* *that blood and water flowed out confirming He was already dead. On the 3ʳᵈ day of His death, He arose again. He met with His disciples who saw His pierced palms and His injured chest. He dined with them, admonished them, and gave them solace, and then the disciples witnessed Jesus Christ rose back to heaven. If anyone believes and puts his/her faith and trust on God's love for all mankind and on Jesus Christ's crucifixion and death as the atoning sacrifice for the sins of all men and receives Jesus Christ into his/her heart and life as his/her Lord, God, Savior and Redeemer, all his/her sins are forgiven and cleansed by the blood of Jesus Christ on the cross and is now destined for heaven, - right then and there, the Holy Spirit comes to indwell in this person's heart never to leave nor forsake this person and to walk with him/her and help him/her to be God-abiding, and this person also receives a new birth – he/she becomes spiritually born again as God's child.* Si Hesu Cristo, Dios Anak na mula sa langit ay bumaba sa lupa para Siya ang tumanggap ng parusa sa mga kasalanan ng mga buong nilalang, imbes na tayo ang maparusahan sa ating mga kasalanan. Sinaktan, hinaplitan, sinampal, dinuraan, nilait, kinoronahan ng tinik si Hesu Cristo, at pinabuhat sa Canya ang mabigat na cruz paakyat sa bundok Calvario. Pinako Siya sa cruz at doon Siya namatay. Tinusok ang tagiliran Niya at natiyak na patay na nga Siya. Pagkatapos ng tatlong araw, nabuhay si Hesu Cristo muli, at nakipagkita Siya sa Canyang mga dicipulo at nakita nila ang sugat sa Canyang palad at tagiliran. Nasaksihan nilang pumailanglang si Hesu Cristo pabalik sa langit. Kapag isuko at ipagkatiwala natin ang sarili natin sa Dios at maniwala, manalig a magsampalataya tayo na ang mga pagdurusa at pagkapako ni Hesu Cristo sa cruz ay kabayaran ng lahat nating mga kasalanan, at tanggapin natin si Hesu Cristo sa puso't buhay natin bilang Dios natin at Tagapagligtas natin, ang mga kasalanan natin sa nakaraan, sa kasalukuyan at sa hinaharap ay mapatawad at malinisan na ng dugo ni Hesu Cristo sa cruz, at sa katuparan ng sinabi ng Dios, matira na ang Dios Espiritu Santo sa puso at buhay natin dahil ang Dios ay Immanuel *(meaning God with us)* para tulongan Niya tayong maging maka-Dios, at magkaroon tayo ng bagong kapanganakang *spiritual* at tayo ay maging *spiritual* na anak na ng Dios. Itong regalong kaligtasan sa atin ng Dios ay hindi mawawala kailanman.

Christening binyag; Iloc: bunyag

Christian *(Tag. & Iloc.)* Cristiano-*Sp*

CHRISTMAS Pasko; Iloc: Pascua-*aSp*

CHRISTMAS gift aginaldo-*Sp*, regalo-*Sp*; Iloc: regalo

CHRISTMAS lantern *(Tag. & Iloc.)* farol/parol-*Sp*

Chronic, Recurring pabalik-balik; Iloc: agsubli-subli

Chronological *adj.*, **Chronology** *n.* pag-areglo-*Sp* ng mga nangyayari batay sa fecha-*Sp* magbuhat sa umpisa hanggang sa katapusan o kasalukuyan; Iloc: pag-areglo cadagiti mapaspasamak batay iti fecha agrugi idi immuna inggana iti kapalpasan o iti madama a tiempo-*Sp*

Chubby bilog at mataba; Iloc: timbukel ken nataba

Chuckle pigil na pigil na pagtawa; Iloc: laplap a katawa

Chum matalik na kaibigan; Iloc: nadekket a gayyem

CHURCH simbahan, iglesia-*Sp*; Iloc: simbaan, iglesia

CHURCH mass/Sunday service *(Tag. & Iloc)* misa-*Sp*, *Sunday service*

CHURCH worship, attend magsimba; Iloc: makimisa

Cigar *(Tag. & Iloc.)* tabaco-*Sp*

CIGARETTE *(Tag. & Iloc.)* cigarilyo-*Sp*

CIGARETTE butt upos; Iloc: rungrong

Cinder baga; Iloc: beggang

Circa malapit sa..; Iloc: asideg iti...

Circle bilog, circulo-*Sp*; Iloc: timbukel, circulo
  Correlated words
  Oval hugis itlog, habilog, *oval*; Iloc: forma ti itlog, *oval*
  Square *(Tag. & Iloc)* *square,* cuadrado
  Rectangle *(Tag. & Iloc)* *rectangle*
  Triangle *(Tag. & Iloc.)* *triangle*

Circular pabilog; Iloc: agtimbukel

Circulate ilaganap, ipalaganap, icalat, ilibot; Iloc: iwaras, iwarnak, ilawlaw
  Correlated words
  Broadcast isahimpapawid, ipahayag; Iloc: ipablaak
  Announce i-anuncio; Iloc: ibandilyo, i-anuncio
  Publish ilathala; Iloc: iwarnak
  Report ipaalam; Iloc: ipaammo

Notice, Alert Information noticia, aviso, pabatid, babala; Iloc: noticia, aviso, pangpaamo, pangpaalerto

Circulation, blood circulasyon-*Sp* ng dugo, pag-agos ng dugo sa ugat ng katawan; Iloc: circulasyon ti dara, pagayos ti dara iti urat ti bagi

Circumcision tuli; Iloc: cugit

Circumference palibotang gilid o bibig ng circulo; Iloc: igid a palikaw wenno bibig ti circulo

Circumspect pag-iingat, pagtanto sa mga pangyayari o circumstancia-*Sp* at ang puedeng maging kahihinatnan; Iloc: pagan-annad, pag-amiris cadagiti mapaspasamak o circumstancia ken nu ania ti mabalin a pagbanagan da

Circumstance circumstancia-*Sp*, pangyayari; Iloc: circumstancia, mapaspasamak

Circumstantial *(Tag. & Iloc.)* depende-*Sp* sa circumstancia-*Sp*

Circumvent 1] paligiran o palibutan; 2] nag-aalala ng hindi mabuti kaya para maiwasan ang baticos o pagkabigo o pagkatalo, gumamit ng kabulaanan o kasinungalingan; magtactica na magpasikot-sikot at magpaligoy-ligoy

Citation 1] parangal sa nakakahangang ginawa, 2] utos na humarap sa hukuman; Iloc: 1] pagdayaw ti nakasay-sayaat nga obra-*Sp*, 2] mandar-*Sp* a sumango iti hues-*Sp*

Cite, Quote sipiin; Iloc: mangi-usar-*Sp* ti popular-*Sp* o nasirib a sarita para pang-leksion-*Sp*, pagsurat o pagtungtongan

Citizen mamamayan, taong-bayan; Iloc: tao ti bayan

CITY *city*, lunsod, ciudad-*Sp*; Iloc: *city*, ciudad

CITY government govierno-*Sp* ng ciudad-*Sp* na pinangungulohan ng alcalde-*Sp* o *mayor*

CITY square *(Tag. & Iloc.)* plaza-*Sp*

Civic anomang tungkol sa mamamayan

Civil marespeto at mabuti ang pakikisama nito; Iloc: narespeto ken naimbag ti pakicadcadwa na ti tao

Civilized *(Tag. & Iloc.)* educado-*Sp* at civilisado-*Sp*

Civilization *(Tag. & Iloc.)* civilisasyon-*Sp*, ang proceso-*Sp* na pagbuo o pagyabong ng sociedad-*Sp* sa pag-unlad ng *science*, karunongan, educasyon-*Sp*, larangan ng *arts* at cultura-*Sp*, pagpalakad ng govierno-*Sp* at mga organisasyon-*Sp*, pagbibigay ng importancia-*Sp* sa pagiging mapagkatiwalaan, katapatan, etico-*Sp* at moralidad-*Sp*

Claim mag-*claim* o mag-angkin o maghabol ng karapatan o ng hiniling; Iloc: ag-*claim* ti nayturayan kencuana o iti ingkiddaw na

Clam tulya; Iloc: bennek

Clap palakpak, tampal; Iloc: palakpak, sipat

Clarify ipaliwanag, ipaunawa, linawin, iclaro; Iloc: ilawlawag ken ipaawat a claro-*Sp*

Clarity napakaliwanag o clarong-claro-*Sp* sa ichura-*Sp*, sa pag-iisip, sa mensahe-*Sp* at sa rason-*Sp*

Correlated word

Cogent nakakacumbinsi at nakakapaniwala dahil maliwanag pertinente na may kaugnayan sa paksa at kalagayan, at nasa tamang rason at claro ang pagkaexplica at paglalarawan

Clasp pangcabit, pang-ipit; Iloc: callawit, pang-ipit

Class *(Tag. & Iloc.)* clase-*Sp*, categoria-*Sp*, uri, tipo-*Sp*

Classic *(Tag. & Iloc.)* excelente-*Sp*, primera-*Sp* clase-*Sp*

Classification *(Tag. & Iloc.)* clasificasyon-*Sp*, categorya-*Sp*

Classified 1] naareglo ayon sa categoria; 2] lihim at *confidential* na na-lalaman lamang ng may karapatan dito

Classify pag-uri-uriin, pagbukod-bukodin sa mga uri nito; Iloc: paglasin-lasinen ken pagdumadumaen

Classmate *(Tag. & Iloc.)* kaclase

Classy *(Tag. & Iloc.)* ichura-*Sp* na elegante-*Sp*; may *class*

Clay tumigas na putik; Iloc: timmangken a pitak

CLEAN *adj.* malinis; Iloc: nalinis, nadalus

Correlated words

Sanitary malinis at nadisinfectahan; Iloc: nalinis ken nadisinfectaran

Hygiene kalinisan sa katawan at gawi; Iloc: kalinisan ti bagi ken costumbre

Kempt maareglo, maayos; Iloc: naareglo naurnos

Spick-and-span ayos at napakalinis; Iloc: naareglo ken nakalinlinis

Spotless malinis at wala man lamang mancha

Antonyms

Dirty marumi; Iloc: narugit, namureng, nadungrit, nadugyot

Gross nakakadiri, nakakatayo ng balahibo; Iloc: makaam-amak, makaar-aryek, makasumgar ti dutdot

CLEAN *v.* maglinis; Iloc: aglinis, agdalus

CLEAN a toddler's tushy after he/she used the potty ipatuwad ang puwit ng bata para malinis at mapunasan; Iloc: ipugiit ti ubet ti ubing tapno ma-ilwan ken malinisan

CLEAN bill of health certificasyon-*Sp* sa *doctor* na ang tao ay malusog pagkatapos ng pagsusuri

CLEAN by washing maghugas, banlawan; Iloc: agugas, banlawan, agbuggo, bugwan

CLEAN ear with cotton swab kikigan; Iloc: agkuricor

CLEAN up one's act tanggalin ang masamang ugali at magpakabuti, mas pagbutihin ang pagsasagawa; Iloc: ikkaten iti dakes a costumbre-*Sp* ken agpakasingpet, mas pagsayaaten iti pagobra

Cleaning rag basahan, trapo-*Sp*; Iloc: nisnis, trapo

Cleanse paglinis ng Panginoong Dios sa mga kasalanan ng tao; Iloc: paglinis ni Apo Dios iti basbasol ti tao

CLEAR claro-*Sp*, malinaw, maliwanag; walang calat at walang mabubunggo; Iloc: claro-*Sp*, nalitnaw, nalawag; awan iti nakawaras ken awan ti madalapus o mapad-dekan

CLEAR-sighted napakaliwanag ang paningin at pangturing sa mga pangyayari; Iloc: nakalawlawag a pagkita ken pangbigbig ken pagkaawat cadagiti mapaspasamak

Clearance 1] vacanteng parte na nilaan para daanan, 2] certificasyon-*Sp* na pinawalang-sala; Iloc: 1] vacante-*Sp* nga parte-*Sp* nga indesignar a pagnaan, 2] certificasyon nga impaawan ti basol na

Cleave 1] dumikit ng husto, kumapit; 2] manatiling matapat o *faithful* gaya sa mabuting principio sa buhay kahit na may pagpapahirap sa canya

Clemency *n.*, **Clement** *adj.* nakakapagpakita ng awa o kaluwagan o pagpapatawad sa kapwa pati kalaban o taong masama; Iloc: makapagpakita ti pagliway o asi o pagpakawan iti tattao pati kalaban wenno dakes a tao

Synonyms

Merciful mahabagin, mapang-awa; Iloc: mannangaasi

Mercy awa, habag; Iloc: asi

Clench mahigpit na hawak, capit; Iloc: tenglen, petpetan, cumpet, capet

Clenched fist *(Tag. & Iloc.)* kamao

Clergy *(Tag. & Iloc.)* mga pari (padi) o pastor ng simbahan

Cleric *(Tag. & Iloc.)* 1] mga pari/padi o pastor ng simbahan; 2] miembro-*Sp* ng *clerical staff*

Clerk tagagawa ng trabaho-*Sp* sa oficina-*Sp* sa pamumuno ng superbisor-*Sp*; Iloc: agob-obra-*Sp* ti trabaho iti oficina iti pangigaway ti superbisor

Clever mautak, matalas ang isip, matinik; Iloc: nasirib

Click 1] lagitik, 2] madali silang nagkapalagayang-loob at agad silang naging magkaibigan; Iloc: 1] lagitik, 2] nalag-an ti ricricnaen da maysa ken maysa ken naglaca da nga naggayyem

Client *(Tag. & Iloc.)* cliente-*Sp*

Cliff bangin; Iloc: teppang, derraas

Climate tiempo-*Sp*, clima-*Sp*, panahon; Iloc: tiempo, clima, panawen

Climb umakyat; Iloc: agcalay-at
> *Synonym*
> **Go up** papanhik; Iloc: umuli, ngumato, sumang-at

Cling kumapit; Iloc: cumpet

Clingy person pakapit-kapit; Iloc: naumbi, nacarayo
> *Correlated word*
> **Cleave** magdikit-dikit; Iloc: agpadikkit-dikkit

Clinic *(Tag. & Iloc.)* *clinic*

Clink cumacalansing; Iloc: agcalcalansing

Clip ipit, pangipit; Iloc: sigpit, sipit

Cliique kapisanan o exclusivong grupo na kaunti lamang sila

Clitoris tilin; Iloc: tunggil

Clock (wall) and wristwatch relo-*Sp*, orasan; Iloc: relo

Clog mag-bara; Iloc: ag-barra

Clogged barado; Iloc: barrado

Clogs, Filipino wooden *(Tag. & Iloc.)* bakya

CLOSE isara, sarhan, ipinid; Iloc: i-cerra-*Sp*, rikipan

CLOSE by malapit; Iloc: asideg, adani

CLOSE call, Close shave napakakitid lamang na chansa pero nakatakas at nakaligtas siya sa isang mapanganib na pangyayari.

Closed sarado, nakapinid; Iloc: cerrado-*Sp*, nakarikep

Closure pagkakaroon ng nakakabuntong-hiningang katapusan pagka-tapos ng dinanas na hirap; pagkasara ng isang parte ng buhay; Iloc: maaddaan iti makasennaay ken makabang-ar pagpalpas iti napasaran a rigat; pagkacerra ti maysa a parte ti biag.

Clot nagbuo na dugo at bumara sa ugat kaya hindi na makaagos ang dugo; Iloc: agbalay a dara nga mangbarra idiay urat isu a manglapped ti pagaayos ti dara,

CLOTH tela-*Sp*; Iloc: tela, lupot

CLOTH spread or cover for table, etc. telang pantakip, panaklop, mantel-*Sp*; Iloc: ap-ap, mantel

CLOTHE baro, damit, bestido-*Sp*; Iloc: bado, cawes, arwat, bestido

CLOTHE, hand-me-down segundo-mano-*Sp*, nalakihang damit ni ate o kuya; Iloc: segundo-mano, dinakkelan nga bado ni manang o manong

CLOTHE or dress someone bihisan; Iloc: badwan, cawesan

Clothesline sampayan; Iloc: sallapayan

Clouds ulap; Iloc: ulep

Cloudy, Overcast maulap, kulimlim; Iloc: naulep, nacudrep, nalidem

Clown *clown,* payaso-*Sp*; Iloc: *clown,* bulbullagaw

Club 1] asosasyon o samahan, 2] lugar na pag-ipon-iponan, pag-iinoman o sayawan, 3] kahoy na panghampas o pamalo; Iloc: 1] asosasyon o pagkacadwaan, 2] lugar nga pagtitiponan, pagbartekan o pagsasalaan 3] kayo a pagpang-or wenno pangmalo

Clue bakas, tanda: Iloc: pangtandaanan

Clumsy mali-mali; Iloc: agbiddu-biddut

Cluster cumpol; Iloc: bunggoy

Clutch mahigpit na hawak, capit; Iloc:tenglen, petpetan, capet, cumpet

Clutter magcalat; Iloc: agiwara
   Antonym
   Declutter iligpit; Iloc: idulin, ipakni, agpenpen

Coach *coach,* tagasanay; Iloc: *coach*

Coagulate mamumuo, maglaput; Iloc: agbalay, bimmalay

Coal, live baga; Iloc: beggang

Coalition pagsasama, pag-aanib at pagkakaisa ng mga tao o grupo o ng mga provincia o mga bayan na puedeng hindi naturingan na permanente

Coarse magaspang; Iloc: nakersang, narasi

COAST tabing-dagat, baybay, dalampasigan; Iloc: igid ti baybay

COAST is clear, the walang mga tao o walang nakikita na peligro-*Sp* o nakakahadlang

Coat *(Tag. & Iloc.)* *coat*

Cobra *(Tag. & Iloc.)* *cobra*

Cobweb bahay-gagamba; Iloc: saput

Cock tandang; Iloc: cawitan

Cockfight sabong, pintakasi; Iloc: pallot, pintakasi

Cockpit 1] sabungan, 2] lugar-*Sp* ng piloto-*Sp* sa eroplano-*Sp*; Iloc: 1] galyera-*Sp*, 2] lugar ti piloto diay eroplano

Cockroach *(Tag. & Iloc.)* ipis

Cocky mayabang, malakas ang loob na igiit ang gusto, makasarili

Cocoa *(Tag. & Iloc.)* cacaw-*Sp*

COCONUT *(Tag. & Iloc.)* niyog

COCONUT grater pangkayod, kudkuran; Iloc: igad

COCONUT husk for polishing the floor bunot, lampaso; Iloc: lampaso

COCONUT meat *(Tag. & Iloc.)* macapuno

COCONUT milk *(Tag. & Iloc.)* gata

COCONUT shell with its husk removed and its meat scraped out and made to dry to be used as a scooper or used in a Filipino dance bao; Iloc: bao, buyoboy

COCONUT, young *(Tag. & Iloc.)* buco

CODE codigo-*Sp*, 1] natipon-tipon na mga alituntunin o reglamento ng batas; regulasyon-*Sp*, makatarungang principio; 2] sistema-*Sp* ng palihim na pangcomunicasyon sa pamamagitan ng mga letra-*Sp*, simbolo-*Sp*, tunog at ilaw na nagpapahiwatig ng canilang kahulogan.

CODE word secretong salita na ginagamit na *code name* o *password*

Codfish *(Tag. & Iloc.)* bacalaw-*Sp*

Coed, Female college student *(Tag. & Iloc.)* colehiala-*Sp*

Coerce fuersahin, pahirapan o dominahin para magbago ang asal at paniniwala; Iloc: fuersaen, parigatan o dominaren para agbalbaliw iti custombre-*Sp* ken iti pammati na (fuersa-*Sp*, domina/dominar-*Sp*)

Coexist magkakasama at payapa silang nabubuhay kahit sila ay may pagkakaiba; Iloc: agcacadwa ken natalna da nga agu-ummong uray no adda pagsabalyan da.

Coffee *(Tag. & Iloc.)* café-*Sp*

Coffin ataul, cabaong; Iloc: lungon

Cogent nakaka-cumbinsi-*Sp* at nakakapaniwala dahil maliwanag, tugma sa paksa at pertinente-*Sp* sa kalagayan, at nasa tamang rason-*Sp* at claro-*Sp* pa ang pagka-explica-*Sp* at paglalarawan.

Cognitiveness, Cognition obra-*Sp* ng utak gaya ng pag-isip, pag-alam, pag-ulirat, memoria-*Sp*, pagrason, paghusga, pagkilala o pagturing, pagtanto, kutob o pakiramdam; Iloc: obra ti utek casla ti pagpanunot, pag-ammo, pagkapuot, memoria, pag-rason, paghusgar ken pagbigbig.

Cognizance ulirat, malay; Iloc: puot

Cohabit nagsasama sa bahay na parang mag-asawa pero hindi pa sila casal; Iloc: agkabbalay da a casla agasawa ngem haan da pay casar-*Sp*

Cohere magdikit, kumapit; Iloc: agcapet, agdikkit

Coherent 1] sang-ayon sa *logic*, 2] naturalesang magkasundo, 3] magkadikit

Cohesive magkakasama dahil may elemento o bagay na nakakapagpadikit o makapag-ugnay sa kanila.

Coil pulupotin, ilikaw-likaw; Iloc: iputipot, icawicaw, ipulipol, icunikon

Coin *(Tag. & Iloc.)* centavo-*Sp*, centimo-*Sp*

Coincide magkasabay na mangyari; Iloc: agrinnana, agrana, aggiddan
Synonyms
Simultaneous magkasabay; Iloc: aggiddan, agrinnana
Altogether sabay-sabay; Iloc: aggigiddan, agririnnana, agrarana

Colander salaan; Iloc: sagatan

COLD malamig; Iloc: nalamiis, nalam-ek, nalammin

COLD attitude matamlay makisama, ilag, mailap; Iloc: natamnay a makicadwa, naatap

COLD-blooded walang-wala man lamang kahit kaunting awa o simpatiya o damdamin; Iloc: awan man laeng uray sangkabassit nga asi o simpatiya o pang-ricna

COLD, feel giniginaw; Iloc: malamlammin

COLD feet hindi na maisagawa gaya ng talumpati o canta dahil na-lupig siya ng takot o hiya; Iloc: haanen a makadiscurso o cancion ta naparmek isu ti buteng wenno bain

Colds sipon; Iloc: sipon, panateng

Collaborate *v.*, **Collaboration** *n.* 1] makipagtrabaho sa iba sa isang proyecto-*Sp;* 2] maki-anib sa kalabang lumusob sa bayan bilang traidor sa sariling bayan

Collaborative *adj.,* **Collaborator** *n.* 1] makipagtrabaho sa kapwa; 2] makipagsabwatan sa lumusob sa canyang bayan

Collapse gumuho, nagiba, nabuwal; Iloc: marba, matwang
Correlated words
> **Avalanche** pagguho ng lupa sa bundok; Iloc: daga ti bantay nga agrumek, agrebba ken agregreg
> **Gush** bumulwak, biglang maraming pag-agos; Iloc: agpus-suak, golpe nga nakaad-adu nga pagayos
> **Erode** mayurak; Iloc: marunaw, agrumek
> **Disintegrate** gumuho o magkadurog-durog; Iloc: agrurumek

Collar *(Tag. & Iloc.)* cuelyo-*Sp*

Collarbone balagat; Iloc: tulang ti baba ti tengnged

Collateral ang *security* na kinakailangan sa pag-utang na pangseguridad na mababayaran ang inutang

COLLECT mangolecta; Iloc: ag-colecta-*Sp*

COLLECT a debt magsingil, singilin, mag-cobra-*Sp*; Iloc: agsingir, singiren, ag-cobrar-*Sp*

Collector of debt, Collection agency *(Tag. & Iloc.)* cobrador-*Sp*

COLLEGE *(Tag. & Iloc.)* colehio-*Sp*

COLLEGE degree, with a *(i.e., bachelors, masters, doctorate)* *(Tag. & Iloc.)* educado-*Sp* at titulado-*Sp* nakatapos ng educasyon-*Sp* sa colehio-*Sp* o universidad-*Sp*

Collide magkabanggahan; Iloc: agkabanggaan

Collision banggahan, bunggohan; Iloc: banggaan, agbinnunggoan

Colloquial ordinaryong pag-uusap o ordinaryong pagsusulatan na hindi formal-*Sp*

Collusion dalawang tao o mga grupo na palihim o secretong nagkakasundoan; Iloc: dua a tao wenno maysa a grupo a palimed nga agtulag

Colon parte ng bituka na malaki; Iloc: parte ti bituka a dakkel

Colonel *(Tag. & Iloc.)* coronel-*Sp*

Colonize fuersahang pagpapasok ng mga dayohan sa isang bayan para sila ang maghari dito habang sila ay nakaugnay pa rin sa kanilang inang bayan; Iloc: fuersaan a pagserrek dagiti tagadayo iti maysa a nasyon tapno isuda iti agari ditoy mientras-*Sp* a nakaconectado da pay met laeng iti nasyon-*Sp* a pinaggapuan da

Colony *colony*, coloniang bayan na inagaw at pinamumunohan ng mga dayohan; Iloc: *colony*, colonia nga bayan nga inagaw ken agar-ari dagiti nangngagaw a tagadayo

COLOR culay; Iloc: color-*Sp*

COLOR-bleed magculay o magpusyaw sa laba; Iloc: agali

Column haligi, poste-*Sp*; Iloc: adigi, poste

Comatose walang malay; Iloc: awan poot

COMB *n.* suklay; Iloc: sagaysay

COMB *v.* suklayin; Iloc: sagaysayen, bisngayen

COMB for removing head lice suyod; Iloc: sugod

Combination *(Tag. & Iloc.)* combinasyon-*Sp*

Combine pagsamahin, ipag-combinasyon-*Sp*; Iloc: pagcombinasyonen, pagcadwaen, pagtiponen

Combustible madaling makasunog; Iloc: nalaca a makauram

COME punta dito, dulog, dating; Iloc: umay ditoy

"COME!" *(singular)* "Halika!," Iloc: "Cadtoy!" "Inca ditoy"

"COME!" *(plural)* "Halikayo!," Iloc: "Incayo ditoy" "Umay cayo ditoy"

"COME again." *(Tag. & Iloc.)* "Mag-visita-*Sp* po ulit kayo."

"COME again?" "Paki-ulit mo nga dahil hindi ko narinig/hindi ko naintindihan"

"COME and get it" "Ang pagkain ay handa na, halina't kumain"

COME as you are kung ano ka man, pumarito ka sa natural mo at huwag kang maggayak-gayak o ano pa

COME down with something magkasakit ng isang claseng sakit

COME from galing sa; Iloc: naggapu idiay

"COME here" "Halika didto," Iloc: "Umay ca ditoy"

"COME in" "Tuloy po kayo;" Iloc: "Sumrek kayo"

COME in pumasok; Iloc: sumrek, umuneg

COME in handy magagamit sa oras na kinakailangan; Iloc: may-usar-*Sp* no caano masapul

"COME near" "Lumapit ka," "Parito ka;" "Halika"; Iloc: "Umasideg ka," "Umadani ka", "Cadtoy"

COME near lumapit; Iloc: umasideg, umadani

Antonym

Go far lumayo; Iloc: umadayo

COME to one's senses 1] mataohan, magkamalay; 2] naliliwanagan na ang canyang isip o pag-intindi

COME unprepared hindi man lang handa; Iloc: ima-ima

Antonym

Prepared handa na, preparado; Iloc: preparado, nakarubwaten, nakasaganan

"COME what may!" *(Tag. & Iloc.)* **"Bahala na!"**

Comeback 1] pagbabalik, 2] pagsasagot sa sulat o tawag

Comedian *(Tag. & Iloc.)* comediante-*Sp*

Comedy *(Tag. & Iloc.)* comedy

Comestible ligtas na kainin; Iloc: mabalin nga kanen nga awan peggad na

COMFORT nakakaginhawang kalagayan; Iloc: makabang-ar a kasasaad, nam-ay

COMFORT food pagkaing nakakasaya o nakakaginhawa pagkaing nakakabigay ng alaala sa pagsalo-salo noong kabataan pa

COMFORT someone magmalasakit, mag-simpatiya-*Sp*, bigyan ng consuelo-*Sp*, pagaanin ang kalooban ng iba; Iloc: pabang-aran na iti puso ken nakem ti sabali, mangited iti consuelo, mangisaksakit, agsimpatiya, liwliwaen, ay-aywen

COMFORT zone 1] ito ay nasa lugar-*Sp* o situasyon-*Sp* na ligtas at comfortab-le-*Sp* ang tao at caya niyang kumilos o magsagawa ng gusto niya o ang kinakailangan niyang gawin 2] sa *Medicine*, ito ay nasa temperatura na nanatiling balanse-*Sp* ang init ng katawan at hindi manginig sa ginaw, at ito ay 13° at 21°C o 55.5° o 70°F kung nakadamit, at 28° at 30°C o 82.5° at 86°F kung nakahubad

Comfortable comfortab-le-*Sp*, maginhawa; Iloc: comfortab-le, maka-bang-ar, nanam-ay

Correlated words

In one's element nasa panahon o nasa lugar na canyang naturalesang kalagayan o nasa comfortableng kalagayan o kapaligiran

Comforting nakakapalubag-loob, nakaka-consuelo-*Sp*; Iloc: nakaka-consuelo, nakaliwliwa, makabang-ar,

Command mag-mando-*Sp*, mag-utos; Iloc: ag-mandar-*Sp*, agbilin

Commander *(Tag. & Iloc.)* commander

Commemorate parangal na pang-alaala kay/ng..; Iloc: padayaw a pang-lagip ken/iti...

Commence umpisahan, magsimula; Iloc: rugyan, irugi

Commend kalugoran o magbigay ng papuri sa taong nakagawa ng mabuti; parangalan, magpasalamat; Iloc: ag-apreciar-*Sp* o mangited ti pagdayaw ken pagyaman iti tao a nakaaramid iti nakasaysayaat nga obra-*Sp*

Commensurate magkatumbas sa dami o laki o tagal o halaga; Iloc: ag-kapatag wenno adda uniformidad-*Sp* iti pagkaadu o pagkadakkel o pagkabayag o valor

Comment mag-comentario-*Sp*; Iloc: ag-comentario

Commerce *(Tag. & Iloc.)* comercio-*Sp*
   Correlated words
   Business *(Tag. & Iloc.)* negosio
   Company, Enterprise compania, bahay-kalakal; Iloc: compania
   Trading pangangalakal, pagtitinda

Commercial pangkalakal, *commercial*; Iloc: *commercial*

Commission 1] bigyan ng otorisasyon-*Sp* para isagawa ang tinakda na gawain, 2] sueldong comision-*Sp* sa *sales* o pagveventa; Iloc: 1] ikkan ti otorisasyon nga aramiden na iti naydesignar nga obra-*Sp* na 2] commission a sueldo-*Sp* gapu iti paglaclaco na

Commit decididong isagawa; Iloc: decidido-*Sp* o nag-decidir-*Sp* nga aramiden

Committed marubdob, masugid, decidido-*Sp*, determinado; Iloc: naregget, napasnek, decidido, determinado-*Sp*

COMMON pangcaraniwang ichura-*Sp*, gawain o nagaganap; Iloc: ca-dawyan wenno sigud nga ichura, obra-*Sp* o mapaspasamak

COMMON denominator tao o bagay na nandodoon palagi kung may nangyayaring kakaiba na puedeng siya/ito ang pinagbubuhatan ng kalagayan o pangyayaring iyon; Iloc: tao wenno banag nga adda idiay *canayon* a maka-afectar-*Sp* iti kasasaad wenno mapaspasamak
   Synonym
   Bone of contention ang sanhi ng pagkakaalitan, disgustohan o argumento

COMMON sense *ordinary, practical sound and good judgment in which one can distinguish between right or wrong, good or bad, safe or unsafe. Sometimes it is not taken seriously that "Common sense is not common."*

Commotion kagulohang ingay; Iloc: gulo a naringgor

Commune 1] ilagay ang sarili sa kapaligiran kung saan makapayapa o kasiya-siya, 2] matira sa comunidad-*Sp* na parepareho ang interes-*Sp*,

gawain at kinikita; Iloc: 1] agyan iti arrubayan a maka   ited iti talna
ken nam-ay, 2] agyan iti comunidad nga agpapada ti interes, obra-*Sp*
ken sueldo-*Sp* da

Communicate makipagbalitaan sa pag-uusap o pagsusulat o pagsenyas-*Sp*;
Iloc: comunicasyon-*Sp* iti pagsarita o pagsurat o pag-senyas

Communication comunicasyon-*Sp*, pakikipag-usap, pagpapaliwanagan,
pagpapahayagan, pagkakaintindihan; Iloc: comunicasyon-*Sp*, makilaw-
lawagan, pakipagsarsarita, agin-innawatan, pakitinnarusan,
Correlated words

Letter sulat, liham; Iloc: surat

Memorandum, Memo *(Tag. & Iloc.) memo,* comunicasyon sa mga empleyado ng oficina na caraniwan ay buhat sa pinuno

Email pakipagsulatan sa pamamagitan ng *internet* o *computer* na nangangailangan ng *email address* sa bawat nagsusulatan; Iloc: pagsinnuratan idiay
internet o *computer* nga masapul ti *email address* cadagiti agsisinnurat

Text 1] pagpapadala ng mensahe sa pamamagitan ng *cell phone* at ibang
mobile devices, 2] ang nilalaman ng kasulatan, libro, periodico at iba pa

Facebook ito ay producto ng isang companya ng popular na *website*
na nag-aalay ng servicio na *social networking* kung saan puedeng makipagcomunicasyon sa mga kaibigan at puedeng makahanap ng informasyon
tungkol sa mga bagaybagay

Twitter, tweet ito ay producto ng isang *website* na nag-aalok ng servicio
na *social networking* kung saan puedeng makipagcomunicasyon sa libo-
libong tao

Instagram ito ay simpleng paraan para mailarawan ang kasalukuyang
nangyayari sa mundo at mga letrato at *video* na puedeng ipabahagi sa
familya at mga kaibigan

Communion sacramento-*Sp* ng comunyon-*Sp* sa simbahan; Iloc: sac-
ramento ti comunyon, comulgar-*Sp* idiay iglesia-*Sp*

Communist *(Tag. & Iloc.)* comunista-*Sp*

COMMUNITY comunidad-*Sp*, baranggay; Iloc: comunidad

COMMUNITY cooperation *(Tag. & Iloc.)* bayanihan

Commute 1]-*noun:* papunta't pabalik na viahe, 2]-*verb:* pupunta sa trabaho
at uuuwi, 3] pagpalit ng naunang sentencia ng corte at bigyan ng mas
maluwag na parusa; Iloc: 1]-*noun:* papan ken pagsubli a viahe, 2]-*verb:*
mapan diay trabaho ken agawid, 3] suktan ti immuna a sentencia ti
corte tapno ikkan ti mas nalaca a dusa

Compact siksik na siksik; Iloc: siksikan, agdidippit

Companion kasama; Iloc: cadwa

COMPANY kasama, mga kaibigan, barcada; Iloc: cadwa; dagiti gagay-yem, bunggoy

COMPANY, Firm compania-*Sp*, bahay-kalakal; Iloc: compania-*Sp*

Compare *v.,* **Comparison** *n.,* **Comparative** *adj.* icompara, itumbas, iha-wig, ihambing; Iloc: i-comparar-*Sp*, iyarig
Correlated words
Liken ihambing, iparis; Iloc: ipada, iyarig
Juxtapose pagtabihin para maicompara; Iloc: pagabayin para icomparar
Relatively kung icompara o ihambing sa iba; Iloc: nu icompara o iparis iti sabali

Compassionate mapagmalasakit, mahabagin, maawain, nagbibigay ng lingap; Iloc: mannangaasi, nalukneng ti puso, manangconsuelo

Compatible magkabagay at magkasundo sa isip, damdamin, paniwala at puedeng pati pa sa ibang bagay; Iloc: agkatulag ken agkabagay ti nakem, ricna ken pammati da ken mabalin iti sabali pay ida a banag
Correlated words
Rapport parehong may kapalagayang-loob sa isa'isa; Iloc: agpada da a nanam-ay ti panagricricna da maysa ken maysa caniada
Click madali silang nagkapalagayang-loob at agad silang naging mag-kaibigan; Iloc: naglaca da a naggayyem gapu ta nalag-an ti ricricnaen da maysa ken maysa
Harmonious relationship pagkakasundo, magandang pagsasamahan; Iloc: natalna ken nasayaat nga pagkacaduaan
Cohesive magkakasama dahil may elemento o bagay na nakakapag-ugnay sa kanila
See eye to eye magkapareho ang paniniwala at magkasundo ang pagturing sa mga bagay-bagay o kalagayan

Compatriot *(Tag. & Iloc.)* kababayan, kanasyon

Compel isapilitan o fuersahing isagawa; Iloc: fuersaen o piliten nga ipaaramid

Compensate perang bayad o tumbas sa ginawang trabaho o sa pina-kitang kagandahang loob; Iloc: cuarta a bayad o tangdan iti inaramid a trabaho o ti impakita a kaimbagan

Compensation compensasyon-*Sp*, bayad, tumbas; Iloc: compensasyon, bayad, tangdan

Compete maki-*contest*, makipagpaligsahan, makipagcompetensiahan-*Sp*; Iloc: makisalisal, maki-*contest*, makilumba, makicompetensia
Synonym
Vie makipaligsahan, makipagcompetensia, makipag*contest*; Iloc: maki-salisal, makipa-competensia, maki-*contest*
Competent caya, cayang-caya; Iloc: caya, cabaelan
Competition competensia-*Sp*, paligsahan; Iloc: competensia, lumba, salisal
Competitor *(Tag. & Iloc.)* kacompetensia, karival
Compile manguha ng informasyon-*Sp* sa iba't ibang materiales-*Sp* at pag-ipon-iponin o icumpol ang mga ito para gawing libro-*Sp* o para sa ibang pakay; Iloc: mangala ti informasyon cadagiti agsasabali a *sources* ken pag-ipon-iponen dagitoy wenno icummpol para isurat a libro wenno sabali pay a rangta
Complacent, Cool as a cucumber campante-*Sp* siya sa anoman at sa condisyon-*Sp* na kadalasan ay walang batid o malay sa peligro-*Sp* o defecto-*Sp* o kakulangan
Synonyms
Blithe masaya, campante at hindi nag-aalala; Iloc: narambak, campante ken awan ti pagkadanag na
Easy-going, Laid-back *(Tag. & Iloc.)* campante
Complain ireclamo, magreclamo, umaangal; Iloc: ireclamo, agreclamo-*aSp*
Complainer *(Tag. & Iloc.)* reclamador-a*Sp*
Complaisant pagpapakita na mapagbigay siya o sumasang-ayon o sumusunod at tumutupad
Compleat kahanga-hangang kacayahan, experto-*Sp* sa canyang abili-dad-*Sp* o *skills*; Iloc: nakadaydayaw a cabaelan, experto ti abilidad/ *skills* na
COMPLETE *adj.* completo-*Sp*, buo; Iloc: completo
COMPLETE *v.* icompleto, ibuo, bumuo; Iloc: icompleto, ipalpas, isambut
Complement 1] bilang o clase para magiging buo, 2] ano mang nakakabuo o nakakacompleto o nakakapag-perfecto, 3] culay na nakakacomplimento
(read Compliment in this book to compare with Complement)
Complex magusot at mahirap gawin o ayosin, complicado-*Sp*; Iloc: nagulo ken narigat nga aramiden o urnosen, complicado
Correlated word
Convoluted complicado na patong-patong at pulopot

COMPLEXION *(Tag. & Iloc.)* cutis-*Sp*
    Correlated word
    Skin balat; Iloc: cudil

COMPLEXION, brown- *(Tag. & Iloc.)* kayumanggi, morena-*Sp*

COMPLEXION, dark- maitim; Iloc: nangisit

COMPLEXION, light- maputi; Iloc: napudaw

Complicate gawing mahirap o gawing problema kaysa sa katunayan; Iloc: parigaten o parikuten

Complicated *(Tag. & Iloc.)* complicado-*Sp*

Complication *(Tag. & Iloc.)* complicasyon-*Sp*

Complicit makisangkot sa gawaing labag sa batas at hindi kanais-nais na gawa

Compliment salitang complimento-*Sp*, pang-consuelo-*Sp*, paghanga, pagpuri o pampasaya; Iloc: sarita a complimento pangdayaw o pangraem, pangparagsak o pangconsuelo

Comply tuparin, gampanan; Iloc: agtungpal, tungpalen

Component mga parte-*Sp* o lamang-loob ng isang aparato-*Sp* na nagpapalakad o nagpapa- andar-*Sp* nito

Comport mag-asal o kumilos na tugma; Iloc: usto nga garaw o tignay

COMPOSED matatag; Iloc: natibker

COMPOSED of naglalaman ng, nagsasakop ng; Iloc: aglaon iti
    Synonym
    Contain magcarga, naglalaman; Iloc: agcarga, aglaon

Composure hinahon; Iloc: talna

Comprehend maintindihan; Iloc: maawatan

Comprehensible napakadaling maintindihan; Iloc: nagdaras a maawatan
    Correlated words
    Vivid maliwanag at claro; Iloc: nalawag ken claro
    Cogent nakakacumbinsi at nakakapaniwala dahil maliwanag, pertinente na may kaugnayan sa paksa at kalagayan, at nasa tamang rason at claro ang pagkaexplica at paglalarawan

Comprehension abilidad-*Sp* sa pag-intindi-*aSp*; Iloc: abilidad ti pagawat o makaawat

Comprehensive completo-*Sp* o napakalawak ang sinasacop na informasyon-*Sp*; Iloc: completo o adu ti sacop nga informasyon
    Synonyms
    Indepth sacop lahat ang detalye at tama at completo

Complete *adj.* completo, buo; Iloc: completo

Compress isiksik, isingit; Iloc: isiksik, iselsel, pagdidippitin

Comprise of naglalaman ng; Iloc: aglaon iti

Compromise 1-*noun*: compromiso-*Sp*, kasunduang nakakabuti o nakakasama pero-*Sp* obligado-*Sp* na isagawa, 2-*verb*: magpagitna sa dalawang magkasalungat na tao para tulongan silang makarating sa puede-*Sp* nilang pagkakasundoang tatanggapin
Correlated words
With strings attached puedeng gagawin o pagbigyan sa isang condisyon o obligasyon o compromiso

Compulsion *n.,* **Compulsive** *adj.* taong controlado-*Sp* ng *compulsion*-isang fuersahan at sapilitan na nagpapatulak sa canya na kumilos ng isang asal; Iloc: adda napigsa nga mangduron ti tao a mangaramid ti maysa a garaw

Compulsory bilin na isagawa dahil obligado-*Sp* o sapilitan; Iloc: bilin nga obligado o fuersaan nga aramiden
Synonyms
Mandatory utos na hindi dapat labagin; obligado, sapilitang isagawa; Iloc: mandar nga haan masupyatan; obligado o bilin a mayfuersa nga maaramid
Obligated *(Tag. & Iloc.)* obligado
Antonyms
Voluntary kusang-loob, voluntaryo; Iloc: voluntaryo
Optional hindi obligado at puedeng piliin ang ibang ano man; gawin ang sarili niyang decisyon; Iloc: haan nga obligado ken mabalin latta a pilyen na iti sabali wenno iti cayat na nga aramiden

Compunction naliligalig at nababagabag ang budhi dahil sa nagawa niyang kasalanan, pagsisisi; Iloc: puso ken nakem nga haan a makatalna gapu iti basol na nga inaramid na, pagbab-babawi

Compute i-*compute*, sumahin, magsuma, cuentahin; Iloc: i-*compute*, sumaren, agsumar, icuenta (all –*Sp*: suma, cuenta, sumar)

CON *(Tag. & Iloc.)* contra; ito ay kabaligtaran ng Pro (Pro-ventahe-*Sp*) kaya ito ay hindi maventahe

CON artist manlilinlang, falsificador-*Sp*, balasubas, nagkukunwari para makapanloco at makapag-oportunista-*Sp* sa pagpaniwala at pagtiwala sa canya; Iloc: mangallilaw, falsificador, balasubas, agsinsinan tapno makagulib ken maka-oportunista gapu ti pagpati ken pag-fiar-*Sp* canyana

Concave, Bowl-shaped mangkok; Iloc: sucong

Conceal itago, icubli; Iloc: ilemmeng, isuksok
Correlated words
Hide a secret ilihim; Iloc: ilimed
Hide a thing itago, icubli; Iloc: ilemmeng, isuksok

Concede 1] kilalanin o ituring na tama, wasto, husto, o angkop at akma sa tamang gawain; 2] tanggapin ang pagtagumpay ng kalaban o karival, o ang *score* na natamo niya/nila bago ito ofisyal-*Sp* na pinahayag ang kahihinatnan; tanggapin ang pagkatalo; 3] ipagkaloob ang karapatan o privilehio-*Sp*

Concentrate on nakapirming ituon ang pansin sa isang bagay; Iloc: ifirmi nga iperreng ti mata ken nakem iti maysa a banag
Synonyms
Focus *focus*, nakatitig, nakapirming inaatupag ang pinagkakaabalahan; Iloc: *focus*, nakaperreng a firmi iti ob-obraen na
Engrossed, Absorbed abala, ocupado, subsob na subsob o buhos na buhos sa ginagawa; Iloc: ocupado, nakasubsob unay iti ob-obraen na
Antonyms
Distract ilayo ang baling sa pinaggugugolang pansin; Iloc: iyadayo ti perreng idiay madama na nga ob-obraen
Disturb gambalahin, estorbohin, moleschahin; Iloc: agestorbo, agmolescha

Concept ang pagkaalam o pagkaintindi sa isip, o pananaw sa mga bagay-bagay; Iloc: panunot, pag-awat ken pagbigbig iti bambanag ida

Conceptualize magbuo ng kuro-kuro o pagkaalam o pagkaintindi sa pamamagitan ng pag-observa-*Sp* o pinagdanasang karanasan, o sa pinagsaligan o pinagbatayang mga informasyon-*Sp*

Concern alala, pangamba; Iloc: danag

Concerning tungkol sa, hinggil sa; Iloc: maypanggep iti, maypuon iti, maygapu iti

Concert *(Tag. & Iloc.)* concierto-*Sp*

Concerted effort bayanihang sikap o punyagi; magkakasamang plinano at isinagawa; Iloc: bayanihan nga pakat; agkacadua a plinano ken inaramid

Conciliate *v.,* **Conciliatory** *adj.* magkasundoang itungo nila ang isip at pag-uusap sa *peace* o kapayapaan imbes na magcontrahan para maasahan nilang masusunod ito; Iloc: agtulagan nga iturong da ti

247

nakem ken pagsarsarita iti katalnaan imbes-*Sp* nga agcontraan tapno manamnama da a matungpal daytoy

Concise maikli; Iloc: ababa

Conclude taposin, wakasan; Iloc: palpasen, gibusen

Conclusion napagtuklasan at nakarating sa isang teoria-*Sp* pagkatapos ng pag-uusig; Iloc: napagsukalan ken nakadanon iti maysa a teoria palpas ti panagus-usig

Concoct mag-imbento-*Sp* o gumawa ng bagong-bagong paraan o bagong pagluluto

Concord sumang-ayon, pumayag; Iloc: umannugot, agcanunong, agtunos, agmayat, umayon

Concrete *(Tag. & Iloc.)* concreto-*Sp*

Concur *see Concord above*

Condemn sumpain; Iloc: idadanes

Condemned condenado-*Sp*, nasentenciahan ng parusang bilanggoan o sentenciang mamatay; Iloc: condenado, nasentenciaan isu iti preso o sentencia-*Sp* nga matay nga pangdusa da canyana

Condescend ibaba ang sarili para makihalobilo sa mas mababa sa canya sa estado

Condescending mapagmalaki, mapagmataas

Condiment recado-a*Sp*; Iloc: recado, pang-templa-a*Sp*
Correlated word
Ingredient sangkap, sahog; Iloc: sagpaw

CONDITION condisyon-*Sp*; estado-*Sp*; kalagayan; ang nararamdaman; Iloc: condisiyon; estado; kasasaad; rikriknaen
Synonyms
State estado, condisyon, kalagayan; Iloc: estado, condisyon, kasasaad
Disposition kalagayan ng isip at damdamin, disposisyon, modo; Iloc: kasasaad ti nakem ken ricna, disposisyon, modo

CONDITION, To get accustomed magpasanay, magpabihasa; Iloc: iruam

Conditional puedeng maaaprovahan o mapagkasundoan o magpapatuloy <u>kung</u> sundin ang mga rekisito-*Sp* dahil ito ay may condisyon-*Sp* para sundin ang hinihiling; Iloc: dayta kiddawen ket maaprovaan o mapagtulagan o ituloy-tuloy nu suroten dagiti rekisito ken condisyon ida
Synonym

Contingent ang pagkabuo o pagkasagawa ay nakasalalay sa mga condisyon; Iloc: ti pagkabalin o pagkaaramid o pagkaturpos ket agbatay cadagiti condisyon

Condole v., **Condolence** n. nakikiramay, nakikidalamhati; Iloc: makipagladingit

Condone nagpapamihasa, nagpapalugod; Iloc: ited ti capricho-*Sp* na

Conducive nakakapagbunga ng.., nakakapaglahad ng.., nakakapaggawa ng.., nakakapagyari ng..

Conduct asal; Iloc: tignay

Conduit tubo na pagdaanan ng tubig o electricidad-*Sp* o ano pa man; Iloc: tubo nga pagdalanan ti danum wenno electricidad o sabali pay

Conference conferencia-*Sp*, pulong; Iloc: conferencia

Confess magcumpisal; Iloc: ag-confesar-*Sp*

Confidant *(man)*, **Confidante** *(female)*, pinapanaligang tao, taong pinagkakatiwalaan ng mga lihim o *personal* na bagay; Iloc: catalek, tao nga mapagfiaran (fiar-*Sp*) cadagiti limed o privado-*Sp* a banag

Confide ipagtapat ang problema; Iloc: isawang ti problema

Confidence confiansa-*Sp*, tiwala; Iloc: confiansa, talek, fiar-*Sp*

Confident, self- may confiansa sa canyang sarili at sa canyang kacayahan, comfortableng makiharap canino man, may tapang at confiansa sa pakikibaka sa buhay; Iloc: adda confiansa na iti mismo a bagina ken iti cabaelan na, comfortab-le a makipatang iti siasino man, adda tured ken confiansa na nga mangsolvar cadagiti parikut

Confidential *confidential,* bagay na dapat hindi isiwalat, inililihim; Iloc: *confidential,* banag a masapul nga haan nga isawang, nakalimed

Configuration kung paano na-areglo-*Sp* o naka-forma-*Sp* o nakaconecta-*Sp* ang bagay; Iloc: nu casano nga naareglo wenno nakaforma o nakaconecta iti aparato-*Sp*

Confine iculong; Iloc: iculong, ipupok

Confirm i-confirma-*Sp*, ipagpatutoo; Iloc: i-confirmar-*Sp* nga usto, paneknekan

Confirmation *(Tag. & Iloc.)* confirmasyon-*Sp*

Confiscate icumpisca; Iloc: i-confiscar-*Sp*

CONFLICT may pagkacontra; giyera; Iloc: pagkacontra; gerra-*Sp*

CONFLICT of interest ofisyal o empleyado ng companya o govierno na ginagamit ang puesto nila para mag-oportunista at nakikipag-ugnayan sa taong tagalabas para gumawa ng masamang gawain na hindi makabatas kahit maagraviado ang companya na pinagtatrabahoan niya para lamang sa sariling kasakiman niya.

Conform alinsunod sa alituntunin; Iloc: sumursurot ti reglamento-*Sp*
Correlated words
Obedient masunorin; Iloc: mapagtungpal
Complaisant sumusunod sa utos; Iloc: sumursurot ti mandar
Comply tuparin, gampanan, tumalima; Iloc: agtungpal, tungpalen

Conformity uniformidad-*Sp*, magkakapareho, magkakatugma; Iloc: uniformidad-*Sp*, agpapada da amin

Confront harap-harapang sitahin o usisahin na may galit; Iloc: makisango nga agunget, mang-usisa nga adda pungtot na

Confuse litohin, manligalig, balisahin, i-taranta-*Sp*, mangtorete-*Sp*; Iloc: rirwen, itaranta, allilawen, itorete

Confused nalilito, nababalisa, natataranta, natotorete; Iloc: marirriro, matartaranta, matortorete
Synonyms
Disoriented lito, ligalig, balisa; Iloc: riro, maallilaw
In quandary nababagabag, naliligalig, balisa, lito, matorete; Iloc: marirriro, maringgoran, natotorete

Congeal mamumuo, maglaput; Iloc: agbalay, bimmalay

Congenital kung anomang angkin na niya buhat noon pinanganak siya at lumaking dala pa rin niya ay *congenital*

Congest *v.,* **Congestive** *adj.* 1] sobra sa pagkapuno, umaapaw sa dami; 2] sobrang ipon ng dugo o likido sa ugat o *organ* sa katawan

Congratulate *v.,* **Congratulation** *n.* batiin; Iloc: kablaawan
Correlated words
Pat on the back salita o tapik sa balikat para purihin, batiin, palakasin ang loob, o himoking magtagumpay; kalugorang-pagbati sa tao na nakagawa ng mabuti para mapasigla ang loob niya at magpatuloy siya sa paggawa ng mga nakakahanga, tapik-tapikin ang likod o balikat sa paghanga; Iloc: sarita wenno tapik ti likod tapno bigbigen isu ken patibkeren na ti confiansa ti bagi na ken iti cabaelanna tapno agganas nga agpakasayaat ken agballigi isu
High five pagbati o paghanga sa magandang ginawa sa pamamagitan ng pagtaas ng camay ng dalawang tao (ang bumabati at ang binabati) para ipagtampalan o ipalakpak ang canilang mga bukas na palad sa isa't isa

Fist bumps camao ng dalawang tao na pagtapikin o pagsalatin sa isa't isa bilang pagbati o paghanga sa pagtatagumpay o mabuting asal o pakikipagkaibigan

Thumbs up *(Tag. & Iloc.)* senyas na *"okay"* o *"good job"* o aprobado

Felicitate *v.,* **Felicitation** *n.* 1] binabati dahil sa nanalo o nagtapos sa escuela; 2] magpasaya sa iba

Congregate *v.,* **Congregation** *n.* pagtitipon ng nanalig o congregasyon-*Sp* sa simbahan o relihion para magsamba

Congress *(Tag. & Iloc.)* congreso-*Sp*

Congruent sang-ayon, angkop, nasa tama, alinsunod

Congressman *(Tag. & Iloc.)* diputado-*Sp*

Conjecture bumubuo o pumapahayag ng palagay o kurokuro na walang sapat na prueba-*Sp* o evidencia-*Sp*
Correlated words
Guess hulaan; Iloc: agpugto, pugtoan
Jump to conclusion maghusga o maghatol o magpalagay o magsapantaha o magpasya kahit hindi pa alam lahat ang katotohanan
Assume *v.,* **Assumption** *n.* wari, palagay, kuro-kuro, haka-haka
Presume ipalagay, mag-akala, magkuro-kuro, maghaka-haka, wariin; Iloc: ipagarup, agpatta-patta
Supposition pagpapalagay, mag-akala; Iloc: agpatta-patta
Surmise mag-isip, magkuro-kuro o magpalagay kahit walang sigurado at walang evidencia; haka-haka at hula lamang

Conjoined (i.e., bodies of fruits or vegetables) hugpong; Iloc: siping

Conjugal karapatan at ugnayan sa relasyon-*Sp* ng magasawa

Conjugate 1] magsamang magkapareha o mag-asawa; 2] balaraila o grammar: itanghal o ipakita o ibibigkas ang sari-saring forma-*Sp* ng salita o ng *sentence* sa mga pagkaayos gaya ng ng *verb* o pandiwa para magawa ang forma-*Sp* ng nakaraan, ng kasalukuyan at ng hinaharap

Connect i-conecta-*Sp,* icabit, pagconectahin, pagcabitin; Iloc: iconecta, pagcapeten, pagsilpuen, isilpo
Antonym
Disconnect tanggalin, putolin; Iloc: putden ti conecta o silpo

Connection pagkakaugnay, coneksion-*Sp*; Iloc: coneksion

Connive magsabuat, magsapacat; Iloc: agsabuat

Connote ipahiwatig; Iloc: ipaammo

Conquer supilin, lupigin, sugpoin; Iloc: parmeken

CONSCIENCE concensia-*Sp*, budhi; Iloc: concensia
Correlated words
Scruple pag-aatubili o pag-aalinlangan dahil sa kabig ng conciensia; Iloc: haan a makatalna gapu iti pagkidag iti conciensia
Scrupulous *(Tag. & Iloc.)* may/adda conciensia at principio

CONSCIENCE, clear or clean *If there is accusation, a person who is innocent and not guilty at all has a clean and clear conscience.* Malinis na conciensia-*Sp* o budhi dahil sa katunayan ay hindi siya ang gumawa ng sala o hindi siya ang nagkasala
Synonyms
High-minded nagtataglay ng marangal at dakilang asal at kaisipan na dapat huwaran o ehemplo o pamantayan
Upright matuwid ang pagkatao; Iloc: nalinteg ti katatao na
Scrupulous *(Tag. & Iloc.)* may/adda conciensia at principio
On the up and up, Strictly on the up and up matapat, makatarungan at matuwid

CONSCIENCE-compunction, Conscientious, Conscionable *When you have these 3 mentioned qualities, you are honest and trustworthy because you follow the dictates of your conscience. Conscience gives you a sense of what is right or wrong in all your thoughts, words and deeds, reminds you of right and proper ways, and moral and ethical principles that need to be followed, while it compels you to refuse wrong and evil ways. Compunction nips your conscience that you realize your wrongdoing and brings in remorse and self-accountability of the offensive pain you caused. You neither validate nor justify your wrongdoing, nor lay the blame on people, or on things, or on circumstances, because you discern the damage and pain you inflicted. You apologize for your fault and you accept the ensuing chastisement that you deserve. Unfortunately these qualities are not valued by some people due to pride, alibis, justification, lack of empathy, humility, and good judgment. Hopefully everyone comes to realize the need for these 3 qualities and adopts and practices these in their lives. After all, when we confess our sins to God, He wants us to be truly sorry for our sins.* Ang may budhi o consiencia ay umaamin ng kasalanan niya dahil mayroon siyang katalinohang tumanggap sa sariling pagkakamali, nakakaturing ng nagawang

252

kamalian at kasamaan niya at naaawa at nagmamalasakit siya sa sinaktan niyang tao, humihingi ng patawad at tinatanggap niya ang kahihinatnan o resultang parusa sa sakit at pinsala na dinulot niya. Mga iyan ay kahanga-hanga at napakadakila. Sa kasawiang-palad, dahil sa amor proprio-*Sp* o pagpapataas ng sarili at pangangatwiran at pagpapalusot, ang mga katangiang ito ay hindi pinapahalagahan ng ilan-ilang mga tao. Harinawa, huwag nating gawin iyan, kundi mamulat tayo at isagawa at ipabihasa natin sa buhay natin mga pagtuturo, paggigising at pagpapatnubay ng ating budhi o consiencia. Ang patakaran ng Panginoong Dios ay magsisi tayo sa mga kasalanan natin, at magkaroon tayo ng malinis na conciensia, at **hindi** ipagkaila ang kasalanan natin kundi tanggapin natin ang mga ito dahil sa katotohanan ay may responsibilidad tayo at *answerable* tayo sa lahat na anomang gawain natin - masama man o mabuti.

Conscious may malay, may ulirat; Iloc: adda poot

Consciousness ulirat, malay; Iloc: poot

Consecutively sunod-sunod; Iloc: agsasaruno

Consensual *adj.,* **Consensus** *n.* pag-ayon o pagsang-ayon at pagkakaisa ng mga taong nagkapulong-pulong

Consent sang-ayon, payag, pahintulot, permiso-*Sp*; Iloc: umannugot, umayon, agcanunong, agtunos, palubos, permiso

Consequence kahihinatnan, resulta-*Sp*; Iloc: pagbanagan, resulta

Consequently caya tuloy; Iloc: isu ngarud

Conservative *(Tag. & Iloc.)* conservativo-*Sp*, may moralidad-*Sp*

CONSERVE, Jam, Jelly *(Tag. & Iloc.)* conserva-*Sp*

CONSERVE, Not waste pangalagaan at palagoin, mag-ipon at hindi mag-aksaya, hindi magsayang ng biyaya ng Dios-*Sp*; Iloc: taraknen ken palapsatin, mangilala ken agipon; haan mangsayang iti gracia ti Dios

Consider turingan, wariin ; Iloc: bigbigen, panunoten

Considerable 1] napakalaki at napakadami; 2] importante-*Sp* na kina-kailangan ang pansin at respeto-*Sp*

Considerate *Understanding and have polite and kindly regard for other people's feelings, conditions and experiences that may have affected their circumstances or personality, even perceptions. Being considerate, one also becomes helpful, charitable, compassionate,* *caring and tolerant to others, besides being discreet that he/she sees to it that he/she is not a burden to others.* Pagtuturing at pag-uunawa sa kalagayan ng iba at sinisikap niyang makatulong kung caya niya, at sinisikap niyang hindi siya makakabigat o makahadlang sa kapwa; Iloc: makabigbig ken makaawat ti kasasasad ti dadduma ken ipakat na a makatulong nu cabaelan na ken isigurado na nga haan a makapa- dagsen o makapalapped iti tao

Consideration 1] considerasyon-*Sp*, pagturing sa kalagayan ng iba, 2] pagmumuni-muni o pag-iisip sa pagsuri bago gumawa ng *decision*; Iloc: 1] considerasyon, pagbigbig ti kasasaad ti dadduma, 2] pag- pampanunot a panagusig baro nga ag-*decision*

Consist naglalaman; Iloc: aglaon

Consistent walang pagmamaliw, matatag; Iloc: natibker, awan ti pagbalbaliw

Consolation, Emotional relief consolasyon-*Sp*, consuelo-*Sp*, pagsusuyo at pagpapagaan ng loob; Iloc: consolasyon, consuelo, pagliwliwa ken paglag-an ti barucong ken nakem

Console *alleviates and soothes other people's burdens; comforts, sym- pathizes, consoles, cheers and give encouragement.* Pagin-hawain at pagaanin ang kabigatan ng iba, bigyang consuelo-*Sp*, magmalasakit, magsimpatiya; Iloc: pabang-aran, ikkan ti consuelo, mangisaksakit, ag-simpatiya-*Sp*, liwliwaen, ay-aywen

Consort *(Tag. & Iloc.)* consorte-*Sp*

Consorting with the bad elements of society nakikialyado o nadawit o nasabit sa mga masasamang kasama; Iloc: naki-alyado cadagiti dakes a tao

Conspicuous lantad, halata, litaw, kitang-kita, vistado-*Sp*; Iloc: makitkita, nakaparang, vistado, nalatak

Conspiracy sabwatang manakit o maminsala o manira sa kapwa; Iloc: agsabwat nga mang-perdi-*Sp* o mangsakit iti tao

Conspirator kasabwat, kasapacat, kasangkot; Iloc: kasabwat

Constantly palagi, madalas, malimit; Iloc: canayon, mamin-adu

Constipation tibi; Iloc: tibbil

Constituent 1] parte-*Sp* ng isang buo, 2] residente-*Sp*, 3] mga puede itong magvoto-*Sp*

Constitute *(Tag. & Iloc.)* parte o elemento

Constitution constitusyon-*Sp*, 1] ang pagkagawa ng isang bagay o ang pagkatao ng isang nilalang, 2] ang mga batas at principio-*Sp* na nagdidicta ng pinapahalagaan at ng paraan at limitasyon-*Sp* ng govierno-*Sp* o institusyon-*Sp*

Constrain *v.*, **Constraint** *n.* fuersahin, pilitin, gawing katungkulan
Correlated words
Restrain *v.*, **Restraint** *n.* pigilan, i-control, hadlangan, maglagay ng limitasyon; arestohin, tanggalin ang kalayaan; Iloc: tengngelen, i-control, tipden, mangigawid ta adda limitasyon na; i-aresto, ikkaten iti waya o *freedom* na

Construct magpatayo ng bahay o gusali; Iloc: agpatacder ti balay o facilidad-*Sp*

Constructive nakakatulong para sa pagtubo o pag-unlad o pagbuti; Iloc: makatulong para iti pagtubo, pagsayaat, pagrang-ay o pagballigi

Consult sumangguni, magconsulta; Iloc: agpa-consulta-*Sp*

Consultation consultasyon, sangguni; Iloc: consultasyon

Consume 1] gamitin, kainin, 2] ubosin, simutin, isaid; Iloc: 1] i-usar-*Sp*, kanen, 2] ibusen,

Consummate nagawa, nacompleto, napagbunga, natapos, natamo, nagtagumpany

Consumption *(Tag. & Iloc.)* pagconsumo-*Sp*

Contact *(Tag. & Iloc.)* contakin, tawagan, makipagkita

Consumed wala na, ubos na; Iloc: awanen, naibusen

Contagious nakakahawa, nakakainfecta; Iloc: makaacar, makaalis, makainfectar

Contain mag-carga-*Sp*, naglalaman; Iloc: agcarga, aglaon

Container lalagyan, sisidlan, pagcargahan: Iloc: pagikkan, pagikabilan, pagcargaan

Contempt muhi; Iloc: gura

Contemplate *v.*, **Contemplation** *n.* magmuni-muni, magdili-dili; Iloc: agimatang

Contemporary magkapanahon; Iloc: agkapanawen, agcasadar

Content 1] contento-*Sp*, 2] laman, carga-*Sp*; Iloc: 1] contento, nanam-ay, 2] nagyan, carga

Contentment *(Tag. & Iloc.)* pagkacontento

Contention *n.*, **Contentious** *adj.* madaling makipagsagutan o makipag-away o makipag-discusyonan; Iloc: nadaras makipagsungbatan, apa o discusyonan

Contest paligsahan, timpalak, competencia-*Sp*, *contest;* Iloc: salisal, competensia, *contest*

Context sa pagsasalita/*spoken statement* o sa sulat/*writing*, ito ay puedeng nasa umpisa o nasa huling parte ng *sentence* o pangungusap pinapaliwanag ang ibig sabihin ng isang salitang nandodoon o wala doon pero pinahiwatig doon, o nagbibigay ng halimbawa ng nasabi na salita o sinasabi ang kabaligtaran ng salitang iyon

Contingent *adj.*, **Contingency** *n.* ang pagkabuo o pagkasagawa ay nakasalalay sa mga condisyon-*Sp* o pangyayari o pagkatupad ng kasundoan; Iloc: ti pagbalinan o pagkaaramid o pagkaturpos ket agbatay cadagiti condisyon o mapaspasamak o pagtungpal ti contrata-*Sp*

Continuation karugtong; Iloc: continuasyon-*Sp*

Continue ituloy, patuloy; Iloc: ituloy, i-continuar-*Sp*

Continuous tuloy-tuloy at walang humpay; Iloc: agpatpatuloy nga awan sardeng

Synonym

Incessant walang tigil, patuloy-tuloy; Iloc: awan sardeng, agpatpatuloy laeng

Contort ngiwiin, sirain ang anyo o hugis o forma, baluktotin; Iloc: diwwigen, kiwingen, dadaelen o perdien ti langa o forma (perdi-*aSp*)

Contour hubog, hugis, forma-*Sp*, corte-*Sp*; Iloc: forma, corte

Contraband *(Tag. & Iloc.)* contrabando-*Sp*, hindi makabatas na *smuggled* o naipuslit na mga bagay sa bayan

Contract contrata-*Sp*, kasunduan, kasulatan; Iloc: contrata, pagtulagan, kasuratan

Contradict contrahin, pabulaanan; Iloc: mang-contra-*Sp*, supyatan

Contrast kabaligtaran; Iloc: balictad

Contributing member to society and being an altruist: *An altruist who is considerate to other people and a contributing member to society have compassion and a kind heart to lend a hand to humanity. And being such makes one a hero and an asset to one's country and one's community. When one has civic-mindedness, people appreciate this person for being kindhearted, caring and compassionate. The* *following ways are many but are quite easy and simple. Put purpose and meaning to your life by being the solution and not the problem, working and being a self-sufficient person and not depending on handouts from the government or from others. Put the good of the community above your personal pleasure and greed by giving back to the country and society. Pay taxes and feel good about it because it helps the country's economy and its projects.* **Vote with a conscience** *by casting your vote on the* <u>truly trustworthy candidates who are patriotically, morally, ethically and intellectually fit to manage effectively and honestly the needs of the country and the citizens</u>. **Choose lawful ways to live this life by abiding by the laws of the country**. *Have civic morals by driving with caution and observing traffic laws; refuse bribes for graft and corruption dealings, reject illegal activities, and prevent others from indulging on it by reporting such to authorities.* **Save a life** *by donating blood to people who needs it.* **Give donations to help charities that provide valuable services to the needy** *if you have money to spare or you have things to donate.* **Volunteer in hospitals and charitable organizations** *that are short of staff, and in schools to help students who need help in their lessons.* **Do little acts of kindness** *by* <u>lending a helping hand</u> *to the weak, the disabled and the elderly; and give words of encouragement to the helpless; listen to people who need somebody to talk to; rescue someone when it is safe and you are capable of doing it; give a smile to strangers whether they smile back or not; donate food to organizations or churches that serve the needy; do not throw thrash* <u>just anywhere</u> *but* **initiate or participate in community cleanliness, beautification and correct garbage disposals**; *reuse or* <u>recycle</u> *reusable products like periodicals and boxes so as not to waste them;* **never discriminate or marginalize tribal people or other races**, *including the poor, the elderly, and the physically- and mentally-challenged, and many other useful acts of kindness.*

Contribution *(Tag. & Iloc.)* contribusyon-*Sp*

Contrite *adj.,* **Contrition** *n.* pagsisisi; Iloc: pagbabawi

257

Contrive 1] matalinong paglikha o pagpapanibago, 2] magplano ng masama sa kapwa; Iloc: 1] nasirib nga agparnuay wenno pangbalbaliw, 2] agplano iti dakes iti dadduma

Control magbigay ng otorisasyon-*Sp* ang ofisyal-*Sp* o makabatas na kapangyarihan o karapatang regulasyon na ipamahala at itaguyod, patnugotan, pagalawin, iwasto, ipatuwid, areglohin, sang-ayonan o ayawan, pigilin, siyasatin, at awatin

Controlled *(Tag. & Iloc.)* controlado-*Sp*

Controversial *controversial,* nakakapagbunga ng pagtutol, ng argumento-*Sp* o pagtatalo dahil nakakasalungat sa tamang gawi, layonin at paraan; palacontra at hindi nakikiisa; Iloc: makapagbunga ti pagcontra, argumento, ringgor ken adu pay nga parikut gapu ta haan nga nasayaat nga aramid ken pammati

Controversy alitan, pagtatalo; Iloc: pagringgoran

Contuse *v.,* **Contusion** *n.* sakit o bunggo sa balat pero walang sugat; Iloc: sakit wenno bunggo ti cudil ngem awan sugat

Conundrum hula/bugtong na paglalaro ng mga salita

Convalesce pagbabalik sa lakas at kalusogan pagkatapos ng pagkakasakit; Iloc: pagsubli iti pigsa ken salun-at palpas nga nagsakit

Convenience hindi nagbibigay ng hirap kundi kaginhawaan at kaluwagahan lamang; Iloc: haan a mangited iti dagsen nu di makabang-ar ken makapanam-ay laeng

Convenient libre-*Sp* o maluwag na tiempo-*Sp* na puedeng maginhawa at comfortab-le-*Sp* pa para bumaling sa bagay na kinakailangang balingan; Iloc: libre ken nalawa a tiempo nga mabalin nga nabang-ar ken comfortab-le pay para makaperreng iti masapul nga asecasoen

Convent *(Tag. & Iloc.)* combento-*Sp*

Convention *(Tag. & Iloc.)* combension-*Sp,* formal-*Sp* na pulong-pulong ng mga profesyonal-*Sp* at ibang mataas ang katungkulan

Converse *v.,* **Conversation** *n.* magchatchatan, makipag-usap-usapan; Iloc: makitungtong, makisarsarita, makisao
Synonyms
Chat masayang cuentohan; Iloc: nakaliwliwa nga pagtungtongan
Banter cuentohang masaya na nagkakatuwaan at may kasamang mga biro; Iloc: storiaan a naragsak nga addaan pay ti pagkakatawaan ken angaw

258

Communicate makipagbalitaan sa pag-uusap o pagsusulat o pagsenyas; Iloc: comunicasyon iti pagsarita o pagsurat o pagsenyas

Convert taong nacombinsing magpalit ng paniwala o relihion-*Sp*; Iloc: tao a na-combensir-*Sp* nga agsukat iti pammati na wenno iti relihion na

Convey ipaalam o ipabatid ang mensahe-*Sp* o balita; Iloc: ipakaammo ti mensahe o damag

CONVICT *n.* taong nahatulan ng parusa, taong nakapreso dahil sa crimeng ginawa niya; Iloc: tao nga nasentenciaan iti dusa ti corte-*Sp* ti husticia-*Sp*, tao a nakapreso gapu iti crimen nga inaramid na

CONVICT *v.* hatolan ng parusa; Iloc: dusaen iti nayrebbeng canyana

Convince combinsihin; Iloc: ag-combensir (*Sp:* cumbinsi, cumbinsir)

Convinced (*Tag. & Iloc.*) combensido-*Sp*

Convoluted (*Tag. & Iloc.*) pulopot; complicado-*Sp*

Convulse mag-combulsion-*Sp*, kumikisay-kisay; Iloc: agcombulsion, agbugbugsot

Convulsion (*Tag. & Iloc.*) combulsion-*Sp*

COOK magluto; Iloc: agluto

COOK, Chef (*Tag. & Iloc.*) cusinero/ra-*Sp*

COOK by stirring haloin; Iloc: kiwaren, kiburen

COOK with ingredients or spices recadohan; Iloc: recadoan, sagpawan (recado-*Sp*)

Cooking oil mantica-*aSp*; Iloc: manteca-*Sp*

Cool malamig; Iloc: nalamiis, nalam-ek, nalammin

Coop up nakatira sa maliit na bahay o culongan

Cooperate makisali sa paggagawa; Iloc: maki-participar-*Sp* ti pagobra-*Sp*

Cooperation cooperasyon-*Sp*, bayanihan, magsama-sama na magtulong-tulongan; Iloc: cooperasyon, pagkacadwaan nga agtitinnulongan
Correlated words
    Community cooperation (*Tag. & Iloc.*) bayanihan
    Concerted effort magkakasamang plinano at isinagawa; Iloc: agkacadua a plinano ken inaramid

Coordinate 1] pareho-*Sp* ang ranko-*Sp* o importancia-*Sp*, 2] binabagay at pinagtutugma para magka-angkop ang combinasyon-*Sp*; Iloc: 1] pareho ti ranko ken importancia, 2] aramiden nga agkabagay isu nga i-umno tapno usto-*Sp* iti combinasyon da

Cope, Coping skills, Coping mechanism *In dealing with dilemmas and contentions, find out ways on how to cope with such quandaries in order to achieve solutions and relief. Consider the positive side to a problem like what you have learned from it because hindsight is learning from difficult experiences so as to know how to deal with similar future situations. If it is about a certain a person, rather than keep it to yourself, ponder whether talking to him or her may help or not. Unburdening problems to a counselor or to a family member or to a trusted person usually help. Another ideal way is to cast your burdens upon God for God to handle your problem while He gives you peace that surpasses all understanding, including solutions that may come immediately or later. Also depend and rely on God to always lead and guide you in all your ways, then await and be aware of His <u>peaceful</u> leading and answer. Embarking on activities may also be used as coping mechanisms, like hobbies, sports, crafts, singing, composing songs, playing musical instruments, reading, writing stories and experiences for publication, writing down your to-do lists, planning a good future for yourself, using to the utmost your abilities, skills and talents, being busy with work at your job or chores at home, taking a needed rest, enjoying the company of family or friends, short trips to nice places, joining associations that are fun, beneficial and educational, attending entertainment shows, praying to God, meditating on Bible verses and other good excerpts, and many more. Never, never try tobacco, alcohol and illegal drugs because such* **addictions never solve problems at all,** *but definitely bring more loads of troubles, difficulties and even failures in life.*

Copious sagana, marami; Iloc: adu, wadwad, ruay

Copper *(Tag. & Iloc.)* tanso-*Sp*

COPY *n. (Tag. & Iloc.)* copia-*Sp*

COPY *v.* mangopia, copiahin, ipacopia; Iloc: ag-sacar-*Sp*, ag-copiar-*Sp*, copiaren, icopiar

Copycat taong nanggagaya o tumutulad sa mabuti o masamang gawain ng ibang tao; Iloc: tao nga ag-copiar-*Sp* o tumultulad iti naimbag o dakes nga aramid iti dadduma

Copyright karapatang makabatas o *legal* ng manunulat bilang nag-memay-ari sa isinagawa niyang *manuscript* ng libro-*Sp* o musica-*Sp* at siya lamang ang may karapatan sa tubo ng pagventa ng ito, at kung may mangopya o mang-*plagiarize* nito, ang nangongopya ay mapapasailalim sa parusa ng batas kahit ano pa mang bayan siya naroroon; Iloc: adda *legal* o kalintegan na iti insurat na a libro o musica ken isu laeng ti rumbeng iti tubo iti pagventa cadagiti libro na ken nu adda ag-*plagiarize* o mangcopia iti obra na, maidarum isu iti corte uray nu inchenna man a bayan pay isu ditoy mundo
Correlated word

Patent *legal* na karapatan o titulo sa nag-imbento ng producto; Iloc: *legal* nga katurayan ken titulo iti nang-imbento ti producto

Cord cordon-*Sp*, tali, pisi, lubid, lazo-*Sp* o sintas ng sapatos-*Sp*; Iloc: cordon, tali, siglot, lazo o sintas ti sapatos

Core 1] pinakaloob-looban o pinakagitna o pinakaimportanteng parte ng anomang bagay; 2] fundasyon-*Sp*, puso, diwa, buod, pinagsaligan, pinagbabatayan

Cork tapon-*Sp*; Iloc: sullat, tapon

CORN *(Tag. & Iloc.)* maiz-*Sp*

CORN on one's foot *(Tag. & Iloc.)* calyo-*Sp*

Corner sulok, canto-*aSp*; Iloc: suli, canto

Coronation *(Tag. & Iloc.)* coronasyon-*Sp*, patungan ng corona-*Sp*

Corporation *(Tag. & Iloc.)* corporasyon-*Sp*

Corpse *(Tag. & Iloc.)* bangkay

Corpulent malaki o mataba ang katawan; Iloc: dakkel ti bagi na o buchog isu

CORRECT *v.* isaayos, ituwid, iwasto, itama; Iloc: i-correhir-*Sp*, ilinteg, i-usto-*Sp*

CORRECT *adj.* tama, wasto, tumpak, tunay; Iloc: usto-*Sp*, agpayso

Corrective sinasaayos o nire-remedio-*Sp* ang mali; Iloc: mang-usto o mang-remedio iti haan nga usto-*Sp*

Correlate itatag ang pagsasamahan o pagkaugnayan sa nagdadamayan at sa mabuting tugonan gaya ng *give and take*

Correlative nagcocomplemento sila sa isa't isa

Correspond *v.*, **Correspondence** *n.* pakikipagsulatan, makipagsulatan; Iloc: agsinnurat, makipagsinnuratan

Corresponding 1] magkapareho sa lahat ng *aspect* o diwa; pareho-*Sp* ang puesto-*Sp*, tungkulin, layonin, forma-*Sp* at iba pa; magkaanib sa trabaho-*Sp* at iba pang kaugnayan; magkasundo, magka-pareho, magkatugma; 2] magsulatan

Corridor *(Tag. & Iloc)* *corridor*, pasilyo-*Sp*

Corroborate patunayan, magbigay ng prueba-*Sp*; Iloc: paneknekan, mangited ti prueba

Corrode maagnas, mangalawang; Iloc: marunaw, marunot, agrumek, agburak

Corrupt ginagamit ang canyang puesto-*Sp* (ofisyal-*Sp* man siya o ordinaryong empleyado-*Sp* lamang) para palihim at *illegal* na gumagamit ng pera ng oficina-*Sp* para sa sarili niyang pagpapayaman o siya ay nakikipag-ugnayan sa nagpapagawa sa canya ng labag sa batas na favor-*Sp* para siya ay makatanggap ng *bribe* - ito ay taong *corrupt* na wala man lamang etico-*Sp*, moralidad-*Sp*, dignidad-*Sp* at integridad-*Sp* kaya hindi siya mapagkakatiwalaan

Cortège *[kwartezzh]* procesyon na kasama sa ceremonya

Co-sign mag-firma-*Sp* bilang ang kinakailangang *co-signer* ng documento

Cosmetic para sa pagpapaganda ng ichura-*Sp*; Iloc: para ti pagpapintas ti ichura-*Sp*

COST precio-*Sp*, halaga; Iloc: precio, valor-*Sp*

COST of living ang caraniwang gastos sa bahay, pagkain, damit at iba pang kinakailangang bagay at servicio-*Sp* na binayaran ng tao o familia-*Sp* na tinuturing na pamantayang categorya-*Sp* sa isang grupo

Costly mahal; Iloc: nangina

Cot *(Tag. & Iloc.)* *cot*, tiheras-*aSp*

Cotton bulak, telang *cotton*; Iloc: capas, tela-*Sp* na *cotton*

Cough ubo; Iloc: uyek

Counsel *advice*, payo, balacad, aviso-*Sp*; Iloc: *advice*, aviso, balacad, bagbaga

Counseling ang escuela-*Sp*, govierno-*Sp*, simbahan at iba pa ay mga lugar na pagkuhanan ng payo sa paglutas ng suliranin para makalayo sa problema-*Sp* at panganib dahil *knowledge is power and counseling helps one to discover a right decision that is for his/her best interest. Kinds of Counseling*

Informed decision bago magpasiya ng ano man lalo na sa mga importanteng decisyon, mag-*research* at humiling ng payo para malaman at makagawa ng pinakatamang pasya na makakabigay-ligtas at buti sa buhay, gaya halimbawa kung binabalak magtrabaho sa ibang lugar, kailangang mag-*research* bilang dagdag sa mga ibinabalita sa pahayagan at TV, kung abot-caya mo ang marangyang titirhan doon o simp-le lamang na matuloyan sa sueldo na itatakda sa iyo, kung makakaunlad ka sa empleado mong iyan, kung ano ang mga binibigay na *perks* ng iyong trabaho (*medical-dental coverage*, mga omento, mga matataas na puesto na puede mong maabot doon sa iyong pagpapakitang-gilas, *vacation leave, sick leave* at iba pa), kung hindi magulo ang pook na titirhan mo, kung maayos ang viahe papunta't pabalik sa oficina, *etc.*

Youth counseling ang unang-unang paghingan ng payo ay ang magulang dahil sila ang may pinakamalaking pagmamalasakit sa anak pero kung kailangan pa ang dagdag na payo o kaya may pag-aalangan kang magsabi sa magulang mo ng iyong problema at hindi mo cayang lutasin ito, mayroong lugar na pagtatakbuhan ng mga kabataan o menor-de-edad para makakuha sila ng tulong o payo – magtanong-tanong lamang <u>sa escuela o sa gobierno o sa simbahan</u>.

Pre-engagement background check and guidance *Take early steps to choose the right person for you as going steady can result in marriage which is a lifetime commitment. Get to know at the onset if he/she is single, responsible, trustworthy, reliable, has a good character, a college degree, a job, is law-abiding, a churchgoer, or whether he/she is violent and has a hot temper or is understanding and patient. Always have a frank and honest communications with him/her to get a <u>clear picture of a future official relationship with him/her</u>. Don't emulate what they show in movies, TV shows or romantic books where couples are <u>rushing blindly into romantic relationships without regard of a person's character</u>, a quality that is essential in marriage. Nowadays, even before going steady with anyone, it is necessary to check a person's history that can indicate someone's character. Don't pour out all your heart and soul into a relationship before you make a background check on him/ her.* **Knowledge is power.** *One can make checks on his/her history from police records, internet identity-searches, social media, at the school he/she is/was enrolled, at the church he goes to, and with people who know him/her like friends, co-workers, classmates and relatives. Nowadays if you do <u>not</u> use such inquiry-channels that are available to everyone and the person you fall in love with <u>turns out to be an erroneous choice</u>, you missed the opportunity to know him or her adequately prior to everything that **deep regret may come***

263

too late. Take the right steps always and even find a good counselor to get a good advice from.

Red flag *watch out for **warning signs** of possible future problems that may be hard to endure, i.e. bad character, bad deeds.* Para ligtas ka sa kabigoan sa buhay, bigyang pansin ng husto ang mga kapintasan sa ugali at gawa gaya ng mainitin ang ulo, hindi makatagal sa trabaho, bastos, parating *defensive* kaya *no remorse, no self-accountability on his wrongdoings,* walang conciensia kaya siya ay **unconscionable**, mapagsinungaling, o seloso/sa, irresponsab-le, wala nang intelihente-wala pang etico, at iba pang masasamang signo o babala.

Baggage Ito ang mga puedeng magiging problema sa darating na pagsasamahan ng magkasintahan kung ipagpapatuloy nila ang canilang kaugnayan sa isa't isa gaya kung may asawa sa kasalukuyan ang nakucorsonadahan, o mayroong anak na puedeng mahirap makakasundo kapag mag-asawa na sila, o may *police record* o may masamang vicio gaya ng *drug addiction,* o malakas uminom ng alak, o may malaking utang, at iba pang puedeng mabigat at nakakasira sa pagmamahalan at pagsasamahan. Huwag ipawalang-bahala mga ito kundi ngayon pa man ay dapat pansinin na ang nakikitang problema dahil puedeng makakasira sa pagmamahalan at pagsasamahan ang mga iyan.

<u>**Relationship questions**</u> Para makagawa ng pasyang maganda na *based on informed decision* tungkol sa taong nakucorsonadahan, kailangang maaga pa ay makita at mabatid na ang totoong pagkatao niya para malaman kung magiging payapa at magkasundo ang dadating na pagsasamahan, marami dapat itatanong, at *the following* ay isa sa maraming itatanong: 1] *What is important to you in life/*ano ang importante sa iyo sa buhay? Gusto bang umunlad o campante lamang? 2] *What is your belief in God?* Sumasamba ba sa Dios o walang pakialam sa Dios? Ang taong palasimba ay mabuting *sign*, pero marami pa ring kailangang malaman kung siya nga ay magiging mabuting kabiyak sa buhay. 3] *What would you want to achieve in life or plans in life?* Kung hindi maliwanag ang sagot, magtanong ka pa o hilinging ipaliwanag pa at doon ka mag-isip kung mabuti nga siyang tao, o kung hindi at may kapintasan ba siyang malaki, at mayroon bang pag-asa na magbabago siya?

<u>**Premarital counseling**</u> *If your findings on the person you are dating has an addiction, a police record and a criminal, or has no determination to find a job, has a hot temper, often gets impatient, is unfaithful, untrustworthy, a pathological liar, no moral and ethical values, doesn't have your back, doesn't really love you, has no remorse nor compassion nor conscience-compunction that he is always defensive by justifying and validating his*

264

*wrongdoings or denying them proving he has no personal responsibility and self-accountability to his culpabilities, etc. If you find him/her to have shocking or disappointing character, break off the engagement. While you're **not** yet married, it's **not too late to back out** from the relationship to save you from future problems. See a counselor for a good advise.*

Marriage counseling Ang pag-aasawa ay maraming responsibilidad dahil ito ay panghabang-buhay, kaya't kung may mga problema, pag-usapan at lutasin ninyong mag-asawa ng calmado. Mga responsibilidad sa *marriage* ay suportahan ang familya sa pamamagitan ng paghahanap-buhay ng tatay at kung walang mga anak ang asawang babae ay maghanapbuhay din, sa mga anak – dapat mahalin, arugain, palakihing maging mabait, makabatas, mag-aral, maging masipag at magpaunlad sila, ipagpatuloy ang pagmamahalan at pagmamalasakit sa isa't isa sa buong familya, at iba pa. Nakakabuti rin na humingi ng payo sa *church* o sa *professional counselor* kung kinakailangan.

Counselor consehal-*Sp*, tagapayo; Iloc: consehal-*Sp*, tagaaviso-*Sp*, taga-balacad

Count cuentahin (cuenta-*Sp*), bilangin; Iloc: bilangen

Countenance anyo ng mukha o asal; Iloc: ichura-*Sp* ti rupa ken tignay

Counter 1] lamesa sa tindahan na nakahilera ang mga paninda; mahabang lamesa-*Sp* sa *restaurant* o banko-*Sp* para makapag-*order* ng pagkain o makapag-deposito-*Sp* o *withdraw* ng pera; ibabaw ng *cabinet* sa cusina-*Sp* para sa paghahanda ng pagkain; 2] taong nagbibilang; 3] kabaligtaran; contra-*Sp*; salungat, *opposite*

Counterfeit falsificado-*Sp*, falso-*Sp*, huwad, peke; Iloc: falsificado, falso
Antonym
Genuine, Authentic *genuine*, tunay, puro, lantay, otentico; Iloc: *genuine*, pudno, puro, otentico

Countercharge ang *defendant* o inacusang tao ay gumanti ng paratang, habla o sakdal din sa *plaintiff* o ang nag-acusa sa canya

Counterpart tao o bagay na nakakamukha, pagkahawig o may pagkaka-pareho-*Sp* sa isang kagaya nito halimbawa "Ang presidente namin ay *counterpart* ng inyong hari"

Counterproductive nakakapagpatalo o nakakahadlang sa hinahangad na layonin o sa inaasahang resulta-*Sp*

COUNTRY bansa, bayan, nasyon-*Sp*; Iloc: bayan, nasyon

COUNTRY of birth bayang sinilangan; Iloc: bayan a nakayyanakan

Countryman *(Tag. & Iloc.)* kababayan, kabayan

Countryside, Rural area kabukiran, nayon; Iloc: away, taltalon
Correlated words
Farm bukid; Iloc: talon
Plains, Level land *(Tag. & Iloc.)* kapatagan
Fields parang; Iloc: tanap
COUPLE dalawa; Iloc: dua
COUPLE, married mag-asawa; Iloc: agasawa
COUPLE (engaged or in a relationship) mag-novio-*Sp*, magkasintahan; Iloc: agnovio, agayan-ayat
Courageous *Courageous, brave, intrepid, heroic, gallant.* Bravo-*Sp*, matapang, magiting, bayani; Iloc: bravo, natured, bayani, galante
COURSE, college *(Tag. & Iloc.)* curso-*Sp*
COURSE, Route daan, paglakaran; Iloc: dalan, pagnaan
COURT *(Tag. & Iloc.)* corte-*Sp*
COURT of Justice *(Tag. & Iloc.)* corte-*Sp* ng husticia-*Sp*, hukoman, husgado-*Sp*
COURT trial paglilitis ng crimen-*Sp* sa hukoman; Iloc: pag-usig iti crimen iti corte-*Sp* ti husticia-*Sp*
Correlated word
Hearing panimulang examinasyon ng taong acusado, ang tiempo sa pagkuha ng testimonya ng mga nakakita ng gawaing labag sa batas at itestigo ito sa corte
COURT, Woo ligawan, manligaw, digahan; Iloc: agarem, armen (diga -*aSp*)
Courteous magalang; Iloc: nadayaw
Courtesy cortesiya-*Sp*, magalang na pakikipagcapwa; Iloc: cortesiya, nadayaw a pakicadcadwa
Cousin pinsan; Iloc: casinsin
Couth *(Tag. & Iloc.)* educado-*Sp* at fino-*Sp*
COVER takpan, tapalan; Iloc: abbongan, caluban
COVER for bed *(Tag. & Iloc.)* cubrecama-*Sp*
COVER, Lid takip, taklub; Iloc: calub, taklub, akkub
COVER the mouth to prevent from talking takpan ang bunganga; Iloc: apputan ti ngiwat
COVER the view or screen takpan ang tinitignan o pinapanuod; Iloc: lingidan iti kitkitaen o buybuyaen ti tao
COVER up the ground hole with soil tabunan; Iloc: gaburan

Coverage 1] ang mga balita na pinapahayag ng *reporter* sa *TV* o sa periodico-*Sp*, 2] ang mga beneficio-*Sp* na sinasacop ng *insurance plan* sa pagpapagamot at pagpapanatili ng kalusogan; Iloc: 1] dagiti informasyon-*Sp* nga iwarwarnak ti *reporter* ti *TV* o periodico, 2] dagiti beneficio nga mayyusar iti *insurance plan* ti pagpaagas ken pag-mentener-*Sp* ti salun-at

Covered by an insurance *covered*, naka-*insure*, sacop; Iloc: *covered*, naka-*insure*, nakasacop

Covert tago, lihim; Iloc: lemmeng, limed

Covet inggit at pag-aasam sa pag-aari ng iba; Iloc: agagum ti cucua ti sabali

Cow *(Tag. & Iloc.)* vaca/baka-*Sp*

Coward duwag, cobarde-*Sp*; Iloc: takrot, cobarde

Coy kimi at nag-aalangang makihalobilo, mahiyain; Iloc: naulimek ken maam-amak a makitiptipon ti tao

Cozy maginhawa; Iloc: makabang-ar

CRAB *(Tag. & Iloc.)* alimango, alimasag

CRAB egg and fat *(Tag. & Iloc.)* aligi

CRAB, small *(Tag. & Iloc.)* talangka

Crabby bugnotin, yamotin, sumpongin, mapagpuna, mapaghanap ng mali; Iloc: mapagdillaw, agsipsipot ti basol, nalaca a marurod, agsumsumro

CRACK basag; Iloc: buong
Correlated word
Cut putol; Iloc: tukkol

CRACK one's finger-knuckles ilagitik, ilagutok ang mga daliri; Iloc: irittuok, ilittuok dagiti ramay

Crackdown stricto-*Sp* at mahigpit na pagpapatupad sa regulasyon-*Sp*, alituntunin o batas para matanggal ang mga pag-a-abuso-*Sp* o para malutas ang problema-*Sp*

Cracklings *(Tag. & Iloc.)* chicharon-*Sp*

Cradle catre-*Sp* ng sanggol; Iloc: cama-*Sp* o catre ti tagibi

Craft gawaing camay na mga palamuti sa bahay o tao; Iloc: aramid ti ima a pang-arcos ti balay o tao

267

Crafty hindi mapagkakatiwalaan dahil nanlinlang habang wala kamu-ang-muang ang vinivictima; Iloc: haan mapagfiaran ta agcusit nga haan mapupuotan

Crag bangin; Iloc: teppang, derraas

CRAM mag-aral ng mabilisan para sa examinasyon-*Sp*

CRAM things in isiksik, isingit; Iloc: isiksik, iselsel, pagdidippitin

Cramp makitid na lugar-*Sp*; Iloc: nailet a lugar

Cramps, leg- *(Tag. & Iloc.)* pulikat

Cranky bugnotin, yamotin, sumpongin, mapagpuna, mapaghanap ng mali; Iloc: nalaca a marurod, mapagdillaw, agsipsipot ti basol, agsumsumro

Crap 1] tae, 2] salitang bastos-*Sp* o panlinlang; Iloc: 1] takki, 2] sarita a bastos o pang-allilaw

CRASH malakas na pagkabunggo; Iloc: napigsa a pagkabunggo
Synonym
Ram banggahin, bunggohin; Iloc: banggain, bunggoen

CRASH helmet matigas na pamproteksion ng ulo na ginagamit kapag nagmo-motorciclo-*Sp* o nagbi-bisicleta-*Sp*

Crater bunganga ng vulcan-*Sp*; Iloc: ngiwat ti vulcan

Crave *v.*, **Craving** *n.* pinananabikan, sabik, inaasam-asam, ninanasa; Iloc: agpappapaos, agag-agum

CRAWL gumapang; Iloc: agcaradap

CRAWL of a snake gumagapang; Iloc: agcarayam

Crayons *(Tag. & Iloc.)* crayola

Craze pinagkakalocohang moda o uso o laro o iba pa; Iloc: paggaggagaran a moda o uso o ay-ayam *(sports)* o sabali pay (loco-*Sp*, moda-*Sp*)

Crazy ulol, baliw, loco-loco-*Sp*; Iloc: loco-loco, agmuryot, bagtit, agmauyong

CREAM *(Tag. & Iloc.) cream.* crema-*Sp*

CREAM of the crop ang pinakamahusay at pinakamagaling o pina-kamayaman o pinakamagandang categoria-*Sp*

Create maglikha, bumuhay; Iloc: mangparsua, mangbiag
Correlated words
Make gumawa, magyari; Iloc: agaramid, agparnuay
Engender makapaglikha, makapaggawa, makapagsanhi

Generate maglikha, umimbento, gumawa ng bagong bagay; Iloc: agparnuay, umimbento, mangaramid ti baro a banag

Contrive 1] matalinong paglikha o pagpapanibago, 2] magplano ng masama sa kapwa; Iloc: 1] nasirib nga agparnuay wenno pangbalbaliw, 2] agplano iti dakes iti dadduma

Creation 1] lahat ng claseng nilalang na nilikha ng Panginoong Dios; 2] likha, producto-*Sp*; Iloc: 1] dagiti amin a clase nga imparsua ni Apo Dios, 2] parnuay, producto

Creative may abilidad at dunong sa mas pagpapapabisa o pagpapaganda ng bagay na tinatangi niya at puede rin siyang marunong mag-imbento ng bagong kagamitan; Iloc: adda abilidad na ken sirib nga mas mangpabileg wenno mangpapintas iti banag nga valoran na ken mabalin met nga ammo na ti agimbento iti baro nga maar-aramat
Synonym
Ingenious *adj.,* **Ingenuity** *n.* mapaglikha at matalas ang intelihensia sa pag-iimbento

Creator lumikha, nagyari; Iloc: nangparsua, nangaramid

Credential testimonia-*Sp* o evidencia-*Sp* ng pagka-otoridad-*Sp* o pagti-tiwala sa cacayahan ng tao

Credibility *Being honest, reliable, believable, trustworthy and transparent.* Ang katangian kung saan ang tao ay kilala at lantad at bukas ang pagka**totoo** ng buhay at gawa niya kaya napagkakatiwalaan at pinapaniwalaan siya; Iloc: Ti katatatao ti tao nga nakaparang ken makitkita ti pagka**pudno** na isu nga mamati ken agfiar ti tattao canyana
Correlated word
Honest mapagkatiwalaan at mapanaligan sa pera at iba pa; Iloc: mapagtalkan ken mapagfiaran iti cuarta ken sabali pay

Credible *This is when a person is honest, reliable, sincere, believable, and trustworthy; and may even have transparency by being open about his/her ways and words.* Mapaniwalaan at mapagkatiwalaan dahil nasubokan na ang katapatan ng pagkatao at salita niya; Iloc: Mapatpati ken mapagfiaran ta naypakita na ti kapudnoan ti pagkatao ken sarita na
Correlated word
Honest mapagkatiwalaan at mapanaligan sa pera at iba pa; Iloc: mapagtalkan ken mapagfiaran iti cuarta ken sabali pay

Credit 1] reputasyon-*Sp* na napagkakatiwalaan dahil may paniwala sa canya at sa canyang mahusay na pakita; papuri o parangal dahil sa mahusay na katangian o canyang napagsagawa; 2] utang

Creditor ang nagpapautang; Iloc: ti agpapautang

Credulity *n.*, **Credulous** *adj.*, naniniwala o nagtitiwala kaagad kahit walang sapat na evidencia-*Sp*

Creek batis; Iloc: waig

Creep gumapang; Iloc: agcarayam, agcaradap, agarudok

Cremate sunogin ang bangkay; Iloc: uramen ti bangkay

Crest taluktok, tugatog, ulo ng bundok; Iloc: tuktok, ulo ti bantay

Crevice butas o pahabang biyak sa lupa o sa dinding

Crick sakit sa leeg at batok; Iloc: sakit ti tengnged ken teltel

CRIME *is an extremely evil deed towards others that unfairly put them into devastation, harm, injury or death, or deprive them of the blessings they worked so hard for. Crime invites karma because the wicked deeds criminals do to others **eventually come back to them**. Also the saying "**If you do the crime, you do the time**" is very true - **jail** is deservingly yours **where you LOSE all opportunities that are available to every law-abiding person**. And these opportunities are having a happy life and the chance to advance oneself in life, acquiring a job and being promoted to a higher position because of your having a work ethic which would definitely make you and your family proud of, you can also travel and enjoy going to beautiful places, get married, have a spouse and children who'd love you unconditionally and admire you for being the most important person in their life, you also can become a person respected by the community, and many more rewarding and productive things. So if you do the crime, you can no longer do any of these and more because you have destroyed all your bright promising opportunities and potentials. Besides that, no decent person wants to be your friend that you become a despised outcast/pariah/persona non grata to good people, and realize that you brought shame to your family, that you, yourself, gets to hate the person you have become. So before you commit a crime, reflect first if it is worth it, and consider this: if such unfair, cold-blooded crime happened to you, would you like it? As the* *saying goes:* **Don't do to others what you don't want others do onto you. For your very best interest, be a law-abiding individual and be part of the solution, <u>never, never the problem.</u>**

Criminal *criminal,* salarin, tulisan; Iloc: *criminal,* bandido-*Sp*

Criminals and Bullies: How Society Regard Them

Sadistic taong malupit at walang puso at consiencia; Iloc: tao nga nauyong ken awan puso ken consiencia na

Detestable kasuklam-suklam, kamuhi-muhi; Iloc: nakakapagura, nakabusbusor

Despicable kasuklam-suklam, napakasama; Iloc: makadisgusto unay, nakadakdakes

Obnoxious, Outrageous napakalaswa, nakaririmarim, kahalay-halay, karumaldumal, nakaka-disgusto; Iloc: nakadakdakes, nakaal-alas, nakamad-madi, makadisgusto unay

Heinous masama, makademonyo; Iloc: dakes, makasatanas

Atrocious nakakapatayong-balahibo/nakakadiri na masamang gawain; Iloc: makapatacder ti dudot a dakes nga aramid

Vicious, Vile napakasama; Iloc: nakadakdakes

Lurid napakasama, napakalaswa; Iloc: nakadakdakes

Notorious tanyag sa kasamaan; Iloc: agdindinnamag iti pagkadakes na

Egregious lantad na lantad ang pagkasama at pagkamakapinsala; Iloc: nakaparang ti pagkadakes ken ranggas na

Repugnant nakakarimarim at sobrang nakakadisgusto; Iloc: makasumgar ti dutdot ken makadisgusto

Outrageous napakalaswa, nakaririmarim, kahalay-halay, karumal-dumal, garrafal; Iloc: nakadakdakes, nakaal-alas, nakamadmadi, garrafal

Abject pinakamababa, pinaka-nakakadisgusto, napakasama; Iloc: nakadakdakes, makaaryek ti pagkaalas

Flagrant lantad ang pagkamasama; Iloc: vistado't pagkadakes

Ill-fated nakadestino o nakatakda siya sa kahirapan, kasamaan o bilangguan

Outcast taong itinakwil ng mga tao; Iloc: tao nga laisen ken nakadisdisgusto cadagit tattao isu nga adaywan da isuna

Anathema excomunicadong tao, kinamumuhian at sinusumpa; Iloc: excomunicado a tao, kagurgura, ilalais ken idadanes

Pariah *(see Outcast above)*

Reprobate 1] sinumpa na tao, 2] napakasamang tao; Iloc: 1] indadanes a tao, 2] nakadakdakes a tao

Ostracized taong itinakwil; Iloc: tao nga inlaksid, tao nga haan bigbigen o icascaso

Avaricious katacawan sa pera; Iloc: sarabusab iti cuarta

Chip on one's shoulder parating makipagtalunan o makipaglabanan dahil sa puot; Iloc: canayon a makipagdiscusyonan wenno makilaban gapu ti pungtot ti puso

Contentious *adj.,* **contention** *n.* madaling makipag-argumento, makipagsagutan o makipag-away; Iloc: nadaras a makipag-argumento wenno maki-apa wenno makipagsungbatan

Untrustworthy ones sinungaling, nagnanakaw, nagdidisfalco, nanlilinlang, criminal, falsificador, mandaraya, venggativo, traydor, mapagkunwari, nakikipagtalik sa hindi niya asawa; Iloc: ulbod, agtatakaw, agdesdesfalco, mangallilaw, criminal, falsificador, cusit, manggulgulib, venggativo, traidor, agsinsinan, maki-abig ti haan na nga asawa

Cringe mapakislot o mapatigtig dahil sa gulat o pandidiri o sakit; Iloc: cumpes wenno agtigerger gapu ti aryek o kigtot o sakit

Crippled baldado-*Sp,* may kapansanan, lumpo; Iloc: adda defecto-*Sp* na, bullo, baldado

Crisis kagipitan, crisis-*Sp*; Iloc: parikut, crisis

CRISPY malutong; Iloc: nasarangsang, narasi

CRISPY pork rinds *(Tag. & Iloc.)* chicharon-*Sp*

Criteria, Criterion rekisito-*Sp* o calificasyon-*Sp* na pambatay para maaprovahan

CRITICAL *adj.,* **Critic** *n.* madalas na palapintas, palalait, suspechoso at mapaghanap ng mali dahil malamang siya mismo ay masasama ang gawain kaya naghahanap ng kasama o nag-aakala na lahat ay kapareho niyang masama

CRITICAL condition kalagayan na puedeng mapanganib o lalala; Iloc: kasasaad nga mabalin a napeggad wenno ag-grabe-*Sp*

Criticize pintasan o mamintas; Iloc: agdillaw, aguyaw

Critique comentario-*Sp* tungkol sa likha ng *arts* at literatura-*Sp*

Crochet *(Tag. & Iloc.)* ganchilyo-*Sp*

CROCODILE *(Tag. & Iloc.)* buwaya

CROCODILE tears iyak o pagluha na pagkukunwari lamang; Iloc: sinsinan nga pagsangit o paglua

Cronyism hindi binabatay sa rekisito o qualificasyon-*Sp* kundi sa pagbibigay-favor-*Sp* sa kaibigan o sa taong nagbibigay ng *bribe* sa canya

Crook Ito ay gaya ng lahat ng *criminal*, ang *crook* ay tao na walang conciensia at walang respeto sa sarili kaya parating gumagawa ng masama at nagkukunwari mabait dahit nagfafalsificador para makapanlinlang, makadaya, makapagsamantala at makapanloco para makuha ang pera at ari-arian ng nililinlang nilang tao; Iloc: dagitoy ket tattao nga awan conciensia da ken awan respeto da ti mismo a bagi da isu nga canayon da agaramid iti dakes ken agsinsinan da a nasingpet gapu ta falsificador da ken balasubas a mangallilaw, agcuscusit, agop-oportunista, ken manggulgulib tapno matakaw da ti cuarta ken sanicua iti cuscusiten da a tao

Crooked lico-lico; Iloc: agkillo-killo

Crop, Yield, Produce *(Tag. & Iloc.)* ani

CROSS *(Tag. & Iloc.)* cruz-*Sp*

CROSS-eyed duling; Iloc: pangkis

CROSS-legged *(Tag. & Iloc.)* naka de cuatro-*Sp*

CROSS one's mind kusang pumasok sa isip na hindi inaasahan

CROSS out lagyan ng linya sa nakasulat para tanggalin na

CROSS paths with magkasalubongan o magkatagpo na hindi inaasahan

CROSS the bridge when one comes to it gagawin, aasecasohin o lulutasin kapag nandidiyan na, pero kung hindi pa kinakailangan o wala pang kabulohan na pagbalingan ng pansin ngayon, maghanda lamang at masigasig na antabayanan kung patolan na ang pag-aasecaso.

CROSS the line, Cross the boundary 1] tumawid at lumampas sa linya; 2] lumampas sa pinagbabatayan o pinagsasaligang asal at principio para suwayin ang karapat-dapat na asal o paraan na tanggap ng matinong sangkatauhan; lumampas buhat sa mabuti na ngayon ay masagwa na; kumikilos o nag-uugali na hindi kasiya-siya

CROSS the street, Go to the other side of a river tumawid; Iloc: bumallasiw

Crosshair, in the nasa gitna at puesto-*Sp* ng pansin at ng pagpintas at pag-atake-*Sp*

Crossing *crossing*, tawiran, salicop, bagtasan; Iloc: *crossing*, pagballasiwan

273

Crossroads dalawang calye-*Sp* na nag-cruz-*Sp*; Iloc: dua a calsada-*Sp* a nag-cruz
Synonym
Intersection dalawang calsada na letrang cruz pero apat ang pasukang calsada dito sa *crossing* na may *signal light* para sa paghali-haliling pagdaan ng mga sasakyan sa bawat calsada

Crouch yumukyok, magyukyok; Iloc: agcucot

Crow *(Tag. & Iloc.)* uwak

Crowbar bareta; Iloc: barreta-*Sp*

Crowd nag-ipon-ipong mga tao; Iloc: agu-ummong o agtitipon a tattao

CROWN *n.* *(Tag. & Iloc.)* corona-*Sp*

CROWN *v.* patungan ng corona-*Sp*; Iloc: coronaan

Crucial situasyon-*Sp* na masyadong maselan dahil kailangan ang pang-katapusang decisyon-*Sp* o resulta-*Sp*

Crucible 1] malubha at masakit na pagsubok; 2] bakal o matibay na sisidlan o lagayan na ginagamit na pagpainitan sa napakataas na temperatura-*Sp*

Crucifix anomang hugis cruz-*Sp*; Iloc: aniaman a forma-*Sp* ti cruz-*Sp*

Crucifixion Ito ang pagpapako sa cruz kay Panginoong Dios Hesu Cristo pagkatapos Siyang pinaghahahaplit ng latigo at siniksikan sa ulo ng coronang-tinik at pinabuhat sa Canya ang mabigat na cruz patungo sa malayong bundok ng *Golgotha* o *Calvary* kung saan Siya pinako sa cruz na Canyang binuhat. Maraming mararahas na parusa ang tinanngap ng Dios Anak na si Hesu Cristo para Siya ang magdusa sa parusa ng mga kasalanan ng lahat na nilalang, para maligtas ang mga nilalang sa parusa ng canilang mga kasalanan. Ang sino mang manalig, maniwala, magsampalataya, at magtiwala sa kaligtasang ito at tanggapin niya si Hesu Cristo sa puso't buhay niya bilang Dios niya at Tagapagligtas niya, lahat ng canyang mga kasalanan ay malinisan na ng dugo ni Hesu Cristo sa cruz at mapapatawad na ang lahat ng canyang mga kasalanan at bukas na ang pinto ng langit sa canya *(read God – at the "G" alphabet section of this book)*

Cruel malupit, matigas ang puso, verdugo-*Sp*, salvahe-*Sp*; Iloc: naulpit, verdugo, nauyong, naranggas, narungsot, natangken ti puso
Antonyms
Kind mapagmalasakit, mabait; Iloc: nasingpet, mangisaksakit

Compassionate may malasakit, mahabagin, maawain; Iloc: mangisaksakit, mannangaasi, nalukneng ti puso

Altruist *adj.,* **Altruism** *n.* nagmamalasakit sa kapwa at hindi siya makasarili; Iloc: mangisaksakit iti dadduma ken haan man laeng a bagbagi ti pampanunoten na

Cruelty kalupitan, katigasan ng puso, walang awa; Iloc: uyong, ulpit, tangken ti puso, awan ti asi na

Antonym

Clemency nakakapagpakita ng kaluwagan o awa o pagpapatawad sa kapwa pati sa kalaban o masamang tao; Iloc: makapagpakita ti pagliway o asi o pagpakawan iti tattao pati ti kalaban wenno dakes a tao

Cruise 1] maglayag o sumakay sa barco-*Sp* para sa masaya at nakalilibang na viahe-*Sp*; 2] maglayag o magmaneho ng coche-*Sp* o magpalipad ng eroplano-*Sp* o mag-*cruise* sa *internet* para sa paghahanap ng mga informasyon o mga tao

Crumble durogin; Iloc: buraken

Crumple cusotin; Iloc: cussoten

Crumpled *(Tag. & Iloc.)* cusot-cusot

CRUSH, Passing infatuation *(Tag. & Iloc.)* *crush,* corsunada, palo

Same pronunciation not same meaning

Crash malakas na pagkabunggo; Iloc: napigsa pagkabunggo

CRUSH things durogin, yurakin; Iloc: irumek, buraken

CRUSH head lice with the fingernail tirisin; Iloc: pis-iten

Crutch aparatong panlakad na itungtung sa kili-kili para makalakad ang pilay; Iloc: aparato-*Sp* a pangpagna nga ipatong iti kili-kili para makapagna ti pilay

CRUX primero-*Sp* at maselan na kalagayan na kinakailangan ang pagtuonan ng pansin

CRUX of the matter ang importanteng parte-*Sp* na puedeng kinakailangan ang pag-a-asecaso-*Sp* o paglutas dito

CRY umiiyak, tumatangis; Iloc: agsangsangit, agib-ibit

Correlated words

Weep, Sob humihikbi, humihibik; Iloc: agsasaibbek, agsasain-nek

Wail humahagulhol; Iloc:agan-anug-og, agdungdung-aw

CRY-baby iyakin, mababaw ang luha; Iloc: marasangit

Crystal *(Tag. & Iloc.)* cristal-*Sp*

Cucumber *(Tag. & Iloc.)* pepino-*Sp*

Cuddle pagmamahal na yakap o yapos; Iloc: naayat nga aracop o rakep

Cue senyas-*Sp*, hudyat; Iloc: senyas

Cuisine mga pagkain at kung paano lutoin ang mga ito; Iloc: dagiti makmakan ken nu casano iluto dagitoy

Culinary tungkol sa pagluluto; Iloc: maygapu iti pagluto

Culminate umabot sa pinakamataas na lugar (*summit*) o pinakamataas na pagbuo o pag-unlad; nakarating sa hangganan; 2] taposin, icompleto na

Culpable nagkasala at tugma ang bintang sa canya; Iloc: nakabasol ken rebbeng daytay naypabasol canyana

Culpability *A wrongdoer's guilt or blame that he/she deserves;* nararapat na paratang sa nagawang kasalanan ng isang tao.

Culprit ang siyang may kagagawan ng masama; Iloc: tay nagaramid iti dakes

Cultivate buhayin, arugain, palusogin, palagoin, pasiglahin; Iloc: biagen, taraknen, pasalun-aten, papigsaen, palapsaten

CULTURE 1] cultura-*Sp*, mga asal, kaisipan, paniwala, pagsasalita, modo, arte at mga obra ng isang panahon o grupo o ng sangbayanan; 2] talinong napaunlad ng *practice*, mataas na patag ng pagkafino dahil sa pagkabihasa sa intelihensia at sa pag-estima ng nakaka-contribusyon sa *fine arts*; 3] matalino at *artistic* na mga gagampanan at obra; 4] i-*cultivate* ang lupang pagtataniman, arugain ang mga hayop para mapabuti ang kanilang uri o *stock*; 5] gumawa ng *culture medium* buhat sa *microorganism*

CULTURE medium malatubig o mala-*gel* na naglalaman ng sustancia-*Sp* para i-*cultivate* ang mga *microorganisms* at *tissues* na gagamitin sa mga pagsusuri o *research*

CULTURE shock pagkasindak at pagkagulat sa natagpoang kakaibang pamumuhay at cultura sa ibang bansa

Cultured 1] educado-*Sp*, marangal at fino-*Sp*; 2] binuo buhat sa arti-fisyal-*Sp* at controlado-*Sp* na elemento-*Sp*

Cup *(Tag. & Iloc.)* tasa-*Sp*

Cumbersome palakad o gawain na mahirap o complicado-*Sp* kaya nawawala ang gana-*Sp* kung pagod na pagod na

Cumulative dumadami o lumalaki dahil sa mga sumusunod na dagdag; Iloc: umad-adu o dumakdakkel gapu iti sumarsaruno a pangnaynayon

Cunning abilidad-*Sp* na ginagamit na patago dahil pandaraya, tuso at panukalang panlilinlang

Curable magagamot, malunasan; Iloc: maagasan

Curb gilid ng bangketa-*Sp*; Iloc: igid ti bangketa

Cure gamotin, lunasan; Iloc: agasan

Cured gumaling, bumuti, naghilom; Iloc: limmaeng, umimbag

Curious mausisa, osyoso-*aSp*; Iloc: nausisa, osyoso

Curl, Curly *(Tag. & Iloc.)* culot

CURRENT *(Tag. & Iloc.)* electricidad-*Sp*, coryente-*Sp*

CURRENT, Water flow napakabilis na baha o agos ng ilog o batis

CURRENT, Present time sa kasalukuyan, ngayon; Iloc: madama o itatta a panawen

Curse, Wish evil on... sumpain; Iloc: mangidadanes

Curtail gupitin o putolin kaagad, paiklihin, paliitin, bawasan

Curtain curtina-*Sp*, tabing; Iloc: curtina

Curtsy ibaluctot ang tuhod na parang nakaluhod ng kaunti at marespetong iyuko ang ulo

Curve curva-*Sp*; Iloc:, killo, curva

Cushion *(Tag. & Iloc.)* cuchon

Cuss magmura; Iloc: manglais

Custard *(Tag. & Iloc.)* leche flan-*Sp*

Custody karapatang legal-*Sp* na mapapasacanya ang pagtira at pag-aalaga ng anak; Iloc: inted ti linteg a legal nga mapan canyana ti pagyan ken pagtaraken ti annak

CUSTOM *n.,* **Customary** *adj.* costumbre-*Sp*, gawi, kabihasnan; Iloc: costumbre-*Sp*, sigud nga aramid, cadawyan, nakayruaman

CUSTOM-built ginawa batay sa specificasyon-*Sp* ng nagpagawa; Iloc: inaramid batay ti specificasyon ti nagpaaramid

Customs 1] aduana-*Sp* na sangay ng govierno-*Sp* na cumocolecta ng buis sa mga bagay na galing sa ibang bansa at pinasok sa bayan; 2] departamento-*Sp* ng *airport* o stasyon-*Sp* ng sasakyan kung saan inuusig ang mga bagahe-*Sp* kung naglalaan ito ng contrabando-*Sp* sa mga pinapasok dito

CUSTOMER *customer,* namimili, cliente-*Sp,* suki; Iloc: *customer,* gumat-gatang canayon, cliente, suki

CUSTOMER, consistent or loyal *(Tag. & Iloc.)* suki

CUT baliin, putolin, hiwain, gupitin, lagotin; Iloc: gupden, putden, iwaen, pisyen, gudwaen, galipen, pugsaten
Synonyms
Break, Snap off baliin, putolin, bakliin, lagutin, patirin; Iloc: pugsaten, pugsoten, tukkolen
Halve hatiin; Iloc: gudwaen
Slice hiwa; Iloc: iwa, pisyen, galipin
Mince tadtarin; Iloc: tadtaden
Shred punit-punitin; Iloc: pigis-pigisen
Hack with a bolo tagain; Iloc: tagbaten

CUT a tree putolin ang punong-kahoy; Iloc: pukanen ti kayo

CUT cloth using a pattern tabasin; Iloc: tabasen

CUT corners tipid sa pagtatrabaho o paggastos kaya magsagawa ng hindi matibay at hindi completo, at gumagamit ng mumurahin at mahina na mga parte kaya hindi makayanang mapaglabanan ang lindol o bagyo at maagang magluma, humina o masira ito

CUT down 1] magtipid at ang pagconsumo ay limitado o kaunti lamang, 2] putolin ang punong-kahoy; Iloc: 1] agin-inot ti paggastos ken pagconsumo tapno haan a gatang nga gatang; 2] pukanen ti kayo
Correlated words
Scrimp, Skimp nagtitipid; Iloc: agin-inot, agkirmet

CUT hair magpagupit, gupitin; Iloc: agpa-cortar-*Sp,* agpapukis

CUT losses paliitin ang pagkalugi; paliitin ang paggamit ng mga bagay-bagay at huwag magsayang para magamit lahat ang nararapat na dami para lumiit ang pagkalugi; Iloc: kissayan ti paggastos ken pagiyusar ken mangilala nga haan nga mangsayang tapno bumassit ti pagkalugi

CUT open saksakin at bukadkarin; Iloc: butchaken

CUT some slack hindi higpitan kundi bigyan ng laya o palibrehin ang kagawian niya o sa gawain na caraniwan ay hindi pinapahintulot

CUT to harvest grain with a sickle maggapas; Iloc: aggapas

CUT to the chase sabihin na agad ang mahalaga at importante na paksa/rason/pangyayari at iyong hindi namang mahalaga ay maya-maya kung may oras pa

CUT with an ax sibaken, palakolin; Iloc: balsigen

CUT with a saw lagarihin; Iloc: ragadien, wasayen

CUT with a scissor gupitin; Iloc: gettengen, cartiben

Cutback pagbabawas, magtipid para mapalakad ng mas mahusay; Iloc: pagkissay, pagin-inot para maypadalan ti mas nasayaat

Cute nakakahangang pagkaakit, pagkagiliw at pagkasiya-siya gaya ng mga *cute* na bata

Cutting edge 1] nasa unang-unang puesto, o nangunguna sa larangan; 2] ang matalim at matalas na parte ng gulok, cuchilyo-*Sp* o lanseta

CYBER- *(Tag. & Iloc.) computer system* o *electronic communications network*

CYBER-attack tao o bayan na may masamang balak kaya walang pahintulot na pagpasok nila sa *computer system* o *electronic communications network* at pahintoin, sirain o gulohin ito

Cycling carerahan sa bisicleta-*Sp*; pagsakay o pag-viahe-*Sp* sa pamamagitan ng bisicleta-*Sp* o motorciclo-*Sp*

Cyclone napakalakas na ipo-ipong hangin o mafuersang hangin na paikot-ikot

Cymbals *(Tag. & Iloc)* pompiang

Cynic *n.,* **Cynical** *adj.* taong nilalait o pinagdududahan ang pakay ng kapwa o at pinapakitang hindi niya matanggap ang batayan ng *honesty* at *morality*; siya ay mapagcontra at *pessimistic*

Cyst butlig, pigsa; Iloc: butlig

D

Dab pahiran ng kaunti, maliit na tapik; Iloc: pilkatan, bassit a tapik

Dabble nagtatrabaho na parang palaro-laro lamang; Iloc: agob-obra a casla agay-ayam laeng

Dad, Daddy tatay, ama; Iloc: tatang, ama

Daft, Daffy stupido, loco-loco, napakahina ang isip

Dagger *(Tag. & Iloc)* punyal-*Sp*

DAILY araw-araw, bawat araw; Iloc: cada-*Sp* aldaw, inaldaw

DAILY grind caraniwang trabaho araw-araw; Iloc: sigud nga inaldaw nga obraen

DAILY, Newspaper *(Tag. & Iloc.)* diaryo-*Sp*, periodico-*Sp*

Dainty maganda at fino-*Sp*; Iloc: napintas ken nafino ken naemma

Dairy pinanggagalingan o pinagveventahan ng gatas at ibang producto ng gatas; Iloc: pinaggapuan o paglakwan ti gatas ken sabali pay a producto ti gatas

Dally campante, walang alala, atrasado at nag-aaksaya ng oras, palacua-lacuacha

Dam panghadlang sa pag-agos ng baha; Iloc: pangbarra ti pagayos ti layos

DAMAGE *n.,* pinsala, sira; Iloc: dadael

DAMAGE *v.* pinsalain, siraen; Iloc: dadaelen

DAMAGE control departamento o grupo na maghadlang o bawasan ang posibilidad ng pagkalugi, pinsala, pagkasira, publicidad na masama, at iba pa

Damn *v.,* **Damnation** *n.* 1] nagtuturing na ang bagay o tao ay masama o hindi angkop, hindi valido-*Sp* at di makabatas; nagsusumpa 2] nakatadhana sa infierno-*Sp*

Damp *(Tag. & Iloc.)* medio basa

Dampen 1] gawing medio basa; 2] magtamlay, palungkotin, bigoin

DANCE sayaw; Iloc: sala, bayle-*Sp*

DANCE moves synchronized with music i-cumpas-*Sp*, iindak; Iloc: icumpas

DANCE partner katambal, pareha-*Sp* sa sayaw; Iloc: pareha ti sala, kasala

Dancer baylarina-*Sp*, mananayaw; Iloc: baylarina, mannala

Dances, ballroom mga sayaw na *waltz, fox trot,* tango, cha-cha, mambo, rumba, polka, samba, salsa, merengue, pasa doble, nae-nae, *line dancing*

Dander *(Tag. & Iloc.)* init ng ulo o galit/pungtot

Dandle laroing itaas-ibaba ang bata o sanggol sa camay o sa tuhod ng magulang

Dandruff balakubak; Iloc: lasi

Danger panganib, peligro-*Sp*, kapahamakan; Iloc: peggad, peligro
Antonym
Safety kaligtasan; Iloc: salaknib

Dangerous mapanganib, peligroso-*Sp*, makapinsala; Iloc: napeggad, peligroso
Correlated words
Risky peligroso, mapanganib; Iloc: peligroso, napeggad
Unsafe mapanganib; Iloc: napeggad
Dicey puno ng peligro o panganib; Iloc: napunno ti peligro ken peggad
Precarious delicado o mapanganib na puesto dahil puedeng matomba, mahulog, masaktan, masira o mamatay; Iloc: delicado ken napeggad a puesto gapu ta mabalin a matomba, matinnag, masaktan, madadael wenno matay
Sitting on a powder keg nasa lugar o situasyon na mapanganib at puedeng may mangyayari na nakakasama ano mang oras
Sitting duck madaling mapuntirya at mavictima; Iloc: nalaca a ma-*target* ken mavictima
Vulnerable 1] taong madaling tablan ng sakit, taong madaling ma-influensia o locohin o dayahin o mapahirapan o masaktan o mapatay, 2] *computer* o *credit card* na madaling ma-*hack* o kaya companya o sangay ng govierno na puedeng tirahin ng mga *hacker*; Iloc: 1] tao a nalaca a maacaran ti sakit, tao a nalaca a mainfluwensia o magulib o maloco o maparigatan o masaktan o mapatay, 2] *computer* o *credit card* a nalaca a ma-*hack* wenno companya o departamento ti govierno a mabalin a tiraen dagiti *hacker*
Too close for comfort napakalapit na puedeng mapanganib o hindi comfortab-le
Gullible madaling maniwala o mahikayat; Iloc: nalaca a mamati wenno maawis
DANGLE nakatiwangwang, nakalawit; Iloc: nakatiwwatiw
DANGLE swayingly nag-iindayog; Iloc: agoy-uyaoy
Dare hamunin, kanchawan, udyokan, utoin; Iloc: kanchawan
Daresay or Dare say magpalagay na tutuo
Daring pangahas, atrevido-*Sp*; Iloc: atrevido
DARK color itim, maitim, negro-*Sp*; Iloc: ngisit, nangisit, negro
DARK, getting gumagabi na, dumidilim na; Iloc: sumipsingeten, rumabiin
Darling giliw, irog, mahal; Iloc: ay-ayaten, dungdungwen
Darn magsulsi; Iloc: ag-sursi-*Sp*
Dart maliit na palaso na hinahagis sa puntirya; Iloc: bassit a pana nga ipalladaw diay puntirya-*Sp*
Dash 1] humampas o sumalpok ng malakas; 2] golpeng pagsugod o pagtakbo; 3] kaunti o katiting gaya ng asin sa pagluto; 4] gitling o *hyphen*

Dashboard *panel* sa harap ng *driver* na nagbibigay ng direksion sa pagpaandar ng sasakyan

Dastard duwag na masama at palihim manlinlang

Data informasyon-*Sp* na mahalaga sa trabaho-*Sp* at buhay; Iloc. informasyon nga navalor ti trabaho ken biag

DATE *(Tag. & Iloc.)* fecha-*Sp*

DATE rape nanggahasa ng babae o ginahasang victima sa pakikipag-*date* sa oportunista

DATE someone *(Tag. & Iloc.)* makipag-*date*

Daub pahiran o pintahan ng kaunti; Iloc: paidan o sapsapoan wenno pintaan ti bassit

DAUGHTER anak na babae; Iloc: anak a babai

DAUGHTER- or Son-in-law *(Tag. & Iloc.)* manugang

Daunt natakot, nabantahan; nawalan ng tapang, sirain ang lakas ng loob; Iloc: nabutngan, nadadael ti pigsa ti nakem na

Dauntless *Courageous, brave, daring, unflinching even when threatened, intrepid, resolute in purpose.* Matapang, walang takot, malakas ang loob, hindi umuurong kahit tinatakot, matibay kung magpasia

Dawdle mag-aksaya ng oras-*Sp*, nagtutunganga lamang, naglalacuacha; campante-*Sp* at mahinang kumilos

DAWN madaling araw, bukang-liwayway; Iloc: bigbigat, parbangon, bannawag, aglawag, agsapa

DAWN on, Come to mind sumaisip o naalaala

DAY araw; Iloc: aldaw

DAY, all maghapon; Iloc: entero-*Sp* nga aldaw

Daybreak madaling araw, bukang-liwayway; Iloc: bigbigat, parbangon, agsapa, aglawag, bannawag

DAYLIGHT araw hindi gabi; Iloc: aldaw haan nga rabii

DAYLIGHT savings time panahon kung kailan ang planetang init ay tumatawid sa ecuador ng mundo kaya ang gabi at araw ay magkapareho ng haba sa buong mundo at nangyayari ito sa Marso 21 *(vernal equinox or spring equnox)* at Septiembre 22 *(autumnal equinox)*

Daze tuliro, natulig, mamangha; Iloc: nakigtot

Dazzle 1] nasisilaw ang mata sa marahas na liwanag, 2] magpa-*impress* para humanga sila sa canya; Iloc: 1] mapurar ti mata nga aggapu iti naranggas a ranyag o silaw, 2] agpa-*impress* tapno dumayaw da canyana

De facto 1] ang katotohanan/katunayan; 2] sinang-ayonan o tinanggap kahit walang makabatas na otoridad-*Sp*

Deacon puesto na mas mababa sa pari o pastor

Deactivate hintoin ang pag-andar, tanggalin ang pagka-efecto-*Sp*

DEAD patay, yumao, sumakabilang-buhay; Iloc: natayen

DEAD-end 1] *cul-de-sac* o daan na walang labasan kundi sa pinasukan lamang; 2] walang posibilidad o walang progreso o makaavante

Deaden matanggal ang ramdam o ang sigasig o fuersa

Deadline tinakdang pinakahuling araw sa pagbabayad ng utang o pag-entrega-*Sp* ng kinakailangang papeles

Deadly nakakamatay; Iloc: makapatay

Deaf bingi; Iloc: tuleng, sul-ot
Synonym
Hard of hearing mahinang pandinig; Iloc: bengngeg

Deafen maging bingi; matorete sa lakas ng ingay

Deafening sound nakakabingi; Iloc: makatultuleng

DEAL makisama, makipag-negosio-*Sp*; Iloc: makicadwa, makipagnegosio

DEAL-breaker, Last straw ang gawain o ugali na pagbabatayan kung ipagpatuloy pa o putolin na ang relasyon-*Sp* o negosio-*Sp* o kasundoan; Iloc: aramid o ugali a pagbatayan nu ituloy pay o putden itattan ti relasyon o negosio o pinagtulagan

Dealer negosianteng bumibili ng mga bagay at iventa ito

Dear mahal, irog, giliw; Iloc: ay-ayaten, dungdungwen

DEATH kamatayan; Iloc: pagkapatay

DEATH door, on naghihingalo, nasa bingwit ng kamatayan; Iloc: agbugbugsot, asidegen iti patay

DEATH trap hindi ligtas na lugar at puedeng malagay sa panganib o mamatay sinoman dito; Iloc: lugar nga asideg ti peggad ken mabalin pay a matay

Debacle biglang pagguho o pagkatalo; Iloc: golpe a marba o pagkaatiw

Debase minamata at minemenos ang pagkatao; Iloc: men-menosen ken parwaren a nababa ti pagkatao na

Debate *(Tag. & Iloc.) debate,* debate-*Sp*

Debauch *[dih-bawch]* i-*corrupt* o pasamahin ang asal; gawing *pervert* o iligaw o ilulong sa kalaswaan

Debilitated *adj.,* **Debility** *n.* kahinaan at walang lakas at sigla; Iloc: pagkapsut ken pagkapoy ta naawanan ti pigsa ken enerhia-*Sp*

Debit *(Tag. & Iloc.)* utang

Debrief 1] alamin sa mga sundalo ang ginawa at ang kahihinatnan ng kanilang *mission*, magtanong para malaman ang lihim na kaalaman at plano-*Sp* ng *army*; 2] sa pag-alis niya sa trabaho, pagsabihan siya na hindi ibunyag ang mga privadong informasyon-*Sp* ng oficina-*Sp*; Iloc: 1] amoen cadagiti soldado iti inaramid da ken resulta iti *mission* da, agsaludsod tapno maamwan ti limed nga ammo ken plano ti *army*; 2] iti pagpanaw na idiay trabaho-*Sp*, bagbagaan da isu nga haan na ipaammo dagiti informasyon a privado-*Sp* iti companya-*Sp*

Debris labi o pira-piraso o durog-durog buhat sa nasira o nabasag na anoman

Debt *(Tag. & Iloc.)* utang

Debtor *(Tag. & Iloc.)* ang nakautang

Debunk bucohin, ipabulaan ang kasinungalingan o sobra na pagyayabang ng iba; Iloc: bucoin, ipalibak ti ulbod ken sobra a paglastog ti sabali

Decadence *n.,* **Decadent** *adj.* patungo o nasa tiempong pabulok, pasama, pasira o paghina o pagkababa ng clase-*Sp* nito batay sa *standard* o pamantayan, moralidad-*Sp* at cultura-*Sp*

Decapitate pugotan ng ulo; Iloc: putden ti ulo

Decay mabulok; Iloc: agbulok

Synonyms

Rot mabulok; Iloc: agbukbuk

Spoil mabulok, mapanis, pasira na, mabukbuk; Iloc: aglaes, malungsot, mabangles

Corrode maagnas, mangalawang; Iloc: marunaw, marunot, agrumek

Deceased, Decedent patay, yumao, sumakabilang-buhay; Iloc: natayen

Deceit panlilinlang, balatkayo, daya; Iloc: panggulgulib, allilaw

Deceitful mandaraya, manloloco, manlilinlang; Iloc: mangallilaw, manglocloco, manggulgulib, cusit

Deceive linlangin, locohin, dayain; Iloc: guliben, allilawen, lukwen, cusiten

December *(Tag. & Iloc.) December,* Diciembre-*Sp*

Decent *adj.,* **Decency** *n.* decente-*Sp,* may moralidad-*Sp;* Iloc: decente, addaan iti moralidad

Deception *see Deceit above*

Deceptive mandaraya, manloloco, manlilinlang; Iloc: mangallilaw, manglocloco, manggulgulib, cusit

Decertify tanggalin o bawiin ang *certificate* o *certification* ng tao o ng *organization*

Decide magpasia, mag-decisyon-*Sp;* Iloc: ag-decidir-*Sp,* ag-decisyon, agkeddeng

Decided napagpasiahan, nadecisyonan, decidido-*Sp;* Iloc: napagdecisyonan, decidido

Decipher inuusig at iniintindi ang lihim na *code* o secretong kasulatan

Decision decisyon-*Sp,* pasia; Iloc: decisyon, keddeng

Declare *v.,* **Declaration** *n. formal* na iproclama-*Sp,* ipahayag; Iloc: *formal* nga isawang, iproclamar-*Sp*

Decline 1] magalang na tanggihan ang gawin o ang kasundoan at ipagtapat ang dahilan; 2] *slope* o libis; pababa ang daan o ang precio; 3] humihina ang lakas ng katawan, ang custombre o ang halaga

Declutter magligpit, mag-ayos; Iloc: mangidulin, agpakni, agpenpen

Decode suriin ang lihim na *code* at isalin sa naiintindihan na salita ito; Iloc: sukisoken ti limed nga *code* ken ipatarus iti maawatan a sarita daytoy

Decompose mabulok; Iloc: agbulok

Decompress paginhawain ang bigat/tindi/*pressure*; bumalik sa kalagayang normal mula sa kagipitan o sa kahirapan

Decorate mag-decorasyon-*Sp,* gayakan; Iloc: agdecorasyon, arcosan

Decoration decorasyon-*Sp,* palamuti, gayak; Iloc: arcos, decorasyon
 Correlated word
 Frill, Frills *(Tag. & Iloc.)* burloloy ng decorasyon

Decorum *v.,* **Decorous** *adj.* nag-aasal ng tamang asal; Iloc: aggaraw iti respetado a gunay

Decoy taong nagpapain ng kapwa para mapunta ang victima sa panganib o silo/bitag

Decrease kumokonti, nababawasan, lumiliit; Iloc: bumasbassit, kumiskissay
 Synonym

Peter out kumokonti hanggang maubos; Iloc: agin-inot nga bumassit inggana't maibus

Decrement kung gaano kumoconti-conti at gaano katagal ang pagconti
Antonym
Increment kung gaano dumadami-dami ito at kung gaano katagal ang pagdami

Decry lantarang tutolan/salungatin/pintasan/hamakin

Dedicate alang-alang, ihandog, i-alay; Iloc: ipaay, isagut, idaton

Dedicated nakatalaga, nakaukol o nakaalay ang puso sa..; Iloc: nacaydaton ti puso iti...

Dedication alay; Iloc: pannacaidaton

Deduce makarating sa pangwakasang pasya; Iloc: makadanon iti pangpalpas a decisyon

Deduct *v.*, **Deduction** *n.* bawasan, caltasan, mag-menos-*Sp*; Iloc: kissayan, ipamenos

Deductible 1] puedeng ibawas sa *tax* o buwis gaya ng binibigay sa *charity*; 2] ang parte na bayaran ng paciente na hiwalay sa bayaran ng canyang *medical coverage*

DEED gawa, obra-*Sp*; Iloc: aramid, obra

DEED, Title *(Tag. & Iloc.)* titulo-*Sp*

Deem nagmumuni-muni o ipaalam niya ang canyang kurokuro; Iloc: agpampanunot iti nauneg wenno mangisawang iti *opinion* o iti pangbigbig na

DEEP malalim; Iloc: adalem, nauneg
Antonym
Shallow mababaw; Iloc: ababaw

DEEP pocket napakaraming pera at malawak ang pag-aari; Iloc: adu cuartana ken iti sanicua na

DEEP-seated nakatanim na matatag at matibay

Deepen palalimin, hukayin para lumalim; Iloc: calyen para mas umadalem

Deer usa; Iloc: ugsa

Deescalate ibaba o bawasan ang tindi o laki sa panganib o kagipitan o kahirapan o sakit at iba pa

Deface papangitin o sirain ang ichura-*Sp*; Iloc: perdien (perdi-*aSp*) o dadaelen ti ichura, palaaden, paalasen

Defamation *n.,* **Defame** *v.* paninirang-puri; Iloc: pangdadael ti reputasyon-*Sp*

Default palya, delinquente-*Sp*; Iloc: nagliway, deliquente

Defeat dinaig, tinalo; Iloc: inabak, inatiw
> Important: In order for a learner to NOT be confused, here are examples of the differences of configurations on Win or Won, and Lose/Be defeated or Lost/Defeated that unfortunately both use the same root words although not in the same form.
> **Win**: *daiginm, talonin;* Iloc: *abaken, atiwen*
> **Lose/Be defeated**: *madaig, matalo;* Iloc: *maabak, maatiw*
> **Won**: *dinaig, tinalo;* Iloc: *inabak, nangabak, inatiw*
> **Lost/Defeated**: *nadaig, natalo;* Iloc: *naabak, naatiw*

DEFECT *(Tag. & Iloc.)* defecto-*Sp*, diferencia-*Sp*

DEFECT, Desert lisanan o layasan ang isang layonin o bayan para maki-anib sa iba

Defective may defecto-*Sp*, may diferencia-*Sp*; Iloc: adda defecto, adda diferencia

Defend defensahan, ipagtanggol; Iloc: i-defensa-*Sp*, isalakan, salakniban
> *Correlated words*
> **Protect** ipagtanggol, defensahin; Iloc: isalakan, salakniban, idefensa
> **Rescue** sagipin, saklolohan; iligtas, hangoin sa panganib; Iloc: arayaten, isalvar, salakniban
> **Safeguard** ipagtanggol, pinangangalagaan at pinakaiingatan para malayo sa panganib; Iloc: salakniban, ay-aywanan ken al-alwadan tapno adayo iti peggad
> **Safe** nasa mabuting kamay, ligtas, protectado; Iloc: nakasalvar, naysalaknib, adayo ti dakes ken peggad, protectado

Defendant ang nasasakdal; Iloc: iti naydarum
> *Antonym*
> **Plaintiff** ang nagsakdal; Iloc: ti nangidarum

Defender *(Tag. & Iloc.)* defensor-*Sp*

Defense *(Tag. & Iloc.)* defensa-*Sp*

Defensive 1] pagtatanggol o pangdefensa sa atake o panganib, 2] pag-iiwas ng kasalanan o pintas sa pamamagitan ng pangangatwiran o pagfifilosofo o anomang panglihis; Iloc: 1] pangsalaknib o pang-defensa contra ti atake wenno peggad, 2] panglisi ti basol wenno uyaw isu nga agrasrason wenno agfilfilosofo

Defer *v.*, **Deferment** *n.* 1] ipagpaliban, 2] respetong pag-ayon; Iloc: 1] itantan, 2] respeto-*Sp* a pag-annugot

Deference *(Tag. & Iloc.)* cortesia-*Sp* at respeto-*Sp*

Deferment pagpapaliban, pag-aantala; Iloc: taktak, tantan

Defiance *n.*, **Defiant** *adj.* pag-protesta-*Sp* o pag-contra-*Sp* sa otoridad-*Sp* o sa nilabas na plano-*Sp* o paksa o paraan

Deficiency kakulangan; Iloc: kakurangan

Deficient kulang; Iloc: kurang

DEFICIT kakulangan; Iloc: kakurangan

DEFICIT spending paggastos hindi mula sa buis kundi sa pangungutang

Defile dungisan; Iloc: rugitan

Define ilarawan; Iloc: ipresentar ti nalawag nga itchura o ti napasamak (presentar-*Sp*, itchura-*Sp*)

Definite claro-*Sp* at exactong pagkalarawan; sigradong-sigurado

Definitive nagsisilbing pagpaliwanag, pagpasya o sa wakas ay sa pagkasundoan o pakipag-ayosan, makarating sa *conclusion*; 2] pinakamapagkakatiwalaan, naaasahan, pinakamaotoridad, pinakacompleto,

Deflate *v.*, **Deflation** *n.* 1] palabasin ang hangin o gas sa bola-*Sp*, 2] paliitin ang laki o importancia-*Sp*

Deflect *v.*, **Deflection** *n.* 1] lumihis sa caraniwang paraan o matuwid na rason o daanan; 2] yumukoo tumagilid

Deforest magkaingin o tanggalin ang mga punong-kahoy

Deform ngiwiin, sirain ang anyo o hugis o forma-*Sp*, baluktotin; Iloc: diwwigen, kiwingen, dadaelen o perdien ti langa o forma

Deformed ngiwi; Iloc: kiwing

Defraud estafa-*Sp*, manguha ng cuarta sa panlilinlang, pagfafalsifica, panlinlang, panloloco, pandaraya; Iloc: estafa, mangala ti cuarta iti panggugulib, mangloco, pag-allilaw, agfalsificar, pangcusit

Defray taya, magtagabayad; Iloc: taya, tagabayad ti gastos

Defrost ilabas sa *freezer* bago lutoin at patunawin ang lamig na kumapit na yelo-*Sp*; Iloc: iruar diay *freezer* baro lutwen ken patunawen ti lamiis nga kimpet a yelo

Defunct nawalan na ng buhay, wala na; Iloc: immawanen iti biag, awanen

Defy labagin, mag-rebelde-*Sp*; Iloc: cariten, agrebelde

Degenerate naging masama o labis na bumaba mula sa *normal* o mula sa mabuting kalagayan ng katawan, isip, etika o alituntunin ng moralidad; Iloc: bimmaba o kimmapoy o dimmakes ti kasasaad

Degrade bumaba ang grado-*Sp* o ranko-*Sp* o estado-*Sp* o halaga; bumaba mula sa *normal* dahil sa kalumaan o sa kalawang

DEGREE patag, grado, ranko, sukat, tindi; Iloc: patag, grado, ranko, rukod, pigsa, caro

DEGREE, college ang curso-*Sp* na napagtapusan sa universidad-*Sp* o colehio-*Sp*

College degrees -

Associate degree ang dalawang taong curso na natamo sa *junior college* na puedeng ipagpatuloy para sa apat na taong curso

Bachelors degree pagcompleto ng *undergraduate curriculum* o apat na taong pag-aaral na tinapos sa colehio o universidad

Masters degree pag-aaral lampas pa sa *bachelors degree*; Iloc: pagadal a mas nangato ngem iti *bachelors degree*

Post graduate pag-aaral na lampas pa sa *bachelors degree*; Iloc: pagadal a nalabes pay iti *bachelors degree*

Doctorate degree pagcompleto ng *doctorate degree* na lampas pa sa *masters degree*

Post doctoral pag-aral na lampas pa sa *doctorate degree*; Iloc: pagadal nga nalabes pay ngem iti *doctorate degree*

Dehydrated nawalan ng kinakailangang tubig sa katawan ng tao o ng halaman; Iloc: naawanan iti kasapulan a danum iti bagi ti tao wenno iti tanem

Deign mag-isip ng nakakaangkop o alinsunod sa canyang dignidad-*Sp*; magpakumbaba

Deity *(Tag. & Iloc.)* pagka-Dios-*Sp*

Dejected nasira ang lakas ng loob na magsagawa; nasira ang confiansa-*Sp* sa sarili at sa canyang kacayahan; Iloc: nadadael ti tured nga agobra; nadadael ti confiansa na iti bagi ken cabaelan na

Delay antalahin, ipagpaliban, nagpapaluwat; Iloc: itaktak, taktaken, itantan, ibaybayag

Delayed *(Tag. & Iloc.)* atrasado-*Sp*

Delectable masarap; Iloc: naimas

DELEGATE *n.* taong tinakda o hinirang na gumanap na representante-*Sp* nila na gaganap ng katungkulan at kapangyarihan dito

DELEGATE work ipagawa o isugo ang trabaho-*Sp* sa iba; Iloc: ipaaramid ti trabaho iti sabali a tao

Delete *v.,* **Deletion** *n.* caltasin, tanggalin, alisin, borahin; Iloc: ikkaten, boraen (bora-*Sp*)

Deliberate sinadya, kusa; Iloc: inggagara

Delicate *(Tag. & Iloc.)* delicado-*Sp*

Delicious masarap, katakam-takam; Iloc: naimas

Delight in nawiwili; Iloc: aglinglingay

Delightful kinawiwilihan, kinagigiliwan; Iloc: aglinglingay

Delineate 1] kinocopia o binabakas ang *outline*; nilalarawan sa ginuhit; 2] nilalarawan sa salita; nagsasalin/*translate* ng husto at kasali pa ang detalye-*Sp*

Delinquent delinquente-*Sp*, pumapalya sa obligasyon-*Sp* na magbayad ng canyang utang; Iloc: delinquente, haan na tungpalen ti obligasyon-*Sp* na nga bayadan iti utang na

Delirious nagde-delirio-*Sp*, nahihibang; Iloc: agam-amangaw, agdeldelirio

Deliver magdala; Iloc: mangipan
> *Correlated word*
> **Bring** dalhin, magdala, maghatid; Iloc: iyeg, mangipan, mangikuyog

Delivery *delivery,* pagdadala ng bagay sa patutungohan; Iloc: *delivery,* pangipan ti banag idiay pagturongan na

Delude 1] linlangin ang isip o *judgment*/panghusga; 2] bigoin ang inaasahang resulta o ang pag-asa

Deluge, Flood baha, diluvio-*Sp*; Iloc: layos, diluvio

Delusion matinding maling-akala; Iloc: allilaw ti nakem a napalalo

Delusions of grandeur guni-guni sa sarili na siya ay napakadakila o may karapatan sa mga bagay-bagay na sa Ingles ay *sense of entitlement* kahit hindi siya *entitled*

Deluxe *(Tag. & Iloc.)* elegante-*Sp* at ma-luho-*Sp*
> *Correlated word*
> **Luxury** *(Tag. & Iloc.)* luho

Demagogue, Demagoguery taong politico-*Sp* na nakakatamo ng popularidad-*Sp* sa pamamagitan ng pakikipag-ugnay niya sa emosyon-*Sp* at kagustohan ng mga tao, at pagma-manipulasyon-*Sp* gaya ng pakikipag-ugnay niya sa *prejudice* ng mga tao

Demand demanda-*Sp*, sapilitang mando-*Sp*; Iloc: demanda, mandar-*Sp* nga ipilit a tungpalen

Demarcate markahan ang hangganan ng pag-aaring lupa; Iloc: markaan ti patinggana ti minoyongan o solar-*Sp* na
Correlated word
Boundary landmark *(Tag. & Iloc.)* mohon-*Sp*

Demeanor asal, galaw, kilos, ugali; Iloc: garaw, ugali, gunay, tignay

Demerit markahan ng mababa ang tao dahil sa masama niyang asal, at mga pagkukulang at pagpalya niya; napupunang kasalanan at kaparusahan na kinakailan ng *censure*

Demijohn dambuhalang botelya-*Sp* na gawa sa cristal-*Sp* o kaya finormang putik na tumigas; Iloc: damajuana-*Sp*

Democracy *(Tag. & Iloc.)* democrasia-*Sp*

Demographic pag-aaral tungkol sa populasyon-*Sp* ng comunidad-*Sp* hinggil sa kanilang gawi, estado-*Sp*, pagsilang at pagdami ng tao, pagaasawa, sakit, pagkamatay at iba pa na may kinalaman sa canilang pagiging *consumers* at paggastos; Iloc: pagadal iti populasyon ti comunidad maypanggep ti ug-ugali da, estado, pagpasngay ken pagadu iti tao, pati pagcasar-*Sp*, sakit, pagkapatay da ken sabali pay tapno maamoan ti pagka-*consumers* da o ti paggatgatang ken paggastos da

Demolish gibain, guhoin; Iloc: rakraken, rebbaen, ipamarba

Demon *(Tag. & Iloc.)* demonio-*Sp*, satanas-*Sp*, diantre-*Sp*, diablo-*Sp*

Demonstrate ipakita, ipamalas, itanghal; Iloc: i-presentar-*Sp*, ipakita

Demonstration *(Tag. & Iloc.)* demonstrasyon-*Sp*

Demoralize sirain ang lakas ng loob na magsagawa o magsikap; sirain ang confiansa-*Sp* sa sarili at sa canyang kacayahan; Iloc: dadaelen ti tured nga ag-obra-*Sp* ken agpakat; dadaelen ti confiansa iti bagi na ken cabaelan na

Demote *(Tag. & Iloc.)* ibaba ang/ti rangko-*Sp* o puesto-*Sp*

Demure mayumi, mahinhin; Iloc: naemma

DENIAL pagtanggi, pagkaila; Iloc: paglibak

DENIAL, in nagmamaang-maangan at hindi niya tanggapin ang kasalanan niya kundi isisi ang mga ito sa iba't ibang pagdadahilan - ito ay dahil hindi siya nagtuturing ng sariling responsibilidad niya at *accountability* niya sa canyang mga kamalian niya.

Denim *(Tag. & Iloc.) denim,* maong

Denote ipahiwatig; Iloc: ipaammo

Denounce lantad at bukasang isumpa o laitin sa harap ng publico-*Sp*; ihabla o paratangan sa corte-*Sp* ng husticia-*Sp* o sa *police*; Iloc: laisen ken idadanes diay sango iti publico wenno diay sango ti husticia o *police*

Dense macapal; Iloc: napuskol

Density pagkacapal; Iloc: pagkapuskol

Dent kaunting lubog gaya sa mahinang pagkabunggo; Iloc: lennek
   Correlated words
   Dint, Ding kaunting lubog gaya sa mahinang pagkabunggo Iloc: bassit a lennek
   Warped nayupi; Iloc: nacuppit

Dental tungkol sa ngipin; Iloc: maypanggep ti ngipen

Dentist *(Tag. & Iloc.) dentist,* dentista-*Sp*

Denture *(Tag. & Iloc.)* postiso-*Sp*

Deny hindi aminin, magtanggi, ipagkaila, pabulaanan; Iloc: aglibak, ilibak

Deodorize *v.,* **Deodorizer** *n.* pagtanggal ng mabaho; Iloc: pagikkat iti bangsit

Depart aalis, luluwas, papanaw, lilisan; Iloc: pumanaw ag-larga-*Sp*

Department departamento-*Sp*, kawanihan, sangay; Iloc: departamento

Departure paglisan, pagpanaw, pagluwas, pag-alis; Iloc: pagpanaw

Depend depende-*Sp*, nakasalalay, segun-*Sp*; Iloc: depende, conforme-*Sp*, segun

Dependent *adj.,* **Dependence** *n.* nagdedepende sa tulong ng iba; Iloc: agdepdepende iti tulong ti sabali

Depict ilarawan; Iloc: iladawan

Deplete kumokonti, nababawasan, lumiliit; Iloc: bumasbassit, kumiskissay

Deplore nananaghoy, nananangis; sinisiwalat ang lungkot tungkol sa...; pagtutol, pagpintas

Deploy ipuesto, ihanda ang mga sandatahang sundalo para handang makilaban; Iloc: i-puesto-*Sp* ken i-preparar-*Sp* dagiti soldado-*Sp* nga armado-*Sp* tapno nakasagana da a makilaban

Deport palayasin dahil sa paglabag ng batas ng bansa (gaya ng crimen) kaya pabalikin siya sa bayang pinanggalingan niya; Iloc: papanawen gapu ti pagsupyat na iti linteg ti nasyon (casla iti crimen) isu nga pagsublien da isuna idiay pinaggapuan na a nasyon

Deportation *(Tag. & Iloc.)* deportasyon-*Sp*

Depose *v.*, **Deposition** *n.* 1] tanggalin sa oficina-*Sp* o sa puesto-*Sp*; 2] magsumpa para ibigay ang testigo-*Sp* lalo na sa kasulatan

Deposit mag-deposito-*Sp* ng pera sa banko-*Sp*; Iloc: agdeposito ti cuarta

Depot 1] stasyon-*Sp* ng tren-*Sp* o bus, 2] bodega-*Sp* ng militar-*Sp* na pinaglalagyan ng kanilang mga panlabang armas-*Sp*

Deprave *v.*, **Depravation** or **Depravity** *n.* gawaing napakamalaswa o pagkademonyong sama, kawalan ng moralidad-*Sp*; *corrupt*

Depreciate *v.*, **Depreciation** *n.* pagbaba ng precio-*Sp* o halaga; Iloc: pagbaba ti precio ken valor-*Sp*

Depress palungkotin, papighatiin, bigoin, lumbayin

Depression 1] kapansanan sa emosyon na kung saan hindi makaacecaso ng husto sa mga dapat acecasohin at hindi makatulog o walang ganang kumain, nalulungkot, nawalan na ng pag-asa, gustong saktan ang canyang sarili, 2] lugar na lubak o mas mababa kaysa sa kapaligiran 3] pagbaba ng economiya dahil sa hindi mabungang negocio, pagbaba ng mga precio at maraming hindi naka-empleo *(all Sp:* emosyon, husto, economiya, negosio, precio, gana, gusto, lugar, empleo)

Deprive hindi ibigay ang nararapat sa isang tao - ipagcait at pagdamutan ng angkop sa taong kinararapatan; Iloc: haan nga ited ti rebbeng iti maysa a tao, mangpaidam, ipaidam o imutan iti mismo a nayrebbeng iti piman pay a tao

Depth sukat ng pagkalalim; ang kalalimlaliman; Iloc: rukod ti pagkaadalem; iti kaadalem-daleman
Correlated word
Breadth sukat ng kalaparan, pagkalapad; Iloc: rukod ti kaacaba, pagkaacaba

Deputy *(Tag. & Iloc.)* diputado-*Sp*

Derail nalihis sa riles-*Sp* ang tren-*Sp* na puedeng mayroon o walang napinsala

Deregulation tanggalin ang reglamento o *government regulatory control* na nakatatag

Derelict *adj.,* **Dereliction** *n.* kusang paglayas o pag-iwan sa obligasyon-*Sp* o sa principio-*Sp*

Deride *v.,* **Derision** *n.* katuwaang panunuya para pagtawanan ang victima-*Sp*; Iloc: ay-ayam a sutil tapno pagkakatawaan da tay victima

Derivative anomang natamo o nakamtan buhat sa pinagmulan

Derived from hango sa, galing sa; Iloc: aggapu diay, nagtaud idiay

Dermal tungkol sa balat; Iloc: maygapu ti cudil

Derogate *v.,* **Derogatory** *adj.* minamaliit, panghamak, laitin; pagmemenos, panglait, paninira

Descend bumaba, pumanaog; Iloc: bumaba, umulog, sumalog
Antonym
Ascend mag-akyat; Iloc: ngumato, agsang-at, umuli

Descendant mga supling, anak, apo; Iloc: dagiti annak ken appo na
Correlated words
Ancestors ninuno; Iloc: poon
Ancestry kanuno-nunohan; Iloc: poon, kaputot-putotan

Descent pababa; Iloc: agsalog, agpababa

Describe ilarawan ang itchura-*Sp* o pangyayari; Iloc: i-presentar-*Sp* a nalawag ti itchura-*Sp* wenno iti napasamak

Descriptive *adj.,* **Description** *n.* ang paglalarawan sa sinasabi sa salita o sa sulat

Desecrate manglapastangan sa mga sagradong imahen at paniwala

Desensitize *v.,* **Desensitizer** *n.* pampamanhid; Iloc: pangbibineg para haan makaricna

DESERT lugar na mabuhangin na tigang at mainit ang clima at walang makitang tubig na maiinom, ni halaman at kahoy na tumutubo maliban lamang sa *cactus*; Iloc: panay darat a lugar a napudot ken namaga nga awan makita a danum nga mainom, ni tanem wenno cayo nga agtubtubo malaksid laeng iti *cactus (Desert should not to be mistaken for Dessert)*

DESERT (someone or something) takasan, layasan, iwanan; Iloc: talawan, baybay-an
Antonym
Remain mamalagi, manatili; Iloc: agbati, agtalinaed, agfirmi ti sigud a lugar

Deserve nakakarapatan, naaangkop; Iloc: gunggona, naysaad, rebbeng, umno

Synonyms

Worthy karapat-dapat, nararapat; Iloc: umno, rebbeng

Merit naaangkop, nakararapat, karapat-dapat; Iloc: gunggona, naykarian, naysaad, umno

Design *(Tag. & Iloc.)* *design,* disenyo-*Sp*

Designate hirangin, ihirang, italaga, i-puesto-*Sp*; Iloc: i-designar-*Sp*, ipuesto

Desire kagustohan, nais, hangad, mithi; Iloc: gusto, essem, tarigagay, calicagum, cayat

Desist maghinto, tumigil; Iloc: agsardeng

Desolate lugar na walang katao-tao, abandonado-*Sp*

Despair *n.,* **Desperate** *adj.* desperado-*Sp*, nawalan ng pag-asa o *hope*; Iloc: desperado, naawanan ti namnama o *hope*

Despicable kasuklam-suklam, napakasama; Iloc: makadisgusto, nakadakdakes

Despise laitin, pintasan, kamuhian; Iloc: laisen, uyawen, kagurgura

Despite kahit na, maski pa; Iloc: uray nu, uray pay

Dessert *dessert,* himagas, matamis na kinakain pagkatapos ng *meal* o *regular* na kainan; Iloc: *dessert,* nasasam-it nga kanen palpas ti regular-*Sp* nga pannangan

Destabilize pagpapalit/*change* o paninira ng kalaban para ang mabuting takbo ng bayan o companya ay masira o huminto; Iloc: pagbalbaliw o pagdadael ti kalaban tapno ti nasayaat nga operasyon ti nasyon o companya ket agsardeng o maperdi

Destine *v.,* **Destiny** *n.* naitadhana o naitalaga para sa layonin o kapalaran

Destination destinasyon-*Sp*, patutungohan, puntahan; Iloc: destinasyon, pagturongan, papanan

Destiny destino-*Sp*, kapalaran, hantungan; Iloc: destino, gasat, pagtungpalan

Destitute *(Tag. & Iloc.)* pobre-*Sp*

Destroy sirain, wasakin; Iloc: dadaelen, perdien, rauten, mang-perdi-*aSp*, agraut

Destructive makakasira, maka-disgracia-*Sp*, mapanganib; Iloc: maka-disgracia, maka-perdi-*aSp*, makadadael

Correlated words

Harmful makapinsala, puedeng nakakamatay, nakakasama; Iloc: makasakit, mabalin a makapatay, makadakes

Injurious makasugat, makasakit; Iloc: makasugat, makadunor, makasakit

Bane nakakasugat o nakakasira o nakakapatay o nakakaproblema o nakakagambala o nakakahadlang

Dangerous mapanganib, peligroso, makapinsala; Iloc: napeggad, peligroso

Detach something bakbakin, tuklapin; Iloc: lekkaben, latlaten

Detail *(Tag. & Iloc.)* detalye-*Sp*
Correlated words
Nitty-gritty *(Tag. & Iloc.)* ang diwa, mga detalye
Ins and outs mga detalye ng ano mang bagay-bagay o pangyayari

Detain temporaryong iculong at pagbawalang lumabas; Iloc: temporario-*Sp* nga ipupok/iculong ken igawid

Detect mahalata, mapansin, mapuna; Iloc: maductalan, masucalan

Detention panatiliin na bilanggo at pagbawalang lumabas; Iloc: ipagtalinaed diay preso-*Sp* ken iparit nga rumuar

Deter hadlangan; Iloc: lappedan

Detergent sabong pan-laba-*Sp*; Iloc: sabon a panlaba

Deteriorate humihina, rumurupok, sumasama, lumalala, lumulubha na, pasira na; Iloc: kumapcapsot, agrukrukop, dumakdakes, kumarkaro, lumallalo, madaddadaelen

Determination *(Tag. & Iloc.)* determinasyon-*Sp*

Determined determinado-*Sp*, masigasig, marubdob, decidido-*Sp*; Iloc: determinado, decidido

Deterrent panghadlang; Iloc: panglapped

Detest nasusuklam; Iloc: kabusbusor

Detestable nakakasuklam, nakakamuhi, nakakadisgusto; Iloc: makapagura, nakabusbusor

Detour lumihis, magtaliwas; Iloc: naglisi, umadayo

Detox panggamot para matanggal ang lason sa katawan gaya ng sa alak o sa droga-*Sp*

Detrimental makapasira o makapabagal o makapahinto o makabigay ng sama; Iloc: makadadael o makapabayag o makapasardeng o makapadakes

Devalue tanggalin o bawasan ang halaga; Iloc: ikkaten o kissayan iti valor-*Sp*

Develop magyabong o tumubo o sumulong sa pagbuo; sumisibol sa patutunguhang pagkatao o kahihinatnan na puedeng ito ay sa pagkabuti

o pagkasama; Iloc: agrang-ay o agrusing o agtubo iti pagbalinan iti pagkatao na nu dayta ket pagimbagan wenno pagdaksan
Correlated word
Evolve nagbabago at kadalasan ay bumubuti habang dumadaan ang panahon; Iloc: agbalbaliw ken canayon ket agsay-sayaat mientras nga agpaspasar ti panawen

Deviant ibang-iba sa sa caraniwang asal ng sociedad-*Sp*; Iloc: nakasabsabali iti sigud ugali iti sociedad

Deviate lumihis, tumaliwas o umiba sa caraniwang gawa o patungohan; Iloc: lisyan, sabalyan ti sigud nga aramid o pagturongan

Device 1] bagay o makina-*Sp* o aparato-*Sp* na nakakagawa ng isa o mahigit pang simpleng trabaho, 2] gumawa ng paraan kung paano maisagawa, 3] bomba, 4] manlinlang; Iloc: 1] banag o makina o aparato nga makaaramid ti maysa o mas adu pay a simple nga ob-obra-*Sp*, 2] agaramid ti padalan nu casano maaramid, 3] bomba, 4] manggulgulib

Devil *(Tag. & Iloc.)* demonio-*Sp*, satanas-*Sp*, diantre-*Sp*, diablo-*Sp*

Devious hindi tapat kundi nagpapaligoy-ligoy sa pag-iwas na ipahayag ang katotohanan; Iloc: haan a pudno nu di agpalpalusot iti paglisi iti pagsawang iti kaagpaysuan

Devoid wala, sin-*Sp*, ni-*Sp*, ni isa; Iloc: awan, sin, ni, ni maysa

Devote i-ukol ang oras at pansin at sarili at gawa para sa matimtimang paniwala sa isang doctrina o para sa tinakdang layonin; Iloc: ipaay ti oras ken estimar ken bagi ken aramid para iti nauneg a pammati iti doctrina wenno para iti naikeddeng a rangta

Devotee, Devotion *(Tag. & Iloc.)* devoto-*Sp*, devosyon-*Sp*

Dew tulo ng hamog; Iloc: tedted ti linnaaw
Correlated word
Moisture hamog; Iloc: linnaaw

Diabolical *(Tag. & Iloc.)* obra o asal o salita o bagay na makademonyo o maka-satanas

Diagnose pagsusuri sa uri ng sakit at pinagmulan ng sakit; Iloc: panangusig iti clase ti sakit ken poon ti sakit

Diagram *sketch*/guhit, *outline*/balanghas at plano na nagpapakita ng forma-*Sp* at paraan ng paggawa sa isang *project*

Dialect isa sa mga maraming wika o lengguahe-*Sp* ng isang lugar-*Sp* o bayan, ciudad-*Sp*, provincia-*Sp* wenno nasyon-*Sp*; Iloc: maysa iti adu a sarita wenno lengguahe iti maysa a lugar, ili, ciudad, provincia wenno nasyon

Synonym

Vernacular katutubo o sariling wika ng isla o ng *region* o provincia o ng bayan; Iloc: bukbukod a sarita iti isla, ti *region*, ti provincia wenno iti ili wenno nasyon

Diamond *(Tag. & Iloc.)* diamante-*Sp*, brilyante-*Sp*

Diaper *(Tag. & Iloc.)* *diaper*, lampin

Diarrhea nagtatae, kurso; Iloc: *diarrhea*, agtakki, agburis

Dicey puno ng peligro-*Sp* o panganib; Iloc: napunno ti peligro wenno peggad

Dictate mag-dicta-*Sp*; Iloc: ag-dictar-*Sp*

Dictator *(Tag. & Iloc.)* dictador-*Sp*

Dictionary *(Tag. & Iloc.)* diksionaryo-*Sp*

Didactic palaturo / palasermon; Iloc: parasermon / parasuro

DIE mamatay, matodas; Iloc: matay

DIE-hard nakakapit ng husto sa kinahuhumalingan o sa paniwala; Iloc: nakacumpet nga usto iti mapuspusoan na o iti pammati na

Diet *(Tag. & Iloc.)* *diet*, dieta-*Sp*

Dietetics pag-aaral ng pagkain at *nutrition*; Iloc: pagadal iti makmakan ken *nutrition*

Differ kaiba, hindi pareho-*Sp*; Iloc: duma, haan pareho

Difference pagkakaiba, kaibhan; Iloc: pagkadumaan, pagsabalyan

Different iba, kakaiba, magkaiba; Iloc: sabali, agsinnabali, agduma

Synonym

Far cry kaibang-kaiba sa pinagcocomparaan o pinagbabasehang bagay o tao

Differentiate ituring ang pagkakaiba ng mga bagay; Iloc: bigbigen ti pagkasabalyan dagiti bambanag

Difficult mahirap; Iloc: narigat

Difficulty kahirapan; Iloc: karigatan

Diffident *adj.*, **Diffidence** *n.* mahiyain, kimi, umid; Iloc: managbabain, naulimek, naemma, mikki

DIG with hands magducal; Iloc: agcutcot

DIG with a tool hukayin, dungcalin; Iloc: agcali, calyen

Digest *v.*, **Digestion** *n.* pagtunaw ng pagkain sa bituka; Iloc: pagtunaw iti kinnan idiay bituka

Dignified may dignidad at dangal dahil siya ay nabubuhay ng maetico at may moralidad at mapagkakatiwalaan na hindi siya lalabag sa batas at sa tamang asal

Dignitary *(Tag. & Iloc.)* dignitaryo-*Sp*, taong may mataas na katungkulan

Dignity *(Tag. & Iloc.)* dignidad-*Sp*

Digress sa pagsasalita o pagsusulat, siya ay nalilihis o napapalayo sa pinakamahalagang paksa o layonin

Dilate palakihan, palaparin; buksan o idilat ang mata; Iloc: padakkelen, lucatan iti mata

Dilemma napakahirap o nakakalito na situasyon-*Sp* o problema-*Sp*; situasyon-*Sp* na kailangang mamili sa dalawang parehong hindi kalugod-lugod o hindi kasiya-siya na pagpipilian

Diligent *Industrious, assiduous, persistently and painstakingly working, dynamically busy in accomplishing a task or a purpose.* Masipag, masigasig; Iloc: nagaget, trabahador-*Sp*

Dilute pahinain, haloan, tubigan; Iloc: pacapsuten, laokan, danuman

Diluted malabnaw, matubig; Iloc: nalabnaw, nalasaw

Dim kulimlim, madilim-dilim; Iloc: nasipnget, nalidem

Dimension laki at luwang; sukat ng haba, lapad at kapal

Diminish kumokonti, nababawasan, paliitin; Iloc: bumasbassit, kumiskissay

Diminutive munti; Iloc: balabattit

DIMPLE on cheeks biloy; Iloc: callid

DIMPLE on chin or jaw *(Tag. & Iloc.)* lubo

Dimwitted *(Tag. & Iloc.)* torpe-*Sp*, loco-loco-*Sp*, gago/ga-*Sp*, bobo-*Sp*, tanga, gunggong

Din ingay; Iloc: ariwawa, ringgor, tagari, riri

Dine kumain ng hapunan, kumain sa eleganteng *restaurant*; Iloc: mangan ti pangrabii wenno diay elegante nga *restaurant*

Dinner pinakamabigat na kainan na puedeng sa tanghali o gabi; bankete-*Sp* o formal-*Sp* na kainan para sa parangal sa isang tao

Dint, Ding kaunting lubog gaya sa mahinang pagkabunggo; Iloc: bassit a lennek gapu ti bunggo

Dip 1] sawsawan, salsa-*Sp*, 2] sumisid at sandaling maglangoy sa *pool*, 3] gulod; Iloc: 1] sawsawan, sarsa-*aSp*, 2] agbatok ken apagbiit nga aglangoy diay *pool*, 3] darisdis

DIPLOMA *(Tag. & Iloc.) diploma*

DIPLOMA mill madaya o mababang claseng institusyon na nagbibigay ng *diploma* para sa isang *degree* ng educasyon-*Sp* sa canilang estudiante-*Sp* kahit hindi naman calificado-*Sp* sila at hindi nararapat na magka-*diploma* dahil hindi sapat ang napag-aralan nila dito

Diplomacy *Knowledge in managing and negotiating with people in a polite, tactful, formal and official way to prevent alienation*

Diplomatic *Fraternize in a good-natured, peace-making, tactful, and statesmanship way to initiate cooperation and brotherhood.* May diplomacia-*Sp* o etiqueta-*Sp*; mabuting asal makihalobilo; maingat makibagay at marespeto-*Sp* maki-ugnay sa kapwa; Iloc: adda diplomacia, etiqueta ken nasayaat iti gunggonay na; naannad ken narespeto a makicadwa ken makibagay iti tattao

Dipper sandok; tabu-*Sp* na paglagyan ng tubig para sa pagpawpaw o *hygiene* ng babae; Iloc: aklo; tabu nga pagtaco ti danum para ti pagpawpaw o *hygiene* ti babai

Dire, **Direly** nakakasanhi ng malaking pangamba, takot o pagdurusa; nagpapahiwatig ng problema-*Sp*, kapahamakan, kasamaang-palad; desperado-*Sp*, at kailangan ang madaliang paglutas

DIRECT, Guide magpatnubay; ituro kung paano gawin o kung saan ang daan; Iloc: mangpaturong; isuro nu casano ti mangpamay-an wenno nu inchenna ti dalan

DIRECT, Straight *(Tag. & Iloc.)* derecho-*Sp*

Direction direksion-*Sp*, tungohan, papunta kung saang daco; Iloc: direksion, pagturongan

Directive *(Tag. & Iloc.)* bilin *(See Last Will & Testament, Living Will or Advanced (Medical) Directive and Informed Medical Consent)*

Director patnubay; Iloc: mangiturturong

Dirt dungis, dumi, batik; Iloc: rugit, mureng, dungrit

DIRTY *adj.* marumi, madungis; Iloc: narugit, namureng, nadungrit, nadugyot

DIRTY *v.* dungisan, dumihan, batikan; Iloc: dungritan, rugitan

DIRTY habits salaula, kadiri kagawian; Iloc: makaaryek a rugit a cadawyan na; cochino-*Sp*

DIRTY laundry mga *personal* na bagay na maging kahihiyan kung nalaman ito ng publico; Iloc: dagiti *personal* a banag a nakababain nu maamuan ti publico-*Sp* daytoy

Disable nagpapahina o sumira ng capabilidad-*Sp* o cacayahan na puedeng sanhi ng labanan o accidente-*Sp*

Disability *n.,* **Disabled** *adj. (Tag. & Iloc.)* nasalanta o paralisado o inutil sa katawan o parte ng katawan; baldado-*Sp,* paralisado-*Sp,* paralitico-*Sp*

DISADVANTAGE ang makakabigat o makakasama o makaagraviado-*Sp*; Iloc: ti makadagsen o makadakes o makaagraviado

DISADVANTAGE, at a *(Tag. & Iloc.)* agraviado-*Sp*

Disagree magtutol, magsalungat, mag-contra-*Sp*; Iloc: agsupyat, agsalangad, madi nga umannugot, agcontra
Correlated words
Contradict contrahin; Iloc: mangcontra
Dissenter, Dissident mangprotesta, mangcontra; Iloc: mangprotesta, mangcontra

Disappear mawala; Iloc: agawan, umawan
Synonym
Vanish maglaho, mapawi; Iloc: agpukaw
Antonym
Appear lumitaw, sumulpot, magpakita, sumipot, umahon; Iloc: agparang, agpakita sumanglad, ngumato, lumtaw

Disappoint bucohin, idismaya, hindi pagbigyan; Iloc: ibuco, idismaya, di pagustoan

Disappointed dismayado-*Sp,* nasira ang gana-*Sp,* tumamlay, nasawi, nabigo, nanlumo; Iloc: dismayado, nadadael ti ganas-*Sp,* nagtamnay

Disapprove hindi aprobahan, ipawalang saysay; Iloc: haan nga aprobaran (aproba/aprobar-*Sp*)

Disarrange gulohin, i-desareglo-*Sp*; Iloc: culcolen, idesareglo

Disarray calat, magulo; Iloc: nawara

Disassemble tangga-tanggalin, hiwa-hiwalayin, iwatak-watak; Iloc: pagsinasinaen, watak-wataken

Disassembled *(Tag. & Iloc.)* watak-watak

Disaster calamidad-*Sp*, kapahamakan; disgracia-*Sp*; Iloc: calamidad, disgracia

Disavow pinahayag na wala siyang alam o kinalaman; Iloc: prinoclemar nga haan na ammo o awan ammo na

Disband malansag, mabuwag o maglaho ang organisasyon-*Sp*; magkawasak at magkahiwa-hiwalay

Disbelieve hindi naniniwala; Iloc: haan a mamati

Disburse ibigay ang bayad; Iloc: ited ti bayad

Discard itapon; Iloc: ibelleng

Discern *v.,* **Discernment** *n.* matanglaw at maliwanag na pag-aninaw sa kapwa at mga pangyayari; matalas ang utak sa pagtanto, matinding pagkaalam at pagkatanto; Iloc: nasirib ti nakem nga makaamiris, napigsa nga pagkaammo ken maamiris
Correlated words
Precognition pagka-makinikinita, sagimsim; Iloc: amiris
Detect mahalata, mapansin; Iloc: masucalan, maductalan
Predict nakikini-kinita ang dadating; Iloc: maamiris iti mapasamak iti sumangpet nga aldaw
Perceive nakikinita, naiintindihan, nakikilala, nalalaman, natuturing, natatanto, nararamdaman, nahuhuna; Iloc: maamiris, maawatan, am-ammo, mabigbig, maricna, maylasin
Perspicacious matalas ang utak na siya ay nakakatanto; Iloc: nasirib ti nakem nga makaamiris isu
Shrewd matalino at matanto niya ang kalagayan o katatao ng iba; Iloc: nasirib ken maamiris na ti kasasaad wenno kababalin ti tao
Intuition *n.,* **Intuitive** *adj.* agad-agad at matalas na pakiramdam o paningin ng mga katunayan kahit hindi maipaliwanag ng rason o *reasoning*

Discernible nakikita, nawawari, nakikilala; Iloc: makitkita, mabigbig, maricricna

Discharge 1] palabas na agos, 2] palabasin sa culongan, 3] tanggalin sa trabaho; Iloc: 1] agayos a rumuar, 2] parwaren diay preso, 3] i-cesante-*Sp* isu idiay trabaho

Disciple *(Tag. & Iloc.)* dicipulo-*Sp*

Discipline *Before disciplining a child, the parent needs to explain the reason for the punishment. For ages 1 to 5, they are disciplined only after the third same misbehavior, and if it continues, timeouts are usually the way to discipline very young children to let them know*

the result of misbehaviors. Timeout is having the child sit alone in a corner facing it with no toys or anything with him/her, and the length of time may be from 1 minute to 5 with younger kids given the shortest time. For older children, take away things that are near and dear to them like stuffed animals, toys or cell phones. If earlier discipline fell on deaf ears, take those favorite items again, but this time on a longer time. Having the kids <u>redo</u> the misbehavior <u>this time to a good, kind way or to more friendly words</u> will also teach them the right ways to behave from then on. For teen-agers, <u>talking to them and reminding them now and then</u> about moral and ethical values will help in directing their path in life.

Disclaimer pang-alertong noticia-*Sp* o pahayag na wala silang pananagutan o coneksion-*Sp* sa resulta-*Sp* ng producto-*Sp* o contrata-*Sp*; Iloc: pang-alerto-*Sp* a noticia o mang-proclemar-*Sp* nga isuda ket awan responsibilidad-*Sp* da iti resulta ti producto o contrata

Disclose *v.,* **Disclosure** *n.* ipagtapat, isiwalat, ibunyag, ihayag; Iloc: isawang, ipaammo

Discolor magpusyaw; Iloc: agali

Discomfit litoin, ligaligin o gawing di mapakali; hadlangang makagawa

Discomfort hindi comfortab-le-*Sp* sa isip o sa pakiramdam o sa katawan; Iloc: haan a comfortab-le ti nakem o ti ricna wenno ti bagi

Disconcert *see Discomfit above*

DISCONNECT-*verb* i-disconecta-*Sp*, tanggalin ang coneksion-*Sp*, putolin ang dugtong; Iloc: putden ti coneksion, i-disconecta, putden ti silpo

DISCONNECT-*noun* pagkawala ng kasunduan at comunicasyon-*Sp* dahil hindi magkaintindihan o magkaiba sila sa pag-iisip; Iloc: pagkaawan ti nag-ayonan a tulag ken comunicasyon gapu ta haan da agkaawatan ken agsinnabali ti panunot da

Disconsolate parang hindi makaraos sa pighati o pananakit ng loob; Iloc: casla haan maka-pasar-*Sp* iti pagsagaba na wenno sakit ti nakem na

Discontent na-discontento-*Sp*, hindi contento-*Sp*; Iloc: nadiscontento, haan a contento

Discontinue itigil na; Iloc: isardengen

Discord nagsasalungatan, pagtatalo; Iloc: agsupsupyatan, pagsalangadan

Discount *(Tag. & Iloc.)* discuento-*Sp*

Discourage bigohin o sirain ang gana-*Sp* at balak na makapagkamit, bigoin ang loob; Iloc: patamnayen, i-dismaya-*Sp* o dadaelen ti ganas-*Sp* ken pakat nga makagun-od

Discourse *(Tag. & Iloc.)* discurso-*Sp*, conversasyon-*Sp*, comunicasyon-*Sp*, *lecture*, sermon-*Sp*

Discourteous *(Tag. & Iloc.)* bastos-*Sp*

Discover ma-discobre-*Sp*, matuklasan; Iloc: madiscobre, maductalan

Discredit 1] ayaw paniwalaan, 2] hindi pagkatiwalaan, 3] sirain ang reputasyon-*Sp*; Iloc: 1] madi na patchen, 2] haan na pagfiaran (fiar-*Sp*), 3] dadaelan na ti reputasyon

Discreet maingat; Iloc: naannad

Discrepancy ang pagkakaiba ng katotohanan at ang pinahayag; Iloc: ti pagsabalyan iti agpayso ken iti improclemar

Discretion *n.,* **Discretionary** *adj.* paggamit ng sariling pag-iisip at sariling pasya; Iloc: pagiyusar (usar-*Sp*) ti bagbagi a panunot ken desisyon-*Sp*

Discriminate *v.,* **Discrimination** *n.* imbes-*Sp* na parepareho ang turing sa lahat, may tinakdang pinapanigan o kinacampihan at mayroon namang binabalewala; Iloc: imbes nga parepareho ti pag-estimar-*Sp*, adda fabfaboran na ken adda met haan na pulos bigbigen wenno estimaren

Antonyms

Fair makatarungan, walang pinapanigan; Iloc: nalinteg, awan fabfaboran na
Impartial, Neutral walang kinacampihan, walang pinapanigan; Iloc: awan ti fabfaboran

Discriminating 1] mahusay ang pagtanto at nakikita ang katunayan at ang kaibahan at maingat sa paghatol, 2] fino-*Sp* ang mga pinipili; Iloc: 1] nalaeng nga agamiris ken makita na dagiti kaagpaysuan ken pagsabalyan ken naannad nga ag-husgar-*Sp*, 2] fino dagiti pilyen na

Discuss magtalakayan, magdiscusyonan; Iloc: agdiscusyonan, agpatang

Disease sakit, karamdaman; Iloc: sakit

Disembark umibis, bumaba; Iloc: agdissaag, dumsaag, bumaba

Disencumber paginhawain sa hirap; Iloc: pabang-aran para umawan ti rigat

Disenfranchise pagdamutan o ipagcait o hindi ibigay ang karapatan na mag-voto-*Sp*, privilehio-*Sp*, licensia-*Sp* sa tao, grupo-*Sp* o companya-*Sp*;

Iloc: imutan o ipaidam wenno haan nga ited iti linteg ken rebbeng nga agvoto, privilehio, licensia iti tao, grupo o companya

Disengage 1] kumalas sa pakikitungo, 2] tigilan ang pagpa-andar-*Sp*; Iloc: 1] sumina iti pagcacadwa, 2] isardeng ti pagpaandar

Disentangle magkalas sa pagkaconecta; calagan, i-alpas; Iloc: agwaya iti pagkaconecta; warwaren, lapso-lapsoten

Disfigure sirain ang anyo o hugis; Iloc: dadaelen ti itchura-*Sp* o forma-*Sp*

Disgrace kahihiyaan; Iloc: pagkababainan

Disguise balatkayo, *disguise*; Iloc: *disguise*

Disgust disgustohin; Iloc: i-disgusto-*Sp*

DISH *(Tag. & Iloc.)* pinggan, plato-*Sp*

DISH plate, big oblong *(Tag. & Iloc.)* bandehado-*Sp*

Disheartened nabigo ang loob, dismayado, nanlata; Iloc: nadadael o naperdi ti tured ken ganas na, dismayado

Dishonest hindi mapagkatiwalaan dahil sinungaling o nagnanakaw; Iloc: di mapagtalkan ta ulbod ken agtatakaw

Dishonor bastosin, lapastanganin; Iloc: bastosen, laisen

Disinclined hindi interesado dahil walang ganang gawin; Iloc: haan nga interesado gapu ta awan ganas na nga mangaramid

Disinfect disinfectahin, patayin ang microbio; Iloc: disinfectaran, patayen ti microbio

Disinherit tanggalin na tagapagmana para wala na siyang mamanahin; Iloc: ikkaten iti erencia-*Sp* para awanen iti matawid na

Disintegrate gumuho o magkadurog-durog; Iloc: ag-rumek

Dislike ayaw, hindi gusto; Iloc: haan nga cayat, haan a gusto, madi

Dislocate buto ng katawan na nalinsad o natanggal sa kabitan; Iloc: tulang ti bagi a naikkat diay pagkabitan

Disloyal hindi matapat sa kaibigan niya dahil chinichismis niya siya sa likod; Iloc: haan a pudno diay gayyem na gapu ta ichischismis na isu iti likod

Dismantle tangga-tanggalin, hiwa-hiwalayin; Iloc: pagsina-sinaen

Dismay na-dismaya-*Sp*, nasira ang gana-*Sp*; Iloc: nadismaya, na-perdi-*aSp* ti ganas-*Sp*

Dismember hiwa-hiwain o putol-putolin ang katawan gaya sa manok bago lutoin; Iloc: iwa-iwaen o putdeputden iti bagi casla iti manok baro lutwen

Dismiss 1] alisin sa tungkolin, cesantehin, itiwalag, despachahin, 2] pauwiin na, 3] limotin o iwaksi sa isip; 4] ipawalang-saysay; Iloc: 1] ikkaten diay puesto-*Sp* na iti trabaho-*Sp*, papanawen, despacharen, 2] pagawidenen, 3] lipaten wenno iwaksi iti panunot, 4] bigbigen nga awan valor-*Sp* na (cesante-*Sp*, despacha/despachar-*Sp*)

Dismissal time oras ng uwian; Iloc: oras ti pag-larga-*Sp*

Disobey magsuway, magsuwail; Iloc: agsupring, agsupyat, agsukir

Disobedient *adj.,* **Disobedience** *n.* mapagsuway, suwail; Iloc: sukir, mapagsupyat

Disorderly desareglado, magulo; Iloc: desareglado, magulo, naculcol

Disorganized desareglado-*Sp*, hindi malinis at hindi handa; Iloc: desareglado, haan a nalinis ken haan a nakasagana

Disoriented lito, ligalig, balisa; Iloc: riro, maallilaw

Disown itakwil, hindi kilalanin; Iloc: haan nga bigbigen, laksiden
Correlated word
Renounce itaboy, itakwil; Iloc: ilaksid, haan bigbigen

Disparage hamakin, cutchain, laitin, tuyain; Iloc: laisen

Disparate *adj.,* **Disparity** *n.* hindi pantay-pantay o hindi pareparehong pagturing; Iloc: haan nga agpatag o haan agpapada ti pag-estimar-*Sp* o pag-trato-*Sp*

Dispatch papuntahin, ipadala; Iloc: ibaon, baonen, ipatulod

Dispel 1] iwaksi sa isip, 2] iwisik para cumalat; Iloc: 1] ikkaten idiay panunot, 2] ipurwak tapno agwaras

Dispensable puedeng hindi pagtuonan ng pansin dahil hindi importante; Iloc: uray haan nga asecaswen ta haan nga importante

Dispensary lugar-*Sp* na pagkukunan ng libre-*Sp* o mura na gamot; Iloc: lugar a pagalaan ti libre o nalaca nga agas

Dispense 1] mamigay, mag-entrega, 2] palibrehin sa trabaho o sa kasalanan; Iloc: 1] mangited, ag-entrega, 2] ipalibre ti trabaho o iti basol na (*all Sp:* entrega, libre, trabaho)

Disperse icalat, isabog, ihasik; Iloc: iwarsi, iwaras

Display ipakitang-tao; Iloc: ipakita, ipabuya, iparang

Displease yamutin, inisin, saktan ang damdamin; Iloc: paluksawen, suronen, ruroden

Disposable ito yong bagay na kapag nagamit na, kailangang itapon na at hindi na gamitin muli; Iloc: daytoy ti producto nga nu palpas a mausar, masapul nga ibelleng ta haanen nga iyusar manen.

Dispose itapon; Iloc: ibelleng

Disposed to gawi o fuersa na nakakapagtulak sa tao na mag-asal, gumawa o magturing dahil naging bihasa na kaya nakagawian na kahit hindi muna pinag-isipan kung ito ay tama at nakakabuti o nakakasama at nakakasakit.

Disposition kalagayan ng isip at damdamin, disposisyon-*Sp*, modo-*Sp*; Iloc: kasasaad ti nakem ken ricna, disposisyon, modo

Disprove iprueva na kasinungalingan ito; Iloc: i-prueva-*Sp* ti kaulbodan

Dispute makikipag-argumento-*Sp* o debate-*Sp*; magdiscusyon-*Sp* dahil sa pagkakaiba sa paniwala o pagturing; sagutan sa pagcocontra o pagsasalungat

Disqualify dahil sa kakulangan ng rekisitog qualificasyon-*Sp*, mawalan ng oportunidad-*Sp* o chansang makapasok, sumali o maaprovahan; Iloc: gapu ta kurang ti calificasyon-*Sp* umawan ti oportunidad o chansa a makastrek o makasali o ma-aprovar-*Sp*

Disregard ipawalang-cuenta-*Sp*, hindi pansinin, hindi estimahin; Iloc: haan icascaso, haan nga bigbigen o i-estimaren (estimar-estima-*Sp*), awan cuenta o pateg canyana

Disrepute tao na nasira ang reputasyon-*Sp*; Iloc: tao nga nadadael iti reputasyon

Disrespect hindi respetohin (respeto-*Sp*), bastosin, lapastanganin; Iloc: haan nga respetoen, mang-bastos-*Sp*

DISROBE maghubad; Iloc: aglabos, agussob

DISROBE someone hubaran; Iloc: labosan, ussoban

Disrupt gambalain, antalahin; Iloc: mang-estorbo-*Sp*, mangitaktak

Dissatisfaction *n.*, **Dissatisfy** *v.* hindi nasiyahan o nacontento; Iloc: haan a nagustoan o nacontento

Diss, Dis mam-bastos-*aSp*, mang-insulto-*Sp*, mamintas; Iloc: mangbastos, mang-insulto, manguyaw

Disseminate ipalaganap, icalat; Iloc: iwaras, iwarnak

Dissension pagkakaiba ng paniwala

Dissenter *n,* **Dissident** *adj. (Tag. & Iloc.)* protesta, contra

Disservice nakakasira, nakakasama, nakakaagraviado

Dissimilar magkaiba; Iloc: agsinnabali

Dissipate maglaho, mawala na lamang gaya ng *fog*

Dissolute *adj.,* **Dissolution** *n.* 1] walang moralidad-*Sp* kaya malaswa ang gawa; 2] nadudurog, magkapira-piraso

Dissolve tunawin sa tubig, palabnawin, lusawin; Iloc: tunawen ti danum, labnawan, lusawen
Correlated word
Dilute tubigan; Iloc: danuman

Dissuade himoking huwag gawin; Iloc: bagbagaan nga haan aramiden

Distance distancia-*Sp,* gaano kalayo; Iloc: distancia-*Sp,* casano caadayo

Distant malayo; Iloc: adayo

Distaste *(Tag. & Iloc.)* disgusto-*Sp*

Distinct, Distinctive bukod-tanging uri na hindi kapareho ng iba; Iloc: bukbukod a tipo-*Sp*
Synonym
Unique bukod-tangi; Iloc: sangsangayan

Distinguish makilala; Iloc: mabigbig, maylasin

Distinguished tanyag sa puesto o sa importanteng katangian at katatao niya; Iloc: natan-uk ken nadayaw ti puesto wenno ti importante a kababalin ken katatao na

Distort ngiwiin, sirain ang anyo o hugis o forma-*Sp,* baluktotin; Iloc: diwwigen, kiwingen, dadaelen o perdien iti langa o forma

Distract nilalayo ang baling ng kapwa sa pinaggugugolang gawa o pansin niya; Iloc: storboen na ti tao tapno tay madama nga ob-obran daytoy ket haan na maasecaso

Distress namemerhuisio dahil sa bigat ng damdamin; Iloc: agperper-huisio-*Sp* gapu ti dagsen ti ricna na

Distribute mag-distribusyon-*Sp,* maglaan at magpabahagi sa kapwa; Iloc: agdistribusyon, mangilasin, mangipalak-am ken mangibingay iti dadduma a tattao

Distribution *(Tag. & Iloc.)* distribusyon-*Sp*

District pook; Iloc: purok

DISTRUST walang tiwala, suspechahan, pagdudahan; Iloc: awan ti fiar na, suspechaan, agduda (*all Sp:* suspecha, duda, fiar)

DISTRUST what is being said, Take it with a grain of salt Ito ay nakikinig ng cuento o paliwanag pero mayroon siyang pagdududa; Iloc: agdengdengngeg ngem haan nga mamati ta agdudduda

Disturb gambalahin, estorbohin, moleschahin; Iloc: ag-estorbo-*Sp*, ag-molescha-*Sp*

Disunity wala silang pagkakaisa; Iloc: awan ti pagkaykaysa da

DITCH *n.* *(Tag. & Iloc.)* canal-*Sp*

DITCH *v.* layasan o palayasin para mahiwalay sa taong ito; Iloc: panawan o papanawen tapno agsina da

Diva 1] hinahangaang kumakantang babae, 2] *prima donna*, 3] lalakeng mahilig magdamit at mag-ayos na babae, lalakeng *transvestite*

Dive or into the water sumisid, mag-*dive*; Iloc: agbatok, ag-*dive*

Diverge *v.,* **Divergent** *adj.* umiba o lumihis sa asal na *normal* o kina-gagawian; kakaiba ang isip o asal

Divergence *n.* pagkakaiba sa *normal*; lumilihis sa kagawiang asal; Iloc: pagkasabali iti cadawyan nga aramid; aglisi iti sigud

Diverse *adj.,* **Diversity** *n.* iba't iba, sari-sari; Iloc: saba-sabali, naduma-duma

Divert *v.,* **Diversion** *n.* 1] dibersion-*Sp* na ginagawa ng kaaway para malihis o malito ang kalaban, 2] pangpabaling sa makakalibang para maginhawaan sa dami ng trabaho o problema; Iloc: 1] dibersion nga inaramid ti kacontra tapno maylaw-an wenno mariro ti kalaban, 2] pang-imatang iti paglinglingayan tapno makabang-ar iti kaadu ti trabaho wenno problema.

Divest 1] tanggalin ang suot o damit o balabal; alisin ang palamuti o decorasyon-*Sp*; 2] bawiin o alisin ang canyang pag-aari sa ari-aryan niya; ibenta ang ari-arian

Divide pare-pareho-*Sp* na paghati-hatian, ibaha-bahagi; Iloc: pagbibi-ngayan nga agpada-pada, paglasin-lasinin

DIVINE katangian ng Panginoong Dios, sagrado-*Sp*, nadiosan, banal, mabathala; Iloc: kababalin ni Apo Dios, sagrado, adda divinidad-*Sp* na, nadiosan, maka-Dios

DIVINE Providence pagpapatnubay at pagbibiyaya ng Panginoong Dios-*Sp*; Iloc: pangigaway ken pangiturong ni Apo Dios

Divinity, Study of God pag-aaral tungkol sa Panginoong Dios-*Sp* at divinidad-*Sp*; Iloc: adal maygapu kenni Apo Dios ken divinidad,

Division *division;* dinding o bakuran; Iloc: alad o diding

Divisive nagpapahiwalay ng pagkakaibigan o pagkakaisa ng mga tao o pagkaka-socio-*Sp*

Divorce *(Tag. & Iloc.) divorce*, divorcio-*Sp*

Divulge ibunyag, ipagtapat, isiwalat; Iloc: ipaammo,, isawang

Dizzy nahihilo; Iloc: maulaw
> *Correlated words*
> **Giddy** medio nahihilo; Iloc: medio maulaw
> **Faint** mahimatay; Iloc: matalimudaw

Do isagawa, magsagawa, gawin, gampanan; Iloc: aramiden, agobra (obra-*Sp*)

Doc doctor, manggagamot; Iloc: doctor, mangngagas

Docile handang matuto; payag na magpasailalim sa nakakataas sa canya; madaling pakisamahan

Dock *pier*, muelye, pagdaongan ng sasakyang-pandagat; Iloc: pagsangladan ti pantaaw a lugan, *pier*, muelye-*Sp*

Doctor *doctor,* manggagamot; Iloc: *doctor,* mangngagas

Doctor's visit magpatingin sa *doctor*, magpa-*check-up*, magpaconsulta; Iloc: agpa-*check-up* ti doctor, agpaconsultar (consulta/consultar-*Sp*)

Doctrine doctrina-*Sp*, mga paniwala ng relihion-*Sp*; Iloc: doctrina, dagiti pammati ti relihion

Document *(Tag. & Iloc.)* documento-*Sp*

Dodge ilagan, lihisan, iwasan; Iloc: aglisi, lisyan

DOG *(Tag. & Iloc.)* aso
> *Correlated words*
> **Pup, Puppy** tuta; Iloc: uken

DOG-eat-dog napakamalalang pagkasakim dahil umaangkin ng pag-aari ng iba na wala man lamang pagsisisi dahil binale-wala niya na naagraviado ang nagmemay-ari noon; Iloc: grabe a pagkasarabusab na ta alaen na ti sanicua ti sabali nga awan pagbabawi na ken awan canyana ti asi nga naagraviado na ti makincucua idiay

DOG's bark tahol; Iloc: taol

Doggedness tigas ng determinasyon-*Sp*; Iloc: tibker ti determinasyon

Doghouse maliit na bahay para sa aso; asawa na nakapagpayamot kaya hindi siya puede sa *bedroom* matulog

Dogma doctrina-*Sp*, mga paniwala ng relihiyon-*Sp*; Iloc: doctrina, dagiti pammati ti relihiyon

Doldrum walang kakilos-kilos o galaw gaya sa negocio-*Sp*; malungkot o namimighating kalagayan

Dole magbigay ng abuloy; Iloc: mangited ti donasyon-*Sp*

Doleful nagdadalamhati, Iloc: agladladingit

Doll manica; Iloc: munyeca-*Sp*

Domain *(Tag. & Iloc.)* teritoryo-*Sp*

Dome pabilog na bubong; Iloc: atep nga timbukel

Domestic pang-familia-*Sp*, pantahanan, pangmag-anakan; Iloc: pang-familia

Domesticate gawing maamo ang hayup; Iloc: ipaamo ti animal

Domicile bahay; Iloc: balay

Dominant dominante-*Sp*, naghahari; Iloc: dominante, agar-ari

Dominate mag-dominante-*Sp*, mangibabaw; Iloc: ag-dominar-*Sp*
  Correlated words
  Reign, Rule mamuno, maghari, mamayani, mangibabaw, manaig; Iloc: agturay, agar-ari

Domineer *see Dominate above*

Dominion *(Tag. & Iloc.)* teritoryo-*Sp*, sacop na lugar-*Sp*

Don magsuot, magbihis, magdamit; Iloc: agbado, agbestido (bestido-*Sp*), agarwat, agcawes

Donate mag-*donate*, mag-abuloy, mamigay, ipamigay; Iloc: agsagut, ag-*donate*, agrangkap

Donation *(Tag. & Iloc.)* donasyon-*Sp*

Done gawa na, naganap na, tapos na, yari na; Iloc: nalpasen, naaramiden

Donor nagbibigay ng donasyon-*Sp*; Iloc: mangidon-donasyon

"DON'T!" "Huwag!"; Iloc: "Alto-*Sp*!"
  Correlated words
  "Stop!" "Hinto!" "Huwag!" Iloc: "Alto!"
  "Wait!" Teka! Sandali lang!" "Hintay!" Iloc: "Aguray ka!", "Alto ka!"

DON'T let somebody pull you down *There may be people who intentionally mislabel people even though they do not know them too well. If someone* <u>*wrongfully*</u> *characterizes you in a bad and unfair way, do not let them hurt you - do not give them permission to hurt you.* <u>*Be the better person*</u> *and not go down to the mud where mean* *people are wading. With gentle self-respect, just turn away unscathed from them. Or you may tell them in a tactful way that you are a worthy human being who is capable of handling any challenges in life. Yes, <u>anyone in this world is worthy and truly matters</u>, and anyone can <u>strive and accomplish anything</u> with the mental capabilities and body strength that God has equipped us all.*

DON'T like ayaw, hindi gusto; Iloc: madina cayat

"DON'T mention it" "Walang anoman"; Iloc: "Awan aniaman na"

"DON'T worry" "Hindi bale," "Huwag kang mag-alala" Iloc: "Haan ka nga agdanag", "Haan a bale"

Doofus *(Tag. & Iloc.)* bobo/ba-*Sp*, gago/ga-*Sp*, torpe-*Sp*, tanga

Door puerta-*Sp*, pinto; Iloc: puerta, ruangan, ridaw
   Synonyms
   Egress pagpasokan at paglabasan, daang papalabas; Iloc: pagserkan ken pagruaran, dalan para rumuar
   Entrance pasukan; Iloc: pagserkan
   Exit labasan; Iloc: ruaran

Doorbell *(Tag. & Iloc.)* timbre-*Sp*

Doorman *(Tag. & Iloc.)* bantay, guardia-*Sp*

Doormat kuskusan o pahiran ng sapatos; Iloc: pagpigadan

Doorstep paanan; Iloc: pagserkan

Doozie, Doozy tao o bagay na mahalaga, napakainam at *superior* pa

Doppelgänger hindi kadugo o kaano-ano pero magkamukha parang kakambal

Dosage, Dose kung ilang cucharita-*Sp* o ilang tableta-*Sp* ang inuming gamut at ilang beses-*Sp* inumin ito sa isang araw; Iloc: nu mano a cucharita o mano a tableta ti inumin a medicina-*Sp* ken mano a beses tomaren (tomar-*Sp*) daytoy iti maysa nga aldaw

Dose of one's medicine ano mang masamang ginawa mo na nakasakit o nakaagraviado ka sa iba ay babalik din sa iyo

Dossier naipon-ipong documento tungkol sa isang paksa o tao

Dot, Period *(Tag. & Iloc.)* tuldok

Dote on carinyohin, nilalambing; Iloc: ag-carinyo-*Sp*, agdungngo, aglailo

DOUBLE *(Tag. & Iloc.)* dob-le-*Sp*

DOUBLE-cross, Double-dealing mag-traydor-*Sp*; Iloc: agtraydor

DOUBLE standard ito'y pagbibigay ng mas maraming privilehio-*Sp* o favor-*Sp* sa finafaboran na tao **kaysa sa iba** na naagraviado sila kahit may karapatan din sila sa parehong mga favor

DOUBLE talk 1] mabilis na pagsasalitang kadalasan ay walang katalinohan o hindi relevante; 2] malabo at walang katiyakang salita ng isang *politician* na puedeng panlinlang o pandaya

Doubt mag-duda-*Sp*; Iloc: agduda

Doubtful nakakaduda, walang katiyakan, nakakapaalinlangan; Iloc: nakakasuspecha, nakakaduda

Douche magpawpaw; Iloc: agpawpaw

Doughnot pangmeryendang pagkain na frinito at hugis circulo-*Sp*

Douse buhosan, saboyan; Iloc: suyyatan, sebseban

Dove, Pigeon *(Tag. & Iloc.)* calapati

DOWN sa baba; Iloc: diay baba

DOWN-and-out kawalan o hindi sapat ang pera at gamit at wala nang lakas o caya para makaahon pa

Downcast nabigo ang loob, dismayado, nanlata; Iloc: nadadael o naperdi ti tured ken ganas na, dismayado

Downer 1] droga na masyadong nagpapalungkot o nagpapalumbay; 2] nakakalungkot o nakakalumbay na pangyayari o kalagayan

Downfall 1] pagbagsak, 2] pagkawala ng pag-asa; Iloc: 1] pagbarsak, 2] napukawan iti gasat

Downgrade bumaba ang buti, husay o pagka-efecto-*Sp*

Downhearted *see Downcast above*

Download *download,* i-carga-*Sp* o ilipat ang *information* o programa-*Sp* sa memoria-*Sp* ng maliit na *computer* na nagbubuhat sa malaking *computer*; Iloc: *download,* icarga o iyacar iti informasyon-*Sp* o programa idiay *memory* ti bassit a *computer* nga naggapu iti dakkel a *computer.*

Downplay paliitin o ipawalang-halaga gaya ng kasalanan niya kapag nagpapalusot siya; Iloc: pabassitin o ipaawan na ti valor-*Sp* casla nu i-*justify* na dagiti dakes nga aramid na

Downpour malakas na ulan; Iloc: napigsa nga tudo

Downright completo, buo, lubos-lubos na tiyak; franko at tapat

Downside clase-*Sp* o uri na hindi nakakabuti

Downsize paliitin ang dami ng mga empleyado-*Sp* sa pamamagitan ng pag-*lay-off* o pagcesante

Downstairs sa baba; Iloc: diay baba

Downtime oras na di masyadong ocupado ang empleyado; ito rin ay oras sa trabaho na nasira at hindi makaandar ang makina kaya huminto ang trabaho

Downtown *downtown,* poblasyon-*Sp,* bayan, kabayanan; Iloc: *downtown,* ili, poblasyon

Downtrodden *(Tag. & Iloc.)* inapi, inabuso, minaltrato
Synonym
Aggrieved *(Tag. & Iloc.)* minaltrato, naagraviado

Downward pababa; Iloc: agpababa

Doze umidlip, magsiesta; Iloc: agtuglep, agridep, agsiesta

Dozen isang dozena-*Sp*; Iloc: sangadozena, maysa dozena

Drab 1] hindi nakakalibang, 2] kulay na hindi matingkad; Iloc: 1] haan a makalinglingay, 2] color-*Sp* a haan nabiag

Draft 1] haplos ng hangin sa loob ng bahay o gusali, 2] *rough draft* o pang-una sa pagbubuo ng sulat o plano-*Sp* ng proyecto-*Sp* na puedeng aayosin pa o dadagdagan pa

DRAG caladcarin; Iloc: guyoden, uloden

DRAG linen or one's gown is made to trail on the floor *(Tag. & Iloc.)* sayad, isayad, magsayad

Dragonfly tutubi; Iloc: towwato

Drain ipaagos, ipabuhos, ipalagos; Iloc: pagayosen, ipaarubos, ipaaruyot

Drainage lagosan, agosan ng tubig; Iloc: pagayosan ti danum

Drama *(Tag. & Iloc.)* dula, *drama*

Drastic kilos na marahas, sobrang ma-fuersa-*Sp*

Draw mag-*drawing*, magguhit, iguhit; Iloc: ag-*drawing*, ag-ugis ti ladawan

Drawback anomang makasagabal; Iloc: aniaman a makalapped

Dread takot; Iloc: buteng

Dream panaginip, pangarap; Iloc: tagtagainep, darepdep, arapaap

Dreary hindi nakakalibang; Iloc: haan a makalinglingay

Drench *v.,* **Drenched** *adj.* naulanan o pinalubog sa tubig at basang-basa na, tagas na tagas ng tubig, babad na babad; Iloc: natudoan o inyuper ti danum ket nakabasbasan, banag a nasagepsep ti danum

314

DRESS damit, baro, bestido-*Sp*; Iloc: bado, bestido, cawes

DRESS up magdamit, magbaro, magbihis, magbestido; Iloc: agbado, agbestido, agcawes, agarwat

DRESS up someone damitan; Iloc: badwan

Dressed up formal-*Sp* na nakabihis, nakadamit ng canyang pinakamagara; Iloc: *formal* a nakacawes

Dresser *(Tag. & Iloc.)* tocador, aparador-*Sp*

Dressmaker modista-*Sp*, costurera, mananahi; Iloc: modista, costurera, agdadait

Correlated word

Tailor *(Tag. & Iloc.)* sastre

Dried or wilted vegetable or leaves tuyot; Iloc: nagango

Drift maanod o itangay ng agos ng tubig o pinadpad o nililipad ng hangin; Iloc: mayyanod ti pag-ayos iti danum o itayab iti angin

Drill pag-*practice* o *exercise* na paulit-ulit

DRINK inomin, higopin; Iloc: inomin, igopen

DRINK medicine uminom ng medicina/gamot; Iloc: ag-tomar-*Sp* iti medicina/agas

DRINK the animal way, Lap, Lick in liquid to drink *(Tag. & Iloc.)* laklak

Drip tumutulo, pumapatak; Iloc: agtartaredted, agub-ubo, agtedted

DRIVE a car mag-maneho-*Sp* ng coche-*Sp*; Iloc: agmaneho ti coche

DRIVE a taxi or jeepney for livelihood magpasada-*Sp*, mag-angkas ng pasahero-*Sp*

DRIVE away, Shoo bugawin, itaboy; Iloc: bugawen

DRIVE fast magpacascas, magpabilis; Iloc: agpacascas

DRIVE in, Drive through oficina-*Sp* o *restaurant* na hindi ka kailangang bumaba sa sasakyan mo para makiusap sa empleyado-*Sp* o mag-*order* ng pagkain

DRIVER of a car *(Tag. & Iloc.)* chofer-*Sp*

DRIVER of a horse-drawn carriage *(Tag. & Iloc.)* cochero-*Sp*

Drizzle ambon; Iloc: arbis

Drone 1] lalaking bubuyog, 2] maliit na aparatong pinapalipad sa himpapawid ng taong nasa lupa na nilalaro niyang parang *kite* pero ito ay nakakaletrato habang nasa taas o puede ring nakakaespia at pinapakita ang mga tanawin.

Drool naglalaway; Iloc: agcatcatay

Droop lumoyloy; Iloc: agyudyod; agrucob

DROP ihulog, ilaglag; Iloc: iregreg, itinnag

DROP accidentally mabitiwan, mahulog, malaglag; Iloc: maibbatan, maregreg, matinnag

DROP due to a bump natiwalag; Iloc: matippay

DROP by dumaan para bumisita; Iloc: agvisita

DROP by to fetch someone daanan; Iloc: dagasen

DROP heavily bagsak, lagpak; Iloc: barsak

DROP in kahit walang *appointment* ay dumating pero puedeng asicasohin (gaya ng gamotin ng doctor, ayosan siya ng *beautician,* at iba pa)

DROP in the bucket, Drop in the ocean kaunting-kaunti lamang at hindi sapat

DROP into a container ihulog, ilaglag; Iloc: ipisok, itinnag
   Correlated words
   Pour into a container ibuhos, ibulos; Iloc: ipakbo, ipattog, ibukbok

DROP-off lugar-*Sp* kung saan umibis ang tao o kung saan ihulog ang mga donasyon-*Sp* o mga sulat o hiniram na libro-*Sp* sa *library*

Droplet patak; Iloc: tedted

Drought tuyot, tuyong-tuyo dahil sa kawalan ng ulan o labis na kakulangan ng ulan; Iloc: nakamagmaga gapu ti kaawanan ti tudo o sobra a kurang ti tudo

Drown malunod; Iloc: malmes, lumned, aglenned

Drowsy inaantok; Iloc: makaturog

Drug medicina-*Sp*, gamot; Iloc: medicina, agas

Drug addiction *Immersing oneself in illegal drugs is a CRIME and it is the reason for MANY FAILURES IN LIFE as it is extremely addictive that you may wake up every morning solely craving for the drugs that you become a burden to your family and useless and inutile to yourself and everyone else because drugs are all that matters to you. Drug addiction **traps you throughout your lifetime** with its powerful hold and its damaging effects that **you may die quite early**. While you are still alive, drug addiction weakens and **shuts down** your energy and strength, makes you fragile and sickly, causes hand tremors and seizures, makes you **age earlier** that you **look old**, gaunt, and haggard* *prematurely, makes you looking unkempt and ugly, filthy and stinky, shatters and banishes all your intelligence, abilities, skills and talents, endows you with a bad reputation, criminal record, wasted life and ruined future, **ends** <u>all your opportunities and advancements to success</u>, hits you with inability and helplessness to work or do anything, or even to be set free from the addiction and from its ugly consequences, and you become vulnerable and an easy prey to criminals and human traffickers who would take advantage of your helplessness and inutile condition. **So the** RULE OF THUMB is: Avoid illegal drugs at all cost and never give in to persuasions, otherwise you will No Longer Function as a Normal Human Being and You Will Hate the Person You Have Become. **Instead have a firm, powerful determination <u>in a strong dominant way</u> to resolutely stay away from illegal drugs** no matter how insistent somebody entices you to try it, because <u>immediately before you even know it, drugs transform you into a weakling, a good-for-nothing inutile</u> as it <u>damages your body, soul and spirit, and even gets worse and worse as you'd be helplessly trapped and imprisoned in its **addictive power**. **Illegal drugs' destruction** is immense that all will be gone from your life before you even know it.** You'll **<u>lose</u>** your strength, healthy-normal life, sanity, intelligence, wise judgment, ambitions, goals, your happiness, good looks, values and principles, advancements and progress in life, educational attainments, flourishing careers, <u>love-life, enjoying comfort and contentment with your spouse, being a happy parent to your children</u>, excursions and picnics with your family, <u>having freewill - the will to select beneficial and fun-filled choices, the will to strive and do whatever you want in life like productive and useful deeds and accomplishments</u>, triumphs and success, joy and delights, hobbies, sports, travels, appearance enhancements, and of course, hygiene and sanitary practices. <u>If you are a drug addict, no business will want to hire you. Good people will shun and avoid you because no decent person wants you as a friend. To get hold of drugs, you may steal, rob or do other crimes to get the money to buy drugs, even become a prostitute because morals are no longer important to you as drugs are all that matters. You brought shame and deep disappointment to your family that you, yourself,*</u>

hates the person you have become. **Your problems and deep regret comes much sooner.** *So don't be a problem to yourself, to your family and to society by resolutely avoiding addictive drugs.* **Be the solution, not the problem.** *Be a contributing member to society, not a person who merely depends on hand-outs if there are any that's available.* **Enjoy life as a healthy normal human being.** *(Also, read "Activities that are healthy, lawful, enjoyable that promote advancements and success" in this book)*

Drugstore *(Tag. & Iloc.)* farmacia-*Sp*, botica-*Sp*

DRUM tambol; Iloc: tambor-*Sp*

DRUM up nagkakamit ng mabungang *business* o mga cliente-*Sp* o suporta-*Sp* o venta-*Sp* sa pamamagitan ng masugid na pagtatrabaho at mabuting pakipag-ugnayan

Drunkard lasing, lasenggo; Iloc: bartek, mannanginom, mammartek, bartikero

DRY tuyo; Iloc: namaga
Synonym
Parch tuyong-tuyo; Iloc: nakamagmaga

DRY goods paninda na mga tela-*Sp* o mga kasuotan; Iloc: laco a tela ida wenno arwaten

DRY it by hanging outdoors ibilad; Iloc: ibilag

DRY out by evaporation naigahan; Iloc: maachanan

DRY run *(Tag. & Iloc.)* *rehearsal,* ensayo-*Sp*

Dual dalawa na caraniwan ay magkapareho; Iloc: dua a canayon ket ag-kapada o pareho-*Sp*

Dubious *(Tag. & Iloc.)* nakaka-sospecha-*Sp*, nakaka-duda-*Sp*, nakaka-descomfiado-*Sp*

DUCK *n.* pato-*Sp*, itik; Iloc: pato

DUCK *v.* ilagan, umilag, lihisan, iwasan; Iloc: aglisi, lisyan, liklikan

Duckling *(Tag. & Iloc.)* bibi, batang pato

Duct 1] tubo-*Sp* o canal-*Sp* na dinadaanan ng *fluid* o gas-*Sp* o cab-le-*Sp* ng electricidad-*Sp* o *wires* na kinakailangan sa pag-andar-*Sp*; 2] *tube* sa katawan para daanan ng *body fluid* o ng nilulong pagkain

Dud mintis-*Sp*, paltos; Iloc: mintis

DUE nararapat; Iloc: naturayan, rebbeng

DUE, Payable dapat bayaran sa tinakdang fecha-*Sp*; Iloc: masapul bayadan iti fecha nga in-designar-*Sp* nu caano ti pagbayad

DUE process paraan ng govierno para sa *protection* ng makabatas na karapatan/*legal right* ng tao; Iloc: padalan ti govierno para ti *protection* iti kalintegan o katurayan ti tao

Duet dalawang tao na magkasabay o magparehang cumanta o tumogtog ng musica-*Sp*; Iloc: dua nga tao nga ag-kapareha-*Sp* nga ag-cancion-*Sp* wenno ag-tocar-*Sp* ti musica

Dull mapurol; Iloc: namudil

Dumb pipi; Iloc: umel

Dumbbell 1] mabigat na hawakan para pang-*exercise* ng baraso, 2] bobo; Iloc: 1] nadagsen nga pang-iggem para pang-*exercise* ti takkiag, 2] nengneng

DUMP i-basura-*Sp*, itapon; Iloc: ibasura, ibelleng

DUMP on tambakan, buntonan, tabunan; Iloc: gaburan, buntonan, tambakan

Dung tae o dumi ng hayop; Iloc: lugit, takki ti *animal*

Dungeon cueva-*Sp* sa ilalim ng lupa; Iloc: cueva iti uneg ti daga

Dunk into a dip or a sauce *(Tag. & Iloc.)* isawsaw sa *dip* o sawsawan

Duo dalawang magkasama; Iloc: dua nga agcadwa

Duplicate *(Tag. & Iloc.) duplicate,* copia-*Sp*

Durability pagkatibay kaya matagal na magagamit; Iloc: pagkalagda isu a napaut nga may-usar-*Sp*

Durable matibay; Iloc: nalagda
> *Antonym*
> **Flimsy, Delicate** marupok; Iloc: narukop, nalaca a madadael o mabuong o mapigis

Duration hangganan; tagal; Iloc: paut, bayag

Duress sapilitan o fuersahang babala

During nang, habang, samantala; Iloc: mientras-*Sp*, bayat

Dusk takipsilim, agaw-dilim; Iloc: apagsipnget, sumipnget

Dust alikabok; Iloc: tapok

DUTCH *(Tag & Iloc.) Dutch,* Olandes-*Sp*

DUTCH treat *(Tag. & Iloc.)* KKB *or* kanya-kanyang bayad

DUTY 1] pananagutang katungkulan, responsibilidad-*Sp* o obligesyon-*Sp* sa batas o sa trabaho-*Sp* na inaasahang gampanan, 2] respetadong asal sa pagsusunod sa magulang, at sa mga may edad at sa mas mataas ang ranko-*Sp* o puesto-*Sp*, 3] buis na sinisingil ng govierno-*Sp* lalo na sa mga bagay na pinasok sa bansa.

DUTY, Tariff *(Tag. & Iloc.)* buis

Dwarf 1] mas maliit sa pandak na tao pero ang mga camay at paa ay hindi tugma o kapantay sa laki at forma ng katawan, 2] unano, duende; Iloc: 1] mas bassit ngem iti pandak a tao ngem dagiti saka ken ima na ket haan nga umno wenno maybagay iti kadakkel ken forma ti bagi na, 2] ansisit

Dwarfish bulilit, pandak; Iloc: balabattit, ansisit

Dwell nakatira; Iloc: agyan

Dwelling tahanan, bahay, tirhan; Iloc: balay, pagyanan

Dwindle kumokonti, nababawasan, lumiliit; Iloc: bumasbassit, kumiskissay

Dye culayan, itina; Iloc: coloran, itina (color-*Sp*, tina-*Sp*)

Dynamic, Dynamical masigla at mabisa sa pagkaliksi o pagka-*active*; masigasig sa sipag at sikap; enerhia na nakakagawa ng *motion* o galaw.

Dynamics 1] sangay ng *mechanics* na may kaugnayan sa fuersa o enerhia sa pagbabago o paglilikha ng galaw (hindi nakapigil na walang kagalawgalaw); 2] ang proceso ng pagtubo/*growth*, pagbago/*change* at pagbuo/*develop* sa anomang larangan/*field*; tungkol sa fuersa/*force* at lakas kasamang bisa/*power* sa galaw/*motion*

Dynamite *(Tag. & Iloc.)* dinamita

Dynamo 1] *generator,* 2] taong napakasigasig at puno ng fuersa sa paglikha at pagsagawa; Iloc: 1] *generator,* 2] tao nga nasagiksik ken napunno ti fuersa-*Sp* nga ag-trabaho-*Sp* ken agparnuay

Dynasty matagalang sunod-sunod na nangungulo sa isang bansa na galing sa isang familia lamang

Dysfunction hindi *normal* o hindi mabuting gawaing caraniwan ay sa isang familia-*Sp*

E

Each bawat isa, tig-isa; Iloc: tunggal maysa, cada-*Sp*, cada maysa, saggaysa

Eager *adj.,* **Eagerness** *n.* sabik, sabik na sabik; Iloc: aggag-gagar, magagaran
Synonyms
Ardent mainit, masugid; Iloc: nasged, regget
High-spirited *(Tag. & Iloc.)* vivong-vivo, vivang-viva
Eagerness and determination, short-lived *(Tag. & Iloc.)* ningas-cogon
Synonym
Flash in the pan ningas-cogon, maganang-magana pero hindi matagalan ang pagkagana dahil naglalaho agad
Eagle *(Tag. & Iloc.)* agila-*Sp*
EAR, Ears tainga, tenga; Iloc: lapayag
Correlated word
Otic tungkol sa tenga; Iloc: maygapu ti lapayag
EAR, clean ears with q-tips kikigan; Iloc: curicoran
Ear lobe pidit; Iloc: riting
EAR lobe hole for earrings butas ng tenga; Iloc: tebbeng
EAR pus nana sa tenga; Iloc: duric
EAR tweak on a naughty child pingotin; Iloc. lapigosen
EAR wax or Earwax *(Tag. & Iloc.)* tuli
EARLIER mas maaga; Iloc: nasapsapa
EARLIER, a little, A while ago kanina lamang, bago ngayon; Iloc: itay laeng, antes-*Sp* itatta
EARLY maaga; Iloc: nasapa
EARLY bird gets the worm, the Ang unang-una o ang maagang mag-umpisa ng anomang gawain ay nakakalamang at may ventahe-*Sp* dahil nagagantipalaan ng tagumpay o magandang kahihinatnan
Earmark kasundoan na ang tinakdang fondo-*Sp* ay itabi at inatasan para sa isang proyecto-*Sp* o layonin o organisasyon-*Sp*
Synonyms
Allocate maglaan, mambahagi sa kapwa; Iloc: manglasin, manglak-am, mangibingay ti cacadwa
Allot, Allotment nilaang pera o fondong panggugol para sa tinakdang layonin; Iloc: inlasin a cuarta o fondo nga naysaad para iti maysa a rangta
EARN kumikita, nag-susweldo-*Sp*; Iloc: agsapsapul, agsusweldo
EARN, Deserve nakakarapatan, naaangkop; Iloc: makaala ti gunggona, umno, rebbeng

EARN one's keep 1] tumulong sa mga gawaing bahay para kapalit ng pagkain at pagtira doon; 2] magtrabaho ng tama para karapat-dapat sa canya ang canyang kinikitang suweldo

Earnest sabik, masigasig; Iloc: aggagar, napasnek

Earnings sweldo-*Sp*, kita; Iloc: sweldo, sapul

Earring, Earrings hikaw; Iloc: arritos

EARTH, Soil, Land lupa; Iloc: daga

EARTH, World mundo-*Sp*, daigdig; Iloc: mundo, lubong
Correlated words
Terra firma matigas at tuyong lupa; Iloc: natangken ken namaga a daga
Terrestrial tungkol sa mundong ito at ang mga nilalang dito
Subterranean sa baba ng lupa gaya ng cueva, yungib at minahan

Earthquake lindol; Iloc: ginggined

Earthworm linta; Iloc: alinta

EASE, Soothe paginhawain; Iloc: pabang-aran

EASE, Facility paggamit na madali, mabilis o simp-le; Iloc: pagiyusar ken pagaramid ket nalaca, nadaras ken simple

Easier said than done may mga mas madaling sabihin pero may kahirapang gawin dahil puedeng magastos o mahirap gawin o nakakaalangan o nakakalikha ng away o galit o gulo

East *east,* silangan; Iloc: *east,* daya
Correlated words
West *west,* kanluran; Iloc: *west,* laud
North *north,* norte, hilaga; Iloc: *north,* norte, amianan
South *south,* timog, sur; Iloc: *south,* abagatan, sur
Oriental east, silangan; Iloc: east, daya
Occidental *west,* kanluran; Iloc: *west,* laud

Easter *Easter Sunday,* Domingo Santo-*Sp*, Domingo de Resurecsion-*Sp* or de Pascua-*Sp*

EASY madali; Iloc: nalaca, cascari
Synonym
Facile madali; Iloc: nalaca, cascari

EASY come, easy go kadalasan nawawala agad ang bagay na madali lamang na matamo at hindi pinaghirapan dahil sa pagkamadali nito ay hindi binibigyang halaga

EASY-going *(Tag. & Iloc.)* campante

EAT kumain; Iloc: mangan

Correlated words

Bite cagatin; Iloc: cagaten, kittaben

Nibble, Small bite cagatin ng maliliit; Iloc: kitteban, curiban, kinnetan

Chew nguyain; Iloc: ngalngalen

Gnaw ngatngatin; Iloc: ngutngoten

Chomp nguya-nguyain, ngalotin; Iloc: caremkemen

Munch ngatain; Iloc: caremkemen

Masticate ngangain; Iloc: mamaen

Suck food (i.e. candy, lollipop) simsimin, supsopin; Iloc: supsopen, mulmolen

Snap on food tuklawin, sakmalin; Iloc: tukmaen

Satisfied eating busog; Iloc: nabsog, bussog, napnek

EAT-all-you-can *restaurant* na isang precio-*Sp* lamang pero-*Sp* kumain ka ng kumain hanggang caya mo; Iloc: *restaurant* a maysa a precio laeng ngem kaan ka nga kaan ingganat macayam

Correlated words

Smorgasboard (Swedish) *buffet, all-you-can-eat*

Buffet *restaurant* na isang precio lamang pero kumain ka ng kumain hanggang caya mo; Iloc: *restaurant* a maysa a precio laeng ngem kaan ka nga kaan ingganat macayam

EAT entrée without rice magpapak; Iloc: agalunos

EAT leftovers between meals i-meryenda-*aSp* ang natirang ulam; Iloc: agcallong

EAT one's words bawiin ang mga sinabi, magcumpisal na ang dating binanggit niya ay hindi tama; Iloc: ibabawi ti insawang na, agconfesar-*Sp* nga tay naybaga na ket haan nga usto-*Sp*

EAT rice with soup kumain ng sinabawang kanin; Iloc: aglabay

EAT snacks mag-meryenda-a*Sp*; Iloc: ag-meryenda

EAT together at the dining table salo-salong kumain sa lamesa-*Sp*; Iloc: aggigiddan nga mangan diay lamesa

EAT using hands only camayang-kumain; Iloc: agcammet

Eatery *(Tag. & Iloc.) restaurant (buffet, cafeteria, coffeehouse, fine dining, pub, ethnic eatery)*

Eavesdrop lihim na nakikinig; Iloc: palimed nga agdengngeg

Ebb umontos, lumiit, kumonti; Iloc: bimmassit

Ebola galing sa RNA *virus* na madaling mahawaan kung madampi ang balat sa pawis, dugo, ihi o tae ng paciente na may Ebola at marami ang namamatay sa sakit na ito sa Africa noong 2013-2014

EBook *electronic book,* na puedeng i-*download* sa aparatong madadala kung saan-saang lugar-*Sp*

Ebon, Ebony itim; Iloc: nangisit

Ebonics pagsalita ng African-Americans o Blacks sa Ingles

E-commerce negosiong nangangalakal sa *internet*

Eccentric kakaiba sa caraniwan ang asal na puedeng makapatayo ng balahibo; Iloc: nakasabsabali ngem iti cadawyan a tignay isu nga mabalin a makasumgar ti dutdot

Echo alingawngaw; Iloc: aweng

Eclat lantad na tagumpay at kabantugan; lantad na *display*; paghanga ng mga publico

Eclectic 1] pagpipili sa sari-saring pagpipilian; arkitectura, decorasyon, tanawin, at iba pa na nagmula sa iba't ibang panahon ng *history*; pagpipili ng pinakamahusay sa lahat

Eclipse saglit o maikling tiempo-*Sp* kung kelan ang buwan ay tinatakpan ng ibang malaking planeta-*Sp*

Economical matipid; Iloc: nakirmet

Economize magtipid; Iloc: mangin-inot, agkirmet

Economy mahusay at matipid na pamamahala ng bayan sa pera, ari-arian at kawanggawa dahil umaasa na ang resulta nito ay sapat sa kinakailangan at pag-impok ng bayan

Ecstasy *n.,* **Ecstatic** *adj.* napakatinding kaligayahan

Ecumenical buong mundo-*Sp*; pinagkakaisa ang lahat na iglesia-*Sp* ng Cristiano-*Sp* sa buong mundo

Eczema *eczema*; Iloc: *eczema*, curad

Edema *(Tag. & Iloc.)* manas

Eden *(Tag. & Iloc.)* paraiso-*Sp*

EDGE gilid, bingit; Iloc: igid

EDGE, Upper hand *(Tag. & Iloc.)* may lamang o *advantage*

Edible ligtas na kainin; Iloc: mabalin a kanen nga awan peggad na
　Correlated words
　Comestible ligtas na kainin; Iloc: mabalin a kanen nga awan peggad na
　Potable ligtas na inumin; Iloc: mabalin a mainom nga awan peggad na

Edification *n.*, **Edify** *v. Enlightenment, wisdom and improvement in moral and spiritual uplifting.* Maliwanagan at pagbubuo ng kabutihang puso, isip at gawa; pagpapakabuti sa moralidad-*Sp*, dignidad-*Sp*, integridad-*Sp* at pagpapatnubay ng Espiritu Santo para maging maka-Dios

Edifice *(Tag. & Iloc.)* gusali, *building*

Edit suriin kung saan iwasto o mas ipabuti ang ginawang kasulatan; Iloc: sursoren nu inchenna ti masapul nga i-correhir-*Sp* wenno mas ipaimbag pay iti inaramid na a sursurat
Correlated words
Finishing touch tapos na pero maghanap ng puedeng mali para maayos at mapabuti at dagdagan pa ng informasyon para maging mas macompleto

Edition 1] isang dagdag sa naunang pinublicidad na libro o kaya dagdag sa ilan nang *editions/printing*; 2] gaano kadaming libro-*Sp*, diaryo-*Sp* o ibang pang publicidad sa isang paglalathala

Editor *editor,* patnugot ng pahayagan

Educate paaralin, turoan; Iloc: paadalen, isuro, surwan

Educated *(Tag. & Iloc.)* educado-*Sp*

Education *Do not think pursuing an education is difficult because **having no education** is much harder as life would be extremely problematic, complicated and tough for you since **without education**, you cannot find a good job, a comfortable life and success. Actually education is 1] **fun and delightful** because school is where you find new and old friends that you can enjoy and socialize with; and 2] **inspiring** and **enlightening** because education opens your eyes to new knowledge, which sharpens your mind and makes you wise, well-informed and intelligent to enable you to attain a victorious and rewarding life; 3] education is the **road to success** because you can reach your goals, success, triumphs and happiness.* Huwag mong isipin na ang pagtatamo ng educasyon ay mahirap dahil bale wala iyang apat na taong pagtapos mo ng carera kung ihambing mo sa habang-buhay na paghihirap dahil sa kawalan ka ng educasyon, kaya wala ka ring makuhang trabahong may mataas at sapat na sahod, at tagumpay at paghanga.

Educe iponin at pagsama-samahin ang mga *facts*/katotohanan at dito mag-umpisa na magsagawa o magpasya

Eel *(Tag. & Iloc.)* igat

Eerie anoman na nakakapagparamdam ng hindi maipaliwanag na pag-katakot o ang hindi makapakali

Efface punasan, borahin (bora-*Sp*), tanggalin, maglinis-pahid

EFFECT efecto-*Sp*, resulta-*Sp*, bunga, kahihinatnan

EFFECT, take *(Tag. & Iloc.)* umefecto, nag-efecto-*Sp*

EFFECTIVE mabisa, tumatalab, nagkakaefecto; Iloc: nabisa, agmamaay, agtaltalab, agef-efecto

EFFECTIVE date fechang mag-umpisa na ang *coverage* at pagkasacop sa canila o maging miembro-*Sp* na; Iloc: mangrugi a fecha-*Sp* nga agbalinen a miembron

Effectual nakakagawa ng inaasahang efecto o pagbuo; Iloc: makaar-aramid iti namnamaen a bunga o efecto-*Sp*

Effeminate, Sissy *(Tag. & Iloc.)* binabae, binabai, bakla

Effervesce *v.,* **Effervescent** *adj.* nagbubuga ng bula

Efficacious *adj.,* **Efficacy** *n.* nakakagawa ng inaasahang efecto o pag-completo-*Sp*; Iloc: makaar-aramid iti namnamaen a bunga o efecto-*Sp*

Efficient cayang-caya ang gawa at puedeng higit pa diyan, nakaka-completo ng trabaho at napakahusay pa; Iloc: cayang-caya na ti obra-*Sp* ken mabalin a labes pay dita, makacompleto ti trabaho ken nakalalaeng pay

Effigy malaking manica o forma ng kinamumuhiang tao para sunogin nila sa kanilang pagpupulong

Effort sikap; Iloc: pakat

Effrontery pagkawalang-hiya, bastos-*Sp*, walang respeto

EGG *(Tag. & Iloc.)* itlog
　　Correlated words
　　Yolk pulang parte ng itlog; Iloc: nalabbaga a parte ti itlog
　　Albumen puti ng itlog; Iloc: puraw ti itlog
　　Glair puting ng itlog

EGG, boiled *(Tag. & Iloc.)* malasado

EGG, fried *(Tag. & Iloc.)* strilyado-*Sp*

EGG glair puti ng itlog; Iloc : puraw ti itlog

EGG of a fish puga; Iloc: bugi

EGG of duck embryo, boiled *(Tag. & Iloc.)* balut

EGG or roe of a crab or shrimp *(Tag. & Iloc.)* aligi

EGG, scrambled binating itlog; Iloc: nabatil nga itlog

EGG yolk pula o *yellow* na parte ng itlog

Eggplant talong; Iloc: tarong

EGO 1] ang sarili, 2] ang pagtuturing ng labis na importancia sa sarili; Iloc: 1] ti bagi, 2] ti pangbigbig nga labes ti importancia ti mismo-*Sp* a bagi

EGO trip isang karanasan o tiempo-*Sp* na nagpapalugod-saya o bigay-capricho-*Sp* sa mismong sarili

Egocentric, Egoist, Egotist makasarili, sarili at kapakanan niya ang pinakamahalaga sa canya, at dapat makuha niya ang mga gusto niya at siya ay pinagbibigayan; Iloc: bagbagina na ken iti ventahe na laeng iti pinakanapateg canyana ken masapul nga maala na ti cayat na ken ited ti tao canya dagita

Egregious lantad na lantad ang pagkasama at pagkamakapinsala; Iloc: nakaparang ti pagkadakes ken ranggas na

Egress pagpasokan at paglabasan, daang papalabas; Iloc: pagserkan ken pagruaran, dalan para rumuar

EIGHT *(Tag. & Iloc.) eight,* walo, otcho-*Sp*

EIGHT hundred *eight hundred,* walong daan; Iloc: *eight hundred,* walo gasut

EIGHT o'clock *eight o'clock,* alas ocho-*Sp*

EIGHT thousand *eight thousand,* walong libo; Iloc: *eight thousand,* walo ribo

Eighteen *eighteen,* labing walo; Iloc: *eighteen,* sangapulo ket walo

Eighth ikawalo; Iloc: ikawalo

EIGHTY *eighty,* walompo, ochenta-*Sp*; Iloc: *eighty,* walo pulo, ochenta

EIGHTY one, 82, 83, 84, etc. *(English numbers are commonly used by almost all Filipinos)*

Either...or ang..o; Iloc: ti..o

Ejaculate *v.,* **Ejaculation** *n.* ang lumalabas na *semen* sa lalake sa pagtatalik niya sa babae

Eject 1] ibuga, itapon ng fuersa, 2] alisin, 3] mag-*emergency* na palabas sa eroplano-*Sp* sa pamamagitan ng *ejection* na upuan o *capsule* o *parachute*

Eke dagdagan, damihan, mangsuplemento, lakihan, pahabain, unatin o banatin pa

Elaborate mayaman sa detalye-*Sp* na plano sa paggawa o pagpapaliwanag nito

Elan kasiya-siyang bugso o simbuyo na pagkagana

Elapse lumipas, dumaan; Iloc: limmabas, ag-pasar-*Sp*

Elastic nababanat, lastico; Iloc: mabennat, lastico

Elate magpapagalak, magpapasaya; Iloc: agparagsak

ELBOW *n. (Tag. & Iloc.)* sico

ELBOW *v.* sicohin, tabigin; Iloc: kidagen

ELDER matatandang miembro ng familiao comunidad o simbahan; Iloc: mas lakay/baket, dagiti adda edad da a miembro ti familia, comunidad o iglesia

ELDER brother kuya; Iloc: manong

ELDER sister ate; Iloc: manang

Elderly taong nakalampas ng sesenta'y singco-*Sp* anyos-*Sp* at pataas

Elect ihalal, i-boto-*Sp*; Iloc: iboto

Election *election*, halalan, botohan; Iloc: *election*, pagboto

Electric fan *(Tag. & Iloc.) electric fan,* ventilador-*Sp*

Electricity *(Tag. & Iloc.)* electricidad-*Sp*, coryente-*Sp*

Electrocute kapag na-electricidad-*Sp* ang tao, mamatay ito

Electronic aparato-*Sp* na gumagamit ng electricidad-*Sp* at controlado-*Sp* ng *computer* o ibang makina-*Sp*

Elegant elegante-*Sp*, magara; Iloc: elegante, na-estilo-*Sp*

Element elemento-*Sp*, bahagi o parte-*Sp* na nagpapatakbo o nagpapalakad ng aparato-*Sp* o makina-*Sp*; Iloc: elemento, parte nga mangpapagna o mangpa-andar-*Sp* iti aparato wenno makina

Elementary simp-le-*Sp* at pinakaunang parte; Iloc: simp-le ken primero-*Sp* nga rimmuar a parte-*Sp*

Elevate ilagay sa taas o palakasin ang tunog o bisa; Iloc: icabil diay ngato o papigsaen ti timek o bisa

Elevation 1] pagkataas, ang lugar na mataas; 2] maharlika o dakila dahil sa kataasan ng pag-iisip

ELEVEN *eleven*, labing isa; Iloc: *eleven*, sangapulo ket maysa

ELEVEN o'clock *eleven o'clock*, alas onse-*Sp*

Eleventh hour, At the last minute ultimo ora-*Sp*, pinakahuling oras

Elf *(Tag. & Iloc.)* duende-*Sp*

Elicit 1] udyokin, ilabas, ilitaw, isulpot; 2] makarating sa *conclusion* o pasya batay sa *logic* o tamang pag-rason-*Sp*

Eligible *(Tag. & Iloc.)* *eligible, qualified,* qualificado-*Sp*, calificado-*Sp* dahil may katangian na kinakailangan at karapat-dapat sa puesto na ina-*apply*-an niya

Eliminate alisin, tanggalin; Iloc: ikkaten

Eliminated eliminado-*Sp*, natanggal; Iloc: eliminado, naikkat

Elite mga grupo-*Sp* na ang clase-*Sp* ay mataas sa sociedad-*Sp* o ang intelihensia-*Sp* o may kayamanan

Elixir *Pharmacology* preparasyong ginawa na pinapaniwalaang makakatagal ng buhay o nakakagamot ng lahat/karamihan na sakit

Correlated words

Panacea, Cure-all remedio o panlunas sa lahat ng sakit, at ng nakakasama at nakakahirap; Iloc: remedio wenno pangngagas iti amin a sakit, pagdaksan ken pagrigatan

Elocution talumpati, estilo-*Sp* ng pagtatalumpati

Elongate pahabain; Iloc: paatiddogen

Elope magtanan; Iloc: agtanan

Eloquent *Speaks meaningfully with fluency and intelligence;* Malinaw, mahusay at napaka-intelihente-*Sp* ang pagsalita.

Else iba pa; Iloc: sabali pay

Elsewhere sa ibang lugar-*Sp*; Iloc: diay sabali a lugar

Elucidate pag-explica-*Sp* na napakaliwanag; Iloc: pag-explicar-*Sp* nga nakalawlawag

Elucubrate magsulat ng libro-*Sp* o ibang publicidad-*Sp* na matagal na nilikha ng masidhi at masinsinang pagsisikap

Elude iwasan, layoan; Iloc: lisyan, aglisi, adaywan

Elusion pag-iiwas o pagtatakas; Iloc: aglisi, agtammeng

Elusive may kahirapang madakip o maalaala o maintindihan; Iloc: narigat a matiliw o malagip o maawatan

Emaciate mangayayat, manghina; Iloc: kumuttong, agkapoy

Emaciated buto't balat ang pagkapayat at mahina pa; Iloc: pagkakuttong ket tulang ken cudil ti ichura-*Sp* ken nacapoy pay

Email pakipagsulatan sa pamamagitan ng *internet* o *computer* na nangangailangan ng *email address* sa sumusulat at sinusulatan; Iloc:

pagsinnuratan idiay uneg ti *internet* o *computer* nga masapul ti *email address* iti agsursurat ken iti sursuratan

Emanate lumabas buhat sa pinanggalingan; Iloc: rimwar naggapu diay naggapuan

Emancipate pagpapalaya buhat sa pagcocontrol ng magulang o buhat sa kulongan o pagkaalipin

Emasculate pagkawala ng pagkalalake, at lakas at sigla; Iloc: pagkaawan ti pagkalalaki, ken pigsa ken sagiksik

Embalm *(Tag. & Iloc.)* embalsamo-*Sp*

Embank *v.,* **Embankment** *n.* mga bato o lupa para maprotectahan ang daan sa baha

Embargo pagbabawal ng govierno-*Sp* na ang comercianteng barco-*Sp* ay hindi aalis at hindi papasok sa puerto/*port*/daungan

Embark sumakay sa bapor; Iloc: agsakay ti bapor

Embarrass pahiyain; Iloc: pabainan

Embassy *(Tag. & Iloc.)* embahada-*Sp*

Embattle maghanda, magpatibay, magpabisa, at magpalakas para sa giyera o labanan

Embattled nakalamang o may lamang kaya handang makipag-giyera o makipaglabanan; nilulusob sa pag-atake

Embed isimpa ng husto-*Sp* ang aparato-*Sp* o makina-*Sp*; itatag sa tao ang magandang ugali; Iloc: isimpa ti usto-*Sp* iti aparato o makina; mangitanem iti tao ti singpet iti pagkatao

Embellish 1] maglagay ng decorasyon-*Sp,* 2] dagdagan ang anomang paksa kahit pangpasikat o pangpahanga lamang o kahit na kasi-nungalingan ito; Iloc: 1] mangicabil ti decorasyon; 2] mangnayon iti ania man iti storya uray nu pangpasikat wenno pangpadayaw laeng wenno uray nu kaulbodan pay

Ember, Burning coal baga; Iloc: beggang, agdardarang nga uging

Embezzle mag-desfalco-*Sp*, mangupit, manglustay ng pera ng oficina-*Sp* o ibang tao; Iloc: agdesfalco, agcupit, mangiyusar ti cuarta-*aSp* ti oficina o ti sabali a tao

Emblem sagisag, simbolo-*Sp*; Iloc: *emblem,* simbolo

Embody may katawan na puedeng naforma at nahihipo at hindi gu-niguni lamang; kumakatawan o humahalimbawa sa isang *ideology* sa pamamagitan ng kilos at gawa

Embolden palakasin ang loob at tapang; Iloc: papigsaen iti nakem ken tured

Emboss decorasyon sa tela-*Sp* o cuadro-*Sp* na hindi *flat* kundi nahihipo dahil ito ay nakaalsang decorasyon

Embrace yakapin, yaposin, mag-abrazo-*Sp*; Iloc: aracupen, ag-abrazo

Embroider mag-borda-*Sp*; Iloc: agborda

Embroil *(Tag. & Iloc.)* nakikipag-argumento-*Sp* o nakikipagtalo o nakikipaglabanan

Embryo kauna-unahang forma gaya ng itlog bago bumuo sa tamang forma o katauhan

Emend *editing,* itama, iwasto o bagohin ang kasulatan

Emerald *(Tag. & Iloc.) emerald,* esmeralda-*Sp*

Emerge sumulpot, sumipot, lumitaw; Iloc: agpakita, agparang, sumang-lad, lumtaw

EMERGENCY *(Tag. & Iloc.) emergency*

EMERGENCY phone numbers *when needing help, call **911** if you are in the Philippines, in the USA and Canada; **000** in Australia; **112** in most European countries but the **911** may be redirected to **112** there; **111** in New Zealand; and **999** in the UK (Great Britain).*

Emergent 1] lumilitaw, tumutubo; 2] nangyayari bilang kahihinatnan; 3] kinakailangan ang agad-agad na pag-aasecaso-*Sp*

Emerita, Emeritus kareretiro lamang pero mayroon pa ring pampadangal na titulo na may kinalaman sa dati niyang puesto-*Sp*

Eminent 1] mataas ang ranko-*Sp*, puesto-*Sp* o pagkakilala; matanyag, mabantog; 2] lantad, kapansin-pansin, kapuri-puri; 3] prominente-*Sp*, nakausli at nakalabas; Iloc: natan-uk ken nangato iti puesto o ranko o popularidad-*Sp*

Eminence *(Tag. & Iloc.)* superioridad-*Sp*

Eminent domain ang karapatan ng bayan na confiscahin ang lupa na pag-aari ng mamayan para sa pangpublicong gamit at binabayaran ng govierno-*Sp* ang may-ari ng karapat-dapat

Emissary representanteng pinasugo o pinapunta para sa gagawing trabaho; Iloc: representante nga imbaon para iti maysa a trabaho nga aramiden na

Emit *v.,* **Emission** *n.* singaw, buga; Iloc: pugso, sang-aw

Emoji salitang Hapon na maliliit na letrato o simbolo na nagpapahiwatig ng bagay, damdamin, kaisipan, at iba pa na ginagamit sa mensaheng *text* at iba pang comunicasyong *electronic* at ito ay sama-sama sa tinakdang pulutong o *set* kung saan pumili dito ng gagamitin na forma ng mga ito gaya ng guhit-masaya o guhit-umiiyak

Emollient pangpalambot at pangpakinis sa balat

Emote, Over-acting or OA pagganap sa cine-*Sp* o TV na sa pagpakita ng emosyon-*Sp* ay kailangang may kalabisan para matanto o maramdaman ito ng mga nanonood

Emotion damdamin, emosyon-*Sp*; Iloc: ricna, emosyon

Emotional intelligence or Emotional quotient *Being able to perceive, understand and manage feelings and moods; being aware of one's own emotions and those of others, thus, is able to deal, cope and handle people's feelings appropriately and acceptably.* Ang capabilidad ng tao na makilala ang mismong sarili at pagkatao niya pati pagkakamali niya, at pagkilala ng damdamin ng kapwa; at dito ay tamang maturingan niya ang iba't ibang damdamin, at ginagamit niya ang kaalaman at pag-intindi niya sa mga sari-saring damdamin para mapamahala niya ang sarili niya sa tamang pag-ugnay at tamang pagasal, pati pagbabagay niya ng canyang pagtuturing sa mga pangyayari sa kapaligiran niya

Empathy *n.,* **Empathic** *adj.,* **Empathize** *v. Can understand and identify another person's feelings and feeling it on oneself; experience vicariously what one visualizes as the other person's condition.* Nagmamalasakit sa kapwa sa pagkilala at pag-intindi niya sa katayoan o dinaranas nitong kapwa na nararamdaman din niya

Emphasis *n.,* **Emphatic** *adj.,* **Emphasize** *v.* bigyan ng *emphasis* o fuersa-*Sp* ang isang paksa para maging mas lantad at prominente-*Sp* at para makaseguro na mapansin ito

EMPLOY, Use gamitin; Iloc: usaren, aramaten

EMPLOY, Hire i-*hire*, tanggapin bilang empleyado-*Sp*; Iloc: i-*hire*, pastreken bilang empleyado

Employee empleyado-*Sp*, kawani; Iloc: empleyado
Synonyms
Worker manggagawa, trabahador; Iloc: trabahador
Grassroots ordinaryong mga tao, mga empleyado o *rank-and-file* na walang puestong ma-otoridad sa oficina
Rank-and-file sa *military*, sila ang mga sundalo maliban lamang ang mga pinuno; sa oficina, sila ang mga empleyado maliban lamang ang mga pinuno nila

Employment *(Tag. & Iloc.)* empleo-*Sp*, trabaho-*Sp*

Empower bigyan ng kapangyarihan; Iloc: ikkan ti bileg wenno otoridad-*Sp*

EMPTY walang laman, nasaid, sagad; Iloc: awan ti nagyan

EMPTY-handed hindi handa o walang dala; Iloc: haan a nakasagana wenno ima-ima

EMPTY nest yugto ng buhay ng mga magulang kapag mga anak ay umalis na at hindi na nakatira sa canila

EMPTY place, residence *(Tag. & Iloc.)* vacante-*Sp*

EMPTY out contents ibuhos; Iloc: ipattog, ipakbo

Emulate *v.,* **Emulation** *n.* sikapin o minimithing pantayan, tularan o lampasan

En masse magkakasama lahat; masa; grupo

En route *[ahn root]* nasa daan na papunta sa canyang destinasyon

Enable bigyan ng permiso; Iloc: ikkan ti permiso

Enabler nagpapamihasa, mapagbigay-layaw o luho, nagpapalugod, consentidor-*Sp*; Iloc: mangipalubos ti sobra-*Sp* a capricho-*Sp*, consentidor

Enact *v.,* **Enactment** *n.* batas, gawing batas, isabatas; Iloc: aramiden a linteg

Enamor ligawan; Iloc: armen, agarem

Encamp magtayo ng tolda para tirhan sa campo

Enchant gayumahin para maakit; Iloc: igayuma tapno maawis ken ma-tentar-*Sp*,

Encircle pinapaligiran, pinapalibotan, pinapaikotan; Iloc: lawlawan, likawan, palibotan

ENCLOSE, Insert isilid, isingit, ilakip; Iloc: ipastrek, iyuneg, iserrek

ENCLOSE, Fence in palibotan sa lahat ng gilid; Iloc: aladan ti liklikaw

Enclosure 1] kulongan ng hayop, binakuran sa palibot, 2] nakasilid o nakalakip sa sulat; Iloc: 1] kulongan cadagiti animal, inaladan nga aglawlaw, 2] naypastrek iti *envelop*/sobre-*Sp* a cadwa ti surat

Encounter makasalubong, maka-encuentro-*Sp*, magsagupa; Iloc: masabat, ag-encuentro, agsarak

Encourage *v.*, **Encouragement** *n.* i-enganyo-*aSp*, pasiglain ang confiansa-*Sp* sa sarili at sa canyang kacayahan, bigyan ng pag-asa o ganang magpakabuti o magtagumpay; Iloc: i-enganyo, patibkeran ti confiansa iti bagi na ken iti cabaelan na, papigsaen ti ganas-*Sp* nga agpakasayaat o agballigi

Correlated words

Motivate bigyang ganang umunlad o magbago; Iloc: ikkan ti ganas nga agballigi o agprogreso o agbalbaliw

Incentive, Motivate hangarin o ano mang nakakabigay ng gana o pampasigla para umunlad o magpakabuti; Iloc: essem wenno ania man a mangted iti ganas nga agballigi, agprogreso o agpakasayaat

Bolster, Brace palakasin ang loob; Iloc: patibkeren ti nakem para agtured

Embolden palakasin ang loob at tapang; Iloc: papigsaen iti uneg ken tured

Encroach 1] sumulong o umavante lampas sa tinakdang hangganan, 2] unti-unti at palihim na dumaan o pumasok o makialam sa karapatan ng o ari-arian ng iba na walang pahintulot

Encumber *v.*, **Encumbrance** *n.* mabigat na gambala o panghadlang sa ginagawa; Iloc: nadagsen nga estorbo ken panglapped iti as-asecasoen

Encyclopedia libro-*Sp* na naglalaan ng napakaraming paksa at larangan para pagconsultahan ng mga tao at makakuha ng tamang informasyon-*Sp*

END *v.* magwakas, matapos, tapusin; Iloc: aggibus, ipalpas, malpas

END *n.* katapusan, wakas; Iloc: gibus, panaglippas

Endanger ilagay sa panganib o peligro-*Sp*; Iloc: ikabil iti peggad o peligro

Endear *v.*, **Endearment** *n.* minamahal at tinatangi, pagmamahal; Iloc: ay-ayaten ken dungdungoen, ayat

Endeavor *Strive or make a strenuous effort to undertake something.* Magsikap, magpakasigasig, magpursigi, magpunyagi na magsagawa; Iloc: ikarkarigatan, ipamuspusan, agpakat nga agobra

Endemic sakit na laganap lamang sa isang lugar-*Sp* o sa maliit na comunidad-*Sp*

Correlated words

Epidemic sakit na <u>mabilis</u> na lumaganap sa mga tao sa malaki at maraming lugar

Pandemic sakit na laganap sa malaki at maraming lugar

Plague peste, kalat na calamidad o nakahahawang sakit

Endless walang katapusan; Iloc: awan ti gibus na

Endorse *v.,* **Endorsement** *n.* 1] otorisasyon-*Sp* o pagbabawal; pag-firma-*Sp* ng lagda, paglagay ng tagubilin sa documento-*Sp*, itaguyod, suportahan, tangkilikin; Iloc: suportaran (suporta/suportar-*Sp)*

Endow *v.,* **Endowment** *n.* pagkalooban, pamigay; Iloc: mangisagot, sagot

Endurance tiis; Iloc: ibtur, kired

Endure *Withstand or bear bravely and patiently; accept and survive hardships.* Sikmurain, tiisin; Iloc: an-anosan, ibturan, iturtured
Correlated words

Withstand tiisin; Iloc: anosan, iturtured, ibturan

Bear tiisin; Iloc: anosan

Cope magsikap at magpakasigasig lalo na sa kahirapan ng buhay; Iloc: agpakat, mang-ibtur o mangsolvar aglal-lalo iti rigat ti biag

Fare pagtanggap at mapacenciang pagpangasiwa at mahusay na makibaka sa anomang dumadating sa buhay

Enduring matagal at permanente; matibay, pacensiosa sa pagtitiis; Iloc: agbayag, maka-ibtur

Enema *(Tag. & Iloc.)* labativa-*Sp*

Enemy kalaban, kaaway, kagalit; Iloc: kalaban, kaapa
Synonym

Adversary, Foe kalaban, kaaway, kagalit; Iloc: kalaban, kaapa
Antonym

Advocate, Backer mangsuporta, tagapagtaguyod, tagapagtanggol; Iloc: mangsuporta, mangsalaknib, mangtakder

Energetic masigasig, puno ng sigla; Iloc: nasagiksik, napunno ti ganas, alisto

Energy enerhia-*Sp*, sigla, lakas at cacayahang magcompleto ng mabigat at patuloy-tuloy na trabaho; Iloc: enerhia, siglat, pigsa ken adda cabaelan na a i-completo ti nadagsen ken agtultuloy nga ob-obra-*Sp*

Enervate ipahina; Iloc: ipacapsut, ipacapoy

Enfeeble ipahina; Iloc: ipacapsut, ipacapoy

Enforce fuersahing ipatupad; Iloc: fuersaen nga ipatungpal (fuersa-*Sp)*

335

ENGAGED *engaged,* nagkasundong sila'y magpapacasal; Iloc: agtulag da nga ag-casar-*Sp, engaged*

ENGAGED in *(Tag. & Iloc.)* ocupado, inaatupag ang...

Engender makapaglikha, makapaggawa, makapagsanhi

Engine *(Tag. & Iloc.)* motor-*Sp,* makina-*Sp*

Engineer *(Tag. & Iloc.)* inhinyero-*Sp*

English *(Tag. & Iloc.)* English, Ingles-*Sp*

Engrave *(Tag. & Iloc.)* ukit

Engrossed abala, ocupado-*Sp,* subsob na subsob o buhos na buhos sa ginagawa; Iloc: ocupado, nakasubsob unay iti ob-obraen na

Enhance ayosin para mas-*Sp* humusay at mas ma-ventahe-*Sp* o mas efectivo-*Sp* o magtaglay ng makabagong obra-*Sp*

Enigma pangyayaring nakapagtataka at mahirap o hindi maipaliwanag; taong nakakapagtataka sa kakaibang ugali; salita, tanong o retrao na may nakatagong kahulogan

ENJOY maglibang, mag-aliw, magsaya; Iloc: agpapas, agragragsak, agramrambak

Synonym

Delight in naaliw; Iloc: aglinglingay

Exult *v.,* **Exultation** *n.* labis na pagpapakasaya

Jubilate maglibang, mag-aliw, magsaya; Iloc: agpapas, agragragsak, agramrambak

ENJOY the fruit of one's labor tamasahin ang tagumpay dahil karapat-dapat sa iyo ito pagkatapos kang nagsikap; Iloc: agpaimas iti balligi iti pinagpakatan

Enjoyable nakalilibang, nakakaaliw, nakakasaya, nakakatuwa; Iloc: nakaramrambak, nakaragragsak, nakaling-lingay

Enjoyment katuwaan, kasiyahan; Iloc: pagragsakan, pagrambakan

Enlarge palakihin, laparan, palawakin, paluwangin, pahabain; Iloc: padakkelen, lawaan, i-acaba

Enlighten maliwanagan ang intelihensia-*Sp* o ang pagka-spiritual-*Sp*; pagtuturo at pagpapakabuti sa katalinohan, moralidad-*Sp,* etico-*Sp,* dignidad-*Sp,* integridad-*Sp* at sa pagkamaka-Dios

Enlist 1] magpatala, magpa-lista-*Sp,* 2] sumali, lumahok, maki-alyado, makisapi, umanib; Iloc: 1] agpalista, 2] makisali, maki-alyado, makitipon

Register magparehistro; Iloc: agparehistro

Enliven pagalakin; Iloc: paragsaken

Enmity matinding galit, poot, muhi, suklam; Iloc: busor, gura, rurod, pungtot, uyong

Ennui walang kalatoy-latoy ni gana-*Sp* kaya hindi interesado-*Sp*

Enormity 1] napakalaki sa sukat, lawak, *scope,* o influensia-*Sp*; 2] nakakakilabot sa pagkamasama

Enormous higante-*Sp*, napakalaki; Iloc: higante, nakadak-dakkel

ENOUGH kasya, sapat, bastante-*Sp*; Iloc: makaanay, bastante

ENOUGH to go around mga bagay o pagkain na bastante-*Sp* o sapat para sa lahat na nandodoon

Enrich 1] magpayaman, 2] gawing mas mahusay o mas ma-sustancia-*Sp*; Iloc: 1] agpabaknang, agparang-ay, 2] aramiden a mas nalaeng o mas masustancia

Enroll *(Tag. & Iloc.) enroll*

Enroute nasa daan na papunta sa...; Iloc: adda diay dalan a mapan idiay...

Ensue sumunod, ang kasunod; Iloc: sumaruno, ti mangsaruno

Ensure *Assure, reassure, give surety, guarantee, ascertain certify.* Segurohin (seguro-*Sp*), maniguro; Iloc: seguradwen, mangseguro

Entail kailangang magawa o magkaroon dahil talagang pangangailangan ito; Iloc: masapul a maaramid wenno masapul a maaddaan gapu ta necesario-*Sp* daytoy

Entangled *(Tag. & Iloc.)* nagkabuhol-buhol, nagkapulo-pulopot

ENTER pumasok; Iloc: sumrek, umuneg

ENTER forcibly, Force-entry lusobin, sacopin, magsira ng pinto o vintana para makapasok; Iloc: fuersa-*Sp* a serreken, mangdadael ti puerta-*Sp* wenno ventana-*Sp* para makaserrek

ENTER, let papasokin; Iloc: pastreken

Enterprise inaasecasong nakatayong negosio-*Sp* o proyecto-*Sp*

Entertain aliwin, libangin; Iloc: parambaken, liwliwaen, linglingayen

Entertaining nakakalibang, nakakaaliw; Iloc: makalinglingay, makaliwliwa

Entertainment libangan, aliwan, palabas; Iloc: paglinglingayan, pagrambakan, pabuya

Enthrall 1] akitin o ibighani; 2] bihagin, supilin

Enthused, Enthusiastic maganang-magana; Iloc: aggang-ganas, maga-nasan unay (gana/ ganas-*Sp*)

Synonyms

Animated, Spirited *(Tag. & Iloc.)* vivo, viva

Vibrant masaya, masigla, maliksi, masigasig, ganado, alisto Iloc: naragsak, nasagiksik, ganado, alisto

Spry activo at punong-puno ng buhay; Iloc: activo ken napno ti biag

Gung ho *(Tag. & Iloc.)* ganadong-ganado at dedicado

Lively, Sprightly *(Tag. & Iloc.)* galawgaw, calog

Bubbly masigla at nakakasiya; Iloc: ganado ken naragsak

Vivacious maaliw, masaya at ang kasayahan niya ay nakakahawa; Iloc: nakalinglingay, naragsak ken ti ragsak na ket makaacar ti dadduma

Enthusiasm *n. (Tag. & Iloc.)* pagkaganado

Entice akitin, magkiri, mag-alembong; Iloc: sulisogen, itentar-*Sp*

Entire *adj.*, **Entirety** *n.* entero-*Sp*, lahat; Iloc: entero, am-amin

Entirely lahat-lahat, lubosan, todo-todo-*Sp*; Iloc: pulos, am-amin, todo-todo

Entitle bigyang-karapatan, bigyan ng permiso-*Sp*; Iloc: ikkan ti turay, ikkan ti permiso

Entitled nakakarapatan niya, nabigyang-karapatan, naaangkop sa canya; Iloc: nayturayan na, nayrebbengan na

Entitlement, sense of pinapaniwalaan niyang may karapatan at pri-vilehio-*Sp* siya na mag-angkin o gumawa ng kahit anomang gusto niya kahit wala siyang karapatan o privilehio; Iloc: patchen na nga addaan isu ti rebbeng ken privilehio nga agsanicua isu o mabalin na aramiden ti ania man a cayat na uray nu haan usto-*Sp*

Correlated words

Delusions of grandeur guni-guni sa sarili na siya ay napakadakila o may karapatan sa mga bagay kahit wala

Presumptuous may *sense of entitlement* siya kaya inaakala niya na mayroon siyang karapatan kahit wala o umaasta siya na nakucorsunadahan siya kahit hindi; Iloc: adda *sense of entitlement* isu nga pammati na ket adda linteg na o rebbeng na uray no awan, wenno macurcursonadaan isu uray nu haan

Entity ito'y puedeng companya, organisasyon o tao

Entrails, Internal organs mga lamang-loob; Iloc: lalaem ti uneg ti bagi

Entrance pagpasokan, pinto, entrada-*Sp*; Iloc: pagserkan, entrada, puerta-*Sp*

Entrap silohin, bitagin, dayain para masilo, patibungin

Entreat dibdibang nagsusumamo; Iloc: naregget nga agkidkiddaw

Entree, Main dish ulam; Iloc: sida

Entrepreneur *(Tag. & Iloc.)* negosiante-*Sp*

Entrust ipagkatiwala; Iloc: ipag-fiar-*Sp*, ipatalek

Entry 1] aplicasyon-*Sp* para sumali, 2] mga nakasulat at ang dinadagdag na informasyon-*Sp* sa *record* o *log book*; Iloc: 1] aplicasyon para makasali, 2] dagiti nakasurat ken iti inaynayon nga informasyon iti *record* o *log book*

Entwine ipulopot ang pisi, lubid o pantali sa pagpupulopotan

Enumerate baybayin, isa-isang banggitin; Iloc: isawang a maysa-maysa

Enunciate magbigkas at magsalita ng maliwanag; magpahayag at magpatalastas ng mahusay

Envelope *(Tag. & Iloc.) envelope*, sobre-*Sp*

Enviable *Superior and desirable that it is worthy of envy.* Tunay na mahusay at kawili-wili na nakakainggit

Environment, Environs kapaligiran, kalawakan; Iloc: arrubayan
  Correlated words
  Expanse kalawakan, Iloc: dagiti solar
  Surroundings kapaligiran, paligid, palibot; Iloc: arrubayan, iti aglawlaw
  Neighborhood kapaligiran, kapit-bahayan; Iloc: karkarruba
  Atmosphere 1] ang hangin o clima o ang kapaligran ng isang lugar, 2] ang nakakahawang modo o pag-iisip ng kapaligiran; Iloc: 1] ti angin o clima o arrubayan ti maysa a lugar, 2] ti makaacar a modo o pagpampanunot iti arrubayan
  Firmament himpapawid; Iloc: tangatang
  Sky himpapawid, langit; Iloc: tangatang, langit

Envision ilarawan sa isip; Iloc: i-retrato-*Sp* ti panunot

Envoy sugo; mas mababa sa embahador na nagtatrabaho sa *embassy*

Envy mainggit; Iloc: umapal, agagum, agimon

Epic *n. & adj.*, 1] makamaharlika, marangal, kahanga-hanga; 2] mahabang kasaysayan o tula na nagsasalaysay ng isang tao at mga dakila at makabayaning nagawa niya at iba pang pangyayari na nakasulat sa *elevated style*

Epidemic sakit na mabilis na lumaganap sa mga tao sa malaki at maraming lugar

Epilepsy *epilepsy*, mangaligkig; Iloc: *epilepsy*, kissiw

Epitaph kasulatan sa lapida-*Sp* na alaala sa yumaong tao na nakalibing doon; Iloc: panglaglagip a kasuratan diay lapida iti nakapumpon a tao idiay

Epithet 1] tawag sa tao na panglarawan sa canya gaya ng *The Great Emancipator* kay Abraham Lincoln; 2] pero kadalasan ay ginagamit na pang-abuso o kamuhi-muhing pantawag

Epitome *n.,* **Epitomize** *v.* larawan, kumakatawan; Iloc: retrato-*Sp*, pang -representante-*Sp*

Epoch isang panahon sa nakaraan na tinuturing na mahalaga at karapat-dapat na gunitain

EQUAL katumbas, pantay, patas, tabla; Iloc: tabla, patas, patag, agpada

EQUAL opportunity caraniwan sa trabaho o empleo na pantay-pantay lahat ang turing at walang binabale-wala o walang finafavoran ano man ang kulay ng balat, *race* o lahi, *ancestry* o lipi, edad, babae o lalake, relihion, may kapansanan o wala

Equalize pagparehoin; tumbasan; Iloc: pagpadaen

Equate gawing kapantay o magkatumbas o magkapareho; ituring o itrato o ilarawan na ito ay kapantay o kapareho

Equation ang pagkakapareho o pagiging kapantay o kapareho

Equilibrium 1] kalagayang pahinga/ginhawa; matatag na kalagayan; balansiado ang isip at karamdaman; 2] may balanse ang bisa/lakas, kapangyarihan, influwensia, at iba pa

Equinox *daylight savings time,* panahon kung kailan ang planetang init ay tumatawid sa ecuador ng mundo kaya ang gabi at araw ay magkapareho ang haba sa buong mundo at nangyayari ito sa Marso 21 *(vernal equinox or spring equnox)* at Septiembre 22 *(autumnal equinox).*

Equip bigyan, dulotan, magtustos sa tao, lugar-*Sp*, organisasyon-*Sp* ng ano man na kinakailangan nila gaya ng kagamitan, pagkain, pera at iba pa; magdulot ng panustos para sa intelihensia-*Sp*, abilidad-*Sp*, emosyon-*Sp*, pag-intindi at iba pa.

Equipage kagamitan, mga cargamento-*Sp*; Iloc: alicamen, cargamento, maar-aramat

Equipment *n.* 1] mga kagamitan na dinulot gaya ng mga *tools* at *kits* na kinakailangang magagamit sa paggawa, o mga armas-*Sp* ng mga sundalo na kinakailangan nila; 2] ang kaalaman at abilidad-*Sp* ng isang tao para sa tungkulin niya o sa ocupasyon-*Sp* niya

Equitable pantay-pantay ang turing, makatwiran at makatarungan

Equity 1] ang pagkamakatarungan at pagkamakatwiran at pantay-pantay ang turing; 2] ang halaga ng ari-airan o negosio pagkatapos na pag-usapan ang *mortgage* at mga detalye nito at kung mayroong obligasyon na bayaran.

Equivalent kapantay, katumbas, pareho-*Sp*; Iloc: agpada, pareho

Equivocal malabo at nakakasuspecha na parang iligaw o manlinlang dahil bukas ito sa maraming kahulogan o iba't ibang interpretasyon.

Equivoque or Equivoke *[equavok]* 1] pinaglalaruan ang salita; hindi maintindihang salita o ang ibig sabihin; 2] pangungusap na may dalawang kahulogan

Eradicate alisin, gawing maglaho o maparam; bunotin sa puno o ugat para mawala na

ERASE borahin (bora-*Sp)*, *erase*-in; Iloc: boraen, *erase*-in

ERASE from one's memory iwaksi sa isip; Iloc: iwaksi ti panunot

ERECT nakatayo o nakaupo na derecho-*Sp* ang katawan; Iloc: nakatacder o nakatugaw a derecho ti bagi

ERECT, Build magpatayo, magtatag, mag-puesto-*Sp*; Iloc: mangpatacder, mangplastar-*Sp*, mangsimpa, mangpuesto, mangbangon

Ergonomics ang aplicadong siencia-*Sp* ng makina o ibang aparato-*Sp* na nilikha para makadami, makabilis, makagawa ng maximo-*Sp* sa trabaho-*Sp* pero nakakaginhawa at mas kaunti ang sikap, pagod at *stress.*

Erode mayurak; Iloc: marunaw, agrumek

Err magkamali, magkasala; Iloc: agbasol, agbiddut

Errand lumabas ng bahay para may gagawing tungkulin; Iloc: rumuar ti balay para mangaramid iti masapul nga maaramid.

Erratic taliwas, lumilihis sa caraniwang gawain; Iloc: agsabsabali iti cadawyan nga aramid

Error kamalian, pagkakamali, Iloc: biddut

Ersatz anomang artifisyal-*Sp* o imitasyon-*Sp* na kadalasan ay mumurahin

Erudite, *adj,* **Erudition** *n.* maraming napag-aralan at maraming ka-alaman; Iloc: adu ti naadal ken adu ti ammo

Erupt sumabog; Iloc: agbettak, agpugso ti napudot a pitak

Escalate tumindi o dumami o lumaki; Iloc: cumaro o umado wenno dumakkel

Escalator hagdanan na gumagalaw paakyat o pababa; Iloc: agdan a gumargaraw nga agpangato o agpababa

Escape tatakas, magtalilis, magpuslit; Iloc: agtammeng, aglibas, agpuslit
Correlated word
Abscond umalis na palihim at biglaan at caraniwan ay para makalihis sa reglamento ng batas

Escaped nakatakas, nakapuslit, nakatalilis; Iloc: nakabulos, nakatalaw, nakatammeng, nakapuslit, nakalibas

Escargot suso; Iloc: bisukol

Eschew iwasan, layoan; Iloc: lisyan, adawyan

ESCORT *n. (Tag. & Iloc.)* consorte-*Sp*

ESCORT *v.* samahan; Iloc: kuyogen, cadwaen

Escrow contrata-*Sp*, titulo-*Sp*, *bond* o kasulatang kasundoan na naka-deposito sa ikatlong partido-*Sp*, para siya ang magbigay sa pina-ngakoan kapag ang pinagkasundoang condisyon-*Sp* ay natupad na

Esophagus lalamunan; Iloc: carabukob

Esoteric alam at naiintindihan ng isang grupo-*Sp* lamang at secreto o lihim na hindi nila pinapaalam sa publico-*Sp*

Especially lalo na; Iloc: nangnangruna, aglallalo

Espionage lihim na pagmanman ng espia-*Sp* para makakuha ng kinakailangang informasyon-*Sp*; Iloc: nalimed a pagsipsiput ti espia para makaala ti masapul nga informasyon

Essence buod, diwa; Iloc: amad

Essential *Absolutely required, totally necessary and indispensable; primarily needed.* Kailngang-kailangan, lubhang kailangan, ma-kabulohan masyado-*aSp;* primerong kinakailangan para sa pag-usbong at pagparoon sa progreso at sa kabutihan; Iloc: primero-*Sp* a kasapulan para iti pagrusing ken pag-avante iti progreso ken kaimbagan
Synonyms
Fundamental 1] fundasyon, elementarya, 2] importante, kinakailangan para sa pagsasagawa
Vital kailangang-kailangan, napakahalaga at napakaimportante para ma-kabuo o makapagsagawa

Imperative kinakailangang mangyari o magkaroon; Iloc: masapul nga mapasamak wenno maaddaaan

Indispensable kailangan pagtuonan ng pansin dahil ito ay kinakailangan at hindi maipaubaya dahil obligasyon ito; Iloc: masapul nga asecaswen ta daytoy ket kasapulan ken haan a liwayan ta obligasyon daytoy

Establish magpatayo, magtatag, mag-puesto-*Sp*; Iloc: mangbangon, mangpatacder, mang-plastar-*Sp*, mangpuesto, mangsimpa

Established person nakapagtatag na makilala siya sa canyang ka-pakipakinabang na katatao o gawain o proyecto-*Sp*; Iloc: nakapagsimpa ti popularidad-*Sp* gapu ti navalor ken makapaimbag a katatao na wenno obra-*Sp* wenno proyecto na

Estate lahat ng ari-arian pati bahay at lupa at utang at iba pa; Iloc: amin a cukcukua pati balay ken dagdaga ken ut-utang ken dadduma pay

Esteem estimahin, hangaan; Iloc: estimaren, dayawen (estima/estimar-*Sp*)

Estimable 1] puedeng matancha o macalcula; 2] karapatdapat na hangaan o purihin

Estimate *v.*, **Estimation** *n.* 1] paghahatol at paghuhusga o palagay at kuro-kuro; 2] calcula, tancha

Estrange 1] magpakita ng pagkawalang malasakit at pagkawalang halaga; 2] pag-alis sa dating tinitirhan o sa dating kasama

Et al at ang mga iba; Iloc: ken dagiti dadduma

Etc., Etcetera at iba-iba pang kapanig ng mga ito; Iloc: ken saba-sabali pay a kacadua nadagitoy

Etch *(Tag. & Iloc.)* ukit

Eternal *adj.*, **Eternity** *n.* walang umpisa at walang wakas, walang hangganan at katapusan; Iloc: awan rugi ken awan gibus na, awan patinggana o kapalpasan na
Correlated words
Perpetual tumatagal at walang wakas; Iloc: agpaut ken awan gibus na
Lifelong sa buong buhay, habang buhay; Iloc: ingganat patay, mientras a sibibiag

Ethical *adj.*, **Ethics** *n. a moral person; in accordance with moral principles and values; dealing with morality and right-and-wrong conducts; also the ethics and correct conduct that are the expected practices of a professional career.*

Ethnic *adj.*, **Ethinicity** *n.* lahi na parepareho ang canilang wika at punto ng pananalita, puno't dulo o pinagsimulan, ichura-*Sp*, kaugalian, kagawian, custombre-*Sp* cultura-*Sp*; tradisyon-*Sp* o relihion na magkasama-sama sa isang lugar-*Sp* o bansa; bukod-tanging clase-*Sp* o uri ng isang bayan at mga mamamayan nito

Etiquette, Rules in behaving in a well-mannered society *(Tag. & Iloc.)* etiketa-*Sp*

Synonym

Good manners kabutihang asal; Iloc: ma-etiketa a paggaraw

Euphemism *n.*, **Euphemistic** *adj.* palitan ang maamong salita para maging marahas at nakakasakit na salita; Iloc: sukatan iti naamo a sarita iti naranggas ken makasakit a sarita

Euphony *n.*, **Euphonious** *adj.* magandang pakinggan, napakainam na tono o salita

Euphoria lubhang napakalaking ligaya at galak; Iloc: sobra ken dakkel a ragsak

Evacuate lisanan ang lugar-*Sp* at lumipat sa lugar na ligtas na walang peligro-*Sp*

Evade *v.*, **Evasion** *n.* ilagan, lihisan, iwasan; Iloc: lisyan, aglisi, aglinged

Evaluate calculahin, tanchahin, mag-evaluar-*Sp*

Evangelize pagpapahayag tungkol sa kabanalan, kapangyarihan at pagmamahal sa mga nilalang ng Panginoong Dios sa langit, batay sa Biblia na banal na salita ng Dios.

Evaporate sumingaw at maigahan; Iloc: sumngaw ken maachan

Eve or day before an event *(Tag. & Iloc.)* visperas-*Sp*

EVEN *(Tag. & Iloc.)* pati

EVEN, Tied *(Tag. & Iloc.)* amanos, tabla, patag, patas

EVEN though kahit na, kahit pa, maski na, "Basta!"; Iloc: uray nu, uray pay, "Basta!"

Evening mga primero-*Sp* o unang oras-*Sp* ng gabi gaya ng alas seis-*Sp* o alasiete-*Sp*

EVENT *(Tag. & Iloc.)* ocasyon-*Sp*

EVENT arrival sumapit; Iloc: dumanon

Eventually magaganap sa dadating na panahon; Iloc: mapasamak cadagiti sumangpet a panawen

EVER sa lahat ng panahon; Iloc: iti amin a panawen

EVER since sapul pa noon, mula noon, buhat noon; Iloc: manipud idi, agsipud idi

Every bawat, tuwing, pawang; Iloc: cada-*Sp*, cada maysa

Everyday araw-araw; Iloc: cada-*Sp* aldaw, inaldaw

Everyone, Everybody lahat at bawat isa; Iloc: amin ken tunggal maysa, amin ken cada-*Sp* maysa

Everything lahat-lahat, lahat, todo-todo-*Sp*; Iloc: amin-amin, am-amin, todo-todo

Everywhere sa lahat ng lugar-*Sp*; Iloc: idiay amin a lugar

Evict paalisin sa bahay na tinitirhan, palayasin; Iloc: papanawen diay balay a pagyanan na
Synonym
Oust paalisin, palayasin, despachahin; Iloc: papanawen, despacharen

EVIDENCE *(Tag. & Iloc.)* evidencia-*Sp*
Synonym
Proof prueba, pagpapatotoo, katibayan, pagpapatunay, pagpapatiyak, patunay; Iloc: prueba, pangpaneknek

EVIDENCE is proof, Where there is smoke, there is fire kung may prueba-*Sp* o may evidencia-*Sp*, malaking posibilidad-*Sp* na katotohanan o tutoong-tutoo ito

Evident lantad, halata, litaw, kitang-kita, vistado-*Sp*; Iloc: makitkita, nakaparang, vistado, nalatak

Evil masama, demonyo, satanas; Iloc: dakes, demonyo, satanas, sairo, diablo, diantre

Evitable puedeng maiwasan at malihisan; Iloc: mabalin a malisyan
Synonym
Avoidable puedeng maiwasan at malihisan

Evoke 1] pukawin sa memoria ang isang alaala; 2] tawagan o hugitin; magmungkahi o magsagawa ng guniguni o imahinasyon-*Sp* na kagaya ng tunay sa buhay

Evolve nagbabago at kadalasan ay bumubuti habang dumadaan ang panahon; Iloc: agbalbaliw ken canayon ket agsaysayaat mientras-*Sp* nga agpaspasar ti panawen

Ex dating (sa nakaraang panahon) asawa o novia o matalik na kasambahay o *mistress* o querida-*Sp*

Exacerbate palubhain, palalain, lalong gawing mas grabe ang tindi o hinanakit o pagkapusok (ng sakit, damdamin na nasaktan, at iba pa); galitin, yamotin; gawing malala, malubha at mabigat; Iloc: padagsenen, aramiden a grabe-*Sp*, aramiden a problema-*Sp*

Exact exacto-*Sp*, tamang-tama, tumpak, hustong-husto-*Sp*; Iloc: us-usto-*Sp*, exacto

Exacting mahigpit o mabigat na kautosan o rekisito-*Sp* sa kinakailangang katangian at abilidad-*Sp* para maging karapat-dapat o maging angkop; 2] kinakailangan ang matinding pag-ukol ng pansin at pag-asecaso-*Sp* at pagsasagawa o pagpapairal

Exaggerate palakihin kaysa sa katunayan; Iloc: padakkelen uray ti ka-agpaysuan ket haan

Exalt bigyan ng mataas na pagpupuri at pagdangal at pagsamba; Iloc: iglorificar ken mangited iti dakkel a pagyaman ken pagdayaw

Examination examinasyon, examen, *test*, pagsusulit; Iloc: examinasyon, *test*, examen, sukimat

Examine suriin, pag-aralan, usisain, usigin, siyasatin; Iloc: sukimaten, sukisoken, adalen, usigen, usisaen

EXAMPLE *example*, halimbawa; Iloc: *example*, ehemplo

EXAMPLE, for halimbawa, *for example*, gaya ng; Iloc: casla ti, *for example*, por ehemplo-*Sp*

Exasperate yamotin, consomihin, suyahin, i-perhuisio-*Sp*; Iloc: iconsomi, pasuyaen, sairwen, iperhuisio

Excavate hukayin; Iloc: calyen

Exceed lampasan, higitan; Iloc: ipalabes, pasuroken

Excel mas-*Sp* labis ang natatamo kaysa natatamo ng caraniwang tao; Iloc: mas nalalaeng iti magungun-od na ngem iti cadawyan a tao

Excellent, Excellence *(Tag. & Iloc.)* excelente-*Sp*, *superior*

Except; Exception of, with the maliban sa, hindi kasali ang, huera-*aSp* lang sa; Iloc: malaksid iti, fuera-*Sp* lang iti

Exceptional katangi-tangi, natatanging ugali o gawa na canya lamang; Iloc: aramid o katatao nga bukbukod awan ti kapada na

Excerpt isang maikling parte na hinango sa mahabang kasulatan

Excess lampas, sobra-*Sp*, labis, higit; Iloc: sobra, surok, labes

Excessive palalo, malabis; Iloc: napalalo, nalabes, nacaro

EXCHANGE magpalitan, ipalit; Iloc: agsinnukat, isukat
Correlated words
Substitute palitan, kapalit; Iloc: sukatan, kasukat
Swap magpalitan; Iloc: agsinnukat
EXCHANGE of views magtalakayan, magpalitan ng *opinion*; Iloc: agpinnatang
Excitement buhay na buhay ang saya o pagkasabik o pagkaasam; Iloc: nasged a sibibiag ti ragsak na o gagar na wenno papaos na
Exciting nakakatuwa at nakakalibang; Iloc: nakaramrambak ken nakalinglingay
Exclaim, Blurt biglang magbulalas; Iloc: golpe-*aSp* nga agsawang
Exclude hindi isali, hindi isacop, iliban; Iloc: haan iraman, ilaksid
Excluding maliban lamang, huera lang ang..; Iloc: fuera-*Sp* laeng iti, malaksid laeng ti
Exclusive *exclusive*, para lamang o binubukod lamang sa tinakdang grupo-*Sp* at hindi sinasali ang iba; Iloc: *exclusive*, ibukbukod lang iti naysaad a grupo ken haan a isali ti dadduma
EXCREMENT, Excreta tae, dumi; Iloc: takki
EXCREMENT of birds & lizards dumi, tae; Iloc: lugit
Excrete ilabas o ibuga ng katawan gaya ng dugo o pagdumi, pagtae, pag-ihi
Excruciating sakit na napakatindi; Iloc: sakit a napalalo
Exculpate ipawalang-sala; Iloc: ilaksid iti basol
Excursion *excursion*, isang araw na pasyal o viahe-*Sp* sa malapit na lugar; Iloc: *excursion*, maysa aldaw nga pasiar-*Sp* o viahe iti asideg a lugar-*Sp*
EXCUSE *v.*, bigyan ng paumanhin; Iloc: dispensaren
EXCUSE *n.*, **Alibi** pagdadahilan; Iloc: pambar
"EXCUSE me" "Pardon me" "Ipagpatawad po," "Paumanhin po"; Iloc: "Dispensaren apo" (dispensar-*Sp*)
Execute *v.*, **Execution** *n.* 1] maglikha, ganapin, pairalin, gampanan, asecasohin; 2] ifirma ang signatura-*Sp* para maging valido-*Sp* ang documento-*Sp*; 3] bitayin, ibigti
Executive, Boss *boss*, puno, amo-*Sp*; Iloc: *boss*, pangulo, amo
Exemplary uliran, *role model*; Iloc: nasayaat nga ehemplo-*Sp*
Exemplify magpakita ng mabuting halimbawa para tularan; Iloc: mangipakita ti naimbag nga ehemplo-*Sp* tapno tuladen

Exempt *v.*, **Exemption** *n.* pinili at binukod na hindi isali sa rekisito-*Sp* o alituntnin; Iloc: inlasin nga haan isali iti rekisito-*Sp* o regulasyon

Exercise 1] *exercise*, maliksing paggamit ng fuersa-*Sp* at kilos/galaw ng katawan para sa *training* o pagpapabuti ng kalusogan o para mabihasa o para maisa-condisyon-*Sp* ang katawan o ang tinakdang parte-*Sp* ng katawan; gawaing pang-*practice* o *training;* 2] ipairal o gamitin ang karapatan o kapangyarihan

Exert magsikap, magpakasigasig, magpursigi, magpunyagi; Iloc: ikarkarigatan, ipamuspusan, agpakat

Exertion pagsisikap, pagpupunyagi, pagpupursigi

Exfoliate <u>tanggalin</u> ang kaliskis, kaliskisan; bakbakin o tuklapin ang balat o ano mang nasa parteng-labas gaya ng *bark* ng kahoy o *flakes* at iba pa

EXHALE humingang palabas; Iloc: agsang-aw
Correlated word
Inhale lumanghap, sumamyo; Iloc: aglang-ab

EXHALE and Inhale, Breathe huminga; Iloc: aganges

EXHAUST 1] gamitin lahat, 2] usok na lumalabas sa motor; Iloc: 1] iyusar amin, 2] asok nga rumuar diay motor

EXHAUST pipe *(Tag. & Iloc.)* tambucho

Exhausted pagod, hapo; Iloc: nabannug

Exhibit mag-*exhibition*, magpalabas, magpakita; Iloc: ag-*exhibition*, ag-presentar-*Sp*
Correlated word
Display ipakitang-tao; Iloc: ipakita, ipabuya, iparang

Exhibition *exhibition,* pagtatanghal; Iloc: *exhibition*, pag-presentar-*Sp*, pabuya

Exhilarate magpasaya at magpasigla; Iloc: agparagsak ken agpasagiksik

Exigency *n.*, **Exigent** *adj. Urgent that it requires immediate action, attention, aid, and even a great deal of efforts.* Kinakailangan ang malaking sikap at dali-daling paggalaw o pag-remedio-*Sp*; Iloc: masapul iti dakkel a pakat ken dagdagos a paggaraw o pagremedio

Exile ifuersang paalisin sa lugar o bayan; Iloc: ifuersa nga papanawen iti lugar o bayan

Exist sa tao-nabubuhay; sa mga *things* o bagay, o *values* o namamalagi; Iloc: iti tao-sibibiag, iti banag-addaan ditoy

Exit labasan; Iloc: ruaran

Exonerate i-absuelto-*Sp*, ipawalang sala; Iloc: i-absuelto, paawanen ti basol

Exorbitant *adj.,* **Exorbitance** *n.* 1] asal o custombre-*Sp* na hindi tama o mabuti, 2] preciong napakamahal; Iloc: 1] custombre-*Sp* nga haan usto-*Sp* o nasayaat, 2] precio-*Sp* a sobra-*Sp* ti ngina na

Expand *v.,* **Expansion** *n.* palawakin, pagpalawak, palakihin, pahabain; Iloc: pagpadakkel, palawaen, pagpaacaba
Synonym
Enlarge palakihin, laparan, palawakin, paluwangin, palakihin, pahabain; Iloc: padakkelen, lawaan, iyacaba

Expanse kalawakan, Iloc: dakkel a solar-*Sp*

Expat, Expatriate taong umalis sa sariling bayan para matira sa ibang bayan bilang mamamayan doon; Iloc: tao nga taga sabali nga bayan ngem talawan na para agyan iti sabali nga bayan
Antonym
Repatriate 1] pabalikin ang isang tao (gaya ng isang bilanggo o *refugee*) sa dating pinanggalingang bayan o sa canyang bayang sinilangan; 2] tubong kinita o ari-arian na ipadala sa sariling bayan; 3] pagbabalik sa pinanggalingang bayan

Expect inaabangan, asahan; Iloc: expectaren, namnamaen, agabang, seggaan (expectar-*Sp*)

Expectorate idura, i-ubo; Iloc: itupra, ipugso

Expedience *n.,* **Expedient** *adj.* nararapat o naaangkop o tugma sa isang layonin; tama o wasto para sa circumstancia; alinsunod sa gamit

Expedite padaliin, pabilisan, i-apura-*Sp*; Iloc: padarasen, dagdagen, ipartak, papartaken, ipardas, ipaspas, i-apura

Expedition paglalakbay ng isang grupo na caraniwan ay para sa isang pakay

Expeditious ginaganap o nilikha ng bilis at kahusayan

EXPEL *v.,* **Expulsion** *n.* patalsikin sa escuela-*Sp* bilang parusa sa pag-labag ng alituntunin; Iloc: dusa nga mangpatalsik iti estudiante-*Sp* gapu ti pagsupyat na iti regulasyon-*Sp* ti escuela-*Sp*

EXPEL, Expectorate ibuga; Iloc: ipugso

Expendable para paggamit ng minsan at ubosin na, hindi na iligpit – hindi mahalagang itago o gamitin pang muli

Expenditure ang mga binibili at binabayaran; Iloc: dagiti gatgatangen ken baybayadan

Expense of someone or something, at the sa pagkaagraviado ng tao o ng oficina o ng isang bagay

Expenses *(Tag. & Iloc.)* gastos-*Sp* ng familia

Expensive mahal; Iloc: nangina
Antonym
Inexpensive, Cheap mura, baratilyo; Iloc: nalaca

EXPERIENCE *n.* expiryensa-*Sp*, karanasan, pinagdaanan sa buhay gaya ng trabaho; mga dinanas at napag-aralan sa buhay; Iloc: expiryensa, dagiti nalasatan iti biag
Correlated words
Hard knocks ang mga bagay at pangyayari na napagdadaanan gaya ng paghamon at pagsubok sa buhay, kahirapan at pagpupursigi na dinanas

EXPERIENCE, Undergo *v.* dumadanas, nararanasan, nalalasap; Iloc: malaslasatan, mapaspasaran (pasar-*Sp*), maramramanan

Experienced expiryensado-*Sp* sa mga gawa-gawa at sa kabuhayan dahil sa mga naranasan, mga nakuhang kaalaman dahil sa pagdanas, pagtrabaho at pagsanay sa gawain; Iloc: expiryensado-*Sp* cadagiti ob-obra ken pagbibiag gapu cadagiti nalasatan na ken napagpasaran na, naala a sirib gapu iti pagtrabaho, pagsalsali ken pagsanay na nga usto cadagiti maar-aramid

Experiment *(Tag. & Iloc.)* experimento-*Sp*

Expert *(Tag. & Iloc.)* experto-*Sp*

Expertise *Special skill, prowess or knowledge. (Tag. & Iloc.)* Pagka-experto-*Sp* at pagkadalubhasa sa spesyal na paggawa o kaalaman

Expiate gumawa ng mabuti gawa para ipatuwid ang sariling kamaliang nagawa niya; Iloc: mangaramid iti nasayaat tapno maikaro na ti mismo a naaramid na a basbasol

Expiration date ang fecha-*Sp* na magiging paso na o pasado-*Sp* na; Iloc: fecha nga agbalin a pasadon o nagpasaren (pasar-*Sp*)

EXPIRED yumao na, namatay na; Iloc: natayen

EXPIRED, Out-of-date *expired*, paso, pasado-*Sp*, lipas na; Iloc: *expired*, nagpasaren

Explain ipaliwanag, i-explica-*Sp*; Iloc: ilawlawag, i-explicar-*Sp*

Explanation paliwanag, explicasyon-*Sp*; Iloc: pangpalawag, explicasyon

Expletive malaswang salita, mura; Iloc: nakaal-alas o dakes a sarita

Explication *see Explanation and Interpretation*

Explicit ganap at maliwanag na sinabi o pinakita at malinaw na pinatunayan; matatag na pagtubo at pagbuo gaya ng *explicit knowledge* at *explicit belief;* buong-buo (walang tinagong detalye kahit hindi kasiya-siya), tunay na tunay at napakaliwanag na inexplica o nilarawan o niretrato o finorma.

Explode pumutok, sumabog; Iloc: nagbettak, bumtak, lumtuog

EXPLOIT saliksikin, tahakin; Iloc: sukimaten

EXPLOIT, Manipulate magsamantala, pukawin; Iloc: agoportunista-*Sp*, uyotan

EXPLORE saliksikin, tahakin; Iloc: sukisoken

EXPLORE opportunities makipagsapalaran; Iloc: makigasang-gasat

Explosion sabog; Iloc: bettak

Exponent *n.*, **Exponential** *adj.*, taong nagpapaliwanag ng lahat-lahat pati detalye-*Sp*, nag-e-explica-*Sp*, nagbibigay-kahulugan o nagsasalin ng dayuhang lengguahe-*Sp* sa katutubong wika; tao na kumakatawan o representante-*Sp* o promotor-*Sp* o mang-suporta-*Sp*; simbolo-*Sp* ng isang *ideology*, layonin o pag-iisip.

Exportation, Selling to other countries exportasyon-*Sp*, magventa sa ibang bayan; Iloc: exportasyon, aglako diay sabali a nasyon-*Sp*

Expose *v.* ilantad, ipakita, i-*expose*; Iloc: iparang, ipakita

Exposé *n.* panglantad, pagbunyag ng mga lihim, pangpavisto; Iloc: pangsawang o pangbutaktak cadagiti limed, pangvisto

Exposed, In full view lantad, kitang-kita, nakalabas, nakabilad; Iloc: nakaparang, makitkita, nakaruar, nakabilag

Expound madetalye na paliwanag o explicasyon-*Sp*; Iloc: na-detalye-*Sp* a pangpalawag wenno pang-explicar-*Sp*

Correlated words

Indepth sacop lahat ang detalye at tama at completo

Explicit buong-buo (walang tinagong detalye kahit hindi kasiya-siya), tunay na tunay, at napaka-liwanag na inexplica o nilarawan o niretrato o finorma

Elaborate mayaman sa detalye na plano sa paggawa o pagpapaliwanag nito

Stipulate ipahayag ang mga condisyon at rekisitos para sa kasunduan o contrata; Iloc: isawang dagiti condisyon ken rekisitos para iti pagtulagan o contrata

EXPRESS umimik; Iloc: aguni

EXPRESS pent-up emotions idaing, itaghoy, maghimutok, itangis; Iloc: agsennaay, iyasog, agun-unoy

Expression bukambibig, kasabihan; Iloc: *expression*

Extemporaneous *adj.,* **Extemporize** *v.* kaunti o walang paghahanda para sa talumpati niya at wala rin siyang binabasang codigo-a*Sp*; Iloc: pagsagana para ti discurso-*Sp* na ken awan pay codigo a basbasaen na
Correlated word
Reference paper is codigo *(Tag & Iloc)*

Extend 1] banatin, pahabain, 2] palawakin, 3] mag-alok, 4] magpalugit, iwatiwat

Extension of time palugit; Iloc: watiwat

Extent ang laki, lapad, haba, lawak, luwang, tagal, layo, distancia-*Sp*

Exterior labas; Iloc: ruar

Exterminate puksahin o lipolin lahat-lahat; Iloc: patayen am-amin

External labas; Iloc: ruar

Extinct hayop o halaman na hindi na nabubuhay

Extinguish hipan para patayin ang apoy; Iloc: iddepen, puyotan tapno maiddep

Extort, Obtain by threat magbanta na pipinsalain kung hindi magbigay ng pera, mangkikil; Iloc: agcarit wenno agcarit iti peggad nu haan mangited ti cuarta, mangkikil

Extra sobra-*Sp*, labis; Iloc: sobra, surok

Extract *(Tag. & Iloc.)* bunotin gaya ng (casla ti) ngipin

Extraordinary hindi pangcaraniwan, mas mataas pa sa ordinario-*Sp*; Iloc: haan a cadawyan, nangatngato ngem iti ordinario

Extravagant gastador-*Sp*, waldas, magastos; Iloc: gastador, nakagasgastos

Extreme napaka-masyado-a*Sp*, malabis, sukdolan, sakdal; Iloc: masyado, napalalo unay, nalabes

Extremities mga camay at paa; Iloc: dagiti ima ken saca

Extremity dulo; Iloc: murdong

Extricate palayain o pakawalan sa coneksion, sa sangkot o problema

Extrovert mahilig makihalo-bilo o makipagsosyalan sa mga kapwa-tao; Iloc: magustuan na ti makipag-ummong ken makipagsosyalan iti tattao

Exuberant *adj.*, **Exuberance** *n.* matindi at hindi controlado ang galak at gana; magastos at magara, abundancia

Exude *aura*, ang lumilitaw sa pagkatao o sa damdamin

Exult *v.*, **Exultation** *n.* labis na pagpapakasaya; Iloc: napalalo a pagragsakan

EYE, Eyes *(Tag. & Iloc.)* mata
Correlated words
    Optic tungkol sa mata; Iloc: maygapu ti mata
    Vision paningin; Iloc: pagkita
    Visual may kinalaman sa paningin; Iloc: maygapu iti panagkita

EYE contact tuminging derecho sa mata at walang pikit-pikit o tingin sa baba o taas o sa tabi-tabi kundi derecho lamang

EYE, foreign speck flown into napuwing; Iloc: napulingan

EYE mote muta; Iloc: mukat

EYE poked by someone or something nasundot; Iloc: nasulek

EYE, sore sulyak; Iloc: kamata

EYE sty *(Tag. & Iloc.)* culiti

EYE wink kindat; Iloc: kidday

Eyebrow kilay; Iloc: kiday

Eyeglass salamin, antipara-*Sp*, anchohos-*Sp*; Iloc: sarming, antiparra; anchohos

Eyelash pilikmata; Iloc: curimatmat

Eyelid takipmata; Iloc: tallucob ti mata

EYES blinded by sun or glare masilaw, nasisilaw; Iloc: mapurar ti mata
Correlated words
    Dazzle nasisilaw ang mata sa marahas na liwanag; Iloc: mapurar ti mata nga aggapu iti naranggas a ranyag o silaw
    Glare marahas na ilaw na nakakasilaw sa mata; Iloc: naranggas a ranyag a makapurar ti mata
    Squint ipikit ng konti ang mata dahil nasisilaw ng araw; Iloc: mapakidem a bassit ti mata na gapu ta napurarar ti mata iti silaw ni apo init

EYES blinking kukurap-kurap; Iloc: agkirem-kirem, agkuridemdem

EYES closed nakapikit; Iloc: nakakidem

EYES open wide dilat; Iloc: mulagat

EYES opened by reality namulat; Iloc: nalawagan

EYES, sleepy- *(Tag. & Iloc.)* mapungay

EYES swollen from crying namumugto; Iloc: balucot a mata

Eyesight paningin, *vision*; Iloc: pagkita, *vision*
Synonym
Vision paningin; Iloc: pagkita

F

Fable 1] mga alamat na storia, 2] kasinungalingan

Fabric tela-*Sp*; Iloc: tela, lupot

Fabricate 1] pagsama-samahin ang magkakaibang elemento-*Sp* para makapagtayo o makapagbuo, 2] magsinungaling

Fabulous 1] napakabuti na hindi kapani-paniwala

Façade 1] harap ng gusali, 2] artifisyal o nakakapanlinlang na harapan

FACE *n.* mukhâ; Iloc: rupa, langa

FACE harapin; Iloc: sangwen

FACE chin/jaw supported by both palms while elbows are resting on the table sinasalo o buhat ng dalawang camay ang panga o baba; Iloc: nakatapaya

FACE lift magpa-*cosmetic surgery* o *plastic surgery* para maalis ang mga culobot at bumata ang itchura; gumawa ng pag-aayos sa bahay o *town* para gumanda ito

FACE, make a threatening ngiwian, magngiwi; Iloc: guyaban, agguyab

FACE-saver paraan para maiwasan ang pagkawala ng mabuting pagtingin sa canya

FACE the music harapin at tanggapin ang kahihinatnan (bunga, parusa) ng iyong kamalian; Iloc: sangoen ken akceptaren ti resulta-*Sp* (bunga, dusa) iti dakes nga inaramid mo.

FACE-to-face magkaharap, *personal* na magkaharapan; Iloc: agkasango, agsinnango a *personal*

FACE towel *(Tag. & Iloc.)* labacara-*Sp*, dimpo

FACE value kung ano ang nakalantad na tinuturing na katotohanan-tama man o mali; Iloc. nu ania iti nakaparang nga mabigbig nga daytoy ket kaagpaysoan-husto man wenno haan.

Facetious nakakatawa, libangang katuwaan

Facile madali; Iloc: nalaca, cascari

Antonym

Hard, Difficult mahirap; Iloc: narigat

Facilitate paluwagin o padaliin ang gawa o kalagayan; Iloc: palacaen ken pabiiten ti obra o kasasaad

Facility 1] facilidad-*Sp*, gusali, *building*, 2] pagkamadali o pagkabilis o pagkasimp-le ng paggawa o paggamit; Iloc: 1] facilidad, *building*; 2] laca o daras o pagkasimp-le-*Sp* iti pag-usar-*Sp*

Facsimile *fax, duplicate*, exactong copia-*Sp* ng documento-*Sp*; Iloc: exacto-*Sp* nga copia iti documento

FACT katotohanan; Iloc: kaagpaysuan

FACT of life buhay ng tao na nangyayari sa lahat gaya ng pagpanganak at pagtanda ng tao; 2] <u>*Facts of life*</u>: paano nabuo at sumilang ang sanggol na puedeng isagot sa tanong ng anak na puedeng sagotin na ng tama kapag nasa tamang edad na siya

Faction 1] ito ay isang grupo-*Sp* sa loob ng malaking grupo-*Sp*, 2] forma ng pagsusulat o pelicula-*Sp* kung saan ginagawa ang mga tunay na tao o tunay na pangyayari sa storya-*Sp* pero gawang-isip lamang, 3] pagtatalo o salungatan o hindi pagkakasundo at hiwa-hiwalayan sa isang grupo-*Sp*.

Factoid tama o kasinungalingan pero tinanggap na tutoo dahil sa paulit-ulit na pagpahayag sa *media*; Iloc: usto o kaulbodan ngem inakceptar nga agpayso gapu iti pagpaulit-ulit nga pagwarnak iti *media*.

Factor bagay o tao na nakakatulong sa pagsasagawa o pagbuo o pag bunga; Iloc: banag o tao nga makatulong ti pagparnuay o pagbu-kel o pagbunga.

Factory *(Tag. & Iloc.)* fabrica-*Sp*, pagawaan, planta-*Sp*

Factual tutoo, katotohanan; Iloc: agpayso, kaagpaysuan

Faculty 1] pinanganak na may bisa at abilidad-*Sp* ang katawan at pag-iisip, 2] mga guro at mga namumuno sa escuela-*Sp*; Iloc: 1] inyanak nga addaan bileg ken abilidad-*Sp* ti bagi ken nakem, 2] entero-*Sp* maestra-*Sp* ken *principal* ken *assistants* idiay escuela.

Fad (fashion or practice) *(Tag. & Iloc.)* uso-*Sp*, moda-*Sp*

Fade mangupas, magkupas; Iloc: agkupas, agusaw

FAIL mabigo, masawi; Iloc: agmintis, mapalpak

FAIL test lumagpak, hindi naka-pasa-*Sp*, bumagsak sa examen-*Sp*; Iloc: haan naka-pasar-*Sp*

Synonym
Flunk bagsak; Iloc: nacalabasa

Failure bigo, hindi naisakatuparan; Iloc: mintis, awan pinagbalinan
Synonyms
Fiasco napakalaking pagkabigo o pagkamintis o disgracia
Downfall, Flop, In vain walang kahihinatnan, hindi macacompleto, hindi maisagawa; Iloc: haan a maycompleto o maaramid, awan ti resulta nga inexpectar a bunga ditoy
Antonym
Success tagumpay, katuparan, unlad, pagwagi, sikat, bunga, pagcompleto, pagkayari; Iloc: balligi, pagturpos, naytungpal, bunga, pagcompleto

FAINT mahimatay; Iloc: matalimudaw

FAINT-hearted kulang sa tapang at determinasyon-*Sp* dahil puede na mayroon siyang kapansanan o *inferiority complex* kaya huwag siyang pintasan o laitin

FAIR 1] makatarungan, walang pinapanigan, 2] kaayaayang ichura-*Sp*, 3] kung sa pag-grado-*Sp*, mabuti naman at puede na, 4] isang ocasyon-*Sp* na may mga palabas, competisyon-*Sp* at pagbeventa ng kung ano-ano; Iloc: 1] nalinteg, awan ti fabfavoran na, 2] nakarayrayo nga ichura, 3] nu ti paggrado, nasayaat met ken mabalinen, 4] maysa nga ocasyon nga adda ida pabuya, competisyon ken tienda-*Sp*

FAIR-skinned maputi; Iloc: napudaw

FAIR-weather friend kaibigan pero hindi na siya kaibigan kapag may kahirapan o problema ka o nangangailangan ka ng tulong

Fairground malawak na lupain kung saan ginaganap ang mga *fairs* at *exhibitions*

FAITH pananampalataya, pananalig, paniniwala; Iloc: pammati ken pagfiar

FAITH in God Sa relihiong Cristiano, ang *faith* ay paniniwala, pagtitiwala, pananalig at pagsampalataya sa Dios bilang *Holy Trinity* o Santisima Trinidad (isang Dios sa tatlong banal na persona na Dios Ama, Dios Anak na si Hesu Cristo, at Dios Espiritu Santo) at paniniwala at pananalig sa tinakda ng Dios na kaligtasan ng buong nilalang sa pamamagitan ng pagbaba ni Hesu Cristo sa lupa para Siya ang tumanggap ng parusa sa mga kasalanan ng mga nilalang, imbes na ang nilalang ang maparusahan at mapunta sa infierno. Kapag may *faith* tayo sa pagpaniwala natin na ang napakahapdi at napakasakit na pagpapahirap, pagdurusa at pagkapako kay Hesu Cristo sa cruz ay paraan ng paglinis at pagpatawad ng mga kasalanan ng buong nilalang, at tanggapin natin si Hesu Cristo sa puso't buhay natin bilang Dios natin at Tagapagligtas natin, matatamo na natin ang gracia ng *salvation*-kaligtasan at papunta na tayo sa langit. Sa pagmamahal ng Dios sa mga nilalang para makapunta lahat sa langit, ginawa ng Dios na ang kaligtasan natin ay napakadali - maniwala, pagtiwala at manalig lamang tayo sa libreng kaligtasan na pinagdusahan ni Hesu Cristo, pati pagtanggap natin kay Hesu Cristo sa ating puso at buhay bilang Dios at Tagapagligtas natin at dito mapatawad at malinisan na ang mga kasalanan natin ng dugo ng Panginoong Dios Hesu Cristo sa cruz at nakatakda na tayo sa langit. Papasok na rin ang Espiritu Santo sa puso natin at mamalagi dito mamalagi para patnubayan at gabayan tayo na mabuhay ng maka-Dios. Magkakaroon din tayo ng *new birth* at tayo ay *spiritual* na mapanganak na anak ng Dios. Nagiging *work-in-progress* tayo kung gamitin natin ang *spiritual growth* na inaalay ng Espirito Santo para ang mga masama ay mas madali nang maging mabuti at ang mabuti ay lalo pang bumubuti kung magpagabay tayo sa Espiritu Santo. Ipagdasal natin na ang Dios na ang iiral sa isip, damdamin, asal, salita at buhay natin parati. Magpacumbaba din tayo sa Dios at icumpisal natin sa Dios ang mga nagagawa nating mga kasalanan, kahit na pinatawad na tayo ng Dios ng lahat ng ating mga kasalanan noong tinanggap natin ang Dios Anak na si Hesu Cristo sa puso't buhay natin bilang Dios at Tagapagligtas natin dahil sa pagdurusa Niya alang-alang sa atin.

Faithful *adj.,* **Faithfulness** *n. 1] People who are dedicated, loyal and true to their spouse. Also true to one's words, promises and vows; loving, affectionate, sincere, conscientious; reliable, honest and truthful; dutifully and efficiently performing one's duties and responsibilities; 2] "the faithful" are the believers of the Christian doctrine.*
Correlated words
Fidelity *devoted and faithful to one's spouse; true to friends; adherence to a cause, facts, promises, dulies, obligations, truth and accuracy; reliable; patriotic.*
Sincerity *n.,* katapatan; Iloc: pagkapudno

Dedicated *adj.* nakatalaga (nakaukol, nakaalay) ang puso niya sa/kay; Iloc: nacaydaton ti puso na iti/kenni...

Loyal *adj.,* tapat sa relasyon, tapat sa kaibigan o sa canyang obligasyon; Iloc: usto ken napudno ti pakipagrelasyon na, napudno iti gayyem na wenno iti obligasyon na

Fake *adj.,* **Fakery** *n.,* falsificado-*Sp*, huad; Iloc: falsificado

FALL mahulog, malaglag; Iloc: matinnag, maregreg

FALL for 1] nabitag siya dahil nilinlang siya; 2] nagkagusto at umibig siya

FALL guy taong pinatungan ng sala kahit siya ay inocente-*Sp*, taong pinasubo; Iloc: tao a naypatung ti basol canyana uray no inocente isu, tao nga impasubo

FALL flat mapahiga, mapabulagta, mapahandusay, madapa; Iloc: naypakleb, maypaidda, maypasubsob

FALL hard bumagsak, lumagpak, masadlak; Iloc: naytupak, nabarsak a natinnag

FALL off (hair, petals, leaves) malagas, nacacalvo; Iloc: aglagas, ma-calvo-*Sp*

FALL on deaf ears hindi pinapakinggan, binabale-wala

FALL short 1] may mga kakulangan kaya hindi maituring na sapat, 2] hindi matamo ang hangarin o balak dahil hindi niya naabot ang rekisito-*Sp* o katangiang hinahanap

FALL while erect or standing (i.e., bldg., person) matomba, mabuwal; Iloc: matomba, matwang

Fallacy *n.,* **Fallacious** *adj.* salita na buhat sa maling pagrarason o paniwala; Iloc: sarita a naggapu iti haan usto nga pagrasrason wenno haan a husto a pammati

Fallible nagkakamali at nagkakasala; Iloc: agbidbiddut ken agbasbasol

Falling-out pagkakahiwalay na o pagkakawala na ng pagkakaibigan o pagmamahalan

Fallout, Fall-out 1] ang pagdapo sa lupa ng mga dala ng hangin buhat sa pagsabog ng volcan-*Sp* o *nuclear explosion* o sunog at iba pa, 2] ang hindi inaasahang efecto-*Sp* o bunga o kahihinatnan

FALSE *(Tag. & Iloc.)* falso-*Sp*, falsificado-*Sp*, hindi tutoo

FALSE alarm alarma o pangbabalang hudyat pero lumabas na pagkakamali pala at wala namang panganib

Falsehood kasinungalingan, gawa-gawa lamang; Iloc: parbo, ulbod, lastog, salawasaw

Falsify i-falsifica-*Sp*; Iloc: i-falsificar-*Sp*

Falter 1] nawawalan ng tapang o confiansa kaya urong-sulong siya o nagkakamali-mali siya sa pagsagawa ng kailangan niyang gawin, 2] nauutal o banayad o pahinto-hintong magsalita

Fame pagkabantug, pagka-popular-*Sp*; Iloc: pagkatan-ok, pagkapopular

Familiar *familiar* o namumukhaan o nakikilala dahil dating nakikita niya o napupuntahan o naaamoy niya; Iloc: *familiar* o maylasin o mabigbig na gapu ta dati ket makitkita na o napanan na o maang-angot na
Correlated words
Ring a bell bagay o tunog na nagbibigay ng pagpapakilanlan o nakakapaalaala ng dating naganap o nakita niya

Familiarity 1] hindi masyado at sapat lamang na pagkakilala o pagkaalam, 2] pagchachancing o paggawa ng *sexual advances*; Iloc: 1] haan masyado ta medio am-ammo na laeng ngem haan unay, 2] agchachansing o pagaramid ti *sexual advances*

Familiarize, Get the hang of it magpasanay, magpabihasa; Iloc: iruam tapno ma-ammoan unay

FAMILY, Clan familia-*Sp*, mag-anak, angkan; Iloc: familia

FAMILY leave pagpapayag ng oficina na hindi pumasok ang empleyado ng ilang araw o ilang linggo o buwan para alagaan ang bagong pinanganak na sanggol o alagaan ang may sakit na ka-familia

FAMILY man lalaking may asawa't mga anak

FAMILY name *(Tag. & Iloc.)* apelyido-*Sp*

FAMILY values pangaralin ng magulang ang mga anak ng *moral and ethical values* at iba pang marangal na custombre at masipag na gawain para maitanim sa canila ang mga kabutihan at kaligayahan ng pagkakaroon ng principio sa buhay, dahil ang mabuhay na napakabuti, makabatas, mahusay at magalang ay nagbubuo ng busilak at malinis na pagkatao na mangpatnubay sa canila sa maunlad, mapaya at maligayang kinabukasan.

Famine pagkagutom, taggutom; Iloc: bisin

Famished gutom na gutom; Iloc: mabisbisin

Famous bantog, tanyag, kilala, sikat, popular-*Sp*; Iloc: amammo ti adu a tao, popular, natan-ok, agdindinamag isu

FAN *n.* abanico-*Sp*, pamaypay; Iloc: abanico, paypay

FAN *v.* magpaypay; Iloc: agpaypay, agabanico

FAN, electric *(Tag. & Iloc.) electric fan,* ventilador-*Sp*

FAN of a celebrity tagahanga; Iloc: tagasuporta

Fanatic *(Tag. & Iloc.)* fanatico-*Sp*

FANCY *imagination* o likhang-isip lalo na kung natutuwa o nasisiyahan siyang makipagbiroan o magyabang

FANCY-free binata o dalaga at walang asawa o kasintahan, walang pananagotan dahil hindi pa nakatali

Fanfare pagtatanghal na pasikatang pakitang-taong; publicidad-*Sp* at *advertisement* na panghalina ng cliente-*Sp*; maikling pang-umpisang senyal-*Sp* sa ceremonya-*Sp* ng militar-*Sp* sa pagtugtog ng *trumpet, brass* at iba pa

Fang pangil; Iloc: saong

Fantisize *v.,* **Fantastic** *adj.,* **Fantasy** *n.,* magguni-guni o mag-*imagine* ng mga maluho, mamahalin at kasiya-siya na minimithing pinapangarap at capricho

FAR malayo; Iloc: adayo

FAR cry kaibang-kaiba sa pinagcocomparahan o pinagbabasehang sa tinutukoy na bagay o tao, wala man lamang o kaunting pagkapareho

FAR-fetched hindi kapani-paniwala dahil sa may mga bagay na nagpapahiwatig na kasinungalin lamang ito

FAR-flung napakalayo; ang laki ay napakalawak hanggang sa gilid-gilid

Faraway malayo at nasa kabukiran o katubigan na nakabukod o *remote*

FARE 1] bayad ng pasahero sa paglulan niya sa sasakyan; 2] paano ang pakikibaka sa karanasan o pangyayari–maayos at mabuti ba, o hindi?; 3] pagkain

FARE, bill of listahan ng mga ulam; Iloc: lista cadagiti sida, *menu*

FARE of passengers *(Tag. & Iloc.)* pasahe-*Sp*, flete-*Sp*

FAREWELL pamamaalam, despedida-*Sp*; Iloc: pagpacada, despedida

FAREWELL, bid magpaalam; Iloc: agpacada

FARM, Farmland bukid, bukiran, taniman, sakahan, nayon; Iloc: taltalon, pagtaneman
Correlated word
Agriculture agricultura, pagsasaka; Iloc: agricultura, pagmulmula, pagtanem

FARM helper katulong sa bukid; Iloc: kasamac

Farmer magsasaka; Iloc: mannalon

Farsighted 1] mas claro siyang nakakakita sa malayo kaysa sa malapit; 2] matalas at may pagtanto sa hinaharap at pinaghahandaan pa niya

Fart utot; Iloc: uttot

Farther mas malayo; Iloc: mas adayo, ad-adayo

Farthest, Farthermost pinakamalayo; Iloc: pinakaadayo

Fascinated namamalikmata sa pagkaakit at matinding pagsusubaybay; Iloc: masiddaawan ken maaw-awis ken sigagagar a maamwan iti sumaruno

Fascinating kawili-wili; Iloc: nakaaw-awis

Fashion *(Tag. & Iloc.)* moda-*Sp*, uso-*Sp*

Fashionable posturioso/sa-*Sp*, sunod sa uso-*Sp* at moda-*Sp*; Iloc: posturioso/ sa, sumursurot ti uso ken moda, naimis
Synonyms
In vogue *(Tag. & Iloc.)* mauso, mapagmoda
Hoity-toity nagpapakitang-tao na mataas siya o elegante at hindi siya huli sa moda o *fashion*
Vain vanidoso/sa, pagpapaganda niya ay napaka-importante sa canya, mapostura; Iloc: vanidoso/sa, naimis, ti pagpapintas na ket napakaim- portante canyana, napostura

FAST mabilis, matuling, listo-*Sp*, cascas; Iloc: napartak, napardas, nadaras, paspas, cascas, alisto-*aSp*

FAST for religious purposes or for medical procedure or surgery, Fasting 1] hindi kakain para sa pagsamba o sa dasal na hinihiling sa Dios, 2] hindi kakain at iinom ng ilang oras para sa operasyon o *procedure* na gaganapin sa canya sa ospital o clinic

Fasten higpitan; Iloc: pairutan, reppetan, ipailet

"Faster!" "Dalian mo!" Iloc: "Agawaam!" "Darasem!"

Fastfood turo-turong *restaurant* kung saan magturo ka ng napiling pagkain sa *array*/mga nakalatag na pagkain at dalhin mo ang iyong in*order* sa lamesa; sa cafeteria, mag-*order* ka sa *cashier* ng gusto mong pagkain at dalhin mo rin yang pagkain sa iyong lamesa

Fastidious 1] meticuloso-*Sp*, mapagbutingting, mapagpansin ng mga detalye-*Sp*, 2] maselan o maramdamin; Iloc: meticuloso, nabusisi, managbutingting

Fasting *see Fast for religious purposes... (above)*

FAT mataba, tabachoy; Iloc: nataba, nalukmeg, tabachoy

FAT of meat *(Tag. & Iloc.)* taba

Fatal *(Tag. & Iloc.)* may namatay, nakakamatay

Fatality namatay sa accidente-*Sp* o calamidad-*Sp* o sunog

Fate kapalaran, tadhana; Iloc: gasat

FATHER tatay, ama, papa, *dad*, *daddy*; Iloc: tatang, *dad*, *daddy*, papang, papa

FATHER and child mag-ama; Iloc: agama

FATHER and children mag-aama; Iloc: agaama

FATHER-in-law biyenang lalake; Iloc: katugangan a lalaki

Fatherland bayang pinanganakan; Iloc: bayan nga nay-yanakan

Fatherly relasyon ng tatay sa mga anak na pagmamahal, tagataguyod at tagasustento, tagapagtanggol, mahabagin, mapacensia, pinapamalas at tinuturo ang marangal na asal at mabuti at makabatas na gawain para tularan siya, maunawain, katapatan /*faithfulness* at lambing sa asawa-nanay ng mga bata para ang pagmamahal sa isat'isa sa familya ay lumalago, at pagtatrabaho para sa kabuhayan ng buong familia. Ang nakakabuti sa anak at familia ang dapat pinakaimportante sa tatay.

Fathom 1] *6 feet* ang *unit* o ang *volume* para masukat ang lalim ng tubig (*nautical measure*) o ang *ore bodies* (*mining*) o ang dami ng kahoyan (*forestry*); 2] masinsinang unawain para madiscobre ang katotohanan

Fatigue pagkapagod; Iloc: pagkabannog

Fatty oil, cooled and congealed *(Tag. & Iloc.)* sebo-*Sp*

Faucet *(Tag. & Iloc.)* gripo-*Sp*

FAULT kasalanan, kamalian; Iloc: basol, biddut

FAULT, to a *(Tag. & Iloc.)* sobra, masyado

Faultfinding, Nitpicking reclamador, palapuna, palapintas kahit maliliit o walang kabulohang mga bagay

Faulty may defecto o sira o kakulangan, hindi maasahan

Fauna mga hayop; Iloc: dagiti animal-*Sp*
> *Correlated word*
> **Flora** mga halaman; Iloc: dagiti tantanem
> **Animal** *animal*, hayop; Iloc: *animal*, animal-*Sp*

FAUX peke, artifisyal at hindi tutoong bagay

FAUX pas *[fopah]* mali o nakakahiyang kilos na asal o etiqueta-*Sp* sa publico-*Sp* o sa pakikipagsosyalan

Favor *(Tag. & Iloc.) favor,* favor-*Sp*

Favorable nakakabigay ng kabutihan; Iloc: makaited ti pagimbagan

Favored tinuturing at trina-trato-*Sp* ng mas favorito-*Sp* at mas pinagbibigyan

Favorite *(Tag. & Iloc.) favorite,* favorito-*Sp*

Favoritism may finafoborang tao o grupo kaysa sa iba; hindi pantay-panay ang pagturing

Fawn 1] batang usa; 2] culay dilaw-café o *light yellow-brown* na hindi matingkad; 3] manganak ng usa; 4] nagpapakita ng kabutihan, nagsisipsip, nagsisilbi, o nambobola gaya ng *people-pleaser* para siya ay maging kasiya-siya at mabigyan siya ng favor-*Sp*

Fax, Fax machine makina-*Sp* na nagpapadala't tumatanggap ng mga sulat o larawan sa pamamagitan ng linya-*Sp* ng telefono-*Sp*

Faze nanglilito, nangtaranta, nananakot

Fear takot; Iloc: buteng

Fearful nakakatakot; Iloc: nakabutbuteng

Fearsome takot o manakot, walang lakas-loob

Feasible *Effective, capable of being done and accomplished; suitable, appropriate; possible, likely.* 1] nagagawa, nagagamit, nakaka-efecto-*Sp*; 2] naaangkop, naaakma; 3] malamang o puedeng mangyayari

Feast marangyang pulong, piging, bankete-*Sp*; Iloc: ponsion, padaya, nadayag a *party*, bankete

Feat *Extraordinary and remarkable deed or stunt wielding skills and expertise.* Pambihira at dakilang gawa na hindi lahat ng tao ay nakakagawa

Synonym

Compleat kahanga-hangang kacayahan, experto sa abilidad niya; Iloc: nakasidsiddaaw a cabaelan, experto ti abilidad na

Feather balahibong manok o ibon; Iloc: dutdot ti manok o billit

Feature 1] katangian ng isang bagay, 2] buong ichura-*Sp* ng mukha gaya ng mata, ilong, bibig, 3] pelicula-*Sp* o spesyal-*Sp* na storia-*Sp* sa periodico-*Sp*; Iloc: 1] kababalin ti maysa a banag, 2] ichura ti rupa casla mata, agong, bibig, 3] pelicula o spesyal nga storya ti periodico

Featured na-publicidad-*Sp* o nalathala para mabigyan ng tanyag o pansin

February *(Tag. & Iloc.)* *February,* Febrero-*Sp*

Feces *n.,* **Fecal** *adj.* tae; Iloc: takki

Fed-up sawa na, suya na; Iloc: mauman, nasuyan

Federal ang forma ng govierno kung saan ang mga estados/*states* na sumasakop dito ay tinatanggap, tinutupad at ginagalang ang centro ng kapangyarihan habang pinapamalagi nila ang sarili nilang kapangyarihan

Fee *(Tag. & Iloc.)* bayad sa servicio

FEEBLE walang lakas at fuersa at napakahina dahil sa sakit o sa edad, lampay, nanlulumo; Iloc: nacapsut, nacapoy, lampay

FEEBLE-minded kulang sa *normal* na cacayahan ng isip, kulang sa magandang pagkatwiran o *judgment* kaya kung minsan o kadalasan, nagkakaroon siya ng mali-maling pagturing sa mga bagay o pagpapasya

FEED pakainin; Iloc: pakanen

FEED, spoon- **(i.e., a baby or a patient)** subo, suboan; Iloc: subwan

Feedback ang bumabalik na informasyon-*Sp* bilang resulta-*Sp* ng isang gawain, producto-*Sp* o plano para pang-evaluar-*Sp* kung tinanggap ng publico-*Sp* o hindi

FEEL ramdam, damahin, hipoin; Iloc: ricna, ricnaen, carawaen

"FEEL at home" "Maging comfortab-le ka dito sa bahay namin"

FEEL awkward at doing something maasiwa; Iloc: maamak, maycawa

FEEL lazy tinatamad; Iloc: agsasadut

FEEL out of place asiwa o hindi mapakali dahil parang hindi siya nababagay doon

Feeling, Feelings sentimyento-*Sp*, damdamin, pakiramdam ng katawan, pagdamdam na emosyon-*Sp*; Iloc: sentimyento, ricna ti bagi, pagricna ti emosyon

FEET, Foot paa; Iloc: saca

FEET stomping while marching or dancing *(Tag. & Iloc.)* pumapadyak

Feign magkunwari; Iloc: agincucuna

Feint kilos na huwad o pekeng anyo o palabas para malinlang ang kalaban para lusobin o masalakay nila sila

Feisty matapang at mataray; Iloc: nacarit ken tarabitab

Felicitate *v.,* **Felicitation** *n.* 1] binabati dahil sa nanalo o nag-*graduate* sa escuela; 2] magpasaya ng iba

Felicitous mahusay ang pagkapili, tugma; may nakakasiyang stilo; marka ng kaligayahan o nakakayari kaligayahan

Felicity pagkamasayang-masaya, felicidad-*Sp*

Feline familia ng pusa, leon-*Sp* at tigre-*Sp* at iba pa

Fellow lalake; Iloc: lalaki

Fellowman kapwa-tao; Iloc: kapada a tao, kacadwa

Fellowship 1] pagkakaaniban dahil sa pareho-*Sp* ang canilang pinang-galingang bayan o parehong relihion-*Sp* o profesyon-*Sp* o parehong kinawiwilihan; 2] ang *financial grant* o tulong sa isang kasamahan sa colehio o universidad; fundasyong nagpapagantimpala ng *financial grant*

Felon criminal-*Sp* na taong gumawa ng napakabigat na crimen-*Sp*

Felonious *adj.,* **Felony** *n.* malaking crimen-*Sp* gaya ng pagpatay ng kapwa, paggahasa, pagnanakaw o ilang beses-*Sp* na gumawa ng *misdemeanor* na crimen na ang hatol sa *felony* ay pagkatagal-tagal sa bilibid o *death sentence*

Female babae; Iloc: babai

Feminine pambabae, babaeng-babae, mahinhin; Iloc: pangbabai, naemma

Femininity katangian ng babae gaya ng malambot ang puso, mahinhin at mapakumbaba pero napapanindigan niya ang wasto; decente sa pagkilos, pagsalita at pagbihis; hindi mainggitin, hindi palaaway, contento sa kasalukuyang estado pero alam niyang dapat magsikap pa para mas umunlad, ginagampanan niya ang *moral and ethical values* na principio niya, at tinuturing na ang pag-aasawa ay panghabang-buhay kaya maingat siyang pumili ng kabiyak na marangal, mabuti ang kalooban, at may *conscience-compunction.*

FENCE bakod, bakuran; Iloc: alad

FENCE-sitter siya ay walang pinapanigan o *neutral* siya sa *controversy* o pagtatalo

Fencing escrima-*Sp;* Iloc: arnis

Fend magsikap mabuhay, manatili o macaya lahat kahit walang tulong ng iba; Iloc: agpakat nga agbiag, makamentener wenno maypasar amin uray awan tulong ti dadduma

Feral makahayop ang bangis; Iloc: rungsot ti animal ti adda canyana

Ferment 1] *yeast, mold* at microbio na nagsasanhi ng *fermentation*; 2] gulo, ligalig, magpagalit

Ferocious simaron, salbahe, makahayop ang bangis; Iloc: simaron, nauyong, naranggas, rungsot ti animal

Ferocity, Ferity malahayop ang pagkabangis, pagkalupit, at pagkabagsik

Ferris wheel *(Tag. & Iloc.) ferris wheel,* chobibo

Ferry daongan ng mga *ferryboats*, bapor-*Sp*, barco-*Sp* at banka para ipatawid ang mga pasahero-*Sp* sa kabila ng ilog o laok; Iloc: pagsangladan dagiti *ferryboats*, bapor, barco ken banka para iballasiw dagiti pasahero idiay bangir ti carayan

Ferryboat maliit na bapor-*Sp* na nagpapatawid ng mga pasaherong papunta sa kabila ng ilog o laok; Iloc: bassit a bapor-*Sp* nga mangibalballasiw cadagiti pasahero idiay bangir ti carayan o danaw

Fertile mataba na lupa kung saan madaling tumubo at lumago ang mga tanim; Iloc: mataba a daga nga nalaca nga agpatubo ken aglapsat dagiti mulmula

Fertilizer *(Tag. & Iloc.)* abono-*Sp*

Fervent *v.,* **Fervor** *n.* marubdob na pagmamahal o pagsamba; Iloc: napasnek nga ayat o pangdayaw

Fester 1] magkaroon ng nana o ulcer, 2] nabubulok, 3] bumibigat o pinapairal ang sakit ng loob dahil kinikimkim at hindi binubunyag

Festival, Festivity pista, pistahan; Iloc: fiesta-*Sp*

Festoon decorasyon-*Sp* na naka-cadena-*Sp* na mga bulaklak o laso na naka-curva-*Sp*

FETAL katangian ng *fetus* o sanggol sa sinapupunan

FETAL position nakayukyok habang nasa tiyan ng nanay; Iloc: nakacucot diay chan

Fetch kaonin, sundoin; Iloc: alaen

Fete pistahan o piging o malaking pagdiriwang na caraniwan ay sa labas o sa parke kung saan nag-iipon ang mga tao para sa pagparangal ng tagumpay o ng tao

Fetid mabaho; Iloc: nabangsit

Fetish or Fetich *[fet-ish, fee-tish]* bagay na kinalolocohan

Fetus sanggol na nasa tiyan at ipapanganak pa lamang ng tao o ng hayop

Feud maliit na awayan o alitan; Iloc: bassit a pagap-apaan o riri

Fever lagnat, sinat, mainit ang nuo; Iloc: gorigor, nabara ti muging

FEW konti, kaunti, bahagya; Iloc: manmano, bassit, haan nga adu

FEW times bihira, pambihira, madalang, bahagya; Iloc: manmano, sagpaminsan

Fiancé *(Tag. & Iloc.)* novio-*Sp*, binabalak na, na mag-aasawa sa novia niya

Fiancée *(Tag. & Iloc.)* novia-*Sp* *(see Fiance above)*

Fiasco napakalaking pagkabigo o pagkamintis o problema

Fib kasinungalingan; Iloc: ulbod

Fiber or Roughage hilacha-*Sp* o malasinulid na parte ng gulay at frutas na nakakapaglusog sa katawan at nakakahadlang sa mga sakit; *fiber ay nasa apple & skin, beans & green beans, oatmeal, oranges, okra, onion, broccoli, cabbage, sprouts, spinach, corn, coconut, carrot, yam, turnips, guava, mango, piña, papaya, prunes, peanuts*

Fickle pabago-bago, salawahan; Iloc: agsaba-sabali, agsukat-sukat, agbaliw-baliw

Fiction *n.*, **Fictitious** *adj.* istoryang gawa-gawa ng kaisipan; Iloc: istorya-*Sp* a pinarbo

Fidelity *devoted and faithful to one's spouse; true to friends; adherence to a cause, facts, promises, dulies, obligations, accuracy and truth; reliable; patriotic.*

Fidgety *adj.*, **Fidget** *v.* nababagabag, balisa, nagugusot ang isip, hindi mapakali; Iloc: haan nga makatalna, madanagan, maringgoran

Fiduciary, *noun* trustee o taong pinagkakatiwalaan at obligadong mamahala ng ari-arian para sa kabutihan at kabuhayan ng cliente; *adj.* relasyon ng namamahala at ang canyang inaarugaan at binabatay ito sa tiwala at confiansa

FIELD of science, arts, etc. *(Tag. & Iloc.)* larangan

FIELD day tiempo-*Sp* ng malaking kasayahan o malaking ocasyon-*Sp* o araw ng magandang oportunidad-*Sp*
Correlated words
Festival, Festivity pista, pistahan; Iloc: fiesta
Holiday araw ng pahinga sa trabaho at pagpaalaala o pagpaparangal ng importanteng tao, pangyayari o bagay; pista ofisyal; Iloc: aldaw nga pag-inana iti trabaho ken paglaglagip wenno pagdayaw iti importante a tao, napasamak o banag; fiesta ofisyal

Fields bukid, nayon; Iloc: talon, tanap

Fierce *(Tag. & Iloc.)* simaron

Fiery 1] mainit at nasusunog; 2] madaling magsumpong at bara-barang magalit; Iloc: 1] napudot ken agap-apoy, dagdagos nga agsumro ti pungtot na

Fifteen *fifteen*, labing lima; Iloc: *fifteen*, sangapulo ket lima

Fifth *(Tag. & Iloc.)* ikalima

FIFTY *fifty*, singcuenta-*Sp*, limampu; Iloc: *fifty*, singcuenta, lima pulo

FIFTY one, 52, 53, 54, etc. *(English numbers are more commonly used by Filipinos)*

FIGHT bakbakan, laban, away; Iloc: bakbakan, laban, ringgor

FIGHT against time magmadali para magawa niya bago mag*deadline* o magawa man lamang niya sa *deadline*

Figment gawa-gawa o imbento lamang ng kaisipan at hindi tutuo

FIGURE 1] forma-*Sp*, hugis; 2] tarokin, alamin

FIGURE of speech isang expresyon-*Sp* na ginagamit na pangpaliwanag ng kaisipan gaya ng "Kabutihan ay nagdadala ng Kapayapaan" na nagpapahiwatig na ang malinis at mabuting pamumuhay ay malayo sa gulo at gusot ng buhay

FIGURE out maintindihan, malutas, masuma, macalcula

Filch nakawin; Iloc: takawin

FILE, Queue mag-pila-*aSp*; Iloc: agpila

FILE an application or file a complaint mag-*file;* Iloc: ag-*file*

FILE documents itago sa *cabinet* ang mga mahalagang papeles-*Sp* sa mga *folder* na naareglo ng alfabeto mula sa A to Z para madaling hanapin; Iloc: idulin diay *cabinet* dagiti importante-*Sp* a papeles iti *folders* a naareglo ti alfabeto para nalaca a masapulan

FILE to smoothen the nail kikilin ang kuko; Iloc: kikiren ti kuko

Filibuster 1] makigiyera sa ibang bayan, 2] paghadlang sa pamamagitan ng pag-antala

FILL punoin; Iloc: punwen

FILL up, Complete a form i-*fill up*, isulat ang sagot sa mga nakasulat na tanong; Iloc: i-*fill up*, isurat ti sungbat iti nakasurat a saludsod

Filled to the brim sagad; Iloc: napumpunno

Correlated words

Overflow umaapaw, sagad; Iloc: agliplippias, umap-apaw

Congest punong-puno, magtipon-tipon, umaapaw sa dami

Full puno, punong-puno, tigib, busog; Iloc: napumpunno, napunno, napno, nabsog

Fillet piraso ng isda o carne (manok, baboy, vaca, carnero) na walang tinik o buto

Film *(Tag. & Iloc.)* cine-*Sp,* pelicula-*Sp*

Filter, Filtrate salain; Iloc: sagaten

Filth dumi na nakakadiri; Iloc: rugit a makaar-aryek

Final *(Tag. & Iloc.) final,* final-*Sp*

Finale ang parteng katapusan ng opera-*Sp* o musical-*Sp* na palabas

Finalize ilagay sa aregladong ayos o kasulatan kapag natapos na ang lahat na dapat gawin

Finance kung paano gamitin ang pera gaya ng kinita at gana, fondo-*Sp,* *capital* o utang; Iloc: nu casano nga iyusar ti cuarta casla iti kinita ken ganancia, fondo-*Sp, capital* o utang

Financial loss *(Tag. & Iloc.)* lugi

FIND, Locate hanapin; Iloc: sapulen, biroken, saraken

FIND out alamin; Iloc: amwen

Findings ang kahihinatnang napag-alaman pagkatapos ng lahat ng imbestigasyon o pagsusuri

FINE mabuti; Iloc: nasayaat

FINE (material) fino-*Sp,* manipis; Iloc: fino, naingpis

FINE arts sining, arte-*Sp*; Iloc: arte, *fine arts*

FINE, Penalty *(Tag. & Iloc.)* multa-*Sp*

FINE print parte-*Sp* ng documento-*Sp* o contrata-*Sp* na ang sinasabi ay napakaliit ang mga prenta o letra-*Sp* at may iba-ibang interpretasyon-*Sp* o informasyon-*Sp* na kailangang babasahin para matuklasan kung ito ay ikabubuti at kapakinabangan o pagkaagraviado

FINE tooth comb, with a alamin o hanapin sa lahat ng lugar, todo-todong tuntonin ng maingat at mahusay; Iloc: sukisoken a todo-todo pati igid-igid para maamwan amin

FINE tune mas pahusayin para mas efectivong gamitin o mas maganda ang tunog

Finery fino at magandang borda o decorasyon sa damit

Finesse fino-*Sp* at magandang asal; Iloc: fino ken nadignidad nga aggaraw

FINGER daliri; Iloc: ramay

FINGER knuckle buco ng daliri; Iloc: buco ti ramay

FINGER, little, Pinkie kalingkingan; Iloc: kikit

FINGER, pointer, Index finger, Forefinger hintuturo, Iloc: tammud, ramay a pangtudo

FINGER-pointing nagtuturo sa pambibintang, pagpapasisi sa iba, pagpaparatang; Iloc: agtudtudo iti pagpabpabasol, pagbabalaw

FINGER, thumb hinlalaking daliri; Iloc: tangan

Fingernail *(Tag. & Iloc.)* cuco

Fingerprint tatak ng daliri; Iloc; lemma ti ramay

Finicky, Finical maselan; Iloc: delicada/do-*Sp*

FINISH taposin, icompleto; Iloc: leppasen, palpasen, ileppas, iturpos, i-completo-*Sp*

FINISH it in... (duration) gawin o taposin sa loob ng {...isang oras, isang araw, isang buan, isang taon}; Iloc: aramiden o palpasen iti uneg ti {... maka-domingo, makabulan, makatawen}

FINISHED naisagawa, nayari, tapos na; Iloc: naaramiden, naypalpas, nalpasen, naysambuten, nayturpos

FINISHED, just, Just done katatapus lamang; Iloc: kalkalpas laeng

Finishing touch tapos na pero suriin kung meron pang babagohin para bumuti o gumanda lalo, o kung dagdagan para mas completo o mas maliwanag bago matapos

Finite tiempo-*Sp* na may hangganan o limitasyon-*Sp*

FIRE *n.* sunog, apoy; Iloc: apoy, puor, uram

FIRE *v.* sunogin; Iloc: puoran, uramen

FIRE alarm sirena o alarma na pangbabala para ipaalam para makatakas at makaligtas ang tao sa sunog

FIRE out an employee or worker from his/her job cesantehin, despachahin, alisin sa tungkolin, itiwalag; Iloc: icesante, idespachar, ikkaten diay puesto-*Sp* na iti trabaho-*Sp* (despacha/despachar-*Sp*, cesante-*Sp*)

FIRE at, Shoot tirahin, barilin; Iloc: tiraen, paltogan (tira-*Sp*)

FIRE escape pintong labasan kapag may sunog; Iloc: puerta-*Sp* o ruaran no adda puor

FIRE extinguisher pamatay-apoy

FIRE insurance biniling seguro-*Sp* laban sa sunog sa bahay at ari-airan na nagbibigay ng compensasyong-bayad sa pina-*insure* na halaga;

Iloc: ginatang a seguro-*Sp* laban iti puor iti balay ken sanicua nga mangited iti compensasyon-*Sp* a bayad nu mano iti naka-*insure* amin nga napukaw gapu iti puor

FIRE, lit a sindihan, apoyan; Iloc: seggedan, apoyan
 Correlated word
 Ignite a match kuskosin ang fosforo para magsindi; Iloc: cur-iten iti fosforo para agsindi

FIRE proof hindi nasusunog; Iloc: haan a mapuoran

Firearm baril; Iloc: paltoog

Firecracker *(Tag. & Iloc.)* leventador-a*Sp*, cuitis

Firefly alitaptap; Iloc: culintaba

Fireman, Firefighter *(Tag. & Iloc.)* bombero-*Sp*

Firewall 1] pader na hindi nasusunog para mapigilan at mahadlangan ang paglaganap ng sunog; 2] sa computer, *security system* ito para mahadlangan ang gustong pumasok na naninira

Firewood panggatong; Iloc: sungrod

Firework palabas ng pagsabog ng mga leventador sa gabi para makita ang magagara at magandang stilo, hugis, at kulay

Firing squad mga sundalong pinili para bumaril sa taong hinatulang mamatay sa pagputok ng baril nila

FIRM, Stiff matigas, maganit; Iloc: nasikkil, natangken

FIRM, Corporation *(Tag. & Iloc.)* corporasyon-*Sp*

Firmament langit, himpapawid; Iloc: langit, tangatang

FIRST una, unang-una, nauna, pinakauna, primero-*Sp*; Iloc: umuna, kaunaan, primero, diay damo, immuna

FIRST aid 1] dali-daling panggamot sa simpleng sakit o sugat 2] o kung grabe, pampabalik ng malay gaya ng CPR bago dumating ang ambulancia; Iloc: 1] dagdagos a pangngagas para iti simp-le a sakit o sugat 1] nu grabe, pagpapaungar casla iti CPR baro sumangpet tay ambulancia

FIRST and foremost 1] unang-una, primero; 2] pinakaimportante; 3] bago ang lahat

FIRST born child panganay; Iloc: kaunaan

FIRST-class *(Tag. & Iloc.) first-class,* primera clase-*Sp*

FIRST come, first served para makatarungan, ang unang dumating ay ang unang silbihan; Iloc: ti immuna a simmangpet, isu iti umuna a servian

371

FIRST edition kauna-unahang paglathala ng libro-*Sp* o periodico-*Sp*; Iloc: umun-una a pagprenta iti libro-*Sp*

FIRST-hand nalaman ang balita mula sa pinagmulan o sa mismong orihinal-*Sp* o sa puno't dulo

FIRST things first ang mga importante at mga mahalaga na bagay ang dapat unahing acecasohin muna

FIRST time kauna-unahang beses-*Sp*; Iloc: agdamdamo, umun-una a beses-*Sp*

FIRST time to use i-buena-*Sp* mano-*Sp*; Iloc: agbuena mano

FIRST timer bagohan; Iloc: agdamdamo

FISCAL 1] tungkol sa pera o *financial,* tungkol sa perang nakaipon gaya ng mga kinita, utang, at fondo-*Sp* ng comunidad-*Sp* o govierno-*Sp*; 2] *fiscal* o abogadong nagdedemanda o naglalabas ng prueba-*Sp* ng kasalanan ng taong pinaratangan sa corte-*Sp* ng husticia-*Sp*

FISCAL year 12 buwan mula kadalasan sa Hulyo-*Sp* hanggang sa dadating na Hunyo-*Sp* para iplano ng gobierno-*Sp* o privadong negosio-*Sp* ang paggamit ng fondo-*Sp*

FISH isda; Iloc: lames, ican

FISH bones tinik; Iloc: siit

FISH farm, Fishpond palaisdaang lawa o mga tanke-*Sp* para magpaanak at magparami ng mga isda na pagmemay-ari ng negosiante-*Sp*

FISH fins *(Tag. & Iloc.)* palikpik

FISH gills hasang; Iloc: asang

FISH scales kaliskis; Iloc: siksik

Fisherman mangingisda; Iloc: tagatiliw ti ican

Fishing hook bingwit, pain; Iloc: banniit, silo

Fishy 1] amoy-isda, 2] nakakaduda

Fissure pahabang biyak sa lupa o sa dinding o sa ibang bagay
    Correlated word
      Hole butas, hukay; Iloc: abut

FIST camao; Iloc: gemgem

FIST bumps camao ng dalawang tao na pagtapikin o pagsalatin sa isa't isa bilang pagbati o paghanga sa pagtatagumpay o mabuting asal o pakikipagkaibigan

Fistfight magsuntokan, magbuntalan; Iloc: agdinnanog, agsinnulong
    Correlated word

Wrestle magbunohan; Iloc: aggabbo

FIT casyang-casya, tamang-tama, hustong-husto; Iloc: us-usto, agkascasya

FIT, Flare-up sumpong; Iloc: muryot, sumro

FIT, Healthy malusog; Iloc: nasalun-at, nakaradkad

Fitness kalusogan; cacayahan ng katawan na ikalat ang nahinga niyang *oxygen* sa mga parte ng canyang katawan

Fitting angkop, akma, bagay, relevante-*Sp;* Iloc: umno, agparbeng, relevante

FIVE *(Tag. & Iloc.) five,* lima, singko-*Sp*

FIVE hundred *five hundred,* limang daan; Iloc: *five hundred,* lima gasut

FIVE o'clock *five o'clock,* alas sinco-*Sp*

FIVE thousand *five thousand,* limang libo; Iloc: *five thousand,* lima nga ribo

FIX, Organize ayosin, areglohin; Iloc: tarimaanen, urnosen, aregloen

FIX, Repair kumponihin, i-*repair,* ifirmi sa lugar; Iloc: tarimaanen, i-*repair,* ifirmi

Fixate 1] nakapako ang isip at pansin at kahit pandinig sa isang pinagkakaabalahan o pinagkakainteresan, 2] obsesyon-*Sp*, marubdob na pagkagiliw sa isang bagay o tao

Fixed 1] nakafirmi, tinatag ng husto, naayos, nakumpuni, napag-ugnay, napagconecta, nakakabit, nakadugtong, nakadikit, naitatag, naitakda, naareglo; 2] **hindi** na mapalitan

Fixer-upper biniling mura na bahay o gusali o bodega pero kinakailangan ang pagpaayos o pagcumpuni

Fixture muebles-*Sp* o *appliance* na nakafirmi sa lugar-*Sp*

Fizz, Fizzle pagbubula o tumutunog na bula; Iloc: aglablabutak wenno agun-uni nga labutab

Flabby *adj.,* **Flab** *n. (Tag. & Iloc.)* taba na lumaylay, taba

Flaccid ang laman o *muscle* ng katawan na kulang sa lusog, tigas at lakas, malambot at lumalaglag; Iloc: lasag o *muscle* ti bagi nga kurang iti salun-at ken tangken ken pigsa isu nga nalukneng ken agregregreg

Flabbergast, Flummox taranta, lito, mangha, gilalas o gawin sa iba mga ito; Iloc: mapanganga, mataranta, masdaaw iti kigtot

Flack publicidad; ahente ng *press*

FLAG 1] bandila, watawat, 2] markahan ng maliit at maculay na papel-*Sp* ang pahina-*Sp* ng libro-*Sp*, 3] humihina; Iloc: 1] bandera-*Sp*, 2] markaan ti *page* iti libro iti bassit a papel nga adda color na; 3] kumapcapsot

FLAG of truce bandilang puti na tinataas at winawagayway na simbolo ng pagsuko o paghiling na makipagkasundoan ng pansamantalang paghinto o temporaryong pagpaliban ng alitan o labanan

Flagellant nagpepenitencia sa pamamagitan ng paghaplit ng canyang sarili sa publico-*Sp* kapag cuaresma-*Sp*; Iloc: agpenpenitencia-*Sp* isu a saplitan na ti bagi na a makitkita ti tattao nu cuaresma

Flagging lumiliit, humihina, sobrang pagod, mahina, lupaypay

Flagrant lantad ang pagkamasama; Iloc: nakaparang ti pagkadakes

Flail or flap clothes or linens to shake off dirt, thread, hair, etc. from it ipagpag; Iloc: ipagpag, iwagwag

Flair 1] natural-*Sp* na talento-*Sp* o abilidad-*Sp*, talas ng utak 2] lantad na pagkaelegante at magandang stilo-*Sp*

Flak sa labanan, pagbomba buhat sa eroplano

Flake maliit, pantay at manipis na nabakling parte ng pagkain o nabakbak na lumang pinta sa dinding o kapiraso ng *snow*

Flamboyant mapagpakitang-tao, mapagdamit ng makakabigay ng pansin; Iloc: mapagpakitang-tao, mapagcawes ti makaawis ti talyaw

Flame alab, liyab, ningas, siklab, apoy; Iloc: apoy, gillayab

Flammable, Inflammable madaling mag-apoy o masunog; Iloc: nalaca nga agapoy wenno aguram
Correlated words
Incendiary *chemical* na nakakasanhi ng sunog
Combustible madaling makasunog; Iloc: nalaca a makauram

Flank 1] parte ng katawan ng tao o ng hayop napapagitan ng pina-kamabababang buto ng tadyang hanggang sa balakang, 2] carne na nanggaling sa parte na ito ng katawan ng hayop

Flannel delana-*Sp*; Iloc: delana, franela-*Sp*, burburan

FLARE biglang pagsilakbo ng sunog o ilaw

FLARE up pagsumpong o bagbubuga ng galit; Iloc: golpe-*aSp* nga sumro ti pungtot

FLASH maikling kislap; Iloc: apagbiit a silap

FLASH in the pan ningas-cogon; ganang-ganang magsagawa pero hindi tumatagal ang pagkagana dahil maglaho ito kaagad

FLASH mob, Flashmob grupo na nagtakdang magkita sa isang lugar gaya ng parke, plaza-*Sp, playground,* tabi ng lansangan, *shopping mall* at *airport* o stasyon ng *train* para magtanghal ng palabas gaya ng sayaw o canta o pagtugtog ng mga musicong instrumento na hindi inaasahan ng mga taong naroroon o dumadaan

Flashback 1] ang nakaraang pangyayari na sinisingit sa pelicula o novela; 2] *Psychiatry*: ang *abnormal* at paminsan-minsang alaala sa nakaraang *traumatic* na pangyayari

Flashforward or Flash forward ang sinisingit sa storya-*Sp* o sa pelicula-*Sp* tungkol sa dadating na panahon

Flashlight *flashlight,* hawakang aparato-*Sp* para ilawan ang lugar o ang daan

Flashy maculay, kapansin-pansin at mumurahin

Flask botelya-*Sp*; Iloc: botelya, frasco-*Sp*

Flat 1] patag, pantay, 2] *apartment* sa isang palapag ng gusali; Iloc: 1] patag, patad, 2] *apartment* iti maysa a palapag iti *building*

Flatten gawing pantay; tapak-tapakan o yurak-yurakan para pumantay, iplastado-*Sp*; Iloc: iplastado-*Sp*, badde-baddekan para mapitpit o agdippig

Flatter *v.,* **Flattery** *n.* nagdidilang bulaklak, pambobola; Iloc: pagbolbola, mangar-archok

Flatterer *(Tag. & Iloc.)* bolero

Flatulence, Flatus utot; Iloc: uttot

Flaunt *v.,* **Flaunty** *adj.* ipakitang-tao ang canyang magagarang taglay; Iloc: pasindayag nga iparang dagiti nangina ken napipintas a sanicua

Flavor lasa; Iloc: raman, nanam

Flaw defecto-*Sp,* kapintasan, kakulangan, diferencia-*Sp*; Iloc: defecto pagkauyawan, kacurangan, diferencia

Flawless skin makinis na cutis-*Sp*; Iloc: nalamuyot nga cutis

Flea pulgas-*Sp*; Iloc: timel
  Other bugs
  Bedbug surot; Iloc: kiteb
  Mites that get into armpits or into navels of humans *(Tag. & Iloc.)* tungaw

Flee tatakas; Iloc: agtammeng

Fleet 1] mga bapor panlaban, 2] mga *taxi,* 3] sasakyang pandagat sa mga nagbabayad na pasahero-*Sp*

Fleeting dumadaan ng mabilis at sandalian lamang; Iloc: agpasar ti nadaras ken nabiit laeng

FLESH, Muscles laman; Iloc: lasag
Correlated words
Meat *(Tag. & Iloc.)* carne
Skin balat, cutis; Iloc: cudil, cutis

FLESH and blood 1] buhay na tao; 2] kadugo o kamag-anak gaya ng anak at kapatid; Iloc: 1] sibibiag a tao; 2] kadara o kabagyan casla iti anak ken kabsat

FLEX pagbaluctot, pagcurva-curva at pag-unat-unat ng mga buto at laman-laman ng katawan

FLEX time mga empleyado-*Sp* ay puedeng mag-<u>umpisa</u>-a*Sp* sa ano mang oras na maluwag sa canila na hindi maagraviado ang trabaho sa oficina-*Sp* basta-*Sp* lang isiguradong <u>ocho oras</u>-*Sp* sa isang araw ang <u>buong tagal ng pagtrabaho</u> nila sa oficina.

Flexible, Flexile 1] nacucurva, nababaluctot, nauunat, nahuhubog, 2] puedeng gawin sa ano mang oras-*Sp* o ano mang fecha-*Sp* o saan mang lugar-*Sp*

Flick calabit, tapik, pitik; Iloc: calbit, tapik, pitik, cur-it

Flickering light kukurap-kurap, aandap-andap; Iloc: ag-kudrep-kudrep, agkilap-kilap, agkuri-kuridemdem

Flight lipad ng ibon o eroplano-*Sp*; Iloc: pagtayab ti billit wenno eroplano

Flimsy marupok, madaling masira o mabasag o mapunit; Iloc: narukop, nalaca a madadael o mabuong o mapigis

Flinch mapakislot o mapatigtig dahil sa gulat o pandidiri o sakit; Iloc: cumpes wenno agtigerger gapu ti aryek o kigtot o sakit

Fling 1] ihagis, iitcha, ibato, 2] atrevidong ilagay ang sarili sa bagay na walang kaingat-ingat, 3] romansa-*Sp* na maikli; Iloc: 1] ipalladaw, ibato, ipallato, 2] atrevido-*Sp* nga ikabil na ti bagi na iti maysa a banag nga awan pagal-alwad, 3] nabiit a romansa-*Sp*

FLIP 1] iitcha pataas gaya ng *head-or-tail coin flip*, 2] magcirco pabalintong; Iloc: 1] ipallato nga pangato, 2] pabalintuag a circo

FLIP-flop 1] paatras na balintong, 2] pabago-bago, salawahan; Iloc: 1] paatras a balintuag, 2] agsukat-sukat, agbaliw-baliw

Flippant walang intindi at pabaya at nagpapasaya lamang na walang pakialam

Flirt landi, kiri, harot, alembong; Iloc: garampang, appak, alembong

Flit bigla at maliksing gumalaw o umalis; Iloc: alisto nga aggaraw o pumanaw a dagdagos

FLOAT lumutang; Iloc: agtumpaw, lumtaw

FLOAT on a parade *(Tag. & Iloc.)* carosa-*Sp*

Floater hindi marka ng batik sa mata ito kundi ang gumagalaw na batik na nakikita ng mata sa gilid ng paningin niya nito

Flock 1] grupo ng hayup na nag-iipon-ipon at nagliliwaliw at kumakaing samasama, 2] congregasyon-*Sp* ng simbahan; Iloc: 1] grupo-*Sp* ti animal-*Sp* nga agtipon-tipon ken agkacadua nga agliblibot wenno mangmangan, 2] congregasyon ti iglesia-*Sp.*

Flog haplitan, hampasin, latigohin; Iloc: saplitan, ablatan, i-latigo-*Sp*, basnotan.

Flood baha; Iloc: layos

FLOOR sahig, suelo-*Sp*; Iloc: datar, suelo

FLOOR or story of a building *(Tag. & Iloc.)* palapag

FLOOR-polishing task *(Tag. & Iloc.)* lampaso-*aSp*

Flop 1] mahulog o mapahiga ng matindi at maingay, 2] mintis, paltos

Flora mga halaman; Iloc: dagiti tantanem

Floss tanggalin ang mga tinga sa pagitan ng mga ngipin, mag-*dental floss*

Flotsam pagtatapon ng mga carga para pagaanin ang barco kung may panganib na lumunod ang barco

Flounder matomba-tomba o papilay-pilay sa pagsikap na tumayo o magbalanse habang nakatindig o lumakad

Flour *(Tag. & Iloc.)* arina-*Sp*

Flourish lalago; Iloc: agruay, aglapsat, agrang-ay

Flout pinapakita ang muhi at galit; Iloc: ipakita ti rurod o gura

FLOW mag-agos, dumaloy; Iloc: agaruyot, agayos

FLOW profusely dumadanak, bumubuhos; Iloc: agarubos agbulbulos
    Correlated words
    Gush golpeng pag-agos ng marami; Iloc: golpe nga agayos ti adu
    Drip tumutulo, pumapatak; Iloc: agtedtedted, agubo

FLOWER bulaklak; Iloc: sabong

FLOWER, Philippine national *(Tag. & Iloc.)* sampaguita

FLOWER pot *(Tag. & Iloc.)* masetera-*Sp*

FLOWER vase *(Tag. & Iloc.) flower vase,* florera-*Sp*

Flowery 1] halamanang mabulaklak, 2] nambobola/nanglalangis o magwiwikang mabulaklak o maraming salita na hindi pertinente-*Sp* sa paksa

Flu *(Tag. & Iloc.) flu,* trangkaso

Fluctuate panay taas-baba; Iloc: panay ngato-baba

Fluent mahusay siya sa lengguahe-*Sp* na sinasalita niya at claro-*Sp* pa at madaling intindihin

Fluff *n.,* **Fluffy** *adj.* balahibo o malambot na plumahe-*Sp* ng batang ibon; 2] damit na napakalambot na hipong bulak

Fluid *(Tag.& Iloc.) fluid,* likido-*Sp,* malatubig

Fluke akcidenteng kasuertehan; chambang pangyayari

Fluky masuerte, nakatamo sa chamba hindi sa abilidad; walang kasiguradohan

Flunk bagsak at hindi nakapasa; Iloc: haan a nakapasar

Fluoride ito ay may *fluorine* at sinasali sa *toothpaste* para maiwasan ang bukbok sa ngipin

Flush mag-*flush* ng tubig para mabilis umagos pababa ang tae sa casilyas; Iloc: i-*flush* ti danum para napardas nga agayos pababa ti takki idiay casilyas

Fluster nervioso/sa-*Sp,* ninenervios; Iloc: nervioso/sa, agnernervios

Flutter (i.e., fowl) pumapagaspas, pumapagaypay; Iloc: agcurcuripaspas, agcurcuripagpag, agpayakpak

FLY lilipad; Iloc: agtayab

FLY (insect) langaw; Iloc: ngilaw

FLY, large *(Tag. & Iloc.)* bangaw

FLY on a plane to travel lilipad, sasakay sa eroplano; Iloc: agsakay o aglugan ti eroplano

FLY-by-night tactica ng manloloca na antemano pa lamang ay humihingi na ng maagang bayad at pagkatapos ay hindi niya ginagawa ng husto ang tinakdang trabaho sa canya o hindi na sisipot o biglang mawala na lang at hindi tinapos ang trabaho

Flying colors, in madali, matanyag at excelente-*Sp*

Foam bula; Iloc: labutab

Focus *n. & v.,* **Focal** *adj. focus,* nakapakong pagbaling o pagtitig, matimtiman na inaatupag at pinagkakaabalahan; Iloc: *focus,* nakaimatang, nakalansa ti perreng iti maysa a banag, nakaperreng a firmi iti ob-obraen na,

Fodder 1] damo na kinakain ng mga cabayo o cambing; 2] pagkain na mura pero mababang uri na popular-*Sp* na nabibili

Foe kalaban, kaaway, kagalit; Iloc: kalaban, kaapa

Fog *n.,* **Foggy** *adj.* makapal na hamog; Iloc: napuscol a linnaaw,
Correlated word
> **Haze** sumisingaw na usok, alikabok o hamog na nakakakulimlim ng pook o kapaligiran
> **Mist, Misty** hamog, mahamog; Iloc: linnaaw, nalinnaaw

Foible maliit na pagkakamali; Iloc: biddut

FOIL hadlangan niya ang iba na maisagawa o maisakatuparan nila ang ginagawa, hadlangan ang pagpapabuti ng gawa; Iloc: lappedan na iti dadduma tapno haan da maicompleto o mapasayaat ti aramid da

FOIL paper manipis na malapilak o mala-plata-*Sp* na papel na pambalot; Iloc: naingpis nga malapilak o malaplata a papel a pambungon

Fold itiklop, tiklopin; Iloc: cupinen culpien, iculpi
Antonyms
> **Unfurl** iladlad; Iloc: ukraden, ukagen
> **Spread out** ilapag, ilatag; Iloc: iyaplag, iplastar

Foliage mga tumutubo gaya ng mga halamanan at punong-kahoy; Iloc: dagiti agtubtubo casla mulmula ken kaykayo

Folk taong-bayan, magulang; Iloc: dagiti tattao ti ili, nagannak

Folklore *(Tag. & Iloc.)* alamat

Folksy, Folkish simp-le-*Sp* at mapakumbaba at walang pagkukunwari at madaling makapalagayang-loob; Iloc: simp-le ken napacumbaba ken natural-*Sp* laeng ken nalaca a makicadcadwa iti tao

FOLLOW, Abide by tuparin, tumutupad sa utos, sumosunod sa utos; Iloc: agtungtungpal ti bilin, sumursurot ti mandar-*Sp*

FOLLOW behind bumubuntot, sumusunod; Iloc: sumarsaruno, sumursurot

FOLLOW in someone's footsteps sumunod o gumaya sa pagkatao o sa narating ng isang tinitingalang tao; Iloc: tumulad iti ehemplo-*Sp* iti maysa a daydayawen a tao

FOLLOW up *follow up,* magsubaybay, alamin ang kalagayan at kahi-hinatnan; Iloc: *follow up,* agsubaybay, amwen iti kasasaad ken resulta

379

Follower alagad, tagasunod; Iloc: buyot, tagasurot

Following 1] ang kasunod ay.., 2] mga tagahanga, dicipulo o tagasunod

Folly kahangalan; Iloc: kinamauyong

Foment magsulsol para lumaki ang gusot; Iloc: mangsungsong tapno dumakkel ti problema

Fond mahilig, gusto-*Sp*, ibig, nais, cursonada; Iloc: magustoan, cayat, mayat, cursonada

Fondle haplosin, himasin; Iloc: aprosan

FOOD pagkain; Iloc: makmakan
> *Synonym*
> **Victual** mga pagkain; Iloc: dagiti makan

FOOD, bring-along baon; Iloc: balon

FOOD, burnt sunog; Iloc: nakset

FOOD caught on one's throat that prompts one to cough it out nabilaokan, nabulonan, nahirinan; Iloc: naltutan

FOOD course, Menu potahe-a*Sp*, mga ulam; Iloc: potahe, dagiti sida

FOOD eaten with beer or wine pulotan, kilawin; Iloc: kilawen

FOOD for thought pangungusap na natatandaan dahil ito ay may kahalagaan at nakakatulong sa tao

FOOD being taken out from pot or pan and be served on the table ihain; Iloc: adawin, aggao

FOOD scraps fallen on dining table nalaglag o nacalat na pagkain; Iloc: murkat

FOOD, spoiled nabulok, napanis; Iloc: nabangles, nalungsot

FOOD stamp *coupon* o tarheta-*Sp* na binibigay ng USA na govierno-*Sp* sa mga maliit o walang sueldo-*Sp* para magamit nila na pambili ng kanilang pagkain

FOOD starting to get spoiled pasira na; Iloc: aglaesen

FOOD stucked between teeth *(Tag. & Iloc.)* tinga

FOOD-taking excessively & when done eating, some are wasted and thrown away *(Tag. & Iloc.)* takaw-mata, takaw-tingin

FOOD, thin, liquidy malabnaw; Iloc: nalasaw, nalabnaw

FOOD turning cold from hot maligamgam na; Iloc: nabaawanen

Fool *v.* 1] man-loco-*Sp*, 2] *see crazy, insane*; Iloc: mangloco

Foolhardy pangahas, atrevido-*Sp*; Iloc: atrevido

Foolish *(Tag. & Iloc.)* torpe-*Sp*, loco-loco-*Sp*, gago/ga-*Sp*, bobo-*Sp*, tanga, gunggong

Foolishness kahangalan; Iloc: pagkabagtit

FOOT paa; Iloc: saka

FOOT idioms:

FOOT on the door nasa paanan ng puerta ng oportunidad

Best FOOT forward pagpapakita ng kabutihan o kagalingan sa utak at abilidad

On the right FOOT gumalaw sa makaventaheng paraan

On the wrong FOOT gumalaw sa makakabigo o makakasamang paraan

FOOT heel sakong; Iloc: mucod

FOOT shin *(Tag. & Iloc.)* lulod

FOOT sole talampakan; Iloc: dapan

FOOT pointing to the other side while on top of the other knee while lying down or seated on a chair *(Tag. & Iloc.)* naka de cuatro-*Sp*

FOOT the bill taya sa babayaran, tagabayad ng pasahe, pagkain at iba pa; Iloc: taya, tagabayad ti gastos

Footage *demo* o parte ng palabas sa *video* o pelicula-*Sp*

Footing 1] matibay at matatag na tuntongan ng paa, 2] mahusay na batayan o fundasyon-*Sp* para sa pag-unlad o pag-avante-*Sp* sa buhay

Footloose atrevidong gumawa ng anomang gusto niya at walang makapigil sa canya

Footnote tala o nota-*Sp* sa babang-baba ng pahina-*Sp* na nagbibigay ng batayan o comentaryo-*Sp* ng mga naisulat

Footprint bakas ng paa; Iloc: lamma ti saka o dapan

Footsteps yabag; Iloc: paddek

FOR para-*Sp*, kay; Iloc: para, maipaay ken/iti

FOR fear that baka kung; Iloc: baka nu, amangan nu

FOR good, For keeps panghabang-buhay, permanente; Iloc: para inggana't sibibiag

FOR kicks para sa kasayaan, katuwaan at libangan kahit walang mabuting rason

FOR show *(Tag. & Iloc.)* pakitang-tao

FOR the sake of.. alang-alang sa/cay.., para sa kapakanan ni/ng; Iloc: iti paglaengan ti/ni.., para ti kaimbagan

Antonym

381

At the expense of sa pagkaagraviado ni/ng; Iloc: ti pagkaagraviado ni/iti

Forage 1] pagkain ng mga hayop, 2] maghalungkat para sa paghahanap ng pagkain

Forbear *v.*, **Forbearance** *n.* *Abstain, forego, refrain from, restrain oneself, curb, avoid, shun.*

Forbid ipagbawal, pigilan, hindi payagan; Iloc: iparit, haan nga ipalubos, ipagel

Forbidding 1] nakakapigil ng pag-unlad, 2] nakakadisgusto

Forecast sa tulong ng *technology* at ibang sistema-*Sp*, nalalaman na o nacacalcula ang dadating gaya ng clima, kalagayan at pangyayari

FORCE fuersahin, pilitin, giitin; Iloc: ifuersa, piliten

FORCE-entry lusobin ang bahay at puedeng (puede-*Sp*) manira ng pinto o vintana para makapasok; Iloc: serreken a fuersa-*Sp* ti balay ken mabalin nga dadaelen na pay tay puerta-*Sp* o ventana-*Sp* para makaserrek

FORCE into a controversial or difficult situation *(Tag. & Iloc.)* ipasubo

FORCE of habit dahil bihasa na sa para-parating gawi o ugali, hindi na namamalayang ginagawa-gawa niya o nag-aasal siya nito, at kadalasan ay hindi mapigilang patuloy pa rin niyang ginagawa ito kahit mayroon nang bagong sistema sa paggawa

Forcefully ifuersa, ipursigi; Iloc: ifuersa, ipakat

Fore nasa harap o nasa una, nakaavante; Iloc: adda idiay sango o umuna, nakaavante

Forearm 1] ihanda sa pakikibaka kaya bigyang armas-*Sp* o gawing armado-*Sp*, 2] parte-*Sp* ng camay sa pagitan ng sico at galang-galangan

Forebode *v.*, **Foreboding** *n.* kutob na nakakabalisa; Iloc: kebba nga makapadanag

Foreclose *v.*, **Foreclosure** *n.* palayasin at tanggalin ang canyang titulo o pag-aari sa bahay dahil sa pagkadelinquente sa pagbayad niya ng canyang *mortgage*
Correlated words

Forfeit *v.*, **Forfeiture** *n.* isuko ang ari-aryan dahil hindi na niya cayang bayaran ang *mortgage*

Forego mauna, magpauna; Iloc: umuna, agpauna

Forehead nuo; Iloc: muging

Foreign dayo, sa ibang bansa; Iloc: diay dayo, diay sabali a nasyon-*Sp*

Foreigner dayohan, banyaga; Iloc: tagadayo, taga sabali a nasyon-*Sp*

Correlated words
Immigrant *(Tag. & Iloc.)* imigrante
Stranger *(Tag. & Iloc.)* estranhero
Foreknowledge pagkaalam o kaalaman bago ito mangyari; premonisyon
Foremost una sa lahat, una sa posisyon at sa tiempo-*Sp* at sa lugar-*Sp*
Forensic sa corte-*Sp* ng husticia-*Sp* o pangpublicong debate-*Sp*, discusyon-*Sp* o argumento-*Sp*, ito'y pinag-uusapan at pinagsusurian
Foresee *v.,* **Foresight** *n.* 1] may ***prescience****/kaalaman bago mangyari; nakikita o nalalaman ang hinaharap, bago pa dadating; talino sa paghahanda at pagfondo ng kinabukasan kahit ano man ang mangyayari; 2] pag-iingat at paghahanda para sa darating na panahon gaya ng panustos; Iloc: makitkita na ti masakbayan
Foreshadow ipakita o nagpapahiwatig ng dadating
Forest kakahoyan, kagubatan, gubat; Iloc: kabakiran, bakir
Forestall antalahin, hadlangan, isagabal, pigilan; Iloc: tipden, itaktak, itantan, ibaybayag, ipasardeng, lappedan, teppedan
Correlated word
Filibuster paghadlang sa pamamagitan ng pag-antala
Forethought considerasyon-*Sp* at paghahanda bago dumating ang kinabukasan para maalagaan ang pangangailangan sa panahong iyan
Forever walang hangganan, walang wakas; Iloc: awan iti kalpasan na, awan gibus na
Forewarn magbabala, mag-alerto-*Sp*; Iloc: mang-alerto, mangiyal-alwad
Forewarned is forearmed *Advance warning is beneficial because one can prepare to deal with it competently and effectively, or to prevent it to happen, or to avoid it.* Kung maaga pa ay malaman ang babalang di mabuti, ikaw ay nakahandang makibaka
Forfeit *v.,* **Forfeiture** *n.* isuko ang ari-aryan dahil hindi na niya cayang bayaran ang *mortgage*
Forgery *n.,* **Forge** *v.* crimen na pagcopia ng sinulat ng ibang tao dahil ang tunay na manunulat ay may *copyright* o *protection* sa goiverno kaya ang nangongopia ay maisasakdal sa corte ng husticia sa ginawa niyang pagcopia niya sa pinaghirapang sinulat ng manunulat
Forget makalimutan, makaligtaan; Iloc: malipatan
Synonyms

Slip one's mind nawala sa isip, nakalimutan; Iloc: nagpukaw iti panunot, nalipatan

Lose one's train of thought nawala na lamang o nakalimutan ang paksa na gusto niyang pag-usapan

Forgetful malilimutin, uliyanin; Iloc: managlilipat, agcabcabaw

Forgive patawarin; Iloc: pakawanen, dispensaren

Forgiveness pagpapatawad; Iloc: dispensar-*Sp,* pagpakawan

FORGIVING mapagpatawad; Iloc: mapagpakawan

Synonym

Magnaninous taong mabuting isip at puso at di nagkikimkim ng kasamaan kundi mapagpatawad siya

FORGIVING offenders and managing the hurts they inflicted *God the Son Jesus Christ said, "He that is without sin among you, let him first cast a stone at her"-John 8:7* **(KJV)**, *and one by one, the accusing crowd left the adulterous woman without casting a single stone. Jesus Christ who never had a sin at all, took and endured all the punishments of mankind's sins, and was agonizingly assaulted, flogged, slapped, spitted on, crowned with thorns, crucified and died in order to free every mankind from the punishments of all our sins. God the Son Jesus Christ also stated, "Father, forgive them for they know not what they do." Let us forgive because all of us humans are flawed and imperfect, although people who ruin or rob other people's properties, deprive others of their inheritance, are heartlessly wicked, maliciously slander, mercilessly harm or disable people, murder, commit adultery, and do other egregious things are beyond normal and are in the terribly vile and depraved category of transgressors.*

1. Still, God wants us to forgive all offenders because God's words, the Bible, state, "God commendeth His love towards us in that while we were yet sinners, Christ died for us"-Romans 5:8 **(KJV)**. *Forgive because God has forgiven us of <u>all our lifetime sins</u> through His sacrifices on the cross – so how could we refuse to forgive others on one or a few wrongdoings? God said, "Forgive seventy times seven"-Matthew 18:22* **(NIV)** *which means to forgive offenders as often as we can. The Lord's Prayer in the Bible states, "Forgive us our sins as we forgive those who sin against us"-Luke 11:4* **(NIV)**. *So we need to ask God to help us forgive the offenders and to help us set them free from the offenses they inflicted on us, which actually would release us from bitterness, and even set us free from the emotional pains* *wreaked upon us. And being free from all those, the offender no longer has a hold on us.*

2. *Let us consider that the offender may have begotten their hostile nature from untoward circumstances in life. Did they experience poverty, maltreatments and abuses? were they likewise bullied, disowned and harshly rejected? Also, a lot of times people ignore or take for granted consideration for others, compassion, moral values, and ethical principles that these are not taken seriously or even forgotten that they no longer are aware such qualities exist. Some wrongdoers also have creepy beliefs that everybody is just like them so they attribute their wrongdoings on others. The victim usually is taken aback especially when he/she is not aggressive but unassertive, so the victim gets to consider if he/she should cut the offender some slack, give the offender a pass in order to endure with tolerance, which is a good reaction. It also pays to lift such unmerited hurts to God because God is the judge, not us. Since humans are flawed and imperfect, we may also be a part of the problem like being too sensitive to invectives, censures, tirades and assaults, so let us cast our burdens upon God for God to help us in such vulnerability that is common among humans, yet God blesses us with peace.*

3. *God even wants us to love our enemies as He said, "Love your enemies and pray for those who persecute you," also "Bless those who persecute you, <u>bless and do not curse</u>." Never consider revenge nor wish terrible consequences on the offender. Let us obey God's command to love and pray for the offender saying "Lord God in heaven, forgive me for my resentment on so-and-so (name of offender) and **please make me forgive** so-and-so (offender) and bless (offender) to become a better person" which makes our forgiveness on the offender sincere and unconditional. We are no longer reactive to the offense inflicted on us, as we have become proactive by releasing the pains and resentments from our hearts and even choose gentleness to obey God's command.*

4. *The offenses that the offender inflicts on people usually hurts, yet we need to cast away and eradicate from our heart and memory those offenses including the pains, resentments and grudges that such offenses have created. And when those offenses come to mind, we must ask forgiveness from God for the sins of resentments or grudges that came out from it, and we also ask God to cleanse our hearts and mind from both the pains and the sins that ensued. We can say, "I have released so-and-so (name of offender) from his/her offenses. The pain and the resentment no longer have a hold on me – thank You Lord God in heaven for sanctifying me." When we* *forgive, we set the offenders free, but in actuality, it is us who are set free and liberated from the burden of resentments, grudges and pains. When we forgive and cast away the offenses, the offender's control has no more effect on us. Then all is well in our souls including on our regard for the offender and the "Peace of God that passes all understanding shall keep our hearts and minds through Christ Jesus"-Philippians 4:7* **(KJV)**. *So forgiveness is pleasing because we become pleasing to God.*

5. *Forgiveness is reconciliation but it may not necessitate frequent contacts with the offender as in previous times. If there is toxicity in associating with the offender like more exposure to hurts and injustices, which may hinder a person from obeying God in maintaining peace, kindness and godliness, then it is better to avoid constant associations with the offender. We may talk to the offender or we may not, and whether the offender is alive or already deceased, we say, "**I forgive you** so-and-so (name of the offender)." Let God work in us and let us ask God if we need to talk to the offender or not, and our intention should be to reveal the hurt, not to accuse. However one may send some friendly gestures if he/she feels the need to, like birthday or holiday greeting cards, or a little booklet of inspiring Bible verses, etc., which is practicing agapé love - God's divine love. The truth is when a person knows another human being cares, it creates an uplifting feeling, the same feeling as when a person chooses to be God-abiding and be a hero in patience, in understanding, in gentleness even in the midst of being attacked unfairly and repulsively. Besides our obeying God, forgiveness is also calming and pleasant as it brings wellbeing, liberation, tranquility and joy.*

Forgo 1] talikuran at pabayaan, 2] ipagkait sa sarili; Iloc: 1] tallikudan ken baybay-an; 2] ipaidam iti bagi

Fork *(Tag. & Iloc.)* tinidor-*Sp*

Forlorn malungkot, mapanglaw, nalulumbay; Iloc: naliday, naladingit, naleddaang

Form hugis *(Tag. & Iloc.)* forma-*Sp*, corte-*Sp*

Formal sumsunod sa tamang asal o regulasyon-*Sp*, kung pangceremonya naman, ito ay *formal* o magarbo; Iloc: sumursurot iti nasayaat nga tignay ken regulasyon, nu pangceremonya met, daytoy ket *formal* ken naarcos

Formality *(Tag. & Iloc.)* formalidad-*Sp*

Former, Formerly dati; Iloc: sigud, dati, idi

Formula *(Tag. & Iloc.) formula*

Fornicate *v.,* **Fornication** *n.* pagtatalik ng *sexual* kahit hindi sila casal

Forsake iwanan, lisanan, layasan, kalimotan na; Iloc: panawan, baybay-an, talawan, lipatanen

Foresight matalinong pagturing, pagtanto at paghahanda sa hinaharap

Fort campo ng sundalo na gawa ng makapal, malakas at matibay na pader na mahirap lusobin ng mga kaaway

Forte katangian ng isang tao kung saan siya magaling, mahusay at nangingibabaw

Correlated words

Expertise experto sa nakakabuti o nakakaventaheng kaalaman at abilidad; Iloc: experto iti makasayaat ken makaventahe nga sirib ken abilidad

Capability mga kacayahan at mga talento at mga kaalaman; Iloc: dagiti cabaelan ken dagiti talento ken sirib

Knack talento na may kahusayan at bilis sa paggawa ng sang bagay

Prowess abilidad na mas mahusay kaysa ordinaryo; Iloc: abilidad a mas nalaeng ngem ti ordinario

Flair natural na talento o abilidad, talas ng utak

Mettle pinanganak na may tapang, chaga at pagpupursigi sa anomang kalagayan

Forthcoming 1] darating na, 2] nandidiyan o *available* para matupad ang pangako o kung kakailanganin

Forthright franko/ka-*Sp,* nagsasalita ng frankahan; Iloc: franko/ka

Fortify gawing malakas at matibay; Iloc: aramiden a napigsa ken nalagda

Fortitude *Mentally and emotionally strong in being able to courageously face problems, dangers, difficulties, disasters, misfortunes, temptaions, etc.* Lakas ng isip at damdamin na matapang na harapin at makibaka sa problema, panganib, kahirapan, calamidad-*Sp,* kasawian, gulo, tentacion-*Sp* at iba pa.

Fortress pook o stasyon-*Sp* ng *army* na pinaligiran ng makapal at mataas na cementong bakod

Fortunate mapalad, ma-suerte-*Sp*; Iloc: nagasat, masuerte

Fortune suerte-*Sp,* malaking pag-aaring pera o ari-arian

Forty *forty,* cuarenta-*Sp,* apat napo; Iloc: *forty,* cuarenta, uppat apulo

Forty one, 42, 43, 44, etc. *(English numbers are commonly used by Filipinos)*

Forward 1] paavante, 2] fresco at mapagpalagay na cursonada siya

Foster arugain, palagoin, pasiglahin; Iloc: taraknen, papigsaen, palapsaten

FOUL *(Tag. & Iloc.)* nakakadisgusto, bulok, vulgar, mabaho/nabangsit

FOUL play gawaing madaya, katraidoran at marahas na puedeng makarating sa patayan

FOUL-up kamalian dahil sa pagkalito o taranta o kaculangan ng *common sense*

FOUND, Establish mag-fundar-*Sp*, magbangon, magtatag, magtayo, mangpapuesto; Iloc: agfundar, agsimpa, mangbangon, mang-puesto-*Sp*

FOUND, Located nahanap, natagpoan, natunton; Iloc: nasapulan, nasa-rakan, nabirokan

Foundation fundasyon-*Sp*, batayan, saligan; Iloc: fundasyon, pagtakderan

FOUR *four*, apat, cuatro-*Sp*; Iloc: *four*, uppat, cuatro

FOUR hundred *four hundred*, apat na daan; Iloc: *four hundred*, uppat a gasut

FOUR o'clock *four o'clock*, alas cuatro-*Sp*

FOUR thousand *four thousand*, apat na libo; Iloc: *four thousand*, uppat a ribo

Fourteen *fourteen*, labing apat; Iloc: *fourteen*, sangapulo ket uppat

Fourth ikaapat; Iloc: ikauppat

Fowl mga nilalang na may pakpak gaya ng manok, pato, ibon at iba pa; Iloc: dagiti parsua nga adda payak da casla ti manok, pato, billit ken adu pay

Fraction kapiraso o kabahagi, parte ng buong bilang; Iloc: kapisi o kaparte, parte iti amin a bilang.

Fracture bali, putol; Iloc: tukkol

Fragile marupok, madaling masira o mabasag o mapunit; Iloc: narukop, narasi, nalaca a madadael o mabuong o mapigis

Fragment parte-*Sp* ng aparato o ng isang bagay na hindi nakaconecta; Iloc: pisi ti aparato-*Sp* o banag nga naysina

Fragrance bango, halimuyak; Iloc: banglo

Fragrant mabango; Iloc: nabanglo

Frail *adj.*, **Frailty** *n.* kahinaan sa katawan; kahinaan sa moralidad kaya hirap tumalikod sa tentacion-*Sp*

FRAME, picture *(Tag. & Iloc.)* cuadro-*Sp* ng letrato

FRAME up gumawa ng pagpabintang at pagpalabas na ang inocenteng tao ay ang may kagagawan ng kasalanan; Iloc: agaramid ti pagpabasol ken paruaren nga iti inocente-*Sp* a tao ket isu ti nakabasol

Franchise 1] ang pinunong companya-*Sp* ay nagbibigay ng otorisas-yon-*Sp* sa mga sangay/*branches* nito na iventa nila ang producto-*Sp* ng companya o ialay nila ang servicio-*Sp* ng companya sa mga cliente-*Sp*; 2] privilehio-*Sp* o *exemption* o pagpaliban na igawad ng govierno-*Sp* sa isang tao o grupo-*Sp* o companya-*Sp*; 3] karapatan o licensia-*Sp* na ibinigay ng companya sa tao o grupo-*Sp* para iventa ang canilang producto o servicio sa isang tinakdang lugar-*Sp* o teritoryo-*Sp*; 4] ang karapatang magvoto

Frank franko/ka-*Sp*, nagsasalita ng frankahan; Iloc: franka, agsao ti frankahan
Synonym
Forthright franko/ka, nagsasalita ng frankahan; Iloc: franko

Frantic takot at natataranta; Iloc: mabuteng ken matartaranta

Fraternal pagkakapatid na lalake

Fraud panlilinlang, pag-falsifica-*Sp*, panggaganso, panloloco, panda-raya, pagkukunwari para pagkatiwalaan sila at makuha ang pera o ari-arian ng vini-victima-*Sp* nila; Iloc: pangallilaw, pang-falsificar-*Sp*, panggulgulib, pangloc-loco-*Sp*, pangsinsinan tapno isuda ket mapag-talkan tapno makaala da ti cuarta o sanicua ti vicvictimaen da

Fraught puno, dala-dala, carga-*Sp*; Iloc: napunno

Frazzle 1] pagod na pagod sa katawan at sa emosyon; 2] pudpod na pudpod lalo na sa mga tupi o gilid

Freak, Freaky 1] tao o bagay o pangyayari na *abnormal* at hindi man lang caraniwan kundi kaibang-kaiba, 2] hindi controladong asal na hindi makatwiran dahil puedeng nakadroga

Freckles *(Tag. & Iloc.)* pekas-*Sp*

FREE malaya; Iloc: nawaya

FREE-for-all *(Tag. & Iloc.)* labo-labo, bakbakan

FREE, Gratis libre-*Sp*, walang bayad; Iloc: libre, awan bayad na

FREE lance taong gumagawa ng servicio-*Sp* sa companya o govier-no-*Sp* pero hindi siya nakacontrata bilang empleyado-*Sp* kundi independente-*Sp* at tagalabas lamang na nakikipagtrabaho lang ng panandalian

FREE-range mga hayop gaya ng manok na hindi nakakulong kundi palaboy-laboy lang ang mga ito sa labas

FREE, set, Release pakawalan, palayain; Iloc: pabulosan, ibulos, wayaan

FREE speech malayang ibunyag, ipagtapat, isiwalat ang paniwala na walang pagbabawal basta hindi crimen

FREE will malayang gumawa ng piniling gawain, layonin o asal basta hindi labag sa batas ang mga ito; Iloc: nawaya nga agaramid iti pinili na nga aramiden, rangta, garaw o ugali basta haan nga *illegal* dagitoy

Freebie bagay o servicio-*Sp* na libre-*Sp*; Iloc: banag o servicio nga libre

Freedom kalayaan; Iloc: wayawaya

Freeway, Expressway malawak na daan na walang *intersection* at mabibilis ang takbo ng mga sasakyan (65 mph); Iloc: acaba nga dalan nga awan *intersection* ken nacascas ti taray ti luglugan (65 mph)
Correlated words
Superhighway malawak na daan na naglalaan ng anim na *lanes*; Iloc: acaba a dalan nga addaan ti innem a *lanes*
Highway daan na nagcoconecta ng mga ciudad at bayan
Ramp calzadang pasukan o labasan ng *freeway* o *expressway*; Iloc: calzada a pagserrekan wenno pagruaran iti *freeway* wenno *expressway*
Merging road ang dalawang *lane* na calsada (ang isa ay galing sa *ramp* at ang isa ay sa *freeway*) na nagiging isa na lamang
Overpass calsadang tulay at sa baba nito ay hindi tubig kundi calsada rin; Iloc: calsada a rangtay ken iti baba na ket haan a danum nu di calsada met

Freewheeling walang pagpigil o pamaraan o patakaran at hindi nababahala sa kalabasan, kahinatnan o kasapitan

Freeze 1] ipalamig ng sobra sa *freezer* na kung minsan ay nagbabalat-yelo ito, 2] isang *appliance* o parte ng *refrigerator* na nakakapagpapreserva ng pagkain para hindi masira

Freight *(Tag. & Iloc.)* cargamento-*Sp*

French *(Tag. & Iloc.)* French, Frances-*Sp*

Frenzy temporaryong nasisiraan ng ulo at dito siya nagsisiklab ng lupit at rahas

Frequency kung gaano kadalas o ilang beses-*Sp* na gawin o nangyayari; Iloc: nu mano nga beses nga aramiden o mapaspasamak

Frequently, Frequent palagi, parati, madalas; Iloc: canayon

FRESH fresco-*Sp*, sariwa gaya ng frutas, gulay o carne; Iloc: fresco a makmakan

FRESH (one disposed to taking liberties) fresco-*Sp*, pangahas, bastos-*Sp*; Iloc: fresco, nadarasudos, bastos

Freshman unang taon sa *high school* o sa colehio-*Sp* o universidad-*Sp*; Iloc: umuna a tawen diay *high school* o colehio o universidad

Fret mag-alboroto-*Sp*; Iloc: agalboroto

Friction 1] magkiskisan ang dalawang balat o taklub sa isa't isa, 2] pagkadisgusto ng dalawang tao dahil sa alitan o pagkakaiba ng kanilang paniwala at gusto; Iloc: 1] agradradan iti dua a cudil o calub, 2] agkadisgustoan ti dua nga tao gapu ti apa o pagsabalyan ti pammati ken ti gusto da

FRIDAY *(Tag. & Iloc.)* *Friday,* Viernes-*Sp*

FRIDAY, good *(Tag. & Iloc.)* *Holy Friday,* Viernes Santo-*Sp*

FRIEND kaibigan; Iloc: gayyem
Synonyms
Buddy, Pal kaibigan; Iloc: gayyem
Chum matalik na kaibigan; Iloc: nadekket a gayyem

FRIEND in need is a friend indeed tunay na kaibigan na tumutulong kapag ikaw ay nagigipit, nagdadalamhati o napagkakatiwalaang pagsingawan ng problema
Antonym
Fair-weather friends kaibigan pero hindi na siya kaibigan sa oras ng kahirapan o problema o pangangailangan ng tulong

FRIENDLY palakaibigan; Iloc: nalaeng makigayyem

FRIENDLY fire sa labanan, pagpapaputok ng sundalo na hindi sinasadya ay tumama sa kaanib niyang sundalo at itong kaanib niyang nabaril ay nasugatan o namatay

Friendship pakikipagkaibigan; Iloc: pakigaygayyem

Frighten takotin; Iloc: butngen

Frightful nakakatakot; Iloc: nakabutbuteng

Frigid 1] malamig na kasing lamig ng yelo-*Sp*, 2] matigas at malamig ang asal; Iloc: 1] nalamiis nga kasinlamiis ti yelo, 2] nasikkil ken nalam-ek ti pakipagtrato

Frills, Fringe *(Tag. & Iloc.)* burloloy

Fringe benefit maliban sa sueldo-*Sp* na binabayad ng companya-*Sp*, ito ay mga beneficio-*Sp* na inaalay sa canilang empleyado-*Sp* para matulongan sila at para masiyahan sila at mas-*Sp* pagbutihin nila ang canilang trabaho-*Sp*

Frisbee itcha-salo na laruan; Iloc: ibato-sippaw nga ayayam o abalbalay
Not to be mistaken for -
Freebie bagay o servicio na libre; Iloc: banag o servicio nga libre

Frisk 1] sumayaw, palukso-lukso, patalon-talon, magpasaya sa sarili, makipagtuwaan; 2] saliksikin ang tao sa pagcapcap ng canyang damit at katawan kung mayroon siyang tinatagong armas-*Sp* o droga-*Sp*; capacapain, rikisahin; Iloc: 1] agsala, aglagto-lagto; 2] capcapan, aricapen, rikisaen nu adda armas na o droga
Correlated words
Pat down, Patdown kapkapan ang damit na suot ng tao para matutop kung mayroong nakatagong armas o droga

Fritter 1] aksayahin pakonti-konti, 2] *cake* na naglalaman ng frutas o gulay o isda

Frivolous *adj.,* **Frivolity** *n.* hindi makabulohan at di gaanong mahalaga para pagtuonan ng pansin

Frizzy *(Tag. & Iloc.) African curls,* maliit/babassit a culot

Frog palaka; Iloc: tucak

Frolic aliwang libangan at saya; Iloc: pagpapas ti ragsak ken rambak

FROM (person) mula kay, galing kay, buhat kay; Iloc: aggapu ken

FROM (place) mula sa, galing sa, buhat sa; Iloc: aggapu idiay, mangrugi idiay

FROM now on mula ngayon, buhat ngayon; Iloc: agrugi itattan, manipud itatta

FROM the start noong mula't mula pa, buhat pa sa umpisa; Iloc: manipud pay idi rugi

"FROM where?" "Taga-saan?", "Galing saan?"; Iloc: "Taga-ano?", "Naggapuan na?"

Front, Frontal harap, harapan; Iloc: sangwanan, sango
Antonym
Back likod; Iloc: likod, bukot

FROST hamog na naging yelo-*Sp* dahil sa sobrang kalamigan; Iloc: linnaaw a nagbalin a yelo

FROST bite sugat o pagkasira ng balat at laman dahil sa matagal na pagkababad o pagkabilad sa nieve-*Sp/snow*

Frosting *icing* o masarap na pinapahid para pantakip o pambalat ng buong *cake*

Froth bula; Iloc: labutab

FROWNING face simangot, ngusoan; Iloc: misuot, muregreg, rupanget

FROWNING forehead noong cunot-nuo; Iloc: curetret a muging

Frozen nagbalat-yelo-*Sp* dahil sa sobrang lamig, napreserva sa yelo; Iloc: sobra ti lamiis ket nagcudil ti yelo

Frugal matipid, kuripot; Iloc: kuripot, nakirmet, nainut

FRUIT *(Tag. & Iloc.)* frutas, bunga

FRUIT, bear magbunga; Iloc: agbunga

FRUIT, spoiled nabulok; Iloc: nalungsot

FRUIT skin, Peel balat; Iloc: ukis

Fruition tagumpay, pagtatamo ng bunga sa mga pinagsikapan; Iloc: balligi, makagun-od iti bunga gapu iti pinagpakpakat

FRUITS harvested with a pole sungkitin; Iloc: sucdalen

FRUITS being plucked from the trees mamitas, magpitas; Iloc: puros, agpuros, buras, agburas

Frustrate 1] bigoin at sirain ang gana, 2] hadlangang maisagawa o maitapos; hadlangang maging efectivo

FRY mag-frito-*Sp*; Iloc: agfrito

FRY rice magsangag, magluto ng sinangag; Iloc: agkirog, agluto iti kinirog

Frying pan palayok; Iloc: paryok

Fuel ito ay langis o gas o *coal*/carbon-*Sp* na nakakapa-andar-*Sp* ng makina-*Sp*

Fugitive nakatakas at nagtatago na taong kadalasan ay bilanggo buhat sa bilibid at pinaghahanap siya; Iloc: nakatammeng ken aglemlemmeng a tao nga canayon ket balud a rimwar diay preso-*Sp* nga sapsapulen da isu

Fulfill tuparin, gampanan; Iloc: tungpalen, agtungpal

FULL puno, punong-puno, tigib; Iloc: napunno, napno, napumpunno

FULL-blood pareho-*Sp* ang tatay at nanay nila, magkapatid; Iloc: pareho ti tatang ken nanang da, agkabsat

FULL-fledged yumabong at sumapit sa buong pagkabuo ng lubos at ganap na kalabasan

FULL stomach busog; Iloc: nabsog, napnek

FULL swing, High gear andar o kilos na mabilis, maefectivo at matagumpay; pagsasagawa o *action* na masigla

Fulminate 1] malakas na pagsabog; 2] matindi o marahas na pagsumpa o pagparatang

Fumble 1] kinacapa-capa sa paghahanap, 2] ninenervios na nagraramdam, 3] nag-aatubiling sumige o sumulong; Iloc: 1] agcarcarawa nga agsapul 2] agnernervios nga mangricricna, 3] maam-amak a mapan wenno agtuloy

Fume usok; Iloc: asok

Fumigate magpausok ng pangpatay ng mga insecto

FUN *n.* kasayahan; Iloc: pagrambakan, pagragsakan

FUN *adv.* nakakasaya, nakakalibang, nakakaaliw; Iloc: nakaramrambak, nakalinglingay, nakaliwliwa

Function, Usage gamit, tungkulin; Iloc: usar-*Sp*, obra-*Sp*

Functional *adj.,* **Functioning** *v.* gumagana, umaandar; Iloc: agob-obra-*Sp*, agan-andar-*Sp* *(also see Implementing or In force)*

FUND *n. (Tag. & Iloc.)* fondo-*Sp*

FUND *v.* fondohan, gugolan, tustosan: Iloc: mangfondo, gastosan, suportaan (fondo-*Sp*, gastos-*Sp*, suporta-*Sp*)

FUND-raising mangolecta ng donasyong pera para pantulong sa kapwa o sa layonin

Fundamental 1] fundasyon-*Sp*, elementarya-*Sp*, 2] importante-*Sp*, kinakailangan para sa buhay o pagsasagawa

Funeral libing; Iloc: pumpon, tabun

Funeral parlor *(Tag. & Iloc.)* funerarya-*Sp*

Funnel balisungsong, tubong-patulis para paglagusan o pag-agosan ng likido-*Sp* sa bibig ng botelya-*Sp*

Funny nakakatawa; Iloc: nakakatkatawa
Synonyms
Laughable nakakatawa; Iloc: nakakatkatawa
Comical *(Tag. & Iloc)* comico

Facetious nakakatawa, libangang katuwaan

Fur 1] mabalahibong suot, 2] balahibo ng hayop; Iloc: 1] burbur a cawes, 2] buok ti animal-*Sp/Eng*

Furbish linisan at kuskosan para maging maliwanag at makintab; ibalik sa maganda, sa nagagamit at sa napapakinabangan na namang kalagayan

Furious sobrang pagkagalit, nangangatal o nanggigigil o nananakit sa iba sa galit niya; Iloc: napalalo ti unget na, agngarngaryet ken agcabcabil gapu ti sobra-*Sp* a pungtot na

Furl balumbonin; Iloc: lucoten

Furlough *leave of absence* o vacasyon ng mga sundalo

Furnish bigyan, dulotan; Iloc: ikkan

Furnishing *(see furniture below)*

Furniture muebles-*Sp*, kasangkapan; Iloc: muebles, alicamen ida

Furor malaking karahasan o kagulohan sa publico-*Sp*, malupit na galit o siklab

Furrow inararo, kulobot; Iloc: inarado, curibetbet

Furry mabalahibo; Iloc: burburan

Further dagdag pa; Iloc: nayon pay

Furtherance pagtiagang umavante para makaventahe o umacenso (avante-*Sp*, ventahe-*Sp*, ascenso-*Sp*)

Furthermore at saka, chaka, isa pa; Iloc: chaka, maysa pay

Furtive palihim o pasecretong kumilos

Fury poot, malaking galit; Iloc: rungsot, sobra a pungtot

Fusion 1] tunawin sa init, 2] pinagsama ang iba't ibang elemento para magkaisa gaya ng *metal* at *alloy*, 3] bago at kakaibang pagluto gaya ng pagsama-samahin ang mga recado at mga uri ng pagluto ng iba't ibang cultura o lahi; Iloc: 1] tunawin iti init, 2] pinagkay-kaysa dagiti elemento casla *metal* ken *alloy*, 3] baro ken nakasabsabali a pagluto casla ti paglalaoken dagiti recado ken tipo ti pagluto ti sabasabali a cultura-*Sp* wenno lahi

Fuss, Fussy *(Tag. & Iloc.)* makuscos-balungos, mabusisi, maalboroto

Futile hindi gumagana o hindi maisagawa kahit paanong pagsisikap ang ginagawa; Iloc: haan nga agandar wenno haan agbalin uray no aniaman a pakat ti aramiden

Future ang mga kinabukasang panahon sa hinaharap; Iloc: cadagiti masangwanan/masakbayan a panawen

Futon, Thin mattress manipis na *mattress* na puedeng ilatag sa sahig para matulog o pag-upuan

Futz mag-aksaya ng sikap at panahon sa mali-maling asal o nakakapag-alinlangan at nakakadudang gawain

Fuzz *n.*, **Fuzzy** *adj.* maliliit na buhok o sinulid o ano pa man na dumidikit sa mga damit at muebles-*Sp* at *carpet*

G

GAB *v.*, **Gabby** *adj.* salita ng salita na wala namang kabulohan; Iloc: sarita nga sarita ngem awan met valor-*Sp* na

GAB, gift of mahusay at magaling sa paggamit ng lengguahe, magaling magcumbinsi

Gabble mabilis magsalita na hindi maintindihan; Iloc: napardas nga agsarita nga narigat a maawatan
Synonym
Jabber magsalita ng mabilis at hindi maintindihan

Gadget aparato-*Sp* o maliit na kasangkapan na pinapaandar ng makina-*Sp* o electricidad-*Sp*

Gaffe asiwang kamalian habang nakikihalobilo sa mga tao; Iloc: biddut a makasumgar ti dutdot mientras-*Sp* nga makipagsosyal isu iti tattao

GAG ifuersang takpan ang bunganga para hindi makasigaw o maka-pagsalita; Iloc: ifuersa nga caluban iti ngiwat tapno haan a makariaw wenno makasarita

GAG order, Gag rule mando-*Sp* ng corte-*Sp* na hindi ipapahayag o ibabalita ang tungkol sa caso-*Sp* na kasalukuyang inaatupag sa corte; reglamento-*Sp* na di pag-uusapan o pagdebatehan ang paksa

Gaga 1] ganadong-ganado, libang na libang, gustong-gusto; 2] gaga

Gaiety kasayahan, kagalakan, katuwaan, kasiglaan

Gain tubo, gana; Iloc: ganancia-*Sp*, tubo

Gainful *(Tag. & Iloc.)* matubo, mabunga

Gainsay magsalita o kumilos na pacontra; magpabulaanan, contrahin, makipagtalunan

Gait ang paraan ng paglakad, paghakbang, o pagtakbo; pagyagyag o lakad ng cabayo

Gala *(Tag. & Iloc.)* celebrasyon-*Sp* o fiesta-*Sp*; marangya

Gale malakas na hangin na ang bilis ay 32-63 mph

Gall 1] *(Tag. & Iloc.)* mapait na likido ng/ti apdo/apro, 2] inis, suklam, 3] gasgas sa balat

Gallant galante, marangal, maginoo sa babae; Iloc: narespeto cadagiti babbai, galante

Gallbladder apdo; Iloc: apro

Gallon sukat ng isang *gallon* ay apat na *quarts*

Gallstone *(Tag. & Iloc.)* bato sa apdo/apro

Galore napakadami, abundancia-*Sp*; Iloc: abundancia, nakaad-adu,

Galvanized iron *(Tag. & Iloc.)* galva, yero-*Sp*, sim

Gam binti ng babae; Iloc: gurong ti babae

Gambit pambukas na comentario sa pakikipag-usap, pang-umpisa o pagbating salita

Gamble *(Tag. & Iloc.)* sugal
  Correlated words
  Make a bet *(Tag. & Iloc.)* magpusta, magtaya

Gambler *(Tag. & Iloc.)* sugalero

Gambol naglalarong tatalon-talon; Iloc: agay-ayam nga aglagtolagto

GAME laro; Iloc: ay-ayam

GAME board (Filipino), wooden *(Tag. & Iloc.)* sungka

GAME (Filipino entry blockage) patintero; Iloc: araya

GAME plan tactica na plinano para maisagawa ang layonin
  Synonym
  Modus operandi kung paano ang pagpapatakbo ng balak o hanapbuhay o ng pangangalakal

GAME show paligsahang palabas sa TV; Iloc: salisal a programa-*Sp* diay *television*

Gamut *(Tag. & Iloc.)* entero at completo na laki o dami

Gang barcada-*aSp* o grupo-*Sp* ng mga *teen-ager* na kung minsan, mayroon sa canila'y hindi ginagamit ang talino at nagpapalulon sa masama sila; Iloc: barcada, bunggoy

Gangbang sumali sa masama at mapusok na crimen ang grupo gaya ng gahasa o grupong *rape* na magpare-pareha-*Sp* pero ang kasapitan nila parati ay bilanggo o mapatay sila mismo sa sarili nilang kasamaan

Gangbuster mga *police* na manghiwa-hiwalay o mangwatak-watak ng samahan ng gang

Gangland secretong mundo-*Sp* ng samahan ng mga gang

Gangling, Gangly napakamatangkad at mahaba ang paa; Iloc: nakataytayag ken atiddog ti saksaka na

Gangrene pagkabulok ng laman o *tissue* ng balat dahil sa kakulangan ng dugo sa parteng iyon

Gangster miembro ng grupong criminal

GAP puwang, butas, patlang; Iloc: blanko, abut, patlang

GAP in age agwat ng edad-*Sp* nila; Iloc: nagbaeten ti edad

Gape tumunganga sa gulat o pagtataka o pagkamangha na hindi makakilos; Iloc: mapamulengleng gapu ti kigtot ken siddaaw nga haan makakuti

Garage *(Tag. & Iloc.)* garahe-*Sp*

Garb kasuotan; Iloc: cawes

Garbage *(Tag. & Iloc.)* basura-*Sp*

Garbage collector *(Tag. & Iloc.)* basurero-*Sp*

Garble 1] nakakalito at hindi maintindihan dahil sa pagkadefecto ng aparato; 2] iniiiba ang pagsalin ng pahayag o kasulatan para iligaw, o iligaw sa pamamagitan ng paglaktaw o hindi pagsalin ng lahat na informasyon

Garden *garden*, hardin-*Sp*; Iloc: *garden*, hardin

Gardener *(Tag. & Iloc.)* *gardener*, hardinero-*Sp*

Gardenia rose *(Tag. & Iloc.)* rosal-*Sp*

Gargantuan sobrang napakalaki; Iloc: nakadakdakkel

Gargle magmumog; Iloc: agmulomog

Gargling, Gargly sound *(Tag. & Iloc.)* gumagaralgal

Gargoyle nakakatakot na ichura ng estatua sa gilid ng bubungan ng gusali

Garish matingkad at kumikinang ang mga culay at decorasyong kapunapuna pero mumurahin; Iloc: naranyag nga colcolor nga agparparang la unay

Garland bulaklakang quintas; Iloc: sabsabong a quentas

Garlic *(Tag. & Iloc.)* bawang

Garment kasuotan; Iloc: cawes

Garner 1] makatamo, makaangkin, 2] hakotin at imbakin, mangolecta at mag-ipon; Iloc: 1] makaala, 2] agbunag ken agkamkam, agcolecta ken agurnong

Garnish 1] gayakan ng palamuti, 2] haloan ng pampasarap; Iloc: arcosan, 2] recadoan (recado-*aSp*)

Garnishment mando ng corte na ang ari-aryan at depositong pera at sueldo ng nakautang ay mapunta sa pinagkakautangan upang mabayaran ang canyang utang

Garrulous *adj.*, **Garrulity** *n.* mabunganga, bungangera, madaldal, daldalera; Iloc: tarabitab, daldalera, nadaldal

Garth madamo na patio-*Sp* o *quadrangle* na may bakod o napaligiran ng mga gusali

GAS pampaandar ng makina-*Sp* na likidong gasolina-*Sp*; gas na hindi nakikitang usok na puedeng nakakamatay o makapahirap huminga

GAS mask pantakip na aparato-*Sp* na sinasala ng *charcoal* at *chemicals* na sinasagip ng hangin kaya nagsusuot ng *gas mask* para maprotectahan ang baga niya sa nakakasama o nakakalason na usok *gas*

GASH sugat o hiwa na malalim at mahaba; Iloc: sugat o laslas o iwa nga adalem ken atiddog

Gasp (for air) maghabol ng hininga, magsinghap; Iloc: aglung-ab
Correlated word
Pant humahangos, humihingal, hapo; Iloc: agas-asog, agalal-al

GATE *gate*, pasukan at labasang bakuran; Iloc: *gate*

GATE-crasher puslit, dumadalo sa *party* pero hindi siya imbitado-*Sp*, Iloc: puslit

Gated community lugar na tinitirhan o pinagtatrabahoan na hindi bastabasta makakapasok kung walang pahintulot o tulong ng taong-looban

GATHER by scooping salukin; Iloc: acupen

GATHER dried clothes from the laundry line pupolin; Iloc: akasen

GATHER things to bring to another place hakotin; Iloc: bunagen

GATHER together or meet together magtipon-tipon, magkitakita, magsama-sama; Iloc: agsasarak, agtipon-tipon

Gathering pagtitipon-tipon ng mga tao sa isang lugar; Iloc: pagu-ummong iti tattao ida

Gauche *[gohsh]* walang magandang asal, walang delicadesa-*Sp;* walang kapinohan sa pakiki-ugnay, siya'y magaspang, bastos-*Sp* o saliwa

Gaudy color matingkad at kumikinang ang mga culay at decorasyong culay matingkad pero mumurahin; Iloc: makapurar a color, naranyag nga colcolor nga agparparang unay (decorasyon-*Sp,* color-*Sp*)

Gauge sukatan; Iloc: rukoden

Gaunt buto't balat ang pagkapayat at hihina-hina; Iloc: tulang ken cudil ti pagkakuttong na ken agcapoy-capoy

Gauze gaza-*Sp* na pangtakip ng sugat; Iloc: gaza, pangcalub ti sugat tapno maprotectaan

Gawk *[gawk]* titig ng tanga; tungangang titig

Gay 1] masaya; 2] nakikipagkasintahan o nakikipagtalik na *sexual* sa kapwa lalake o kapwa babae

Gaze titigan; Iloc: mingmingan, perrengen

Gazillion napakadami na walang hangganan; Iloc: naggadu ken awan patinggana

Gear 1] ngipin ng makina-*Sp,* 2] paghahanda para sa dadating na gawain o gaganapin; Iloc: 1] ngipin ti makina-*Sp,* 2] pagsagsagana para iti sumangpet nga maaramid

Geek 1] taong tanga, mali-mali at saliwa, 2] taong magaling sa siencia-*Sp* o *technology* pero **di** sanay makihalobilo sa mga tao

Gel parang *gelatin* o *jelly* ang katangian nito, hindi buo at hindi matubig kundi para lamang crema o yong pangmasahe ng sakit sa katawan

Gelatin pagkaing *gelatin;* Iloc: kanen a *gelatin*

Gem perlas-*Sp* o *mineral* na ginawang pulido-*Sp,* isang binigyang halaga dahil sa kagandahan at pagkaperfecto nito

Genealogy *record* o talaan ng mga ninuno o angkang pinagmulan ng familiia at mga sumunod na supling nito hanggang sa mga huling nakatalang supling; linya ng familya buhat sa umpisa hanggang sa kasalukuyan

Gender kung babae o lalake; Iloc: nu babai wenno lalaki

Genes ito ay namamana sa magulang o ninuno

General heneral-*Sp,* aplicado-*Sp* sa lahat; Iloc: heneral, aplicado iti amin

Generalize pahayag na ang pinag-uusapang gawain o katatao o katangian ay panlahatan at walang pagkakaiba

Generate maglikha, umimbento, gumawa ng bagong bagay; Iloc: agparnuay, umimbento, mangaramid ti baro a banag

GENERATION *(Tag. & Iloc.)* henerasyon-*Sp*

GENERATION X mga napanganak noong 1966 hanggang 1979; Iloc: dagiti nayyanak idi 1966 inggana 1979

Another generation

Baby boomers mga napaanganak noong 1946 hanggang 1965; Iloc: dagiti nayyanak idi 1946 inggana 1965

GENERATION Y, Millennials napanganak noong 1980's hanggang 1990's; Iloc: nayyanak idi 1980 ingana 1990

GENERIC pangcaraniwan o panglahatan; Iloc: pang ordinario-*Sp* o para iti amin

GENERIC medicine *generic* ay aprovadong pangalan ng gamot at kadalasang nirereceta ng mga doctor at lalong sinasakop ng *insurance* ng medicina. Ang *generic medicine* ay mas mura kahit na ang mga gamot na ito ay magkapareho sa *brand medicine* sa bisa at calidad o *quality*

Generosity *n.,* **Generous** *adj. Willingness and plentiful giving; hospitable, kind; noble, good, compassionate, philanthropic, charitable.* Mapagbigay, bukas ang palad sa mga nangangailangan, handang magbigay ng caya niyang ibigay; Iloc: manangisagot, managpaay, naparabur, nakasagana nga mangited ti cabaelan na nga ited

Synonyms

Largess, Largesse pagbibigay ng regalo gaya ng pera at iba pa

Bounty abundanciang pamimigay; Iloc: abundancia a pangited

Genetics siensia tungkol sa namamana *genes* sa magulang o ninuno, mga pagkakahawig na resulta ng *genes*

Genial 1] magandang makipagkaibigan, magiliw; 2] nakakabuti sa buhay, sa pagyabong, sa ginhawa

Genital, Genitalia parte-*Sp* ng katawan na kung saan nagtatalik ang magasawa at dito umuusbong ang mga anak; Iloc: parte ti bagi nga ditoy ag-romansa ti agasawa ken pagrusingan ti annak da

Genius *genius,* taong napakataas ang talino o intelihensia na wala sa ordinaryong tao, at puede-*Sp* pang mayroong talento-*Sp* o abilidad-*Sp* gaya ng pag-imbento-*Sp* o paglikha; Iloc: *genius,* tao nga nakangatngato ti intelihensia na nga awan cadagiti ordinaryo a tao, ken mabalin pay addaan iti talento, abilidad casla pag-imbento ken parnuay

Genome *[jee-nohm]* lahat ng *DNA* o *chromosomes* na namamanang *traits* o pagkatao ng nilikha ng Dios

Genre *[zhan-ruh]* 1] clase-*Sp* o categoria-*Sp* sa larangan ng sining o arte-*Sp* na may forma-*Sp* o nilalaman gaya halimbawa ng pintang larawan ng tutoong pang-araw-araw na kabuhayan; 2] tungkol sa isang nabubukod na tipo-*Sp* ng panunulat o literatura-*Sp*

Genteel finong-fino at maganda ang asal

Gentility mabuting pagpalaki sa mga supling na magresulta ng fino at kagandahang-asal at marangal na buhay

Gentle *adj.*, **Gentilesse** *n.* mahinahon, tahimik, maamo, mayumi, malumanay; Iloc: naemma, naulimek, naamo,

Gentleman *gentleman,* maginoo; Iloc: *gentleman,* natakneng

Gentleman's agreement contratang hindi nakasulat kundi bumabatay lamang sa usapang kasundoan

Genuflect pagluluhod ng dalawang tuhod o isang tuhod lamang at nakatango ang ulo sa pagparangal; Iloc: agparintumeng ti dua a tumeng wenno maysa a tumeng laeng ken nakadumog ti ulo nga agpadayaw

Genuine *genuine,* tunay, puro-*Sp,* lantay, otentico, dalisay; Iloc: pudno, puro, *genuine*

Geography *(Tag. & Iloc.) geography*

Geometry *(Tag. & Iloc.) geometry*

Geriatrics pagsusuri at paggamot ng sakit ng mga *seniors* o matatanda sa larangan ng medicina-*Sp*

Germs *(Tag. & Iloc.)* microbio-*Sp*

German *(Tag. & Iloc.)* Aleman-*Sp, German*

Germane pertinente, relevante at naangkop

Germicide pumapatay ng microbio, *disinfectant*

Germinate umusbong, tumubo, sumibol; Iloc: agsaringit, agrusing, agtubo

Germs *(Tag. & Iloc.)* microbio-*Sp, bacteria*

Gestate *v.*, **Gestation** *n.* 1] pagbubuntis hanggang manganak; 2] magplano, isipin at lumikha ng mahalagang diwa

Gesticulate nagsasalita at ginagamit ang camay at mukha niya para bigyang-diin ang sinasabi; Iloc: agsarita nga iyus-usar-*Sp* ti ima ken rupa na tapno may-presentar-*Sp* na a fuersa-*Sp* iti ibagbaga na

Gesture galaw ng anomang parte-*Sp* ng katawan para ipahiwatig ang gustong sabihin; Iloc: garaw ti ania man nga parte ti bagi para i-presentar-*Sp* na ti cayat na nga ibaga

GET kunin, kuhanin; Iloc: alaen

GET a handle on *Get to know all about it and understand to be able to handle it or deal with it.* Alamin at indindihin para malaman kung paano tratuhin, gawin o sacopin.

GET a break nagkaroon ng suerte o magandang chansa o maunlad na kapalaran

"GET a life!" "Magpakatino ka at humanap ka ng mabuting layonin at gawain sa buhay mo!"

GET along marunong makipagkaibigan, makisama ng mabuti sa kapwa; Iloc: ammo na iti makigayyem

GET along on a shoestring nakacayang mabuhay sa napakakaunting pera; Iloc: caya na iti agbiag iti bassit laeng nga cuarta-*aSp*

GET by 1] nakakayang mabuhay sa napaka-kaunting pera o kahit may kapansanan o mahirap ang kalagayan niya; 2] nakayang maabot ang unang *requirement*; 3] nakagawa ng masama pero hindi nahuli ng *police* o naparusahan

"GET down to the facts" "Sabihin mo lamang ang mga katotohanan at ang may kabulohan"

GET-go sa kaumpisahan; Iloc: diay rugi

GET it off one's chest, Get it out in the open ilabas ang kinikimkim na nakakabalisa, nakakabahala o sakit ng loob
Correlated phrases
Vent out, Express pent-up emotions idaing, itaghoy, maghihimutok, itangis; Iloc: iyasog, agunnoy, agsennaay

GET off bababa; Iloc: agdissaag
Synonyms
Descend bumaba, manaog; Iloc: bumaba, umulog, sumalog
Alight, Disembark umibis, bumaba; Iloc: agdissaag, bumaba

GET off on the wrong foot, Get off to a bad start mag-umpisa sa maling-maling kilos o gawain o pasya

GET one's foot on the door umpisahan ng maaga at ilagay na ang unang hakbang sa proceso-*Sp* ng pagtatamo ng pagkabuo ng isinasagawa pati ventahe-*Sp* at favor-*Sp* na kasama sa tagumpay

GET one's money's worth kunin ang halaga ng binayaran gaya ng pagkatibay at pagkahusay ng pagkagawa

GET over bumuti o nagtagumpay sa pagsugpo niya ng canyang sakit; nakahanap na ng ginhawa at payapa pagkatapos ng kahirapan o dalamhati o paghihiwalay sa dating kasintahan o asawa

GET the better of magkaroon ng kapangyarihan sa tao itong bagay o katangian, o kaya nagiging matagumpay ito sa tao

GET the hang of it natutuhan kung paano gawin o ayosin ang bagay o paano paandarin ang makina o paano magmahala ng tungkulin o negosyo-*Sp*

GET the picture maintindihan na ang buong situasyon-*Sp*

GET to the bottom of it alamin at intindihin lahat ng dahilan o sanhi, at kung bakit nangyari o nalikha ang anoman na situasyon-*Sp* o pangyayari

GET-together magtipon-tipon mag-*get-together;* Iloc: agtipon-tipon, ag-*get-together*

GET-up or Getup 1] bumangon; 2] kasuotang damit

Ghastly nakakatakot, nakakarimarim; Iloc: nakabutbuteng

Ghetto lugar-*Sp* sa isang bayan o ciudad-*Sp* na halatang mahihirap ang nakatira, *slum*

Ghost multo, mumo; Iloc: al-alya

Ghoul taoing interesado sa mga nakakadisgusto, mahalay, malaswa at masama

Giant *(Tag. & Iloc.)* higante-*Sp*

Gibber *v.,* **Gibberish** *adj.* nagsasalita na walang kahulugan o hindi relevante sa paksa o hindi maintindihan

Giblet parte ng manok gaya ng atay, puso at balunbalunan

Giddy medio-*Sp* nahihilo; Iloc: medio maulaw

GIFT regalo-*Sp*; Iloc: regalo, parabur, sarabu, pasagot

GIFT that is best and greatest are unconditional love and acceptance ang regalo na pinakamakahalaga sa lahat ay ang pagmamahal at pagtanggap sa kapwa kahit ano pa man siya o sila

Gig reservang pagtatanghal ng musikero o mga musikero

Gigantic higante-*Sp*, napakalaki; Iloc: higante, nagdakkel

Giggle hagikhik; Iloc: ayek-ek, umlek

Gigolo lalaking patuloy na nakikipagtalik ng *sexual* sa babae at tumatanggap ng pangsuportang pera pa

Gild *(present)*, **Gilt** *(past)* balat-ginto o pinalubog sa ginto

Gill hasang; Iloc: asang

Gimmick, Gimmickry *(Tag. & Iloc.) gimmick*, tactica-*Sp*

Gin *(Tag. & Iloc.)* hinebra-*Sp*

GINGER luya; Iloc: laya

GINGER brew to cure sore throat *(Tag. & Iloc.)* salabat

Gingivitis pamamaga sa gilagid

Gird 1] maghanda sa inaasahang pakikibaka o gagawin, 2] ano man na bagay para pang-cinturon-*Sp*

Girdle masikip pero nauunat na suot sa tiyan para mapitpit at lumiit ito at maitago ang matabang puson; Iloc: nareppet a cawes iti chan para mapitpit ken bumassit dayta ken mailemmeng iti nataba a pus-ong

GIRL babae; Iloc: babai

GIRL friend kasintahan, novia-*Sp*, kaibigang babae; Iloc: kaayan-ayat, kaliwliwa, novia, gayyem a babai

Gist buod, diwa; Iloc: amad, bagas
   Synonyms
   Issue, Theme, Topic, Essence paksa, punto ng salita, diwa, bagay; Iloc: paksa, banag, punto ti pagsarsaritaan

GIVE magbigay, dulotan, ipagkaloob; Iloc: ikkan, mangited, mangisagot, mangiparangkap, mangipaay
   Synonyms
   Bestow ipagkaloob, ibigay; Iloc: ipaay, rangkap, ited
   Supply, Provide tustosan, pagkalooban, dulotan; Iloc: mangited, mangted
   Furnish bigyan, dulotan; Iloc: ikkan
   Dispense mamigay, mag-entrega; Iloc: mangited, ag-entrega
   Correlated words
   Accept tanggapin; Iloc: akceptaren
   Receive tanggapin, kunin; Iloc: awaten
   Refuse, Decline tanggihan, mag-ayaw; Iloc: agmadi
   Return a thing ibalik; Iloc: isubli, ipulang

GIVE away 1] galaw, salita o ichura na nagpapalantad ng pagkatao, 2] bagay na libreng pamigay, regalo-*Sp*, donasyon-*Sp*

GIVE a hard time nagbibigay ito ng hindi kinakailangan at hindi nararapat na kahirapan dahil walang pacensia, o umiinit ang ulo, o pinapalaki o pinapagrabe ang usapan o gawain o plano

GIVE birth magsilang, manganak, magluwal; Iloc: agpasngay, iyanak

GIVE credit where credit is due *Acknowledge the good input and praise the source of it who deserves tribute even though you are reluctant to do it.* Bigyang puri o pasasalamat sa nararapat makatanggap kahit nag-aatubili ka

GIVE importance estimahin, bigyan ng halaga; Iloc: estimaren, ikkan ti valor (estima/estimar-*Sp*, valor-*Sp*)

GIVE in pagbigyan, paunlakan; Iloc: pagustoan (gusto-*Sp*), palubosan

GIVE it a shot *Try or do something; make an effort to do something.* Subokan para malaman kung ano ang kahihinatnan.

GIVE it your best shot *Take efforts, determination and your best skills to pursue and accomplish what you aspire for in order to achieve it.* Gamitin mo ang lahat ng iyong sikap, kakayahan, abilidad, talino, kaalaman at pinakamahusay na hakbang para maicompleto at magtagumpay; Iloc: iyusar iti am-amin nga nakasaysayaat a dalan ken pamuspusan, abilidad, intelihesia o sirib ken amin nga ammo tapno agturpos ken agballigi

GIVE up 1] sumuko, 2] nawalan ng pag-asa o gana kaya huminto na ng husto sa pagsasagawa, 3] ipamigay na

GIVE way paraanin; Iloc: padalanen

Given 1] binigay, ibinigay, 2] inaasahang mangyari, nakatalagang mangyari o magkatutuo

Gizmo ano mang aparatong *mechanical*

Gizzard balumbalunan; Iloc: battikuleng

Glad nagagalak, galak, masaya; Iloc: maragsakan

Gladden pasayahin; Iloc: paragsaken

Glair puting parte ng itlog; Iloc: puraw ti itlog

Glamor *n.,* **Glamorous** *adj.* suot-suot ang pinakauso o modang-moda kasuotan, at naka-*make-up* ng maganda kaya marilag at elegante

Glance sulyapan, balingan; Iloc: talyawan

Glare *n.,* **Glaring** *adj.* 1] marahas na ilaw na nakasisilaw sa mata, 2] nanlilisik na tingin, irap; Iloc: 1] naranggas a ranyag a makapurar ti mata, 2] naranggas a cusilap

GLASS *glass,* salamin, cristal-*Sp*; Iloc: *glass,* sarming, cristal-*Sp*
Correlated words
Vitreous *adj.,* **Vitrify** *v.* ichura ng o gawa sa cristal o salamin

GLASS, drinking *(Tag. & Iloc.)* baso-*Sp*

Glaucoma *(Tag. & Iloc.)* glaucoma, diferencia ng mata

Gleam bigla at madaliang kislap sa kadiliman; Iloc: apagdarikmat a silap iti sipnget

Glean *v.,* **Gleanings** *n.* mag-ani o maghimalay-*gather,* mamulot, manguha ng mga giik-*grains;* mangolecta ng anoman na hinay-hinay o mabagal at unti-unti lamang

Glee masayang canta-*Sp* ng grupo-*Sp*; Iloc: naragsak a canta ti grupo

Gleeful masaya; Iloc: naragsak

Glen maliit, makitid at nakatagong *valley* o lambak

Glib 1] pagsasalita na hindi pinag-isipan, hindi nababahala at hindi pinaghandaan, 2] mahusay magsalita o magsulat pero hindi tapat sa puso ang sinasabi

GLIDE magpadulas; Iloc: agpakaglis

GLIDE down magpadagusdos, magpadausdos; Iloc: agpadarusdos, ag-karuskos pababa

Glimmer bigla at madaliang kislap sa kadiliman; Iloc: apagdarikmat a silap iti sipnget

Glimpse silayan ng sandali; Iloc: kitaen ti nabiit

Glint bigla at madaliang kislap sa kadiliman, malabong pahiwatig; Iloc: apagdarikmat a silap iti sipnget, sawang nga haan nalawag

Glisten, Glister pakurap-kurap na kislap o mahinang kinang ng ilaw; Iloc: agsileng-sileng a ranyag

Glitch magdefecto o pagtigil ng pag-andar na kailangang i-*repair* o icumpuni; golpe at saglit na pagkagambala

Glitter kumikinang; Iloc: agkilap-kilap

Gloat napakagandang pakiramdam dahil sa saya at pagkacontento sa mabuting pagkatao at gawa niya mismo

Global entero-*Sp* o buong mundo-*Sp,* formang bola-*Sp*

Globe *(Tag. & Iloc.)* mundo-*Sp*, planeta-*Sp*

Gloom *n.*, **Gloomy** *adj.* panahong madilim o medio-*Sp* madilim na nakakalatoy at nakakatamad o nakakawalang gana o nakakalungkot, matamlay; Iloc: natamnay, naliday, haan a maganasan

Glop 1] malambot at basang-basang pinaghalong pagkain; 2] kasulatan na walang kabulohan

Glorify purihin, sambahin, luwalhatian; Iloc: dayawen, i-glorificar-*Sp*, i-sagrado-*Sp*

Glorious puno ng gloria; maluwalhati, masagrado, napakadakila, sina-samba, kapuri-puri, pinaparangalan

Glory luwalhati, *(Tag. & Iloc.)* sagrado-*Sp*, gloria-*Sp*

Gloss *n.*, **Glossy** *adj.* kintab; Iloc: sileng

Glove *(Tag. & Iloc.)* guantes-*Sp*

Glow sumikat, kumislap, kumintab; Iloc: agranyag, agsilap

Glower marahas na ilaw na nakakasilaw; Iloc: naranggas a ranyag a makapurar

Glue *(Tag. & Iloc.)* cola-*Sp*
Correlated word
Paste pandikit; Iloc: pangpigket, pangdekket

Glum walang gana, lumbay na lumbay at nalulongkot

Glut kumaing labis sa kinakailangan, matakaw na kumain; Iloc: adu ken sobra-sobra a mangan

Glutton *n,*, **Gluttonous** *adj.* matakaw; Iloc: bukatot, narawet, sarabusab

Gnash kumukoskos ang ngipin habang natutulog o nagngingitngit sa sobrang galit; Iloc: agngarngaryet nga maturog wenno nu agunget

Gnat maliit na langaw; Iloc: bassit a ngilaw

Gnaw ngatngatin; Iloc: ngutngoten

GO pupunta; Iloc: mapan

"GO!" "Sugod!" Iloc: "Ingkan!"
Antonym
"Come!" "Halika!" Iloc: "Cadtoy!"

"GO ahead" "Sige"-*Sp*; Iloc: "Sige", "Ala ngarud"

GO across tumawid; Iloc: bumallasiw

GO around umikot, ikotan, mag-ronda; Iloc: aglikaw, likawan, aglibot, ag-ronda-*Sp*

GO backward mag-atras-*Sp*, umurong; Iloc: ag-atras, agsanud

GO-between siyang nagpakilala sa dalawa at siya ring nagreto at naging tulay para maging magkasintahan sila

GO down papanaog, bababa; Iloc: umulog, agdissaag, agsalog

GO forward mag-avante-*Sp*, sumulong; Iloc: ag-avante

GO-getter *An energetic, enthusiastic, eager beaver ambitious person who seeks for opportunities, works like a live wire using his diligence, abilities, skills and talents, and strives to succeed.*

GO home uuwi; Iloc: agawid

GO immediately sumibat; Iloc: dagdagos nga mapan

GO in pumasok; Iloc: sumrek

GO in one ear and out the other narinig pero hindi inintindi o nabale-wala

GO near lumapit; Iloc: umasideg, umadani

GO outside lumabas; Iloc: rumwar

GO out of one's way kahit ocupado-*Sp* na sa mga dating ginagawa, maglaan pa rin ng tiempo-*Sp* para makabigay tulong o makagawa ng iba pang kinakailangan

GO over *(Tag. & Iloc.)* examinin, inspeksionin

GO overboard 1] mahulog sa tubig buhat sa bapor o bangka, 2] magtrabaho ng sobra-sobra, 3] gumastos ng sobra-sobra

GO to any length, Go the extra mile gawin ang anoman na kina-kailangang gawin at lampasan pa sa tinakdang hangganan

Go through a passage tumagos; Iloc: agsalpot, agsulpot

GO up papanhik, umakyat; Iloc: umuli, ngumato, agsang-at

Goal balak, layonin, sanhi, tangka; Iloc: pakay, panggep,

Goat cambing; Iloc: calding

Gobble lumamon ng mabilis o ng malalaking subo; Iloc: mangan ti paspas wenno dadakkel a subo

GOD: *God is the Holy Trinity, one God in three divine persons - God the Father, God the Son Jesus Christ, and God the Holy Spirit. God is the creator of the universe and everything that is in the universe. God is eternal: He has no beginning and no end. God is omnipotent (all-powerful), omniscient (all-knowing including our thoughts and feelings), omnipresent (is everywhere). God is divine, holy, sacred, righteous, perfect and sinless. God is all-good, all-kind, all-merciful,* *all-forgiving, all-loving, all-caring, all-charitable, all-giving, all-generous, all-helpful, all-trustworthy, all-faithful, all-reliable, all-real, all-true.* **God loves us, all humans, that He provided the grace (free gift) of salvation to all of us so as to be freed from the punishments of all our lifetime sins, past, present and future sins.** *God sent His one and only begotten Son, Jesus Christ, to do the supreme sacrifice for the* **salvation of our souls.** *God the Son Jesus Christ took and endured the agonizing sufferings, crucifixion, death, and resurrection to save us-mankind from being punished in hell for all our sins. So if we believe and put our faith and trust in God's deep love for us, and receive Jesus Christ into our heart and life as our Lord God, Savior and Redeemer because He took and endured the punishments of all our lifetime sins, instead of us-mankind being punished in hell for our sins, then all our sins are forgiven and cleansed by Jesus Christ's most precious blood on the cross and now we are destined for heaven. The Holy Spirit also comes to indwell in our hearts, and we also have a new birth – we are spiritually born-again as God's children. Everything that we have comes from God, even our faith and trust in God comes from Him.* Ang Dios ay Santisima Trinidad: isang Dios sa tatlong banal na persona: Dios Ama, Dios Anak na si Hesu Cristo at Dios Espiritu Santo. Nilikha ng Dios ang buong universo at lahat na nasa universo. Ang Dios ay walang umpisa at walang katapusan. Pinakamakapangyarihan ang Dios. Walang lihim sa Dios dahil alam Niya lahat ang mga nangyayari sa sanlibutan, pati isip at damdamin ng bawat nilalang. Naroroon ang Dios sa lahat ng parte ng universo. Ang Dios ay perfecto na wala man lamang sala kahit isa. Ang Dios ay puno ng kabanalan, gloria, gracia, kabutihan at kabaitan. Siya ay sagrado, mapagpala, maluwalhati, mapagpatawad, mapagmahal, mahabagin, maawain, matulongin, mapagkaloob at tapat. Kahit tayo ay makasalanan at hindi karapat-dapat sa pagmamahal ng Dios ay mahal pa rin Niya tayo. Nagtakda ang Dios ng makakaligtas sa parusa ng ating mga kasalanan sa pamamagitan ng pagsugo sa Dios Anak na si Hesu Cristo para Siya ang magdusa sa mga parusa ng ating mga kasalanan, imbes na pagdusahan natin sa infierno ang mga kasalanan natin. Kung manalig tayo at tanggapin natin si Hesu Cristo na Dios natin at Tagapagligtas natin, ang lahat ng ating mga kasalanan ay mapapatawad na at malinisan na ng banal na dugo ni Hesu Cristo sa cruz at nakatakda na tayong papunta sa langit. Ang Espiritu Santo ay papasok na rin sa puso natin para gabayan tayo na maging maka-Dios. Magkaroon din tayo ng bagong kapanganakan na espiritual at tayo ay nagiging espiritual na anak na ng Panginoong Dios.

John 3:16 For God so loved the world that He gave His one and only begotten Son, that whoever believes in Him shall not perish but have eternal life. **(KJV)**

Romans 5:8 God showed His great love for us by sending Christ to die for us while we were still sinners. **(NLT)**

1 John 4:10 This is love: not that we loved God, but that He loved us and sent His Son as an atoning sacrifice for our sins **(NIV)**

1 John 5:11 And the witness is this, that God has given us eternal life, and this is in His Son. **(NASB)**

GOD the Son, Jesus Christ: *Jesus Christ obeyed God the Father and came down to earth to save mankind from the punishments of all our sins, instead of us-mankind being punished in hell for our sins. Jesus Christ is perfect and has no sin at all, but He took and endured the punishment of the sins of all mankind. He was beaten, flogged, demeaned, spitted upon, slapped, crowned with thorns, made to carry a heavy cross on His trek to Mount Calvary/Golgotha where He was crucified and then died on that cross. A soldier slashed His side with a spear that water and blood flowed out confirming He has died. His dead body was laid in a sepulcher and blocked with a big heavy stone. After three days, Mary Magdalene, Mary, and Joanna went to the sepulcher to daub spices on Jesus Christ's dead body, but they found the sepulcher open and His body was no longer there. So the ladies ran to inform the disciples about their findings, and the disciples also rushed to the sepulcher to check it out. The disciples at first forgot the statement of Jesus Christ that He will arise from His death on the 3rd day and now, Jesus Christ's words came true. Then Jesus Christ appeared to the disciples and they saw His hands that were pierced with nails and His chest that was slashed. They also witnessed Jesus Christ's ascent to heaven after He blessed them and told them to spread His words. All the prophecies for centuries* *of the coming Messiah came true in Jesus Christ like His birth, His life, His earthly family lineage, His sacrifice and death, and many more.* **If we believe and trust that all the sacrifices of Jesus Christ's sufferings, crucifixion, death and resurrection is the only way for us to go to heaven, and we receive Jesus Christ into our heart and life as our Lord, God, Savior and Redeemer, all our past, present and future sins are forgiven and cleansed by the precious blood of Jesus Christ on the cross.** *And right there and then, the Holy Spirit comes to indwell in our heart to walk with us and help us live a God-abiding life. We also have a new birth as we become spiritually born-again as God's children. God wants us to have conscience-compunction and humility to confess our sins to God whenever we commit a sin, even though all our sins have been forgiven and cleansed by the blood of Jesus Christ on the cross when we received Him into our heart and life as our Lord, God, Savior and Redeemer.* Ang Dios Anak na si Hesu Cristo ang tumanggap ng parusa sa mga kasalanan ng lahat ng mga nilalang, imbes na ang mga nilalang ay magdusa sa parusa ng canilang mga kasalanan sa impierno. Tiniis ni Hesu Cristo ang mga dinanas Niyang pananakit sa Canya, mga paglait-lait, paghaplit-haplit ng latigo, sampal at pagdura, pagsiksik sa ulo Niya ng mga tinik na corona, pinabuhat pa Siya ng mabigat na cruz paakyat sa bundok ng Calvario/Golgotha kung saan Siya pinako sa mismong cruz na binuhat Niya. Namatay Siya sa cruz ngunit nabuhay Siya sa ikatlong araw ng Canyang pagkamatay gaya ng dati Niyang sinabi sa nakaraang mga araw. Nakipagpulong Siya muli sa Canyang mga dicipulo at nakita nila ang mga kamay ni Hesu Cristo na sugatang-tuhog ng pako noong ipinako Siya sa cruz, at ang tagiliran Niyang tinusok ng sibat. Nasaksihan din nila si Hesu Cristo na pataas pabalik sa langit. Natupad lahat kay Hesu Cristo ang mga profesia ng mga profeta tungkol sa dadating na *Messiah* gaya ng pagkapanganak Niya, ang buhay Niya, ang angkan ni Santa Maria na nagsilang sa Canya, ang mga pagdurusa Niya dito sa mundo, at marami pang iba. Kapag maniwala, magtiwala, manalig at magsampalataya tayo sa lahat ng pagdurusa ng Dios Anak na si Hesu Cristo, pagkapako sa cruz, pagkamatay Niya, pagkabuhay Niyang muli at pagtaas na pagbalik Niya sa langit ay para sa kaligtasan ng kaluluwa natin, at tanggapin natin si Hesu Cristo sa puso't buhay natin bilang Dios natin at Tagapagligtas natin, ang lahat ng kasalanan natin sa nakaraan, sa kasalukuyan at sa darating na panahon ay mapatawad at malinisan na ng banal na dugo ni Hesu Cristo sa cruz, at mapapasalangit na tayo. Papasok na rin ang Dios Espiritu Santo sa puso natin para gabayan tayo sa buhay. Magkaroon din tayo ng bagong kapanganakan dahil tayo ay nagiging espiritual na anak na ng Panginoong Dios.

Romans 5:8 But God demonstrate His own love for us in this: while we were still sinners, Christ died for us. **(NIV)**

John 1:29 Behold the lamb of God who takes away the sins of the world. **(NASB)**

Matthew 26:28 For this is My blood of the covenant, which is to be shed on behalf of many for the forgiveness of sins. **(NIV)**

Hebrews 9:22 Without the shedding of blood, there is no forgiveness of sins. **(NASB)**

1 John 1:7 The blood of Jesus His Son cleanses us from all sins. **(NASB)**

1 Corinthians 6:11 Your sins are washed away, and you are set apart for God, and He has accepted you because of what the Lord Jesus Christ and the Spirit of our God have done to you. **(NKJV)**

Matthew 1:21 He shall save His people from their sins. **(KJV)**

Ephesians 1:7 In whom we have redemption through His blood, the forgiveness of sins according to the riches of His grace. **(KJV)**

Revelation 1:5 To Him who loves us, and releases us from our sins by His blood. **(NASB)**

Titus 3:7 That being justified by His grace, we might be made heirs according to the hope of eternal life. **(KJV)**

John 8:36 So if the Son sets you free, you will be free indeed. **(NIV)**

Ephesians 2:8 Because of His kindness, you have been saved through trusting Christ. And even trusting is not of yourselves; it is a gift from God. **(NIV)**

2 Corinthians 5:17 Therefore if any man be in Christ, he is a new creature: old things are passed away; behold, all things become new. **(KJV)**

Titus 3:5-7 When the kindness and love of God our Savior appeared, He saved us, not because of righteous things we had done, but because of His mercy. He saved us through the washing of rebirth and renewal by the Holy Spirit, whom He poured out on us generously through Jesus Christ our Savior, so that having been justified by His grace, we might become heirs having the hope of eternal life. **(NASB)**

Matthew 6:33, Luke 12:31 Seek ye first the kingdom of God and His righteousness and all these things will be added onto you. **(KJV)**

Philippians 4:13 I can do all things through Christ who strengthens us. **(NKJV)**

Philippians 1:6 He who began a good work in you will carry it on to completion. **(NIV)**

GOD the Holy Spirit: *He is also known as the Holy Ghost, the Spirit of God, the Spirit of Jesus Christ. God the Holy Spirit inspired and helped the prophets and the disciples to write the Bible, the holy words of God. When we receive Jesus Christ as our Lord, God, Savior and Redeemer into our heart and life in order that we are forgiven and cleansed from our sins, the Holy Spirit then comes to indwell in our heart because **God is Emmanuel meaning "God with us" so that we become a temple of God the Holy Spirit**. The Holy Spirit never leaves us nor forsakes us, and He walks with us and guides us when we surrender ourselves to Him and depend and rely on Him to help us live a God-abiding life. If we ask the Holy Spirit, He purifies us to become obedient to God, pleasing onto God, a good testimony of God, and a blessing to others. The Holy Spirit is the great shepherd who leads, guides, and helps us in any way we ask Him like directions, guidance, assistance, counsel, and solutions. After the Holy Spirit comes to indwell in us, we also acquire a new birth – we become spiritually born-again as God's children.* Ang Dios Espiritu Santo ay Espiritu ng Dios, Espiritu ni Hesu Cristo. Ang Dios Espiritu Santo ang pumukaw sa mga profeta at mga dicipulo para bigyang-sigla silang isulat ang Biblia, ang banal na salita ng Dios. Kapag tinanggap natin si Hesu Cristo sa puso't buhay natin bilang Dios at Tagapagligtas natin, ang Espiritu Santo ay papasok na sa puso natin at templo na tayo ng Espiritu Santo. Hindi Niya tayo iiwanan o lalayasan kahit kailanman dahil ang Espiritu Santo ang tutulong na magpaka-Dios tayo sa pamamagitan ng paggagabay at pagpatnubay Niya sa atin. Kaya tuwing maalaala natin ay magdasal tayo para patnubayan at gabayan tayo ng Dios Espiritu Santo na sumunod sa mga utos ng Panginoong Dios para kasiya-siya tayo sa Dios.

Ezekiel 36:27 I will put My spirit within you so that you will obey my laws and you do whatever I command. **(NASB)**

414

Proverbs 1:23 Behold, I will pour out My spirit unto you. I will make known my words unto you. **(KJV)**

John 16:13 When He, the Spirit of truth, is come, He will guide you unto all truth. **(KJV)**

John 8:32 You will know the truth, and the truth will set you free. **(NIV)**

Ephesians 1:13 In Him, you also, after listening to the message of truth, the gospel of salvation - having also believed, you were sealed in Him with the Holy Spirit of promise. **(NASB)**

1 Corinthians 3:16 Do you not know that you are the temple of God and that the Spirit of God dwells in you? **(NKJV)**

Romans 8:11 If the Spirit of Him who raised Jesus from the dead, dwells in you, He who raised Christ Jesus from the dead will also give life to your mortal bodies through His Spirit who indwells in you. **(NASB)**

1 Corinthians 2:12 Now we have received, not the spirit of the world, but the Spirit which is of God; that we might know the things that are freely given to us of God. **(KJV)**

Romans 8:14-15 For those who are led by the Spirit of God are the **children of God**. The Spirit you received does not make you slaves so that you live in fear again; rather, the Spirit you received brought about your adoption to son-ship. And by Him we cry "Abba Father." The Spirit Himself testifies with our spirit that we are **God's children**. **(NASB)**

Titus 3:7 That being justified by His grace, we might be made **heirs** according to the hope of eternal life. **(NASB)**

Galatians 3:26 For now we are all **children of God** through faith in Jesus Christ. **(NLT)**

1 John 5:4 Whatever is born of God overcomes the world; and this is the victory that has overcome the world – our faith. **(NASB)**

GOD's Salvation for All Mankind, the Importance of FAITH: *God's words, the Bible, states in Romans 1:17 and Galatians 3:11, "The just shall live by faith." **(NKJV)** And in Ephesians 2:8-9, God says "For by grace you have been saved through faith in Jesus Christ, and that not of yourselves. It is the gift of God, not of works lest anyone should boast." **(NASB)** And in Romans 1:16, God's words state, "I am not ashamed of the gospel of Christ; for it is the power of God onto salvation to every one that believeth." **(KJV)** Our faith must be believing and trusting that the sufferings, crucifixion, death and resurrection of Jesus Christ saves mankind from the punishments of* *all of mankind's sins.* ***Jesus Christ's blood on the cross cleanses and forgives all our past, present and future sins where we then become saved and destined for heaven.*** Ang faith ay pag-alam, paniniwala, pagtiwala, pagpanalig at pagsampalataya natin na ang Panginoong Dios ay malaki ang pagmamahal Niya sa atin, kaya nagtakda Siya ng kaligtasan para hindi natin pagdusahan ang parusa ng ating mga kasalanan sa impierno. Ginawa ng Dios na ang kaligtasan natin ay napakadali – ito ay **faith** at ang **faith** ay paniwala, pagtiwala, pananalig, at pagsampalataya sa pagmamahal ng Dios sa atin at ang pagsacrificio ng Dios Anak na si Hesu Cristo, pagkapako Niya sa cruz, pagkamatay Niya at pagbangon muling mabuhay si Hesu Cristo ay para sa ating kaligtasan sa parusa ng ating mga kasalanan. Kaya tanggapin natin sa puso't buhay natin si Hesu Cristo bilang Dios natin at Tagapagligtas natin dahil si Hesu Cristo ang nagdanas sa parusa ng mga kasalanan ng lahat ng sanlibutan, upang ang mga kasalanan natin ay mapatawad at malinisan ng dugo ni Hesu Cristo sa cruz at nakadestino na tayong papunta sa langit. At dito rin papasok ang Espiritu Santo sa puso natin upang dito mamalagi para patnubayan tayong mabuhay na maka-Dios. Magkaroon din tayo ng bagong kapanganakang espiritual kaya nagiging spiritual na anak na tayo ng Dios.

Romans 1:17 For in it the righteousness of God is revealed from faith to faith, as it is written, "The just shall live by faith." **(NKJV)**

Romans 5:12 Therefore since we have been justified by faith, we have peace with God through our Lord Jesus Christ. Through Him, we have also obtained access by faith into grace in which we stand, and we rejoice in hope of the glory of God **(NASB)**

Romans 10:17 Faith comes from hearing, and hearing by the word of Christ. **(NASB)**

GOD's Salvation for All Mankind - the Importance of GRACE: *Grace is a gift that we have not earned nor deserved. The grace of salvation from God is a **free gift** to all mankind because He loves us deeply that God the Father sent His one and only begotten Son Jesus Christ to do the most supreme sacrifice for all mankind. Jesus Christ endured all the sufferings, crucifixion and death in order to carry upon Himself all our sins and have our sins forgiven and cleansed by His most* *precious blood on the cross. In Titus 3:5-7, God says <u>"Not by works</u>* <u>*of righteousness which we have done, but according to His mercy*</u> <u>*He saved us, through the washing of regeneration and renewing*</u> <u>*of the Holy Spirit whom He poured out on us abundantly through*</u> <u>*Jesus Christ, our Savior, that having been justified by His **grace**, we*</u> <u>*should become **heirs** according to the hope of eternal life"*</u>. **(NASB)** *God loves the good works man does to be good individuals and to be in obedience to God's command. But the good works that man does is **not** the divine plan for the salvation of our souls, otherwise we make ourselves our own savior which contradicts God's divine plan for men's salvation. **Salvation is from God alone and He made this free gift** (the grace of salvation) easy, simple and doable for us by believing and putting our faith and trust on God's deep love for us and on Jesus Christ's crucifixion, death and resurrection as the only way for all our sins to be forgiven and cleansed because it is God the Holy Trinity in God the Son Jesus Christ's crucifixion that forgives us, with Jesus Christ's blood on the cross that totally cleanses all our sins. We must admit that we need God to save us from the penalties of our sins while confessing our sins to God. We must receive Jesus Christ into our heart and life as our Lord, God, Savior and Redeemer, giving tribute to what He did for us on the cross, and we are now destined for heaven. The Holy Spirit then comes to indwell in our heart, and we now have a new birth that we become spiritually born-again children of God. Grace* o gracia ay libreng regalo ng Dios sa atin kahit hindi natin pinaghirapan o nakakarapatan ito. Itong gracia ay kaligtasan na itinakda ng Dios para maligtas tayo sa parusa ng ating mga kasalanan sa pamamagitan ng pagsacrificio ng Dios Anak na si Hesu Cristo sa cruz - Siya ang tumanggap ng parusa sa ating mga kasalanan, imbes na pagdusahan natin ang parusa ng ating mga kasalanan sa infierno. Napakadali ang gracia ng kaligtasan ng Dios - maniwala, magsampalataya at magtiwala lamang tayo na ang pagkapako sa cruz, pagkamatay Niya at pag-*resurrect* ni Dios Anak na si Hesu Cristo sa langit ay para sa kaligtasan ng ating kaluluwa, at isuko natin ang puso't buhay natin sa Dios at tanggapin natin si Hesu Cristo bilang Dios natin at Tagapagligtas natin, para lahat ng ating mga kasalanan sa buong buhay ay mapatawad at malinisan na ng dugo ni Hesu Cristo sa cruz. Papasok na rin ang Espiritu Santo sa puso natin para mamalagi at gabayan tayong mamuhay na maka-Dios, at tayo ay magkaroon din ng bagong kapanganakan – tayo ay maging *spiritually born-again* na anak na ng Dios.

Ephesians 2:8-9 For by grace you have been saved through faith. And this is not your own doing; it is the gift of God, not a result of works, so that no one may boast. **(NASB)**

Romans 3:24 All are justified freely by His grace as a gift, through the redemption that is in Christ Jesus. **(NKJV)**

Romans 6:23 The gift of God is eternal life through Christ Jesus our Lord. **(NIV)**

2 Timothy 1:9 Who saved us and called us to a holy calling, not because of works but because of His own purpose and **grace**, which He gave us in Christ Jesus. **(NASB)**

Romans 11:6 If it is by grace, it is no longer on the basis of works; otherwise grace would no longer be grace. **(NASB)**

Hebrews 9:14 The blood of Christ, who through the eternal Spirit, offered Himself without blemish to God, cleanse your conscience from dead works to serve the living God. **(NIV)**

2 Corinthians 9:8 And God is able to make grace abound to you, so that having all sufficiency in all things at all times, you may abound in every good work. **(NASB)**

Titus 2:11 For the **grace** of God has appeared, bringing salvation for all people. **(NLT)**

Titus 3:7 So that being justified by His **grace**, we might become heirs according to the hope of eternal life. **(NLT)**

GOD's Salvation For All Mankind – Bible Verses Illustrate Why and How To Receive God's Salvation For All Mankind: *If you die today, do you know where you are going? God's holy words, the Bible, state in John 8:32, "Ye shall know the truth, and the truth shall make you free" **(KJV)** so the following Bible verses illustrate how we can go to heaven, and not to be cast into hell.* Kung ikaw ay sumakabilang-buhay ngayon, alam mo ba kung saan ka paroroon? Basahin ang mga sumusunod na **banal na salita ng Panginoong Dios** para maligtas tayo at maiwasang mapunta tayo sa apoy ng infierno.

Romans 3:*23 For all have sinned and come short of the glory of God.* **(NIV)**
Mga Taga-Roma 3:23 Ito ay sapagkat ang lahat ay nagkasala at hindi nakaabot sa kaluwalhatian ng Dios.

Romans 6:23 *For the wages of sin is death, but the gift of God is eternal life in Christ Jesus, our Lord.* **(NIV)**
Mga Taga-Roma 6:23 Ito ay sapagkat ang kabayaran ng mga kasalanan ay kamatayan, ngunit ang walang bayad na kaloob ng Dios ay buhay na walang hanggan kay Cristo Hesus na ating Panginoon.

1 John 4:10 *In this is love, not that we loved God, but that He loved us and sent His Son to be the propitiation for our sins.* **(NASB)**
1 Juan 4:10 Ganito ang pag-ibig, hindi sapagkat inibig natin ang Dios kundi dahil Siya ang umibig sa atin at sinugo ang Kanyang Anak bilang kasiya-siyang handog para sa ating mga kasalanan.

John 3:16 *For God so loved the world that He gave His only begotten Son that whoever believeth in Him should not perish but have everlasting life.* **(NASB)**
Juan 3:16 Ito ay sapagkat sa ganitong paraan inibig ng Dios ang sanlibutan kaya ipinagkaloob Niya ang Kanyang bugtong na Anak upang ang sinumang sumampalataya sa Kanya ay hindi mapahamak kundi magkaroon ng buhay na walang hanggan.

Romans 5:8-10 *But God proves His love for us in that while we still were sinners, Christ died for us. Much more surely then, now that we have been justified by His blood, will we be saved through Him from the wrath of God. For if while we were enemies, we were reconciled to God through the death of His Son, much more surely, having been reconciled, will we be saved by His life.* **(NASB)**
Mga Taga-Roma 5:8-10 Ngunit ipinakita ng Dios ang Kanyang pag-ibig sa atin na nang tayo ay makasalanan pa, si Cristo ay namatay para sa atin. Higit pa riyan, tayo ngayon ay pinaging-matuwid sa pamamagitan ng Kanyang dugo. Kaya nga tayo ay maliligtas sa poot sa pamamagitan Niya. Ito ay sapagkat nang tayo ay kaaway ng Dios, pinagkasundo tayo sa Kanya sa pamamagitan ng kamatayan ng Kanyang Anak. Higit pa riyan, ngayong tayo ay ipinagkasundo, tayo ay maliligtas sa pamamagitan ng buhay ng Kanyang Anak.

Ephesians 2:8-9 *For by grace you have been saved through faith in Jesus Christ, and that not of yourselves. It is the gift of God, not of works lest anyone should boast.* **(NASB)**
Mga Taga-Efeso 2:8-9 Ito ay sapagkat sa biyaya, kayo ay naligtas sa pamamagitan ng pananampalataya, at ito ay hindi sa inyong sarili, ito ay

kaloob ng Dios. Ito ay hindi dahil sa gawa upang hindi magmalaki ang sinuman.

Titus 3:5-7 *Not by works of righteousness which we have done, but according to His mercy He saved us, through the washing of regeneration and renewing of the Holy Spirit whom He poured out on us abundantly through Jesus Christ, our Savior, that having been justified by His grace, we should become heirs according to the hope of eternal life.* **(NASB)**

Kay Tito 3:5-7 Nang mahayag ito, iniligtas Niya tayo, hindi sa pamamagitan ng mga gawang katuwiran na ating ginawa kundi sa Kanyang kahabagan. Ito ay sa pamamagitan ng muling kapanganakang naghuhugas sa atin at sa pamamagitan ng Banal na Espiritung bumabago sa atin. Masagana Niyang ibinuhos ang Banal na Espiritu sa atin sa pamamagitan ni Hesu Cristo na ating tagapagligtas. Ginawa Niya ito upang sa pagpapaging-matuwid sa atin sa pamamagitan ng biyaya ayon sa pag-asa, tayo ay maging tagapagmana ng buhay na walang hanggan.

2 Corinthians 6:2 *I tell you, now is the time of God's favor, now is the day of salvation.* **(NIV)**

2 Mga Taga-Corinto 6:2 Narito ngayon ang panahong katanggap-tanggap. Narito ang araw ng kaligtasan.

Hebrews 3:7 *Today if ye hear His voice, harden not your hearts.* **(KJV)**

Hebreo 3:7-8 Ngayon kung inyong marinig ang Kanyang tinig, huwag ninyong pagmatigasin ang inyong mga puso.

Revelation 3:20 *Behold I stand at the door and knock. If any man hears My voice and opens the door, I will come in to him.* **(NASB)**

Pahayag 3:20 Narito Ako na nakatayo sa pintuan at patuloy na kumakatok. Kapag marinig ang sinuman ang Aking tinig at magbukas ng pinto, Ako ay papasok sa kanya.

GOD's Salvation for All Mankind Granted To Us By Praying a Similar Prayer as this Sample Prayer: *You can use your own words that come truthfully and sincerely from your own heart, so here is a sample prayer to guide you in receiving God's grace of salvation.*

"Lord God in heaven, I am imperfect and a sinner. I am sorry that I have sinned against You and against my fellowmen. I would like to confess my sins to You, o God (confess your sins here). Thank You for Your love, Father God, that You sent Your one and only begotten Son to undergo the most supreme sacrifice for me. Thank You, God the Son Jesus Christ that You took and endured the punishments of my

sins, instead of me being punished in hell for all my sins. I receive You now Jesus Christ as my Lord, God, Savior and Redeemer. I thank You that through Your sufferings, crucifixion, death and resurrection, all my sins are forgiven and cleansed by Your most precious blood on the cross, and I am now destined for heaven. Thank You, o Holy Spirit, that You now come to indwell in my heart, never to leave me nor forsake me, but to walk with me always and give me a desire to pray to You always, read and learn Your holy words, the Bible, so that I can have a spiritual growth and become obedient onto You, o God, even become a good testimony of You, and a blessing to others. Thank You that I also have a new birth and I am now spiritually born-again as Your child, o God. Thank You that You opened my eyes to let me know Your grace of salvation and gave me faith to receive God the Son Jesus Christ as my Lord, God, Savior and Redeemer because everything that I have including my faith, trust and love for You came from You."

God's Advice on How to Pray: *The start of the ten commandments of God in Exodus 20:2-5 goes this way, "<u>I am the Lord thy God. Thou shalt not have other gods before Me. Thou shalt not make unto thee any graven image, or any likeness of any thing that is in heaven above, or that is in the earth beneath, or that is in the water under the earth. Thou shalt not bow down thyself to them, nor serve them</u>,"* **(NASB)** *and in John 4:23-24, the Bible states "<u>The true worshippers shall worship the Father in spirit and in truth: for the Father seeketh such to worship Him. God is a Spirit: and they that worship Him must worship Him in spirit and in truth</u>."* **(NASB)** *So we must NOT worship nor kneel down before statues or pictures. God's holy words, the Bible, does NOT STATE that we must pray to His earthly mother, nor to angels, nor to anointed saints.* **We must pray and worship God alone, God who is the Holy Trinity, one God in three divine persons: God the Father, God the Son Jesus Christ and God the Holy Spirit. And we must worship God in spirit and in truth.** *Also in Isaiah 29:13, the Bible states, "<u>These people draw near with their mouths, and honor Me with their lips, while their hearts are far from Me, and their worship of Me is a human commandment learned by</u>*

rote", **(NASB)** *and in Matthew 6:7, it states, "<u>But when ye pray, use</u> <u>not vain repetitions as the heathen do: for they think that they shall be</u> <u>heard for their much speaking.</u>"* **(NASB)** *So when we pray, we must pray to God with reverence, devotion, respect, affinity, allegiance and dedication. Our feelings while praying should be with sincerity in accordance with our heart and mind; and should also be with praise, worship, exaltation, honor, and gratitude to God. Our prayers must not be merely moving of our lips with memorized prayers or "learned by rote" as God says because that would only be a lip-service. When we pray with memorized prayers, our eyes and thoughts even wander away and around, on surroundings, on people, incidents, plans, or things. We must pay attention and take note on what God says, then obey Him on what He says in His holy words, the Bible.*

GOD's Help and Blessings Are Achieved When We Depend and Rely on God *After praying a similar prayer as the sample prayer printed above, we receive God's gift of salvation in which all our sins are cleansed and forgiven through God the Son Jesus Christ's blood on the cross when He was crucified. Now the most effective way to become our best self in being a good Christian and living a life for God is relying on God the Holy Spirit to lead us and guide us always because as humans, we transgress often. It is also essential to pray to God often or everyday because God wants us to have a close relationship with Him by our communicating with Him in prayers, in worship, in gratitude, and in reading His words, the Bible. God said in Matthew 4:4, "<u>Man shall not live by bread alone, but by every word</u> <u>that proceedeth out of the mouth of God</u>"* **(NKJV)** *and in John 8:32, "<u>Ye shall know the truth, and the truth shall make you free.</u>"* **(KJV)** *It is through the Bible where God communicates with us and gives us directions, as well as when we pray fervently for His leading, He communicates with us in peacefully showing us His guidance and/ or answer. We can also cast our problems and difficulties onto God so as for Him to carry our burdens and for Him to give us relief and solutions because He said in Psalms 55:22, "<u>Cast your burdens upon</u> <u>the Lord, and He shall sustain thee</u>"* **(NASB)** *and in Matthew 11:28,*

He said *"Come onto Me, all ye that labor and are heavy laden, and I will give you rest."* **(KJV)** *Also, with us being human and imperfect, we need to ask God to heal us body, soul and spirit – in all aspects of our whole being and in all aspects of our life because God said in 2 Corinthians 5:21,"For our sake, He made Him to be sin who knew no sin so that in Him we might become the righteousness of God."* **(ESV)** *So we need to* **ask God to purify** *our thoughts, words, deeds, emotions, attitudes, intentions, decisions, desires, aspirations, in our daily life and work, in our hurts and pains, in our dealings with people, in our reactions towards them, in our using His blessings on us of intelligence, abilities, skills, talents, expertise, and many more. After a short while, we would notice our nature improving. We also become much more aware of our sins because God wants us to have* **conscience-conviction, remorse** *and* **humility** *so that we ask God to forgive us whenever we sin, even though our sins have all been forgiven and cleansed by the blood of Jesus Christ on the cross when we prayed to receive Jesus Christ as our Lord, God, Savior and Redeemer. With our steady prayers to God and our sincere intentions and deeds to be God-abiding, the bad habits, bad intentions, sinful acts, even addictions that we may have had, are now leaving us. By our obedience to God and by God's grace, we also forgive offenders easily as we likewise get freed from the stings of resentments that were lodging in our heart (read Forgiving offenders and managing the hurts they inflicted). We can also ask God to cover us with His most precious blood on the cross and use us today and throughout our life for His purpose and glory.*

GOD's Help and Blessings Are Achieved When We Stand on and Claim His Promises In the Bible: *After we received the cleansing and forgiveness of all our sins when we prayed to receive into our heart and life God the Son Jesus Christ as our Lord, God, Savior and Redeemer, we are now bestowed to claim and stand on the promises of God so that God's words would come true in our life. Some of God's loving promises are "Seek ye first the kingdom of God and His righteousness and all these things shall be added onto you" (Isaiah*

423

64:8) **(KJV)**; *"God shall supply all your needs according to His riches in glory by Christ Jesus" (Philippians 4:19)* **(KJV)**; *"And we know that to them that love God, all things work together for good" (Romans 8:28)* **(KJV)**; *"The righteous cry and the Lord heareth, and delivereth them out of all their troubles" (Psalm 34:17)* **(KJV)**; *"The Lord is my rock and my fortress, and my deliverer, my God, my strength in whom I will trust, my buckler, and the horn of my salvation, and my high tower" (Psalm 18:2)* **(KJV)**; *"In all these things, we are more than conquerors through Him that love us" (Romans 8:37)* **(KJV)**; *"I can do all things through Christ who strengthens me" (Philippians 4:13);* **(KJV)** *"Trust in the Lord with all your heart and lean not on your own understanding. In all your ways acknowledge Him, and He shall direct thy paths." (Proverbs 3:5-6)* **(KJV)**; *"That ye might walk worthy of the Lord unto all pleasing, being fruitful in every good work, and increasing in the knowledge of God" (Colossians 1:10)* **(KJV)**; *"Commit thy works onto the Lord, and thy thoughts shall be established" (Proverbs 16:3)* **(KJV)**; *and "Let us therefore come boldly onto the throne of grace that we may obtain mercy and find grace to help in time of need" (Hebrew 4:16)* **(KJV)**

Godchild inaanak; Iloc: ihado/da-*aSp*

Godfather *(Tag. & Iloc.)* ninong

Godfather's relationship to parents of the godchild magcompadre-*Sp*; Iloc: ag-compadre

Godly *(Tag. & Iloc.)* maka-Dios-*Sp*

Godmother *(Tag. & Iloc.)* ninang

Godmother's relationship to parents of the godchild magcomadre-*Sp*; Iloc: ag-comadre

Godsend ang biglang pagkakatotoo o pagbunga o pagdating ng kina-kailangang bagay o pangyayari

Godspeed tagumpay o kasuertehan; Iloc: balligi o suerte

Goggle 1] may culay na salamin ng mata; 2] tinging dilat

Goings-on pangyayari na nakakabigat o kaya nakakasakit; Iloc: nadagsen o narigat o nasakit a mapaspasamak

Goiter buklaw, bosyo; Iloc: bekkak, akak

GOLD ginto; Iloc: balitok

GOLD-digger babaeng nakikipagtalik sa lalakeng makakabigay sa canya ng mga mamahaling regalo-*Sp* at pera

GOLDEN gawa sa ginto; Iloc: inaramid iti balitok
Correlated words
Gild *(present),* **Gilt** *(past)* balat-ginto o pinalubog sa ginto

GOLDEN rule *Do unto others as you would have them do unto you.* Gawin mo sa iba ang gusto mong gawin nila sa iyo.

GONE, Consumed ubos na; Iloc: awanen, naibusen

GONE, Left umalis na, lumuwas na; Iloc: pimmanawen, nagtalawen

Gonorrhea *(Tag. & Iloc.) gonorrhea*

Goo *n.,* **Gooey** *adj.* malaput at malagkit na bagay; Iloc: napalet ken napigket

GOOD mabuti, mabait, mahusay; Iloc: nasingpet, nasaya-at, naimbag, nalaeng

"GOOD afternoon" "Magandang hapon, po"; Iloc: "Naimbag nga malem yo, apo"

"GOOD bye" "Paalam na, po"; Iloc: "Agawidacon, apo"

GOOD bye, bid magpaalam; Iloc: agpacada

"GOOD day" "Magandang araw po"; Iloc: "Naimbag nga aldaw yo, apo"

"GOOD evening" "Magandang gabi, po"; Iloc: "Naimbag nga rabii yo, apo"

GOOD-for-nothing *(Tag. & Iloc.)* aparato, gamit o taong inutil-*Sp* o hindi nakakatulong o nakakabigay ng mabuty

GOOD Friday *(Tag. & Iloc.)* Viernes Santo-*Sp*

GOOD-hearted napakabait, mapagmalasakit, maawain at mapagbi-gay; Iloc: nasingpet, mangisaksakit, mangas-asi, manangisagot, manangipaay

GOOD-humored mapagpasaya at nagpapatawa ng mga birong decente; Iloc: ammo na ti mangparangsak

GOOD-looking maganda, makisig, guapo/pa-*Sp*; Iloc: napintas, nalibnos, guapo/pa

GOOD manners kabutihang asal; Iloc: ma-etiketa-*Sp* iti paggaraw

"GOOD morning" "Magandang umaga, po"; Iloc: "Naimbag a bigat yo, apo"

GOOD-natured napakabait ang puso, mapagmalasakit at magandang makisama; Iloc: nasingpet, mangisaksakit, mangas-asi, manangisagot, manangipaay

GOOD quality pagkagawa o pagkatao na magaling, mahusay, mabuti at matibay; Iloc: pagkaaramid o pagkatao a nalaeng, nasayaat, naimbag ken nalagda

GOOD traits mabuting costumbre-*Sp* o pag-uugali; Iloc: nasayaat a costumbre

1. Examples of Good Traits

Ethical maetico, napagkakatiwalaan sa pera at trabaho dahil siya ay sumusunod sa principio ng moralidad, ng batas at ng tamang asal at mabuti ang pagkatao at may awa, integridad at dignidad

Integrity integridad, pagkakaroon ng etico at moralidad at dignidad sa buhay niya; Iloc: integridad, addaan iti etico ken moralidad ken dignidad iti biag na

Conscientious, Conscionable sumusunod sa malinis na conciensia at patakaran ng batas at ng Panginoong Dios; mayroon siyang malinis na budhi at siya ay may pagsisisi kung siya ay nagkasala at hindi niya pinagkakaila ito kundi tinatanggap niya ang canyang sala dahil sa pagkakaroon niya ng pagka-responsab-le sa ano mang gawain niya – masama man o mabuti

Scrupulous *(Tag. & Iloc.)* may/adda conciensia at principio

Dignified may dignidad at dangal dahil siya ay nabubuhay ng maetico at mapagkakatiwalaan na hindi siya lalabag sa batas at sa tamang asal

Diligent masipag, masigasig; Iloc: nagaget, trabahador

Responsible responsab-le, marunong tumupad at managot sa canyang mga obligasyon; Iloc: responsab-le, agtungpal cadagiti obligasyon na

Faithful tapat, matapat sa asawa o kaibigan; Iloc: pudno ti puso iti asawa na ken gayyem na

Moral may moralidad at decente at hindi gumagawa ng kataksilan sa asawa o sa kasintahan, at nabubuhay siya ng mabuti na tama sa batas at sa mata ng Dios

Humble mapagpacumbaba, mababang-loob; Iloc: napacumbaba, umilde, naamo

Gentle mahinahon, tahimik, maamo; Iloc:, naamo, naemma, naulimek, natalna

Magnaninous mabuti sa isip at sa puso at hindi nagkikimkim ng sama kundi mapagpatawad siya at hindi makasarili

Courteous magalang; Iloc: nadayaw

Modest mahinhin, decente; Iloc: naemma, decente

Civil marespeto at mabuti ang pakikisama; Iloc: narespeto ken naimbag ti pakicadcadwa na

Couth *(Tag. & Iloc.)* educado at fino

Generous mapagbigay, bukas ang palad sa mga nangangailangan, handang magbigay ng caya niyang ibigay; Iloc: manangisagot, managpaay, nakasagana nga mangited iti cabaelan na nga ited

2. *Outcomes of Good traits*

Harmonious relationships mapayapa at magandang pagsasamahan; Iloc: natalna ken nasayaat nga pagkacadduaan

Blessings mga pagpapala at biyaya ng Panginoong Dios, biyayang hulog ng langit sa mga mababait at maka-Dios; Iloc: dagiti bendisyon ken gracia ni Apo Dios

Goodness kagandahang loob at kabutihang puso at gawa; Iloc: singpet ti puso ken ricna, nakem ken aramid

Goods mga paninda; Iloc: dagiti laclaco

Goodwill kabutihang balak; Iloc: nasayaat a panggep

Gooey malagkit at malapot

Goof, Goof off nakatunganga lamang, nag-aaksaya ng panahon sa walang pagkilos o pagsasagawa, nagbabatugan lamang; Iloc: agmulmulagat laeng nga awan ar-aramiden na, nakabeldang laeng

Goofy nagpapatawa parati, palabiro

Goon basag-ulero o butangero na kung minsan ay inuupahan para pumatay ng kapwa dahil walang talinong tao

GOOSE *(Tag. & Iloc.)* ganso-*Sp*

GOOSE bumps, Goose pimples tumatayo ang balahibo dahil sa pagkadiri o pagkatakot o sa pagkaginaw; Iloc: sumgar a dutdot gapu ti pagkaaryek o buteng o lam-ek

Gore pagsuwag ng calabaw, toro o *hippopotamus*; Iloc: pagsangdo ti nuang, toro o *hippopotamus*

Gorge bangin sa lambak o *valley* na may ilog sa baba; Iloc: derraas diay lambak nga adda carayan iti baba na

Gorgeous lantad ang kagandahan; Iloc: nakaparang unay ti pintas na

Gory dugoan; Iloc: dara-dara, napno ti dara

Gospel ang tawag sa *gospel* ay *good news* o magandang balita dahil ito ay nagpapahayag tungkol sa pagmamahal ng Panginoong Dios sa mga nilalang kaya nagtatag Siya ng kaligtasan sa parusa ng mga kasalanan ng lahat ng nilalang para hindi sila mapunta at magdusa sa apoy ng infierno. Ito ay sa pamamagitan ng pagsugo ng Dios Ama sa

Dios Anak na si Hesu Cristo upang si Hesu Cristo ang tumanggap at magdanas ng parusa ng mga kasalanan ng sanlibutan, imbes na ang mga nilalang ay magdusa sa infierno. (Basahin ang *God's Salvation for All Mankind* dito sa librong ito.)

GOSSIP mag-chismis-*Sp*, magbulong-bulongan; Iloc: ag-chismis

GOSSIP-monger chismoso/sa-*Sp*, taong nagkakalat ng chismis

Gotcha 1] naintindihan ang sinabi sa canya, 2] tinalo niya ang kalaro o kalaban niya, 3] nahuli niya ang tao na palihim na gumagawa ng bagay

Gouge 1] tanggalin sa pamamagitan ng pagsalok; 2] sumingil o singilan pero mas mahal sa dapat

GOURD, Squash calabasa-*Sp*, Iloc: carabasa

GOURD, white club-shaped upo; Iloc: tabungaw

Gourmand mahilig sa pagkaing pangmayaman

Gourmet ang mga pagkain at inuming pangmayaman

Gout piyo, sakit sa kasukasuan *(bone joints)*; Iloc: sakit ti pagsilpuan ti tulang iti bagi

Govern mamuno, mamahala, mangasiwa, magtangkilik, magpalakad; Iloc: ipangulwan, mangigaway, mangiturong, mangpapagna

Government pamahalaan, govierno-*Sp*; Iloc: govierno

Governor *(Tag. & Iloc.)* governador-*Sp*

Gown *(Tag. & Iloc.)* terno/na-*Sp*, *gown*

Grab sunggaban, dakmain, agawin; Iloc: sibbaruten, agawen, gammatan, rabsuten, rabnuten

GRACE kilos na fino-*Sp* at elegante-*Sp*; Iloc: tignay nga fino ken elegante

GRACE from God Ang gracia ay libreng regalo ng Dios para maligtas tayo sa parusa ng ating mga kasalanan. Itong gracia ay napakasimp-le at madali at hindi man lamang natin paghihirapan dahil ito ay regalo ng Dios at libreng binibigay ito sa atin dahil sa napakalaking pagmamahal ng Dios sa atin, kahit hindi tayo karapat-dapat nito dahil bawat tao ay makasalanan. Ang gracia ay paraan ng Dios para maiwasan natin ang parusa ng ating mga kasalanan at maiwasang mapunta tayo sa impierno. Mapapasaatin ang gracia ng Dios kapag naniniwala, nagtitiwala, nananalig at nagsasampalataya tayo na ang mga sacrificio at pagkapako kay Hesu Cristo sa cruz ay kabayaran ng ating mga kasalanan, kasama *rin* ang pagtanggap natin kay Hesu Cristo sa puso't buhay natin bilang Dios natin at Tagapagligtas natin dahil sa sacrificiong ginawa Niya para sa atin.

GRACE period tinakdang tiempo-*Sp* at fecha-*Sp* na palugit sa pagbayad ng utang o *insurance premium* na wala man lamang interes o multa-*Sp* na nakapatong at activo-*Sp* o *in force* pa rin ang *insurance policy* o ng anomang *coverage* kahit atrasado-*Sp* ang bayad; Iloc: naykeddeng nga tiempo o fecha iti pagbayad iti utang nga awan ipatong nga interes o multa ken activo o *in force* pay met laeng uray atrasado-*Sp* ti bayad

Gracious gracioso/sa-*Sp*, mabuti at masayang makibagay sa kapwa-tao; Iloc: gracioso/sa, nasayaat ken naragsak a makibagay cadagiti tattao

Gradate *v.*, **Gradation** *n.* dahan-dahan o mahina at hindi mahalata na pagbabago, bahagyang pagyabong o pagprocesong pagbabago; bahagyang pagkakaiba ng culay, tunog o tono

Grade grado-*Sp*, baytang; Iloc: grado, *grade*

Gradual patuloy-tuloy ang pagbabago pero hindi ito agad-agad o mabilisan; Iloc: agcontinuar ti pagbalbaliw ngem haan nga ensegida-*Sp* ken nadaras

GRADUATE *v.*, **Graduation** *n.* mag-*graduate*; Iloc: ag-*graduate*, agturpos

GRADUATE school institusyon-*Sp* ng mas mataas na pag-aaral na ang mga nakatapos dito ay pinaparangalan ng *masters degree* at *doctorate degree*

Graffiti mga pader at bakod na may mga sulat at mga larawang-guhit na kagagawan ng mga taong hindi sumusunod sa batas dahil nakakadumi, nakakapangit, at nakakapababa ng clase sa lugar

Graft 1] paggamit ng posisyon para magpayaman na labag sa batas pero gawain ito ng mga materioso-*Sp* at magnanakaw, at hindi makabatas na ofisyal-*Sp* o may importanteng katungkulan (gaya ng pamamahala ng pera ng companya) o may mga proyecto at nasa politco-*Sp*; 2] operasyon-*Sp* ng *doctor* para maglagay ng balat sa parte-*Sp* ng katawan na nasira sa sakit o sunog, 3] pagdugtong o pagconecta ng isang halaman sa ibang clase na halaman

Grain *grain*, grano-*Sp*, buto, butil, binhi; Iloc: *grain*, bukel, bin-i, grano

Grammar balarila; Iloc: *grammar*

Grand, i.e. party *(Tag. & Iloc.)* engrande-*Sp*

GRANDCHILD *(Tag. & Iloc.)* apo

GRANDCHILD, great apo sa tuhod; Iloc: apo ti tumeng

Grandeur malaki at nakaka-*impress*, elegante-*Sp* at ma-dignidad-*Sp*

Grandfather lolo; Iloc: lolo, lelong, apong

Grandiose *adj.,* **Grandiosity** *n.* 1] dakila ang katangian o ang pakay 2] pagka-elegante na pangpakitang-tao

Grandmother lola; Iloc: lola, lelang

Grandstand lugar-*Sp* kung saan nakatayo o nakaupo ang mga nanonood habang may competencia-*Sp* o parada-*Sp*

Grant ipagkaloob, ibigay; Iloc: ipaay, irangkap, ited

Grapefruit suha; Iloc: sua, cahel

Grapes *(Tag. & Iloc.)* ubas-*Sp*

Graph letratong *graph* na panglarawan para pangpa-explica-*Sp* ng kalagayan o estado-*Sp*

Graphic mga linya, kasulatan o larawan na pangpaliwanag at panglarawan

Grapple 1] magdakma at magsunggab, 2] dakmaan at sunggaban sa bunohan o *wrestling*; Iloc: 1] aggammat, agsibbarut, 2] gammatan bayat nga makigabbu

Grasp mahigpit na hawak, capit; Iloc: capet, cumpet, tenglen, petpetan

GRASS damo; Iloc: ruot

GRASS roots ordinaryong mga tao, mga empleyado-*Sp* o *rank-and-file*

Grasses, tall cogon, talahib; Iloc: cogon, sical, pan-aw

Grasshopper tipaklong; Iloc: dudon

Grassland parang; Iloc: tanap

Grate cayurin, cudcorin; Iloc: igaden, garugaden

Grateful pagkilala o pagtanaw ng utang-na-loob, mapagpasalamat; Iloc: ammo na ti agyaman, managyaman iti nayted nga sayaat canyana

Grater pangkayod, cudcuran; Iloc: igad, garugad

GRATIFICATION pagtatamo- o pagbibigay-kasiyahan; Iloc: paggun-od o pagited iti ragsak

GRATIFICATION, immediate mga halimbawa ng *immediate gra-tification* ay pagkakaroon ng canyang gustong-gustong anoman kahit <u>hindi</u> pinaghirapan muna; gustong mapatawad agad sa canyang kasalanan kahit <u>hindi</u> man lamang humingi ng paumanhin o patawad kundi nagdadahilan o pagalit pa na binanggit ang kasalanan niya at hindi man lamang nagpakita ng pagsisisi o *remorse* sa masamang ginawa niya

Gratify papagsawain, pacontentohin; Iloc: pacontentoen, penneken, pacapneken

Gratis libre-*Sp*, walang bayad; Iloc: libre, awan bayad na

Gratitude pasasalamat; Iloc: pagyamyaman

Gratuity _tip_, pera na pagpasalamat o pangpalubag-loob sa pagsilbi ng servidor-*aSp* o trabahador-*Sp*

GRAVE *(Tag. & Iloc.)* grabe-*Sp*

GRAVE, Tomb libingan, nicho-*Sp*; Iloc: panchon, nicho

Gravel pinagsama-sama at pinaghalo-halo na binasagbasag na malalaking bato at maliliit na bato sa daan

Gravestone, Tombstone *(Tag. & Iloc.)* lapida-*Sp*

Gravitate *v., ***Gravitation** *n.* nahahalina o naa-*attract* kaya napapalapit; Iloc: adda makapaduron o makaawawis canyana nga umasideg

Gravity 1] ang fuersa na nagpapanatili sa atin sa lupa imbes-*Sp* na mahulog tayo sa himpapawid kahit bilog ang mundo; 2] ang pagkagrave ng kalagayan o paksa o sakit

Gravy *sauce* na mas lusaw kaysa *gel* at binubuhos o pinapahid sa pagkain gaya ng *steak;* sarsa o salsa

GRAY *gray,* culay abo; Iloc: *gray,* color-*Sp;* dapo

GRAY hair puting buhok, Iloc: uban

Graze 1] pag kumakain ng damo ang mga hayop; 2] masagi habang dumadaan; magasgasan o makayud

Grease 1] mantica, 2] langis ng sasakyan o makina

GREAT dakila, excelente; Iloc: natakneng, excelente, natan-ok

GREAT grandchild apo sa tuhod; Iloc: apo ti tumeng

Greatness pagkadakila; Iloc: pagkatakneng

GREEDY, food- matakaw; Iloc: bucatot, narawet, sarabusab, butot

GREEDY, money- sakim, mukang-pera; Iloc: pinakanapateg canyana ket cuarta

Greek *(Tag. & Iloc.)* Greco, *Greek*

GREEN *green,* luntian; Iloc: *green,* verde-*Sp*

GREEN horn 1] baguhan; 2] hindi masyadong experiensado-*Sp* na madaling mapagsamantalahan

Greet batiin; Iloc: kablaawan

Gregarious mahilig makihalo-bilo o makipagsosyalan sa mga kapwa-tao; Iloc: magustoan na ti makipag-ummong ken makipagsosyalan iti tattao

Grenade *(Tag. & Iloc.)* granada-*Sp*

Griddle pantay na bakal para magluto sa tuyong init gaya ng *pancake*

Gridlock *traffic* na huminto o mahina ang takbo dahil sa accidente-*Sp* o may nakabara sa daan

Grief *n.,* **Grieve** *v.* may lumbay, pighati o dalamhati; Iloc: adda ladingit, liday, leddaang

Grievance karaingan, reclamo-*Sp*; Iloc: reclamo

Grievous nakakabigay ng dalamhati, pighati at sakit ng loob at katawan

Grill 1] lutoang pang-ihawan, 2] mag-ihaw, ihawin, 3] pang-*cross-examination* kapag ini-imvestiga-*Sp*; Iloc: 1] pagtunwan, 2] ituno, agtuno, 3] *cross-examination*
Correlated word
Griddle pantay na bakal para magluto sa tuyong init gaya ng *pancake*

Grim malagim; Iloc: makasumgar ti dutdot

Grimace pagngiwi ng mukha dahil sa sakit o yamot o pagkabigo; Iloc: agdiwwig ti rupa gapu ti sakit o rurod wenno pagkadismaya

Grin ngisi; Iloc: musiig

Grind gilingin; Iloc: gilingen

Grinder *(Tag. & Iloc.)* gilingan

Grip humahawak ng mahigpit, cumapit; Iloc: agcapet, cumpet, tenglen, petpetan

Gripe parating nagmamaktol, nagrereclamo, nagpapayo; Iloc: agrek-reclamo, agtanta-nabutob ken mangbagbaga cancanayon

Grisly nakakatakot, nakakapatayo ng balahibo

Grit 1] determinasyon-*Sp*, 2] *gravel*/graba, *stone*; Iloc: 1] determinasyon, 2] graba, bato

Groan umuungol; Iloc: agung-ungor

Groceries, buy mag-*grocery*; Iloc: ag-*grocery*

Grocery malaking tindahan na nagveventa ng marami at sari-saring pagkain at mga gamit sa bahay gaya ng sabong panligo at panlaba, *toiletries*, pati medicina-*Sp*, halaman at iba pa

Groggy inaantok at parang lasing ang pakiramdam; Iloc: makaturog ken casla nabartek ti ricna

Groin singit; Iloc: sellang

Groom 1] ikakasal na lalake, 2] ayosin at pakisigin ang ichura-*Sp*, 3] ihanda para sa isang bagay

Grope capain; Iloc: carawaen, aricapen

GROSS 1] napakahalay, nakakadiri, nakakarimarim, karumaldumal, 2] halaga ng sueldo-*Sp* bago binawas ang mga bayad sa buis, *health coverage* at iba pa; Iloc: 1] makaam-amak, makaar-aryek, 2] sumar-*Sp* ti sueldo-*Sp* baro inkissay ti buis ken dadduma pay

GROSS out nangangalisag o tumatayo ang balahibo sa pandidiri; Iloc: sumgar ti dutdot na gapu ti pagkaamak

Grotesque hindi caraniwan o *normal* na ichura-*Sp* kundi nakakatakot at nakakarimarim

Grotto *(Tag. & Iloc.)* grotto

Grouchy bugnotin, yamotin, sumpongin, mapagpuna, mapaghanap ng mali; Iloc: mapagdillaw, agsipsipot ti basol, nalaca a marurod, agsumsumro

GROUND lupa; Iloc: daga

GROUND floor silong, unang palapag ng *building*; Iloc: sirok, *first floor* ti gusali

GROUND meat *(Tag. & Iloc.)* giniling na carne-*Sp*

Groundless walang pagbatayan o pagbasehan

Group grupo-*Sp*, pangkat; Iloc: grupo, timpuyog, bunggoy

Grovel magpakumbaba at kumilos na bigay-paglingkod o kilos na may takot; mahiga na parang sanggol sa sinapupunan o gumapang na parang alipin

GROW tumubo, umusbong, lumaki; Iloc: tumubo, dumakkel

GROW robustly lumalago; Iloc: agtubo a nalapsat, agruay

Growl umuungol na ang tunog ay galing sa lalamunan; Iloc: ungor ti carabucob

Grown-up buhat sa edad 21 at pataas; Iloc: nataenganen

Growth proceso-*Sp* ng paglaki, pagdami, paglapad, paghusay; pagyabong o pag-unlad sa dapat na kahihinatnan

Grudge hinanakit, sama ng loob, pinag-iinitan ng ulo; Iloc: naypempen a rurod o luksaw, rurod

Grueling ano mang marahas na dinadanas gaya ng paraan, nakakahapo, nakakapanlata

Gruesome nakakatakot, nakakapatayo ng balahibo

Gruff 1] mababa at garalgal na boses; 2] tao o asal na brusco at *hostile* o halata ang poot o galit

Grumble nagmamaktol, bumubulong-bulong; Iloc: agtantanabutob, agdaydayamudom

Grumpy bugnotin, yamotin, sumpongin, mapagpuna, mapaghanap ng mali; Iloc: mapagdillaw, agsipsipot ti basol, nalaca a marurod, agsumsumro

Grunt umuungol na ang tunog ay galing sa lalamunan; Iloc: ungor ti carabucob

G-string bahag; Iloc: baag

Guacamole *(Tag. & Iloc.)* nalamas na avocadong may kahalong iba pa

Guaranteed *(Tag. & Iloc.)* garantisado-*Sp*

Guaranty *(Tag. & Iloc.)* garantiya-*Sp*

GUARD *n.* tanod, bantay, guardia-*Sp*; Iloc: bantay, guardia

GUARD *v.* bantayin, guardiahin; Iloc: bantayan, guardiaen

Guardian tagapag-alaga, tagasustento; Iloc: tagasustento, mangaw-awir, mangay-aywan

Guava *(Tag. & Iloc.)* bayabas

Guerrilla *(Tag. & Iloc.)* gerilya-*Sp*

Guess hulaan; Iloc: agpugto, pugtoan

Guest visita-*Sp*, panauhin; Iloc: visita, sangaili

Guffaw halakhak; Iloc: garakgak, paggaak

GUIDE *n.* kagabay; Iloc: bagnos

GUIDE *v.* patnubayan, gabayan, akayan; Iloc: idalan, iturong, ibagnos, igaway

Guideline ano mang pagpapatnubay o pagpahayag ng paraan ng tinakdang kilusan o *action* na isasagawa

Guile tacticang pangtraidor o panlinlang

GUILT sala, kasalanan; Iloc: basol, biddut

GUILT-trip ipaalaala o ikintal ang kasalanan ng kapwa kahit hindi na kailangan o wala nang kabulohan

Guilty salarin; Iloc: nakabasol
Synonym
Culpable nagkasala, nakarapatan niya ang bintang sa canya Iloc: nagbasol, rebbeng na tay acusar o naypabasol canyana

Guinea pig maliit na daga na hindi makita ang buntot na ito ay ginagawang *pet* o alagang-hayup at kung minsan ay ginagamit sa experimento-*Sp* o *laboratory study*

Guitar gitara-*Sp*; Iloc: gitarra-*Sp*

Gullible madaling maniwala o mahicayat; Iloc: nalaca a mamati wenno maawis
Synonym
Naïve inocente, madaling maniwala o mahikayat; Iloc: inocente, nalaca a mamati o maawis

Gulp lagokin; Iloc: sultopen

GUM gilagid; Iloc: gugot

GUM, bubble *(Tag. & Iloc.)* *bubble gum*

GUM disease, Pyorrhea *(Tag. & Iloc.)* *pyorrhea*

GUM zit or Lip zit *(Tag. & Iloc.)* singaw

GUN baril; Iloc: paltoog, paltug

GUN, pull the trigger of a calabitin ang baril; Iloc: calbiten ti paltoog

Gunfight magbarilan; Iloc: agpinnaltogan

Gung ho *(Tag. & Iloc.)* ganadong-ganado at dedicado

Gunk malaput at malangis na dumi

Gurgle magmumog; Iloc: agmulomog

Gush biglang dumaloy ang maraming pag-agos; Iloc: agpussuak ken golpe nga agayos ti nakaad-adu

GUST *n*, **Gusty** *adj.* biglang malakas na pagsugod ng hangin, ulan o usok; Iloc: golpe nga pagsangpet iti napigsa nga angin wenno napigsa nga tayab ti asok wenno napigsa a tudo

GUST, Gustation 1] ang panlasa ng tao, 2] hilig at kagustohan

Gusto maganang-maganang pagkawili, gusto; Iloc: magusgustoan, cay-cayat, gusto

Gut, Guts 1] bituka o tiyan, 2] sirain ang loob ng facilidad, 3] damdamin; 4] batayan o kailgangan paksa

Gutsy *adj.* lakas ng isip na nagbibigay ng katapangan at pagtitiis sa sakit ng katawan at bigat ng buhay

Guttural pagsasalita na galing sa lalamunan

Gymnastics *(Tag. & Iloc.) gymnastics* na kadalasan ay ginaganap sa gymnasium o gym

Gynecology paggamot sa mga condisyon ng babae

Gyp dayain para maipagkait ang ari-aryan ng may-ari sa pamamagitan ng *fraud* o *swindle*; Iloc: cusiten tapno maypaidam ti cukua ti makinsanicua gapu ta inaramidan da isuna ti *fraud* o *swindle*

Gyrate, Gyral, Gyratory, Gyre umiikot, gumugulong; Iloc: agpusipos, agtayyek, agtulatid, aglikos-likos

H

Habile nag-aangkin ng sari-sari at malawak na abilidad-*Sp*

HABIT kagawi na custombre-*Sp*; Iloc: nakayruaman nga custombre

Habits can form and direct your being, so be sure your habits are good and useful. Kailangang magtaglay ka ng kagawiang napakabuting custombre dahil ito ang makakaunlad at makakapagpaligaya sa iyo, umpisa sa kalinisang pagpaligo at pagsisipilyo hanggang sa maayos, matalino at maka-Dios na pamumuhay. Ang kagawiang masama gaya ng pagsisinungaling, masama na asal, pananakit ng kapwa, paggumon sa droga, crimen, katamaran, karumihan sa bahay at pamumuhay ay magiging bihasa sa iyo na naghuhubog at nagbubuo sa pagkatao mo na mahirap tanggalin o iwaksi, at magiging masama sa iyo at sa kapwa mo (ang publico, asawa, kamag-anak, *in-laws*, katrabaho) at makakasira o puedeng *downfall* mo pa sa iyong kapalaran at tiyak na makapagpalayo ng kaibigan, kaligayahan, kaunlaran at pagpapala ng Dios sa iyo.

HABIT-forming ang nakakagumon o nakakapapusakal gaya ng alak, droga-*Sp*, cigarilyo-*Sp* o sugal na napakahirap kumalag sa mga ito

Habitable puede at naangkop na matirahan o pagtirhan

Habitat, Habitation ito ang natural-*Sp* na lugar-*Sp* at pagtirhan ng tao, hayup, isda at insecto-*Sp* at kung saan sila ay caraniwang nakikita

Habitual kagawian, bihasa; Iloc: nayruam, naycadawyan, naysigud

Habituate sanay o bihasa dahil sa parating pagsasagawa o dahil sa pagkababad sa tanging situasyon-*Sp* niya

HACK with a bolo or machete tagain; Iloc: tagbaten

HACK online pumasok sa *server website* para sirain o kumuha ng privadong informasyon para canyang gamitin sa canyang masamang pakay; Iloc: sumsumrek iti *server website* tapno dadaelen o alaen na dagiti privado nga informasyon

Hag 1) matandang babae na pangit o nakakatakot, mangkukulam; 2] isang maliit na lugar na maputik

Haggard mukhang pagod na pagod; Iloc: nabambannog ti ichura-*Sp* na

Haggle, Negotiate for a bargain tumawad, magtawaran; Iloc: agtawar, agtinnawar

Correlated words

Got a bargain nakamura, nakatawad; Iloc: nakatawar

HAIL 1] bati, saludo-*Sp*, 2] mga malabatong yelo-*Sp* na nahuhulog buhat sa himpapawid; Iloc: 1] kablaaw, saludo, 2] dagiti malabato nga yelo nga matintinnag naggapu idiay tangatang

HAIL Mary "Ave Maria," ang pagbati ng Anghel Gabriel kay Santa Maria o Mother Mary upang ipaalam sa canya na siya ang pinakamapagpala sa lahat ng mga dalaga dahil pinagpala siya na nasa sinapupunan niya ang Dios Anak na si Hesu Cristo, at si Santa Maria ay nagtaka dahil siya ay virhen, puro at banal at wala pa siyang nakapiling na lalake kahit mayroon na siyang katipan na si Joseph o San Jose, pero dahil si Santa Maria ay maka-Dios na dalaga, tinanggap niya ang kalooban/ *will* ng Dios sa canya.

Pinaalam din ni Anghel Gabriel kay San Jose sa panaginip ang pagdadalang-tao ng canyang kasintahang si Santa Maria, na pangalanin nila ang Dios Anak na Hesus (ang ibig sabihin ng Hesus ay Tagapagligtas ng bawat nilalang) at Cristo (ang ibig sabihin ng Cristo ay ang Napakapinagpalang Tao o *Messiah).*

HAIL Mary *(slang for last attempt)* ang kahuli-huliang sikap o pagpurbang manalo bago matapos ang larong competensia-*Sp* o bago matapos ang ano mang nagaganap; Iloc: iti kaudian nga pakat o pangpurbar nga agballigi baro malpas ti competensia-*Sp* wenno baro malpas ti ania man a mapaspasamak

Hails from *(Tag. & Iloc.)* taga- (i.e., taga-America, taga-Luzon, taga-Visayas)

HAIR buhok; Iloc: buok

HAIR, body balahibo; Iloc: dutdot

HAIR clip or pin ipit; Iloc: sigpit

HAIR, curly *(Tag. & Iloc.)* culot

HAIR fixed in a chignon/bun pusod; Iloc: pinggol

HAIR, gray *(Tag. & Iloc.)* uban

HAIR hang loosely nakalugay; Iloc: nakalaylay

HAIR lice *(Tag. & Iloc.)* cuto

HAIR nit (egg of lice) lisa; Iloc: lis-a

HAIR, pubic bulbol; Iloc: urmot

HAIR-pulling fight sabunotan; Iloc: agpinnungot

HAIR whorl or cowlick at the top of the head puyo; Iloc: aligusgos

Hairbrush *(Tag. & Iloc.)* hairbrush

Haircut gupit; Iloc: pukis, cortar-*Sp*

Hairy balbon, mabalahibo; Iloc: burburan, barbon-*aSp*

Hale 1] malusog at walang sakit, 2] hilain, kaladkarin; Iloc: 1] nasalun-at ken nakaradcad nga awan saksakit na, 2] guyoden, uloden

HALF kalahati; Iloc: kagudwa

HALF-breed or of inter-racial parents (one is White) *(Tag. & Iloc.)* mestizo/za-*Sp*

HALF-cooked meat savored by guys with wine or beer kilaw; Iloc: kilaw, kilawen

HALF-hearted *(Tag. & Iloc.)* walang kalatoy-latoy, pumayag o sumige pero walang gana o hindi todo-todo ang kalooban

HALF-mast, Half-staff bandilang naiyangat hindi sa kataas-taasan kundi sa kalagitnaan lamang ng *flagpole* na simbolo-*Sp* ng pagdalamhati sa taong namatay

HALF-truth hindi sinabi ang lahat kundi may hindi ibinunyag na mga mahalagang informasyon-*Sp*

Halitosis mabahong hininga; Iloc: nabangsit a sang-aw

Hall 1] bulwagan, 2] lugar na pagpupulongan ng mga tao, 3] daanan sa bahay o gusali

Hallelujah "Sinasamba ko Kayo Yahweh" (Yahweh ay pangalan ng Panginoong Dios sa Hebrew)

Hallow, Hallowed sagrado at banal; pinupuri, pinaparangalan at sinasamba

Hallucinate *v.*, **Hallucination** *n.* nahihibang sa pagguguni-guni dahil hindi maliwanag ang isip; Iloc: agam-amangaw

Hallway *(Tag. & Iloc.)* *corridor*, pasilyo-*Sp* ng bahay o gusali, pasukan sa gusali

Halo ang coronang ilaw sa taas ng ulo ng anghel-*Sp*; Iloc: silaw nga corona-*Sp* iti ulo ti anghel

Halt 1] hinto, 2] pag-suspindi-*Sp* o pansamantalang paghinto ng gawain; Iloc: 1] sardeng, 2] pag-suspender-*Sp* o pagsardeng ti obra-*Sp* iti nabiit

Halve hatiin; Iloc: gudwaen, pisyen

Ham *(Tag. & Iloc.)* hamon-*Sp*

HAMMER martilyo-*Sp*, pamukpok; Iloc: martilyo

HAMMER down *(Tag. & Iloc.)* pukpokin ng martilyo-*Sp*

Hammock duyan; Iloc: indayon

Hamper 1] pigilan o isagabal ang paggalaw o pagprogreso, 2] *laundry basket*, malaking buslo na may takip na paglagyan ng mga labahang damit

HAND camay; Iloc: ima

HAND-dance of babies to imitate Filipino dances *(Tag. & Iloc.)* arimunding-munding, kumintang

HAND, give a 1] magpalakpak para sa mabuting pinakita sa pagganap; 2] tulongan; Iloc: 1] agpalakpak a pang-apreciar-*Sp* ti impabuya; 2] tulongan

HAND-me-down pinagsawahan na bagay o pinaglakihan na suot na ipamigay caraniwan sa nakakabatang kapatid.

HAND over i-abut, ibigay, i-entrega-*Sp*; Iloc: iyawat, ited, idatag, i-entrega

HAND palm *(Tag. & Iloc.)* palad

HAND rail *(Tag. & Iloc.)* pasamano-*Sp*

Similar Filipino words

Window sill *(Tag. & Iloc.)* pasamano

Ledge *(Tag. & Iloc.)* pasamano

HAND-to-mouth existence dahil sa maliit na sueldo, tamang-tama lamang na pambayad ng mga kinakailangan para makakain at makasilong siya at ang canyang familya-*Sp* hanggang kikita o magsuweldo siya ulit.

Handbook libro-*Sp* na nagbibigay ng iba't ibang informasyon-*Sp* gaya ng trabaho-*Sp*, responsibilidad-*Sp*, obligasyon-*Sp*, paraan, at iba pa

Handcuff *(Tag. & Iloc.)* posas-*aSp*
Correlated word
Chain cadena, posas; Iloc: cadena, kawar

Handful 1] sandakot, 2] anoman o sino man na mahirap pakibagayan dahil walang *control* sa kagustohan niya o dahil may galit siya; Iloc: 1] sangarakem, 2] ania man o sinno man nga narigat pakibagayan gapu ta awan isu ti *control* ti cayat na wenno gapu adda pungtot na.

Handicap *n.,* kapansanan; Iloc: defecto a mangpalapped ti cabaelan

Handicapped *adj.,* baldado-*Sp*, may kapansanan, lumpo; Iloc: adda defecto-*Sp* o diferencia-*Sp* na, baldado, bullo

Handily ang mandaling paggawa na experto-*Sp*, ma-abilidad-*Sp* at maluwag o maginhawa o madali

Handiwork bagay o producto-*Sp* na ginawa sa kamay; Iloc: banag o producto-*Sp* nga aramid ti ima
Synonyms
Handmade yaring camay; Iloc: aramid ti ima
Manual isagawa sa pamamagitan ng camay; Iloc: ima iti iyusar a pagaramid

Handkerchief, Hankie *(Tag. & Iloc.)* panyo-*Sp*, panyolito-*Sp*

HANDLE mangasiwa, asecasohin; Iloc: igaway, mang-asecaso-*Sp*

HANDLE of a cup, pitcher, etc. tangnan, tanganan, hawakan; Iloc: pagiggaman

HANDLE on, have a controlado-*Sp* at may kaalaman at pag-intindi sa bagay na ginagampanan; Iloc: caya na nga asecasoen gapu iti sirib ken nabayag nga pag-obra-*Sp* na ditoy

HANDLE to hold or to grip for one's safety (bus, stairs, etc.) hawakan, capitan; Iloc: pagiggaman, pagcapetan

Handling 1] hipoin, ramdamin, formahin o asecasohin sa pamamagitan ng camay, 2] sa mga in*order*, ito ay ang pag-empake-*Sp*, pagpapaingat, at pagpadala

Handmade yaring camay; Iloc: aramid ti ima

Handout 1] libreng pamigay na pagkain o damit o pera sa mga nangangailangan, 2] *flyers* o pahayag sa papel na ineentrega sa mga dumadating o dumadaan; 3] copia-*Sp* o kasulatan ng talumpati, *policy* ng oficina-*Sp*, pahayag na pinababahagi sa mga dumalo sa *meeting*; Iloc:

1] libre a kankanen wenno bado o cuarta nga ited cadagiti makasapul, 2] *flyers* o informasyon nga pang-entrega cadagiti simmangpet o lumaslasat; 3] copia iti surat wenno discurso-*Sp*, dagiti *policy* iti oficina, informasyon nga ipaammo cadagiti nag-atender iti *meeting.*

Handpick 1] pulotin o dampotin ng camay, 2] ang tanging pinili

Handrail *(Tag. & Iloc.)* pasamano-*Sp*
Correlated words
Windowsill *(Tag. & Iloc.)* pasamano

HANDS akimbo nakapamewang, mamewang; Iloc: nakabanyikis, agbanyikis

HANDS-off ihadlang ang paghawak o paghipo para hindi papakialaman; Iloc: iparit nga iggaman wenno sagiden tapno haan a biangan

HANDS-on sariling ginagampanan; sarili at tanging pag-aacecaso; Iloc: isu mismo-*Sp* iti agas-acecaso nga agob-obra-*Sp* ken mangar-aramid

Handshake camayan, makipagcamayan; Iloc: alamano-*aSp*, maki-alamano

Handsome makisig, guapo-*Sp*; Iloc: nataer, guapo

Handwash the laundry maglabang-camay; Iloc: lab-an iti ima, gelgelen iti malab-an

Handwriting sulat-kamay, *penmanship;* Iloc: surat-ima

Handy maluwag at madaling makuha o maabot; kung kailan kinakailangan, nandidiyan lamang; nagagamit, madaling mani-obra-*Sp* o patakbohin, paandarin, patalabin

Handyman maabilidad sa pagtrabaho ng anoman gaya ng *maintenance,* pagcumpuni sa bahay o oficina at iba pa; mahusay sa paggamit ng canyang kamay

HANG magbitin, maglambitin; Iloc: agbitin

HANG around 1] umaali-aligid, nag-iistambay, 2] ginugogol ang oras sa bahay at kung minsan ay nasasayang ang oras na dapat sana ay nakakatapos ng gawa

HANG clothes, etc. ibitin, isampay, isabit, ilawit; Iloc: ibitin, isallapay, isab-it, ikallawit, ibalaybay

HANG, Execute *(Tag. & Iloc.)* bitayin

"HANG in there" *"Keep on going, don't give up because the outcome is valuable to you."* "Kung makabulohan para sa iyo, magpatuloy ka at huwag kang sumuko."

HANG on 1] cumapit ng mahigpit, 2] magpatuloy na magpursigi, 3] maghintay ng sandali sa telefono; Iloc: 1] agcapet ti napigsa, 2] agananos nga agpatpatuloy, 3] agur-uray ti nabiit diay telefono-*Sp*

HANG-out *(Tag. & Iloc.)* lugar na pinag-iistambayan

HANG out with someone nagkikita at nagsasamahan sila

HANG together nagkakaisa sila, nagsasamahan, nagkakasayahan, nagtutulongan

HANG tough *Keep on with your diligent pursuits/good purpose even when there are difficulties, even when there are oppositions because if it is advantageous and beneficial for you or for everyone, it is all worth the effort.* Ipagpatuloy mo ang pagpupursigi kahit mahirap, kahit may tumututol, dahil kung makabubuti o makapaunlad sa iyo o sa lahat, ang pagsisikap mo/layonin mo ay napakamarangal.

HANG up 1] tapusin ang pakikipag-usap sa telefono, 2] may diferencia-a*Sp* sa emosyon-*Sp* na puedeng sobra-*Sp* ang pag-aalangang makihalobilo o may hindi maintindihang takot sa isang bagay

Hanger *hanger,* sabitan ng mga damit; Iloc: *hanger,* sablay ti badbado

Hangover *(Tag. & Iloc.)* efecto-*Sp* ng sobrang pag-inom ng alak/arak

Hanker pinananabikan, ninanasa, inaasam-asam; Iloc: agag-agum, agpappapaos

Hanky-panky pagtatalik ng *sexual* pero hindi naman sila casal

Haphazard bara-bara o padalos-dalos lamang sa paggawa o pag-areglo kaya hindi maayos ang obra-*Sp*
Synonyms
Slipshod hindi maingat ang pagkagawa at mumurahin pa ang ginagamit
Harum-scarum bara-bara, padalos-dalos, pangahas, kawalang-ayos o *disorganized,* mali-mali o *erratic,* hindi mawari ang gagawin o *unpredictable,* at walang pagkaresponsab-le
Antonym
Well-made *(Tag. & Iloc.)* pulido

Happen mangyari, maganap; Iloc: mapasamak

Happening pangyayari, nagaganap; Iloc: mapaspasamak, maypatpatang
Synonyms
Circumstance *(Tag. & Iloc)* circumstancia
Incident *(Tag. & Iloc.)* incidente

HAPPINESS kaligayahan, kasayahan; Iloc: karagsakan, karambakan
Synonyms

442

Joy galak, saya, tuwa; Iloc: ragsak, rambak

Bliss malaking kaligayahan, kaligayahang espiritual; Iloc: dakkel a ragsak, ragsak nga espiritual

Felicity pagkamasayang-masaya, felicidad

Exult *v.*, **Exultation** *n.* labis na pagpapakasaya

Ecstasy *n.*, **Ecstatic** *adj.* napakatinding kaligayahan

Euphoria lubhang napakalaking kaligayahan at kagalakan

Hilarious *adj.*, **Hilarity** *n.* malaking pagkasaya; Iloc: dakkel a ragsak

HAPPINESS-triggers to use or put to mind anytime: *recalling happy and funny moments; counting one's blessings (like one's loved ones, health, strength, job, finished tasks, safety, health, shelter, etc.); refreshed for having a well-deserved rest; being an asset and a solution to family, to the job and to the community; being nice to someone with smiles (whether they smile back or not), laughter, happy dance, claps, smiles and waving to people, thumbs up or high five as a gesture for a "great job!"; random acts of kindness; and forgiving offenders while releasing the offenses he/she inflicted by asking God to help to be freed from those hurts and resentments, and many more.*

HAPPY maligaya, masaya; Iloc: naragsak, narambak

Synonyms

Joyful, Joyous galak na galak, masayang-masaya, tuwang-tuwa; Iloc: nakaragragsak, nakaramrambak

Vivacious maaliw, masaya at ang kasayahan niya ay nakakahawa; Iloc: nakalinglingay, naragsak ken ti ragsak na ket makaacar ti dadduma

Jovial masaya, maaliw, madaling magpatawa o magpasaya; Iloc: nakalinglingay, naragsak, nalaeng nga agpakatawa o agparagsak

Jolly nagagalak, natutuwa; Iloc: maragsakan

Gloat napakagandang pakiramdam na kadalasan ay sa pagkacontento sa sariling mabuting pagkatao o sa sariling nagawa

Excitement buhay na buhay ang saya o pagkasabik o pag-asam o pag-aasa; Iloc: sibibiag ti ragsak o gagar o papaos wenno namnama

"HAPPY birthday" *(Tag. & Iloc.) "Happy birthday,"* "Maligayang cumpleanyo-*Sp*," at "Maligayang kaarawan"

HAPPY-go-lucky masaya, campante-*Sp* at hindi nag-aalala; Iloc: narambak, campante ken awan ti danag

443

HAPPY medium compromiso-*Sp* ng dalawang tao o dalawang grupo-*Sp* para makarating sa kalagitnaan kung saan sila makahanap ng pagkakasundoan

"HAPPY New Year" *"Happy New Year,"* "Manigong Bagong Taon"; Iloc: *"Happy New Year,"* "Narang-ay nga Baro a Tawen"

Harangue mahabang paggalit o pag-atake; mahabang, malakas at maingay na talumpati na namemuersa o nagfuefuersa

Harass galitin o inisin ng madalas; Iloc: ruroden canayon

Harbinger babala o tanda ng dadating na pangyayari

Harbor 1] puerto-*Sp*, parte-*Sp* ng dagat na daongan ng barco-*Sp*, bapor-*Sp*, 2] cupcopin, pasilongin at tulongan; Iloc: 1] puerto, sangladan ti barco, 2] ipacamang, linongan ken tulongan

HARD, Difficult mahirap; Iloc: narigat

HARD, Firm matigas; Iloc: natangken
Synonym
Rigid, Stiff maganit; Iloc: nasikkil
Antonym
Soft malambut; Iloc: nalukneng

HARD-bitten tumigas o nagkalakas-loob dahil sa mga napagdaanang hirap at pagsubok sa buhay

HARD core 1] napakatapat at dedicado o devoto sa canyang grupo-*Sp* o organisasyon-*Sp*, 2] tutol na tutol at hindi pumapayag sa mga pagbabago, 3] masyadong malaswa

HARD cover ang labas ng libro-*Sp* na yari sa katad o balat cuero-*Sp* o sa napakatigas na carton-*Sp*

HARD-hearted matigas na loob at walang malasakit o pakialam sa iba, at walang pagsisisi sa mga ginawang kasalanan o pananakit sa iba, matigas ang ulo; Iloc: natangken ti puso ken awan asi o pakibiang iti dadduma ken awan ti pagbabawi na iti inaramid na a basbasol ken iti inted na a sakit ken liday iti tattao, natangken ti ulo

HARD-hit masyado-*Sp* na naafectohan; Iloc: masyado a naafectaran (afecto/afectar-*Sp*)

HARD knocks ang mga bagay at pangyayari na napagdadaanan sa buhay gaya ng paghamon o *challenges* at pagsubok o *trials*, kahirapan o *hardships* at pagpupursigi o *persevering work*

HARD-pressed, Hardpressed 1] mabigat na pasanin, kahirapan dahil sa sobra-*Sp* ang trabaho-*Sp* o utang o ang pangangailangan ng pera; 2] makikipag-competensiya-*Sp* o makikipag-paligsahan na may kahirapan; nasasailalim ng matinding pag-atake ng kalaban; 3] masugid siyang hinahabol o tinutugis

HARD sell pagbe-venta-*Sp* na napaka-agresivo-*Sp* at matactica para makahikayat ng mga suki o bumibili

Harden manigas, patigasin; Iloc: tumangken, patangkenen

Hardening naninigas, gumaganit; Iloc: agtangtangken, agsiksikkil

Hardliner taong tagataguyod o nakakapit sa pagsunod ng doctrina o teoria o paniwala

Hardly halos hindi o halos wala; Iloc: ngang-ngani haan, ngang-ngani awan

Hardness katigasan; Iloc: pagkatangken

Hardship kahirapan; Iloc: rigat

Hardy malusog, malakas ang katawan, matapang at cayang buhatin o tiisin ang hirap at bangis ng panahon

Harelip bingot, sungi; Iloc: gusing

Hark pakinggan; Iloc: denggen

Harlot *(Tag. & Iloc.)* puta-*Sp*

Harm saktan ang katawan o damdamin; Iloc: saktan ti bagi wenno ricna

Harmful makapinsala, nakakasama, puedeng nakakamatay; Iloc: makadakes, makasakit, mabalin a makapatay

Harmonica *(Tag. & Iloc.)* cilindro-*Sp*

Harmonious *adj.,* **Harmony** *n.* **Harmonize** *v.* pagkakasundo, mabuting pagsasamahan; Iloc: naimbag a pagkacadua ken paggagayyeman

Harp *(Tag. & Iloc.)* *harp,* arpa-*Sp*

Harsh mabagsik at stricto-*Sp*; Iloc: naranggas ken stricto

Harum-scarum bara-bara, padalos-dalos, pangahas, kawalang-ayos o *disorganized*, mali-mali o *erratic*, hindi mawari ang gagawin o *unpredictable*, at **ni** pagkaresponsab-le

Harvest mag-ani, maggapas; Iloc: agani, aggapas, agapit
Correlated words
Crop, Yield, Produce ani; Iloc: ani

HAS, Have may, mayroon; Iloc: adda
Correlated word

445

Own nag-aari, nag-aangkin; Iloc: cuckua, akinkucua

HAS-been *(Tag. & Iloc.)* laos na

HAS to/Have to.. kailangan na.., Iloc: masapul nga..

Hash 1] pagkaing tinadtad o putol-putol na carne at gulay na frinito o nilutong magkakasama; 2] disaregladong gulo o sirain ang ayos; 3] pag-usapan ng matagalan o paggunitang pagsusuri, gamitin ulit o ayosin ang dati nang nagawang kasulatan

Hassle argumento-*Sp*, labanan, problema-*Sp* o panggambala

Haste pagmamadali, pag-aapura; Iloc: pagap-apura-*Sp*, pagdardaras

Hasten padaliin, bilisan, i-apura-*Sp*; Iloc: dagdagen, padarasen, ipartak, papartaken, ipardas, ipaspas, i-apura

Antonym

Slow down bagalan; Iloc: bayagen

Hasty *adj.* nagmamadali, nag-aapura-*Sp*; Iloc: agap-apura, agdardaras

HAT, man's sumbalilo, sombrero-*Sp*; Iloc: callugong, sombrero

HAT, woman's or man's hat, wide-brimmed hat made of reeds or other materials *(Tag. & Iloc.)* salakot

Hatch egg mamisa; Iloc: agpessa

HATE nasusuklam, namumuhi; Iloc: kagura, kabusor, karurod

Antonym

Love ibigin, mahalin, itangi, gusto; Iloc: ayaten, dungwen, gusto

HATE crime pananakit *(physically or emotionally)* sa isang grupo o lahi-*race* ng tao dahil sa hindi pantay-pantay ang pagturing nito sa lahat ng *races* o nilalang.

Correlated word

Racial discrimiation pagtuturing na mababa o masama ang isang tao/ grupo/lahi at ipawalang-pansin ang pagkahalaga nila; Iloc: bigbigen a nababa wenno dakes ti tao/grupo/lahi ken haan na bigbigen ti valor da.

Hateful puno ng pagkamuhi; Iloc: napunno ti gura

Hatred matinding galit, poot, muhi, suklam; Iloc: gura, rurod, busor, pungtot, uyong

Haughty mayabang, mapagmalaki at mapagmata sa kapwa; Iloc: lastog, pangas

Haul 1] ifuersang hilain ang sasakyan, 2] hakutin, ilulan at dalhin sa pagdadalhan

Haunt 1] pagmultohan, 2] lugar-*Sp* na parating pinupuntahan

Haute couture *[oht-koo-toor]* namumunong tindahan o tagadisenyo o *designers* na nagveventa o lumilikha ng mga magaganda at mamahaling kasuotan

HAVE, Has, There is/are may, mayroon; Iloc: adda

HAVE a ball nagtamasa siya ng kasiyahan, nagalak at nalibang ng husto

HAVE a lot of promise *You are likely to become successful if you possess or develop any of these and capitalize on them: intelligence, good judgment, great effort, diligence, perseverance, determination, ingenuity, creativity, reliability, trustworthiness, credibility, expertise, abilities, skills, talents, and other useful traits.* Nakikinita ang promesa-*Sp* sa pagkakaroon ng mga nasabing katangihan para magiging matagumpay ang kinabukasan.

HAVE a lot on one's mind ocupado ang isip sa mga bagay-bagay, nababalisa o nababahala ang canyang isip

HAVE a weakness for... gustong-gusto sa isang bagay o pagkain na hindi niya cayang matiis na hadlangan o labanan ang canyang pagkasabik; Iloc: agpap-papaos iti cayat na unay

HAVE a word with someone makipag-usap sa tao na caraniwan ay privado-*Sp*

HAVE-not *(Tag. & Iloc.)* pobre-*Sp*

HAVE seen better days, Worn out pudpod na, gasgasado, gastado; Iloc: rutrot, rutay-rutay, gorudgod, gasgasado

HAVE something in common dalawa o mahigit pa sa dalawang bagay o tao na mayroon silang pagkakaparehoan

HAVE the upper hand mataas ang posisyon-*Sp* o nasa puesto-*Sp* na may ventahe o may lamang

HAVE what it takes, Very Capable *Read "Have a lot of promise" above.*

Haven sanctuario, silongan, tuloyan, lugar na ligtas

Havoc laganap na pagkasira o pagkawasak; malaking gulo; Iloc: dadael ken gulo nga afectado ti dakkel a lugar

Hawk lawin; Iloc: cali

Hawker tindero na hinihikayat ang mga bumibili sa maingay niyang pagveventa

Hay damo at iba pang halaman na pinutol-putol at pinatuyo para sa pagkain ng mga hayop

Correlated word

Fodder 1] damo na kinakain ng mga cabayo o cambing; 2] pagkain na mura pero mababang uri na popular na nabibili

Hazard panganib, peligro-*Sp*; Iloc: peggad, peligro

Hazardous waste mga basura-*Sp* o mga lumalabas na panapon ng industria-*Sp* o *nuclear plant* na puedeng makasira at makapinsala sa kapaligiran at sa karagatan at sa mga tao at hayop at isda at ibon at iba pa

Haze sumisingaw na usok, alikabok o hamog na nakakakulimlim ng pook o kapaligiran

Hazy malabo; Iloc: nacudrep, nacusnaw

He/She siya; Iloc: isu, isuna

HEAD *(Tag. & Iloc.)* ulo

HEAD cover for ladies talukbong, *bandana*, velo-*Sp*, *scarf*; Iloc: *bandana*, velo, *scarf*, dalungdong, abungot, abbong ti ulo

HEAD, bent magyuko; Iloc: agdumog

HEAD, bump one's maumpog, mauntog; Iloc: maytimog

HEAD count binibilang kung ilan ang taong nandodoon o dumalo o kasali sa grupo-*Sp*

HEAD crown or head top bumbonan; Iloc: tuktok ti ulo

HEAD movement to indicate "No" iiling-iling; Iloc: agwingiwing

HEAD movement to indicate "Yes" tatango-tango; Iloc: aglingaling, agtang-ed

HEAD nodding due to being sleepy magyukayok; Iloc: agtuglep, agdungsa

HEAD of an office or a business *(Tag. & Iloc.)* pangulo, boss, amo-*Sp*

HEAD-on magkasalungatang-ulo o magkabunggohan

HEAD start or Headstart maunang pag-umpisa na nakakabigay ng lamang o ventahe-*Sp*

Headache sakit ng ulo; Iloc: sakit ti ulo

Heading pamagat; Iloc: *title*, titulo-*Sp*

Headquarters ang *main* o pinakacentro ng operasyon-*Sp* ng *military* o ng comercio-*Sp*

Heads up 1] avante o pa-unang noticia o panghanda ng dadating na magaganap o tungkulin, 2] babala sa puede na maganap dahil may

448

hirap, problema o panganib; Iloc: 1] umuna o avante a noticia o pangsagana iti sumangpet nga mapasamak wenno obraen, 2] pangalwad iti mabalin a mapasamak a rigat wenno peggad

Headstrong, Hardheaded matigas ang ulo; Iloc: natangken ti ulo

Headway mga hakbang na ginagawa para makamit ang layonin; Iloc: dagiti addang nga ar-aramiden para magunod ti panggep ken calicagum na

Heal gumagaling, bumubuti, naghihilom; Iloc: agim-imbagen, aglalaengen
Correlated words
> **Convalesce** pagbabalik sa lakas at kalusogan pagkatapos ng pagkakasakit; Iloc: pagsubli iti pigsa ken salun-at palpas a nagsakit
>
> **Rejuvenate** sumisigla at may frescong liksi at kalusogan; Iloc: lumaplapsat ken adda fresco a sagiksik ken salun-at na
>
> **Revitalize** bigyan ng bagong lakas at sigla; Iloc: ikkan ti baro a pigsa, bileg ken kired
>
> **Invigorate** gumagaling na at nagkakaroon na ng lakas, sigla, sigasig at lusog sa katawan; Iloc: umim-imbagen ken maaddaanen iti pigsa, sagiksik, lapsat ken salun-at ti bagi
>
> **Recuperate** nagpapagaling, nagpapalakas, tinutubos uli ang kalusogan; Iloc: agim-imbag, aglalaeng, agsaysayaat, subboten manen iti caradcad
>
> **Recover health** gumaling at bumalik ang lusog; Iloc: umimbag ken nagsubli ti salun-at na
>
> **Getting cured** gumagaling, bumubuti, naghihilom; Iloc: aglalaeng, umim-imbag

Health kalusogan; Iloc: salun-at, caradkad

Healthy malusog; Iloc: nasalun-at, nalapsat, nacaradcad
Correlated word
> **Wholesome** 1] decente, 2] pampalusog, masustancia; Iloc: 1] decente, 2] pangsalun-at ken pangkaradkad, masustancia

HEAP bunton, tumpok; Iloc: bunton

HEAP on tambakan, buntonan, tabunan; Iloc: gaburan, mangbunton

Hear marinig; Iloc: madengngeg, mangngeg
Correlated words
> **Hark** pakinggan; Iloc: dengngen
>
> **Listen** makinig, pakinggan; Iloc: agdengngeg, dumngeg, dengngen

HEARING, sense of pandinig; Iloc: pagdengngeg

HEARING, hard of mahinang tenga, mahinang pandinig; Iloc: bengngeg

HEARING, court panimulang imbestigasyon-*Sp* ng tao na acusado-*Sp*; ang tiempo-*Sp* sa pagkuha ng testimonya-*Sp* ng mga nakakita ng gawaing labag sa batas at itestigo ito sa corte-*Sp*

Hearken, Harken makinig, pakinggan ang sinasabi

Hearsay balitang nalaman sa iba na puedeng tutoo o hindi; Iloc: sao-sao nga haan usto o usto

HEART *(Tag. & Iloc.)* puso

HEART, by naisaulo dahil sa pagmememoria o sa pagbanggit ng paulit-ulit o pirming pagdinig ng canta

HEART of gold mapagbigay, matapat at mapagkaibigan

HEART of stone malupit, walang habag, at walang conciensia

HEART-to-heart talk privado-*Sp* na usapan o matalik at matapat na pag-uusap

HEARTBEAT tibok ng puso, pintig ng puso; Iloc: kebba, pitik ti puso

HEARTBEAT, fast (due to fear or worry) kumokutobkutob, kacaba-caba; Iloc: agtibtibbayo, agkebba-kebba

Heartbreaking nakakabigay ng matinding pighati o hapis

Heartburn, Gas pain sinisikmura, cabag; Iloc: agrusrusok

Hearten magbigay ng lakas-loob, confiansa-*Sp* sa sarili at saya; Iloc: papigsaken ti nakem ken ricna

Heartfelt buong-puso na galing sa isip at damdamin; Iloc: impuswan ken naggapu iti nakem ken ricna

Heartstring napakalalim na pagmamalasakit at pagmamahal; Iloc: nauneg nga panangsaksakit ken pagayat

Heartwarming nakakasiya, magantimpalang bati o pagturing; nakaka-bigay ng pagpasalamat, kasiyahan, kalugoran, at kaginhawahan

Hearty 1] masinta, mairog, magiliw, masiglang pagkasaya; tapat, tunay, taos-puso at buong puso, devoto; 2] masigla ang pagkasaya gaya sa tawa; malakas at malusog

HEAT *n.* init; Iloc: pudot, bara, darang

HEAT *v.* ipainit, uminit; Iloc: ipainit, ipapudot, pumudot, idadang, ipadarang

HEAT stroke sa katagalang nakabilad sa init, nagkakaroon ng malalang condisyon na paglalagnat, paghihinto ng pagpapawis at nawawalan ng ulirat

HEAT, sweltering maalinsangan; Iloc: nadagaang

HEAT wave napakainit na panahon sa *summer* o tag-init ng Estados Unidos

Heathen miembro ng relihion na <u>hindi kinikilala</u> ang Dios ng mga Cristiano, Judaism, Islam at iba pa

Correlated words

Pagan taong walang relihion o sumasamba sa *nature* o *earth*

Infidel ang tawag ng mga Islam o Muslim sa mga hindi Muslim o hindi kaanib

Heave 1] i-angat o ihagis ng buong lakas, 2] humangos dahil sa nararamdamang sakit o sa pagsisikap; Iloc: 1] ingato wenno ipalladaw iti amin nga pakat ken pigsa, 2] umasog gapu iti sakit a maricricna wenno iti pagpakat na ti usto

HEAVEN *(Tag. & Iloc.)* langit

HEAVEN-sent ang dumating na sagot sa panahon ng tunay na pangangailangan

Synonym

Godsend ang kinakailangan na biglang sinagot o dumating

HEAVY mabigat; Iloc: nadagsen, nabantut

Antonym

Light weight magaan; Iloc: nalag-an

HEAVY-duty matibay at matagalang mabisa at magamit dahil nacacayanan ang madalas at magusot at maruming paggamit

HEAVY-laden mabigat ang canyang mga pasanin; nababagabag, nababalisa, naliligalig at nag-aalala

Hebrew, Jew *(Tag. & Iloc.)* Hudjo

Heckle ginagambala at sinusupalpal ang nagsasalita sa entablado-*Sp*

Hectare *(Tag. & Iloc.)* ectaria-*Sp*

Hectic pagkakaroon ng maraming gagawin na kinakailangan ng bilis pero nakakabigay ng kagipitan at *stress*

Hedge 1] nakahilera na mga palumpong o pandak na halaman na ginawang bakuran, 2] kusang magbigay ng pampalusot na pahayag gaya ng "Seguro", "Posib-le"...

Heed makinig at sumusunod; Iloc: agdengngeg ken mangtungpal

HEEL sakong; Iloc: mukod

HEEL, shoe takong; Iloc: takon

Hefty mabigat; Iloc: nadagsen, nabantut

Height tangkad, pagkataas; Iloc: tayag, pagkangato
Correlated word
Weight timbang, pagkabigat; Iloc: dagsen, pagkabantut

Heinous masama, makademonyo; Iloc: dakes, makasatanas

Heir tagapagmana; Iloc: eredero-*Sp*, mangtawid

Heist pagnanakaw; Iloc: pagtakaw

Hell impierno-*Sp*; Iloc: infierno-*Sp*

Hello sagot sa telefono-*Sp* o pagbati sa kasalubong na kakilala
Correlated word
Hi! pangbati sa kasalubong na tao

Helm *(Tag. & Iloc.)* puesto-*Sp* ng otoridad-*Sp* o ng pangulo

Helmet makapal na pangprotecsiong ng ulo para sa mga nagbibisicleta, nagmomotorsiclo o nag-*skateboard*

HELP tulong, ayuda-*Sp*; Iloc: tulong

HELP, ask for magpatulong; Iloc: agpatulong

"HELP!" "Saklolo" *"Help"*; Iloc: "Arayatendac", *"Help"*

HELP, house- *(Tag. & Iloc.)* muchacho/a-*aSp*, achay, katulong, muchacho/ *cha*, achoy,

Helper *(Tag. & Iloc.)* katulong

Helpful matulongin, makakatulong; Iloc: mapagtulong, makatulong

Helping along with others bayanihan, makipagtulongan; Iloc: makipagtinnulong
Synonym
Community cooperation *(Tag. & Iloc.)* bayanihan

Hem 1] laylayan; 2] itupi, ililip; Iloc: itupi, ililip, ilupi

Hemoglobin pula ng dugo; Iloc: nalabbaga ti dara

Hemorrhage nagdudugo; Iloc: agdardara

Hemorrhoid *(Tag. & Iloc.)* almoranas-*Sp*

Hemp, Manila *(Tag. & Iloc.)* abaca

Hen inahing manok; Iloc: dumalaga

Hence kaya, kung ganon; Iloc: isu ngarud nga

Henpecked *(Tag. & Iloc.)* *under-the*-saya

Hepatitis sakit sa atay; Iloc: sakit ti dalem

HER/His canya, niya, ni; Iloc: cuana

HER/Him, to, Through her/him, On her/him sa canya; Iloc: canyana

Herald tagapahayag ng noticia; Iloc: tagabandilyo

Herb doctor *(Tag. & Iloc.)* erbolaryo-*Sp*

Herd grupo o magkakasamang isang claseng hayop

HERE dito, rito, narito, nandito; Iloc: ditoy, idtoy

"HERE it is" "Heto;" Iloc: "Daytoy", "Adtoy"

Hereabout dito sa mga lugar dito; Iloc: ditoy arrubayan

Hereditary *adj,* **Heredity** *n.* mga ari-aryan o ichura at katangian na namamana sa magulang o ninuno; Iloc: dagiti sanicua wenno ichura ken katatao nga impatawid ti nagannak wenno ti pupoon

Hereon, Hereupon mula ngayon, buhat ngayon; Iloc: manipud itatta

Heretic, Heretical miembro-*Sp* ng relihion-*Sp* pero contra-*Sp* ang paniwala niya sa doctrina-*Sp* ng canyang relihion

Heritage *n.* mana, ari-aryan na puedeng ipamana o mapunta sa mga sumusunod na henerasyon-*Sp*; Iloc: tawid, erencia-*Sp*

Hermaphrodite ang nilalang, caraniwan ay insecto-*Sp*, na may *genitals* o organo-*Sp* sa panganganak na parehong sa lalake at sa babae

Hernia *(Tag. & Iloc.)* luslos

Hero *(Tag. & Iloc.)* bayani, bida

Heroism kagitingan, pagkabayani; Iloc: pagkabayani

Heron tikling, tagak; Iloc: tikling, kannaway

Hers, His sa canya; Iloc: cuana

Herself, Himself siya mismo-*Sp*; Iloc: isu mismo, isuna mismo

Hesitant *adj.,* **Hesitate** *v.* atubili, pag-aayaw-ayaw, pagdadalawang-isip; Iloc: pagmadi-madi, pagduadua

Synonyms

Falter 1] nawawalan ng tapang o confiansa kaya urong-sulong siya o nagkakamali-mali siya sa pagsagawa ng layonin, 2] nauutal o mabagal o pahinto-hintong magsalita

Wary nagdadalawang-isip, hindi mapakali; Iloc: agdudua, maam-amak

Antonyms

Embolden palakasin ang loob at tapang; Iloc: papigsaen iti uneg ken tured

Daring pangahas, atrevido; Iloc: atrevido

Heterogenous ang pinagmulan o kanunohan ay iba; hindi galing sa sariling katawan kundi galing sa katawan ng iba

Heterosexual tungkol sa magkaibang *sexes* o *gender* gaya ng babae at lalake; taong nagkakagusto o nakikipagtalik sa ibang *gender* gaya ng lalake sa babae o ang babae naman ay nagkakagusto o nakikipagtalik sa lalake

Antonym

Homosexual *gay* o bakla o *lesbian*; taong nagkakagusto o nakikipagtalik sa kapwa lalake o kaya kapwa babae

Heyday kasicatan; Iloc: pinakangato a dayaw iti tao

Hiatus patlang o puwang o pansamantalang pagtigil ng gawain o pagpalakad

Hibiscus *(Tag. & Iloc.)* gumamela

Hiccup sinok; Iloc: saiddek

Hidden tago, nakacubli, lingid; Iloc: nakalemmeng, naylinged, naysuksok

HIDE tago, cubli; Iloc: lemmeng, suksok, linged

HIDE, Animal skin katad, cuero; Iloc: lalat

HIDE-and-seek game *hide-and-seek,* tagoan; Iloc: *hide and seek*

HIDE a secret ilihim; Iloc: ilimed, i-secreto-*Sp*

HIDE-out, Hiding place pagtagoan para hindi mahuli o madakip; Iloc: paglemmengan

Hideous pangit na pangit; Iloc: nakaal-alas nga ichura-*Sp*

Hie agad-agad na pumunta; Iloc: dagdagos a mapan

HIGH mataas, matayog; Iloc: nangato

Correlated words

Lofty mataas; Iloc: nangato

Tall matangkad, mataas; Iloc: natayag

Height tangkad, pagkataas; Iloc: tayag, pagkangato

HIGH-and-mighty pag-iisip na mas magaling o *superior* siya kaysa sa iba kaya mapagmata siya sa kapwa

HIGH blood pressure mataas ang presyon o may altapresyon-*Sp;* Iloc: nangato ti presyon, adda altapresyon na

Correlated word

Blood pressure presyon ng dugo; Iloc: presyon ti dara

HIGH chair *toddler's chair;* upoan ng sanggol; Iloc: tugaw ti tagibi

HIGH five pagbati o paghanga sa magandang gawa at asal o sa pagtatagumpay sa pamamagitan ng pagtaas ng camay ng dalawang tao (ang bumabati at ang binabati) para pagtampalin o ipalakpak ang canilang mga bukas na palad sa isa't isa

HIGH-hat mapagmalaki, suplado/da-*Sp,* hindi nagpapansin sa ayaw niyang tao; Iloc: ipangpangato ti bagi na, suplado/da, haan na estimaren ti tao nga dina cayat

HIGH horse, get on a umasta na parang mas mabuti, mas mahusay a mas-*Sp* intelihente-*Sp* siya kaysa sa iba

HIGH maintenance 1] makina na nanganailangan ng maraming sicap at parating pagre-*repair,* 2] mademandang tao na nangangailangan ng madalas na pag-estima o pera at sicap

HIGH-minded *Practice and maintain high and virtuous principles and intentions; conscientious, righteous, moral, ethical, honorable, chivalrous.* Nagtataglay ng marangal at dakilang asal at kaisipan na dapat huwaran o ehemplo o pamantayan

HIGH on something nasa influwencia ng droga o alak

HIGH-pitched matinis, matulig; Iloc: nasinggit, natileng

HIGH road, take the *Lots of emerging influences have degenerating values, uncanny, creepy ideas, expanding addictive products, and strange lifestyles. Occurrences also show increasing number of crimes, risks, threats and accidents. All these can cause discomfort and fear. But our shield and weapon to these is **not** to immerse into those emerging mores nor to blend with those who practice them. If we haven't yet, **this is the time to take the high road.** <u>Taking the high road is focusing on the higher calling and greater good, requiring more of ourselves and raising ourselves to a higher standard by engaging on righteous activities and carrying these out in life consistently, aspiring to reach our potentials and utilizing our intelligence, abilities, skills and talents into good and noble use while at the same time praying always to God to help us fulfill all these.</u>*

HIGH school *(Tag. & Iloc.)* high school

HIGH-spirited *(Tag. & Iloc.)* vivong-vivo, vivang-viva

HIGHER mas mataas; Iloc: mas nangato

HIGHER-up taong ang *position* o ranko-*Sp* ay mas mataas kaysa sa iba

Highest pinakamataas; Iloc: kangatuan

Highfalutin mapagmataas, mapagkunwari, mayabang, palalo

Highlight ipalantad para kapansin-pansin; Iloc: aramiden a nakaparang tapno nalaca a makita

Highway daan na nagcoconecta ng mga ciudad at bayan

Hijack marahas at mabagsik na kunin ng *hijacker* o terorista-*Sp* ang pamamahala o *control* ng sasakyan (na kadalasan ay eroplano-*Sp*) para palihisan sa ibang ang direksion-*Sp* at papuntahin sa destinasyon-*Sp* na gusto ng *hijacker*

HIKE 1] *exercise* o libangan na lakad, 2] biglang pagtaas ng precio-*Sp*

HIKE, take a umalis o pinaaalis dahil hindi siya kailangan doon

Hilarious *adj.,* **Hilarity** *n.* malaking pagkasaya; Iloc: dakkel a ragsak

Hill burol; Iloc: turod

Hillside libis; Iloc: sikig ti bantay

Hilt, to the nakarating sa limitasyon, nacompleto na

HIM, Her siya; Iloc: isu

HIM/Her canya, niya, ni; Iloc: cuana

HIM/Her, to, Through her/him, On her/him sa canya; Iloc: canyana

Himself, Herself siya mismo-*Sp*; Iloc: isu mismo

Hinder hadlangan, isagabal, pigilan; Iloc: igawid, awiden, ipasardeng, lappedan, tipden, teppedan

Hindsight *After an experience or occurrence, having hindsight is acquiring a lesson and wisdom from it opening his eyes to procedures, solutions, measures, preventions, possibilities, requirements, etc. that would make such circumstance manageable, beneficial and productive.* Pagkakaroon ng leksion pagkatapos ng isang pangyayari, at ngayon alam nang dapat gawin kung mangyari uli, at magkaroon din ng abilidad-*Sp* na umintidi kung ano dapat ang gawin, kung ano ang dahilang nangyari iyon; ang pagkilala sa mga katotohanan at kahalagahan ng pangyayari, ang posibilidad-*Sp* na pupuedeng mangyari uli, at mga kinakailangan ng isang situasyon-*Sp* para malutas, at iba pa

Hint malabong pahiwatig o pangparamdam, pangpaalaala; Iloc: nacudrep a pangpaammo o pangparicna, pampalagip, singasing
Synonym
Imply nagpapahiwatig na hindi derechohan ang tinutukoy

HIP 1] matalas ang pagkaalam sa mga kasalukuyang nangyayari, 2] sumusunod sa uso at pinakabagong moda-*Sp* ng pananamit

HIP bone sinili; Iloc: pading

Hips balakang; Iloc: patong

Hipster taong interesado sa mga pinakabagong uso-*Sp* at moda-*Sp*

HIRE *(Tag. & Iloc.)* upa, arkila-a*Sp*
Correlated word
Rent magrenta, mag-upa; Iloc: agrenta, agabang

HIRE an employee tanggapin bilang empleyado-*Sp*; Iloc: akceptaren (akceptar-*Sp)* nga ag-empleyado, i-puesto-*Sp* iti trabaho

His, Her canya, niya, ni; Iloc: cukuana, cuana, kenni, kencuana, agpaay canyana

Hispanic taga Latin-America *(South at Central America* gaya ng *Chile, Peru* at iba pa*)* na ang wika ay Espanyol; Iloc: dagiti taga Latin America *(South* ken *Central America* casla *El Salvador, Argentina, Nicaragua* and others*)* nga agsarita iti Castila

History *n.,* **Historical** *adj.* pagsalaysay ng mga pangyayari ng lumampas na panahon; Iloc: storya-*Sp* iti kasasaad ken naaramid iti limmabas a panawen ida

HIT banggahin, bunggohin, golpehin, suntokin, buntalin, saktan, bug-bogin, sapukin, hampasin; Iloc: bugbogen, banggain, bunggoin, golpien (golpe-*Sp)*, danugen, saktan, sulongen, disnogen, cabilen

HIT-and-miss puedeng matamaan o magtagumpay o puedeng hindi; Iloc: mabalin a matukmaan o agballigi wenno mabalin a haan

HIT-and-run makabunggo ng sasakyan o makasagasa ng tao pero tumakas para iwanan ang nabunggo o nasagasaan

HIT bottom lumubog siya sa pinakamababa at pinakamasamang ka-lagayan; Iloc: matinnag wenno malmes iti pinakanababa o pina-kanarigat a kasasaad

HIT by something *(Tag. & Iloc.)* natamaan

HIT many times *(Tag. & Iloc.)* bugbogin ng bugbogin, tamaan ng tamaan

HIT on the nape by someone *(Tag. & Iloc.)* batukan, dagukan, sapukin

HIT the hay, Hit the sack mahiga sa cama-*Sp* at matulog na; Iloc: agidda diay cama-*Sp* ken maturogen

HIT the head with a shaft or bat pukpokin; Iloc: pang-uren, pak-ulen

HIT the spot tumugma at tamang-tama

Hitch nakakahadlang, nakakatali o magkakabuhol-buhol; Iloc: maka-lapped o makasiglot o makapulupot

Hitched, get *(Tag. & Iloc.)* mag-asawa

Hitchhike pupunta sa ibang lugar pero isenyas ang canyang *thumb* para makikisakay lamang siya sa kung sinong magpasakay sa canya at caraniwan ay sa taong hindi niya kakilala

Hoard, Being a pack rat sobra-sobrang magkamkam, mag-ipon at mag-imbak; Iloc: sobra-sobra nga agkamkam, agipon ken agurnong

Hoarse voice paos, malat; Iloc: agpaparaw

Hoax panlilinlang na disimulado-*Sp* o hindi nahahalata at hindi napupuna; Iloc: panggugulib a disimulado o haan a maductalan o masucalan

Hobble hirap at mabagal lumakad, parang pilay; Iloc: marigatan wenno nainnayad a magna, casla agpilay-pilay

Hobby kinahihiligan, libangan, gustong-gustong dibersion; Iloc: paglinglingayan, pasatiempo-*Sp*, gustong-gusto nga dibersion-*Sp*

Hobnob nakikiha-lobilo sa mga tao, makipagsosyalan; Iloc: makitiptipon cadagiti tattao, makipagsosyalan

Hodgepodge pinaghalo-halo ang magkakaibang laman at recado

Hoe asarol; Iloc: gabyon

Hog lahat ng clase ng baboy na puedeng maamo o mabangis

Hogwash salita o kasulatan na walang halaga o walang katapatan sa puso na hindi mapaniwalaan

Hoi poloi mga caraniwang tao; Iloc: dagiti ordinaryo a tattao

Hoist iyangat, ipataas, itaas, i-alsa-*Sp*; Iloc: ipangato, isagpat, isang-at

Hoity-toity nagpapapakitang-tao na mataas siya o elegante siya at hindi siya huli sa moda-*Sp* o sa *fashion*

HOLD hawakan, tanganan, captan; Iloc: tengngelen, iggaman, cumpet, capeten, agcapet

HOLD all the aces nasa puesto na maventahe o nakakabigay ng favor-*Sp* sa canya, nasa puestong siya ay namumuno o may kapangyarihan
    Synonym
    Have the upper hand mataas ang posisyon o nasa puesto na may ventahe o kalamangan

HOLD back pigilin, hadlangan, controlan; Iloc: gawiden, tipden, teppedan, tenglen, tengngelen, i-*control*

HOLD hands magkahawak; Iloc: agkibin

HOLD off pag-antala; Iloc: i-atraso-*Sp*

HOLD on 1] mahigpit na pisil o hawak; pinapanindigan o manatili sa canyang pasia o paniwala; 2] magpahintay sandali at babalikan ang kausap sa telefono

Correlated word

On hold naghihintay habang nasa temporaryong pagtigil

HOLD out 1] patuloy ang buhay; 2] ipagkait ang bagay na inaasahan o nakatakda o nararapat na ibigay; umayaw o tumangging ibigay o ayaw sumunod

HOLD the fort habang wala ang magulang o kaya ang *boss*, siya ang may responsibilidad-*Sp* na mamahala sa lugar-*Sp* at pangangailangan, gaya ng oficina-*Sp*, tindahan o bahay; Iloc: isu iti mangigaway o mangipaturong iti lugar-*Sp* casla iti oficina-*Sp*, tienda-*Sp* wenno iti balay

HOLD tight, Grip hawakang mahigpit, cumapit; Iloc: agcapet ti nareppet, cumpet, tenglen, petpetan

HOLD up 1] nakawan sa pamamagitan ng pagtutok ng baril; 2] i-antala, i-atraso-*Sp*; 3] ipataas ang bagay para ipakita at ipaalam

HOLD with both legs idantay; Iloc: icawil

HOLE in the ground bungkal, lupang nahukay; Iloc: abut, nacali a daga

HOLE on a cloth or furnishing butas; Iloc: butbot, lubbot, lussok

HOLE made by a needle, Prick turok; Iloc: tudok

HOLE up somewhere nagsisilong, nakatira o nagtagtago siya sa isang lugar

Holiday pista ofisyal, araw na pahinga sa trabaho at pagpaalaala o pagdidiwang ng importanteng tao, pangyayari o bagay; Iloc: fiesta ofisyal, aldaw nga pag-inana iti trabaho ken paglaglagip wenno pagpadaya iti importante a tao o napasamak

Holier-than-thou nagpapahayag na mas mabuti siya na tao kaysa sa kaharap niya o kaysa sa ibang tao

Holiness pagkabanal, pagkasagrado, pagkamaka-Dios, pagkasantisimo

Holler magsigaw, maghiyaw; Iloc: agriaw, agpukkaw

Hollow butas, puwang, patlang, hukay; Iloc: abut, cali, butbot

Holograph kasulatan o documento-*Sp* na nakasulat sa camay at may firma-*Sp* o signatura-*Sp* ng sumulat

HOLY ang katangian ng Dios, sagrado-*Sp*, divinidad-*Sp*, pinagpapala, banal, nadiosan, nasantoan; Iloc: ti katatao ni Apo Dios, sagrado, divinidad, nadiosan, nasantoan

Synonym

Hallow sagrado at banal; pinupuri, pinaparangalan at sinasamba

HOLY Friday *(Tag. & Iloc.)* Viernes-*Sp* Santo-*Sp*

HOLY Saturday *(Tag. & Iloc.)* Sabado-*Sp* Santo-*Sp*

HOLY Spirit Ang Espiritu Santo ay Espiritu ng Dios, Espiritu ni Hesu Cristo bilang isang Dios sa tatlong banal na persona ng *Holy Trinity/ Santisima Trinidad* (Dios Ama, Dios Anak na si Hesu Cristo at Dios Espiritu Santo). Ang Espiritu Santo ang naghimok sa mga profeta at dicipulo para isulat ang Biblia, ang banal na salita ng Dios. Kapag taos-pusong tanggapin natin ang Dios Anak na si Hesu Cristo sa puso't buhay natin bilang Dios natin at Tagapagligtas natin dahil sa pagpatawad Niya ng lahat ng ating mga kasalanan sa pamamagitan ng dugo Niya sa cruz sa pagdurusa at pagkapako Niya sa cruz, ang Espiritu Santo ay papasok na sa ating puso para tayo ay maging templo ng Espiritu Santo dahil ang Dios ay Immanuel *(God with us)*. Hindi Niya tayo iiwanan o lalayasan kahit kailanman. Kung hilingin natin sa Espiritu Santo, bibigyan Niya tayo ng pagnanasa na basahin ang Biblia, ang banal na salita ng Dios, at matutupad ang mga maluwalhating pangako ng Dios sa Biblia kung ipagdasal natin iyan. Ang Espiritu Santo ay maaasahan nating gabayan at patnubayan tayo sa ating mga palakad sa buhay kung hihilingin natin ito sa Canya para mabuhay tayong maka-Dios.

HOLY Thursday *(Tag. & Iloc.)* Hueves-*Sp* Santo-*Sp*

HOLY Trinity *Holy Trinity,* Santisima Trinidad-*Sp,* *isang Dios sa tatlong banal na persona*: Dios Ama, Dios Anak na si Hesu Cristo, at Dios Espiritu Santo na Siya ang lumikha ng bunong universo at lahat ng nasa universo. Siya ang Panginoong Dios sa langit.

HOLY week *(Tag. & Iloc.)* semana-*Sp* santa-*Sp*

Correlated words

Lent *(Tag. & Iloc.)* cuaresma

Easter Sunday *easter,* Domingo Santo, Domingo de Pascua o de Resurescion

Holy Friday or Good Friday *(Tag. & Iloc.)* Viernes Santo

Holy Saturday *(Tag. & Iloc.)* Sabado Santo

Homage espesyal-*Sp* na parangal sa karapat-dapat na tao sa harap ng madla o publico-*Sp*

HOME bahay, tahanan, tinitirhan; Iloc: balay, pagyanan, pagtaengan
Correlated words
Dwelling tirhan; Iloc: pagyanan
Lodging tuloyan; Iloc: pagdagusan
Shelter canlongin, silongan; Iloc: pagcamangan
Hut bahay kubo, dampa; Iloc: balay a nipa, calapaw
Shanty barong-barung; Iloc: rutrot a balay

HOME-made gawa sa bahay at hindi binili; Iloc: inaramid diay balay, haan nga ginatang

HOME school programa-*Sp* na pang-educasyon-*Sp* na ginagampanan sa sariling bahay para magkapag-aral ang mga anak na kapareho sa educasyon sa escuela-*Sp*

HOME study curso-*Sp* na ang mga leksion-*Sp* ay pinapadala sa bahay para pag-aralan

Homebody contento na siya na sa bahay lamang siya

Homecoming piniling fecha-*Sp* para sa ocasyon-*Sp* para magkita-kita, maghalobilo at magtipan ang dating magkakamag-aral sa escuela-*Sp*, colehio-*Sp* o universidad-*Sp* kahit matagalan na silang nag-*graduate* doon

Homeland bayang sinilangan; Iloc: bayan a nakayyanakan

Homemaker nanay na nag-aalaga sa mga anak sa bahay at nagtatrabaho sa pangfamilia at pambahay

Homely hindi nagpapaganda at hindi mapostura kundi simp-le lamang siya

Homeowner ang nagmemay-ari ng bahay; Iloc: isu iti makincua iti balay

Homesick nasasabik sa sariling bayan o familia-*Sp*; Iloc: mail-iliw

Hometown ang bayan kung saan napanganak o lumaki o nakatira; Iloc: ili nu inchenna a nayyanak wenno dimmakkel wenno aggigian

Homicide *(Tag. & Iloc.)* ang pagpatay ng tao

Homogenous *adj.,* **Homogeny** *n.,* alinsunod sa o ayon sa natural-*Sp* na pinagmulan o kanuno-nunohan

Homograph dalawa o mahigit pang dalawa na salita na magkapareho ang baybayin/*spelling* at ang pagbigkas o *pronunciation* pero magkaiba ang ibig sabihin (halimbawa ang ibig sabihin ng "<u>bunyag</u>" sa Tagalog ay *reveal* samantala, "<u>bunyag</u>" sa Ilocano ay *baptism;* ang "<u>poot</u>" sa Tagalog ay *anger* samantalang "<u>poot</u>" sa Ilocano ay *consciousness)*

Homosexual nakikipagtalik ng *sexual* sa kapwa-lalake o kapwa-babae at ang mas kilalang tawag ngayon ay *gay* at *lesbian* pero sa Filipinas ginagamit pa rin ang "bakla" na tawag sa lalakeng *homosexual*

Hone hasain, ihasa, tasahin; Iloc: asaen, tasaren

HONEST *adj.,* **Honesty** *n. Principled, honorable, respectable, virtuous, sincere, genuine, true, frank, trustworthy and reliable; honest dealings and honest acquisition of assets; upright in intentions and actions; conscientious, ethical, fair, high-minded.* Mapagkatiwalaan at mapanaligan sa maraming bagay pati sa pera; Iloc: mapagtalkan ken mapagfiaran (fiar-*Sp*) iti adu a banag pati iti cuarta
Correlated words

Transparency *Transparent like a glass are the ways, intentions and nature of a person who has transparency.* Katatao, buhay at gawa niya ay lantad at mapagkatiwalaan ang katapatan niya dahil wala man lang siyang nililihim; Iloc: kababalin, biag ken aramid na ket nakaparang nga husto ken mapagfiaran isu ta awan man laeng ti limed iti bagi na

Honesty is not just the most excellent policy, it must be always practiced katapatan at pagkatotoo ay hindi lamang ito ang pinaka-excelente at pinakamahusay na policiya o paraan kundi ang pagkatotoo ay panay-panay na susundin

HONEST and aboveboard *Honest, open, visible to the public, has transparency in deeds and in giving account and enlightenments;* Tapat at tunay at kitang-kita ng publico, hindi madaya at hindi manloloco

Honeymoon maikling viahe-*Sp* ng bagong casal para patuloy na ipagdiwang ang bagong buhay nila bilang mag-asawa

Honk pagbo-bosina-*Sp* kung kinakailangan habang nagmamaneho-*Sp* ng sasakyan
Correlated words

Horn of vehicle *(Tag. & Iloc.)* bosina

HONOR *n.* karangalan; Iloc: dayaw

HONOR *v.* parangalan, purihin; Iloc: padayawan, raeman

HONOR system, Honesty/Trust system *Participants of this system are expected to be bound by their <u>honor</u> to comply with regulations. To*

ensure compliance, there is a random check on the participants, and the fear of getting checked will coerce them into compliance. Cheating or non-compliance can include, loss of status, public shame, and even expulsion from the country. Paraan na pagkakatiwalaan mga tao kahit walang *supervision* at kahit may tentaciong magnakaw o mandaya
Correlated words

Gentleman's agreement contratang hindi nakasulat kundi bumabatay lamang sa usapang kasundoan at tiwala

Honorable marangal, dakila, kagalang-galang; Iloc: nataer, maday-dayaw, nakararaem

Hood 1] panakip ng ulo at batok na parte ng jacket, 2] tao na masama at gumagawa ng crimen, 3] ang takip ng *engine* ng sasakyan

Hoodlum butangero, basag-ulero; Iloc: butangero

Hoodwink estafa-*Sp*, manguha ng cuarta sa panlilinlang, panloloco, linlang, falsifica-*Sp*; Iloc: estafa, mangala ti cuarta iti panggulgulib, pangloco ken falsificar-*Sp*

HOOK cawit, sungkit; Iloc: callawit, cawit, sab-it, sukit

HOOK and eye, Clasp for a jewelry *(Tag. & Iloc.)* cawit

HOOK for fishes bingwit; Iloc: banniit

Hooker *(Tag. & Iloc.)* puta-*Sp*

Hooky, play *absent* o hindi pumasok sa escuela na wala man lang pasabi sa escuela at walang malay ang magulang

Hooligan *(Tag. & Iloc.)* barumbado, basag-ulero

Hoopla 1] maingay at magulo na kasayahan; 2] magastos at malawak na publicidad-*Sp*; Iloc: 1] naariwawa ken naringgor nga pagragragsakan, 2] nangina ken naywaras o naywarnak a publicidad-*Sp*

HOP magkandirit, magaan na talon o lukso sa isang paa lamang; Iloc: agkingking

HOP in *(Tag. & Iloc.)* makisakay ng libre

HOPE *n.* pag-asa; Iloc: namnama

HOPE *v.* umaasa; Iloc: agnamnama

HOPE, give bigyang pag-asa; Iloc: pagnamnamaen

Hopefully sana, harinawa; Iloc: sapay cuma, barbareng

Hopeless walang pag-asa; Iloc: awan namnama na

Hopscotch kandirit; Iloc: kingking *(see Hop above)*

Horde pagdagsa o pagdumog ng mga tao; Iloc: agaribongbong nga tattao

Horizon ang abot-tanaw na pagitan ng mundo at langit

Horizontal pahiga; Iloc: paidda

   Antonym

   Vertical patayo; Iloc: patacder

HORN sungay; Iloc: sara

HORN of vehicle *(Tag. & Iloc.)* bosina-*Sp*

Hornet putakti; Iloc: alumpipineg

Horrendous hindi matitiis, terib-le; Iloc: haan a maibturan, terib-le

Horrible nakakatakot, napakasama; Iloc: nakabutbuteng, nakadakdakes

Horrify takotin; Iloc: butngen

Horror malagim at nakakatakot; Iloc: makasumgar ti dutdot iti pagka-buteng ken pagdakes daytoy

Hors d'oeuvre *[orderve]* *crackers* o maliliit na *sandwich* (sukat ay isang pulgada sa apat o lahat na gilid) na may iba't iba ang palaman o patong gaya ng isda, carne o keso na sinisilbi sa *party*

HORSE cabayo-*Sp*; Iloc: cabalyo-*Sp*

HORSE, young batang cabayo-*Sp*; Iloc: urbon

Horseradish malunggay; Iloc: marunggay

Hosanna, Hosanah "Sinasamba ko Cayo, o Dios", Iloc: "Daydayoen ko Cayo, Apo Dios"

Hose 1] *stockings*, 2] gomang tubo na pagdaloyan ng tubig-pandilig

Hosiery *(Tag. & Iloc.)* *stockings* ng babae

Hospital *hospital*, ospital-*Sp*, pagamutan; Iloc: *hospital*, ospital

Hospitable *adj.*, **Hospitality** *n.* mainam na pagtanggap sa visita o sa mga dayohan; Iloc: naimbag a pagtrato iti visita wenno iti tagadayo

Hospitalization *n.*, **Hospitalize** *v.* pumunta o dinala sa ospital-*Sp* para magamot doon; Iloc: napan o impan da idiay ospital para maagasan cada aldaw nga agyan idiay

Host 1] kung sino ang nagpa-*party*, 2] ang nagbabalita o nag-i-*interview* sa TV, 3] oscha sa *Holy Communion*

Hostage fuersang nabihag na tao na gagawin siyang pangdefensa o pagtaklub sa sarili o pangdemanda ng paghuthot ng *ransom* (fuersa-*Sp*, defensa-*Sp*, demanda-*Sp*)

HOSTILE *adj.*, **Hostility** *n.* asal at pananalita na masasakit dahil puno siya ng suklam at galit ang puso; Iloc: pagsarita ken tignay a nakasaksakit gapu ta napunno ti gura ken rungsot iti puso na

HOSTILE look nanlilisik ang matang tumingin; Iloc: cusilap a napunno iti rurod

HOT mainit, maalinsangan; Iloc: napudot, nasalimuot, nadagaang, nabara

HOT air pagyayabang na nakaka-duda-*Sp*, promesa-*Sp* na hindi maaasahan

HOT charcoal nagbabagang uling; Iloc: agbarbarang nga uring

HOT with fever nilalagnat; Iloc: aggorgorigur

HOT-headed mapusok, mainisin, mainitin ang ulo, yamotin, walang pasencia pero pikon; Iloc: alipunget, nalaca a makapungtot, napudot ti ulo, naunget, awan pasencia ngem pikon

HOT spot lugar kung saan may panganib o kagulohan o labanan

HOT stuff 1] tao o bagay na di-pangcaraniwang clase at kahusayan; 2] kakaiba, kagila-gilalas, walang takot na may pagkapangahas

Hotel *(Tag. & Iloc.)* hotel

Hound 1] isang claseng aso 2] himokin ng himokin

Hour *(Tag. & Iloc.)* oras-*Sp*

Hourly oras-oras, tuwing oras; Iloc: cada-*Sp* oras-*Sp*

HOUSE bahay, tahanan, tinitirhan; Iloc: balay, pagyanan, pagtaengan

HOUSE arrest sentencia-*Sp* ng husticia-*Sp* na mapreso sa sariling bahay imbes-*Sp* na sa bilanggoan

Houseboy/Housegirl *(Tag. & Iloc.)* muchacho/a-*aSp*, alila

Housebreaking 1] turoan at sanayin ang aso na tumai o umihi sa labas ng bahay, 2] pagpasok ng criminal sa tahanan na hindi canya para magnakaw

Housemate kabahay, kasama sa bahay; Iloc: kabbalay

Housetop bubungan; Iloc: tuktok ti balay

Housewife maybahay, asawa na hindi namamasokan sa oficina kundi sa bahay lamang siya nagtatrabaho; Iloc: asawa nga haan nga agof-oficina nu di idiay balay laeng
Synonym
   Homemaker nanay na nag-aalaga sa mga anak sa bahay at gumagawa ng pangfamilia at pambahay na trabaho

Hover lilipad-lipad at aali-aligid sa isang lugar-*Sp*; Iloc: agtayab-tayab ken aglibot-libot iti maysa a lugar

"HOW?" "Paano?" "Papano?" Iloc: "Casano?"

"HOW are you?" *(Tag. & Iloc.)* "Comosta?" o "Comosta ka?"; *(if addressing elders and giving respect to them, it would be)* "Comosta kayo?"

465

"HOW are you related?" "Magkaano-ano kayo?" Iloc: "Agkaano-ano kayo?"

"HOW big?" or "What size?" "Gaano kalaki?" Iloc: "Casano kadakkel na?"

"HOW is this done?" "Paano ang paggawa nito?" Iloc: "Casano ti pagaramid ditoy?"

"HOW many?" "Ilan?" Iloc: "Mano?"

"HOW many times?" "Ilang veses-*Sp*?" "Gaano kadalas?" Iloc: "Mano a veses?" "Maminmano?"

"HOW much?" "Magkano?" Iloc: "Sagmamano?"

"HOW sad of him/her" "Kawawa naman" Iloc: "Piman met"

HOW-tos mga leksion at paraan kung paano ang paggawa ng mga bagay-bagay

However gayun man, pero-*Sp*; Iloc: ngem, uray casta/pay

Howl alulong na tahol ng aso; Iloc: sangit a taul ti aso

Hub centro-*Sp* ng kasiglaan at mahalaga o masayang mga pangyayari; Iloc: centro ti pag-u-ummongan ken iti importante-*Sp* ken naragsak a mapaspasamak

Hubby *(Tag. & Iloc.)* asawa na lalake

Huddle together nagsisiksikang mga tao, nag-uumpokan; Iloc: agsisik-sikan a tatttao, aguum-mongan
Correlated words
    Cramped together nagkakadikit-dikit ang mga tao; Iloc: agdedekket o agdedennet dagiti tao

Hug yakapin, mag-abrazo-*Sp*; Iloc: aracopen, agabrazo
Correlated words
    Embrace yakapin, yaposin, mag-abrazo; Iloc: aracopen, rakepen, agabrazo
    Caress yacap na macarinyo at maconsuelo at may pagmamahal; Iloc: aracop nga macarinyo ken maconsuelo ken naayat
    Cuddle pagmamahal na yakap o yapos; Iloc: naayat nga aracop wenno rakep
    Fondle haplosin, himasin; Iloc: aprosan
    Nestle pagmamahal na yakap o yapos; Iloc: naayat nga aracop wenno rakep

Huge malaki, napakalaki, malaking-malaki; Iloc: dakkel unay nakadakdakkel

Hum higing, humiging; Iloc: ag-canta-*Sp* nga cerrado-*Sp* ti bibig, ag-*hum*

HUMAN, Human being *(Tag. & Iloc.)* tao

HUMAN rights mga karapatan ng tao na may kalayaan na mabuhay, karapatan na may pagkakapantay sa turing, karapatan na pagpahayag ng paniwala at isip at iba pang mga karapatan

Humanitarian *This person has a heart for others as he/she is considerate of others, compassionate, helpful, generous if within his/her means (he/she knows a person does not have to have money in order to be of help to others), gives solace and relief to those who are sick or in difficulties, in pain or in poverty, and many more, all for the sake of human welfare.*
Correlated words

To be a humanitarian is to find a need and fill it; find a hurt and heal it, find a problem and solve it para maging dakilang mapagmalasakit na tao ay humanap ng pangangailangan at handogan ng tugon, humanap ng sugat at lunasan para magamot, humanap ng suliranin at talakayan ang kalutasan

Humane *This person has a heart for all creations like men and animals. He/she has mercy, sympathy, compassion, especially when the one that needs help is old and weak, sick or disabled, hungry, cold and needs clothes or shelter, suffering, grieving for a deceased loved one, and other predicaments.*

Humanity, Human race sangkatauhan; Iloc: tattao ti mundo-*Sp*

Humble *adj.,* **Humility** *n.* mapagpacumbaba, mababang-loob, maamo; Iloc: umilde-*Sp*, napacumbaba, naamo
Synonym

Folksy simp-le at walang pagkukunwari at madaling makapalagayang-loob

Humdrum nakakaantok o nakakainip dahil hindi nakakalibang; Iloc: makapaturog o mangpatektek gapu ta haan a makalinglingay

Humid nagkakaroon ng maraming tubig o hamog; Iloc: addaan iti adu a danum wenno linnaaw

Humidifier aparato-*Sp* na nagbibigay ng tubig o hamog na hangin sa cuarto-*Sp* o *greenhaouse*

Humidity hamog; Iloc: linnaaw

Humiliate pahiyain, laitin; Iloc: pabainan, laisen

Humongous sobrang-sobrang malaki; Iloc: sobra ti kadakkel na

Humor *n.,* **Humorous** *adj.* katatawanan; Iloc: katawaan

Hunch 1] may pakiramdam na may mangyayari, 2] nakayuko o baluktot ang katawan

Hunchback cuba; Iloc: cubbo

Hundred daan, raan; Iloc: gasut
Correlated words
Thousand libo; Iloc: ribo
Million *(Tag. & Iloc.) million*

Hunger *n.,* **Hungry** *adj.* gutom, nagugutom; Iloc: bisin, mabisin
Antonym
Full stomach busog; Iloc: nabsog, napnek

Hunk *(Tag. & Iloc.)* masculadong lalake

Hunky-dory *adj.* nakakasiya at nakakacontento; Iloc: makaliwliwa ken makapagcontento

Hunt paghagad o pagtugis ng hayop

Hurdle panghadlang sa mga nagcacarera o *running-a-race* na kailangan ay luksohan at tumalon sa mga bara para hindi ito tumomba

Hurl ihagis, ibato, iicha; Iloc: ipalladaw, ipallato, ibato, ipurwak

Hurricane napakalakas na bagyo; Iloc: napigsa a bagyo

Hurry up magmadali, mag-apura; Iloc: agdardaras, agapapura-*Sp*

HURT (bodily) saktan, sugatan, nasaktan, nasugatan; Iloc: saktan, cabilen, nasaktan, nacabil

HURT (feelings) magtampo, magdamdam; Iloc: paluksawen, suronen

Husband asawang lalake; Iloc: asawa nga lalaki
Synonym
Spouse *(Tag. & Iloc.) asawa*

Hush 1] patahimikin, pacalmahin o hangoin sa sama ng loob, 2] sawayin ang pagbubunyag

Husky *(Tag. & Iloc.)* masculadong lalake

Hustle 1] itulak o ipagmadali, 2] masigasig na pagsisikap, agresivo-*Sp* sa pagnenegosio

Hut bahay kubo, dampa; Iloc: balay a nipa, calapaw

Hybrid 1] mestisong tao dahil ang magulang ay magkaiba ang nasyon-*Sp*, 2] anak ng dalawang magkaibang hayop o bunga ng magkaibang halaman

Hydrate bigyan ng inoming tubig para makabalik ang nawala na kinakailangang tubig sa katawan dahil sa init o dahil sa walang mainom

HYGIENE *n.,* **Hygienic** *adj.* pagkagawi na kalinisan sa katawan; Iloc: cadawyan a kalinisan ti bagi

HYGIENE wash after using the toilet (Filipino custom) magpawpaw;
Iloc: agpawpaw

Hymn himno-*Sp*, cantang pagsamba at pagpasalamat sa Panginoong
Dios; Iloc: himno, canta-*Sp* o cancion-*Sp* para iti pag-glorificar-*Sp* ken
pagyaman kenni Apo Dios

Hype 1] labis na publicidad na sinusundan ng pagcarambola ng mga
tao bilang madamdaming-sagut dito, 2] pakana ng *advertisement* na
sobrang ipagparangal ang canilang producto o servicio-*Sp*, 3] *addict*
na nagumon sa droga o alak, 4] *syringe* o carayom ng inyecsion

HYPER labis ang paglabas ng emosyon-*Sp* gaya ng nervios-*Sp*, tuwa at
takot

HYPER- *(prefix in English, not in Filipino)* labis-labis, sobra-sobra

Hyperbole kasabihan na mas malabis pa kaysa sa katotohanan para
lamang mabigyang-diin o mas may efecto ang sinasabi, gaya ng
"hahalikan kita ng libo-libo" o "maghintay ako hanggang eternidad"

Hypertension alta-presyon-*Sp*, mataas ang presyon; Iloc: altapresyon,
nangato ti presyon

Hypnosis *n.,* **Hypnotize** *v.* mapamalikmata, i-*hypnotize*

Hypochondriac paniwala na siya ay may sakit o may iba't ibang sakit na
puedeng guni-guni lamang

Hypocrite hipocrito/ta-*Sp*, mapagkunwari; Iloc: hipocrito/ta; aginkukuna,
aginsisingpet, agsinsinan

Hypothesis *n.,* **Hypothetical** *adj.* panukala na ginagamit bilang palatandaan o pagpapalagayan o pagpaliwanag ng isang pangyayari
para makatulong sa imbestigasyon-*Sp*; palagay, kuro-kuro o hula;
para magamit sa imbestigasyon-*Sp*, bigyang considerasyon ang mga
napansin, sinabi, naobserva at ang puedeng nangyari o *scenario* kahit
walang kasegurohan

Hysterical hindi controladong pag-iyak o pagtawa
Correlated word
    Hyper labis ang paglabas ng emosyon gaya ng nervios, tuwa at takot

I

I ako; Iloc: siac

I. e. iyan ay...; Iloc: dayta ket...

I am ako ay/ang; Iloc: siac ni/ti

"I bet" "Tutoo", "Sigurado ako" Iloc: "Usto", "Siguradoac"

"I don't know" "Aywan ko," "Ewan," "Hindi ko alam;" Iloc: "Haan ko ammo"

"I don't like" "Ayaw ko;" Iloc: "Mandiak," "Madic cayat", "Mandiac"

"I don't like you" "Ayaw ko sa 'yo;" Iloc: "Madic kenca"

"I know" "Alam ko;" Iloc: "Haan ko ammo"

"I like" "Gusto ko;" Iloc: "Gustok" (gusto-*Sp*), "Cayat ko"

"I like you" "Gusto kita"; Iloc: "Mayatac kenca"

"I love you" "Iniibig kita," "Mahal kita;" Iloc: "Ay-ayatenca"

ICE *(Tag. & Iloc.)* yelo-*Sp*

ICE cream *(Tag. & Iloc.)* *ice cream,* sorbetes-*aSp*

Icebreaker 1] pagbati na pampaluwag ng formalidad at makapagbukas ng pag-uusap sa parehong hindi magkakilala; 2] aparato, makina o barco na ginawa para baklibakliin, wasak-wasakin at durog-durogin ang yelo-*Sp*

Icing *(Tag. & Iloc.)* *icing* o *frosting*

Icon 1] imahen-*Sp* o letrato ng sinasamba, 2] simbolo sa *computer* na i-*click* para mapasukan ang *website*

Iconoclast 1] taong nagpipintas o umaatake sa mga paniwala, tradisyon at iba pa na ang pang-atake niya ay mali at *superstition* lamang; 2] nambabasag at naninira sa mga imahen na sinasamba ng relihion

ID, ID card tarheta-*Sp* na nagpapatunay na ikaw nga ang nakaletrato sa *card* na nakaulat ang fecha ng pinanganakan mo, ang taas o tangkad mo, culay ng mata at buhok, *address* at iba pa

Idea *(Tag. & Iloc.)* *idea,* diwa/amad

Ideal ginagawang pamantayan o huwaran ito ng pagkaexcelente; tinuturing na pinakamabuti at pinakamagaling na katangian, na tao, na bagay o lugar-*Sp*

Idealist taong tinatangi at sinusunod ang mga matataas at dakilang pricipio/*principle*, layonin at paniwala

Idealize tinitingala ang isang tao o bagay bilang huwaran o ehemplo ng pagkadakila o kabutihan o pagka-*superior*

Identical magkamukha, magkawangis, magkatulad; Iloc: agkaruprupa, agkaingas, agkalanga

IDENTIFICATION *identification,* pangpatibay o evidencia na ikaw talaga ang pinapahayag mo na ikaw, na meron kang letrato at iba pang informasyon tungkol sa iyo na ang pagpapatunay na ito ay buhat sa govierno na puedeng *ID card* na may retrato o pasaporte at iba pang-verificasyon-*Sp* o pagpapatunay kung ikaw nga ang sinasabi mo

IDENTIFICATION card *(Tag. & Iloc.) ID card*

Identify kilalanin, ipamukhaan, ituro; Iloc: bigbigen, ilasin, itudo
Synonym
Recognize mamukhaan, makilala; Iloc: mabigbig, mailasin

IDENTITY *I.D.,* pagpapatunay kung sino ang tao talaga. Ang buong katatao niya ay ang ichura-*Sp,* asal, custombre-*Sp* marka ng daliri at marka sa katawan gaya ng taling/*mole,* peklat o tattoo, at iba pa na nagpapatunay na siya ang pinapahayag niyang siya, pati ang kabuhayan, ocupasyon at nakalipas niya, at kasama din dito ang numero-*Sp* na tinakda ng govierno-*Sp* sa canya na tanging canya lamang, at *I.D. card* na may retrato siya na pangpapatunay pa rin na siya nga iyon.

IDENTITY theft nakawin ang informasyong *financial* (numero-*Sp* ng *bank account* o *credit card*) at informasyong *personal* (pangalan, fecha-*Sp* ng pinanganakan, tinitirhan, numero ng *Social Security Number* o *Department of Motor Vehicles card*) para magamit at manakaw ang mga pera at ari-aryan ng ninakawan

Ideology ang doctrina, paniwala, alamat o gawa-gawa na pumapatnubay sa tao o grupo o organisasyon o institusyon para ipairal o ipatakbo o ipakilos ito.

Idiosyncrasy ang kakaibang gawi o asal ng isang tao na tanging canya

Idiot taong sobrang mababa ang cacayahan ng canyang utak, isang stupido-*Sp*

Idle, Idling away nagtutunganga para makakabuntunghininga o dahil sa katamaran; Iloc: agbaybayanggudaw tapno mabang-aran wenno gapu ti pagkasadut.
Correlated words

Lazy tamad; Iloc: sadut

Passing the time unproductively nagtutunganga; Iloc: agmulmulengleng, agmutmuttaleng

Idolatry sumasamba sa <u>iba</u> kaysa sa Dios; Iloc: agdglorificar-*Sp* iti <u>sabali</u> nga haan ken ni Apo Dios

Idolize pagsamba at pagdevoto sa idolo; sambahin na parang Dios

Idyll *n.,* **Idyllic** *adj.* 1] maganda at simpleng tanawin, 2] tula na naglalarawan ng nakakaakit na kabukiran

If kung sakali, kapag, pag, kung; Iloc: nu caspagarigan, bareng nu, nu

Ignite sindihan; Iloc: isindi, seggedan

    Correlated word

    Ignited umapoy; Iloc: immapoy, simged

Ignominious *adj.,* **Ignominy** *n.* ang napakatinding kahihiyan at pagkasira ng puri; nakakasuka sa kalaswaan na asal, ugali, pagkatao o pangyayari

Ignorance *n.,* **Ignorant, Ignoramus** *adj.* ignorante-*Sp*, kulang sa pagkaalam o pagkadunong; Iloc: ignorante-*Sp*, kurang ti ammo na o ti sirib na

Ignore hindi pansinin, hindi ituring o estimahin, ipawalang-cuenta; Iloc: haan nga icascason haan nga bigbigen wenno estimaren, ipaawan iti cuenta o pateg na

Iguana bayawak; Iloc: banyas

Ilk *(Tag. & Iloc.)* familia, clase, uri

ILL may sakit; Iloc: agsakit

ILL-bred nakakadisgusto ang ugali dahil sa pabaya na pagpapalaki sa canya ng canyang mga magulang na salat sa mabuting pangangaral at dala niya itong kakulangan hanggang sa canyang paglaki at pagkatanda

ILL-equipped walang-wala sa canya ang katangiang magpakabuti o magpakaunlad sa tama o mabuting paraan

ILL-fated nakadestino o nakatakda siya sa kahirapan, kasamaan o bilangguan

Ill-feeling damdaming poot, galit, yamot o hinanakit sa isang tao o grupo

ILL-gotten anomang ari-aryan niya na nakuha niya sa hindi mabuting paraan gaya sa pagnanakaw o suhol o panlilinlang

ILL-mannered *(Tag. & Iloc.)* bastos-*Sp*

ILL-natured pagkatao, ugali at gawi na napakasama

ILL-will, Ill-wisher 1] masamang tangka, 2] nagmimithi ng kasamahan sa kapwa

Illegal labag sa batas; Iloc: contra ti linteg, haan a naturay

Illegible sulat na hindi mabasa o sinulat na hindi maintindihan

Illegitimate 1] labag sa batas, 2] napanganak na hindi casal sa isa't isa ang magulang

Illicit labag sa batas; Iloc: contra ti linteg, haan a naturay

Illiterate *adj.*, **Illiteracy** *n.* hindi marunong magbasa o magsulat; Iloc: haan na ammo ti agbasa ken agsurat

Illness karamdaman; Iloc: sakit

Illogical pahayag o pag-aasal na hindi tugma sa husto at makatarungang rason at lohica at sa pagkapertinente at relevanteng intelihensia-*Sp*

Illuminate *v.*, **Illumination** *n.* ilawan; Iloc: silawan

Illuminati mga tao na nagpapahayag na sila'y nag-aangkin ng mataas, nakahihigit at superior-*Sp* na liwanag ng pag-iisip

Illusion isang nakakapanlinland na naglalarawan ng nakakadaya, nakakaligaw at huwad o pekeng ichura; panlilinlang lamang

Illustrate *v.*, **Illustration** *n.* ilarawan sa pagpapaliwanag o pagpakita; Iloc: i-presentar-*Sp* iti panglawlawag o pagpakita, iladawan ti itchura-*Sp* wenno ti napasamak

Illustrious kilala na experto-*Sp* sa importanteng bagay, matanyag at marangal; Iloc: popular-*Sp* isu gapu iti pagkaexperto na iti importante a banag, natan-ok ken nadayaw

IMAGE *(Tag. & Iloc.)* imahen-*Sp*

IMAGE, graven, Statue *(Tag. & Iloc.)* rebulto

Imaginary guniguni; Iloc: arapaap

Imagine *v.*, **Imagination** *n*, **Imaginative** *adj.* ilarawan sa isip, likhang-isip o guni-guni; Iloc: iretrato iti panunot
Synonyms
Envision, Visualize ilarawan sa isip; Iloc: iretrato iti panunot

Imbecile taong sobrang mababa ang cacayahan ng utak niya at kaisipan, isang stupido-*Sp*

Imbed i-puesto-*Sp* o itatag ng husto-*Sp* sa tao o sa makina-*Sp* (i.e. aparato-*Sp*, magandang ugali); Iloc: icabil o isimpa ti usto-*Sp* iti tao wenno iti makina (i.e., aparato, singpet iti pagkatao)

Imbibe *(Tag. & Iloc.)* *drink, swallow*, uminom

Imbroglio complicado-*Sp* at nakakalitong situasyon-*Sp*, kagusotan; Iloc: complicado ken nakarirriro nga situasyon, gulo

Imbue magkintal o magtanim ng damdamin, palagay, paniwala at iba pa; ibabad sa tubig, pangkulay at iba pa

Imitate gayahin, tularan, tumulad, copiahin; Iloc: tuladen, suroten, copiaren (copia/copiar-*Sp*)

Imitation *(Tag. & Iloc.)* imitasyon-*Sp*

Immaculate busilak; Iloc: puro ken nalinis

Immaterial walang kabulohan, hindi importante; Iloc: awan servi, haan nga importante

Immature isip-bata hindi pa masyadong nakakaintindi ng buhay-buhay

Immediately agad-agad; Iloc: ensegida-*Sp*, dagdagus

Immemorial napakatagal na na lampas pa sa memoria o alaala o kasulatan/ *record*s o kaalaman

Immense *adj.*, **Immensity** *n.* napalaki, napakalawak; Iloc: nakadakdakkel, nakalawlawa

Immerse *v.*, **Immersion** *n.* ibabad, ilubog sa tubig, ilublob; Iloc: itabnaw ti danum, iyuper

Immigrate *v.*, **Immigrant** *n.* sumakabilang-bansa at doon na matira ng permanente-*Sp*, imigrante-*Sp*

Imminent malapit nang mangyari; Iloc: asidegen a maaramid

Immobilize ipirmi sa lugar at hindi pagalawin; hadlangan ang gamit, paggawa o kilos

Immoral *adj.*, **Immorality** *n.* hindi decente-*Sp* at walang moralidad-*Sp* at etico-*Sp* at dignidad-*Sp* at integridad-*Sp* at nakikita ito sa pagpalakad ng canyang buhay

Immortal walang kamatayan, buhay magpakailanman

Immovable firme-*Sp* sa lugar-*Sp* at <u>hindi</u> mailipat at maikilos gaya ng bahay, gusali at punong kahoy

Immune ang katawan niya ay mayroong malakas na panlaban at resistancia-*Sp* sa sakit kaya hindi siya tinatablan; Iloc: ti bagi na ket addaan iti napigsa a panglaban ken resistancia ti sakit isu nga haan isu a maacaran.

Immunity 1] pagkakaroon ng resistancia-*Sp* sa sakit; 2] sa batas, siya ay ipagpaliban sa pagsakdal, multa-*Sp* at pananagutan para kapalit ng canyang testimonya-*Sp*

Immunize turokan ng vacuna-*Sp* para hindi makasagap ng sakit; Iloc: agpavacuna

Imp *n.*, **Impish** *adj.* pilyong bata, maliit na demonyo-*Sp*; Iloc: pilyo, alicuteg

Impact 1] ang malaking fuersa-*Sp* o ang malakas na bunggohan o banggahan o hampasan sa isa't isa, 2] mafuersang efecto ng bagong kaisipan o paniniwala o cultura o tecnolohia-*Sp* o clima-*Sp* gaya ng *impacted area*; 3] influwensa-*Sp*, efecto-*Sp*

Impair sirain o pahinain o gawing hindi na efectivo-*Sp*

Impart ipaalam, ipahayag; Iloc: ipaammo, isawang

Impartial *adj.*, **Impartiality** *n.* walang kinacampihan, walang pinapanigan; Iloc: awan ti fabfaboran (fabor-*Sp*)

Impassable hindi puedeng padaanan dahil sa *landslide* o mga nieve-*Sp* o *snow* sa daan; hindi puedeng ipasa o aprovahan dahil sa may diferencia-*Sp* sa negosasyon-*Sp*

Impasse 1] daanan na walang labasan, 2] situasyon-*Sp* na walang magawang progreso-*Sp*

Impassion punoin o pairalin ang silakbo o simbuyo o pagpalabas o pagbulalas ng matinding damdamin

Impatient walang pasencia, naiinip; Iloc: awan pasencia-*Sp*, matektekan
Antonym
Patient pacencioso/sa, mapagtiis; Iloc: pacencioso/sa, nakaan-anos

Impeach acusahan ang mataas na pinuno sa govierno-*Sp* o pamahalaan sa hindi tamang ginawa at puede na siya ay tanggalin sa katungkulan ng corte-*Sp* husticia-*Sp* kung mapatunayan ito

Impeccable *perfect*, perfecto-*Sp* at walang defecto-*Sp*

Impede hadlangan, pigilan; Iloc: lappedan, igawid

Impediment hadlang, bara, sangga; Iloc: barra-*Sp*, sangga

Impel isapilitan o fuersahing isagawa; Iloc: piliten o fuersaen (fuersa-*Sp*) nga ipaaramid

475

Impend, Impending ang signo-*Sp* kung ano ang darating gaya ng kulog at kidlat, o malakas na ulan na nagpapahiwatig ng bagyo o baha, at iba pang signo-*Sp*

Impenetrable imposibleng makapasok o matusok o maintindihan

Impenitent wala man lang pagsisisi sa mga ginawa niya na kasalanan at sa pananakit sa iba; Iloc: awan ti pagbabawi na iti inaramid na a basbasol ken iti inted na a sakit ken liday iti dadduma

Antonyms

Apologize magpaumanhin; Iloc: agpadispensar

Repent *v.,* **Repentant** *adj.* magsisi, ikalulongkot; Iloc: agbabawi

Remorse taos na pagsisisi; Iloc: pagbabawi ti puso ken nakem

Imperative kinakailangang mangyari o magkaroon; Iloc: masapul nga mapasamak wenno maaddaaan

Imperceptible, Impercipient imposibleng makita o maintindihan o marinig

Imperfect <u>hindi</u> perfecto-*Sp*, may defecto-*Sp*

Imperil, Endanger ilagay sa panganib o peligro; Iloc: ikabil iti peggad o peligro-*Sp*

Impersonate 1] mag-ichura at gumanap na gaya ng iba na tao para mapaniwala niya ang iba na siya iyong ginagampanan niyang tao dahil ito ay panlilinlang, 2] artista sa pelicula o TV na gumaganap ng ibang tao

IMPERTINENT, Ill-mannered bastos-*Sp*, walang modo-*Sp*; Iloc: bastos, awan modo na

IMPERTINENT, Irrelevant impertinente-*Sp*, hindi tugma sa diwa o pangyayari; Iloc: impertinente-*Sp*, haan nga umno iti paksa ken mapaspasak

Imperturbable calmado-*Sp* at campante-*Sp*; hindi nababagabag o nagugulohan; halos hindi napupukaw o nayuyogyog ang damdamin

Impervious 1] hindi puedeng matagos o matarakan, hindi puedeng masugatan o masira; 2] hindi puedeng mainfluwensiahan o mahimok o maaffectahan

Impetus *n.,* **Impetuous** *adj.* fuersa-*Sp* na nagtutulak sa sarili na gumawa ng isang bagay, pabigla-bigla; Iloc: fuersa nga mangiduron ti bagi nga agaramid ti maysa a banag, nadursok

Impiety *n.,* **Impious** *adj.* hindi relihioso, kulang sa pagsamba o hindi nagsasamba sa Dios; hindi nagdadasal o nagsasamba

Impinge 1] magkintal ng marka o bakas; 2] manghimasok, makialam

Implant *v.,* **Implantation** *n.* itanim ng matatag; sa paggagamot, ano man ang ipasok-ilakip o ihugpong-idugtong sa katawan para malunasan ang sakit o palitan ang parteng hindi na gumagana sa katawan

Implement *v.,* **Implementation** *n.* isagawa, gamitin sa paggawa; Iloc: aramiden, iyusar iti pagaramid

Implicate *v.,* **Implication** *n.* 1] isang pahiwatig sa nakikitang kilos at hindi sa salita o sa anomang pagpahayag na dito nabubuo ang palagay; 2] idawit o isangkot ang kapwa o ng bagay sa isang pangyayari

Implicit 1] pahiwatig lamang at hindi sa sinabi o pahayag 2] hindi pinag-aalinlanganan o hindi pinaglilihim kundi tinuturing na tiyak

Implore magmakaawa at humingi ng tulong ng puspusan; Iloc: agpacaasi ken pamuspusan nga dumawat ti tulong

Implosion paloob sumabog; Iloc: pauneg nga agbettak

Imply nagpapapahiwatig ng hindi derechohan ang tinutukoy

Impolite *(Tag. & Iloc.)* bastos-*Sp* at walang respecto-*Sp*

Import *v.,* **Importation of foreign goods brought into the country** *(Tag. & Iloc.)* importasyon-*Sp*

Important *adj.,* **Importance** *n.* importante-*Sp,* mahalaga, kahalagahan; Iloc: importancia-*Sp,* napateg

Importune nagkukulit na humingi ng tulong; Iloc: mangdagdagdag nga agpatulong

Impose *v.,* **Imposition** *n.* isapilitan, mag-utos, magmando-*Sp,* magiit, maglapat o magpataw ng alituntunin o ng dapat susundin bilang isang obligasyon-*Sp* o pasanin; Iloc: i-obligar-*Sp,* i-mandar-*Sp;* ipilit

Impossible *(Tag. & Iloc.)* imposib-le-*Sp*

Impostor *impostor,* manlilinlang na nagpapanggap; Iloc: *impostor,* suitik

Imposture panlilinlang na pagpataw o paglapat sa kapwa ng *burden* o pasanin

Impotent 1] walang bisa, 2] hindi makaanak, baog; Iloc: 1] awan bisa, awan ti bileg, 2] baog

Impoverished pobre-*Sp,* dukha, maralita, gipit; Iloc: pobre, napanglaw, marigrigat

Impractical walang kabulohang gamitin dahil walang maibigay na tulong kaya sayang lamang ang oras-*Sp* na igugol dito

Impregnable 1] napakalakas at matatag na <u>hindi</u> madadaig o malupig o masupil o mapabulaan; 2] puedeng mabuntis

Impresario nagtatatag o namamahala ng mga palabas na nakakaaliw gaya ng *ballet, opera* at mga concierto-*Sp*

Impress pahangain niya ang iba sa sarili niya; Iloc: padayawan na ti bagi na cadagiti tattato

Impression 1] ang lumantad na pangkilala sa tao na bumuo sa pag-o-observa-*Sp* o pakikihalobilo sa taong ito; 2] bahagyang efecto-*Sp* o imahen-*Sp* ng isang bagay o letrato, 3] kusang idiniin na marka o marka-*Sp* na hindi sinadyang naiwang evidencia-*Sp* para sa crimen-*Sp*

Impressive kahanga-hanga; Iloc: nakadaydayaw

Imprint 1] diniing marka; 2] pahina kung saan ang pangalan, titulo, fecha ng paglathala o publicidad ng libro at iba pang informasyon

Imprison iculong, ibilanggo; Iloc: iculong, ibalud, ipupok, i-preso

Imprisoned nakaculong, nakabilanggo, nakabihag; Iloc: nakaculong, nakabalud, nakapupok, naka-preso-*Sp*, naka-calaboso-*Sp*
Correlated words
Prison bilangguan, bilibid, piitan, culongan; Iloc: pagbaludan, bilibid, carcel, pagculongan, calaboso
Prisoner bilanggo, preso; Iloc: balud, preso

Improbable malaking chansa na hindi tutoo o hindi mangyayari

Impromptu kaunti o walang preparasyon-*Sp* o biglaan lamang; Iloc: balabassit o awan preparasyon-*Sp* wenno dagdagos laeng

Improper hindi mabuti, hindi karapat-dapat, hindi tugma sa mabuting asal; Iloc: haan nga naimbag, haan nga rebbeng, haan nga umno iti nasayaat nga ugali

IMPROVE oneself nagpapakabuti; Iloc: agpakaimbag, agpakasayaat
Synonym
Reform magpakabuti sa pamamagitan ng pagtanggap ng kamalian niya para matanto ang sarili niyang pagkatao at ipasyaha niyang iwaksi ang canyang mga kasamaan; Iloc: agpakaimbag isu nga mang-acceptar iti madi nga ugali na mismo tapno aglucat ti mata na iti usto a katatao na ken irangta na nga iwaksi dagiti dakes nga aramid na

IMPROVE work husayan at pagbutihin ang trabaho; Iloc: palaengen ken paimbagen ti trabaho

Improvise kahit hindi sapat ang gamit at paghahanda at ginagamit lamang ang anomang materiales na nandoon, siya/sila ay nakakapagsagawa pa rin, nakakacompleto, makapagtanghal, tumotugtog

Imprudent *adj.*, **Imprudence** *n.* atrevido/da-*Sp*, hindi ginagamit ang isip at di nag-iingat, bara-bara

Impudent pilyo, salvahe, walang hiya, bastos, pangahas, fresco, walang galang

Impugn pintasan, batikosin at hamonin na ang salita, pakay, layonin ng iba ay falso o kaduda-duda

Impulse *n.*, **Impulsive** *adj.* sumisige siya sa fuersa-*Sp* na nagtutulak sa canya kaysa sa paggamit niya ng canyang isip; hindi sinasadyang biglaang pagsugod sa isang kilos nakakagiit o nakakahimok na fuersa sa kilos na basta na lamang lalabas; Iloc: agsumro iti dursok na

Impunity hindi binibigyan o napapalaya siya sa dapat niyang pananagutang sakdal, multa-*Sp* o parusa sa canyang kasalanan

Impure *adj.*, **Impurity** *n.* hindi puro o hindi malinis dahil nahaloan na o nahawaan na ng ibang elemento

Impute *v.*, **Imputation** *n.* pagturing o pagdangal na iukol o igawad sa nakakarapat; Iloc: pagbigbig o pagdayaw nga ipaay o isaad diay rebbeng a tao

IN sa, nasa, nasa loob; Iloc: idiay uneg, idiay

IN a bind, In a jam, In a fix, In a pickle, In a tight spot nasa masikip at mahirap na kalagayan, napailalim siya sa gusot at problema-*Sp*

IN black and white nakasulat o nakaprenta, *recorded* at ofisyal-*Sp* na documento-*Sp*

IN case sakali mang..., kung sakaling..., kung; Iloc: nu cas pagarigan, nu amangan nga

IN character tugma sa kagawiang asal o ugali at tunay na pagkatao niya

IN compliance to sumusunod sa/kay, alinsunod sa; Iloc: sumursurot iti/kenni

IN deep water nasa situasyon na mapanganib

IN due course, In due time magaganap sa inaasahang o tinakdang panahon

IN force gumagana pa, efectivo pa, *covered* pa, sacop pa; Iloc: may bisa pay, efectivo pay, *covered* pay, sacop pay

IN full swing kasalukuyang nagaganap at panay at patuloy na walang humpay ang pagsasagawa o pagkikilos o pag-aandar

IN good shape, In good condition (tungkol sa tao at sa malaki o maliit na mga kasangkapan) magaling, malakas at nakakagawa o ginagawa ng mahusay

IN hot water nasa kalagayang napahamak siya

IN kind kagamitan o ari-arian imbes na pera

IN lieu of something or somebody gumaganap o sumasagot para sa isang tao/grupo

IN one's element nasa canyang naturalesa at comfortableng kalagayan o kapaligiran o comfortableng lugar-*Sp* at panahon

IN progress nagaganap o nangyayari na ngayon sa kasalukuyang ito

IN re tungkol sa; Iloc: maygapu iti

IN season kung nasa kapanahumang puedeng mabili, mag-ani ng palay, o maggapas sa panahon ng lanzones, o manghuli ng alimango o ulang/ *lobster*

IN the same boat nasa parehong kalagayan o situasyon-*Sp*

IN the work hinahanda, pinaplano, isinasagawa

Inability walang cacayahan, kulang ng lakas, capacidad, abilidad at kaparaanan

Inaccessible *adj.*, **Inaccessibility** *n.* hindi puedeng matamo o magamit o mapasukan; Iloc: haan a mabalin nga maala o maaramat wenno maserkan

Inaccurate *adj.*, **Inaccuracy** *n.* hindi tama, hindi tutoo, mali; Iloc: haan nga usto, haan nga agpaypayso

Inaction wala man lang pag-aacecaso, walang kaobra-obra; walang ginagawa kahit mag-umpisa; Iloc: haan man lang nga agacecaso, haan man laeng nga agobra wenno agkuti wenno mangrugi

Inactivate hindi pagalawin, hindi paandarin

Inactive hindi kumikilos; Iloc: haan nga aggargaraw

Inadequacy *n.*, **Inadequate** *adj.* kakulangan, kulang; Iloc: kakurangan, kurang

Inadvertent nangyari o nagawa kahit hindi kinusang mangyari

Inane walang diwa at kahulogan; walang talino

Inappeasable hindi mapalubag ang loob, hindi maaliw o mapaginhawa, hindi mapahinahon o hindi napapayapa

Inappreciative hindi nakakaramdam ng kasiyahan sa kasiya-siyang bagay; hindi marunong kumilala ng utang na loob; walang pasalamat; hindi nalulugod o natutuwa sa karapat-dapat na kalugoran

Inappropriate hindi angkop o tama, hindi akma, mali; Iloc: haan a rebbeng wenno umno, haan nga usto-*Sp*
Antonym
Appropriate akma, angkop, bagay; Iloc: umno, naytutop, us-usto, rebbeng

Inaptitude walang cacayahan, ni abilidad, ni expiryensa o kaalaman

Inarticulate kulang o walang cacayahang magsabi, magpahayag o magpahiwatig ng maliwanag o naiintindihan na pananalita

Inasmuch as dahil sa ganyan; yamang ganyan; kung ganon ay; Iloc: nu casta, gapu ta casta

Inattentive pabaya at hindi nakikinig; walang-ingat kaya walang kamuang-muang kung nasa ligtas siyang lugar o mapanganib; nag-i-*imagine* o nagguguni-guni na walang siyang malay o hindi naririnig ang nangyayari

Inaudible hindi marining; Iloc: haan a mangngeg

Inborn pinanganak na ganyan; Iloc: nayyanak a casta

Incapable hindi caya; Iloc: haan na a cabaelan
Antonym
Capable caya, cayang-caya; Iloc: caya, cabaelan

Incapability *n.,* **Incapable** *adj.* kulang sa kinakailangan na abilidad o cacayahan at bisa, hindi makasagawa ng nararapat na husay; Iloc: kurang o haan na pulos caya.

Incapacitate salantahin, pinsalahin, sirain, ibaldado; Iloc: ibaldado, igawid wenno ipasardeng, dadaelen, aramiden nga haan nga ag-efecto-*Sp*

Incapacity kulang sa kinakailangang lakas o cacayahan; defecto-*Sp* o baldado; Iloc: kurang ti pigsa o cabaelan, adda defecto na

Incarcerate ibilanggo, iculong; Iloc: ibalud, ipreso

Incarnate <u>pagkatawang-tao</u> ni Dios Hesu Cristo noong tinanggap at tiniis Niya ang mga parusa ng mga kasalanan ng buong nilalang dahil sa pagmamahal Niya sa lahat ng tao

Incendiary *chemical* na madaling makasunog

Incense 1] pagalitin, 2] isang pampabango na nilalagay sa sasakyan o bahay o cuarto para kasiya-siya ang amoy ng lugar

Incentives *Now and then, incentives and opportunities come to light so be quick to notice those and grab them. However, you do not have to wait for incentives to emerge - you, yourself, can create an incentive on anything. This can be an incentive to live a happy life (have a happy disposition by considering the positive side of anything, greet or smile at anyone whether they smile back or not, be pleasant always, etc.), or incentive to raise yourself to a higher standard (i.e., pursue a higher education, reading good books, taking work seriously by being competent, efficient and learning more to establish expertise on the job, etc.), or become productive (i.e., using all your abilities, skills, talents, and expertise and even raising these to an excellent degree, etc.), or become a person with dignity and integrity (i.e., being God-abiding, practicing moral and ethical values always, being honest, trustworthy and reliable, being considerate of others, etc.).*

Inception kaumpi-<u>umpisa</u>hang fecha-*Sp* o fechang pagbubukas ng isang negosio-*Sp*, o pagtrabaho sa oficina, o ang pagkasakop ng naka-*insure* sa canyang *insurance policy*

Incessant walang tigil, patuloy-tuloy; Iloc: awan sardeng, agpatpatuloy laeng

Incest *n.*, **Incestuous** *adj.* crimen-*Sp* na pakikipagtalik ng *sexual* sa anak o kamag-anak at bawal ito sa batas at sa principio-*Sp* ng lahat ng tao sa buong mundo-*Sp*

Inch *(Tag. & Iloc.)* pulgada-*aSp*

Incident incidente-*Sp*, pangyayari; Iloc: incidente, pasamak

Incidental pangyayari na hindi binalak at walang kamuang-muang na mangyari

Incidentally siyanga pala...

Incidentals *minor expenses* o gastos na hindi makabulohan

Incise *v.*, **Incision** *n.* ang paghiwa sa balat o laman ng katawan na kinakailangan sa operasyong *medical*

Incite udyokin, ibuyo; Iloc: sulisogen, uyotan

Inclement 1] bagyo, 2] walang awa; Iloc: 1] bagyo, 2] awan asi

Incline tagilid, itagilid; Iloc: patingig, batwag, ipatingig, ibatwag

Inclined *adj.,* **Inclination** *n.* gawi o hilig na nakakapagtulak sa tao sa isang kilos o pagturing na naging bihasa na sa canya ito kahit hindi muna pinag-isipan kung ito ay nakakabuti o nakakasama

Include isali, isama, isacop, ibilang; Iloc: iraman, naybilang, nainayon, naysacop
Antonym
Exclude hindi isali, hindi isacop, iliban; Iloc: haan nga iraman, ilaksid

Including kabilang, kasali, contodo-*Sp,* pati; Iloc: kabilang, agraman, contodo, pati
Antonym
Excluding maliban ang, huera ang; Iloc: fuera ti, malaksid

Inclusive sinasaklaw o pinapalibutan o nilalaan ng lahat na nasabi; kasali lahat, sinasacop, nilalaman lahat-lahat na puedeng masacop nito
Synonyms
Comprehensive completo o napakalawak ang sinasacop; Iloc: completo wenno nakalawlawa ti sacop
Indepth sacop lahat ang detalye at tama at completo
Antonym
Exclusive exclusivo, binubukod lamang sa tinakdang bagay at hindi sinasali ang iba; Iloc: exclusivo, ibukbukod laeng iti naysaad a banag ken haan nga isali ti sabali

Incogitant walang considerasyon, walang pakialam; pabaya at hindi mapag-isip o mapagturing ng mga bagaybagay o ng kapwa; Iloc: awan ti biang na iti sabali ida

Incognito tinatago ang tunay na katauhan niya para hindi siya makilala; Iloc: ilemmeng na ti usto nga katatao na tapno haan isu a mabigbig

Incognizant walang kaalam-alam o pagkabatid; Iloc: haan na pulos ammo

Incoherent hindi angkop sa kasalukuyang situasyon-*Sp* o sa naturalesa-*Sp,* walang diwa, walang karason-rason, hindi maintindihan

INCOME sueldo-*Sp,* sahod, kinikita, compensasyon-*Sp;* Iloc: sueldo, kita, sapul, compensasyon

INCOME tax buis ng sueldo o kinita na dapat mapunta sa govierno

Incoming 1] ang dadating, ang sasapit; 2] ang susunod na kapalit ng umalis, ang kahalili

Incommensurate ang pagsisikap o tagal ng trabaho ay <u>hindi</u> kasukat o kapantay ng sueldo-*Sp*

Incommunicado walang karapatan o walang paraang makipagcomunicasyon o makipag-usap

Incommunicative tahimik, kimi, hindi mapagsalita, mahiyain

Incomparable hindi matutularan, walang kahambing, walang kaparis, walang kapantay, walang kawangis walang katulad; Iloc: haan a matulad, awan kapada na

Imcompatible hindi magkasundo kundi magkasalungat sila; Iloc: haan da nga agcanunong maysa ken maysa nu di agkacontra ti pammati wenno ugali da

Incompetent hindi makatupad ng tungkulin, hindi macayanan o kulang ang cacayahan; Iloc: haan a makatungpal ti trabaho, haan na macaya o kurang ti macaya na, haan na mabalinan

Incomplete *(Tag. & Iloc.)* hindi/haan completo-*Sp*

Incompliant hindi sumosunod, hindi tumutupad, mapagsuway; Iloc: agsupyat, madi nga agtungpal

Incomprehensible hindi maintindihan o napakahirap intindihin; Iloc: narigat o haan maawatan

Incomprehensive *adj.*, **Incomprehension** *n.* hindi makaintindi o hindi maintindihan

Inconceivable hindi maisip o mailarawan; hindi kapanipaniwala; Iloc: haan na mayretrato ti nakem na, haan a mapatpati

Inconclusive walang narating na resulta o kahihinatnan; walang kasagutan ang mga tanong at duda kaya walang pasya o kalutasan

Incondite masama o mahina o mali ang pagkayari, pagkapatayo; Iloc: nakapsut o madi ti pagkaaramid

Inconsiderate walang pakialam sa ikabubuti o pangangailangan ng kapwa; Iloc: salabusab, awan ti biang na iti makaimbag wenno iti kasapulan ti dadduma

Inconsistent hindi matatag kundi pabago-bago; Iloc: haan a natibker nu di agbaliw-baliw

Antonym

Consistent walang pagmamaliw, matatag; Iloc: awan ti pagbalbaliw, natibker

Inconspicuous hindi nakikita, hindi napapansin, hindi lantad; Iloc: haan a makita, haan a nakaparang

Incontinent *adj.,* **Incontinence** *n.* hindi mapigilan ang pag-ihi o pagtae dahil basta na lang lumalabas

Inconvenience abalahin, estorbohin, gambalahin, moleschahin; Iloc: mang-estorbo-*Sp*, mang-molescha-*Sp*

Incorporate isali o idagdag sa isang nakatatag nang bagay; Iloc: isali wenno inayon idiay maysa a sigud a nakasimpan a banag
Correlated word
    Integrate sumali sa o isali sa isang nakatatag nang bagay; Iloc: sumali idiay o isali daytoy idiay sigud a nakasimpan a banag

Incorrigible hindi maiwasto o di mabago, ni mareforma; Iloc: haan a maiyusto, ni maybalbaliw ken ni mareforma

Increase damihan, dagdagan; Iloc: nayonan, paadwen, ipaado, surokan
Synonym
    Add dagdagan, idagdag; Iloc: nayonan
Antonyms
    Decrease bawasan; Iloc: kissayan
    Subtract tanggalan, bawasan; Iloc: ikkatan, kissayan

Increased dumami; Iloc: immadu

Incredible hindi kapanipaniwala; Iloc: haan nga mapatpati

Increment dumadagdag sa dami o sa laki o sa lawak at kung gaano ang pagkatagal ng proceso-*Sp* ng mga ito

Incriminate *(Tag. & Iloc.)* acusahan/acusaren ng/iti crimen-*Sp*

Incubation 1] pag-aalaga ng manok sa canyang mga itlog para magpisang maging sisiw, 2] ang tiempo-*Sp* buhat sa mahawa hanggang lumabas ang sintoma-*Sp* ng infeksion-*Sp* sa katawan

Inculcate itanim sa isip (i.e., ng mga bata) sa pamamagitan ng firming pagtuturo at paghahalimbawa; Iloc: itanem ti panunot ti ubbing ti firme a pagisuro ken pag-ehemplo-*Sp*

Incumbent 1] ang kasalukuyang nakaupong ofisyal-*Sp* ng govierno-*Sp* o companya-*Sp;* 2] obligadong gawin

Incur magkaroon; Iloc: macaala

Incurable hindi na malunasan o gagaling; Iloc: haanen nga umimbag o maagasan
Correlated word
    Irremediable imposibleng maremedio o mapatama o mapaayos; Iloc: imposib-le a maremedioan o macorrehir o maareglo
Antonym

485

Curable magagamot, malunasan; Iloc: maagasan

Indebted *(Tag. & Iloc.)* nakautang

INDECENT hindi decente-*Sp*, walang *moral*, malaswa, mahalay, bastos; Iloc: haan nga decente-*Sp*, awan ti *moral*, bastos-*Sp*

INDECENT exposure ang crimeng paglalantad sa tao o sa publico ng parteng *sexual* sa katawan na labag sa batas at mabilanggo ang gumagawa nito

Indeed tutuo, talaga, husto-*Sp*, siempre-*Sp*; Iloc: talaga, usto-*Sp*, siempre

Indefatigable walang pagkapagod; Iloc: awan ti pagkabannog

Indefinite hindi claro-*Sp*, malabo, walang kasiguradohan, di decidido-*Sp*

Indemnify *v.*, **Indemnity** *n.* bilang proteksion kung may kapahamakang mangyari, ito ay compensasyon-*Sp* na pagtumbas na bayad sa nawala dahil sa sunog o accidente-*Sp* o pinsala o kamatayan o sa nawalang sahod
Correlated word
Insurance *insurance*, seguro, contrata para magkaroon ng compensasyon kung kailangan ang pagpapagamot sa katawan o compensasyon laban sa pagkasunog o pagkawala o pagkasira ng bahay o ari-arian o negosio o sasakyan

Independence *(Tag. & Iloc.)* independencia-*Sp*

Independent nagdedepende lamang sa sariling at walang tulong sa iba; Iloc: agdepdepende laeng iti bagi nga awan tulong ti sabali
Synonym
Stand on one's own two feet hindi magdepende sa iba kundi sinisiguro na sapat ang kinikita para caya lahat-lahat ng pangagailangan kaya nagsisikap at nagtitipid siya

Indepth sacop lahat ang detalye-*Sp* at tama at completo-*Sp*

Index finger *pointer finger*, hintuturo; Iloc: tammudo, ramay a pangtudo

Indicate *v.*, **Indication** *n.* ipahiwatig, pagpahiwatig; Iloc: indicasyon-*Sp*, ipaammo

Indicative nagpapahiwatig, nagpapaliwanag, binabanggit ang, hinggil sa

Indict ihabla o acusahan ng crimen-*Sp* sa husticia-*Sp*

Indifferent may pag-asta na malamig at walang pakialam at hindi interesado; Iloc: adda *attitude* na nga awan aniaman canyana ken awan biang na, haan nga interesado-*Sp* pay

Indigence *n.*, **Indigent** *adj.* *(Tag. & Iloc.)* pagkapobre

Indigenous pinagmulan o pinakaunang tao sa isang lugar-*Sp* o nasyon-*Sp*; katangian ng isang lugar o bayan; likas, katutubo, natural-*Sp*

Indigestion empacho-*Sp*, sakit ng chan; Iloc: empacho-*Sp*, sakit ti chan
Correlated word
Heartburn sinisikmura; Iloc: agrusrusok

Indignance *n.,* **Indignant** *adj.* galit, poot; Iloc: pungtot, rungsot

Indiscernible malabo, disimulado-*Sp*; Iloc: nacusnaw, disimulado

Indispensable kailangan pagtuonan ng pansin dahil ito ay kinakailangan at hindi dapat pabayaan dahil importante o obligasyon ito; Iloc: masapul nga asicaswen ta daytoy ken masapul nga haan nga liwayan ta importante daytoy wenno obligasyon.

Indisposed medio nakakaramdam ng sakit sa katawan na hindi caya ang magtrabaho; hindi payag

Indisputable ito ay valido-*Sp* o tunay ito kaya hindi dapat tanggihan o salungatan

Indistinct malabo, disimulado-*Sp*, mahirap makita; Iloc: nacusnaw, disimulado-*Sp*, narigat makita, nacudrep.
Correlated words
Undetected *(Tag. & Iloc.)* disimulado

Indiscernible malabo, disimulado; Iloc: disimulado

Individual isang tao; Iloc: maysa a tao

Indolent *adj.,* **Indolence** *n.* tamad; Iloc: sadot

Indomitable mahirap o imposibleng matalo dahil hindi sumusuko, hindi masupil o di malupig ang katapangan, at ang kalooban/ *will* o amor propio-*Sp*/*pride* ng tao o sundalo.

Indoor, Indoors loob ng bahay o gusali; Iloc: uneg ti balay wenno *building*

Induce udyokan, ibuyo; Iloc: sulisogen, uyotan

Indulge *v.,* **Indulgent** *adj.* pinagbibigyan ang sarili o mga anak sa canilang capricho-*Sp*; nagpapalugod

Industrious *Diligent; indefatigable; actively, conscientiously and eagerly working hard; vigorously busy in accomplishing a task or a purpose.*
Napakasipag, masigasig; Iloc: nakagaggaget, trabahador-*Sp*

Industry *(Tag. & Iloc.)* industriya-*Sp*

Indwell matira sa loob; Iloc: agyan diay uneg

Inebriate maglasing, lasingin; Iloc: agbartek, barteken

Ineffective, Ineffectual walang bisa, hindi tumatalab, hindi nag-e-efecto-*Sp*; Iloc: awan bisa, haan nga agtalab, haan nga ag-efecto
Antonym
Effective mabisa, tumatalab, umeefecto; Iloc: nabisa, agmamaay, agtaltalab, agef-efecto

Inefficient hindi macaya o walang cacayahan, hindi makagawa o makacompleto o makatulong; Iloc: haan na a macaya o awan ti cabaelan na, haan a makaaramid wenno maka-completo-*Sp* o makatulong
Antonyms
Efficient, Competent cayang-caya ang gawa at puedeng higit pa diyan, nakakatulong ng husto, nakakacompleto; Iloc: cayang-caya na ti obra ken mabalin a labes pay dita, makatulong ti usto, firmi a makacompleto

Inept walang kacayahan o abilidad-*Sp* o karanasang trabaho-*Sp* o kaalaman para matupad ang mahusay na paggawa; hindi naangkop sa gawain; Iloc: haan a makatungpal ti trabaho-*Sp*, haan na macaya o kurang ti macaya na, haan na mabalinan.

Inequality hindi pantay-pantay o hindi pare-parehong pagturing at pag-trato-*Sp*; Iloc: haan nga agpatag o haan agpapada ti pag-estimar-*Sp* o pagtrato

Inevitable hindi mailagan dahil seguradong mangyayari; Iloc: haan nga malisyan ta adda kaseguradoan na nga mapasamak

Inexcusable hindi puedeng patawarin o ipagpaumanhin; Iloc: haan mabalin a mapakawan o ma-dispensar-*Sp*

Inexpensive mura, barato-*Sp*; Iloc: nalaca
Antonym
Expensive mahal; Iloc: nangina

Inexperienced bagito, bagohan; Iloc: agdamdamo, kabarbaro
Synonym
Unaccustomed nababaguhan dahil hindi niya kagawian; Iloc: maycawa gapu ta haan na nakayruaman
Antonym
Experienced expiryensado sa mga obra at sa kabuhayan dahil sa mga naranasan at mga nakuhang kaalaman dahil sapat sa pagsasagawa ng mga gawain; Iloc: expiryensado cadagiti ob-obra ken pagbibiag gapu cadagiti nalasatan ken napagpasaran na ken nakaala iti sirib gapu iti pagob-obra na cadagiti maar-aramid

Infallible perfecto na katangian ng Dios, hindi nagkakamali, hindi nagkakasala kaya buong mapagkakatiwalaan Siya

Infamy *n.,* **Infamous** *adj.* nakakahiya at napakasamang pagkakakilala o reputasyon-*Sp*

Infant, Infancy sanggol, musmos; Iloc: tagibi

Infanthood pagkamusmos; Iloc: pagkatagibi

Infatuation may *crush* o may cursonada sa babae o sa lalake na napupusoan

Infect mainfectahan, hawaan, makasagap ng sakit; Iloc: maacaran, nayyalis, infectaran (infecta/infectar-*Sp*)

Infection *(Tag. & Iloc.) infection*

Infectious nakakahawa, nakakainfecta; Iloc: makaacar, makaalis, maka-infectar-*Sp*
Correlated word
Virulent sobrang nakakahawa, nakakalason o napakamaligno

Infer ipahiwatig, pagpahiwatig; Iloc: indicasyon-*Sp*

Inferior mas mababa ang ranko, mumurahin, mababang uri, pangit ang pagkagawa, kaunti ang naibibigay na ventahe-*Sp*

Inferiority complex mababa ang turing sa sarili, walang confiansa sa sarili

Inferno impierno-a*Sp*; Iloc: infierno-*Sp*

Infertile hindi makaanak, baog; Iloc: baog

Infidel ang tawag ng mga Islam o Muslim sa mga hindi Muslim o kaanib

Infidelity ang pangangaliwa-*cheating* ng may asawa dahil sa paki-kipagtalik niya sa iba

Infiltrate pagpasok ng tao bilang miembro sa isang grupo para mag-espia o para gumawa ng pinsala sa grupo

Infinite walang hanggan, walang katapusan; Iloc: awan ti patinggana, awan ti gibus na

Infirm mahina at may sakit; Iloc: nacapsot ken agsakit

Inflammable, Flammable madaling masunog o mag-apoy; Iloc: nalaca nga agapoy wenno aguram
Synonyms
Incendiary *chemical* na nakakasanhi ng sunog
Combustible madaling makasunog; Iloc: nalaca a makauram

Inflate 1] lagyan ng hangin o gas, 2] palakihin o ipataas ang turing kahit hindi tunay

Deflate 1] palabasin ang hangin o gas sa bola, 2] paliitin ang laki o importancia

Inflection 1] pag-iba-iba ng tono ng boses-*Sp* - tumaas o bumaba; 2] ang pagbabago ng forma ng salita gaya ng *"s"* na *plural* sa Ingles o *"'s"* na *possessive* sa Ingles o "-ed" na *past tense* sa Ingles; *paradigm* ng salita

Inflict saktan ang kapwa sa katawan o sa kalooban

Influence mag-influwensia-*Sp,* hikayatin, himokin, sulsolan; Iloc: suliso-gen, awisen, influwenciaan, isungsong

Influential nakakahimok at nakakahikayat sa mga tao

Influenza, Flu *(Tag. & Iloc.)* trangkaso-*Sp, flu*

Influx pagdagsa, dumogin; Iloc: agcarambola, aribongbongan

Inform ipaalam, ipabatid, ipahayag, ibalita; Iloc: ipakaammo, ipadamag
Synonyms
Reveal ipagtapat, isiwalat, ibunyag; Iloc: isawang
Publicize ilathala; Iloc: iwarnak, isurat diay periodico
Impart ipaalam, ipahayag; Iloc: ipaammo, isawang

Informal usapang pangcaraniwan na hindi gaya ng pagsusulat na *formal*, kung pangceremonya naman, ito ay *"come as you are"* o magbihis pang-araw-araw na kasuotan o damit na pangcaraniwan lamang
Antonym
Formal sumusunod sa tamang asal o regulasyon; kung pangceremonya naman, ito ay *formal* o magarbo magdamit; Iloc: sumursurot iti nasayaat a tignay ken regulasyon; nu pangceremonya met, daytoy ket *formal* ken naarkos

Information imformasyon-*Sp,* balita, pahayag; Iloc: informasyon, damag

INFORMED decision *Decision made after **learning** about **relevant** **facts** and **information** on a subject or on one that one wants to make a consideration on. This can be about a medical treatment one needs to undergo; or what career to pursue; or what house or car to buy; or if relocation to another community or country is advisable, etc. Since ailments and medical treatments have <u>time constraints</u>, information from the doctors and learning more about the disorder and treatment would suffice, so the scheduled treatment set up by the doctor has to be complied with. If there is no time constraints, the subject matter has to be studied, researched and scrutinized, thought of in details*

490

*and evaluated before one comes to a verifiably wise decision. With
all that, one still has to consider safety, affordability, manageability
and convenience, and if it is right time and the most rational course
to undertake.* Bago magpasiya ng mga importanteng decisyon,
mag-*research* at humiling ng payo para malaman at makagawa ng
pinakatamang pasya na makakabigay-ligtas at buti sa buhay, gaya
halimbawa kung binabalak magtrabaho sa ibang lugar, kailangang
mag-*research* bilang dagdag sa mga ibinabalita sa pahayagan at TV,
kung abot-caya ang marangyang titirhan doon o simp-le lamang
na matuloyan sa sueldo na itatakda, kung makakaunlad sa pag-
ka-empleado, kung ano ang mga binibigay na *perks* ng companya
(*medical-dental coverage, vacation leave, sick leave,* mga omento,
mga *promotion* na puedeng maabot sa pagpapakitang-gilas at iba pa),
kung hindi magulo ang pook na titirhan doon, kung maayos ang viahe
papunta't pabalik sa oficina, *etc.*

INFORMED medical consent isang forma-*Sp* na pinipirmahan ng
paciente-*Sp* na nagpapahiwatig na sumasang-ayon siya sa operasyon-*Sp*
o *procedure* (*colonoscopy, blood transfusion, appendectomy, knee* o
hip replacement) o iba pa na gagawin sa canya, at pinapaalam sa canya
sa pagpapahayag at sa babasahing papel ang mga panganib-*risk* na
puedeng mangyayari gaya ng pagdudugo, infeksion, o posibilidad na
may mahiwa o matusok na *body organ* o kamatayan kahit na maliit
lamang na magkatutoo iyon o posibleng malaki.

Informer nagsusuplong ng informasyon sa otoridad

Infraction gawaing labag sa batas o sa alituntunin, pumasok na walang
pahintulot; Iloc: aramid nga haan nalinteg wenno haan sumursurot iti
reglamento, sumrek nga awan ti palubos

Infrequent bihira, pambihira lamang, madalang, bahagya; Iloc: manmano,
sagpaminsan

Infringe labag sa batas o sa alituntunin na pumasok, mangopia, o
umangkin na walang pahintulot; Iloc: haan a nalinteg wenno haan
sumursurot iti reglamento a sumrek, mangala o agcopiar nga awan ti
palubos canyana

Infuriate pagalitin, pasiklabin ang poot; Iloc: papungtoten

Ingenious *adj.*, **Ingenuity** *n.* mapaglikha at matalas ang intelihensia-*Sp* sa pag-iimbento

Ingénue *[an-zhuh-noo]* inocenteng dalagita; Iloc: inocente-*Sp* a balasitang

Ingrate ingrato-*Sp*, walang utang na loob, walang pagpapasalamat; Iloc: ingrato, awan ti pagyamyaman na

Ingratiate tacticang pagpapakita ng kasiya-siya para babalik sa canya ang favor

Ingredient sangkap, sahog; Iloc: sagpaw

Inhabit dumating para doon matira; Iloc: sumangpet tapno agtaeng ken agyan idiay

Inhabitant ang nakatira doon, residente-*Sp*

INHALE lumanghap, sumamyo; Iloc: aglang-ab
  Antonym
  Exhale humingang palabas; Iloc: agsang-aw

INHALE and exhale huminga; Iloc: aganges

Inhaler aparato-*Sp* na paluluwagin ang paghinga sa mga may sakit na hika o *asthma*

Inherent *(Tag. & Iloc.)* naturalesa-*Sp*, natural-*Sp*, katutubo, katatao, likas

Inherit *v.* manahin; Iloc: matawid, ma-erencia-*Sp*

Inheritance mana; Iloc: tawid, erencia-*Sp*

Inhibit hadlangan, pigilan, hindi payagan

Inhibited alam man o walang kamalay-malay dahil sa bihasang gawi o pagkamahiyain, tinitimpi ang sarili, kinikimkim, sinusugpo, at pinipigilan ang sarili

Inhibition 1] paghahadlang, pagbawalan; 2] hindi makapagsiwalat ng kanyang damdamin gaya ng mga daing at taghoy kundi kinikimkim na lamang niya sa loob; Iloc: 1] pagbarra, haan agpalubos; 2] haan a makasawang iti ricricnaen na casla iti sennaay ken pag-asug nu di ipempen na laeng diay uneg na

Inhuman, Inhumane walang awa, ni simpatiya, ni habag; malupit

Iniquity kasalanan; Iloc: basol

Initial *n.*, **Initialize** *v.* maikling firma o lagda na isulat lamang ang mga tatlong pangunahing letra ng pangalan at dalawang apelyido-*Sp*, halimbawa ang *initial* ni John Fitzgerald Kennedy ay JFK (FK ay ang dalawang apelyido)

Initially una, nauna, sa umpisa; Iloc: umuna, immuna, diay rugi

Initiate pambungad na iharap at ipaalam ang bagong kagampanan, bagong kakayahan, bagong pagsasagawa para makapag-umpisa na dito sa bagong larangan

Initiation sa pagtanggap ng gustong magmiembro sa *fraternity*, pinapadanas muna sila sa *hazing* na pagsusubok o *test* sa canila pero kung minsan labag-sa-batas dahil nasosobrahan ang karahasan ng pagsubok

Initiative anomang nakakatulak o nakakabigay-gana-*Sp* para maisagawa

Inject mag-iniksion; Iloc: ag-*injection*

Injure *(Tag. & Iloc.)* saktan at sugatan

Injury sugat, galos; Iloc: dunor, sugat

Injurious makasugat, makasakit; Iloc: makadunor, makasugat, makasakit

Injustice kawalang-katarungan; Iloc: awan ti kalintegan

Ink *(Tag. & Iloc.)* tinta-*Sp*

Inkling muang, malinggit na pagkaalam; Iloc: balabassit nga pagkaammo

Innate natural-*Sp*, pinanganak na ganoon o meron na noon; Iloc: natural, nay-yanak nga casdiay wenno addaan ti casdiayen idi pay ubing

Inner kalooban, sa loob ng katawan o ng bahay o gusali o cueva-*Sp*; Iloc: diay uneg ti bagi o balay o stractura o cueva

Innermost, Inmost pinakaloob-looban; Iloc: kaunegan

Innocence *(Tag. & Iloc.)* pagka-inocente-*Sp*

Innocent *(Tag. & Iloc.)* inocente-*Sp*

Innovate *v.,* **Innovation** *n.,* **Innovative** *adj.* mag-imbento o mag-umpisang gamitin ang paraan o *idea*; unang pagpakilala sa publico-*Sp* ng bagong-bagong na-imbento-*Sp*

Innuendo parinig na paninira at panglait; Iloc: pasagid a pangpasakit o panglais

Inpatient pacienteng ginagamot sa ospital; Iloc: paciente-*Sp* nga masapul nga maospital para agasan *(not to be mistaken with Impatient)*
Correlated word
Outpatient nagpapagamot na paciente na <u>hindi</u> kinakailangan na maospital; Iloc: agpapaagas a paciente nga <u>haan</u> a masapul a maospital

Input 1] sikap, aparato-*Sp*, enerhia-*Sp* na pinapasok para tumakbo ang makina ng mahusay, 2] contribusyon-*Sp* na informasyon-*Sp* o comentario-*Sp* na puedeng magamit sa paghayag

Inquire magtanong, mag-usisa; Iloc: agsaludsod, agusisa, agdamag

Inquisitive osyoso, pakialamero; Iloc: osyoso, mapagbibiang

Ins and outs mga detalye-*Sp* ng ano mang bagay-bagay o pangyayari

Insane *adj.,* **Insanity** *n.* baliw, pagkabaliw; Iloc: bagtit, balla, pagkaballa

Inscribe *(Tag. & Iloc.)* prenta, ukit, sulat/surat

Inscription 1] kasulatan, marka o larawan sa lapida-*Sp*; 2] ang kasulatang pag-aalay sa isang libro-*Sp*

Insect *insect,* kulisap, insecto-*Sp*; Iloc: *insect,* insecto

Insecure *adj.,* **Insecurity** *n.* 1] walang confiansa-*Sp* sa sarili at sa canyang kacayahan at nag-aalangang makisama sa mga tao; 2] hindi matatag, umuuga; Iloc: 1] awan confiansa na ti mismo-*Sp* a cabaelan na ken maycawa a makicadcadua iti tattao; 2] haan a natibker, nalucay

INSERT isilid, isingit, ilakip; Iloc: iyuneg, ipastrek, iserrek

INSERT through a hole isulot, isilid; Iloc: isullot

INSIDE sa loob; Iloc: diay uneg

INSIDE out, Inverted baligtad, balintuad; Iloc: balictad

Insidious disimulado-*Sp* o lihim na gumagawa at nagpapalaganap ng nakakasama o nakakapatay o nakakapinsala o nakakasira

Insight *n.,* **Insightful** *adj.* nalalaman kaagad ang tunay na naturalesa o kalikasan o katutubong ugali sa pamamagitan ng katalinohan; malalim na paningin ng utak; kacayahang makita ang kaloob-loobang ugali o ang katotohanang hindi lantad sa iba; nalalaman sa sarili o sa kapwa ang pinagmulan ng problema ng emosyon at ang palakad ng pag-iisip, at nakikita ang fuersa na nakakaudyok para gumawa; intelihenteng mag-isip o mag-asal; may paningin at panturing at pangdamdam ng kalooban ng iba, matalas na pagpapalugod at pagpapahalaga ng nararapat, at matinik na pagkakakilala ng mabuti sa masama

Insincere hipocrito/ta-*Sp,* nagsasalita o umaasal o nakikipag-ugnayan na contra-*Sp* sa canyang damdamin at isip; Iloc: hipocrito/ta, agsarsarita o agtigtignay o makigayyem nga contra ti ricna na ken panunot na

Insinuate nagpapahiwatig, at nagpaparamdam; Iloc: mangpaammo iti pagpasagid.

Correlated words

Innuendo parinig na paninira at panglait; Iloc: pasagid a pangpasakit o panglais

Imply nagpapahiwatig na hindi derechohan ang tinutukoy

Subtle malabo at hindi disimuladong pananalita na mahirap maintindihan na misterio o panglait o makatraidor

Hint malabong pahiwatig o pangparamdam; Iloc: nacudrep a pangpaammo wenno pangparicna

Insipid 1] hindi nakakabigay ng gana-*Sp* o interes-*Sp*, 2] walang lasa; Iloc: haan makaited ti interes o raman

Insist igiit; Iloc: ipapilit

Insistent mapilit, namimilit, makulit; Iloc: napilit, makulit

Insolvent *adj.*, **Insolvency** *n.* hindi makabayad ng utang, *bankrupt*

Insomnia hindi makatulog; Iloc: di makaturog

Inspect mag-*inspection*; Iloc: ag-*inspection*

Inspection *(Tag. & Iloc.) inspection*

Inspiration *(Tag. & Iloc.)* inspirasyon-*Sp*

Inspired *(Tag. & Iloc.)* inspirado-*Sp*, ganado-*aSp*

Inspiring nakakabigay-ganang tularan; Iloc: maka-ganas nga tuladen (gana/ ganas-*Sp*)

Inspite of bagamat, bagaman; Iloc: uray pay

Install itayo, i-puesto-*Sp*; Iloc: isimpa, i-plastar-*Sp*, i-puesto

Instant, Instantaneous kaagad-agad; Iloc: dagdagos

Instead sa halip, imbes-*Sp*; Iloc: imbes

Instigator tagasulsol; Iloc: tagasungsong

Instill <u>ikintal o itanim</u> sa mga bata ang pinagsasandigang mabuting gawi ng familya, at harinawang sila ay sumonod upang matuwid ang pag-iisip nila at mapagmahal ang puso nila at responsab-le at marangal ang gawi at asal nila para makakabuti sa canila.
Correlated word
Inculcate itanim sa isip (i.e., ng mga bata) sa pamamagitan ng firmi at patuloy na pagtuturo at paghahalimbawa

Instinct natural-*Sp* o katutubo o kalikasan o pinanganak na asal at pagturing at damdamin at pagkatao.

Instinctive natural-*Sp* o katutubong asal na pinanganak, likas at kusa pero walang *premeditation* o pagpaplano o paghahanda.

Institute magpatayo, magtatag, mag-puesto-*Sp*; Iloc: agpatacder, mang-plastar-*Sp*, mangsimpa, mangbangon, mang-puesto-*Sp*

Institution *(Tag. & Iloc.)* institusyon-*Sp*, lugar-*Sp* ng educasyon-*Sp* o lugar-*Sp* ng mga kailangang alagaan/taraknen.

Instruct turoan; Iloc: surwan

Instruction *instruction,* tagubilin, leksion-*Sp*; Iloc: *instruction,* leksion, bilin

Instrument(s) *apparatus,* aparato-*Sp,* kagamitan, kasangkapan, instrumento-*Sp*; Iloc: *apparatus,* aparato, instrumento

Insubordinate mapagsuway, suwail; Iloc: nasupring, nasukir

Insufficient kulang, hindi sapat, hindi kasya; Iloc: kurang, haan makaanay
Antonyms
Sufficient, Adequate sapat, casia; Iloc: umanay, bastante

Insulate *v.,* **Insulation** *n.* paglagay ng materyales-*Sp* sa pader ng bahay para hindi pumasok o lumabas ang init o lamig o ingay

Insult insultohin, hamakin, laitin, supalpalin; Iloc: laisen, insultoen (insulto-*Sp*)

Insurance *insurance,* seguro-*Sp,* contrata-*Sp* para magkaroon ng compensasyon-*Sp* kung kailangan ng pagpapagamot sa katawan o compensasyon-*Sp* laban sa pagkasunog o pagkawala o pagkasira ng bahay o ari-arian o negosio-*Sp* o sasakyan

Insurrection *n,* **Insurgency** *n.,* **Insurgent** *adj.* pag-alsa na pagrebelyon, pag-rebelde-*Sp* sa otoridad-*Sp* o govierno-*Sp*

Intact buo, buong-buo, completo-*Sp* lahat; Iloc: sibubukel nga entero-*Sp,* completo amin
Synonym
Solid buong-buo at walang butas o basag; Iloc: sibubukel ken awan pulos ti abut, awan butbot wenno buong

Intangible hindi nakikita o nahahawakan o naririnig o natitikman o naamoy; hindi maipaliwanag o isalin, hindi magampanan o matupad

Integral tungkol sa parte/kasapi na nakakapagbuo at kapag wala ito ay hindi nabubuo

Integrate 1] sumali sa o isali sa isang nakatatag na ano man, 2] tanggapin ang isang lahi o grupo-*Sp* na maging miembro-*Sp* ng bayan o ng kanilang lipunan; Iloc: 1] sumali idiay o isali daytoy idiay sigud a nakasimpa nga aniaman, 2] akceptaren ti maysa nga lahi wenno grupo nga agmiembro iti bayan wenno iti asosasyon-*Sp.*

Integrity integridad-*Sp,* pagkakaroon ng etico-*Sp* at moralidad-*Sp* at dignidad-*Sp,* marangal na nabubuhay; Iloc: integridad, addaan etico ken moralidad ken dignidad, nadayaw ti pagbibiag na.

Intellect *n.,* **Intellectual** *adj.* ang abilidad-*Sp* na matuto at magrason; maraming kaalaman at mataas na pag-intindi

Intelligence *n.,* **Intelligent** *adj.* 1] intelihensia-*Sp,* talino, katalinohan, karunongan, dunong, 2] lihim na kaalaman at plano ng *security* ng bayan; Iloc: 1] intelihensia-*Sp,* kasiriban, sirib, kaammoan; 2] lihim na kaalaman at plano ng *security* iti nasyon.

Correlated words

Wisdom maraming kaalaman at karunongan; Iloc: adu a kaamoan ken sirib

Knowledge kaalaman, karunongan, talino, muwang, dunong Iloc: sirib, dagiti ammo

Acumen, Keen intellect katalasan ng isip; Iloc: kasiriban

Perspective perspectivo, pananaw at pagturing sa mga pangyayari at paligid at tao; Iloc: perspecivo, pagkita ken pangbigbig cadagiti kasasaad ken arrubayan ken tattao

Common sense talinong nakakakilala kung ano ang ligtas at makakabuti sa tao o kalagayan; pero kung minsan sa caraniwang tao, *"Common sense is not common"*; Iloc: sirib nga mangbigbig nu ania ti adayo ti peggad ken pagimbagan iti tao ken ti situasyon, ngem nu dadduma agliwliway iti tattao

Insight *n.,* **Insightful** *adj.* intelihenteng pagkaalam, paningin at panturing at pangdamdam ng kalooban ng iba, matalas na pagpapalugod at pagpapahalaga ng nararapat, at matinik na pagkakakilala ng mabuti at masama

Hindsight ang abilidad na pag-intindi, pagkatapos ng isang pangyayari, kung ano ang dapat na ginawa o kung ano ang dahilan na nangyari ang pangyayari; ang pagkilala sa mga katotohanan at kahalagahan ng pangyayari, ang posibilidad o pupuedeng mangyari, at mga kinakailangan (*requirements)* ng isang situasyon, decisyon at iba pa na nangyari na noong nakaraan

Intelligent napakatalino, napakataas ang pag-obra-*Sp* ng canyang utak, intelihente-*Sp,* matalino; Iloc: nakasirsirib, nakangatngato ti pag-obra ti utek na, intelihente, nasirib

Correlated words

Smart 1] madaling makapag-isip ng mabuti at makapagtugma sa pabago-bagong circumstancia; 2] smarte, pusturioso, elegante

Clever mautak, matalas, matinik; Iloc: nasirib

Wise matalino, mautak, matalas, matinik; Iloc: nasirib, intelihente

Knowledgeable marunong, maraming kaalaman; Iloc: nasirib, adu ti ammo

Versatile maraming kaalaman at kacayahan o abilidad at talento; Iloc: addaan iti adu nga sirib ken cabaelan o abilidad ken talento

Erudite, *adj,* **Erudition** *n.* maraming napag-aralan at maraming kaalaman; Iloc: adu ti naadal ken adu ti ammo na

Perspicacious matalas ang utak na siya ay nakakatanto; Iloc: nasirib ti nakem nga maka-amiris isu

Pundit maraming alam at matalinong tao; Iloc: adu ti ammo ken nasirib a tao

Genius *genius,* taong napakataas ang intelihensia na wala sa caraniwang tao; Iloc: *genius,* tao nga nakangatngato ti intelihensia na nga awan cadagiti ordinaryo a tao

Foresight 1] talino sa paghahanda at pagfondo ng kinabukasan kahit ano man ang mangyayari; 2] may *prescience* o kaalaman bago dumating

Prudent maingat at magaling magturing ng karapat-dapat at magaling din maghanda sa hinaharap, iniisip muna bago magsalita o bago sumige sa dapat gagawin

Shrewd matalino at matanto niya ang kalagayan o katatao ng iba; Iloc: nasirib ken maamiris na ti kasasaad wenno kababalin ti tao

Judicious nararapat na pagturing o paghatol, napakaingat, matalino at makatwiran

Intend tangkain; Iloc: panggepen

Intended for para, naukol sa/kay, nakalaan sa/kay; Iloc: para, agpaay ti/ken ni, naytutop para ti/ken, naysaad para ti/ken ni

Intense matindi, masidhi; Iloc: nacaro, napalalo

Intensity tindi, sidhi; Iloc: nauneg ti pagkacaro

Intent, Intention intension-*Sp,* balak, kusa, tangka, layonin; Iloc: intension, pakay, panggep, rangta

Intentionally sinadya, nagkusa; Iloc: inggagara
> *Correlated words*
> **Deliberate** sinadya, kusa; Iloc: inggagara
> **Will** kagustuhan, kalooban; Iloc: kagustoan, *intention*
> **Volition** kusa; Iloc: intension, gagara
> **Purposefully** sinadya, kusa; Iloc: inggagara

Interact pag-ugnayan o pagtugonan sa asal, pakikisama, pakikitungo; Iloc: maki-annugotan, makibagay

Interest *(Tag. & Iloc.)* interest

Interested *(Tag. & Iloc.)* interesado-*Sp*

Interesting kawili-wili; Iloc: makalinglingay

Interfere makialam, manghimasok; Iloc: makibiang, ag-meter-*Sp*

498

Interim 1] pagitan ng dalawang tiempo-*Sp*, 2] panahon kung kelan kaaalis lamang ang dating nasa puesto-*Sp* at ngayon ay ang pagkuha ng temporaryong kapalit habang wala pang itinakdang permanenteng uupo sa puestong iyon

Interior *see Internal below*

Interlope pumasok o sumali na walang karapatan gaya ng querida-*Sp* ng palikerong asawa; Iloc: sumrek o sumali nga awan linteg o rebbeng na

Interment libing, burol; Iloc: pamumpon, tabun

Intermission patlang o puwang o pansamantalang pagtigil ng gawain o pagpalakad

Intermittent naghahaliling huminto at pagkatapos mag-umpisa uli; Iloc: agsinnublat nga agsardeng ken agrugi

INTERNAL kalooban, sa loob ng katawan o bahay/gusali o cueva-*Sp*; Iloc: diay uneg ti bagi o balay/facilidad-*Sp* o cueva
Antonym
External, Exterior sa labas; Iloc: adda ti ruar

INTERNAL organs *entrails,* mga lamang-loob; Iloc: e*ntrails,* lalaem ti uneg ti bagi

International tungkol sa dalawa o mas marami pa sa dalawa na mga nasyon

Internet napakalaking *computer telecommunication network* na conectado sa mas maliliit na *computer networks* sa buong mundo na ang mga ito ay iba't iba gaya ng comercio, educasyon, govierno at iba pa

Interpolate 1] ipakilala o isingit o ipasok ang ano man sa pagitan ng mga bagay o parte-*Sp* nito; 2] gumawa ng pagbabago sa pamamagitan ng pagsingit ng bagong bagay para makapanlinlang na walang otorisasyon-*Sp*

Interpret *v.,* **Interpretation** *adj.* interpretasyon-*Sp*, pagpapaliwanag para maintindihan ng husto-*Sp* kung ano ang kahulogan ng sinasabi, o pagsasalin sa sariling wika ang ibang wika
Correlated words
Paraphrase pag-explica o pagsasalin ng salita o kasulatan o ibang wika para maintindihan; Iloc: pag-explicar wenno pagpatarus ti sarita o ti naysurat o ti sabali a lengguahe tapno maawatan
Translate namamagitan sa dalawang taong magkaiba ang wika o lengguahe para isalin sa bawat wika ang ibig sabihin ng bawat isa

Interrelation mabuting paggagantihan sa mabuting pag-uugnayan at pagsapi-sapi nila sa isa't isa

Interrogate usisahin, kilatisin, usigin; Iloc: usisaen, usigen

Interrupt magsabad, gambalain, antalahin, estorbohin; Iloc: agmeter-*Sp*, estorbohin (estorbo-*Sp*), taktaken

Intersection *crossroad,* dalawang calsadang may apat na pasokan sa gitna o *crossing* na nagletrang cruz (letra-*Sp*, cruz-*Sp*) na magbagtasan at magsalubongan sa gitna nito na may *signal lights* para sa paghali-haliling pagdaan ng mga sasakyan sa bawat calsada

Correlated word

Junction dalawang calye na nagletrang "T" kung saan sila magkacabit o magkasalubong pero ang isa dito ay doon na ang hangganan o katapusan; Iloc: dua a calsada nga agletra nga "T" nga agkacabit o agsabat da ngem maysa a calsada ket ditoyen ti patinggana nan

Interstate *highway* na dumadaan sa malalaking bayan ng 48 na *states* ng USA *(i.e., I-80 or Interstage-80)*

Interval pagitan; Iloc: nagbaetan

Intervene mang-awat sa pagtatalo ng dalawang panig; Iloc: mang-anawa iti pag-argumento-*Sp* ti dua a panig

Interview makipanayam para mag-*interview*; Iloc: makipatang para ti *interview*

Intestate walang *legal will* o *last will and testament* na iniwan sa familya-*Sp*

Intestine bituka; Iloc: bituka, bagis

Intimacy *n.,* **Intimate** *adj.* napakamalapitang relasyon-*Sp* sa isa't isa, napaka-*personal* na pag-uugnayan; Iloc: nakaper-*personal* nga relasyon caniada a dua

Intimidate inisin, suyain; Iloc: ruroden, paguraen

Intimidation *(Tag. & Iloc.)* intimidasyon-*Sp*, pananakot na may kasamang pagbabala; Iloc: mangcarit tapno agbuteng

Intolerant hindi nagpaparaya o nagpapahintulot; Iloc: mangiparparit

Intoxicate lasingin, maglasing; Iloc: barteken, agbartek

Intravenous pinapasok sa sa loob ng ugat; Iloc: iserrek iti uneg ti urat

Intrepid walang takot; Iloc: awan ti buteng na

Intrigue *arouse*/pukawin ang *interest* o *curiosity*; intrigahin; gumamit ng tacticong panlinlang

Introduce ipakilala, magpakilala; Iloc: iyam-ammo, maki-am-ammo

Introvert contento-*Sp* siyang mag-isa dahil siya'y mahiyain o hindi mapakali na makipag-halobilo sa tao

Antonym

Extrovert, Gregarious mahilig makihalobilo sa mga kapwa-tao; Iloc: magustuan na ti maki-ummong ken makipagsosyalan iti tattao

Intrude makialam, mag-meter-*Sp*, manghihimasok; Iloc: agsampitaw, ag-meter-*Sp*, makibiang

Intrusive entremetido/da-*Sp*, pakialamero/ra, mapanghimasok; Iloc: entre-metido/da, miron-*Sp*, agbibiang

Intuit *v.*, **Intuition** *n.*, **Intuitive** *adj.* agad-agad at matalas ang paki-ramdam o paningin sa mga katotohanan kahit hindi maipaliwanag ito at hindi caraniwan sa tao; malaman o madiscob-re-*Sp* sa pamamagitan ng *intuition*

Inundate magbaha; Iloc: aglayos

Inure pasanayin, magpabihasa; Iloc: iruam

Inutile inutil-*Sp*, walang silbi; Iloc: inutil, awan servi-*Sp*

Invade *v.*, **Invasion** *n.* lusobin, sacopin, pasoking sapilitan ng fuersa-*Sp*; Iloc: sacopin, serken a fuersa

Invalidate ipawalang bisa; Iloc: ikkaten wenno paawanen ti bileg o turay

Invaluable walang halaga, hindi makabigay ng buti; Iloc: awan servi na, awan mayted na nga imbag

Invasive 1] paglusob o panghimasok na labag, pagpasok na fuersa-*Sp* na walang pahintulot; 2] *Medical* pagpasok ng carayom o *cathether* o ibang instrumento-*Sp* sa loob ng katawan para sa examinasyon-*Sp* at pagsusuri ng kalagayan ng paciente-*Sp*

Invective pagmumura; Iloc: panglalais

Inveigle *arouse*-pukawin at hikayatin at himokin at udyokan at sulsolan ang canyang victima-*Sp* sa paggamit niya ng canyang tactica-*Sp* at pagkukunwari at pagbabalat-kayo para maisagawa niya ang canyang layonin na nakakaventahe-*Sp* lamang sa canya kahit nakakaagraviado sa victima-*Sp*; Iloc: mangisungsong tapno makapag-oportunista-*Sp* iti victima na.

Invent mag-imbento-*Sp*, maglikha; Iloc: ag-imbento, agparnuay

Invention imbension-*Sp*; Iloc: imbension, parnuay

Invert baligtarin; Iloc: balictaden

Invest mag-*invest*, mamuhonan; Iloc: mag-*invest*, agpuonan

Investigate magsiyasat, siyasatin, mag-imbestiga-*Sp*, magsuri, mag-usisa, mag-usig; Iloc: ag-imbestigar-*Sp*, agusig, sukimaten, sukisoken, agusisa

Investigation *(Tag. & Iloc.)* imbestigasion-*Sp*

Investigator *(Tag. & Iloc.)* imbestigador-*Sp*

Invigorate gumagaling na at nagkakaroon na ng lakas, sigla, sigasig at lusog sa katawan; Iloc: umim-imbagen ken maaddaanen iti pigsa, sagiksik, lapsat ken salun-at

Invigorating mafresco, maginhawa; Iloc: na-fresco-*Sp*, makabang-ar

Invincible hindi matalo; Iloc: haan a maabak

Invisible *(Tag. & Iloc.)* hindi/haan makita

INVITE-*verb:* cumbidahin, imbitahin, anyayahan, yakagin, cumbida-hin; Iloc: cumbidaren, imbitaren, awisen (cumbida/cumbidar-*Sp*, imbita / imbitar-*Sp*)

INVITE-*noun,* **Invitation**-*noun: (Tag. & Iloc.)* imbitasyon-*Sp*

Involve isama, ibilang, isangkot, idawit; Iloc: iraman, isacop, ibilang

Iota katiting, malinggit; Iloc: battit, balabattit

   Synonym

   Very little napakamunti, napakaliit, malinggit; Iloc: bassiusit, battit unay

IPad tabletang *computer* na gaya ng IPhone ay kayang maglaman ng iba't ibang aplikasyon-*Sp* (*read App*); Iloc: tableta-*Sp* a *computer* nga casla ti Iphone ket mabalin a makalaon cadagiti agsabasabli nga aplicasyon-*Sp*

IPhone telefono-*Sp* na hindi nakasaksak sa *plug* maliban lamang kung ipa-*recharge* ito at puedeng dalhin kung saan-saan at puedeng maglaman ng iba't ibang aplikasyon-*Sp* at mag-*text* o tignan ang ba't ibang larawan o pumunta sa iba't ibang *website* ng buong mundo-*Sp*; Iloc: telefono-*Sp* nga haan nga nakaconecta iti *plug* malaksid laeng nu ipa-*recharge* daytoy ken mabalin nga ikuyog ti aniaman a lugar-*Sp* ken aglaon ti saba-sabali nga aplicasyon para kitaen dagiti agsasabali a clase-*Sp* ken retrato ken makaserrek iti saba-sabali a *website* iti amin ditoy mundo.

IPod bagay na puedeng i-*download* ang mga canta dito na galing sa *internet* o CD para sa sariling pakikinig habang dinadala kung saan-saan; Iloc: banag nga mabalin i-*download* dagiti cancion-*Sp* idtoy a naggapu diay *internet* wenno CD para mismo a denggen bayat nga ikoykoyug uray inchenna a lugar-*Sp.*

Ire *n.,* **Irate** *adv.* galit, nagagalit; Iloc: rungsot, makapungpungtot,

Irk consumihin, yamotin, inisin; Iloc: suronen, ruroden

Iron bakal; Iloc: landok

Ironic *adj.*, **Irony** *n.* salita na kabaligtaran ang sa binigkas; Iloc: sarita a balictad ti naibaga

Irrational hindi tugma sa rason-*Sp* o *logic*, walang karason-rason, hindi makatwiran; Iloc: haan umno iti rason, <u>awan</u> ti *common sense*

Irrationality kahangalan; Iloc: pagkabagtit

Irreconcilable hindi na puedeng magkaisa o magkasundo o magkaayosan pa; sila o isa sa canila ay hindi pumapayag sa pagpalubag-loob o makipag-compromiso-*Sp*

Irrefutable imposibleng itanggi, ipagkaila o ipabulaan

Irregular <u>walang</u> pagkakaparis o *uniformity*; <u>hindi</u> patag o walang pagkakaparehong hugis o forma-*Sp*; walang firmi-*Sp* o permanenteng paraan, principio-*Sp*, pananatili o pamamalagi, o presyo-*Sp*, halaga, bilang, tulin, bilis; taliwas o lumilihis sa normal-*Sp*; hindi tumatalima-*conform* o sumusunod sa reglamento-*Sp*, etiqueta-*Sp*, custombre-*Sp* o moralidad-*Sp*; may diferencia-*Sp* o sira o hindi makaabot sa tinakdang pamantayan ng pagkagawa; may pagkaimperfecto.

Irrelevant *adj.*, wala man lamang kinalaman sa kasalukuyang pinag-uusapan o pangyayari; Iloc: haan nga umno iti madama nga pag-sasaritaan o mapaspasamak

Irremediable imposibleng ma-remedio-*Sp* o mapatama o mapaayos; Iloc: imposib-le-*Sp* a maremedioan o macorrehir-*Sp* o ma-areglo-*Sp*

Irreplaceable hindi mapapalitan dahil ito ay ang uri na bukod-tangi o *unique*

Irrespective hindi bale iyan/iyon, ito ang gagawin

Irresponsible irresponsab-le-*Sp*, pabaya at wala man lamang pakialam; Iloc: irresponsab-le-*Sp*, agliway ken awan biang na
Antonym
  Responsible responsab-le, marunong tumupad at managut sa canyang mga obligasyon; Iloc: responsab-le, agtungpal cadagiti obligasyon na

Irretrievable hindi mapapanumbalik, hindi maibabalik, hindi mababawi, di mapanauli, di makuha uli, hindi matubos

Irrevocable hindi puedeng magkaroon ng bisa o saysay na naman; hindi mababago ang hatol o pasya dito

Irrigation irigasyon-*Sp*, umaagos na batis para sa pampatubig ng mga taniman; Iloc: irigasyon-*Sp*, agay-ayos nga waig para pampadanum cadagiti mulmula

Irritate consumihin, yamutin, inisin; Iloc: i-consumi-*Sp*, ruroden, suronen, sairwen, paluksawen

Irritable bugnotin, yamotin, sumpongin; Iloc: alipunget, agpungpungtot

"Is that so?" "Talaga?" "Tutoo," Iloc: "Talaga?"

Island *(Tag. & Iloc.)* isla-*Sp*, pulo

Isolate ihiwalay at ibukod para mag-isa; Iloc: isina nga bukbukod tapno agmaymaysa

Issue 1] mag-agos, ipasa, mamigay, pumunta, lumabas; 2] ilathala, iprenta, ikalat, ilibot, ipalaganap, 3] isang copia ng periodico, o isang grupo ng libro na may dagdag o pagbabago sa iba kahit magkaparehong libro, 4] pinakahuling resulta ng conclusion-*Sp* o pasya gaya ng paglutas ng problema, 5] ang paksa, diwa, buod, punto ng pinag-uusapan o pinagtatalunan

IT ang; Iloc: ti, iti

IT takes only seconds to hurt someone but it can take years for them to heal from it napakamadaling saktan ang ating kapwa pero kadalasan ay napakatagal na maghilom sila sa sakit ng loob o sakit ng katawan na nilikha natin

"IT'S a deal!" "Payag ako!," "Sang-ayon ako!"

"IT'S a pity" "Kawawa naman;" Iloc: "Piman met"

IT'S high time oras na dapat nandito o mangyari na para hindi tatagal pa

Italian *(Tag. & Iloc.)* *Italian*, italiano-*Sp*

Itch cati; Iloc: gatel, budo

Itchy macati; Iloc: nagatel, nabudo

Itemize ilista isa-isa na kasama ang mga detalye-*Sp* o mga importanteng bagay na namumukod-uri ng mga ito gaya ng kinita, gana, bayad, utang, bawas, pagkalugi, *etc.*

Itinerant taong palipat-lipat ang lugar-*Sp* ng pinagtatrabohan gaya ng mag-trabaho-*Sp* ng isang panahon sa isang lugar at pagkatapos ay lilipat sa ibang lugar para magtrabaho

Itinerary ang tinakdang lilibotin o lalakbayin sa isang viahe-*Sp*, pati kung anong lugar-*Sp*, kung gaano katagal doon, anong magagandang tanawin o gagawin doon, nilalarawan ang makikita sa dinadaanan o *route*, at iba pa

Itself *(Tag. & Iloc.)* mismo-*Sp*

Ivory 1] ang puting nakalabas na ngipin o pangil ng elefante-*Sp*; 2] ang mga *keys* ng piano at iba pang instumento-*Sp* na may *keyboard*

J

Jab duldol, sundot; Iloc: tudok, tugkel

Jack, Jack up 1] magpalubag loob, pasayahin o palakasin ang loob; 2] iyangat o ilipat ang lugar; 3] mag-omento-*Sp* sa sueldo-*Sp* o itaas ang precio-*Sp* o ipabilis ng pagpatakbo ng sasakyan

Jackfruit langka; Iloc: nangka

Jaded 1] nawalan na ng gana dahil napagbibigyan ng husto sa canyang mga capricho-*Sp*; 2] sirang-sira sa kagagamit o katatrabaho

Jagged may mga kutab, gatgat o ngipin gaya ng lagari o magaspang ito at magalasgas at hindi pantay-pantay; uka-uka, lubak-lubak, bako-bako o tulis-tulis

Jail, Jailhouse bilanggoan, piitan, carcel-*Sp*; Iloc: pagbaludan, calaboso-*Sp*, carcel

Jam 1] *jam* na nilalagay sa tinapay 2] mag-empake-*Sp* ng punong-puno at siksik na siksik, 3] mabunggo, 4] bigla na huminto at hindi na gumagana, 5] baradong daanan 6] situasyon-*Sp* na mahirap lutasin

Jammies, PJ *(Tag. & Iloc.)* pajama

Jampack mga taong nagsisiksikan upang mag-ipon-ipon at magpulong-pulong sa isang lugar-*Sp* na hindi sapat sa kadamihan nila

JAR, wide-mouthed glass bottle *(Tag. & Iloc.)* garrapon
Correlated words
Bottle bote; Iloc: botelia
Demijohn dambuhalang botelya na gawa sa cristal o kaya finormang putik at pagkatapos ay tumigas; Iloc: damajuana

JAR, earthen banga, tapayan, calamba; Iloc: burnay, banga, caramba-*aSp*

Jargon sulat o pananalita na hindi maintindihan at hindi relevante man lamang at kaulolan o kunwari-kunwari

JAW panga, baba; Iloc: sangi

JAW, long *(Tag. & Iloc.)* babalo

Jaywalk tumawid ng calsada sa hindi tawiran ng tao

Jealous seloso/sa-*Sp*, mag-selos-*Sp*, manibugho; Iloc: agimun, seloso/ sa, agselos

Jeepney, Jitney *jeep* na nagsasakay ng mga pasahero-*Sp* sa murang bayad

Jeer ginagambala at sinusupalpal ang nagsasalita sa *stage*

Jeopardize isapanganib, ipasama; Iloc: ipapeggad, idadael

Jeopardy sapalaran na may panganib o may peligro-*Sp* na masaktan, mapinsala, mawalan, mapreso o mamatay

Jerk 1] haltakin, hatakin, 2] biglang galaw ng katawan na hindi sinasadya at hindi voluntaryo; Iloc: 1] pag-uten, 2] golpe nga garaw iti bagi nga haan nga igaggagara o haan a voluntaryo

Jesus Christ *is God, the Holy Trinity – __one__ God in three divine persons: God the Father, God the Son Jesus Christ, and God the Holy Spirit. God has no beginning and no end. He created the whole universe and everything that is in the universe. God is sinless, perfect, holy, sacred and divine. He loves us, all mankind, so much that He came down to earth to save mankind from hell where unpardoned sins are condemned and punished. Jesus Christ descended in the form of a man to take and endure upon Himself the agonizing punishments of the sins of all mankind. This is God's grace of salvation, a free gift from God so that those who receive it would not be doomed in hell. This grace of salvation which makes us heaven-bound, is easy, simple and doable: we simply believe and put our faith and trust in God that the sufferings, crucifixion and the blood of Jesus Christ on the cross makes all our lifetime sins forgiven and cleansed and with this belief, we must receive Jesus Christ into our heart and life as our Lord God, Savior and Redeemer. Right there and then, the Holy Spirit comes to indwell in our heart to walk with us and help us live a God-abiding life, and we also acquire a new birth where we become spiritually born again as God's children. God wants us to have a close relationship with Him by constantly reading His words, the Bible, praising Him in worship and gratitude, and lifting up and communicating to Him our petitions and prayers (read more about **God** in the letter **G** section of this book).* Ang Dios Anak na si Hesu Cristo ay walang umpisa at walang katapusan – Siya ay magpakailanman *(eternal)*. Ang Panginoon Dios Hesu Cristo ang nagdusa sa parusa ng mga kasalanan ng lahat ng nilalang, imbes na ang mga nilalang ang maparusahan sa infierno dahil sa canilang mga kasalanan. Kapag maniwala, manalig, magtiwala at magsampalataya tayo na ang pagdurusa sa cruz ni Hesu Cristo ay kabayaran ng ating mga kasalanan at tanggapin natin si Hesu Cristo sa puso't buhay natin bilang Dios natin at Tagapagligtas natin, lahat ng kasalanan natin ay mapatawad at malinisan na ng dugo ni Hesu Cristo sa cruz, at matira na ang Dios Espiritu Santo sa puso at buhay natin dahil ang Dios ay Immanuel *(God with us)* para tulongan tayong maging maka-Dios at magkaroon tayo ng bagong kapanganakan at tayo ay nagiging *spiritual* na anak na ng Dios. Hindi mawawala and kaligtasang binigay na libre ng Dios sa atin, at hindi rin tayo iiwanan o lalayasan ng Espiritu Santo.

Jetlag pagkaantok pagkatapos ng viahe-*Sp* na galing sa ibayong lugar-*Sp* na ang oras-tulogan nila ay iba

Jetsam, Jettison pagtatapon ng mga carga-*Sp* para pagaanin ang barco pag may problema-*Sp* baka lumunod ang barco-*Sp*

Jewel, Jewelry alahas-*Sp*, hiyas; Iloc: alahas

Jibe magkaangkop; Iloc: agkayarig

Jiffy saglit, sandali, napakaikling tiempo-*Sp*

Jiggle saglit-saglit siyang kumilos ng pababa at pataas, paurong-pasulong, pakaliwa-pakanan

Jilt biglaang pagtakwil ng kasintahan

Jingle cumacalansing; Iloc: agcalcalansing

Jinxed *(Tag. & Iloc.)* minamalas

Jitters (one have with an unfamiliar activity or when at an unfamiliar environment or when served with an unfamiliar food) naninibago; Iloc: maam-amak

Jittery ninenervios; Iloc: agnernervios

Jocose mapagbiro; Iloc: mapag-angaw

Jocular nakakatawa; Iloc: nakakatkatawa

Jocund maginhawang makisama; Iloc: maconsuelo a makicadwa

Jog, Jogging *(Tag. & Iloc.) jogging*

JOIN, Ally with *v.* sumali, lumahok, maki-alyado, makisapi, umanib; Iloc: makisali, makitipon, maki-anib

JOIN, Connect iconecta, icabit, pagconectahin, ipagcabit; Iloc: iconecta, pagcapeten, pagconectaen, isilpo

Joint 1] *see body joints*, 2] lugar-*Sp* o daan na magkacoconectado 3] pagmemay-ari ng dalawang tao o mas mahigit pa sa dalawa sa *account* sa banco-*Sp* o bahay o negosio-*Sp*, 4] *slang word for* lugar na mumurahin at may masamang reputasyon-*Sp* o kaya bilanggoan

Joke, Jest *joke*, biro; Iloc: *joke*, angaw

Joker, Jester palabiro, comikero-*Sp*; Iloc: naangaw, comikero

Jolly nagagalak, natutuwa; Iloc: maragsakan

Jolt 1] napalundag sa gulat, 2] haltakin, hatakin; Iloc: 1] agculagtit ti kigtot, 2] pag-uten

Josh biroin o magbiroan; Iloc: angawin o aginnangaw

Jostle magtulak o magsico para makadaan

Jot 1] magsulat ng maikli o mabilisan, 2] pinakamaliit na anomang bagay

Journal *diary*, *record* ng mga pangyayari o ng mga pinagdadaanan o dinadaranas

Journalism pangongolecta ng mga balita para ilathala sa periodico-*Sp*; mga balita na sinusulat sa diaryo-*Sp* at iba pang pahayagan

Journey mag-viahe-*Sp*, maglakbay magliwaliw; Iloc: agviahe

Jovial masaya, maaliw, palatawa; Iloc: nakalinglingay, naragsak, mapagkatawa

Jowl pinapagitan ito ng panga sa babang tabi ng bibig; Iloc: pagbaetan ti panga

Joy galak, saya, tuwa; Iloc: ragsak, rambak

Joyful, Joyous galak na galak, masayang-masaya, natutuwa; Iloc: nakaragragsak, nakaramrambak

Jubilatnt *adj.*, **Jubilation** *n.* damdamin ng galak, saya, ligaya; Iloc: agramrambak

JUDGE *n. judge*, hues-*Sp*, hurado-*Sp*, hukom, tagahatol; Iloc: *judge*, hues, hurado, hukom, husgado-*Sp*

JUDGE *v.* hatolan; Iloc: mang-husgar-*Sp*

Judgment hatol; Iloc: husgar-*Sp*

Judgmental palapintas, palapuna, mapaghanap ng mali dahil puede na siya mismo ay may masasamang ginawa kaya nag-hahanap ng kasama o nag-aakala na lahat ay kapareho niyang masama

Judicial *adj.,* **Judiciary** *n.* tungkol sa paghusga o paghatol ng mga caso sa corte ng husticia

Judicious mabuting pagturing o paghatol na napakaingat, matalino at makatwiran

Juggle 1] maglaro o magtanghal ng pagsasalamangka sa pag-itcha-*Sp* at pagsalo ng mga bola-*Sp*; 2] *multi-tasking* o magsagawa ng marami ng halinhan o sabay-sabay

Juggler *(Tag. & Iloc.)* salamangkero

Jugular parte ng leeg at lalamunan; Iloc: parte ti tengnged ken carabucob

Juice katas; Iloc: tubbog

Juicy makatas; Iloc: natubbog

Juul, Juuling or Vape, Vaping *This is an e-cigarette using a juul pod with flavors to mask the nicotine in it. Debates are still ongoing and since it's a recently made product, its risk whether, big or small, is still unknown. But as always, <u>if in doubt, it's much better and safer never to use it and never to try it</u>, because some products when they come into your system, <u>its hold on you is quite difficult to get free from it</u>. And <u>regret will come at the end</u>. There are safer and more valuable activities to do than this.* **Rule of thumb: never exploit and use questionable products because they usually come with risks.** Ito ay may *nicotine* pero napakaaga pa ngayon na malaman kung nakaka-gawa ng malaki o maliit na panganib ito, kaya para hindi **sa huli ang pagsisisi**, mas mabuting layoan ito at ang mga iba pang nakaka-suspechang producto. Napakaraming napakabuting pag-ukolan ng pansin, kaya layoan ang puedeng mapanganib *(read Addiction and Drugs, illegal in previous pages).*

JUMP lumukso, tumalon, lumundag; Iloc: aglagto, laktaw

JUMP at the opportunity *Welcome and seize with promptness, rea-diness, eagerness and enthusiasm to take full advantage of this chance, opening, opportunity, and prospect.* Samantalahin na habang may oportunidad-*Sp*, sunggaban ang nakakabuti at nakakaunlad

JUMP-start paandarin ang sasakyan o paandarin ang makina na basta na lang huminto (andar-*Sp*, makina-*Sp*)

JUMP to conclusion maghusga o maghatol o magpalagay o magsapantaha o magpasya kahit hindi pa alam lahat ang katotohanan

Junction dalawang calye-*Sp* na nagletrang "T" kung saan sila magkacabit o magkasalubong pero ang isa dito ay doon na ang hangganan o katapusan; Iloc: dua a calsada nga agletra ti "T" nga agkacabit o agsabat da ngem maysa a calsada ket ditoyen ti patinggana nan

Juncture sandalihang parte-*Sp* ng tiempo-*Sp*; Iloc: bassit a parte ti tiempo

June *(Tag. & Iloc.)* *June,* Hunyo-*Sp*

Jungle kakahoyan, kagubatan, gubat; Iloc: kakaywan, kabakiran, bakir

JUNIOR kapangalan ng bata ang canyang ama kaya lang ang tatay ay *senior* at siya naman ay *junior*

JUNIOR college ang institusyon-*Sp* na nag-aalok ng dalawang taong curso-*Sp* *(Associate degree)* na puedeng ipagpatuloy para sa apat na taong curso-*Sp* na *Bachelors degree*

JUNK mga panapon gaya ng basura-*Sp* at mga *junk mail*

JUNK food pagkaing mura at masarap pero nakakataba at mababa ang sustancia at nakakataas ng *blood pressure* o presyon ng dugo

JUNK mail mga sulat o babasahin na walang interes para sa iyo. Sa ibang tao ang mga sulat na humihingi ng tulong ay binibigyan nila ng pansin pagkatapos na matiyak na ito ay valido o tunay na *charitable organization*, kaya nagbibigay sila paminsan-minsan o ng regular

JURISDICTION 1] ang katarungan at kapangyarihan na pinapairal ng batas, 2] otoridad

JURISDICTION, within sacop, nakasacop; Iloc: sacop

JUST a while ago kani-kanina lamang; Iloc: itattay lang

JUST because palibhasa, yamang; Iloc: gapu laeng

"JUST imagine" "Biro mo" Iloc: "Agasem"

JUST now ngayon lamang; Iloc: itatta laeng

JUST, Only, Merely lamang, lang; Iloc: laeng, lang

JUST, Proper, Fair, Truthful makatarungan, pantay-pantay sa lahat ang karapatan; Iloc: nalinteg, agpapada iti gundaway

JUST right tamang-tama lang, katamtaman lamang; Iloc: kalalaengan na, kaus-ustoan na

Justice katarungan, hukoman; Iloc: linteg

Justifiable *adj.*, **Justification** *n.* tama, tumpak, makatwiran at nasasabatas

Justify mangatwiran, magpalusot, nagdadahilan, magrason-rason; Iloc: agpampambar, agras-rason, agpalusot

Jut out umuusli, lumalawit; Iloc: agdawdawidaw, agusli

Juvenile ang kabataan <u>bago dumating</u> ng mayor-de-edad-*Sp*; Iloc: ti ubing baro nga ag-mayor-de-edad

Correlated words

Kid bata; Iloc: ubing

Teen-ager *(Tag. & Iloc.) teen-ager*

Adolescent boy binatilyo; Iloc: bumarito

Adolescent girl, lass, maiden dalaginding, dalagita; Iloc: balasitang

Ingénue inocenteng dalagita; Iloc: inocente a balasitang

Youth kabataan, menor de edad; Iloc: pagkaubbing, menor de edad

Juxtapose pagtabihin para mai-compara-*Sp*; Iloc: pagabayin tapno icomparar-*Sp*

K

Kale or Kail gulay na malarepolyo na medio alon-alon at kulubot ang dahon at ka-uri ng familyang mustasa-*Sp*

Kapok mala-seda-*Sp* na bulak na ginagamit na palaman ng unan o gawing sinulid

Kaput wasak at sira na kaya kailangang igiba na; ang sabi ng *"**go kaput**"* ay hindi na umaandar o nag-*break down* na

Karaoke aparato-*Sp* na pangcanta o kaya sa TV rin kung saan ang mga canta-*Sp* ay nakasulat at may kasaliw na tugtoging musica-*Sp*

Karma mula sa *Hindu* at *Buddhist*, ito ay parusang kahihinatnan ng anomang masamang asal at gawain

Kayo, Kayos pinaikling tawag sa *knockout (KO)* sa labanang *boxing*

KEEL pag-ikot o pagtagilid sa maling tabi; matomba o bumagsak

KEEL, on an even matatag na balansiado

KEEL over mapataob

KEEN matinik; Iloc: nasirib

KEEN on gusto; ibig; Iloc: gusto, cayat

KEEP itago; Iloc: idulin

Antonyms

Throw away, Dispose itapon; Iloc: ibelleng

KEEP abreast of... *Keep informed, stay up-to-date with something important to you, your family or your work.* Patuloy na nakakaalam sa importanteng bagay sa inyo; Iloc: itultuloy nga amwen ti importante a banag cadacayo.

Synonyms

Hip 1] matalas ang pagkaalam sa mga kasalukuyang nangyayari, 2] sumusunod sa uso at pinakabagong moda ng pananamit

Up-to-date alam ang pinakabagong balita at siya ay alinsunod sa kasalukuyang kaisipan o gawain o uso; Iloc: ammo na ti pinakabaro a damag ken agbatay isu iti madama nga kasiriban ken aramid ken uso

KEEP an account ilista o i-*record* sa *log book*

KEEP as one's possession angkinin, taglayin; Iloc: isanicua

KEEP, Maintain ipamalagi, ipanatili; Iloc: i-mantener-*Sp*

KEEP one's distance from someone or something layoan; Iloc: adaywan

KEEP one's head above water *Survive and endure while struggling to not be overwhelmed by difficult financial problems; keep up with your responsibilities at work, and at home.* May problema or may mga katungkulan ka, patuloy na magpursigi at masipag sa pagsisigasig ng lutas sa mga kinakailangan ninyo o sa mga problema mo.

KEEP one's word *Honor your words; do what you promised so that people will find you to have credibility because you are trustworthy.* Igalang mo at gampanan at tuparin ang pinangako mo para paniwalaan ka ng tao dahil napagkakatiwalaan ka.

KEEP someone in line tinitiyak na ang tao - bata man o taohan - ay nag-aasal ng mabuti at tama

KEEP the ball rolling umpisahan at sige ng sige ang pagsagawa para naisasagawa lahat at nagbubunga

KEEP up with someone sumulong para makaabot at makapareho ng takbo o pag-unlad ng iba

Keepsake bagay na pang-alaala; Iloc: banag a pakalaglagipan

Kempt maareglo, maayos; Iloc: naareglo, naurnos

Ken pag-unawa sa situasyon at sa kapwa at tumutugon ng tama; Iloc: pagawat iti situasyon ken tao ken mangipaay ti nasayaat

Keratin himaymay o *fiber* na may *protein* at mahalagang bahagi ng buhok, kuko, *feathers*, paa ng hayop at iba pa

Kerchief panyo o pantalukbong sa ulo ng babae

Kernel ang malambot at nakakain na parte-*Sp* sa loob ng *shell* ng *nut*; ang buong *seed*/binhi ng *grain* o butil gaya ng mais o *wheat*

Kettle caldero-*aSp* na pinagpapakulohan ng tubig

Keyboard ang hilera-*Sp* ng mga *keys* sa piano, *organ* at iba pa para pangtugtog ng musica-*Sp*; ilang *rows* o hilera ng mga letra-*Sp* at numero-*Sp* sa *computer, ipad,* o *cell phone* para makapagsulat o *text*

Key susi, liave-*Sp*; Iloc: liave, tulbek

Khaki *(Tag. & Iloc.) khaki*

Kibitz 1] osyosong-miron-*Sp*, 2] basta na lang nagpapayo kahit hindi kailangan

Kibosh kahangalan; Iloc: kabagtitan

KICK sipain, tadyakin; Iloc: cugtaran, icusay

KICK-off or **Kickoff** 1] ang umpisa o kauna-unahang yugto o hakbang; 2] pagsipa ng bola-*Sp* sa mga larong *football* o *socce*r

KICK the bucket *(Tag. & Iloc.)* mamatay

Kickback 1] pagsusuhol o *bribery* kung saan may porcientong pera at ventahe-*Sp* na pinagkasundoan ng grupo o ng dalawang tao; 2] biglang hindi controladong galaw ng makina-*Sp* o ibang aparato sa pag-umpisa ng andar-*Sp* o dahil may nakapasok na problema

KID, Child bata; Iloc: ubing

KID, Tease magbiro, biroin, manukso; Iloc: agsutil-*Sp*, agangaw
   Correlated words
   Josh biroin o magbiroan; Iloc: angawin o aginnangaw
   Jocose, Jocular mapagbiro; Iloc: mapag-angaw

Kidnap dukotin, *kidnap;* Iloc: agcumaw, *kidnap*

Kidnapper nandudukot ng tao na kadalasan ay bata o babae; Iloc: cumaw

Kidney bato; Iloc: bato, biel
   Correlated word
   Renal tungkol sa bato o *kidney*; Iloc: maygapu iti biel

Kill patayin, paslangin; Iloc: patayen

Killjoy taong sumisira ng kasayahan, kaligayahan at kagalakan ng iba

Kimona kasuotang Filipina *(Filipino costume)* na bordadong pantaas at kacombinasyon ang saya o *long skirt*

Kimono kasuotang Haponesa *(Japanese costume)* na mala-bata de baño

Kin kamag-anak; Iloc: kabagyan, parientes-*Sp*

KIND clase-*Sp*, uri, tipo-*Sp*; Iloc: clase, tipo

KIND, in kagamitan o ari-arian imbes-*Sp* na pera

KIND of medio, puede na

KIND person maawain, mahabagin, may malasakit; Iloc: mannangaasi, nasingpet, nalukneng ti puso

Kindle sindihan; Iloc: sindian, seggedan

Kindness (spreading kindness has its blessings) *When you are kind to others, take mercy and help, being understanding, supportive, considerate and charitable to others, sympathize, and do other humanitarian deeds, you are considered a hero and a role model and you will be blessed by God.*

Kindred magkakamag-anak; *clan* o tribo na nanggaling sa pareho na ninuno

Kinetic tungkol sa galaw o kilos; tungkol sa/likas sa/sanhi sa paggalaw

King hari; Iloc: ari

Kingdom kaharian, palacio-*Sp*; Iloc: castilyo-*Sp*, palacio

Kink 1] defecto na nakakahadlang ng tagumpay o ng pagpalakad; 2] *crick* o sakit sa batok at likod ng katawan; 3] malaswa o kakaibang pagtatalik ng lalake't babae

Kinky 1] maliliit na culot gaya ng afro, 2] asal na *sexual*

Kinship conecsion-*Sp* sa pamamagitan ng dugo, casalan o pag-ampon, pagka-relasyon-*Sp* sa ugali o katutubo

Kinsman or Kinswoman 1] magkamag-anak sa pagkakadugo ng familia-*Sp*; 2] taong parehong nacionalidad-*Sp*

Kiosk kiosko-*Sp* o *gazebo* na caraniwan ay nasa gitna at pinaligiran ng pagdaanan ng sasakyan o nasa gitna ng parke

KISS halikan, hagkan, beso-*Sp*; Iloc: bisongen, ungwen, ag-anggo, beso
Correlated words
Smooch halik; Iloc: bisong
Smack 1] icera at buksan ang bibig ng maingay, 2] maghalik ng maingay; Iloc: 1] icerra ken luktan ti bibig a natagari, 2] natagari nga agbisong

KISS the hand of an older person or dab on one's forehead (forehead of younger person) to greet and show respect to an elder (Filipino custom) mag-mano-*Sp*; Iloc: agmano

Kit maliit o manipis na pakete-*Sp*

KITCHEN *(Tag. & Iloc.)* cucina-*Sp*

KITCHEN towel trapo-*Sp*, basahan; Iloc: trapo, nisnis

Kite *(Tag. & Iloc.)* saranggola, *kite*

Kith and Kin magkakakilala o magkakamag-anak

Kitsch decorasyon na hindi magkaangkop o nababagay sa bahay o sa ibang kasangkapan
Synonym
Out-of-place wala sa lugar, hindi bagay o karapat-dapat sa lugar; Iloc: haan bagay o umno iti lugar

Kitten kuting; Iloc: muning

Knack napakahusay na galing, spesyal na talento, abilidad o *skill*

Knapsack *bag* na pinapatong o binubuhat sa balikat

Knave walang principiong tao na <u>hindi</u> tapat o *honest* at <u>hindi</u> napagkakatiwalaan

Knead lamasin, lamutakin; Iloc: ramasen, masaen
Synonym
Mash magmasa, magligis; Iloc: limugen, imasa-masaen

Knee tuhod; Iloc: tumeng

Kneecap bayugo; Iloc: lipay

Kneel luhod; Iloc: parintumeng
Synonym
Genuflect pagluluhod ng dalawang tuhod o isang tuhod lamang at nakatangong nagpaparangal at nagsasamba sa Panginoong Dios; Iloc: agparintumeng ti dua a tumeng wenno maysa a tumeng laeng ken nakadumog ti ulo na a mangdaydayaw ken mang-glorificar ken ni Apo Dios

Knickknack mga abubot; Iloc: dagiti arcos

KNIFE lanseta-*Sp*, patalim; Iloc: lanseta-*Sp*
Correlated words
Large knife bolo, gulok, itak, tabak; Iloc: bolo, buneng
Dagger *(Tag. & Iloc.)* punyal
Machete, Philippine *(Tag. & Iloc.)* balisong
Philippine moslem sword *(Tag. & Iloc.)* kris

KNIFE, pocket *(Tag. & Iloc.)* cortapluma-*Sp*

KNIFE, serving *(Tag. & Iloc.)* cuchilyo-*Sp*

Knight in shining armor isang lalaking tutulong sa panahon ng kagipitan

Knit *(Tag. & Iloc.)* mag-ganchilyo-*Sp*

Knob tanganan o pihitan para buksan o sarhan ang pinto

KNOCK magcatok, tuktokin; Iloc: agcatok, agtuktok

KNOCK-kneed piki; Iloc: sallakung

KNOCK out tinalo sa boksing, nawalan ng malay pagkatapos na nasuntok o nahampas ng kung ano

KNOT tali; Iloc: siglot, galut, tali

KNOT, entangled *(Tag. & Iloc.)* nagkabuhol-buhol

KNOT, entwined ipulopot; Iloc: iputipot

KNOW-how alam, batid; Iloc: ammo

KNOW someone, Acquainted kilala; Iloc: am-ammo

KNOW, to alamin, kilalanin; Iloc: ammuen

KNOW, not hindi alam, hindi kilala; Iloc: haan na ammo

Known kilala, sicat, tanyag, popular-*Sp*; Iloc: natan-ok, am-ammo ti adu a tao, popular-*Sp*

Knowledge kaalaman, karunongan, talino, dunong, pagkabatid, pagkaunawa, muwang; kaalaman sa mga katotohanan, principio-*Sp* at *facts* sa pamamagitan ng pag-aaral, pagsasakob sa mga aralin at imbestigasyon, at karanasang pag-aasecaso na mga ito; kaalaman sa isang *branch of learning* o sangay ng kaalaman o mga sakop ng kakaibang mga larangan at informasyon-*Sp*; Iloc: sirib, dagiti amin nga ammo.

Knowledgeable maraming kaalaman; Iloc: adu ti ammo
Synonym
Erudite *adj.*, **Erudition** *n.* maraming napag-aralan at maraming kaalaman

Knuckle dugtong sa mga daliri na nababaluktot; dugtong ng mga daliri sa kamay na kitang-kita kapag gumawa ng *fist* o kamao

Koala oso na katutubong Australia; Iloc: oso ti Australia
Correlated word
Panda oso na katutubong China; Iloc: oso ti China

Kosher 1] angkop na kainin alinsunod sa batas ng *Judaism*; 2] *informal*: wasto, tama at nauukol; *genuine*, dalisay, *authentic* o tunay na tunay

Kowtow 1] magluhod at magbigay ng respeto-*Sp*, 2] magsilbi o sumunod sa utos; Iloc: agparintumeng ken mangited iti respeto; 2] ag-servi-*Sp* ken agtungpal ti mandar-*Sp*

Kudo, Kudos pagparangal, pagpupuri, pagtanggap at pagsang-ayon

Kvetch *[k-vetz]* panay ang reclamo at angal; Iloc: reclamador-*aSp*

Synonyms
Complainer *(Tag. & Iloc.)* reclamador
Querulous *(Tag. & Iloc.)* reclamador

L

Label *label,* tatak, marka; Iloc: *label,* marka

LABOR pagtrabaho, pagsisikap para makasagawa; Iloc: pagtrabaho, pagpakat para makaaramid

LABOR pains during childbirth kirot sa panganganak; Iloc: agpasikal

Laboratory *(Tag. & Iloc.)* laboratorio-*Sp*

Laborer trabahador-*Sp*, manggagawa; Iloc: trabahador

Laborious kinakailangan ng maraming obra-*Sp* at sikap, at patuloy na pagtiyaga at pagsunod sa tamang paraan

Labyrinth libangang lugar na pasikot-sikot ang daan na pinapaligiran ng matataas na halaman o pader na mahirap hanapin ang labasan

Lace 1] lazo-*Sp*, 2] tela-*Sp* na fino-*Sp* na bordado-*Sp* o may magagandang decorasyon-*Sp*

Lacerate laslasin, hiwain; Iloc: sugatan, iwaen

Laches sa *legal case*, hindi nagawa ito sa tamang tiempo-*Sp* at ang atrasong ito ay makakahadlang sa canya para magsakdal o magdemanda-*Sp*

Lack kakulangan, hindi sapat, hindi kasya; Iloc: kurang, haan makaanay
Correlated word
    Bereft wala sa canya ang kinakailangan niya; Iloc: awanan isu ti masapul na

Lackluster, Lackaidaisical walang kalatoy-latoy, walang sigla; Iloc: awan ganas na
Synonym
    Ennui walang kalatoy-latoy ni gana dahil hindi interesado

Laconic paliwanag sa pinakaconting salita pero completo na at claro pa

Lactate may lumalabas nang gatas kaya nakakapagpasuso na ng sanggol

LAD binata; Iloc: baro

LAD, young binatilyo; Iloc: bumarito

Ladder hagdan, hagdanan; Iloc: agdan

Lade *(Tag. & Iloc.)* 1] icarga para sa *shipment*; 2] magbigay ng pasanin sa kapwa, magpabigat sa kapwa

Laden nagcacarga o nagpapasanin ng problema-*Sp*

Ladle sandok; Iloc: aklo

LADY babaeng nakaabot na ng edad-*Sp* beinte-*Sp* uno-*Sp* o mahigit pa; Iloc: babae nga nakadanonen ti edad beinte uno wenno labes pay dita

LADY, single dalaga; Iloc: balasang

Ladylike *Well-bred*, ugali ng mabuti at respetadong dalaga

Lag atrasado-*Sp* o nahuhuli parati at hindi makahabol sa tinakdang oras-*Sp* o fecha-*Sp* para tapusin dahil mabagal siya

Lagoon *(Tag. & Iloc.)* laguna-*Sp*

Laid-back *(Tag. & Iloc.)* campante-*Sp*, walang alala

Lair 1] bahay ng hayop, 2] bahay na pinagtataguhan

Lake lawa na napaligiran ng lupa; Iloc: danaw a nalawlawan ti daga

Lam nagtatago dahil tumakas sa bilanggo o culongan

Lamaze paraan para ang pagluluwal ng sanggol ay mas madali at mas ligtas sa buntis na ina at sa sanggol

Lamb cordero-*Sp*; Iloc: carnero-*Sp*

Lambaste 1] hampasin, haplitan, 2] pagalitan ng grabe; Iloc: 1] saplitan, 2] ungetan ti napalalo

Lame *(Tag. & Iloc.)* pilay

Lament nananaghoy, nananangis; Iloc: agladladingit

Lamp *(Tag. & Iloc.)* lampara-*Sp*, ilaw/silaw

Lampoon *roast*, katatawanang pang-atake sa isang tao o sa isang grupo na pumapayag na maatake para sa katatawanan

Lanai *patio* o lanai na tawag sa Hawaii sa *veranda* gaya ng Lanai na isla sa Hawaii

Lance *(Tag. & Iloc.)* sibat

LAND lupa, lugar-*Sp*, bayan, bansa, nasyon-*Sp*; Iloc: daga, lugar, nasyon, bayan

LAND on lumapag, mag-*landing*; Iloc: agdisso, ag-*landing*
Synonyms
Perch on, Roost, Alight on dumapo; Iloc: agdapo

Landholder ang nagmamay-ari ng lupa

Landlord, Landlady *(Tag. & Iloc.)* 1] ang nagmemay-ari ng bahay o gusali at pinapaupahan niya ito, 2] tumatanggap ng mag-casera-*aSp* o ng uupa ng matirhan

LANDMARK *(Tag. & Iloc.)* 1] ang kilalang monumento-*Sp* o stractura-*Sp* o tanawin sa isang bayan

LANDMARK, boundary *(Tag. & Iloc.)* mohon-*Sp*

Landscape 1] malawak na tanawin o natatanaw na lugar, 2] *gardening,* pagpapaganda ng bakuran o hardin

Landslide *landslide,* lupang gumuho; Iloc: *landslide,* daga nga aguyas pasalog nga aggabur

LANGUAGE salita, lengguahe-*Sp,* wika; Iloc: lengguahe, sarita, sao,

LANGUAGE, use strong nanlalait, nang-iinsulto, nambabanta at iba pang mapang-abuso na salita

Languid mahina, lampay at matamlay; Iloc: nacapsut ken awanan ti ganas na

Languish 1] nanlulumo, nanlalata at wala nang lakas, 2] abandonado-*Sp* at masaklap ang kalagayan sa pinag-iwanan sa canya

Languor mahina; Iloc: nacapsut

Lank, Lanky matangkad at payat; Iloc: tayag ken cuttong

Lantern *(Tag. & Iloc.)* parol-*Sp*

LAP 1] calungang hita, candungan; 2] ginagamit ang dila para kumain o uminon gaya ng aso; Iloc: 1] luppo a saklutan, 2] iyusar ti dila tapno mangan wenno uminom casla ti aso

LAP, Lick in liquid with the tongue to drink *(Tag. & Iloc.)* laklak

Lapse 1] lipas na o paso na sa tinakdang *deadline,* 2] naging masama o bumaba ang *standards* kaysa sa dati

Laptop *computer* na madala saan man at puedeng ipatong sa candungan ng hita; Iloc: *computer* nga maiyeg uray ania a lugar-*Sp* nga mabalin ipatong iti saklutan ti luppo

Larceny ang crimen na pagkuha ng pagmemay-ari ng iba at tanggalin na permanente ang karapatan ng dating may-ari dito

Large malaki; Iloc: dakkel

Largess, Largesse *[lar-jes] Generosity;* pagbibigay ng regalo gaya ng pera at iba pa

Lark 1] kumacantang ibon; 2] lakarang masaya na may biroan at larong *prank*

Larva higod; Iloc: itlog ti igges

Laryngitis sakit sa lalamunan; Iloc: sakit ti carabucob

Larynx lalamunan; Iloc: carabucob

Laser aparato-*Sp* na may *radiation* na ginagamit sa larangan ng *Medicine* at sa *facelift* na pampabata

Lascivious masyadong malibog; Iloc: masyado nga nauttog

Lash haplitan, hampasin; Iloc: saplitan, ablatan, basnotan

Lass dalaginding, dalagita; Iloc: balasitang

Lasso *(Tag. & Iloc.)* laso-*Sp*

LAST kahuli-hulian, panghuli, sa huli, kulelat, ultimo-*Sp*; Iloc: naudi, kaudian, diay udi, kutit, ultimo
Synonym
Ultimate sa kahulihulian, sa huling kahihinatnan; Iloc: iti kaudianan, iti naudi a pagbanagan
Antonym
First una, pinakauna, primero; Iloc: umuna, kaunaan, primero

LAST ditch pinakahuling hakbang o sikap para maiwasan ang kagipitan

LAST judgment ang *final* o ang pinakahuling paghusga ng Dios sa lahat ng mga nilalang

LAST long magluwat, malaon; Iloc: agpaut, agbayag

LAST minute ultimo ora-*Sp* magsagawa dahil may hadlang o pagpaliban na usbong ng katamaran

LAST month itong nakaraang buan; Iloc: daytoy napalabas a bulan

LAST name *(Tag. & Iloc.)* apelyido-*Sp*

LAST night kagabi; Iloc: idi rabii
Correlated word
Yesterday kahapon; Iloc: idi calman

LAST resort, as a kung lahat-lahat ay hindi gumana o umobra, may huling paraan na siyang gagamitin; pinakahuling dulogan o takbuhan o paraan kung pagkatapos ng lahat na sikap o pagpapagamot ay nagawa na pero wala pa ring asenso.

LAST straw pinakahuling pagpapacensia sa mga kamalian o kasalanan ng asawa, kaibigan, kanegosio o empleyado, kaya <u>pinuputol na</u> niya ang pakikipagkapwa at pakikitungo sa taong ito.
Synonym
Deal-breaker gawain o ugali na pagbabatayan kung ipagpatuloy pa o putolin na ang relasyon o negosio o kasundoan; Iloc: aramid o ugali nga pagbatayan nu ituloy pay o putden ti relasyon o negosio o ti pinagtulagan itattan

LAST supper ang pinakahuling hapunan ng Dios Anak na si Hesu Cristo at ng Canyang mga dicipulo bago Siya dusahin at ipako sa cruz.

LAST week/ month/ year itong nakaraang lingo / buwan / taon; Iloc: daytoy napalabas nga dominggo / bulan / tawen.

LAST will and testament lahat ng tao ay may katapusan at karamihan ay nangangailangan ng kasulatang bilin para sa kagustohang mangyayari lalo na kung may mga magmamana o *beneficiaries*, at para siguradong makabatas ito, kinakailangang ipanotarya ito o magpatulong sa abogado sa bilin an ito.

LAST year itong nakaraang taon; Iloc: daytoy napalabas a tawen

Lasting matagalan, magluwat, malaon; Iloc: napaut, nabayag

Late atrasado-*Sp*, huli; Iloc: atrasado, naladaw

Lately kamakailan lamang; Iloc: di pay nabayag

LATENT katangian o cacayahan na tago at natutulog at lingid sa ibang tao at puedeng ring lingid sa mismong taong may angkin nito hangga't mag-umpisa siyang magsagawa at madiscobre niya ang talino at abilidad niyang ito

LATENT period nasa pagitan sa pagkahawa sa sakit hanggang sa magyabong na yung sakit sa canya

Later mamaya, maya-maya; Iloc: madamdama, intunokua, itattanto

Latest pinakahuli, pinakabago; Iloc: pinakabaro, kabaroan

Lather bula ng sabon; Iloc: labutab ti sabon
  Correlated words
  Froth, Foam bula; Iloc: labutab

Latin-America lugar ng *South America, Central America* at *Mexico* at sa islas ng Caribbean na ang wika ay Espanyol o Portugesa

Latrine casilyas o cubeta sa campo o sa *barracks* ng mga sundalo

Latter dito nagbabanggit ng dalawang paksa, at ang *latter* ay iyung ikalawa (medio kapareho ng *later*) at yung *former* ay yung unang binanggit

Laud purihin at hangaan; Iloc: dayawen ken ipateg

LAUGH tumawa; Iloc: agkatawa
  Correlated words
  Smile ngiti, ngumiti; Iloc: isem, umisem
  Guffaw halakhak; Iloc: garakgak, paggaak
  Grin nakangisi; Iloc; musiig
  Giggle hagikhik; Iloc: ayek-ek, umlek-*secret giggle*

Banter cuentohang masaya na nagkakatuwaan at may kasamang mga biro; Iloc: storiaan a naragsak nga addaan iti pagkakatawaan ken paginnangawan

Risibility *n.,* **Risible** *adj.* napapatawa ng madalas, madaling tumawa; Iloc: makakatkawa canayon, nalaca nga agkatawa

Chuckle pinipigil na pagtawa; Iloc: laplappedan nga katawa

Snicker tumawa ng palihim; Iloc: agcatawa a palimed, laplappedan na nga katawa, um-umlek

LAUGH often bungisngis; Iloc: agkarakatawa

Laughable nakakatawa; Iloc: nakakatkatawa

Laughing stock taong pinagtatawanan o pinagpapatungan ng biro

Laughter tawa; Iloc: katawa

Launch magbunsod ng bagong proyecto-*Sp,* ganadong mag-umpisa; Iloc: mangbangon ti baro a proyecto, ganado nga mangirugi

Launder maglaba; Iloc: aglaba

Laundry labada; Iloc: labada, dagiti malab-an ida

Lava ang umuusok at mainit na putik na sinabog ng pumutok na vulcan

Lavatory *(Tag. & Iloc.)* lavatorio-*Sp,* cubeta-*Sp,* casilyas-*Sp, ladies'* o *men's room*

Lave maghugas, maligo; Iloc: agugas, agdigos

Lavish 1] bagay o ocasyon-*Sp* na napakagara at ginastosan ng husto-*Sp;* 2] mamigay o magdulot ng abundancia-*Sp*

LAW batas, ordinanza-*Sp,* reglamento-*Sp,* kautosan ng batas; Iloc: linteg, turay, ordinanza, reglamento, mandar-*Sp* ti linteg
Synonyms
Regulation regulasyon, reglamento; Iloc: regulasyon, reglamento, mandar
Ordinance ordinansa Iloc: ordinansa
Order mando; Iloc: mandar
Rule patakaran, reglamento, alituntunin; Iloc: reglamento
Mandate kautosan ng batas; Iloc: mandar ti linteg
Mandatory utos na hindi dapat labagin; Iloc: mandar nga haan masupyaten

LAW-abiding sumusunod sa batas, makatarungan; Iloc: sumursurot ti linteg, nalinteg, naturay

Lawful *legal,* makatarungan, makabatas; Iloc: *legal,* naturay, nalinteg
Synonyms
Legal, Legitimate, Licit *legal,* makatarungan, makabatas, makatwiran, nasasabatas; Iloc: *legal,* naturay, nalinteg
Antonym

Unlawful labag sa batas, hindi makatarungan; Iloc: haan a nalinteg

Lawn madamong lugar-*Sp* sa loob ng bakuran o paligiran (harap at/o likoran) ng bahay; Iloc: solar-*Sp* a karuotan iti lawlaw (sango ken/ wenno likod) ti balay

Lawsuit *(Tag. & Iloc.)* demanda-*Sp*, asunto-*Sp*

Lawyer *(Tag. & Iloc.)* abogado-*Sp*

Lax pabaya, maluwag; Iloc: haan nga stricto, agliwliway

Laxative laxante-*Sp*, purga-*Sp*, gamot o *prunes* na frutas o *juice* na pang-palambot ng tae o pangtulong para makatae
> *Synonym*
> **Purgative** purga, pangtulong para makatae; Iloc: purga, pangtulong para makatakki

LAY ilagay; Iloc: icabil

LAY egg mangitlog; Iloc: agitlog

LAY-off pagtanggal ng mga trabahador-*Sp* o empleyado-*Sp* dahil sa kahi-naan ng negosyo-*Sp* o pagbabago ng organisasyon-*Sp* ng companya-*Sp*

LAY-out, Layout ang mga *chart* at *diagram* ng plano-*Sp* at mga detalye-*Sp* nito

Layer *(Tag. & Iloc.)* patong

Layover maikling pagtigil ng eroplano o *cruise ship* sa isang lugar sa pagviahe bago magpatuloy sa paglipad sa patutunguhan

Laziness katamaran; Iloc: pagkasadot

LAZY tamad, batugan; Iloc: sadot

LAZY feeling tinatamad; Iloc: agsasadot

LEAD igabay; Iloc: igaway
> *Synonym*
> **Guide** patnubayan; Iloc: idalan, iturong, igaway

LEAD by hand akayan; Iloc: akayen, kibinen

LEAD, metal *(Tag. & Iloc.)* tingga

Leader namumuno; Iloc: bagnos

Leading 1] nananalo, 2] kung sino ang pinuno

Leaf dahon; Iloc: bulong

League kapisanan, asosasyon-*Sp*, samahan, katipunan; Iloc: asosasyon, timpuyog

Leak 1] tulo, daloy, tagas, 2] pagbubunyag ng informasyon-*Sp* na walang otorisasyon-*Sp* o pahintulot ng batas o companya-*Sp*; Iloc: 1] agubo, tedted, agtaredted, 2] mangisawang ti informasyon-*Sp* ngem awan otorisasyon-*Sp* na wenno awan palubos iti linteg o companya-*Sp* canyana

LEAN 1] magsandal, magsandig, 2] halos walang taba, 3] kaunti at hindi mabunga; Iloc: 1] agsanggir, agsadag, 2] ngangngani awan taba a carne, 3] bassit laeng ken haan a nabunga

LEAN on, soft shoulders to sandalang masimpatiya na tao, maconsuelong paghingaan ng problema; Iloc: pagsanggiran a nasimpatiya a tao, maconsuelo a tao

LEARN malaman, matuto, mabatid; Iloc: makasursuro, maammuan, makaadal

Synonyms

Study mag-aral, pag-aaralan; Iloc: agadal, adalen

Know alamin, magbatid, kilalanin; Iloc: amwen

LEARN the hard way, Learn from your mistakes *Also read hindsight in thie book.* Dito dapat natututo ng leksion pagkatapos na nakagawa ng pagkakamali at harinawa maalala parati para hindi maulit muli

LEARN the ropes pag-aaral at pag-eensayo para malaman ang pagsagawa

LEARN the tricks of the trade aralin lahat ng paraan ng pagpapatakbo ng negosio o ng departamento pati ang mga detalye, ang mga bagay na nakakaprogreso, ang mga iwasan dahil hindi efectivo o hindi nakakabigay ng ventahe - lahat ito at iba pa ay alamin para madaling umunlad sa trabaho o sa negocio.

Learned a lesson after an eye-opening experience *Read Hindsight in this book.*

Lease contrata-*Sp* para ipaupa ang bahay o sasakyan o ibang bagay

Leashed, On leash nakatali; Iloc: nakagalut

Least pinakamaliit sa laki; pinakakaunti sa dami, pinakamababa sa tindi o sa importancia

Leather katad, cuero-*Sp*; Iloc: lalat, cuero

LEAVE lilisan, aalis, maglayas; Iloc: pumanaw, agtalaw, agawid, ag-larga-*Sp*

LEAVE behind iwan; Iloc: ibati

"LEAVE it to God" "Ipaubaya sa Panginoong Dios;" "Bahala na (Bathala na)" Iloc: "Ited kenni Apo Dios", "Adda kenni Apo Dios"

LEAVE no stone unturned *Make all efforts, do all that one can, use all available resources, try all possible courses of action, search in all places to find, achieve or obtain something, solve a problem or complete a task.*

LEAVE quickly, Bolt out sumibad; Iloc: agtalaw a dagdagus

LEAVE someone behind iwanan, lisanan, layasan; Iloc: talawan, panawan

LEAVE something behind mag-iwan; Iloc: mangibati

LEAVE something for someone maglaan; Iloc: mangilasin

LEAVE-taking pagpapaalam, despedida-*Sp*; Iloc: pagpacada, despedida

Lecherous *adj.,* **Lechery** *n.* naglululon sa gawaing *sexual,* malibog; Iloc: masyado nga nauttog

Lector tagabasa sa simbahan o escuela-*Sp*

Lecture pagpapapahayag ng informasyon o payo at iba pa sa mga nakikinig o sa escuela-*Sp*

Led by sa pangunguna ni..; Iloc: iti pangiturong ni...

Ledge *(Tag. & Iloc.)* pasamano-*Sp*

Ledger libro-*Sp* o *record* tungkol sa pagpasok at paglabas ng pera

Leech linta; Iloc: alimatek

Leer sulyap sa tagiliran na tinging-duda o *sexual;* Iloc: talyaw ti sikigan nga talyaw-duda o *sexual*

Leery nagsususpecha at hindi maniwala; Iloc: agsususpecha ken haan nga mamati

Leeway 1] ang pinapahintulot na laya sa asal, capricho-*Sp* o kahinaan ng kapwa; 2] *extra o dagdag* na oras, pagitan o *gap* at iba pa para sa pagpatakbo o pag-andar-*Sp*

LEFT caliwa; Iloc: cannigid
Antonym
Right canan; Iloc: cannawan

LEFT, Gone umalis na, lumuwas na; Iloc: pimmanawen, nagtalawen

LEFT-handed caliwete; Iloc: cannigid nga ima iti primero-*Sp* nga iyusar caslat iti pagsurat

LEFT out unintentionally nawaglit, na-*omit*; Iloc: nagliway, na-*omit*

LEFT undone *Irresponsibly leaving the work unfinished.* Nakati-wangwang; Iloc: pinanawan nga haan a naypalpas

Leftover tira; Iloc: tidda, natda

LEG ankle buol; Iloc: lansalansa

LEG calf (back, fleshy part) binti; Iloc: gurong

LEG knee tuhod; Iloc: tumeng

LEG shin (front part from knee to ankle) lulod; Iloc: ballawas, lulod

LEG thigh hita; Iloc: luppo

LEG of pig or cow, sliced for cooking *(Tag. & Iloc.)* pata-*Sp*

LEG room luwang na puedeng i-unat ang mga paa

Legacy pamana; Iloc: patawid

LEGAL *legal*, makatarungan, makabatas; Iloc: *legal,* naturay, nalinteg

LEGAL right karapatan at katarungan ng mamamayan; Iloc: katurayan ken kalintegan iti tagabayan

Legality *(Tag. & Iloc.)* legalidad-*Sp*

Legalism *n*, **Legalist** or **Legalistic** *adj. Legalism is adherence to a religious law by doing good works to be saved from one's sins. God loves good works and advices mankind to practice it, but God's salvation does not depend on one's good works, otherwise he/she is his/her own savior. Salvation comes from God and it is a **divine plan** provided to all mankind, and it is the grace (free gift) of salvation, which frees men from the deserved punishments of all their lifetime sins. God loves mankind deeply that He sent His only begotten Son, Jesus Christ to do the supreme sacrifice for the salvation of mankind by Jesus Christ's sufferings, crucifixion, death, and His resurrection. If a person believes that Jesus Christ took and endured the punishments of all men's lifetime sins, and receives Jesus Christ into his/her heart and life as his/her Lord God, Savior and Redeemer, all his/her past, present and futures sins are forgiven and cleansed by the blood of Jesus Christ on the cross, and he/she is now destined for heaven. Right there and then, the Holy Spirit comes to indwell in his/her heart never to leave nor forsake him/her as God is Immanuel, meaning God with us, to walk with us and help us live a God-abiding life; and he/she also acquires a new birth and becomes spiritually born again as God's child. Legalism* ay pagsunod sa reglamento ng batas pero hindi sa salita ng Dios na nag-uulat na ang kaligtasan ng tao ay hindi natatamo lamang sa mabuting gawain. Nasisiyahan ang Dios sa mabuting gawain at hinihimok Niyang mamuhay tayong mabait at mabuti parati, pero hindi iyan ang kaligtasan ng ating *souls* dahil may *divine plan* ang Dios para sa kaligtasan ng ating kaluluwa. Ang kaligtasang itinakda ng Dios ay pagtanggap sa Dios Anak na si Hesu Cristo sa buhay at puso natin bilang Dios natin at Tagapagligtas natin dahil si Hesu Cristo ang nagdusa sa mga parusa ng ating lahat na kasalanan, imbes na tayo ang magdusa sa infierno. Ang mga kasalanan natin ay napapatawad at nalilinisan sa pamamagitan ng pagdurusa, *crucifixion* at dugo ng Dios Hesu Cristo sa cruz, at dito ay makakapunta na tayo sa langit, at dito ay tumitira din ang Dios Espiritu Santo sa puso natin para gabayan tayong mamuhay ng maka-Dios, at nagkakaroon pa tayo ng bagong kapanganakan kaya nagiging espiritual na anak na tayo ng Dios.

Legend mga sari-saring cuentong pinamana pa ng mga ninuno

Legible nababasa at kung mga simbolo, puedeng matanto ng mga ito

Legislate ipasasabatas; Iloc: aramiden a linteg nga reglamento-*Sp* iti husticia

Legitimate *legal*, makatwiran; Iloc: *legal*, nalinteg

LEGS paa; Iloc: saka
Correlated words
Bow-legged sakang; Iloc: pakkang
Knock-kneed piki; Iloc: sallakung

LEGS astride or wide apart while seated nakabucaca, bukangkang, nakahandusay; Iloc: nakakayang, nakabukangkang, nakabeldang

LEGS moving to and fro while seated nag-iindayog ang paa; Iloc: agkoycuyakoy dagiti saksaka

Lei bulaklakang quintas sa leeg; Iloc: quentas a sabsabong

Leisure tiempo-*Sp* ng pahinga; Iloc: tiempo ti paginana

Leisurely banayad, campante-*Sp*, at walang man lang pagmamadali

Lemon *(Tag. & Iloc.)* calamansi, dalanghita at iba pang frutas na maaasim/ naalsem

Lemonade *(Tag. & Iloc.)* lemonada-*Sp*

LEND magpahiram, ipahiram, magpautang; Iloc: agpautang, agpabulod
Correlated words
Borrow hiramin; Iloc: buloden
Owe mangutang; Iloc: agutang
Return a thing ibalik; Iloc: isubli, ipulang

Pay *(Tag. & Iloc.)* mag-/ag-bayad

LEND an ear, Give ear makinig; Iloc: agdengngeg

Length haba; Iloc: kaatiddog

Lengthen pahabain; Iloc: paatiddogen, gayadan
Correlated word
Stretch banatin, unatin; Iloc: bennaten, unnaten
Antonyms
Shorten paiklihin, paigsihin; Iloc: pakitingin pabassiten
Truncate paigsihin, paiklihin o bawasan kaya putolan ang isang parte nito

Lenient pabaya, maluwag; Iloc: haan nga stricto, agliwliway
Synonym
Lax pabaya, maluwag; Iloc: haan nga stricto, agliwliway
Antonym
Strict stricto, mahigpit; Iloc: stricto

Lens *(Tag. & Iloc.)* lente-*Sp*

Lent *(Tag. & Iloc.)* cuaresma-*Sp*

Leper *adj.*, **Leprosy** *n. (Tag. & Iloc.)* may ketong

Lesbian babae na ang gustong asawa o kasama sa buhay ay kapwa babae

Lesion *(Tag. & Iloc.)* sugat

Less mas kaunti; Iloc: mas bassit, basbassit

Lessee ang umuupa; Iloc: iti agup-upa

Lessen bawasan, pakontihin; Iloc: kissayan, pabassiten

Lesson *(Tag. & Iloc.)* leksion-*Sp*

Lessor ang nagpapaupa; Iloc: iti agpapaupa

Lest baka kung, sakali mang..; Iloc: baka nu, amangan nu

LET pahintulotan; Iloc: palubosan

LET it go, Let it pass *When there is violence, report it to the authorities. But if it is just a petty offense by somebody, take the high road and cut him/her some slack by letting it pass.*

"LET it go," "Let it pass" "Hayaan mo na" Iloc: "Bay-amon," "Pagpasaremon"

"LET us eat" "Kumain na tayo" Iloc: "Mangan tayon"

"LET us go!" "Tena!" Iloc: "Intayon!"

Lethal nakakamatay; Iloc: makapatay

Lethargic tulog ang pakiramdam na parang walang malay; Iloc: turog ti ricna nga casla awan puot na

LETTER sulat, liham; Iloc: surat

LETTER, alphabet letra-*Sp*, titik; Iloc: letra

Lettuce *(Tag. & Iloc.)* lechugas-*Sp*

Leukemia *(Tag. & Iloc.)* lukemya

Levee estero-*Sp*, canal ng tubig na may pinataas na bakod sa magkabilang gilid bilang sangga para hindi umapaw ang tubig at bahain ang labas

LEVEL ipatag, ipantay; Iloc: ipatag

LEVEL with someone maging matapat at nagsasabi ng katotohanan sa isang tao

Leverage ang pagkakaroon ng katangian o nasa *position* siya na makakabigay ng lamang o ventahe-*Sp* sa canya; Iloc: addaan isu iti kababalin wenno iti puesto a makaited canyana iti gundaway o lamang o ventahe
Correlated words
Edge, Advantage *(Tag. & Iloc.)* lamang
Hold all the aces nasa puesto na maventahe, nasa puesto na siya ang namumuno
Outguess nagkakaroon ng lamang dahil sa mismo niyang katalasan ng isip at pagtuturing sa kinabukasan at puedeng paghahanda pa nito at naaantabayanan ang tama at husto na gawain o layonin

Levitate tumaas na walang tulong - basta lumulutang lamang

Levy ifuersang colectahin ang buis; (British): ipasok na magsilbi sa *military*

Lewd bastos-*Sp*, malaswa, mahalay, walang moralidad-*Sp* at etico-*Sp* at dignidad-*Sp* at integridad-*Sp*, hindi decente-*Sp*; Iloc: bastos, haan a decente, awan ti moralidad ken etico ken dignidad ken integridad

Lexicography proceso-*Sp* ng paggawa ng dictionaryo-*Sp* sa pamamagitan ng pananaliksik o *research*, pagsasalin ng kahulugan, pagsulat at ma-ingat na pag-aayos o *editing*

Lexicon, Lexis *(Tag. & Iloc.)* vocabulario-*Sp*

Liability responsibilidad, obligasyon-*Sp*, pananagutan

Liable mananagot, responsab-le-*Sp*; Iloc: mangsungbat, responsab-le

Liar sinungaling, bolero/ra-*Sp*; Iloc: naulbod, agparparbo, bolero/ra

Liaison 1] matalik na pagkakaugnay o coneksion-*Sp*, 2] *adulterous* na relasyon-*Sp*

Libel manirang-puri, pasamahin ang reputasyon-*Sp*; Iloc: mangpadakes ti reputasyon, mang-perdi-*Sp* ti dayaw,

Liberal bukas siya sa mga bagong proposisyon-*Sp* at hindi siya nakatali sa tradisyon-*Sp* ng bayan o sa mga paniniwala ng relihion-*Sp* at iba pa

Liberate pakawalan siya sa pag-aapi sa canya o sa culongan o sa *control* ng ibang bayan

Liberty kalayaan; Iloc: wayawaya

Libido pag-aasam na *sexual*

Library *(Tag. & Iloc.)* library

Libretto mga salita o pangungusap na ginanagmit sa musica-*Sp* o *opera*

Lice *[plural],* **Louse** *[singular]* *(Tag. & Iloc.)* cuto
  Correlated word
  Egg of lice lisa; Iloc: lis-a

License *(Tag. & Iloc.)* licensia-*Sp*

Licensed *(Tag. & Iloc.)* licensiado-*Sp*

Licentious hindi nagkakaroon ng *moral* na diciplina-*Sp* o hindi pina-pansin ang mga makabatas na pinagbabawal kundi nakatuon ang pansin sa mga *sexual* na gawain

Licit legal-*Sp*, nasasabatas; Iloc: *legal*, nalinteg

LICK talonin; Iloc: abaken

LICK with tongue himodin, dilaan; Iloc: dilpatan, dildilan

Lid, Cap cover takip; Iloc: calub

LIE kasinungalingan, magsinungaling, magbulaan, bulaan, mambola; Iloc: ulbod, agulbod, agparbo, mangbola
  Synonym
  Far-fetched hindi kapani-paniwala dahil sa may mga bagay na nagpapahiwatig na kasinungalin lang

LIE down mahiga; Iloc: agidda

LIE in state (viewing before the funeral) *viewing,* nakaburol

LIE low tahimik para hindi mapansin, tinitiyak niyang hindi siya lantad

LIE next to another magsiping; Iloc: agcaidda

LIE prostrate, face down magdapa, maghandusay; Iloc: agpakleb, agdeppa

LIE supine flat, face up bulagta, tihaya; Iloc: agidda a nakatangad ti langit/ngato

Lien ang makabatas na pag-aangkin ng *claimant* sa ari-arian ng isang nakautang para mabayaran at matupad ang obligasyon ng nakautang

Lieu of, in *[in loo of]* gaganap para kay/sa

Lieutenant *(Tag. & Iloc.)* tenyente-*Sp*

LIFE buhay; Iloc: biag

LIFE insurance seguro na naggagarantiya na ang tinakda na perang halaga ay mapunta sa *beneficiary* kapag ang

LIFE jacket, floater *(Tag. & Iloc.)* salvavida-*Sp*

LIFE support mga paraan at aparato-*Sp* na ginagamit ng mga manggagamot para mapanatiling buhay ang paciente at inaasahang lumakas at gumaling na naman

Lifeguard expertong lumalangoy na nagtatrabaho na magmanman ng ibang lumalangoy at sagipin sila kung sila'y nalulunod

Lifelong sa buong buhay, habang buhay; Iloc: ingganat patay, mientras-*Sp* a sibibiag

Lifestream, Lifecast icuento o i-*record* ang iba't ibang *topics* o nilalaman at pakikipagsosyalan sa *internet* sa isa lamang na *website* mula sa kauna-unahang fecha-*Sp* hanggang sa kasalukuyan o sa kahuli-hulihang fecha

Lifetime *see Lifelong above*

LIFT i-angat, i-alsa-*Sp*, ipataas; Iloc: isagpat, ipangato

LIFT a finger *(Tag. & Iloc.)* tumulong, magsagawa

Ligament litid, Iloc: piskel, pennet

LIGHT *n.* ilaw, tanglaw; Iloc: silaw

LIGHT *v.* ilawan; Iloc: silawan

LIGHT a candle magsindi ng candila-*aSp*; Iloc: agsindi ti candela-*Sp*

LIGHT at the end of the tunnel sa dulo ay may nakikitang tulong o pagkakataon o pag-asa o oportunidad-*Sp* o labasan para makaahon sa kasalukuyang problema-*Sp*

LIGHT bulb *(Tag. & Iloc.)* bombilya-*Sp*

LIGHT-headed parang nahihilo o mahihimatay

LIGHT, switch on the buksan ang ilaw; Iloc: luktan silaw

LIGHT, switch off the patayin ang ilaw; Iloc: patayen ti silaw

LIGHT weight magaan; Iloc: nalag-an
Antonym

Heavy mabigat; Iloc: nadagsen, nabantut

Lighted maliwanag; Iloc: nalawag

Lighten the load pagaanin; Iloc: palag-anen

Lightning kidlat, kumikidlat; Iloc: kimat, agkimat-kimat

Lightning and thunder kidlat at kulog; Iloc: kimat ken gurrood

LIKE, Be fond of gusto-*Sp*, ibig, nais, cursonada-*Sp*; Iloc: gusto, cayat, mayat, cursonada

LIKE, Resembling parang; Iloc: casla

"LIKE that" "Ganyan"; Iloc: "Casta"

"LIKE this" "Ganito"; Iloc: "Castoy"

Likely, Likelihood malamang, seguro-a*Sp*; Iloc: nalabit, mabalin, seguro

Liken ihambing, iparis; Iloc: ipada, iyarig

Likewise gayundin; Iloc: casta met

Lily *(Tag. & Iloc.)* lily, lirio-*Sp*

Limb bisig o paa; Iloc: takiag wenno saka

Limber nacucurva, nababaluctot; Iloc: maycurva

Lime dayap, calamansi; Iloc: dalayap, calamansi

Limit hangganan, taning; Iloc: paginggaan, patinggana

Limitation limitasyon-*Sp*, hangganan; Iloc: limitasyon, patinggana

Limited limitado-*Sp*, may hangganan, may taning; Iloc: limitado, adda patinggana

Limn i-*drawing* o ipintura para mailarawan; ilarawan sa pamamagitan ng pagsalaysay

Limp *(Tag. & Iloc.)* pipilay-pilay

Limpid *(Tag. & Iloc.)* maaninag, claro, calma, walang gulo

LINE linya-*Sp*, pila/fila-*Sp*, guhit; Iloc: linya, pila/fila
  Correlated word
  Row *(Tag. & Iloc.)* hilera-*Sp*

LINE, draw the maglapat ng limitasyon o hangganan o pangtakda

LINE, in nasa tuwid na linya, derecho; sumasang-ayon o alinsunod sa alituntunin; controlado ang asal at may timpi sa ugali; preparado at handa

Lineage angkan ng tao, ninuno hanggang sa kasakuyan o hanggang sa nabubuhay na famillia; Iloc: kaputotan o pinagtaudan ti familya inggana't iti cadara da a tattao itatta

Linger manatili pa ng konti, hindi nag-aapurang umuwi; Iloc: agtaed wenno agbati ti nabiit, haan nga agap-apura

Lingerie damit-panloob ng mga babae

Lingua franca anomang wika na ginagamit para magkaintindihan ang mga taong may iba't ibang katutubong salita at may kahalo na ibang dayuhang lengguahe-*Sp*

Linguist taong nakakapagsalita ng iba't ibang lengguahe-*Sp*
Correlated words
   Multilingual or Polyglot marunong magsalita ng mahigit pa sa dalawang lengguahe; Iloc: makasarita iti mas adu pay ngem ti dua a lengguahe
   Bilingual nakakapagsalita ng dalawang lengguahe; Iloc: makasarita iti dua a lengguahe
   Monoglot nagsasalita ng isang lengguahe lamang

Liniment medicinang minamasahe sa balat para matanggal ang sakit at ang paninigas

Link 1] dugtongan, cabitan, icabit, idugtong; 2] ano mang makipag-dugtong o magconecta sa iba; 3] sumali, makipag-isa; Iloc: isilpo, pagcapeten, maki-alyado

Lint himaymay, hibla o buhok na dumidikit sa kasuotan o sa muebles-*Sp*

Lion *(Tag. & Iloc.)* leon-*Sp*

LIP, Lips labi, nguso, bibig; Iloc: bibig

LIP service panlabas na salita pero hindi tapat o taos-puso sa kalooban

Liquid *(Tag. & Iloc.)* *liquid, fluid,* likido-*Sp,* fluido-*Sp,* malatubig

Liquidate 1] bayaran ang mga utang o obligasyon, 2] patayin

Liquidity ang pagkadali na ma-*convert* ang *asset* sa pera kahit kelan kung kinakailangan

Liquify natutunaw at nagiging tubig; Iloc: matuntunaw ken agdanumen

Liquor alak; Iloc: arak

Lisp defecto sa pagsalita na kadalasan ay hindi nabibigkas ang salita ng tama; Iloc: abul

Lissome nacucurva, nababaluctot; Iloc: maycurva

LIST *n.* lista-*Sp,* listahan; Iloc: lista, listaan

LIST *v. (Tag. & Iloc.)* ilista

Listen makinig, pakinggan; Iloc: agdengngeg, denggen

Lit, Lighted maliwanag, nailawan; Iloc: nalawag, nasilawan

Liter *(Tag. & Iloc.)* litro-*Sp*

Literal tama at tugma sa kahulugan at wala man lang dagdag

Literary may kinalaman sa *literature* o sa mga kasulatan at mga libro-*Sp*

Literate marunong magbasa at sumulat, educado o may kaalaman sa isa o iba't ibang larangan

Literati matatalino sa panunulat, o may maraming kaalaman sa isa o maraming larangan; Iloc: nalaeng iti pagsurat, wenno adu iti kaamwan na iti maysa wenno adu a larangan

Literature mga kasulatan sa isang lengguahe at sa isang panahon at sa isang cultura-*Sp* at lahi, mga kasulatang tinuturing na may kahalagahan sa larangan ng arte-*Sp*, o mga kasulatan ng mga *scholars* at mga *researchers*

Litigant siya ang nag-a-acusa-*Sp* o *plaintiff* na kasali sa caso-*Sp* na iharap sa corte-*Sp*

Litigate pagharap sa corte-*Sp* ng hukoman dahil sa paglilitis o demanda-*Sp*; Iloc: pagsango ti corte-*Sp* ti hukoman gapu ti demanda-*Sp* o caso

Litter 1] mga kalat-kalat, 2] mga batang hayop

LITTLE (size) maliit, munti; Iloc: bassit, pandak

LITTLE (quantity) kaunti, konti, bahagya; Iloc: manmano, haan nga adu, bassit
Correlated word
Pittance napakakonti; Iloc: nakabasbassit

LITTLE, very napakaliit, malinggit; Iloc: bassi-usit, bala-battit, battit unay
Synonym
Iota, Whit katiting; Iloc: battit, balabattit

LITTLE by little pakonti-konti; Iloc: bassi-bassit

LIVE, Exist buhay, mabuhay, nabubuhay; Iloc: biag, agbiag, sibibiag

LIVE, Reside nakatira sa; Iloc: agigian idiay, agtaeng idiay, agtaed idiay

LIVE and let live *Be open-minded and accepting of others even when they are different from you. Live the way you choose to live and let people do the same regardless of what others think of them; be tolerant of other people's opinions, beliefs, behavior as long as those are not harmful and destructive.* Mabuhay ka ng mapayapa at pabayaang mabuhay rin ng mapayapa ang iba.

LIVE by your wits mabuhay ka na ginagamit ang iyong katalinohan at mga kaalaman at matuto ka sa leksion ng iyong pinagdadaanan sa buhay

LIVE-in 1] nakatira sa lugar na pinagtatrabahoan; 2] magkasama na sa bahay na kahit hindi pa sila casal

LIVE stream or Livestream ipahayag sa *internet* ang *event* o pangyayari o pagdiriwang habang ito ay nagaganap

LIVE together magpisan, magsambahayan; Iloc: agkabbalay

LIVE within your means *Cut your expenses and spend less than what you bring in; stop relying on credit cards and stop keeping up with the Joneses; carefully budget your earnings; and save for the future.* Magtipid ka para may natitira pa sa sweldo mo para mayroon kang nabubunot sa bolsa-*Sp* mo kapag nangangailangan ka sa darating na kinabukasan; huwag kang umutang kahit sa paggamit ng *credit card* dahil nakakadagdag ng babayaran at nakakabigat lalo sa iyo.

Livelihood pinagkakakitahan, hanapbuhay, kabuhayan; Iloc: pagsapulan, pagkakitaan

Lively *(Tag. & Iloc.)* galawgaw, calog

LIVER atay; Iloc: dalem

LIVER spot batik sa balat na culay *brown* na kadalasan ay lumalabas kapag matanda na

Livestock mga alagang hayop gaya ng baka, cabayo at iba pa na puedeng mapagnegosyohan

Livid 1] nangitim na pasa o bugbog, 2] maputlang ichura, 3] sobrang galit; Iloc: 1] aglitem; 2] agbessag; 3] sobra a napungtot

LIVING, Alive buhay pa; Iloc: sibibiag

Synonym

Exist nabubuhay; Iloc: agbibiag

LIVING room *(Tag. & Iloc.)* salas, sala

LIVING Will, Advanced (Medical) Directive Ito ay napanotario na kasulatang bilin ng isang tao tungkol sa kagustohang paggamot sa canya kung sakaling sa dadating na araw ay paciente siya at hindi na siya makapagsalita para isabi ang pasya niya, gaya halimbawa na dapat gawin lahat ng doctor ang canyang makacaya para sa pagpapatagal pa ng canyang buhay at paggamit lahat ng *life support* gaya ng *CPR, blood transfusion, oxygen,* medicina at iba pa, o kaya kaunti lamang ang gagawin o wala man lamang gagawin at hintayin na lamang kung mabuhay siya o mamatay. Ang kasulatang ito ay nakukuha sa ospital

o sa *nursing home* at ang orihinal nito ay dapat binibigay sa canyang anak o malapit na kamag-anak, at kung gusto niya ay may copia rin ang canyang doctor; puede rin magtakda ng kamag-anak na magsalita para sa canya at ito rin ay nakasulat sa documentong ito
Correlated words

Informed medical consent isang forma na pinipirmahan ng paciente na nagpapahiwatig na sumasang-ayon siya sa operasyon o *procedure (colonoscopy, blood transfusion, appendectomy, knee* o *hip replacement)* o iba pa na gagawin sa canya, at pinapaalam sa canya sa pagpapahayag at sa papel na ito ang mga panganib na puedeng mangyayari gaya ng pagdudugo, infeksion, may mahiwa o matusok na parte ng katawan o kamatayan kahit na maliit lamang na magkatutoo iyon o posibleng malaki.

LIZARD, gecko *(Tag. & Iloc.)* tuko

LIZARD, house (small) butiki; Iloc: saltek, alutiit

LIZARD, large bayawak; Iloc: banyas

LIZARD, medium size bubuli; Iloc: alibut

LOAD *n.* *(Tag. & Iloc.)* cargamento-*Sp*, carga-*Sp*

LOAD *v.* magcarga, cargahan; Iloc: agcarga, cargaan

LOAD, Burden pasanin; Iloc: dagsen a bakbaklayen

Loaf 1] tinapay o pan de unan, 2] magtunganga o gumalagala

LOAN *n.,* **Lend** *v.* *(Tag. & Iloc.)* utang, umutang, magpautang

LOAN shark nagpapautang pero napakataas ang ipatong na *interest rate* na bawal sa batas

Loathe nasusuklam, namumuhi; Iloc: kagura, kabusor, karurod

Lobby 1] bulwagan, paghintayan, 2] grupo na nanghihikayat sa mga ofisyal-*Sp* ng govierno-*Sp* na ipasa o aprovabahan ang hinihiling nila

Lobster ulang; Iloc: udang, kappi

Local *adj.* 1] tungkol sa uri ng isang lugar o kung saan ito makita; 2] hindi laganap kundi para dito lamang sa lugar na ito; 3] <u>*noun*</u>: mamamayan ng isang lugar

Locale lugar kung saan naganap ang pangyayari

Locality pook, purok, distrito-*Sp* o kapitbahayan

Locate hanapin; Iloc: sapulen, biroken, saraken
Synonyms
Seek hanapin; Iloc: sapulen, biroken, saraken

Search hanapin, saliksikin, magtunton; Iloc: biroken, sursoren, agsursur, tuntonen, agsukain

Trace back, Track down bakasin, tuntonin; Iloc: sursoren, tuntonen
Correlated words

Found, Located nahanap, natagpoan, natunton; Iloc: nasapulan, nasarakan, nabirokan

Discover madiscobre, matuklasan; Iloc: madiscobre, maductalan

Location *(Tag. & Iloc.)* locasyon-*Sp*, lugar-*Sp*

LOCK i-candado-*Sp*, susian; Iloc: i-candado, tulbekan
Correlated word

Key susi, liave-*Sp*; Iloc: liave, tulbek

LOCK-up *(Tag. & Iloc.)* iculong sa bilibid, ipreso

Locket quintas na may letrato-*aSp*; Iloc: quentas nga addaan retrato-*Sp*

Locomotion pagpunta-punta o paglipat-lipat sa mga lugar

Locomotive sasakyan para makapunta kung saan

Lodge 1] tuloyan, 2] magcasera, matira, 3] nafirme sa isang lugar; Iloc: 1] pagyanan, 2] agcasera, agyan, 3] nagfirme iti maysa a lugar

Lofty mataas; Iloc: nangato

LOG parte-*Sp* ng pinutol na kahoy; Iloc: parte ti pinuted a kayo

LOG in, Sign in 1] paraang pagpasok sa trabaho para makapag-umpisa na, 2] paraang pagpasok sa *computer* kung saan ilagay ang *username* at *password*

LOG off, Sign off paraang pagpaalam kapag maghinto na siya sa gawain at paalis na siya; Iloc: padalan pagpalpas ken pagsardeng ti trabaho tapno agawiden

Logic pag-aaral ng mga principio ng pagrarason, mga sistema ng pagrarason

Logical pahayag o pag-aasal na tugma sa matuwid at matalinong rason na tunay at tutoo

Logistic, Logistics 1] ang siencia-*Sp* at pagpagalaw, pag-*supply*, paggamit at pagpanatili ng *military forces* sa larangan; 2] pangangasiwa ng paggamit ng materiales-*Sp* sa pagpalakad ng organisasyon-*Sp* buhat sa *raw materials* hanggang sa *finished goods*; ang madetalyeng plano-*Sp* at pangangasiwa ng malaking *complex*.

Logo marka na kilalang simbolo ng isang companya

Loin lomo-isang parte ng carne; Iloc: nalukneng a lasag iti carne

Loiter pagala-gala; Iloc: aglibot-libot

Loll gumalaw o umupo o tumindig na tamad ang kilos

LONE mag-isa, walang kasama; Iloc: agmaymaysa, awan cadwa na

LONE wolf 1] lobo na aso na hindi sumasali sa pangkat; 2] taong miembro-*Sp* ng teroristang grupo-*Sp* na inutosang gumawa ng patayan sa lugar na itinakda sa canya

Lonely, Lonesome nalulungkot, nalulumbay, namamanglaw; Iloc: naliday, agladladingit

LONG (duration) matagal, malaon, maluwat; Iloc: nabayag, agpaut
Antonym
Short (duration) maikli, sandali; Iloc: nabiit

LONG (length) mahaba; Iloc: atiddog, nagayad
Antonyms
Brief maikli, maigsi; Iloc: ababa
Short (length) maikli, maigsi; Iloc: ababa, nakiting

LONG for nag-aasam; Iloc: agcarayo, agpapaos
Correlated words
Yearn nananabik, nag-aasam; Iloc: aggaggagar, agcarayo, agpapaos, agil-iliw
Hanker pinananabikan, ninanasa, inaasam-asam; Iloc: agagagum, agpappapaos
Homesick nasasabik sa sariling bayan o familia; Iloc: mailiiliw

LONG haul matagal na panahon o malayong distancia-*Sp*

LONG, very napakahaba, panghabang panahon; Iloc: nakaat-atiddog, napaut, nawatiwat

LONG-winded napakahabang magtalumpati o magcuento o magpayo na nakakaantok na tuloy; Iloc: discurso o storia o balacadan o *advice* nga atiddog ken nabayag

Longevity katagalan, kahabaan ng tagal; Iloc: pagkabayag

Longing kasabikan; Iloc: pagpappapaos

LOOK tingnan, malasin, silayan; Iloc: kitaen

LOOK afar tanawin; Iloc: agtan-aw, tan-awen

LOOK-alike magkamukha; Iloc: agkaruprupa

LOOK back lingonin; Iloc: talyawen

LOOK briefly sulyapan, balingan ng sandali; Iloc: tumalyaw nabiit

LOOK downward from one's window dumungaw; Iloc: agcalumbaba

LOOK for hanapin; Iloc: biroken, sapulen

LOOK forward to something masugid na nag-aabang; Iloc: aggag-gagar nga agur-uray ken agsirsirpat

LOOK hostile irapan; Iloc: kusilapan

LOOK lengthily tititigan; Iloc: mingmingan

LOOK-out 1] taga-bantay o guardia, 2] mataas na lugar kung saan nakikita ang buong tanawin

LOOK out expectantly for someone nag-aabang; Iloc: sirsirpaten

LOOK-see madaliang pagsusuri o pag-*survey*

LOOK side by side to be aware of one's surroundings palinga-linga; Iloc: kumitakita nga agsinnumbangir

LOOK upward tumingala; Iloc: agtangad a kumita

Looks *(Tag. & Iloc.)* ichura-*Sp*

LOOP ano mang bilog o bilogan; tinaling pisi, lubid o lazo-*Sp* na pabilog; Iloc: silo

LOOP, in or out of the kung *IN* ka, kasali ka sa nakakaalam sa *information* ng matataas na rangko ng departamento-*Sp*, kung *OUT* ka, hindi ka kasali

Loophole ang mga makakapagpatakas o makakapagpalaya ng sarili sa obligasyon-*Sp* ng contrata-*Sp* gaya ng pagtanggal ng nakakabitag na salita o gawing malabo o paiba-iba ang kahulugan

LOOSE maluwag; Iloc: nalawa, nalucay
Antonym
Tight masikip, makipot, mahigpit; Iloc: nairut, nailet, nareppet, nakipot

LOOSE change barya, sukli, cencilio-*Sp*; Iloc: cencilio, supli

LOOSE ends 1] hindi nalulutas o naayos o nacompleto sa pakikitungo sa negocio; 2] parte o piece na nakabitin, hindi nakaconecta, hindi nagamit

LOOSE-lipped salita ng salita na hindi ginagamit ang isip at puedeng nabubunyag ang mga privadong informasyon

LOOSE, Untied calas, calag, natanggal ang tali; Iloc: nakawaya, nawarwar ti galot na

Loosen luwagan; Iloc: lawaan, palucayen

Loot mga mahalagang bagay na fuersahang nakuha sa mga victima sa labanan

Lop-sided tiwas, liblib, tabingi, hindi pantay; Iloc: bangking, haan a patag

Lord 1] ang Panginoong Dios, 2] titulo ng pangulo o ang may kapangyarihan sa maharlika o *nobility*

LOSE a competition or a battle *—In order for a learner to NOT be confused, here are the differences of Win or Won, and Lose or Lost that unfortunately both use the same words although not in the same form.*

(Future tense)

Will lose madadaig, **matatalo**; Iloc: maatiw tu, maabak tu

Will win dadaigin, **tatalonin**; Iloc: atiwen tu, abaken tu

(Present tense)

Losing nadadaig, **natatalo**; Iloc: maat-atiw, maab-abak

Winning dinadaig, **tinatalo**; Iloc: at-atiwen, ab-abakin

(Past tense)

Lost nadaig, **natalo**, natodas; Iloc: naatiw, naabak

Won dinaig, **tinalo**; Iloc: inabak, inatiw

LOSE a thing mawala; Iloc: mapukaw

Correlated words

Misplaced nawaglit; Iloc: naywawa

Find, Locate hanapin; Iloc: sapulen, biroken

Search hanapin, saliksikin, magtunton; Iloc: biroken, sursoren, agsursur, tuntonen, agsukain

LOSE money in business *(Tag. & Iloc.)* malugi

LOSE one's train of thought nawala na lamang o nakalimutan ang paksa na gusto niyang pag-usapan

LOSE one's way maligaw ng landas; Iloc: mayyaw-awan

Synonym

Get off course nalihis; Iloc: naywawa

LOSE touch with someone nawala ang *contact* o pakikipagbalitaan sa kaibigan o kamag-anak

Loser 1] natalo, natepok, natodas; 2] taong parating hindi mabuti ang kalabasan ng canyang gawa; Iloc: 1] naabak, naatiw, natepok, natodas; 2] tao nga canayon a madi iti pagbalbalinan iti aramid na

LOSS pagkawala, pagkatalo; Iloc: pagkapukaw, pagkaatiw

LOSS ratio panumbas o pagtumbas ng *premiums* na binayad ng nag-paseguro sa *insurance company* katumbas sa *claims* na binabayaran nila sa nakaseguro

Lot lote-*Sp*; Iloc: solar-*Sp*, lote

Lotion *lotion*, pamahid sa cutis ng mukha o ibang parte ng katawan

Loud malakas na voses-*Sp* o tono-*Sp* o tinig; Iloc: napigsa a voses o tono o uni

Correlated words

High pitch matinis; Iloc: nasinggit

Noisy maingay, nakakabingi; Iloc: natagari, nariri, naringgor, naariwawa

Louder, make the voice/tone volume lakasan mo ang voces/tono; Iloc: pigsaan ti voces/ tono

Lounge 1] nagpapalipas ng oras para maginhawaan at makapagpahinga, 2] bulwagan, napakalaking salas

Lousy 1] pangit o mumurahin ang pagkagawa, 2] hindi nakakaaliw ang pagganap, 3] matamlay ang pakiramdam

Lovable kaakit-akit, kaibig-ibig, kagiliw-giliw; Iloc: nakaay-ayat, nakalinglingay

LOVE *n.* pag-ibig; Iloc: ayat

Correlated words

Heartstring napakalalim na pagmamalasakit at pagmamahal

Real humane love is helping someone who can never return the favor ang tunay na pagmamahal sa kapwa ay tumulong sa iba na hindi nila cayang gumanti sa tulong na natanggap nila

LOVE *v.* ibigin, mahalin, itangi, gustohin, nagtatangi; Iloc: ayaten, dung-wen, gustoen (gusto-*Sp*)

Synonyms

Endear mahalin at tinatangi; Iloc: ayaten ken dungdungoen

Like, Be fond of, Want gusto, ibig, nais, cursonada; Iloc: gusto, cayat, mayat, agrayo, cursonada

LOVE, fading nagmamaliw na pag-ibig; Iloc: kumapcapsot nga ayat

LOVE handle taba sa baywang; Iloc: taba iti siket

LOVE, pure matimyas at dalisay na pagmamahal; Iloc: puro-*Sp* ken usto-*Sp* a pagayat

LOVE seat sofa na dalawa lamang ang puedeng umupo

LOVE, show carinyohin, lambingan, maglambing; Iloc: ag-carinyo-*Sp*, agdungngo, aglailo

Lovely kaakit-akit, kanais-nais, kabigha-bighani, guapa-*Sp*, kagiliw-giliw; Iloc: guapa, nakaliwliwa, napintas, nakaay-ayat

Lovemaking *see Sexual intercourse*

Lovers magkasintahan, magnovio't novia-*Sp*; Iloc: agayan-ayat, agnovio-*Sp* ken agnovia

Lovey-dovey dalawang nagkacarinyohan; Iloc: dua nga agdindinnungngo

Loving malambing, macarinyo, carinyoso/sa; Iloc: nadungngo, mapag-carayo, carinyosa, nalailo, nacarinyo

LOW mababa; Iloc: nababa
Antonym
High mataas, matayog; Iloc: nangato

LOW beam ilaw ng sasakyan na mahina na maikling layo lamang ang iniilawan

LOW brow mga hilig at kagustohan ay nagpapahiwatig na siya ay hindi intelihente

LOW-key simp-le at maamo at mapacumbaba at mahinhin, asal na simp-le at wala man lamang siyang paghahambog o pagpapasikat; Iloc: simp-le-*Sp*, na-emma at umilde-*Sp*

LOW profile *(same as Low-key above)*

LOWER *adj.* mas mababa; Iloc: mas nababa

LOWER *v.* ilagay sa baba; Iloc: ibaba

Lowest part pinakamababa, kailalimlaliman; Iloc: kababaan, kasirok-sirokan

Lowlife taong walang moralidad o taong pobre

Lowly mapagpakumbaba, simp-le-*Sp* at hindi imikin

Loyal *adj.,* **Loyalty** *n. Faithful to a cause, responsibilities, commitments, one's country, friend or spouse by means of trustworthiness, sincerity, reliability, adherence, honor, patriotism, devotion, truthfulness, support, bond and other good traits.*

Lube, Lubricate langisan; Iloc: lanaan (lana-*aSp*)

Lucid 1] madaling maintindihan, intelihente, tama ang pagrarason, 2] naaaninag o claro

Luck suerte-*Sp*; Iloc: suerte, gasat
Correlated words
Fluke *(Tag. & Iloc.)* kasuertehan
Fortunate mapalad, masuerte; Iloc: nagasat, masuerte

Lucky masuerte, mapalad; Iloc: suerte, nagasat

Lucrative maunlad; *(Tag. & Iloc.)* kumikita, gumagana

Lucre pera o malaking balik-puhunan

Ludicrous nakakatawa dahil sa halatang hindi relevante o hindi tugma sa kawastoan o sa tamang rason

Luggage *(Tag. & Iloc.)* maleta-*Sp*, bagahe-*Sp*

Lukewarm maligamgam; Iloc: nabaaw, haan unay nga napudot

Lull 1] nakakacalma o antok, nakakaginhawa, nakakapahinga; 2] pagitan o sandaling pagtigil dahil sa paghina ng bagyo o trabaho

Lullaby mahinahong canta-*Sp* para patulogin ang sanggol

Lumbago sakit sa likod ng balakang dahil sa *strain* sa laman o kaya *slipped disk*

Lumber negosyong pagputol ng mga punong-kahoy para sa pagpagawa ng mga bahay, muebles-*Sp* at iba pa

Luminous maliwanag, masinag; Iloc: nalawag, nasillag, naranyag

LUMP bukol, pigsa; Iloc: bukol, busali
  Correlated word
  Cyst *(Tag. & Iloc.)* butlig

LUMP sum minsanang pagbigay ng pera na tinuturing na completong bayad na

Lumpy sauce namuo-muo; Iloc: agtutukel

Lunacy *n.,* **Lunatic** *adj.,* baliw, pagkabaliw; Iloc: bagtit, balla, pagkaballa

Lunch pananghalian; Iloc: pangngaldaw

Luncheon formal o eleganteng kainan

Lungs baga; Iloc: bara

Lure hikayatin at iligaw; Iloc: awisen ken ilawlaw-an
  Synonym
  Induce addiction ilulong, ipalulong

Lurid napakasama, napakalaswa

Lurk, Lurk around aali-aligid; Iloc: aglibot-libot
  Correlated word
  Loiter pagagala-gala; Iloc: agpalibot-libot

Lush malagong dumahon; Iloc: nalapsat nga agbulong

Lust libog, kalibugan; Iloc: kauttugan

Lustful masyadong malibog; Iloc: masyado nga nauttog

Luster, Lustrous kinang, kintab, ningning; Iloc: sileng

Luxuriant tumutubong malago; Iloc: agtubtubo a nalapsat ken naruay

Luxury *(Tag. & Iloc.)* *luxury,* luho-*Sp*

Lynch pagbibitay na sinuportahan ng mga tao pero walang pahintulot ng batas

Lyric *n.,* **Lyrical** *adj.* tula at musica na nagpapahayag ng emosyon at observasyon

M

Ma'am or sir pô; Iloc: apo

Macabre nakakatakot, tungkol sa patay at pagkabulok nito

Machete, Philippine *(Tag. & Iloc.)* balisong, bolo

Machine *(Tag. & Iloc.)* makina-*Sp*, motor-*Sp*

Machismo, Machoism paniwala at evidencia-*Sp* na ang lalaki ay mas dominante-*Sp* kaysa sa babae dahil mas malakas, mas matangkad, mas matapang, at mas matibay ang katawan

Macho lalakeng nagpapakita ng pagka-*machoism or machismo*

MAD, Angry galit; Iloc: makaunget

MAD, Crazy baliw; Iloc: mauyong

Madden pagalitin, pasiklabin ang poot; Iloc: papungtoten

Madam *(address for a woman)* po, ate, ale, tita-*Sp*; Iloc: apo, manang, nana, tita

MADE in gawa sa, yari sa; Iloc: aramid idiay, aramid iti

MADE-to-order hindi binili sa tindahan o sa catalogo-*Sp* kundi pinagawa para masunod ang kagustohang stilo-*Sp*

Magazine *(Tag. & Iloc.) magazine*

Maggot mga uod na galing sa langaw na lumalabas buhat sa patay at nabubulok na hayop

Magisterial 1] naaangkop sa *master*, may otorisasyon-*Sp*, importancia-*Sp*, influwencia-*Sp*; dominante-*Sp*, dictador-*Sp*, *superior*; 2] nasa puesto-*Sp* ng mahistrado

Magistrate ofisyal-*Sp* na nagpapalakad ng administrasyon-*Sp* ng batas; hues-*Sp*

Magnanimous *Noble, high-minded, altruist, always a do-gooder; willingly forgive offender's offenses; selfless, kindly, considerate and has a philanthropic heart.* Taong mabuti ang isip at puso at ayaw gumanti o hindi nagmimithi ng masamang mangyari sa nanakit sa canya kundi mapagpatawad siya.

Magnate taong may influwensia-*Sp* sa negosio-*Sp* at industria-*Sp*

Magnet *(Tag. & Iloc.)* batumbalani

Magnificense karilagan at ganda; Iloc: naranyag ken napintas

Magnify palakihin kaysa sa katunayan; Iloc: padakkelen ngem iti kaagpaysuan
Synonyms
  Aggrandize palabasin na mas malaki ang estado o influwensia o reputasyon
  Exaggerate palakihin kaysa sa katunayan; Iloc: padakkelen uray ti kaagpaysuan na ket haan
  Embellish dagdagan ang salaysay ng anoman kahit pangpasikat lamang o kasinungalingan; Iloc: mangnayon ti aniaman iti storya uray nu pangpasikat laeng wenno kaulbodan

Magnitude pagkadakila sa ranko-*Sp*, puesto-*Sp*, lawak, laki, impor-tancia-*Sp* influwencia-*Sp*

Maid 1] virhen at walang asawa na babae; 2] *housemaid, maid* - muchacha, alila, achay, katulong sa bahay

MAIDEN dalaginding, dalagita; Iloc: balasitang

MAIDEN name ang apelyido ng babae bago siya nag-asawa

MAIL *v.* ipadala sa coreo-*Sp*; Iloc: i-buzon-*Sp*, ipatulod diay coreo

MAIL box *(Tag. & Iloc.)* buzon-*Sp*

MAIL order mga in*order* na binili mula sa ibang lugar ay naipapadala sa eroplano o truck at hinahatid sa paanan ng bahay ng nag-*order*

MAIL, Post Office service *mail,* coreo-*Sp*; Iloc: *mail,* correo

Mailman *(Tag. & Iloc.)* cartero-*Sp*

Maim napinsala at puedeng nabaldado o nawalan ng parte ng katawan gaya ng paa o camay

Main ito'y pangunahin at may malaking importancia-*Sp*

Mainstream kasalukyan at naghahari na tinanggap ng marami na pag-iisip, kaugalian at kagawian; Iloc: inakceptar a pagpampanunot, ugali ken ar-aramid

Maintain ipanatili, ipamalagi; Iloc: i-mentener-*Sp*

Maintenance pangangalaga, pagsuporta, pagpreserva at pagkumpuni para sa matagalang paggamit nito

Maize *(Tag. & Iloc.)* mais-*Sp*; culay *yellow*

Majesty 1] ang supremong pagkadakila at pagkamapangyarihan at kabutihan ng Panginoong Dios; 2] ang pagkadakila ng maharlika

Major *(Tag. & Iloc.)* *major*, importante-*Sp* na tao o bagay o ocasyon, mataas na ranko-*Sp*

Majority *majority*, karamihan, mayoria-*Sp*; Iloc: *majority*, kaadduan, mayoria

MAKE gumawa, magyari; Iloc: agaramid, agparnuay

MAKE a big deal of something, Make a mountain out of a molehill maliit at simp-le-*Sp* lamang ang paksa o nagawa, pero ituring na napakalaki o napakamatindi o napakaseryoso o napakalabis

MAKE a clean sweep 1] nakakamangha na pagpanalo; 2] <u>completong</u> paglilinis na <u>walang</u> pinabayaan o iniwasan

MAKE a fast buck, Make a quick buck kumita ng malaking pera sa magaang sikap lamang

MAKE a killing malaking tagumpay lalo na sa pagpatubo ng pera

MAKE a living kumikita ng nakakasapat mabuhay

MAKE do kinacayang magsagawa o mabuhay sa kahit na anomang naroroon na magagamit o ikabubuhay

MAKE both ends meet *Budget your wage so that it is sufficient to pay your needs until the next payday; earning and spending should be in the same amount so as **not** to have debts and retain your peace of mind.* Pagkasyahin ang maliit na kinikita sa pagtitipid at simpleng pamumuhay na walang utang para nandiyan pa rin ang payapa at saya sa inyong mag-anak.

MAKE hay while the sun is shining *Take advantage of the sunny days before the storm comes and the opportunities while available before they are gone; grab the chance to pursue or accomplish something while conditions are good.* Habang maganda ang panahon, lumabas ka't maghanap ng mga oportunidad; habang bata ka na malakas at malusog, samantalahin at gamitin mo mga iyan para matamo mo ang mga hangarin mo, makapagcarera, at magtagumpay ka

MAKE nothing of it binabale-wala; hindi pinopuna o pinapansin na parang wala lang o hindi nangyari

MAKE-or-break ang resulta nito ay puedeng tagumpay o kabigoan

MAKE something from scratch magsagawa ka hindi sa pamamagitan ng pera kundi sa anomang bagay na mayroon diyan o nasa kapaligiran, o sa anomang magagamit mo sa pamamagitan ng iyong talino, abilidad, talento at lakas

MAKE the grade naabot ang kinakailangan requisito-*Sp*, naturingang kasiya-siya para pumasa

MAKE the most of something gawing napakabuti sa iyo kahit ano mang situasyon ka nandodoon, gamitin ang talino at maghanap ng paraan kung ano ang marangal na makakapuno ng kakulangang sa kalagayan

MAKE time mag-ukol ng panahon; Iloc: mangilasin iti tiempo-*Sp*

MAKE-up 1] *make-up* gaya ng crema-*Sp*, pulbos-*Sp*, *lipstick*, colorete-*Sp*, *eyebrow pencil* at iba pang ginagamit sa mukha ng babae para gumanda lalo, 2] pagkagawa ng ano mang bagay o bahay, 3] spesyal na *examination* para sa estudiante-*Sp* na hindi nakapag-examen-*Sp* dahil sa nagkasakit o primero, hindi nakapasa sa *examination*

MAKE up one's mind magpasiya, magdecisyon, at kung may mga opciones-*Sp* o paraang-pagpipilian, pasiahan kung ano ang pina-kamabuti at pinakaligtas; Iloc: ag-decidir-*Sp* ken nu adda pagpilyan, masapul nga panunotem nu ania iti pinakanaimbag ken nasalvar, ken isu dagita ti masapul a pilyen

"MAKE yourself at home" "Ituring na bahay mo ito at maging comportab-le ka dito"

Maker ang maygawa; Iloc: iti nangaramid

Makeshift ang ginawang pansamantalang matitirhan o magamit

Malady sakit ng katawan na pabalik-balik at matindi

Malaise matamlay; Iloc: natamnay o madi ti rikricnaen

Malapropos wala sa lugar, hindi relevante-*Sp*

Malaria *(Tag. & Iloc.) malaria*

Male lalake; Iloc: lalaki

Correlated word

Masculine tungkol sa mga lalake, malalake, panlalake

Maleficence *n.,* **Maleficent** *adj.* demonyo at gawaing malademonyo at makakasama

Antonym

Beneficent magandang loob at maawain at mapagbigay ng tulong; Iloc: naimbag ti puspuso na ken mannangaasi ken mapag-ited ti tulong

547

Malevolence *n.,* **Malevolent** *adj.* ang pagkakaroon ng masamang tangka, nakaka-influwensia ng masama
Antonym
Benevolence ang pagiging mapagbigay ng tulong at awa at kabutihan; Iloc: ti pagit-ited ti tulong ken asi ken kaimbagan
Malfeasance pagsasagawa ng ofisyal-*Sp* ng govierno-*Sp* na hindi maka-tarungan, nakakapinsala at contra-*Sp* sa batas; gawain na sumuway sa *public trust* o tiwala-*Sp* ng publico-*Sp*
Malfunction nagmamali-mali o hindi umoobra ng tama o hindi umaandar
Correlated words
Glitch magdefecto o pagtigil ng pag-andar na kailangang i-*repair* o icumpuni; golpe at saglit na pagkagambala
Defect *(Tag. & Iloc.)* defecto, diferencia
Malice *(Tag. & Iloc.)* malicia-*Sp*
Malicious *(Tag. & Iloc.)* malicioso/sa-*Sp*
MALIGN *adj. (Tag. & Iloc.)* maligno-*Sp*, masama/dakes
MALIGN *v.* hamakin, cutchain, laitin, tuyain; Iloc: laisen
Malignant *(Tag. & Iloc.)* maligno o grabeng sakit
Malinger nagkukunwaring may sakit; Iloc: aginsasakit
Mallet, wooden palo-*Sp*, pamalo; Iloc: malo
Malnourish efecto-*Sp* ng walang sapat na pagkain o hindi masustanciang pagkain
Malpractice hindi maingat o hindi tamang paggawa gaya ng paggagamot na humantong ng pagkagrabe o pagkamatay ng paciente
Maltreat maltratohin, abusohin, apihin, pagmalupitan; Iloc: i-maltrato, abusoen, idadanes
Malversation gawaing *corrupt* na bawal sa govierno-*Sp* o privadong companya
Mammary glands *(Tag. & Iloc.)* suso
Manacle cadena-*Sp*, posas-*Sp***,** rehas-*Sp*; Iloc: cadena, kawar, rehas
MAN mamá, lalake, tao; Iloc: lalaki, tao
MAN in addressing him with respect ginoo, kuya, tiyo-*Sp*, tito-*Sp*; Iloc: manong, tiyo, tito, tata
MAN, married lalaking may asawa; Iloc: lalaki nga adda asawa na
MAN, single binata; Iloc: baro

Manage mamahala, mangasiwa, magtangkilik, magpalakad; Iloc: ipangulwan, mangigaway, mangiturong, mang-acecaso, mangpapagna, mangimaton
Correlated words
> **Supervise** *v.,* **Supervision** *n.* mamahala, mangasiwa, mangpatnubay; Iloc: mangigaway, mangimaton

Manageable puedeng mapangasiwaan o ma-*control*; Iloc: mabalin a maigaway o mai-*control*

Management pamahalaan, pangasiwaan, tangkilikan

Manager *boss,* tagapamahala, puno, amo-*Sp*; Iloc: *boss,* amo

Mandate kautosan ng batas; Iloc: mandar-*Sp* ti linteg

Mandatory utos na hindi dapat labagin; Iloc: mandar nga haan masupyaten
Correlated word
> **Obligatory, Compulsory** obligasyong gawin, responsibleng tungkulin na dapat ganapin

Maneuver *[muh-noo-ver]* plinano at pinamahalang kilusan ng mga sundalo, *warships* at iba pa; patuloy na karugtong ng pagsasanay na *tactical* na ginagampanan ng maraming tropa sa malawak na *fields* na ginagaya ang kalagayan ng giyera; maniobra-*Sp*

Mango *(Tag. & Iloc.)* mangga

Manhandle tratohin siya ng kabangisan, kalupitan, kabruscohan at galit; Iloc: tratwen isu iti uyong, ulpit, ranggas ken pungtot

Manhunt laganap na paghahanap ng taong caraniwan ay nakatacas na criminal-*Sp* o tumakbong *suspect*

Manifest 1] ipakita, ilantad, 2] listahan ng mga carga-*Sp* o pasahero-*Sp*; Iloc: 1] ipakita, nakaparang, 2] lista-*Sp* ti carga ken pasahero ida

Manipulate *v.,* **Manipulator** *adj., n.,* **Manipulation** *n.* manipulasyon-*Sp*, tactica-*Sp* ng pang-uudyok, ito ay taong mapag-oportunista-*Sp* na gumgamit ng tactica para pukawin at hikayatin at himokin at udyokan at sulsolan ang canyang victima sa paggamit niya ng pagkukunwari at pagbabalat-kayo para maisagawa niya ang canyang layonin na nakakaventahe sa canya lang pero nakakaagraviado sa canyang victima

Mankind ang mga tao sa mundo, mga nilalang

Manliness *(Tag. & Iloc.)* pagkalalake

Manner ito ay lahat ng sumusonod: asal at kilos at salita at isip at dam-damin, modo-*Sp*; Iloc: sarita ken ricna ken nakem, modo ken garaw
Synonym
Behavior asal, ugali, salita; Iloc: garaw, ugali, salita

Mannerism hindi caraniwan sa maraming tao ito pero ito ay asal na natatangi lamang sa nag-aangkin nito gaya ng kagawian niyang pagkagat-kagat ng canyang daliri, pagsasalita na ginagamit ang camay sa pagpapaliwanag, pagsuyod-suyod sa buhok ng canyang camay, madalas na pagta-*tap* ng paa o daliri o ano mang kagawian niya na hindi caraniwan o hindi madalas na asal ng karamihan.

Mannerly maganda ang pag-aasal, pitagan at magalang

Mansion *(Tag. & Iloc.) mansion,* napakalaking bahay

Manual isagawa sa pamamagitan ng camay; Iloc: ti ima ti iyusar nga agaramid

Manufacture pagbuo ng producto-*Sp* na gamit ang *raw materials* gaya ng punong-kahoy, balat ng hayop, mga *minerals* ng lupa at tubig at iba pa

Manufacturer fabrica-*Sp*, ang maygawa, planta-*Sp*; Iloc: fabrica, iti nangaramid

Manure dumi o tae ng hayop na kung minsan ay ginagamit na *fertilizer* o abono-*Sp*

Manuscript isang libro-*Sp* o documento-*Sp* o ibang composisyon-*Sp* na sinulat ng camay sa *computer* o sa *typewriter* na pinadala para ipaprenta at mapalathala at ipasasa-publicidad-*Sp*

Many marami; Iloc: adu

Map *(Tag. & Iloc.)* mapa-*Sp*

Mar ito ay gawain ng taong salat at kapos sa katalinohan at kawalan ng mabuting puso at pag-iisip kaya siya ay naninira sa mapayapang kalagayan ng comunidad o sa mahusay na pagpapalakad ng buhay o paninira sa reputasyon ng taong kinamumuhian niya o nandudumi gaya ng *graffiti* at *vandalism*

Marble *(Tag. & Iloc.)* marmol-*Sp*

Marble game holen; Iloc: holen, bulintik

MARCH *(Tag. & Iloc.) March,* Marso-*Sp*

MARCH *v.* mag-marcha-*Sp*; Iloc: ag-marcha

Margarine mantikilya-*Sp*; Iloc: mantekilya-*Sp*

Margin parte ng kasulatan sa tabi-tabi at blanko

Marginalize minamaliit, tinuturingang hindi importante at walang bisa; tinatabi sa labas na *margin*

Marinade *n.,* **Marinate** *v.* pagbabad ng carne-*Sp* o isda ng ilang oras sa recado-*Sp* o templa-*Sp* ng suca o alak at *oil* at iba pa

Marine tungkol sa dagat; Iloc: maygapu iti taaw
Correlated words
Nautical, Naval pandagat; Iloc: pangtaaw

Mariner *(Tag. & Iloc.)* marinero-*Sp,* marino-*Sp*

Marital tungkol sa pag-asawa o sa mag-asawa

Maritime tungkol sa dagat at paglayag dito

Mark marka-*Sp,* tanda, palatandaan; Iloc: marka-*Sp,* pangtanda, pangilasinan, pangbigbig

MARKET palengke; Iloc: mercado-*Sp*

MARKET value precio-*Sp* ng kasalukuyan o precio buhat sa *book value* o halaga ng negosio-*Sp,* ng ari-arian at iba pa alinsunod sa ventahan sa *open market*

Marketing gawaing *buy-&-sell* o pagbili sa lumilikha ng producto-*Sp* at iventa sa mga mamimili na kasama ang *advertising, shipping* at *storing*

MARRIAGE casalan, matrimonio-*Sp*; Iloc: matrimonio, panag-casar-*Sp*

MARRIAGE counseling ang pag-aasawa ay maraming responsibilidad dahil ito ay panghabang-buhay at kinakailangang suportahin ang familya sa pamamagitan ng paghahanap-buhay, at mga anak ay dapat arugain, palakihing maging mabait at maunlad na tao, kaya't kung may mga problema, pag-usapan at lutasin ninyong mag-asawa ng calmado. Nakakabuti rin na humingi ng payo sa *church* o sa *professional* na tagapayo kung kinakailangan

MARRIED may asawa, casal na; Iloc: adda asawa na, nagcasaren (casar-*Sp*)

MARRIED couple mag-asawa; Iloc: agasawa

Marrow *(Tag. & Iloc.)* bulalo

Marry mag-aasawa, magpacasal, pacasalan; Iloc: agasawa, agpacasar, agcasar

Martyr 1] taong pumapayag magdusa kahit kamatayan kaysa tatalikuran ang canyang relihion-*Sp* o paniwala o *ideology* o layonin; 2] taong naghahanap ng awa o suporta sa pamamagitan ng pagkukunwari o pagpapalabis sa dinanas niyang sakit o panghahamak sa canya

Marvel *v.,* **Marvelous** *adj.* 1] taka, 2] kahanga-hanga, nakapagtataka; Iloc: 1] siddaaw, agsiddaaw, masdaaw, 2] nakadaydayaw

Marzipan *(Tag. & Iloc.)* marsapan

Masculine tungkol sa mga lalake, malalake, panlalake

Mash imasa, iligis gaya ng patatas; Iloc: limugen, imasa

Mask *(Tag. & Iloc.)* mascara-*Sp*

MASS misa-*Sp* sa simbahang Catolico, pagtitipon-tipon ng mga tao
Correlated words
Sunday Service misa o pagsasamba sa simbahan ng Protestante gaya sa iglesia ng Baptist o Pentecostal

MASS (Catholics in the Philippines) at dawn 9 days before Christmas midnight mass *(Tag. & Iloc.)* misa del galyo-*Sp*, simbang-gabi

Massacre pagpapapatay ng maraming tao

MASSAGE masahein, hilotin; Iloc: i-masahe-*Sp*, iloten

MASSAGE body with oil or lotion pahiran, himasan o haplosan at masahein ng lana o *lotion* ang katawan; Iloc: sapsapoan, aprosan ken masahein (masahe-*Sp*) ti lana o *lotion* ti bagi

Master amo-*Sp*, panginoon; Iloc: amo, apo

Mastermind ang utak at nagplano ng gawain nila; Iloc: utek ken ti nag-plano iti aramid da

Masterpiece *(Tag. & Iloc.)* obramaestra-*Sp*, ang pinakamahusay na ginawa ng isang *artist*

Master's degree isa pang *degree* na natapos sa colehio-*Sp* o univer-sidad-*Sp* pagkatapos na nakatapos na ng apat na taong *Bachelor's degree*

Mastery pagkaexpertong kacayahan sa isa o higit pa sa isa sa larangan ng kaalaman

Masticate ngangain; Iloc: mamaen

Mat, nipa banig; Iloc: icamen

MATCH, Fit bagay, magkabagay, akma; tumbasan; Iloc: agkabagay, umno; pagpadaen

MATCH, ignite a kuskosin ang fosforo-*Sp* para magsindi; Iloc: cur-iten ti fosforo-*Sp* para agsindi

MATCH, phosphorous *(Tag. & Iloc.)* fosforo-*Sp*

MATCH a couple romantically *(Tag. & Iloc.)* i-reto-*aSp,* pinagrereto

Mate isa sa dalawang magkapareha gaya ng asawa, matalik na kaibigan, kasamahan, kabahay

Material *(Tag. & Iloc.)* *material, (plural)* materiales-*Sp*

Materialistic mukang-pera; Iloc: importante unay canyana ket cuarta
   Synonym
   Avaricious katacawan sa pera; Iloc: sarabusab iti cuarta

Materialize maisakatuparan, magkatutuo, magbunga, naisagawa, bumuo; Iloc: napagbalin, nagbunga, naiturpos, nay-completo-*Sp*

Maternal 1] tungkol sa katangian ng ina o angkop sa isang ina; 2] nakuha o namana sa ina; may relasyon-*Sp* na mula sa canyang ina

Maternity tungkol sa pagka-ina o sa pagbubuntis

Matinee palabas na musical gaya ng *opera* na tinatanghal sa araw, caraniwan ay sa hapon

Matrimony casalan, matrimonio-*Sp*; Iloc: panag-casar-*Sp*, matrimonio

Matrix *sing.,* **Matrices** *plural,* 1] kung saan umusbong o nagkabuo o tumubo ang sustancia-*Sp,* situasyon-*Sp,* circumstancia-*Sp* at kalagayan ng kapaligiran; ang pinakamahalaga o pangunahing bahagi; 2] matris

Matron *(Tag. & Iloc.)* matrona-*Sp*

Matter 1] bagay na nakikita, 2] diwa, 3] may halaga

Mattress *(Tag. & Iloc.)* cuchon, *mattress*

Mature dahil nasa hustong gulang na, completo na ang pagkayabong ang katawan at isip
   Correlated word
   Grown-up nakarating na sa mayor-de-edad; Iloc: adda ti mayor-de-edad, adda iti usto nga edad itattan

Maul 1] mahabang martilyo, 2] saktan ng grabe-*Sp* gaya ng pagbugbog

Maverick 1] bakang hindi natarakan o hindi namarkahan; 2] isang politico o isang taong kilalang matalino na tumututol sa mga bagay na sa canya ay hindi tama, at independenteng tumayong mag-isa sa pagpapatnubay niya sa sariling paniwala at pag-iisip

Maxim kasabihan, kawikaan, salawikain; Iloc: pagsasarita a makapabang-ar wenno mangpaleksion, popular-*Sp* a kungkuna
   Correlated word

Quotation mga hinangong mahahalagang mensahe ng mga dakila o matatalinong tao; Iloc: dagiti inadaw a napateg nga mensahe nga insarita dagiti natan-uk wenno nasirib a tattao

Maximize gawing puno o napakalaki at napakadami; turingan ng pinakamataas na importancia-*Sp*

Maximum maximo-*Sp*, pinakamalaki, pinakamarami; Iloc: maximo-*Sp*, kadakkelan, kaadwan iti amin

MAY *(Tag. & Iloc.)* *May,* Mayo-*Sp*

MAY, Might, Can puede-*Sp*, maari; Iloc: mabalin

"MAY I pass" "Makiraan nga po;" Iloc: "Magnaak man apo"

Maybe seguro-*aSp*, yata, marahil; Iloc: seguro, ngata, sa, nalabit. *Note: "Seguro" meaning Maybe in Filipino, has been in long and customary usage despite the fact that in Spanish, "Seguro" means Sure, Certain*

Mayhem napakalupit na pananakit at marahas na panggugulo at pagsisira

Mayonnaise *(Tag. & Iloc.)* *mayonnaise, mayo*

Mayor *(Tag. & Iloc.)* *mayor,* alcalde-*Sp*

Maze, Labyrinth libangang lugar na pasikot-sikot ang daan na pinapaligiran ng matataas na halaman o pader na mahirap hanapin ang labasan

ME ako, ko; Iloc: siac, -ac

ME, to, On me, Through me sa akin; Iloc: canyak

Meadows parang; Iloc: tanap

Meager kaunti, kulang na kulang; Iloc: bassit, nakakurkurang

Meal kainan, pagkain; Iloc: pannangan, makan

Meals, in-between *(Tag. & Iloc.)* merienda-*Sp*, chichiria

MEAN, Meaning kahulogan, ibig sabihin; Iloc: katarusan, ipataros

MEAN, Unkind masungit; Iloc: naulpit

Meander 1] gumalaw na campante at parang walang direksion-*Sp*, 2] daan o ilog na pacurva-curva

Meaning kahulogan, ibig sabihin; Iloc: katarosan, kaipapanan, cayat na nga sawen

Meaningful makahulogan; Iloc: napateg

Means 1] paraan o cacayahan o instrumento na naisasagawa ang isang bagay, 2] pera, ari-arian o kayamanan

Meant for nakalaan kay/sa, para kay/sa, nakalaan sa/kay; Iloc: agpaay kenni/iti, para kenni/iti

Synonym

554

Intended for para, naukol sa/kay; Iloc: para, agpaay ti/kenni, naytutop para ti/kenni, naysaad para ti/kenni

Meanwhile, Meantime, While samantala, habang; Iloc: mientras-*Sp*, bayat

Measles tigdas; Iloc: camuras
  Other ailments that is evident on the skin
  Chicken pox bulutong-tubig; Iloc: tuko
  Smallpox bulutong; Iloc: burtong

Measure sukat; Iloc: rukod
  Synonym
  Gauge sukatan; Iloc: rukoden, agrukod

MEAT carne-*Sp*, laman; Iloc: carne, lasag

MEAT, tough or leathery makunat na carne-*Sp*; Iloc: naculbet nga carne, nakinnit

MEAT, tender malambot na carne-*Sp*; Iloc: nalukneng nga carne

Meaty, Fleshy malaman; Iloc: nalasag

Mechanic *(Tag. & Iloc.)* mekanico-*Sp*

Mechanical 1] makinang aparato; 2] dahil sa patuloy-tuloy o bihasang paggawa o sa bihasang pamaraan, parang makina-*Sp* na tuloy siyang magsagawa; Iloc:1] makina; 2] gapu ta patuloy-tuloy o cadawyan nga obra iti sigud a pagaramid o pagpadalan, isu ket casla makina nga agobra itattan

Medal *(Tag. & Iloc.)* medalya-*Sp*

Meddle nakikialam, sumasabad; Iloc: agsampitaw, agmetmeter-*Sp*, agbi-biang, agmir-miron-*Sp*

Media mga paraan ng comunicasyon-*Sp* at libangan gaya ng *radio, television*, mga periodico-*Sp* at Internet na nakakarating at nakakaabut sa karamihan ng mga tao; Iloc: dagiti pangdalan ti comunicasyon-*Sp* ken pagliwliwaan casla iti radio-*Sp*, TV, dagiti periodico ken Internet nga makapan ken makaabut iti kaadduan a tattao

Medial nasa puesto-*Sp* na gitna o tungkol sa *middle*

Mediate, Act as go-between mamagitan para ayosin ang pagkaka-diferencia ng dalawang panig; Iloc: agtengnga tapno aregloen iti pagkadiferencia iti dua a panig
  Correlated words

Middle ground ang dalawang magkaiba o magkasalungat na pag-iisip ay puedeng magkasalubongan sa kalagitnaan para doon sila maghanap ng mapagkasundoan nila

Intervene mang-awat sa pagkadiferenciahan ng dalawang panig; Iloc: manganawa iti pagkadiferenciaan ti dua a panig

Medic manggagamot, miembro-*Sp* ng *medical corps* ng *military*

Medical tungkol sa pagpapagamot at pagsusuri ng sakit at pagreceta ng medicina na nasasa-camay ng *doctor* o sa ospital at laboratoryo

Medicate paggamot sa pamamagitan ng medicina-*Sp*

MEDICINE, Medication medicina-*Sp*, gamot; Iloc: agas, medicina
Kinds of Medicine, Medication

Prescription medicina na nireceta ng doctor para sa paggamot ng sakit ng canyang paciente

Over-the-counter medicinang hindi nireceta ng *doctor* kundi kusang pinili at binili sa mga naka-hilerang mga gamot sa *shelf*

Generic medicine *generic* ay aprovadong pangalan ng gamot at kadalasang nirereceta ng mga doctor at lalong sinasakop ng *medical insurance coverage.* Ang *generic medicine* o *medication* ay mas mura kahit na ang mga gamot na ito ay magkapareho sa *brand medicine* sa bisa at calidad o *quality*

Brand name medicine ginawa itong *brand name medicine* para madaling maalaala at ibigkas at ibaybay o i-*spell*. Ang *brand name medicine* ay, kung minsan, may combinasyon na ibang medicina at mga ito'y nakasulat sa cahon o botelya nito

Mega-vitamins sobra o mas labis sa kinakailangang dami para manatiling malusog

MEDICINE, take uminom ng gamot/medicina-*Sp*; Iloc: ag-tomar-*Sp* ti agas/medicina

Mediocre caraniwan ay ordinaryo-*Sp* na uri o clase-*Sp* o puede ring medio-*Sp inferior* o medio-*Sp* mababang clase kung i-compara-*Sp* sa pinakamahusay

Meditate *v.*, **Meditative** *adj.* nagmumuni-muni, nagdidilidili, nag-iisip ng mabuti; Iloc: agpampanunot

Meditation *(Tag. & Iloc.)* meditasyon-*Sp*

Medium 1] mas maliit sa *large* at mas malaki sa *small*, 2] taong kinilalang may comunicasyon-*Sp* sa mga espirito-*Sp*; Iloc: 1] mas bassit diay *large* ken mas dakkel ngem iti *small*, 2] tao nga naypaammo nga mabalin na makipagcomunicasyon-*Sp* cadagiti spirito

Meek tahimik, kimi, maamo; Iloc: naulimek, naemma, kimmi, naamo

Meet magsalubong, salubongin, magtagpo, magtipan, magkita; Iloc: agsabat, sabaten, agsarak, agkita

Synonym

    Encounter makasalubong, makaencuentro, masagupa; Iloc: masabat, agsabat, ag-encuentro

Meeting pulong-pulong, pagtipon-tipon, *meeting*; Iloc: pagtitipon, *meeting*

Meeting place pagtagpoan; Iloc: pagsasarakan

Mega- mas labis sa mga kapareho

Mega-vitamins sobra o mas labis sa kinakailangang dami para manatiling malusog

Melancholic *adj.,* **Melancholy** *n.* mapanglaw, malungkot at parating maiyak-iyak na parang may *depression*; Iloc: naliday, naladingit ken makasangsangit nga casla adda *depression* na

Mélange iba't-ibang pinagsama-sama, halo-halo; Iloc: agsaba-sabali nga pinaglalaok

Meld pag-isahin o pagsamahin; Iloc: pagmaymaysaen

Melee *(Tag. & Iloc.)* bakbakan, labo-labo

Mellow mahinahon; Iloc: natalna

Melody himig ng awit; Iloc: tono-*Sp* ti cancion-*Sp*

Melt tunawin, matunaw; Iloc: tunawen, matunaw

Correlated word

    Liquify natutunaw at nagiging tubig; Iloc: matuntunaw ken agdanumen

Meltdown 1] grabeng sumpong ng emosyon-*Sp*, 2] sobra na pag-init ng *nuclear reactor core* kaya natunaw at lumabas ang *radiation*

Melting pot 1] caldero-*Sp* na gawa sa metal-*Sp*; 2] lugar-*Sp* o rehion-*Sp* o bansa kung saan nagbabagayan at nag-aangkop para magkaisa ang iba't ibang grupo-*Sp* kahit halo-halo ang canilang lahi, cultura-*Sp* at tradisyon-*Sp*

Member miembro-*Sp*, kasapi; Iloc: miembro, kasali

Correlated word

    Ally kaalyado, kaanib, kacampi, kasapi; Iloc: katimpuyog, kaalyado, kabuyot,

Meme *[Mim]* pananalita, pag-iisp o asal na madalas na pinapabahagi, inuulit, ginagaya at tinutularan ng madla na nagiging parte ng canilang kagawian, kataohan o cultura

Memento bagay na nagdudulot ng pang-alaala; Iloc: banag a paglaglagipan

Memorabilia mga bagay na importante-*Sp* dahil may ugnay sa lahi, sa cultura-*Sp* o sa *history* kaya mga ito ay pang-alaala ng mahalaga sa bayan at sa mahahalagang panahong lumipas

Memorable makakapaalaala; Iloc: makakapalagip
Synonym
Unforgettable hindi makakalimotan; Iloc: haan a malipatan

Memorandum, Memo *(Tag. & Iloc.)* *memo,* comunicasyon-*Sp* sa mga empleyado-*Sp* ng oficina-*Sp* na caraniwan ay buhat sa pinuno

Memorize isaulo, i-cabesa-*Sp*, memoryahin; Iloc: icabesa, i-memoria-*Sp*

Memorized *(Tag. & Iloc.)* cabesado-*Sp*, namemoria

Memory memoria-*Sp*, ang parte ng utak na nagpapaalaala ng mga nakalipas sa kamakailan lang at sa kasalukuyan; Iloc: memoria-*Sp*, parte ti utek a mangpalagip iti napalabas ida iti kalkalpas ken itatta

Menace may pagkamasama, banta; Iloc: adda pagkadakes

Menagerie 1] palabas kung saan makikita ang iba't ibang hayop, 2] lugar kung saan pinatira at inaalagaang mga hayop, 3] grupo-*Sp* na magkakaiba

Mend, Darn magsulsi; Iloc: ag-sursi
Correlated word
Patch *(Tag. & Iloc.)* tagpi

Mendicant nagpapalimos; Iloc: agpalpalimos, agpalpalama

Meningitis *(Tag. & Iloc.)* *meningitis*

MENSTRUATION regla-*Sp*; Iloc: regla, agsangaili, agcadawyan

MENSTRUATION pain *(Tag. & Iloc.)* disminoria

MENTAL tungkol sa utak at isip

MENTAL health ang condisyon-*Sp* ng utak at pag-iisip kung ito ay *normal* o hindi, kung ito ay matino o hindi o kung ito ay matibay pa ang memoria-*Sp* o hindi na

Mentality kung ano ang cacayahan ng utak at isip, kung paano gumagana ang utak at isip

Mention mabanggit, masambit, masabi; Iloc: maybaga, maisao, maysawang

Menu, Food course *(Tag. & Iloc.)* potahe-a*Sp*

Mercantile *adj.,* **Mercantilism** *n.* tungkol sa mga taong nagcocomersio o nagnenegosio

Mercenary mercenario, sa pag-aasam niya ng salapi, madaling maudyok kung saang lugar siya magkakaroon ng pagkakakitaan; pumapasok sa ibang bayan at sumali sa *army* nito para kumita ng pera

Merchandise, Goods for sale mga paninda; Iloc: dagiti laclaco

Merciful mahabagin, mapang-awa; Iloc: mannangaasi

Merciless walang awa, walang habag; Iloc: awan asi

Antonyms

Sensitive to people's needs/feelings, With empathy mapagdamdam, intelihensia at kabaitan sa pan-dama sa kapwa at tumutugon sa ikabubuti ng situasyon at payapang pagsasamahan; Iloc: intelihensia ken singpet nga panricna iti tao ken mangsubsubalit iti usto para ti pagimbagan ti situasyon ken natalna a pakikicadwa, mapangricna iti tao ken situasyon

Soft-hearted malambot ang puso, maawain, may considerasyon sa kapwa; Iloc: nalukneng ti puso, mannangaasi, adda considerasyon na iti dadduma

Mercy awa, habag; Iloc: asi

Mere, Merely lang, lamang; Iloc: laeng, lang, latta

Merge ang dalawang kalakal o mahigit pa sa dalawa ay pinag-isa o pinagsama bilang isang compania

Merging roads ang dalawang *lane* na calsada (ang isa ay galing sa *ramp* at ang isa ay sa *freeway* mismo) na nagiging isa na lamang

Merit 1] *verb:* naaangkop, nakararapat, karapat-dapat, 2] *noun:* katangian na nakakatamasa ng paghanga o pag-aprova-*Sp*; Iloc: 1] *verb:* gung-gona, umno, rumbeng, naykaryan, naysaad, umno, 2] *noun:* katatao a makagun-od ti pagdayaw wenno pag-aprovar-*Sp*

Meritorious karapat-dapat ang pagpupuri o paghanga at pagtangi o ng gantimpala

Mermaid *(Tag. & Iloc.)* serena-*Sp*

Merriment kasayahan; Iloc: pagragsakan

"Merry Christmas" "Maligayang Pasko"; Iloc: "Naragsak a Pascua-*aSp* yo"

Mesmerize napamalikmata o na-*hypnotized*

Mess disareglado-*Sp*, calat, ginulogulo na mga gamit o lugar-*Sp*; Iloc: disareglado, warawara, culcol, nagulogulo nga alicamen o lugar

Message *(Tag. & Iloc.)* message, mensahe-*Sp*

Messenger sugo; Iloc: naybaon, *(Tag. & Iloc.)* messenger, mensahero-*Sp*

Messiah *Messiah*, ang hinihintay ng mga Hudyo at mga Cristiano na tagapagligtas ng mga nilalang na nagkatutuo lahat na profesiya buhat sa pagkapanganak hanggang sa buong kabuhayan ng Dios Anak na si Hesu Cristo

Messy burara, salaula, disareglado-*Sp*, macalat, magulo; Iloc: burara, nawara, disareglado, magulo

Metal *metal,* bakal; Iloc: *metal,* landok
Other metals
Iron, Steel bakal; Iloc: landok
Copper *(Tag. & Iloc.)* tanso
Gold ginto; Iloc: balitok
Lead *(Tag. & Iloc.)* tingga
Silver pilak, plata; Iloc: pirak, plata

Metaphor isang pananalita o *expression* na nagsasaad ng hindi caraniwang kahulogan pero may katotohanan gaya ng "Ang pagkakaroon ng conciensia ay makapagpatuwid ng buhay"

Mete maglaan, mambahagi; Iloc: manglasin, manglak-am, mangibingay

METER *(Tag. & Iloc.)* metro-*Sp*

METER for electric or water usage *(Tag. & Iloc.)* contador-*Sp*

Method sistema-*Sp*, pamaraan, paggamit; Iloc: sistema, kapamay-an, pagaramid o pagiyusar

Methodology ang mga tinatanggap ng *scientific community* gaya ng pag-iisip, batayang palagay, sistema-*Sp* ng pagsasagawa gaya ng pamaraan, palakad, patakaran o alituntunin, kautusan o reglamento-*Sp*

Meticulous 1] meticuloso-*Sp*, mabusisi, mapagbutingting, mapagpansin ng mga detalye, 2] maselan; Iloc: 1] meticuloso, nabusisi, managbutingting; 2] delicado/da-*Sp*

Metro *train* na dumadaan sa ilalim ng lupa na tawag nito ay *subway* o *tunnel*

Metropolitan napalaking ciudad-*Sp* na caraniwan ay kasama ang kalapit- o kacapit-ciudad gaya ng Metropolitan Manila na magkakasama ang Manila, Quezon City, Pasay, Makati, Pasig, Mandaluyong, Caloocan, at iba pa

Mettle may tapang, chaga at pagpupursigi sa anomang kalagayan

Miasma nakakadisgustong modo-*Sp* o influwensia-*Sp* ng kapaligiran, mabaho o nakakalason na amoy na puedeng galing sa mga *canal*; Iloc: nakakadisgusto nga modo o influwensia iti arrubayan, nabangsit o makasabidong nga angot nga mabalin ket naggapu iti *canal*

Correlated word

Pollution lugar, tubig o himpapawid na nasalinan ng masasamang bagay na galing sa mga fabrica, sasakyan at *chemicals* na mapanganib sa mga nilalang at kapaligiran, pati buong mundo; Iloc: lugar, danum o tangatang nga naacaran iti dakes a banag a naggapu iti fabrica, luglugan ken *chemicals* a napeggad cadagiti amin a nayparsua ken iti arrubayan ken iti mundo

Mice *plural,* **Mouse** *sing.* daga, mga daga; Iloc: bao, dagiti bao

Microbe *(Tag. & Iloc.)* microbio-*Sp, bacteria*

Microclimate clima ng magkakalapit at magkakacabit na mga bayan pero magkakaiba ang temperatura *(i.e., San Francisco Bay Area's various weather-temperatures)*

Micromanage pamamahala o pagco-*control* na sobrang bigay-pansin sa mga hindi naman masyadong importanteng bagay o detalye-*Sp*

Microphone *microphone,* microfono-*Sp*

Microscope *microscope,* pang-imbestiga-*Sp* na instrumento-*Sp* na may mga *lenses* sa mata para mapalaki ang tinititigang mga sulat o mga bagay

Mid gitna, centro-*Sp*; Iloc: tengnga, centro

Midday tanghali; Iloc: tengnga ti aldaw

MIDDLE centro-*Sp*, kalagitnaan, gitna; Iloc: centro, akintengnga, tengnga

MIDDLE ground ang dalawang magkaiba o magkasalungat na paniwala o pag-iisip ay puedeng magkasalubongan sa kalagitnaan para doon sila maghanap ng mapagkasundoan nila

Midget mas maliit sa pandak na tao pero tugma o nababagay ang laki ng mga paa at kamay niya sa canyang katawan

Midnight hatinggabi; Iloc: tengnga ti rabii

Midst nandodoon sa posisyon-*Sp* ng kalagitnaan o pagitan

Midwife comadrona-*Sp*, hilot; Iloc: comadrona, ilot

Might lakas, sigla, bisa, fuerza-*Sp*; Iloc: pigsa, bileg, bisa, anib, kired, fuerza

Migrate dadayo, mangibang-bayan para doon na matira; Iloc: agdayo, mapan sabali a nasyon-*Sp* ken idiay agyanen

Mild *(Tag. & Iloc.)* sua-ve-*Sp*

Mildew *(Tag. & Iloc.)* amag, buot

Mile *(Tag. & Iloc.)* milia-*Sp*

Milestone 1] batong haligi na nagpapakita ng distancia-*Sp in miles* papunta sa isang lugar buhat dito sa may bato; 2] makahulogang *event o stage in life or in history* ng isang bayan o ng tao na may kinalaman sa progreso-*Sp* at iba pang mahalagang pangyayari

Millieu lugar-*Sp* o kapaligiran

Militant agresivo, masigasig at masugid lalo na sa pagsuporta ng isang layonin; nakikipaglaban na pang-giyera

Military *(Tag. & Iloc.) military,* military-*Sp*

MILK *n. (Tag. & Iloc.)* 1] gatas; 2] *v.* magmakinabang, hindi makatarungan o panlilinlang na makakuha o manghikayat ng bagay lalo na ang pera

MILK bottle boteng pandede ng sanggol; Iloc: botelya-*Sp* nga pangdede ti tagibi

Milkfish *(Tag. & Iloc.)* bangus

Millennials mga napanganak sa mga taong 1980 at 1990; Iloc: dagiti nayyanak cadagiti tawen ti 1980 ken 1990

Millennium isang libong taon, mil-*Sp*

Million *(Tag. & Iloc.) million*

Millionaire *(Tag. & Iloc.)* milyonario-*Sp*

Mimic kinocopia o tinutularan ang pagsalita o asal o galaw o ichura

Mince tadtarin; Iloc: tadtaden

MIND isip; Iloc: nakem

MIND other people's business nakikialam, sumasabat; Iloc: agsampitaw, agmetmeter, agbibiang, ag-miron-*Sp*

Mindful *(Tag. & Iloc.)* mapag-asecaso

MINE minahan; Iloc: mina-*Sp*

MINE, My akin, ko; Iloc: cuak, cucuak, bagik, -ac

Mineral bato o uling na galing sa lupa o tubig na matigas at may *chemical* at puedeng culay cristal at nakakatulong sa tao, hayop at halaman

Mingle makihalobilo, makitungo sa tao, makipagkaibigan; Iloc: makilaok cadagiti tattao, makigayyem
Synonym
Hobnob nakikihalobilo sa mga tao, makipagsosyalan; Iloc: makitiptipon cadagiti tattao, makipagsosyalan

Miniature copia o halimbawa ng isang bagay na pinaliit

Minimize paliitin; Iloc: pabassitin

MINIMUM pinakakonti, pinakamaliit; Iloc: kabassitan

Maximum pinakamalaki, pinakamarami; Iloc: kadakkelan, pinakaadu

MINIMUM wage pinakamababang puedeng ipasueldo na alinsunod sa utos ng batas

Minister 1] pari o pastor ng relihion o simbahan, ministro-*Sp*, pastor-*Sp*, 2] asecasohin ang pangangailangan ng iba

Ministry *(Tag. & Iloc.)* ministrio-*Sp*, ang pagsisilbi/pagservi-*Sp* sa Dios at sa kapwa

Minor mas kaunti o mas maliit o mas mababa ang ranko-*Sp* o halaga o importancia-*Sp*

Minority *minority*, minoria-*Sp*, ang mas kaunti sa buong mamamayan; Iloc: *minority*, minoria, ti mas bassit iti entero a tattao
Antonym

Majority *majority*, karamihan, mayoria; Iloc: *majority*, kaadduan, mayoria

MINT 1] halaman na ang langis at lasa nito ay masarap; 2] lugar-*Sp* kung saan ginagawa ang sencilyo-*Sp* o barya ng bayan na napapasailalim sa pahintulot at otorisasyon-*Sp* ng govierno-*Sp*

MINT condition napakahusay o perfecto-*Sp* ang pagkagawa; Iloc: nagsayaat ken perfecto ti pagkaaramid

Minus menos-*Sp*, bawasan ng..; Iloc: menos, ikkatan ti...

Minute *(Tag. & Iloc.)* minuto-*Sp*

Minutes ago kani-kanina lamang; Iloc: itattay laeng

Miracle milagro-*Sp*, himala; Iloc: milagro

Mirror salamin; Iloc: sarming, espeho-*Sp*

Mirth katuwaan at kagalakan na nalalantad sa halakhakan

Misappropriate mag-desfalco-*Sp*, mangupit, manglustay ng pera ng oficina-*Sp* o ibang tao; Iloc: agdesfalco, agcupit, mangi-usar-*Sp* iti cuarta ti oficina o sabali a tao

Misbehave mag-asal ng hindi tama o nakakasakit o nakaksugat

Miscarriage *n,* **Miscarry** *v.* 1] nakunan o nahulog ang pagkabuntis, 2] maling pagpatakbo ng administrasyon; Iloc: 1] naalisan, natinnag ti sicog, 2] haan a nasayaat a pagpaturong iti administrasyon-*Sp*

Miscellaneous *adj.,* **Miscellany** *n.* iba't iba; Iloc: agsasabali

Mischief *n.,* **Mischievous** *[mis-chi-voos]* *adj.* malisyosong palabiro pero nakakayamot, pilyo-*Sp*, gumagawa ng nakakasakit o gulo

Misconceive *v.,* **Misconception** *n.* maling akala; Iloc: pagarup a haan usto

Misconduct kilos, salita at gawa na masama at hindi sumusunod sa tamang asal at sa utos ng batas

Misdeed masamang gawa, maling gawa; Iloc: dakes nga aramid, haan usto nga aramid
Correlated words
Sin, Iniquity kasalanan, masamang gawain; Iloc: basol, dakes nga aramid
Shortcoming, Defect kakulangan, kapintasan; Iloc: kakurangan, pagkauyawan

Misdemeanor crimen-*Sp* na hindi kasing serioso-*Sp* ng *felony* at mas maikli ang parusa

Misdirect, Mislead iligaw; Iloc: iyaw-awan, ilaw-an
Antonyms
Lead by hand akayan; Iloc: kibinen
Guide patnubayan, gabayan, akayan; Iloc: idalan, iturong, igaway

Miserable miserab-le-*Sp*, aba; Iloc: miserab-le

Misfit hindi akma; Iloc: haan a rumbeng

Mishap disgracia-*Sp*, accidente-*Sp*, sacuna; Iloc: disgracia, accidente

Misjudge *v.*, **Misjudgment** *n.* maling paghusga, paghatol at pagturing, hindi makatarungan

Mislead *see Misdirect above*

Mismatched pair hindi magkapares; Iloc: pangis

Misnomer maling pangalan ng tao o lugar

Misogynist *adj.*, **Misogyny** *n.* taong galit sa babae

Misplace tinabi sa ibang lugar kaya hindi mahanap; Iloc: naywawa, naywagat, inkabil iti sabali a lugar-*Sp* isu a haan masapulan

MISS Binibini, BB. *(abbrev)*, *Miss*; Iloc: *Miss*

MISS the point hindi maintindihan ang buod o paksa

Missing nawawalang tao o bagay; Iloc: haan a masapulan a tao o banag
Correlated word
Posse grupo na hinilingan ng policia na tumulong sa paghanap ng nawawalang tao at pagpahayag sa periodico, TV at sa *boards* sa *highway* para mabasa ng mga nagmamaneho at mga pasahero; Iloc: grupo nga kiniddawan ti policia nga tumulong iti pagsapul iti tao ken inwarnak da idiay periodico, TV ken *boards* idiay *freeway* para makita dagiti lumab-labas

Mission trabaho sa ibang bayan na kadalasan ay para sa Dios o pagtulong o paggamot sa mga may sakit at may kapansanan; Iloc: trabaho sa ibang bayan nga canayon ket para ken ni Apo Dios o pagtulong o mangngagas cadagiti agsakit ken baldado

Missionary ang nagtatrabaho sa *mission*

Missive sulat; Iloc: surat

Mist *n.,* **Misty** *adj.* hamog, mahamog; Iloc: linnaaw, nalin-naaw

Mistake mali, kamalian, pagkakamali, Iloc: biddut

Mistaken for mapagkamalan...; Iloc: biddut ti pagarup...

Mister, Mr. Ginoong, *Mister*; Iloc: *Mister*

Mistreat *(Tag. & Iloc.)* i-maltrato-*Sp*

Mistress querida-*Sp,* cabit; Iloc: querida

Mistrust duda-*Sp,* walang tiwala; Iloc: duda, haan ag-fiar-*Sp,* haan nga agtalek

Misunderstanding hindi pagkakaunawaan; Iloc: haan nga agkinnaawatan

Mites that get into armpits and into navels of humans *(Tag. & Iloc.)* tungaw

Mitigate pagaanin ang kahirapan o kabigatan; Iloc: palag-anen iti rigat o dagsen

Mix pagsama-samahin, haloin; Iloc: paglalaoken, kiwaren, kiburen

Mnemonic *[ni-mon-ik]* tungkol sa o anomang nakakatulong sa memoria

Moan daing, taghoy, himutok, tangis; Iloc: unnoy, asog, sennaay
    Correlated word
    Lament naghihimutok; Iloc: agun-unnoy

MOBILE nalilipat-lipat o nadadala saanman; Iloc: may-yacar-acar ken maytugtugot uray inchenna

MOBILE device maliit na makina-*Sp* na may gamit at nadadala saan-saan; Iloc: bassit a makina-*Sp* nga adda usar-*Sp* na nga maikuyog uray ichenna

Mobilize pakilosin; Iloc: pagarawen
    Synonyms
    Launch magbunsod, magtatag; Iloc: mangbangon
    Initiate mga pinakaunang hakbang para maumpisahan ang pagsagawa at para ang iba ay tumulad o sumali
    Start magsimula, mag-umpisa, umpisahan; Iloc: mangrugi irugi, rugyan

Mock cuchain; Iloc: insultoen (insulto-*Sp*)

Model 1] huwaran, 2] modelo-*Sp*; Iloc: 1] ehemplo-*Sp,* 2] modelo

Moderate kalagitnaang uri lamang, katamtaman, malumanay; Iloc: agtengnga a clase laeng, haan a narigat wenno nalaca, haan a naamo wenno narungsot

Modern 1] makabago, 2] anomang bagong uso o moda o bagong labas na aparato-*Sp* o ang bagong clase nito
Correlated word
State-of-the-art pinakabagong labas na nagtataglay ng pinakabagong likha, imbento at pag-unlad sa larangan ng tecnolohia, siencia at arte na puede ring pinakamahusay ang pagkagawa at pinakamaraming gamit ang binibigay

Modest mahinhin, decente-*Sp*; Iloc: naemma, decente

Modify ibahin ang forma o uri

Modus operandi ang paraan ng pagpapatakbo ng pangangalakal, paghahanapbuhay at pagpapalakad

Moist *(Tag. & Iloc.)* medio-*Sp* basa

Moisten basahin ng tubig ng konti; Iloc: basaen ti bassit

Moisture hamog; Iloc: linnaaw

Moisturizer ginagawa na ang cutis ay magkaroon ng kinakailangang cremang pang-*hydrate* sa cutis para makinis at hindi matuyo at magculubot ng maaga
Other skin care
Emollient panglambot at pangpakinis sa balat

Molasses pulot, panocha-*Sp*; Iloc: tagapulot, panocha

MOLD, Mildew *(Tag. & Iloc.)* amag, buot

MOLD, Form *(Tag. & Iloc.)* i-forma-*Sp*

Mole nunal, taling; Iloc: siding

Molest manghalay o gawan ang babae o bata ng masama gaya ng *sexual*

Mollify pacalmahin, ipahinahon, papayapain, awatin, palubagin ang loob; Iloc: pacalmaen, patalnaen, aganawa, ay-aywen, anawaen, paulimeken, pabang-aran

Mollusk, 1" or 2" long with thin wrinkled and bumpy-coned body cuhol; Iloc: agurong

MOMENT ilang minuto lamang ang tagal

MOMENT ago, a kanina lamang; Iloc: itay laeng

Momentarily, Momentary sandali lamang; Iloc: apagbiit laeng

Momentum bilis o fuerza-*Sp* ng galaw; Iloc: pardas wenno fuerza ti garaw

Monday *(Tag. & Iloc.)* *Monday,* Lunes-*Sp*

Monetary tungkol sa pera o fondo-*Sp*; Iloc: maygapu iti cuarta/fondo

MONEY pera, cuarta, salapi; Iloc: cuarta, pirak

MONEY-scarce, Can't make both ends meet kinakapus, gipit sa pera; Iloc: agkurkurang ti cuarta

Monitor pagsubaybay, pagrepaso, pag-ayos, pagsiyasat o pag-observa ng tao o makina

Correlated word

Observe inoobservahan, minamatyagan, minamanmanan, minamasdan, pinupuna, pinapansin; Iloc: agob-observar, agsipsipot, agsisiim, agmingmingming

Monkey unggoy, matching *(small ape)*, bakulaw *(big ape)*; Iloc: chonggo

Monogamy pagkakaroon ng isa lamang na asawa

Monoglot alam at nagsasalita ng isang lengguahe lamang

Monogyny pagkakaroon ng isa lamang na asawang babae

Monolith 1] malaking estatuang monumento-*Sp* o isang malaking haligi na patulis gaya ng *pyramid*; 2] isang malaking bato na hugisang pang-estatua-*Sp*; 3] malaki at may pagka-uniformidad-*Sp* sa matibay na calidad-*Sp* o ugali na hindi nababaluktot

Monolithic 1] gawa sa isang malaking bato na buong-buo 2] malaki, may pagkakaisa o uniformidad-*Sp*, matibay, matatag at hindi tinatablan o hindi nababaluktot

Monopolize sinasarili lamang, binubukod lamang niya ang mga bagay; Iloc: bukbukoden na laeng, ibagbagi na laeng

Monotonous pare-pareho na at paulit-ulit pa; Iloc: agparepareho langaruden ken paulit-ulit pay

Month buan; Iloc: bulan

Monthly buanan, buan-buan, tuwing buan; Iloc: binulan, cada-*Sp* bulan

Monument *(Tag. & Iloc.)* monumento-*Sp*, bantayog

Mood *(Tag. & Iloc.)* modo-*Sp*, disposisyon-*Sp*

Moody sumpongin; Iloc: agmuryot

Moon buan; Iloc: bulan

Same Filipino word, different meanings

Month buan; Iloc: bulan

Moonlight liwanag ng buan; Iloc: sellag ti bulan

Moot hindi relevante-*Sp*, walang halaga; Iloc: haan a relevante, awan valor-*Sp* na

Mop magkuskos-punas ng sahig; Iloc: agnasnas ti datar
   Correlated words
   Sweep magwalis; Iloc: agcaycay, agsagad
   Polish wooden floor maglampaso; Iloc: aglampaso
Mope malungkot at matamlay dahil sa pagtampo
MORAL may moralidad at decente at hindi gumagawa ng kataksilan sa asawa, ni kalaswaan at nabubuhay siya ng mabuti na tama sa batas at sa mata ng Dios.
MORAL and ethical values *To have moral and ethical values, one can distinguish between right and wrong and chooses to do what is right and ethical despite any difficulties. Having moral and ethical values is evident in one's character and personality manifesting indisputable qualities of integrity, dignity, honesty, trustworthiness, credibility, truthfulness, reliability, faithfulness, loyalty, morality, work ethic, goodwill, altruism, compassion, kindness, helpfulness, cooperation, pleasant dealings with people, showing respect and graciousness, respecting people's rights and spaces at whatever age, and many more. A person who has these can be relied on and can be trusted.*
Morale disposisyon ng tao na napapamalas sa canyang confianza-*Sp*, pagkasaya, pagkagana at diciplina-*Sp*
Morality *Virtous conduct, speech, intentions and goals conforming to chastity, decency, purity, faithfulness, righteousness, and other moral values;* (*Tag. & Iloc.*) moralidad-*Sp*
Moratorium *n.*, **Moratory** *adj.* 1] pagsuspende ng gawain; 2] legal-*Sp* at may otorisasyon-*Sp* na pag-antala o pagpaliban muna na bayad dahil sa *emergency* o ang paggawa muna ng ibang legal-*Sp* na obligasyon
Morbid 1] tungkol sa mga sakit at pagkamatay, 2] walang lusog at lakas
MORE mas-*Sp*, lalo, higit; Iloc: mas, nasurok
   Correlated word
   Over lampas, sobra, labis; Iloc: surok, labes, sobra
MORE or less humigit kumulang; Iloc: agsurok agkurang
MORE than one way to skin a cat *There are many ways, known, little known and still to be discovered methods to achieve and reach your goals.* May iba't ibang paraang makapagsagawa, makacompleto, makabuo para matamo mo ang pangarap mo

MORE to it than meets the eye, there's mayroon pang iba pang bagay na hindi lantad o nakikita

Moreover isa pa, at, atchaka; Iloc: ken maysa pay

Mores costumbre-*Sp* o moralidad-*Sp* ng isang grupo-*Sp* o bayan; Iloc: costumbre-*Sp* o moralidad-*Sp* ti maysa a grupo-*Sp* o bayan

Morgue lugar kung saan dinadala ang katawan ng mga patay bago maihanda ang kanilang pagpapalibing o bago makilala kung sino sila

Morning umaga; Iloc: bigat, agsapa

Moron taong may defecto-*Sp* ang utak at kahit matanda na sila, ang isip-kaedad nila ay sa 7 o 12 taong gulang

Morose malungkot; Iloc: naliday

Morph 1] pagbabago sa ibang imagen-*Sp* sa pamamagitan ng *computer*; 2] pagbabago ng todo-todo sa ichura-*Sp* o sa ugali

Morphology 1] pag-aaral ng forma at stractura ng salita sa lengguahe contodo punto at kung saan ang pinanggalingan, 2] sangay ng *biology* tungkol sa forma at stractura ng nilalang na organismo; Iloc: 1] pagadal ti forma ken stractura ti sarita iti lengguahe contodo ayug ken nu inchenna ti pinaggapuan na, 2] sangay ti *biology* maygapu ti forma ken stractura iti imparsua nga organismo

Mortal 1] namamatay at may hangganan na gaya ng mga nilalang, 2] nakamamatay

Mortgage utang sa banko-*Sp* para makabili ng bahay at lupa; Iloc: utang diay banko para makagatang ti balay ken lote-*Sp*

Mortification *n.,* **Mortify** *v.* 1] pinahiya siya kaya nawalan siya ng paghanga sa mismo niyang sarili, 2] pagkamatay ng isang parte ng katawan

MOSLEM-Filipino from the Mindanao provinces *(Tag. & Iloc.)* moro/ra-*Sp*

MOSLEM Filipino ruler *(Tag. & Iloc.)* sultan, datu

MOSQUITO *(Tag. & Iloc.)* lamok

MOSQUITO net kulambo; Iloc: moskitero-*Sp*

Moss *n.,* **Mossy** *adj. (Tag. & Iloc.)* lumot, malumot

Most halos lahat, karamihan; Iloc: ngangngani amin, dandani amin, kaaduan

Mote maliit na bagay, *i.e.,* muta

Moth gamugamo; Iloc: simut-simut

MOTHER nanay, ina, mama, *mommy*; Iloc: mamang, nanang, inang, mama, *mommy*
Synonym
Maternal tungkol sa pagiging ina

MOTHER and child mag-ina; Iloc: agina

MOTHER and children mag-iina; Iloc: agiina

MOTHER-in-law biyenang babae; Iloc: katugangan

MOTHER tongue ang kinagisnang wika na lengguahe ng magulang

Motherhood ang pagiging ina; Iloc: ti pagka-ina

Motherland bayang sinilangan, bayan kung saan ipinanganak

Motherly pagpapakita o pagbibigay ng pagmamahal na taos-puso gaya ng pagmamahal ng ina

Motif ang piniling arte-*Sp* o ichura-*Sp* o forma-*Sp* para sa ocasyon-*Sp* o stractura-*Sp* o bahay

Motion galaw, kilos; Iloc: garaw, kuti

Motionless walang kagalaw-galaw; Iloc: awan pulos garaw na

Motivate bigyang ganang umunlad o magpakabuti o umunlad; Iloc: ikkan ti ganas-*Sp* nga agballigi o agsayaat o ag-progreso-*Sp* o agbalbaliw

Motivation hangarin o ano mang nakakabigay ng gana o pampasigla para umunlad o magpakabuti; Iloc: essem wenno aniaman a mangted iti ganas nga agballigi, agprogreso o agpakasayaat (gana/ ganas-*Sp*, progreso-*Sp*)

Motive motivo-*Sp*, rason-*Sp*, balak, layonin, tangka; Iloc: motivo, rason panggep, pakay, rangta

Motor *(Tag. & Iloc.)* motor-*Sp*

Motorboat *(Tag. & Iloc.)* *motorboat,* bancang de motor-*Sp*

Motorcycle *(Tag. & Iloc.)* *motorcycle,* motorciclo-*Sp*

Motorist isang nagmamaneho o sumasakay sa sasakyan

Motorized *(Tag. & Iloc.)* de makina-*Sp*

Motto maikling pananalita na nagpapahiwatig ng layonin o principio-*Sp* o mahalagang pangpaalaala

Mound bunton, punso; Iloc: bunton

Mount, Get on top of magsampa; Iloc: agsampa

MOUNTAIN bundok; Iloc: bantay
Correlated word

Hill burol; Iloc: turod

MOUNTAIN top taluktok, tugatog; Iloc: tuktok ti bantay

Mourn nagluluksa, nagdadalamhati; Iloc: agladladingit, agledleddaang, agdungdung-aw
Synonym
    Grieve naglulumbay, namimighati, Iloc: agladingit, agliday, agleddaang

Mourning attire luto-*Sp*, itim na suot; Iloc: nakapanes

Mouse daga; Iloc: bao

Moustache *(Tag. & Iloc.)* bigote-*Sp*

MOUTH bunganga, bibig, nguso; Iloc: ngiwat, bibig

MOUTH, open nganga, buka ang bibig; Iloc: nakanganga

MOUTH, put into one's langgain; Iloc: sakmulen

MOUTH, put words into my pinahayag niya na may bagay daw akong sinabi pero hindi ko man lamang sinabi iyon o hindi iyon ang ibig kong sabihin

MOUTH rash *(Tag. & Iloc.)* singaw

MOUTH-to-mouth resuscitation *first aid* na paraan para makahinga uli ang nahinto ng paghinga at para bumalik uli ang malay at mabuhay

Mouthful isang subo; Iloc: sangkasakmol

Mouthwash pangmumog; Iloc: pangmulomug

MOVE gumalaw, kumilos; Iloc: aggaraw, agtignay

"MOVE a little, please" "Paki-usog po"; Iloc: "Agpadengdeng kayo man bassit, apo"

MOVE, Relocate lumipat, manibagong-bayan; Iloc: umacar, umalis

MOVE sidewise, i.e. to give someone space to be seated umusog; Iloc: agpadengdeng

MOVE up, Move up in the world umavante ka para umunlad at ma-katamo ka ng magandang kapalaran at tagumpay

MOVEMENT galaw, kilos, kibo; Iloc: garaw, tignay, gunay, kuti

MOVEMENT with a stirring or rustling sound kumakaluskos; Iloc: agkarkarasakas

Movie *(Tag. & Iloc.)* cine-*Sp*, pelicula-*Sp*

Moviehouse cinehan; Iloc: cine-*Sp*

Mrs. *Mrs.*, Ginang; Iloc: *Mrs.*

MUCOUS, Phlegm flema-*Sp*, uhog, sipon; Iloc: flema, buteg, anged, sipon

MUCOUS, blow out magsinga; Iloc: agpangres

MUCOUS, dried, Booger kulangot; Iloc: duggong

MUCOUS, inhale or suck in singhotin; Iloc: singluten

Mud putik; Iloc: pitak, lutlot

Muddle 1] gawing parang maputik o malabo, 2] nalilito at natataranta, 3] pagkadisareglo o kagulohan

Muddy maputik; Iloc: napitak, nalutlot

Mudsling paninirang-puri o pag-aacusa ng masama o malisyosong bintang

Muff sira ang ginawa dahil sa hindi nag-ingat o bara-bara lamang ang paggawa o kaya wala o kaunti lamang ang kaalaman sa ginagawa; Iloc: nadadael ti inaramid gapu ti kaawanan ti pagannad o bara-bara laeng ti pag-aramid wenno awan wenno bassit laeng iti pagkaammo na iti ar-aramiden na

Muffle takpan para humina o hindi marinig ang tunog

Muffler 1] *scarf* sa leeg para hindi ginawin, 2] aparato-*Sp* para humina ang tunog

MUG inuman na hubog tubo-*Sp* at mas malaki sa tasa-*Sp*; parte ng mukha; Iloc: pang-inom nga forma-*Sp* ti tubo-*Sp* ken mas dackel pay ngem ti tasa; parte iti rupa

MUG shot letrato ng mukha ng *suspect* na kinuha sa departamento-*Sp* ng policia-*Sp*; Iloc: retrato ti rupa ti *suspect* nga innala idiay departamento ti policia

Mugger nananakit ng tao na caraniwan ay para nakawan; Iloc: mangsaktan ti tao para takawan

Muggy weather maalinsangan, init na nakakapawis; Iloc: makaling-et a pudot

Mull matinding pinag-iisipan at pilit na inaalaala ang mga pangyayari o detalye-*Sp*

MULTI- iba't iba; Iloc: agsaba-sabali

MULTI-tasking sabay-sabay na gumagawa ng mas marami pa sa isa gaya ng minamasdan ang sanggol habang nagpapalambot ng carne sa lutoan o nakikinig ng leksion o balita sa television habang naghuhugas ng pinggan, nag-e-*exercise* na lakad na pinapasyal din ang aso o habang naglalakad ay gumagawang *exercises* sa balikat o *wrists* at mga daliri at batok

One example of Mutlti-tasking

Kill two birds with one stone *This needs* <u>*proficiency and skillfulness,*</u> *yet it is quite possible to tackle and accomplish two tasks with only one effort; achieve two ends or objectives by a single action; solve two problems with one solution; use only one effort to finish two tasks; or complete two things at the same time.* Lutasin ang dalawang problema-*Sp* sa isang sikap lamang pero-*Sp* kinakailangang tiyaking <u>mahusay ang pagsasagawa at buo at completo</u>-*Sp*

MULTI-vitamins iba't ibang vitamina para sa kalusogan

Multilingual, Polyglot marunong magsalita ng mahigit pa sa dalawa na lengguahe; Iloc: makasarita iti mas adu pay ngem ti dua a lengguahe

Multinational 1] sa dalawa o mas marami pa sa dalawa na nasyon, may mga oficina, *branches*, operasyon-*Sp*, *investments*, kasocio sa mga ito; 2] tungkol sa higit pa sa dalawang nasyon-*Sp*

Multiple mas marami pa sa isa na tao o parte-*Sp* o elemento-*Sp*

Multiplication *(Tag. & Iloc.) multiplication*

Multiply i-*multiply*; Iloc: ag-*multiply*

Multiracial iba't ibang lahi

Multitude napakarami; Iloc: nakaad-adu

Multitudinous sobra at labis-labis ang dami; Iloc: sobra unay ti kaadu

Mum walang imik; Iloc: awan uni

Mumble mababang voses at hindi maintindihan, paliitin ang voses para hindi marinig ng lahat

Mumbo jumbo 1] ceremonyang walang kahulogan, ni saysay, ni kahalagahan; 2] isang idolong sinasamba dahil sa *superstition*; 3] malabo o pagpapanggap na pananalita para malito ang kausap

Mumps biki; Iloc: cabbi, bikki

Mundane ordinaryo, karaniwan, pangkaraniwan, makamundo, *common*

Munch ngatain; Iloc: caremkemen

MUNICIPAL pambayanan; Iloc: pagilyan

MUNICIPAL government govierno-*Sp* ng municipalidad-*Sp* o bayan na pinangungulohan ng alcalde-*Sp* o *mayor* na ang oficina ay sa municipio-*Sp*

Municipality *(Tag. & Iloc.)* municipalidad-*Sp*, municipio-*Sp*

Mural *painting* o obra-pinta na pininta sa pader o kisame

Murder crimeng pagpatay ng tao; Iloc: crimen a pumatay ti tao

Murderer mamamatay-tao; Iloc: mangpatay ti tao

Murk *n.,* **Murky** *adj.* nakakalungkot at madilim; maulap at hindi maliwanag na parang may usok o *fog*; malabo at nakakalito

Murmur 1] bumubulong-bulong, umaangal, 2] maghuning marmar ang puso; Iloc: 1] agtantanabutob, agan-aneng-eng, 2] adda uni a marmar ti puso
Synonym
Mumble, Mutter mababang boses at hindi maintindihan, paliitin ang boses para hindi marinig ng lahat; Iloc: nababa a boses nga haan a maawatan, bassit a boses para haan a mangngeg ti sabali

Muscle *muscle,* laman-laman ng katawan, laman ng balat; Iloc: *muscle,* piskel, laslasag ti bagi, lasag ti cudil

Muscular *(Tag. & Iloc.)* masculado-*Sp*

MUSE paraluman, lakambini, mutya; Iloc: *muse,* musa-*Sp*

MUSE, Ponder nagmemeditasyon, nagdidili-dili, o tahimik at malalalim na nag-iisip; tumitig ng malalim o ng pagtataka

Museum *(Tag. & Iloc.)* *museum*

Mush ang kaining malapot-lapot gaya ng *cereal, oatmeal,* lugaw, champorado at malapot na arroz caldo

Mushroom kabute; Iloc: uong

MUSIC *(Tag. & Iloc.)* musica-*Sp*
Correlated word
Song awit, canta; Iloc: canta, cancion

MUSIC, dance with the 1] i-cumpas-*Sp* ang canta-*Sp,* iindak, 2] makibagay sa kagawian; Iloc: 1] icumpas ti cancion-*Sp,* 2] makibagay iti ar-aramiden ti kaadoan
Synonym
Synchronize *(Tag. & Iloc.)* icumpas

MUSIC, play tumogtog (sa *piano,* violin-*Sp,* gitara-*Sp, flute, drum...*); Iloc: ag-tocar-*Sp* (iti *piano,* violin, gitarra-*Sp, flute, drum..*)

MUSICAL *(Tag. & Iloc.)* *musical*

MUSICAL note *(Tag. & Iloc.)* nota-*Sp* ng musica-*Sp*

Musician *(Tag. & Iloc.)* musikero-*Sp*

Mussel halaan; Iloc: cabibi, kaong

Must kailangan, dapat; Iloc: masapul

Mustache *(Tag. & Iloc.)* bigote-*Sp,* balbas/barbas-*Sp*

Mustard *(Tag. & Iloc.) mustard,* mustasa

Muster pagtipon-tiponin, pagpulong-pulongin ang mga sundalo na may kinalaman sa servicio, inspeksion, paghahanda, giyera, utos o *order,* discharge at iba pa

Mutate *v.,* **Mutation** *n.* kapag may pagbabago ng *chromosomes* o *genes* ng *cell,* pag-usbong at pagbuo ng anak ay naaafectohan; ang *chromosomal change* ay may pagbabago sa ichura ng tao

Mute pipi; Iloc: umel

Mutilate pagsugat, sugatan, bagohin ang ichura, gawing hindi na dati sa pamamagitan ng pagtanggal o ng wala ng remediong pagsira; pagputol: ipagkait sa hayop o tao ang paa at camay at puedeng iba pang mahalagang parte ng katawan

Mutter mababang boses-*Sp* na hindi marinig at parang kinakausap ang sarili; bumubulong-bulong parang umuungol o dumadaing

Mutual magkatuwang o magkapareho sa pag-aari o sa relasyon-*Sp* o kagustohan at iba pa; Iloc: agsinnaranay o agkapareho ti sanicua da o relasyon da o ti gusto da ken dadduma pay

My akin, ko; Iloc: cuak, cucuak, bagik, -ac

"MY way only," "Shut up" *(Tag. & Iloc.)* "Basta!," "Ah, basta!"

Myriad napakadami at iba't iba; Iloc: adu ken nadumaduma

Myself ako mismo-*Sp*; Iloc: siac mismo

Mysterious *adj.,* kababalaghan, himala, mahiwaga, misterioso-*Sp*; Iloc: nakasidsiddaaw, misterioro

Mystery misterio-*Sp*, hiwaga; Iloc: misterio, datdatlag

Myth mga kilalang cuento-*Sp* na gawang-isip lamang o may kaunting pagkatotoo tungkol sa mga ninuno, mga bayani, o kababalaghan na tugma sa lahi o cultura-*Sp* ng lugar-*Sp*

N

Nab arestohin, dakpin, huliin; Iloc: tiliwen, iyaresto

Nag cheche-bureche, paraparating pagrereclamo, pagpapayo o paghi-hikayat na nagiging nakakaperhuisio; Iloc: cheche-bureche,

cana-canayon nga agrekreclamo, pagbagbaga ken pagsulsulisog nga makaperhuisio
Correlated word

Didactic palaturo o palasermon; Iloc: parasuro wenno parasermon

NAIL pako; Iloc: lansa

NAIL on finger and toe *(Tag. & Iloc.)* cuco

Nailed it nagtagumpay o ayos-na-ayos dahil perfecto-*Sp* ang pagsagawa niya

Naïve *adj.,* **Naivete** *n.* inocente-*Sp* siya sa kabuhayan pati sa mga makapanlinlang o mapanganib; Iloc: inocente isu cadagiti kabibiag pati dagiti makaallilaw o makapeggad

Naked hubad; Iloc: labus, ussob

Namby-pamby *sentimental* at mahina, pipichugin

NAME pangalan; Iloc: nagan

NAME addressed endearingly to the youth when the name is not used *(Tag. & Iloc.)* (boys) Nonoy, Iho-*Sp*, Totoy, anak, nakkong; (girls) Iha-*Sp*, Neneng, Nene, anak, nakkong

NAME addressed to adults *Mr.*, Ginoong, *Mrs.*, Ginang

NAME addressed to strangers (*man*) mama, (*woman*) ale, (*girl*) nene, iha; Iloc: (*elders-man & woman*) apo, (*girl*) neneng, (*man*) manong, tata, (*woman*) manang, nana

NAME-drop nagbabanggit ng mga pangalan ng mga popular-*Sp* na tao na nakakahalobilo niya na kadalasan ay para humanga ang mga nakakarinig sa canya

Namesake tocayo-*Sp*, kapangalan; Iloc: tocayo, agkanagan

Nanny *(Tag. & Iloc.)* yaya

Nap umidlip, mag-siesta-*Sp*; Iloc: rumidep, agsiesta

Nape batok; Iloc: teltel

NAPKIN *(Tag. & Iloc.)* *napkin*, servilyeta-*Sp*

NAPKIN (menstruation), sanitary *(Tag. & Iloc.)* pasador

Narcissism *n.,* **Narcissistic** *adj.* matinding pagmamahal sa sarili at pinakamahalaga sa canya, makikialam o tumulong lamang siya sa iba kung favor sa canya; Iloc: dakkel a pagayat iti mismo a bagi ken daytoy iti pinakanapateg canyana, estimaren na dagiti sabali nu dayta ket makapagfavor canyana

576

Narcotic ang mga droga na nakaka-*addict* gaya ng *opium cocaine, heroin, morphine, marijuana* at iba pang mga lumalabas na droga na igumon ka sa pagnanasa at aasam-asamin mong <u>mapapasaanib nito</u> dahil nawala na ang pagkalalake mo para matapang mong tanggihan ito at nawala pa ang talino mo para matanto mo na ang *narcotic* ay sisirain ang buong pagkatao mo at ang kahihinatnan mo kaya para ka nang *moron* o walang utak, at napakahirap na makawala ka sa higpit na capit sa 'yo.

Narrate magsalaysay, mag-cuento-*Sp*; Iloc: ag-storia-*Sp*

Narration, Narrative salaysay, cuento-*Sp*, kasaysayan; Iloc: storia-*Sp*

Narrow makitid, makipit; Iloc: akikid

    Antonym

    Broad malapad, malawak; Iloc: nalawa, naacaba

Nasal tungkol sa ilong; Iloc: maygapu iti agong

Nascent mag-umpisang mabuhay o magyabong

Nasty 1] malaswa at malicioso o nakakasuklam at nakakainis, 2] naka-kadisgustong amoy at dumi

Natal tungkol sa pagsilang o panganganak

Nation bansa, bayan; Iloc: nasyon, bayan

National pambansa; ano mang caraniwan sa mga tao sa isang nasyon-*Sp*

Nationalism *patriotism* o pagmamahal, pagmamalasakit at katapatan sa sariling bansa; espiritu ng nasyon pati ang adhika sa kapayaan at pag-unlad nito; pagsuporta at pagtataguyod sa nasyon at ang mga *policy*, patakaran, paniwala, aspirasyon at *history* nito

Nationality kung anong lahi naipanganak; kung anong nasyon nakaanib o nakasapi

Native katutubong tao o bagay; Iloc: tao o banag a tubo iti ili o nasyon

Nativity tungkol sa pagsilang o pagpapanganak ng sanggol na ang pinakakilalang *nativity* ay ang pagkapanganak sa Panginoong Dios Hesu Cristo

NATURAL natural-*Sp*, likas, katutubo, katatao; Iloc: natural-*Sp*, katutubo, katatao

NATURAL resources natural na angkin ng isang bayan gaya ng lupa, tubig, gubat, deposito sa mga minahan, at mga bunga ng mga halaman at iba pa

Naturalize igawad o ipagkaloob sa isang legal-*Sp* na banyaga o dayuhan o imigrante-*Sp* ang karapatan at privilehio-*Sp* ng isang tunay na mamayan pagkatapos na naipasa niya ang mga pagsusuri at *interview* at limang taong pagtira sa bayang ito at pati pag-angkin at maki-angkop sa salita, asal, gawi at *values* ng pinasukang bayan gaya ng isang tunay na mamayan

Naturally natural-*Sp*, siempre naman at walang duda

NATURE ang mundo at mga nandidito, buhay o patay na, mga nakikita dito, ang mga nakakabuhay at nakakaventahe at nakakapinsala (bagyo o pagputok ng vulcan), at iba pa; mga uri o katangian ng mga tao, hayop, at iba pang nilikha gaya ng punong kahoy, tubig, himpapawid; naturalesa-*Sp*, naturalidad-*Sp*, kalikasan

NATURE, by likas at katutubo at pinanganak na ganyan

NAUGHT wala kahit ano; Iloc: awan pulos

NAUGHT, come to mauwi sa wala; Iloc: awan pulos pag-balinan na

Naughty pilyo-*Sp*; Iloc: pilyo, cohino-*aSp*

Nauseous nakakalula; Iloc: makasarwa

Nautical, Naval pandagat; Iloc: pangtaaw

Navel pusod; Iloc: puseg

Navigate 1] maglakbay sa lupa o tubig o himpapawid habang nasa sasakyan, barco o eroplano; atasan o mangasiwa ng rota o gagawin sa paglakbay; 2] *Computer*: mag-*cruise* o liwaliw sa paghanap at pagbasa ng kinakailangang informasyon sa mga balita, *website* at iba pa

Navy hukbong pandagat; Iloc: militar ti taaw

Near malapit; Iloc: asideg, adani
  Antonym
  Far, Distant malayo; Iloc: adayo

Nearby malapit, dito lang sa paligid; Iloc: asideg, ditoy la lawlaw

Nearly muntik na; Iloc: nagistayan
  Synonym
  Almost halos, halos lahat, muntik na; Iloc: ngangngani, dandani, nagistayan

Nearest pinakamalapit; Iloc: kaasitgan
  Antonym
  Farthest pinakamalayo; Iloc: kaadaywan

Neat maayos, malinis, areglado-*Sp*; Iloc: nadalimanek, areglado, nalinis ken naurnos

Neaten mag-ayos, mag-areglo-*Sp*; Iloc: agdalimanek, agareglo, agurnos ken agpenpen cadagiti alicamen

Necessary kailangan, kinakailangan; Iloc: masapul, kasapulan
Synonyms
Must kailangan, dapat; Iloc: masapul
Behoove kailangan na gawin; Iloc: masapul nga aramiden
Indispensable kailangan pagtuonan ng pansin dahil ito ay kinakailangan at hindi dapat pabayaan dahil importante ito; Iloc: masapul nga asicaswen ta daytoy ket kasapulan nga haan a liwayan ta importante daytoy
Imperative kinakailangang mangyari o magkaroon; Iloc: masapul nga mapasamak ken maaddaan

Necessities mga pangangailangan; Iloc: dagiti kasapulan

Neck leeg; Iloc: tengnged

Necklace quintas; Iloc: quentas

Necktie *(Tag. & Iloc.)* corbata-*Sp*

Nee pangalan at apelyido-*Sp* ng babae bago ikinasal, noong dalaga pa

Need kailangan, kinakailangan; Iloc: masapul, kasapulan

Needle karayom; Iloc: dagum

Needs mga pangangailangan; Iloc: dagiti kasapulan

Needy nangangailangan; Iloc: makasapul

Negate pabulaanan, ipagkaila; Iloc: mangpalibak

Negative *adj.*, **Negativism** *n.* negativo at pesimismo; mapag-isip na baka mabigo o mahirap o makakasama; hindi tumuturing o nag-papalagay ng magandang mangyayari; tumututol sa mungkahi, at payo; inaasahan at gagawa ng pangontra o hindi kikilos man lamang

Neglect magpalya; Iloc: liwayan

Neglectful, Negligent pabaya, pumapalya, irresponsab-le-*Sp*, hindi nag-aasicaso; Iloc: agliwliway, irresponsab-le, mangbaybay-an, haan nga mangicascaso

Negligible puedeng ipagwalang bahala; Iloc: mabalin a liwayan
Synonym
Dispensable puedeng hindi pagtuonan ng pansin dahil hindi importante; Iloc: uray haan nga asecaswen ta haan nga importante

Negotiate makipagtalakayan, makipagkasundo sa contrata tungkol sa fondo o sa reglamento o mga makakabuti; Iloc: makipatang ken makitulag iti contrata maygapu iti fondo o reglamento o iti magun-od a nasayaat

Negotiation *(Tag. & Iloc.) negotiation,* negosasyon-*Sp*

Neighbor kapitbahay; Iloc: carruba

Neighborhood kapaligiran, kapitbahayan; Iloc: arrubayan, kakarrubaan

Neither...nor hindi ang...ni-*Sp*; Iloc: haan ti...ni

Nemesis karival o kacompetensia o kalaban na hindi caya ng tao na talonin o supilin

Nephew pamangking lalake; Iloc: kaanakan a lalaki

Nephrology ang siencia-*Sp* o larangan ng medicina-*Sp* na sumusuri o gumagamot sa mga sakit sa bato o *kidney*

Nepotism sa politica-*Sp*, ito ang pinasok na miembro ng familya-*Sp* o kamag-anak o kaibigang matalik para makakatamo ng suporta-*Sp*, privilehio-*Sp* o favor-*Sp* dito pero hindi ito makatarungan at labag sa batas ito sa maraming *countries* sa mundo-*Sp*

Nerve ugat ng nervios-*Sp*; Iloc: urat ti nervios

Nervous nervioso/sa-*Sp*, ninenervios-*Sp*; Iloc: nervioso/sa, agnernervios

NEST pugad; Iloc: umok

NEST egg pera na nirereserva para sa mga *emergency* o dadating na pangangailangan

Nestle pagmamahal na yakap o yapos; Iloc: naayat nga aracop wenno rakep

Netizen parating nakatuon ang pansin sa *internet*

Network sa TV at radyo, ito ay grupo ng mga stasyon na nakaanib sa *wire relay* para ang mga programa ay maipahayag o maipakita nila; sa telecomunicasyon, ito ay sistema na naglalaon ng mga combinasyon ng *computer terminals* at iba pa para magpalitan ng informasyon at magdamayan ng *resources* o tulong na nagagamit kahit kelan kinakailangan; sa mga telefono, ito ay conectado sa *telecommunication equipment* na cab-le na ginagamit na ipadala o tumanggap ng informasyon

Neurology siensia-*Sp* ng medico-*Sp* na may kinalaman sa nervios-*Sp* at ang mga sakit dito; Iloc: siencia ti medico nga maygapu iti nervios ken dagiti sakit ditoy

Neurosis *n.*, **Neurotic** *adj.* diferencia-*Sp* sa isip at damdamin gaya ng *depression* o sobrang pagkanervios

Neutral walang kinacampihan, walang pinapanigan; Iloc: awan ti fab-favoran (favor-*Sp*)

Neutralize 1] gawing walang pinapanigan; 2] gawin ang isang bagay na walang efecto-*Sp* o walang bisa

NEVER hinding-hindi kailanman; Iloc: haan pulos ingganat caano man

"NEVER mind" "Di bale" Iloc: "Haan a bale"

Nevertheless kahit na, kahit pa; Iloc: uray pay

NEW bago; Iloc: baro

NEW, brand- bagong-bago; Iloc: kabarbaro
> *Antonym*
> **Old (thing)** luma; Iloc: daan

Newborn, Neonate bagong panganak na sanggol

Newcomer baguhan sa trabaho, bagito; Iloc: kaserserrek iti trabaho, kabarbaro, agdamdamo

News balita; Iloc: damag

Newsman *(Tag. & Iloc.)* periodista-*Sp*

Newspaper pahayagan, diaryo-*Sp*, periodico-*Sp*; Iloc: periodico

NEXT kasunod, susunod; Iloc: sumaruno

NEXT of kin pinakamalapit na kamag-anak ng tao

Nibble magcagat ng maliit; Iloc: agkitteb, agkinnet, agcurib

NICE mabuti, mainam, mahusay, mapayapa, kasiya siya; Iloc: nanam-ay, nasayaat, naimbag, natalna, naay-ayo

NICE person mabait, kasiya-siya, mapayapa; Iloc: nasingpet, nasayaat, natalna

NICK pingas, lamat, bitak, nabungihan; Iloc: birri, tipping

NICK of time ang pinakahuling oras; bago dumating ang oras na mapanganib o malala

Nickname *nickname*, palayaw; Iloc: *nickname*, birngas

Niece pamangking babae; Iloc: kaanakan a babai

NIGHT gabi; Iloc: rabii

NIGHT, all magdamag; Iloc: agpatnag

NIGHT, last kagabi; Iloc: idi rabii

Nightly gabi-gabi, tuwing gabi; Iloc: cada rabii, rinabii

Nightmare *(Tag. & Iloc.)* bangungot

Nihilism *[nahy-uh-liz-uhm]* buong pagtanggi o pag-ayaw sa batas o alituntunin o otoridad-*Sp* o *values* o paniwala o katotohanan; pagrebolusyon o terorismo

NINE *(Tag. & Iloc.)* nine, siam, nueve-*Sp*

NINE hundred *nine hundred,* siam na daan; Iloc: *nine hundred,* siam a gasut

NINE o'clock *nine o'clock,* alas nueve-*Sp*

NINE thousand *nine thousand,* siam na libo; Iloc: *nine thousand,* siam a ribo

Nineteen *nineteen,* labing siam; Iloc: *nineteen,* sangapulo ket siam

Ninety *ninety,* siam na po, noventa-*Sp*; Iloc: *ninety,* siam nga pulo, noventa

Ninth *(Tag. & Iloc.)* ikasiam

NIP ipitin o curotin para matanggal; Iloc: sipiten wenno piddilen tapno maikkat

NIP it in the bud *Put a stop to a bad demeanor and bad habit at the beginning in its early stage before it becomes fixed, deeply rooted, and unalterable.* Sugpoin ang gawaing masama habang maaga pa para hindi maging bihasa at kagawian na mahirap na tuloy masugpo; Iloc: masapul a parmeken iti dakes nga aramid mientras-*Sp* nga nasapa pay tapno haan nga agbalin a sigud nga aramid nga narigat tun nga ikkaten ken isardeng

Nipple, Teat utong; Iloc: mungay

Nit, Egg of a lice lisa; Iloc: lis-a

Nitpicker *n.,* **Nitpicking** *v.* nampupuna at namamansin ng lahat na kapintasan pati ang mga puedeng ipagpaubaya na maliliit na bagay; Iloc: mapagdillaw uray iti babassit a banag ida nga mabalin baybay-an

Nitty-gritty mga bagay na katotohanan at may kabulohan, ang diwa, mga detalye-*Sp*; Iloc: ti amad ken dagiti detalye-*Sp*

NO, Not hindi, di; Iloc: haan, saan, di

NO-brainer napakasimp-le at napakadali na hindi kailangan ang intelihensia para malaman ito

NO pain, no gain *Work hard to get what you want, even progress to success; hard work promises expertise, excellence and great rewards.* Ang hindi magsikap ay walang matatamo

"NO sweat", **"No problem"** "Bale wala," "Huwag kang mabahala," "Okay lang"

"NO wonder" "Hindi nakakapagtaka dahil may rason at malaking posibilidad na mangyayari iyan dahil kagawian iyan"

Noble may dignidad at integridad, may dangal, marangal, dakila; Iloc: adda dignidad, integridad, nadayaw, natakneng, nataer

NOD to agree magtango; Iloc: aglingaling, agtung-ed

    Antonym

    Head movement to indicate "No" iiling-iling; Iloc: agwingiwing

NOD drowsily magyukayok; Iloc: agtuglep, agdungsa

Noise ingay; Iloc: ariwawa, ringgor, tagari, riri

Noisy maingay, nakakabingi; Iloc: natagari, nariri, naringgor, naariwawa

Nomenclature ang *terminology* o mga pangalan o pantawag na ginagamit sa siencia, *arts, subject,* larangan, at iba pa na ginagamit ng tao o comunidad

Nomination *(Tag. & Iloc.)* nominasyon-*Sp*

Non sequitur hindi tugma o hindi angkop o di relevante sa nangyayari o sa pinag-usapan sa kasalukuyan at mga sumusunod sa mga ito

Nonchalant *[non-shuh-lahnt]* payapa at campante-*Sp* na hindi balisa, walang pag-alala, lubag ang loob

None, Not one wala, ni isa, sin-*Sp*, ni-*Sp*; Iloc: awan, ni maysa, sin, ni

Nonsectarian magkakasama at hindi limitado-*Sp* sa isang denomi-nasyon-*Sp* ng relihiyon-*Sp*

Noon tanghali; Iloc: tengnga ti aldaw

Noose tali na may bilog na pansilo para pangbitag ng hayop; Iloc: silo nga adda timbukel a tali ti murdong na

Nor *(Tag. & Iloc.)* ni-*Sp*

Normal *(Tag. & Iloc.)* *normal*

North *north,* norte-*Sp,* hilaga; Iloc: *north,* norte, amianan

NOSE ilong, nguso; Iloc: agong

    Correlated words

    Nasal tungkol sa ilong; Iloc: maygapu iti agong

    Snout ang pahabang parte ng mukha ng hayop gaya ng ilong; Iloc: ti paatiddog o paacaba a parte ti rupa ti *animal* casla ti agong

NOSE, flat *(Tag. & Iloc.)* pango

NOSE, pointed *(Tag. & Iloc.)* matangos

Nosebleed halingoyngoy; Iloc: daringongo

Nostalgia sabik o nagmimithi na bumalik ang nakaraang buhay o lugar o ang familia o mga mahal sa buhay na nakakasiyang alalahanin

Nostril butas ng ilong; Iloc: abut ti agong

Nosy osyoso, pakialamero; Iloc: osyoso, mapagbibiang

NOT, No hindi, di; Iloc: haan, saan, di

NOT out of the woods mas bumuti-buti na pero hindi pa gumaling o hindi pa bumuti ang kalagayan, o hindi pa nakaahon sa problema

Notary public taong may *legal* na otorisasyon na magnotaryo, magpatutoo ng contrata, *deeds, affidavits,* at iba pa

Notch hiwang hugis V; Iloc: iwa nga forma iti V

Nothing walang-wala; Iloc: awan pulos

Notice mapuna, mapansin; Iloc: madlaw, masiputan

Noticeable kapansin-pansin, napupuna; Iloc: madmadlaw

Notify, Inform magbigay alam, ipaalam; Iloc: ipaammo

Notorious tanyag sa kasamaan; Iloc: agdindinnamag iti pagkadakes na

Nourish buhayin, arugain, palusogin, palagoin, pasiglahin; Iloc: biagen, taraknen, pasalun-aten, papigsaen, palapsaten

Novel *(Tag. & Iloc.)* novela-*Sp*

November *(Tag. & Iloc.)* *November,* Noviembre-*Sp*

Now ngayon, kasalukuyan; Iloc: itatta, itatta mismo-*Sp*

Nowadays sa panahong ito; Iloc: kadagitoy nga panawen
> *Correlated words*
> **In the past** noong lumipas na panahon; Iloc: idi limmabas a panawen
> **In the future** sa hinaharap, sa mga kinabukasang panahon; Iloc: cadagiti sumangpet a panawen

Noxious nakakapinsala o nakakasama sa katawan at kalusogan ng tao; nakakasira, nakaka-*corrupt* o bulok sa moralidad-*Sp*

Nuance mahina at halos hindi mahalata na pagbabago, bahagyang pagyabong o pag-proceso-*Sp* ng pagbabago; bahagyang pagkakaiba ng culay, tunog o tono-*Sp*

Nude hubad; Iloc: labus, ussob

Nudge sicohin, tabigin, kabigin; Iloc: kidagen

Nugget maliit na buo pero mahalaga at excelente gaya ng ginto o mamahaling bakal o *metal*

Nuisance *(Tag. & Iloc.)* estorbo-*Sp*, molescha-*Sp*, sairo

Null and void na-*cancel* o napawalang-bisa kaya wala nang halaga

Nullify ipawalang-bisa, ipawalang saysay; Iloc: ikkaten ti bileg o turay na
Synonyms
Invalidate ipawalang bisa; Iloc: ikkaten wenno paawanen ti bileg o turay
Overrule 1] ipawalang-bisa, hindi magpahintulot ng mga argumento o gawain, 2] maghahari o magdomina

Numb walang pakiramdam, manhid; Iloc: agbibineg, agpipikel, haan nga makarikna

NUMBER *(Tag. & Iloc.)* numero-*Sp*, bilang

NUMBER one 1] numero uno ang ano mang prayoridad o nakakabuti o favor-*Sp* sa kalusogan at kapakanan ng isang tao; 2] tao, companya at iba pa na nangunguna o pinakamataas sa rangko, *scale/order*/antas, o *quality/calidad-Sp*, o importancia, o katanyagan, o kabantugan; 3] *urination* o pag-ihi

NUMBER two 1] ikalawa o segundo lamang sa importancia o calidad; 2] *defecation/ bowel movement* o pagtae

Nun *(Tag. & Iloc.)* madre, mongha-*Sp*

Nurse *(Tag. & Iloc.)* *nurse*

Nurture buhayin, arugain, palusogin, palagoin, pasiglahin; Iloc: biagen, taraknen, pasalun-aten, papigsaen, palapsaten

Nutrient sustancia-*Sp*, pampalusog; Iloc: sustancia, pangsalun-at ken karadkad

Nutrition *(Tag. & Iloc.)* *nutrition*

Nutritious *(Tag. & Iloc.)* masustansia

O

Oar sagwan; Iloc: tagwan

Oasis 1] maliit na lugar-*Sp* sa *desert* o desierto-*Sp* na may damo at tubig; 2] anomang nakakabigay ng ginhawa sa gitna ng kapaguran o pagdurusa *(don't confuse it with dessert)*

Oath, Vow sumpa, panata; Iloc: sapata

OB/GYN doctor na nagpa-*practice* ng combinasyon ng dalawang larangan sa *Medicine* na mga ito ay *obstetrics* o pagpapanganak ng sanggol at *gynecology* o pagpanatili na malusog ang babae, pagsusuri at paggamot sa sakit ng mga babae

Obdurate hindi mahimok kahit pinipilit o kinacarinyo; matigas ang loob at hindi magpahintulot

Obedient masunorin; Iloc: mapagtungpal

Obeisance asal o galaw ng tao na nagpapahiwatig ng paggalang; Iloc: tignay ti tao nga mangipakita iti pagdayaw, ken respeto

Obese *(Tag. & Iloc.)* matabang-mataba, tabachoy

Obey tuparin, tumutupad sa utos, sumusunod sa utos; Iloc: agtungtungpal ti bilin, sumursurot ti bilin
Synonyms
Comply, Fulfill tuparin, gampanan; Iloc: tungpalen, agtungpal
Conform alinsunod sa alituntunin; Iloc: sumursurot ti reglamento

Obfuscate *v.,* **Obfuscation** *n.* balisahin, litohin, gawing hindi maliwanag, padilimin

OBJECT, Be against contrahin, magtutol, mag-oposisyon, magprotesta; Iloc: agcontra, agoposisyon, agsupiat, agsalangad (contra-*Sp*, oposisyon-*Sp*, protesta-*Sp*)

OBJECT, Thing bagay; Iloc: banag

OBJECTIVE, Aim balak, tangka, sanhi, layonin, adhika, intension-*Sp*; Iloc: pakay, panggep, rangta, intension

OBJECTIVE viewpoint *It is not based from the person's experiences, feelings and opinions. It is based on facts and figures, not based on his/her views.*
Antonym
Subjective viewpoint *It is based on the person's character, feelings, experiences and opinions.*

Oblation ang pag-alay sa Panginoong Dios ng tinapay at alak sa Eucharist; ang pag-aalay sa Panginoong Dios sa langit.

Obligate ipasagawa na dapat gampanan at sundin, ipaobliga, gawin na obligasyon; Iloc: ipaaramid a masapul a tungpalen ken suroten, ipa-obligar (obliga/obligar-*Sp*)

Obligation obligasyon-*Sp*, responsibilidad-*Sp*, tungkulin; Iloc: obligasyon, responsibilidad

Obligated *(Tag. & Iloc.)* obligado-*Sp*

Oblige 1] i-obliga sa pamamagitan ng principio-*Sp* ng batas, *ethics* at *society*/sociedad- *Sp*, 2] magbigay ng servicio-*Sp* o favor-*Sp*

Obliging payag o magaan ang loob na magbigay ng tulong o favor; matulungin at nag-aalok ng tulong o servicio; maluwag, pabaya

Oblique 1] pahilis, pasandal, pasandig, 2] hindi mapagkatiwalaan dahil sinungaling o nagnanakaw; Iloc: 1] darisdis, nakatingig, 2] haan a mapagtalkan ta ulbod ken agtatakaw

Obliterate borahin o tanggalin o itapon para wala man lamang bakas nito; Iloc: boraen o ikkaten o ibelleng tapno awan pulos ti pagkakitkitaen daytoy

Oblivion walang kaalam-alam o alintana o kamalayan o nalimutan ng husto; Iloc: awan poot na o pagkaammo wenno completo a nalipatan na

Oblivious walang malay o pagkaalam, o kaya limot na limot na niya; Iloc: awan iti poot na wen no nalipatan nan o haan na talaga ammo

Oblong *(Tag. & Iloc.) oblong,* formang itlog

Obnoxious napakalaswa, nakaririmarim, kahalay-halay, karumaldumal, garrafal-*aSp*; Iloc: nakadakdakes, nakaal-alas, garrafal, nakamad-madi

Obscene hindi decente-*Sp*, napakasama, nakaririmarim, napakalaswa at nakakadiri; Iloc: haan a decente, nakadakdakes, nakaal-alas ken makaaryek

Obscure 1] malabo at hindi claro; mahirap intindihin; hindi malinaw sa paningin at sa ibang *senses* gaya ng pandamdam, amoy, lasa, o tinig; madilim o hindi mahalata; 2] hindi kilala, tago o hindi kapansin-pansin; 3] gawing madilim o malabo

Obsequious, People-pleaser mapagsipsip, masilbi o mapagdilang-bulaklak para maging kasiya-siya siya sa tao; Iloc: mapagsipsip, agap-apreciar o agser-servi-*Sp* para nakaay-ayat isu cadagiti tattao.

Observant mapuna, mapagmasid; Iloc: mapagmingming, mapagsiim, mapagsipot

Observatory lugar-*Sp* o gusali kung saan magmanman o magmasid ng mga planeta, bituin at ibang bagay sa langit na gumagamit ng mabisang telescopio-*Sp*

Observe inoobservahan, minamatyagan, minamanmanan, minamasdan, pinupuna, pinapansin; Iloc: agob-observar-*Sp*, agsipsipot, agsisiim, agmingmingming

Obsessed *adj.*, **Obsession** *n.* nahuhumaling sa tao, sa idolo-*Sp*, sa diversion o bagay at dahil diyan, maraming oras-*Sp* ang ginugogol niya sa pag-aatupag nito at madalas na laman ng canyang isip; Iloc: agpappapaos iti mapuspusoan na a tao, nga idolo, nga diversion-*Sp* o banag isu nga panay-panay a pagpaspasaran na ti tiempo-*Sp* ditoy ken pampanunoten na cancanayon.

Synonyms

Die-hard nakakapit ng husto sa kinahuhumalingan; Iloc: na-kacumpet nga usto iti mapuspusoan na

Fixate 1] nakapako ang isip at pansin at kahit pandinig sa isang pinagkakaabalahan, 2] obsesyon, marubdob na pagkagiliw sa isang bagay o tao

Obsession *obsession*, marubdob na pagkagiliw sa isang bagay o tao

Obsessive-compulsive disorder ang condisyon na ito sa meron nito ay matagalang *disorder* na caraniwan at kagawian kaya madalas na ginagawa o iniisip ito at hindi mapigil dahil may malakas na simbuyo na nagbibigay ng *urge* na gawin o isipin ito paulit-ulit, halimbawa ang madalas na paghugas ng kamay ng ilang beses

Obsolescent halimbawa nito ay salitang nagiging *obsolete* kaya hindi na ginagamit; *outmoded* at *outdated* nang makina kaya hindi na kai-langang gamitin

Obsolete sira na, luma na, makaluma na o wala nang bisa kaya hindi na ginagamit

Obstacle hadlang, sagabal; Iloc: maka-barra-*Sp,* makalapped

Obstetrics larangan ng panganganak; Iloc: larangan ti pagpapaanak

Obstinate matatag na nakakabig o nakakapit sa canyang pakay o palagay kaya hindi pasasakop sa iba kahit pinipilit siya; mahirap siyang masupil, mapasailalim o masakop; sakit na mahirap malunasan o gumaling

Obstruct *v.,* **Obstruction** *n.* harangin, magsagabal, sanggahin, sarhan; Iloc: sanggaen, pasardengen, serraan, mang-barra-*Sp*

Obtain magkaroon; Iloc: makaala

Obtrude ifuersa sa tao ang canyang sarili at paniwala kahit hindi mga ito *welcome*; Iloc: ifuersa na ti bagi na ken pammati na iti tao uray nu haan da cayat o kasapulan

Obtuse hindi matalas kundi mahina sa pag-unawa, pagintindi, pag-damdam at pagturing

Obviate nakakaturing siya ng antemano-*Sp* kaya naiiwasan niya ang mga hirap, pinsala at hindi maventaheng kahihinatnan sa pamamagitan ng paraang mabuti at mahusay at pag-iwas sa hindi kinakailangan; sinasalubong at alisin o gawing hindi makabulohan ang problema o anomang nakakabigat sa pamamagitan ng efectivong paraan

Obvious kitang-kita, lantad; Iloc: makitkita, nakaparang

Occasion *(Tag. & Iloc.)* ocasyon-*Sp*

Occasionally pana-panahon; Iloc: tiempo-tiempo-*Sp*
Correlated words
> **Once in a while** kung minsan; Iloc: sagpaminsan
> **Sometimes** paminsan-minsan; Iloc: no dadduma, pasaray

Occidental *west,* kanluran; Iloc: *west,* laud
Antonym
> **Oriental** *east,* silangan; Iloc: *east,* daya

Occult misterio-*Sp*, lampas sa gilid o bingit ng ordidnaryo na kaalaman o pag-intindi; tago at lihim maliban lamang sa mga kasapi

Occupant naninirahan, residente-*Sp*; Iloc: aggigian, residente

Occupation ocupasyon-*Sp*, hanapbuhay, pagkakakitahan; Iloc: ocupasyon, pagsapulan

OCCUPIED, Absorbed in abala, ocupado-*Sp*, subsob, buhos na buhos, inaatupag ng husto; Iloc: ocupado, nakaperreng iti madama na nga as-asecaswen
Synonym
> **Rapt** abala, subsob, buhos na buhos sa ginagawa; Iloc: nakasubsob ti ar-aramiden na

OCCUPIED, Lived in may nakatira, ocupado-*Sp* at hindi vacante-*Sp*; Iloc: adda aggigian, ocupado, haan a vacante

Occupy ocupahin, i-ocupa-*Sp*; Iloc: i-ocupar-*Sp*, agyan

Occur mangyari, maganap; Iloc: mapasamak

Occurrence pangyayari, nagaganap; Iloc: mapaspasamak

OCEAN / SEA karagatan, dagat; Iloc: baybay, taaw
Correlated words
> **Lake** lawa na napaligiran ng lupa; Iloc: danaw a nalawlawan ti daga

Bay look na napaligiran ng lupa at may labasan at pasukan ang tubig na galing sa dagat; Iloc: danaw a nalawlawan ti daga nga adda pagserkan ken pagruaran ti danum a naggapu diay taaw

River ilog; Iloc: carayan

Brook, Creek batis; Iloc: waig

Spring batis o maliit na ilog; Iloc: bassit a carayan

City or town levee *(Tag. & Iloc.)* estero-*Sp*

Reservoir lawa na gawang-tao para sa kinakailangang tubig at inomin ng comunidad; Iloc: danaw nga aramid iti tao para iti danum ken inomin ti comunidad

OCEAN / SEA, Middle of nasa laot, nasa karagatan; Iloc: diay tengnga ti taaw o baybay

OCEAN / SEA tides *(Tag. & Iloc.)* alon

OCEAN / SEA big waves daluyong; Iloc: dalluyong

OCEAN / SEA tidal waves *(Tag. & Iloc.)* *tsunami*

October *October,* Octobre-*Sp*

Octopus pugita; Iloc: curita

Ocular nauukol sa mata; Iloc: maypapan iti mata

Odd iba sa caraniwan o sa ordinario o sa inaasahan; kakaiba at hindi pangcaraniwan

ODDS 1] <u>malamang na mangyayari</u> kaysa hindi, gaya ng pag-ulan *(The odds are it will rain)*; 2] sa dalawang magkacompetensia, <u>ang odds ay yung may ventahe o mas mahusay</u> sa kalaban ang makatulong sa pagpanalo; pagkakaiba na ang isa ay mas mabuti o mas masama

ODDS, at pagkakaiba ng palagay; hindi pagkakasundo, walang pagkakaisa

Odious *adj.*, **Odium** *n.* naglilikha ng galit, kasuklam-suklam, kamuhi-muhi, nakakadisgusto

ODOR amoy; Iloc: angot

Correlated words

Scent amoy; Iloc: angot

Olfactory tungkol sa pang-amoy; Iloc: maygapu ti pagangot

Osmics siencia sa pang-amoy at *olfactory sense*; Iloc: siencia iti pagangot ken ti *olfactory sense*

ODOR, bad mabaho, mabantot; Iloc: nabangsit, naangdud

ODOR, drifting sumisingaw, umaalingasaw; Iloc: agalingasaw, agsangsang-aw

ODOR, fishy malansa; Iloc: nalangsi

ODOR, fragrant mahalimuyak; Iloc: nabanglo

ODOR, overwhelming perfume masansang; Iloc: napalalo ti angot a bangbanglo

ODOR, spoiled food amoy sira na; Iloc: nabangles, nalang-es, nalang-esen

ODOR, sweaty armpit anghit; Iloc: anglit

ODOR, urine mapanghi; Iloc: naangseg

Odoriferous maamoy; Iloc: nakaang-angot

Odorous malakas ang amoy; Iloc: nakaang-angot

OF ni, ng *(pronounced "nang")*; Iloc: kenni, ni, iti, ti

"OF course" *(Tag. & Iloc.)* "Siempre"-*aSp*

OFF wala man lang, kaunti o hindi tama o mali; Iloc: awan man laeng, bassit wenno haan nga usto

OFF color 1] hindi exacto-*Sp* ang kulay o maling culay; 2] malaswa, vulgar-*Sp*, bastos-*Sp*

OFF course nalihis; Iloc: naiwawa
Same pronunciation, different spelling & meanings
"Of course" *(Tag. & Iloc.)* "Siempre"

OFF-guard, Off one's guard walang kamalay-malay kaya hindi handa

OFF-key wala sa tono-*Sp*; Iloc: awan ti tono

OFF-limits bawal pumasok; Iloc: mayparit ti sumrek

OFF-the-record hindi panglathala o hindi ipagsabi at hindi rin ipaalam ang pinagmulan; Iloc: haan nga ipawarnak o haan isawang ken haan met nga ipaammo nu sinno ti pinagguapoan na

Offend inisin, yamotin, consumihin, suyahin, iperhuisio, saktan ang damdamin; Iloc: suronen, ruroden, paluksawen, i-consumi-*Sp*, suyaen, sairwen, i-perhuisio-*Sp*

Offended nasaktan ang damdamin, naghihinakit; Iloc: masuron, maluksaw

Offensive nakakahinanakit, nakakadisgusto; Iloc: makapasuron, maka-paluksaw, makadisgusto

Offer iyalay, ihandog, i-alok, idulot; Iloc: isagut, idatag, i-ofrecer-*Sp*

Offering alay; Iloc: sagut, daton

Office *office*, oficina-*Sp*, tanggapan; Iloc: *office,* oficina

Officer *officer*, mataas ang katungkulan sa pinagtatrabahoan niya; Iloc: *officer*, nangato ti posisyon-*Sp* diay pagtrabahoan na

Official *official,* may otorisasyon-*Sp* ng oficina-*Sp*; Iloc: *official* gapu ta adda otorisasyon ti oficina

Officiate gampanan ang tungkulin ng miembro-*Sp* sa simbahan bilang serviciong divinidad-*Sp*; gampanan ang tungkulin sa companya o sa ano mang trabaho-*Sp* sa iba't ibang departamento-*Sp* sa oficina-*Sp*

Officious pangahas na basta na lang nag-aalok ng servicio o payo o pagpakialam kahit hindi humingi ng payo o anoman sa canya

Offish *aloof, unapproachable* dahil hindi mapagkibo at lumalayo sa mga tao; Iloc: haan nga agun-uni ken umad-adayo cadagiti tattao

Offset ano man ang kulang o wala ay tinutumbasan

Oshoot 1] tangkay sa sanga ng kahoy; 2] bunga o supling

Often palagi, madalas, malimit; Iloc: canayon, mamin-adu
  Correlated word
  Always tuwina, tuwing beses, firmi, parati, palagi, panay-panay; Iloc: cada beses, firmi, agnanayon, pasig

Ogle tumititig na mapanghalina o parang may cursonada; Iloc: kumitkita nga casla mangaw-awis wenno adda cursonada-*Sp* na

"Oh my!", "Gosh!" "Ay naku!"; Iloc: "Ay sus!"

OIL langis, lana; Iloc: lana

OIL, cooking mantica-*aSp*; Iloc: manteca-*Sp*

Ointment *ointment,* pang-hilot o -masahe sa balat na puedeng maka-gamot, magpakinis o pangpaganda; Iloc: *ointment,* pang-ilot o masahe ti cudil a mabalin a pangngagas, panglamuyot o pangpapintas

Okay *(Tag. & Iloc.)* ok

OLD luma; Iloc: daan

OLD age matanda, katandaan; Iloc: lakay, baket

OLD-fashion *(Tag. & Iloc.)* makaluma
  Antonym
  Modern *(Tag. & Iloc.)* makabago

OLD maid *spinster,* nakakasakit na tawag sa babaeng hindi nag-asawa hanggang siya'y tumanda

OLD person matanda; Iloc: lakay *(old man)*, baket *(old woman)*
  Antonym
  Young person bata; Iloc: ubing

OLD thing luma; Iloc: daan
  Antonym

New bago, Iloc: baro

OLD timer matanda, napakatagal na sa trabaho; Iloc: lakay o baket, nakabaybayagen diay trabaho

OLDER mas matanda, mas may edad-*Sp*; Iloc: mas adda edad-*Sp*, *older man:* laklakay, mas lakay, *older woman:* bakbaket, mas baket
Antonym
Younger mas bata; Iloc: mas ubing

OLDER brother kuya; Iloc: manong

OLDER sibling mas matandang kapatid; Iloc: kabsat a mas lakay, kabsat a mas baket
Antonyms
Younger mas bata; Iloc: mas ubing, ub-ubing
Younger sibling nakakabatang kapatid; Iloc: ading

OLDER sister ate; Iloc: manang

OLDER thing mas luma; Iloc: mas daan

OLDEST offspring/child panganay; Iloc: inauna
Antonym
Youngest offspring/child bunso; Iloc: buridek, inaudi

OLDEST person/animal pinakamatanda; Iloc: kalakayan, kabaketan, kaunaan,
Antonym
Youngest person/animal pinakabata; Iloc: kaubingan

OLDEST thing pinakaluma; Iloc: pinakadaan

Olfactory, Olfaction tungkol sa pang-amoy; Iloc: mayga-pu ti pagangot

Olio ulam na nilutong marami ang sahog; halo-halong mga bagay o musica o programa na sari-sari ang palabas

Ombudsman empleyado-*Sp* ng govierno-*Sp* na nag-iimbestiga-*Sp* ng mga reklamo ng mamayan contra-*Sp* sa isang *official* ng govierno, o kaya sa empleyado contra sa oficina-*Sp* niya, o estudiante-*Sp* contra sa univesidad

"OMG!", "Goodness gracious!" *(Tag. & Iloc.)* *"Ayyayyay!"*

Omelet *(Tag. & Iloc.)* torta-*Sp*, binating itlog, *scrambled egg*

Omen pangitain, signos-*Sp*; Iloc: senyal-*Sp* iti sumangpet a mapasamak

Ominous 1] nagpapahiwatig ng masama o nakakapanganib; nagbababala; 2] pangitain, nagpapahiwatig ng dadating na pangyayari na puedeng mabuti o masama

Omit laktawan; Iloc: liwayan, laktawan

Omission *(Tag. & Iloc.)* palya, paglaktaw

Omnipotent, All-powerful Dios na pinakasupremo at pinakamakapangyarihan sa lahat na Siya ang lumikha ng universo at lahat na nasa universo

Omnipresent, All-present Dios na nasa lahat ng lugar

Omniscient, All-knowing Dios na nalalaman ang lahat na gawain, isip, pakiramdam at pagkatao ng bawat nilalang at lahat ng nangyayari sa buong universo

ON sa, nasa; Iloc: idiay

ON and of, or Off and on naghahalinhan na gumana at maghinto, paandarin at ihinto; nandodon at wala

ON board 1] nakasakay sa bapor o bus o eroplano; 2] empleyadong nagtatrabaho sa tinutukoy na oficina-*Sp*

ON call handang magsilbi o magtrabaho kapag tawagin

ON duty kasalukuyang ginagawa ang katungkulan niya

ON-guard, On one's guard nakahanda, alisto at maliksi sa pagtatanod

ON par *(Tag. & Ilog.)* kapantay/kapatag o kapareho

ON second thought nagdalawang-isip; Iloc: agdudua ti nakem na
  Correlated word
  Waver mag-urong-sulong; Iloc: agavante-agatras

ON the go kumikilos dito't doon sa pagtatrabaho, ocupadong-ocupado-*Sp*

ON the heels of kasunod agad, sumusunod agad

ON the house bigay-libre ng tindahan o *restaurant*

ON the other hand sa kabilang dako; Iloc: iti bangir a panig

ON the tip of my tongue nasa dulo ng dila ko, hindi ko lang masabi o maalaala

ON the up and up, Strictly on the up and up matapat, makatarungan at matuwid

ON thin ice mapanganib na situasyon-*Sp*

ON top of the world, Sitting on top of the world napakasayang pakiramdam, napakagalak, napakaligaya

ONCE minsan, isang beses-*Sp*; Iloc: maminsan, maysa a beses

ONCE in a while kung minsan; Iloc: nu sagpaminsan

ONE isa, *one*, uno-*Sp*; Iloc: maysa, *one*, uno

ONE after the other isa-isang magkakasunod; Iloc: maysa-maysa nga agsasaruno

ONE and only, Solely kaisa-isa; nag-iisa, iisa lamang, bugtong, tangi; Iloc: agmaymaysa, kaykaysuna laeng, bugbugtong

ONE each tig-isa; Iloc: saggaysa

ONE hundred *one hundred,* isang daan; Iloc: *one hundred,* sangagasut

ONE-liner maikling biro; nakakatawang maikling cuento

ONE o'clock *one o'clock,* ala una-*Sp*

ONE thousand *one thousand,* isang libo; Iloc: *one thousand,* maysa nga ribo

ONE-track iisang landas lamang; hindi caya ang mas marami sa isa na paksang-isip o gawain dahil kailangan na isa lamang ang canyang pagkakaabalahan

Onerous ang obligasyon nito ay mas lampas at mas mabigat kaysa sa ventahe, mabigat na pasanin

Oneself sarili, mismo-*Sp* ang sarili; Iloc: iti bagi, mismo a bagi

Ongoing nagpapatuloy at walang paggambala o paghinto, kasalukuyang nagaganap; Iloc: agranrana, madama nga mapaspasamak

Synonyms

In the works hinahanda, plinaplano, isinasagawa

In progress nangyayari na ngayon, kasalukuyang nagaganap

In full swing kasalukuyang nagaganap at panay ang andar na walang balakid

Onion cibuyas-*Sp*; Iloc: cebolyas-*Sp*, lasuna

Online pumasok sa *internet* o nakaconecta sa *computer* o sa *computer network*

Onlooker *(Tag. & Iloc.)* miron-*Sp*, osyoso/sa-a*Sp*

Only lang, lamang; Iloc: laeng, lang, latta

Onset sa umpisa; Iloc: diay pagrugi

Onslaught bugbog o lait na napakarahas na pang-atake; Iloc: bugbog o lais nga sobra a nakarangranggas a pang-atake

Onus mahirap at hindi kasiya-siyang obligasyon o tungkulin o pasanin; responsibilidad-*Sp* at sisi

Onward pa-avante-*Sp*, pagsulong; Iloc: paavante

Antonym

Backward, paatras, paurong, Iloc: agpaatras

Oodles napakadami; Iloc: nakaad-adu

Ooze daloy, tulo, tagas; Iloc: ubo, tedted

Op-ed pahina ng periodico na itinakda para sa mga comentario, *essays*, katatawanan, *opinions*, kuro na may signatura ang sumulat

OPEN *adj.* nakabukas, nakabuklat; Iloc: nakalukat, nakaukrad, abierto-*Sp*

OPEN *v.* buksan; Iloc: luktan, lukatan, i-abre-*Sp*

OPEN a book buklatin; Iloc: ukraden

OPEN and aboveboard *honest, open, visible to the public, has transparency in deeds and in giving account, enlightenments and information;* Tapat at tunay at kitang-kita ng publico, hindi madaya at hindi manloloco

OPEN-minded makinig at tinuturingan ang mga diwa at pag-iisip ng mga iba; Iloc: agdengngeg ken estimaren na ti amad ken pampanunot ti sabali

Opera *(Tag. & Iloc.)* opera-*Sp*

Operate, Do surgery operahin, mag-operasyon-*Sp*, mag-opera-*Sp*; Iloc: operaren, ag-operar-*Sp*, ag-operasyon

OPERATION of a government or private business institution pamamahala; Iloc: pangigaway

OPERATION, Surgery *(Tag. & Iloc.)* operasyon-*Sp*

Operator ang nagpapalakad ng makina-*Sp* o ng negosio; Iloc: iti mangpapagna ti makina-*Sp* wenno ti maysa a negosio-*Sp*

Ophthalmologist *adj.,* **Ophthalmology** *n.* sangay ng siencia-*Sp* ng Medicina-*Sp* na may kinalaman sa *anatomy*-pagkabuo ng mata, sa *function*-obra at kahalagahan nito, at ang mga sakit sa mata

Opine pagkaroon ng palagay at pagbunyag at pagpapanindig nito

Opinion *opinion*, hubog ng pag-iisip at pagturing sa mga ano man; Iloc: *opinion*, panagbigbig wenno pagpanunot iti ania man a kasasaad o banag

Opinionated nakacapit siya sa sarili lamang niyang diwa at pag-iisip at sarado siya sa ibang diwa; Iloc: nakacapet isu ti mismo na nga amad laeng ken pagpampanunot ken cerrado isu iti sabali nga amad

Opponent *(Tag. & Iloc.)* kalaban, kacompetensia

Opportune tamang-tama sa panahon para sa tinakdang balak; Iloc: us-usto-*Sp* ti tiempo para iti naykeddeng a rangta

Opportunist *(Tag. & Iloc.)* oportunista-*Sp*

Opportunity oportunidad-*Sp*, chansa na nakakaventahe

Oppose mangontra, magprotesta, manghadlang

OPPOSITE kabaligtaran, kasalungat; Iloc: balictad

OPPOSITE SIDE sa kabila; Iloc: diay bangir

OPPOSITE SIDE, turn to the tumagilid sa kabila; Iloc: agballikid

OPPOSITE sides magkabilahang panig; Iloc: agsinnumbangir

Opposition oposisyon-*Sp*, protesta-*Sp*; Iloc: oposisyon, protesta, salangad

Oppress isiil, apihin; Iloc: parmeken

Opt pumili at magdecisyon; Iloc: agpili ken agdecisyon

Optic tungkol sa mata; Iloc: maygapu ti mata

Optician pagsukatan ng paningin at pagkuhanan ng antipara-*Sp*; Iloc: pagrukodan ti pagkita ken pagalaan ti antiparra-*Sp* o anteohos-*Sp*

Optimal pinakamaventahe, nakakasiya ng husto; Iloc: pinakanaventahe, nakaay-ayat

Optimism pagkapositivo, malarosas ang pagtuturing sa ano man sa buhay at nag-aasa ng kabutihan; Iloc: malarosas ti pangbigbig iti ania man iti biag ken agnamnama ti kaimbagan.
Correlated word
Positivism nagpapahiwatig ng kasegurodohan at pagtanggap, may confianza at walang pagdududa; Iloc: 1] mangisawang iti kaseguroan ken pag-akceptar, adda confianza na ken awan iti pagkaduda.

Optimistic *(Tag. & Iloc.)* optimista-*Sp*

Optimize gawing pinakaperfecto at pinakaefectivo; gawing pinakamaventahe

Optimum, Optima nasa pinakamataas ang nagagawang ventahe, kabutihan, unlad, kabulohan, pinakamabunga

Optional hindi obligado-*Sp* at puedeng pumili ng iba, o mag-decisyon-*Sp* siya mismo at hindi tanggapin ang bilin ng iba; Iloc: haan obligado ken mabalin nga agpili ti sabali ken isu ti agdecidir ti cayat na

OPTIONS pagpipiliang mga paraan o bagay; Iloc: dagiti pagpilyan a pamay-an o banag

OPTIONS are plenty whether things to choose from or to do for advancement or for peaceful living, or people to associate with. *There are many fishes in the waters* napakamarami ang pagpipilian kaya piliin mo ang pinakamaventahe at makakapayapa sa iyo - tao man o bagay - hindi basta-basta o bara-bara lamang pumili kundi ingat lang at gamitin ang talino sa pagpili

Optometrist *adj.*, **Optometry** *n.* profesyon-*Sp* sa pag-examen-*Sp* ng mata, kung ano ang grado ng mata para marecetahan ng tama at angkop na bisa-*Sp* ng salamin, anteohos, antiparra-*Sp*; o kung minsan ay may matuklasang diferenciang sakit ng mata na pinapayoan ang paciente-*Sp* na magpatingin sa doctor sa *ophthalmology*
Correlated words
Ophthalmologist *adj.*, **Ophthalmology** *n.* sangay ng siencia ng Medicina na may kinalaman sa *anatomy* (pagkabuo ng mata), sa *function* (tungkulin at kahalagahan nito), at ang mga sakit sa mata

Opulence kayamanan, abundancia; Iloc: pagkabaknang, abundancia

Or o; Iloc: o, wenno

Oral sinasalita, hindi sinusulat; Iloc: isarsarita

ORANGE dalandan, dalanghita; Iloc: naranghita-*Sp*

ORANGE color *(Tag. & Iloc.)* *orange*

Oratory kahusayan at kagalingan sa pagtatalumpati; Iloc: nakalalaeng nga agdiscurso iti publico

Orb globo parang sa mundo o planeta; buong mata; bilog, circulo-*Sp*

Orchard lugar-*Sp* ng mga kahoy na nagbubunga ng frutas-*Sp*; Iloc: minuyongan ti frutas

Orchestra *(Tag. & Iloc.)* *orchestra*

Orchestrate *v.*, **Orchestration** *n.* 1] kumatha at ayosin ang musica-*Sp* para magamit sa *orchestra*, 2] areglohin at pangasiwaan para gawing controlado-*Sp* ang mga elemento-*Sp* at makagawa ng mabuting resulta-*Sp* o efecto-*Sp*

Ordeal mahirap na pagsubok sa buhay; Iloc: parikut o rigrigat nga baklayen nga mang-purbar-*aSp* iti anos ti tao

ORDER 1] mag-utos, magmando-*Sp*, 2] kaayosan, areglo-*Sp*; Iloc:1] agmandar-*Sp*, agbaun, agbilin, 2] urnos, areglo

ORDER from (i.e, catalog) mag-*order*; Iloc: ag-*order*

Orderly maayos, malinis, areglado-*Sp*; Iloc: nadalimanek, areglado, nalinis ken naurnos

Ordinance *(Tag. & Iloc.)* ordinansa-*Sp*

Ordinary caraniwan, regular-*Sp*, ordinario-*Sp*; Iloc: cadawyan, regular, ordinario
Synonyms

Common pangcaraniwang nagaganap o gawain; Iloc: cadawyan o sigud a mapaspasamak wenno obra

Average caraniwan, regular, ordinario; Iloc: cadawyan, regular, ordinario

Run-of-the-mill caraniwan, ordinario

Generic pangcaraniwan o panglahatan; Iloc: pang-ordinario o para iti amin

Banal ordinaryo, caraniwan; Iloc: ordinaryo

General heneral, aplicado sa lahat; Iloc: heneral, aplicado iti amin

Organ 1] pianong organo-*Sp* na may mga pipa-*Sp* o tubo-*Sp*, 2] organo-*Sp* na nasa loob ng katawan; Iloc: 1] organo a piano-*Sp* nga addaan ti pipa o tubo, 2] organo nga adda ti uneg iti bagi

Organize i-*organize*, mag-areglo o magpalakad ng mahusay at itatag ang pagsasamahan; Iloc: i-*organize*, agareglo wenno agpadalan iti nasayaat, mangtimpuyog iti pagkacadwaen

Organized na-*organized* na, naareglo na; Iloc: na-*organized*-sen, naareglon

Organization *(Tag. & Iloc.)* organisasyon-*Sp*

Orient *east*, silangan; Iloc: *east,* daya

Orientate matuto para mabihasa sa kapaligiran o circumstancia; Iloc: adalen tapno mayruam

Oriental *oriental*, taga-silangan o taga-oriente-*Sp*; mga bayan na nasa *geography* ng Asia at *Malay Archipelago* gaya ng Filipinas, Borneo at Indonesia; Iloc: taga-daya

Orientation bilang pambungad na pagpapakila, inaakay at pinapatnubayan para maka-*adjust* o makasanay sa bagong paligiran, trabaho, kaganapan at iba pa

Oriented ano mang pinagsasandigan o nakasanayang paniniwala at costumbre-*Sp*

Origin pinagmulan, pinanggalingan, puno't dulo; Iloc: pinaggapuanan, pinagtaudan, poon

Original *original*, pinakauna; Iloc: *original*, kaunaan

Originality pinakauna at matatag, hindi tumutulad sa iba; Iloc: kaunaan ken natalinaed, haan nga tumulad ti sabali

Originate from nanggaling sa, nagmula sa; Iloc: naggapu idiay

Ornament *(Tag. & Iloc.)* ornamento-*Sp*, decorasyon-*Sp*

Ornate labis ang paglagay ng decorasyon

Ornery pangit at nakakadisgusto ang ugali o asal

Orphan *(Tag. & Iloc.)* ulila

Orphanage bahay ampunan; Iloc: pag-amponan ti ubing

Ort tira-tirang pagkain sa plato o sa mesa; Iloc: murkat

Orthodox sumusunod sa naaprovahang forma ng doctrina-*Sp*, filoso-fiya-*Sp*, paniniwala, kaisipan at asal

Osmatic kalakasan ng pang-amoy; Iloc: pagkapigsa ti pag-angot

Osmics siencia sa pang-amoy at *olfactory sense*; Iloc: siencia iti pag-angot ken ti *olfactory sense*

Ostentation *v.*, **Ostentatious** *adj.* pangpasikat at pangpamalas, pakitang-tao; Iloc: pangpasikat ken pangiparang, pakitang-tao

Ostracized taong itinakwil; Iloc: tao nga inlaksid, tao nga haan bigbigen o icascaso

OTHER ang iba; Iloc: tay sabali

OTHER side sa kabila, kabila, sa kabilang panig; Iloc: bangir, diay bangir, diay bangir a sibay

Others mga iba; Iloc: dadduma, dagiti sabsabali

Otherwise kung hindi; Iloc: nu haan

Otic tungkol sa tenga; Iloc: maygapu ti lapayag

Ouch! Aray!; Iloc: Annay!

Ought dapat; Iloc: masapul

OUR, OURS amin, namin; Iloc: cuami, cucuami

OUR, OURS (yours & mine) atin, natin; Iloc: cuatayo, cuata

Ourselves tayo, tayo mismo-*Sp*; Iloc: datayo, datayo mismo

Oust paalisin, palayasin, despachahin; Iloc: papanawen, despacharen (despacha-*Sp*, despachar-*Sp*)

OUT sa labas; Iloc: diay ruar

OUT of character iba sa kagawiang kilos o ugali niya

OUT-of-date laos na, makaluma; Iloc: nagpasaren

OUT of place 1] hindi sa tamang lugar-*Sp*; 2] masagwa o mahalay o impertinente-*Sp* o hindi nababagay o hindi relevante-*Sp*; Iloc: 1] haan umno iti lugar, 2] dakes, bastos, impertinente-*Sp*

OUT-of-pocket expenses kung hindi babayaran ng *medical insurance* o *car insurance*, ito ay ang parteng babayaran ng naka-*insure*

OUT of sight, out of mind kung ang dadalhin ay nakalagay sa hindi kitang-kita bago umalis o lumabas o magviahe, puedeng maiwanan ito dahil sa limot o pagmamadali

OUT of the hole, Out of the red nabayaran na ang lahat na utang

OUT-of-the way ilang na lugar-*Sp*, libliban; Iloc: adayo ken nakalinged a lugar

OUT of the woods nakalampas na sa maselan at malubha na kalagayan at gumaling na

Out-of-whack wala sa tamang linya o lagay; hindi wasto, hindi angkop

Outage pansamantalang walang electricidad sa sangkabayanan o parte ng bayan; Iloc: temporario nga awan electricidad iti entero nga ili o parte ti ili

Outbreak golpeng gulo, siklab, sabog, insureksion-*Sp*

Outburst silakbo, bulalas; sabog; Iloc: sumro, bettak

Outcast taong itinakwil ng mga tao; Iloc: tao nga inlaksid ken adaywan dagiti tattao

Outcome kinalabasan, resulta-*Sp*, bunga, kahihinatnan; Iloc: pagbanagan, pagmaayan, resulta, gunggona, bunga

Outcry maingay na galit o protesta sa publico-*Sp*

Outdo higitan, malampasan, daigin; Iloc: abaken, maartapan, malabsan, atiwen

Outdoor sa labas ng bahay o gusali; Iloc: idiay ruar ti balay wenno iti *building*

Outer panlabas; Iloc: akinruar

Outfit 1] anomang suot at mga gamit na kinakailangan sa pagsagawa; 2] isang negosio-*Sp*

Outgoing 1] mahusay makihalo-bilo sa mga tao, 2] magretiro na o iiwanan na ang canyang *position*; Iloc: 1] naimbag a makilaok cadagiti tattao, 2] agretiron wenno panawan nan ti puesto-*Sp* na

Outgrow malakihan ang hilig o ang damit; Iloc: madakkelan na ti magusgustoan na wenno ti bado na

Outguess nakakalamang sa pag-antabayanan niya ng tamang magaganap dahil sa paggamit niya ng talas ng canyang isip at pagpansin/pagpuna niya ng asal at galaw at gawain ng kapwa o kalaban o situasyon

Outing *outing, picnic*, pasyal, *excursion*; Iloc: *outing, picnic*, pasiar-*Sp, excursion*

Outlast nabubuhay o tumatagal ng mas matagal kaysa sa; Iloc: mas nabayag ti biag na ngem ti

Outlet 1] bukas ang daanan papalabas; paraan para mailabas o maipahayag ang nasasaloob; 2] tindahan para sa mga producto; 3] TV o radio para magpabalita

Outlive nabubuhay o tumatagal ng mas matagal kaysa sa; Iloc: mas nabayag ti biag na ngem ti

Outlook 1] lugar na pagtatanawan ng kapaligiran, 2] pananaw o pagturing sa mga ano man sa buhay; Iloc: 1] lugar a pagtan-awan iti arrubayan, 2] pagkita o pagbigbig cadagiti ania man iti biag

Outmoded laos na, makaluma; Iloc: nagpasaren

Outpatient nagpapagamot na paciente na hindi kinakailangan na maospital; Iloc: agpapaagas a paciente nga haan a masapul a maospital

Output bunga ng paggamit ng sikap at abilidad-*Sp* o intelihensia-*Sp*; producto-*Sp* ng ginagawa sa fabrica-*Sp*; Iloc: bunga ti pagiyusar ti pakat ken abilidad-*Sp* o intelihensia-*Sp*; producto-*Sp* ti maar-aramid diay fabrica

Outrageous napakalaswa, nakaririmarim, kahalay-halay, karumal-dumal, garrafal-*aSp*; Iloc: nakadakdakes, nakamadmadi, garrafal, nakaal-alas

Outreach pagbibigay ng tulong hanggang sa labas ng teritorio-*Sp* o bansa; Iloc: pagited ti tulong inggana ti ruar ti teritorio o bayan

Outright 1] bukas at walang tinatago at completo-*Sp* at entero, 2] derecho at agad-agad

Outset sa umpisa; Iloc: idiay rugi

Outshine lampasan sa liwanag o sa pagkaganda o pagkaexcelente

Outside sa labas; Iloc: diay ruar

  Synonym

  Alfresco sa labas kung saan fresco ang hangin; Iloc: diay ruar nu inchenna ti fresco nga angin

Outsider tagalabas, hindi kaanib; Iloc: haan a miembro

Outsmart utakan para matalo niya o maloco niya, nanlalamang sa pagkukunwari o sa panlilinlang; Iloc: siriban para maatiw na wenno maloco na, makaoportunista gapu iti pagsinsinan na ken iti panglocloco

Outsource ipadala ng USA o ng nasyon sa Europe sa *branch* nito o fabrica-*Sp* na nasa labas ng canilang bansa para makamenos sa gastos-*Sp*; Iloc: ipatulod iti USA wenno iti nasyon idiay Europe iti *branch* da o fabrica iti ruar ti bayan para makamenos ti gastos

Outspoken *(Tag. & Iloc.)* franko/ka-*Sp*

Outstanding superyor-*Sp*, excelente-*Sp*

Outward papalabas ang tungohan; Iloc: agparuar ti pagturongan

Outwear *see Outlast*

Outweigh mas mataas ang halaga, importancia-*Sp*, influwensia-*Sp*, mas kilala at iba pa; mas mabigat, napakabigat na buhatin

Outwit maging mas mabuti sa pamamagitan ng mas magaling na katalinohan at katalasan ng isip; daigin o lampasan sa kaalaman at karunogan; utakan para matalo niya o maloco niya, nakakalamang dahil sa pagkukunwari o sa panlilinlang; Iloc: siriban para maatiw na wenno maloco na, makaoportunista gapu iti pagsinsinan na ken iti panglocloco

Oval *oval*, hugis-itlog, habilog; Iloc: *oval*, forma ti itlog

Ovary matris-*Sp*, sinapupunan, bahay-bata; Iloc: matris

Ovation matagal na pagpalakpak at caraniwan ay nakatayo pa sila para parangalan ang talumpati o ang palabas

Oven *(Tag. & Iloc.)* horno-*Sp*, orno-*Sp*, pugon

OVER sa taas; Iloc: diay ngato

OVER, Finished tapos na; Iloc: nalpasen

OVER-easy strilyadong itlog na frinito sa magkabilaan - sa taas at baba

OVER-the-counter medicinang hindi nireceta ng *doctor* kundi kusang binili ang gamot para manatiling malusog o lumakas pa batay sa nababasa nila

OVER the long haul sa matagalang panahon

Overall ito ay ang laki, taas, haba at daming nilalaman ng bagay o paksa

Overalls suot na parang *jumper* ang taas at may pantalon sa baba na pangsuot ng magsasaka at ng nag-aalaga ng baboy o manok, at iba pang mga hayop

Overbearing naghahari, dominante-*Sp*; Iloc: agar-ari, dominante

Overboard 1] mahulog sa tubig buhat sa bangka o bapor 2] sobra na magsagawa o sobrang gumastos

Overcast maulap, kulimlim; Iloc: naulep, nacudrep, nalidem

Overcharge magsingil ng mas sobra sa dapat

Overcome masupil, malupig at masugpo ang kalaban o ang sakit; Iloc: maparmek ti kalaban wenno ti sakit

Overdo labis-labis na magsagawa o kumain o magluto at iba pa

Overdose nadamihan masyado o nasobrahan ang pag-inom ng medicina o droga

Overdraft ito ay kung magbayad ng cheke-*Sp* na labis sa nakadeposito-*Sp* sa bangko-*Sp*, nagkulang kaya ma-*overdraft*; Iloc: daytoy ket nu agbayad iti cheke-*Sp* a labes iti nakadeposito-*Sp* diay bangko-*Sp* isu a macurangan ken ma-*overdraft* langarud

Overdue atrasado dahil hindi ginawa ang obra o hindi binayaran ang utang sa tinakdang araw o sa palugit na tiempo-*Sp*; Iloc: atrasadon gapu ta haan na inaramid ti obra na o ti pagbayad ti utang na iti aldaw a naykeddeng wennoo ti naywatiwat a tiempo

Overestimate lumabis ang paghalaga; Iloc: nalabes iti pagvalor

Overflow umaapaw, sagad; Iloc: agliplippias, umap-apaw

Overload nagcarga ng sobra sa dapat cargahin

Overkill gawa o salita na napakalabis sa dapat gawin o sabihin; Iloc: aramid o sarita nga sobra wenno sobra iti usto wenno iti kasapulan

Overhear maulinigan; Iloc: nangngeg, nakangngeg

Overlap pagpatong-patungin; Iloc: pagtuon-tuonen

Overlook nakaligtaan, nalingatan; Iloc: naliwayan

Overpass calsadang tulay at sa baba nito ay hindi tubig kundi calsada-*Sp* pa rin; Iloc: calsada a rangtay ken iti baba na ket haan a danum nu di calsada met pay

Overpower gapiin, supilin, lupigin, sugpoin; Iloc: parmeken

Overrate lumabis ang paghalaga; Iloc: naglabes ti pagvalor

Override umiiral, mamayani, mananaig; Iloc: agturay, mangabak

Overrule 1] ipawalang-bisa, hindi magpahintulot ng mga argumento o gawain, 2] maghahari o magdomina

Oversee mamahala, mangasiwa, mangpatnubay, manghimatong, mamatnugot; Iloc: mangipaturong

Overseer *(Tag. & Iloc.)* superbisor-*Sp*, capatas-*Sp*

Oversight hindi sinasadyang nakaligtaan o nalaktawan; Iloc: naliwayan nga haan nga inggagara

Overstep gawa o salita na napakalabis sa dapat; Iloc: aramid o sarita nga sobra ken aglabes ngem iti usto wenno iti kasapulan

Overstock labis ang pag-imbak o sobrang napuno ng *provision* o *supplies*; Iloc: nalabes nga pagipon o napunno ti *provision* o *supplies*

Overt bukas, lantad at hindi lihim; Iloc; nakalucat, nakaparang ken haan
a nakalimed

Overtake malampasan, maabutan; Iloc: maabutan

Overthrow lupigin, ibagsak

Overtime *overtime*, dagdag na pagtrabaho pagkalampas ng tinakda na
ocho oras na trabaho sa isang araw

Overturn tumaob, bumaligtad, tumiwarik; Iloc: nagbalinsuek, nag-
balictad, nagpattog, nagbattuag
Synonyms
   Capsize tumaob, magbaligtad, tumiwarik; Iloc: agbalinsuek, agbalictad
   Upside down taob, tumbalik, tiwarik; Iloc: balinsuek

Overweight *(Tag. & Iloc.)* tabachoy

Overwhelm 1] ma-*stress* sa isip at katawan, 2] talunin, daigin; Iloc: 1] ma-
stress iti nakem ken bagi, 2] abaken

Owe mangutang; Iloc: agutang

Owl *(Tag. & Iloc.)* kuwago

OWN *adj.* ari, angkin; Iloc: cucua, akincucua
Synonym
   Possess nagtataglay, nag-aangkin, nag-aari; Iloc: makincucua, akincucua,
   addaan

OWN *v.* ariin, angkinin; Iloc: mangcucua

OWN and admit a wrongdoing or a shortcoming *Owning and admitting
a **wrongdoing** shows you have a sense of guilt and conscience-compunction. You are using your conscience and that is very commendable
and dignified since nowadays, conscience is being ignored. You can
distinguish what is right and wrong and that is cognition. You have
emotional intelligence to discern your own wrongdoings and you
take responsibility and accountability of the transgressions you
have done, and you accept the consequences. You are courageous,
noble, dignified and reliable. If you have **shortcomings** like physical,
intellectual or integrity deficiency, you do not have to announce that
to people but admitting it to yourself is the best way to deal with it
because being awakened to reality, you would make steps to rise
above it and be victorious. It usually takes a mere owning of your
wrongdoings and shortcomings to conquer it and become a much
superior person.*

Taking responsibility and self-accountability of one's errors and mistakes, Taking ownership of one's errors and mistakes Pag-aamin o pangungumpisal ng ginawang kasalanan o kamalian na nagpapahayag na ang katatao nito ay mabuti at may budhi

Confess magcumpisal; Iloc: agconfesar

Tell the truth magsabi ng tutoo; Iloc: agpudno

Avow matapang na isabi o aminin sa harap ng mga tao; Iloc: natured a bigbigen o akceptaren ti sango ti tattao

Swallow one's pride kalimutan ang pagmamalaki at tanggapin ang pagpapacumbaba na nakakapayapa

Owner may-ari, nag-aangkin; Iloc: makinkucua

Ownership sariling pag-aari, pagmemay-ari; Iloc: pagsanicua

Oxygen ito ay elemento na caraniwan ay *gas* na 1/5 nito ay nasa *atmosphere* o hangin ng kapaligiran. Ang oxygen ay *molecule* na gawa sa dalawang *atoms.* Kapag tayo ay humihinga ng *oxygen*, ito ay dinadala ng *hemoglobin* sa ating dugo sa lahat ng parte ng ating katawan, kung saan ito lumilikha ng kalakasan ng katawan

Oyster *(Tag. & Iloc.)* talaba

P

Pace sukat ng hakbang, sukat ng bilis sa paglakad o pagtakbo; Iloc: rukod ti addang, rukod ti daras ti pagna o pagtaray

Pacific mapayapa at calmado; Iloc: natalna, calmado

Pacific Ocean ang pinakamalaking dagat sa buong mundo na sacop ang kanlurang Estados Unidos at silangang Asia hanggang sa Australia

Pacifier, baby's *(Tag. & Iloc.) pacifier,* chupon, bibiron

Pacify *v.,* **Pacifism** *n.* ayaw sa giyera kundi kapayapaan kaya nag-papahinahon, nagpapacalma, nagpapayapa, nagpapatahimik, nang-aawat; Iloc: madi na ti guerra-*Sp* isu nga agpacalma, agpatalna, agpaulimek, manganawa, ay-aywen, ken pabang-aran

Correlated words

Mollify pacalmahin, ipahinahon, papayapain, awatin, palubagin ang loob; Iloc: pacalmaen, patalnaen, aganawa, ay-aywen, anawaen, paulimeken, pabang-aran

Appease, Placate magpalubag-loob na makipagkasundoan para bumuti ang kanilang pagsasamahan, pacalmahin, ipahinahon, papayapain, awatin, palubagin ang loob; Iloc: mangpatalna nga makitinnulag tapno agsayaat iti pagkacadwaan da, pacalmaen, patalnaen, aganawa, ay-aywen, anawaen, paulimeken, pabang-aran

PACK mag-empake-*Sp*; Iloc: ag-empake

PACK tight, Fill up isiksik punoin; Iloc: isedsed, iselsel, punwen

Package *(Tag. & Iloc.) package*

Packet *(Tag. & Iloc.)* pakete-*Sp*

Pact, Treaty kasunduan ng mga nasyon; Iloc: pagtulagan dagiti nasyon

Pad 1] maliit na cutchong-unan; 2] papeles na pinagsama-sama ng pandikit sa taas na dulo nito pero natatanggal kapag kumuha ng papel; 3] titirhan gaya ng *apartment* o cuarto

Paddle 1] sagwan ng bangka; 2] pamalo; 3] mallit na formang sagwan na panghalo o pambati

Paddy bukirin o sakahang tinataniman ng bigas

Padlock *(Tag. & Iloc.)* candado-*Sp*

Page 1] pahina-*Sp* ng papeles o libro, 2] pagtawag ng magulang o anak sa *loudspeaker* pag hindi sila magkahanapan o magkatagpoan sa *shopping mall*, hotel o casino; Iloc: 1] pahina ng libro o documento, 2] awag ti nagannak o anak iti *loudspeaker* nu haan da nga agkasapulan wenno agkasarakan idiay *shopping mall*, hotel o casino;

Paid bayad na; Iloc: nabayadanen

Pail *(Tag. & Iloc.)* timba-*Sp*, balde-*Sp*

PAIN *(Tag. & Iloc.)* sakit
Correlated word
Pang biglang kirot sa katawan o biglang sulpot ng pag-alala, pagkabagabag o pagkabalisa; Iloc: golpe nga sakit ti bagi wenno golpe a pagsumro ti danag, ringgor wenno riro

PAIN, sharp, biting makirot, mahapdi; Iloc: naapges, nasanaang

PAIN, throbbing makirot; Iloc: naut-ot

PAIN-reliever pamawi ng sakit; Iloc: makaikkat ti sakit

Painful masakit; Iloc: nasakit
Synonym
Sore masakit; Iloc: nasakit

Paint mag-pinta-*Sp*, mag-pintura-*Sp*; Iloc: agpinta/agpintura

Painter *(Tag. & Iloc.)* pintor-*Sp*

Pair magka-pares-*Sp*, magka-pareha-*Sp*; Iloc: agkapares, agka-pareha
Antonym
> **Mismatched pair** di magkapares; Iloc: pangis, agpangis

Pajama, PJ *(Tag. & Iloc.)* *pajama*

Pal kaibigan; Iloc: gayyem

Palace *(Tag. & Iloc.)* palacio-*Sp*
Correlated word
> **Castle** *(Tag. & Iloc.)* palacio, castilyo

Palatable masarap, malasa; Iloc: naimas, naraman

Palate ngalangala; Iloc: ngadas

Pale maputla; Iloc: bessag
Correlated word
> **Wan** maputla, nandidilaw; Iloc: puraw ti pagkabessag na a casla awan dara nan

Pallid sobra-*Sp* at *abnormal* ang pagkaputla; Iloc: sobra ken *abnormal* ti pagkabessag a color-*Sp* na

Pallor sobra o kakaibang pagkaputla dahil sa takot, o sa sakit o patay na

PALM *(Tag. & Iloc.)* nipa-*Sp*, palma, palmera-*Sp*

PALM of hand *(Tag. & Iloc.)* palad

PALM fruit *(Tag. & Iloc.)* sago

Palpable lantad at kitang-kita at naririnig at nadadama

Palpate i-examen sa paghipo para masuri ang sakit

Palpitate tumitibo, pumipintig; Iloc: agkebba-kebba, agpitik-pitik

Palpitation of the pulse or the heart *(Tag. & Iloc.)* pitik ng pulso-*Sp*, palpitasyon-*Sp*

Palsy-walsy lantad ang pakikipagkaibigang matalik niya

Palter umasal o magsalita na hindi *sincere* o taos-puso; Iloc: agtignay ken agsarita nga awan kaagpaysuan iti puso ken nakem na

Paltry nakakatawa o nakakainsulto dahil kaunting-kaunti lamang at walang kabulohan

Pamper nagpapamihasa, mapagbigay-layaw, nagpapalugod na consentidor-*Sp*, mapagbigay-luho; Iloc: consentidor nga mangpagpagustoan a mangited amin a capricho

PAN 1] cawali, 2] salain ang buhangin o lupa para makuha ang ginto dito *(gold panning)*; Iloc: 1] paryok, 2] sagatan ti darat ken daga para makaala ti balitok ditoy

PAN out, Turn out or **Work out all right** nabuo, nayari, nacompleto na mabuti at kasiya-siya

Panacea, Cure-all remedio-*Sp* o panlunas sa lahat ng sakit, kasamaan at kahirapan; Iloc: remedio o pangngagas iti amin a sakit, dakes ken rigat

Pancreas *pancreas*, lapay; Iloc: *pancreas*, yusi

Pandemic nagkahawaan sa sakit ang mga tao at laganap ito sa malaki at maraming lugar-*Sp*; Iloc: nagi-innacar iti sakit ken naiwaras iti tattao iti adu ken nalawa a lugar

Pandemonium infierno-*Sp*; malaking kagulohan na hindi maawat o masaway

Pander taong nang-aalok sa mga cliente-*Sp* ng mga babaeng puta-*Sp* o *prostitutes*; taong nagsasamantala sa kahinaan o vicio-*Sp* ng iba; namamagitan siya sa pag-iibigan

Pandora's box kung saan lumalabas ng napakadami at hindi inaasahang mga problema

Pane salaming parte-*Sp* ng vintana; Iloc: sarming nga parte-*Sp* ti ventana-*Sp*

Panel 1] grupong mga tao para sa discusyon-*Sp* sa publico-*Sp* o tagapayo o maghatol sa mga patimpalak; 2] bahagi ng pader

Pang biglang kirot sa katawan o biglang sulpot ng pagkabalisa o pagkabagabag o pag-alala; Iloc: golpe-*aSp* a sakit ti bagi o golpe a pagsumro ti danag, ringgor o riro

Panhandle nakatayo sa dinadaanan ng mga tao, o nilalapitan ang mga tao para humingi ng limos-*aSp*; Iloc: nakatacder idiay paglablabsan iti tattao, wenno umasideg iti tao tapno dumawat ti limos

Panic, in takot at natatataranta; Iloc: mabuteng ken taranta

Panorama malawak na tanawin ng kalawakan; Iloc: nalawa a matan-aw iti arrubayan

Pant humahangos, humihingal, sumasagap ng hininga; Iloc: agas-asog, agal-al-al

Pants *(Tag. & Iloc.)* pantalon-*Sp*

Panty salawal, *panty*; Iloc: calson-*Sp*, sapin, *panty*

Pantry maliit na cuarto-*aSp* sa cocina-*Sp* para paglagyan ng mga *groceries* at iba pa; Iloc: bassit a cuarto diay cocina para pagdulinan ti *groceries* ken sabali pay

Pap 1] malambot na pagkain ng mga sanggol; 2] mga *invalid* at masasakiting tao; 3] suso or utong, chupon; 4] paksa, pag-uusap, libro at iba pa na walang kahalagahan

PAPER, Papers *(Tag. & Iloc.)* papel-*Sp*, papeles-*Sp*

PAPER trail kasulatan gaya ng *transactions* o evidencia ng hukuman na magagamit sa paghusga ng crimen-*Sp*

PAR 1] magkapantay, magkapareho, magkatumbas; 2] caraniwan, *normal, standard*, ang pagsaligan; 3] dami ng pagtira sa *golf*

PAR excellence ang halimbawa ng excellence at *superior;* pinaka-excelente na walang makapantay

Parable simpleng storia na nagbibigay ng *moral lesson* o magandang leksion

Parade *(Tag. & Iloc.)* parada-*Sp*

Paradigm 1] halimbawa, modelo-*Sp*, huwaran, ehemplo-*Sp;* 2] ang mga tinatanggap ng *scientific community* gaya ng pag-iisip, batayang palagay, sistema-*Sp* ng pagsasagawa gaya ng pamaraan, palakad, patakaran, alituntunin, kautusan o reglamento-*Sp*; 3] sa *grammar*, ito ay pangkat ng salita kung ito ay ginagamit sa iba't ibang areglo ng salita gaya ng boy, boys, boy's, boys'

Paradise *(Tag. & Iloc.)* paraiso-*Sp*

Paradox paghahayag/*statement* o mungkahi/*proposition* na parang kabalictaran o kahangalan pero sa tutuo lang ay nagsasabi ng posibleng katotohanan; *self-contradictory and false proposition*; palagay o pahayag na contra sa caraniwang tinatanggap na *opinion*

Paragon *noun:* modelo ng *excellence*; larawan ng kabutihan at kabaitan; *verb*: makipantay o higitan; icompara, turingan na *paragon*

Parakeet *(Tag. & Iloc.)* culasisi

Parallel magkapareho at magkapantay ang uri sa lahat ng bagay pero hindi magkalapit

Paralysis *(Tag. & Iloc.)* *paralysis*

Paralyzed, Paralytic *(Tag. & Iloc.)* baldado-*Sp*, paralisado-*Sp*, paralitico-*Sp*

Paramedic taong tumutulong sa mga mangggamot sa oras ng *emergency* dahil siya ay nag-aral at nakapagsanay sa paggagamot; Iloc: tao a tumultulong cadagiti mangngagas iti oras iti *emergency* gapu ta nagadal ken nakalasat ti *training* ti pag-agas

Paramilitary ordinaryong mamamayan na puedeng sumali o tumulong sa militante-*Sp* kung kinakailangan; Iloc: tao ti bayan a mabalin a sumali wenno tumulong ti militante/*army* nu makasapulan

Paramount pinakamataas sa importancia o influwencia; kataas-taasan, dakilang-dakila; pinakamataas sa ranko o sa otoridad; *supreme ruler, overlord*

Correlated words

Executive *boss,* puno, amo; Iloc: *boss,* pangulo, amo

Head of an office or a business *(Tag. & Iloc.)* pangulo, boss, amo

Boss tagapamahala, amo, pinuno, pangulo; Iloc: amo, apo, pangulo

Manager *boss,* tagapamahala, puno, amo; Iloc: *boss,* amo

In-charge pinuno, nangungulo, hefe, cabesa; Iloc: cabesa, hefe

Call the shots siya ang mamumuno; Iloc: isu ti mangigaway

Supervisor *(Tag. & Iloc.)* superbisor

Paranoid madalas na naniniwalang pinagmamalupitan at nilalait siya ng iba; Iloc: canayon a patchen na nga ul-ulpitan ken ilalais da isuna

Paraphernalia ari-arian, pagaaring kagamitan at kasangkapan; Iloc: sanicua, cukcukua nga alicamen ken muebles-*Sp* ken dagiti maar-aramat

Paraphrase pag-explica o pagsasalin ng salita o kasulatan o ibang wika para maintindihan; Iloc: pag-explicar wenno pagpatarus ti sarita o ti naysurat o sabali a lengguahe tapno maawatan (explica/ explicar-*Sp*, intindi-*aSp*)

Paraprofessional empleyadong na-*train* para tumulong sa manggagamot, abogado-*Sp*, guru at iba pa, pero wala siyang licensia-*Sp* sa pagtrabaho sa mga *profession* na tinutulongan niya

Parasite 1] microbio-*Sp* na tumitira sa katawan ng tao o hayup, 2] taong umaasa sa pagsuporta ng iba kahit puede siyang kumayod ng husto; Iloc: 1] microbio nga aggigian iti bagi ti tao wenno animal-*Sp*, 2] tao nga agdepdepende iti suporta ti sabali uray no caya na ti agobra ti usto

Parboil ipakulo ng sandali lamang; Iloc: ipaburek ti nabiit laeng

Parcel 1] pakete-*Sp*, 2] hindi malawak na laki ng lupa, 3] pagbahaba-haginan; Iloc: 1] pakete, 2] bassit a solar ti daga, 3 pagbingay-bingayan

Parch tuyong-tuyo; Iloc: nakamagmaga

Pardon *n.,* **Pardon** *v.* 1] pagpapatawad, 2] patawarin; Iloc: 1] dispensar-*Sp*, pagpakawan, 2] dispensaren, pakawanen

Pare balatan ang frutas-*Sp* o gulay sa pamamagitan ng cuchilyo-*Sp*; Iloc: ukisan ti frutas wenno nateng nga iyus-usar-*Sp* ti cuchilyo

Synonym

Peel balatan, talupan; Iloc: ukisan

Parent, Parents magulang; Iloc: nagannak

Parental management: Ang sabi ng Panginoong Dios sa Biblia, *"Train up a child in the way he should go, and when he is old, he will not depart from it."* Ang numero uno na *job* at obligasyon ng magulang – ang tatay at ang nanay - ay ang mga anak nila. Kinakailangang patnubayan at turoan ang mga anak parati sa tamang *direction* upang matuto silang mabuhay na marangal, makabatas at maka-Dios para sa canilang kapayapaan/*peace*, kabutihan, kaligayahan at kaunlaran. 1] *Show them your love for them often, allot quality time for them, and praise them for their good ways to mold their self-esteem* Ipakita at ipadama ng mga magulang ang pagmamahal nila sa canilang mga anak para malaman ng mga anak na ginigilaw sila, pâti ang maarugang paglalaan sa canila ng tiempo-*Sp*, at hangaan ang canilang mga asal at gawa na tama, mahusay at mabuti, para magkaroon sila ng *self-confidence* sa sarili nila at nakakabuo ng confiansa at lakas ng loob sa pakikibaka ng anoman sa buhay; 2] *Nip wrongdoings in the bud at its early stage* Huwag pagtawanan ang mga mali nila para hindi nila isipin na nakakatuwa at tama ang mga mali nila, kundi mahinahong iwasto para masugpo ang masama at maling gawa, salita o ugali habang maaga pa para hindi mabihasa at magiging kagawian, na mahirap na tuloy tanggalin; 3] *Be vigilant parents* Alerto sa pagtatanod at pagpapatnubay para malaman nila ang ligtas, mabuti at matuwid na daan sa buhay; 4] *Let God be a constant part in their life* Ipaalam ang *blessings* at ventahe ng malapit sa Dios at payoan silang parating magdasal, magsamba/*praise*, humingi ng *direction* sa Dios para matuwid ang lakad araw-araw lalong-lalo na kung may kahirapan, at huwag kalimutang magpasalamat sa Dios sa malaki at maliit Niyang mga biyaya; 5] *Instill a strong foundation of moral and ethical values to establish a dignified, lawful, peaceful, happy, rewarding, and blessed life* Magtanim ng <u>strong foundation</u> ng *moral and ethical values* sa mga anak para kahit ano mang pagsubok sa buhay ay manatili pa rin silang makabatas, marangal, busilak, mapayapa, masaya, maunlad, maka-Dios, at maayos; 6] *Walk the talk to be good role models to the children* Ihalimbawa ng mga magulang sa *action* at ugali ang kabutihang-puso, kabaitan, kasipagan, pagsisikap, pagi-ging maka-Dios, mapagbigay, mapag-intindi sa kalagayan ng kapwa at iba pang mga asal na makakapagpabait at makakapagpabuti sa mga anak para tularan nila ang mga halimbawa ng mga magulang; 7] *Hold oneself to a higher standard for a better and rewarding tomorrow* I-angat ang sarili nila sa marangal na pagkatao at katalinohan (pag-aaral, pagbabasa ng *beneficial and edifying informations*, taposin ang colehio at carera, magprogreso) at huwag na huwag ibaba ang sarili sa kasamaan at katamaran; at ipaalam din na <u>magpaumanhin at aminin</u> ang kasalanan kung nagkasala at mahigpit na iwasan ang pagpapalusot dahil nagpapamalagi at nagpapabihasa sa kasalanan ang pagpalusot kaya uulitin ang mga iyon. 8] *Use one's strength, knowledge, intelligence, abilities, skills, talents and other assets so that these won't be forgotten and vanish by non-usage* Turoang gamitin ang canilang *assets* gaya ng kalusogan at lakas ng katawan, katalinohan, kaalaman, mga abilidad at talento at iba pa <u>para hindi makalimutan, hindi maglaho at mawala</u> ang mga ito; 9] *Use time productively* Turoang gamitin ang oras nila sa makabulohang gawa gaya ng mag-aral, magbasa ng mga libro, magdasal, tumulong sa bahay at sa kapwa, mag-*exercise* para sa kalusogan ng katawan, pansaman-talang mag*volunteer* (walang bayad) sa municipio o sa mga *charitable institutions* para matuto pa sila ng ibang *skills* na magagamit sa kina-bukasan, at nagiging makabayani pa sila sa pagiging *contributing members to society;* 10] *Be the solution, never the problem* Ipaalam na dapat maging kalutasan sila at hinding-hindi maging problema kahit minsan; 11] *Morals prevent problems and risks* Maraming marangal na lalaking marespeto sa babae, pero may mga lalake na walang pagpipigil sa canilang *libido* o libog kaya dapat malaman ng babae ito para hindi siya walang kamuang-muang na magahasa tuloy; hindi kasiya-siya ang magahasa at may mga problema pa gaya ng pagbubuntis kahit hindi kasal at baka mahawaan pa ng *venereal diseases.* Kaya ang babae ay dapat mag-ingat sa pakikipag-*date* at kumapit parati sa moralidad. 12] ***Tell them never, never go into drug addiction, never even try it no matter how persistent the persuasions are because it only brings devatating failures in life,*** *like loss of good sense-good judgment-and-intelligence, neglect of hygiene practices that one smells so disgustingly, it also generates ugly and unkempt appearance, old-age wrinkles even at a young age, weakness and frailty, illness and pains, and even an early death.*

PARENTS-in-law (male or female) mga biyenan, Iloc: dagiti katugangan

PARENTS (male or female) of a son or daughter-in law to the other parent balae; Iloc: abalayan

Pariah taong itinakwil ng mga tao; Iloc: tao nga inlaksid ken adaywan dagiti tattao

PARK *(Tag. & Iloc.) park,* parke-*Sp*
Correlated word
Fairground malawak na lupain kung saan ginaganap ang mga *fairs* at *exhibitions*
Playground *(Tag. & Iloc.) playground*

PARK a car iparada ang coche-*Sp*; Iloc: iparada ti coche

Parlor cuarto para tumanggap at makihalo-bilo sa mga visita; lugar na makipagpulong tungkol sa negosio o politico

Parole palayain ang bilanggo pero may nakapatung na condisyon-*Sp* na dapat niyang sundin kung hindi ay ibilanggo uli siya; Iloc: parwaren iti balud ngem adda condisyon nga masapul a tungpalen na nu haan ket ipreso da manen isu

Parrot *(Tag. & Iloc.)* loro-*Sp*

Parry ilagan, umilag, lihisan; Iloc: lisyan, liklikan

Part parte-*Sp*, bahagi; Iloc: parte

Partake makilahok, lumahok, sumali, bumahagi; Iloc: ag-participar-*Sp*, makisali, makiraman

Partial 1] parte lamang hindi buo, 2] finafavoran ng mas mahigit ang isang tao/grupo kaysa sa iba, 3] pagkakagusto o pagkakahilig sa isang bagay o isang tao

Particle piraso o maliit o katiting na bagay

Particular 1] tungkol sa isang tanging tao, bagay, grupo-*Sp*, clase-*Sp*, ocasyon-*Sp*; hindi sa marami o lahat, kundi bukod-tangi lamang; 2] pihikan at maselang tao

Participant kalahok, kasali; Iloc: kasali, participante-*Sp*

Participate makilahok, lumahok, sumali, bumahagi; Iloc: agparticipar-*Sp*, makisali, makiraman

Partisan makapartido at makalapi; mahigpit na pumapanig sa *political party* o sa tao, grupo o layonin

Partition *partition*, pader, dingding; Iloc: *partition*, diding

PARTNER *(Tag. & Iloc.)* 1] pareha-*Sp*, kapareha, 2] kasocio sa negocio, 3] ka-*partner* sa sayaw, kasayaw

Party *party*, handaan, piging; Iloc: *party*, padaya
Correlated words

Potluck *potluck*, pagtitipon kung saang bawat visita ay nagdadala ng ulam, salo-salo; Iloc: *potluck*, padaya nga tagmaysa a visita ket mangitugot ti makan

Banquet bankete, piging, marangyang pulong; Iloc: bankete, ponsion, dakkel ken naragsak a *party*

Fete pistahan o piging o malaking pagdiriwang na caraniwan ay sa labas o sa parke kung saan nag-iipon ang mga tao para sa pagparangal ng tagumpay ng tao

PASS dadaan, dumaan; Iloc: lumabas, labsan, lumasat

PASS away *(Tag. & Iloc.)* namatay

PASS for/as puedeng maipagpalagay na kagaya; Iloc: mabalin a maytutop nga kapareho

PASS, let someone paraanin, tumabi para paraanin; Iloc: palasaten, papagnaen, umigid tapno palasaten

PASS out mahimatay, mawalan ng malay; Iloc: matalimudaw

PASS something to someone i-pasa-*Sp*, iyabot; Iloc: iyawat, i-pasa, iyabot

PASS a test maka-pasa-*Sp*; Iloc: makapasar-*Sp*

PASS the time nagpapalipas ng oras-*Sp*; Iloc: mangpaspasar ti oras (pasar-*Sp*, oras-*Sp*)

PASS through a tight narrow place lumusot; Iloc: lumsot

PASS up tanggihan o palampasin at ipagpabaya; Iloc: agmadi wenno itantan para iti sabali nga aldaw

Passable 1] puedeng daanan o tawiran; 2] valido, sapat at matatanggap; 3] pasadong ipasa-batas

Passage 1] daanan, 2] ginawang batas ng *legislature*; Iloc: 1] lasatan, 2] inaramid a linteg ti lehislativo

Passé *(Tag. & Iloc.)* laos na

Passed, Past lumipas na; Iloc: napalabasen

Passed, long matagal nang nangyari, malaon na; Iloc: idi pay laeng a napasamak, nabayagen

Passenger *(Tag. & Iloc.)* pasahero-*Sp*

Passerby or Passer-by taong dumaraan; Iloc: tao nga lumablabas, lumaslasat

Passing the time unproductively nagtutunganga at sinasayang ang oras imbes na makagawa ng makakabuti o makabunga; Iloc: agmulmu-lengleng o agmutmuttaleng ken sayangen na iti oras imbes nga makaaramid iti makapaimbag o makabunga

Passion makapangyarihang damdamin gaya ng pag-ibig, saya, galit at poot; Iloc: nakapigpigsa a ricna casla ti pagayat, ragsak, pungtot ken gura

Passionate 1] may malakas na damdamin sa pagturing ng mga bagay-bagay, 2] matindi ang damdaming *sexual*; Iloc: 1] adda napigsa a ricna na iti pagbigbig cadagiti bambanag ida, 2] napalalo ti *sexual* a ricna na

Passive hindi tumutugon sa pananakit at iba pang pinapadanas sa canya; Iloc: haan nga agsubalit iti pangpasakit wenno aniaman a ipalpalasat canyana

Passport *(Tag. & Iloc.)* *passport,* pasaporte-*Sp*

Password maikling salita na lihim para siya lamang ang makapasok sa bukod-aring *bank account* niya o *internet site* niya

PAST ang nakaraan, ang nakalipas, ang lumipas na panahon; Iloc: ti napalabas, idi limmabas a panawen

PAST, bring back the ungkatin ang nakalipas; Iloc: ungkaten ti napalabas

PAST, in the noon, lumipas na panahon; Iloc: idi pay nagpasar nga tiempon

PASTE *n.* pandikit, cola-*Sp*; Iloc: pangpigket, pangdekket, cola

PASTE *v.* idikit, i-cola-*Sp*; Iloc: ipigket, idekket, icola

Pasteurize ipadarang ang pagkain gaya ng gatas, *yogurt*, queso-*Sp*, cerveza-*Sp* o alak ng nakatakdang araw o oras na sapat para mamatay ang mga *microorganism* na nakakabigay ng sakit

Pastiche literatura-*Sp* o musico-*Sp* o bagay ng arte-*Sp* na gawa sa forma-*Sp* o paksa o stilo-*Sp* na hiniram sa isa o mahigit sa isa na pinagmulan

Pastime kinahihiligan, libangan, dibersion-*Sp*; Iloc: paglinglingayan, pasatiempo-*Sp*

Pastor *(Tag. & Iloc.) pastor*

Pastry kakaning pangmeryenda; Iloc: baduya, saramsan

Pasture madamong kaparangan; parang na puno ng damo at iba pang mga halaman kung saan kumakain at nagpapastol ang mga hayop

PAT *(Tag. & Iloc.)* tapik

PAT on the back salita o tapik sa balikat para purihin, batiin, palakasin ang loob, o himoking magtagumpay; kalugorang-pagbati sa tao na nakagawa ng mabuti para mapasigla ang loob niya at magpatuloy siya sa paggawa ng mga nakakahanga, tapik-tapikin ang likod o balikat sa paghanga; Iloc: sarita wenno tapik ti likod tapno bigbigen isu ken patibkeren na ti confiansa ti bagi na ken iti cabaelanna tapno agganas nga agpakasayaat ken agballigi isu

PATCH 1] tagpian ng tapal, 2] kapirasong lupa; Iloc: 1] tacupan, 2] bassit a pisi ti daga

PATCH up magkaayusan, magbalikan, maging magkaibigan ulit o magkasintahan o magkasundoan; Iloc: agsubli iti pagcacaduaan, paggagayyeman, o paginnayan-ayatan da manen

Patdown, Pat down kapkapan ang damit na suot ng tao para matutop kung mayroong nakatagong armas-*Sp* o droga-*Sp*

Pate *(Tag. & Iloc.)* ulo, utak/utek, tuktok ng/ti ulo

Patent *legal* na karapatan o titulo sa nag-imbento ng producto na kapag ang iba ay nagcopia nito, sila ay lumabag sa batas at maisakdal sila sa corte ng husticia; Iloc: *legal* nga *protection* nga turay ken liteg iti nang-imbento ti producto nga nu adda agcopiar ditoy, isuda ket maydarum iti corte ti husticia

Paternal may kinalaman sa ama, katangian ng ama; Iloc: maygapu iti tatang o ama, katatao iti ama

Paternity ang pagiging ama at ang pagpapatunay nito; Iloc: ti pagbalbalinan nga ama ken iti pangpaneknek na daytoy

Path daanan, daan; Iloc: dalan, pagnaan

Pathetic nakakaawang-nakakadisgusto dahil sa kasamaan niya; Iloc: nakakaasi a nakakadisgusto gapu ti pagkadakes na

Pathological *adj.,* **Pathology** *n.* kagawian at nakakafuersang asal

Pathos nagbibigay ng damdaming lungkot o awa

Patience pacencia-*Sp,* chaga; Iloc: pacencia, anos
Correlated word
> **Forbear** 1] nagpapasencia kahit hinahamon, 2] pagpipigil; Iloc: 1] agpaspasencia uray nu carcariten da, 2] pagtepped

PATIENT pacencioso/sa-*Sp,* mapagtiis; Iloc: pacencioso/sa, naanos

PATIENT, medical *(Tag. & Iloc.)* paciente-*Sp*

Patriach lalaking namumuno ng familia-*Sp* o tribo-*Sp;* Iloc: lalaki nga agdominar-*Sp* iti familia o tribo

Patriotic *v.,* **Patriotism** *n. patriotic,* patriotismo-*Sp,* pagmamahal, pagtatanggol at pagsuporta sa sariling bayan; pagkadevoto, makabayan; Iloc: *patriotic,* pagay-ayat, pagdefensa ken pagdevoto iti bayan

Patrol, Squad watch *(Tag. & Iloc.)* ronda-*Sp, patrol*

Patron *(Tag. & Iloc.)* suki, madalas na cliente-*Sp*

Patronize itaguyod, suportahan, tangkilikin; ibaba ang sarili sa mas mababa sa canya; Iloc: mangsuporta

Patsy *sucker* o taong madaling maloco, malinlang, maakit, mahikayat, mapilit; *scapegoat* o taong pinagpapatungan ng sala kahit hindi siya ang gumawa ng kasalanan

Pattern 1] *pattern* o pangtabas ng damit na tatahiin; 2] desenyong decorasyon-*Sp* sa tela-*Sp,* sa platong china o pader; 3] bihasa o paraparating gawi, kagawian

Pauper nagpapalimos; Iloc: agpalpalimos

Pause patlang o puwang o pansamantalang pagtigil ng gawain o pagpalakad
Synonym
> **Intermission, Hiatus** patlang o puwang o pansamantalang pagtigil ng gawain o pagpalakad

PAVE takpan o patongan ang calsada o lakaran ng concreto-*Sp*, cemento-*Sp*, bato, *bricks, tiles*, kahoy o anomang nakakapagtigas, nakakapaglakas at nakakapagpantay ng daanan

PAVE the way to/for ipatnubay at ihanda para magaan at madali ang pagpasok o papunta doon o pag-umpisa

Pavement ibabaw ng calsada gaya ng cemento-*Sp* o asfalto-*Sp*; daanan, bangketa-*Sp*; Iloc: rabaw ti calsada casla iti cemento o asfalto; pagnaan, bangketa

Paw paa ng hayup; Iloc: saca ti animal

Pawn magsangla; Iloc: ag-salda-a*Sp*

PAY magbayad, bayaran; Iloc: agbayad, bayadan

PAY-off 1] buong bayad ng sweldo; 2] kalutasang pangwakas na bayad; kahihinatnang nararapat na parusa o gantimpala

Payable dapat bayaran na o sa fechang tinakda; Iloc: masapul bayadanen o iti fecha nga indesignar

Payment *(Tag. & Iloc.)* bayad, kabayaran

Pea *(Tag. & Iloc.)* gisantes-*Sp*

PEACE kapayapaan; Iloc: talna, pia

PEACE sign inaangat ang mga daliri na nakaforma ng "V" na senyas-*Sp* ng payapa; Iloc: ingato iti ramay a nakaforma iti "V" a senyas ti talna
Another Peace sign
Wave white flag simbolo ng pagsuko o kaya hiling na makipagkasundoan ng pansamantalang paghinto ng labanan o temporaryong pagpaliban ng alitan

Peaceful mapayapa, tahimik; Iloc: natalna, naulimek, nalinnaay, napia

Peacekeeping pagpanatili ng kapayapaan, katahimikan, katatagan at kaligtasan ng buong mundo sa pamamagitan ng pagtatag ng militante/ *army* sa mga itinakdang lugar

Peacemaker tagagawa ng kapayapaan; Iloc: tagaaramid iti talna

Peach *(Tag. & Iloc.) peach*, melocoton-*Sp*

Peak taluktok, taas ng bundok; Iloc: tuktok, ngato ti bantay
Correlated words
Acme tugatog, pinakamataas na parte ng bundok
Apex pinakamataas na lugar, patulis na forma sa ulo ng bundok; Iloc: kangatuan a lugar, natirad a forma diay ulo ti bantay

Peal ibatingaw ang campana-*Sp*; Iloc: ipatit ti campana

Peanut *(Tag. & Iloc.)* mani-*Sp*

Pear *(Tag. & Iloc.)* peras-*Sp*

Pearl *(Tag. & Iloc.)* perlas-*Sp*

Peat pasirang pagkain gaya ng gulay na magamit na fertilizer o abono-*Sp* ng halaman o panggatong; Iloc: agdadaelen a kanen casla ti natnateng nga maaramid nga abono iti tanem wenno pangsungrod

Pebble batong maliit; Iloc: bassit a bato

Peck tuka ng ibon, mabilisang halik sa pisngi

Pecking order hilera-*Sp* ng mga ibon na ang nasa harap ay ang naghahari sa lahat at tumutuka sa kasunod na katabi na mas mababa ang ranko sa kanya pero may kataasan din, at ito rin ay tumutuka sa kasunod niyang katabi na mas mababang rangko, at patuloy-tuloy ang pagtuka sa mas mababa sa canila hanggang ito ay makarating sa pinakamababa at pinakahuli sa lahat at ang tawag sa canya ay *the last of the pecking order*, at ito'y ginagamit din kung minsan sa pagtrato sa tao o sa *race*.

Peculiar *adj.*, **Peculiarity** *n.* kaugalian na kakaiba na ito ay natatangi sa isang tao o isang grupo-*Sp* lamang; Iloc: costumbre-*Sp* nga naydumduma nga bukbukod ti maysa a tao o maysa a grupo laeng
Correlated word
Idiosyncrasy ang kakaibang gawi o asal ng isang tao na tanging canya

Pecuniary tungkol sa pera o pagbabayad; ito rin ay tungkol sa multa-*Sp*, o tungkol sa parusa dahil sa pera

Pedagogue *teacher*, maestra-*Sp*, guro; Iloc: maestra

Pedal *pedal*, parte-*Sp* ng sasakyan o makina-*Sp* kung saan ang paa ang nagpapaandar; Iloc: *pedal*, parte ti lugan wenno makina nga ditoy ket saca ti agpaandar

Peddle naglilibot para magventa; Iloc: agliblibot tapno aglaco

Pedestal 1] patungan, fundasyon-*Sp* na pangsuporta ng poste-*Sp*, 2] ito ay lugar o puesto-*Sp* ng karangalan at pagmamahal; Iloc: 1] pagbatayan, fundasyon nga mangsuporta ti poste, 2] lugar o puesto ti dayaw ken ayat

Pedestrian taong tumatawid at naglalakad papunta sa paroroonan, hindi nakasakay sa sasakyan

Pedophile binata o may asawa na naaakit at gustong makipagtalik sa mga bata kaya nakakakilabot na *weird* at nakakadisgusto

Pee iihi; Iloc: umisbo

Peek sumilip; Iloc: agsirip

PEEL a fruit balatan, talupan; Iloc: ukisan

PEEL off from a hard surface bakbakin, watakin, tuklapin; Iloc: lekkaben, cuplaten

PEELING balat, talup; Iloc: ukis

PEELING off nagtutuklap; Iloc: agcuplacuplat

Peep sumilip; Iloc: agsirip

Peeping Tom palasilip; Iloc: mannirip

PEER 1] kapantay, magkaparehong katayuan, 2] titigan; Iloc: 1] kapatag, kapada, agkasadar, 2] mingmingan, perrengen

PEER pressure para matanggap at maging karapat-dapat, tupdin ang mga utos ng mga mas makapangyarihan, gawin ang tinakdang kilos, at sumang-ayon sa mga patakaran at principio-*Sp* nila.

Peeve yamotin, consomihin, suyahin, i-perhuisio-*Sp*; Iloc: iconsomi, pasuyaen, sairwen, iperhuisio.

Peeved naghinanakit, magdamdam; Iloc: maluksaw, makasuron

Peevish masungit, bugnotin, antipatico/ca-*Sp*, mahilig mangontra, suplado/da; Iloc: natangsit, nasaur, makarurrurod, managsupyat, antipatico/ca, suplado/da-*Sp*

Pell-mell 1] pagmamadali na magulo, taranta at bara-bara; 2] *crowd* o mga taohan o kilos o paraan na nakakalito o magulo.

Pelt 1] balat ng mabalahibong hayop, 2] pagsususuntokin o pagbabatohin; Iloc: 1] cudil ti nabuok nga animal, 2] danog-danogen wenno uboren iti bato

Pelvis, Hips balakang; Iloc: patong

Pen *(Tag. & Iloc.) pen,* pluma-*Sp*

Penalize *v.,* **Penalty** *n.* parusahan, multahan; parusa, multa-*Sp;* Iloc: dusaen, castigaren (castigar-*Sp*)

Penance dasaling pangpenitencia para sa absolusyon-*Sp* o patawad ng mga kasalanang ikinumpisal sa *priest* o pari; Iloc: penitensia-*Sp* nga ilualo para iti absolusyon iti basbasol nga in-confesar-*Sp* iti padi o *Catholic priest*

Penchant hilig, kinasasabikan; Iloc: paggagaran, pagpapaosan
Correlated words
    Have a weakness for... gustong-gusto sa isang pagkain o isang bagay na hindi niya cayang labanan o matiis; Iloc: agpap-papaos iti...
    Gusto maganang-maganang pagkawili, gusto; Iloc: magusgustoan, caycayat, gusto
Pencil *(Tag. & Iloc.)* lapis-*Sp*
Pending pansamantalang nakabitin habang naghihintay na magaganap o maaprovahan; Iloc: nakabitin nga ur-urayen mientras-*Sp* nga haan pay a mapasamak o maaprovaran
Penetrate tusokin, itusok, tagusin; Iloc: tudoken, itudok, tugkelen
Penicillin *(Tag. & Iloc.) penicillin*
Penis bayag, titi; Iloc: buto, titing
Penitent nagsisisi sa ginawa niyang kasamaan o kasalanan; Iloc: agbabbabawi cadagiti inaramid na a dakes o basol
Penitentiary preso, carcel-*Sp*, bilangguan, kulongan para ibilanggo ang mga *criminal*
Penmanship pagsulat; Iloc: pagsurat
Pension *(Tag. & Iloc.) pension*
Pensioner *(Tag. & Iloc.)* pensionado-*Sp*
Pensive taimtim sa pag-iisip; Iloc: agpampanunot ti nauneg
Correlated words
    Ponder magmuni-muni; Iloc: agpampanunot
    Contemplate magdili-dili, magmuni-muni; Iloc: agimatang
    Reflect pagdili-dili kung ano ang tama o macaya o makapabuti; Iloc: nauneg a pagpampanunot nu ania ti usto o ti macaya o makapaimbag
    Mull matinding pinag-iisipan at inaalaala ang mga pangyayari o detalye
Pent-up emotions kinikimkim na sakit o sama ng loob, bumibigat o pinapairal ang sakit ng loob dahil kinikimkim lamang niya at hindi niya binubunyag; Iloc: napempen a rungsot o sakit ti puso, dumagdagsen ken agpatpatuloy gapu ta ipempempen na laeng ken haan na nga isennaay
Penury labis-labis na karalitaan o pagkapobre, sobrang kakulangan
People mga tao, ang publico, mga mamamayan; Iloc: ti publico-*Sp*, dagiti tattao iti ili, iti nasyon-*Sp*, iti lubong
Pep sigla, liksi; Iloc: sagiksik, listo

Pepper sili-a*Sp*, paminta-a*Sp*; Iloc: sili, pimienta-*Sp*

Peppy listo-*Sp*, masigla, maliksi; Iloc: alisto, nasagiksik

PER 1] sa bawat isa, 2] sa pamamagitan, 3] ayon sa/kay; Iloc: 1] cada-*Sp* maysa, 2] iti pagiyusar iti.., 3] cuna ni, cunada

PER se siya mismo, ang sarili niya; Iloc: isu mismo, iti bagbagi na

Perceive nakikinita, naiintindihan, nalalaman, natatanto, nararamdaman, nahuhuna; Iloc: maamiris, maawatan, mabigbig, maricna, maylasin

Percent *(Tag. & Iloc.)* porciento-*Sp*

Perception *n.*, **Perceptive** *adj.* kacayahang malaman o makilala agad sa pamamagitan ng paningin, pandamdam, pangtanto, pandinig, pang-amoy at pag-intindi; intelihensiang pandama at pangtanto sa kapwa at tumutugon sa ikabubuti ng situasyon at payapang pagsasamahan; Iloc: intelihensia nga maamoan, maamiris, maricna, maawatan ken makita ti tao ken situasyon-*Sp* ken mangsubalit iti usto para ti pagimbagan ti situasyon ken natalna a pagkacadwa.

PERCH 1] pinagdadapoan ng ibon gaya ng punong kahoy, sanga, bakod, *electric pole* at iba pa; 2] plataforma o mataas na lugar na puedeng hingaan o pag-upo-upoan, puesto na maventahe at ligtas.

PERCH on dumapo; Iloc: agdisso

Perchance kung sakali, kapag, pag, kung; Iloc: nu caspagarigan, bareng nu, nu

Peregrinate paglilibot na karaniwan ay paglakad papunta't pabalik, pataas at pababa, pa-*zigzag* at patabi at patawid; Iloc: ti pagliblibot a canayon ket magmagna papan ken pagsubli, pangato ken pababa, pa-*zigzag* ken paigid ken pagballasiw.

Peremptory 1] nakakahinanakit na agresivong pagdidicta sa mga tao na parang mayroon siyang kapangyarihan, kahit puedeng wala, na dapat susundin at wala man lamang pangogontra; 2] mandong panay-panay ang pangangailan ng pansin at kilos para maiwasan ang giyera.

Perennial patuloy sa buong taon o patuloy na walang hangganan - ganyan katagal nito; Iloc: agtultuloy iti entero-*Sp* tawen wenno agtultuloy nga awan patinggana na - casta ti kabayag na daytoy.

Perfect *(Tag. & Iloc.)* perfecto-*Sp*

Synonyms

Impeccable *perfect*, walang defecto

Paragon halimbawa ng pagkaperfecto ng isang bagay; Iloc: ehemplo ti pagkaperfecto ti maysa a banag

Mint condition napakahusay o perfecto ang pagkagawa; Iloc: nagsayaat ken perfecto ti pagkaaramid

Perforate tusokin, turokin, tuhogin, sundotin; Iloc: tudoken

Perform gampanan, gawin, isagawa; Iloc: aramiden

Performer ang nagsasagawa, artistang gumagampana ng *role* niya sa pelicula-*Sp* o entablado-*Sp*

Perfume pabango; Iloc: babanglo

Perfunctory dahil sa firme at patuloy-tuloy na gawain o bihasang gawi o pamaraan, nawala na tuloy ang *interest* o kaunti na lang ang pagkagana niya sa paggawa; Iloc: gapu ta firme o canacanayon a pagaramid iti cadawyan ken sigud nga aramid o pagpadalan, isu ket naawan langaruden isu ti *interest* o bassit laengen ti ganas na iti pag-obra.

Perhaps marahil, seguro; Iloc: nalabit, seguro, ngata

Peril *n.,* **Perilous** *adj.* panganib, mapanganib; Iloc: peggad, napeggad

Period 1] tuldok; 2] isang parte ng panahon - mahaba o maikli man itong panahong ito

Peripheral *adj.,* **Periphery** *n.* 1] hindi ang pinakaimportanteng parte kundi tabi-tabi o kaugnay lamang o menor-*Sp* lamang, ang labas na parte ng lugar-*Sp* o ng katawan o gilid-gilid ng lugar-*Sp*, circumferencia-*Sp, borders, boundary;* 2] kaugnay ng *computer* na hiwalay dito gaya ng *printer, keyboard* at *monitor*

Perish mamatay at maglaho o magdanas ng pagkasira dahil sa pinsala, rahas o karalitaan o may kakulangan

Perishable pagkain na madaling mabulok; Iloc: kanen a nadaras a mabulok

Perjure maging *guilty* o may kasalanan dahil sa pagsumpa niya ng kasinungalingan sa hukoman

Perjury pagsisinungaling sa corte-*Sp* ng husticia-*Sp*; Iloc: pagulbod diay corte ti husticia

Perk sigla, liksi; Iloc: ganaygay, sagiksik

Perks see Perquisite below

Perky masigla, vivo at masayang asal; Iloc: nasagiksik, vivo ken naragsak a costumbre

PERMANENT *(Tag. & Iloc.)* permanente-*Sp*

Temporary pansamantala *(Tag/Iloc)* temporaryo, *temporary*

PERMANENT (hair curl) *(Tag. & Iloc.)* pagpaculot

Permeable puedeng matagasan o magtagas

Permeate dumadaan at pumapasok sa loob at sa buong parte; tumu-tusok, tumatagos, tumutulo; lumalaganap, kumakalat; bumababad at umaagos; Iloc: aglabas ken sumrek iti uneg ken amin a parte; tudoken, lussoken, agsalpot, agwaras, agsagepsep ken agayos

Permit *v.,* **Permission** *n.* bigyan ng permiso-*Sp,* pahintulotan, payagan; Iloc: palubosan, ikkan iti permiso

Permissive mapagparaya, mapagpaunlak; Iloc: mangibaybay-an

Perpendicular patayo o *vertical*

Perpetrate *v.* **Perpetrator** *n.* magsulsol at ipasagawa ang masama; Iloc: agsungsong ken agpaaramid ti dakes

Perpetual tumatagal at walang wakas; Iloc: agpaut ken ni gibus na

Perpetuate may kagagawan o pananagutan ito sa pagpairal ng canyang gustong pairalin

Perplexed nababagabag, naliligalig, balisa, lito, torete; Iloc: marirriro, maringgoran, torete

Perplexing nakapagtataka, nakakalito, nakakataranta; Iloc: makasidsid-daaw, makariro, makataranta

Perquisite or Perks sa empleo-*Sp* o pinagtatrabahoan, mga ito ay dag-dag na beneficio-*Sp* o privilehio-*Sp* o *bonus*, bukod pa o karugtong ng regular-*Sp* na sueldo-*Sp* at *overtime pay*; Iloc: iti empleo, dagitoy ket nayon a beneficio o privilehio o *bonus*

Persecute pagmamalupitan at nilalait; Iloc: pag-ul-ulpitan ken ilalais

Perseverance *n.,* **Persevere** *v. Resolute and continued working for a living or for a purpose despite difficulties, obstacles and discouragement.* Nagpapatuloy, nagpupursigi at nagchachaga kahit mahirap at may hadlang; Iloc: agpatpatuloy, agpampamuspusan ken agan-anos uray narigat ken adda makalapped

Correlated words

To the best of one's ability hangga't caya, magpupursigi ng husto; Iloc: inggana't caya ket sige laeng nga agpamuspusan

Pursue pagsisikap at pagpupursigi para matamo ng hangaring pinupuntirya; Iloc: pagpakpakat ken tibker ken anos nga agpatpatuloy tapno magun-od na ti calicagum na

Stability matatag at manatiling magpatuloy sa dating kagawian o kalagayan; Iloc: tibker ti pagmentener nga isu met la nga isu iti sigud nga aramid wenno kasasaad

Continue ituloy, patuloy; Iloc: ituloy, icontinuar

Determined *(Tag. & Iloc.)* determinado

Determination *(Tag. & Iloc.)* determinasyon

Resolute deteminado, tibay sa paniwala o tibay sa pagsasagawa ng balak; Iloc: determinado, tibker iti pammati o tibker iti pagturpos iti pakay

Grit, Doggedness *(Tag. & Iloc.)* tigas ng/tibker ti determinasyon

Persist panay ang pursigi; Iloc: panay ti pagpatpatuloy

Persistent *(Tag. & Iloc.)* panay-panay at sigue-sigue sa paggawa

Persnickety 1] meticuloso-*Sp* sa pagpansin ng mga detalye-*Sp*, 2] maselan o maramdamin

Person *(Tag. & Iloc.)* tao

PERSONA grata taong tinatanggap ng govierno

PERSONA non grata taong hindi tinatanggap ng govierno

Personable kasiya-siya ang ichura-*Sp*; kasiya-siya ang pakikibagay sa tao; Iloc: nakaay-ayo ti ichura ken ugali

Personal *personal,* tungkol sa sarili at pagkatao; Iloc: *personal,* maypapan ti bagi ken katatao

Personality *(Tag. & Iloc.)* personalidad-*Sp*, asal, modo-*Sp* costumbre-*Sp*

Personnel *(Tag. & Iloc.)* taohan, mga empleyado-*Sp*, mga pinuno, mga trabahador-*Sp*, mga taohan sa trabaho-*Sp*

Perspective *adj.,* **Perspectiveness** *n.* 1] ang pananaw na nakikita lahat ng detalye na relevante o may kaugnayan sa bagay, sa balita, paksa o nagaganap, at ang kahalagaan o importancia ng mga ito; ang pagturing sa mga pangyayari at informasyon-*Sp* o balita batay sa kahalagahan ng mga ito; ang tama at tumpak o angkop na pag-iisip at pagturing; 2] tanawing nakikita ang buong kalawakan, layo at himpapawid nito
Correlated word

Viewpoint *perspective,* pananaw at pagturing sa mga tao at pangyayari o paligid; Iloc: *perspective,* panagkita ken pangbigbig cadagiti tattao o kasasaad o ti arrubayan

Help to have the right outlook: pray to God to give you the bigger picture so as to have a sharp understanding and a right perspective on situations and issues

Perspicacious *adj.*, **Perspicacity** *n.* matalas ang paningin at pag-intindi, ang utak niya ay nakakatanto at nakakapag-aninaw ng hindi pang-caraniwan, may *vision;* Iloc: nasirib ti nakem nga makaamiris isu

Perspire nagpapawis; Iloc: aglingling-et
Synonyms
Sweat, Perspiration pawis; Iloc: ling-et

Persuade *v.*, **Persuasion** *n.* icumbinsi, himokin, udyokin, hikayatin, pilitin; Iloc: i-cumbinsir-*Sp*, mangsulisog, uyotan, pilitin

Pert masigla, maliksi; Iloc: listo, nasagiksik

Perturb labis itong mang-estorbo at mambahala at mambalisa; litohin, manligalig, balisahin, itaranta, mangtorete; Iloc: mangrirriro, mang-taranta, mangallilaw, agtorete

Pertaining to tungkol sa; ang tinutukoy na; hinggil sa; Iloc: maypuon ti, maypanggep ti

Pertinacious nakakapit siya sa layonin, sa paniwala at sa paraan ng matatag at walang humpay

Pertinent *(Tag. & Iloc.)* pertinente-*Sp*, relevante-*Sp*

Peruse magbasa ng maingat, ng masusi at madetalye

Pervade *v.*, **Pervasive** *adj.* *influence* o asal, o amoy na ito ay puede na kakalat, papalibot at lalaganap; Iloc: nay-acar a pammati ken angot, ugali nga dagitoy ket mabalin nga aglawlaw ken agwaras

Perverse, Pervert taliwas/*deviant/aberrant* na kasamaan at kalaswaan at nakakadiri; Iloc: taliwas ti pagkadakes ken pagkaalas ken maka-tigerger iti aryek

Perverted nabago at nasira ang anyo o hugis o diwa; Iloc: nabalbaliwan ken nadadael ti langa o forma ken amad

Pescetarian, Pescevegetarian taong kumakain ng gulay at isda lamang, walang carne; Iloc: tao nga mangmangan laeng iti nateng ken ikan, ken awan man laeng carne

Pesky molescha-*Sp*, estorbo-*Sp*; Iloc: sairo, molescha, estorbo

Pessimist, Pessimism pesimista-*Sp*, ang parating nakikinita o inaasahan niya'y negativo-*Sp* gaya ng hirap, kabigoan, kamalian; Iloc: pesimista, canayon a nakaperreng o ag-expectar-*Sp* ti negativo casla iti rigrigat o pagdaksan

Antonyms

Optimist optimista, madalas na positivo at kabutihan ang pagtuturing at pagkita; Iloc: optimista, canayon nga positivo ken pagkasayaat ti pagbigbig na ken pagkita

Sanguine masayang-masayang nag-aasa ng mabuti, optimista, may tiwala, may pananalig at pag-asa

Pest 1] insecto na nakakatayo ng balahibo o nakabigay ng sakit, 2] molescha-*Sp*, peste-a*Sp*, estorbo-*Sp*; Iloc: 1] insecto a makapasumgar ti dutdot o makaited iti sakit, 2] sairo, molescha, estorbo

Pesticide *(Tag. & Iloc.)* *chemical* na pampatay ng insecto

Pester *(Tag. & Iloc.)* kulitin, moleschahin, estorbohin

Pet alagang hayup; Iloc: taraken nga animal

Petal talulot; Iloc: *petals* ti sabong

Peter out kumokonti hanggang maubos; Iloc: agin-inot a bumassit inggana't maibus

Petite mababa at balingkinitang babae; Iloc: babai a nababa ken narapis

Petition *petition*, kahilingan, hiling; Iloc: *petition,* kiddaw

Petty 1] maliit lang ang importancia, 2] masama, madamot, maramdamin at mababa ang pag-iisip; Iloc: 1] bassit laeng ti importancia, 2] dakes, naimot arinsagid ken nababa laeng ti pagpampanunot na

Pew banco-*Sp* o upuan sa simbahan; Iloc: tugaw diay iglesia-*Sp*

Phalanx *[fey-langks]* grupo ng tao na nagkakaisa sa isang layonin o mga layonin

Pharmacist *(Tag. & Iloc.)* farmaciotica-*Sp*

Pharmacy *(Tag. & Iloc.)* farmacia-*Sp*, botica-*Sp*

Pharynx lalamunan, lalagukan; Iloc: carabucob

Phase 1] isang tiempo sa pagproceso o pagtubo o pagbuo o panahon ng pagsibol sa buhay, 2] yugto, aspecto, parte; Iloc: 1] maysa a tiempo ti pagproceso o pagtubo, o panawen a pagrusing ti biag, 2] aspecto, parte

Phenomenon kababalaghan; Iloc: datdatlag

Phenomenal kakaiba, kataka-taka; Iloc: nakasidsiddaaw

Philander, Philanderer lalaking nambobola at nagkacarinyo at nag-papahanga dahil gusto lang makipagtalik sa babaeng hindi niya asawa at hindi niya pakakasalan

Philanthropist, Philanthropy nagsisikap para i-ukol ang *goodwill* (kabutihang-loob, maawain, mahabagin, mabait at may malaki na pagkaintindi sa kapwa, matulongin, mapagbigay, mapagkaloob) at tumutulong para sa pag-unlad ng kapwa; mapagmalasakit at hindi siya makasarili kaya nagbibigay ng donasyon-*Sp* at servicio-*Sp*; Iloc: mangisaksakit iti dadduma ken agdondonasyon ken tumultulong para iti pagprogreso ti tultulongan na

Philippines Filipinas

PHILIPPINE citizen Filipino

PHILIPPINE man Filipino

PHILIPPINE woman Filipina

PHILIPPINE currency *peso,* piso; Iloc: *peso,* pisos

Phish tao o grupo na may masamang balak sa pagkuha ng informasyong privado-*Sp* (gaya ng *password)* at informasyong *financial* (gaya ng depositong pera) ng mga *internet users* sa pamamagitan ng pagpadala ng *email* at *news* na ginagamit ng *impostor* kahit na mukhang galing sa tunay o *legitimate* na institusyon-*Sp* pero naglalaman ng coneksion-*Sp* sa falsificadong *website*

Phlegm flema-*Sp,* uhog, sipon; Iloc: flema, buteg, sipon, anged

PHONE *(Tag. & Iloc.) telephone,* telefono, *cell phone, smart phone*

PHONE (cell phone, smart phone) Obsessive Focus *This obsession has its harms. It can cause accidents because of one's being unaware of people and one's surroundings, and also can make one vulnerable to criminals, thus become an easy-target to them. Driving while talking on the phone is <u>distracting,</u> even with a hands-free phone, as it presents <u>attention-lapses and reaction-failures</u> like fail to stop at red lights, fail to maintain the required speed, stray away from the lane that one is in, fail to step on the brake at a safe time or at a safe distance, fail to see peripheral areas like other incoming vehicles on the side - all of which can cause accidents <u>like bump other cars or run over pedestrians.</u> It can also damage the eardrums when listening to loud music; it ruins one's posture or causes backaches.*

*Being glued to one's phone while at social gatherings can cause disconnection to others, and such disregard to friends and family are considered rude. Text messaging that uses abbreviations and codes impair language cognition. Texting generates forgetfulness or procrastination on necessary tasks and school lessons, i.e. forgo studying for the exams in favor of phone absorption. Healthwise, it can cause burns or cancer risk since some phones emit radiations. There is a report that for young people, focusing obsessively and addictively on one's phone makes one obese by the time he/she reaches age 35; and **what's worst is, one does <u>not</u> even realize one's phone dependence or addiction** despite always holding the phone for quick response to callers, or info-checking on the phone, even while eating one's meals. **<u>Nip it in the bud and free yourself from phone addiction by</u>** 1] being in control of your life, have a to-do list reminder to use your time productively by putting priorities on exigent deeds that are constructive and beneficial, which rewards you with achievements, fulfillments, superior results, self-esteem, self-confidence, satisfaction and much gratification; 2] <u>don't blend</u> with others who are <u>trapped</u> on phone addictions - only use your phone when urgent and necessary – nip in the bud any inclination to use the phone unnecessarily <u>so as not to get worse like its turning into addiction</u>; 3] be happy and feel fulfilled while focusing on other things like contributing your share of work at home, being an asset and the solution (never the problem), reading good books, and face-to-face dealings with friends and family while avoiding cyber-bullying, trolls or inflammatory messages that mobile device networking presents; 4] get a hobby that is valuable and healthy to your body, mind, spirit, life and career like exercise, book-reading, doing honest and humanitarian acts to contribute goodness to your job and to society; 5] give a smile and mingle with friends, family, schoolmates, churchgoers, co-workers and neighbors, instead of telephone networking; 6] enjoy the beauty of nature: the flowers and gardens; the trees, meadows and hills; the sunshine that brightens the day, the beautiful sunrise and sunset, the lovely colors of the sky; the exhilarating air; the flowing streams and rivers, the graceful tides of the sea, even imposing buildings and mansions, and tranquil,* *modest homes; 7] pray for help and guidance; and 8] count your blessings taking into consideration the good things and good people in your life with a thankful heart.*

Phony mapagkunwari; Iloc: mapagsinsinan, agincucuna

PHOTO, Photograph *picture,* letrato, larawan; Iloc: *picture,* retrato-*Sp,* ladawan

PHOTO shoot tipanan para magparetratong pang-*commercial* o kaya para ilabas sa periodico-*Sp* o *magazine*

Photographer *(Tag. & Iloc.) photographer,* retratista-*Sp*

Photoshop *trademark* o marka-*Sp* ng *computer* para ibahin o bagohin ang letrato *digitally*

Physical *physical,* tungkol sa katawan o tungkol sa kabuohan o pagkabuo; Iloc: *physical,* bagi o dagup/*entirety*

Physician doctor, manggagamot; Iloc: doctor, mangngagas

Physique ichura ng katawan; Iloc: ichura ti bagi

Piano *(Tag. & Iloc.) piano*

Pianist *(Tag. & Iloc.) pianist,* pianista-*Sp*

PICK pulotin, dampotin; Iloc: pidoten

PICK magpili; Iloc: agpili

PICK out nits and lice from hair maghinguto, cotohan; Iloc: mangicuto, cotwan

PICK up the tab siya ang tagabayad kapag lumabas kumain o sa pasahe-*Sp* o sa ibang babayaran ng grupo-*Sp* o ng magkakaibigan

Picky pihikan; Iloc: napili

Pickle *(Tag. & Iloc.)* achara-*Sp*

Pickpocket tumatangay o dumudukot ng pera sa *handbag* o *bag* na hindi namamalayan ng nagmemay-aring ninanakawan; Iloc: mangpag-ut ti cuarta iti *handbag* o uneg ti *handbag* o *bag* nga haan a marikna ti makin-*bag*

Picture *picture,* letrato, larawan; Iloc: *picture,* retrato-*Sp,* ladawan

PIECE piraso, pedazo-*Sp,* piesa-*Sp*; Iloc: piraso, kapirgis

PIECE, music *(Tag. & Iloc.)* piesa, composisyon-*Sp*

PIECE de resistance 1] ang pinakamahalagang ulam sa kainan; 2] ang matagumapy at napakaexcelente na gawa

PIECE of cake 1] napakadaling gawin, 2] kapirasong *cake*; Iloc: 1] nakalaclaca nga aramiden, 2] kapiraso ti *cake*

Piecemeal unti-unti at hiwa-hiwalay na natatamo o binibigay o ginagawa sa pagdaan ng panahon

Pier *pier*, muelye-*Sp*, pagdaongan ng sasakyang pandagat; Iloc: *pier*, muelye, pagsangladan dagiti pangtaaw a lugan

Pierce tusokin, turokin, tuhogin, sundotin; Iloc: tudoken
  Correlated words
  Penetrate tagusin; Iloc: tudoken
  Puncture butasan; Iloc: lussokan
  Perforate tusokin, turokin, tuhogin, sundotin; Iloc: tudoken
  Stab saksakin; Iloc: bagsolen
  Poke duldol, sundot; Iloc: tudok, tugkel
  Thrust into the ground itirik; Iloc: itugkel
  Prick tusokin ng maliit na carayom; Iloc: tudoken ti bassit a dagum

Piety paggalang, pagpuri at pagsamba sa Dios bilang devosyon-*Sp* sa Canya para maging kasiya-siya sa Dios; respeto-*Sp* at pagmamahal sa magulang at sa bayan

PIG *(Tag. & Iloc.)* baboy

PIG, roast *(Tag. & Iloc.)* lechon-*Sp*

PIG, suckling biik; Iloc: buryas

Pigeon calapati; Iloc: calapati, pagaw

Piggery *(Tag. & Iloc.)* baboyan

PIGGY-back 1] isakay sa likod o sa balikat; 2] ilagay sa *flatcar* o *train* ang mga coche-*Sp* o *truck trailers,* 3] isali sa pagpapahayag sa malaking lathala

PIGGY bank *(Tag. & Iloc.)* alcansia-*Sp*, maliit na pag-iponan ng pera na hugis baboy at may butas para paghulogan ng cencilyo-*Sp*

Pigtail tirintas; Iloc: sallapid

PILE bunton, tumpok; Iloc: bunton

PILE over tambakan, buntonan, tabunan; Iloc: mangbunton, gaburan

Pilfer, Filch/steal money sneakily over and over mangupit; Iloc: agcupit

Pill, medicine *(Tag. & Iloc.)* tableta, *pill*

Pillage maghalughog sa pagnakaw; Iloc: agraut nga agtakaw

Pillow unan; Iloc: pungan

Pillowcase *(Tag. & Iloc.)* funda-*Sp*

Pilot *(Tag. & Iloc.)* piloto-*Sp*, aviador-*Sp*

Pimple taghiyawat; Iloc: taramidong

PIN *v.*, ipitin; Iloc: ipitin, sipiten

PIN *n. (Tag. & Iloc.)* aspili

PIN, safety *(Tag. & Iloc.)* imperdib-le-*Sp*

Pinch curotin; Iloc: cuddoten
  Correlated word
  Squeeze pisilin; Iloc: pis-iten, pispisen, pisilen

Pinchers, Clip for papers or hair ipit; Iloc: sigpit

Pine pananabik at pagmimithi; Iloc: pagpapas, paggagar

Pineapple *(Tag. & Iloc.)* pinya-*Sp*

Pink *(Tag. & Iloc.)* *pink*, derosas, malarosas

Pinkie kalingkingan, pinakamaliit na daliri ng camay; Iloc: kikit, pina-kabassit a ramay ti ima

Pinnacle 1] pinakamataas na lugar-*Sp*, 2] patulis na forma sa ulo ng bun-dok; Iloc: 1] kangatuan a lugar, 2] natirad a forma diay ulo ti bantay

Pinpoint 1] anumang napakaliit, 2] ituro ang tamang sagot o ang hinahanap na bagay o lugar; Iloc: 1] aniaman a nakabatbattit, 2] itudo iti usto nga sungbat o ti sapsapulen a banag o lugar

Pious madevoto sa Panginoong Dios; Iloc: nadevoto kenni Apo Dios

PIPE, Tube *(Tag. & Iloc.)* tubo-*Sp*

PIPE, tobacco pipa-*Sp*, cuaco; Iloc: pipa, suaco

Piquant maanghang; Iloc: nagasang, naarang

Pique masaktan ang damdamin, maghihinakit; Iloc: masuron, maluksaw

Pirate *pirate*, tulisan sa dagat; Iloc: *pirate,* tulisan ti taaw

Pirouette umikot; Iloc: agpusipos

Piss, Pee *(slang)* umihi; Iloc: umisbo

Piss off pagalitin; Iloc: papungtoten

Pit 1] malalim na butas sa lupa, 2] lugar ng pagminahan, 2] buto ng frutas-*Sp* gaya ng sa *prunes*; Iloc: 1] adalem nga abut iti daga, 2] lugar ti pagminaan, 3] bukel ti frutas casla iti *prunes*

Pitch 1] ihagis ang *baseball* na bola-*Sp*, 2] kung mababa o mataas ang tinig o tono, 3] maglagay ng masilongan o *tent*; Iloc: 1] ipalladaw ti *baseball* a bola, 2] nu nangato o nababa nga timek wenno canta, 3] mangicabil ti paglinongan wenno *tent*

Pitcher *(Tag. & Iloc.) pitcher*

Pitfall 1] hindi nalaman o nakikinitang panganib o kahirapan, 2] butas sa lupa na pangpain o pambitag; Iloc: 1] haan a naamwan o naamiris nga adda peggad o rigat, 2] abut ti daga nga pangbitag

Pitieous, Pitiable nakakapagtatag ng awa, lungkot, hapis, bagabag at pagkabahala

Pitiful kaawa-awa; Iloc: nakakaasi

Pittance napakakonti; Iloc: nakabasbassit

Pity kaawaan, kahabagan; Iloc: kaasian, isalakan

Pivot *n.,* **Pivotal** *adj.* 1] parte o dulong tusok o tulis na nagpapaikot o nagpapaduyan; 2] bagay o tao kung saan nakasalalay ang sigla at bisa at pagpaganap o pagpaandar; 3] *pivotal* - kinakailangan at importante

Placard malaking puting carton-*Sp* na nakasulat ang layonin o payo na pinapakita at pinapahayag sa publico-*Sp*; Iloc: dakkel ken puraw a carton nga nakasurat iti *advice* o balakad o rangta da nga iparparang ken iwarnak da iti publico

Placate magpalubag-loob na makipagkasundoan para bumuti ang pagsasamahan nila; pacalmahin, ipahinahon, papayapain, awatin Iloc: mangpatalna nga makitin-nulag tapno agsayaat iti pagkacadwaan da; pacalmaen, patalnaen, aganawa, ay-aywen, anawaen, paulimeken, pabang-aran

PLACE, Location *(Tag. & Iloc.)* lugar-*Sp,* pook, puesto-*Sp, location*

PLACE, Put ilagay, ilagay, i-puesto-*Sp*; Iloc: i-plastar-*Sp*, ipuesto, icabil, isimpa

Synonyms

Lay on ilagay sa ibabaw; Iloc: iparabaw

Set ilatag; Iloc: isimpa

Spread out (cloth) ilatag; Iloc: iyaplag, ilapag, iplastar

PLACE slammingly idabog; Iloc: ibugtak

PLACE, well-ventilated or airy and comfortable maaliwalas; Iloc: napariir ken comfortab-le

Placebo effect ang nakakagaling na efecto-*Sp* sa paciente-*Sp* dahil sa malaking paniwala sa bisa-*Sp* ng nireceta sa canya o sa tipo-*Sp* ng pagpapagamot sa canya kahit na wala siyang kamuang-muang na ang pinapainom sa canya ay *placebo* lamang; Iloc: ti makapaagas ti usto iti paciente gapu iti dakkel a pammati na nga nabileg tay nireceta canyana wenno daytay tipo ti pangngagas canyana ket haan na ammo nga daytoy inreceta ket *placebo* laeng

Placid calmado-*Sp* lamang kahit sa kalagitnaan ng kapahamakan at gulo; Iloc: calmado laeng uray iti tengnga ti riro ken gulo

Plagiarize *v.*, **Plagiarism** *n.* <u>crimen na pagcopia sa sinulat ng iba;</u> pagkuha at paggamit ng kasulatan, diwa o pag-iisip ng ibang manunulat dahil ang kinopyahang manunulat ay may *copyright* o *protection* sa goiverno, kaya ang gumawa ng crimeng pangongopia ng sinulat ng iba ay maisasakdal sa corte ng husticia at mapaparusahan
Correlated word
Infringe labag sa batas o sa alituntunin na pumasok, mangopia, o umangkin na walang pahintulot; Iloc: haan a nalinteg o haan sumursurot iti reglamento a sumrek, mangala o agcopiar nga awan ti palubos canyana

Plague peste-*Sp*, calat na calamidad o nakakahawang sakit

PLAIN 1] simp-le at maliwanag kaya madaling maintindihan, 2] walang kahalong ano-anoman sa pagkain, 3] simple lang ang ichura na walang decorasyong burloloy; Iloc: 1] simp-le ken nalawag, isu nga nalaca a maawatan, 2] awan iti laok nga aniaman ti makan, 3] simp-le laeng iti ichura nga awan ti arcos nga iparparang

PLAIN clothes or Plainclothes *(also see Undercover) police* na suot ay hindi yong uniforme-*Sp* ng *police*

Plains, Level land kapatagan; Iloc: tanap

Plaintiff ang nagsakdal; Iloc: ti nangidarum
Synonym
Litigant siya ang *plaintiff* na nagsakdal ng caso na haharap sa corte; Iloc: nagidarum
Antonym
Defendant ang nasasakdal; Iloc: ti naydarum

PLAN plano-*Sp*; Iloc: plano, gandat

PLAN, evil pakana; Iloc: dakes a plano

Planet *(Tag. & Iloc.)* planeta-*Sp*

Plank *(Tag. & Iloc.)* tabla-*Sp*

PLANT magtanim; Iloc: agmula, agtanem
Correlated words
Plow araro; Iloc: arado
Till the land ararohin ang lupang taniman; Iloc: mangarado
Sow magtanim; Iloc: agmula, agtanem

Water the plants diligan; Iloc: sibugan

Fertilizer *(Tag. & Iloc)* abono

PLANT bud or sprout usbong; Iloc: saringit, rusing

Plantation bukid, taniman, hacienda-*Sp*; Iloc: pagtaneman, minuyongan, tanap, hacienda
Correlated words
Agriculture agricultura, pagsasaka; Iloc: agricultura, pagmulmula
Farms nayon, bukid; Iloc: talon
Garden *(Tag. & Iloc.)* hardin

Planter pot *(Tag. & Iloc.)* macetera-*aSp*

PLANTS halamanan, mga pananim; Iloc: mulmula, tantanem ida

PLANTS, flowering *(Tag. & Iloc.)* macetas-*aSp*

Plastic *(Tag. & Iloc.)* plastic

Plate *(Tag. & Iloc.)* pinggan, plato-*Sp*

Plateau bundok na pantay ang ulo gaya ng lamesa; Iloc: bantay nga patag iti ulo a casla lamesa

Platform *(Tag. & Iloc.)* en tablado-*Sp*, entablado-*Sp*

Platonic mabuting pagkakaibigan na walang *sexual* sa gawa o sa dam-damin; Iloc: nakaim-imbag a paggayyeman nga awan *sexual* nga aramid wenno ricna

Platter *(Tag. & Iloc.)* bandehado-*Sp*

Plausible katotohanan man o hindi, parang lumalabas na totoo at kapani-paniwala; Iloc: kaagpaysoan man o haan casla agparang nga usto-*Sp* ken nakapatpati

PLAY maglaro; Iloc: agay-ayam

PLAY catch up magsikap para makaabot o malampasan ang inaasahang paglikha para makaahon sa atrasadong pag-umpisa o pagkaag-graviado, o para madaig ang lamang o ventahe-*Sp* ng iba

PLAY hard to get magpakipot, aayaw-ayaw, "hele-hele bago quiere-*Sp*"; Iloc: agpasenggel, agpakipot, "hele-hele baro quiere"

PLAY hooky *absent* o hindi pumasok sa escuela na walang pasabi sa escuela at walang malay ang magulang

PLAY house *(Tag. & Iloc.)* magbahay-bahayan

PLAY it safe *Be careful and take precautions. Avoid any risk or danger.* Mag-ingat ka at layoan mo ang mga panganib para ligtas ka at mga kasama mo.

PLAY music tumutogtog; Iloc: ag-tocar-*Sp*

PLAY with fire walang-ingat magsagawa kahit may posibilidad na problema

Playbook 1] kasulatan na ginagamit ng mga artistang gaganap sa dula; 2] libro-*Sp* na nagtataglay ng mga kasulatan para sa mga dula; 3] *notebook* o cuaderno-*Sp* na inilalarawan lahat ng mga paraan at mga tactica-*Sp* na dapat gamitin ng *team* o pangkat, gaya sa *football, insurance selling* at iba pa

Playboy mahilig sa babae, palikero; Iloc: naarem, palikero

Player manlalaro; Iloc: makicompetensia

Playground *(Tag. & Iloc.) playground*

Playing card *(Tag. & Iloc.)* baraha-*Sp*

Playmate kalaro; Iloc: kaay-ayam

Plaza plaza-*Sp*, pagpapasyalang lugar-*Sp* sa gitna ng bayan; Iloc: plaza -*Sp*, pagpaspasiaran (pasiar-*Sp*) nga lugar iti tengnga iti ili

Plea *n.*, **Plead** *v.* magsumamo, nakiki-usap; Iloc: agpakpacaasi, maki-cacaasi, agkiddaw
Correlated words
Entreat dibdibang nagsusumamo; Iloc: naregget nga agkidkiddaw
Request humiling, makisuyo, makipaki-usap; Iloc: makifavor, agkiddaw ti favor
Solicit maghiling; Iloc: agkiddaw
Implore magmakaawa at humingi ng tulong ng puspusan; Iloc: agpacaasi ken dumawat ti tulong a pamuspusan

PLEASANT personality may magandang-loob, kaaya-aya, magandang makitungo sa kapwa, may pakikisama; Iloc: napintas ti puso na, nacaay-ayo, nasayaat makibagay iti tattao
Synonyms
Nice person mabait, mapayapa, kasiya-siya; Iloc: nasingpet, nakaay-ayo, natalna
Folksy simp-le at walang pagkukunwari at madaling makapalagayang-loob
Jocund maginhawang makisama; Iloc: maconsuelo a makicadwa

PLEASANT weather maaliwalas; Iloc: naalinnaay

"PLEASE" "Makisuyo po," "Paki-*(+ root word),*" "Puede po ba...*"*; Iloc: "Paki-*(+ root word),*" "...man", "Pangngaasi yo"

PLEASE, Delight suyoin; Iloc: mangay-ayo, mangrayrayo

Pleasing kasiya-siya; Iloc: nakaay-ayat

Synonyms

Nice mabuti, mainam, mahusay, mapayapa, kasiya-siya; Iloc: nanam-ay, nasayaat, naimbag, nalaeng, natalna, naay-ayo

Hunky-dory nakakasiya at nakakapacontento; Iloc: maka-liwliwa ken makapagpacontento

Relaxing maginhawa, nakakapahinga; Iloc: makabang-ar, makapainana

Pleasure kaligayahan, kasiyahan, katuwaan, kalugoran, paglilibang, maganda at kasiya-siyang damdamin

Pleats or folds of an attire *(Tag. & Iloc.)* tupi, pleges-*Sp*

Plebiscite ang *plebiscite* ay hindi *election* dahil wala ni isang candidato dito - ito ay pagboboto ng buong bayan o ng isang malaking partido para malaman ang turing sa napakaimportanteng mungkahi o balak o paksa, sa pamamagitan ng pagsagot ng *yes or no.*

Pledge sumpa, panata; Iloc: sapata

Pleistocene period ito ay noong unang panahon na bago-bago pa ang mundo kung kelan may mga pagdadaanang yelo sa mga dagat, ang mga dayohan ay lumalakad sa mga yelong daanang iyan para makarating sa iba't ibang bansa

Plentiful, Plenteous napakarami; Iloc: nagadu, nawadwad

Plenty marami; Iloc: adu, nawadwad

Pliable, Pliant 1] madaling macurva o maforma o mapabago, 2] madaling mainfluwensia o mahikayat; Iloc: 1] nalaca a macurva o maforma o mabalbaliw, 2] nalaca a mainfluwensia o madominar o maisungsong

Correlated words

Limber nacucurva, nababaluctot; Iloc: maycurva

Flexible, Flexile 1] nacucurva, nababaluctot, nauunat, nahuhubog, 2] pupuedeng gawin sa anomang oras o fecha o saan mang lugar o anomang gawain

Antonym

Rigid, Stiff maganit; Iloc: nasikkil

Plier *(Tag. & Iloc.)* *plier*, pla-is, malaking chani

Plight 1] mahirap na situasyon-*Sp*, 2] magsumpa o magpanata; Iloc: 1] narigat a situasyon-*Sp*, 2] agsapata

Plot 1] lupang maliit na tinataniman ng halaman, 2] ang buod ng storya, 3] lihim na plano-*Sp* para sa kasamaan at crimen; Iloc: 1] daga a bassit nga pagtaneman, 2] iti amad ti storya, 3] nalimed a plano a dakes ken para pagarmid iti crimen-*Sp*

Plow araro; Iloc: arado

Ploy tactica para matalo ang ka-competencia-*Sp* o makakuha ng ventahe-*Sp* kadalasan ay sa lihim na paraan

Pluck bakbakin, watakin, tuklapin; Iloc: lekkaben, cuplaten

Plumber ang nag-aayos ng mga nasirang gripo-*aSp* o pag-agosan ng tubig sa cusina-*Sp* o banyo-*Sp*; Iloc: ti mangtarimaan iti nadadael a gripo ken tubo-*Sp* ti danum idiay cusina ken banyo

Plummet mahulog na paderecho sa baba; Iloc: matinnag a paderecho pababa

Plump *(Tag. & Iloc.)* taba, tabachoy

Plunder fuersahang pag-agaw o pagnakaw ng mga ariarian at mga pagkain sa panahon ng giyera; Iloc: fuersaan a pag-agaw o pagtakaw cadagiti sanicua ken makmakan iti tiempo-*Sp* ti gerra-*Sp*

Plunge 1] biglang mahulog o lumundag, sumisid o maglublob; 2] saksak, manaksak

Plural mahigit sa isa, maramihan; Iloc: mas adu ngem maysa, adu

Pneumonia *(Tag. & Iloc.)* *pneumonia*

Pocket *(Tag. & Iloc.)* bolsa-*Sp*

Pockmark bulutong; Iloc: burtong

Poem tula; Iloc: daniw

Poet makata; Iloc: agdandaniw

Poignant *sentimental*, nakakapaluha; Iloc: *sentimental*, makapalua

POINT parteng matulis na kadalasan ay matalim at matalas; Iloc: parte-*Sp* nga natirad nga cadawyan ket natadem

POINT out ituro; Iloc: itudo, isuro

Pointed patulis; Iloc: natirad

POINTER, nominative (before a masc. or fem. name) si (*i.e. si Maria*); Iloc: ni (*i.e. ni Juan*)

POINTER, nominative (before 2 or more names) sina (*i.e. sina Maria at Juan, o si Maria at si Juan*); Iloc: da (*i.e. da Maria ken Juan, o ni Maria ken ni Juan*)

POINTER finger *pointer finger*, hintuturo; Iloc: tammudo, ramay a pangtudo

Poise kung paano magdala ng sarili; Iloc: nu casano na awiten ti bagi na

Poised, With poise may confiansang magdala ng sarili; Iloc: adda confiansa na iti pagtignay a nadayaw

Poison lason, kamandag; Iloc: lason, sabidong

Poke duldol, sundot; Iloc: tudok, tugkel

Polarity, Polar attribute taong may mga asal o paniniwala na sobrang magkacontra; ang pagkakaroon o ang pagpapahayag o pagpapakita ng dalawang magkasalungat o magkacontrang asal o hilig o *ideology*; mayroon ding *polarity* sa *science* at sa *medicine* na may tanging kahulogan

Polarization *n.,* **Polarize** *v.* 1] marahas na pagkahiwalay o *division* ng mga mamamayan o grupo; 2] mayroon din ibang kahulogan ng *polarization* sa *medicine* at sa *physics* gaya ng galaw ng electricidad-*Sp* at ilaw

Pole haligi, poste-*Sp*; Iloc: adigi, poste

Police *(Tag. & Iloc.) police,* policia

Policeman *(Tag. & Iloc.) police, policeman*

Policy *(Tag. & Iloc.) policy,* policiya

POLISH 1] alisin ang mga defecto-*Sp* at gaspang at gawing pulido-*Sp,* 2] pakintabin; Iloc: 1] ik-katen ti defecto ida ken kersang ken aramiden a pulido, 2] pasilengen

POLISH wooden floor maglampaso; Iloc: aglampaso

Polished *(Tag. & Iloc.)* pulido-*Sp*

Polite magalang; Iloc: naraem, nadayaw

Political party *(Tag. & Iloc.)* partido-*Sp* ng politica-*Sp*

Politician *(Tag. & Iloc.)* politico-*Sp*

Politics *(Tag. & Iloc.)* politica-*Sp*

Polling place lugar-*Sp* para-*Sp* mag-boto-*Sp*; Iloc: lugar para agboto

Pollution lugar, tubig o himpapawid na nasalinan ng masasamang bagay na galing sa mga fabrica-*Sp,* sasakyan, at *chemicals* na mapanganib sa nilalang at sa kapaligiran pati buong mundo; Iloc: lugar, danum o tangatang a naacaran iti dakes a banag a naggapu iti fabrica, luglugan ken *chemicals* a napeggad cadagiti nayparsua ida ken iti arrubayan ken iti mundo

Polygamy ang pagkakaroon ng maraming asawa; Iloc: ti pagkaadda ti adu nga asawa

Pomade *(Tag. & Iloc.)* pomada-*Sp*

Pomelo suha; Iloc: sua, lukban

Pompous pakitang-tao sa ganda o rangya o importancia

Pond maliit na lawa sa daanan o sa parang; Iloc: bassit a danaw iti calsada wenno diay tanap

Ponder magmuni-muni; Iloc: agpampanunot

Ponzi scheme panlinlang na puhunan na nagpapangako ng mataas na tubo mula sa gawa-gawa lamang o hindi tutoong mga pinanggagalingan

Pooh-pooh magpakita ng kayamutan o kawalang pacensia-*Sp*; Iloc: pagpakita ti rurod wenno kaawan pacensia

Poop, Poo tae; Iloc: takki

Pooper-scooper ang panghakut ng tae ng alagang aso; Iloc: ti pang-acup ti takki ti taraken nga aso

POOR pobre-*Sp*, dukha, maralita, gipit; Iloc: marigrigat, pobre, napanglaw

POOR grade mababang grado-*Sp* sa escuela-*Sp* o sa *test* o examen-*Sp*; Iloc: nababa a grado diay escuela o *test* o diay examen

"POOR guy!" "Kawawa naman siya", Iloc: "Piman pay!"

POOR (very) but please realize that you have opportunities in life Kahit ikaw ay pobre, marami ka pa ring oportunidad para umunlad. **Gamitin mo ang mga kacayahan mo** (huwag mong sayangin ang mga kacayahan mo at ang oras mo sa tutunga-tunganga lamang) dahil mayroong mga trabaho na puede kang mag-umpisa na doon ka magsikap o magpakita ng gilas para magtagumpay ka, dahil lahat ng tao sa buong mundo na kapareho sa kalagayan mo ay ganyan ang ginagawa para maging maunlad at maligaya. Mga **kagalang-galang na trabaho** ay **pagsasaka** at **pangingisda**. Ganun din ang pag-*janitor* sa shopping mall o pag-*houseboy* o *housegirl* at huwag mahiya, tanungin mo sa amo mo kung puedeng pumasok sa paaralan para mag-aaral para sa iyong kinabukasan at kinabukasan ng magiging familya mo; magpakita ka ng sipag at kabaitan para sumang-ayon ang amo mo. Kung mahusay kang **mag-*drawing***, ipagpatuloy mong **magguhit** lalo na sa mga magagandang tanawin at letrato ng tao, at mga araw-araw na pamumuhay ng tao at ipaalam at ipakita mo sa *mayor* at sa periodico ang mga ginuhit mo at baka diyan ka makilala. Kung maganda ang boses mo, mag-*volunteer* kang **kumanta** sa fiesta o mga *party* ng tao hangga't ikaw ay mahangaan at madiscobre. Kung gusto mong **mag-artista**, sulatan mo ang mga *television stations* at *producers* ng pelikula. Igala mo ang mata mo o **magtanong-tanong** ka para malaman mo ang iba't ibang mapapasokan. Humiram ka ng mga libro sa *library* at **magbasa** ka sa mga *for sale* na libro sa mismong *bookstore*, para madagdagan ang kaalaman at talino mo na kinakailangan at hinahanap ng maraming oficina.

Pope papa, pinakamataas na puesto-*Sp* sa relihiong Catolico Romano; Iloc: papa, ti kangatwan a puesto iti relihion a Catolico Romano-*Sp*

Populace lahat ng mamamayan sa bayan; mga ordinaryo na taong nakatira sa comunidad o nasyon-*Sp* na hindi sila kasing tanyag ng mga nasa taas na baytang ng buhay
Synonym
Hoi poloi mga caraniwang tao; Iloc: dagiti ordinaryo a tao

Popular *adj.*, **Popularity** *n.* popular-*Sp*, tanyag, kilala, bantog; Iloc: popular, natakneng, agdindinnamag, natan-ok

Population *(Tag. & Iloc.) population*, populasyon-*Sp*, ang lahat ng mga mamayan ng isang lugar at gaano kadami sila
Correlated word
Citizen mamamayan, taong-bayan; Iloc: katutubo a tao, tao ti bayan

Porcelain *(Tag. & Iloc.)* porcelana-*Sp*

Porch balconahe-*Sp*; Iloc: balconahe, bangsal

Pore labasan ng pawis; Iloc: pagruaran ti ling-et

PORK carne-*Sp* ng baboy; Iloc: carne ti baboy

PORK belly *(Tag. & Iloc.)* liempo

Pornography, Porn mga letrato o palabas na mga hubad na tao at ang gawain nilang *sexual*; Iloc: dagiti retrato-*Sp* o pabuya iti nakalabus a tattao ida nga aramid da ket *sexual*

PORRIDGE, chocolate *(Tag. & Iloc.)* champorado

PORRIDGE, rice *(Tag. & Iloc.)* lugaw, arroz caldo-*Sp*

PORT puerto-*Sp*, daungan ng barco-*Sp*; Iloc: puerto, sangladan ti barco
Correlated words
Pier *pier*, muelye, pagdaongan ng sasakyang pandagat; Iloc: *pier*, muelye, pagsangladan dagiti pangtaaw a lugan
Ferry daongan ng mga *ferryboats*, bapor, barco at banka para ipatawid ang mga pasahero sa kabila ng ilog o laok; Iloc: pagsangladan dagiti *ferryboats*,

bapor, barco ken banka para iballasiw dagiti pasahero idiay bangir ti carayan o danaw

PORT of call daongan ng barco-*Sp* kung saan sila magcarga-*Sp* at discarga-*Sp* ng mga bagay-bagay at kung saan magpacumpuni ng sira sa barco; Iloc: pagsangladan ti barco nu inchenna da nga agcarga ken discarga cadagiti bambanag ida ken nu inchenna nga ipa-*repair* da iti ania man a masapul tarimaanen ditoy barco

PORT of entry dito umibis o umakyat ang mga naglalayag na turista; Iloc: ditoy ti pagdissaagan wenno pagluganan dagiti turista ida

Portable nabubuhat at nadadala saanman; Iloc: mabitbit ken mayyal-alis-alis
Correlated word
Mobile nalilipat-lipat o nadadala saanman; Iloc: mayyacaracar ken may-tugtugot uray inchenna

Portal pinto, pasukan; Iloc: puerta-*Sp*, pagserkan

Portend *v.,* **Portent** *n.* nagpapahiwatig ng dadating, pangitain ng dadating, babala na nakakabalisa o nakakaligalig

Portfolio 1] *portfolio, flat* na *bag* na paglagyan ng mga documento-*Sp* na kinakailangan sa trabaho-*Sp*; 2] grupo-*Sp* ng *investments* ng isang negociante-*Sp*

Portion parte-*Sp* ng isang buo, bahagi; Iloc: parte, parte ti maysa a banag

PORTMANTEAU maraming gamit o clase, bagahe

PORTMANTEAU word salita na pinaghalo ang dalawang salita

Portrait larawan ng tao; Iloc: retrato-*Sp* ti tao

PORTRAY, Illustrate ilarawan; Iloc: i-presentar-*Sp* ti itchura-*Sp* o ti napasamak

PORTRAY as gumaganap na..; Iloc: umar-arte a cas...

Pose 1] magpostura para sa pintura o para makunan ng letrato, 2] gumaganap o nagkukunwari; Iloc: 1] agpostura para iti retrato o pintura, 2] agsinsinan o umar-arte a casla sabali a tao
Antonym
Candid tunay na asal na hindi pinaghandaan at hindi kaartehan; Iloc: usto a tignay nga haan pinagsaganaan ken haan a kaarteaan

Poseur hindi natural-*Sp* na asal at may pagkukunwari; Iloc: haan a natural nga tignay na ken adda pagincucuna

POSITION posisyon-*Sp*, puesto-*Sp* sa trabaho-*Sp*, katayuan, estado-*Sp* sa sociedad-*Sp;* lugar-*Sp* na inoocupa o tinitirhan; Iloc: posisyon, puesto, estado, balay a ocuparen

POSITION of, in the bilang isang...Iloc: bilang maysa a...

Positive 1] nagpapahiwatig ng pagtanggap at magandang pagturing sa mga bagay-bagay; 2] may confianza at walang pagdududa, 3] sa larangan ng *Medicine*, ito ay *positive test result* na nagpapahiwatig na buntis o pagkakaroon ng sakit o organismo na makabigay-sakit; Iloc: 1] mangisawang iti pag-akceptar ken nasayaat a pagbigbig, 2] adda confianza na ken awan iti pagkaduda, 3] iti larangan ti *Medicine*, daytoy ket *positive test result* nga masicog wenno adda sakit na o *infection*

Posse mga mamamayan na hinilingan ng policia na tumulong sa gawaing batas gaya ng paghanap ng nawawalang tao at pagkilanlan ng nakalarawang criminal; Iloc: tattao ti bayan nga kiniddawan ti *police* nga tumulong iti linteg a servicio casla iti pagsapul ti tao a nagpukaw ken panglasin iti nakaretrato o impabuya ti TV a criminal

Possess nagtataglay, nag-aangkin, nag-aari; Iloc: makincucua, akincucua, addaan canyana

Possessions ari-arian, pagaaring kagamitan at kasankapan; Iloc: sanicua, cukcukua nga alicamen ken muebles-*Sp* ken dagiti maaramat

Possibility *(Tag. & Iloc.)* posibilidad-*Sp*

Possible, Feasible posib-le-*Sp*, puede-*Sp*, maisagawa, maaari; Iloc: posible-*Sp*, mabalin

POST 1] ipasok o ilista sa *record* o *ledger* o *journal*, 2] ilagay ang anuncio-*Sp* sa lugar-*Sp* na maraming makakabasa, 3] haligi, poste-*Sp*, 4] pagpadala ng mga sulat o *package* sa coreo-*Sp*; 5] *base* ng *army*; Iloc: 1] iserrek o ilista idiay *record* o *ledger* o *journal*, 2] icabil ti anuncio iti lugar nga adu ti makabasa, 3] adigi, poste, 4] pagpatulod iti surat ken *package* idiay coreo o pagbuzonan, i-buzon-*Sp*; 5] *base* ti *military*

POST doctoral pag-aral na lampas pa sa *doctorate degree*; Iloc: pagadal nga nalabes pay ngem iti *doctorate degree*

POST graduate pag-aaral lampas pa sa *bachelors degree;* Iloc: pagadal a nalabes pay iti *bachelors degree*

POST Office *(Tag. & Iloc.)* *post office*, coreo-*Sp*

POST script, PS dagdag na mensahe-*Sp* sa liham sa baba ng signatura-*Sp*; Iloc: nayon a mensahe iti surat idiay baba iti firma-*Sp*

Postage stamp *(Tag. & Iloc.) stamp,* selyo-*Sp*

Postdate cheke-*Sp* na nakaavante sa dadating na fecha-*Sp* imbes-*Sp* na fecha ng kasalukuyang pag-firma-*Sp*; Iloc: cheke nga nakaavante iti sumangpet a fecha imbes nga fecha iti pag-firma

Posterior puit; Iloc: ubet

Posterity ang mga dadating na *generation*/henerasyon-*Sp*; lahat ng mga supling at apo

Posthumous 1] napanganak pagkatapos na namatay ang tatay niya, 2] publicasyon-*Sp* na lumabas pagkatapos na namatay ang sumulat, 3] nagaganap pa rin pagkatapos ng pagkapatay niya; Iloc: 1] naiyanak palpas ti pagkapatay ni tatang na, 2] publicasyon-*Sp* a rimmuar palpas a natay tay nagsurat, 3] maar-aramid pay laeng uray nu natayen isu

Postman *(Tag. & Iloc.)* cartero-*Sp*

Postmark marka-*Sp* ng *Post Office* sa celyo-*Sp* at sobre-*Sp* kung kelan at saan hinulog itong sulat o pakete-*Sp*; Iloc: marka ti *Post Office* ti celyo ken sobre nu caano ken inchenna i-buzon-*Sp* daytoy surat o pakete

Postpone ipagpaliban, ipagpapabukas; Iloc: itantan, iladladaw, ibaybayag
Correlated words
  Delay antalahin, ipagpaliban; Iloc: itaktak, taktaken, itantan, ibaybayag
  Abeyance pagpapaliban, pagpaibang-araw; Iloc: itantan para ti sabali nga aldaw, iladladaw

Postpositive salita o *suffix* na nakalagay pagkatapos ng ibang salita para ipakita ang kaugnayan sa pinapahiwatig dito; Iloc: sarita wenno *suffix* nga naycabil palpas iti sabali a sarita para ipakita iti relasyon-*Sp* na iti isawsawang ditoy

Posture postura-*Sp*, tindig; Iloc: postura, takder

POT-bellied may malaking puson, malaking tiyan, may buyong, buchog; Iloc: agpus-ong, buchog, agbuy-ong

POT, cooking *(Tag. & Iloc.)* caldero-*Sp*, caserola-*Sp*

POT, earthen *(Tag. & Iloc.)* banga

POT-holed road lubak-lubak o baco-baco; Iloc: abut-abut

Potable ligtas na inumin; Iloc: awan peggad nga inumin

POTATO *(Tag. & Iloc.)* patatas-*Sp*

POTATO, sweet *(Tag. & Iloc.)* camote-*Sp*

Potency lakas, sigla, bisa, virtud, talab, fuerza-*Sp*; Iloc: bileg, bisa, pigsa, anib, kired, virtud, fuerza

Potent mabisa, malakas, tumatalab; Iloc: nabisa, nabileg, naanib, napigsa, agtaltalab

Potential 1] maaasahan na puedeng mangyayari o magkabunga; 2] may posibilidad-*Sp* na nagtataglay ng cacayahan, kapangyarihan, pagunlad at pagtagumpay; Iloc: 1] manamnama nga mabalin a maaramid o agbunga, 2] adda posibilidad nga addaan ti caya, macabalin, asenso-*aSp* ken balligi

Potluck *potluck*, salo-salo, handaan kung saang bawat bisita'y nagdadala ng ulam; Iloc: *potluck*, padaya nga cada bisita ket mangitugot ti sida

Potshot pangpintas o salitang pang-*bully* sa cayang-caya na tao; Iloc: pangdillaw o sarita a pang-*bully* iti cayang-caya na a tao

Potty, toddler's *(Tag. & Iloc.)* orinola-*Sp*

Pouch maliit na supot na *bag* na may tali; Iloc: bassit a supot a *bag* nga adda siglot na

Poultry *(Tag. & Iloc.)* manokan

POUND bayohin, pukpokin, dikdikin; Iloc: baywen, palpalen, dekdeken, taltalen

POUND (weight) *(Tag. & Iloc.)* libra-*Sp*

POUR out into a container ibuhos, ipaagos, itulo; Iloc: ipakbo, ipattog, ibukbok
Correlated words
Drop into a container ihulog; Iloc: ipisok

POUR out on a container overflowingly that it spills over ibubo; Iloc: aglipyas

POUR water on buhosan, ibubo, ibugso; Iloc: buyyatan, suyyaten

POUT, Frown simangot, ngusoan; Iloc: misuot, muregreg, rupanget

POUT with lower lip out umismid, ismiran, magtami, maglabi; Iloc: agtammi, aglibbi

Poverty kadukhaan, karalitaan, kagipitan, pagka-pobre-*Sp*; Iloc: kina-panglaw, kina-pobre

POWDER *(Tag. & Iloc.)* polvos-*Sp*

POWDER puff *(Tag. & Iloc.)* polvera-*Sp*

Power kapangyarihan, kalakasan, bisa; Iloc: kabalinan, katurayan, bileg, pigsa

Synonyms

Potency bisa, lakas, talab, virtud; Iloc: virtud, bileg, pigsa, anib, bisa

Prowess abilidad na mas mahusay kaysa ordinaryo; Iloc: abilidad a mas nalaeng ngem ti ordinario

Powerful makapangyarihan; Iloc: mannakabalin

Practicable nagagawa, nagagamit, nakaka-efecto-*Sp* sa pamamagitan ng mga bagay na meron ito o naririyan

Practical 1] <u>sa paggawa</u> ang pagka-efectivo-*Sp* o pagtalab nito, <u>hindi</u> sa teoria-*Sp* o kuro-kuro; 2] matino ang pag-iisip at <u>mahusay mag-obra</u>-*Sp* at hindi magpakuro-kuro lamang; Iloc: 1] <u>pag-obra</u> ti pagkaefectivo ken pagkabileg na daytoy, <u>haan</u> nga teoria o patta-patta; 2] nasirib ti pagpampanunot ken <u>nalaeng nga agobra</u> nga haan nga agpatta-patta laeng

PRACTICE 1] *practice,* mag-ensayo-*Sp,* magsanay para mas lalong humusay *(Practice makes perfect),* 2] ginagampanan; Iloc: 1] *practice,* agsanay, iruam ti bagi o memoria tapno mas lumaeng, 2] ar-aramiden

Correlated word

Inure pasanayin, magpabihasa; Iloc: iparuam ti bagi

PRACTICE what you preach, Walk the talk *whatever rigtheous things you teach or advice, exemplify those in your ways, especially in your character so that such refinements can be perceived and admired while its good consequences can also be witnessed making children and others accept and abide by your teachings*

Pragmatic 1] sumosoporta at tinataguyod ang *practical* o nakikita na katibayan gaya sa kilos at asal kaysa sa teoria o doctrina; tungkol sa araw-araw na gawain; kumakalinga sa kapakanan ng bayan at comunidad; 2] tumuturing sa mga pangkaraniwang nangyari sa history sa dahilan at resulta nito gaya ng kalagayan noon

PRAISE, Admire magbigay ng papuri sa taong nakagawa ng mabuti, parangalan, magpakalugod, magpasalamat; Iloc: mangited ti pagda-yaw ken pagyaman iti tao nga nakaaramid iti pagimbagan ken tulong

PRAISE, Reverence para sa Panginoong Dios ay purihin Siya, ilu-walhati, sambahin, ipagbunyi, parangalan, pasalamatan, hangaan;

Iloc: para kenni Apo Dios ket daydayawen, agyaman, i-glorificar-*Sp*, ikkan ti respeto-*Sp*

Praiseworthy kapuri-puri, kahangahanga, ang dangal-dangal; Iloc: madaydayaw, nakaresrespeto

Prawn *(Tag. & Iloc.)* sugpo
Synonym
Shrimp hipon; Iloc: pasayan

Pray magdasal, magdalangin; Iloc: agcararag, aglualo

Prayer dasal, dalangin; Iloc: cararag, lualo

Praying mantis insecto na samba-samba; Iloc: wasaywasay

Preach magpahayag ng pagmamahal ng Panginoong Dios sa mga nilalang at mga katotohanan tungkol sa Canya lalo na ang gracia ng kaligtasan; mag-evanghelio; Iloc: ipaammo iti pagayat ken dungngo ni Apo Dios ti amin a tattao ken ito kaagpaysuan maygapu Canyana lallalo iti gracia a pangsalvar ti basbasol ida; ag-evanghelyo-*Sp*
Synonym
Sermon magsermon, mangaral; Iloc: agsermon, agbagbaga

Precarious delicado-*Sp* o mapanganib na lugar-*Sp* dahil puedeng matomba, mahulog, masaktan, masira o mamatay; Iloc: delicado o napeggad a lugar gapu ta mabalin a matomba, matinnag, masaktan, madadael wenno mabalin ti matay dita

Precaution pag-iingat; Iloc: pag-annad, pagal-alwad

Precede, Preceding mangungunang mangyari; Iloc: umun-una a maaramid
Antonyms
Succeeding, Following ano mang sumusunod

Precedent naunang nangyari kaya ginawang panghalimbawa sa mga sumusunod na kapareho; Iloc: immuna a naaramid isu nga inaramid nga ehemplo-*Sp* cadagiti sumarsaruno a kapada na
Synonyms
Arche type ang pinaka-orihinal na modelo o tipo kung saan gumaya ang iba; Iloc: ti pinakaimmuna a modelo o tipo nga tinuladan dagiti sumaruno
Precursor tao o bagay na nakagawa ng unang-unang paraan o bagay; Iloc: tao wenno banag nga nakaaramid iti umun-una a padalan o banag

Precinct *(Tag. & Iloc.)* precinto-*Sp*

Precious pinapapahalagahan, minamahal, minumutya, sinisinta; Iloc: ival-valor-*Sp*, ipatpateg

Precipice *n.,* **Precipitous** *adj.* bangin, gilid ng bundok na derechong pababa; Iloc: teppang, derraas igid ti bantay a derecho-*Sp* nga pababa
Correlated words
Cliff, Crag bangin; Iloc: teppang, derraas
Ravine, Gorge bangin sa lambak *(valley)* na may ilog sa baba; Iloc: derras iti tanap *(valley)* nga adda carayan iti baba
Slope gulod, libis; Iloc: darisdis, agsalog

Precipitate 1] ipagmadali o ipalabas ng sobrang aga at biglaan; 2] ihagis pababa, magtalon; 3] pag-uulan.

Precipitous matarik na bundok; Iloc: derecho-*Sp* agpababa nga derraas ti bantay, nasang-at

Precise exacto-*Sp,* tamang-tama, tumpak, hustong-husto-*Sp;* Iloc: ususto-*Sp,* exacto

Precision, with *(Tag. & Iloc.)* exactong-exacto

Preclude hadlangan ang pagdalo o na mangyari o mabuhay; gawing imposib-le; Iloc: lappedan nga agatender o agpasamak o agbiag, aramiden nga impo-sib-le

Precognition abilidad na makakini-kinita ang dadating, salagimsim, sagimsim; Iloc: amiris

Precursor tao o bagay na nakagawa ng unang-unang paraan; tao o bagay na nangunguna sa paggawa o pagbuo ng paraan

Predator, Predatory hayup o tao na naghahanap ng mavivictima; Iloc: animal-*Sp* o tao nga agsapsapul iti mavivictima na

Predecessor dating nagtrabaho sa isang puesto-*Sp* na ngayon ay mayroon nang pumalit

Predestine *v.,* **Predestination** *n.* bago dumating ito, naitakda na ito; Iloc: baro nga sumangpet, naidesignaren

Predicament magusot na kalagayan o suliranin na may kahirapang lutasin; Iloc: complicado-*Sp* a situasyon-*Sp* o problema-*Sp* a narigat nga i-solvar-*Sp*

Predict nakikini-kinita ang dadating; Iloc: maamiris iti mapasamak iti sumangpet nga aldaw
Correlated word
Forecast sa tulong ng *technology* at ibang sistema, nalalaman na ang dadating gaya ng clima at temperatura

Predictable inaasahan at nakatalagang mangyari o magkatutuo

Given inaasahang mangyari, nakatalagang mangyari o magkatutuo

Prediction pangitain; Iloc: amiris

Predispose *v.*, **Predisposition** *n.* 1] madaling mahawa o kapitan; 2] puedeng gagawin dahil nakagawian na

Predilection ang gusto at tinatangi, ang kinakagawihan, ang pinapanigan at finafavoran

Predominant mas marami o mas naghahari o mas laganap; Iloc: mas adu o mas agar-ari o mas nakawaras ken inakceptar ti tattao ida

Preempt *v.*, **Preemptive** *adj.* 1] ang oportunidad o karapatan na ariin bago ariin ng iba dahil siya'y unang-unang nandoon at unang -unang mag-*claim* o mag-angkin; 2] ginawang paraang pangcontra sa nakikinitang nakakakabang mangyayari kaya gumawa ng pandefensa, panghadlang at pampigil

Prefer *(Tag. & Iloc.)* mas gusto-*Sp*, mas favor-*Sp*

Preference *(Tag. & Iloc.)* tinatangi sa buhay, finafavoran

Pregnancy with craving for a certain food naglilihi; Iloc: agininaw

Pregnant buntis, nagdadalang-tao; Iloc: masicog

Prejudice pagtuturing na mababa o masama ang tao/grupo/lahi at ipa-walang-pansin ang pagkahalaga nila; Iloc: bigbigen a nababa wenno dakes ti tao/grupo/lahi ken haan nga bigbigen ti valor da

Preliminary pang-unang alamin ang paraan o proyecto-*Sp* at pangpakilala nito

Premature maaga pa at di pa oras o di pa napapanahon; Iloc: nasapa pay ken haan pay oras o haan pay panawen

Premise 1] salita na pinapalagay na tutoo para pag-usapan at makarating sa conclusyon; plano o mungkahi na makakatulong o makakasuporta o makakapagpaliwanag ng conclusyon o pasya o palagay; 2] isang gusali kasama ang lupaing paligid nito, ang bakuran at ano pa man na kasali sa ari-ariang iyon; 3] batayan o saligan kung saan pagmumulan ng pagrarason; ang kasulatan ng pangyayari kung saan binabatay ang reklamo

Premonition kutob, caba sa dadating na anoman; Iloc: kebba, tibbayo iti sumangpet nga aniaman

Correlated words

Hunch 1] may pakiramdam na may mangyayari, 2] magyuko at ibaluktot ang katawan

Precognition abilidad na makakini-kinita, salagimsim, sagimsim; Iloc: amiris

Fast heartbeat due to fear or worry kumokutob-kutob, kacaba-caba; Iloc: agtibtibbayo, agkebba-kebba

Foreboding kutob na nakakabalisa; Iloc: kebba nga makapadanag ken makariro

Prepare maghanda, ihanda, mag-prepara-*Sp*; Iloc: agrubwat, irubwat, agsagana, isagana, ag-preparar-*Sp*

Prepared handa na, preparado-*Sp* na; Iloc: preparadon, nakarubwaten, nakasaganan

Prerequisite, Requisite rekisito-*Sp* sa pagka-qualificado-*Sp*; Iloc: rekisito a maka-calificado

Presage nagpapahiwatig o naghuhudyat o nakakapagparamdam o naki-kinita ang mangyayari sa hinaharap

Prescribe 1] magtatag ng pamaraan o reglamentos-*Sp* para sa dapat gagawin; 2] magreceta ang doctor ng medicina-*Sp* para sa paciente-*Sp*; Iloc: 1] mangaramid ti padalan wenno reglamentos para iti masapul nga aramiden, 2] ag-receta-*Sp* ti doctor ti medicina para iti paciente

Prescription medicina-*Sp* na ni-receta-*Sp* ng *doctor* para sa paggamot ng sakit ng canyang paciente-*Sp*

PRESENCE 1] kasa-kasama sa lugar, 2] pagdalo o kinaroroonan; Iloc: 1] cadwa idiay lugar, 2] pag-atender-*Sp*

PRESENCE of mind calmadong isip na nakakasuri ng tama at mabuting hakbang na gagawin kapag may kagipitan o panganib o *emergency*

PRESENT regalo-*Sp*; Iloc: regalo, parabur, sarabu, sagot

PRESENT a show itanghal, ilahad, magtampok, magpamalas, mag-palabas; Iloc: mang-presentar-*Sp*, mangipabuya, mangiparang

PRESENT, In attendance dumalo; Iloc: ag-atender-*Sp*

PRESENT time ngayong kasalukuyan, ngayong mga panahong ito; Iloc: dagitoy a panawen, itatta mismo-*Sp*

Correlated words

Past ang lumipas na panahon, noon pa; Iloc: iti napalabas a panawen, idi pay

Future ang hinaharap, ang mga kinabukasang panahon; Iloc: iti ma-sangwanan, cadagiti sumangpet a panawen

Presentable presentab-le-*Sp*, magandang paglalahad; Iloc: presentab-le, naimbag nga pakita wenno pabuya

Presentation, Performance pagtatanghal, palabas, *presentation*; Iloc: pabuya, *presentation*

Preserve mag*preserve* at hindi sayangin, mag-conserva-*Sp*; Iloc: i*preserve* tapno haan a masayang, mangilala, agconserva

Preside magpangulo sa pagtitipon; Iloc: mangpangulwan iti pagtitipon ti tattao

President presidente-*Sp*, pangulo; Iloc: presidente

PRESS pindotin, idiin; Iloc: deppelen, ital-meg

PRESS down a box to flatten pisain; Iloc: pitpiten
> *Correlated words*
> **Flatten, Compress** tapak-tapakan o yurak-yurakan para pumantay at magplastado; Iloc: badde-baddekan para mapitpit o agdippig o agplastado

PRESS down into container to stuff more things isalya, isiksik; Iloc: isedsed, isiksik
> *Correlated words*
> **Push to sink something, i.e. in mud** ipasak, iduldol; Iloc: ilumlom, ilupak

Pressed for time kapus sa tiempo, gahol, gipit sa oras; Iloc: agkurkurang ti tiempo

Pressing iron to smoothen washed clothes *(Tag. & Iloc.)* plancha-*Sp*

Prestige mataas na turing sa isang tao dahil sa canyang puesto-*Sp* o rangko-*Sp* o sa magandang reputasyon-*Sp*, o sa canyang pagkaimportante niya sa bayan o sa canyang pagkarespetado o pagkadignidad niyang tao o sa pagkaexperto niya sa isang larangan

Presume ipalagay, mag-akala, magkuro-kuro, maghaka-haka, wariin; Iloc: ipagarup, agpatta-patta

Presumptive may rason-*Sp* na mangyayari, malamang na magkatutoo

Presumptuous galaw o salita na mayroon siyang karapatan o may *sense of entitlement* kahit kadalasan ay wala o hindi tutuo, o kaya cursonada siya o may gusto sa canya kahit sa isip niya lamang; Iloc: gunay o sarita nga addaan isu ti turay wenno adda *sense of entitlement* isu uray nu awan wenno haan nga agpayso wenno cursonada da isu uray nu panunot na laeng dayta.

PRETEND magkunwari, magpanggap; Iloc: agingcucuna, agsinsinan

PRETEND "participant" (i.e, a kid to please him/her) salingpusa; Iloc: salimpusa

Pretentious mapagkunwari, mapagpanggap; Iloc: aginkukuna ken agsinsinan

Pretext pagdadahilan; Iloc: pambar

PRETTY maganda, marikit, marilag, maalindog, guapa-*Sp;* Iloc: napintas, nakaay-ayat, guapa

"PRETTY much" halos lahat; Iloc: ngangngani amin

Prevail umiiral, mamayani, mananaig; Iloc: mangabak
   Synonym
   Reign mamuno, maghari, mamayani, nangingibabaw, manaig; Iloc: agturay, agar-ari

Prevalent calat, laganap, tanggap ng marami; Iloc: nakawaras, in-akceptar-*Sp* ti adu

Prevaricate magsinungaling; Iloc: agulbod

Prevent hadlangan, iwasan; Iloc: lappedan, teppedan

Previous, Previously noong nakaraan, noong nakalipas, dati-rati; Iloc: idi napalabas

Prey 1]-*verb*: hayop gaya ng tigre na nagmamanman o nagsusubaybay ng *prey* na makain niyang hayop; 2] *noun*: taong madaling mavictima o i-*bully*; Iloc: 1] *verb*: sipsiputan ken palimed nga sursuroten na ti *prey* tapno kanen na daytoy, 2] *noun*: tao a nalaca a mavictima o ma-*bully*

Price precio-*Sp*, halaga; Iloc: precio, valor-*Sp*

Prick masundot ng maliit na carayom; Iloc: matudok iti bassit a dagum

Prickle tinik; Iloc: siit

PRICKLY nakakatinik, makasundot; Iloc: makatudok

PRICKLY heat bungang-araw; Iloc: bagas-ling-et

Pride amor propio-*Sp*, pagmamalaki, pagpapahalaga sa sarili o sa canyang puesto o iba pa; Iloc: amor propio, pagpanpannakkel, pangpatpateg iti mismo a bagi wenno ti dayaw na
   Correlated word
   Smug kasiyahan sa mismong sarili; Iloc: ragsak ti mismo bagi

Priest *(Tag. & Iloc.)* pari/padi, padre-*Sp*, *priest*, sacerdote-*Sp* ng simbahang Catolico

Prima donna 1] pangunahing kumacanta sa opera, 2] tao na naglulublob sa aliw at inaakala niyang may karapatan siya parati sa privilehio at sa mahusay na trato pero namumuhi siya kapag pinipintasan o inaabala siya

Primal 1] kauna-unahan, katutubo; 2] puno, pinono, pinakaimportante

Prime time of life, In one's prime nasa pinakamahusay at pinaka-mabunga at pinakamabuting panahon sa buhay; Iloc: kasayaatan ken nabunga a parte o tiempo-*Sp* iti biag

Prince *(Tag. & Iloc.)* principe-*Sp*

Princess *(Tag. & Iloc.)* princesa-*Sp*

Principal *(Tag. & Iloc.) principal*

Principle *(Tag. & Iloc.)* principio-*Sp*

Print *(Tag. & Iloc.) print,* prenta-a*Sp,* imprenta-*Sp*

Prior to now kararaan lamang, bago ngayon; Iloc: daytoy laeng a napalabas, baro laeng a napasamak

Priority pinapauna at binibigyang panahon o sikap dahil mahalaga at prayoridad-*Sp* ito; Iloc: iyun-una ken ikkan ti oras ken pakat gapu ta bigbigen da a napateg ken prayoridad daytoy

Prison bilanggoan, bilibid, piitan, culongan; Iloc: pagbaludan, bilibid, carcel-*Sp*, pagculongan, calaboso-*Sp*

Prisoner bilanggo, preso-*Sp*; Iloc: balud, preso

Pristine taglay ang katutubong pagkapuro, walang dungis

Private *(Tag. & Iloc.) private,* privado-*Sp*

Privilege privilehio-*Sp*; Iloc: privilehio, gundaway

Prize gantimpala, premio-*Sp*; Iloc: gunggona, premio

Proactive *Initiating effective and anticipatory work, not responding to it after it happened. Acting in advance to deal with expected difficulties; preparing, mediating, intervening, restraining, curbing and controling to prevent potential problems.*

Probable malaking chansa na tutoo o mangyayari

Probably malamang, seguro-a*Sp*, baka; Iloc: baka, nalabit, seguro, sa, ngata

Probe usigin, usisahin, siyasatin; Iloc: sukimaten, usigen, usisaen, sukisoken

Problem suliranin, problema-*Sp*; Iloc: problema, parikut
  Synonyms
  Imbroglio complicado at nakakalitong situasyon, kagusotan Iloc: complicado ken nakarirriro nga situasyon, gulo

Predicament magusot na kalagayan o suliranin na may kahirapang lutasin; Iloc: complicado a situasyon o problema a narigat nga isolvar

Proclivity natural o kagawian na gawa o kahiligan

Procrastinate antalahin, ipagpaliban; Iloc: itantan

Procedure mga pamaraan gaya ng paggawa para makabuo ng producto o makapatayo ng gusali; sa medicina para magamot ang sakit, sa pag-aral para makatamo ng katalinohan at abilidad; sa paglutas ng mga suliranin, para makahango sa hirap; sa siencia para makadiscobre pa ng dapat madiscobre; sa tecnologia para makaimbento ng mga bagong kinakailangan para umaavante ang mundo, sa pamaraan ng tagumpay at kapayapaan at iba pa

Process paraan, proceso-*Sp* o pagbubuo o pagtubo; Iloc: kapamay-an, proceso-*Sp* o pagtubo o pag-completo

Procession *(Tag. & Iloc.) procession,* procesyon-*Sp,* paglibot ng mga relihiong imahen sa bayan
Synonym
Parade *(Tag. & Iloc.) parade,* parada

Proclaim ipahayag, i-proclama-*Sp,* mag-anuncio-*Sp*; Iloc: isawang, i-proclamar-*Sp,* ag-anuncio

Prodigy 1] tao na kadalasan ay bata na nagkakaroon ng talento-*Sp* o abilidad-*Sp* na pambihira at kahanga-hanga ang gilas; 2] isang nakakapagtaka o nakakamangha

Produce nagagawa ang isa o mas marami pa sa mga sumusunod na ito - magyari, maglikha, magsagawa, mamunga, maglahad, magdulot, magtubo, magpa-usbong, magpasibol

Product *(Tag. & Iloc.)* producto-*Sp*

Productive *Capable of producing, generating and creating things, especially products and services that yield favorable effects and results. It is being fertile with valuable outcomes.* Mabunga, nakakasagawa o nakakabuo ng mabuting bagay; Iloc: nabunga, makaobra o makaaramid iti naimbag a banag

Profession *profession,* hanapbuhay; Iloc: *profession,* pagsapulan
Synonym
Occupation ocupasyon, hanapbuhay, pagkakakitahan; Iloc: ocupasyon, pagsapulan

Professional *professional,* tungkol sa pag-aacecaso o pangangasiwa ng sariling hanapbuhay o profesyon na alinsunod sa karapat-dapat at matuwid na pagpapalakad nito

Proficient *adj.,* **Proficiency** *n. Experienced, accomplished, trained, and well advanced in science, art and other fields; capable, competent, efficient, intelligent, skillful, adept, talented, gifted, and an expert.* Experto-*Sp* dahil sa kaalaman at abilidad-*Sp* na galing sa expiryensa-*Sp* at karunongan; Iloc: experto gapu iti kasiriban ken abilidad nga naggapu iti expiryensa ken intelihensia-*Sp*
Correlated words
Efficient cayang-caya ang gawa at puedeng higit pa diyan, nakakacompleto ng trabaho at napakahusay pa; Iloc: cayang-caya na iti obra ken mabalin a labes pay dita, makacompleto iti trabaho ken nakalalaeng pay

Effectual, Efficacious nakakagawa ng inaasahang efecto o pagkabuo; Iloc: makaar-aramid iti namnamaen a bunga o efecto

Proactive nakahanda sa mga inaasahang magaganap lalo na sa mga complicado para maisagawa niya o controlado niya; Iloc: nakasagana cadagiti expectaren a mapasamak o maaramid lallalo cadagiti complicado tapno maaramid na ken controlado na

Reliable mapagkakatiwalaang tutupdin ang canyang obligasyon at trabaho at pangako na maaasahan at mapapanaligan siya; Iloc: mapagtalkan nga tungpalen na ti obligasyon ken trabaho ken ti incari na a manamnama ken mapagfiaran

Competent caya, cayang-caya; Iloc: caya, cabaelan

Resourceful laging naghahanap ng mga pamaraan o sistema para makapagsagawa o makapaglutas, marunong magdilihensia; Iloc: agbirbirok ti dalan o sistema tapno makaturpos wenno makasolvar, ammona ti agdilihensia

Profit tubo, kinita; Iloc: tubo, ganansia-*Sp*

Profitable malaki ang kinikita dito, matubo; Iloc: dakkel iti ganancia-*Sp* ditoy

Profound ang lalim ay kahanga-hanga; Iloc: iti kaadalem ket nakasidsiddaaw

Program programa-*Sp*, palatuntunan; Iloc: programa

PROGRESS *n. progress,* progreso-*Sp*, kaunlaran, asenso-*aSp*; Iloc: *progress,* progreso, panagrang-ay, asenso

PROGRESS *v.* magprogreso, mag-unlad; Iloc: agprogreso, agrang-ay *(see Success also)*

Correlated words

Flourish lalago; Iloc: umadu

Thrive umunlad, magprogreso, mabuhay, tumubo; Iloc: agrang-ay, agprogreso, agtubo, agbiag

Progressive maunlad, maprogreso, ma-asenso-a*Sp*; Iloc: nakaas-asenso, naprogreso, narang-ay

Prohibit pagbawalan; Iloc: ipagel, iparit

Project *(Tag. & Iloc.) project*, proyecto-*Sp*, Iloc: gandat

Proliferate tumubo at lumago ng maraming sanga at nagbubunga; maglaganap ng marami at mabilis

Prolific *Producing much fruits, many offsprings. Abundant productivity, inventiveness, and frequent successful results.* Mabunga, maraming anak o bunga o gawa o resulta; Iloc: nabunga, adu iti anak o bunga o aramid o resulta

Prolong patagalin pa: Iloc: pabayagin
Synonym
Extend the deadline, Allow longer time to comply his/her obligation palugitan; Iloc: ipawatiwat

Promenade pasyal sa lugar-*Sp* ng publico-*Sp*, marcha-*Sp* ng grupo-*Sp* sa isang pagdiriwang

PROMISE *n. promise,* promesa-*Sp*, pangako; Iloc: promesa, *promise,* kari
Correlated words
Oath, Vow, Pledge sumpa, panata; Iloc: sapata
Swear magsumpa, magpanata o mangako caraniwan sa husticia o sa simbahan; Iloc: agsapata o agkari iti sango ti husticia wenno iti simbaan

PROMISE *v.* mangako, mag-*promise*; Iloc: ag-*promise*, agkari

Promised naipangakoan, pinangako; Iloc: naykarian, ingkaryan

Promissory note kasulatan na ipangako na babayaran ang tinakdang halaga na pera sa loob ng tinakdang tiempo o sa sapilitang pangolecta

Promote tulongang lumago o umunlad at magprogreso; umabante sa susunod na patag o *level*; tumaas ang rangko o puesto; itaguyod ang isang patakaran o isang producto

Promoter *(Tag. & Iloc.)* promotor-*Sp*

Promotion *(Tag. & Iloc.) promotion*, asenso-a*Sp*

Prompt maagap, empunto-*Sp*; Iloc: empunto

Prone 1] nakadapa na ang mukha ay harap sa lupa o cama, 2] *tendency* o nagagawi o nahihilig na gumawa o mag-asal ng nakabihasnan; Iloc: 1] nakapakleb nga ti rupa ket nakasango ti daga o cama, 2] *inclination* o maytuptutop nga agaramid wenno agtignay it naysigudan na

Pronounce *v.,* **Pronunciation** *v.* bigkasin, i-*pronounce*; Iloc: i-pronunciar-*Sp,* ibalikas, balikasen, i-*pronounce*

Proof prueba-*Sp,* pagpapatotoo, katibayan, pagpapatunay, pagpapatiyak, evidensia-*Sp,* patunay; Iloc: prueba, evidensia, pangpaneknek, pangpa-sigurado
Synonym
Evidence *(Tag. & Iloc.) evidence,* evidencia

Propaganda *n.,* **Propagandize** *v.* pagpapalaganap

Propagate 1] magkaanak para dumami ang tao sa mundo-*Sp,* 2] ipaalam ang kinakailangan sa isang henerasyon-*Sp* at sa susunod na henerasyon, o ipalaganap sa malaki na madla o sa kabayanan; Iloc: 1] aganak tapno umadu ti tao iti mundo, 2] ipaammo iti henerasyon ken ti sumaruno nga henerasyon wenno iwaras cadagiti publico-*Sp*

Propensity *n.,* **Propend** *v.* natural o kagawian na gawa o kahiligan

Proper tugma sa magandang asal at sa batas; Iloc: umno iti na-etico a biag ken iti linteg

Property ari-arian, aring bahay at lote; Iloc: sanicua, cukua a balay ken lote

Prophet *(Tag. & Iloc.)* profeta-*Sp*

Prophecy pangitain ng profeta

Propitiate gumagawa ng mabuting paraan para matamo ulit ang magandang pagsasamahan at ang tiwala sa canya, nagpapahinahon; Iloc: nasayaat a mangipadalan tapno agsubli manen ti nasayaat nga pakicadcadwa ken iti pagfiar canyana; mangpatalna

Propitious *Presenting favorable conditions and a good chance of success. Favorably disposed, merciful, kindly and gracious.* Nagbibigay ng magandang circumstancia-*Sp* na makakabigay ng kabutihan, pati tagumpay; Iloc: mangpresentar iti napintas a circumstancia a makaited iti kaimbagan wenno balligi pay

Proponent taong makipag-discusyon-*Sp* para suportahan ang isang diwa; Iloc: tao a makipatang o makidiscusyon para suportaran da ti maysa nga amad wenno rangta

Proportionate parte-*Sp* na magkaka-pareho-*Sp* o magkakaangkop sa ibang parte; Iloc: parte nga agpapada wenno agparbeng cadagiti sabali a parte

Proposal *n.*, **Propose** *v.*, **Proposition** *n.* mungkahi, panukala, *proposition*; Iloc: singasing, *proposition*

Proprietary *personal* o tanging pagmemay-ari, tungkol sa pagiging *proprietor*

Proprietor nagmemay-ari ng malaking ari-arian; Iloc: akincukua iti dackel a sanicua

Propriety sumasalig o bumabatay sa magandang asal at pananalita; Iloc: agsanggir ken agbatbatay iti naimbag a tignay ken pagsarita

Pro rata calculahin na batay sa pagkakaangkop sa halaga sa lugar, sa bagay at sa iba pa

Prorate magbaha-bahaginan ng pare-parehong parte; Iloc: agbibingayan nga agpapada a parte

Proscribe isumpa, ipagbawal, ipahayag na masamang tao at dapat ipailalim sa batas; Iloc: idadanes, iparit, ipaammo nga dakes a tao ken masapul nga sumungbat iti husticia wenno otoridad

Prosecute magdemanda ng *legal* na parusa; Iloc: agdemanda ti *legal* a dusa

Proselytize 1] hikayatin para sumali sa samahan nila, 2] magpahayag tungkol sa Panginoong Dios o i-*convert* sa isang relihion-*Sp*; Iloc: 1] sulisogen para sumali iti pagkakaduaan da, 2] mangipaammo may-gapu kenni Apo Dios o i-*convert* iti maysa a relihion

Prospect 1] puedeng maging suki o cliente-*Sp*, 2] maghalukay ng lupa para humanap ng ginto o iba pang mahalagang *mineral*; Iloc: 1] mabalin nga agbalin a cliente o suki, 2] agcali tapno agsapul ti balitok o aniaman a mabirokan nga navalor a *mineral*

Prospective maasahan at puedeng mangyari; Iloc: manamnama ken adda posibilidad-*Sp* nga agbalin

Prosper mag-unlad, magsagana; Iloc: agrang-ay

Prosperous maunlad, malago, mariwasa; Iloc: narang-ay

Prostate parte ng katawan ng lalake na may kinalaman sa pag-ihi at pagpapabuntis ng babae; Iloc: parte ti bagi ti lalaki nga mang-efecto-*Sp* ti pag-isbu ken pangpasicog ti babai

Prostitute *(Tag. & Iloc.)* puta-*Sp*

Protagonist 1] bida sa storya-*Sp* o *drama*, 2] namumuno o sumosuporta sa isang layonin; Iloc: 1] bida ti storya o *drama*, 2] bagnos o mang-supsuporta ti maysa a rangta

Protect ipagtanggol, defensahin; Iloc: salakniban, i-defensa-*Sp*

Protection *protection*, pagtanggol; Iloc: *protection*, salaknib
   Correlated word
   Security *(Tag. & Iloc.)* seguridad

Protest contrahin, magtutol, mag-oposisyon-*Sp*, magprotesta-*Sp*; Iloc: agcontra, ag-oposisyon, agprotesta, agsupyat, agsalangad

Protestant *(Tag. & Iloc.)* protestante-*Sp*

Protocol 1] ceremonia-*Sp* at etiketa-*Sp* na sinusunod ng mga *diplomats* at pinuno ng bayan, 2] isang sinusunod na pamaraan para sa tama at mahusay na sistema, 3] paraan para sa pagpagaling sa sakit o paggawa ng experimento-*Sp* sa siencia-*Sp*

Protract patagalin, pahabain, unatin; Iloc: pabayagen, paatiddogen, un-naten

Prostrate 1] nakahiga na nakadapa; 2] nakadapa sa pagparangal o pag-samba na custombre ng ibang *religion*; Iloc: 1] agidda a nakapakleb; 2] nakapakleb nga agdayaw ken agcararag nga custombre ti dadduma a *religion*

Protruding umuusli, lumalawit; Iloc: agdawdawadaw, agusli

Proud mapagmalaki, mapagmataas, mata-pobre-*Sp*, hambog, suplado/da-*Sp*; Iloc: napangas, mapagpannakkel, suplado/da

Prove patunayan, ipakita ang prueba-*Sp*; Iloc: paneknekan, ipakita ti prueba
   Synonyms
   Verify ipagpatutoo, patibayin; Iloc: ipakita ti kaagpaysuan, iverificar
   Substantiate patunayan, magbigay ng prueba; Iloc: mangited ti prueba o pangpaneknek
   Uphold panindigan; Iloc: itacder, paneknekan
   Testify magpatunay, magtestigo, magsaksi; Iloc: agtestigo, agsaksi, ipaammo ken patalgedan ti usto ken kinaagpayso

Provide gugolan, tustosan, dulotan, gastosan, pagkalooban, suportahan: Iloc: suportaran, gastosan, mangited

Synonyms

Fund fondohan; Iloc: mangfondo

Donate mag-*donate,* mag-abuloy, mamigay, ipamigay; Iloc: ag-*donate,* agabuloy, agsagut, agrangkap

Supply tustosan, pagkalooban, dulotan; Iloc: mangited

Propitiate nagbibigay ng nakakabuti; Iloc: mangited iti makapaimbag, nagundaway

Provident *adj,* **Providence** *n. Protective care and divine love of God towards all men; God's caring guidance to men. Someone having prudence and foresight.* 1] pag-aalaga at pagpapatnubay ng Panginoong Dios sa lahat na nilalang; 2] pagkakaroon ng *foresight* at naghahanda sa mga kailangan sa hinaharap.

Province *(Tag. & Iloc.)* provincia-*Sp*

Provincial government govierno-*Sp* ng provincia-*Sp* na pinangungulohan ng *governor* o governador-*Sp*

PROVISION 1] *provision,* pagbibigay, pagdulot, 2] mga pangangailangan sa buhay gaya ng pagkain at damit; Iloc: 1] *provision,* paay, pangited, sagot, 2] dagiti kasapulan ti biag casla iti kanen ken cawes

PROVISION to bring along on a trip baon; Iloc: balon

Provocateur taong nanghahamon, nang-iinis; Iloc: tao nga agcarcarit, agcatcatil, agparparurod

Provoke *v.,* **Provocation** *n.* hamon, pang-inis; Iloc: carit, catil, pangparurod

Prowess abilidad-*Sp* na mas mahusay kaysa ordinaryo-*Sp*; Iloc: abilidad a mas nalaeng ngem ti ordinario

Prowl naglilibot sa paghahanap ng magawan niya ng masama; Iloc: aglawlaw nga agsapul ti maaramidan na ti dakes

Proximity pagkalapit sa isang lugar o pagkalapit sa tinakdang numero o dami; Iloc: pagkaasideg iti maysa a lugar wenno pagkaasideg iti numero wenno kaadu

Prude *n.,* **Prudish** *adj.,* isang taong labis-labis na mahinhin at mabuting mag-asal at magsalita, ganon din sa pananamit, sa tindig at *attitude*

Prudent *adj.,* **Prudence** *n. Has wisdom and discretion and takes precautionary and careful steps in managing life and resources to prepare for future contingencies/unforeseen events.* Pag-iingat at matalinong pamamahala ng kapakanan at kapakinabangan sa paghahanda sa hinaharap.

Correlated word

Foresight talino sa paghahandang pagfondo ng kinabukasan

Prune off (i.e. veggie leaf) talbusan; Iloc: uggotan

Prunes *(Tag. & Iloc.)* frutas na *prunes*

PRY manilip; Iloc: agsirip

PRY open tuklapin, baklasin; Iloc: lekkaben, ungaten

Psalms *(Tag. & Iloc.)* *Psalms*, sagradong canta sa Biblia

Pseudo *(Tag. & Iloc.)* peke, falsificado

Pseudonym *pen name* dahil hindi ginagamit ang tunay na pangalan, falsificadong pangalan

Psyche ang utak na nagpapalakad ng isip, emosyon-*Sp* at asal na dito nakikita ang pagkatao o kaluluwa o spiritu-*Sp* ng tao

Psychology *(Tag. & Iloc.)* *psychology*

Psycopath *n.*, **Psychopathic** *adj.* ayaw niyang makihalobilo sa tao dahil may diferencia ang katatao niya at lantad ito sa canyang pagkaagresivo at hindi niya makilala ang masama sa mabuti at siya ay nakakagawa ng crimen pero wala man lamang siyang pagsisisi o pagkaawa

Psychosomatic nararamdamang sakit pero sa kaisipan lamang; Iloc: maricricna na a sakit ngem iti pagpampanunot na laeng

Psychotherapy paggagamot sa diferencia-a*Sp* ng isip at damdamin o sa nararamdaman ng katawan sa pamamagitan ng *psychology*; Iloc: pag-agas ti diferencia ti nakem ken *emotion*, pagpaagas iti maricna iti bagi nga *psychology* ti makaagas nu dadduma

Puberty nasasa-edad na puede nang magkaanak; Iloc: addaan iti edad nan a mabalinen nga aganac

Pubic hair bulbol; Iloc: urmot

PUBLIC 1] mga mamamayan na nakatira sa comunidad-*Sp* o sa bayan; publico-*Sp*, mga tao, madla, kabayanang tao; 2] panlipunan, bukas sa lahat ng tao - pang-servicio-*Sp* ng buong mamamayan; Iloc: 1] dagiti tattao nga aggigian iti comunidad wenno bayan; publico, tao ti bayan; 2] para iti amin a tao - pangservicio iti am-amin

PUBLIC assistance tulong na inaalay sa mga nangangailangan, sa mga may edad na, at sa mga dinapuan ng salot gaya ng nakakasira na bagyo o lindol

PUBLIC domain 1] lupain na pag-aari ng bayan o *state*, 2] ang estado ng *publication* o mga lathala, o producto o paraan na hindi protectado ng *patent* o *copyright*

PUBLIC relations ito ang nagtatatag at nagtataguyod ng magandang pagkakaugnayan ng publico

PUBLIC school escuela-*Sp* na nasa pamamahala ng govierno-*Sp*, Iloc: escuela nga igaway ti govierno

Publication paglalathala ng libro-*Sp* o ng ibang babasahin gaya ng periodico-*Sp*; Iloc: iprenta dagiti libro ken dad-duma pay a mabasa casla iti periodico

Publicity *(Tag. & Iloc.)* publicidad-*Sp*

Publicize, Publish ilathala, i-publicidad-*Sp*; Iloc: iwarnak, ipublicidad

Publisher nag-aasecaso ng paggawa ng mga kasulatan, balita o babasahing libro at nilalathala niya ito

Puddle putik na lubak sa daan; Iloc: lutlot nga abut wenno lubnak iti dalan

PUFF 1] tunog ng maliit na sabog, 2] mabilis na hihip o pagbuga ng hininga; Iloc: 1] uni ti bassit a bettak, 2] nadaras nga puyot wenno pagpug-aw iti anges

PUFF up when soaked in water mamintog; Iloc: bumlad

Pug-nosed *(Tag. & Iloc.)* pango

Puke magsuka; Iloc: agsarwa, agvacuar

PULL hilain; Iloc: guyoden
Correlated word
Yank haltakin, hatakin, batakin; Iloc: fuersa a guyoden, paguten
Antonym
Push itulak; Iloc: iduron

PULL a fast one biglaang pagtatagumpay ng *criminal* sa pagsasagawa niya ng canyang crimen-*Sp* o panlilinlang

PULL forcefully haltakin, hatakin, batakin; Iloc: pag-uten

PULL it off magtagumpay datapwat mahirap o hindi inaasahan

PULL out bunotin, hilain, batakin, haltakin; Iloc: paroten, rabnoten
Synonym
Uproot halbutin, labnutin; Iloc: paruten, rabnoten

PULL out something from a hole or a hollow jar ducotin, hugotin; Iloc: ducoten, caoten

PULL out with a hook from a bottle or hole sungkitin, cawitin; Iloc: sukiten, cawiten

PULL over Kapag dumadaan ang nagsasaklolong ambulansia-*Sp* o sasakyan ng bombero o *firefigther,* o *police,* o kung pinapahinto ka mismo-*Sp* ng *police,* dapat mag-*exit* ka o umalis sa daanan ng mga sasakyan at pumunta ka sa gilid ng calsada-*Sp* at huminto.

Pulled meat hinilang laman-laman ng carne-*Sp* na pagsahog sa sopas-*Sp* o palaman sa *sandwich*; Iloc: naguyodguyod nga lasag ti carne nga isagpaw ti sopas o ti iyuneg iti *sandwich*

Pulp laman ng frutas-*Sp* o gulay na malambot at may katas; Iloc: lasag ti frutas o nateng nga nalukneng ken natubbog

Pulsate tumitibok, pumipintig; Iloc: agpitpitik

Pulse *(Tag. & Iloc.)* pulso-*Sp*

Pulverize durogin, dikdikin, yurakin, gawing pulvos-*Sp*; Iloc: runawen, buraken, dikdiken, aramiden a pulvos

Pummel *(Tag. & Iloc.)* pukpokin, pamukpok, pangpukpok

Pump 1] makina o aparato-*Sp* na pampaalsa o pangdiin o pampiga o pampasalin o pampalipat ng likido; 2] ang pusong pumipintig

Punch 1] golpehin, suntokin, saktan, buntalin, bugbogin, sapukin, hampasin, 2] alak at *juice* na pinaghalo; Iloc: 1] golpien, danugen, saktan, sulongen, disnogen, bugbogen cabilen, 2] arak ken *juice* nga pinaglaok

Punctilio mainam o mabuting paksa o detalye-*Sp* o asal o pamaraan o ceremonia-*Sp*; tumpak, exacto-*Sp*, at stricto na pagsunod ng mga formalidad-*Sp* o nakakacomfortable sa buhay.

Punctual, On time maagap, empunto-*Sp*; Iloc: empunto

Puncture butasan; Iloc: lussokan

Pundit maraming alam, matalino at experto na nagcocomentario o naghuhusga ng ma-otoridad; Iloc: adu ammo na, nasirib, experto

Pungent maanghang; Iloc: nagasang

Punish parusahan; Iloc: dusaen, castigaren
Synonyms
   Convict *v.* hatolan ng parusa; Iloc: ikkan ti rebbeng na a dusa
   Chastise dusahin; Iloc: dusaen

Punishment parusa; Iloc: dusa, castigar-*Sp*

Punitive maglapat ng parusa, ipasailalim sa parusa

Pupil mag-aaral, estudiante-*Sp*; Iloc: agad-adal, estudiante

Puppeteer taong nagpagalaw at nagsasalita pero kunwari ang canyang mga manica o *puppets* ang kusang gumagalaw at nagsasalita; Iloc: tao a mangpagpagaraw ken agsarsarita ngem sinsinan a dagiti munyeca-*Sp* wenno *puppets* na ti mismo-*Sp* nga agargaraw ken agsarsarita

Puppy, Pup tuta; Iloc: uken

Purchase bumili; Iloc: gumatang

Pure puro-*Sp*, busilak; Iloc: puro ken nalinis

Puree malapot na sopa-*Sp* na gawa sa nadikdik na gulay; Iloc: napalet a sopas nga aramid iti nadikdik a nateng

Purgative purga-*Sp*, pangtulong para makatae; Iloc: purga, pangtulong para makatakki

Purgatory *(Tag. & Iloc.)* *purgatory*, purgatorio-*Sp*

Purge 1] linisan at tanggalin ang mga dumi o kasalanan; 2] ipawalang-sala, ipalaya sa bintang; 3] purgahan (purga-*Sp*) para makatae

Purify gawing puro-*Sp* at hindi haloan ng iba; gawing hindi magkaroon ng nakakasira o nakakadumi o nakakasama o anomang hindi kanais-nais na katangian

Purity kalinisan at pagkadalisay; Iloc: pagkalinis ken pagkapuro

Purple *purple*, culay na pinaghalo ang pula at azul-*Sp*; Iloc: *purple*, color-*Sp* a pinaglaok ti nalabbaga ken azul

Purport 1] nagpapahiwatig, nagbibigay ng kahulogan o pakay; 2] nagmumungkahi, nagpapakita ng ano man na kadalasan ay hindi tutoo

Purpose balak, tangka, layonin, sanhi, adhika, pakay, intension-*Sp*; Iloc: pakay, rangta, panggep, intension

Purposefully sinadya, kusa; Iloc: inggagara

Purse *(Tag. & Iloc.)* *purse*

Pursuant sumusunod batay sa; Iloc: tunpalen batay iti

Pursue *v.*, **Pursuit** *To tackle and strive to attain, accomplish and gain an objective. To chase to overtake or to capture a suspect.* 1] pagsisikap at pagpupursigi para matamo ang hangaring pinupuntirya; 2] habulin para arestohin; Iloc: 1] pagpakpakat ken tibker ken anos nga agpatpatuloy tapno magun-od na ti calicagum na, 2] camaten para arestoen

Purvey tao, servicio-*Sp* o negocio-*Sp* na nagsu-*supply* ng pagkain at ibang pangangailangan

Pus *(Tag. & Iloc.)* nana

PUSH itulak; Iloc: iduron

PUSH away isalya; Iloc: iwalin, iwadag

PUSH to deliver one's baby during childbrith mag-iri; Iloc: ag-iri

PUSH to sink something, i.e. in mud ipasak, iduldol; Iloc: ilumlom, ilupak

PUSH up *exercise* para lumakas ang baraso at camay; Iloc: *exercise* para pumigsa ti takkiag ken ima

Pushy makadisgustong pagkaagresivo at pagkadominante dahil akala niya ay kailangan mong sundin ang canyang gusto; Iloc: makadisgusto a pagkaagresivo ken pagkadominante gapu ta pagarup na nga masapul mo nga suroten ti cayat na

PUT, Place ilagay, ipuesto; Iloc: icabil, ipuesto, isimpa

PUT all one's eggs in one basket ilagay ang lahat-lahat na pera o mga naipon sa <u>isa</u> lang na lugar-*Sp* o *investment* kaya kung malugi o bumagsak ito, lahat-lahat na mga iyon ay mawawala na

PUT aside something to clear the way itabi para maluwag ang lugar-*Sp*; Iloc: iwalin, iwadag tapno nu nalawa ti lugar

PUT down ibaba, ilapag; Iloc: idiso

PUT down or Putdown salitang panglait sa kapwa; Iloc: sarita a panglais iti tao

PUT in a good word for someone magpahayag ng magandang salita tungkol sa isang tao para pangsuporta sa canya gaya ng *reference* sa *resume*

PUT it on, Wear isuot; Iloc: icawes, agbado

PUT-on, Put on an act magpanggap kahit pagkukunwari lamang; Iloc: aginkukuna uray nu haan agpaypayso

PUT oneself on someone else's shoes *Consideration and compassion that leads one to try to <u>understand other people's situation</u>.* Isipin kung ano at paano ang pinagdadanasan ng kapwa.

PUT something over something daganan, isampa; Iloc: pandagan, battoonan

PUT things in perspective Ito ay tamang pagtuturing sa nangyayari sa iyo at kung hirap ka, hindi iyon ang *the end of the world* dahil malamang mas mabuti ang kalagayan mo kaysa sa mga nasa lugar ng giyera na namamatay, nasusugatan, napipilayan o hindi na makakilos o makapagsalita; chaka kaysa sa mga *homeless* na walang matuloyan o makain; o kaya kung hindi ka pa nakatapos ng pag-aaral, ay walang hadlang na matatapos mo ang carera mo kung ipagpatuloy mo sa ano mang edad na makapag-aral ka muli; o kung nakipaghiwalay ka sa mahal mo, isipin mong mas marunong ka na ngayong pumili ng mas nakakatugma sa ugali at pananaw mo sa buhay; o kung wala kang trabaho, alamin mo ang kacayahan at abilidad mo at ipaalam mo tuwing mag-*apply* ka ng trabaho at anoman ang puesto mo - pang-umpisa o mataas na - pag-aralan mo ang trabaho mo, husayan mo para humanga sa iyo at pagkakatiwalaan ka para mai-angat at mapaunlad mo ang sarili mo doon o sa iba na paglilipatan mo.

PUT to a higher place iyangat, itaas, iyalsa-*Sp*; Iloc: ipangato, isagpat, isang-at

PUT to a lower place ibaba, ilagay sa baba; Iloc: ibaba, iyulog

PUT together things pagsama-samahin lahat, pagbuobuohin; Iloc: pag-cacadwaen nga entero-*Sp*

Putrefy nabubulok at nag-aamoy nang bulok

Putrid 1] bulok na bulok na at amoy na bulok pa; 2] ugaling malaswa at kamuhi-muhi

Putter 1] taong abala pero palaro-laro lamang na wala o kaunti lamang ang sikap o ang nagagawa; 2] taong naglalaro ng *golf* o nagpa-*putt*

Puzzle palaisipang bugtong; Iloc: pagpampanunotan nga pugpugto

Puzzling nakapagtataka, nakakalito, nakakataranta; Iloc: makasidsiddaaw, makariro, makataranta

Pygmy or Pigmy mga pandak o napakamababa ang tangkad na mga tao sa Africa; taong ang mga katangian ay tinuturing na maliit

Python sawa; Iloc: beklat

Q

Quack 1] huni ng pato; 2] taong nagpapahayag sa publico na may *university diploma* kaya *professional* siya at may abilidad at kaalaman pero wala siya ng mga iyon at nagpapanggap lamang siya; gumagamot siya na parang doctor pero *quackery* lamang at wala siyang alam sa tunay na *medical practice* ng doctor

Quadrangle *quadrangle* sa isang gusali gaya ng *gym* na malawak na kuadradong may apat na gilid kung saan ginaganap ang larong *sports* o kung sa escuela, dito ginaganap ang *physical education* ng mga estudiante

Quaff galak na galak siyang umiinom ng maraming alak

Quagmire 1] lupa na ang ibabaw ay malambot na putik, 2] napaka-delicadong situasyon na kahit anong oras ay puedeng may pinsala o masira; Iloc: 1] daga nga iti rabaw na ket nalukneng nga lutlot, 2] nakadeldelicado a situasyon nga uray no ania oras ket mabalin nga adda disgracia wenno madadael

Quail *(Tag. & Iloc.)* pugo

Quaint kakaiba, hindi pangcaraniwan; Iloc: nakasabsabali, haan a cadawyan

Quake yumayanig; Iloc: aggingined

Qualification *qualification*, calificasyon-*Sp* gaya ng kacayahan, ka-talinohan, kaalaman, *experience*, abilidad-*Sp*, *skills*, talento-*Sp*, personalidad-*Sp*, at educasyon-*Sp*; Iloc: *qualification*, casla dagiti cabaelan, sirib, kaammoan ida, *experience*, abilidad, talento, per-sonalidad, educasyon ken sabali pay

Qualify suriin kung siya'y calificado-*Sp*; Iloc: kitaen ken usisaen nu isu ket qualificado-*Sp*

Qualified *(Tag. & Iloc.)* *qualified*, qualificado-*Sp*, calificado-*Sp* dahil may katangian na angkop o labis pa na karapat-dapat sa puesto na ina-*apply*-an niya

Quality *(Tag. & Iloc.)* calidad-*Sp*, clase-*Sp*, uri

Qualms biglang hindi mapakali at hindi comfortab-le o nakakaramdam ng pag-alala o pagkatakot dahil sa hindi pagsunod ng tama o mabuti; Iloc: golpe nga haan a makatalna ken haan a comfortab-le o makaricna ti pagdanag wenno pagkabuteng gapu ti haan na pagsurot iti usto ken nasayaat a padalan

Quandary, in nababagabag, naliligalig, balisa, lito, matorete; Iloc: marirriro, maringgoran, matortorete

Quantify alamin o ipahayag ang bilang; ipahayag ang dami nito gaya ng numero ng bilang o salitang lahat o wala o ilan lamang; Iloc: amuen ken ipaammo no mano iti bilang o sarita a amin o awan o mano laeng.

Quantity dami, bilang; Iloc: caadu, bilang, sumar-*Sp*

Quarantine *quarantine*, hindi payagang lumabas ang tao o bagay dahil ito ay may dalang sakit na nakakahawa; Iloc: *quarantine*, haan a palubosan nga rumuar ti tao o banag gapu ta addaan daytoy iti sakit a makaacar

Quarrel mag-away, mag-alitan, maglabanan, basag-ulo; Iloc: agapa, agringgoran, agrin-niri, aglaban

Quarrelsome palaaway, nanggugulo, mapaglaban, basagulero; Iloc: mannaki-apa, mangrirriro, mannakilaban, mannakiribribok, agrir-riri
Synonym
Contentious *adj.,* **Contention** *n.* madaling makipagdiscusyon o maki-pagsagutan o makipag-away; Iloc: nadaras a makipagdiscusyonan o maki-apa o makipagsungbatan

Quarter isa sa mga apat na magkakaparehong dami gaya ng 25 centimo sa piso; Iloc: maysa cagagiti uppat nga agkakapareho ti kaadu casla 25 centavo iti pisos

Quarterly tuwing tatlong buwan sa isang taon; Iloc: cada tallo bulan ti maysa a tawen

Quash 1] otorisasyong ipahinto at ipagbawal o fuersang sugpoin, 2] i-controlado-*Sp* ang galaw, damdamin pati pananabik, 3] ipagbawal ang pagpapapahayag, 4] sa larangan ng medicina ay pagpahinto ng pagdudugo, pagubo at iba pa

QUASI nagkakahawig, nagkakatulad, nagkakaanyo

QUASI- halos pero hindi talaga, nakakahawig lamang pero hindi talaga

Quaver nanginginig ng husto; nangangatal na magsalita; kumacanta na parang nanginginig o iba-iba ang *pitch*

Queasy nasusuka; Iloc: makasarsarwa
Correlated words
Nauseous nakakalula; Iloc: makasarwa
Seasickness hilo at nalulula; Iloc: maulaw ken makasarwa

Airsickness hilo at nalulula; Iloc: maulaw ken makavacuar

Vomit magsuka, sumuka, lumula; Iloc: agsarwa, agvacuar

Queen *(Tag. & Iloc.)* reyna-*Sp*

Queer kakaiba sa caraniwan ang ichura o asal; Iloc: sabali iti cadawyan ti ichura wenno garaw

Quell 1] sugpoin o patigilin ang gulo; lupigin at talonin ang kagulohan; 2] papayapin ang taong nagdurusa o nababalisa

Quench 1] mangpatid-uhaw, bigyan ng kasiyahan ang pananabik ng damdamin; 2] sugpoin ang sunog

Querulous *(Tag. & Iloc.)* reclamador-a*Sp*

Quest paghahanap; Iloc: pagbirok

QUESTION tanong; Iloc: saludsod

QUESTION someone about a possible infraction *(Tag. & Iloc.)* citain (cita-*Sp*)

Questionable nakakaduda ang saysay o kahalagahan o otorisasyon-*Sp*, nakakaduda ang katapatan, moralidad-*Sp*

Queue 1] nakapila o nakalinya na mga taong naghihintay ng canilang torno; nakalinyang mga *computer data* para madaling makuha; 2] buhok na nakatirintas

Quibble pagsisinungaling o nagdadahilan; nagpapalusot sa argumento para makaiwas ng responsibilidad-*Sp* o *self-accountability* kaya nag-sisinungaling o lumilihis siya sa paggamit ng hindi relevanteng diwa

QUICK agad-agad, mabilis, matuling, madali, listo-*Sp*; Iloc: napardas, nadaras, napartak, alisto-*aSp*

QUICK on the uptake madaling makaintindi at makatugma sa ibig sabihin ng mga bagay-bagay

Quiddity *[kwid-i-tee]* **or Haecceity** *[hek-ci-ye-tee]* ang katangian na nagbubuo ng isang bagay; ang naturalesa ng isang bagay

Quilescent nagpapahinga, payapa, tahimik, hindi kumikilos; kusa na pinapabayaang hindi activo ang sarili

Quiet tahimik; Iloc: naulimek

Antonym

Noisy maingay, nakakabingi; Iloc: natagari, nariri, naringgor, naariwawa

Quilt cubrecama-*Sp* o sobrecama-*Sp* na *bedspread* o pantakip ng cama o catre na may dalawang patong na tela na may malambot na panloob sa pagitan ng dalawang tela; pangkumot kapag natutulog o magpasarap sa loob nito habang nakahiga lalo na kung malamig ang panahon

Quintessence *n.*, **Quintessential** *adj.* pinakatamang halimbawa; Iloc: pinakausto nga ehemplo-*Sp*
Correlated words
Good role model uliran; Iloc: nasayaat nga ehemplo
Ideal tinuturing na pinakamabuti at pinakamagaling kaya ginagawang pamantayan o huwaran ng kabutihan
Exemplary uliran; Iloc: nasayaat nga ehemplo
Paragon halimbawa ng pagkaperfecto ng isang bagay; Iloc: ehemplo ti pagkaperfecto ti maysa a banag

Quip matalinong pangungusap; Iloc: nasirib a comentario-*Sp*

Quirk kakatwa o hindi pangkaraniwang gawa, asal, custombre-*Sp* o kagawian o personalidad-*Sp*; ang hindi inaasahang pangyayari o kahihinatnan gaya ng *quirk of fate*

Quit magbitiw, tumiwalag; Iloc: umikkat
Synonym
Resign magbitiw, tumiwalag; Iloc: umikkat

Quitclaim pagbitiw o pagsuko sa *claim* o pag-angkin ng ari-arian at ng karapatan dito na ito ay *formal* na pagtalikod sa angking bagay; paglipat lahat ng sariling *interest* o kapakinabangan o *benefit* na gaya ng lote na *real estate* lalo na kung walang hawak na titulong garantiya

Quiver nanginginig, nangangatog; Iloc: agtigerger

Quixotic 1] simbuyo/*urge*, pabigla-bigla at golpeng pabara-bara; 2] nakatuon sa hindi makatotohanang *optimism* o malarosas na uma-asa, at makabayani at *idealistic* dahil may matataas na principio-*Sp* kapareho ni Don Quixote

Quiz pagsusulit; Iloc: pangsukimat

Quorum kinakailangan ang tinakdang bilang ng mga miembro-*Sp* ng grupo-*Sp* o organisasyon-*Sp* na obligadong (obligado-*Sp*) dumadalo sa pagtitipon bago sumapit ang makabatas na *transaction* ng negocio-*Sp*

Quota kung gaano kadami ang dapat ibigay o gaano kadami ang dapat abutin na paninda; Iloc: nu kasano kaadu ti mabalin nga ited wenno mano ti masapul nga abotin nga ilaco

Quotation mga hinangong mahahalagang mensahe-*Sp* ng mga dakila o matatalinong tao; Iloc: dagiti inadaw nga napateg nga mensahe nga insarita dagiti natan-uk o nasirib a tattao
Correlated words
Adage kasabihan, kawikaan, salawikain; Iloc: pagsasarita a makapabang-ar wenno mangpaleksion, popular a kungkuna
Bon mot intelihenteng kasabihan; Iloc: nasirib a bagbaga
Cite sipiin; Iloc: adawen ti popular o nasirib a sarita tapno maiyusar iti pagsurat o pagtungtong
Maxim kasabihan, kawikaan, salawikain; Iloc: pagsasarita a makapabang-ar wenno mangpaleksion, popular a kungkuna
Quote sipiin ang mga salitang nakakabigay ng leksion-*Sp*; Iloc: adawen ti popular-*Sp* o nasirib a sarita tapno maiyusar iti pangleksion, pagsurat o pagtungtong

R

Rabbit *(Tag. & Iloc.)* coneho-*Sp*
RACE *(Tag. & Iloc.)* lahi, *race*
RACE, Running competition magcarerehan, *running a race*; Iloc: agcareraan, aglumba, *running a race*
Racial discrimination pagtuturing na mababa o masama ang tao/ grupo/ lahi at ipawalang-pansin ang pagkahalaga nila; Iloc: bigbigen a nababa wenno dakes ti tao/ grupo/lahi ken haan nga bigbigen ti valor da
RACK 1] *cabinet* na lagayan ng mga gamit o mga pang-*display*, 2] paglagyan ng mga pagkain ng mga hayop, 3] napakasakit na kalagayan ng katawan; Iloc: 1] *cabinet* a pangicabilan ti maar-aramat o dagiti pang-*display* ida, 2] pangicabilan iti kanen iti animal ida, 3] nakasaksakit a ricricnaen iti bagi
RACK up magpadami ng bilang o mga gamit; Iloc: agpaadu ti bilang wenno maar-aramat
Racket 1] pamalo sa *tennis ball*; 2] biglang ingay, 3] negosiong labag sa batas

Racketeer taong nanghuhothot ng pera o sumusuhol, nangkikikil o nambabanta kung hindi ibigay ang pera, nagpapautang na may napakataas na *interest rate*, at iba pang gawaing hindi makabatas

RADAR paraan para sundin ang kilos o malaman ang clima-*Sp* o *aircraft* at kung saan ito, ang bilis, at itchura na pinapakita sa alon ng radyo o *radio waves*

RADAR, off the (or not on the radar) hindi alam o hindi tinuturing, hindi pinapansin

RADAR, on the nasasaisip o nalalaman ito

RADAR, under the nagsasagawa na walang nakakahalata at nakakaalam ng canyang ginagawa

Radiatte sumisikat, kumikislap, sumisinag, nagniningning; Iloc: sumilsilap, agranranyag, agkirkirap

Radical 1] sobrang tindi kung gagawa ng pagbabago mula sa kagawian o caraniwang forma; pinapanigan ang marahas na reforma sa politico o economia o panlipunan; 2] taong sumusunod ng malakas na paniniwala o napakalabis na *ideology*; taong tamataguyod ng pampolitico, pang-economia o panlipunang reforma na ayaw makipagkasundo o makipagcompromiso

Radio *(Tag. & Iloc.)* *radio*

Radish labanos; Iloc: rabanos-*Sp*

Raft *(Tag. & Iloc.)* balsa-*Sp*

Rag trapo-*Sp*, basahan; Iloc: trapo, nisnis

Rage poot o galit na matindi at hindi controlado; Iloc: rungsot a napalalo ken uyong nga haan a controlado

Raid lihim at biglang panlulusob; Iloc: palimed ken dagdagos ken nafuersa a pagserrek ken pag-aresto

Railway *(Tag. & Iloc.)* riles ng tren-*Sp*

Rain ulan; Iloc: tudo
  Correlated words
  Downpour malakas na ulan; Iloc: napigsa nga tudo
  Storm, Typhoon *(Tag. & Iloc.)* bagyo
  Drizzle ambon; Iloc: arbis
  Hurricane napakalakas na bagyo; Iloc: nakapigpigsa nga bagyo
  Torrent *n,,* **Torrential** *adj.* ulan o agos ng ilog na napakalakas; Iloc: tudo wenno pagayos ti carayan nga nakapigpigsa

Rainbow bahaghari; Iloc: bullalayaw

Raincoat *(Tag. & Iloc.)* capote-*Sp*

Rainy maulan; Iloc: agkaratudo, agtudtudo

RAISE iyangat, ipataas, itaas; Iloc: ipangato, isagpat, isang-at

RAISE in pay *(Tag. & Iloc.)* omento-*Sp*

RAISE some eyebrows sa hindi kanais-nais na asal niya o salita niya, ito ay nakapagpanganga ng bibig at nakakapagtaas ng kilay dahil sa sindak, gulat o disgusto-*Sp*

Raisins *(Tag. & Iloc.)* pasas-*Sp*

Rake calaykay; Iloc: caraykay

Rally 1] pag-ipon-ipon ng mga tao para suportahan ang isang layonin, 2] biglang pagbabalik sa kahusayan ang economiya-*Sp*, 3] biglang pagbabalik sa kalusogan o kasayahan sa buhay; Iloc: 1] agiipon ti tattao tapno suportaan ti maysa a pakay, 2] golpe-*Sp* a pagsubli ti pagsayaat ti economiya, 3] golpe a pagsubli ti salun-at o ragsak ti biag

Ram banggahin, bunggohin; Iloc: banggaen, bunggoen

Ramification *n.*, **Ramify** *v.* 1] maghati-hati at maglaganap ng iba't ibang sanga; 2] magyabong o magbunga ng complicadong kahihinatnan

Ramp calzadang papasok sa *freeway* o labasan ng *freeway*; Iloc: calzada nga sumrek diay *freeway* wenno rumuar iti *freeway*

Rampage biglang marahas o magulong labanan

Rampant laganap at madalas na nagaganap; Iloc: canayon a maar-aramid ken iti adu a lugar-*Sp*

Ranch *(Tag. & Iloc.)* rancho-*Sp*, hacienda-*Sp*

Random basta lamang mangyari kahit walang tinakdang oras-*Sp* o fecha-*Sp* o tao o lugar-*Sp* at kung minsan ni rason-*Sp*; Iloc: basta laeng maaramid uray nu awan indesignar-*Sp* nga oras o fecha o tao o lugar ken pasaray ni rason

Range laki, lawak, iba't ibang categoria-*Sp*, mga serye-*Sp*, sacop, solar-*Sp*

RANK *(Tag. & Iloc.)* ranko-*Sp*

RANK-and-file sa *military*, sila ang mga sundalo maliban lamang ang mga pinuno; sa oficina-*Sp*, sila ang mga empleyado-*Sp* maliban lamang ang mga pinuno

Ransack halughogin; Iloc: ukag-ukagen, agsuksukain

Ransom pantubos sa kinidnap na tao; Iloc: pangsubbot iti kinidnap nga tao

RAPE gahasa; Iloc: aradas

RAPE offender *How do you spend your time? Is it watching porno-graphy on videos, movies or TV? or reading pornography books? or exchanging sexual encounters with friends? or looking at women with sexual thoughts in your mind? So when you rape somebody as the <u>end product of your focus on pornography and uncontrolled libido</u> that you get imprisoned for it, <u>was it worth it</u>? Of course, the answer is a big **NO!** because <u>it is not only jail time that will be imposed on you</u>, but you will also be <u>listed and regarded</u> as a sex offender throughout your lifetime, and after jail time, you are considered a <u>persona non grata</u> (**outcast**) in job employments and among your friends, and realize that you have also brought shame onto your family. No one will like you working at their business office, and no decent person will want you to be his/her friend. Consider that if the person who was raped was your sister or your mother or your daughter, would you like that? It is such a pitiful and offensive assault on the victim of a rape, isn't it? Nowadays, girls and women are now empowered to come to court have the rapist be imprisoned for many years. **Be a real man** because taking advantage of girls just because females are weaker than man shows that you are <u>not a real man but a coward and an obnoxious opportunist</u>. **A real man is a gentleman who protects the weak and respects girls and women**. So stay away from pornography and transform your thoughts **mainly** into pursuing decency and uprightness through a relationship with God, and using your energy to get a college degree, and to live a decent, honorable, and productive life that you yourself will be proud of, as well as your family who loves you and wishes the best life for you.*

RAPE Prevention *there are many good, moral and decent men who are righteous in character, in principles and in deeds, but a few are **not** who use their strong libido (sex drive) to sexually assault women. Women are not always aware that there is one dissimilarity between a man and a woman that may be risky and this is a man's strong libido. <u>So females must take precautions so that they are out-of-the-way from sexually-inclined daredevil men and far-off from being sexually assaulted. Women should find out the character of a</u>*

*man before trusting him to go on solo dates. Women should avoid men who are fresh and take liberties on women because they are **not** decent and moral. Group-dating or with a chaperon is a good practice. Unfortunately, when a woman is raped, she feels damaged and dirty, while some mean people who come to know about the rape, one-sidedly disparage and humiliate her **unfairly.*** Maraming babae ay walang kamalay-malay na may pagkaka-iba ang pagkatao ng lalake sa babae. Maraming mababait na lalake pero dapat mag-ingat at lumayo ang babae sa makasarili, malibog at mapag-oportunista na lalake dahil mas malakas ang *libido* ng lalake. Mas mahina rin sa katawan ang babae na puedeng malupig at mapabagsak siya ng lalake. Kaya makipag-*date* ng grupo o may *chaperon* para mas ligtas, kaysa sa makipag-*date* ng *solo* lamang. Kung sa kasamaang-palad ay nagahasa (*raped*) ka, natural na napasakit sa loob mo na pinagsamantalahan ka at iniisip mo na *damaged* ka na at marumi pa. Natural ang pagdamdam mo, pero iwaksi ang isip na iyan dahil pinilit ka lamang at hindi mo nakayanang iligtas ang sarili mo dahil sa kalakasan ng nanggahasa sa iyo. Huwag ring sisihin ang sarili mo dahil wala kang kamuang-muang na mangyayari iyon sa iyo - ikaw ay sinupil. May mga babaeng kapareho sa dinanas mo kaya sinusuplong nila ito sa batas para huliin ang salarin, at maculong sa preso. Kahit nangyari iyan sa iyo, magpatuloy kang mamuhay ng **maprogreso at decente** – namuhay kang **may moralidad at integridad** dahil dito mo maibalik ang kalakasan ng loob mo. At mula diyan ay **mag-iingat ka nang** pumili ng napakabuting mga kaibigan at kasama, lalo na ang magiging kabiyak mo sa buhay, habang pinagdarasal mo ang tulong at *protection* ng Dios.

Rapid mabilis; Iloc: napardas

Rapport dalawang tao o mahigit pa diyan na pare-parehong mag-kapalagayang-loob sa isa'isa; Iloc: dua a tao o mas adu pay ti dua nga agpapada da a nanam-ay ti panagricricna da cada maysa canyada

Rapt abala, subsob, buhos na buhos sa ginagawa; Iloc: nakasubsob ti ar-aramiden

Rapture espiritual na kasayahan sa pagpunta na sa langit; Iloc: espiritual a ragsak a pagpapanen idiay langit

Rare kaunti, bihira madalang, matumal; Iloc: bassit, man-mano, sagpaminsan

RASH, Reckless *(Tag. & Iloc.)* bara-bara

RASH and daring *(Tag. & Iloc.)* atrevido/da-*Sp*

RASH on skin butlig-butlig; Iloc: supot-supot

Rasp, File kikil; Iloc: kikir

Rat daga; Iloc: bao

Rather kaysa sa; Iloc: ngem ti

Ratify aprovahan at bigyan ng otorisasyon-*Sp* para maging valido-*Sp*; Iloc: aprovaran ken ikkan ti otorisasyon para agbalin a valido (aprova/ aprovar-*Sp*)

Ration *(Tag. & Iloc.)* rasyon-*Sp*

Rational 1] ginagamit ang abilidad niya sa pagrason, 2] may matinong pag-iisip, may *logic* ang pag-iisip at pagtuturing niya; Iloc: 1] iyus-usar na ti abilidad na ti pagrason, 2] adda sirib ti pagpampanunot na, adda *logic* ti pagbigbig na

Rattan yantok; Iloc: uway

Ravage marahas na pagsisira at pagnakaw ng lahat-lahat na ari-arian

Ravine bangin sa lambak (*valley*) na may ilog sa baba; Iloc: derraas diay bantay nga adda carayan idiay baba na

RAW hilaw, mapakla, hindi luto, hindi hinog; Iloc: naata, naganus, nasugpet, haan a naluto, haan a naluom

RAW deal *unfair* o madaya, hindi mabuting turing at hindi makatarungan sa pakikipag-ugnay o sa gawain

RAW fish served for eating *(Tag. & Iloc.)* sushi
Correlated words
Half-cooked meat relished by guys during their wine or beer session kilaw; Iloc: kilaw, kilawen

Ray sinag; Iloc: sinamar

Raze gibain, guhoin; Iloc: rakraken, rebbaen, marbaen

Razor labaha; Iloc: labahita

REACH, Arrive makarating, nakasapit, nakaabot; Iloc: makadanon, makasangpet

REACH for abutin; Iloc: abuten, gaw-aten

Reachable naaabut; Iloc: maabut, magaw-at

React *v.,* **Reaction** *n.* pagtugon sa kahalobilo dahil sa pinahayag sa canya na salita o asal; Iloc: pagsubalit iti kapatang na gapu iti impaammo canyana a sarita wenno tignay

Reactive napapakilos o nasasalat ang damdamin; nagkakaroon ng efecto sa damdamin o sa pagkilos

Read magbasa; Iloc: agbasa

READY handa na, preparado-*Sp*; Iloc: sisasagana, nakasaganan, preparado, nakarubwaten

READY, get maghanda, mag-prepara-*Sp*; Iloc: agsagana, agrubwat, ag-preparar-*Sp*

REAL tunay, totoo, husto-*Sp*; Iloc: pudno, agpayso, usto

REAL estate bahay o gusali at lupa; Iloc: balay, *building* o facilidad-*Sp* ken daga

Reality katotohanan, katunayan; Iloc: kaagpaysoan, kapudnoan

REALIZE mamulat ang mata, maunawaang-lubos; Iloc: malawlawagan ti pagawat
Correlated words
Learned a lesson after an eye-opening experience *(Tag. & Iloc.)* natuto ng husto, nadala na

REALIZE a goal naisakatuparan, natupad, naisagawa, nayari; Iloc: naytungpal, naaramid, nayturpos,
Correlated word
Materialize maisakatuparan, magkatutuo, magbunga; Iloc: agbunga, agbalin, agturpos

REALLY tutuong-tutuo; Iloc: agpaypayso

REALLY? Tutuo?, Talaga? Iloc: Agpayso?, Cadi?, Talaga?

Realm larangan; Iloc: solar-*Sp*, minoyongan, larangan

Realpolitik ginaganap ang puesto niya sa politico batay sa kapangyarihan, hindi sa *ideals*; pagkaoportunista at marahas siya sa trabaho niyang *public affairs,* imbes na batay sa etico at moralidad

Realty *see Real Estate*

Reap mag-ani, gapasin; Iloc: agani, aggapas, agapit

Rear 1] palakihin ang bata, 2] likod; Iloc: 1] padakkelen ti ubing, 2] likod

Reason rason-*Sp*, dahilan, sanhi; Iloc: rason

Reasonable makatwiran; Iloc: nalinteg

Reassure bigyan ng prueba-*Sp* para makita ang katotohanan; Iloc: ikkan ti prueba tapno makita iti kaagpaysoanan

Rebate isauli ang parte-*Sp* ng binayad gaya ng discuento-*Sp;* Iloc: isubli ti parte ti binayad casla ti discuento

Rebel *(Tag. & Iloc.)* rebelde-*Sp*

Rebellion *rebellion*, paghihimagsik; Iloc: *rebellion*, pagsupring, pag-alsa

Rebound tumalbog dahil sa malakas na salpok o *impact*; gumaling o manumbalik ang lakas at lusog ng katawan; manumbalik ang pag-asa pagkatapos ng pagkabigo; tumalbog ang bala sa mismo na nagpaputok o kaya *backlash o counter attack* sa nagkusang gumawa ng masama

Rebuff ayawan, laitin; Iloc: agmadi, laisen

Rebuke pagalitan, pagsabihan, sermonan; Iloc: ungtan, agunget, correhiren (correhir-Sp), bagbagaan sermonan

Rebuttal pabulaanan sa argumento-*Sp* o debate-*Sp*; Iloc: ipalibak iti argumento o debate

Recall 1] gunitain, isipin, tandaan, 2] pagpahayag ng *manufacturer* na ibalik ang nilikha nilang producto-*Sp* dahil may defecto-*Sp*; Iloc: 1] lagipen, tandaan, 2] ipablaac iti *manufacturer* nga isubli iti imparnuay da nga producto ta adda defecto na

Recant iyurong, bawiin ang sinabi; Iloc: ibabawi ti sinao
Synonyms
Retract bawiin ang sinabi; Iloc: ibabawi ti sinao
Renege on a promise pagtalikod sa pangako; Iloc: babalawen ti kari, haan nga agtungpal iti ingkari na
Antonym
True to one's words tinutupad ang canyang promesa; Iloc: agtungtungpal iti ingkari na

Recap *n.,* **Recapitulate** *v.* sumarya-*Sp,* maikling pang-ulit sa binalita; Iloc: sumarya, ababa a pang-ulit iti kaybagbaga a damag

Recede 1] kumokonti, 2] paurong na papalayo; Iloc: 1] kumiskissay, 2] agatras nga agpaadayo

Receipt *(Tag. & Iloc.)* recibo-*Sp*

Receive tanggapin; Iloc: awaten

Recently kamakailan lamang, di pa natatagalan, kagaganap lamang; Iloc: nabiit pay laeng, kapaspasamak laeng

Recession humina ang galaw ng economiya-*Sp*; Iloc: kimmapsot ti garaw ti economiya

Recidivate *v.,* **Recidivism** *n.* pagbabalik sa dating gawi lalo na sa gawing crimen-*Sp*; Iloc: pagsubli iti dati nga aramid lallalo iti pagka-*criminal*
Correlated word
   Backslide pagbalik sa mali o masamang gawa; Iloc: pagsubli iti haan nga usto o iti dakes nga aramid

Recipe *recipe*, paraan ng pagluto; Iloc: *recipe*, padalan nu casano ti pagluto

Reciprocal pasasalamat na pagganti sa pinakitang kagandahang-loob; Iloc: pagyaman nga pagsubalit iti impakita nga asi o pagimbagan

Reciprocate gantihan ng magkasingbuti o higit pang mabuti sa natanggap pero kung hindi caya, ang taos-puso na pasasalamat ay sapat at kasiya-siya na; Iloc: agsubalit iti cas kaimbag wenno mas naimbag pay ngem iti naawat, ngem nu haan na cabalinan ket iti napusoan a pagyam-yaman ket umanayen ken nakaliwliwa pay

Recital 1] palabas ng mga estudiante-*Sp* sa musica-*Sp* at sayaw, 2] *formal* na pagbasa ng tula o *poetry*; Iloc: 1] pabuya ida ti estudiante iti musica ken pagsala, 2] *formal* a pagbasa ti daniw o *poetry*

Reckless barumbado-*aSp;* padalus-dalos; Iloc: bara-bara, barumbado

Reckon magbilang o magsuma, magturing o magpalagay; Iloc: agbilang wenno agsumar, mangbigbig wenno mangpagarup

Reckoning 1] pagbilang o pagsuma; 2] *statement* kung ano at magkano ang babayaran; 3] ang pagbabayad ng utang o kasalanan *(i.e., day of reckoning)*

Reclusive gustong mag-isa at ayaw makihlobilo sa mga tao; Iloc: cayat na ti agmaymaysa ken madi na ti makilaok iti tattao ida

RECOGNIZE, Acknowledge kilalanin, ituring; Iloc: bigbigen, akuen

RECOGNIZE, Identify mamukhaan, makilala; Iloc: maylasin, mabigbig

Recognition pagkilala, pagturing; Iloc: panangbigbig, panglasin,

Recoil 1] mapaatras dahil sa disgusto o takot o pandidiri, 2] ang pag-talbog ng baril kung minsan sa pagpaputok; Iloc: 1] mapaatras gapu ti disgusto o buteng o aryek, 2] pagtalbog ti paltug nu dadduma nu ipaltoog

Recollect *v.,* **Recollection** *n.* gunitain, isipin, tandaan; Iloc: lagipen

Recommend i-recomenda-*Sp*; Iloc: i-recomendar-*Sp*
Synonym

Suggest imungkahi; Iloc: isingasing

Recommendation recomendasyon-*Sp*, mungkahi, panukala; Iloc: recomendasyon, singasing

Recompense compensasyon-*Sp*, perang bayad o perang pantumbas sa ginawang trabaho o pinakitang kagandahang-loob; Iloc: compensasyon, cuarta a bayad o cuarta a tangdan ti inaramid a trabaho o ti impakita a kaimbagan

Reconcile magkaayusan, magkasundoan, magbalikan; Iloc: agsubli iti pagcacaduaan o paggagayyeman wenno paginnayan-ayatan da manen

Recondite labis sa ordinaryong kaalaman o pag-intindi; kaunti ang nakakaalam dahil malalim at mahirap intindihan

Reconnaissance pangunahing *survey* o panaliksik ng isang lugar-*Sp*; Iloc: umuna a *survey* o pangsukimat iti maysa a solar-*Sp*

Record 1] informasyon-*Sp* ng tao na nakatala, 2] rehistro-*Sp*, 3] i-*tape* o itala/*record*/*list* ang sinabi o palabas sa pamamagitan ng *magnetic recorder* para marinig ulit o mapanood; Iloc: 1] informasyon ti tao a nakasurat iti *file*, 2] rehistro, 3] i-*tape* ti bagbaga o pabuya nga iyusar ti *magnetic recorder* tapno denggen wenno buyaen manen

Recount 1] icuento, isalaysay; ipahayag isa-isa kasama ang mga detalye-*Sp*; 2] bilangin ulit gaya ng mga *ballots*; Iloc: 1] agistoria; agisawang cada maysa contodo-*Sp* dagiti detalye; 2] bilangen manen casla dagiti balota

Recourse 1] bumaling sa iba para humingi ng tulong o *protection* sa iba; tao o samahan na pumayag tumulong o nagtanggol; 2] pagbaling sa kinakailangang *support* at kahalili; Iloc: pumadas iti dadduma para dumawat iti salaknib ken tulong; *option, alternative*

RECOVER bawiin, mabawi; Iloc: maysubli, maala manen, maybabawi

RECOVER health gumaling at bumalik ang lusog; Iloc: umimbag ken nagsubli ti salun-at ken caradcad

RECOVER an investment *(Tag. & Iloc.)* masulit

Recreation libangan at aliwan pagkatapos ng pagsisikap; Iloc: paglinglingayan o pagrambakan palpas ti pagpakpakat

Recruit *verb*: mangasiwa sa paghanap at paghimok ng bagong kasapi, kaanib, manlalaro, estudiante at iba pa; pagtanggap ng mga bagong miembro para mag-servicio sa hukbo; *noun:* bagong *enlisted* o *drafted* na miembro ng *armed forces*

Rectangle rectangulo-*Sp*, formang <u>pahiga</u> at may apat na sulok at dinding; Iloc: rectangulo, forma-*Sp* nga <u>naca-idda</u> ken adda uppat a suli ken diding na
Correlated word
Square *(Tag. & Iloc.) square,* cuadrado na parepareho ang sukat sa lahat ng panig

Rectify itama, ayosin, itumpak, ituwid, i-balanse-*Sp*, i-remedio-*Sp*

Rectum puwit, tumbong; Iloc: ubet, kimmut

Recuperate nagpapagaling, nagpapalakas, bumabalik na naman sa kalusogan; Iloc: agim-imbag, aglalaeng, agsay-sayaat, agsubli manen iti salun-at ken caradcad

Recur muling maganap, maulit na naman; Iloc: mapasamak manen, agulit manen

Recurring pabalik-balik; Iloc: agsubli-subli

Recuse umurong o mag-*withdraw* sa puesto ng paghahatol para maiwasan ang pagkawari o pagkawangis ng pagkampi o pagpapanig (*prejudice or partiality*)

Recycle pagsama-samahin ang mga panapon na mga papel-*Sp*, carton-*Sp*, bote at delata-*Sp* at ihiwalay sa basura at ilagay ang mga ito sa *recycling bin* o hakotin at dalhin ang mga ito sa *recycling center* para hindi naaaksaya at nasasayang sa paggamit pa muli na ikabubuti ng buong mundo-*Sp* at lahat ng nilalang

RED pula, *red*; Iloc: nalabbaga, nalabbasit, *red*

RED tape ang kawalan ng asecaso sa kinakailangang gawin kaya hindi natatapos sa tinakdang fecha dahil sa katamaran, pag-antala o pagpaliban; Iloc: awanan ti pag-asecaso iti masapul nga aramiden isu nga haan a maypalpas iti inkeddeng a fecha gapu iti pagkasadot, pangtaktak ken pangyur-uray inton makaganas nga agobra
Correlated word
Lag atrasado o nahuhuli parati at hindi makahabol sa tinakdang oras o fecha para tapusin dahil mabagal siya

Redact gawing panliteratura, umaka o sumulat ng mabuti para sa publicidad-*Sp*; i-*edit* o iwasto, ayosin o pagbutihin ang text bago ang paglathala o *publication*

Redeem tubosin; Iloc: subboten

682

Redeemer Dios Anak na si Hesu Cristo na ating *redeemer* at tagapagligtas sa lahat ng nilalang para hindi ang mga nilalang ay maparusahan sa kanilang mga kasalanan sa infierno. Sa awa ng Dios, si Dios Anak na si Hesu Cristo ang tumanggap ng parusa sa kasalanan ng sanlibutan para hindi maparusahan ang mga nilalang sa mga kasalanan nila. Sa pagmamahal ng Dios, Siya ang nagtiis sa paghahahaplit ng latigo sa Canya, paglait-lait, pagdura-dura, paglait-lait sa Canya, pagsampal-sampal at pagcorona ng masasakit na tinik sa Canya, at pagkatapos ay pinabuhat sa Canya ang mabigat na cruz papunta sa bundok ng Calvario kung saan Siya doon ipinako sa mismong cruz na binuhat Niya. Ang sinomang manalig, maniwala, magtiwala at magsampalataya na ang sacrificio ng Dios Hesu Cristo ay para sa kaligtasan ng lahat ng tao at tanggapin niya si Hesu Cristo sa puso't buhay niya bilang Dios niya at Tagapagligtas niya, siya'y mapatawad at malinisan na ng dugo ni Hesu Cristo sa cruz sa lahat ng canyang mga kasalanan at makakapunta na siya sa langit. Hindi mawawala ang kaligtasang ito na pinaghirapan ng Dios sa atin pero magpacumbaba tayo sa Dios sa pagsisisi ng lahat nating mga kasalanan at icumpisal mga ito sa Dios, at pagkatapos icumpisal muli tuwing nagkakasala tayo, kahit napatawad at nalinisan na lahat ng ating mga kasalanan ng dugo ng Dios Hesu Cristo sa cruz.

Reddish mapula-pula; Iloc: labbasit

Redress 1] maginhawang remedio-*Sp* sa paghihirap, 2] paraan at posibilidad-*Sp* na makakuha ng remedio-*Sp*, 3] compensasyon-*Sp* sa canyang sacuna at ang nawala sa canya; Iloc: 1] nabang-ar a remedio para maawanan iti rigat, 2] pangdalan nga posibilidad nga makaala ti remedio, 3] compensasyon iti pagkadisgracia na ken iti napukaw canyana

Reduce paliitin, pakontihin, mag-menos-*Sp*, tanggalan; Iloc: pabassitin, agmenos, kissayan

Redundant paulit-ulit at napakahabang pagpaliwanag o pagpahayag; Iloc: iyulit-ulit ken nakaat-atiddog nga pangilawlawag ken pangpaammo

Reek mabahong amoy, umaalingasaw, umaalisangsang; Iloc: angot a nabangsit ken umal-alingasaw pay

Reel gumulong; aparato na pangpulopot; Iloc: agkarolig; aparato nga pangpusipos o pangcawicaw/cunikon

Reeling humapay-hapay o ugoy-ugoy habang nakatayo o mapatomba dahil sa hilo, pagkalasing o pagkasuntok sa canya

Refer 1] maghanap o magsangguni sa libro o sa *online* ng mga kinakailangang malaman, 2] tumutukoy sa tao o bagay; Iloc: 1] biroken o agconsulta cadagiti libro o idiay *online* ti makasapulan nga informasyon, 2] mangigapu iti tao wenno banag

Referee *referee*, tagahatol sa pangcompetensiang laro; Iloc: tagahusgar iti pang-competensia-*Sp* nga ay-ayam

References *reference* o recomendasyon-*Sp* tungkol sa katangian o kahalagahan o pagka-calificado-*Sp* ng kakilala na tao na nagbubuhat sa nangrecomenda-*Sp* na puedeng makakatulong ito sa pagtanggap sa canya sa trabaho-*Sp*.

Correlated words

Put in a good word magpahayag ng magandang salita tungkol sa isang tao para pangsuporta sa canya

Referral, doctor's ang *personal* na doctor ng paciente ay pinapadala siya sa ibang doctor - sa specialistang doctor na dalubhasa sa sakit nitong paciente para magamot ang paciente ng tama

Refill 1] lagyan o punoin na naman, 2] *refill* ng dati nang niresetang gamot na kukunin sa farmacia-*Sp*; Iloc: 1] cargaan wenno punwen manen, 2] *refill* ti dati a nayreseta nga agas nga alaen idiay farmacia

Refinance bagohin ang *mortgage* ng bahay para maging abot-kaya ang bayad tuwing buwan; Iloc: balbaliwan ti *mortgage* ti balay tapno maaramid nga abot-caya ti bayad cada-*Sp* bulan

Refined *(Tag. & Iloc.)* fino-*Sp*, pulido-*Sp*

Refinement finong-asal, salita at galaw, may yumi at delicadeza-*Sp*; Iloc: fino-*Sp* ang ugali ken tignay ken sarita, addaan delicadeza

Reflect 1] aninag o anino na larawan, 2] pagdili-dili sa isip kung ano ang tama o macaya o makakabuti

Reflection aninag; Iloc: anninaw

Reform magpakabuti sa pamamagitan ng pagtanggap ng kamalian niya para matanto ang sarili niyang pagkatao at ipasyaha niyang iwaksi ang canyang mga kasamaan; Iloc: agpakaimbag isu nga mang-acceptar-*Sp*

iti madi nga ugali na mismo tapno aglucat ti mata na iti usto a katatao na ken irangta na nga iwaksi dagiti dakes nga aramid na

Refrain pigilin o ipagkait sa sarili ang hindi makakatulong o hindi makakalusog para sa ikabubuti ng sariling niyang pagkatao; Iloc: ipagel ken ipaidam iti bagi iti haan a makatulong o haan a makasalun-at canyana para ti kaimbagan ti mismo a katatao na

Refresh magpa-refresco-*Sp*; Iloc: agpa-refresco

Refreshment pangrefresco, pamatid-uhaw; meryenda-a*Sp*; Iloc: inumin nga pangikkat ti uwaw; meryenda

REFUGE, give, Shelter *v.* cupcopin, canlongin; Iloc: ipa-camang

REFUGE, seek maghanap ng masilongan niya; Iloc: agsapul ti pag-camangan na

REFUGE, Shelter pagsilongan; Iloc. pagcamangan, paglinongan

Refund binayad na isauli; Iloc: binayad nga isubli

Refuse tanggihan, magtutol, mag-ayaw, ayawan; Iloc: agsupyat, ag-madi, agsalangad

Refute pabulaanan sa pamamagitan ng evidencia-*Sp* o argumento-*Sp*; Iloc: manglibak nga mangipakita ti evidencia wenno makipag-argumento

REGAIN bawiin, mabawi; Iloc: ibabawi, maybabawi

REGAIN consciousness magkamalay, mataohan; Iloc: agsubli ti puot, agungar

Regard ituring, ibilang; Iloc: bigbigen, ibilang

Regarding tungkol sa, hinggil sa; Iloc: maypanggep iti, maypuon iti, maygapu iti, maypapan iti

Regime govierno-*Sp* na kasalukuyang naghahari sa isang bayan; Iloc: govierno nga madama nga agar-ari iti maysa nga bayan

Regimen mga hakbang o paraan sa pagpagamot o sa *training*; Iloc: dagiti addang wenno padalan iti pangngagas ken iti *training*

Region *(Tag. & Iloc.)* region

Register magpa-rehistro-*Sp*, magpa-lista-Sp, magpatala; Iloc: agparehistro, agpalista

Registration, Registry talaan, pagparehistrohan, pagpalistahan; Iloc: pagparehistroan, pagpalistaan

Regress *v.*, **Regression** *n.* 1] umatras, bumalik; 2] bumalik sa dati na mas mababa o *inferior* na estado-*Sp* o forma-*Sp* o modo-*Sp* na asal;

pagbabalik sa dating mas mababang clase, pag-iisip at katatao; paurong at pumapalayo sa pag-unlad at pagpapakabuti; Iloc: pagsubli iti dati a mas nababa a clase o panagpampanunot ken pagkatao; pa-atras-*Sp* nga umadayo iti progreso-*Sp* ken kaimbagan
Antonym

Upgrade mas pagbutihin ang pagkagawa, itaas ang *standard* Iloc: mas pasayaaten ti pagkaaramid; ingato ti *standard*

REGRET magsisi, manghinayang, ikalulongkot; Iloc: agbabawi
Synonyms

Contrite *adj.,* **Contrition** *n.* pagsisisi; Iloc: pagbabawi

Remorse *n.,* **Remorseful** *adj.* dahil meron siyang budhi o conciensia, nagsisisi at nababagabag siya sa canyang nagawang kasalanan; Iloc: gapu ta adda conciensia na, agbabbabawi ken haan isu a makatalna gapu iti naaramid na a basol

Repent *v.,* **Repentant** *adj.* magsisi, ikalulongkot; Iloc: agbabawi

Sorry magsisi, ikalulongkot; Iloc: agbabawi
Correlated words

Forgive patawarin; Iloc: pakawanen, dispensaren

Pardon *n.,* **Pardon** *v.* 1] pagpapatawad, 2] patawarin; Iloc: 1] dispensar, pagpakawan, 2] dispensaren, pakawanen

REGRET comes at the end "Sa huli ang sisi;" Iloc: "Diay udi iti pagbabawi"

Regular caraniwan, regular-*Sp,* ordinario-*Sp;* Iloc: cadawyan, regular, ordinario

Regulate ayosin para umandar o maging tama ang kalagayan; Iloc: tarimaanen tapno umandar o usto ti kasasaad

Regulation regulasyon, alituntunin, reglamento-*Sp;* batas, patakaran, pamamalakad, Iloc: regulasyon, reglamento, linteg
Synonym

Rules patakaran, pamamalakad; Iloc: pangpaturong, pangpadalan

Rehabilitate ipabalik ang kalusogan o mabuting pagpalakad ng buhay sa pamamagitan ng *therapy*

Rehabilitation, Rehab *(Tag. & Iloc.)* rehabilitasyon-*Sp,* lugar kung saan ipanumbalik ang kalusogan o sa mga may mga suliranin, ipanumbalik ang buhay na mahalaga at matuwid at makabatas o *lawful*

Rehearsal *(Tag. & Iloc.) rehearsal,* ensayo-*Sp*

Reign mamuno, maghari, mamayani, nangingibabaw, manaig; Iloc: agturay, agar-ari

Reimburse isauli ang binayad; Iloc: isubli ti ginastos
Synonym
Refund binayad na isauli; Iloc: binayad nga isubli

Reinstate ibalik sa dating puesto-*Sp* o kalagayan; Iloc: isubli ti sigud a puesto wenno kasasaad

Reject tanggihan, magtutol, mag-ayaw; Iloc: agmadi, agsupyat, agsalangad

Rejoice masayang pakiramdam, magpakasaya; Iloc: naragsak a ricna, agragsak

Rejoinder dagdag sa sinabi niya o ng sinabi ng iba; Iloc: nayon ti imbaga na wenno iti imbaga ti sabali

Rejuvenate sumisigla at may bagong liksi at kalusogan; Iloc: lumaplapsat ken adda baro a sagiksik ken salun-at

Relapse mabinat; Iloc: agbignat

Relate i-cuento-*Sp*; Iloc: i-storya-*Sp*

Related 1] kamag-anak; 2] kaugnay, pertinente-*Sp*; Iloc: 1] kabagyan; 2] umno, pertinente

Relation *(Tag. & Iloc.)* relasyon-*Sp*

RELATIONSHIP kaugnayan; Iloc: pagkarelasyon

RELATIONSHIP, harmonious pagkakasundo, maganda na pagsa-samahan; Iloc: natalna ken nasayaat nga pagkacaduaan

Related magkaugnay, magkamag-anak; Iloc: agkaconecta, agkabagyan

Relative kamag-anak; Iloc: kabagyan, parientes-*Sp*

Relatively kung icompara o ihambing sa iba; Iloc: nu icompara o iparis iti sabali

Relatives magkakamag-anak; Iloc: agkakabagyan
Correlated words
Kindred magkakamag-anak, *clan* o tribo na nanggaling sa parehong ninuno
Kinship coneksion sa pamamagitan ng dugo, casalan o pag-ampon, pagkarelasyon sa ugali o pagkatutubo o lahi
Affinity damidaming pagkakaugnay; Iloc: ricna a pagkakabsatan

Relax luwagan, ipahinga; Iloc: agpabang-ar, painanaen

Relaxing maginhawa, nakakapahinga; Iloc: makabang-ar, makapainana

RELEASE pakawalan, palayain; Iloc: pabulosan, ibulos

RELEASE from one's grip bitiwan; Iloc: ibbatan

Relevant pertinente-*Sp*, akma o may kaugnayan sa kasalukuyang pinag-uusapan o pangyayari; Iloc: pertinente o umno iti madama a pagsasaritaan o situasyon-*Sp*

Correlated words

Pertinent *(Tag. & Iloc.)* pertinente

Applicable aplicado, angkop, may kinalaman; Iloc: aplicado, umno, maytutop, adda pagkayarigan na

Appropriate akma, angkop, bagay; Iloc: umno, naytutop, us-usto

Germane pertinente, relevante at naangkop

Terse sagot o salita na maikli pero franka at tugma sa paksa; Iloc: sungbat wenno sarita nga ababa ngem franka ken umno iti punto ti pagsasaritaan

Suitable angkop, akma, bagay, relevante; Iloc: umno, agparbeng, relevante

Expedience *n.*, **Expedient** *adj.* nararapat o naaangkop o tugma sa isang layonin; tama o wasto para sa circumstancia; alinsunod sa gamit

Reliable mapagkakatiwalaang tutupdin ang canyang obligasyon-*Sp* at trabaho-*Sp* at ang pangako din niya ay maaasahan at mapapanaligan siya; Iloc: mapagtalkan nga tungpalen na iti obligasyon ken trabaho na ken iti incari na a manamnama ken mapagfiaran (fiar-*Sp*)

Relic bagay na natagpuan na galing sa panahong napakatagal nang lumipas; Iloc: banag a nadiscobre nga naggapu iti panawen nga nakabaybayagen a nag-pasar-*Sp*

RELIEF ginhawa, pahinga; Iloc: bang-ar, inana

RELIEF, sigh of buntong-hininga; Iloc: sennaay nga makabang-ar

RELIEVE paginhawain; Iloc: pabang-aran

RELIEVE someone from his work shift manghalili sa trabaho, mangrelyevo-*Sp*; Iloc: mangrelyevo o mangsukat o tagasublat isu iti trabaho,

Relieved naginhawaan, makapabuntong-hininga, gumaan ang kalooban; Iloc: nabang-aran, nakainana, limmag-an iti barucong na

Reliever, Alternate worker relyevo, kahalili; Iloc: relyevo, mangsublat

Religion *(Tag. & Iloc.) religion*, relihion-*Sp*

Relinquish isuko, bitiwan, iwanan, ipaubaya, talikdan; Iloc: isuko, ibbatan, panawan

Relocate lilipat, ilipat; Iloc: umacar, iyacar, agalis, iyalis

Rely umasa, mag-depende-*Sp*; Iloc: agdepende

Remain mamalagi, manatili; Iloc: agbati, agtalinaed, agfirmi-*Sp* ti sigud a lugar-*Sp*

Remainder tira; Iloc: tidda, natda

Remark magcomentario, punahin; Iloc: ag-comentario-*Sp*

Remedial nagbibigay ng remedio-*Sp*, anomang may defecto-*Sp* puede na maremediohan; Iloc: mangited ti remedio, mabalin a maremedioan

Remedy remedio-*Sp*, remediohan, lunasan; Iloc: remedio, iremedio, agasan

Remember maalaala, matandaan, magunita, alalahanin; Iloc: malagip, lagipen, tandaan

Synonyms

Reminisce gunitain, isipin, tandaan; Iloc: lagipen, tandaan

Retrospect gunitahin o sariwain ang mga nakaraan; Iloc: lagipen dagiti napalabas

Antonym

Forget malimutan, makaligtaan; Iloc: malipatan

Remembrance pang-alaala; Iloc: pakalaglagipan

Remind ipaalaala; Iloc: ipalagip

Reminder pangpaalaala; Iloc: pangpalagip

Reminisce gunitain, isipin, tandaan; Iloc: lagipen

Remiss pumalya sa dapat niyang gawin kahit obligasyon niya; Iloc: agliway iti masapul nga aramiden na pati obligasyon na

Remit magpadala ng cuarta; Iloc: agipaw-it ti cuarta

Remnant *(Tag. & Iloc.)* mga naiwang bagay; mga piraso

Remorse *n.*, **Remorseful** *adj.* dahil meron siyang budhi o conciensia-*Sp*, nagsisisi at nababagabag siya sa canyang nagawang kasalanan; Iloc: gapu ta adda conciensia na, agbabbabawi ken haan isu a makatalna gapu iti naaramid na a basol

Remote ilang na lugar-*Sp*, libliban; Iloc: adayo ken nakalinged a lugar

Remove alisin, tanggalin; Iloc: ikkaten

Remunerate compensasyon-*Sp*, perang bayad o perang pantumbas sa ginawang trabaho o kagandahang-loob; Iloc: compensasyon, cuarta a bayad o cuarta a tangdan ti inaramid a trabaho o ti impakita a kaimbagan

Renal tungkol sa bato o *kidney*; Iloc: maygapu iti biel

Rend punitin para maghiwalay; Iloc: pigisen tapno agsisina

Render pagkaloob o pagbigay ng servicio-*Sp* o paggaganap ng palabas; Iloc: pagaramid ti servicio o pag-presentar-*Sp* iti pabuya

Rendezvous tipanan; Iloc: pagsinnarakan

Rendition palabas sa entablado-*Sp* ng *drama*, musica-*Sp* ng mga instrumento-*Sp*, canta-*Sp*, o pagsasalin ng cuento-*Sp* buhat sa libro-*Sp*

Renegade 1] taong takasan o lisanan o talikuran ang partido-*Sp* niya para sumali sa iba; 2] traydor-*Sp* o rebelde-*Sp*

Renege pagtalikod sa pangako; Iloc: babalawen ti ingkari, haan na tungpalen ti kari na

Renew *v.,* **Renewal** *n.* mag-umpisa ulit o magpanibago na magparehistro-*Sp* ng licensia-*Sp* o contrata-*Sp*; magpanibagong ipagpatuloy ang *insurance policy* o ng contrata ng servicio-*Sp* o ng upa ng bahay o tindahan o sasakyan, o sa pakikipag-anib sa grupo-*Sp* o asosasyon-*Sp*; Iloc: baro manen nga pagparehistro ti licensia wenno ti contrata ken dadduma pay

Renounce itaboy, itakwil, hindi ituring; Iloc: ilaksid, haan a bigbigen

Renovate cumpunihin, ayosin at bagohin para manumbalik sa dati o mas mabuti pang kalagayan ng bahay o gusali o sasakyan; Iloc: tarimaanen, ayosin ken barbarwen tapno agsubli iti dati o mas nasaysayaat pay nga estado-*Sp*

Renown bantog, tanyag, kilala, sikat, popular-*Sp*; Iloc: popular, am-ammo ti amin o iti kaaduan a tao, natakneng

Rent *(Tag. & Iloc.)* arkila-*aSp*, renta-*Sp*, abang, upa
Synonyms
Hire, Lease mag-arkila; Iloc: ag-arkila

REPAIR cumpunihin, ayosin; Iloc: tarimaanen
Synonyms
Retrofit lagyan ng bagong parte o aparato o makina at ayosin; Iloc: mangikabil iti baro nga parte o aparato wenno makina ken tarimaanen
Fine tune mas pahusayin para mas efectivo at mas mabuti sa paggamit

REPAIR shop *(Tag. & Iloc.)* talyer-*Sp*

REPAIR by scrutinizing item by item *(Tag. & Iloc.)* cutingtingin

Reparation 1] magpakita ng kabutihan para makapagpalubag-loob dahil sa nakagawa siyang mga kasalanan o pananakit sa kapwa,; 2] *repair* o pagkukumpuni; 3] compensasyon-*Sp* na pera o mga bagay o pagtrabaho bilang bayad sa pinsala na ginawa sa kapwa, o bayad ng nagtagumpay o nanlusob na bayan sa tinalong bayan dahil sa mga pinsala at resulta-*Sp* ng giyera

Repartee matalas at nakakalibang na sagot; Iloc: nasirib ken naka-linglingay a sungbat

Repast ang pagkain sa almusal, pananghalian o hapunan

Repatriate 1] pabalikin ang isang tao (gaya ng isang bilanggo o *refugee*) sa dating pinanggalingang bayan o sa canyang bayang sinilangan; 2] tubong kinita o ari-arian na ipadala sa sariling bayan; 3] pagbabalik sa pinanggalingang bayan

Repay bayaran o i-*refund*; magbigay din ng ngiti o complimento sa nagbigay nito; gantihan din ang tulong na ibinigay

Repeal ipawalang-bisa, ipawalang-saysay; hindi na puedeng magpatuloy dahil binawi na ang karapatan

Repeat ulitin; Iloc: uliten

Repel ayawan at layuan, madisgusto; Iloc: adaywan ken agmadi, madisgusto

Repent *v.*, **Repentant** *adj.* magsisi, ikalulongkot; Iloc: agbabawi

Repercussion efecto-*Sp* o resulta-*Sp* sa ano mang ginawa – mabuti man o masama

Repertoire lista ng drama, opera, parte, piesa at iba pa na ang companya, artista o kumacanta ay handang gampanan; ang buong abilidad, sistema o aparato na ang isang ocupasyon o larangan ay tinataglay o minamahala

Repetition *n.*, **Repetitious** *adj. (Tag. & Iloc.)* paulit-ulit

Repetitive *(Tag. & Iloc.)* sige lang na paulit-ulit

Replace palitan; Iloc: sukatan

Replacement palitan, kapalit; Iloc: sukatan, kasukat

Replay patugtogin uli; Iloc: patocaren (tocar-*Sp*) manen

Replenish maglaan at mag-imbak na naman ng mga kinakailangan o *supplies;* magdagdag, maglagay o tustusan para mapuno o completo na naman; Iloc: mangicabil manen iti masapsapul a *supplies*

Replete labis ang pag-imbak o sobrang napuno ng *provision* o *supplies*; Iloc: sobra nga pagipon o pinunno ti *provision* o *supplies*
Correlated word

Abundance abundancia, sagana, dami; Iloc: abundancia, adu, wadwad, ruay

Replicate 1] ulitin o gumawa ng panibago o gumawa ng katulad; 2] patalikod na magbaluktot o matiklop o iyupi

Reply sumagot; Iloc: sumungbat, agsubalit

Repo 1] kasunduang bumili uli; 2] bawiin ang sasakayan o ano mang bagay dahil sa hindi cayang magpatuloy magbayad

REPORT *(Tag. & Iloc.) report*, ulat
Correlated word
Dossier naipon-ipong documento tungkol sa isang paksa o tao

REPORT a news i-ulat, ipahayag; Iloc: iwarnak

REPORT a wrongdoing isumbong; Iloc: ipulong

Reporter tagaulat sa periodico-*Sp*; Iloc: tagasurat iti periodico

Repose 1] nakahigang nagpapahinga, 2] nakahigang patay na; Iloc: 1] nakaidda nga agin-inana, 2] nakaidda a natayen

Repossess makuha ulit at maibalik na naman sa canya; Iloc: maala na manen, maisanicua na manen

Reprehensible naaangkop siyang mapintasan at kayamutan dahil sa canyang kawalang-hiyaan o pagkasama

Represent *v.*, **Representation** *n.* kumakatawan, gumaganap bilang, inilalarawan, magsilbi bilang...

Representative representante-*Sp*, kinatawan; Iloc: representante

Repress 1] ipagbawal ang karapatan, 2] patahimikin ang protesta-*Sp*, 3] tanggalin sa isip; Iloc: 1] iparit ti katurayan, 2] iparit ti protesta, 3] iwaksi diay panunot

Reprimand pagalitan, pagsabihan, sermonan; Iloc: ungtan, agunget, i-correhir-*Sp*, pagsawsaw-an, ag-sermon-*Sp*

Reprieve temporaryong ipagpalugit o ipagpaliban ng husticia ang parusa ng criminal

Reprisal maghiganti, vengganza-*Sp*, parusa o kahihinatnan ng kasamaan, paghihiganti; Iloc: mangibales, vengganza

Reproach sisihin, paratangan, pagsabihan; Iloc: pabasolen, babalawen, i-correhir-*Sp*

Reprobate 1] sinumpa na tao, 2] napakasamang tao; Iloc: 1] indadanes a tao, 2] nakadakdakes a tao

Reprobation malakas na pagkasuklam, pagsumpa; Iloc: napigsa nga gura, pagidadanes

Reproduce gumawa ulit ng productong nagawa na; gumawa ng copia-*Sp* o ng katulad; mag-usbong ulit sa natural-*Sp* na proceso-*Sp* gaya ng pagtubo o pagsibol ng tangkay

Reprove pagsabihan para matuto ng tama o pintasan ang masamang gawain

Repudiate itakwil, hindi kilalanin; Iloc: haan nga bigbigen, ilaksid

Repugnant *adj.*, **Repugnance** *n.* nakakarimarim at sobrang nakaka-disgusto; Iloc: makaar-aryek ken makadisgusto

Repulse *v.*, **Repulsion** *n.* madisgusto kaya lumayo; Iloc: madisgusto isu nga umadayo

Repulsive nakakapagpakita siya at nakakasanhi siya ng suklam, muhi at disgusto-*Sp*

Reputable maganda ang reputasyon-*Sp*; Iloc: napintas ti reputasyon

Reputation reputasyon-*Sp*, puri, dangal; Iloc: reputasyon, dayaw

Repute paniwala o pagtingin o pagkilala o pagturing sa paningin ng ibang tao; karangalan, mabuting pangalan

Request pakiusapan, maghiling, makisuyo; Iloc: makica-caasi, agkiddaw, maki-favor-*Sp*

Require, Requirement rekisito-*Sp* sa kinakailangang mga kacayahan o katangian para maaprovahan; Iloc: rekisito a kasapulan nga cabaelan ida ken katatao para maaprovaran (aprova/aprovar-*Sp*)

Requisite, Prerequisite *(Tag. & Iloc.)* rekisito-*Sp* sa/ti pagka-qualificado-*Sp*

Requite *v.*, **Requital** *n.* magbayad o tumogong-kabutihan sa ginawa na tulong, servicio, *benefits,* at iba pa; magganti sa ginawang kasamaan sa canya

Rerun uliting ipakita na naman sa *television* ang naipakita nang palabas o nailathala nang balita

Rescind ipawalang-bisa, ipawalang-saysay; tanggalin, hindi puede na magpatuloy dahil binawi na ang karapatan

RESCUE sagipin, saklolohan; iligtas, hangoin sa panganib; Iloc: arayaten, i-salvar-*Sp*, salakniban

RESCUE someone iligtas, saklolohan, sagipin; Iloc: i-salvar-*Sp*, arayaten

Rescued, ask to be magpasaklolo; Iloc: agpaarayat, agpasalvar-*Sp*, agpasalaknib

Research pananaliksik; Iloc: sukimat

Resemblance kahawig, magkamukha, kawangis; Iloc: agkaruprupa, agkaing-ingas, agkalanga

Resemble nakakamukha, nakakatulad, pareho-*Sp* ang ichura-*Sp* o gawi; Iloc: agkayarig

Resent *v.*, **Resentment** *n.* hinanankitt, tampo, naghinanakit, magdamdam; Iloc: sakit tii ricna ken nakem, maluksaw, makasuron

Reservation magpa-reserva-*Sp* ng lamesa-*Sp* sa *restaurant* o upuan sa palabas o *shows* o eroplano-*Sp* o cuarto-*Sp* sa matutuloyang *hotel*; Iloc: agpareserva ti lamesa iti *restaurant* o tugaw iti pabuya o ti eroplano o cuarto iti pagdagusan nga *hotel*

Reserve 1] maglaan, 2] magpareserva; Iloc: 1] agpalakam, 2] agpareserva

Reserved 1] nakareserva na, 2] walang kibo, kimi; Iloc: 1] nakareservan, 2] haan a maun-uni, naulimek

Reservoir *[rezer-vuahr]* lawa na gawang-tao o *man-made* para sa kinakailangang tubig at inomin ng comunidad-*Sp*; Iloc: aramid iti tao nga danaw para iti danum ken inomin ti entero-*Sp* comunidad

Reset patakbohin o paandarin o pagalawin ulit

Reside nakatira; Iloc: agigian, agtaeng, agtaed

Residence bahay, tahanan, tirahan, residencia-*Sp*; Iloc: balay, pagyanan, residencia

Resident *(Tag. & Iloc.)* residente-*Sp*, nakatirang tao

Residual 1] mga natira, 2] bayad ng artistang gumaganap o ng manunulat sa patuloy na pagtatanghal ng *recorded* na gawa nila, 3] ang mga patuloy na kasunod na kalagayan o pangyayari; Iloc: 1] dagiti natidda, 2] bayad ti artista wenno mannurat iti itultuloy a pangiparang iti *recorded* nga obra-*Sp* da, 3] iti agtultuloy a sumarsaruno a kasasaad wenno napasamak

Residue ang tira; Iloc: ti natidda

Resign magbitiw, tumiwalag; Iloc: umikkat

Resilience *Ability to recover promptly from trauma, illness, hardship, calamities, failures, threats, stresses, depression, etc. without being overwhelmed by such experiences or without wallowing in pity, but rather stand up and continue living life as usual. Resilient people may have mental toughness and fortitude, which means they are strong enough to bear difficulties and even bear such with tranquility and nonchalance, or they may also have* *grit, which is withstanding struggles on a longer period.* 1] kacayahang bumalik agad sa dating lakas o saya o pagkacontento pagkatapos ng hirap o problema-*Sp* o sakit na karamdaman, at kahit na nandodoon pa rin ang mga problema ay may giting at katapangan kasama ang kapayapaan at kabutihang loob sa canya, 2] puedeng makabalik sa dating forma kahit pinilipit o binaluktot; Iloc: 1] cabaelan nga agsubli ensigida-*Sp* iti dati a pigsa o ragsak wenno pagkacontento palpas ti rigat o problema-*Sp* ken saksakit ti bagi, ken uray nu adda pay laeng dagiti rigrigat mamentener na iti tured, talna ken singpet; 2] mabalin a makasubli iti sigud a forma uray no natiritir wenno nacurva

Correlated words

Guts *n.,* **Gutsy** *adj.* lakas ng isip na nagbibigay ng katapangan at pagtitiis sa sakit ng katawan at bigat ng buhay

Fortitude giting at katapangan kasama ang lakas ng pag-iisip at damdamin at tiyagang magpatuloy sa paglutas at sa pagharap ng kahirapan, panganib, pati kaharap na muhi at galit at tentacion

Resist mangontra na walang pagbabago; Iloc: ag-contra-*Sp* nga haan pulos agbalbaliw

Resistance 1] resistancia-*Sp*, lakas ng katawan na makipaglaban sa sakit at microbio-*Sp*, 2] secretong samahan na may sariling secretong layonin; Iloc: 1] resistancia, pigsa ti bagi nga manglaban ti sakit ken microbio, 2] limed a grupo-*Sp* nga adda rangta da a limed met

Resolute *Firmly set on one's goal or purpose; determined, decided, uncompromising, serious, staunch, unwavering.* Determinado-*Sp*, masigasig, decidido-*Sp*, marubdob, tibay sa paniwala o tibay sa pagsasagawa ng balak; Iloc: determinado, decidido, tibker iti pammati o tibker ti pagturpos iti rangta

Resolve mag-decisyon-*Sp*, decisyonan sa pamamagitan ng votohan para makarating sa pasya na sang-ayon sa lahat; maghanap ng solusyon-*Sp*; Iloc: agdecidir-*Sp*, agvotoan para macadanon iti decisyon-*Sp* nga cayat iti amin; agsapul ti pang-solvar-*Sp*

Resonate tumugon, umalingawngaw; Iloc: sumungbat, umaw-aweng

Resort 1] lugar-*Sp* na nakakalibang, 2] patuloy na maghanap ng ibang lutas kung hindi nagtagumpay ang mga dating sinubokan o ginawa; Iloc: 1] lugar nga makalinglingay, 2] agpatuloy nga agbirok ti sabali a *solution* nu haan a nagballigi dagidi pinadas o inaramid da

Resound mag-*echo* o umalingawngaw *(see Resonate above)*

Resource ang mga pinagsama-samang kayamanan ng bayan gaya ng mga mineral, lupa, capital, obra ng mga trabahadores o mga nag-oficina, mga makina-aparato-at iba pang *equipment*, pera, ari-arian na madaling ipagpalit sa pera, kakayahan, intelihencia, dunong sa pag-imbento o pagdilihencia, pagkaganang makapagsagawa at makapaglutas at anomang makuha at magamit agad sa oras ng pangangailangan; pinanggagalingan ng pangtustos sa pangangailangan o pangsuporta lalo na sa madali lang na makuhanan

Resourceful *Diligent at promptly researching and finding ways to solve problems, or deal with new situations and dilemmas; ingenious at formulating ways and means to deal with complexities, and many more.* Laging naghahanap ng mga pamaraan o sistema-*Sp* para makapagsagawa o makapaglutas, marunong magdilihensia-*Sp* na makabatas; Iloc: agbirbirok ti dalan o sistema tapno makaturpos wenno maka-solvar-*Sp*, ammo na ti agdilihensia a *legal*

Respect *(Tag. & Iloc.) respect*, respeto-*Sp*
Synonym
Deference *(Tag. & Iloc.)* cortesia at respeto

Respectable respetado-*Sp*, marangal, dakila, kagalang-galang; Iloc: nataer, respetado, madaydayaw, naraem
Synonyms
Dignified, Noble may dignidad, marangal, dakila; Iloc: adda dignidad na, nadayaw, natakneng, nataer
With integrity may integridad, pagkakaroon ng etico at moralidad at dignidad; Iloc: addaan iti integridad, addaan ti etico ken moralidad ken dignidad

Respected nire-respeto-*Sp*, ginagalang, tinitingala bilang kagalanggalang na tao; Iloc: iresrespeto, iraraem, tangtangaden a madaydayaw a tao

Respectful marespeto, magalang; Iloc: narespeto, mapagdayaw, naraem

Respective relevante-*Sp* o angkop sa isang tao, o sa maraming tao

Respiration paghinga; Iloc: paganges

Respire *v.*, **Respiration** *n.* huminga; Iloc: aganges

Respite 1] pinagitang tiempo-*Sp* para makapahinga at maginhawaan, 2] temporaryong pag-antala o pagpaliban gaya sa sentenciang-mamatay or *death sentence* ang isang bilanggo; Iloc: 1] pagbaetan a tiempo para makainana ken makabang-ar; 2] temporaryo-*Sp* a pagtantan casla iti sentencia-*Sp* nga matay wenno *death sentence* ti maysa a balud

Resplendent masikat, makislap, masinag, maningning, maluningning; Iloc: nasilap, nasillag, naranyag

Respond sumagot, tumugon; Iloc: agsubalit, agsungbat

Response tugon o sagot sa salita, sa kilos o sa sulat; Iloc: sungbat nga sarita, tignay wenno surat

Responsibility responsibilidad-*Sp*, katungkulan, pananagutan, obligasyon-*Sp*; Iloc: responsibilidad, karbengan, rebbeng, obligasyon
Correlated words
You are the cause of everything that happens to you. Be careful what you cause ikaw ang dahilan ng ano mang mangyayari sa'yo - pag-ingatan mo na ang gawa mo at pagsisikap mo ay kabutihan at kadakilaan para makapagbunga mga ito ng kadakilaan at kaunlaran sa iyo
Avoiding one's responsibility never brings good results, rather it brings problems. Ang paglihis o pagtakas sa iyong pananagutan o obligasyon ay walang mabuting kahihinatnan at walang dudang magbibigay pa sa iyo ng hirap o problema

Responsible *Fills a position where he has responsibilities, control and authority. He/she has to be trusted and relied on because he is answerable, accountable and responsible with a lot of things and people. In his/her <u>duty as a **person**</u>, he must be law-abiding and a good citizen; <u>as a **parent**</u>, he/she must love, take care and support the spouse and children; <u>as an **employee**</u>, to work diligently and efficiently; <u>as an **executive** in an office</u>, is responsible of managing the business and employees. He is held responsible for the growth and success of the business, as well as its failure.*

Responsive handang umunawa sa katayoan ng kapwa, handang tumanggap ng mungkahi; handang sumagot o kumilos sa inaasahang *response* o pagtugon

Rest magpahinga; Iloc: aginana

Restaurant *(Tag. & Iloc.) restaurant (buffet, cafeteria, coffeehouse, pub, ethnic, fine dining)*

Restful maginhawa, makabigay ng pahinga; Iloc: makapabang-ar, makaited ti inana, makanam-ay

Restitution pagsasauli sa nagmamay-ari; Iloc: pagisubli idiay makincukua

Restless nababagabag, balisa, nagugusot ang isip, hindi mapakali, hindi makatulog; Iloc: alicuteg, haan nga makatalna, madanagan, maringgoran, haan makaturog

Restore ibalik sa dating kalagayan; Iloc: isubli a sigud a condisyon-*Sp*

Restrain *v.*, **Restraint** *n.* pigilan, i-control, hadlangan, maglagay ng limitasyon; i-aresto, tanggalin ang kalayaan; Iloc: tengngelen, i-control, tipden, mangigawid ta adda limitasyon na; i-aresto, ikkaten iti waya o *freedom* na

Restroom *(Tag. & Iloc.)* banyo, *ladies room* o *men's room*

Restrict higpitan, strictohan, bigyan ng limitasyon-*Sp*; Iloc: strictoan, ikkan ti limitasyon (stricto-*Sp*)

Result resulta-*Sp*, kinalabasan, kinasapitan, kahihinatnan; Iloc: resulta, pagbanagan, pagmaayan, gunggona

RESUME pag-umpisa na naman pagkatapos ng paghinto o pag-antala; Iloc: pagrugi manen palpas ti pagsardeng wenno pagtantan

RESUMÉ, Summary of work experiences and qualifications *resumé*, sumaria ng karunongan, pinag-aralan, expiryensang trabaho, abilidad, mga parangal na natanggap sa kahusayan sa pagtrabaho at talino sa escuela, at iba pang nakakabigay ng favor sa aplicante

Resurrection *God resurrected from the dead because He is God and He had to return to His kingdom in heaven, after lovingly sacrificing and suffering for all mankind. Jesus Christ's resurrection was on the 3ʳᵈ day after His death from being crucified on the cross. Prior to His ascension to heaven, He met with His disciples to give them blessings and good counsels. The disciples saw His pierced hands where the nails penetrated through when He was nailed on the cross, and they also saw His chest that was punctured by a spear that gave proof that He was already dead. And then the disciples witnessed Jesus Christ rose back to heaven.* Pagkatapos na ginampanan ng Dios Anak na si Hesu Cristo ang pinakadakilang sacrificio para sa kaligtasan ng lahat na nilalang kung saan Siya nilait-lait, sinaktan-saktan, kinoronahan ng mga tinik, pinabuhat ang mabigat na cruz paakyat sa Golgotha/Calvario, at binitay at pinako Siya sa cruz, ang Dios Anak na si Hesu Cristo ay namatay. Sa ikatlong araw ng pagkamatay Niya, maagang pumunta sina Maria Magdalena, Maria, at Joanna sa puntod

Niya pero bukas na ang cuevang puntod at wala na ang katawan ng Panginoong Dios Hesu Cristo doon. Dali-daling tumakbo sina Maria Magdalena para ipaalam sa mga dicipulo, kaya pumunta ang mga dicipulo sa cueva para matiyak ang sinabi nina Maria. Nagtataka ang mga dicipulo dahil nawala sa isip nila sa limot ang sinabi ng Panginoong Dios Hesu Cristo na mabubuhay Siyang muli sa ikat-long araw ng pagkamatay Niya. Namangha ang mga dicipulo noong lumitaw at nakipagkita at nakipagpulong ang Panginoong Dios Hesu Cristo sa canila. Nakita ng mga dicipulo ang sugatang butas sa mga kamay ni Hesu Cristo kung saan Siya naipako sa cruz, at ang sugat sa tagiliran Niya kung saan Siya sinaksak ng sibat. At pagkatapos ay malinaw nilang nakita si Hesu Cristo na pumailanglang pataas sa pagbabalik Niya sa langit.

Resuscitate *v.,* **Resuscitation** *n.* paggawa ng paraan para mabuhay o bumalik uli ang malay gaya ng CPR o *first aid*; Iloc: pagaramid ti pangpasubli iti poot ken biag casla iti CPR wenno *first aid* iti paciente-*Sp*
Synonym
Revive mataohan muli at mabuhay; Iloc: agungar

Retail pagveventa ng tingi-tingi lamang at ang bumibili ay tingi-tingi din, hindi pakyawan; Iloc: aglaco iti haan nga adu ken dagiti gumatang ket haan nga adu, haan a casla iti *wholesale*
Antonym
Wholesale pakyaw, maramihang bili para iventa

Retain ipanatili sa puesto-*Sp* at manatiling hawak-hawak niya ito sa pag-iingat at pag-alaga at dahil sa pinagkakatiwalaan siya dito

Retainer 1] katulong sa familia ng marami nang taon; 2] bayad sa servicio-*Sp* ng abogado-*Sp*; 3] sa *Orthodontics*, nagpapapantay sa mga ngipin na natatanggal-tanggal

Retaliate tumugon ng pareho-*Sp* o gumaganti sa hindi mabuting pag-trato-*Sp* sa canya; Iloc: agsubalit wenno mangibales iti dakes a pagtrato canyana

Retard gawing mabagal o i-antala o i-atraso ang pag-*develop* o pagbuo o pag-unlad

Retarded taong mabagal o huminto na ang pag-*develop* ng utak niya pero hindi naman loco-loco

Reticent sarado ang bibig, hindi mapagpahayag o mapagbigay ng informasyon-*Sp*; Iloc: cerrado-*Sp* ti bibig, haan a mapagsawang o haan mangmangted ti informasyon
Correlated words
Uncommunicative hindi siya palasalita o palasulat o hindi siya mapagbunyag ng informasyon
Stonewall ayaw sumagot at makipagcoaperasyon; Iloc: madi sumungbat ken madi a makipag-coaperasyon

Retire mag-retiro-*Sp*; Iloc: agretiro

Retort magsagot; Iloc: agsungbat

Retouch *(Tag. & Iloc.)* retoque-*Sp*

Retract bawiin ang sinabi; Iloc: ibabawi ti sinao

Retreat umurong, umatras para hindi na lalaban; Iloc: agsanud, umatras para haanen a lumaban (atras-*Sp*)

Retrench *v.*, **Retrenchment** *n.* magbawas, magtipid, lagyan ng *limit* o strictohan ang hangganan ng paggastos

Retribution kahihinatnan ng kasamaan; parusa, bumalik na ganti sa masamang gawain
Synonym
Karma mula sa *Hindu* at *Buddhist*, ito ay parusang kahihinatnan ng anomang masamang asal at gawain

Retrieve bawiin o mabawi, panumbalikin sa dati o sa mas mabuting kalagayan sa pamamagitan ng pagcumpuni at pag-aayos; *atone, amend* o pagbayaran ang ginawang kasalanan; Iloc: maysubli, maala manen, maybabawi

Retroactive ang efectivo-*Sp* na fecha-*Sp* ay <u>mas maaga sa kasalukuyang fecha</u>; Iloc: iti efectivo a fecha nga inkeddeng ket <u>mas nasapa</u> ngem itatta

Retrofit lagyan ng bagong parte o aparato-*Sp* o makina-*Sp* at ayosin; Iloc: mangikabil ti baro nga parte o aparato o makina ken tarimaanen

Retrograde paurong at nagiging mas masama ang condisyon-*Sp*; Iloc: paatras-*Sp* ken agbalin nga mas agdakes ti condisyon

Retrogression pagbabalik sa dating mas mababang clase, pag-iisip at katatao; paurong at pumapalayo sa pag-unlad; Iloc: pagsubli iti dati a mas nababa a pannakabalin, panagpanunot ken pagkatao; pa-atras-*Sp* nga umadayo iti progreso-*Sp*

Retrospect paggugunita o sinasariwa ang mga nakaraan; Iloc: paglaglagip cadagiti napalabas

RETURN a thing ibalik, isauli; Iloc: isubli, ipulang

RETURN the favor, Reciprocate tumogon ng kasingbuti dahil sa ginawang kabutihan sa canya; Iloc: agsubalit iti pada a naimbag gapu iti inaramid a kaimbagan canyana
Correlated word
Reciprocal pagganti na pasasalamat sa pinakitang kagandahang-loob; Iloc: pagsubalit nga pagyaman iti impakita nga asi o pagimbagan

RETURN (to a place) bumalik, mag-vuelta-*Sp*; Iloc: agsubli, agvuelta

Reunion *(Tag. & Iloc.) reunion*

Rev paandarin; mas bilisan; Iloc: paandaren (andar-*Sp*), mas pacascasen

Revamp gawin ulit o bagohin o mas pagbutihin; panumbalikin sa dating mabuting kalagayan ng bahay, gusali o sasakyan sa pamamagitan ng pagcumpuni at pag-aayos

Reveal ipagtapat, isiwalat, ibunyag, ihayag; Iloc: isawang, ipaammo

Revel 1] masiyahan at ma-contento-*Sp*, 2] magsaya sa maingay na *party*; Iloc: 1] agragsak ken macontento, 2] agrambak iti naariwawa nga *party*

REVENGE *v.* maghiganti; Iloc: mangibales

REVENGE *n.* vengganza-*Sp*, paghiganti; Iloc: vengganza, panangibales

Revengeful mapaghiganti, venggativo-*Sp*; Iloc: manangibales, venggativo

Revenue ang kinikita ng govierno buhat sa buis, *customs* o adwana, at iba pa; ang suweldo-*Sp* o sahod na regular-*Sp* na palagiang dumarating

Reverberate mag-*echo* o mag-alingawngaw
Synonym
Echo alingawngaw; Iloc: aweng

Revere magsamba sa Panginoong Dios, magdasal, magpuri, maghanga, magbunyi, maggglorificar, isagrado at parangalan Siya, pasalamatan at tingalain Siya dahil sa Canyang kabanalan, kabutihan, pagkapuno ng gloria at gracia at dahil Siya ang lumikha sa universo at lahat-lahat ng nasa universo at dahil sa pagmamahal Niya sa bawat tao kahit hindi karapat-dapat ang tao dahil lahat ay makasalanan, pero gumawa ang Dios ng paraan para maligtas tayo sa parusa ng ating mga kasalanan sa pamamagitan ng sacrificio ng Dios Anak na si Hesu Cristo sa cruz.

Reverse ibaligtad; baligtad, tumbalik, saliwa; Iloc: ibalictad; balictad, ballikid

Reversible attire baligtaran, damit na angkop/*appropriate* na suot pa rin kahit ibaligtad; Iloc: cawes nga pareho-*Sp* nga may-usar-*Sp* ti ruar ken ti uneg, uray nu ibalictad

Revert *v.,* **Reversion** *n.* 1] pagbabalik sa dating gawi, paniniwala, condisyon o iba pa; pagbabalik sa isip o pakikipag-usap o sa dating paksa o *topic*; 2] ibalik sa dating nagmemay-ari o sa mga tagamana nito

Review mag-*review*, mag-repaso-*Sp*; Iloc: ag-*review*, agrepaso

Revile magsalitang pang-abuso-*Sp* at pang-insulto-*Sp*

Revise bagohin at ayosin; Iloc: baliwan ken urnosen

Revitalize bigyan ng bagong lakas at sigla; Iloc: ikkan ti baro a pigsa, bileg ken kired

Revive mataohan muli at mabuhay; Iloc: agungar

Revoke ipawalang-bisa, ipawalang-saysay; hindi na puedeng magpatuloy dahil binawi na ang karapatan; Iloc: ikkaten ti turay ken bileg

Revolt *(Tag. & Iloc.)* protestang pag-rerebelde sa otoridad

Revolution revolusyon-*Sp*, himagsik; Iloc: revolusyon, pag-alsa

Revolve umikot; Iloc: agpusipos

Revolver *(Tag. & Iloc.) revolver*

Reward gantimpala, premio-*Sp;* Iloc: gunggona, premio

Rewind ipulopot, likawin; i-*reverse* pabalik ang *tape*; Iloc: ipulipol, icunikon

Rhetoric, Rhetorics mahusay at efectivong paggamit ng lengguahe, gaya ng talumpating nakakainfluwensia at nakakahikayat at nakakahimok; paggamit ng lengguahe sa *simile* o dalawang magkaiba pero may pagkapareho gaya ng *metaphor*, simbolo at *emblem*, o ng *antithesis* o magkacontra gaya ng *"Give me liberty or give me death"*; paggamit ng lengguaheng maraming kalabisan (*bombastic, grandiloquent*) o nagkukunwaring makahulogan pero kulang sa tunay na importansia

Rheumatism *(Tag. & Iloc.)* rayuma-*Sp*

Rhyme magkaparehong bigkas o tunog ng tula o canta-*Sp;* Iloc: agkapareho nga balikas o uni iti daniw o cancion-*Sp*

Rib tadyang; Iloc: paragpag

Ribald nakakatawa pero kabastusan; Iloc: nakakatkatawa ngem kabastusan, salawasaw

Ribbon *(Tag. & Iloc.)* *ribbon*, laso-*Sp*

RICE, cooked kanin, sinaing; Iloc: innapoy

RICE, fried sinangag; Iloc: kinirog

RICE, leftover tirang kanin; Iloc: kilabban

RICE mill *(Tag. & Iloc.)* kiskisan

RICE, overcooked tutong, sunog; Iloc: nakset, ittip

RICE paddy palayan; Iloc: kapagayan, taltalon

RICE, porridge *(Tag. & Iloc.)* lugaw, arroz-*Sp* caldo-*Sp*

RICE, uncooked or raw bigas; Iloc: bagas

RICE, undercooked kanin na di pa luto; Iloc: nacusel

RICE, unhusked palay; Iloc: irik, pagay

Ricefields palayan; Iloc: kapagayan

Rich mayaman; Iloc: nabaknang, rico-*Sp*

Riches kayamanan, yaman; Iloc: rico o baknang a sanicua

Ricochet talbog, tumira pero bumabalik; Iloc: talbog, nagtira ngem nagsubli

Rid of, get iwaksi, itapon; Iloc: iwaksi, ibelleng

Riddance pagpalayas, pagpaalis, iwala, ipaglaho

Riddle bugtong; Iloc: pugpugto, burburcha
  Correlated word
  Guess hulaan; Iloc: agpugto, pugtuan

RIDE maglulan, magsakay; Iloc: aglugan, agsakay

RIDE, bumpy matagtag; Iloc: natagtag

RIDE wth someone *(Tag. & Iloc.)* makisakay, maki-angkas
  Correlated word
  Transport isakay, ilulan; Iloc: ilugan, isakay

Ridicule katuwaang panunuya para pagtawanan ang victima-*Sp*; Iloc: ay-ayam a sutil tapno pagkakatawaan da daytoy victima

Rife 1] abundancia, napakadami; 2] caraniwan o paraparating nangyayari o laganap ito

Rig bagohin ang paraan o makina-*Sp* o *election* para makapandaya; Iloc: balbaliwan ti pamay-an o makina o *election* tapno makacusit

RIGHT tama, wasto, tumpak; Iloc: usto, agpayso

RIGHT (direction or side) canan; Iloc: cannawan
  Antonym
  Left side caliwa; Iloc: cannigid

RIGHT, legal karapatan, katarungan; Iloc: katurayan o kalintegan, gundaway, turay

RIGHT hand canang camay; Iloc: cannawan nga ima

RIGHT now! Ngayon na!, Agad-agad!; Iloc: Itat-tan!, Ensegida-*Sp*!

RIGHT time napapanahon na, panahon na, oras na; Iloc: orasen, panawenen

Synonyms

Timely, It's about time napapanahon na; Iloc: orasen, tiempon

Opportune tamang-tama sa panahon para sa tinakdang balak; Iloc: us-usto ti tiempo para iti inkeddeng a rangta

Antonyms

Untimely hindi pa panahon; Iloc: haan pay a tiempo

Premature maaga pa at di pa napapanahon; Iloc: nasapa pay ken haan pay a panawen

Righteous maka-Dios, *honest*, tapat at matuwid, mabait, mapacumbaba, mahabagin, mapagbigay; Iloc: maka-Dios, nasingpet, nalinteg, napacumbaba, mannangaasi, mapagited ti tulong

Rightful makatarungan; Iloc: naturay

Rigid maganit; Iloc: nasikkil

Rigorous strictong pagsunod ng exacto o tamang-tamang paraan; Iloc: stricto-*Sp* a pagsurot ti exacto-*Sp* ken us-usto-*Sp* nga pagaramid

Rile galitin, inisin; Iloc: ruroden, paguraen

Rim gilid, bingit, labi; Iloc: igid

Rind *[rahynd or rind]* labas na takip ng mga fruitas

RING *(Tag. & Iloc.)* singsing

RING a bell ang dating limot nang pangalan o tunog o amoy o bagay na naulinigan o nakita muli ay nagpapasariwa o nagpapakilanlan o nakakapaalaala ng dating *event*

Correlated word

On the tip of my tongue nasa dulo ng dila ko, hindi ko lang masabi o maalaala

RING the doorbell mag-timbre-*Sp*; Iloc: agtimbre

RING or peal the belfry ibatingaw ang campana-*Sp*; Iloc: ikililing o ipatit ti campana

RINSE clothes balnawan, Iloc: banlawan

RINSE dishes hugasan; Iloc: ugasan, bugwan

RINSE plate or glass by flapping back and forth on a water-filled basin ihughog; Iloc: ikawkaw, igawgaw

Riot kagulohan o labanan ng maraming tao; Iloc: dakkel a gulo, aglablaban a tattao

RIP punitin; Iloc: pigisen, pirgisen

RIP off siningil ng mahal kahit mumurahin lamang, bumili ng imitasyon-*Sp* sa pag-aakalang tunay ito; Iloc: siningir ti nangina uray nalaca laeng daytoy, nakagatang ti imitasyon gapu ta ti pagarup na ket *genuine* daytoy

Ripe hinog; Iloc: naluom
  Antonym
  Raw hilaw, mapakla; Iloc: naata, naganus, nasugpet

Ripen mahinog; Iloc: agluom

RISE *(Tag. & Iloc.)* bumangon
  Antonym
  Lie down mahiga; Iloc: agidda

RISE to the occasion *The world or the community or the family or a group needs a hero, so be the hero like be the patient or understanding one when there is contention, be of help when there is a need for it, be the consoler or the one who gives cheer to someone who is dejected or disheartened, and many more good deeds. Also live an honorable, exemplary and productive life.* Kahit pobre ka o anomang nakakahadlang sa'yo, umangat ka sa mga iyan dahil may lakas at abilidad ka. Magsagawa ka ng nakakabuti sa iyo at sa mga mahal mo sa buhay, mag-asal ng mabuti at marangal, magpaunlad ka sa pagtapos mo ng pag-aaral dahil iyan ang makakahango sa iyo, makakabigay ng magandang trabaho; gamitin mong anomang abilidad at talento mo para di maglaho at mawala mga iyan sa hindi paggagamit; lumayo ka sa mga gumagawa ng masama at nagdodroga dahil nagdadalang bwisit, kabigoan at bilanggoan lamang ang mga yan.

Risibility *n.,* **Risible** *adj.* napapatawa ng madalas, madaling tumawa; Iloc: makakatkawa canayon, nalaca nga agkatawa

Risk panganib, peligro-*Sp*; Iloc: peggad, peligro

Risky peligroso-*Sp*, mapanganib; Iloc: peligroso, napeggad

Risque hindi tamang asal, hindi decente-*Sp*; Iloc: haan nga nasayaat a garaw, haan a decente

Ritual parating kagawiang ceremonia-*Sp*; Iloc: sigud maar-aramid a ceremonia

Rival *(Tag. & Iloc.)* karival, ka-competensia-*Sp*
   Synonym
   Opponent *(Tag. & Iloc.)* kalaban, kacompetensia

Rive punitin o hampasin ng patalim para maghiwalay

RIVER ilog; Iloc: carayan

RIVER current agos ng ilog; Iloc: ayos ti carayan

Riverside tabing ilog, pampang; Iloc: dammang
   Correlated word
   Seashore tabing-dagat, dalampasigan; Iloc: igid tibaybay

ROAD calsada-*Sp*, calye-*Sp*, daan; Iloc: calsada, calye, dalan

ROAD, pot-holed lubak-lubak o baco-bacong daan; Iloc: abut-abut a dalan
   Correlated words
   Bumpy road, Bumpy ride matagtag; Iloc: natagtag

ROAD rage galit na galit at nakaka-accidente na asal ng nagmamaneho dahil sa napakasama niyang ugali

Roadside tabing-daan; Iloc: igid ti dalan

Roam pagala-gala, palibot-libot, maglacuacha, magbulakbol; Iloc: aglib-libot, aglacuacha, agbulbulakbol, agbalballog

Roamer *(Tag. & Iloc.)* lacuachero, bulakbol; Iloc: ballog

ROAST mag-ihaw; Iloc: agtuno

ROAST, Lampoon katatawanang pang-atake sa isang tao o sa grupo na pumapayag na maatake para sa katatawanan

Rob tumotutok ng armas at nagbabanta sa victima para makapagna-kaw siya; Iloc: manglayat iti armas wenno agcarit iti victima para makatakaw isu

Robber magnanakaw; Iloc: agtatakaw

Robe 1] bata de banyo-*Sp*, 2] toga-*Sp* na gamit sa ceremonia-*Sp* gaya sa corte-*Sp* o *graduation*; Iloc: 1] bata de banyo, 2] toga nga i-usar-*Sp* ti ceremonia casla diay corte o diay *graduation*

Robust growth malago; Iloc: nalapsat, naruay

ROCK malaking bato; Iloc: dakkel a bato

ROCK the cradle iduyan; Iloc: indayonen

ROCK the boat manggulo o mangpabagabag sa pagtitipon na dating mapayapa at mahinahon

ROCKET sasakyan o stractura-*Sp* na naglalakbay sa *space* o sa lampas pa ng himpapawid ng mundo-*Sp*

ROCKET science larangan kung saan kinakailangan ang malaking kaalaman o intelihensia-*Sp* at abilidad-*Sp* sa teknolohia-*Sp*

Rod tungkod, palo-*Sp*; Iloc: sarrukod, pang-ur

Roe, Egg of fishes or other water creatures puga, aligi; Iloc: bugi

Rogue 1] hindi mapagkatiwalaan dahil siya ay sinungaling, mandaraya, manloloko, manlilinlang o magnanakaw, taksil at traydor; lumalabag siya sa batas; 2] taong masama ang reputasyon-*Sp*, 3] hampaslupa at palaboylaboy, lagalag; 4] makahayop na hindi matanto ang gagawin sa iyo; 5] *Biology*: isang *organism* o buhay na halaman o insecto na kakaiba sa caraniwan

ROLE ang gaganaping responsibilidad at puesto sa trabaho; ang gaganaping pagkatao sa pelicula-*Sp*; Iloc: iti obligasyon na ken puesto na iti trabaho; iti iladawan na a pagkatao bilang artista iti pelicula o drama

ROLE model uliran; Iloc: nasayaat nga ehemplo-*Sp*

ROLL gumulong, umikot; Iloc: agtulatid, agkarolig
Synonym
Rotate, Spin, Whirl umikot; Iloc: agpusipos, agtayyek

ROLL a bandage around *(Tag. & Iloc.)* i-benda-*Sp*

ROLL of cords, tissue, etc. *(Tag. & Iloc.)* rolyo-*Sp*

ROLL or wind a thread or string puloputin, balumbonin; Iloc: cunikonen, icunikon, pulipolen
Synonym
Coil pulupotin, balumbonin; Iloc: iputipot, icawicaw
Antonym
Unwind calagin; Iloc: warwaren

ROLL up, i.e. to put away the sleeping bag or mat balumbonin; Iloc: lucoten

ROLL up one's sleeves ilislis ang manggas-*Sp* ng damit at mag-umpisa-*aSp* nang mag-trabaho-*Sp*

Rollback gumulong pabalik; pagbabalik sa dating mababang precio-*Sp* bilang utos ng govierno-*Sp*

Romance *(Tag. & Iloc.)* romansa-*Sp*

Romantic *(Tag. & Iloc.)* romantico/ca-*Sp*

Roof atip, bubongan; Iloc: atep, bobida-*Sp*
Correlated word
   Ceiling *(Tag. & Iloc.)* kisame
Rookie baguhan; Iloc: agdamdamo
ROOM silid, cuarto-*Sp*; Iloc: siled, cuarto
Correlated words
   Bedroom silid tulogan; Iloc: cuarto a pagturogan
   Living room *(Tag. & Iloc.)* salas, sala
   Dining room silid kainan; Iloc: cuarto a panganan
   Bathroom *(Tag. & Iloc.)* banyo
   Kitchen *(Tag. & Iloc.)* cusina
ROOM, cozy, bright and airy maaliwalas na lugar; Iloc: napariir ken nalawa ken nalawag a lugar, makabang-ar a lugar
ROOM and board upa na ang bayad ay para sa pagkain at cuarto na matitirhan
ROOM, living *(Tag. & Iloc.)* salas-*Sp*, sala
ROOM mate magka-cuarto-*Sp*; Iloc: agkacuarto
Roost mataas na lugar kung saan dumadapo ang mga ibon; Iloc: nangato a lugar nu inchenna nga agdisso dagiti billit
ROOSTER tandang; Iloc: cawitan
ROOSTER crow magtilaok; Iloc: agtarauk
Root 1] ugat, 2] malakas na palakpak at malugod na sigaw ng tagahanga sa pinakitang nakakahanga; Iloc: 1] ramut, uggot, 2] napigsa a palakpak ken naragsak a pukkaw ti tagasuporta iti idolo wenno iti favorito-*Sp* a *team* na
Rope lubid, tali; Iloc: galut, siglot
Correlated words
   Cord cordon, sintas, pisi, lazo ng sapatos; Iloc: cordon, sintas, tali, lazo ti sapatos
   Noose tali, tali na may bilog na pansilo para pangbitag ng hayop; Iloc: silo nga adda timbukel a tali ti murdong na
Rosary, Rosary beads *(Tag. & Iloc.)* rosario-*Sp*
Rose *(Tag. & Iloc.)* rosas-*Sp*
Roster *(Tag. & Iloc.)* lista ng mga empleyado
Rot mabulok; Iloc: agbulok, agbukbok
Rotate umikot; Iloc: agpusipos
ROTATION pagulong-gulong, paikot-ikot; Iloc: pagtultulatid, paglikoliko

ROTATION, Work shifts *(Tag. & Iloc.)* rotasyon-*Sp*, relyebohan, halinhinan

Rote *routine*, permanente-*Sp* at regular-*Sp* na paraan at palakad na nagiging parang *mechanical* na

Rotund *(Tag. & Iloc.)* mataba, bilog

Rotunda *(Tag. & Iloc.)* rotonda-*Sp*

Rouge *(Tag. & Iloc.)* colorete-*Sp* para sa pisngi

ROUGH 1] anomang mahirap, nakakabigat o puedeng makakapinsala, 2] taong malupit o bastos-*Sp* at wala man lang kafinohan

ROUGH surface 1] baco-bacong daanan, 2] magaspang na labas o balat; Iloc: 1] dalan nga abut-abot wenno narumek-rumek a bato, 2] nakersang o narasi a cudil wenno ti ruar na

Roughage *fiber* na pagkain, magaspang na pagkain gaya ng gulay na tumutulong sa magandang pagdumi o *bowel movement*

Roulette *(Tag. & Iloc.)* ruleta-*Sp*

ROUND, Circle bilog; Iloc: agtimbukel

ROUND off something 1] pabilogin ang isang bagay o hugis, 2] ilagay ang numero sa pinakamalapit na bilang gaya ng 47 ay magiging 50, ang 22 ay magiging 20

ROUND-trip ticket fare flete-*Sp* para sa viaheng papunta at pabalik, fleteng-balikan: Iloc: flete para mapan ken agsubli, flete a vueltaan (viahe-*Sp*, vuelta-*Sp*)

Route pagdaanan; Iloc: pagdalanan

Routine kinagawiang gawa, kaugaliang pamaraan; Iloc: sigud o cadawyan nga aramid o sigud a pamay-an

Rove *(Tag. & Iloc.)* paglibot-libot

ROW *(Tag. & Iloc.)* hilera-*Sp*

ROW a boat magsagwan; Iloc: agtagwan

RUB body maghilod, hiloran; Iloc: lidlidan

RUB body on a surface due to an itch ihilod ang katawan; Iloc: iilad ti bagi

RUB elbows with.. nakikipaghalo-bilo kay/sa, nagkakaugnayan sa pagtatrabaho o sa isang proyecto-*Sp*, magkasama-sama

RUB off dirt from body maghilod, hiloran o hagorin ang libag; Iloc; lidlidan iti cabcab

RUB off dirt or stain from a thing kayurin, kiskisan, kuskosin; Iloc: isisoan, kiskisin, kuskosin

Scour to clean dirt or scum kuscosin, kiskisin, is-isin; Iloc: kuscosen, kiskisen, is-isuan, radradan

RUBBER *(Tag. & Iloc.)* goma-*aSp*

RUBBER band *(Tag. & Iloc.)* lastico-*aSp*

RUBBER-necker *(Tag. & Iloc.)* miron-*Sp*, osyoso/sa-a*Sp*

Rude bastos-*Sp*, malaswa, mahalay, hindi decente-*Sp*; Iloc: bastos, haan a decente,

Rudiment ang unang-unang principio-*Sp* ng paksa; ang hindi masya-dong nabuong *version* ng isang bagay; *organ* na nasa pinakamaagang matantong forma-*Sp* gaya ng embryo

Rue magsisi, ikalulongkot; Iloc: agbabawi

Ruin maninira gaya ng tatamad-tamad at bara-bara lang para mawalan ka ng pera at trabaho, gumawa ka ng masama para masira ang pagkatao mo't mabilanggo ka, mambabae o manlalake ka para masira ang familia mo, maging *addict* ka ng droga at alak para sira na ang isip, buhay, ichura at kinabukasan mo

RULE, Law batas, patakaran, pamamalakad, alituntunin; Iloc: linteg, reglamento-*Sp*

RULE, Reign mamuno, maghari, nangingibabaw, manaig; Iloc: agturay, agar-ari, ag-dominar-*Sp*

RULE of thumb ito ay pambabala na iwasan ang masama at mali, at <u>kagawiang ipako lamang ang pansin at gawa sa makakabuti, makakaligtas at makakagaan</u> gaya ng *"**Rule of thumb: Never exploit and use questionable products because they are usually full of risks"** para hindi mabitag sa *drug addiction* at iba pang matagalang nakakasamang kalagayan, at *"A place for everything and everything in its place"* at *"Out of sight, out of mind"* para madaling hanapin at walang makalimutang dalhin, at hindi nagtatarantang maghanap-hanap kapag nagmamadaling lumabas sa bahay.

Rummage halughogin; Iloc: ukag-ukagen, agsuksukain

Rumor chismis-*Sp*, usap-usapang makapanira; Iloc: chismis, pagsasaritaan nga makadadael

RUN tumakbo; Iloc: agtaray

RUN/Operate an office mamahala at mangasiwa ng oficina-*Sp*; Iloc: mangigaway ken mangipaturong ti oficina
Synonym
Manage mamahala, mangasiwa, magtangkilik, magpalakad; Iloc: ipangulwan, mangigaway, mangiturong, mang-acecaso, mangpapagna
RUN after habolin; Iloc: camaten
Correlated words
Chase habolin; Iloc: camaten, tiliwen
Catch up mahabol, maabutan; Iloc: camacamen, macamacam, macamatan
RUN into by chance hindi inaasahan pero nagkataong nagkita; Iloc: agtumpongan
RUN-of-the-mill caraniwan o ordinaryo-*Sp* lamang
RUN over by a vehicle nasagasaan, makasagasa; Iloc: mapilidan
Runabout *teen-ager* na palibot-libot sa lugar o palipat-lipat ng grupong makasama niya; maliit na banca o coche
Runaround pagdadahilan at pangagatwiran, pag-iiwas, pag-aantala, pagtuturoan kung sino ang dapat bibintangan o kakausapin; Iloc: pambar ken paglislisi ti responsilidad-*Sp*, pagtaktak, pagitudotudo nu sinno iti mabalin da a kasarita
Runaway 1] tao na lumayas sa bahay at familya; tumakas na bilanggo o nagpoprotesta sa grupo o gawain o mga gawi na kadalasan para magtayo ng karival na grupo; cabayo na nagwawala at mahirap macontrolado; 2] malaking diferencia o lamang sa pagpanalo sa competensia; preciong laganap at hindi mahadlangan
Rundown 1] sumaria ng *report* na kapapahayag lamang tungkol sa mga importanteng detalye-*Sp*, 2] bahay na sira-sira na, 3] pagod na pagod o kaya hindi mabuti ang kalagayan ng katawan; Iloc: 1] sumaria ti *report* nga kaybagbaga laeng maygapu cadagiti importante a detalye, 2] balay nga adu dadael na, 3] nabannog unay o madi ti kasasaad ti bagi na
Rung of the stairs or ladder baytang ng hagdanan; Iloc: pagaddangan ti agdan
Runs in the family, it katangian ng isang familya-*Sp* na nagsalin-salin sa mga miembro-*Sp* nitong familya
Runway *strip*/daan na daongan ng eroplano, kung saan mag-*landing* mga ito
Rural bukid, barrio; Iloc. away, taltalon, barrio

Ruse tactika-*Sp* para malinlang, maloco o makuha nila ang pera o alahas mo

Rush madaliang pagkilos na parang may hinahabol na importante at mahalaga

Russian *(Tag. & Iloc.) Russian,* Ruso

Rust calawang, mangalawang; Iloc: lati, aglati

Rustic bukid, barrio; Iloc. away, taltalon, barrio

Ruthless walang awa; Iloc: awan asi na

RV, Recreational Vehicle *van* na ginagamit sa *camping* na may tulogan, lutoan at banyo-*Sp*; Iloc: *van* na iyus-usar-*Sp* iti pagcamping nga adda pagturogan, paglutoan ken banyo

S

Sabbath *(Tag. & Iloc.) Saturday,* Sabado-*Sp*

Saber *(see Sword)*

Sabotage makatraydor na gawain gaya ng pagsira sa mga gamit o paghadlang ng mahusay na pamaraan para hindi na gumagana; Iloc: makatraydor nga aramid casla ti pagdadael cadagiti aramat ken ilapped iti naimbag nga operasyon para haanen nga umandar o makabalin

Saboteur taong pahamak, naninira at nanghahadlang ng magandang operasyon ng bayan o companya; Iloc: tao a mangdadael, mangpadakes ken manglapped

Sack, jute sako-*Sp*, custal; Iloc: sako, custal, langguchi

Sacred banal, sagrado-*Sp*; Iloc: sagrado

Sacrifice *(Tag. & Iloc.)* sacrificio-*Sp*

Sad malungkot, mapanglaw, nalulumbay; Iloc: naliday, naladingit, naleddaang

Sadden palungkotin, patamlayin; Iloc: palidayen, patamnayen

Sadistic taong walang-walang awa at malupit at walang puso at consiencia-*Sp*; Iloc: tao nga awan asi uray nu sangkabassit ken nauyong ken awan puso ken consiencia na

Safe ligtas, nasa mabuting kamay, malayo sa panganib, protectado-*Sp*; Iloc: salvar-*Sp*, nakasalaknib, adayo ti dakes ken peggad, protectado

Safeguard pagtatanggol, pag-aalaga, pag-iingat at pagsisigurado na malayo sa panganib; Iloc: salakniban, pagaywan, pang-alwad ken pagsisigurado nga adayo iti peggad

Safekeeping pagligpit ng bagay para ligtas at hindi mawala dahil nasa kamay ng pag-aalaga at pag-iingat

Safety kaligtasan; Iloc: pannakasalaknib, pagkasalvar

Safety tips

Be careful, be safe mag-ingat ka, sigurohing ligtas ka, protectado na kasama ang napagkakatiwalaang tao para nasa mabuting kamay ka at malayo sa panganib; Iloc: agannad ka, sigurwen nga salvar ka, protectado nga adda caduam a mapagfiaram tapno nakasalaknib ka ken adayo iti dakes ken peggad

Be certain that you are safe *It is better to be safe than sorry, so we must take our safety and the family's safety seriously anytime and anywhere. Day or night, in urban streets or remote places, try not to be alone, and be aware of your surroundings. Don't focus on your phone as you may be run over or sideswiped by vehicles, or be vulnerable to bag snatchers, robbers, kidnappers, muggers, or wild animals. If you summon for a ride, be sure it's really an uber or lyft or a taxi, and don't take a lift on the car of somebody you just came to know. In social media online, be careful going into relationships as there are catfishes or people pretending to be someone simply to dupe others. When putting down your pin numbers in ATM machines, cover these up. These are just a few precautions to remember.*

SAFETY net ito'y lambat na pansalo na nasa baba upang sumalo sa nahuhulog na cirkero-*Sp* o trabahador-*Sp* buhat sa taas ng gusali

SAFETY pin *(Tag. & Iloc.)* imperdib-le

Sag luyloy; Iloc: yudyod

Sagacious *adj.,* **Sagacity** *n.* utak na matalas ang pag-aninaw o pananaw, mahusay at tama ang paghusga

Sage matalino ang pagturing at paghusga at pagpayo; Iloc: nakasirsirib ti pangbigbig ti tao ken situasyon-*Sp*

Sail maglayag, sasakay ng barco-*Sp* o banka; Iloc: aglayag, agsakay ti bapor o banka

Saint *(Tag. & Iloc.)* santo-*Sp,* santa-*Sp,* san-*Sp (i.e., San Pablo)*

Sake ikabubuti, pakinabang, magandang mahita o mapala

Salacious sulat, letrato at iba pa na napakalaswa, napakahalay, bastos-*Sp,* hindi decente-*Sp*

Salad *(Tag. & Iloc.) salad*, ensalada-*Sp*

Salary suweldo-*Sp*, sahod, kita; Iloc: suweldo, kita

Sale venta-*Sp*, tinda; Iloc: venta, laco

Saleable maive-venta-*Sp*, handang iventa

Salesman tagaventa, tagatinda; Iloc: tagaventa; tagalaco

Salient 1] lantad, nangingibabaw; 2] nakausli palabas

Saliva dura, laway; Iloc: tupra, catay

Salt *(Tag. & Iloc.)* asin

SALTED fish, dried *(Tag. & Iloc.)* tuyo, daing

SALTED fish sauce patis, alamang, bagoong; Iloc: aramang, bagoong, patis

Salty maalat; Iloc: naapgad

Salutary makakalusog, pampalusog, makaventahe o ano pang makakabuti

Salutation pagsasaludo, pambating salita, sulat o gawa; ang parteng *"Dear Sir"* sa sulat

Salutatory sa umpisa ng *commencement exercises*, ito ay talumpating nakaukol sa lahat ng mga nandodoon upang batiin sila ng pagtanggap at pag-*welcome*

Salute *(Tag. & Iloc.)* saludo-*Sp*

Salvage sagipin para hindi masira o masayang; Iloc: subboten para haan a madadael o masayang

Salvageable tubosin o impokin dahil mapapakinabangan pa kaya huwag itapon para hindi maaksaya o masayang

SALVATION kaligtasan; Iloc: pagka-salvar-*Sp*

SALVATION from God Ito ang regalong kaligtasang gracia na itinakda ng Panginoong Dios para maligtas tayo sa parusa ng ating mga kasalanan sa pamamagitan ng pagbaba ni Dios Hesu Cristo sa lupa bilang tao. Ang Dios Hesu Cristo ang nagdusa sa ating mga kasalanan, imbes na tayo ang magdusa sa infierno. Hindi natin paghihirapan itong *grace of salvation* na ito dahil ito ay libreng regalo ng Dios para sa kaligtasan ng lahat ng nilalang - *come as you are,* pero maniwala, mgtiwala at magsampalata lamang tayo na ang sacrificiong pinagdusahan ng Dios Hesu Cristo sa cruz ay para sa kaligtasan ng *soul* natin, at tanggapin natin si Hesu Cristo sa puso't buhay natin bilang Dios at Tagapagligtas natin, at magsamba tayo sa Canya. Ang lahat ng ating mga kasalanan - kasalanan sa nakaraan, sa kasalukuyan at sa hinaharap – lahat nito ay mapapatawad at malinisan na ng dugo ni Dios Hesu Cristo sa cruz. Papasok na rin ang Dios Espiritu Santo sa puso natin at hindi tayo iiwanan o lalayasan, at magkaroon din tayo ng *new birth* na *spiritual*—tayo'y espiritual na anak na ng Dios. Sa ating pagsisimba, pagdadasal, pagbabasa ng Biblia na banal na salita ng Dios, at paghiling na gabayan tayo ng Dios, <u>tayo'y madali nang bumuti at bumait.</u> Kapag binubuyo ng demonyo tayo para gumawa ng masama at magkasala, magdasal tayo sa Dios para hindi tayo mahulog sa tentacion. Ang Dios ang dapat maghari sa buhay natin parati - magdepende parati tayo sa paggabay ng Dios sa atin para mamuhay tayong maka-Dios. Hindi mawawala itong *gift of salvation* sa atin ng Dios. Magpacumbaba tayo at icumpisal natin sa Dios kapag nagkakasala tayo, kahit pinatawad na lahat ng ating mga kasalanan sa *crucifixion* na pinagdusahan ng Dios Hesu Cristo..

Salve pamahid na pampagaling ng sugat o pamawi ng sakit sa katawan

SAME pareho, ganun din; Iloc: pareho, isu met la nga isu

SAME age magkasing-edad-*Sp,* magkaedad; Iloc: agcasadar, agkaedad

SAME height magkasintangkad; Iloc: agkasintayag

SAME looks magkamukha; Iloc: agkaruprupa, agkalanga, agkaingas

SAME name *(Tag. & Iloc.)* tocayo-*Sp*

SAME time magkasabay, sabay-sabay; Iloc: aggiddan, agrinnana

SAME weight magkasintimbang, magkasimbigat; Iloc: agkasindagsen, agkasimbantut

Sample 1] *sample* ng producto-*Sp;* 2] subokan o tikman kung ito'y ma-gugustohan; Iloc: 1] *sample* ti producto; 2] padasen wenno ramanan tapno maammoan nu magustoan daytoy

Sanative mabisang panglunas o pangpagamot

Sanctify gawing banal, santohin; Iloc: bendisyonan, isagrado, pasantoen

Sanction 1] ang paraan na pinagkasundoan ng mga nasyon para mafuersang ipasunod sa isang nagkakasala at namiminsalang nasyon para hindi ipagpatuloy ang ginagawang panlulupig at pagsasacop ng ibang nasyon, pangbabala para ipatupad na sundin ang batas, 2] permiso o pagsang-ayon o pahintulot na binibigay na otorisasyon ng batas para sa ikabubuti ng lahat

Sanctity i-pagkamaka-Dios, gawing banal, gawing sagrado

Sancturary 1] sagradong lugar; 2] lugar na kanlungan o kublihan para makaiwas ng bilanggo o pagpa-*deport;* 3] silongan ng mga ibon at hayop para ligtas sila sa mga *hunters* o mangangaso

Sand buhangin; Iloc: darat

Sandals *(Tag. & Iloc.)* sandalya-*Sp*

Sandpaper *(Tag. & Iloc.)* papel-*Sp* de liha-*Sp*

Sandwich *(Tag. & Iloc.) sandwich*

Sandwiched or squeezed between two objects or persons *(Tag. & Iloc.)* naipit

Sane matino; Iloc: nanakem, normal ken claro ti panagpampanunot

Sanguine 1] masayang-masayang nag-aasa ng mabuti, optimista-*Sp*, may tiwala, may pananalig at pag-asa; 2] pula na gaya ng dugo; madugo o *sanguinary*

Sanitary malinis at nadisinfectahan; Iloc: nalinis ken nadisinfectaran (disinfecta/disinfectar-*Sp*)

Sanitation sanidad-*Sp*, kalinisan; Iloc: sanidad, kinadalus

Sanitize panglinis ito para mamatay ang mga microbio-*Sp*

Sanity kaliwanagan at katinohan ng isip; Iloc: lawag ken sirib iti nakem

Sans wala, hindi kasama; Iloc: awan, haan a naycadwa

Sap katas; Iloc: tubbog

Sapid malasa, masarap; kasiya-siya; Iloc: naimas

Sapient matalino ang pagturing at paghusga

Sapor ang elemento na nakakaafecto ng panlasa

Sarcasm *n.*, **Sarcastic** or **Sarcastical** *adj.*, sarcastico, ordinaryong salita pero pangtuya, panglait at pangpintas sa kapwa

Sardines *(Tag. & Iloc.)* sardinas-*Sp*

Sardonic kutyaan ang kapwa para bastosin

Sash bigkis; Iloc: barikes

Sashay lumakad na pakendeng-kendeng

Sass bastos-*Sp* o pang-insultong salita o sagot

Satan *(Tag. & Iloc.)* satanas-*Sp*, demonyo-*Sp*, diablo-*Sp*, diantre-*Sp*

Satiate, Satiety, Sate busogin; Iloc: bussogen, penneken

Satire *n.*, **Satirize** *v.*, paglalantad ng vicio-*Sp* o kamangmangan sa pamamagitan ng *irony* o kabaligtaran sa katunayan; Iloc: pangiparang ti vicio-*Sp* o pagkanengneng nga mangiyusar ti *irony* o balictad ti kaagpaysuan

Satisfaction pagkasaya kasama ang pagkacontento; Iloc: pannacapnek, pannakacontento

Satisfactory nandoon lahat ng kinakailangang katangian kaya pasado at nakakasiya; Iloc: dagiti rekisito ket adda amin canyana isu nga pasado ken maragsakan

SATISFIED nasiyahan, contento-*Sp*; Iloc: naragsakan, napennek, contento

SATISFIED eating busog; Iloc: nabsog, bussog, napnek

Satisfy papagsawain, pacontentohin; Iloc: pacontentoen, penneken, pacapneken (contento-*Sp*)

Synonym

Gratify papagsawain, pacontentohin; Iloc: pacontentoen, penneken, pacapneken

Saturate *v.*, **Saturation** *n.* 1] punoin o maglaganap ng producto-*Sp* o ibang kinakailangan; pangangailangan; 2] ibabad hanggang tumagos at mabasa lahat-lahat

Saturated basang-basa, tagas na tagas ng tubig, babad na babad sa tubig; Iloc: nakabasbasa, nagsagepsep ti danum

Correlated words

Immerse ilubog sa tubig, ibabad; Iloc: iyuper, itabnaw ti danum

Soak ibabad, ilubog sa tubig, ilublob; Iloc: iyuper, ilenned, itabnaw ti danum

Drenched basang-basa, tagas na tagas ng tubig, babad na babad sa tubig; Iloc: nakabasbasa, nagsagepsep ti danum

Saturday *(Tag. & Iloc.)* *Saturday,* Sabado-*Sp*

Sauce salsa-*aSp*, sawsawan; Iloc: sarsa

Saucer *(Tag. & Iloc.)* platito-*Sp*

Saunter mamasyal o maglakad ng kawalang-bahala

Sausage *(Tag. & Iloc.)* longganisa-*Sp*, chorizo-*Sp*

Sauté mag-gisa-*aSp*; Iloc: ag-gisar-*aSp*

Savagery, Savage trait *(Tag. & Iloc.)* salvahe-*Sp*

Savant taong napakalawak ang pinag-aralan

SAVE iligtas; Iloc: agsalvar

SAVE for a rainy day *Reserve or stock funds aside to provide contingency funds to be used in time of unforeseen tough times or emergency needs like school needs or future medical bills.* Mag-ipon, mag-impok, magtabi ng pera na pang-ipon para sa dadating na mga panahon kung kinakailangan ang pambayad sa importanteng bagay, para mayroong binubunot-bunot na pera

Synonyms

Scrimp, Skimp nagtitipid; Iloc: agin-inot, agkirmet

Set aside for future needs ibukod para sa pangangailagan sa mga kinabukasan; Iloc: ilasin para ti pakasapulan cadagiti masangwanan

Nest egg pera na nirereserva para sa mga *emergency* o dadating na pangangailangan

Saved naligtas sa kapahamakan; Iloc: naysalvar iti peggad

Savings ang naipon, ang naimpok; Iloc: ti naipon, ti naurnong

Correlated words

A penny saved is a penny earned Ang pera na naimpok dahil sa pagtitipid ay pareho sa pera na kinikita sa empleo o trabaho

SAVIOR taong tagapagligtas para hindi masaktan o mamatay ang nililigtas niya; Iloc: tao nga mangsalvar para haan a masaktan wenno matay ti i-salvar-*Sp* na

SAVIOR Jesus Christ Dios Anak na si Hesu Cristo na tagapagligtas ng lahat na nilalang para hindi maparusahan ang mga nilalang sa kanilang mga kasalanan dahil ang Panginoong Dios na si Hesu Cristo na ang tumanggap ng canilang mga parusa. Pinaghaplit-haplit si Hesu Cristo ng latigo, hinampas-hampas, dinuraduraan, sinampal -sampal, nilait-lait, kinoronahan ng mga tinik, at binuhat Niya ang mabigat na cruz papunta sa bundok ng Golgotha o Calvary kung saan Siya doon ipinako sa mismong cruz na binuhat Niya. Ang sinomang manalig, magtiwala, maniwala at magsampalataya sa sacrificio ni Hesu Cristo at tanggapin niya si Dios Hesu Cristo sa puso at buhay niya bilang Dios niya at Tagapagligtas niya, siya ay mapatawad at malinisan na sa lahat ng canyang mga kasalanan at makakapunta na siya sa langit.

Savory malasa, malinamnam; Iloc: naraman

Savvy nakakaalam ng husto pati ang mga detalye; Iloc: ammo na unay pati dagiti detalye

Saw for carpentry lagari; Iloc: ragadi

Saxophone *(Tag. & Iloc.) saxophone*

Say sabihin, magwika; Iloc: ibaga, ikuna, isao

Scab langib; labas ng nahihilom na sugat; Iloc: gudgod

Scabby, psoriasis-like on the skin galis; Iloc: gaddil

Scalawag tampalasan, oportunista-*Sp* para sa tanging-sarili lamang kaya gumagawa ng kasamaan

Scald mapaso sa mainit na tubig; Iloc: masinit ti napudot a danum

SCALE for weighing timbangan; Iloc: pagbatayan nga pangrucod ti dagsen

SCALE of fish kaliskis; Iloc: siksik

Scallop 1] pagkaing galing sa tubig na may balat o talakup na *shell*; 2] ang decorasyon na kalahating circulo-*Sp* o curba sa gilid ng damit o mantel

Scalp anit; Iloc: cudil ti ulo

Scam gawain ng taong walang conciensia at ni respeto sa sarili at ni considerasyon sa vinivictima niya kaya gumagawa ng masama gaya ng panlilinlang sa kapwa at pandadaya at panloloco para makapagsamantala at makuha ang pera at ari-arian ng vinivictima niya; Iloc: aramid ti tao nga awan conciensia na, ni respeto ti mismo a bagi na o ni considerasyon iti vicvictimaen na isu nga agaramid iti dakes casla iti pangallilaw ken panggulib ken pangcusit ken pangloco para maala na ti cuarta ken sanicua ti victima

Scamper papunta o tumakbo ng bigla o mabilis; tumakbo na palaro gaya ng bata

Scan basahin at suriin ang informasyon at mga detalye

Scandal *(Tag. & Iloc.)* escandalo-*Sp*

Scandalous *(Tag. & Iloc.)* escandaloso/sa-*Sp*

Scant, Scanty limitadong bilang kaya kulang; halos hindi sapat o hindi kasya, bahagya lamang; Iloc: ngangngani awan pulos wenno haan nga umanay

Scapegoat taong pinatungan ng sala kahit siya ay inocente, taong pinasubo; Iloc: tao nga napabasol uray no inocente-*Sp* isu, tao nga impasubo

Scar peklat; Iloc: piglat

Scarce kaunti, konti, bahagya; Iloc: manmano, haan nga adu, bassit

Scare takotin; Iloc: butngen

Scaredy-cat matatakotin; Iloc: managbutbuteng

Scarf *[single]*, **Scarves** *[plural]* *(Tag. & Iloc.)* *scarf*

Scary nakakakilabot, nakakasindak, katako-takot; Iloc: nakabutbuteng, makasumgar ti dutdot

Scat pumunta agad-agad; Iloc: mapan ensegida-*Sp*

Scatter icalat, isabog; Iloc: iwara, iwaras

Scavenge mangurakot; Iloc: agcurakot

Scenario storya-*Sp* ng *drama* na nilalarawan ang lugar-*Sp,* mga taohan sa dula, mga situasyon-*Sp* o pangyayari at iba pa

Scene 1] tanawin; 2] situasyon o pangyayari sa tunay na buhay; 3] lugar kung saan ang palabas o paligsahan o pagtitipon

Scenery, Beauty of nature maganda at kasiya-siyang kalikasang tanawin ng kalawakan; Iloc: napipintas a naturalesa-*Sp* ti arrubayan a matantan-aw

Correlated word

Panorama malawak na tanawin ng kalawakan; Iloc: nalawa a matan-aw ti arrubayan

Scenic naturalesang tanawin; magandang tanawin; letrato ng tanawin

Scent amoy; Iloc: angot

Schedule an appointment itakda ang araw at oras at lugar ng pagkikita ng magkaibigan o sa pagpaconsulta sa doctor o *interview* sa trabaho; Iloc: i-calendario-*Sp* ti aldaw ken oras ken lugar nga makipagkita iti gayyem na wenno iti pagpaconsultar iti doctor o *interview* iti trabaho

Scheme 1] plano-*Sp,* detalye-*Sp* o programa-*Sp* o *line-ups* ng gagawin para sundin o para ipagbuo ng mga ito; 2] pinangarap pa lamang na proyecto-*Sp*; 3] palihim na sabwatan na nakakasama

Schlep, Schlepp, Shlep, Shlepp *[shlep] slang*: 1] kaladkarin o buhatin; 2] kumilos ng mabagal, lampa at hindi *normal*

Schlock, Shlock *[shlok] slang* mababang-clase-*Sp,* mumurahin, basura-*Sp*; producto-*Sp* na gawa sa mura at mababang uri

Schmooze *[shmooz] slang* makipagcuentohan o makipag-chismisan para magpalipas ng oras, para pasatiempo-*Sp* lamang

Scholar estudiante-*Sp* lalo na ang nagbigyan ng scholarship; taong mataas ang kaalaman; Iloc: estudiante lallalo iti naikkan ti *scholarship*; tao nangato ti ammo na

Scholarship 1] ang natamo ng mapag-aral na estudiante, 2] pera na igantimpala sa karapat-dapat na estudiante para tulongan siya sa pag-aaral; Iloc: 1] ti nagun-od ti nagaget agadal nga estudiante, 2] cuarta nga ited ti agrebbeng nga estudiante a pangtulong iti pagadal na

SCHOOL escuela-*Sp,* paaralan; Iloc: escuela, pagadalan

SCHOOL of hard knocks ang karanasan sa buhay lalo na sa mga kahirapan at kabigoan na nakakabigay ng aral at kaalaman

Schoolmate kamag-aral; Iloc: ka-escuela-*Sp*

Schoolyear panahon ng pasukan; Iloc: panawen ti pag-escuela-*Sp*

Sciatica nararamdamang sakit sa balakang hanggang sa likod ng hita at sa paligid dito; Iloc: sakit idiay patong inggana likod ti luppo

SCIENCE *(Tag. & Iloc.) science,* siensia-*Sp*

SCIENCE, practical or applied diciplina sa pag-uugnay at paggamit ng kaalaman sa siencia para sa paglutas ng mga problema

Scientist *(Tag. & Iloc.) scientist*

Scissors gunting; Iloc: getteng, cartib

Sclerosis pamamaga ng *organ* o lamang-loob ng katawan gaya ng *tissues* o daanan ng dugo dahil sa pagtigas o pagkapal sa parteng may inflamasyon-*Sp*

Scoff 1] mag-insulto; 2] matakaw at mabilis na kumain

Scold pagalitan, pagsabihan, sermonan; Iloc: ungtan, correhiren (correhir-*Sp*), pagsawsaw-an

Scoop out salokin; Iloc: acupen

Scooper pangsalok; Iloc: pangacup

Scoot biglang pagtakbo; Iloc: golpe a pagtaray

Scope laki, lawak, capacidad, ang puedeng masacop

Scorch mapaso; Iloc: masinit

    Correlated words

    Singe, Sear mapaso; Iloc: masinit

    Burn masunog; Iloc: mauram, mapuoran

    Scald mapaso sa mainit na tubig; Iloc: masinit ti napudot a danum

Score *(Tag. & Iloc.)* puntos

Scorn pagkamuhi; Iloc: rurod

Scorpion alakdan; Iloc: manggagama

Scot-free malaya dahil pinawalang-sala, hindi binilanggo at hindi pinarusahan

Scour 1] kuscosin, kiskisin, is-isin at lampasohin, linisan, sabonan at hugasan para maalis ang mga kinuskos; 2] magsaliksik sa kapaligiran para maghanap; Iloc: kuscosen, kis-kisen, is-isuan, radradan; 2] agsukimat

Scourge 1] parusahan, 2] haplitan, hampasin, latigohin; Iloc: 1] dusaen, 2] saplitan, ablatan, basnotan, i-latigo-*Sp*

Scowl magkunot-noo o magmukhang galit o nagbabanta; Iloc: agmuregreg a casla agunget wenno agcarit

"Scram!" "Umalis ka!" Iloc: "Fuera!-*Sp* ka ditoy"

Scramble hastily among a group to grab a valued thing, i.e., a ball magcarambolang agawan; Iloc: ag-carambola-*aSp* nga aginnagawan

Scrap piraso-*Sp*, retaso-*Sp*, panapong bagay; Iloc: piraso, retaso, pangbelleng a banag

SCRAPE, skin scratch *(Tag. & Iloc.)* gasgas

SCRAPE, skin bruise *(Tag. & Iloc.)* galos

SCRAPE out coconut meat cayorin; Iloc: carusen

SCRATH on an appliance or a car *(Tag. & Iloc.)* gasgas

SCRATCH with one's nails magcamut, magcalmut; Iloc: agcaramot, agcudcod

Scratchy 1] tunog ng nagcacamut o kahig-manok; 2] makati kaya kinakamot

Scrawl sumulat ng mabilis at bara-bara lamang; Iloc: agsurat iti napaspas ken bara-bara laeng

Scrawny napakapayat; Iloc: nakakutkuttong

Scream tumili; Iloc: agikkis

Screech tunog na parang umaandar na gulong na biglang pinapahinto

Screen 1] salamin ng *television* o *computer*, 2] pangtakip o pangprotecta; Iloc: 1] sarming ti *television* wenno *computer*, 2] pang-abbong o protecta

SCREW *n. (Tag. & Iloc.)* tornilyo-*Sp*, roscas-*Sp*

SCREW *v.* pihitin; Iloc: tiritiren

SCREW, loosen with a pihitin para paluwagin; Iloc: tiritiren para mapalukay

SCREW, tighten with a pihitin para higpitan; Iloc: tiritiren para mapairut

Screwdriver aparatong pangpihit ng tornilyo-*Sp* pag higpitan ito o paluwagin

Scribble sumulat o mag-*drawing* ng mabilis at bara-bara lamang at walang kahulogan; Iloc: agsurat o *sketch* a napaspas ken bara-bara laeng nga awan iti kaipapanan na

Scribe manunulat sa periodico-*Sp*, *journalist*; Iloc: mannurat iti periodico, *journalist*

Scrimp magtipid ng husto-*Sp*; Iloc: agin-inot ken agkirmet ti usto-*Sp*

Script sinulat sa kamay, kasulatan; Iloc: insurat ti ima, kasuratan

Scripture *(Tag. & Iloc.)* 1] *Bible*, Biblia-*Sp*, 2] libro ng reli*gion* na tinuturing na sagrado

Scroll balumbon; Iloc: nalucot

Scrounge humiram na walang balak isauli o bayaran ito; humiram ng maliit na bagay pero hindi masahang ibalik; tungkol sa taong palahiram; 2] magsaliksik para makaipon ng kinkailangan

SCRUB 1] kuskusin ng madiin sa pamamagitan ng *brush* para matanggal ang mga dumi; 2] mababang punong-kahoy o halaman gaya ng *shrubs*

SCRUB skin maghilod; Iloc: agludlod

Synonym

Rub off dirt from body maghilod, hiloran ang libag; Iloc: ludlud, lidlid, lidliden ti cabcab

Scruff 1] batok, likod ng leeg; 2] taong madungis; 3] dumi o *scum* na dumikit na dahil sa matagalang hindi paglinis

Scruple pag-aatubili o pag-aalinlangan dahil sa kabig ng conciensia-*Sp*; Iloc: haan a makatalna gapu iti pagkidag iti conciensia

Scrupulous may budhi conciensia-*Sp* at principio-*Sp*

Scrutinize *v.*, **Scrutiny** *n.* usisahin o suriing mabuti; masusing sinisiyasat at iniimbestiga; pagmamanman o pagbabanta; matalas na pagtingin na parang naghahanap; Iloc: usigen o usisaen ti naimbag, sukisoken, sukimaten

Scum tumigas na dumi na dumikit sa *shower wall* o ibang lugar dahil sa matagalang di nalinisan; 2] tumigas na bula o mabahong bula sa taas ng likido; 3] masamang tao

Scurrility *n.*, **Scurrilous** *adj.* nakakadiri, malaswa, pang-abuso, panglait, pang-insulto

Scurry kumilos o pakilosin ng kaagad-agad at mabilis; Iloc: aggaraw o pagarawin ensegida-*Sp* ken napardas

Scurvy pamamaga at pagdudugo ng gilagid, maculay na batik-batik sa cutis, at iba pa dahil sa kaculangan ng vitamina C; 2] masama, ka-muhi-muhi at nakakasuklam

SEA dagat, karagatan; Iloc: baybay, taaw

SEA waves alon, daluyong; Iloc: dalluyong

Seal 1] ipinid ng husto, 2] napakalaking isda, 3] tatak ng kalakal; Iloc: 1] rikpan ti usto, 2] nakadak-dakkel a lames, 3] celyo-*Sp* o marka-*Sp* ti compania-*Sp*

Seam tiklop sa gilid ng kasuotan na itatahi, linya-*Sp* na tatahiin

Seamstress *(Tag. & Iloc.)* modista

Sear mapaso; Iloc: masinit

SEARCH hanapin, saliksikin, magtunton; maghalughog at magsaliksik sa paghahanap; magmanman, makiusap, magtanong, mag-discobre-*Sp*; Iloc: biroken, sursoren, agsursur, tuntonen, agsukain, mangdiscobre
Correlated word

Quest paghahanap; Iloc: pagbirok

SEARCH blindly by groping in the dark cacapa-capa habang humahagilap; Iloc: agar-aricap mientras nga mangsapsapul

SEARCH (body) by frisking or patting down capcapan, capain; Iloc: capcapan, aricapen

SEARCH rummagingly by taking out contents halungkatin, bulatlatin; Iloc: ukagen, bukitkiten

Seashore tabing-dagat, baybay, dalampasigan; Iloc: igid ti baybay

Seasickness hilo at nalulula; Iloc: maulaw ken makasarwa

SEASON tiempo-*Sp* o panahon gaya ng tag-init, taglamig at tag-ulan, clima-*Sp*; Iloc: tiempo wenno panawen, clima

SEASON the food timplahan; Iloc: templaan

Seasonal pana-panahon; Iloc: panapanawen

Seasoning recado-*aSp*, panimpla; Iloc: pang-templa-*Sp*, recado

Seat upoan, silya-*Sp*; Iloc: tugaw, silya

Secede *v.*, **Secession** *n.* umalis sa asosasyon-*Sp* o federasyon-*Sp* o ano mang kinaaniban alinsunod sa tamang patakaran

Seclude *v.*, **Seclusion** *n.* ihiwalay sa kapwa o sa mga publico-*Sp*; gawin siyang mag-isa na lamang

SECOND ikalawa, segundo/da-*Sp*; Iloc: maykadua, segundo/da

SECOND-guess gamitin ang *hindsight* o ang pagkilala sa mga katotohanan/*facts* at posibilidad-*Sp* at mga kinakailangan/*requirements* ng isang situasyon-*Sp* at tamang *decision* at iba pa sa tangkang ilagay sa katuwiran o ituring ang halaga o ituro ang mali; tangkang hulaan ang mangyayari o mag-*outguess*/hintayin at asahan ng husto ang pagkilos o galaw o pakay na dadating

SECOND nature katangian na nakatanim at natural-*Sp* lamang sa isang taong nagtataglay niyan

SECOND thought, on nagdadalawa ang isip; Iloc: agdudua

Secondary hindi primero kundi yung segundo-*Sp* o ikalawa lamang; ito ay yung kasunod ng nauna; mas mababa hindi kasing importante sa primero-*Sp*

SECRET secreto-*Sp*, lihim; Iloc: secreto, limed, limed, liiw
Correlated words
Hide a secret ilihim; Iloc: ilimed
Hide a thing itago, icubli; Iloc: ilemmeng, isuksok
Esoteric alam at naiintindihan ng isang grupo lamang at secreto o lihim na hindi nila pinapaalam sa publico
Conceal itago, icubli; Iloc: ilemmeng
Hidden tago, nakacubli, lingid; Iloc: nakalemmeng, nakalinged, nakasuksok

SECRET service sangay ng govierno para sa *intelligence* at *counter-intelligence operations* na nagi-imbestiga-*Sp* tungkol sa lakas ng *army* ng ibang bansa, pati ang pag-aalam at pagdakip ng mga gumagawa ng mga falsipikadong pera; at pinoprotectahan din nila ang presidente-*Sp* ng bayan at ng canyang familya-*Sp*; at iba pa na palihim na trabaho-*Sp* gaya ng pag-e-espia-*Sp*
Correlated word
Undercover espia, gumaganap ng palihim; Iloc: espia, agobobra a palimed

Secrete pagdaloy o paglabas ng likido-*Sp* o sustancia-*Sp* sa katawang-laman o *body organ* bilang *normal* na gawain nito

Secretive malihim; Iloc: nalimed, naliiw

Sectarian tungkol sa paniwala at mga principio-*Sp* o uri ng pangkat ng sumusunod ng mga ito

Section *n.*, **Sectional** *adj.* 1] parte na tinanggal sa katawan ng buo na kung ibalik ay kasang-ayon pa rin; 2] parte o bahagi ng bagay, bayan, comunidad, clase at iba pa; 3] ang pagbaha-bahagi o paghati-hati ng isang bagay; 4] tungkol sa mga pinaghiwa-hiwalay na parte gaya ng *sofa* na puedeng magkakasama o magkakahiwalay

Sector *(Tag. & Iloc.)* sector, panig

Secular tungkol sa maka-mundo at hindi tungkol sa mga relihion-*Sp*, espiritual-*Sp* at sagrado-*Sp*

SECURE, Fix firmly naka-puesto-*Sp* ng mahusay, nakatalaga o naka-tayong matatag, nakatakip o sarado ng mabuti; Iloc: naka-plastar-*Sp* a nalaeng, natibker ti tacder, naka-cerra-*Sp* nga usto-*Sp*

SECURE, Free from risk ligtas at malayo sa panganib; Iloc: adda seguridad-*Sp* o *security or safety* na, adayo ti peggad

SECURE person malaking confiansa-*Sp* sa sariling kacayahan, com-fortab-le-*Sp* na makisama sa mga tao; Iloc: dakkel ti confiansa na ti mismo-*Sp* a cabaelan na, comfortab-le a makisango ti tattao

SECURITY *(Tag. & Iloc.)* seguridad-*Sp*

SECURITY-taker, Not a chance taker *(Tag. & Iloc.)* segurista-*Sp*

Sedate *v.*, **Sedation** *n.* calmado-*Sp*, tahimik at payapa; bigyan ng *sedative* para mailagay sa ganyang condisyon-*Sp* para mawala ang hapis o pagkabagabag ng loob

Sedentary kaunting pagkikikilos lamang gaya ng nakaupo lamang

Sedition sa salita at gawa, mag-udyok na magrebelde sa kapayapaan ng bayan o govierno-*Sp*, at mag-alsa ng *public disorder,* paghihimagsik

Seduce *v.*, **Seduction** *n.* i-*corrupt*, hikayati at piliting makipagtalik ng *sexual*; himokin na pabayaan ang tungkulin, kabutihan, katapatan o *allegiance* sa principio-*Sp* o paniwala sa Dios, at sa iba pa

Sedulous masipag at matiyaga; nakapako ang tingin at maingat na pagsunod sa tamang pagsagawa

SEE tingnan, silayan, malasin, makita, mabanaag, masinag; Iloc: makita, kitaen

Synonyms

Look tingnan, malasin, silayan; Iloc: kitaen

Look afar tumatanaw; Iloc: agtantan-aw, tan-awen

Look sidewise or back lingonin sa magkabilaan o sa likod; Iloc: tumalyaw nga agsinnumbangir wenno diay likod

Look downward from one's window dungawin; Iloc: agcalumbaba

Glance sulyapan, balingan; Iloc: tumalyaw

Glimpse silayan ng sandali; Iloc: kitaen ti nabiit

Focus on nakatitig ng firmi; Iloc: perrengen

Stare titigan; Iloc: mingmingmingan

Glare at irapan; Iloc: mulmulagatan

Hostile look nanlilisik ang matang tumingin; Iloc: cusilapan

Ogle tumititig na mapanghalina o parang may cursonada; Iloc: kumitkita nga casla mangaw-awis wenno adda cursonada na

Watch a show panoorin; Iloc: buyaen

Observe inoobservahan, minamatyagan, minamanmanan, minamasdan, pinupuna, pinapansin; Iloc: agob-observar, agsipsipot, agsisiim, agmingmingming

View *v.* pagmasdan, tignan; Iloc: agtan-aw, kitaen

Notice mapuna, mapansin; Iloc: madlaw, masiputan

Surveill *v.,* **Surveillance** *n.,* pagtatanod, pagmamachag; Iloc: panangsipsiput, pagsisiim, palpaliiwan

Spy on nanunubok, naniniktik, nagmamanman, nagsusubaybay; Iloc: agsipsiput, sipsiputan, agpalpaliiw, agsisiim

SEE eye to eye magkapareho ang paniniwala at magkasundo ang pagturing sa mga bagay-bagay o kalagayan

SEE the light at the end of the tunnel pagkatapos ng mga panahon ng kahirapan at pagsisikap, may nasisilayan na maasahang ginhawa o gantimpala

SEE-through naaninag; Iloc: maan-anninag

Seed buto, butil, binhi, semilya-*aSp*; Iloc: bukel, bin-i, semilya

Seedling punla; Iloc: bunobon

Seedy 1] mabunga at ma-abundancia; 2] sira-sirang titirhan dahil sa pabaya; 3] pagod na pagod o may sakit; 4] sira ang puri o karangalan

Seek *see Search*

Seem, Seem like parang, tila, wari, mistulang; Iloc: casla, agparang a casla

Seep through magtagos; Iloc: agsagepsep

Seesaw *(Tag. & Iloc.) seesaw*

Seethe 1] kumukulo o nagpapakulo; 2] may *excitement* o nasa kataasan ang damdamin na puedeng sa kagulohan o sa kasiyahan

Segment *see Section*

Segregate 1] ihiwalay, 2] paghiwa-hiwalayin batay sa lahi; Iloc: 1] isina, 2] pagsisinaen batay ti *race* o lahi

Seismic tungkol sa lindol at pagyanig nito

SEIZE, Grab sunggaban, dakmain, agawin; Iloc: rabsuten, rabnoten, gammatan, agawen, sibbaruten

SEIZE a place/country to takeover forcefully sacopin, lupigin; Iloc: parmeken

SEIZE the opportunity *Act quickly and take advantage of an opportunity when available or offered, as opportunities are not on hand all the times.* Huwag mong pabayaang lumampas ang oportunidad-*Sp* habang nandidiyan - dakmain mo at sunggaban mo baka nakabukas iyan para sa iyo.

Seizure mangaligkig; Iloc: kissiw

Seldom bihira, pambihira, madalang, matumal, bahagya; Iloc: manmano, sagpaminsan
Antonyms
Often palagi, madalas, malimit; Iloc: canayon
Successive sunod-sunod; Iloc: agsasaruno

Select piliin; Iloc: pilyen

Selection *(Tag. & Iloc.)* pagpipilihan, *menu, options*
Correlated word
Choice *(Tag. & Iloc.)* napili

SELF sarili; Iloc: bagi
Synonym
Body katawan; Iloc: bagi

SELF-assured may confiansa-*Sp* sa canyang sarili at sa canyang ka-cayahan, at comfortab-le-*Sp* na makiharap canino man; may tapang at confiansa sa cacayahang makibaka sa anoman sa buhay; Iloc: adda confiansa na ti bagi na ken ti cabaelan na, comfortab-le a makipatang ti siasino man; adda tured ken confiansa na iti cabaelan na a mang-solvar-*Sp* cadagiti parikut ken problema.

SELF-centered makasarili, sarili lamang ang inuuna at binibigyan niya ng kapakanan; Iloc: mismo-*Sp* ti bagbagi laeng ti un-unaen na ken pagpagustoan na (gusto-*Sp*)
Antonym
Altruist nagmamalasakit sa kapwa at hindi siya makasarili; Iloc: ma-ngisaksakit iti dadduma ken haan a bagbagi laeng ti pampanunoten na

SELF-confident *adj.,* **Self-confidence** *n.* may confiansa sa canyang sarili at sa canyang kacayahan, at comfortab-le-*Sp* na makiharap canino man; may tapang at confiansa-*Sp* sa cacayahang makibaka sa anoman sa buhay; Iloc: adda confiansa na ti bagi na ken iti cabaelan na,

comfortab-le a makipatang iti siasino man; adda tured ken confiansa na iti cabaelan na a mang-solvar-*Sp* cadagiti parikut/problema
Correlated word
Morale disposisyon ng tao na napapamalas sa canyang confianza, pagkasaya, pagkakaroon ng diciplina at pagkagana na magagampanan niya ang gawaing itinakda o hinirang sa canya

SELF-control *Self-control is the same as self-discipline. It is controlling, restraining and stopping oneself from doing things one wants to do that are not in one's best interest. It needs self- control on actions, emotions, words, reactions, desires, greed, temper, impulses, recklessness, haste, etc. because without self-control, one may do offensive things that are damaging to oneself and detriment to one's success. It also needs self-denial like refusing cakes and pastries when one is on diet. Presence of mind is also needed to be resolute in controlling onself.*
Synonym
Forbear *v.,* **Forbearance** *n. Abstain, forego, refrain from, restrain oneself; curb, avoid, shun things that are detrimental.*

SELF-defense pagtatanggol at pang-defensa-*Sp* sa sarili; Iloc: pang-salvar-*Sp* ken pangdefensa iti bagi

SELF-denial hindi pagbigyan at pagkaitan ang sarili sa mga luho lang na hindi nakakabuti sa canya; Iloc: haan a pagustoan o ipaidam iti bagi na dagiti carinyo a haan makatulong canyana

SELF-employed pagkakaroon ng sariling pagkakakitaan

SELF-esteem respeto-*Sp* sa sarili at sa mabuting pagkatao niya; Iloc. respeto iti bagi na ken iti a nasingpet a pagkatao na

SELF-explanatory hindi kailangan ang pag-explica dahil nakikita, lantad at maliwanag ang pahiwatig

SELF-indulgent caprichoso/sa-*Sp*, maluho, magpalugod sa sariling ka-gustuhan, mapagbigay ng layaw sa canyang sarili, mapamihasa, nagsasariling nagpapasarap; Iloc: caprichosa/so, agpapas ti mismo-*Sp* a kagustoan na, agbukbukod nga agpapaimas cadagiti cayat na

SELF-interest para sa sariling kapakanan; Iloc: para ti kaimbagan ti bagi na

SELF-liquidating 1] puedeng iventa at ipalit sa pera sa madaling panahon o bago dumating ang fecha-*Sp* na ang tagagawa ng producto-*Sp* ay dapat mabayaran; 2] utang na ginagamit para fondohan ang mga *transaction* na ang bayad dito ay naaasahang lumaki bago dumating ang fecha na bayaran ang utang

SELF-made nagtagumpay sa pamamagitan ng sariling pawis at sicap; Iloc: nagballigi gapu ti bukbukod a linget ken pacat

SELF-perception matalas ang utak at nakikila ang sarili niya ng husto, nalalaman ang resulta ng canyang asal at gawa, nalalaman kung ano ang nararamdaman o naiisip ng iba sa canyang sinasabi o pakikitungo sa canila, nalalaman kung may gagawin siyang paliwanag o pagmamagandang-loob kung nagkasala siya at iba pa

SELF-reliance *adj., This is relying on one's own capabilities, skills, strength, resources, decisions, abilities, etc. He/she should be able to cook his meals, manage his money efficiently like making __no__ credit card debts, know how to take care of his health and safety, etc. At times however, getting feedback from others like the family may be necessary when discussing some important decisions to find out other favorable alternatives.*

Correlated words

Independent nagdedepende lamang sa sariling cacayahan at walang tulong sa iba; Iloc: agdepdepende laeng iti cabaelan na nga awan tulong ti sabali

Stand on one's own two feet hindi magdepende sa iba kundi sinisiguro na sapat ang kinikita niya o nagtitipid siya para hindi mangutang at caya pa ring mabayaran ang mga pangangailangan niya at familia niya

Fend sikaping mabuhay, manatili o macaya lahat kahit walang tulong ng iba; Iloc: agpakat nga agbiag, makamentener o maypasar na amin uray awan tulong ti dadduma

Get by nacacaya kahit may kapansanan o pobre o mahirap ang kalagayan; Iloc: maypaspasar na uray nu adda diferencia ti bagi na o pobre isu wenno narigat ti kasasaad

SELF-respect may respeto sa sarili dahil siya ay gumagawa ng mabubuti at maganda ang canyang asal parati; Iloc: adda respeto na ti bagi na gapu ta agar-aramid isu ti naimbag ken nasayaat ken addaan isu ti napintas nga ugali canayon

SELF-restrained mahinahon, mapagtimpi, controlado ang asal at damdamin at pananalita; Iloc: natalna, controlado - matengngel na ti garaw, ricna ken ti pagsasao na

SELF-service sa *cafeteria, gas station* at iba pang facilidad-*Sp*, sini-silvihan ang sarili na walang sinoman tumutulong o nagsisilvi sa canya

SELF-serving ocupado siya sa pagpamihasa o pagbigay ng layaw sa canyang sarili lamang

SELF-sufficient cayang-cayang sustentohan ang canyang sarili pati lahat ng canyang pangangailangan nilang mag-anak dahil sa pagkasipag niya, pagkaresponsab-le at paggastos ng pera ng tama para hindi mangutang niya

Selfie kinukuhanan ng letrato ang sarili niya o siya at mga kasamahan niya sa pamamagitan ng hawak-hawak na *digital camera* o *phone camera* na ang tangka ay i-*upload* sa *social networking website*; Iloc: iret-retrato-*Sp* na ti bagi na wenno isu ken kacadwa na nga iyus-usar-*Sp* na ti ig-igaman na a *digital camera* o *phone camera* nga ti panggep na ket i-*upload* na idiay *social networking website*

Selfish sakim, makasarili, sinasarili lamang at di nagpapadamay, madamot; Iloc: naimot, napaidam, bagbagi na laeng ti pagpagustoan na ken haan nga mangiraman ti sabali
Antonym
Generous mapagbigay, bukas ang palad sa mga nangangailangan, handang magbigay ng caya niyang ibigay; Iloc: manangisagot, mangipaay, nakasagana nga mangited iti cabaelan na nga ited

SELL mag-venta-*Sp*, magtinda; Iloc: aglaco

SELL out 1] iventa lahat-lahat, 2] ipasubo niya ang kapwa niya sa canyang pagtatraidor; Iloc: 1] ilaco aminamin, 2] ipasubo ti cadwa na iti pangtraidor na

Semantic ang kahulugan o interpretasyon-*Sp* ng salita o ng isang *sentence*; Iloc: ti katarusan wenno interpretasyon-*Sp* iti sarita o iti *sentence*

Semblance panlabas na ichura-*Sp* tutoo man iyan o pakita lamang; pagkapareho o copia ng isang bagay

Semen *(Tag. & Iloc.)* tamud

Seminary *(Tag. & Iloc.)* seminario

Senate *(Tag. & Iloc.)* senado-*Sp*

Senator *(Tag. & Iloc.)* senador-*Sp*

SEND ipadala ihulog sa coreo-*Sp*; Iloc: ipaw-it, i-buzon-*Sp*, ipatulod ti coreo

SEND-off parangal sa pag-alis, despedida-*Sp*; Iloc: padaya a pammalubos, despedida

Senile palatandaan ng katandaan; paghina na ng katawan o ng pag-obra-*Sp* ng utak gaya ng pagka-uliyanin

Senior 1]matandang tao, 2] taong mas mataas ang ranko-*Sp*, 3] nasa huling baytang na ng *high school*; Iloc: 1] baket o lakayen, 2] tao nga mas nangato ti ranko, 3] addan iti kaudian a baytang ti *high school*

Seniority sa pareho-*Sp* ang posisyon-*Sp*, siya ay iyong mas matagal na sa puesto-*Sp*; Iloc: nu agkapareho ti puesto da, isu iti daytay mas nabayagen iti puesto

Sensation 1] normal-*Sp* na tungkulin ng iba't ibang *senses* ng tao gaya ng pag-obra ng isip, pang-amoy, pandinig, pagsalita, pangkain, panlasa, chan, damdamin, lakas at iba pa; 2] *sensation* o *excited feelings* o madidiin na damdamin na ginigising ng napapanood at ng mga pangyayari sa kapaligiran

Sensational nagpapagising ng pananabik o pag-aasamasam; Iloc: mangriing iti paggagar ken pagpapaos

Sensationalize magpahayag (sa salita, periodico-*Sp*, *reports*, *events*, at iba pa) na ang pangyayari ay mas maculay o mas nakakakilabot <u>kaysa</u> sa katunayan

SENSE 1] abilidad at capabilidad ng katawan gaya ng paningin, pandinig, pang-amoy, panglasa, pandamdam; 2] nakakaramdam pero malabo at hindi mawari; *discern*; 3] makatarungang intelihencia dahil sa mahusay na pag-obra ng utak; 4] ang diwa; 5] ang kahulogan ng salita o *statement* o pagpapahayag

SENSE, make makatwiran, naiintindihan dahil ito ay pertinente at tunay na nangyayari sa buhay

Senses, come to one's manumbalik ang tamang pagturing o katunayan sa buhay kaya nagiging makatwiran na

Sensibility nakakaramdam sa hipo o pandamdam kaya tumutugon dito; mabilis at matalas na pagtugon ng isip sa nakikita, naririnig, nararamdaman, naaamoy at nalalasahan; madaling tablan o maramdaming *senses* na tumutugon; intelihenteng paningin at pagturing, pagtanto at pangdamdam, matalas na pagpapalugod at pagpapahalaga ng nararapat, at matinik na pagkakakilala ng mabuti't masama

Sensible matino, mabait at maingat; Iloc: nasirib, nanakem, nasingpet ken naannad agaramid ti pagimbagan

SENSITIVE, Thin-skinned balat-sibuyas, maramdamin, pikon; Iloc: arinsagid, pikon

SENSITIVE to people's needs/feelings, With empathy mapagdamdam, intelihensia at kabaitan sa pandama sa kapwa at tumutugon sa ikabubuti ng situasyon at payapang pagsasamahan; Iloc: intelihensia ken singpet nga panricna iti tao ken mangsubsubalit ti usto para ti pagimbagan ti situasyon ken natalna a pakicadcadwa; mapangricna iti tao ken situasyon-*Sp*
Correlated word

Soft-hearted malambot ang puso, maawain, may considerasyon sa kapwa; Iloc: nalukneng ti puso, mannangaasi, adda considerasyon na iti dadduma

Sensor aparato-*Sp* na nakakaramdam at tumutugon ito ng pang-alerto-*Sp*; o aparato sa *signal light* sa *intersection* ng calsada na nagpapa-*go-signal* o *stop-signal* at tutugon naman ang mga sasakyan kung aavante na o hihinto

Sensual nahihilig sa pagbibigay-kasiyahan sa *senses* gaya ng *sex*; walang moralidad-*Sp* dahil hindi niya pigilin ang pagnanasa niya sa *sex*

Sentence 1] pangungusap; grupo ng mga salita na nagpapahiwatig ng completong kaisipan; 2] parusa na hinahatol ng hukom ng husticia-*Sp*

Sentiment sentimyento-*Sp*, pagdamdam na emosyon-*Sp*; Iloc: sentimiento, pagricna nga emosyon

Sentimental cuento o palabas na *sentimental* o nakakaiyak; Iloc: storya o pabuya nga makapagpalua, *sentimental* o makapasangit
Synonym

Poignant *sentimental*, nakakapaluha; Iloc: *sentimental*, makapalua

SEPARATE hiwalay; Iloc: agsina
Synonym

Apart hiwalay, magkalayo, Iloc: nakasina, naysina, agsina

SEPARATE the men from the boys maraming mga katangian na nagpapatunay kung ang lalake ay lalaking-lalaki nga o pipichugin lamang dahil ang tunay na lalake ay **hindi** nananakit o nambu-*bully* sa babae o sa mas maliit at mas mahinang lalake sa canya - hindi siya duwag na nanakit sa cayang-caya niyang tao. Ang tunay na lalake ay may malinis na budhi kaya kung nagkasala siya, lalaking-lalaki niyang aminin ang sala niya at hihingi ng tawad – hindi siya nagdadahilan o binibintang ang sisi sa iba kaya respetado ang pagkatao niya. Ginagampanan niya ang obligasyon niya bilang marangal at makabatas na mamayan kaya nag-aaral siya para umasenso, pinipili ang mabuting tao na kaibigan at tinatalikdan ang mga *bad influence* (nagdodroga, walang ambition, may napakasamang ugali o gawi). Ginagamit lahat ng canyang lakas, abilidad, talento at karunongan niya para umunlad at para sa kabutihan niya at sa kapwa at sa bayan.

Separated and disassembled *(Tag. & Iloc.)* watak-watak

Septagenarian taong nasa edad-*Sp 70s*; Iloc: tao nga adda ti edad *70s*

September *(Tag. & Iloc.)* *September,* Septiembre-*Sp*

Sequel of a story yugto ng storya-*Sp*

Sequence nagkakasunod; nakaareglo na patuloy na magsunod-sunod sa isa't isa buhat sa pinakauna hanggang sa pinakahuling bagay; buhat sa pinakaunang numero-*Sp* hanggang sa pinakahuling numero-*Sp;* at ganon ding magkakasunod ang mga fecha-*Sp,* pangyayari, resulta at kahihinatnan

Sequester tanggalin at ihiwalay, i-*exile,* palayasin, iwaksi; ihiwalay sa kapwa o sa mga publico-*Sp* at gawin siyang mag-isa na lang; Iloc: isina, ibukod

Serenade mangharana, magtapat; Iloc: agharana

Serene mapayapa, tahimik; Iloc: natalna, nalinnaay, naulimek

Sergeant *(Tag. & Iloc.)* sarhento-*Sp*

Serial *n.,* **Serialize** *v.* anomang lathala sa pahayagan o pagpasahim-papawid o *broadcast* na lumalabas sunod-sunod at may pagitan na mga yugto o *series*

Serious serioso-*Sp,* malubha, malala; Iloc: serioso
Synonyms
Acute malala, malubha; Iloc: nacaro
Grave *(Tag. & Iloc.)* grabe
Malign *(Tag. & Iloc.)* maligno
Severe matindi, grabe; Iloc: nacaro, grabe
Terrible terib-le; Iloc: terib-le

Sermon mag-sermon-*Sp,* mangaral; Iloc: agsermon, agbalacad

Serpent ahas; Iloc: uleg

Serrate may mala-lagaring ngipin na aparato

Servant katulong, alila, achay, utusan, muchacho/cha-*aSp*; Iloc: katulong, muchacha/cho, tagabu

Serve magsilbi, maglingkod, manungkolan; Iloc: ag-servi

Server *(Tag. & Iloc.)* servidor/ra-*Sp*

Service servicio-*Sp*, silbi, paglilingkod, panungkulan; Iloc: servicio, panagservi

Servile labis na nagpapailalim at nagpapasakop at sumusunod at tumutupad sa mga utos; nagpapaalipin, sumusuyo na parang sa alipin

Servitude *slavery* o pagsusupil; sapilitan o fuersahang servicio-*Sp* o trabaho-*Sp* bilang parusa sa mga *criminal*

Session *(Tag. & Iloc.) session, meeting*

SET 1] ilagay sa isang lugar-*Sp* o lalagyan o ilatag sa tamang *position*; 2] itakda ang oras-*Sp* o fecha-*Sp* o precio-*Sp*; 3] gawin na ang *alarm clock* ay tumunog sa oras ng pagbangon; 4] grupo-*Sp*, pangkat; 5] lagyan ng *rollers* ang buhok; 6] ang lugar na mag-*filming* ng pelicula-*Sp* o ang entabladong pagpalabasan ng *opera*; 7] lumapot o manigas ang *gelatin*; 8] isang bagay na may kasa-kasamang mga bagay na magkakaugnay sa pagsagawa gaya ng *computer, keyboard, monitor* at *printer,* o ibang aparato-*Sp* gaya ng kasangkapan ng carpintero-*Sp* o sa pagtatahi, pagluto at iba pa

SET aside, Set aside for someone or something ibukod; Iloc: ilasin

SET the table (with food) maghain; Iloc: agdasar

SET-up 1] i-areglo, ihanda, 2] dahil masamang pakay, ilagay ang tao sa mahirap na kalagayan o kapahamakan

Setback makaantala, makahadlang, makapahinto, makasira; Iloc: makatantan, makalapped, makapasardeng, makadadael

Setting 1] ang lugar na mag-*filming* ng pelicula-*Sp* o ang entabladong pagpalabasan ng *opera* o lugar ng pagdiriwang o ng pang-alaalang pangyayari sa *history*; 2] kung saan nakapatong ang alahas

Settle 1] matira ng permanente sa isang lugar, 2] nakapagkasunduan sila, 3] mabayaran na niya ang utang; Iloc: 1] agyan iti maysa a lugar a permanente-*Sp*, 2] nagkatulagan dan, 3] mabayadan ti utang nan

SEVEN *(Tag. & Iloc.) seven,* pito, siete-*Sp*

SEVEN hundred *seven hundred,* pitong daan; Iloc: *seven hundred,* pito agasut

SEVEN o'clock *seven o'clock,* alas siete

SEVEN thousand *seven thousand,* pitong libo; Iloc: *seven thousand,* pito nga ribo

Seventeen *seventeen,* labing pito; Iloc: *seventeen,* sangapulo ket pito

Seventh *(Tag. & Iloc.)* ikapito

Seventy *seventy,* pitompo, settenta-*Sp*; Iloc: *seventy,* pitopulo, settenta-*Sp*

Seventy one, 72, 73, 74, etc. *(English numbers are commonly used by Filipinos)*

Sever tanggalin, ihiwalay; Iloc: ikkaten, isina

Several marami; Iloc: adu

Severe matindi, grabe-*Sp*; Iloc: nacaro, grabe

SEVERANCE pagpatid, paglagot, pagputol; Iloc: pagtukkol, pagputed

SEVERANCE pay kapag ang empleyado-*Sp* ay tinanggal o na-*lay-off* sa trabaho-*Sp*, ang suweldo-*Sp*, *back pay* at iba pa na nararapat sa empleyado ay dapat ibayad sa canya

Severity 1] kalupitan, kahigpitan o kabagsikan; 2] labis-labis na pag-kasimp-le sa asal, stilo o pagkahilig; 3] napakatalas o napakatindi gaya ng sakit o lamig; 4] grabe na efecto-*Sp*

Sew magtahi; Iloc: agdait

Correlated words

Darn magsulsi; Iloc: agsursi

Embroider magborda; Iloc: agborda

Hem ilupi, ililip; Iloc: agtupi, aglilip

Unstitch tastasin; Iloc: agtastas, satsaten

Knit *(Tag. & Iloc.)* ganchilyo

Thread sinulid; Iloc: sinulid, panait

Sewage canal *(Tag. & Iloc.)* imbornal-*aSp*

Sewer 1] mananahi; 2] tubong nasa ilalim ng lupa para pagdaluyan ng mga dumi na galing sa paligoan at casilyas at sa lababo o *sink* ng cusina-*Sp*

SEX, Gender kung babae o lalake; Iloc: no babai wenno lalaki

SEX, Sexual intercourse hindut, cantot; Iloc: iyot

SEX abuse gahasa/*rape*, atakeng *sexual*, fuersang pangmolescha o panligalig na *sexual*

SEX crime labag sa batas na gawaing *sexual* na ginawa sa paggahasa, sa pagfuersa dahil mas malakas siya kaysa sa victima, at ginawa din sa pagbabanta at pananakit

Sexually transmitted diseases, STD mga sakit na nakukuha sa pagtatalik ng *sexual* sa may sakit o sa pagtatalik sa iba't ibang tao; Iloc: dagiti sakit a maala iti pakipagrelasyon a *sexual* iti tao nga adda sakit na wenno iti agsaba-sabali a tattao

Shabby gusgosin; Iloc: narugit ken rutay-rutay

SHACK bahay sa lugar ng *squatters* o sa *slum*

SHACK up makapiling sa bahay at sa cama kahit hindi pa mag-asawa

Shackle bakal na pang-ipit sa galang-galangan/*wrist* o sa bukong-bukong/*ankle* para hindi makalaya at para siya ay maawat at masugpo ang paglaban at pagsaway niya

Shade lilim, pagsilongan; Iloc: linong

Shadow anino; Iloc: anniniwan

Shaft poste, sinag, silahis; Iloc: poste, sinamar

SHAKE yumayanig; Iloc: agginggined

SHAKE a tree, pole or a movable shed yugyogin, ugain; Iloc: gunggonen, yugyogen

SHAKE a container alog-alogin, calogin, tagtagin; Iloc: tagtagen

SHAKE hands makipagcamayan; Iloc: makialamano

SHAKE out or flail a linen *(Tag. & Iloc.)* ipagpag, wagwagen

SHAKE, Quiver due to fear or cold weather nanginginig, nangangatog; Iloc: agtigerger, agtagirgir

SHAKE violently and uncontrollably pumapagaspas; Iloc: agculipagpag, agcuripaspas

Shaky 1] nanginginig, nangangatog, nangangatal; umuuga, umaalog 2] hindi matatag at matibay kaya nakakaduda at tuloy hindi mapagkatiwalaan o mapanaligan o maasahan

Shall gagawin sa dadating na araw o panahon; Iloc: maaramid iti sumangsangpet nga aldaw o panawen

Shallow mababaw; Iloc: ababaw, narabaw

Antonym

Deep malalim; Iloc: adalem, nauneg

Sham huwad, peke; Iloc: sinsinan, peke

SHAMBLE, Place of destruction lugar kung saan pinatay ang mga tao; lugar na katayan ng hayop o ventahan ng mga carne at isda at iba pa; lugar na sobrang dis-areglado

SHAMBLE, Shuffle asiwang paglakad na nakabukangkang ang mga paa, o kapit-tuhod/*bow-legged*, o kaya kinakaladkad ang paa

SHAME *n.* kahihiyaan; Iloc: pakababainan

SHAME *v.* pahiyain; Iloc: pabainan

Shameful kahiya-hiya; Iloc: nakababain

Shameless walang hiya, makapal ang mukha; Iloc: awan ti bain, nabeng-beng ti rupa na

Shampoo *shampoo,* maggugo; Iloc: *shampoo,* aggulgol

Shank paa ng tao buhat sa hita hanggang pababa ng buong paa; parte-*Sp* ng mga aparato-*Sp, devices* at *tools* na puedeng magconecta sa iba

Shanty barung-barong, dampa; Iloc: rutrot a balay

Shape hubog, hugis, forma-*Sp*, corte-*Sp*; Iloc: forma, corte

SHARE *n.* bahagi; Iloc: bingay

SHARE *v.* magpamudmod, bahaginan, nagpapamahagi, damayan, magdamay; Iloc. mangbingay, mangiramay, mangibagi, mangiraem, mangilak-am

SHARE the umbrella with somebody magpasucob; Iloc: mangpalinong

SHARE one's winnings magbalato; Iloc: agbalato

Shari'a o **Sharia** o **Shariah** *law* o batas na nagmula sa Koran, hadith, ijma', at qiyas; buong nilalaman nito ang *canonical law* na bumabatay sa Koran na naglalahad ng mga tungkulin at parusa ng mga Muslim

Shark *(Tag. & Iloc.)* pating

Sharp matalas, matalim; Iloc: natadem

Sharpen hasain, ihasa, tasahin; Iloc: asaen, tasaren

Sharpener pantasa; Iloc: pangtasar (tasa/tasar-*Sp*)

Shatter mawasak, mabasag, sumabog; Iloc: maburak, mabuong, agbettak

Shave the beard mag-ahit ng balbas; Iloc: agi-barbas-*Sp*

Shaving 1] pag-aahit ng balbas; 2] mga katiting na piraso o pinaggilitan ng *carpenter's tool*

Shawl *(Tag. & Iloc.)* mantilya-*Sp*, balabal, capa-*Sp*, cagay

She/He siya; Iloc: isu

Shear, Shears 1] gunting o matalim na instrumento-*Sp*, 2] tanggalin o putolin, putolin ang buhok o balahibo
Correlated words
Cut hair magpagupit, gupitin; Iloc: agpacortar, agpapukis

Sheath *n.*, **Sheathe** *v.* bakal na lagayan o pantakip ng gulok at ng espada-*Sp*; isalong o ikaluplop sa loob ang espada

Shebang ang *structure* o pagkabuo at pagkayari gaya ng sa isang likha, organisasyon, plano at iba pa

Shed 1] maliit na bahay, 2] itapon, 3] maglagas, 4] umagos; Iloc: 1] bassit a balay, 2] ibelleng, 3] agtinnag wenno aglagas, 4] agayos

Sheen kinang; Iloc: sileng

SHEEP, fully grown *(Tag. & Iloc.)* carnero-*Sp*

SHEEP, young, Lamb *(Tag. & Iloc.)* cordero-*Sp*

Sheer 1] manipis at maliwanag na naaninag na tela; 2] walang kahalo at mismong completo na

Sheet 1] papel-*Sp*; 2] pansapin ng cama-*Sp*; Iloc: 1] papel; 2] pang-akkub ti cama

Shelf *(Tag. & Iloc.)* estante-*Sp*, aparador-*Sp*

Shell 1] bahay ng itlog, talaba, suso, tulya, pagong at iba pa 2] bahay ng bala-*Sp*; Iloc: 1] balay ti itlog, talaba, bisukol, cabibi, pag-ong ken sabali pay, 2] balay ti bala

Shelled marine creatures or bivalves

    Clam, small tulya; Iloc: cabibi

    Clam, medium size halaan; Iloc: bennek

    Oyster *(Tag. & Iloc.)* talaba

    Mollusk, 1" or 2" long with thin wrinkled and bumpy-coned body cuhol; Iloc: agurong

    Mussel *(Tag. & Iloc.)* tahong

    Snail, Escargot suso; Iloc: bisukol

    Shrimp hipon; Iloc: pasayan

    Lobster ulang; Iloc: udang, kappi

SHELTER *v.*, cupcopin; Iloc: ipacamang

SHELTER, Housing *n.*, pagsilongan, pagtuloyan; Iloc: paglinongan, pagdagusan, pagcamangan

Shelve 1] ilagay sa estante; 2] i-antala o itabi muna; kalimutan o ipawalang-bahala

Shenanigan *deceit*, asal o salita na nakakalinlang; *prank* o kapilyohang panlilinlang para sa katatawanan; Iloc: tignay o sarita a makaallilaw; kapilyoan a pang-allilaw

Shepherd 1] *The Shepherd* ay si Panginoong Dios Hesu Cristo; 1] nagpapastol ng mga cordero-*Sp*; taong pinagtatanggol, pinapatnubayan at inalagaan ang bawat tao

Sherbet sorbetes-*Sp* na puedeng may halong gatas o wala

Shiatsu masahe sa pamamagitan ng katamtamang bigat na dampi ng palad at hinlalaking daliri ng camay

Shibboleth 1] bukod-tanging pagbigkas, asal, pananamit at iba pa na nagpapahiwatig ang lahi ng tao; 2] *slogan*; kasabihan o paniwala na kaunti lang ang kahulogan o katotohanan

Shield gamit na makapagtanggol o makapanaklub; Iloc: may-usar-*Sp* a pangsalaknib wenno pangtaklub

Shift 1] magpalit ng *direction* o *position*, 2] mga trabahador-*Sp* na naghahalinhinan ng oras sa pagtrabaho; Iloc: 1] agsukat o balbaliwan ti *direction* o *position,* 2] dagiti trabahador nga agsisinnukat wenno agrelyevoan ti oras-*Sp* nga pagtrabaho

Shin of leg (front part from knee to ankle) lulod; Iloc: sango ti saka, ballawas

Shine sumikat, kinang; Iloc: agranyag, sileng

Shingles 1] mahapding sakit na mga buga sa cutis na lumalabas kapag may edad na ang tao; 2] manipis na patpat na kahoy, bakal, *asbestos* at iba pa na formang oblong at inilalagay ito na magsanib-sanib o *overlap* sa bubong at pader ng gusali, 3] tabing-ilog o tabing-dagat na natabunan ng mga maliliit na bato

Shiny makintab, makinang; Iloc: nasileng, nasilap

Ship *(Tag. & Iloc.)* barco-*Sp*, bapor

Shipping pagpadala ng mga pakete o ari-arian o paninda; Iloc: pagpatulod ti pakete o sanicua wenno dagiti ilaco

Shipshape malinis at maayos ang pagkaareglo; Iloc: nalinis ken nakaurnos ti pagkaareglo

SHIRT, long-sleeved *(Tag. & Iloc.)* camisadentro-*aSp*

SHIRT, short-sleeved *(Tag. & Iloc.)* shirt

SHIRT-under, T-shirt or sleeveless *(Tag. & Iloc.)* camiseta

Shit 1] dumi, tae, *diarrhea*; mapatae o mapaihi sa damit dahil sa sakit o gulat; 2] pagkukunwari, pagpapanggap, kasinungalingan, pagpapalabis ng katotohanan at kaulolan; 3] mababang uri, walang saysay o walang halaga; 4] makasarili, sakim, maramot, masama, kamuhi-muhi, kasuklam-suklam; 5] mga hindi *legal* na mga droga

Shiver nanginginig, nangangatog; Iloc: agtigtigerger, agtagtagerger

Shock 1] bigla at malakas na pagyayanig, 2] efecto-*Sp* ng na-electricidad-*Sp*, 3] malaking pagkagulat; Iloc: 1] golpe-*aSp* a tagtag, 2] efecto ti maelectricidad, 3] dakkel a kellaat

Shocking sobrang nakakagulat, nakakadisgusto, nakakatakot at napa-kasama; Iloc: makakellaat

Shoddy mababang uri, masama o pangit ang pagkagawa; bastos at walang pagmamalasakit

SHOE *(Tag. & Iloc.)* sapatos-*Sp*

SHOE brush *(Tag. & Iloc.)* escoba-*Sp*

SHOE heel *(Tag. & Iloc.)* tacon-*Sp*

SHOE lace *(Tag. & Iloc.)* sintas-*Sp*

SHOE sole *(Tag. & Iloc.)* suelas-*Sp*

SHOE, wooden *(Tag. & Iloc.)* bakya

Shoemaker or Shoe repairer *(Tag. & Iloc.)* sapatero-*Sp*

Shoestring 1] napakakonting pera, 2] cordon-*Sp* o sintas-*Sp* ng sapatos-*Sp*; Iloc: 1] nakabasbassit a cuarta, 2] cordon wenno sintas ti sapatos

Shoo bugawin, itaboy; Iloc: bugawen, iyabug

Shoot barilin; Iloc: paltoogan

Shop pamilihan, talyer-*Sp* o maliit na pagawaan; Iloc: tienda-*Sp*, agrep -*repair* o bassit a fabrica-*Sp*

Shopping mamili, mag-*shopping*; Iloc: mapan aggatang, ag-*shopping*

Shoplift magnakaw ng nakalantad na mga paninda sa tindahan

Shore tabing-dagat, baybay, dalampasigan; Iloc: igid ti baybay

SHORT (duration) sandali; Iloc: nabiit, nadaras
> *Antonym*
> **Long (duration)** matagal; Iloc: nabayag, agpaut

SHORT (height) mababa, maliit, bulilit, pandak; Iloc: nababa, bassit, bulilit, pandak
> *Correlated words*
> **Dwarf** unano; Iloc: ansisit
> **Midget** mas maliit sa pandak na tao pero hindi gaya ng *dwarf* dahil ang *midget* ay tugma o nababagay ang laki ng mga parte ng katawan niya sa canyang pagkaliit

Tall matangkad, mataas; Iloc: natayag

Giant *(Tag. & Iloc.)* higante

SHORT (length) maigsi, maikli; Iloc: ababa, nakiting
Antonym
Long (length) mahaba; Iloc: atiddog, nagayad

SHORT-handed kulang ng mga trabahadores

SHORT-tempered madaling magalit, magagalitin

SHORT-term maikling panahon lamang

Shortage kakulangan; Iloc: kacurangan

Shortchange magsukli ng kulang; mandaya sa pera

Shortcoming defecto-*Sp*, kapintasan, kakulangan, diferencia-*Sp*; Iloc: defecto, kacurangan, pagkauyawan, diferencia

Shorten paiklihin, paigsihin, paliitin; Iloc: pakitingen
Antonym
Lengthen pahabain; Iloc: paatiddogen

Shortening mantekilya-*Sp*, manteca-*Sp*; at iba pang *fat* na ginagamit sa *pastry* at tinapay

Shortness of breath hirap huminga; Iloc: marigatan nga aganges

Shot 1] nabaril, 2] *injection*; Iloc: 1] napaltogan, 2] *injection*

Should dapat, kailangan; Iloc: masapul, rebbeng

SHOULDER, Shoulders balikat; Iloc: abaga

SHOULDER blades paypay; Iloc: aklo-aklo

SHOUT magsigaw, maghiyaw; Iloc: agriaw, agpukkaw
Synonyms
Scream tumili; Iloc: agikkis
Yell magbulyaw, magsigaw, maghiyaw; Iloc: agbugkaw, agriaw, agpukkaw

SHOUT at, Rebuke harshly bulyawan; Iloc: bugkawan

SHOUT-out pagpasalamat na maikli pero pam-publicong malakas

Shouting distance malapitan lamang; Iloc: asideg laeng

SHOVE itulak ng marahas; Iloc: iduron ti napigsa

SHOVE it down on one's throat magbigay ng balita o payo na ang tangka niya ay para mapilit niya ang iba na paniwalaan siya

Shovel *(Tag. & Iloc.)* pala-*Sp*

SHOW *n.*, palabas; Iloc: pabuya

SHOW *v.*, **Present** magpakita, magpamalas, magtanghal; Iloc: ipakita, mangiparang, ipabuya, i-presentar-*Sp*
Correlated word
Display ipakitang-tao; Iloc: ipakita, ipabuya, iparang
SHOW-off, Lavish display irangya, ipakitang-tao, ipasicat o ihambog ang canyang magagarang taglay; Iloc: ipasindayag, mangipakitang-tao, ipangas o ipasicat na dagiti nangina ken napipintas a sanicua na
SHOW one's true colors sadya man o hindi, nakikita o pinapakita ang tunay na pagkatao
SHOW up dumating, dumalo; Iloc: agatender, dumteng, sumangpet
Showcase *noun* salaming na aparador na panglantad sa mga madla ang mga bagay-bagay gaya sa museo-*Sp* at tindahan o isang lugar-*Sp* na paglantad ng mga coche-*Sp*; *verb:* itanghal o ilandad ang mga pina-kahihintay na producto-*Sp* o kinagigiliwang palabas; *adj:* tinuturing na espesyal-*Sp* na pagtatanghal
Shower 1] ambon, hindi malakas na ulan, 2] pagpaligong parang ulan sa banyo-*Sp*, 3] *party* na ang tangka ay pangregalo-*Sp* sa ikacasal na babae o sa isisilang na sanggol; Iloc: 1] arbis, haan a napigsa nga tudo, 2] pagdigos nga casla tudo diay banyo, 3] *party* nga ti rangta ket pagited ti regalo iti iti agcasar nga babai wenno para iti ipasngay nga tagibi
Shred punit-punitin; Iloc: pigis-pigisen
Shrew magaliting babae; Iloc: naunget a babai
Shrewd matalino at matanto niya ang kalagayan o katatao ng iba; Iloc: nasirib ken maamiris na ti kasasaad wenno kababalin ti tao
Shrewish bugnotin, yamotin, sumpongin, mapagpuna, mapaghanap ng mali; Iloc: mapagdillaw, agsipsipot ti basol, nalaca a marurod, agsumsumro
Shrill matinis at nakakabinging tunog; Iloc: nasinggit ken makapatuleng nga uni
Shrimp hipon; Iloc: pasayan
Shrink *v.*, **Shrinkage** *n.* mangurong, umikli, lumiit; Iloc: agkumbet, agkebbet
Shrivel mangurong at magkulobot; Iloc: agkumbet ken agcuribetbet
Shrub palumpong; Iloc: pandak a cayo

Shrug shoulders magkibit ng balikat; Iloc: agkuyet iti abaga

Shuck upak o talupak - balat at takip ng *beans, nuts* at maiz-*Sp*

Shudder due to fear mangilabot, mangalisag o tumayo ang balahibo; Iloc: sumgar ti dutdot gapu ti buteng

SHUFFLE maglakad na hindi inaangat ang paa kundi parang kinakayod lamang sa sahig

SHUFFLE cards balasahin; Iloc: ibalasa

Shun iwasan, layuan; Iloc: lisyan, aglisi, adaywan

Shush patahimikin, magpatahimik

SHUT i-sara; Iloc: i-cerra-*Sp*

"SHUT up" "Tumigil ka sa pagsalita"; Iloc: "Agsardeng ka nga agsarita"

Shutdown sandaling pagtigil muna dahil sa *emergency* o pagtatapos at pagsara na ng operasyon-*Sp* o pagpatakbo ng fabrica-*Sp*, makina-*Sp*, at iba pa

Shuttle 1] transportasyong pampubliko gaya ng bus, tren, eroplano na bumaviahe papunta't pabalik ng regular-*Sp* na pagitan sa regular na ruta-*Sp* o daanan; 2] parte-*Sp* ng *sewing machine*; aparato-*Sp* sa pagtrabaho ng loom

Shy mahiyain; Iloc: managbabain, kimmi, mikki

SIBLING (no gender) kapatid; Iloc: kabsat, kabagis

SIBLING, step- kinakapatid; Iloc: kashuman a kabsat

SIBLINGS magkapatid; Iloc: agkabsat

SIBLINGS, All magkakapatid; Iloc: agkakabsat

SICK may sakit, may karamdaman; Iloc: agsakit
  Correlated words
  Bed-ridden may sakit at nakaratay sa cama; Iloc: agsakit ken nakadasay iti cama
  Infirm mahina at may sakit; Iloc: nacapsut ken agsakit
  Stricken with ailment dinapuan ng sakit; Iloc: nadiswan ti sakit
  Under the weather may sakit; Iloc: agsakit

SICK leave hindi makapasok sa oficina o sa trabaho dahil may sakit pero may bayad pa rin

Sicken 1] magkasakit o gawing magkasakit; nagkakaroon ng sintoma ng sakit; 2] nasusuka o nadidisgusto

Sickly sakitin; Iloc: managsaksakit, agkarasakit

Sickness sakit, karamdaman; Iloc: sakit

SIDE tabi, gilid; Iloc: abay, dinna, igid

SIDE (body) tagiliran; Iloc: bakrang, sikigan, sikig

SIDE by side magkatabi, magkapiling, magkasiping; Iloc: agkadinna, agkaabay

SIDE effect efecto-*Sp* o resulta-*Sp* na kakaiba datapuwat makakalunas daw; Iloc: efecto wenno ricna nga nakasabsabali uray nu makaagas cano

SIDE, other kabila; Iloc: bangir

SIDE saddle upong babae na magkatabi ang paa kapag nakasacay sa cabayo-*Sp* o sa calabaw; Iloc: pagtugaw ti babai nga agkadinna ti saka nu nakasacay iti cabalyo-*Sp* o nuang

SIDE with campihan, panigan; Iloc: favoran, umalyado

Sideburns *(Tag. & Iloc.)* patilya-*Sp*

Sideline 1] linya sa tabi o gilid; 2] may isa pang trabaho na dagdag sa primero-*Sp* niyang trabaho-*Sp*

Sides, both magkabilaan, magkabila; Iloc: agsinnumbangir

Sideshow *see Donut-driving or donut show*

Sidestep 1] humakbang sa isang tabi para hindi makaharang; hakbang ng sayaw o boksing; 2] iwasan o lihisan ang decisyon-*Sp*, problema-*Sp*

Sideswipe nabunggo sa tabi; nasagi sa tabi kaya naiba ang posisyon-*Sp* o nahulog, mabunggo sa tabi; Iloc: mabunggo ti sikigan

Sidetrack maligaw o malihis sa paksa o buod

Sidewalk *(Tag. & Iloc.)* bangketa-*Sp*

Sideways, lie or stand patagilid; Iloc: agpasikig

Sidle umusog; Iloc: agpadengdeng

Siesta umidlip, magsiesta; Iloc: rumidep, agsiesta

SIEVE *v.* salain; Iloc: sagaten

SIEVE *n.* panala, pansala; Iloc: pagsagatan

Sift salain; Iloc: sagaten

Sigh buntong-hininga; Iloc: sennaay, anges a makabang-ar

Sight paningin, *vision*; Iloc: panagkita, *vision*

Sightseeing magliwaliw para makita ang mga maganda at kagiliw-giliw na kalikasang tanawin ng kalawakan at paligid; Iloc: aglawlaw o ag-viahe-*Sp* para makita ti napipintas ken makalinglingay a naturalesa-*Sp* ti arrubayan a matantan-aw

SIGN *(Tag. & Iloc.)* signo-*Sp*, senyas-*Sp*, palatandaan, marka-*Sp*, simbulo-*Sp*, caratula-*Sp*; Iloc: panglasin, pangbigbig

SIGN (write one's signature) ilagda ang signatura-*Sp*, mag-firma-*Sp* ng buong pangalan; Iloc: agfirma ti signatura nga entero-*Sp* a nagan
Correlated word
Initialize maikling firma o lagda na isulat o ifirma lamang ang mga <u>tatlong pangunahing letra na mga ito ay pangalan</u> at dalawang apelyido; Iloc: ababa a firma nga isurat laeng ti <u>tallo nga umuna a letra ti nagan</u> nga dagitoy ket dagiti dua nga apelyido

SIGN in, Log in 1] pagfirma pagpasok sa trabaho para makapag-umpisa na, 2] paraang pagpasok sa *computer* kung saan ilagay ang *username* at *password*

SIGN off, Log off pagfirma kapag maghinto nang magtrabaho at paalis na

Signal senyal-*Sp*, senyas-*Sp*, hudyat; Iloc: senyal, senyas

Signature firma-*Sp*, lagda, signatura-*Sp*; Iloc: firma, signatura

Signboard *(Tag. & Iloc.)* caratula-*Sp*

Significance *n.*, **Significant** *adj.* 1] importante-*Sp*, importancia-*Sp*, kahalagahan, bantog; 2] nagbibigay ng kahulogan, nagpapahiwatig, nagpapakilala

Signify pagpahiwatig sa salita, kilos o signo; Iloc: ipaammo iti panagsarita, garaw o signo

Silence silensio-*Sp*, katahimikan; Iloc: silensio, ulimek

Silent tahimik, walang ingay; Iloc: naulimek, awan uni

Silk *(Tag. & Iloc.)* seda-*Sp*

Sill kahoy sa baba ng vintana-*Sp* o pinto; Iloc: kayo ti baba ti ventana-*Sp* wenno puerta-*Sp*

Silver pilak, plata-*Sp*; Iloc: pirak, plata

Silverware *(Tag. & Iloc.)* cubiertos-*aSp*

Similar *adj.*, **Similarity** *n.* magkawangis, magkahawig, magkamukha, magkatulad, magkagaya, magka-uri, pareho-*Sp*; Iloc: agkapada, agkapareho, agkaruprupa, agkalanga, agpadpada, agka-tipo, agkaingas, agkayarig
Correlated words
Alike magkagaya, magkatulad, pareho; Iloc: agpada, agkayarig, pareho
In the same boat nasa parehong kalagayan o situasyon

Have something in common sa dalawa o mahigit pa sa dalawa na bagay o tao, mayroon silang pagkakaparehoan

Similitude pagkakamukha, may pagkakapareho

Simmer pahinain ang init sa paglutoan pagkatapos na kumulo; Iloc: pacapoyen ti init palpas a nagburek.

Simper ngiting kimi, may hiya o asiwa; ngisi

SIMPLE simp-le-*Sp*, walang luho-*Sp*; Iloc: simp-le, haan a nagarbo

SIMPLE-minded simp-le-*Sp*, walang arte-*Sp* o pagkukunwari; tapat at walang panlilinlang; kulang sa katalasan ng isip

Simpleton *(Tag. & Iloc.)* ignorante-*Sp* at tanga

Simplify gawing simple-*Sp* para hindi complicado-*Sp*; Iloc: aramiden a simple tapno haan a complicado.

Simply *(Tag. & Iloc.)* basta

Simulate *v.*, **Simulation** *n.* maglikha ng kapareho (sa uri, ichura-*Sp*, sistema-*Sp*, situasyon-*Sp*); tularan, magkunwari

Simultaneous magkasabay, sabay-sabay; Iloc: agrinnana, aggiddan

Sin sala, kasalanan masamang gawain; Iloc: basol, biddut, dakes nga aramid

SINCE, Ever since mula noon, buhat noon; Iloc: manipud idi, agsipud idi

SINCE, In as much as yamang.., Iloc: idinto ta...

Sincere *adj.* **Sincerity** *n.*, taos-puso; Iloc: naggapu ti puso ken nakem ken ricna

Sincerity katapatan; Iloc: pagkapudno

Sinew *tendon* na dito nanggagalingan ang lakas, bisa-*Sp*, fuersa-*Sp* at capabilidad-*Sp* na makaangkop o makabagay sa anomang kalagayan; litid; Iloc: pennet, piskel

Sinful makasalanan; Iloc: managbasol

Sing awit, canta-*Sp*; Iloc: cancion-*Sp*, canta

Singe mapaso; Iloc: masinit

Singer manganganta; Iloc: taga-canta-*Sp*, taga-cansion-*Sp*

SINGLE isa, Iloc: maysa

SINGLE-handed isinagawa at tinapos ng isa lamang na tao at buhat sa canyang sariling pagsisikap

SINGLE man, unmarried binata, soltero-*Sp*, walang asawa; Iloc: baro, soltero, awan asawa

SINGLE woman, unmarried dalaga, soltera-*Sp*, walang asawa; Iloc: balasang, soltera, awan asawa

Singular isa; Iloc: maysa

Antonym

Plural marami, mahigit sa isa; Iloc: adu, mas adu ngem maysa

Sinister parang may kademonyohan; Iloc: casla adda pagkademonyo

SINK lumubog; Iloc: lumned

Correlated word

Drown malunod; Iloc: malmes, aglemmes, lumned, aglenned

SINK for washing *(Tag. & Iloc.)* lavabo-*Sp*, banyera-*Sp*

Sinkhole lugar na nakakagawa ng butas ng lupang nalulusaw at natutunaw na kapag napalakad ka dito, lulubog ka dito at mahirap ang umalis o makaahon dahil palubog ka ng palubog

Sinner makasalanan; Iloc: managbasol

Correlated word

Fallible nagkakamali at nagkakasala; Iloc: agbidbiddut ken agbasbasol

Sip sipsipin, supsopin; Iloc: sepsepen, susopen

Sir, Madam *(addressing adults)* po; Iloc: apo

Sire lalaking magkakaroon ng anak

SIREN, Mermaid *(Tag. & Iloc.)* serena-*Sp*

SIREN, Warning alarm *(Tag. & Iloc.)* sirena-*Sp*

SISTER kapatid na babae; Iloc: kabsat nga babai

SISTER-in-law hipag; Iloc: ipag, abirat

SISTER, older ate; Iloc: manang

SISTER, younger batang kapatid na babae; Iloc: adding, adi

SIT umupo; Iloc: agtugaw

SIT on floor or ground with feet spread out lupasay; Iloc: agdalupisak

Correlated word

Squat *squat*, magtingkayad; Iloc: *squat*, agdalupakpak

Site lugar-*Sp*; Iloc: lugar, solar-*Sp*

SITTING duck madaling mapahamak o mapuntirya-*Sp* at mavictima; Iloc: nalaca a maypeggad o mapili nga victima

SITING on a powder keg puedeng wala siyang kamuang-muang o kaalam-alam pero siya'y nasa lugar-*Sp* o situasyon-*Sp* na mapanganib at puedeng ma-disgracia-*Sp* anomang oras-*Sp*

Synonym

Precarious delicado o mapanganib na puesto dahil puedeng matomba, mahulog, masaktan, masira o mamatay; Iloc: delicado wenno napeggad a puesto gapu ta mabalin a matomba, matinnag, masaktan, madadael wenno matay isu

Situate ilagay sa tinakdang lugar-*Sp* o puesto-*Sp*; Iloc: icabil iti indesignar-*Sp* a lugar o puesto

Situation situasyon-*Sp*, kalagayan; Iloc: situasyon, kasasaad

SIX *six,* anim, seis-*Sp*; Iloc: *six,* innem, seis

SIX hundred *six hundred,* anim na daan; Iloc: *six hundred,* innem agasut

SIX o'clock *(Tag. & Iloc.) six o'clock,* alas seis-*Sp*

SIX pack nakabukod na anim na delata-*Sp* o botelya-*Sp* ng *beer* sa isang carton-*Sp*; Iloc: nakabukod nga innem a botelya o delata ti cerveza-*Sp* iti carton

SIX thousand *six thousand,* anim na libo; Iloc: *six thousand,* innem nga ribo

Sixteen *sixteen,* labing anim; Iloc: *sixteen,* sangapulo ket innem

SIXTH ikaanim; Iloc: ikainnem

SIXTH sense ang limang *senses* ng tao ay 1-kita, 2-dinig, 3-isip, 4-emosyon o ramdam at 5-pagsalita, at ang <u>dagdag na ika-anim ay pantanto at pandama na bukod-tangi ng nagmemay-ari at ipinanganak siyang mayroon nito na hindi lahat ay mayroon niyan</u>; Iloc: ti lima a *senses* ti tao ket 1-kita, 2-dengngeg, 3-panunot, 4-emosyon o ricna ken 5-pagsarita, ngem iti nayon nga <u>ika-innem ket pangamiris</u> nga bukbukod ken nayyanak nga addaan daytoy nga iti dadduma ken awanan daytoy

Sixty *sixty,* anim napo, sisenta-*Sp*; Iloc: *sixty,* innem a pulo, sisenta

Sixty one, 62, 63, 64, etc. *(English numbers are commonly used by Filipinos)*

Size anomang laki, pagkalaki; Iloc: pagkadakkel

Sizeable sobra ang pagkalaki

Sizzle tunog ng frinifrito sa mantica-*Sp*; Iloc: uni ti ifritfrito iti manteca-*Sp*

Skates ginagamit sa paang may sapatos na *roller skate* o *skateboard* para gumulong sa daanan o calsada, at *ice skate shoes* para magpadulas sa mayelong sahig

SKELETON calansay, bungo; Iloc: tulang ti bagi ti natay a tao

SKELETON in the closet nakatagong lihim na napakasama at nakakahiya

Skeptic *n.,* **Skeptical** *adj.* nagdududa, nag-aalinlangan, suspechoso-*Sp* at hindi makapaniwala hangga't makakita ng patotoo; Iloc: adda pag-dududa ken haan a mamati inggana't makakita iti prueba-*Sp*

Sketch gumuhit, maghugis; Iloc: ag-*drawing*

Sketchy 1] guhit-guhitan; 2] kaunti lang ang informasyon

Skew ngiwiin, sirain ang anyo o hugis o forma, baluktotin; Iloc: diwwigen, kiwingen, dadaelen o perdien ti langa o forma

Skewer mahaba at payat na bakal o patpat na pantusok ng *barbecue*; Iloc: atiddog ken naingpis a landok o bislak a pangtudok ti *barbecue*

Ski magpadulas o magpadausdos sa yelong bundok na suot-suot ang pang-*ski* sa paa at hawak-hawak sa magkabilang camay ang *ski poles*; Iloc: agpagpagalis o agpadarusdos iti banta a yelo nga mangiyus-usar ti pang-*ski* iti saka ken agsinnumbangir nga agiggem iti *ski poles*

Skill kakayahan o kahusayan sa canyang napag-aralan sa pamamagitan ng expiryensa o sa pag-aaral gaya ng tecnolohia, medico, *science, education,* musica, arte at iba pa; Iloc: cabaelan wenno kinalaeng nga naggapu ti expiryensa o pagadal diay escuela casla ti tecnolohia, medico, *science, education,* arte, musica ken dadduma pay

Skillful pagkadalubhasa at kahusayan sa canyang abilidad-*Sp* dahil sa expiryensa-*Sp* o matagalang karanasang pagtrabaho niya dito

Skim 1] tanggalin ang nakalutang na bula na gamit ang cuchara o sandok; 2] madaliang basahin o aralin o magmuni-muni o i-*consider* o tratohin; 3] itago o ikubli ang parte ng suweldo o pinanalonan para ang akala niya ay maiwasan niya ang magbayad ng buis

Skimp magtipid ng husto-*Sp*; Iloc: agin-inot ken agkirmet ti usto-*Sp*

Skimpy kaunti lamang; sobrang pagkakuripot

SKIN, Complexion *(Tag. & Iloc.)* cutis-*Sp*

SKIN (of humans and animals) balat; Iloc: cudil
> *Correlated word*
> **Dermal** tungkol sa balat; Iloc: maygapu ti cudil

SKIN, brown *(Tag. & Iloc.)* kayumanggi, morena-*Sp*

SKIN, dark maitim, negro/ra-*Sp*; Iloc: nangisit, negro/ra

SKIN-deep mababaw, panlabas lamang

SKIN discoloration due to bump or beating nangitim, pasa, pantal; Iloc: naglitem, lamma
> *Other skin problems*

White splotches on skin barak sa cutis; Iloc: camanaw

Scabbies galis; Iloc: gaddil, gudgod

Rash butlig-butlig; Iloc: supot-supot

Blotch manchang itim o pula o puti sa cutis o balat ng tao; Iloc: mancha a nangisit wenno labbaga wenno puraw iti cutis o cudil ti tao

Speck maliit na mancha o pasa sa balat; Iloc: bassit a mancha o litem iti cudil

Welt marka ng palo; Iloc: marka ti baut wenno bugbog

Wart culugo; Iloc: tucak-tucak

Scabby, psoriasis-like on the skin galis; Iloc: gaddil, gudgod

Scrape, Skin scratch *(Tag. & Iloc.)* gasgas

Scrape, Skin bruise galos; Iloc: dunor

Wound, Injury, Bruise *(Tag. & Iloc.)* sugat

SKIN, fair maputi; Iloc: napudaw

SKIN, smooth & flawless *(Tag. & Iloc.)* cutis-porcelana-*Sp*

Skinny napakapayat; Iloc: nakakutkuttong

SKIP magkandirit pero sa dalawang paa na naghahalinhinan; Iloc: agkingking ngem iti dua a saca nga agsinsinnublat

SKIP, Leave out 1] laktawan o lumampas na hindi basahin o pansinin; 2] hindi papasok sa escuela-*Sp*, oficina-*Sp* o ibang lugar-*Sp*, 3] takbohan ang canyang utang

SKIRT *(Tag. & Iloc.)* falda-*Sp*

SKIRT, long tapis, saya; Iloc: bidang, pandiling

Skit maikling nakakatawang drama; Iloc: nabiit nga nakakatkatawa a drama

Skull bungo, buto o bao ng ulo; Iloc: banga-banga, bao ti ulo wenno tulang ti ulo

Sky himpapawid, langit; Iloc: tangatang, langit

Synonym

Firmament himpapawid; Iloc: tangatang

SLACK 1] hindi mahigpit kundi maluwag at pabaya at walang ingat; 2] mabagal, walang sigla; 3] mahina, tamad, campante-*Sp*; Iloc: haan nga stricto ken agliwliway, haan nga agan-annad, 3] nacapsut, sadut, campante

SLACK, cut someone some magpaubaya, magparaya, bigyan ng pahintulog

Correlated word

Tolerate pumapayag na magpahintulot, magpaubaya at magparaya

751

Slacken gawing hindi maliksi at masigla; tanggalin ang higpit at gawing maluwag

Slacks pantalon na suot para sa mga paa

Slalom magpa-*zigzag* sa pag-*ski*; Iloc: agpa-*zigzag* nga ag-*ski*

SLAM down things nagbabagsak; Iloc: agbarbarsak, ituptupak

SLAM-dunk tumalon at maipasok niya ang bola-*Sp* sa *basket* sa larong *basketball*; Iloc: aglagto ken maypatupwak na ti bola ti uneg ti *basket* iti *sports* a *basketball*

SLAM things or slam doors magdabog-dabog; Iloc: agbugtabugtak

Slander manirang-puri, pasamahin; Iloc: mang-perdi-*aSp* iti dayaw, mang-padakes ti reputasyon-*Sp*

Slang salitang lansangan, hindi formal-*Sp* na wika na caraniwan ay imbento-*Sp*; Iloc: sarita ti calye-*Sp*, haan a *formal* a sarita nga canayon ket imbento

Slanting pahilis, pasandal, pasandig; Iloc: darisdis, nakatingig
   Synonyms
   Tilt tagilid; Iloc: tingig
   Lean magsandal, magsandig; Iloc: agsanggir, agsadag,
   Oblique pahilis, pasandal, pasandig; Iloc: darisdis, nakatingig

SLAP sampalin, tampal; Iloc: sipaten, tungpaen

SLAP on the wrist hindi sapat o napakagaan at napakahinang parusa sa crimen o sa napakamasamang gawain

Slapstick *comedy* na panay habulan, banggahan at impertinenteng usapan; Iloc: *comedy* nga panay ti panagkikin-namatan, banggaan ken ang-angaw a salawasaw

Slash laslasin; Iloc: laslasen

Slat *(Tag. & Iloc.)* tabla-*Sp*

Slate 1] lista-*Sp* ng mga candidato-*Sp* ng isang partido-*Sp*, 2] lista ng mga dating nagawa; Iloc: 1] lista cadagiti candidato iti maysa a partido, 2] lista iti dati nga inararamid

Slaughter an animal for cooking katayin ang baboy o vaca-*Sp* o cordero-*Sp*; Iloc: agparti ti baboy o vaca, ipugpogan ti carnero-*Sp*

Slavery pag-aalipin; gawin ang tao na canyang alipin na mapasailalim sa canya ang kalayaan nito at sa pagtrabaho sa canya ng fuersa o libre o sa mababang bayad lang

Slay patayin; Iloc: patayen

Sleazy 1] napakarumi at sira-sira; 2] dahil sa pagkasama niya, siya ay nakakasuklam o nakakamuhi

Sleek 1] pantay, makinis at makintab, 2] kahanga-hanga na magdamit; Iloc: 1] patag, nalamuyot ken nasileng, 2] nakamaymayat nga agcawes

SLEEP matulog; Iloc: maturog
Correlated words
Slumber matulog; Iloc: maturog
Nap, Catnap, Siesta, Snooze, Doze off umidlip, magsiesta; Iloc: rumidep, agridep, agsiesta
Wake up gumising; Iloc: agriing, aglukag
Wake someone up gisingin; Iloc: riingen

SLEEP, deep mahimbing na tulog; Iloc: naimas a turog

SLEEP-deprived *(Tag. & Iloc.)* puyat

SLEEP, put baby to *(Tag. & Iloc.)* ihele-hele

SLEEP (shake off sleep upon waking) mag-alimpungat; Iloc: agmurmuray

Sleepy inaantok; Iloc: makaturturog
Correlated words
Drowsy inaantok; Iloc: makaturog
Drowsy nod magyukayok; Iloc: agtuglep, agtungung-ed

Sleeves *(Tag. & Iloc.)* manggas-*Sp*

Slender balingkinitan; Iloc: narapis

Slice hiwain; Iloc: iwaen, pisyen, galipen, gerreten

Slick 1] makinis, makintab at malambot o gawing ganyan; suaveng asal at pagsasalita; matalino at matalas; 2] palihim, tuso at bihasa; ang labas ay nakakahalina at *sophisticated* pero ang laman ay mababaw; matalas, mapaglinlang, madaya; 3] madulas dahil napatungan ng yelo-*Sp* o tubig o langis

SLIDE (at the park or backyard) *(Tag. & Iloc.)* *slide*

SLIDE, Glide down magpadausdos; Iloc: agpadarusdos, agkaruskos

Slight 1] kaunti, mababang antas; payat; maliit ang pagkaimportante, hindi mahalaga, mahina; 2] tratohing hindi mabuti; hindi pansinin; hindi estimahin

Slim maliit; Iloc: bassit

Slingshot tirador; Iloc: palsiit

Slinky patago, palihim na kilos; nakakaakit kumilos gaya ng pagbihis na nakakapit sa katawan

SLIP madulas, madapilos; Iloc: maypagalis

SLIP from one's grasp mabitawan; Iloc: maibbatan

SLIP of the tongue nadulas ang dila at nasabi ang hindi dapat sabihin

SLIP one's mind nawala sa isip, nakalimutan; Iloc: nalipatan, nagpukaw iti panunot

Slipshod bara-bara, mali-mali, mumurahin at ginamit ng hindi ayos, hindi maingat ang pagkagawa o pagbihis at ichura-*Sp*

Slippers *(Tag. & Iloc.)* chinelas-*Sp*

Slippery nakakadulas; Iloc: nagalis, makagalis

Slit hiwa na mahaba; Iloc: iwa nga atiddog

Slither padulas na parang ahas na gumagapang; Iloc: pagna ti uleg, carayam

Slob burara, salaula, busalsal, disareglado-*Sp*, macalat, magulo; Iloc: burara, nawara, disareglado, magulo

Slop 1] pagkain ng baboy; 2] matubig na putik; 3] maglakad sa putik; 4] nabuhos o nagsaboy na tubig

Slope gulod, libis; Iloc: darisdis, agsalog

Sloping tagilid; Iloc: patingig, batwag

Sloppy salaula, busalsal, disareglado-*Sp*; Iloc: disareglado

Slothful, Sluggard *adj.* napakatamad na tao na nagtutunganga lang

Slouch maginhawang nakasandal na umupo o tumayo pero hindi magara; Iloc: makabang-ar nga nakasanggir nga agtugaw o tumacder ngem haan nga naelegante

SLOW mabagal, marahan; Iloc: mabayag, nabuntog
  Synonym
  Slowpoke *(Tag. & Iloc.)* patay-patay, pipichugin
  Antonym
  Fast mabilis, matuling, cascas, paspas; Iloc: napartak, nadaras, napardas, cascas, paspas

SLOW business-wise matumal; Iloc: nakapsut ti venta

SLOW down bagalan, dahan-dahan; Iloc: bayagen, agininnayad

SLOW on the uptake mahinang mag-isip o sumuri, mahinang maka-intindi o makatugma sa ibig sabihin

Slowpoke *(Tag. & Iloc.)* patay-patay, pipichugin

Slug suntokin, pukpokin; Iloc: danugen, pang-uren

Sluggish tinatamad, walang gana; Iloc: aglaladut, agsasadot, awang ganas-*Sp* na

Slumber tulog; Iloc: turog

Slump 1] lumagpak o bumagsak o sumadlak, 2] nakahukot o sumalagmak sa upoan, 3] nalubak sa putik, 4] hindi mabuti at palpak ang pakikibaka o pagsasagawa

Slur 1] hindi maintindihan ang pagsalita, 2] magmura; Iloc: 1] haan maawatan ti pagsarita, 2] agsao ti panglais

Slurp *(Tag. & Iloc.)* laklak, pag-inom ng aso

Slut *(Tag. & Iloc.) prostitute*, puta-*Sp*

Sly nakakatakot makipagkaibigan sa ganitong tao dahil hindi mo mapagkakatiwalaan na puedeng linlangin ka at siraan ka na wala kang kamuang-muang; Iloc: nakabutbuteng ti makigayyem iti castoy a tao ta haan isu mapagfiaran ken mabalin na ka nga cusiten ken laisen nga haan mo man laeng ammo

Smack 1] maingay na sara-at-bukas ang bibig, 2] maghalik ng maingay; Iloc: 1] natagari nga cerra-ken-lucat ti bibig 2] natagari nga agbisong

SMALL (amount) kaunti, konti; Iloc: bassit, haan adu
Antonym
Many, Plenty marami; Iloc: adu

SMALL (size) maliit, munti, pandak; Iloc: bassit, pandak
Synonym
Short *(Tag. & Iloc.)* pandak
Antonym
Tall matangkad; Iloc: natayag

SMALL fry 1] mga bata; 2] maliliit na isda; 3] hindi importante na tao o bagay

SMALL talk cuentohang simp-le-*Sp* at magaan; pinaguusapan ang mga hindi makabulohang paksa lamang

SMALL time *achievement* na turing ay maliit lamang

SMALL, very napakaliit; Iloc: batti-utit, bassit unay

Smallpox bulutong; Iloc: burtong

Smarmy naglalangis at nambobola para maganda ang trato at pagtingin sa canya

SMART 1] mahusay makapag-isip at makapagturing sa pabago-bagong circumstancia-*Sp*; 2] smarte-*Sp*, pusturioso-*Sp*, elegante-*Sp*

SMART aleck mapagfilosong magsalita at mapagdahilan; Iloc: agfilfiloso nga asarita ken mapagpambar

SMASH wasakin, durogin, dikdikin, yurakin; Iloc: runawen, rumeken, buraken, dekdeken
Correlated word
Shatter mawasak, mabasag, sumabog; Iloc: maburak, mabuong, agbettak
SMASH flat pipihin; Iloc: pitpiten, cuppiten
Smatter mag-usap na parang maraming kaalaman
Smear dungisan, dumihan, batikan; Iloc: rugitan, dungritan, pulagidan ti rugit, piltakan
Correlated word
Dirt dungis, dumi, libag, batik; Iloc: rugit, mureng, batik, dungrit
SMELL amoyin, langhapin, samyohin; Iloc: angoten, lang-aben
Correlated words
Snort maingay na paglanghap; Iloc: natagari nga aglang-ab
Sniff amoyin, langhapin, samyohin; Iloc: angoten, langaben
SMELL bad mabaho; Iloc: nabuyok, nabangsit
Synonym
Stink, Reek umaalingasaw Iloc: agal-alingasaw
SMELL good mabango; Iloc: nabanglo
Synonym
Fragrant mahalimuyak; Iloc: nabanglo
SMELL, sense of pang-amoy; Iloc: pang-angot
Correlated word
Olfactory tungkol sa pang-amoy; Iloc: maygapu ti pagangot
Smelly maamoy, nangangamoy; Iloc: naangot, nakaangangot
Smidgen napakakaunti; Iloc: nakabasbassit
Smile ngumiti; Iloc: umisem
Correlated words
Grin nakangisi; Iloc; musiig
Smirch dungisan, dumihan, batikan; Iloc: rugitan, dungritan, pulagidan ti rugit, piltakan
Smirk ngiti hindi sa tuwa kundi *sarcastic;* Iloc: isem nga haan nga gapu ti ragsak nu di *sarcastic*
Smite saktan sa pamamagitan ng buntal, pamukpok o armas-*Sp*; Iloc: saktan ti danug wenno pukpok o armas
Smith trabahador-*Sp* ng mga bakal gaya ng *blacksmith*
Smock maluwag na damit na pang-*protect* sa suot-suot na damit habang nagtatrabaho ito gaya sa ospital-*Sp*

Apron sinusuot kapag nagluluto para hindi marumihan ang damit

SMOKE usok; Iloc: asok

SMOKE cigarette or cigar manigarilyo, mag-tabaco-*Sp*; Iloc: ag-cigarilyo-*Sp*, agtabaco

SMOKE detector *fire alarm* na tutunog kung may natutop na usok

SMOKE screen pangkubli para maitago o makalinlang; balatkayo o *camouflage*

Smoking gun evidencia-*Sp* na nakakapagsangkot, nakakapagdawit o nakakapagdamay sa tao sa nangyaring crimen-*Sp*

Smolder nasusunog na kahoy pero walang alab; Iloc: maur-uram ken agbarbarang a kayo ngem awanen ti apoy

Smooch halik; Iloc: bisong

Smooth makinis, fino-*Sp*; Iloc: nalamuyot, fino

Smorgasboard (Swedish) *(Tag. & Iloc.) buffet, all-you-can-eat*

Smother pigilan ang paghinga; Iloc: lappedan ti paganges

Smudge pahiran ng dumi, dumihan; Iloc: paidan ti rugit, piltakan

Smug kasiyahan sa mismong sarili; Iloc: ragsak iti mismo-*Sp* a bagi

Smuggle magpuslit ng bawal na bagay; Iloc: mangipuslit ti mayparit a banag

Smut *pornography*, malaswang palabas o salita o sulat; Iloc: *pornography*, bastos nga pabuya, sarita o surat

Snacks minindal, meryenda-*aSp*, chichiryas; Iloc: meryenda, saramsam

Snafu gulo na hindi mapigilan at di matimpi; situasyon na punong-puno ng lito at taranta

Snag hindi inaasahang hadlang o sagabal; Iloc: haan nga naseggaan a barra o lapped

SNAIL cuhol, suso; Iloc: bisukol

SNAIL pace napakabagal; Iloc: nakabaybayag

Snake ahas; Iloc: uleg

SNAP a finger pitik, lagitik, lagutok; Iloc: pitik, rittuok

SNAP off, Break baliin, putolin, bakliin, lagutin, patirin; Iloc: pugsaten, pugsoten, tukkolen

SNAP on food tuklawin, sakmalin; Iloc: tukmaen

Snappy 1] bigla at mabilis sa kilos; nag-aaporado; 2] ang pagsakmal ng aso sa bigay na pagkain; 3] yamot at walang paciencia-*Sp*

Snare painin, silohin, bitagin; Iloc: silwen, isilo

Snarl 1] ang pagbantang ungol o kahol ng aso; magsalita na parang nagbabanta; 2] magkabuhol-buhol na lubid, sinulid o buhok; nagka-lito-litong situasyon-*Sp* o usapan

Snatch sunggaban, dakmain, agawin; Iloc: agawen, sibbaruten, gammaten, rabsuten, rabnoten

Snatcher magnanakkaw na nandadakma at nangsusunggab ng *handbag* o pitaca-*aSp* ng iba; Iloc: agtatakaw nga manggammat ken mangrabsut ti *handbag* o pitaca ti tat-tao

Sneak out or Sneak into panakaw na pumasok o lumabas; Iloc: aglimed a sumrek o rumwar

Sneaky palihim, gawa ng nandadaya at nanlilinlang

Sneer ngumiwi, ngumiti, tumawa o magbigkas ng payamot, panglait o galit

Sneeze magbahin, maghatsing; Iloc: agbain, aghatsing

Snicker tumawa ng palihim; Iloc: laplappedan na nga katawa

Snide nanlalapastangan gamit ang malupit na asal at salita

Sniff amoyin o langhapin; samyohin; Iloc: anguten wenno lang-aben

Sniffle pasinghot-singhot sa pag-iyak o dahil siya'y may sipon; Iloc: agsangsang-aw gapu ti pagsangit o sipon

Snip guntingin ng maliit lamang; Iloc: gettengen o cartiben ti bassit laeng

Snippet maliit na tinanggal na piraso

Snitch on someone isumbong; Iloc: ipulong, ipungpong

Snob mapagmalaki, suplado/da, hindi nagpapapansin sa ayaw niya na tao; Iloc: ipangpangato na ti bagi na, suplado/da, haan na estimaren ti tao nga dina cayat

Snoop naninilip sa privadong buhay ng tao; Iloc: agsirsirip ti privado a garaw ti tao

Snoot *(slang)* ilong; Iloc: agong

Snooty: mapagmata sa tao, mapagmataas

Snooze umidlip, mag-siesta-*Sp*; Iloc: rumidep, agridep, agsiesta

Snore naghihilik; Iloc: agur-urok

Snort maingay na paglanghap; Iloc: natagari nga aglang-ab

Snout ang pahabang parte ng mukha ng hayop gaya ng ilong; Iloc: ti paatiddog o acaba a parte ti rupa ti *animal* casla ti agong

Snow *(Tag. & Iloc.)* *snow*, niebe-*Sp*, yelo-*Sp*
  Correlated word
  Ice *(Tag. & Iloc)* yelo-*Sp*

Snowflake or Snow 1] nieve-*Sp*, maliit na bahagi ng *snow*; 2] salita na panlinlang o pandaya; 3] *crystalline narcotic powder* na may *morphine, heroin* at *cocaine*

Snub *see Snob earlier in these two pages*

Snug 1] comfortab-le-*Sp*, maginhawa at mainam; 2] nakatago o ang pagtagoan na ligtas

SNUGGLE comfortab-le at maginhawang nagpapasarap na mamaluktot; Iloc: comfortab-le ken nabang-aran nga agpapaimas nga agkucot

SNUGGLE up comfortably in bed magpasarap sa catre na yumu-yokyok sa loob ng cumot at yakap-yakap ang unan o *teddy bear*; Iloc: agpapaimas idiay catre nga agcumot ti ules ken agaracop ti pungan wenno *teddy bear*

SO para, upang; Iloc: para, tapno

SO-called tinagurian; Iloc: ninaganan

SO far, so good hanggang ngayon, mabuti naman ang kalagayan o ang nangyayari

SO long paalam, *good-bye*

SO-so hindi mabuti at hindi masama - katamtaman lang

SO that para, upang; Iloc: tapno, para

"SO what" "E, ano ngayon"

SOAK ibabad, ilubog sa tubig, ilublob; Iloc: iyuper, ilenned, itabnaw ti danum

SOAK through magtagos; Iloc: agsagepsep

SOAP *(Tag. & Iloc.)* sabonan

SOAP for dishes sabong panghugas ng plato-*Sp*; Iloc: sabon a paginnaw

SOAP for laundry *detergent,* sabong pan-laba-*Sp*; Iloc: *detergent,* sabon a panlaba

Soar 1] lumipad na gaya ng ibon o eroplano; 2] magmithi o mag-ambisyon-*Sp* ng mataas na matatamo

Sob humihikbi; Iloc: agsasaibbek, agsasainnek

Sober *adj., Sobriety n.* 1] hindi lasing dahil pag uminom ng alak, katamtaman lamang; 2] tahimik at calmado-*Sp*; 3] mukhang malungkot ang fachada-*Sp* o *façade* pati pananalita; 4] matino, mababang-loob o mapakumbaba, matiwasay o *self-controlled;* Iloc: 1] nausawanen, 2] calmado ken controlado-*Sp* ti bagi nan, 3] seryoso-*Sp*

Sobriquet palayaw; Iloc: birngas, *nickname*

Sociable mahilig makihalobilo sa tao; Iloc: magustoan na a makilalaok iti tattao

Synonyms

Extrovert, Gregarious mahilig makihalo-bilo o makipag-sosyalan sa mga kapwa-tao; Iloc: magustuan na ti makipag-ummong ken makipagsosyalan iti tattao

SOCIAL tungkol sa relasyon-*Sp* o pagsama-samahang pagkakaibigan; masaya at magalang na pagsama-samahan o pagpupulong-pulong

SOCIAL network *online* sa *computer* o *mobile device* na comunidad-*Sp* ng mga taong nagiging magkakaibigan o naghahalobilo dahil sila ay may parehong *interest* o parehong ocupasyon-*Sp* o parehong educasyon-*Sp* o pareho-*Sp* na lahi at iba pa; nabubuo ito ng mga taong may pagkakaparehoan dahil sa kanilang informasyon-*Sp* na nakakatulong sa isa't isa at iba pa

Socialize makitungo sa tao, makipagkaibigan, makihalobilo; Iloc: makicadua, makigaygayyem, makilaok cadagiti tattao

Synonyms

Associate makipagkaibigan, makitipon; Iloc: makitimpuyog

Hobnob nakikihalobilo sa mga tao

Mingle makihalobilo, makitungo sa tao, makipagkaibigan; Iloc: makilaok cadagiti tattao, makigayyem

Interact mag-ugnayan, magtugonan, magsamahan, magsapi-sapi

Society *society,* lipunan; Iloc: *society,* sociedad-*Sp*

Sociopath taong may diferencia *psychologically* na ayaw sa mga tao at dahil walang conciensia-*Sp*, hindi mapanagutan o di mataggap ang mga kasalanan niya kundi mag-dadahilan at magparatang sa iba

Socket tapon o pagpasakan ng *plug* ng electricidad-*Sp* para isaksak ang *electrical cord* kung gustong gumamit ng *computer* o makina-*Sp*; Iloc: pagsullatan ti *plug* ti aparato nga de electricidad-*Sp*

Socks *(Tag. & Iloc.)* medias-*Sp*

Sofa *(Tag. & Iloc.) sofa*

SOFT malambot; Iloc: nalukneng
Antonym
Hard matigas; Iloc: natangken

SOFT-hearted malambot ang puso, maawain, mapagconsiderasyon sa kapwa; Iloc: nalukneng ti puso, mannangaasi, mapag-considerasyon-*Sp* ti tao

SOFT shoulders to cry on puedeng idaing ang pighati o problema dahil mapagmalasakit, mahabagin, maunawain, maawain at mapag-con-suelo-*Sp*; Iloc: mabalin nga iyasog ti problema ta isu ket mannangaasi, *understanding*, manag-consuelo ken nalukneng ti puso

SOFT-spoken malumanay magsalita; Iloc: naemma

SOFT spot in one's heart for someone or something may malambot na puso at damdamin sa..

Softened by too much handling nalamog; Iloc: napugpog

Soggy binabad kaya tagos na tagos ang tubig sa lahat ng parte

SOIL, Earth lupa; Iloc: daga

SOIL, Make dirty dungisan, dumihan, batikan; Iloc: rugitan, dungritan

Soiled narumihan; Iloc: narugitan

Solace, give bigyang consuelo, magmalasakit, magsimpatiya; Iloc: ikkan consuelo, mangisaksakit, agsimpatiya, mangliwliwa, mangay-aywan

Solar tungkol sa araw o nanggaling sa araw; Iloc: maygapu wenno naggapu idiay init

Soldier sundalo, kawal, militante-*Sp*; Iloc: soldado-*Sp*, buyot, militante

SOLE, Solely bugtong, nag-iisa; Iloc: agmaymaysa, is-isu

SOLE of foot talampakan; Iloc: dapan

SOLE of shoe *(Tag. & Iloc.)* suelas-*Sp*

Solemn taimtim; Iloc: natalna ken impuspuso

Solicit pakiusapan, makisuyo, manghingi ng favor-*Sp*, humiling; Iloc: makicacaasi, makifavor, agdawat, dumawat, agkiddaw

Solicitous masinsinang pag-asecaso-*Sp*, pag-alaga at pag-estima; Iloc: firmi nga pag-asicaso, pagtaraken ken pag-estimar, pagicascaso (estima/estimar-*Sp*, firmi-*Sp*)

Solid buong-buo at walang butas o basag; Iloc: sibubukel ken awan pulos ti abut, butbot wenno buong

Solidarity pagkakaisa sa tangka at responsibilidad-*Sp* ng mga miembro-*Sp* ng grupo-*Sp* o asosasyon-*Sp*, pagkakaisa sa *interest* at simpatia-*Sp*

Soliloquy, Soliloquies pagsasalita na parang mag-isa ay siya lamang; pagsasalita o nagdidiscurso na kausap ang sarili at wala siyang pakialam o hindi niya alam na may mga taong nakakarinig sa canya

Solitaire *(Tag. & Iloc.) solitaire,* larong baraha-*Sp*

Solitary, In solitude mag-isa, walang kabahay; Iloc: agmay-maysa, awan kabbalay na

Solo nagso-solo-*Sp*, mag-isang gaganap; Iloc: agsol-solo-*Sp* nga ag-presentar-*Sp* o agpabuya

Soluble 1] puedeng matunaw o malusaw, 2] puedeng malutas o maipaliwanag; Iloc: 1] mabalin a matunaw o malusaw o marunaw, 2] mabalin a masolvar o mailawlawag
Correlated word
  Liquify natutunaw at nagiging tubig; Iloc: matuntunaw ken agdanumen

Solution solusyon-*Sp*, kalutasan; Iloc: pang-solvar-*Sp*, solusyon

Solvable puedeng at cayang malutas na problema-*Sp*

Solve lutasin, ayosin; Iloc: ag-solvar-*Sp* ti problema-*Sp*

Solvent 1] cayang bayaran ang mga utang; 2] nakakapagtunaw gaya ng tubig

Somber 1] kulimlim o madilim at mapanglaw; maitim at hindi kasiya-siya; 2] serioso-*Sp*, grabe-*Sp*; nakakalungkot, nakakalumbay

SOME people mga ilang tao; Iloc: adda tattao ida

SOME things mga ilang bagay; Iloc: adda bambanag ida

Somebody, Someone may isang tao; Iloc: adda maysa a tao

Somersault mag-circo-*Sp*, magbalintong; Iloc: ag-circo-*Sp*, agbalintuag

Something isang bagay; Iloc: maysa a banag

Sometimes paminsan-minsan; Iloc: no dadduma, pasaray, sagpaminsan

Somewhat *(Tag. & Iloc.)* medio-*aSp*

SON anak na lalake; Iloc: anak a lalaki

SON-in-law, Daughter-in-law *(Tag. & Iloc.)* manugang

SONG canta-*Sp*, awit; Iloc: canta, cansion-*Sp*

SONG, Filipino love *(Tag. & Iloc.)* kundiman, harana

SOON sandali lamang pagkatapos; Iloc: apagbiit pagpalpas
Correlated words

By and by, Later mamaya, maya-maya, chaka na; Iloc: madamdama, intunokua, itattanto tu

SOON as possible sa pinakamadaling panahon; Iloc: iti pinakanabiit a tiempo o oras

Soot *n.*, **Sooty** *adj.* ang dumikit sa *chimney* o pader na maitim dahil sa usok

Soothe hangoin sa hirap, pighati o sakit; bigyan ng consuelo-*Sp* o ginhawa, ipagpalubag-loob, paginhawin, pagaanin ang kahirapan o kabigatan; Iloc: ikkan ti bang-ar, inana wenno consuelo; agsimpatiya, ay-aywen, pabangaran, palag-anen iti rigat ken dagsen

Sophisticated 1] dahil sa educasyon-*Sp*, expiryensa-*Sp* at iba pa siya ay naging madunong sa mga bagay sa mundo-*Sp*; hindi na siya maang; 2] lantad ang pagka-educado-*Sp* niya't maraming kaalaman, kasiya-siya, kalugod-lugod

Soporific nakakaantok at nakakapagpatulog

Sordid walang moralidad-*Sp*; makasarili, mukhang-pera; napakarumi at sira-sira

SORE masakit; Iloc: nasakit

SORE spot maselang paksa na nanggigising ng sama ng loob at pagkamaramdamin

Sorrow dalamhati, kalungkutan; Iloc: ladingit, leddaang

Sorry magsisi, ikalulongkot; Iloc: agbabawi

SORT of *(Tag. & Iloc.)* medio-*aSp*

SORT out pag-uri-uriin, pagbukod-bukodin; Iloc: paglasin-lasinen

SOUL kaluluwa; Iloc: kararwa

Synonym

Spirit *(Tag. & Iloc.)* espirito

SOUL mate or Soulmate taong malapit sa canya na magkapareho sila kung ano ang mahalaga o nakasisiya sa canila o ang paniwala nila o ano pa man

SOUND tunog, imik, tinig; Iloc: uni, timec, ungor

SOUND (click of a finger) pitik, lagitik, lagutok; Iloc: pitik, rittuok

SOUND, droning or buzzing *(Tag. & Iloc.)* ugong

SOUND, falling object *(Tag. & Iloc.)* calabog

SOUND, gun shot putokan; Iloc: uni ti paltog

SOUND, jingling i.e., coins cumacalansing; Iloc: agcalcalansing

SOUND, joggling contents from a container aalog-alog; Iloc: agcalog-calog

SOUND, loud, defeaning nakakabingi na tunog; Iloc: makatultuleng nga uni

SOUND, pounding lumalagapak; Iloc: aglepleppaak

SOUND, raspy *(Tag. & Iloc.)* garalgal

SOUND, rustling caluskos, Iloc: carasakas

SOUND, shrill, high pitch matinis, matulig; Iloc: nasinggit, natileng

SOUND, successive explosions nagsasabugan; Iloc: agcanalbuog

SOUND to call the attention of someone *(Tag. & Iloc.)* sitsit, psst!

SOUND volume, make louder palakasin ang tunog; Iloc: papigsaen ti uni

SOUND volume, make lower hinaan ang tunog; Iloc: pabassiten ti uni

SOUP *(Tag. & Iloc.)* sopas-*Sp*, caldo-*Sp*
   Synonym
   Broth sabaw; Iloc: digo, labay

SOUP, lumpy namumuo-muo ang sopas-*Sp*; Iloc: agbalay-balay ti sopas

SOUP, thick malapot na sopas; Iloc: napalet a sopas

SOUP, thin malabnaw; Iloc: nalabnaw, nalasaw

Sour maasim; Iloc: naalsem

Source pinagmulan, puno't dulo; Iloc: iti poon, pinagtaudan, pinaggapuan
   Synonym
   Origin pinagmulan, puno; Iloc: pinaggapuanan, pinagtaudan, poon

South *south*, timog, sur-*Sp*; Iloc: *south*, abagatan, sur

Souvenir pang-alaala; Iloc: pakalaglagipan

Sow magtanim; Iloc: agmula, agtanem

Space lawak ng lugar; Iloc: lawa ti lugar

Spacious maluwag, malawak; Iloc: nalawa, acaba

Spade *(Tag. & Iloc.)* pala-*Sp*

Spam 1] delatang pagkain; 2] mensahe-*Sp* sa *internet* na nakakaistorbo lamang at hindi makaventahe

Span 1] dangkal-layo sa pagitan ng hinlalaki/*thumb* at ng pinakamaliit na daliri; 2] buhay ng tao sa mundo-*Sp* na may hangganan

Spaniard, Spanish *(Tag. & Iloc.)* Espanyol, Castila

Spanish language *(Tag. & Iloc.)* espanyol, castilyano

Spank paloin (palo-*Sp*); Iloc: bauten

Spar, Sparring partner 1] labanang walang sakitan; ensayo-*Sp* para sa dadating na boksing; alitan o argumento-*Sp*; 2] magkaibigang nagkakatuwaang mag-argumento

SPARE 1] magpabahagi; 2] itago para sa isang pangangailangan; 3] ang natirang sobra-*Sp* pagkatapos na nagawa ang tinakdang pagkabuo; 4] itago at hindi sayangin o aksayahin, magtipid; 5] pigilan o timpihin ang sarili para hindi makakasakit o makasira, iwanang walang masaktan; 6] magkaroon ng considerasyon-*Sp* at hindi bigyan ng bigat o hirap

SPARE tire gulong na nakatago sa *trunk* ng sasakyan para may pangpalit kung ma-*flat tire* ang gamit na gulong

Spark kutitap; Iloc: rissik

Sparkle sumikat, kumislap, kumintab; Iloc: agsilap-silap, agkirap-kirap

Sparrow maya, pipit; Iloc: maya

Sparse napakakaunti; manipis na mga sinabog at kinalat

Spasm biglang sakit sa *muscle* o laman ng katawan na patuloy na maramdaman

Spat maikling away; Iloc: nabiit nga apa
Correlated word
Bicker pag-aaway tungkol sa wala man lang kabulohan; Iloc: apa maygapu ti awan kavalor-valor na

Spawn 1] anak, panganganak, pagkakaroon ng anak; 2] mga itlog na dineposito ng mga isda, cabibe at iba pa

SPEAK *v.*, magsalita, magsabi, magbigkas, magwika; Iloc: ibaga, agsao, agsarita, agkuna
Correlated words
Talk *v.*, magsalita; Iloc: agsarita
Tell *v.*, sabihin, ipaalam, ipamalita; Iloc: ibaga, ipaammo, isawang
Say *v.*, sabihin; Iloc: ibaga, ikuna, isao
Mention mabanggit, masambit; Iloc: masao, maysawang
Comment *v.*, magcomentario, punahin; Iloc: agcomentario
Converse *v.*, makipag-usap; Iloc: makitungtong, makisarita, makisao
Reveal *v.*, ipagtapat, isiwalat, ibunyag, ipaalam, ihayag; Iloc: isawang, ipaammo
Declare, Proclaim *v.*, ipahayag, isabi; Iloc: ibaga, iproclemar
Announce *v.*, ipahayag, iyanuncio; Iloc: ibandilyo, ipablaac, iwarnac

Articulate *v.,* magsalitang claro at madaling maintindihan; Iloc: agsarita nga claro ken nalaca a maawatan

Enunciate *v.,* magbigkas at magsalita ng maliwanag, magpahayag o magpatalastas ng mahusay

Fluent *adj.* magsalitang claro at madaling maintindihan; Iloc: agsarita iti claro ken nalaca a maawatan

Exclaim, Blurt *v.,* biglang magbulalas; Iloc: golpe nga agsawang

Whisper *v.,* ibulong; Iloc: iyarasaas

Voice out *v.,* umimik, ipahayag; Iloc: aguni, agsawang

Express *v.,* umimik; Iloc: agsawang

Express out or unburden oneself from pent-up emotions *v.,* idaing, itaghoy, maghimutok, itangis; Iloc: iyasog, agunnoy, agsennaay

Recommend, Suggest *v.,* imungkahi, irecomenda; Iloc: isingasing, irecomendar

Broach *v.,* ilabas na paksa para pag-usapan; Iloc: iruar a paksa tapno pagsaritaan

Repartee *n.,* matalas at nakakalibang na sagot; Iloc: nasirib ken nakalinglingay a sungbat

Expound *v.,* madetalye na paliwanag o explicasyon; Iloc: nadetalye a pangpalawag wenno pang-explicar

Extemporaneous *adj,* kaunti o walang paghahanda para sa talumpati niya at wala rin siyang binabasang codigo; Iloc: bassit o awan ti pagsagana para iti discurso na ken awan pay codigo a basbasaen na

Laconic *adj.,* paliwanag sa pinakaconting salita pero completo na at claro pa

Rhetoric *n.,* pagsalita o pagsulat ng mahusay; Iloc: pagsarita o pagsurat a nakaim-imbag

Gift of gab *n.,* mahusay at magaling sa paggamit ng lengguahe, magaling magcumbinsi

Gab *v.,* panay ang salita at wala namang kabulohan

Gabble, Jabber *adj.,* nagsasalita ng mabilis na hindi maintindihan tuloy

Gibber *v.,* **Gibberish** *adj.* nagsasalita na hindi maintindihan o walang kahulugan o hindi relevante sa paksa

Loose-lipped *adj.,* salita ng salita na hindi ginagamit ang isip at puede na nabubunyag pa ang mga privadong informasyon

Tell something in secret *v.,* sabihin ng palihim; Iloc: agkissim

Lisp *n.,* defecto sa pagsalita na kadalasan ay hindi nabibigkas ng tama

Stammer, Stutter *v.,* nauutal, nabubulol; Iloc: agum-umel

Sweet talk *n.,* panghikayat o panghimok na salita, pambobola para makuha ang gustong niyang matamo; Iloc: pangsulisog o pangsungsong a sarita, uyotan, pangbobola para magun-od na ti cayat na a maala
Quip matalinong pangungusap; Iloc: nasirib a comentario
Interpretation *adj.,* **Interpret** *v.* interpretasyon, pagsasalin sa ibang wika o lengguahe; Iloc: interpretasyon, pagpatarus iti sabali a lengguahe
Pronounce *v.,* bigkasin; Iloc: ibalikas, balikasen, ipronunciar
Spell *v.,* i-*spell*, baybayin; Iloc: i-*spell*
SPEAK gently malumanay magsalita; Iloc: naemma nga agsasao
SPEAK for mangusap para...; Iloc: agsarita para...
Speaker tagapagsalita; Iloc: tagadiscurso wenno taga-anuncio
Spear sibat; Iloc: pica-*Sp*
Special espesyal-*Sp*, hindi pangcaraniwan; Iloc: espesyal, haan nga ordinaryo-*Sp*
Specialist specialista-*Sp*, dalubhasa; Iloc: specialista
Specialize *v.,* **Specialization** *n.* ang pagiging dalubhasa o experto-*Sp* sa isang profesyon-*Sp* ay pagsikap at pagpunyagi sa pag-aaral para makatapos ng hinahangad na *specialized field* (namumukod na pag-kadalubhasa) at dagdagan ng *experience* o pagsagawa nito para mabihasa at lalaki ang kaalaman dito
Specialty *(Tag. & Iloc.)* specialidad-*Sp*
Specific uri ng isang bagay, bukod-tangi; Iloc: clase-*Sp* ti maysa a banag; bukbukod
Specify para maliwanag at naiintindihan ang kinakailangang malaman at hinahanap, kailangan tukoyin ang pangalan at ang bukod -tanging katangian o detalye
Speck maliit na mancha-*Sp* o pasa sa balat; Iloc: bassit a mancha o litem iti cudil
Spectacle *(Tar. & Iloc.)* anchohos-*Sp*, antiparra-*Sp*, salamin/sarming
Spectacular nakakamalikmata, kawili-wili o kahanga-hanga na palabas; makabagbag-tuwa o pagkasaya dahil sa magara na mga *scenario*, magandang storia-*Sp*, maculay na mga kasuotan at iba pa
Spectators mga nanood; Iloc: dagiti agbuybuya
Correlated word
Audience mga nakikinig; Iloc: dagiti agdengnged

Speculate *v.*, **Speculation** *n.* magmuni-muni, pag-isipan ng husto at timbangin ang ventahe-*Sp* *versus* panganib o *risk* at pananagutan o *liability*

SPEECH talumpati; Iloc: discurso-*Sp*

SPEECH, nasal *(Tag. & Iloc.)* ngongo

SPEECH, stammering utal, bulol; Iloc: abul

Speechless, became natulala, naumid, napatunganga; Iloc: napatunganga

Speed bilis, tulin, cascas; Iloc: pardas, partak, daras, cascas

Speedy driving magpacascas, magpabilis; Iloc: agpacascas

Spell i-*spell*, *spell*ingin, baybayin; Iloc: i-*spell, spell*ingin

Spelunk, Spelunking hilig sa pagsisiyasat ng mga cueva o yungib

SPEND maggasta, maggastos; Iloc: ag-gastar-*Sp*, aggastos

SPEND time on gugolan ng oras o pansin; Iloc: mangilasin ti oras tapno maka-estimar-*Sp* ken makaacecaso

Spew iluwal; Iloc: ipugso

Sphere *(Tag. & Iloc.)* bola, globo

Spice recado-*aSp*, panimpla; Iloc: recado, pang-templa-*Sp*

Spick-and-span napakalinis at ayos na ayos; Iloc: nakalinlinis ken nakaar-areglo-*Sp*

Spicy maanghang; Iloc: nagasang, naarang

Spider gagamba, Iloc: lawalawa

Spike 1] malaking pagdami, paglaki, pagbangon, pagtaas; 2] mala-pako na pangkapit, pangkabit o pang-ugnay

Spill natapon, nabuhos; Iloc: maybuyat, naypakbo, naypat-tog

Spin 1] umiikot, pagulong-gulong; 2] gumawa ng sinulid o hilacha-*Sp* o *yarn*; 3] magpahayag ng balita sa publico-*Sp* na may kaibahan sa totoo; Iloc: 1] agtaytayyek, agpusipos, 2] agaramid ti sinulid o hilacha, 3] iwarnak ti damag iti publico-*Sp* ngem adda pagkasabali iti kaagpaysoan

Spine, Spinal column gulogod; Iloc: dori

Spiny matinik; Iloc: nasiit

Spinster matandang dalaga; Iloc: balasang a baket

Spiral nakapulopot, nakalikaw; Iloc: nakapulipol, nakacunikon

Spirit *(Tag. & Iloc.)* spirito-*Sp*, espirito-*Sp*

Spit iluwa, idura, buga; Iloc: itupra

Correlated words

Spittle, Saliva ang dura; Iloc: ti tupra
Sputum dura at sipon; Iloc: tupra ken buteg
Spitoon pagdurahan; Iloc: pagtupraan
Spite malicioso-*Sp*, masama ang tangka, hangad niyang manakit, mang-insulto, mambuisit, nambibigo; Iloc: dakes a rikricna ken nakem ken rangta nga mangsakit
Spitoon pagdurahan; Iloc: pagtupraan
Spitting image kamukhang-kamukha ng isang tao; Iloc: agkaruprupa unay
Spittle, Saliva ang dura; Iloc: ti tupra
Splash magsaboy, magsabuyan; Iloc: agbuyyat, buy-yatan
Splatter tilamsik, talsik; Iloc: sapri, parsiak
Spleen pali, limpa; Iloc: apro
Splendid kahanga-hanga; Iloc: nakadaydayaw
Splendor karilagan at ganda; Iloc: naranyag ken napintas
Splinter tinik; Iloc: siit
Split 1] hatiin, hiwain, 2] maghiwalay; Iloc: 1] gudwaen, pisyen, putden, 2] agsina
Splurge gumastos ng malaki; Iloc: ag-gastos-*Sp* ti dakkel
SPOIL mabulok, mapanis, pasira na, mabukbok; Iloc: malungsot, ma-bangles, aglaes
SPOIL a child ipamihasa, ibigay ang layaw, consentidor-*Sp*; Iloc: ipalubos iti madi nga aramid, consentidor

1. Correlated ways

Being an enabler nagpapamihasa, mapagbigay-layaw, mapagbigay-luho, nagpapalugod, consentidor; Iloc: mangited ti amin a capricho, consentidor
Permissive mapagparaya, mapagpaunlak, consentidor; Iloc: mangibaybay-an, consentidor
Condone nagpapamihasa, nagpapalugod; Iloc: ited amin a capricho
Pamper nagpapamihasa, mapagbigay-layaw, mapagbigay-luho, nagpapalugod; Iloc: mangited amin a capricho

2. Results of Spoiling a child

Brat batang makasarili at macapricho; Iloc: ubing nga bagbagi na ti pagustoan na ken macapricho
Capricious umaasa lagi o ginigiit ang sariling kagustohan at capricho; Iloc: agur-uray wenno ipilit ti kagustoan na ken capricho na

Self-indulgent caprichoso/sa, maluho, magpalugod sa sariling kagustohan, mapagbigay ng layaw sa canyang sarili, mapamihasa, nagsasariling nagpapasarap; Iloc: caprichosa/so, agpapas ti mismo a kagustoan na, agbukbukod nga agpapaimas cadagiti cayat na

Blasé nasuya na at nawalan na ng gana dahil sa pagpapalugod sa canyang mga gusto at capricho; Iloc: nasuyan ken naawananen ti ganas gapu ti canayon a pangpaganas canyana cadagiti capricho na

Sense of entitlement inaakala o pinapaniwalaan niyang may karapatan at privilehio siya na sa canya ang mga bagay o magawa niya kahit ano mang gusto niya; Iloc: ipagpagarup na o patchen na nga addaan isu ti turay ken privilehio nga agsanicua isu ken mabalin na aramiden ti ania man a cayat na

3. _Instead of spoiling a child, here are some smart and responsible ways_ _(also read_ Parental management _in earlier pages)_

Gentility mabuting pagpalaki sa mga supling na magresulta ng fino at kagandahang-asal at marangal na buhay

Tough love pagmamahal at pag-aalaga pero hindi pagbibigay ng layaw kundi pagtuturo ng tamang asal at diciplina; Iloc: ayat ken pagaywan ngem haan mangited ti capricho ti ubing no di pagisuro iti nasayaat nga ugali ken diciplina

Spoken sinabi, pagsasabi; ipahayag, ipaalam sa pagsalita

Sponge 1] magaspang na _pad_ na pangkuskos ng dumi, 2] makinis na spongha-_Sp_ para sa pulvos-_Sp_ ng mukha; Iloc: 1] nakersang nga _pad_ nga pangkuskos ti rugit, 2] nalamuyot nga spongha nga pangpulvos ti rupa

Sponsor _(Tag. & Iloc.) sponsor_

Spontaneous natural-_Sp_, likas at kusang-loob na hindi binalak o hindi pinagsikapan muna

SPOON (tbsp) _(Tag. & Iloc.)_ cuchara-_Sp_

SPOON, small (tsp) _(Tag. & Iloc.)_ cucharita-_Sp_

SPOON-feed 1] suboan ng pagkain ang bata o ang may sakit, 2] pagtulong sa malusog pero tamad na tao at nagdedepende lamang sa iba; Iloc: 1] subwan ti kanen ti ubing wenno ti agsakit, 2] pagtulong iti napigsa ngem sadut a tao ken agdepdepende laeng iti dadduma

Sporadic pabugso-bugso; Iloc: sagpaminsan

Sports _sports,_ paligsahang laro; Iloc: _sports,_ salisal nga ay-ayam

Spot 1] maliit na dako, 2] patak o mancha, 3] masilayan; Iloc: 1] bassit a lugar, 2] bassit a marka o mancha, 3] nasipotan, nasiiman

Spotless _(Tag. & Iloc.)_ malinis at walang mancha-_Sp_

Spotted *(Tag. & Iloc.)* batik-batik

Spout magsuyot, magbuga; Iloc: agsuyot, agsuyat

Spousal tungkol sa pag-aasawa o pagcasal; tungkol sa mag-asawa

Spouse *(Tag. & Iloc.)* asawa

Sprain sakit sa laman-laman o buto-buto dahil sa golpeng pagkilos ng katawan o pagkabunggo o pagtrabaho ng matagalan; Iloc: sakit ti laslasag o tultulang gapu iti golpe-*Sp* nga pagkiet ti bagi wenno nabunggo o pagtrabaho iti nabayag
Correlated words
Strained for working or being in same position for so long nangangalay, nangangawit; Iloc: mactangan

Sprawl 1] nakaupo o nakabulagta/nakahiga na ang mga paa ay nakahandusay, nakabukangkang; 2] nakakalat, nakalaganap

SPRAY *spray*-an, wisikan; Iloc: *spray*-an
Correlated words
Squirt puswitan; Iloc: pusitsitan, pugsitan, isuyot
Spout magsuyot, magbuga; Iloc: agsuyot, agsuyat, agsaplit
Splatter tilamsik, talsik; Iloc: sapri, parsiak
Sprinkle wisikan, wigwigan, hasikan; Iloc: saprian, warsian
Splash magsaboy; Iloc: agbuyat
Pour water on buhosan; Iloc: buyyatan, suyyaten
Water the plants diligan; Iloc: sibugan

SPRAY clothes with water before ironing wigwigan; Iloc: warsian

SPREAD on (i.e., butter or jam) *spread,* pahiran; Iloc: *spread,* ipaid

SPREAD out, Circulate ilaganap, ipalaganap, icalat; Iloc: iwaras, iwarnak

SPREAD over a cloth ilatag, ilapag; Iloc: ilapag, iyaplag, iplastar-*Sp*

Spree 1] masiglang kasayahan o maikling liwaliw o *outing;* silakbo o bulalas o *outburst* na masigla; 2] nag-iinuman

Sprightly *(Tag. & Iloc.)* galawgaw, calog

Spring 1] biglang pagbangon o pagsulpot, 2] maglukso, 3] batis o maliit na ilog, 4] *springtime* na panahon ay sa buwan ng Marso, Abril at Mayo, 5] pulupot na alambre na kahit ipitin o banatin ay babalik pa rin sa dating forma na parang sa lastico; Iloc: 1] golpe nga agbangon o lumtaw, 2] aglagto, 3] bassit a carayan, 4] *springtime* a panawen iti bulan ti Marso, Abril ken Mayo, 5] agcawicaw nga alambre nga uray

no ipiten wenno unnaten ket absubli pay laeng iti dati a forma a casla
iti lastico

Sprinkle wisikan, wigwigan, hasikan; Iloc: saprian, warsian

Sprint makipagcarera ng pabilisan sa pagtakbo o sa pagtagwanan ng
mga banca

Spritz wisikan, wigwigan, tilamsikan; Iloc: agsapri, agwarsi

Sprout, Germinate umusbong, sumibol, tumubo; Iloc: agsaringit, agtubo,
agrusing

Spruce 1] isang clase-*Sp* ng *pine tree*, 2] linisin at ayosin ang sarili para
magmukang smarte-*Sp*, 3] linisan at ayosin ang lugar-*Sp*; Iloc: 1] maysa
a clase ti *pine tree*, 2] linisan ken urnosen ti bagi tapno smarte ti
ichura-*Sp*, 3] linisan ken urnosen ti lugar

Spry listo-*Sp* at punong-puno ng buhay; Iloc: alisto ken napno ti biag

Spur-of-the-moment kumilos agad dahil sa biglang pangangailangan
kahit walang dating balak; Iloc: aggaraw ensegida-*Sp* gapu ti dagdagos
nga pakasapulan uray nu awan ti dati a rangta

Spurious 1] walang katunayan na ito ay tunay; falsificado-*Sp* 2] bastardo
nga anak; Iloc: 1] awan ti paneknek nga daytoy ket usto ken agpayso,
2] bastardo nga anak

Spurn sipain, tanggihan, pakitahan ng muhi, imaltrato, hamakin

Sputum dura at sipon; Iloc: tupra ken buteg

SPY espia-*Sp*, tiktik; Iloc: espia

SPY on nag-eespia, nanunubok, nagmamanman, nagsusubaybay,
naniniktik; Iloc: ages-espia-*Sp*, agsipsiput, mangsipsiput, agpalpaliiw,
agsisiim
Synonym
Surveillance pagtatanod, pagmamatchag; Iloc: panangsipsiput, pagsisiim,
panagmingmingming

Squabble maliit na away; Iloc: bassit nga apa

Squalid marumi, mabaho at nakakadisgusto dahil sa wala o kulang ang
paglilinis at pag-aayos; pinabayaan; bumaba o sumama ang calidad-*Sp*
o ranko-*Sp*

Squalor nakakadisgusto dahil sa mga calat at dumi

Squander maglustay, magwaldas; Iloc: sobra nga aggastos ken agiyusar
uray no haan a masapul ti sobra kaadu

Square *(Tag. & Iloc.)* cuadrado-*Sp*, *square*

Squash 1] calabasa-*Sp*, 2] pipiin, pisain, 3] labanan at yurakan; Iloc: 1] carabasa-*aSp*, 2] pitpiten, pis-iten, 3] labanan ken dippigen

Squat 1] magtingkayad, 2] matira kahit walang pahintulot sa lugar na hindi canya; Iloc: 1] agdalupakpak, 2] agyan uray nu haan a pinalubosan isu iti lugar-*Sp* nga haan na nga cukua

Squeaky tinig ng pinto kapag binubuksan dahil kailangan ang langis; Iloc: timec ti puerta-*Sp* nu lucatan ta masapul ti *oil*

Squeal 1] isumbong ang kapwa; magreklamo; 2] tumili ng mahabang iyak na parang sa sakit, o sa takot, o sa sorpresa-*Sp*, o sa gulat

Squeamish maselan; madaling magulat, masindak o madisgusto lalo na sa mga malalaswa; Iloc: delicada/do-*Sp*

SQUEEZE pisilin; Iloc: pis-iten, pespesen, pisilen

SQUEEZE, Wring out water from cloth pigain, pilipitin; Iloc: pekkelen, tiritiren

Squeezed or sandwiched between two objects or persons *(Tag. & Iloc.)* naipit

Squid *(Tag. & Iloc.)* pusit

Squint ipikit ng konti ang mata dahil nasisilaw sa araw, o ipikit na may kasamang cunot ng noo dahil nakahalata ng masamang salita o pakay; Iloc: mapakidem a bassit ti mata ta napurarar ti mata na iti silaw ni apo init o mapakidem ken agmuregreg ti muging na ta nakaricna iti dakes a rangta wenno sarita

Squirt magpuswit; Iloc: agpusitsit, agpugsit, agsuyot

Stab saksakin; Iloc: bagsolen, bagkongen, dugsolen

Stabilize *v.,* **Stability** *n.* nananatili sa dati o firming kalagayan o uri; pagiging matatag; matibay na magpanatili o magpamalagi sa gawi o kalagayan niya

STABLE matatag at hindi basta-basta lamang na magturing sa mga pagbabago; malinaw mag-isip at hindi sumasandig sa hindi relevante at sa mga kalocohan, hindi madaling mahikayat o ma-estorbo; mapamalagi at mapagnatili at naasahan o *reliable* siya

STABLE tirahan ng mga cabayo

Stack 1] tumpokan ng mga libro sa *bookshelves*, 2] patung-patong na mga kahoy para panggatong; Iloc: 1] agcacadwa ida a libro a nakaurnos iti *bookshelf*, 2] agpatung-patong a kayo ida para pangsungrod

Stadium *(Tag. & Iloc.)* *stadium*

Staff mga empleyado-*Sp* sa mga oficina-*Sp*, escuela-*Sp*, ospital-*Sp*, gobierno-*Sp* at iba pang bahay-kalakal; Iloc: dagiti empleyado iti oficina, escuela, ospital, gobierno ken sabali pay nga companya-*Sp* ida

STAGE *(Tag. & Iloc.)* entablado-*Sp*

STAGE presentation of a Filipino play *(Tag. & Iloc.)* zarzuela-*Sp*

STAGE scene *(Tag. & Iloc.)* eksena-*Sp*

Stagger 1] lumakad, kumilos o tumayong nangangatog na parang mabubuwal; 2] nag-aalinlangan at nagdududa sa pakay; 3] nag-aatubili, urong-sulong siya

Stagnant *adj.,* **Stagnate** *v.* hindi gumagalaw o hindi umaagos, walang kakilos-kilos at walang pag-unlad; Iloc: haan nga aggargaraw ken haan nga agay-ayos, awan paggaraw na ken awan progreso

STAIN *n.* mancha-*Sp*, libag, bahid, batik; Iloc: mancha, rugit, pilkat

STAIN *v.* dungisan, manchahan; Iloc: manchaan, rugitan

Stairs hagdan; Iloc: agdan

Stake out firming pagmanman ng *police* sa *suspect*

Stale hindi na fresco-*Sp* o hindi na mabisa; Iloc: haanen a fresco o haanen a mabileg

Stalk 1] sanga ng halaman, 2] pagmamasid niya at pagbuntot-buntot sa taong kinahuhumalingan; Iloc: 1] sanga ti tanem, 2] pagmingming-ming o pagsurot-surot iti tao nga pagpappapaosan na

Stalwart malakas, matapang at matipuno; hindi makipagcompromiso-*Sp* dahil matatag at tapat sa layonin siya

Stamina tibay ng katawan at kalusogan na makibaka sa sakit o pagod o hirap at sige lang na magpatuloy-tuloy; Iloc: lagda ken tibker ti bagi ken salun-at nga makilaban iti sakit o bannog o rigat ken sige lang nga agpatpatuloy

Stammer nauutal, nabubulol; Iloc: agum-umel

STAMP tatakan, timbrehan; Iloc: markaan, i-timbre-*Sp*

STAMP, Post Office *(Tag. & Iloc.)* selyo-*Sp*

STAND 1] tumayo, tumindig; 2] aparador-*Sp* na paglagayan ng mga gamit; Iloc: 1] tumacder, 2] aparador

STAND-by taong humahalili at pinagkakatiwalaang makakatulong kapag kinakailangan o kapag may *emergency*; Iloc: tao a pagfiaran a mangsublat nga makatulong nu adda kasapulan wenno nu adda *emergency*

Correlated words

Reliever, Alternate worker relyevo, kahalili, manghalili sa trabaho, mangrelyevo; Iloc: relyevo, mangsublat, tagasublat o mangsukat idiay trabaho, mangrelyevo

STAND-in hinahanda ang sarili para papalit at gaganap ng tungkulin kapag kailangan na

STAND on one's own two feet hindi magdepende sa iba kundi sinisiguro na sapat ang kinikita para sa lahat-lahat ng pangagailangan kaya nagsisikap at nagtitipid siya

STAND on something tumuntong; Iloc: agbatay

STAND out 1] kakaiba ang tindig niya at turing sa canya dahil siya ay kilala na marangal at *superior,* 2] kitangkita at lantad na lantad; Iloc: 1] sabsabali iti tacder na ken pangbigbig canya ta isu ket bigbigen nga natakneng ken *superior,* 2] nakaparang ken vistado unay

Standard 1] saligan, batayan, pamantayan, sukatan, 2] kagawiang paraan o rekisitos-*Sp;* Iloc: 1] saligan, pagbatayan, rucodan, 2] cadawyan o sigud nga pagaramid o rekisitos

Standardize ginagawa at sinusunod ang tinatag o tinakdang laki, bigat, lakas, tibay at iba pang clase nito

Standing order ang tinatag na utos ay dapat sundin at tupdin

Staple 1] mag-staple sa pamamagitan ng *stapler* na ang bala nito ay mangkabit ng mga papeles-*Sp* para magsama-sama ang mga ito; 2] ang kailangang-kailangan na kalahok sa pagkain gaya ng kanin o *rice* sa mga Asians; 3] primerong *raw material* na tanim o gawa sa isang comunidad-*Sp*

STAR bituin, tala; Iloc: bituin

STAR apple fruit *(Tag. & Iloc.)* caimito

STAR, shooting *(Tag. & Iloc.)* bulalakaw

Stare tititigan; Iloc: mingmingmingan

START magsimula, mag-umpisa, umpisahan; Iloc: mangrugi, irugi, rugyan

Antonym

Finish taposin; Iloc: leppasen

START from scratch mag-umpisa sa wala o kaunti lang pero pue-deng marami pa rin ang makamtang kaunlaran sa sariling sigasig, pagsisikap at *resourcefulness*

START the ball rolling simulan ang pagkilos at magtrabaho na, magsagawa na

START with a clean slate kalimutan ang nakaraan at mag-umpisa na naman ng panibago at pagbabago

Startle matulala; Iloc: makellaat

Starve matinding pagkagutom dahil may katagalan nang hindi kumain; Iloc: mabisbisin unay gapu ta nabayagen nga haan nangan

Stash 1] iligpit habang hindi ginagamit at alagaan at ingatan para magamit sa mga dadating na panahon; 2] lugar-*Sp* para sa pag-imbakan/*store/ storage* o pagtagoan ng alahas-*Sp* o *illegal drugs*

STATE estado-*Sp*, condisyon-*Sp*, kalagayan; Iloc: estado, condisyon, kasasaad

STATE government govierno-*Sp* ng *State* ng USA na pinangungulo-han ng *governor* o governador-*Sp*; *state* ay katumbas ng *province* sa Filipinas.

STATE (place) *(Tag. & Iloc.) state*
Correlated words
Province *(Tag. & Iloc)* provincia
Small village *(Tag. & Iloc.)* barrio
Town bayan, municipalidad; Iloc: ili, municipalidad
City *city,* lunsod, ciudad; Iloc: *city,* ili, ciudad
Suburb, Suburbia comunidad sa labas ng ciudad/*city*; Iloc: comunidad iti ruar ti ciudad/*city*
Country bansa, bayan, nasyon; Iloc: bayan, nasyon

STATE-of-the-art pinakabagong labas na nagtataglay ng pinakaba-gong likha, imbento-*Sp* at pag-unlad sa larangan ng tecnolohia-*Sp*, siencia-*Sp* at arte-*Sp* na puede-*Sp* ring pinakamahusay ang pagkagawa at pinakamaraming gamit ang binibigay; moderno

STATE magsalita/sabi, magpahiwatig; Iloc: agsarita/sao, mangpa-ammo

Statement 1] *statement,* pahayag, 2] *account statement* buhat sa banco o sa *credit card* o sa naniningil

Static 1] nakapirmi sa lugar-*Sp* at ni pagkilos, 2] garalgal na ingay sa radyo o telefono; Iloc: 1] nakafirme ti lugar ken awanan ti paggunay, 2] garalgal nga uni diay *radio* o teleforno

Station *(Tag. & Iloc.)* stasyon-*Sp*, himpilan

Stationary nakafirmi at hindi gumagalaw o di mailipat; Iloc: nakafirmi nga haan agcuti o haan a maiyacar

Antonym

Portable nabubuhat at nadadala saanman; Iloc: mabitbit ken mayyal-alis-alis

Stationery magarbong papel-*Sp* para sa pakikipagsulatan; Iloc: na-garbo-*Sp* a papel para ti pakisinnurat

Statue *(Tag. & Iloc.)* estatua-*Sp*, rebulto, bulto

Stature tindig; sukat segun sa *position* o kayamanan na pinagbabasehan ng marami sa pagtingala; Iloc: tacder, rukod segun ti *position* wenno pagkabacnang a pagibatayan tapno matangad da iti tao

STATUS 1] estado-*Sp*, condisyon-*Sp*, kalagayan, 2] kataasan ng puesto-*Sp*; Iloc: 1] estado, condisyon, kasasaad, 2] pagkangato ti puesto

STATUS quo ang kasalukuyang paraan o kagawian; Iloc: iti madama a padalan ken canayon nga iyus-usar

Statute ang batas ng govierno-*Sp* na dapat susundin ng lahat; patakaran o alituntunin ng organisasyon-*Sp* o corporasyon-*Sp* na dapat sundin ng mga miembro-*Sp* o mga empleyado-*Sp*

Staunch tapat at firming matatag sa pagsunod sa principio-*Sp*; katibayan, katatagan, katapatan, hindi malupig

STAY tumira; Iloc: agyan

STAY behind manatili; Iloc: agbati

STAY put mamalagi, manatili; Iloc: agfirmi, agtalinaed nga agyan ti sigud a lugar

Staying power matagalang tibay at tatag, tibay sa pagpupursigi at pagsisikap

Steady 1] matatag na matibay, 2] wala o halos walang pagbabago; Iloc: 1] nakaplastar a firme-*Sp*, 2] awan o ngangngani awan ti pagbalbaliw

Steal *v.*, magnakaw; Iloc: agtakaw

Stealer *n.* magnanakaw; Iloc: agtatakaw

Stealth *n.*, **Stealthily** *adj.* secreto-*Sp*, lihim, patago, panakaw na pumasok o lumabas o manguha; Iloc: aglimed a sumrek o rumwar o mangala

Synonym

Surreptitious, Covert palihim; Iloc: palimed

Steam mainit na usok ng tubig; Iloc: nainit nga asok ti danum

Steel bakal; Iloc: landok

Steep matarik na bundok; Iloc: derecho pababa nga derraas ti bantay, nasang-at

Steeple tore na may campana-*Sp*, campanaryo-*Sp* ng simbahan; Iloc: torre-*Sp* ti campana, campanaryo ti simbaan

STEER patnugutan, patnubayan o mag-navigador-*Sp* para malaman ng tinuturoan ang *direction* o ang pamaraan

STEER clear of kusang lumayo at iwasan

Steering wheel *(Tag. & Iloc.)* manovela-*Sp*

Stem sanga, tangkay; Iloc: sanga

Stench baho, bantot; Iloc: bangsit, buyok, angdud

STEP apak, yabag; Iloc: baddek, paddak, paddek

STEP on tapakan, tuntongan, yapakan, apakan; Iloc: payatan, paddakan, batayan

STEP on someone's toes magsagabal o manghimasok o makakasakit sa damdamin; natapakan ang paa

STEP pace hakbang; Iloc: addang

STEP(s) on stairs or a ladder baytang ng hagdanan; Iloc: pagaddangan ti agdan

Stereotype halimbawa ng pag-*stereotype* ay: ang paraparati at mata-galan nang panlarawan o panturing sa isang lahi na tinuringan pang panlahatan/*generalization* sa bawat taohan nila at hanggang ngayon ay ganon pa rin ang pagkakilala sa canila; itong pag-*stereotype* na ito ay kadalasan ay pilipit, baliktad at mali-mali

Sterile *adj.,* **Sterilize** *v.* patayin ang microbio-*Sp* sa pamamagitan ng pagpakulo o dis-infectahan ng *alcohol* o *sanitizer,* malinis at walang microbio; di makapagsupling; Iloc: patayin ti microbio iti pagpaburek wenno disinfectaran iti *alcohol* wenno *sanitizer*

Stern *(Tag. & Iloc.)* stricto, mahigpit

Stew mag-gisa-*Sp*; Iloc: ag-gisar-*Sp*

Stewed *(Tag. & Iloc.)* nilaga, estofado-*Sp*, gisado-*Sp*

STICK, bamboo patpat; Iloc: bislak

STICK, Cling magdikit, kacapit; Iloc: agcapet, agdikkit

Stickler nakacapit at nakadikit sa paraan at paniwala niya at walang makakapagpabago sa isip niya

STICKY malagkit, nakakadikit; Iloc: napigket

STICKY fingers may pagkagawiang magnakaw

Stiff maganit at matigas; Iloc: nasikkil nga natangken

Stigma batik sa pagkatao; Iloc: mancha-*Sp* ti pagkatao

Stigmatize mamarkahan ng manchang kahihiyaan o mamarkahang tanda ng sakit o kahirapang dinanas; Iloc: maaddaan iti nakababain a mancha wenno mamarkaaan iti pakabigbigan iti sakit wenno rigrigat a nilasatan

Still pa, pa rin; Iloc: pay, pay laeng

Stimulate pukawin; Iloc: parugsoen

Sting kagat ng insecto-*Sp*; Iloc: cagat ti insecto

Stingy matipid, kuripot; Iloc: kuripot, nakirmet, nainut

Stink mabaho, mabantot; Iloc: nabangsit, nabuyok

Stint 1] pagiging kuripot, kinakacayahan sa kaunti lang na pera; limitasyon-*Sp* at paghihigpit; 2] tagal sa pagsagawa ng bagay

Stipend suweldo-*Sp* buhat sa pinagtatrabahoan; panapanahong bayad sa estudiante-*Sp* para sa *scholarship* niya

Stipulate ipahayag ang mga condisyon-*Sp* at rekisitos-*Sp* para sa kasundoan o contrata; Iloc: isawang dagiti condisyon-*Sp* ken rekisitos-*Sp* para iti pagtulagan o contrata

Stir haloin, batihin; Iloc: kiwaren, kiburen, paglaoklaoken

Stock 1] mga gamit na inipon para sa pangangailangan ng kinabukasan, 2] mga tinda ng comerciante-*Sp* na pinapamalagi sa *warehouse* bago iventa, 3] ang *capital* o fondo-*Sp* ng corporasyon-*Sp* na pinapaunlad nila sa pamamagitan ng pag-venta-*Sp* ng *shares*

Stocky malaki o mataba ang katawan; Iloc: dakkel o mataba ti bagi

Stockings *stockings,* mahabang medias ng babae na suot hanggang sa bewang; Iloc: *stockings,* atiddog a medias ti babai

Stoic walang *emotion* kahit pakiramdam na saya, lungkot, aliw, dalamhati at sakit; Iloc: awan *emotion* uray ricna a ragsak, rambak, liday, ladingit ken sakit

Stole, Stolen nagnakaw, ninakaw; Iloc: nagtakaw, tinakaw

STOMACH tiyan, sikmura; Iloc: chan, buksit

Correlated words

Belly, Tummy pusun, bilbil; Iloc: pus-ong, buksit

STOMACH ache sakit ng chan; Iloc: sakit ti chan

STONE *n. (Tag. & Iloc.)* bato

Correlated words

Rock malaking bato; Iloc: dakkel a bato

Pebble maliit na bato; Iloc: bassit a bato

STONE *v.* batohin; Iloc: batwen

STONE continuously pagbabato-batohin; Iloc: uboren

Stonewall ayaw sumagot at makipagcoaperasyon; Iloc: madi sumungbat ken madi makipagcoaperasyon

STOOL, Excrement tae; Iloc: takki

STOOL, Small bench *(Tag. & Iloc.)* banco-*Sp*

Stoop 1] magyuko, tumungo, 2] imbes na i-angat ang sarili sa tama at mabuting gawain, ipababa at laitin ang sarili sa pagsasagawa niya ng mali at masamang gawa na nagpapababa ng pagkatao niya; Iloc: 1] agsucog, 2] ibaba ken laisen ti bagi na iti pagaramid na iti dakes a makababa iti pagkatao na, imbes nga agpakasayaat isu

STOP maghinto, tumigil; Iloc: agsardeng

STOP someone pahintoin, patigilin; Iloc: pasardengen

"STOP!" "Hinto!" "Huwag!" Iloc: "Alto-*Sp*!", "Alto ka !"

"STOP!" (to a driver of a taxi or a bus or a jeepney) *(Tag. & Iloc.)* "Para-*Sp*!"

Storage *storage,* pag-imbakan ng mga naimpok; Iloc: *storage,* pag-ummongan cadagiti naurnong ken dagiti idulin para iti kasapulan ida iti masangwanan/masakbayan

Store tindahan; Iloc: tienda-*Sp*

Storehouse, Warehouse *(Tag. & Iloc.)* bodega-*Sp*, kamalig

Storm *(Tag. & Iloc.)* bagyo

STORY kasaysayan, cuento-*Sp*, nobela-*Sp*, salaysay; Iloc: storya-*Sp*, nobela

STORY, tell a magsalaysay, magcuento; Iloc: agistorya

Stout mataba, tabachoy; Iloc: nataba, nalukmeg, tabachoy

STOVE paglutoan; Iloc: paglutwan

STOVE, earthen calan; Iloc: dalican

STOVE, put pot on a hot isalang; Iloc: isaang

STRAIGHT *straight,* tuwid, derecho-*Sp*; Iloc: *straight,* nalinteg, derecho

STRAIGHT ahead derecho-*Sp*, patungong patuwid; Iloc: derecho, agturong a derecho

Straighten ituwid, iderecho, ayosin, iwasto, itama; Iloc: iderecho, ipa-*straight*, ilinteg, i-usto

Strain 1] magsikap ng labis-labis; magbanat at magsikap ng labis kaya nakasama, nakapinsala at humina at tumigas at humigpit ang laman-laman; sobrang bigat at lubhang nakakapagod na trabaho na magsanhi ng *strain* sa katawan; 2] ma-*strain* dahil napapasailalim sa marami at mahirap na hapis at paghamon/ *challenges* ng buhay at ng profesyon niya; 3] salain ang tubig at nadurog na butil ng café-*Sp*; 4] musica-*Sp* at canta-*Sp*

Strained for working or being in same position for so long nanga-ngalay, nangangawit; Iloc: mactangan

Strainer panala, pansala; Iloc: pagsagatan

Strait, Straits makitid o makipot na daanan ng tubig na nakaconecta sa dalawang malawak tubigan gaya ng dagat o lawa

Strange kakaiba, asiwa o saliwa ang galaw; Iloc: nakasab-sabali, makaam-amak wenno nakasidsiddaaw ti tignay

Stranger di kilalang tao; Iloc: estranhero-*Sp*, haan nga am ammo nga tao

Strangle sakalin; Iloc: bekkelen

Stratagem plano o kabulaanang gawa o kilos para malinlang ang kalabang walang kamuang-muang at para makatamo ng ventahe at makalamang sa kalaban sa competensia

Strategize magplano ng pagkakakitaan at kung paano magpatuloy-tuloy at pag-unlad nito, at pagkatapos, itakda at italaga ito ng pinaka-mahusay na paraan

Strategy ang pagtipon-tipon at paggamit ng kainakailangan sa giyera para sa pagpaplano at pagpapatnugot ng malaking operasyon ng *military*; plano-*Sp* o pamaraan o tactica-*Sp* o mga hakbang na pakana para matamo ang layonin o ang minimithing kahihinatnan gaya ng pagtatagumpay sa negosio-*Sp* o sa politico-*Sp*

Stray mawala, maligaw, malihis, mahiwalay

STREAM 1] umaagos na batis o makitid na ilog; 2] ang patuloy na pag-agos ng tubig o pagtulo ng luha

STREAM, go with the, Drift with the stream makibagay sa itinatag na pamantayan o *standards*

STREAM, Streaming Sa *digital technology,* ito ang paglipat ng informasyong tinataguriang tutuo para mahusay na tanggapin at ipamaraan o ipagpalakad ng mabuti ng patuloy-tuloy gaya ng pag-agos; patuloy na pagdaan o paglayag ng informasyon gaya ng mga balita, pelicula o ang kasalukuyang nangyayaring pinapanood para ipadala ng maayos at patuloy-tuloy na walang patid buhat sa pinangalingan at papunta sa *computer, mobile device* at iba pa.

Correlated words

Lifestream, Lifecast icuento o i-*record* ang iba't ibang *topics* o nilalaman at pakikipagsosyalan sa *internet* sa isa lamang na *website* mula sa kaunaunahang fecha hanggang sa kasalukuyan o sa kahuli-hulihang fecha

Livestream or Live stream ipahayag sa *internet* ang *event* o pangyayari o pagdiriwang habang ito ay nagaganap

Streamline *v.,* bagohin para mas gumana ng mahusay at simp-le lamang; Iloc: tarimaanen para mas agobra a nasaysayaat ken nalaca laeng

Street lansangan, calzada-*Sp,* calye-*Sp;* Iloc: calzada, calye

Synonyms

Path, Way daan, daanan; Iloc: dalan, pagnaan

Road calsada, calye, daan; Iloc: calsada, calye, dalan

Avenue avenida, maluwang na calsada; Iloc: avenida, nalawa a calsada

Trail daan sa ilang na pook; Iloc: dalan idiay kabakiran

Correlated words

Intersection dalawang calsada na magkacruz o letrang cruz pero apat ang pasukang calsada dito sa *crossing* na may *signal light* para sa paghali-haliling pagdaan ng mga sasakyan sa bawat calsada

Junction dalawang calye na nagletrang "T" kung saan sila magkacabit o magkasalubong pero ang isa dito ay doon na ang hangganan o katapusan; Iloc: dua a calsada nga agletra nga "T" nga agkacabit o agsabat da ngem maysa canyada ket ditoyen ti patinggana o gibus nan

Streetside *(Tag. & Iloc.)* canto-*Sp,* pasilyo-*Sp*

Strength lakas, sigla, bisa, fuerza-*Sp;* Iloc: pigsa, bileg, lagda, tibker, fuerza

Correlated words

Vim, Vigor lakas, sigla; Iloc: pigsa, bileg, kired

Vigorous ginagamit ang buong lakas at sigla; Iloc: pagiyusar iti amin a pigsa ken bileg

Stamina tibay ng katawan at kalusogan na makibaka sa sakit, pagod, hirap at sige lang na magpatuloy-tuloy; Iloc: lagda ken tibker ti bagi ken salun-at nga makilaban iti sakit o bannog o rigat ken sige laeng nga agpatpatuloy

Staying power matagalang tibay at tatag, tibay sa pagpupursigi at pagsisikap

Fortitude giting at katapangan kasama ang lakas ng pag-ii-sip at damdamin at tiyagang magpatuloy sa paglutas at pagharap ng kahirapan, panganib, kaharap na muhi at galit, at tentacion

Guts lakas ng isip na nagbibigay ng katapangan at pagtitiis sa sakit ng katawan at bigat ng buhay

Hardy malusog, malakas ang katawan, matapang at cayang makalusot sa kahirapan o bangis ng panahon

Mettle pinanganak na may tapang, chaga at pagpupursigi sa anomang kalagayan

Strengthen palakasin, pagtibayin; Iloc: papigsaen, patibkeren

Correlated words

Fortify gawing malakas at matibay; Iloc: aramiden nga napigsa ken na lagda

Gird 1] ihanda ang mga katangian o kagamitan para sa inaasahang pakikibaka o gagawin

Foster arugain, palagoin, pasiglahin; Iloc: tarak. nen, papigsaen, palap saten

Stress (*see Strain above*) perhuisio-*Sp*; 2] naglalagay ng diin o *stress/ emphasis* kung ang nakasulat na salita ay napakamahalaga para lantad ito sa pamamagitan ng *bold, underline* at iba pa

Stressed nababagabag at namemerhuisio dahil sa mga problema, paghadlang, kadamihan ng trabaho at ibang nakakabigat; Iloc: aborido-*Sp* ken agper-perhuisio-*Sp* gapu ti parikut, panglapped, ken pagkaadu nga trabaho-*Sp* ken sabali pay nga makapadagsen

Synonyms

Distress namemerhuisio dahil sa bigat ng damdamin; Iloc: agperper huisio gapu ti dagsen ti ricna

Frazzle 1] pagod na sa katawan at sa emosyon pa

Into a hectic situation pagkakaroon ng maraming gagawin na kinakailangan ng bilis pero nakakabigay ng kagipitan at *stress*

STRETCH a thing banatin, unatin; Iloc: unnaten, bennat

STRETCH one's body magbanat-ugat, mag-inat; Iloc: aginat

STRETCH the truth nagsasabi ng hindi completong katotohanan para lamang turingan siyang mas mabuti o mas mahusay kaysa sa tunay

Strict stricto-*Sp*, mahigpit; Iloc: stricto

STRIDE maglakad na mahahaba ang hakbang; Iloc: magna nga dakkel iti addang na

STRIDE, take in magtalakay ng calmado-*Sp*; Iloc: gawayan nga calmado

Strife 1] away, labanan; alitan o salungatan, samaan ng loob; 2] competencia-*Sp*, tunggalian; 3] napakabigat na pagsisikap o trabaho

STRIKE golpehin, suntokin, saktan, buntalin, bugbogin, sapukin, hampasin; Iloc: golpien, danugen, saktan, sulongen, disnogen, bugbogen, cabilen

STRIKE, employees on *(Tag. & Iloc.)* welga-*Sp*

STRIKE while the iron is hot habang malakas at bata pa o habang malusog pa o may mga oportunidad-*Sp* na nakabukas, kumilos na at magsikap para matamo ang makakapaunlad at makakalutas at makaka-ventahe-*Sp*

STRING tali, lubid, pisi, cordon-*Sp*; Iloc: galut, siglut, tali, cordon

STRING beads or flowers kwintas na tinuhogan ng butil o bulaklak; Iloc: cuentas-*aSp* nga naubonan ti abalorio-*Sp* o sabsabong

STRING of a violin or guitar *(Tag. & Iloc.)* cuerdas-*Sp*

STRING orchestra *(Tag. & Iloc.)* rondalya-*aSp*

Strings attached, with may kasamang condisyon o obligasyon

Strip 1] hubad; 2] alisin o tanggalin ang sa canya, agawan, bawian, nakawan, ubosin lahat ng ari-arian niya; Iloc: 1] lubos; 2] ikkaten, takawen, babawyen, ibusen

Stripe *stripe,* guhit-guhit; Iloc: *stripe,* garit-garit

Strive *Exert efforts; aim, endeavor, undertake and tackle to attain one's success and propitious things.* Magsikap, magpakasigasig, magpursigi, magpunyagi; Iloc: ikarkarigatan, ipamuspusan, agpakpakat

Synonyms

Ardous gamitin ang lahat ng lakas at tibay at tiis; Iloc: iyusar amin a pigsa ken pakat ken anos

Aspire magmithi ng matayog at magpursigi na matamo ito; Iloc: agcalicagum ti nangato ken ipakat nga maala daytoy

Exigency *n.,* **Exigent** *adj.* kinakailangan ang malaking sikap at dali-daling paggalaw o pagremedio; Iloc: masapul ti dakkel a pakat ken dagdagos a paggaraw o pagremedio

Capacitate gumawa ng paraan para macayanan; Iloc: agaramid ken agpurbar amin tapno macabaelan

Stroke 1] hampasin sa pamamagitan ng kamao ng kamay o armas o pamukpok; 2] pagmamahal na haplos; 3] baradong pag-agosan ng dugo sa utak na tuloy ay biglang naatake at nawawala ng malay o/ at nabaldado ang *muscles* at hindi na maigalaw ang mga afectadong parte ng katawan o pati pagsalita ay hindi na maintindihan

Stroll magpasyal; Iloc: ag-pasiar-*Sp*

STRONG malakas, matibay; Iloc: napigsa, nalagda, nabileg, natibker

STRONG-arm imbes na lumaban siya sa kasing laki niya na tao, nanakit siya sa mas maliit at sa mas mahina sa canya (lalake man o babae), sa pangamba niyang matalo at masaktan siya kung kasing laki niya ang sinasaktan niya dahil siya ay napakaduwag at umiiral ang kasamaan sa canya dahil sa matinding kakulangan niya ng intelihensia at dignidad

STRONG language salitang masama, galit, sumpa, babala

Structure 1] gusali, facilidad-*Sp*, 2] pagpatayo o paggawa ng isang bagay kasama ang lahat na parte nito; Iloc: 1] facilidad, 2] pagpatacder o pagaramid ti maysa nga banag ken amin a parte na daytoy

Struggle magpunyagi, magsikap, magpursigi; Iloc: agkarkarigatan, agpamuspusan, agpakat

Strut gumalaw at lumakad na parang mayabang at para humanga ang tao sa canya; Iloc: aggaraw ken magna nga casla agpangpangas para agdayaw ti tao canyana

Stubborn matigas ang ulo; Iloc: natangken ti ulo

Stuck in mud or sinkhole nalupak; Iloc: naylupak

Student *(Tag. & Iloc.)* estudiante-*Sp*

Studio *(Tag. & Iloc.)* *studio* na lugar

Study mag-aral, pag-aralan; Iloc: agadal, adalen

Stuff 1] hindi ipangalanan na bagay gaya ng gamit sa bahay, gamit na *personal*, pera, droga na *illegal*-hindi makabatas, 2] i-empake at ipasok sa loob ng paglalagyan; Iloc: 1] di ninaganan nga banag casla iti aramat ti balay, aramat a *personal*, cuarta, droga nga *illegal* o haan a makalinteg, 2] i-empake ken iserrek diay uneg ti pagyanan

Stuffing for sandwich or relyeno recipe *(Tag. & Iloc.)* palaman

Stuffy, Hot and humid maalinsangan; Iloc: napudot nga awan angin

STUMBLE madapa; Iloc: maypakleb, maypatakleb

Correlated words

Trip matapilok, natisud, natalisud; Iloc: maytublak

Slip madulas, madapilos; Iloc: maypagalis

Tumble down *(Tag. & Iloc.)* matomba

STUMBLE face down masubsob; Iloc: maydaramudom, maypatakleb

Stun golpeng mawalan ng malay o di makapagsalita dahil sa pagkabugbog o dahil sa gulat o pagkabagbag-damdamin; Iloc: golpe-*Sp* a maawanan ti poot wenno haan makapagsarita gapu iti pagkabugbog wenno gapu iti kigtot ken taranta

Stunt 1] hadlangan ang paglaki o pagprogreso, 2] kamanghamanghang pagpakita sa tao ng canyang gilas; Iloc: 1] lappedan ti pagrusing o pagprogreso, 2] nakasidsiddaaw nga pagpakita ti tao ti abilidad-*Sp* na

Stupidity kamangmangan; Iloc: pagkanengneng

Stutter nauutal, nabubulol; Iloc: agum-umel

Sty pidit ng mata; Iloc: riting ti mata

Style *(Tag. & Iloc.)* estilo-*Sp*, stilo-*Sp*

Stylish *(Tag. & Iloc.)* posturioso/sa-*Sp*, mapag-moda-*Sp*

Suave *(Tag. & Iloc.)* sua-ve-*Sp*

Subdue supilin, lupigin, sugpoin; Iloc: parmeken

Subject matter paksa, diwa; Iloc: amad, punto ti pagsarsaritaan

Subjugate 1] supilin, lupigin, sugpoin, icontrolado ng husto; 2] i-*master* niya at maging dalubhasa; 3] alipinin niya at gawin niya na masunorin o mapagsilbi

Sublime matayog, dakila at marangal na kaisipan, wika at kalagayan; tanyag, bantog; panghimok o inspirasyon-*Sp* para sa kadakilaan, paggalang, pagkamatayog

Subliminal bawat ang limang *senses* ng tao ay parating nagpapadala ng informasyon-*Sp* sa utak. Pero puedeng mayroon ding ibang nagpapadala ng informasyon-*Sp* sa utak: ito ay sa pamamagitan ng *subliminal messages* na tinatanggap ng walang kamalay-malay ng isip at hindi man lamang niya natatanto, gaya ng tunog, *advertisements*, imahen, larawan ng pagkain, frutas at iba pa pero ang kabutihan ay hindi parating nakakaudyok ng kilos o pagsunod.

Submerge sumisid at nakalubog sa ilalim ng tubig, nakalubog; Iloc: agbatok ken nakalenned diay adalem, nakalenned

Submissive nagpapakumbaba, nagpapasailalim, sumusunod sa utos o payo, nagpapasakop

SUBMIT, Hand over i-entrega-*Sp*, ipasok, i-*submit*; Iloc: i-entrega, iserrek, idatag, iyawat, i-*submit*

SUBMIT, Succumb sumuco, magpasailalim, magpacumbaba; Iloc: agpacumbaba, agsuco

Subordinate empleyado-*Sp* o trabahador-*Sp* na nasasailalim ng *boss* o superbisor-*Sp*; Iloc: empleyado o trabahahador nga igawgaway ti *boss* o superbisor na

Subscribe mag-*subscribe* ng mga babasahin para panaypanay ang pag-tanggap niya gaya ng diaryo-*Sp*; Iloc: ag-*subscribe* tapno cada domingo o cada bulan o cada aldaw a sumangpet casla iti periodico-*Sp*

Subsequent, Subsequently *adv.* nangyayari pagkatapos; sumusunod o pagsunod niyan; ang kasunod niyan; pagkatapos niyan; Iloc: sumaruno dita; palpas na dayta

Subservient *see Submissive*

Subside umuntos; Iloc: aglennek, lumnek

Subsidize sa privadong industria-*Sp*, *charity organization* at iba pa, may tulong o abuloy sa canila na caraniwan ay pera at caraniwan ay buhat sa govierno-*Sp*

Subsidy tulong ng govierno sa pagbayad ng gamot o pagpagamot sa mga mababa ang kinikita

Subsist mabuhay at magpatuloy na mabuhay sa pamamagitan ng pag-kain, suweldo-*Sp*, ari-arian at iba pa o may nagbibigay ng sustento-*Sp* o suporta-*Sp* sa canila

Substance 1] sustancia-*Sp*, 2] laman na buo, 3] buod o diwa ng usapan o kasulatan

Substantial 1] marami, malaki, malawak; 2] *substance* kaya tutoo at nahihipo

Substantiate patunayan, magbigay ng prueba; Iloc: paneknekan, mangited ti prueba

Substitute palitan, kapalit; Iloc: sukatan, kasukat

Subterranean sa baba ng lupa gaya ng cueva-*Sp*, yungib/*cavern*/*cave* o minahan

Subtle malabo at hindi disimuladong pananalita na mahirap maintindihan at puedeng misterio-*Sp* o makatraidor

Subtract tanggalan, bawasan, magmenos; Iloc: ikkatan, kissayan, agmenos ikissang

Suburb, Suburbia comunidad-*Sp* sa labas ng ciudad-*Sp*/*city*; Iloc: comunidad iti ruar ti ciudad

Subvert *v.*, **Subversion** *n.* ang pagpapabagsak ng isang govierno-*Sp*; Iloc: ti pagpabarsak iti maysa a govierno

Subway 1] *metro*, riles-*Sp* ng tren-*Sp* na pinapaandar sa ilalim ng lupa sa ciudad-*Sp* o malaking bayan, 2] *tunnel* o *underpass* o daanan sa ilalim ng lupa na para sa mga tao o mga sasakyan

Succeed magtagumpay, naisakatuparan, umunlad, nagwagi, naisagawa, sumikat, nagbunga, na-completo-*Sp*, nayari; Iloc: nagballigi, nagturpos, naytungpal, nagbunga, naycompleto
Correlated words
Consummate nagawa, nacompleto, napagbunga, natapos, natamo, nagtagumpany
Materialize maisakatuparan, magkatutuo, magbunga, naisagawa; Iloc: napagbalin, nagbunga, naiturpos
Attain *v.*, **Attainment** *n.* nakatapos, natamo, nacamit; Iloc: nakaturpos, nakagun-od

Success pagtagumpay, katuparan, pag-unlad, pagwagi, bunga. pagsikat, pagkacompleto, pagkayari, pagkasagawa; Iloc: balligi, pagturpos, pagtungpal, bunga, pagkacompleto
Correlated words
Triumph *v.*, **Triumphant** *adj.* tagumpay, pagwawagi, pagpanalo; Iloc: balligi, pangabak
Victory tagumpay; Iloc: pangabak, balligi
Godspeed tagumpay o kasuertehan; Iloc: balligi o suerte
Eclat tagumpay at kabantugan dahil sa mahusay na ginawa at ipinakita
In flying colors matanyag at excelente
Heyday kasicatan; Iloc: pinakangato a dayaw iti tao
People are all the same - <u>ordinary people</u> - but the successful person attains his success with willpower and persevering efforts lahat ng tao ay pareparehong caraniwan, pero ang matagumpay na tao ay dahil sa matibay niyang pasyang magtamo at matiyaga pagsisikap niya

If others can do it, everyone else can do it kung caya ng iba, caya mo din maging sino ka man

If it is to be, it is up to me kung maisasagawa, ako ang magsasagawa

Value your little successes/attainments – don't ignore them for they are in your path to a bigger success, besides it rewards you with self-confidence, inspiration and motivation Huwag mong ipawalang-bahala ang maliliit mong tagumpay o naisagawa – bigya mo ng halaga dahil ang mga ito ay nasa iyong daan papunta sa mas malaking tagumpay, at nagbibigay pa ng tiwala sa iyong sariling cacayahan, at inspirasyon at pagganyak na magpatuloy kang umangat

Your success is proven by your ability to complete things Ang iyong tagumpay ay <u>napapatunayan</u> sa cacayahan mong taposin mo ang iyong mga gawain

When your greatest effort is not enough, try something else Kung ang pinakamagaling mong sikap ay hindi sapat, subokan mo ang iba pang paraan ng pagsasagawa

If you think you can or you think you cannot, you are always right Kung iniisip mo ay caya mo o hindi mo caya, tama ka parati

We get what we expect Natatanggap natin ang ating inaasahan o ano mang ipapaniwala natin sa ating sarili

Without effort, nothing is gained Kung hindi ka magsikap, wala kang matatamo at kikitain

Successive sunod-sunod; Iloc: agsasaruno

Succinct salita o pahayag na maikli lamang

Succor *(Tag. & Iloc.)* tulong

Succulent puno ng katas ang laman ng frutas-*Sp*

Succumb sumuco, magpasailalim, magpacumbaba; Iloc: agsuco, magpacumbaba

SUCK supsop, higopin; Iloc: nutnoten, susopen, igupen, sultopen

SUCK a candy or lollipop supsopin; Iloc: supsopen, mulmolen

Suckle milk from mom's breast magsuso, magdede; Iloc: agsuso, agdede

Suckling sanggol na hayop na nagdedede pa sa ina; Iloc: tagibi nga animal nga agsus-suso pay iti ina

Sudden bigla, golpe-*Sp*; Iloc: dagdagos, ensigida-*Sp*, golpe

Suddenly biglang..., sa isang iglap; Iloc: apagdarikmat, dagdagos a pagamwan

Suds bula ng sabon; Iloc: labutab ti sabon

Sue mag-demanda-*Sp*, magsakdal, magsuplong; Iloc: ag-demanda, ag-darum, agsaklang
Correlated word
Lawsuit *(Tag. & Iloc.)* asunto, demanda, saklang

Suede *(Tag. & Iloc.)* gamusa-*Sp*

Suffer magdanas ng sakit o sugat sa katawan o hapis sa isip o kalooban; magdanas ng kahirapan; magdurusa, namimighati, nagdaranas ng hirap; Iloc: agsagsagaba, agrigrigat

Suffering pagdurusa, calvaryo-*Sp*; Iloc: pagsagsagaba, calvaryo

Sufficient sapat, kasya, bastante-*Sp*; Iloc: umanay, bastante

Suffocate pigilan ang paghinga, takpan ang ilong, sakalin; Iloc: lappedan ti paganges, caluban ti agong, bekkelen

Suffocating init sa loob ng sasakyan o bahay na parang hindi makahinga ang tao dahil kulang ang hangin sa loob; Iloc: init ti uneg ti lugan o balay ket casla haan makaanges ti tao gapu ta kurang ti angin diay uneg

Sugar asucal-*Sp*; Iloc: asucar-*Sp*

Sugarcane tubo; Iloc: unas

Suggest imungkahi; Iloc: isingasing

Suggestive 1] puno ng pagpahiwatig ng mga *ideas* o tungkol sa ibang tao, kaisipan at iba pa pero hindi derechohang nasasabi; 2] nagpapahiwatig ng hindi decente o hindi wasto

Suicide magpatiwakal, magpakamatay; Iloc: ag-*suicide*

SUIT naaangkop, akma, bagay; Iloc: umno, agparbeng, rumbeng, bagay

SUIT, man's formal *(Tag. & Iloc.)* americana

Suitable angkop, akma, bagay, relevante-*Sp;* Iloc: umno, agparbeng, ag-rebbeng, relevante

Suitcase *(Tag. & Iloc.)* bagahe-*Sp*, maleta-*Sp*

Suitor manliligaw, mangingibig; Iloc: mangar-arem

Sulk magtampo; Iloc: maluksaw

Sulky matampohin; Iloc: malukluksaw

Sully dumihan, manchahan, sirain ang linis o ganda

Sum up *v.,* **Summation** *n.* calculahin, sumahin para malaman ang *total;* magsuma, cuentahin, bilangin; Iloc: sumaren, ag-sumar-*Sp*, cuentaen, bilangen

Summarize sa maikling pangungusap, ipahayag ang mga importanteng sakop o bahagi ng pinag-uusapang paksa para malaman ang pahayag, diwa at buod nito

Summary *(Tag. & Iloc.)* sumarya-*Sp*

Summer tag-araw, tag-init; Iloc: panawen ti pudot

Summit pinakamataas na parte-*Sp* ng bundok o ng puesto-*Sp* *official* sa govierno-*Sp*; Iloc: pinakangatoan a parte ti bantay wenno ti puesto *official* ti govierno

Summon tawagin, palapitin; Iloc: ayaban, awagan, paasitgen

Sumptuous mamahalin, magara, maganda at nakakahanga; napakagastos

Sun araw; Iloc: apo init

Sunbeam, Sun's rays silahis, sinag; Iloc: rayos-*Sp*

Sunday Linggo; Iloc: Domingo-*Sp*

SUNNY maaraw, maliwanag, masinag, sumisikat ang araw; Iloc: nalawag, nasillag, ranyag ti init

SUNNY place sa bilad; Iloc: diay bilag

Sunrise bukang-liwayway, pagsikat ng araw, madaling-araw; Iloc: bannawag, pagngato ti init, bigbigat
Synonym
Dawn, Daybreak madaling araw, bukang-liwayway; Iloc: bigbigat, pagbangon, bannawag

Sunshine sikat ng araw; Iloc: ranyag ti init

Sunset takipsilim, paglubog ng araw, gumabi; Iloc: lumnek ti init, rumabii, sumipnget
Synonyms
Dusk takipsilim; Iloc: apagsipnget, sumipnget
Dark time of day gumagabi na, dumidilim na; Iloc: agsipngeten, rumabiin

Super *(Tag. & Iloc.)* superyor-*Sp*

Superb 1] nakakahangang pagkabuti o pagkaexcelente; lubhang kasiya-siya; 2] marangal na ichura-*Sp* o clase-*Sp*

Supercillious magpakita ng pagkamapagmataas, pagmamalaki, suklam, panghamak o pagkasuplado/da

Superficial *(Tag. & Iloc.)* pakitang-tao lang

Superfluous 1] labis o lampas o higit o sobra-*Sp* sa kinakailangan; 2] hindi kailangan; Iloc: 1] labes o nasurok o sobra ngem ti kasapulan; 2] haan a masapul

Superhighway malawak na daan na naglalaan ng anim na *lanes*; Iloc: acaba a dalan nga addaan ti innem a *lanes*

Superior 1] napakaexcelente at napakalaki ang halaga, 2] mas mataas ang ranko kaysa iba; Iloc: 1] nakaek-excelente ken nakadakdakkel ti valor-*Sp*, 2] mas nangato iti ranko-*Sp* ngem ti dadduma

Superiority *(Tag. & Iloc.)* superioridad-*Sp*

Superlative pinakamataas at mas-*Sp* sobra-*Sp* pa sa ibang matataas; Iloc: pinakanangato ken mas sobra pay ngem iti sabali ida nga nangangato

Supernatural ang hindi maipaliwanag dahil hindi natural-*Sp* o hindi nangyayari ng caraniwan

Supersede gawing pangpalit sa dating pamaraan o ano mang bagay; Iloc: aramiden a kasukat o pangsukat iti dati a padalan, kasuratan o aniaman a banag

Superstition pamahiin; Iloc: *superstition*

Supervise *v.,* **Supervision** *n.* mamahala, mangasiwa, mangpatnubay; Iloc: mangigaway, mangimaton

Supervisor *(Tag. & Iloc.)* superbisor-*Sp*, capatas-*Sp*

Supine nakahiga at nakaharap ang mukha sa kisame; Iloc: nakaidda ken nakasango ti rupa na diay kisame

Antonym

Prone nakadapa na ang mukha ay nasa lupa o catre; Iloc: nakapakleb a ti rupa na ket nakasango iti daga wenno catre

Supper hapunan; Iloc: kanen a pang-rabii

Supplant *v.,* **Supplantation** *n.* 1] tanggalin at palitan sa pamamagitan ng fuersa-*Sp* o sabwatan; 2] palitan ang isang bagay ng ibang bagay

Supple malambot na nababaluktot pero hindi napuputol o hindi masira ang forma-*Sp*

Supplement suplemento-*Sp*, dagdag; Iloc: nayon, suplemento

Suppliant *see Supplicate below*

Supplcate magdasal na mapakumbaba at sumasamo at nagmamakaawa na sagotin ang canyang pinagdarasal

SUPPLY bigyan, dulotan, magtustos sa tao o organisasyon-*Sp* ng ano mang kinakailangan nila

SUPPLY, Stock (i.e., a month's supply of medicine) *(Tag. & Iloc.)* isang buan o isang taon na *supply*

SUPPORT *v.,* itaguyod, alalayan, suportahan, tangkilikin; Iloc: mang -suportar-*Sp*

Correlated words

Endorse *v.,* itaguyod, suportahan tangkilikin; Iloc: suportaran

Patronize *v.,* tangkilikin; Iloc: paggatgatangan canayon

Proponent *n.,* taong makipagdiscusyon para masuportahan ang isang bagay; Iloc: tao a makidiscusyon para masuportaran ti maysa a banag

SUPPORT financially tustosan, sustentohan; Iloc: mangsustento-*Sp*

SUPPORT group grupo na pare-pareho ang mga dinanas at nagsu-suportahan sa pamamagitan ng pagkakaibigan at nagpapayohan ng panglutas para lumakas ang loob na gumawa ng ikabubuti; Iloc: grupo nga pare-pareho ti nilasatan da ken agsuportaran da ken ag-gagayyeman da, agbibinnalakad da para pangsalvar ken pangsolvar para pumigsa ti nakem da tapno maaramid da ti pagimbagan

Supporter katunggali; Iloc: dagiti agsuportar

Supportive nakikiramay at nagbibigay ng pampalubag-loob at con-suelo-*Sp*; Iloc: makikiramay ken mangted ti liwliwa ken consuelo

Suppose magkuro-kuro, maghaka-haka, wariin; Iloc: agpatta-patta

Supposing kung, sakaliman; Iloc: nu, nu cas pagarigan

Supposition palagay, pag-aakala; Iloc: patta-patta

Suppress 1] otorisasyong ipahinto at ipagbawal o fuersa na sugpoin, 2] i-controlado-*Sp* ang galaw, damdamin pati pananabik, 3] ipagbawal ang pagpapahayag, 4] sa larangan ng medicina ay pagpahinto ng pag-dudugo, pag-ubo at iba pa

Supreme pinakamataas ang kapangyarihan at importancia-*Sp*, pinaka-magaling sa gawa at kabutihan; Iloc: pinakanangato ti kababalin ken bileg ken importancia, pinakanasayaat iti aramid ken kaimbagan

Sure *(Tag. & Iloc.)* segurado-*Sp*, tiyak na tiyak

Surely *(Tag. & Iloc.)* segurado-*Sp*, siempre-*aSp*

Surf 1] daluyong o alon ng dagat, 2] sumakay sa *surfboard* sa alon, 3] paghahanap ng *information* sa *internet* o *TV*; Iloc: 1] dalluyong o pagayos ti taaw, 2] agsakay ti *surfboard* diay dalluyong, 3] agsapul ti informasyon idiay *internet* wenno *TV*

Surface labas na parte o ang pinakamataas/ibabaw na parte ng ano mang bagay; Iloc: ruar a parte o ti pinakanangato/ pinakarabaw a parte ti ania man a banag

Surfeit kalabisan sa dami; pagiging matakaw sa pagkain; uminom ng alak kahit lasing na lasing na; kalabisan sa anoman

Surge malakas na sugod o agos o tangay o pagdagsa; biglang pagdami o pagtaas

Surgeon doctor na nag-ooperasyon; Iloc: doctor nga agopopera ti paciente

SURGERY *(Tag. & Iloc.)* operasyon-*Sp*

SURGERY, have a maopera; Iloc: maoperar

Surmise mag-isip, magkuro-kuro o magpalagay kahit walang sigurado at walang evidencia-*Sp*; haka-haka at hula lamang

Surmount mangibabaw, manaig, manalo, umiral/*prevail*

Surname *(Tag. & Iloc.)* apelyido-*Sp*

Surpass higitan, daigin; Iloc: maartapan, malabsan, atiwen

Surplus labis o lampas o higit o sobra-*Sp* sa kinakailangan; Iloc: labes o nasurok o sobra-*Sp* ngem ti kasapulan

Surprise gulat, sorpresa-*Sp*; Iloc: kigtot, sorpresa
> *Correlated words*
> **Jolt** napalundag sa gulat; Iloc: agculagtit
> **Astonish** mapatanga; Iloc: mapanganga
> **Surprising** nakakagulat; Iloc: makapakigtot

Surreal *[seh-reel]* parang hindi tutoo ang pangyayari na parang pana-ginip lamang; Iloc: casla haan nga usto ti mapaspasamak ken casla tagtagainip laeng

Surrender isuko, sumuko, mag-*surrender*; Iloc: agsuko, ag-s*urrender*

Surreptitious palihim; Iloc: palimed

Surrogate diputado-taong hinirang na gumanap para sa iba; kapalit

Surround palibutan, paligiran, ibakuran; Iloc: aribongbongan, lawlawan

Surroundings kapaligiran, paligid; Iloc: arrubayan, lawlaw

Surveillance *n.,* **Surveil** *v.,* pagtatanod, pagmamatchag; Iloc: pagsipsiput, pagsisiim, panagmingmingming

Survey 1] magtanong-tanong at ipagcompara ang mga uri ng pinag-kakainteresang bagay bago magdecisyon kung anong pipiliin, 2] magmasid at mag-inspecta at mag-imbestiga-*Sp* ng husto at maayos para malaman ang kalagayan at halaga at kung saan ang mga gilid-gilid, ano ang kahalagahan, sukat, lawak at kung aplicado-*Sp* ang principio-*Sp* ng *geometry* at *trigonometry*

Surveyor agrimensor-*Sp*, nagsusukat ng lupa; Iloc: agrimensor, mang-rukrukod ti daga

Survival of the fittest para matagumpay, maunlad at ligtas, magkaroon ng pinag-aralan, o malinis na *record* na walang bahid na kasamaan, at may abilidad-*Sp* o talento-*Sp*, o matalino o masipag at napag-kakatiwalaan, at malakas ang determinasyon-*Sp* at pagpupursigi ng sikap

Survive matagumpay na malampasan o mapaglabanan ang grabeng sakit o kahirapan; Iloc: agballigi nga malasatan o maypasaran o malabanan ti grabe-*Sp* a sakit ken rigrigat

Survived nakalampas o nakalusot sa mga hirap o sakit o pagdurusa; Iloc: nakalasat o nakabulos cadagiti rigat o dusa o sakit

Susceptible madaling mahawa ng sakit; Iloc: nalaka a maacaran ti sakit

SUSPECT *n.* ang tawag sa taong gumawa ng crimen bago siya hinatulan ng husticia

SUSPECT *v.* maghinala, mag-suspecha-*Sp*, magduda; Iloc: agsuspecha, ag-duda-*Sp*

Suspend suspindihin; Iloc: i-suspender-*Sp*

Suspenders *(Tag. & Iloc.)* tirante-*Sp*

Suspense nakakapanabik na malaman ang susunod na cabanata; Iloc: makapagagar a maamwan ti sumaruno nga mapasamak

Suspension suspindi-*aSp*, sapilitan na pansamantalang ipatigil ang can-yang trabaho-*Sp* o pag-escuela-*Sp* dahil sa ginawang hindi maipa-hintulot dahil masama o nakakapanira iyon; Iloc: masuspender-*Sp*, kapilitan a temporaryo-*Sp* a pasardengen idiay trabaho wenno idiay escuela

Suspicion *(Tag. & Iloc.)* suspecha-*Sp*; duda-*Sp*

Suspicious *(Tag. & Iloc.)* nakaka-sospecha-*Sp*, nakakaduda-*Sp*, nakaka-descomfiado-*Sp*

Sustain 1] itaguyod na magpanatiling mabuhay; sustentohan ang pangangailangan ng buhay at kalusogan, 2] iconfirma, ipagpatunay at ipagpatutoo

Sustainable cayang sustentohan, suportahan at panatilihin sa pama-magitan ng magandang pamaraan, o mahusay na pagtubo o pag-yabong o pag-unlad na proceso, o sa abot-cayang fondo, o sa mga katutobong *natural resources* na magagamit sa paggawa nitong producto na walang masira o masayang na likas na kayamanan ng bayan

Correlated word

Practicable nagagawa, nagagamit, nakaka-efecto sa pamamagitan ng mga bagay na meron ito o naririyan

Sustenance *(Tag. & Iloc.)* sustento-*Sp*

Suture tahi sa operasyon-*Sp*; Iloc: dait iti operasyon

Svelte *[isvelt, isfelt]* magandang pagkabalingkinitan, kahali-halina

Swagger gumalaw at lumakad na parang mayabang at para humanga ang tao sa canya; Iloc: aggaraw ken magna a casla agpangpangas para agdayaw ti tao canyana

SWALLOW lulonin *(for solids)*, lunokin *(for liquids)*; Iloc: tilmonen *(for solids)*, igopen *(for liquids)*

Correlated words

Drink inumin, higopin; Iloc: inumin, igopen

Gulp lagokin; Iloc: sultopen

Sip sipsipin; Iloc: sipsipen, sepsepen, susopen

Put into mouth langgain; Iloc: sakmulen, sam-ulen

SWALLOW one's pride kalimutan ang pagmamalaki at tanggapin ang pagpapa-cumbaba na nakakapayapa

Swap magpalitan; Iloc: agsinnukat

Swarm pagsugod, sugoran, pagdagsa, dumogin; Iloc: agcarambola-*Sp*, agaribongbong

Swat paghampas ng *swatter* sa langaw; Iloc: pagsaplit ti *swatter* iti ngilaw

Sway 1] indayog, ugoy, 2] magpakembot-kembot o magpakendeng-kendeng habang naglalakad o sumasayaw; Iloc: 1] agoy-uyaoy, ag-indayon; 2] agpakendeng-kendeng nga magna o agsala

Swear 1] magsumpa, magpanata o mangako sa corte o sa simbahan, 2] manakit ng damdamin sa bastos na pananalita; Iloc: 1] agsapata o agkari iti sango ti corte wenno iti simbaan, 2] mangpasakit iti ricna nga mangiyusar iti bastos nga sarita

Sweat pawis; Iloc: ling-et

Sweater *(Tag. & Iloc.)* *sweater*

Sweatshop fabrica sa ibang bansa <u>hindi sa USA</u> kung saan ang mga trabahador ay nagtatrabho ng matagalan araw-araw pero sinesueldohan ng kaunti lamang

Sweep magwalis; Iloc: agcaycay, agsagad

SWEEPER, broom for the home walis; Iloc: sagad

SWEEPER for the yard walis-tingting; Iloc: caycay

SWEET matamis; Iloc: nasam-it

SWEET talk panghikayat o panghimok na salita, pambobola para makuha ang gustong niyang matamo; Iloc: pangsulisog o pangsungsong a sarita, uyotan, pangbobola para magun-od na ti cayat na a maala

SWEET tooth gustong-gusto sa matatamis gaya ng mga *candy* at matatamis na *pastries*

Sweetheart kasintahan, novio-*Sp*, novia-*Sp*; Iloc: kaayan-ayat, kaliwliwaan, novio, novia

SWELL manas, mamaga; Iloc: lumteg, letteg, bumsog, bumlad

"SWELL" "Ang buti!" "Ang galing!"; Iloc: "Nagsayaat!"

Swelter sobrang init ng araw o panahon; Iloc: sobra nga init iti tiempo-*Sp*

Swerve magpalico imbes-*Sp* na dumerecho; Iloc: agpalico imbes nga agderecho

Swift mabilis, matuling, cascas, paspas; Iloc: napartak, napardas, nadaras, nacascas, napaspas

Swim *(Tag. & Iloc.)* langoy
Correlated words
   Dive or go underwater sumisid; Iloc: agbatok

Swindle estafa-*Sp*, manguha ng cuarta sa panlilinlang, panloloco, manlinlang, mag-falsifica-*Sp*; Iloc: estafa, mangala ti cuarta iti panggugulib, mangloco, ag-falsificar

Swindler manlilinlang, falsificador-*Sp*, balasubas, manloloco, nagkukunwari para makuha ang tiwala at pera ng vinivictima; Iloc: mangallilaw, falsificador, balasubas, manggulgulib, agsinsinan tapno maala na ti talek ken cuarta iti vicvictimaen na

SWING duyan; Iloc: indayon

SWING feet while seated nag-iindayog ang paa; Iloc: agcoycoyyakoy ti saca

SWING hands while walking nag-iimbay ang camay; Iloc: agwidwidawid ti ima

Swinging nagduduyan, nag-iindayog; Iloc: agin-indayon

Swipe 1] kung magbayad sa pamamagitan ng ATM *card* o *credit card*, ipadulas sa aparato-*Sp* at ilagda ang pangalan o ilagay ang *password* (ingatang walang nakakasilip ng *password* mo); 2] paloin ng pahampas; 3] mamintas o manlait sa kapwa

Swirl umikot-ikot; Iloc: agpuspusipos

SWITCH 1] *switch*, coryenteng pasakan; 2] palitan

SWITCH off isara, patayin; Iloc: i-cerra-*Sp*, patayen

SWITCH on buksan, paandarin; Iloc: lukatan, luktan, paandaren (andar-*Sp*)

Swivel ang *device* na nakakapagpaikot sa aparato-*Sp* gaya ng *loom* at upoan

Sword, Saber *(Tag. & Iloc.)* espada-*Sp*, sab-le-*Sp*

Sworn tinakda siya sa puesto pagkatapos siyang sumumpa sa harap ng ofisyal-*Sp* ng hukoman at nakatali siya at may pananagutan sa canyang sumpaan

Sycophant *n.,* **Sycophantic** *adj.* mapagsilbi o mapagdilang-bulaklak para maging kasiya-siya siya sa iba; Iloc: agap-apreciar o agserservi-*Sp* para nakaay-ayat isu cadagiti tattao

Syllabic bigkasin ang lahat na pantig gaya sa wikang Filipino at sa wikang Espanyol

Sylvan tungkol sa kagubatan at kakahoyan; Iloc: maygapu iti kabakiran ken kakaywan

Symbiosis 1] relasyon-*Sp* ng dalawang taong nagdedepende at nagtutulongan sa isa't isa na kadalasan ay para sa kabutihan nila pero sa ilan-ilan lamang ay puede-*Sp* rin para sa kasamaan ng iba; 2] ang pagdepende ng sanggol sa ina 3] dalawang magkaibang *organism* na nagsasamahan dahil nakakakuha sila ng ventahe-*Sp* sa isa't isa

Symbol simbulo-*Sp*, marka-*Sp*, tanda; Iloc: simbulo, pangbigbig, panglasin, marka

Synonym

Emblem sagisag, Iloc: *emblem*

Sympathetic *adj.,* **Sympathy** *n.* simpatico/ca-*Sp*, mapagsimpatiya-*Sp*, maawain, kalinga; Iloc: simpatico/ca, mapagsimpatiya, mannangaasi

Sympathize nagsi-simpatiya-*Sp* at nagmamalasakit o nakakaintindi sa hirap at dalamhati ng kapwa kaya pinapalubag-loob niya sila; Iloc: agsimsimpatiya ken mangisakkit ken makaawat ti rigat ken sagaba ti dadduma

Correlated words

Empathize makilala at maintindihan ang katayuan o damdamin o layonin ng kasama; Iloc: mabigbig ken maawatan na ti kasasaad o ricna o rangta iti cadwa na

Care nagmamalasakit; Iloc: mangisaksakit

Console bigyang pampalubag-loob, iconsuelo, magsimpatiya; Iloc: ikkan ti consuelo, agsimpatiya, liwliwaen, ay-aywen

Comfort someone pagaanin ang kalooban, bigyang consuelo, magmalasakit, magsimpatiya; Iloc: mangpabang-ar iti puso ken nakem, ikkan ti consuelo, mangisak-sakit, agsimpatiya, liwliwaen, ay-aywen

Solace, give bigyang consuelo, magmalasakit, magsimpatiya; Iloc: ikkan ti consuelo, mangisaksakit, agsimpatiya, liwliwaen, ay-aywen

Soothe, Alleviate nagpapalubag-loob, hangoin sa hirap o pighati o sakit, bigyang consuelo o ginhawa; Iloc: ikkan ti bang-ar o inana, mangconsuelo, agsimpatiya, ay-aywen

Soft shoulders to cry on nakikinig sa may problema at nagmamalasakit, mahabagin, maawain, mapagconsuelo; Iloc: ag-dengngeg iti adda problema na ken mannangaasi, managconsuelo, nalukneng ti puso

Appease, Mollify, Placate magpalubag-loob; Iloc: mangpatalna, mang pabang-ar

Side with, Take side of makidamay, pumanig; Iloc: makiramay, favoran

A hurting person needs a helping hand, not blaming ang inapi o may sakit na tao ay nangangailangan ng mapagbuntong-hiningaan at consuelo, hindi ang pambibintang, pamimintas at panlalait

Put yourself in someone else's situation turingan kung ano at paano ang pinagdadanasan ng taong inapi o may sakit para maintindihan mo ang canyang problema

A joy shared increases the joy, and a burden shared decreases the burden ang ligaya na sinasapingan ng kapwa ay lalong lumalaking ligaya. ang kabigatang-loob na may nakikiramay ay gumagaan ng husto

Relieved naginhawaan, makapabuntong-hininga, gumaan ang hirap na kalooban; Iloc: nabang-aran, nakainana, limmag-an iti barucong na

Symphony orchestra musical-*Sp* na banda-*Sp* na gamit halos lahat ng instrumento-*Sp* ng musico-*Sp* na tumutogtog sa marangyang pagtatanghalan; Iloc: banda musical nga iyus-usar-*Sp* ngangngani amin nga instrumento ti musico nga agtoc-tocar-*Sp* iti nadayag a pagpabuyaan a lugar

Symptom sintoma-*Sp* o simbolo-*Sp* ng sakit o ang nararamdaman sa katawan na puedeng palatandaan ng isang claseng sakit, Iloc: sintoma o senyal-*Sp* ti sakit o ricricnaen ti bagi nga mabalin a mangitudo ti clase-*Sp* a sakit

Synchronize in music or dance *(Tag. & Iloc.)* i-cumpas-*Sp*

Synonym magkasinghulogan; Iloc: agkapareho ti katarusan
    Antonym *opposite,* saliwa o kasalungat sa kahulugan, kabaligtaran; Iloc: *opposite,* balictad a patarus

Synopsis napakamaikling pagbibigay-informasyon na sacop ang mga importanteng bagay; Iloc: nakaab-ababa a pangpresentar ti informasyon nga aglalaon cadagidiay importante a banag
    Synonyms
    Recap, Recapitulate sumarya, maikling pang-ulit sa binalita; Iloc: sumarya, ababa a pang-ulit iti kaybagbaga a damag

Summary *(Tag. & Iloc.)* sumarya

Synthesis magkakaibang bagay na pinagsama-sama para magbuong isa; Iloc: agsaba-sabali a banag nga pinagkakadua para iforma a maysa

Syringe karayom ng *injection*; Iloc: dagum ti *injection*

Syrup arnibal, malapot at matamis na harabe-*Sp*; Iloc: arnibal, napalet ken nasam-it nga harabe

System sistema-*Sp*, pamaraan, *computer*; Iloc: sistema ti pagaramid o pagiyusar, *computer*

T

TABLE lamesa-*Sp*, mesa-*Sp*; Iloc: lamesa, lamisaan
TABLE, head of *(Tag. & Iloc.)* cabecera-*Sp*
TABLE, set the food on the maghain; Iloc: agdasar
Tablecloth *(Tag. & Iloc.)* mantel-*Sp*
Tablespoon *(Tag. & Iloc.)* cuchara-*Sp*
Tablet *(Tag. & Iloc.)* tableta-*Sp*
    Synonym

Medicine pill *(Tag & Iloc)* tableta, *pill*

Tableware *(Tag. & Iloc.)* cubiertos-*aSp*, cuchara-*Sp*, tinidor-*Sp*, cucharita-*Sp*, plato-*Sp*, platito-*Sp*, baso-*Sp*, tasa-*Sp*, servilyeta-*Sp* o *napkin*

Taboo bawal; Iloc: mayparit

Tacit, Taciturn tahimik, nagkaintindihan kahit walang usapan, pahiwatig na hindi derechohan dahil hindi nagsasalita man lamang o hindi sinasabi ng derechohan o ng mahinang pahiwatig
Correlated word
Unspoken nagkakaintindihan kahit walang salita; Iloc: agkaawatan uray nu awan sarita

Tackle 1] mangasiwa, mamahala, magsagawa, lutasin; 2] ang gamit sa pangingisda o pamimingwit

Tacky walang magandang asal at bastos at mapagdisrespeto; asal at salita na nakakapangalisag o nakakapatayo ng balahibo at makapanginig; Iloc: awan ti nasayaat nga ugali ta bastos ken mangdisdisrespeto; ugali ken sarita a makapatacder ti dutdot ken makapagtigerger ti bagi

Tact *Knowledge of what is appropriate, pleasing, and polite; know how to handle delicate situations; know what to say so as not to be offensive; diplomatic, prudent, discreet, subtle, sensitive, intelligent and respectful.* Marespeto dahil may talino at magandang puso sa pagturing ng tama at masama at pinipili ang tama at mabuti sa pakikipag-ugnay at pakikisama sa kapwa.

Tactful magalang at maingat sa salita at asal para hindi makasakit ng loob ng kapwa; Iloc: naimbag ken naannad iti sarita ken ugali tapno haan a makasakit ti ricna ti tao

Tactic *n.,* **Tactical** *adj.,* tactia-*Sp*, ang pagpaplano, pagmani-obra, pamaraan para matamo ang hinahangad na kalalabasan; calculadong pamaraan

Tactile maramdaman sa paghipo; Iloc: marina ti pagsagid

Tag 1] papel o carton na *label* o etiketa-*Sp* ng producto-*Sp* o pagtatakan ng precio; nakakabit na kapiraso a papel, *plastic*, bakal o cuero-*Sp* o *leather*; 2] bumubuntot o nasa likod siya sa sinusundan niya

TAIL buntot; Iloc: ipus

TAIL, Follow behind bumubuntot-buntot, sumusunodsunod; Iloc: sumurot-surot

Tailor *(Tag. & Iloc.)* sastre-*Sp*

Seamstress *(Tag. & Iloc.)* modista

Attire-alterer mananahi; Iloc: agdadait

Taint manchahan; Iloc: manchaan (mancha-*Sp*)

TAKE kunin, kuha; Iloc: alaen, gun-oden

TAKE advantage magsamantala; Iloc: ag-oportunista-*Sp*

TAKE a hint bigyang pansin ang pahiwatig at kumilos ng nararapat

TAKE after kumuha kay; Iloc: immala kenni

TAKE apart ihiwa-hiwalay, tanggatanggalin; Iloc: pagsina-sinaen, lekka-lekkaben

TAKE a walk, Take a hike 1] mamasyal, 2] paalisin dahil hindi siya nakakabuti sa pagsasamahan o siya mismo ang umalis para hindi siya makapagyamot o magkasala o maapi o maagraviado

TAKE care alagaan, arugahan, asecasohin; Iloc: taraknen, ay-aywanan, asecaswen

TAKE food from the cooking pot to serve on the table maghain; Iloc: agadaw

TAKE for granted hindi bigyang halaga ni pansinin; Iloc: haan nga ikkan ti valor-*Sp,* ni estimaren (estimar-*Sp*)

TAKE-home pay ang *total* ng halaga ng suweldo-*Sp* pagkatapos na tinanggal ang *deductions* sa buis at iba pa

TAKE in stride hindi pansinin kundi <u>calmado</u> lamang niyang tanggapin ang hirap at problema sa buhay, at hindi payagang makahadlang sa kapayapaan at sa patuloy niyang pagsisikap

TAKE it at face value pinapaniwalaan niya at tinatanggap na tutuo ang inilalahad

TAKE it out on ibaling ang sama ng loob sa...; Iloc: ipatong ti sakit ti nakem na iti sabali a tao

TAKE it the wrong way maling akala na kung minsan ay mabuti at kung minsan naman ay masama gaya ng pagaakalang galit o panglalait ang kilos o salita ng iba

TAKE it with a grain of salt makinig ng pahayag o paliwanag pero may pagdududa o di tunay na cumbinsido

TAKE note observahan at alamin ang kahalagahan

TAKE liberties gumagawa o kumikilos ng inaakalang karapatan niya; walang consiencia kaya walang pag-alinlangan o pagkabalisa na manghipo o mang-*take advantage* ng kapwa

TAKE off (or Tilt) one's hat to someone magbigay ng papuri sa taong nakagawa ng mabuti, parangalan, ikalugod, magpasalamat; Iloc: mangited ti dayaw ken pagyaman iti tao nga nakaaramid iti nakasaysayaat nga aramid

TAKE one's medicine 1] inumin ang gamot, 2] tanggapin ang parusa o kahihinatnan ng canyang kasalanan; Iloc: ag-tomar-*Sp* ti agas; 2] akceptaren (akceptar-*Sp*) na ti dusa ti basol na

TAKE-out pagkain na iyuuwi at di kakainin sa *restaurant*; Iloc: kanen nga iyawid nga haan a kanen diay *restaurant*
Synonym
To-go pagkaing in*order* sa *restaurant* na imbes na kainin doon ay iyuuwi

TAKE over siya/sila ang magpatuloy na mamahala at magbuhat ng responsibilidad-*Sp*; Iloc: isu/isuda ti agpatuloy nga mangigaway ken mangbagkat ti responsibilidad

TAKE root mag-umpisang mag-ugat ang halaman; magkabisa o bumunga ang pinagsisikapang gawain

TAKE shelter from rain or shine magsucob; Iloc: aglinong

TAKE someone under one's wings, Give shelter alagaan at protectahan at pasucobin sa bahay; Iloc: ipacamang

TAKE the law into one's hands imbes na ipagpaubaya sa otoridad-*Sp*, siya ang magparusa sa salarin

TAKE the rap/blame for someone inaangkin ang bintang na dapat ay para sa tunay na gumawa ng sala

TAKE the side of campihan, panigan; Iloc: favoran (favor-*Sp*)

TAKE turns salisihan, salit-salit; Iloc: agsinnalisi
Synonym
Alternating torno-torno, naghahalili, naghahalinhan; Iloc: agsisinnublatan, agsinnalisian

TAKE up time nangangailangan ng maraming oras-*Sp* o tiempo-*Sp*; Iloc: masapul ti adu nga oras wenno tiempo

Taken aback natulala, naumid, napatunganga; Iloc: napanganga

Tale 1] cuento-*Sp*, storya-*Sp* tungkol sa tutoo o likhang-isip na salaysay; 2] kasinungalingan; 3] chismis-*Sp* o bulong-bulongan

Talent *talent,* bukod-tanging karunongan o abilidad na natamo na likas pa noong bata o sa pinag-aralan gaya ng pag-imbento-*Sp* o pagcomposisyon ng canta-*Sp* o pagtugtog ng musica-*Sp* o pag-awit o pagpinta-*Sp* o pagsulat

Talented *(Tag. & Iloc.) talented,* matalento

TALK magsalita; Iloc: agsarita

TALK in circles paulit-ulit mag-usap o magsalita

Talkative madaldal, daldalera, daldal ng daldal; Iloc: tarabitab, daldalera

TALL building or tree matayog; Iloc: nangato
> *Antonym*
> **Low** mababa; Iloc: nababa

TALL person matangkad, mataas; Iloc: natayag
> *Antonym*
> **Short person** *(Tag. & Iloc.)* pandak

Tally sumahin, bilangin, calculahin; ipagcompara kung magkatugon; lista-*Sp* ng utang at mga binayad, ang *score* o puntos sa paligsahan at iba pa

Tamarind sampalok; Iloc: salamagi

Tambourine *(Tag. & Iloc.) tambourine*

Tame maamo; Iloc: naamo

Tamper bagohin o cutingtingin pero napapasama tuloy; Iloc: balbaliwan wenno cutingtingin ngem agmadi o agdakes langarud

Tan 1] kayumanggi o culay-Filipino; sa *whites,* ang pagpainit sa araw ay para umitim sila ng bahagya; 2] ibabad ang katad/balat ng hayop sa *tanbark* para maging cuero-*Sp* o *leather* ito

Tang matalas na lasa; maanghang na amoy

Tangible 1] nahihipo, tunay at buo at may katawan; 2] puedeng i-negosio; Iloc: 1] masagsagid, agpayso ken adda bagi na; 2] mabalin nga i-negosio
> *Antonym*
> **Intangible** hindi nakikita, di nahahawakan, di naririnig, di natitikman, di naamoy

Tangle, Tangled magulong napagsama-samang sinulid, lubid, buhok at iba pa na nagkabuhol-buhol, nagkapulupotan, nagkagusot-gusot, sali-salimuot, at sala-salabid

Tank *(Tag. & Iloc.)* tanke-*Sp*

Tantalize sinasabik, manukso at hikayatin ng pang-akit pero gawing hindi matamo

Tantamount ka-pareho-*Sp* sa efecto-*Sp* at valor-*Sp*; Iloc: kapareho ti efecto ken valor

Tantrum, Fit of temper alboroto-*aSp*, sumpong; Iloc: sumro, alboroto

TAP gripo-*aSp*; tapikin para pansinin; sayaw na ang sapatos ay may tunog ng tapik tuwing tumapak sa suelo-*Sp*

TAP or pat somebody's shoulder *(Tag. & Iloc.)* tapikin
Correlated words
Flick somebody's shoulder or arm calabitin; Iloc: calbitin

TAPE 1] *strip* o mahabang *gauze* o gaza-*Sp* na tela para pantali o pantakip ng sugat; 3] *plaster* na nirolyo na pandikit sa pader o *board* ng mga papeles o iba pa

TAPE measure mahaba't makitid na *strip* na may mga numero na pangsukat ng damit, taas/*height* at iba pa

Taper patulis; Iloc: agtirad

Tapeworm bulati sa chan; Iloc: bulati ti chan

Taps sa *military*, ito ay signal ng *drum* o *bugle* sa gabi bilang utos na patayin na ang mga ilaw; tinutugtog din ito sa paglilibing ng yumaong sundalo

Tardy atrasado-*Sp*, huli; Iloc: atrasado, naladaw

Target *(Tag. & Iloc.)* *target*, puntirya-*Sp*

Tariff listahang ofisyal-*Sp* na nakasulat ang mga tungkulin at buis o bayad sa aduana-*Sp* na tinakda ng govierno-*Sp* sa mga angkat/*imports* at mga kalakal panluwas/*exports*; ang mga puedeng napapasailalim ng buis sa tren, bus at iba pa

Tarmac 1] daang paglunsaran at pagliparan ng mga eroplano-*Sp* sa *airport;* 2] maglatag ng pinaghalong durog-durog na mga bato, alkitran at *bitumen* sa calsada, at sa *airport runway*

Tarnish dumihan at alisin pa ang kintab nito; Iloc: rugitan ken ikkaten pay ti sileng na

Taro gabi; Iloc: aba

Tarry 1] atrasado sa paggawa, pag-umpisa o pagdating, 2] maghintay o manatili o matira sa lugar

Tart 1] malakas ang lasa gaya ng asim, sangsang, pait at pakla; 2] ugaling nanunuya at nanlalait; 3] *pie* o pastel-*Sp* na puno ng frutas-*Sp* at pinatungan ng malutong na *crust*; 4] babaeng walang moralidad-*Sp* o puta-*Sp*; Iloc: 1] napigsa nga raman casla alsem, gasang, pait ken sugpet; 2] manguy-uyaw ken manglalais; 3] *pie* nga adda frutas na; 4] puta nga babae

Tartar amarilyo-*Sp* o *yellowish* na tumigas na tinga sa ngipin dahil sa hindi pagsisipilyo o hindi tamang pagsipilyo; kinatatakutang tao

Taser aparatong ginagamit ng *police* na *stun gun*

Task isa sa mga tinakdang trabaho; Iloc: maysa cadagiti indesignar a trabaho

Tassel *(Tag. & Iloc.)* burloloy

Taste tikman, lasahan, simsiman; Iloc: ramanan
Correlated words
   Delicious masarap; Iloc: naimas
   Savory malasa; Iloc.: naraman
   Tasty malinamnam, malasa; Iloc: nananam
   Bland taste matabang; Iloc: nalab-ay, natamnay
   Sweet matamis; Iloc: nasam-it
   Bitter mapait; Iloc: napait
   Sour maasim; Iloc: naalsem
   Tart malakas ang lasa gaya ng asim, sangsang, pait at pakla; Iloc: napigsa nga raman casla alsem, gasang, pait ken sugpet
   Piquant, Spicy maanghang; Iloc: nagasang, naarang
   Salty maalat; Iloc: naapgad
   Ripe hinog; Iloc: naluom
   Unripe hilaw, mapakla; Iloc: naata, naganus, nasugpet
   Gust, Gustation ang panlasa ng tao

Tasteless walang lasa; Iloc: awan raman na

Tasty masarap, malinamnam, malasa; Iloc: nananam, naimas

Tattered punit-punit, gisigisian, gusgosin; Iloc: rutay-rutay, pigis-pigis

Tattle *(Tag. & Iloc.)* magchismis-*Sp*

Taunt cuchain; Iloc: ruroden

Tawdry damit, akcesoria o palamuti na matingkad ang kulay, pampalantad at mumurahin

Tax *(Tag. & Iloc.)* *tax*, buis

Taxi 1] *taxicab, cab* na may metrong nagpapakita ng babayaran ng pasahero-*Sp*; 2] ang pagdaan ng eroplano-*Sp* sa *airport runway* pagkababa at lumulunsod o kaya bago lumipad

Taxidermy sangay ng *arts* kung saan hinahanda at prinepreserva ang balat ng hayop para pasakan ng laman para mag-ichurang buhay na naman

Tea *(Tag. & Iloc.)* cha-a

Teach magturo, turuan; Iloc: mangisuro, surwan
> *Synonyms*
> **Instruct** turoan; Iloc: surwan
> **Guide, Direct** turoan kung paano gawin o kung saan ang daan; Iloc: isuro nu casano ti mangpamay-an wenno nu inchenna ti dalan
> **Enlighten, Edify** paliwanagan ang intelihensia o sa pagkaspiritual; pagtuturo at pagpapakabuti sa katalinohan, moralidad, etico, dignidad, integridadat sa pagkamaka-Dios
> *Correlated words*
> **Study** mag-aral, pag-aaralan; Iloc: agadal, adalen
> **Learn** matuto; Iloc: agadal, makaadal, makasursuro

Teacher *teacher,* maestra-*Sp*, guro; Iloc: *teacher,* maestra

Team pangkat; Iloc: timpuyog

Teamwork pagtulong-tulongan, bayanihan, magdamayan ng trabaho; Iloc: agtitinnulong, bayanihan

Tear punitin; Iloc: pigisen, pirgisen
> *Correlated words*
> **Torn** napunit; Iloc: napisang, napigis
> **Tattered** punit-punit, gisigisian, gusgosin; Iloc: pigis-pigis, rutay-rutay

Teardrop butil ng luha; Iloc: tedted ti lua

Tears luha; Iloc: lua

Teary-eyed napapaluha; Iloc: makalulua

Tease tuksohin, biroin; Iloc: angawen, sutilen (sutil-*Sp*)

Teaspoon *(Tag. & Iloc.)* cucharita-*Sp*

Teat *(Tag. & Iloc.)* utong ng suso

Technic or **Technique** *n.*, **Technical** *adj.* mga sistema-*Sp*, pamaraan, paggamit at alituntunin ng pagganap o pagsasagawa sa mga larangan ng sciencia o ng *arts* na may canya-canyang bukod-tanging paraan o *specialized ways;* gawi at abilidad-*Sp* ng artista-*Sp*, manunulat, mananayaw, *athlete* o manlalaro na gumagamit ng tinakdang sikap sa tinakdang larangan para matamo ang pinupuntiryang magandang kahihinatnan o palabas o efecto-*Sp*; Iloc: sistema, kapamay-an, pagaramid, pagpadalan

Technician *(Tag. & Iloc.) technician, tech*

Technology *technology,* teknolohia-*Sp*, imbensiong makina o aparato-*Sp* na ginagamit para mas mahusay at mas madali ang trabaho sa oficina at *industrial arts* at *practical or applied science* at purong siencia-*Sp*

Tedious *adj.,* **Tedium** *n.* nakakapagod, nakakaantok, nakakainip dahil nakakawalang gana o hindi nakakalibang; Iloc: makapaturog gapu ta haan a makalinglingay

Teem saganang-sagana, abundancia-*Sp*

Teen-ager *(Tag. & Iloc.) teen-ager,* edad na may *"teen"* umpisa sa 13 hanggang sa 19

Teeter hirap gumalaw o hirap lumakad ng husto; Iloc: marigatan nga aggunay o magna iti husto

TEETH mga ngipin; Iloc: dagiti ngipen

TEETH, food stuck between *(Tag. & Iloc.)* tinga

TEETH (gnashing because of anger) nagngingitngit, nanggigigil; Iloc: agngarngaryet ti pungtot

TEETH, sensitive nangingilo; Iloc: naalino

Teethe, Teething pagngingipin na sanggol

Telecast ibalita o ipalabas sa *TV*; Iloc: ipadamag o ipabuya diay TV

Telecommute, Telecommuting nagtatrabaho sa bahay na gumagamit ng *computer terminal* na nakaugnay o naka-*link* sa canyang empleo-*Sp* o oficinang *employment* niya

Telepathy *(Tag. & Iloc.) telepathy*

Telephone mag-telefono-*Sp*, tumawag sa telefono; Iloc: ag-telefono, agawag diay telefono

Telescope *(Tag. & Iloc.)* largavista-*Sp, binocular,* telescopio-*Sp*

Television *(Tag. & Iloc.) television, TV*

TELL sabihin, ipaalam, ipamalita; Iloc: ibaga, ipaammo, isawang

TELL the truth magsabi ng tutoo; Iloc: agpudno

Correlated words

Level with someone maging matapat at nagsasabi ng katotohanan sa isang tao

Reassure bigyan ng prueba para makita ang katotohanan; Iloc: ikkan ti prueba tapno makita iti kaagpaysoan

TELL something in secret sabihin ng palihim; Iloc: agkissiim

Temerarious *adj.*, **Temerity** *n.* walang ingat at bara-bara

Temp taong nagtatrabaho ng *temporary* o pansamantala lamang

Temper 1] kalagayan o lagay ng isip at *emotion*, 2] init ng ulo; Iloc: 1] kasasaad ti panunot ken *emotion*, 2] pudot ti ulo

Temperament ang combinasyon-*Sp* ng isip, katawan at *emotion*/ damdaming katangian ng tao; ang natural-*Sp* na pag-uugali kasama ang bukod-tanging *peculiarities* o kakaibang uri o asal niya

Temperamental magalitin at kulang sa pasencia-*Sp*; Iloc: nalaca nga agpungtot ken kurang ti pasencia

Temperate katamtamang hindi mapagpalabis; may pagtitimpi at pagpipigil sa sarili; katamtamang init o lamig

Temperature *(Tag. & Iloc.)* *temperature*, temperatura-*Sp*

TEMPEST *n.*, **Tempestous** *adj.* marahas na bagyo na may kasama na malakas na ulan o *snow*/nieve-*Sp* o *hail* o mga batong yelo

TEMPEST in a teapot, Storm in a teacup kagulohan o sigawan tungkol sa napakaliit na bagay o sa walang-wala man lamang kabulohan

Temple *(Tag. & Iloc.)* templo-*Sp*

Temporal tungkol sa tiempo-*Sp* o oras-*Sp*; tungkol sa buhay ngayon o tungkol sa mundo-*Sp*

Temporary hindi permanente-*Sp*, tumatagal ng maikling panahon lang; temporaryo-*Sp*, pansamantala

Tempt akitin; Iloc: mang-tentar-*Sp*

Temptation pagpaakit; Iloc: tentasyon-*Sp*

TEN *ten*, dies, sampu; Iloc: *ten*, dies-*Sp*, sangapulo

TEN o'clock *ten o'clock*, alas dies-*Sp*

Tenable puedeng ipanatili at ipagtanggol laban sa atake; naipagtatanggol

Tenacious hinahawakan at tangan-tangang mahigpit; dumidikit, nanatili, namamalagi gaya ng *tenacious memory*

Tenant nangungupa, nangangasero; Iloc: agup-upa, agcascasero-*aSp*

Tend 1] posib-leng mangyari, nahihilig, 2] alagaan, arugahin, asicasohin; Iloc: 1] posib-le-*Sp* a mapasamak, 2] taraknen, asicasuen, aywanan, awiren

Tendency *n.,* gawi o fuersa na nakakapagtulak sa tao na gumalaw, gumawa o magturing dahil naging bihasa na sa canya kahit hindi muna pinag-isipan kung ito ay tama o nakakabuti o nakakasama sa canya o kapwa

Synonyms and correlated words

Inclined *adj.,* **Inclination** *n.,* **Disposed to** *adj.,* gawi o hilig na nakakapagtulak sa tao na gumalaw, gumawa o tumuring dahil naging bihasa na sa canya ito kahit hindi muna pinag-isipan kung ito ay nakakabuti o nakakasama

Oriented *adj.,* ano mang pinagsasandigan o nakasanayang paniniwala at costumbre

Urge, Compelling feeling *n.,* fuersang nagpapatulak sa katawan o damdamin; Iloc: fuersa a mangiduron iti bagi o ricna

Pathological *adj.,* nakagawian at nakakafuersang asal niya; Iloc: nakayruaman ken nakakafuersa nga aramid na

Prone *adj., tendency* o nagagawi o nahihilig na gumawa o mag-asal ng nakabihasnan; Iloc: *tendency* o maytuptutop nga agaramid wenno agtignay it naysigudan nan

Wont *n.,* costumbre, bihasa, kaugalian, gawain; Iloc: costumbre, sigud nga aramid

Tender 1] malambot; 2] mahina at delicado-*Sp* ang uri; 3] mapagmalasakit at maawain; 4] mapagmahal o carinyoso/sa-*Sp;* 5] may considerasyon-*Sp* at hindi nakakasakit magsalita; 6] maramdamin o madaling mabalisa; 7] i-alay o i-entrega-*Sp;* Iloc: 1] nalukneng; 3] mannangaasi; 4] naayat, carinyoso/sa; 5] nakalinglingay agsarita

Tenderize ipakulo ng matagal-tagal o pukpokin gaya ng carne-*Sp* para lumambot

Tendon litid sa katawan na pagcapitan ng laman sa buto; Iloc: piskel nga pagcapetan ti lasag iti tulang ti bagi

Tense nababagabag, balisa; Iloc: maringgoran

Tension magbanat, maghatak, maghila o fuersahin ang katawan; pagalala, pagkabalisa, pananabik ng damdmin o isip; kalamigan ng loob o sama ng loob sa pagitan ng dalawang tao o nasyon-*Sp* o sa mahigit pa sa dalawa

Tenet *(Tag. & Iloc.)* doctrina-*Sp,* paniniwala

Tent *(Tag. & Iloc.) tent*

Tentative may pag-aatubili dahil walang kasiguradohan o katiyakan; sa kasalukuyan, pagsubok o temporaryo muna lamang

Tenth ikasampu; Iloc: ikasangapulo

Tenuous 1] manipis at marupok; 2] kulang sa batayan o katibayan; hindi gaanong makabuluhan; 3] malabo, di claro

Tenure 1] pagmamay-ari; 2] panahon ng panunungkulan sa oficina-*Sp*, sa puesto-*Sp* nito; ang karapatang maging permanente-*Sp* sa empleo-*Sp* hanggang sa magretiro

Tepid maligamgam; Iloc: haan a napudot ken haan met nalamiis
Synonym
Lukewarm maligamgam; Iloc: nabaaw, haan unay napudot

TERM 1] tinaguriang pangalan o tawag, interpretasyon-*Sp* o pangsalin na salita, 2] taning o tinakdang tiempo para sa pagsisilbi ng isang *official*, 3] rekisito o reglamento o condisyon-*Sp* na dapat sundin para maaprovahan o para mabuti ang pakikipag-ugnayan

TERM insurance ang *insurance policy* na nag-aalok ng sakop o *coverage* sa limitadong panahon at mababayaran lamang kung ang pagkawala ay mangyayari sa loob ng limitadong panahon na iyon, kaya walang bayad pagnakalampas na ang panahong iyon

Termagant babaeng mabagsik at nanakit

Terminal hangganan, *terminal*; Iloc: patinggana, *terminal*

Terminate *v.*, **Termination** *n.* nagtatapos, paghinto, nagwawakas, pagtigil; ang panahon, lugar-*Sp* o parte-*Sp* na nagwawakas; Iloc: aggibus, malpas, palpasen

Terminology ang tinaguriang tawag ng ano man sa lengguahe-*Sp*, siencia-*Sp*, negocio-*Sp*, medico-*Sp*, sakit, gamot at iba pa

Termite *(Tag. & Iloc.)* anay

Terra firma matigas at tuyong lupa; Iloc: natangken ken namaga a daga

Terrain lupain na binibigyang-pansin ang *natural features* o katangian gaya ng lamang o pakinabang na makuha ng militar

Terrestrial tungkol sa lupain/*earth* at hindi sa karagatan o himpapawid at tungko sa mga nilalang at halaman na nabubuhay sa lupain; *TV signal* na pinadala sa himpapawid ng mundo pero galing sa *transmitter* sa lupa, hindi sa *satellite*.

Terrible napakasama, terib-le-*Sp*, masiado, palalo; Iloc: terib-le, naka-dakdakes, masiado-*Sp*, napalalo

Terrific sobrang dakila, mabuti at mahusay; nakakatakot, nakakakilabot

Terrified kinilabutan, nasindak, natakot, nangamba, nangalisag; Iloc: nabutngan, simgar ti dutdot na

Terrify takotin; Iloc: butngen

Terrifying nakakakilabot, nakakasindak, katakot-takot; Iloc: nakabut-buteng, nakaam-amak

Territorial tungkol sa teritorio-*Sp* o lupa na nakatakda sa isang distrito-*Sp* o bayan o *ruler*; pinagtatanggol ang angking teritorio-Sp laban sa mga *intruders* o pumapasok na walang pahintulot

Territory teritorio-*Sp*, lupa at karagatan na controlado at nasa otori-zasyon-*Sp* ng isang bansa; Iloc: teritorio, daga ken baybay nga controlado ken adda iti uneg ti otorizasyon ti maysa a nasyon-*Sp*

Terror takot na matindi o nakakakilabot

Terrorism *(Tag. & Iloc.)* terorismo-*Sp*

Terrorist *(Tag. & Iloc.)* terorista-*Sp*

Terrorize tinatakot ng lubha; Iloc: butngen ti napalalo

Terse sagot o salita na maikli pero franka at tugma sa paksa; Iloc: sungbat wenno sarita nga ababa ngem franka ken umno iti amad /*sense* o relevante ti pagsasaritaan

Test *test,* examen-*Sp*, pagsusulit, pagsubok; Iloc: *test,* examen

Testament *(Tag. & Iloc.)* testamento-*Sp*

Testate, Testator gumawa at nag-iwan ng validong testamento-*Sp* o huling bilin

Testicle bayag; Iloc: batillog, lateg

Testify tumetestigo, sumasaksi, nagpapatunay o nagbibigay ng evi-dencia-*Sp* sa harap ng hukoman at formal-*Sp* at mataimtim na nagpapatunay ng katotohanan; Iloc: agtestigo, agsaksi, ipaammo ken patalgedan ti usto ken agpayso

Testimonial kasulatang declarasyon-*Sp* na nagpapatutoo ng ugali, asal at katangian ng tao, o ang halaga ang pagkahusay ng bagay; recomen-dasyon-*Sp*; 2] anomang binibigay o ginagawa bilang pagpapakita ng paghanga, pagpapahalaga o pagtanaw ng utang na loob

Testimony testimonya-*Sp*, pagpahayag o declarasyon-*Sp* ng saksi o testigo-*Sp* sa ilalim ng pagsusumpa at paninindigan; prueba-*Sp* o evidencia-*Sp* na sumusuporta sa katotohanan o pahayag

Tetanus *(Tag. & Iloc.)* tetano-*Sp;* sakit na pinasukan ng microbio-*Sp* ang sugat sa katawan at inafectohan ang paghinga, ang laman-laman at ang panga *(lockjaw)*

Text 1] ang nilalaman ng *manuscript*, libro-*Sp*, periodico-*Sp*, sulat at iba pa; ang orihinal-*Sp* na mga salita ng manunulat; tula o *lyrics* ng canta-*Sp;* 2] magpadala ng mensahe-*Sp* sa *cell phone* at sa ibang *mobile device*

Textile *(Tag. & Iloc.)* tela-*Sp*

Texture ichura-*Sp* at hipo ng balat o labas ng isang bagay; Iloc: ichura-*Sp* ken ricna ti cudil o ruar ti maysa a banag

Thalassic tungkol sa dagat, karagatan, lo-ok, lawa o dagat-dagatan; o anomang nakatira sa mga tubig na ito

Than caysa sa; Iloc: ngem iti

"Thank you" "Salamat pô;" Iloc: "Dios ti agngina," "Agyamanak, apo"
   Correlated words
   "You're welcome" "Walang anoman;" Iloc: "Awan ania man na"

Thankful kumikilala ng utang na loob; Iloc: managyaman

Thankless ingrato-*Sp*, walang utang na loob, walang pagpapasalamat; Iloc: ingrato-*Sp*, awan ti pagyamyaman na

Thanks, give magpasalamat; Iloc: agyaman
   Correlated words
   Appreciate ikalugod; Iloc: apreciaren
   Grateful mapagpasalamat; Iloc: manangyamyaman

Thanksgiving pasasalamat; Iloc: pangyamyaman

THAT iyan; Iloc: dayta, daydiay

"THAT way" (method) "Ganyan ang paggawa," "Ganyan;" Iloc: "Casta ti pagaramid", "Casta"

"THAT way" (route) "Diyan ang daan", "Papunta dian" Iloc: "Dita ti dalan nga mapan idiay", "Agpaturong dita"

"THAT will be the day" "Hindi ako naniniwala na iyan ay magaganap o mangyayari"

Thaw ilabas sa *freezer* ang lulutoin at patunawin ang lamig o ang kumapit na yelo-*Sp*; Iloc: iruar diay *freezer* ti lutwen ken patunawen ti lamiis ken iti kimpet a yelo

THE-*singular* ang, ng ("ng" is *pronounced "nang")*, iyong; Iloc: ti, iti, daytay
  Synonym
  A, ang, ng *("ng" prounced "nang")*; Iloc:ti, iti
THE-*plural* ang mga *("mga" is pronounced "ma-nga")*, ng mga *(pronounced "nang ma-nga")*; Iloc: dagiti
THE daily grind ano mang caraniwan o kinagawiang gawa o trabaho ng isang tao araw-araw
  Correlated word
  Routine kinagawiang gawa, kaugaliang pamaraan; Iloc: sigud o cadawyan nga aramid o sigud a pamay-an
Theater cine-*Sp*, lugar-*Sp* na pagtanghalan ng pelicula-*Sp* o *opera* o *symphony orchestra* at iba pang palabas; Iloc: cine, lugar a pagbuyaan ti pelicula wenno opera wenno *symphony orchestra* ken sabali pay a pabuya
Thee Cayo po (Thee: tawag sa Dios); Iloc: Dacayo apo
Theft pagnanakaw; Iloc: pagtakaw
Their canila, nina; Iloc: cuada
Theirs canila, nila; Iloc: cucuada
THEM sila; Iloc: isuda
THEM, to, On them, Through them sa canila, pamamagitan sa canila; Iloc: canyada
THEME paksa ng talumpati, usapan, discusyon-*Sp*, meditasyon-*Sp* o composisyon-*Sp*; *essay* o *composition* sa escuela-*Sp*; kung sa *arts,* ito ang nagkaisahan at nangingibabaw na diwa, *motif* at iba pa; Iloc: amad, paksa, banag, punto ti pagsarsaritaan; theme, motif
THEME song ang canta-*Sp* o musica-*Sp* na inuulit parati o pinapatugtog sa umpisang-umpisa kaya nangingibabaw ito sa palabas o kaya nagpapakilala ito kung anong programa-*Sp* sa TV o anong palabas sa *opera* at iba pa
Themselves sila mismo-*Sp*; Iloc: isuda mismo
Then 1] noon, sa panahong iyon; 2] pagkatapos niyan, kasunod niyan, maya-maya; Iloc: 1] idi, idi cuan, 2] idi nalpas
Thence 1] buhat sa lugar-*Sp* na iyan; 2] dahil diyan; 3] kung ganon ay... Iloc; 1] nagtaud idiay; 2] gapu dita; 3] nu casta ket...

Theology *theology,* teolohia-*Sp,* pag-aaral tungkol sa relihion-*Sp*; Iloc; *theology,* teolohia, maypapan iti relihion

Theorem diwa, paniniwala, pamaraan o pahayag na kadalasan ay tinatanggap na tutuo o karapat-dapat kahit hindi nagbibigay ng prueba-*Sp*

Theory *n.,* **Theoretical** *adj.* 1] teoria-*Sp;* batay sa teoria at hindi sa gawa; 2] nasubokan nang mga palagay, hakahaka at kuro-kuro na tinuri-ngang tama at puedeng gamiting pangpaliwanag o palatandaan ng isang kakaibang pangyayayari o kababalaghan

Therapy *n.,* **Therapeutic** *adj.* paggamot ng sakit sa katawan o sa isip; tungkol sa pagpapagaling sa sakit

THERE iyon, diyan, doon, naroroon, nandun, nandiyan; Iloc: idiay, diay, dita

THERE is more to it than meets the eye may iba pang bagay sa likod ng nakalantad o nakikita

Therefore kaya, dahil dito, kung ganon; Iloc: gapu dita, isu ngarud

Thermal suot-panloob na nakakabigay ng init sa katawan sa panahon ng taglamig; Iloc: pang-uneg a cawes a makaited ti init iti bagi nu *winter*

Thermometer *(Tag. & Iloc.) thermometer*

Thermos *(Tag. & Iloc.) thermos,* termos-*Sp*

These mga ito; Iloc: dagitoy

Thesis *(Tag. & Iloc.) thesis*

They sila; Iloc: isuda

They said so daw, raw; Iloc: cano
  Synonym
  Was said/stated daw, raw; Iloc: cano, cunada

Thick macapal; Iloc: napuscol, nabengbeng
  Antonym
  Thin manipis; Iloc: naingpis

Thicken pacapalin, palapotin; Iloc: papuscolen, papaleten

Thief magnanakaw; Iloc: mannanakaw

Thigh hita; Iloc: luppo

THIN people payat; Iloc: nakuttong
  Correlated words
  Slender balingkinitan; Iloc: narapis ti bagi

Emaciated, Gaunt buto't balat ang pagkapayat at hihinahina; Iloc: tulang ken cudil ti pagkakuttong ken agcapoycapoy

THIN things manipis; Iloc: naingpis

THIN, very buto't balat, payat na payat; Iloc: nakakutkuttong

Thine ang Inyo, sa Inyo po; Iloc: ti Cuayo apo

Thing ginagamit na salita kung hindi ipangalanan na bagay gaya ng gamit sa bahay, pera, gawain, pangyayari at iba pang bagay-bagay; Iloc: di ninaganan nga banag casla iti aramat ti balay, cuarta, aramid, mapaspasamak ken dadduma pay a bambanag
Correlated words
Object, Stuff, Material ito ang tawag kung hindi nababanggit ang pangalan ng isang bagay; Iloc: daytoy iti awag nu haan nga isawang iti nagan ti maysa a banag

THINK mag-isip, isipin; Iloc: agpanunot, panunoten

THINK outside the box *This is a new way of looking at things; new perspectives, creative thinking, which should be beneficial, appropriate and relevant to people and situations. Read good books, talk to friends and be open to suggestions to find out other useful aspects that are not traditionally or usually implemented.* Huwag magdepende lamang sa kagawian o mga kasalukuyang pamaraan, kundi mag-isip ng mas lampas pa diyan na makalikha at makabuo ng nakakaventahe at napakahusay na *solutions* at *outcomes*

THIRD ikatlo, tercero/ra-*Sp*; Iloc: ikatallo, tercero/ra

THIRD-degree 1] ikatlong antas; 2] malabis at matinding *questioning* o pag-uusisa; o kaya marahas na pag-*grill* ng *police* para makakuha ng informasyon-*Sp* o para mahimok na mangumpisal o umamin ng kasalanan

Thirst pagkauhaw; Iloc: pagkawaw, makain-inom

Thirsty uhaw, nauuhaw; Iloc: makainom, mawaw

Thirteen *thirteen,* labing tatlo; Iloc: *thirteen,* sangapulo ket tallo

Thirty *thirty,* treinta-*Sp*, tatlumpo; Iloc: *thirty,* treinta, tallopulo

Thirty one, 32, 33, 34, etc. *(English numbers are commonly used by Filipinos)*

THIS ito; Iloc: daytoy

THIS, of nito; Iloc: para daytoy

Thorn tinik; Iloc: siit

Thorny matinik; Iloc: nasiit

Those mga iyan, mga iyon; Iloc: dagidiay

Thorough completo at tumpak; Iloc: completo ken usto

Thoroughbred purong lahi; Iloc: puro-*Sp* a lahi

Thoroughfare *highway* o *main road*; calsada o *street* na sa magkabilang dulo ay nakakabit sa ibang *street*.

Thou Cayo po; Iloc: Dacayo apo

Though, Although bagaman, kahit na; Iloc: uray pay

Thought isip; Iloc: panunot

Thoughtful maalalahanin sa kapwa; Iloc: nanakem, makalaglagip ti cadwa

Thoughtless pabaya o walang considerasyon-*Sp* na campante-*Sp* lang siya sa canyang katayoan at hindi nagpatuturing kung ano ang maka-katulong ng husto-*Sp* sa sarili, sa familia-*Sp* o sa kapwa

Thousand libo; Iloc: ribo

Thrash 1] daigin ng husto, 2] umuugoy-ugoy o nahahaltak-haltak habang nasa banka at ang daluyong ay marahas at gumigiwang-giwang; Iloc: 1] abaken iti usto, 2] napigsa nga mayduron-duron bayat nga nakasakay ti banka ken ti dalluyong ket naranggas nga mangin-indayon canyada

Thread sinulid; Iloc: sinulid, panait

Threat *n.*, **Threaten** *v.* pagbabanta, pananakot, pagbabala; Iloc: carit ti peggad

Correlated word

Menace may pagkapeligro, banta; Iloc: adda peggad, carit

Threatening gesture of the hand, raised and ready to strike mag-amba; Iloc: aglayat

THREE *three,* tatlo, tres-*Sp*; Iloc: *three,* tallo, tres

THREE hundred *three hundred,* tatlong daan; Iloc: *three hundred,* tallo gasut

THREE o'clock *(Tag. & Iloc.) three o'clock,* alas tres-*Sp*

Three R's reading-'riting-'rithmetic *(reading-writing-arithmetic)* na sali-gan ng educasyon

THREE thousand *three thousand,* tatlong libo; Iloc: *three thousand,* tallo nga ribo

Threshold paanan, bukana, bungad; Iloc: pagserkan, sango ti balay

Thrice tatlong beses-*Sp* Iloc: tallo nga beses

Thrift *n.,* **Thrifty** *adj.* matipid, kuripot, barat; pagtitipid at pag-iingat sa paggastos para mapag-abot ang buanang suweldo-*Sp* hanggang sa kasunod na suweldo na walang kautang-utang; pagtipid, pag-impok at hindi pag-aksaya o magsayang ng graciang pinagkaloob ng Dios

Thrill nagigiliwan; Iloc: maay-ayatan

Thrive umunlad, mag-progreso-*Sp*, mabuhay, tumubo; Iloc: agrang-ay, agprogreso, agtubo, agbiag

Throat lalamunan; Iloc: carabukob
> *Synonym*
> **Larynx** lalamunan; Iloc: carabucob

Throb tumitibok, pumipintig; Iloc: agpitpitik

Throne *(Tag. & Iloc.)* trono-*Sp*

THROUGH, By means of sa pamamagitan ng; Iloc: iti pangdalan ti, iti pangi-usar-*Sp* ti

THROUGH, Finished tapos na; Iloc: nalpasen

THROUGH thick & thin, Through hell & high water kahit dumanas ng napakahirap na kalagayan, magsasagawa pa rin; kahit mabuti man o masama ang panahon, magpursigi pa rin

Throughout todo-todo buhat sa simula hanggang sa katapusan; Iloc: todo-todo manipud diay rugi inggana't patinggana

THROW, Toss ihagis, i-itcha-*Sp*, ibato; Iloc: ibato, ipalladaw, ipalapal, ipurwak, ipallato
> *Correlated words*
> **Brandish** ipukol; Iloc: iwasiwas
> **Catch a thrown or falling object** salohin, hagipin; Iloc: sippawen

THROW angrily *(Tag. & Iloc.)* ibalibag

THROW away itapon; Iloc: ibelleng

THROW one's weight around/about ginagamit ang kapangyarihan o mataas na katungkolan para matamo ang gusto lalo na sa maling paraan o pang-oportunista lang gaya ng maghari-hari at mangdominante.

Throwback ihagis uli o kaya ibalik ang hinagis.

Thru *(see Through, By means of)*

THRUST into the ground itirik; Iloc: itugkel

THRUST into someone saksakin; Iloc: bagsolen, bagkongen, dugsolen

Thug *(Tag. & Iloc.)* butangero, basag-ulero

THUMB hinlalaking daliri; Iloc: tangan, nataba a ramay

THUMB-suck nagnunotnot ng daliri; Iloc: agnutnot ti ramay

Thumbprint marka-*Sp* ng diniin na hinlalaking daliri; Iloc: marka ti dineppel a tangan a ramay

Thumbs up senyas na *"okay"* o *"good job"* o aprobado-*Sp*

Thunder kulog; Iloc: gurrood

THURSDAY *(Tag. & Iloc.) Thursday,* Hueves-*Sp*

THURSDAY, holy *(Tag. & Iloc.) Holy Thursday,* Hueves Santo-*Sp*

Thus kaya; Iloc: isu ngarud

Thwart pigilin ang pangyayari; contrahin o daigin ang sikap ng iba; Iloc: lappedan iti mar-aramid; contraen o abaken ti pakat ti sabali

Thy, Thyself ang Inyong; Cayo

Tic walang sakit pero bigla at pabugso-bugsong hindi sinasadyang *twitch* o kimbot ng *muscle* sa mukha o ibang parte ng katawan

Tick *(Tag. & Iloc.)* garapata-*Sp*

TICKET *(Tag. & Iloc.) ticket*

TICKET booth *(Tag. & Iloc.)* takilya-*Sp*

Tickle kilitiin; Iloc: kilkilyen

Ticklish kilitiin; Iloc: nalaca a maaryek

Tidbit-*(USA),* **Titbit-***(UK)* konti-konti at pira-pirasong pagkain masarap na pagkain; magandang balita; kawiliwiling chismis-*Sp*; Iloc: naimas a makan nga napirapirao; chismis-*Sp*

Tide *n.,* **Tidal** *adj.* 1] alon, daluyong o tungkol sa mga yan; Iloc: dalluyong, 2] tiempo-*Sp* o panahon gaya ng tag-init, tag-ulan at iba pa

Tidy maglinis at mag-ayos, mag-areglo-*Sp*; Iloc: aglinis ken agpenpen, agpakni, agareglo

Correlated words

Clean maglinis; Iloc: aglinis, agdalus

Neaten mag-ayos, mag-areglo; Iloc: agurnos, agdalimanek, agtarimaa-nen

Declutter iligpit ang mga calat; Iloc: idulin, ipakni, agpenpen cadagiti nakawaras

Kempt maareglo, maayos; Iloc: naareglo naurnos

Orderly maayos, malinis, areglado; Iloc: nadalimanek, areglado, nalinis ken naurnos

Shipshape mahusay ang pagkaareglo; Iloc: nakaur-urnos pagkaareglo

TIE *(Tag. & Iloc.)* corbata-*Sp*

TIE *n. & v.* tali, igapos; Iloc: galot, igalot, siglot, isiglot

Antonym

Untie calagin, i-alpas; Iloc: warwaren, lapso-lapsoten

TIE, Even *(Tag. & Iloc.)* tabla, patas, patag

TIE, Cord tali, lubid, cordon-*Sp*; Iloc: galot, siglot, tali, cordon

TIE the knot magpakasal; Iloc: agcasar

Tier *(Tag. & Iloc.)* baytang

Tiff munting away, alitan, yamotan, sumpongan

Tiger *(Tag. & Iloc.)* tiger, tigre-*Sp*

TIGHT masikip, makipot, mahigpit; Iloc: nakipet, nailet, nareppet, nairut
Antonym
Loose maluwag; Iloc: nalawa, nalucay

TIGHT-fisted *see Thrift, Thrifty*

TIGHT space makitid, masikip; Iloc: nasiksik
Antonym
Spacious maluwag, malawak; Iloc: nalawa

TIGHTEN higpitan; Iloc: pairuten, reppetan, paileten
Antonym
Loosen luwagan; Iloc: lawaan, palucayan

TIGHTEN one's belt, Cut back kung maliit lamang ang sueldo, gumastos lamang ng macacayanan para hindi umutang o maging dukha o pobre-*Sp* at para makaahon sa hirap o pagsubok

Till 1] hanggang..., 2] mag-araro para ihanda ang lupa para sa tanim; Iloc: 1] inggana..., 2] agarado para isagana ti daga para ti tanem

Tilt tagilid; Iloc: patingig, batwag
Correlated words
Lopsided, Uneven tabingi; Iloc: bangking

TIME panahon, tiempo-*Sp*; Iloc: panawen, tiempo
Correlated phrases
"It's about time" "Kapanahonan na;" Iloc: "Panawenen," "Tiempon"
Any time is the right time to do what is right ano mang oras ay napapanahon para gumawa ng tama
Don't waste time, invest it with beneficial and productive deeds huwag mag-aksaya ng oras, gamitin ito ng kapakipakinabang at nakakaventahe gawain para sa iyo, sa kapwa mo at sa mundo
Strike while you can and while there is an opportunity habang may lakas ka at may cacayahan ka, at habang may oportunidad, maliksi kang gumalaw sa pagsasagawa para matamo mo ang matagumapay na gantimpala - huwag mong sayangin ang oportunidad o palampasin

Time is valuable and precious, don't put it to waste ang oras ay mahalaga at kayamanan, gamitin mo ito sa pag-uunlad mo

TIME frame ang tinakdang panahon kung kailan at gaano katagal gaganapin ang isang pangyayari o pagsagawa; *schedule of date and length of an event or of a work development until its completion*

TIME gap pagitan; Iloc: nagbaetan ti dua a panawen

TIME is gold, Every moment counts bigyang halaga ang oras-*Sp* dahil masasayang ito kung hindi gamitin sa kapakanan mo at makakabunga ng kabutihan sa iyo at makakalutas at makakaahon sa iyo mula sa hirap

TIME limit *(Tag. & Iloc.)* taning, *deadline*

TIME out 1] humpay sa pagitan ng larong *sports,* 2] pangdiciplina sa batang anak nagkasala na patayohin o paupohin sa tabi o sulok ng ilan lamang na minuto; Iloc: 1] tiempo-*Sp* a nagbaetan ti ay-ayam nga *sports,* 2] pangdiciplina ti ubing nga anak a patacderen o patugawen iti igid wenno suli iti mano laeng a minuto

Timeline, Time line 1] *schedule* o iba't ibang fecha-*Sp* ng mga pangyayari, paligsahan, pagdiriwang at iba pa; 2] *time frame* kung kelan o gaano katagal gaganapin

Timely nasa oras; napapanahon na; Iloc: adda iti orasen, panawenen

Times, number of *(Tag. & Iloc.)* kadalasan o ilang beses-*Sp*
    Synonym
    Frequency kung gaano kadalas o ilang beses na nangyayari; Iloc: nu mano nga beses nga mapaspasamak

Timetable ang tinakdang panahon o plano na mangyayari o matatapos ito; ang tinakdang ilang beses at oras kung kailan dadating at aalis ang tren, eroplano, *bus* at iba pa

Timid tahimik, kimi, umid; Iloc: ulimek, naemma, mikki

Tin *(Tag. & Iloc.)* lata-*Sp*

Tinder anomang bagay na madaling magsiklab sa tilamsik ng apoy

Tinge malabo o bahagyang bakas o culay; may lasa o amoy pero halos hindi mawari dahil napakabahagya lamang

Tingle kinikilig, kumikilig; Iloc: agpipikel

Tinker *(Tag. & Iloc.)* cutingting

Tint 1] maputlang culay; 2] pangtina sa buhok

Tiny katiting; maliit, kaunti, munti, malinggit; Iloc: balabattit

TIP 1] dulo; 2] kaunting pabuya sa pagsilbi ng servidor-*aSp*; 3] *tip-off*: magbigay ng informasyon-*Sp* kung paano ang paggawa, o magbigay ng babala para maging maingat, o pagpapaalam sa otoridad-*Sp* tungkol sa lihim na masamang gawain; 4] itagilid; 5] tulis; Iloc: 1] murdong; 2] cuarta para ti servicio ti serbidor/ra; 3] mangipulong; 4] ipatingig; 5] tadem

TIP of the iceberg maliit na palatandaan ng mas malaki o mas complicadong caso-*Sp* o kalagayan o iba pa

Tipster taong nagbibigay ng *tip* kung ano ang nakakapagpanalo sa mga *betting* o *horse races*; o ng informasyon-*Sp* tungkol sa crimen o labag sa batas na gawain

Tipsy medio nakainom ng alak kaya hindi masigla ang paggalaw; Iloc: medio nakainom ti arak isu nga haan nga nasiglat gunay na

Tiptoe nakatiyad; Iloc: nakatil-ay

Tirade matagalan at panay-panay na pagbubulalas ng masakit, mapusok, marahas at malupit na pananalita

TIRE pagorin; Iloc: bannogen

TIRE, Car wheel gulong ng sasakyan, goma-*aSp*; Iloc: pilid ti lugan, goma

Tired pagod, hapo, lupaypay, nanlalambot; Iloc: nabannog

Tiredness kapaguran; Iloc: bannog

Tissue *(Tag. & Iloc.) tissue*

Tithe 10% sa sweldo-*Sp* na binibigay sa Panginoong Dios; Iloc: dies-*Sp* porciento-*Sp* ti sweldo nga ited kenni Apo Dios

Titillate *arouse* o pukawing kaaya-aya; hipoin o haplosin ng malumanay

Title *title*, titulo-*Sp*, pamagat; Iloc: *title*, titulo

Titular 1] tungkol sa titulo-*Sp* at mga uri ang mga ito; titulo o ranko-*Sp*; 2] nasa titulo lamang - sa pangalan lang, pero wala siya nuong katungkulang nauugnay sa titulo

TO sa, kay, upang; Iloc: diay, ti, iti, ken, tapno

TO and fro, Back and forth palayo at palapit, papunta't pabalik, paatras-paavante

TO boot maliban diyan, dagdag pa ito; Iloc: daytoy ket nayon na pay dayta

TO date hanggang sa ngayon sa kasalukuyang ito

TO-go pagkaing in*order* sa *restaurant* na imbes-*Sp* na kainin doon ay iyuuwi

TO him/her sa canya; Iloc: canyana

TO me sa akin; Iloc: canyac

TO no avail, Of no avail hindi man lang mangyari o magtagumpay; walang silbi, walang ventahe-*Sp*, hindi efectivo-*Sp*, hindi nakakabunga

TO one's heart's content hanggang sa sariling kagustohan/kalugoran

TO that para diyan; Iloc: para dita

TO the best of one's ability hangga't caya, magpupursigi ng husto; Iloc: inggana't caya ket agpamuspusan

TO the letter akma, tama at tugmang-tugma sa inutos o sa reglamento-*Sp*; exacto-*Sp* sa tinuro o pinagbilin; exacto sa kasulatan

TO the nth degree sa pinakamalaking bilang o cuenta-*Sp*

TO them sa canila; Iloc: canyada, cadacuada

TO these sa mga ito; Iloc: cadagitoy

TO those para doon; Iloc: cadagiti, cadagidiay, cadagita

TO you (singular) sa iyo; Iloc: kenka

TO you (plural) sa inyo; Iloc: cadacayo

Toast *(Tag. & Iloc.)* i-tosta-*Sp*

Toasted *(Tag. & Iloc.)* tostado-*Sp*

Tobacco *(Tag. & Iloc.)* tabaco-*Sp*

Today ngayon, ngayong araw na ito; Iloc: itatta, itatta nga aldaw

Toddler bata na nag-eedad ng isa hanggang tatlo; Iloc: ubing nga ag-edad-*Sp* ti maysa inggana tallo

TOE daliri ng paa, Iloc: ramay ti saka

TOE the line, Toe the mark kailangang sundin o tuparin ang inaasahan o tinakdang gagawin o asal

TOGETHER (2] magkasama; Iloc: agkuyog, agkadua

TOGETHER (3 or more) magkakasama, sama-sama; Iloc: agkukuyog, agkakadua

TOGETHER as lovers magkapiling; Iloc: agcadwa nga agayan-ayat

Toil cumacayod sa trabaho-*Sp*; Iloc: agpakat nga agtrabaho

Toilet *(Tag. & Iloc.)* cubeta-*Sp*, casilyas-*Sp*, *CR, comfort room, ladies'* o *men's room*

Toiletry anomang bagay o gamit sa pagpaligo, paglinis, pagpaayos at pagpaganda o pagpakisig gaya ng sabon, *deodorant, make-up*, at iba pa

Token tanda; Iloc; pakakitaan

Tolerable puedeng maipahintulot, mapagtitiisan, mapapagpacensiahan

Tolerance pagpahintulot, pagparaya; Iloc: baybay-an o palubosan latta iti aramiden na

Tolerant pumapayag na magpahintulot, magpaubaya at magparaya

Tolerate parayain, hayaan, paunlakan; Iloc: baybay-an ken haan biangan

Toll 1] bayad sa pagdaan sa tulay o pagtawag sa telefono-*Sp*, 2] kabigatan o parusa sa buhay; Iloc: 1] bayad ti pagserrek iti rangtay wenno pagiyusar ti telefono; 2] dagsen wenno dusa ti biag

Tomato kamatis; Iloc: tamatis

Tomb libingan, nicho-*Sp*; Iloc: panchon, nicho

Tomboy *(Tag. & Iloc.)* tomboy

Tombstone *(Tag. & Iloc.)* lapida-*Sp*

Tome librong malaki, mabigat at maraming naituturo; o kaya kaugnay o kasama ng ibang libro

Tomorrow bukas; Iloc: nu bigat

Ton *(Tag. & Iloc.)* 2,000 libra

TONE *(Tag. & Iloc.)* tono-*Sp*

TONE down hintoin ang pagkarahas o pagkalupit at magpakahinahon sa kainaman o katamtaman lamang

Tongs *(Tag. & Iloc.)* sipit

TONGUE *(Tag. & Iloc.)* dila

TONGUE sticked out with scorn nandidila, dilaan, Iloc: agdilat, dilatan, agguyab

TONGUE-lashing baticosin, pagalitan; Iloc: pagsawsaw-an

TONGUE-tied hindi makasalita dahil sa takot o pagkataranta; Iloc: haan a makasarita gapu ti buteng wenno pagkataranta

Tonight ngayong gabi; Iloc: nu rabii, itatta rabii

Tonsil *(Tag. & Iloc.)* tonsil

TOO, Also din, rin; Iloc: met

TOO much *(Tag. & Iloc.)* masyado-*aSp*, sobra-*Sp*
    Synonyms
    Much marami, masyado; Iloc: adu, masyado
    To a fault *(Tag. & Iloc.)* sobra, masyado

TOO close for comfort napakalapit na puedeng mapanganib o hindi comfortab-le

TOO good to be true sobrang-sobrang napakahusay at napakabuti na parang hindi kapani-paniwala at caraniwan ay hindi nga tutuo talaga

Tools *apparatus,* aparato-*Sp,* kagamitan, kasangkapan, instrumento-*Sp;* Iloc: *apparatus,* aparato, instrumento

TOOTH ngipin; Iloc: ngipen

TOOTH decay, Tooth cavity bukbok, uka; Iloc: bukbok, ribrib, rucapi

TOOTH, fang *(Tag. & Iloc.)* pangil

TOOTH filling *(Tag. & Iloc.)* pasta

TOOTH food deposit *(Tag. & Iloc.)* tinga

TOOTH, molar bagang; Iloc: sangi

TOOTH plaque tumigas na tinga; Iloc: dikki

TOOTH, sensitive nangingilo; Iloc: naalino

Toothbrush *(Tag. & Iloc.)* cepilyo-*Sp*

Toothless (1 or 2 or all teeth missing) bungi, bungal; Iloc: tuppol

Toothpaste *(Tag. & Iloc.) toothpaste*

Toothpick *(Tag. & Iloc.) toothpick,* palito

TOP, Peak taluktok, tuktok, tugatog; Iloc: tuktok

TOP (toy) *(Tag. & Iloc.)* trompo-*Sp*

Topic paksa, diwa, buod, punto ng salita; Iloc: amad, paksa, banag, punto ti pagsarsaritaan
   Correlated words
   Summary, Gist buod, Iloc: amad

Topmost nasa kataas-taasang lugar-*Sp,* pinakamataas; Iloc: kangatoan

Topnotch, Topflight primera-*Sp* clase-*Sp, first-rate, superior,* pinaka-mataas, pinakabantog, pinakatanyag na puede sa natamo o sa giting o sa kabutihan, excelente-*Sp*

Topple mabuwal at lumagpak; Iloc: agbalintuag

Topsy-turvy taob, napakagulo; Iloc: balinsuek, nakagul-gulo

Torch *(Tag. & Iloc.) torch,* tanglaw

Torment pahirapan, pagdusahin; Iloc: parigatan, i-castigaren (castigar-*Sp*)

Torpid hindi kumikilos o nagsasagawa o tamad, walang kalatoy-latoy, mahina, matamlay

Torrent *n.,* **Torrential** *adj.* ulan o agos ng ilog na napakabilis; Iloc: tudo wenno pagayos ti carayan nga napardas unay

Torrid sobrang init dahil nasa napakainit na lugar-*Sp* ng mundo-*Sp*; napakainit na clima-*Sp*

Torso pinakamalaking parte ng katawan na bumubuo ng balikat, dibdib, likod, chan, bewang at balakang maliban ang ulo, kamay at paa; Iloc: dakkel a parte ti bagi nga manglaon iti abaga, barukong, likod, chan, siket ken patong fuera-*Sp* ti ulo, ima ken saka

Torture *n.*, **Torturous** *adj.* pagpapahirap o pananakit ng labis-labis gaya ng pagparusa o paghihiganti dahil sa mabagsik na kalupitan, o para mahimok na umamin ng kasalanan, o makakuha ng informasyon-*Sp*; magbigay ng iba't ibang mahapding pananakit o pagdurusa sa katawan, sa isip at sa damdmin

Toss 1] ihagis, ibato, iicha; 2] paghalo-haloin ang *salad* gaya ng iba't ibang dahong-gulay, pasas-*Sp* at *nuts*; 3] pag-ugoy at pag-indayog ng bapor-*Sp* dahil sa malakas na hangin o daluyong; 4] hindi mapakali sa pagkabalisa o pag-alala ng problema-*Sp* kaya pabali-baligtad sa cama 5] biglang patagilid na pagtaas ng ulo na lumipad-ladlad ang buhok

Total amount suma-*Sp*, total-*Sp*, cuenta-*Sp*; Iloc: sumar-*Sp*, total, cuenta, bilang

Totalitarian goviernong dictador-*Sp* at may *control* at hindi nagpa-pahintulot ng mga partido-*Sp* dito na magkakaiba ang paniwala't paraan nila; taong dictador at gustong controlado-*Sp* niya ang iba

Tote buhatin, cargahin; Iloc: bagkatin, cargaen

Totter yumayanig at nanginginig ang galaw at lakad; Iloc: mapatigerger ti garaw ken agtiwed-tiwed ti pagna

TOUCH ramdamin, hipoin, dampihin; Iloc: carawaen, sagiden

TOUCH a sore spot, a sore point isang bagay na puedeng makakasakit o nakakaiyak o makakapagpaalaala ng maselan o mahirap na karanasan

TOUCH accidentally madaplis, masagì, masalat; Iloc: masagid, madalapus

TOUCH-and-go 1] peligro-*Sp* at walang kasiguradohan o katiyakan sa kalagayan at sa kahihinatnan; delicado-*Sp* at may panganib; 2] madaliang pagkilos

TOUCH base bihi-bihirang pangungumusta sa pagtawag o sa pag-sulat, magpanibagong makipagcomunicasyon na naman; Iloc: agbaro ti nakem wenno agil-iliw isu nga makipagcomunicasyon manen; sagpaminsan nga mang-comusta iti pag-awag wenno pagsurat

Touchdown paglapag ng eroplano-*Sp*; pagpuntos sa laro ng *sports*

TOUGH 1] matipuno, malakas ang damdamin at cayang tanggapin ang mabibigat na situasyon, 2] agresivong tao na gumagawa ng di tama; Iloc: 1] napuner, napigsa ti bagbagi na ken mabagkat na dagiti nadadagsen a situasyon, 2] agresivo a tao nga agar-aramid iti dakes

TOUGH it out palakasin at patatagin ang kalooban para mapagtiisan ang mga pagsubok

TOUGH love matinding pagmamahal at mahusay na pag-aalaga sa mga anak pero hindi pagbibigay ng layaw kundi pagtuturo ng tamang asal at diciplina para sa ikabubuti at pag-unlad nila sa buhay; Iloc: nadungngo a pagayat ken pagtaraken ti annak ngem haan mangited ti capricho nu di pagi-suro iti nasayaat nga ugali ken diciplina para ti pagsiyaatan ken pagprogreso da

TOUGH meat makunat; Iloc: naculbet
Antonym
Tender meat malambot na carne; Iloc: nalukneng nga carne

TOUGH-minded matibay at hindi madaling mainfluwencia dahil buma-batay siya sa prueba na kilos, gawa at kahihinatnan kaysa sa pag-papahayag/pagpasikat lamang

Tour *sightseeing* at pagliliwaliw na viahe-*Sp* sa iba't ibang lugar-*Sp* ng grupo-*Sp* na may nagpapatnubay na *tour guide*

Tourism *(Tag. & Iloc.)* turismo-*Sp*

Tourist *(Tag. & Iloc.)* turista-*Sp*

Tournament *(Tag. & Iloc.)* *tournament,* torneo-*Sp*

Tourniquet ang ginagamit na pagpatigil ng pagdudugo na mahigpit na ipulopot o mabigat na itapal sa sugat

Tow hilain ang sasakyan; Iloc: guyoden ti lugan

TOWARDS patungo; Iloc: agpaturong, agturong

TOWARDS (pointing) "Banda diyan;" Iloc: "Banda dita"

Towel *(Tag. & Iloc.)* tualya-*Sp*

Tower tore-*aSp*; Iloc: torre-*Sp*

TOWN bayan, municipalidad-*Sp*; Iloc: ili, municipalidad

TOWN hall *(Tag. & Iloc.)* municipio-*Sp*

TOWN proper *(Tag. & Iloc.)* *downtown,* centro-*Sp*

TOWN square *(Tag. & Iloc.)* plaza-*Sp*

TOWN total population bilang ng sambayanan; Iloc: bilang ti entero nga agkakailyan

Townmate(s) kababayan; Iloc: kailyan

Toxic *adj.,* **Toxicity** *n.* lason, nakakalason; Iloc: lason, makasabidong

Toy laroan; Iloc: ay-ayam, abalbalay

TRACE bakas na malabo; Iloc: marka a nacudrep

TRACE back bakasin, tuntonin; Iloc: tuntonen, sursoren

TRACK 1] riles ng tren-*Sp*; 2] bakas ng anomang dumaan gaya ng gulong ng sasakyan, sapatos-*Sp*, paa ng tao o hayop; 3] daanang nabuo dahil sa kalalakad ng mga hayop, *hunters* o magbubukid

TRACK down i-*pursue* o tugisan hanggang mahuli

TRACK, keep masinsinang subaybayan ang mga galaw o pangyayari at mga sumusunod na pangyayari

Tract ang kalawakan ng lupain o dagat o rehion-*Sp*

Trade 1] *buy-and-sell,* bilhin at ibenta, 2] ari-arian na ipagpalit sa ibang bagay; magpalitan; Iloc: 1] *buy-and-sell,* gatangen ken ilaco, 2] sanicua nga isukat iti sabali a banag, makisinnukat

Trademark tatak pangalakal; Iloc: marka-*Sp* ti companya

Tradition *n.,* **Traditional** *adj.* mga kagawian ng bayan o ng ninuno ng angkan na ine-entrega-*Sp* sa mga anak at mga apo para ipamana sa canila ang mga tradisyon-*Sp* ng lahi o ng familya-*Sp* kagaya ng pagmamano sa nakakatandang kamag-anak nila, mga paniwala, custombre-*Sp* gaya ng pagtawag ng "Tao po" pagkatapos kumatok sa pinto, at iba pang kaugalihan

Traffic *(Tag. & Iloc.) traffic*

Tragedy *n.,* **Tragic** *adj.* trahedya-*Sp*; nakakaawa, kahabaghabag; accidente, sakuna o kapahamakan; malaking kapinsalaan, kakila-kilabot, pagkasawi, pagkamatay

Trail daan sa ilang na pook; Iloc: dalan idiay kabakiran

TRAIN, Learn and get accustomed *train,* ensayo-*Sp,* magsanay, matuto para mabihasa

Correlated words

Get the hang of it, Familiarize oneself pag-aralan kung paano gagawin o gagamitin o paano gumaling ng husto

Practice *practice,* mag-ensayo, magsanay para mas lalong humusay

TRAIN (transportation) *train,* tren-*Sp*

TRAIN rail *(Tag. & Iloc.)* riles-*aSp* ng tren-*Sp*

Trainer tagasanay, *trainer*: Iloc: *trainer,* mangpa-ensayo

Trait *(Tag. & Iloc.)* pag-uugali, costumbre-*Sp*, katatao

Traitor traidor-*Sp*, taksil; Iloc: traidor

Trample 1] yurakan o tapakan ng mabigat at kadalasan ay nadudurog at nalulupig; tapak-tapakan, yapak-yapakan 2] magdomina na nanghihimasok ng malupit; Iloc: 1] payat-payatan, bade-baddeken; 2] agarari, ag-dominar-*Sp*

Tranquil *(Tag. & Iloc.)* calmado-*Sp*

Tranquilizer medicinang pangpacalmado o pangpatulog

Transact *v.,* **Transaction** *n.* makipagkasundoan sa ibang companya-*Sp* o sa ibang tao tungkol sa servicio-*Sp* o producto-*Sp* ng negosio-*Sp,* para sa pagpaunlad at patuloy pang pag-unlad

Transcend *v.,* **Transcendent** and **Transcendental** *adj.* 1] papunta lampas sa *limit* o hangganan; *surpassing* o lumalampas, *exceeding* o mas humihigit; *superior, supreme* o pinakamataas, pinakadakila; 2] lampas sa pag-unawa, sa labas ng ulirat o *consciousness*

Transcribe i-*type* o i-makinilya-*Sp* o isulat sa *computer* ang dinicta na sulat o *memo*; copiahin sa *copying machine* ang mga documento na kinakailangang macopia; isalin/i-*translate* sa ibang lengguahe-*Sp* o ibang alfabeto ang mga kasulatan

Transcript, Tanscription ito ang *printed copy*; ang exactong copia-*Sp* ng ofisyal-*Sp* na kasulatan; kasulatang sinalin sa ibang lengguahe-*Sp* o ibang alfabeto

Transfer ilipat; Iloc: iyacar, iyalis

Transfigure *v.,* **Transfiguration** *n.* palitan ang nakalitaw na forma-*Sp* o ichura-*Sp*

Transform *v.,* **Transformation** *n.* pagpapanibago; bagohin ang forma-*Sp,* anyo, pagkayari at pagkagawa; bagohin ang kalagayan, katangian at custombre-*Sp*; bagohin ang diwa, buod, laman at sangkap

TRANSFUSION, blood *blood transfusion,* salinan ng dugo ang paciente-*Sp* para makabawi ang nawalang dugo sa canyang katawan; Iloc: *blood transfusion,* mangiyacar ti dara idiay paciente tapno makaala manen ti dara a nagbulos a rimmuar caniana

TRANSFUSION tube tubong pagdaluyan ng medicina na likido-*Sp* o dugo na kinakailangan ng paciente-*Sp*; Iloc: tubo-*Sp* nga pagayusan ti agas a likido wenno dara nga masapul ti paciente

Transgress magkasala sa Dios dahil sa kasalanan niya sa kapwa-tao, sa batas at sa mismong sarili; Iloc: agbasol kenni Apo Dios gapu ti pagbasol na ti dadduma, iti linteg ken ti mismo a bagi

Transgression sala, kasalanan, masamang gawain; Iloc: basol, biddut, dakes nga aramid

Transient 1] tao o bagay na temporaryong trabahador-*Sp*, temporaryong nagcacasera ng bahay, panandaling visita-*Sp* lamang, at iba pa; 2] hindi permanente-*Sp*, hindi tumatagal, hindi nagluluwat, temporaryo-*Sp*, panandali o pansamantala lamang

Transit paglakbay buhat sa pinanggalingan papunta sa destinasyon-*Sp* sa pamamagitan ng pagsakay ng sasakyan

Transition pagdaan mula sa pinanggalingan papunta sa isang lugar o papunta sa isang kalagayan o sa isang yugto ng buhay

Translate magsalin/*translate* o ipaliwanag ang hindi naintindihang lengguahe-*Sp* sa lengguahe na naiintindihan ng kausap

Translation interpretasyon-*Sp*, pagsasalin sa ibang wika o lengguahe-*Sp*; Iloc: interpretasyon, pangpatarus iti sabali a lengguahe

Transmit *v.*, **Transmittance** *n.* magbalita sa anumang paraan gaya sa telefono-*Sp*, *email, text,* liham/sulat, o talumpati; Iloc: agpadamag ti aniaman a dalan casla diay telefono, *email, text,* surat o discurso-*Sp*

Transmute *v.*, **Transmutation** *n.* bagohin, palitan, pagbabago; Iloc: baliwan, sukatan, pangbalbaliw

Transnational 1] lampas sa dulo o hangganan ng isang bayan/*country*; 2] mga tao, companya-*Sp*, organizasyon-*Sp*, at iba pa na tumatayong representate-*Sp* ng cani-canilang bayan o lahi

Transparency *The quality of being seen through like a glass; do things in an open way without secrets;* Bukas na libro ang canyang buhay at sa pagpapahayag niya ng canyang ginagawa, lantad ang katatao niya kaya mapagkatiwalaan siya

Transparent naaaninag; Iloc: maanninag

Transplant 1] tanggalin ang halaman sa isang lugar-*Sp* at itanim sa ibang lugar; 2] Medicina: ilipat ang isang laman *(organ, tissue, etc.)*

buhat sa isang parte-*Sp* ng katawan at ilagay sa ibang parte nito, o kaya maglagay nito na galing sa ibang tao at ilagay sa paciente na nangangailangan nito

Transport isakay, ilulan, buhatin, o hakotin para dalhin sa destinasyon-*Sp* nito; Iloc: isakay o ilugan para ipan idiay destinasyon na

Transportation transportasyon-*Sp*, sakayan; Iloc: lugan, transportasyon

Transpose bagohin o ibahin ang pagkasunod-sunod na ayos o pagkaareglo o pagkapila o hilera-*Sp/row*

Trap silohin, bitagin; Iloc: silwen, tiliwen

Trappings mga decorasyon-*Sp*, magagandang gayak

Trash *(Tag. & Iloc.)* basura-*Sp*

Trauma *trauma*, 1] efecto-*Sp* ng accidente-*Sp* sa katawan; 2] nabuong damdamin at asal at paningin sa buhay-buhay dahil sa marahas o masakit na dinanas noong batabata siya o dahil sa madalas na kalupitan na dinanas sa buhay niya

Travail mahirap, mabigat at masakit na pasanin; sakit o pagdurusa ng katawan at isip; matinding pagsisikap sa trabaho-*Sp*; ang sakit sa panganganak o pagluwal ng sanggol

Travel mag-viahe-*Sp*, maglakbay magliwaliw; Iloc: agviahe, aglibot

Traverse ang paglibot ng saan mang lugar at papunta't pabalik, pataas at pababa, pa-*zigzag* at patabi at patawid; Iloc: ti paglibot inchenna man a lugar a mapan ken agsubli, pangato ken pababa, pa-*zigzag* ken paigid ken pag-ballasiw

Travesty imitasyon-*Sp* na sobra-*Sp* at nakakasindak; Iloc: imitasyon nga sobra ken nakaam-amak

Tray *(Tag. & Iloc.)* *tray*, **Tray-like bowl** *(Tag. & Iloc.)* bandehado-*Sp*

Treacherous *adj.*, **Treachery** *n.* katraydoran, pagtataksil

Tread on maglakad, tapak-tapakan, yapak-yapakan; Iloc: magna, payat-payatan, bade-baddeken

Treason pagiging traidor-*Sp* sa sariling bansa; Iloc: pag-traidor ti mismo-*Sp* nga bayan na

Treasure estimahin, bigyang halaga, tinatangi, minumutia; Iloc: estimaren, valoran, ikkan ti valor-*Sp*, ilala

Treasurer *(Tag. & Iloc.)* tesorero-*Sp*

TREAT tratohin; Iloc: tratwen, agtrato, mang-trato-*Sp*

TREAT-giver (pays for the meal or for the fun time) *(Tag. & Iloc.)* taya
Correlated words
    Share one's winnings magbalato; Iloc: agbalato
TREATMENT pagtrato sa kapwa; Iloc: pagtrato iti tao
TREATMENT, medical paggagamot sa maysakit; Iloc: pag-agas ti agsakit
Treaty kasunduan ng mga bansa; Iloc: pagtulagan iti nasyon ida
TREE puno, punong-kahoy; Iloc: kayo
TREE, cut down magtroso; Iloc: pukanen ti kayo
TREE, swaying *(Tag. & Iloc.)* naglalawiswis
TREE trunk puno; Iloc: poon
Trek paglalakbay sa pamamagitan ng paglakad; Iloc: magmagna laeng iti pagviahe na
TREMBLE due to fear nanginginig o nangangatog sa takot; Iloc: agtigerger, agtagirgir iti buteng
TREMBLE due to excitement kinikilig; Iloc: makilkilig
Tremendous sobrang pagkalaki, pagkadami o pagkatindi
Tremor yumayanig, yumuyogyog; Iloc: agginggined, ag-yugyugyog
Trench hinukay sa lupa para pagkublihan para ligtas sa kalaban at sa atake-*Sp* nila
Trend kasalukuyang uso-*Sp*; Iloc: madama nga uso
Trepid *adj.*, **Trepidation** *n.* nanginginig sa takot; Iloc: ag-tigtigerger iti buteng
Trespass 1] pumasok o dumaan na walang pahintulot, 2] magkasala sa kapwa; Iloc: 1] sumrek o lumabas nga awan ti palubos canyana, 2] agbasol iti tao o tattao
TRIAL *hearing* sa corte-*Sp* ng husticia-*Sp*; Iloc: *hearing* diay corte ti husticia
TRIAL and error panay ang pagsubok para magtagumpay at matamo ang layonin, hanggang malaman ang secreto ng pagtagumpay
Trials mga mahirap na pagsubok sa buhay; Iloc: parikut o rigrigat nga baklayen nga mangpurbar iti anos ti tao
Triangle *(Tag. & Iloc.)* *triangle*
Tribe *(Tag. & Iloc.)* *tribe*, tribo-*Sp*
Tribunal *(Tag. & Iloc.)* corte ng husticia-*Sp*

Tribute magbigay papupuri, paghanga, pagbubunyi o pagkilala ng tulong o kabutihan; patunay o pagpapakita ng parangal at pagpasalamat ng utang na loob; Iloc: isaad ti pammadayaw, pagyaman
Correlated word
Homage espesyal na parangal sa karapat-dapat na tao sa harap ng madla o publico

Trick katuwaang pagdadaya; Iloc: pagkakatawaan a pag-cuscusit

Trickle 1] tumutulo o pumapatak ng mabagal at konti-konti lamang; 2] dumadating o umaalis o dumadaan ng <u>unti-unti</u> gaya ng mga visita na nag-ti-*trickle* na pauwi

Tricks of the trade mga paraan, kaalaman at kacayahan na kinakailangan para maisagawa ang producto o ang pagpalakad ng negocio-*Sp*

Tricky 1] palihim na nandadaya na puedeng masamang panlinlang o katuwaang *prank* lamang, 2] kailangang pag-ingatang gawin ito dahil may pagkadelicado o kahirapan para maisagawa

TRIED sinubokan, nasubokan; Iloc: pinurbaran, pinadas

TRIED-and-true nasuri at nasubokan na at napatunayang karapat-dapat, maasahan, mapagkakatiwalaan, mahalaga at tutoong maisasagawa

Trigger 1] maliit na nakalabas na parte ng baril na kapag diinan ito, magbuga ng bala, 2] kilos o pangyayari na makapag-udyok ng kilos

Trifle, Trifling 1] pangkatuwaan lamang, hindi gaanong may kabulohan, mababaw; 2] kaunti lang o iilan-ilan lang, 3] halos wala o talagang walang kahalagaan o walang pakinabangan kaya nasasayang lamang ang oras at sikap dito; Iloc: 1] para pagkakatawaan laeng; 2] bassit o manmano laeng; 3] bassit o awan servi na isu a sayang laeng ti pakat ken oras ditoy

Trillion *(Tag. & Iloc.) trillion*

Trimming burloloy; Iloc: arcos

Trinity *Holy Trinity* o Santisima Trinidad-*Sp* o *Blessed Trinity* dahil ito ang <u>isang</u> Dios sa tatlong banal na persona: Dios Ama, Dios Anak na si Hesu Cristo at Dios Espiritu Santo

TRIP matapilok, madapa, natalisud; Iloc: maytublak

TRIP, Journey mag-viahe-*Sp*, maglakbay magliwaliw; Iloc: agviahe, aglibot

TRIP on something natisud, natalisud; Iloc: nasikkarud

Tripe *(Tag. & Iloc.)* goto

Triple *(Tag. & Iloc.)* tatlo, trip-le-*Sp*

Trite nakakawala ng interes dahil sa madalas na paggamit o paulit-ulit na naririnig o napapanood o nararanasan

Triumph *v.*, **Triumphant** *adj.* tagumpay, pagwawagi, pagpanalo; Iloc: balligi, pangabak

Trivia *(Tag. & Iloc.)* bagay-bagay o detalye na hindi importante

Trivial ordinaryo, caraniwan at wala masyadong halaga

Troll, Trolling 1] pagcanta o pagsasalita na parang umiikot na voces-*Sp*; 2] *Fishing*: pangingisda na gamit ang bingwit at iba pa; 3] *Digital technology*: magpatalastas o magsulat gaya sa *internet* ng mga comentario na hindi tama o hindi angkop para lamang makapanakit at makapagbunsod o makapaghimok ng tugon o sagot

Trombone *(Tag. & Iloc.)* *trombone*

Troops hukbo, mga sundalo, tropa-*Sp*, pangkat; Iloc: tropa, dagiti buyot, dagiti soldado-*Sp*

Tropic, Tropics, Tropical ang mga bayan na sinisinagan ng araw na derechohan sa taas nila gaya ng mga bayan sa Southeast Asia at India; sa Central at South America at Mexico; sa Caribbean; at sa Central, East at West Africa

Trouble kapahamakan, gulo, gusot, basag-ulo, away, alitan; Iloc: riri, gulo, ringgor, ribok

Troubled nababagabag, naliligalig, balisa, torete; Iloc: marirriro, maringgoran, matorete

Troublesome nanggugulo, nangpapahamak, basag-ulero; Iloc: mangrirriri, mangribribok, mangringringgor, mannakilaban, manggulgulo, mangipaspasubo

Trounce golpehin, bugbogin o hampasin; parusahan o talonin

Trouser *(Tag. & Iloc.)* pantalon-*Sp*

Trove pinag-ipon-ipon o *collection* na mga bagay

Truant *adj.*, **Truancy** *n. absent* o hindi pumasok sa escuela na walang pasabi sa escuela at walang malay ang magulang

Truce pinagkasunduang pansamantalang paghinto ng labanan o giyera; Iloc: pinagtulagan a temporaryo-*Sp* nga pagsardeng ti laban o gerra-*Sp*

Truck *(Tag. & Iloc.)* *truck*

Trudge pagod na pagod at hirap na hirap na lumalakad; may kahabahan na lakad

TRUE, Truly totoo, tunay; Iloc: usto, agpaypayso, pudno

TRUE colors ang tunay na pagkatao

TRUE to form, What else is new parating nangyayari, o patuloy at parating nag-aasal o ginagawa ang kagawian ng isang tao, exacto sa inaasahan kaya hindi na nagtataka ang mga tao

TRUE to one's word tinutupad ang canyang promesa

Trumpet *(Tag. & Iloc.)* trompeta-*Sp*, torotot

Truncate paigsihin, paiklihin o bawasan kaya putolan ang parte-*Sp* nito

Trunk puno ng kahoy, lacasa; paglagyan ng bagahe sa likod ng coche-*Sp*; Iloc: lacasa, baol-*Sp*; pagikabilan ti bagahe iti likod ti coche

Trust tiwala, panalig; Iloc: talek, fiar-*Sp*

Quotation on Trust

Being trusted is not developed overnight trust is built and established, then maintained every day. Ang tiwala ay hindi nalilikha sa isang gawa o sa isang araw lamang, ang tiwala ay nililikha at tinatatag araw-araw

Trustee 1] tao o grupo-*Sp* na hinirang o inatasan na mangasiwa ng mga tungkulin at gawain ng companya-*Sp*, institusyon-*Sp* at iba pa; 2] tao na humahawak ng titulo-*Sp* ng ari-arian para sa pakinabang ng iba

Trustworthiness *n.,* **Trustworthy** *adj.* mapagkatiwalaan, mapanaligan, tapat; Iloc: mapagtalkan, mapagfiaran, pudno (fiar-*Sp*)

Quotation and correlated words

Trustworthiness is established for many, many years, but it takes only one time and only an instance to damage it. Ang pagiging mapagkakatiwalaan ay nililikha at patuloy na pinapausbong ng napakamaraming taon, pero sa isang gawa lamang at sa isang iglap lamang, ito ay masisira

Transparency bukas na libro ang canyang buhay at maliwanag at lantad ang canyang gawain, buhay at katatao niya kaya napagkatiwalaan ang pagkatapat niya

Honest mapagkatiwalaan at mapanaligan sa pera at iba pa; Iloc: mapagtalkan ken mapagfiaran iti cuarta ken sabali pay

Credibility may katangian, pagkatao at gawain na mapapaniwalaan at mapagkatiwalaan siya, rico man siya o pobre

Reliable mapagkakatiwalaang tutupdin ang canyang obligasyon at trabaho at pangako na maaasahan at mapapanaligan siya; Iloc: mapag- talkan nga tungpalen na ti obligasyon ken trabaho ken ti incari na a manamnama ken mapagfiaran

Responsible responsab-le, marunong tumupad at managot sa canyang mga obligasyon; Iloc: responsab-le, makaammo ken agtungpal cadagiti obligasyon na

Truth kawastohan, katotohanan, katunayan; Iloc: usto ken agpayso, kaagpaysuan, kapudnoan

Truthful nagpapahayag ng wasto, tutoo at husto; Iloc: mangisawsawang iti agpayso, pudno ken usto
Correlated word
Literal tama at tugma sa kahulogan at wala man lang dagdag o panghimok

Try subokan, purbahan, tangkahin; Iloc: padasen, purbaran, ipabpabareng (purba/purbar-*Sp*)
Synonym
Attempt tangkahin; Iloc: padasen

Tryst tipanan, magtagpo at magtipan ang magkasintahan; Iloc: pag-sinnarakan, agsarak ken agkita ti agayan-ayat
Synonym
Rendezvous tipanan; Iloc: pagsinnarakan

T-SHIRT camiseta-*Sp*

T-SHIRT underwear buttoned front neck worn under a barong tagalog *(Tag. & Iloc.)* camisa de chino-*Sp*

Tub *bathtub* o paligoan sa modernong *bathroom*

Tube *(Tag. & Iloc.)* tubo-*Sp*
Correlated word
Conduit tubo na pagdaanan ng tubig o electricidad o iba pa; Iloc: tubo nga pagdalanan ti danum wenno electricidad wenno sabali pay

Tuberculosis *(Tag. & Iloc.)* *tuberculosis, TB*

Tuck 1] isingit sa maliit at lihim na lalagyan gaya ng pera sa *wallet*; 2] takpan na matiwasay at maginhawa gaya ng kumotan ang bata sa cama-*Sp*; 3] isuksok (ang blusa-*Sp* o camisadentro-*Sp*) paloob ng pantalon; 4] gumawa ng pleges-*Sp*

Tuesday *(Tag. & Iloc.)* *Tuesday,* Martes-*Sp*

Tug haltakin, hatakin, hilain, batakin; Iloc: guyoden

Tugboat banca-*Sp* na panghila ng ibang banca na tumirik; Iloc: banca a pangguyod ti sabali a banca nga nadadael

Tuition *(Tag. & Iloc.)* *tuition,* matricula-*Sp*

Tumble down matomba, madapa; Iloc: matomba, matuang

Tummy puson, bilbil; Iloc: buksit, pus-ong

Tumor *(Tag. & Iloc.) tumor*

Tumult ingay at gulo ng nagsama-samang mga tao; Iloc: ariwawa ken gulo ti nag-uummong nga tattao

TUNE tono-*Sp*, himig; Iloc: tono

TUNE out hindi dinggin at di pansinin kundi ituon lang ang pansin sa ibang bagay

TUNE, out of *(Tag. & Iloc.)* desintonado-*Sp*

Turbulent marahas at mapusok; ligalig, balisa at magulo

Turf 1] lupaing madamo at mahalaman; 2] *peat* o tuyong halaman na pang-abono-*Sp* o panggatong; 3] pook kung saan ang *gang* o pangkat ng mga batang mala-*criminal;* 4] kung saan nagaganap ang *horse racing*

Turkey *(Tag. & Iloc.)* pavo-*Sp*

TURN maglico; Iloc: aglico

TURN a deaf ear kusang suwayin at hindi pakinggan

TURN around umikot ng buong ikot o bilog; Iloc: aglikaw ti entero a likaw-timbukel

TURN-by-turn torno-torno, naghahalihalili, halinhinan; Iloc: torno-torno, agsisinnublat

TURN down tanggihan, ayawan; Iloc: haan akceptaren

TURN of the century ang katapusan ng isang siglo-*Sp* at ang umpisa-*aSp* ng kasunod na siglo

TURN-off 1] serhan; 2] mandiri o anomang makapawalan ng *interest* sa bagay na iyon; Iloc: 1] i-cerra-*Sp*, 2] maaryek wenno ania man a maka-awanan iti *interest*

TURN-on 1] paandarin; 2] buhayin ang *interest* o ang makamundong pagnanasa; Iloc: 2] paandaren; 2] biagen iti *interest* o iti makamundo nga pagpap-papaos

TURN one's back magtalikod, talikuran; Iloc: agtallikod, tallikudan

TURN-out 1] dami ng taong dumating, 2] dami ng lumabas na producto-*Sp*; Iloc: 1] mano a tao ti nagatender, 2] mano ti nagbalinan a bunga wenno producto

TURN to the right/to the left maglico sa canan/sa caliwa; Iloc: aglico ti cannawan/ti cannigid

Turncoat taong nagpalit ng lapi, umanib sa karival; Iloc: tao nga agbaliw ti katimpuyog na, kimmadwa ti ka-*rival*

Turnip *(Tag. & Iloc.)* singkamas

Turnover 1] pagtiwarik, pagtaob, pagtumbalik; 2] pagpalit kapag may umalis - sila ang maghahalili (gaya ng nag-uupa ng bahay, empleyado-*Sp* o trabahadores-*Sp*); 3] kung magkano ang kinita ng negocio-*Sp* sa tinakdang panahon; kung ilang producto-*Sp* ang naventa at iba pa

Turtle pagong; Iloc: pag-ong

Turtleneck cuelyo na mala-tubo na panakip ng leeg

Tush *(slang)* puit; Iloc: ubet

Tutelage pagiging *guardian* o privadong guro/*tutor*; aralin, instruksion at pagpapatnubay ng *tutor,* o pagiging tagapag-aral sa pagtuturo at patnubay ng *tutor*

Tutor *(Tag. & Iloc.)* privadong guro

Tutorial mga instruksion-*Sp* para makapag-aral ang gustong matuto

Twang magsalitang kakaiba sa tunog o sa pagbigkas

TWEAK 1] curot, pingot, 2] ayosin ang tunog, 3] tuksohin; Iloc: 1] lapigos, piddil, cuddot, 2] ayosen ti tono, 3] sutilen

TWEAK ear of a naughty child pingotin ang tenga; Iloc. lapigosen ti lapayag

Tweet ito ay *digital technology* buhat sa *Twitter website* na sinulat na mensahe-*Sp* na naglalaon ng *text, keywords,* mga *users* o gumagamit nito, *links,* at *video* sa *website*

Tweezers *(Tag. & Iloc.)* chani

TWELVE *twelve,* labing dalawa; Iloc: sangapulo ket dua, *twelve*

TWELVE o'clock *twelve o'clock,* alas dose

Twenty *twenty,* beinte-*Sp,* dalawampu; Iloc: *twenty,* beinte, duapulo

Twenty one, 22, 23, 24, etc. *(English numbers are commonly used by Filipinos)*

Twerk magsayaw na nakatingkayad at kinekendeng-kendeng ang puit na nakalabas habang bucaca ang mga paa; Iloc: agsala a nakaduriri ken ikendeng-kendeng na ti ubet na nga nakaruar mientras nga naka-bucangcang dagiti saka na

Twice dalawang beses-*Sp;* Iloc: dua beses

Twitch biglang kibot o kislot ng katawan

Twiddle ilaro-laro ang mga daliri

Twig maliit na sanga ng punong-kahoy; Iloc: bassit a sanga ti kayo

Twilight kaunting sinag bago lumabas ang araw o palubog ang araw; oras sa umaga pero caraniwan sa maggagabi na kung kelan may kaunti pang sinag

Twinge biglang matinding kirot sa katawan; kirot sa isip at damdamin

Twinkle kumislap-kislap; Iloc: agsilap-silap, agkirap-kirap

Twins cambal; Iloc: singin

Twirl umiikot; Iloc: agpusipos, agtayyek

TWIST ikotin, ipaliko-liko, pilipitin; Iloc: ipilipit, ilico-lico, tiritiren

TWIST someone's arm fuersahin o bantahan o takotin para mapilitang sumunod; Iloc: fuersaen (fuersa-*Sp*) wenno butngen gapu ti carit iti peggad tapno mapilitan nga agtungpal ken sumurot iti bilin

Twisted pilipit; Iloc: tiritit

TWO *(Tag. & Iloc.)* *two*, dalawa, dos-*Sp*; Iloc: *two*, dua, dos

TWO hundred *two hundred*, dalawang daan; Iloc: *two hundred*, dua gasut

TWO o'clock *two o'clock*, alas dos-*Sp*

TWO thousand *two thousand*, dalawang libo; Iloc: *two thousand*, dua a ribo

TWO-time someone hindi *faithful* o matapat, nakikipagtalik sa iba kahit may asawa na o kasintahan; nagtatraydor sa tao

TYPE *n.* tipo-*Sp*, uri, clase-*Sp*; Iloc: tipo, clase

TYPE *v.* magmakinilya sa *typewriter* o sa *keyboard* ng *computer*

Typhoid *(Tag. & Iloc.)* tipus

Typhoon *(Tag. & Iloc.)* bagyo

Typify gawing maglarawan o magrepresentante ng bagay o tao o tipo o *symbol*

Typical kalikasang kaugalian ng tao o ng mga mamayan sa isang bayan; Iloc: naturalesa-*Sp* nga custombre ti tao o dagiti tattao iti maysa a bayan

Tyranny ang govierno-*Sp* kung saan ang nagpapalakad ay isa lang na pangulo at lahat-lahat ng kapangyarihan ay nasa canyang hawak

Tyrant ang isang pinuno na nagpapalakad at namamahala ng lahat-lahat at walang limitasyon-*Sp* at walang bawal sa canyang magagawa

U

Ubiquitous *omnipresent,* kakayahang nandodoon sa lahat ng parte ng mundo sa parehong tiempo

Ugh! *(Tag. & Iloc.)* Ay naku!, Ay-yay-yay!

Ugly pangit; Iloc: nalaad, naalas nga langa

Ukelele gitara na pinatanyag ng Hawaii; Iloc: gitarra-*Sp* nga pinapopular ti Hawaii

Ulcer *ulcer* na napabayaang galis na grumabeng masyado na puedeng nasa bituka o sa balat ng katawan

Ulterior motive balak na lihim at masama; Iloc: rangta a limed ken dakes

Ultimate sa kahulihulian, sa huling kahihinatnan; Iloc: iti kaudianan, iti naudi a pagbanagan

Ultimatum *ultimatum,* pinakahuli na babala; Iloc: *ultimatum,* kauddian o *final* a pangpaalwad

Umbrella *(Tag. & Iloc.)* payong

Umpire tagahatol sa pangcompetensiang laro; Iloc: tagahusgar iti pangcompetensia nga ay-ayam

Unable hindi niya macaya, hindi niya magawa; Iloc: haan na macaya, haan na maaramid

Unaccustomed nababaguhan dahil hindi niya kagawian; Iloc: maycawa gapu ta haan na nakayruaman

Unanimous pagkakaisa nila sa kanilang balak at isip; Iloc: agkaykaysa da iti pakay ken panunot

Unassailable imposibleng pabulaanan o contrahan, hindi matanggihan dahil walang dudang ito ay napakahusay

Unattached hindi casal at hindi seriosong ka-relasyon; hindi nakacontrata o hindi nag-aasahan sa isa't isa

Unavoidable hindi maiwasan; Iloc: haan a malisyan

Unaware walang kamalay-malay, walang kamuang-muang; Iloc: haan na pulos ammo

Unawares sorpresa, hindi inaasahan; Iloc: sorpresa, haan a naseggaan

Unbearable hindi matitiis; Iloc: di maibturan/maanosan

Unbecoming hindi angkop, di bagay; Iloc: haan a rumbeng, haan a bagay

Unbelievable hindi kapanipaniwala; Iloc: di mapatpati

Unbeknownst walang kamuang-muang; hindi niya alam; hindi niya inaasahan; walang kamalay-malay; Iloc: awan pulos ammo; haan na naseggaan; haan na ninamnama; awan kapuot-puot na

Unbutton tanggalin sa butones, hindi nakabutones; Iloc: ikkaten diay butones, haan a nakabutones

Uncalled for walang kadahi-dahilan o walang karason-rason-*Sp* na isagawa; Iloc: awan ti gapu wenno awan karason-rason-*Sp* nga aramiden
Synonym
    Unwarranted wala man lang rason na isagawa; Iloc: awan man laeng ti rason nga maaramid

Uncertain hindi sigurado; walang katiyakan; Iloc: haan a sigurado; awan ti kaseguradwan

Unchanging walang pagmamaliw; Iloc: awan pagbalbaliw

Uncircumcised hindi natuli; Iloc: supot, haan a nacugit

Uncle tito-*Sp*, tiyo-*Sp*; Iloc: tiyo, tito, uliteg, tata

Unclear malabo, hindi claro-*Sp*; Iloc: haan a nalawag, haan a claro, nacusnaw, nacudrep

Uncomfortable naninibago, hindi comfortab-le-*Sp*, hindi bihasa; Iloc: maykawa, maamak, haan a comfortab-le

Uncommon hindi caraniwan, hindi ordinaryo-*Sp*; Iloc: haan a cadawyan, haan nga ordinaryo
Synonym
    Unusual hindi caraniwan, pambihira Iloc: haan nga cadawyan, haan a sigud

Uncommunicative hindi palasalita o palasulat o hindi mapagbunyag ng informasyon

Unconcerned walang pakialam; Iloc: awan ti pakibiang na

Unconditional pahintulotan o umayon na walang condisyon-*Sp* na pina-tong, hindi nakatali sa obligasyon-*Sp* o reglamento-*Sp*; Iloc: awan con-disyon nga impatong da, haan a naygalot ti obligasyon o reglamento

Unconscious nawalan ng malay; Iloc: naawanan ti poot

Uncontrollable hindi cayang icontrolado, hindi mapigil o maawat o masaway o makatimpi

Uncover alisin ang takip at buksan; Iloc: ikkaten ti calub ken luktan

UNDER, Underneath sa ilalim, sa silong; Iloc: diay sirok, diay baba

UNDER-the-table *illegal* o labag sa batas kaya palihim nilang ginagawa gaya ng suhol o *bribe*; Iloc: *illegal* o haan a sumursurot ti linteg isu nga haan a nalinteg ken palimed daytoy nga obra-*Sp* casla ti pasuksok o *bribe*

UNDER the weather may sakit; Iloc: agsakit

UNDER wraps itago o ilihim muna hanggang kailangan o hanggang napapanahon nang ilabas o ibunyag

Underarm *(Tag. & Iloc.)* kili-kili

Underbite ang ngipin sa baba ay nakausli at hindi kasing-pantay sa ngipin sa taas

Undercover espia-*Sp*, gumaganap ng palihim; Iloc: espia, agob-obra-*Sp* a palimed

Underdog ang pinakamahinang kalaban sa larangan ng *sports* o politica-*Sp*; Iloc: ti pinakanacapoy nga kalaban iti larangan ti *sports* wenno politica

Underdone hindi pa sapat ang pagkaluto

Underestimate tinuturing na kulang ang cacayahan o mababa ang pagtingin sa canya; Iloc: bigbigen da nga haan na a cabaelan wenno nababa ti panagbigbig da canyana

Undergo *v.* dumadanas, nararanasan, nalalasap; Iloc: malaslasatan, mapaspasaran (pasar-*Sp*), naex-expiryensa-*Sp*

Undergraduate taong nagcolehio pero hindi nakatapos ng *4-years Bachelors Degree*; Iloc: tao nga nagcolehio ngem haan nakaturpos ti *Bachelors Degree*

Underground 1] sa ilalim ng lupa; nasa loob ng lupa, 2] dahil organisasyong secreto-*Sp* ang layonin nito sa iba, ito ay *illegal* o masama; Iloc: 1] diay uneg iti daga, adda iti uneg ti daga, 2] gapu nga organisayon a secreto ti rangta ngem ti dadduma, daytoy ket *illegal* wenno makaperdi ken makapatay

Underhanded *illegal* o labag sa batas kaya palihim nila na ginagawa; Iloc: *illegal* o haan a sumursurot ti linteg isu nga palimed da nga ar-aramiden

Underline lagyan ng guhit sa baba ng *sentence*/pangungusap o ng salita; Iloc: ikkan ti linya ti baba ti *sentence* o ti sarita

Undermine ituring na hindi mahalaga o walang kabulohan, mamatahin; Iloc: bigbigen a haan a navalor o awan cuenta na

Underneath sa baba, sa ilalim, sa silong; Iloc: diay baba, diay sirok

Undernourish payat at mukhang lampay dahil sa kakulangan ng pagkain; Iloc: nakuttong ken nacapsut gapu iti kakurangan ti kanen

Understand maunawaan, maintindihan, matalos; Iloc: maawatan, maka-awat, matarosan

Correlated words

Fathom maintindihan ng husto

Figure it out tugmaan; Iloc: tukmaan

Understandable madaling maintindihan at maunawaan; Iloc: nalaca a maawatan

UNDERSTANDING *n.* pag-intindi, pag-unawa, pagtanto; Iloc: pagawat

UNDERSTANDING *adj.* nakakaintindi at nakakaunawa ng kalaga-yan ng kapwa at tumutugon para sa kabutihan at consuelo nito; Iloc: nalawa ti pagawat na; makaaw-awat cadagiti kasasaad ken mangisaad ti consuelo ken pagimbagan

Synonyms

Clear-sighted napakagaling ang paningin at pangturing sa mga pang-yayari; Iloc: nakasirsirib a pagkita ken pangbigbig ken pag-awat cadagiti mapaspasamak

Sensitive, Perceptive, Insightful intelihensia na pandama sa kapwa at tumutugon ng tamang *reaction* sa ikabubuti ng situasyon at payapang pagsasamahan; Iloc: intelihensia nga panricna iti tao ken mangsubsubalit iti usto nga *reaction* para ti pagimbagan ti situasyon ken natalna a pakikicadwa

Considerate nakakaunawa sa kalagayan ng iba at sinisigurado niyang hindi siya makakabigat o makahadlang sa kanila Iloc: makaawat ti kasasaad ti tao ken isigurado na nga haan a makapadagsen o makapalapped canyada

Has empathy makilala at maintindihan ang katayuan o damdamin o layonin ng kasama; Iloc: mabigbig ken maawatan na ti kasasaad o ti ricna o rangta iti cadwa

Kenned or Kent, Having a Ken pag-unawa sa situasyon at sa kapwa at tumutugon ngmabuti; Iloc: pagawat iti situasyon ken tao ket mangisaad isu ti nasayaat

Undertake gagawin, isagawa; Iloc: aramiden, agobra-*Sp*, mangaramid

Undertow alon sa dagat na humihila ng tao papunta sa malalim; Iloc: dalluyong ti taaw nga mangguyod iti tao paturong idiay adalem

Undervalue hindi binibigyan ng valor; Iloc: haan a ipatpateg o ivalvalor

Underway nag-umpisa na at patuloy pa sa pag-aasicaso hanggang sa maisagawa; Iloc: agrug-rugin ken itultuloy nga as-asecasoen inggana't maypalpas

UNDERWEAR, female's panty salawal, *panty*; Iloc: calson-*Sp*, sapin, *panty*

UNDERWEAR, man's brief *(Tag. & Iloc.)* carsonsilyo-*Sp*

UNDERWEAR, man's sleeveless shirt *(Tag. & Iloc.)* sando, camiseta-*Sp*

UNDERWEAR woman's sleeveless chemise *(Tag. & Iloc.)* camison-*Sp*

Underwrite balikatin ang responsilidad na *financial* para sa naka-*insure* at maggarantiya laban sa sunog, accidente at iba pang kapahamakan

Undetected *(Tag. & Iloc.)* disimulado-*aSp*

Undoing, Doing dahilan ng gawaing nakakapanira o nakakapahamak; Iloc: poon ti obra-*Sp* nga maka-perdi-*aSp* o makapeggad

Undress maghubad, hubaran; Iloc: aglabus, labusan, agussob

Undue 1] masyadong sobra sa dapat, 2] hindi tama at di makabatas; Iloc: 1] masyado a sobra ngem iti kasapulan, 2] haan nga nasayaat ken contra iti linteg

Unearth hucayin, dungcalin; Iloc: calyen, cutcoten

Uneasy hindi mapakali, hindi mapalagay; Iloc: maycawa, haan nga makatalna, maam-amak

Uneven hindi patag, tabingi, hindi pantay; Iloc: bangking, haan a patag
Synonym
Lopsided tabingi; Iloc: bangking
Antonym
Flat, Level patag, pantay; Iloc: patag, patad

UNEXPECTED hindi inaasahan; Iloc: haan nga ex-expectaren
Antonym
Expect mag-abang, asahan; Iloc: expectaren, namnamaen, agab-abang, ur-urayen

UNEXPECTED correct guess, Unexpected winning *(Tag. & Iloc.)* naka-chamba, chamba

Unfair 1] hindi makatarungan at di sumusunod sa batas at mali ang pagkilatis 2] hindi pantay-pantay ang pagturing dahil may pina-panigan; Iloc: 1] haan nga sumursurot ti linteg ken agbiddut ti pagvalor na ti tao, 2] haan a parepareho ti pagbigbig o pakicadwa ta adda fabfaboran na

Unfaithful hindi matapat sa kabiyak o asawa dahil nakikipagtalik sa iba; Iloc: haan a pudno iti kaayan-ayat na wenno iti asawa na ta maki-abig ti sabali

Unfinished hindi natapos o nacompleto; Iloc: haan a naypalpas o na-completo-*Sp*
Correlated words
Left undone nakatiwangwang; Iloc: pinanawan nga haan naypalpas

Unfit 1] hindi qualificado-*Sp* dahil sa kakulangan ng abilidad-*Sp* o kaalaman, 2] may sakit at masama ang kalagayan ng katawan; Iloc: 1] haan a calificado-*Sp* gapu ta kurang ti abilidad ken sirib na, 2] agsakit ken haan a nasayaat ti condisyon-*Sp* ti bagi na

Unforgettable hindi makakalimotan; Iloc: haan malipatan

Unforseen hindi inaasahan at di nakikinita na mangyayari; Iloc: haan nga expectaren ken haan na naammoan man laeng nga mapasamak
Correlated word
Unexpected hindi inaasahan; Iloc: haan ex-expectaren

Unfortunate sawi, kapos-palad; Iloc: daksang-gasat

Unfounded walang batayan, walang pinagbasehan; Iloc: awan pagbatayan, awan pagbasean

Unfurl iladlad; Iloc: ukraden, ukagen

Ungrateful ingrato-*Sp*, walang utang na loob kahit pagpapasalamat; Iloc: ingrato, awan ti pagyamyaman na

Unhappy malungkot, hindi maligaya, di masaya; Iloc: naliday, haan a naragsak

Unhealthy hindi malusog; pagkaing hindi makabigay-lusog at baka makasama pa; Iloc: haan a nasalun-at/nakaradcad; haan a maka-salun-at ken mabalin a makadakes pay

Uniform *(Tag. & Iloc.)* uniforme-*Sp*

Unify lahat ay magkaisa; Iloc: amin ket agkaykaysa da

Unintelligent mangmang; Iloc: nengneng, dagmel

Union *(Tag. & Iloc.) union,* unyon-*Sp*

Unique pambihira, bukod-tangi; Iloc: pakaidumaan, sigsigud laeng a kababalin

Unisex puedeng gamitin o isuot ng lalake o babae; Iloc: mabalin nga iyusar o icawes ti lalaki o babai

Unison, in (work, sing, eat, etc.) magkakatugmang sabay-sabay; Iloc: aggigiddan a pada-pada

Unit *(Tag. & Iloc.)* *unit*

Unite magkakaisa; Iloc: agkaykaysa da amin

Unity pagkakaisa; Iloc: panagkaykaysa

Universe *n.,* **Universal** *adj.* sandaigdig at lahat sa universo; Iloc: sanlubongan ken amin iti universo

University *(Tag. & Iloc.)* *university,* universidad-*Sp*

Unkind malupit, matigas ang puso; Iloc: nauyong, natang-ken ti panagpuspuso na, naulpit

Unkempt marumi at gulong-gulong calat; Iloc: narugit ken nagulo a waras

Unknown hindi kilala; Iloc: awan ti macaammo canyana

Unlawful *illegal,* labag sa batas, hindi makatarungan; Iloc: *illegal,* contra ti linteg

Unless maliban lamang kung; Iloc: malaksid nu, fuera-*Sp* laeng nu

Unlikely malamang hindi mangyayari; Iloc: mabalin nga haan mapasamak

Unlivable, Unhabitable hindi nakakabuting matirhan; Iloc: haan nga makapaimbag nga pagyanan

Unload *(Tag. & Iloc.)* discarga-*Sp*

Unlock susihin para mabuksan; Iloc: lukatan nga iyusar ti tulbek

Unlucky malas; Iloc: nadaksang-gasat, malas

Unmoved hindi siya afectado-*Sp*; Iloc: haan nga afectado

Unnecessary hindi kailangan; Iloc: haan a masapul

Unorthodox hindi naniniwala at hindi sumusunod sa naaprovahang forma ng doctrina, filosofiya, kaisipan at asal

Unpaid hindi pa bayad; Iloc: haan pay nabayadan

Unprepared hindi handa, hindi preparado-*Sp*; Iloc: haan a nakasagana, haan a preparado

Unproductive hindi nakakasagawa o nakakabuo ng makakabuting bagay; Iloc: haan a makaobra o maka-aramid iti maka-ventahe-*Sp* a banag

Unqualified hindi qualificado-*Sp*, wala o kulang sa canya ang mga rekisitos-*Sp* na hinahanap para maging calificado-*Sp*; Iloc: haan a calificado, awan o kurang canyana dagiti rekisitos nga masapul para ag-calificar-*Sp* isu

Antonyms

846

Qualified, Eligible *qualified,* qualificado, calificado, akma; Iloc.; *qualified,* qualificado, calificado, rumbeng

Unreasonable hindi akma sa rason-*Sp,* walang karason-rason; Iloc: haan umno iti rason, awan ti *common sense*

Unreliable hindi maasahang gawin ang dapat gawin niya, hindi mapagkatiwalaang magsabi ng tutuo; Iloc: haan a mapagtalkan nga aramiden na ti masapul nga maaramid, haan a mapagfiaran nga agsarita ti kaagpaysoan

Unripe hilaw, mapakla; Iloc: naata, naganus, nasugpet
Antonym
  Ripe hinog; Iloc: naluom

Unruly *(Tag. & Iloc.)* hindi/haan ma-diciplina-*Sp,* hindi/haan ma*control*

Unsafe mapanganib, peligroso-*Sp;* Iloc: napeggad, peligroso

Unsettled hindi matatag; Iloc: haan a nakasimpa ti usto

Unspoken 1] nagkakaintindihan kahit walang salita, 2] hindi pinaguusapan; Iloc: 1] agkaawatan uray no awan sarita, 2] haan nga pagsarsaritaan

Unstable umuuga-uga, gumagalaw-galaw, nagyuyogyog; Iloc: aggunaygunay, aggaraw-garaw, agyogyogyog

Unstitch tastasin; Iloc: agtastas, satsaten

Unsubscribe ipahinto ang pagpadala ng mga informasyon-*Sp* o periodico-*Sp* at ibang pahayagan dahil ayaw nang makatanggap; Iloc: isardeng ti pagpatulod ti informasyon o periodico ken dadduma pay

Unsuccessful hindi nagtagumpay, hindi nakasagawa

Unsullied puro, dalisay, busilak at malinis na walang kabahidbahid; Iloc: puro ken nakalinlinis

Untangle calagan, i-alpas; Iloc: warwaren, lapso-lapsoten

Untapped abilities mawala na abilidad-*Sp* o talento-*Sp* dahil hindi ginagamit; Iloc: agpukaw nga abilidad o talento ta haan nga iyus-usar-*Sp*
Correlated words
  You lose what you don't use maglaho o mawawala ang ano mang lakas, talino, abilidad at talento na hindi mo ginagamit - kung gamitin mo, dadami at huhusay pa iyan

Untidy burara, salaula, busalsal, disareglado-*Sp,* macalat, magulo; Iloc: burara, nawara, disareglado, magulo

Untied calas, calag; Iloc: nakawaya, nawarwar tay galot

Until hanggang sa; Iloc: aginggana ti, inggana ti

Untrue kasinungalingan, hindi tutoo; Iloc: kaulbodan, haan a usto, haan nga agpayso

Untrustworthy ones sinungaling, nagnanakaw, nagdidisfalco, nanlilinlang, falsificador, mandaraya, venggativo, traidor, mapagkunwari, magnanakaw, mamatay-tao, nakikipagtalik sa hindi niya asawa, criminal, terorista; Iloc: ulbod, agtatakaw, agdesdesfalco, mangallilaw, falsificador, cusit, manggulgulib, venggativo, traidor, agsinsinan, agtatakaw, agpatpatay-tao, maki-abig ti haan na nga asawa, criminal, terorista

Unusual pambihira, hindi caraniwan; Iloc: haan nga cadawyan, haan a sigud

Unwarranted walang otorisasyon, hindi nabigyan ng katwiran, walang pangangailangan nito, walang rason na gagawin; Iloc: awan otorisasyon, haan a naikkan iti linteg ken rason nga aramiden

Unwholesome nakakasama sa kalusogan at moralidad-*Sp*; Iloc: makadakes iti caradcad ken moralidad

Unwilling ayaw; Iloc: madi

Unwind calagin; Iloc: warwaren

Unwitting, Unwittingly 1] hindi alam at walang kamuang-muang o walang kamalay-malay; 2] hindi sinasadya, *accidental*; Iloc: 1] haan na pulos ammo; 2] haan na nga inggagara
Synonyms
Unaware walang kamalay-malay, walang kamuang-muang; Iloc: haan na pulos ammo
Oblivious limot na limot o walang kaalam-alam; Iloc: nalipatan na o haan na man laeng ammo

Unbeknownst walang kamuang-muang sa pangyayari, plano o ano man kaya mabibigla na lamang siya kapag malaman niya ang mga ito; Iloc: awan pulos ammo na iti kasasaad, plano wenno ania man isu nga makigtot isu intonu maamwan na dagitoyen
Antonyms
Deliberately sinadya, kusa; Iloc: inggagara
Intentionally sinadya, nagkusa; Iloc: inggagara

Unworthy hindi karapat-dapat; Iloc: haan nga rebbeng

UP sa itaas; Iloc: diay ngato

Antonym
Down sa baba; Iloc: diay baba
UP-and-coming lantad na tumutubo ng mahusay at maventahe; Iloc: nakaparang nga agtubtubo ti nasayaat ken makaventahe
UP for grabs puedeng makuha o mabili o maangkin ng sino man
UP in the air inaasahan pero wala pang balita o wala pang pasya o wala pang kasiguradohan o wala pang katiyakan, hindi pa napagpasyahan
UP-to-date alam ang mga pinakabagong balita o mga kasalukuyang kaisipan o gawain o uso; Iloc: ammo na ti pinakabaro a damag wenno dagiti madama nga kasiriban ken aramid wenno uso
UP to par kasing buti ng ibang matinong tao o ng mga ibang sinasaligan at binabatayang producto-*Sp*
Upbringing kung paano ang pagpalaki ng anak; Iloc: nu casano ti pagpadakkel ti anak
Update i-*record* o ibalita ang pinakabagong informasyon-*Sp*; Iloc: i-*record* o ipadamag ti pinakabaro nga informasyon
Upfront 1] napakafranko/ka-*Sp*, 2] magbayad ng maaga o avante na fecha-*Sp*; Iloc: 1] nakafrangfranko/ka, 2] agbayad iti nasapa o avante a fecha
Upgrade mas pagbutihin ang pagkagawa, itaas ang *standard* o pinag-babatayan; Iloc: mas pasayaaten iti pagkaaramid; ingato iti *standard*
Uphill paakyat; Iloc: agsang-at
Uphold panindigan; Iloc: ipagtacder
Upkeep ang pagsustento para sa pagpapanatili at pagpapamalagi sa buhay
UPON sa ibabaw, sa; Iloc: iti rabaw, iti, idiay
UPON, On the time that nang; Iloc: idi
Upright matuwid at mabuti, nakatayong derecho-*Sp*; Iloc: nalinteg ken nasayaat, nakatacder a derecho
Uprising paghihimagsik; Iloc: tattao nga ag-alsa para ti protesta
Uproot halbutin, labnutin; Iloc: paruten, rabnoten
Ups and downs mga mabuti at mahirap na mga karanasan
Upscale 1] *adj:* may kinalaman sa mga mayayaman at eleganteng kabu-hayan, 2] *verb:* gumawa ng pagbabago para magmukhang mayamang lugar
Correlated word

Uptown 1] mataas na lugar sa bayan o ciudad, 2] may kinalaman sa mayamang pamumuhay o ichura

Upset 1] talonin, bigoin, 2] consomihin, nasaktan ang damdamin, naghihinakit, 3] mapataob; Iloc: 1] abaken, 2] ikkan ti consumisyon-*Sp*, nasaktan ti ricna, maluksaw, masuron, 3] agbalinsuek

Upshot 1] kinalabasan, resulta-*Sp*, bunga, kahihinatnan, 2] buod, diwa, paksa; Iloc: 1] pinagbanagan, pinagmaayan, resulta, gunggona, bunga, 2] amad, diwa, punto ti pagsasaritaan

Upside-down taob, tumbalik, tiwarik; Iloc: balinsuek

Upstairs nasa taas; Iloc: diay ngato

Upstream sa lugar na pinanggalingan ng agos ng ilog; Iloc: diay lugar nga pinaggapuan ti pagayos ti carayan

Uptown 1] mataas na lugar-*Sp* sa bayan o ciudad-*Sp*, 2] may kinalaman sa mayamang pamumuhay o ichura-*Sp*

Upward pataas; Iloc: agpangato

Urban may kinalaman sa o tungkol sa ichura ng *city*/ciudad-*Sp* o bayan

Ureter medicong tubo-*Sp* para pag-agosan ng ihi; Iloc: tubo ti medico para pagayosan ti isbu

URGE, Persuade himokin, hikayatin; Iloc: uyotan, sulisogen

URGE, Compelling feeling fuersang nagpapatulak sa damdamin para umasal o magsagawa; Iloc: fuersa-*Sp* a mangiduron iti ricna tapno agtingnay wenno agaramid

Urgent *v.,* **Urgency** *n.* kinakailangang gawin agad-agad para iremedio o gamotin; Iloc: masapul nga ensigida-*Sp* nga aramiden para remedioan (remedio-*Sp*) o agasan

Synonym

Exigency *n.,* **Exigent** *adj.* kinakailangan ang malaking sikap at dalidaling paggalaw o pagremedio; Iloc: masapul ti dakkel a pakat ken dagdagos a paggaraw o pagremedio

Urinal *(Tag. & Iloc.)* orinola-*Sp*

Urinate, Pee *v.,* **Urine** *n.* umihi, ihi; Iloc: umisbo, isbo

US (you and I) tayo; Iloc: datayo, dacami

US (we) kami; Iloc: sicami, dacami

Usable puedeng magamit; Iloc: mabalin a ma-usar-*Sp*

Usage gamit; Iloc: usar-*Sp*

USE gamitin; Iloc: i-usar-*Sp*, usaren, aramaten

USE all up ubosin, simutin, isaid; Iloc: ibusen, simuten

USE thriftily nagtitipid; Iloc: agin-inot

Useful may silbi, napapakinabangan, magagamit; Iloc: agserbi-*Sp*, mayyus-usar-*Sp*, adda pagtungpalan na

Useless inutil-*Sp*, walang silbi, walang kabuluhan, walang saysay; Iloc: inutil, awan serbi-*Sp*, awan pagtungpalan na

Usual, Usually caraniwan, kinagawian, caraniwan; Iloc: cadawyan, gagangay, sigud nga aramid, canayon
Synonym
Common pangcaraniwang gawain o nagaganap; Iloc: cadawyan, sigud nga aramid o mapaspasamak

Used gamit na, segunda mano; Iloc: nausaren, segunda mano (usar-*Sp*, segunda-*Sp*, mano-*Sp*)

Usurp 1] manghimasok o agawin ng fuersa-*Sp* ang puesto-*Sp* o oficina-*Sp* o kapangyarihan na walang pahintulot; 2] gamitin kahit walang karapatan o otoridad-*Sp*; mali o masamang magsagawa

Usury nagpapautang na may *interest rate* na napakataas at labag sa batas ito; Iloc: agpapautang ngem nakangat-ngato ti *interest rate* nga haan a nalinteg

Uterus, Womb sinapupunan, matris-*Sp*, bahay-bata; Iloc: matris-*Sp*

Utile magagamit; Iloc: may-usar-*Sp*
Synonym
Useful may silbi, napapakinabangan, magagamit; Iloc: agserbi, mayyus usar, adda pagtungpalan

Utilities mga pangangailangan ng familia-*Sp* gaya ng electricidad-*Sp*, tubig, *gas*, telefono-*Sp*; Iloc: dagiti kasapulan ti familia casla ti electricidad, danum, *gas*, telefono

Utilize gamitin; Iloc: usaren (usar-*Sp*)

V

Vacant *adj.*, **Vancancy** *n.* pagka-vacante-*Sp*, hindi ocupado-*Sp*, walang laman

Vacate lisanan, iwanan; Iloc: panawan, talawan

Vacation *(Tag. & Iloc.)* *vacation*, vacasyon-*Sp*

Vacillate 1] urong-sulong sa isip; nag-aatubili, pabago-bago; 2] nag-iindayog, uugoy-ugoy, tataas-bababa

Vaccinate vacunahan, magpa-vacuna-*Sp*; Iloc: mangvacuna, agpavacuna

Vaccine *(Tag. & Iloc.)* vacuna-*Sp*

Vacuity *n.,* **Vacuous** *adj.* 1] vacante-*Sp*, walang kalaman-laman; 2] walang ulirat o malay, matamlay at hindi nakakakilos o nakakaisip

VACUUM walang laman at wala man lang anoman doon

VACCUM cleaner aparatong *electrical* na panglinis ng sahig at mga ibabaw na kailangang linisan

Vagabond taong walang permanenteng tirahan, palibot-libot, pagala-gala; Iloc: tao nga awan permanente a pagyanan na, aglibot-libot

Vagina kiki, puki; Iloc: pepet, uki

Vagrancy *n.,* **Vagrant** *adj. homeless,* pagala-gala, palaboy-laboy, lagalag dahil walang bahay ni trabaho; hampaslupa; Iloc: *homeless,* aggigian idiay calye-*Sp* o calsada, agwalwalang ta awan balay na

Vague malabo; Iloc: nacudrep, nacusnaw

VAIN vanidoso/sa-*Sp*, pagpapaganda niya ang napaka-importante-*Sp* sa canya, mapostura; Iloc: vanidoso/sa, naimis, iti pagpapintas ken postura ti importante canyana

VAIN, in walang kinahinatnan, hindi maka-completo-*Sp*, hindi maisa-gawa; Iloc: haan a maycompleto o maaramid awan ti resulta-*Sp* nga ine-expectar-*Sp* da

Vainglory *n.,* **Vainglorious** *adj.* pagpapasikat; sobra sa galak o yabang sa sariling abilidad-*Sp* o *accomplisments* o gawain niyang natupad

Valedictory ocasyon-*Sp* ng pagpapaalam ng escuela-*Sp* sa mga nag-*graduate* dito

Valedictorian estudianteng nakatamo ng pinakamataas na grado at sa *graduation exercise* ay magtalumpati ng *valedictory address*

Valiant matapang; Iloc: natured

Valid *(Tag. & Iloc.)* valido-*Sp*, makatarungan, *legal*

Validate gawing valido-*Sp* o *official*; Iloc: aramiden a valido o *official*

Valley lambak; kapatagan na nasa gitna ng mga bundok; Iloc: patag a tanap nga adda iti tengnga iti bantay ida

Valor *n.,* **Valorous** *adj.* makabayaning katapangan, kagitingan sa labanan; Iloc: tured, kinatured

Valuable mahalaga, may kabulohan; Iloc: adda valor-*Sp* na, adda pateg na, adda cuenta-*Sp* na

Valuation alamin ang uri, kalikasan at kahusayan para macalcula o matahasan ang halaga

VALUE *v.*, binibigyang kahalagahan, tinatangi, estimahin; Iloc: valoran, ikkan ti valor-*Sp*, estmaren, ilala (estima/estimar-*Sp*)

VALUE *n.* halaga, kabulohan; Iloc: valor, pateg

Values mabubuti at marangal na principio sa pagpalakad ng buhay gaya ng *moral and ethical values*; Iloc: nasayaat ken narespeto a principio nga pagpadalan iti biag casla iti moralidad ken etico

Van *(Tag. & Iloc.) van*

Vandal: taong nagva-*vandalize* o nagsusulat at nagdo-*drawing* sa mga *walls* sa comunidad at mga gusali na nakakadumi o nakakasira ng ichura

Vandalize pinapapangit o dinudumihan ang bakuran, pader, gusali o sasakyan sa pamamagitan ng mga sulat at guhit kahit bawal at labag sa batas ang mga ito; Iloc: ipalaad o rugitan iti alad, diding, lugan ken *building* nga ag-surat ken ag-ugis uray nu contra iti linteg

VANISH maglaho, nagpawi, maparam; Iloc: agpukaw, agawan

VANISH into thin air nawala at parang naglaho na gaya ng hangin; Iloc: nagawan a casla impukaw ti angin

Vanquish lupigin, supilin at talonin sa labanan o sa salungatan o sa competisyon

VANTAGE ventahe-*Sp*, lamang o superioridad-*Sp*

VANTAGE point puesto-*Sp* o lugar-*Sp* kung saan matanaw ang magandang kalawakan

Vapor usok na basa; Iloc: asok nga nabasa

Vaporizer usok na may gamot na langhapin para gumaling ang ubo o sakit sa lalamunan; Iloc: asok nga adda agas na nga lang-aben tapno aglaeng iti uyek wenno sakit ti carabucob

Variable mag-iba-iba o magbago-bago gaya ng clima-*Sp*

Variety, Various iba't iba, sari-sari kahit na nasa isa lang na categorya-*Sp*; Iloc: saba-sabali, naduma-duma

Varnish *(Tag. & Iloc.) varnish* na pinta na walang culay pero pinapakintab ang muebles-*Sp* na gawa ng kahoy

Vary iba't iba, sari-sari; Iloc: saba-sabali, nadumaduma,

Vascular mga ugat sa katawan; Iloc: dagiti urat iti bagi

Vase *(Tag. & Iloc.) vase,* florera-*Sp*

Vast lugar na malawak, malaki at malapad at mahaba; Iloc: solar-*Sp* a dackel ken nalawa ken naacaba

Veer lumihis; Iloc: aglisi, lisyan

Vegan *(see Vegetarian below)*

VEGETABLE gulay; Iloc: nateng

VEGETABLE, leafy, dried and shriveled natuyohang dahon ng gulay; Iloc: nagango nga bulong ti nateng

Vegetarian, Vegan taong kumakain ng gulay lamang at walang carne; Iloc: tao nga mangmangan iti nateng laeng ken awan pulos carne

> *Correlated words*
>
> **Carnivorous** kumakain lamang ng carne; Iloc: mangmangan laeng iti carne
>
> **Pescetarian, Pescevegetarian** taong kumakain ng gulay at isda lamang, walang carne; Iloc: tao nga mangmangan iti nateng ken ikan laeng ngem awan pulos carne

Vehement agresivo-*Sp* at matapang sa pagbibigay-alam niya ng canyang isip at paniniwala at kalooban; Iloc: natured nga ipaammo na ti nakem ken pammati ken ricna na

VEHICLE sasakyan; Iloc: pagsakayan, pagluganan

> *Correlated words*
>
> **Car, Automobile** *(Tag. & Iloc.) coche*
>
> **Bus** *(Tag. & Iloc.) bus*
>
> **Jeepney, Jitney** *jeep* na nagsasakay ng mga pasahero sa kaunting bayad
>
> **Truck** *(Tag. & Iloc.) truck*
>
> **RV** *recreational vehicle, van* na ginagamit sa camping na may tulogan, lutoan at banyo; Iloc: *recreational vehicle, van* na iyus-usar iti pagcamping nga adda pagturogan, paglutwan ken banyo

VEHICLE, stalled tumirik na sasakyan; Iloc: agtirik a lugan

Veil *(Tag. & Iloc.)* velo-*Sp*

Vein ugat; Iloc: urat

> *Synonym*
>
> **Vascular** mga ugat sa katawan; Iloc: dagiti urat iti bagi

Velocity bilis, kabilisan; Iloc: pardas

Venal tumatanggap siya ng *bribe* o suhol, mercenario; madaling talikoran ang kabutihan, obligasyon, principio at consencia o budhi para lamang makatamo ng pera; *corrupt* at madaling masuholan

Vend pagveventa; Iloc: paglaco

Veneer ang dinikit o pinatong sa luma, pangit o mumurahing *plywood* para bumago o mas gumanda ang ichura-*Sp* na gaya ng *brick* o ladrilyo-*Sp* at iba pang pampaganda; artifisyal-*Sp* na ichura

Venerate magsamba sa Panginoong Dios, magdasal, magpuri, maghanga, ipagbunyi at parangalan Siya, pasalamatan at tingalain Siya dahil sa pagkabanal Niya at pagkapuno ng gloria-*Sp* at gracia-*Sp* at unang-una, dahil sa pagmamahal Niya sa bawat tao kahit hindi karapat-dapat ang tao dahil ang tao'y makasalanan; Iloc: agcararag, aglualo, dayawen, agyaman, i-glorificar-*Sp* ken tangtangaden na ni Apo Dios gapu iti pagkasagrado Na ken napunno ti gloria, gracia ken pagayan-ayat Na ti tattao.

Vengeance vengganza-*Sp*, paghihiganti; Iloc: vengganza, panangbales

Venison carne ng usa; Iloc: carne ti ugsa

VENT maliit na butas para labasan at pasukan ng hangin, lagusan

VENT out pent-up emotions, Unburden idaing, itaghoy, maghimutok, itangis; Iloc: agsennaay, iyasog, agunnoy

Ventilation *ventilation*, ventilasyon-*Sp*, pasok-labas ng hangin; Iloc: *ventilation*, ventilasyon, agserrek-agruar ti angin

Venture 1] makipagsapalaran, 2] pumasok sa gawaing walang ka-segurohan o puedeng may panganib; Iloc: 1] makigasang-gasat, 2] sumrek ti aramid nga awan ti pagkaseguroan nga mabalin ket adda pay peggad na

Venue lugar-*Sp* kung saan gaganapin; Iloc: lugar nu inchenna aramiden o agtipon-tipon o ipabuya

Veracity alinsunod o sang-ayon sa katotohanan, katumpakan at kawastohan

Veranda *(Tag. & Iloc.) veranda*, balconahe-*Sp*, balcon

Verbal sinasalita at sinasabi, hindi sinusulat; Iloc: pagsarita, pagsao, isarsarita, haan a surat

Verbatim, Word by word ipahayag o isalin bawat salita na binanggit; Iloc: isawang, ipablaac o ipatarus cada maysa-maysa a sarita

Verdant nagkulay luntian dahil sa malalagong halaman; Iloc: nag-color-*Sp* verde-*Sp* o *green* gapu ti nalalapsat a tanem

Verdict hatol o sentencia-*Sp* ng asunto-*aSp* sa corte-*Sp* ng husticia-*Sp*; Iloc: sentencia ti asunto idiay corte ti husticia

Verge bingit, dulo, gilid; Iloc: igid, murdong

Verification *n.,* **Verify** *v.* tiyakin kung tutoo; evidencia-*Sp* o formal-*Sp* na declarasyon-*Sp* sa pagtatag o pagpatunay ng katotohanan o kawastohan ng bagay; Iloc: i-verificar-*Sp* nu usto; evidencia ken prueba-*Sp* ti kaagpaysuan

Vermin iba't ibang maliliit na hayop gaya ng daga o ipis na nakakasira, nakakabigay ng sakit o nakakapatayo ng balahibo

Vernacular katutubo o sariling wika ng isla-*Sp* o *region* o ng provincia-*Sp* o ng bayan; Iloc: bukbukod a sarita iti isla, ti *region*, ti provincia, ti ili o ti nasyon

Versatile maraming kaalaman at kacayahan at talento-*Sp*; Iloc: addaan iti adu nga sirib ken cabaelan ken talento
Synonyms
Prolific maraming kacayahan; Iloc: adu ti cabaelan na
Talented *(Tag. & Iloc.) talented,* matalento

Verse *(Tag. & Iloc.) verse* na ginagamit sa tula

Version *version*; pagsasalin, interpretasyon-*Sp* o ulat ng isa na puede na kaiba sa iba

Vertebra gulogod; Iloc: dori

Vertical patayo; Iloc: nakatacder
Antonym
Horizontal pahiga; Iloc: paidda

Vertigo nahihilong at parang nawawala ang balanse; Iloc: maam-amak ken maul-ulaw

Very masyado-*aSp*, ubod ng...; Iloc: unay, masyado

Vest *(Tag. & Iloc.)* chaleco-*Sp*

VET, Veteran veterano-*Sp* o sundalong nagretiro pagkatapos magsilvi sa *military* at lumaban sa giyera

VET, Veterinarian, Veterinary *veterinarian,* manggagamot o paggamot sa mga hayop at pag-ooperasyon pa sa mga ito kung kinakailangan; Iloc: *veterinarian,* mangngagas ti *animal*

VET or Vetting usisahin-suriin-at-siyasating husto at masinsinan, i-*scrutinize* na masusing tingin at pagmasdan kung may diferencia, icalcula, siyasatin kung tutoo, valido, tama, tumpak at wastong-wasto na wala man lamang mali

Veto sa pamahalaan, pagtatanggi at hindi pagpapayag na pumasa para hindi maaprovahan ng otoridad

Vex *v.,* **Vexation** *n.* saktan ang damdamin; paghihinakit, pagkainis at pagkayamot; Iloc: masuron, maluksaw

Via papunta o patungo sa..., sa pamamagitan ng..; Iloc: agturong diay, iti pangiyusar iti..

Viable cayang mabuhay, lumaki, lumawak, umunlad; nakarating sa *development* na caya pang magyabong/*develop* lalo kahit walang tulong ang ina

Viand ulam; Iloc: sida

Vibrant masaya, masigla, maliksi, masigasig, ganado, listo; Iloc: naragsak, nasagiksik, ganado, alisto

Vibrate *v.,* **Vibration** *n.* may ritmong panginginig

Vicarious 1] ginawa, tinanggap o tiniis alang-alang sa ibang tao; humalili o pumalit o gumanap para sa iba; 2] naramdaman niya sa guniguni ang pinagdadaanan ng iba

VICE *vice,* vicio-*Sp,* pagkalulong sa masamang gawain o *habit*; Iloc: *vice,* vicio, pagkalublob iti dakes nga aramid o *habit*
Synonym
Addict nalulong sa vicio sa droga o sa alak o sa paninigarilyo o sa pagsusugal o sa iba pang nakakagumon ng sama

VICE (position, i.e., Vice President) *(Tag. & Iloc.)* vise

VICE versa ganun din sa kabila

Vicinity 1] pagkalapit, 2] sa loob ng purok, 3] mahigit-kumulang sa bilang; Iloc: 1] pagkaasideg, 2] iti uneg ti arrubayan, 3] agsobra-agkurang a bilang

Vicious napakasama; Iloc: nakadakdakes

Victim *(Tag. & Iloc.)* victima-*Sp*

Victor *champion,* ang nanalo, campeon; Iloc: *champion,* ti nangabak

Victory tagumpay; Iloc; pangabak, balligi

Victual mga pagkain; Iloc: dagiti makan

Vie makipaligsahan, makipag-competensia-*Sp*, makipag-*contest*; Iloc: makipagcompetensia, makisalisal, maki-*contest*

VIEW *n.* tanawin; Iloc: napintas a matantan-aw iti arrubayan

VIEW *v.* pagmasdan, tignan; Iloc: agtan-aw, kitaen

Viewpoint *perspective*, pananaw at pagturing sa mga tao at pangyayari o paligid; Iloc: *perspective*, panagkita ken pangbigbig cadagiti tattao o kasasaad o ti arrubayan

Vigil lamay; Iloc: pagpuyat para mangbantay

Vigilance *n.*, **Vigilant** *adj.*, pagtatanod, pagbabantay, pagmamanman para mapuna kung may panganib

Vigor lakas, sigla; Iloc: pigsa, bileg

Vigorous ginagamit ang buong lakas at sigla; Iloc: pagiyusar iti amin a pigsa ken bileg

Vile napakasama; Iloc: nakadakdakes

Vilify mag-alipusta, manirang-puri, manglait

Village, small *(Tag. & Iloc.)* barrio

Villager tagabukid; Iloc: taga-barrio, tagatalon

Villain *(Tag. & Iloc.)* contrabida

Vim lakas, sigla; Iloc: pigsa, bileg

Vindicate ipawalang-sala dahil sa pinakitang prueba-*Sp*; Iloc: naawanan iti basol gapu ti impaneknek a prueba

Vindictive mapaghiganti, venggativo-*Sp*; Iloc: manangibales, venggativo

VINE baging; Iloc: lanut

VINE, edible *(Tag. & Iloc.)* pandan

Vinegar *(Tag. & Iloc.)* suká

Vintage 1] pag-ani ng *grapes* sa *vineyeard* para gawing alak; pinaka-*superior* na alak; 2] *collection* o pinagtipon-tipon na *contemporaneous*/magkakaparehong panahong tao o bagay; pinakamahusay sa isang nakaraang panahon

Violate labagin, lumalabag; Iloc: agsupyat, agsukir, agsalangad

Violence grabeng labanan, karahasan, kapangahasan; Iloc: grabe a labanan, ranggasan

Violent *(Tag. & Iloc.)* vayolente-*Sp*, sakitan at patayan

Violin *(Tag. & Iloc.)* viulin-*Sp*

Violet *(Tag. & Iloc.)* *violet*

Virgin *(Tag. & Iloc.)* virhen-*Sp*

Virginity hindi pa nakaranas ng pagtatalik sa lalake o babae; Iloc: haan na pay napasaran iti makiidda ti *sexual* iti lalake o babae

Virile lalaking-lalaki, matipuno; Iloc: malalaki, nalapsat

Virtual 1] nagkakaroon ng bisa o fuersa o diwa at efecto-*Sp* pero hindi sa ichura o forma; tactica ng *computer* kung saan ang tao ay gumagamit ng *headset* o *mask* na nakakabigay ng expiryensa na siya ay nasa isang kapaligiran na nilikha ng *computer* at nakikipagganap dito; 2] nakakagawa ng efecto sa pamamagitan ng tanging lakas o cacayahan

Virtue *n.*, **Virtuous** *adj.* 1] pinapahalagahan ng husto ang moralidad-*Sp* at dignidad-*Sp* at integridad-*Sp* at etico-*Sp* at pagkamaka-Dios, 2] malinis ang pagkatao, maka-Dios; Iloc: 1] ival-valor-*Sp* na unay iti moralidad ken dignidad ken integridad ken etico ken pagkamaka-Dios, 2] nalinis ti pagkatao na ta isu ket maka-Dios

Virulent 1] sobrang nakakahawa, nakakalason o napakamaligno; 2] sobrang antipatico at magalitin

VIRUS clase-*Sp* ng microbio-*Sp* na nakakabigay ng sakit; Iloc: clase ti microbio nga mangited iti sakit

VIRUS protection 1] vacuna-*Sp* contra-*Sp* sa sakit na galing sa *virus*, 2] kung gumagamit ng *windows computer* kinakailangan ng proteksion-*Sp* contra-*Sp* sa *virus* o *malware* dahil puedeng makapasok na di man lamang natin alam ang *virus* at manira sa nilalaman ng *computer*; Iloc: 1] vacuna contra ti sakit a naggapu ti *virus*, 2] nu mangiyus-usar iti *windows computer*, masapul ti proteksion contra ti *virus* wenno *malware* gapu ta haan tayo ammo nga simrek ti *virus* ken mangdadael cadagiti addaan iti uneg ti *computer*

Visa otorisasyon-*Sp* na binigay ng govierno-*Sp* sa pamamagitan ng pasaporte-*Sp* para makapasok sa isang bayan at magliwaliw o matira doon

Vis-à-vis *[viz-a-viz]*, **Face-to-face** magkaharapan, pagkikita sa pagsalubongan o tagpoan

Visible *adj.*, **Visibility** *n.* lantad, halata, litaw, kitang-kita, vistado; Iloc: nakaparang, vistado, makitkita

Correlated words

Evident lantad, halata, litaw, kitang-kita, vistado; Iloc: makitkita, nakaparang, vistado, nalatak

Transparent naaaninag; Iloc: maan-anninag

Exposed, In full view lantad, kitang-kita, nakalabas, nakabilad; Iloc: naka-parang, makitkita, nakaruar, nakabilag

Conspicuous lantad, halata, litaw, kitang-kita, vistado; Iloc: makitkita, nakaparang, vistado, nalatak

Obvious kitang-kita; Iloc: makitkita

Evident halata, litaw, vistado; Iloc: nakaparang, vistado

Overt bukas, lantad at hindi lihim; Iloc: nakalucat, nakaparang ken haan a nakalimed

Antonym

Covert tago, lihim; Iloc: lemmeng, limed

Invisible *(Tag. & Iloc.)* hindi/haan makita

Hidden tago, nakacubli, lingid; Iloc: nakalemmeng, nakalinged, nakasuksok

Undetected *(Tag. & Iloc.)* disimulado-*aSp*

Vision paningin; Iloc: pagkita

Visit mag-visita-*Sp*, dadalaw; Iloc: agsarungcar, agvisita, agdagus

Visitor visita-*Sp*, panauhin; Iloc: visita, sanga-ili

Vista magandang kalikasang tanawin; Iloc: napintas a naturalesa-*Sp* a matantan-aw

Visual tungkol sa paningin; Iloc: maygapu iti panagkita

Visualize ilarawan sa isip; Iloc: iretrato iti panunot

VITAL kailangang-kailangan, napakahalaga at napakaimportante-*Sp*; Iloc: napateg, importante

VITAL signs palatandaan na ang tao ay buhay pa o ano ang kalagayan ng canyang katawan gaya ng temperatura-*Sp*, pintig ng puso at pulso-*Sp*, at paghinga; Iloc: panglasin nu sibibiag pay ti tao wenno ania ti kasasaad ti bagi na casla iti temperatura, pitik ti puso ken pulso, ken paganges

Vitality capacidad-*Sp* na mabuhay at patuloy na sumisibol sa kalusogan na mga ito'y kakaiba sa taong patay

Vitamin *(Tag. & Iloc.)* vitamina-*Sp*

Vitreous *adj.*, **Vitrify** *v.* ichura ng o gawa sa cristal o salamin

Vivacious maaliw, masaya at ang kasayahan niya ay nakakahawa; Iloc: nakalinglingay, naragsak ken ti ragsak na ket makaacar

Vivid maliwanag at claro-*Sp*; Iloc: nalawag ken claro

Vivify bigyang buhay, buhayin; Iloc: biagen

Vlog *blog* na *video* sa *internet* na nagpapakita ng ginagampanan at kung minsan ay may nakasulat

Vocabulary *(Tag. & Iloc.)* vocabulario-*Sp*

Vocal gamit ang voces-*Sp*; Iloc: iyusar ti voces

Vocalist kumacanta, vocalista-*Sp*; Iloc: agcang-canta-*Sp*, agcangcansion-*Sp*, vocalista-*Sp*

Vogue, in *(Tag. & Iloc.)* mahilig sa uso at moda

VOICE voces-*Sp* tinig; Iloc: voces, timec

VOICE, hoarse paos, malat; Iloc: agpaparaw

VOICE out, Express oneself magpahayag, umimik, Iloc: aguni, agsawang

Void ipawalang bisa; Iloc: ikkaten ti turay o bileg

Volcano *(Tag. & Iloc.)* vulcan-*Sp*

Volatile 1] parating pabago-bago; 2] puedeng maging vayolenteng pananakit o pagsabog; Iloc: 1] canayon nga agsaba-sabali, 2] mabalin nga agvayolente a pangpasakit wenno agbettak

Volition kusa, sadya; Iloc: intension-*Sp*, gagara

Volt, Voltage fuersa-*Sp* na nanggagaling sa pag-agos ng electricitad-*Sp*; Iloc: fuersa a naggapu ti pagayos ti electricidad

Volume 1] kung gaano kadami, 2] tinipon-tipon na mga kasulatan na iba't ibang informasyon-*Sp*; Iloc: 1] nu casano kaadu, 2] colecsion-*Sp* ti nakasurat ida a saba-sabali nga informasyon

Voluntary kusang-loob, voluntario-*Sp*; Iloc: voluntario

Voluptuous tungkol sa pagpapalayaw sa katawan hindi sa isip; ito ay luho at *sensual pleasure*, makamundong kasiyahan; *sexy* na pang-akit

Vomit magsuka, sumuka, lumula; Iloc: agvacuar, agsarwa

Voracious matakaw; Iloc: bucatot, narawet, sarabusab

Vortex umiikot na tubig o hangin na dinadala ang nahihigop nito sa kalagitnaan ng tubig o sa lupa; Iloc: agpus-pusipos nga danum o angin nga ipan na iti naigop na idiay katengngaan iti danum wenno iti lugar ti daga

Vote *(Tag. & Iloc.)* voto-*Sp*

Vouch magpatunay, magsuporta, maggarantiya, magcertificar, magsaksi, mangprueba, magdeclarar ng katotohanan tungkol sa tao o bagay at uri o pagkayari nito

Voucher 1] tao na nagpapatunay; 2] kasulatan, recibo-*Sp* o forma-*Sp* tungkol sa mga gastos-*Sp*, utang o bayad o bibilhin sa kinabukasan

Vouchsafe pumayag o magbigay o magkaloob bilang favor o dahil sa kabutihang-loob

Voter *(Tag. & Iloc.)* votante-*Sp*

Vow sumpa, pangako; Iloc: cari, sapata

Voyage paglakbay sa malayong lugar-*Sp*, paglayag sa dagat; Iloc: pagviahe-*Sp* iti adayo a lugar, aglayag iti taaw

Vulgar vulgar-*Sp*, bastos-*Sp*, garrafal-*Sp*, malaswa, mahalay; Iloc: vulgar, bastos, garrafal

Vulnerable 1] taong madaling tablan ng sakit, taong madaling mainfluwensia o locohin o dayahin o mapahirapan o masaktan o mapatay, 2] *computer* o *credit card* na madaling ma-*hack* o kaya companya o sangay ng govierno-*Sp* na puedeng tirahin ng mga *hacker*; Iloc: 1] tao a nalaca a maacaran ti sakit, tao a nalaca a mainfluwensia o magulib o maloco o maparigatan o masaktan o mapatay, 2] *computer* o *credit card* nga nalaca a ma-*hack* wenno companya o departamento-*Sp* ti govierno-*Sp* a mabalin a tiraen dagiti *hacker*

W

Wacko, Wacky kakaiba at hindi *normal*, sinto-sinto

Wad nabalumbon na papel-*Sp*; Iloc: nalucot a papel

Wade magtampisaw sa mababaw na parte ng ilog o dagat; Iloc: agtampisaw diay ababaw a parte iti carayan o baybay

Waddle lakad-pato; Iloc: pagna ti pato

Wafer *(Tag. & Iloc.)* apa

Waft hihip ng hangin, simoy ng hangin, singaw ng hangin; Iloc: puyot ti angin

WAG *(Tag. & Iloc.)* ipagpag, iwagwag, iwagayway

WAG its tail, dog kawag, kinakawag ang canyang buntot

Wage 1] suweldo, kita, sahod, 2] magtaguyod; Iloc: 1] suweldo, kita, 2] irugi ken itultuloy

Waif bata na walang tinitirhan at ni kaibigan; aso o pusa na lumilibot at hindi malaman kung may nagmemay-ari nito; napakapayat na tao na caraniwan ay babae

Wail humahagulhol; Iloc: agan-anug-og, agdungdung-aw

Waist baywang, bewang; Iloc: siket, sibet

WAIT maghintay, mag-abang; Iloc: aguray, urayen, agsirpat, agabang

WAIT! Teka!, Sandali lang!, Hintay!; Iloc: Aguray ka!, Alto-*Sp* ka!

WAIT-and-see attitude payag na maghintay at tingnan ang kasunod o kahihinatnan, bago magpasya

Waiter *(Tag. & Iloc.)* servidor-*aSp*

Waiting place hintayan; Iloc: pagurayan

Waive isuko, bitiwan; Iloc: isuko, ibbatan

Waiver kusang isuko ang karapatan at ang pag-aari at interes-*Sp* sa isang reglamento o condisyon; pinahayag sa salita at kasulatan tungkol sa pagsuko nito

WAKE 1] magising, 2] nakikilamay sa patay; Iloc: 1] makariing, 2] makilamay iti patay

WAKE someone up gisingin; Iloc: riingen, lucagen

WAKE up abruptly gumising ng bigla; Iloc: agbaringkuas

WALK lakad; Iloc: magna

Correlated words

Stroll magpasyal; Iloc: agpasiar

Hike *exercise* o libangan na lakad gaya sa bundok o sa may ilog

Wander naglilibot, pagala-gala, palaboy-laboy, naglalacuacha, nagbulakbol; Iloc: aglaklacuacha, agbulbulakbol, aglib-libot, ballog

Trudge pagod na pagod at hirap na hirap na lumalakad; may kahabahan na lakad

Limp *(Tag. & Iloc.)* pipilay-pilay

Hobble hirap at mabagal lumakad, parang pilay; Iloc: marigatan wenno nainnayad nga magna, casla agpilay-pilay

Teeter hirap gumalaw o hirap lumakad ng husto; Iloc: marigatan nga aggunay o magna iti husto

Flounder matomba-tomba o papilay-pilay sa pagsikap na tumayo o magbalanse habang nakatindig

Totter yumayanig at nanginginig ang galaw at lakad; Iloc: mapatigerger ti garaw ken agtiwed-tiwed ti pagna

WALK-in 1] paciente-*Sp* na makipagkita sa *doctor* kahit walang tinakdang *appointment*; *customer* na kusang pumuntang kumain sa *restaurant* sa araw o oras-*Sp* na gusto-*Sp* niya; 2] cuarto-*Sp* na puedeng mag-*walk-in* gaya ng malaking *closet* o *pantry*

WALK on eggs, Walk on a tight rope, Walk on thin ice dahil naki-kibagay sa maseselan na mga tao, parating nag-aalangan at nag-iingat ng husto sa asal at salita, o nasa kalagayang delicado-*Sp* dahil puedeng may hindi kanais-nais na mangyayari o mapahamak kaya nag-iingat

WALK-out or Walkout 1] pagwe-welga-*Sp* ng mga trabahador-*Sp* o mga empleyado-*Sp*; 2] pinto na para sa mga papalabas na tao

WALK sexily with swaying hips magpakembot-kembot, magpakendeng-kendeng; Iloc: agkinni-kinni

WALK with a wobble uugod-ugod, lumakad o tumayo na parang hirap at mabubuwal; Iloc: uugod-ugod, magna o tumacder a casla marigatan ken matomba-tomba

WALK with a limp pipilay-pilay, titikod-tikod, hihingkod-hingkod; Iloc: agpilpilay, agsiksikkayud, agpakkapakkang

Walking papers papel na nagpapahiwatig na tatanggalin sa trabaho ang empleyado-*Sp*; Iloc: kasuratan nga mangpaammo nga iti empleyado a maikkaten isu iti trabaho

Wall pader, dingding; Iloc: pader, diding

Wallet *(Tag. & Iloc.)* pitaca-*aSp*

Wallow maglublob, maglulong; Iloc: aglubnak

Waltz *(Tag. & Iloc.)* waltz

Wan maputla, nandidilaw; Iloc: agpuraw a casla awan dara na

Wand, Baton *(Tag. & Iloc.)* wand, baton

Wander palibot-libot, pagala-gala, naglalacuacha, nagbubulakbol, pala-boy-laboy; Iloc: agliblibot, aglaclacuacha, agbulbulakbol, agbalballog

Wanderlust matinding pagkagusto na maglibot-libot o paviahe-viahe-*Sp*

Wane humina, kumonti, pawala; Iloc: kumapoy, agpukaw, umaw-awan

Want 1] gusto-*Sp*, ibig, hangad, nais, 2] pangangailangan; Iloc: 1] gusto-*Sp*, cayat, mayat, 2] kasapulan

Wanton walang karason-rason na basta-basta at bara-bara lang kumi-los, na karaniwan ay malaswa, malisyoso, o walang kaingat-ingat o walang hinahon/*restraint*

War labanan, sagupaan, giyera, digmaan; Iloc: gerra-*Sp*, gubat

Ward 1] sangay ng ospital-*Sp*, 2] taong inaalagaan; Iloc: 1] parte-*Sp* ti ospital, 2] tao nga tartaraknen

Warehouse *(Tag. & Iloc.)* almacen-*Sp*, bodega-*Sp*, camarin

Warfare giyera o labanan ng mga hukbo o *army*

WARM maligamgam; Iloc: nabara, haan a napudot ken haan met nalamiis, kaus-ustuanan na latta

WARM up ipainit ng katamtaman; Iloc: ipapudot ti kalalaengan na

WARNING babala, *warning*, pabatid; Iloc: pangpaalwad, pang-alerto -*Sp*, *warning*

Warmth 1] maligamgam na init, 2] maconsuelong pagtrato; Iloc: 1] kalalaengan a pudot, 2] na-consuelo-*Sp* a trato-*Sp*

WARNING expressions Hala!, Hep!, Uh-oh; Iloc: Alla!, Uh-oh

Warp yupi; Iloc: cuppit

Warrant 1] otorisasyong-*Sp* gawin, 2] nakakarapatan, naaangkop; Iloc: 1] otorisasyon nga aramiden, 2] gunggona, umno, rebbeng

Warranty otorisasyon; makabatas na documento na nagsasaad ng katotohanan o paniguro o pangako o garantiya o kautosan kung mayroon o walang karapatan o kapangyarihan

Warrior sundalo; Iloc: soldado-*Sp*

Wart culugo; Iloc: tucak-tucak

Wary nagdadalawang-isip, di mapakali; Iloc: agdudua, maam-amak

Was said/stated daw, raw; Iloc: cano, cunada

WASH maghugas, magbanlaw; Iloc: agugas, agbuggo, bugwan, banlawan

WASH clothes maglaba; Iloc: aglaba

WASH dishes maghugas ng pinggan; Iloc: aginnaw

WASH face maghilamos; Iloc: ag-lavar-*Sp*, agdiram-os

Washstand *(Tag. & Iloc.)* banyera-*Sp*, lavabo-*Sp*

Wasp putakti; Iloc: alumpipinig

Waste mag-aksaya, sayangin; Iloc: sayangen, haan a mangilala
  Antonym
  Save mag-ipon, magtipid; Iloc: agurnong, tiponen, mangìlàla, ilala

Wasted *(Tag. & Iloc.)* nasayang

Wasteful maaksaya, mapaglustay, waldas; Iloc: haan nga mangsayang, haan a mangilala, sobra-*Sp* nga ag-gastar-*Sp* ken mangiyusar
  Antonyms
  Skimp nagtitipid; Iloc: agin-inot
  Set aside for future needs ibukod para sa pangangailangan sa mga kinabukasan; Iloc: ilasin para ti pakasapulan o pang-gastos cadagiti masangwanan nga panawen

WATCH *n.* relong suot sa camay; Iloc: relo-*Sp* nga may-usar-*Sp* ti ima

WATCH *v.* tignan, panoorin; Iloc: kitaen, buyaen

Watcher tagabantay, guardia-*Sp*, tanod; Iloc: agbantay, guardia

Watchful maingat na nagtatanod at nag-oobserva sa kalibutan para sa kaligtasan ng tao at ng lugar; Iloc: naalwad nga agob-observa ken agguar-guardia para nasalaknib ti tao ken ti lugar
Synonym
Guard bantayin, guardiahin; Iloc: guardiaen, agbantay

WATER tubig; Iloc: danum

WATER from a well, draw mag-igib; Iloc: agsakdo

WATER scooper tabu-*Sp*; Iloc: tabu, tacu
Correlated words
Coconut scooper bao; Iloc: boyoboy

WATER the plants magdilig; Iloc: agsibug

WATER under the bridge lumampas na at nakalimutan na rin; Iloc: limmabasen ken nalipatanen

WATER well, dug-out open balon; Iloc: bubon
Correlated word
Artesian well *(Tag. & Iloc.)* pozo

Waterfall *(Tag. & Iloc.) waterfall,* talon

Watermelon pakwan; Iloc: sandia-*Sp*

Waterproof hindi tinatagusan ng tubig; Iloc: haan nga agsipsip wenno serken ti danum

WAVE at someone cawayan, cumaway; Iloc: payapayan, agpayapay

WAVE something to and fro iwagayway; Iloc: ipayapay

WAVE, ocean or sea alon, daluyong; Iloc: dalluyong

Waver mag-urong-sulong; Iloc: agavante-agatras

WAY daan; Iloc: dalan

WAY, Method paraan, *method,* sistema; Iloc: pagaramid, *method,* sistema, kapamay-an
Correlated words
Routine kinagawiang gawa, kaugaliang pamaraan; Iloc: sigud o cadawyan nga aramid o sigud a pamay-an
Strategy pamaraan, tactica; Iloc: pangpapagna, tactica
Maneuver *(Tag. & Iloc.)* maniobra
Modus operandi ang paraan ng pagpapatakbo ng pangangalakal, pag-hahanapbuhay at pagpapalakad

Protocol 1] ceremonia at etiketa na sinusunod ng mga *diplomats* at pinuno ng bayan, 2] isang sinusunod na pamaraan para sa tama at mahusay na sistema, 3] paraan para sa pagpagaling sa sakit o paggawa ng experimento sa siencia

Waylay hintayin o antabayanan para mang-atake-*Sp* sa walang kamuang-muang na mga victima-*Sp*; harangin para hadlangan o salakayin

Wayward tinatalikuran ang tama, wasto at tumpak at mabuting gawain

WE tayo; Iloc: datayo

WE all tayong lahat; Iloc: datayo amin

WE both tayong dalawa; Iloc: sita nga dua

Weak mahina, lampay, lumo; Iloc: nacapsut, nacapoy
  Correlated words
  Languor mahina; Iloc: nacapsut
  Lethargic, Unenergetic matamlay, nanlalata; Iloc: agcapsut ken awan pulos ganas na
  Frail mahina, lampay, nanlulumo Iloc: nacapsut, nacapoy, lampay
  Antonym
  Strong malakas; Iloc: napigsa

Weaken humihina, nanlalambot, nanlulumo, nanlalata; Iloc: agcapcapsut, agcapcapoy, agluplupoy
  Synonym
  Emaciate mangayayat, manghina; Iloc: agkapoy, kumuttong

Weaker mas mahina; Iloc: mas nacapoy, mas nacapsot

Wealth kayamanan, yaman; Iloc: pagkabaknang, pagkarico

Wealthy mayaman, masalapi; Iloc: nabaknang, rico-*Sp*

Wean from breastfeeding ina ay iwalay ang sanggol niya sa pagsuso sa canya; Iloc: ipusing

Weapon armas-*Sp* gaya ng baril, canyon, patalim o lanseta

WEAR magsuot, magbihis, magdamit; Iloc: ag-bestido-*Sp*, agarwat, agbado, agcawes
  Antonyms
  Disrobe, Undress maghubad; Iloc: aglabos, agussob

WEAR and tear matagal na at madalas ang paggamit kaya marupok at pasira-sira

WEAR more than one hat maraming responsibilidad na pinapanagutan; maraming trabaho ang ginagampanan

Weary sa isip o sa katawan, pagod na pagod dahil sa katatrabaho, pagsisikap, *stress*, hirap at pagtitiis

Weather tiempo-*Sp*, clima-*Sp*, panahon; Iloc: panawen, tiempo, clima
Weather conditions
Pleasant weather maaliwalas; Iloc: nalinnaay
Summer *summer,* tag-init; Iloc: *summer,* tiempo ti pudot
Winter sa mga nasyon na may *winter,* ito ang tunay na pinakamalamig sa lahat na tiempo sa isang taon dahil may *snow*
Sunny maaraw; Iloc: naranyag ti init
Rainy maulan; Iloc: agkaratudo
Stormy bumabagyo; Iloc: agbagbagyo
Drizzle, Shower ambon; Iloc: arbis
Windy mahangin; Iloc: naangin
Foggy mahamog; Iloc: nalinnaaw
Cloudy, Overcast maulap, kulimlim; Iloc: naulep, nalidem
Weave maghabi; Iloc: agabel
Web, spider bahay-gagamba; Iloc: saput
Website lugar-*Sp* sa *internet* na ang namamahala ay isang tao o grupo-*Sp* o organisasyon-*Sp* na may *homepage* at puedeng pagkuhanan ng informasyon-*Sp* o ng servicio; Iloc: lugar-*Sp* idiay *internet* nga ti mangigaway ket maysa a tao o grupo o organisasyon nga adda *homepage* na ken pangalaan ti informasyon-*Sp* ken iti servicio-*Sp*
Wed magpakasal; Iloc: agcasar
WEDDING casal; Iloc: casar-*Sp*
WEDDING sponsors *(Tag. & Iloc.)* madrina-*Sp* (female), padrino-*Sp* (male)
Wedge, in or through a ipilit na dumaan sa makipot o makitid na daan
Wednesday *(Tag. & Iloc.) Wednesday,* Miercoles-*Sp*
Wee munti; Iloc: balabattit
Week linggo, semana-*Sp*; Iloc: lawas, dominggo-*Sp*, semana
Weekly tuwing linggo, linggo-linggo; Iloc: cada-*Sp* domingo-*Sp*, cada lawas
Weep humihikbi; Iloc: agsasaibbek, agsasainnek
Weigh timbangin; Iloc: rukoden ti dagsen
  Correlated word
  Scale *(Tab. & Iloc.)* timbangan, itimbang
WEIGHT timbang, pagkabigat; Iloc: kadagsen, kabantut
WEIGHT, light magaan; Iloc: nalag-an
WEIGHT, heavy mabigat; Iloc: nadagsen, nabantut

Weird kakaiba kaysa caraniwan ang ichura at asal na puedeng nakakadiri o nakakatakot; Iloc: nakasab-sabali ngem iti cadawyan iti ichura ken garaw na nga mabalin a makaaryek wenno nakabutbuteng

Welcome tanggapin o salubongin at batiin; Iloc: sabaten ken cablaawan

Welfare kapakanan; Iloc: pagimbagan

WELL mabuti, maayos; Iloc: naimbag, nasayaat

WELL-being, Wellbeing kalagayang malusog, masaya at bastante-*Sp* sa mga kailangan; Iloc: condisyon nga nakaradkad, naragsak ken bastante cadagiti kasapulan

WELL-heeled mayaman, macuarta

WELL-made *(Tag. & Iloc.)* pulido-*Sp*

WELL-off, Well-do-do mayaman, macuarta

WELL-rounded pagkakaroon ng sari-sari at kanais-nais at kasiya-siyang mga abilidad-*Sp*

Wellness malusog sa katawan at sa isip dahil sa pag-aalaga ng husto dito; pagbibigay-diin ng *health care* para maiwasan ang sakit at lalong tatagal ang buhay

Welt marka-*Sp* ng palo-*Sp*; Iloc: marka iti baut wenno iti bugbog

West *west,* kanluran; Iloc: *west,* laud

WET *adj.,* basa; Iloc: nabasa

WET *v.,* basahin; Iloc: basaen

WET, soaking basang-basa; Iloc: nakabasbasa

WHACK 1] paloin na may parang palakpak na tunog; 2] parte ng buo o kabahagi

WHACK, out of sira o hindi gumagana o <u>wala</u> sa *alignment* o pagka-kahanay o hilera; hindi tama ang kalagayan o hindi balanse-*Sp*

WHACK with a bat or club hambalosin; Iloc: pang-oren

Whale *(Tag. & Iloc.)* balyena-*Sp*

Wharf *pier,* muelye-*Sp,* pagdaongan ng sasakyang pandagat; Iloc: *pier,* muelye, pagsangladan dagiti pangtaaw a lugan

WHAT ano; Iloc: ania, ana

"WHAT can I do for you?" "Ano ang maitulong ko sa inyo?" Iloc: "Ania ti maitulong ko cadacayo"

"WHAT else is new", "So what else is new" hindi bago ito dahil nang-yayari nang madalas ito at kagawiang gawain niya/nila ito

"WHAT is your name?" "Ano ang pangalan mo?" Iloc: "Ania ti nagan mo?"

Whatchamacallit cuan, yong ano/cuan; Iloc: tay cua

Whatever ano man, kahit ano; Iloc: uray ania

Whatever you sow, you'll reap now or in the future anomang tinanim o ginagawa mo sa buhay, mabuti o masama, ay siyang babalik sa iyo o aanihin

Wheel gulong; Iloc: pilid

Wheeze, Wheezy paghinga na may huni at may kahirapang huminga pa

WHEN kelan, kailan, nang; Iloc: caano, inton caano, idi

WHEN, If kung; Iloc: nu

WHEN in Rome, do as the Romans do kapag nasa ibang lugar ka, tularan mo ang canilang kilos para hindi ka magmukhang asiwa o kakatwa doon, pero kung hindi mo alam ang gawi nila, basta sumunod ka lamang sa mabuti at makabatas na asal

Whenever kapag, kahit kelan, kung...; Iloc: uray nu caano, nu...

WHERE saan, nasaan; Iloc: inchenna, sadino a lugar

WHERE, from taga saan; Iloc: taga-ano

Whereabouts saan man ang kinaroroonan; Iloc: inchenna man iti ayan na

Wherever kahit saan; Iloc: uray inchenna

Whether maski ano, kahit ano; Iloc: uray ania

Which alin; Iloc: ania cadagita, sinno canyada

Whichever alinman, kahit alinman; Iloc: uray nu ania cadacuada

WHILE nang, habang, samantala; Iloc: mientras-*Sp*, bayat

WHILE ago, a kanina, kanina lamang; Iloc: itay, itay laeng

Whim *(Tag. & Iloc.)* capricho-*Sp*

Whine, Whimper umaangal; Iloc: agan-aneng-eng

Synonym

    Grumble nagmamaktol, bumubulong-bulong; Iloc: agtantanabutob, agdaydayamudom

WHIP 1] latigohin, haplitan, hampasin; 2] magbati gaya ng itlog; Iloc: 1] i-latigo-*Sp*, saplitan, ablatan, basnotan; 2] agbati ti itlog

WHIP the buttocks paloin (palo-*Sp*); Iloc: bauten

WHIP up 1] dali-daling magsagawa o mag-plano-*Sp*; dali-daling magluto o maghalo-halo ng recado; 2] mag-udyok, magsulsol, magbuyo

Whirl umiikot; Iloc: agpusipos, agtayyek

Whirlpool alipuyong tubig sa dagat, alipuyong tubig sa banyo-*Sp*; Iloc: ipo-ipo iti taaw; ipo-ipo idiay banyo

Whirlwind buhawi, ipo-ipo, alimpuyo; Iloc: alipugpog

Whisper ibulong; Iloc: iyarasaas

WHISTLE sumipol; Iloc: agsagawisiw

WHISTLE (instrument) *(Tag. & Iloc.)* pito, silbato-*Sp*

WHISTLE-blower nagsusumbong; Iloc: agipulpulong, agipungpungpong

WHISTLE with fingers into mouth to call someone magsipol; Iloc: agsultip

Whit katiting, malinggit; Iloc: battit, balabattit

White puti, *white*; Iloc: puraw, *white*

Whitewash 1] *whitewash* na pangpaputi ng dinding at mga kahoy; 2] panlinlang na salita o kilos para maitago o mangpalusot sa kanilang kasalanan at masasamang gawain o para makakalag o mapawalang-sala sila; 3] *Sports*: talonin ang ka-competensia-*Sp* para hindi makatamo ng *score*

Whiz-kid batang matalino at *successful*/matagumpay o maunlad at puede pang *influential* o nakakahimok at nakakapaghikayat

WHO sino; Iloc: sinno

WHO are you? Sino po kayo?, Sino po sila?; Iloc: Sinno kayo?

Whoever kahit sino, sinoman; Iloc: uray sinno, uray siasino man

WHOLE buo, lahat, lahat-lahat, todo-todo; Iloc: amin-amin, entero, todo-todo

Correlated words

Entire *adj.*, **Entirety** *n.* entero, lahat; Iloc: entero, am-amin

Complete completo, buo; Iloc: completo

Intact buo, buong-buo, completo lahat; Iloc: sibubukel nga entero, adda amin a parte, completo amin

WHOLE 9 yards buo, lahat, lahat-lahat, entero-*Sp*, todo-todo; Iloc: amin-amin, entero, todo-todo

WHOLE, become magbuo; Iloc: agbukel

WHOLE-hearted buong-puso sa isip at damdamin; Iloc: naggapu ti puso, ricna ken nakem

WHOLE shebang *(see Whole 9 yards above)*

Wholesale pakyaw, maramihang bili para i-venta-*Sp*

Wholesome 1] decente, 2] nakakabigay buti; Iloc: 1] decente, 2] makasayaat

Whom kanino; Iloc: akinkukua

Whop 1] malakas na bugbog, hampas, pukpok o palo-*Sp*; mabigat na bagsak; 2] golpe-*Sp* na paghaltak, bunot, hila o dukot

Whopping sobrang-sobra, labis-labis, napakadami, napakalaki

Whore *(Tag. & Iloc.)* *prostitute*, puta-*Sp*

Whose kanino, sino ang nagmemay-ari; Iloc: makinkukua, akinkukua

Whosoever kahit sino, sino man; Iloc: sinno man

Why bakit; Iloc: apay

Wick micha-*aSp*; Iloc: mecha-*Sp*

Wicked napakalupit, napakasama, walang puso, ang tigas ng puso, napa-kalaswa, nakaririmarim, karumaldumal; Iloc: nakauy-uyong, manag-basbasol, nakadakdakes, nakaul-ulpit, nakamad-madi

Wide malapad, malawak; Iloc: nalawa, naacaba
Antonym
   Narrow makipot, makitid; Iloc: akikid

Widen laparan, palawakin, paluwangin; Iloc: lawaan, i-acaba

Widespread laganap, calat; Iloc: naiwaras ti adu a lugar, nakawaras

Widow *(Tag. & Iloc.)* balo, viuda-*Sp*

Widower *(Tag. & Iloc.)* balo, viudo-*Sp*

Width, Breadth kalaparan, kaluwangan, lawak; Iloc: kaacaba, lawa

Wife asawang babae; Iloc: asawa nga babai

Wig *(Tag. & Iloc.)* peluca-*Sp*

Wild simaron, salbahe, mabangis; Iloc: simaron, nauyong, naranggas

Wilderness kakahuyan, kagubatan, gubat; Iloc: kasikalan, bakir, kakaywan

Will kagustuhan, kalooban; Iloc: kagustoan

Willing sang-ayon, pumapayag; Iloc: agmayat, agayon, cayat na

Wilt malanta, matuyo; Iloc: malaylay, agango

Win, Triumph magwagi, manalo, magtagumpay; Iloc: agballigi, ma-ngabak, mangatiw
   In order for a learner to NOT be confused, here are the differences of Win or Won, and Lose/Be defeated or Lost/Defeated that unfortunately both use the same words although not in the same form.
   Win: *daigin, talonin; Iloc: abaken, atiwen*
   Lose: *madaig, matalo; Iloc: maabak, maatiw*
   Won: *dinaig, tinalo; Iloc: inabak, nangabak, inatiw*
   Lost: *nadaig, natalo; Iloc: naabak, naatiw*

Conquer, Overpower supilin, sugpoin; Iloc: parmeken

Surpass, Outdo higitan, daigin; Iloc: maartapan, malabsan, atiwen

Wince mapakislot o matigtig; Iloc: agcumpes o maaryek o mapatigerger

WIND hangin; Iloc: angin

Correlated words

Whirlwind buhawi, ipo-ipo, alimpuyo; Iloc: alipugpog

Gale malakas na hangin na ang bilis ay puedeng 32-63 mph

Gust, Gusty biglang malakas na pagsugod ng hangin o ulan o usok; Iloc: golpe nga pagsangpet iti napigsa nga tayab ti angin wenno asok

WIND gust hihip o unos ng hangin; Iloc: puyot ti angin

Winder *(Tag. & Iloc.)* cuerdas-*Sp*, roscas-*Sp*

Windfall tiba-tiba dahil nagkaroon ng bigla at hindi inaasahang suerte-*Sp* o dating ng maraming pera; Iloc: suerte gapu ta naaddaan iti haan nga in-expectar-*Sp* nga gracia-*Sp* a cuarta

WINDOW durungawan, vintana-*Sp*; Iloc: ventana-*Sp*, tawa

WINDOW cabinet for chinaware/plates *(Tag. & Iloc.)* banggera

WINDOW sill *(Tag. & Iloc.)* pasamano-*Sp*

Windpipe lalamunan, lalagukan; Iloc: carabucob

Windy mahangin; Iloc: naangin

Wine alak; Iloc: arak, basi

WING, Wings pakpak ng ibon o ng eroplano; Iloc: payak

WING it magsagawa kahit walang sapat na preparasyon o wala siyang karanasan sa pagsagawa nito

Wink kindat, kurap; Iloc: kidday, kirem

Winner ang panalo; Iloc: ti nangabak

Winnings pinanalunan; Iloc: pinangabakan

Winnow magtahip; Iloc: agtar-ap

Winnowing basket bilao; Iloc: bigao

WIPE punasan, pahiran; Iloc: punasan, nasnasan, paidan

WIPE or clean anus linisan ang puit; Iloc: agilo, ilwan

WIPE off or rub off dirt on shoe sole on the floormat ikuskos; Iloc: agpigad, ipulagid

Wire, barbed alambreng may pakong tinik; Iloc: alambre-*Sp* nga adda lanlansa na, barut

Wisdom ang katalasan ng pag-iisip at ng pagkilos na ginagamit ang *knowledge* o kaalaman at karunongan, *experience* o mga dinanas at napag-aralan sa buhay, *understanding* o pag-intindi, pag-unawa at pagtanto, at *discernment* o matanglaw at maliwanag na pang-aninaw na biyaya buhat sa Panginoong Dios; mataas at matalas na katalinohan, karunongan at kaalaman na may tamang paghahatol, pag-aaninaw at pag-unawa; 2] mga matalino at wastong kilos at kasabihan

Wise matalino, mautak, matalas, matinik; Iloc: nasirib, nanakem, intelihente-*Sp*

Wish mithi, gusto-*Sp*, nais, pangarap, hangad; Iloc: essem, calicagum, cayat, tarigagay, gusto

Wishy-washy kulang ang pagpapasya, walang lakas at determinasyon-*Sp* kaya nagdadalawang-isip

Wit intelihenteng pagmamanman, matalas na pandama, mapaghanap ng mga pamaraan (*resourceful*) at mahusay na manlikha; matalas at matalinong pag-iisip at pandama na pinapahayag para makapagpasaya

Witch bruha-*Sp*, mangkuculam, aswang; Iloc: bruha, mannamay

Witchcraft, pagculam; Iloc: pagtamay

WITH contodo-*Sp*, kasama, de-*Sp* (i.e., de armas); Iloc: contodo, caddua, de

WITH flying colors buo at nagniningning na tagumpay

WITH strings attached puedeng gagawin o pagbigyan basta sa isa na condisyon-*Sp* at obligasyon-*Sp;* alinsunod sa compromiso-*Sp*

WITHDRAW from (i.e. a case, an agreement) bawiin o i-urong ang kasundoan o ang caso; Iloc: ibabawi ti caso wenno ti pinagtulagan

WITHDRAW money maglabas o mag-*withdraw* ng pera sa banko; Iloc: mangiruar ti cuarta diay banko

Wither malanta, matuyo; Iloc: malaylay, agango

Withhold 1] ibawas sa sweldo-*Sp* o sa *account* sa banko-*Sp*; 2] ihinto ang pamimigay; Iloc: 1] ikkatan idiay sueldo wenno diay *account* diay banko, 2] isardeng ti pagited

WITHIN (place) sa loob; Iloc: diay uneg

WITHIN (a certain time) sa loob ng..isang lingo..isang buwan.. dalawang taon; Iloc: iti uneg iti..makadomingo…makabulan... makatawen

Without wala, sin-*Sp*, ni-*Sp*; Iloc: awan, sin, ni

Withstand tiisin; Iloc: anosan, iturtured, ibturan

Witness magsaksi, nakasaksi, mag-testigo-*Sp*, nakakita; Iloc: agsaksi, nakasaksi, agtestigo, nakakita

Wobbly umuuga-uga, gumagalaw-galaw, nagyuyogyog; Iloc: aggaraw-garaw, aggunay-gunay, agyogyogyog
Antonyms
Stable, Securely installed naka-puesto ng mahusay, nakatayong matatag; Iloc: napigsa ti tacder ta nakaplastar nga nalaeng

Woe pagdurusa, pighati, aba, kapos-palad; Iloc: sagaba, rigrigat, daksang-gasat

Woke 1] *past tense* ng *wake*; 2] inaabangan o inaantabayanan ang mga balita tungkol sa gawaing hindi makabatas o makatarungan at pagmemenos sa kapwa

Wolf in sheep's clothing mukhang mabait na tao o mabuting bagay pero balatkayo lamang at ang katotohanan ay siya o ito ay masama

WOMAN babae na nakaabut ng veinte-uno-*Sp* anyos-*Sp* sa edad-*Sp* o mahigit pa diyan; Iloc: babai a nakaabut ti veinte-uno anyos nga edad o mas labes pay dita

WOMAN in addressing her with respect ginang, ate, tiya-*Sp*, tita-*Sp*; Iloc: manang, tiya, tita, nana

WOMAN, single dalaga; Iloc: balasang

Womanhood kababaihang di na bata; Iloc: babbabai nga nataenganen

Womanizer *(Tag. & Iloc.)* lalaking palikero, babaero

Womb sinapupunan, matris-*Sp*, bahay-bata; Iloc: matris

Wonder magtaka; Iloc: siddaaw, agsiddaaw, masdaaw

Wonderful kahanga-hanga; Iloc: nakadaydayaw

Wont costumbre-*Sp*, bihasa, kaugalian, gawi, gawain; Iloc: costumbre, kanayon nga aramid

Woo ligawan; Iloc: armen, agarem

WOOD kahoy; Iloc: kayo

WOOD, insect-eaten *(Tag. & Iloc.)* bukbok

WOODEN yari sa kahoy; Iloc: naaramid ti kayo

WOODEN board, Plywood *(Tag. & Iloc.)* tabla

WOODEN clogs, Filipino *(Tag. & Iloc.)* bakya

Woods gubat, kakahoyan, kagubatan; Iloc: kakaywan, bakir

Wool lana-*Sp*; Iloc: lana, franela-*Sp*

Woolen blanket delana-*Sp*; Iloc: delana, franela-*Sp*, burburan nga ules

WORD salita; Iloc: sarita

WORD of honor binibigyang dangal ang pinangako, tinutupad ang sinabi; Iloc: ikkan ti dayaw ti ingkari, agtungpal ti imbaga na o ti ingkari na

WORD of mouth ipaalam sa lahat sa pamamagitan ng pagsabi-sabi; Iloc: ipaammo ti amin nga iyusar ti pagsao-sao o pagibaga-baga a pagpadamag

WORK nag-tatrabaho-*Sp*, nagsasagawa, naglilingkod, namamasukan; Iloc: agtrabtrabaho, agob-obra-*Sp*, agar-aramid, agser-servi-*Sp*

WORK ethic *A person with work ethic has high standard of professionalism as his demeanor and work are above and beyond what is expected in the job. He/she is determined to succeed in the job; comes to work on time, ready to start his/her work shift and do the job efficiently and productively all day. He/she gets more work done because he/she organizes tasks in time ranges and accomplishes them at the end of the day. Being resourceful, he/she doesn't wait for someone else to handle work troubles, but calls for the right authority to remedy the problem. He/she updates or exchanges important job information with co-workers and foster teamwork and cooperation among them. He/she is always reliable to do the right thing in whatever task he/she handles, no matter how big or urgent those are.*

Workers mga manggagawa; Iloc: dagiti trabahador-*Sp*

Workmanship pagkakagawa; Iloc: pagkaaramid, obra-*Sp*

Workshop *(Tag. & Iloc.)* talyer-*Sp*

World mundo-*Sp*, daigdig; Iloc: mundo, lubong

Worldly *(Tag. & Iloc.)* maka-mundo-*Sp*

Worldwide 1] *worldwide*, pandaigdig; 2] laganap sa buong mundo-*Sp*; Iloc: 1] *worldwide*, para ti entero-*Sp* mundo, 2] nakawaras ti entero mundo-*Sp*

Correlated words

National *(Tag. & Iloc.)* pambansa

International *international,* tungkol sa dalawa o mahigit pa sa dalawa na nasyon

WORN, Used gamit na, segunda-*Sp* mano-*Sp*; Iloc: nausaren, segunda- mano

WORN OUT (person) pagod na pagod, nanlulupaypay; Iloc: nabambannog, lupoy

WORN OUT (thing) pudpod na, gasgasado, gastado; Iloc: rutrot, rutay-rutay, gorudgod, gasgasado

Worse mas masama, mas malala, masahol; Iloc: mas dakes, napalpalalo

Worsen sumasama, lumalala, gumagrabe; Iloc: kumarkaro aggrab-grabe-*Sp*, dumakdakes

Worship minamahal tayo ng Dios kahit tayo ay makasalanan, kaya magpasalamat tayo sa Canya, magsamba tayo sa Panginoong Dios, magdasal, magsampalataya, magpuri, maghanga, ipagbunyi at parangalan Siya, pasalamatan at tingalain natin Siya dahil sa pagkabanal Niya at pagkapuno ng gloria at gracia, at bigyang halaga ang Canyang banal na salita, ang Biblia, sa pamamagitan ng pagbabasa nito para malaman natin ang mga bilin ng Panginoong Dios at magkatutuo sa buhay natin ang mga magagandang pangako ng Dios.

Correlated words

Faith pananampalataya, paniniwala pananalig, paniniwala sa Dios; Iloc: pammati ken fiar kenni Apo Dios

Pray magdasal, magdalangin; Iloc: agcararag, aglualo

Glorify purihin, sambahin, luwalhatian ang Panginoong Dios; Iloc: dayawen, iglorificar, isagrado ni Apo Dios

Attend church services isa sa *10 Commandments* ay ang pagtuturing ng araw ng *Sabath* na araw ng pagsamba sa Dios caya magsimba at sambahin ang Dios sa araw ng linggo, pero huwag kalimutang sambahin pa rin ang Panginoong Dios sa ibang araw o sa araw-araw maliban pa sa linggo

Exalt bigyan ng mataas na pagpupuri at pagdangal sa pamamagitan ng pagsamba sa Dios; Iloc: iglorificar ken mangted ti nangato a pagyamyaman ken pagdayaw kenni Apo Dios

Praise purihin, iluwalhati, sambahin, ipagbunyi, parangalan, hangaan ang Dios; Iloc: daydayawen, agyaman, iglorificar ni Apo Dios

Fervent *v.,* **Fervor** *n.* marubdob na pagmamahal o pagsamba; Iloc: napasnek nga ayat o pangdayaw kenni Apo Dios

Bible-reading kusang basahin ang banal na salita ng Panginoong Dios, ang Biblia, para sundin ang Canyang mga payo at bilin, at malaman ang mga magagandang pangangaral at pangako Niya sa bawat nilalang

Bible Study Group sumali sa grupo na nag-aaral ng banal na salita ng Dios, ang Biblia, at makihalobilo sa kapwa Cristiano para lumakas ang pagsasamba sa Dios at pagpapatuloy na mabuhay na maka-Dios

Prayer Meetings sumali sa grupo sa pagdadasal nila sa Panginoong Dios sa mga hinihiling nilang tulong, pagpapala at bendisyon sa bawat isa sa grupo

Esteem estimahin, hangaan ang Dios; Iloc: estimaren, dayawen

Worst pinakamasama, pinakamalala, pinakamasahol; Iloc: pinakadakes, kadaksan iti amin

Antonym

Best pinakamabuti, pinakamagaling, pinakamahusay, pinakamatalino, pinakamabait; Iloc: kangatwan ti sayaat ken imbag, kalaengan, kasayaatan, kaimbagan ti amin

WORTH halaga, cabulohan, saysay; Iloc: pateg, valor-*Sp*

WORTH a shot makabulohang subokan dahil may kahalagahan at makakabigay ng buti o unlad

Worthless walang cuenta-*Sp*, walang silbi; Iloc: awan cuenta, awan servi-*Sp*

Worthwhile may pakinabang; Iloc: adda ventahe-*Sp* na

Worthy karapat-dapat, nararapat; Iloc: umno, rebbeng

Would have kung sana; Iloc: nu cuma

WOUND sugat, galos; Iloc: dunor, sugat

WOUND heals naghihilom; Iloc: aglaengen

WRAP balotin; Iloc: bungonen, balkoten

WRAP-around cloth or cape *(Tag. & Iloc.)* balabal

Wrapper pambalut; Iloc: pangbungon

Wrapping bandage benda-*Sp*, gaza-*Sp*; Iloc: benda, bedbed

Wraps, under itago o ilihim muna hanggang kailangan o napapanahon nang ilabas o ibunyag

Wreck wasakin, lansagin, sirain; Iloc: dadaelen, i-perdi-*aSp*

Correlated word

Demolish gibain, guhoin; Iloc: rakraken, rebbaen

Wrestle magbunohan; Iloc: aggabbo

Wretched kahabag-habag, pinakamababa, pinadisgusto; Iloc: kakaasi, pinakamababa, pinakamakadisgusto

Wriggle 1] kilos ng uod o ahas; 2] mamilipit o mag-alumpihig para makalabas o makalusot sa makitid na lugar-*Sp*

WRING pilipitin; Iloc: tiritiren

WRING out water from cloth pigain; Iloc: pekkelen

Wrinkle culubot, lucot, cunot; Iloc: curibetbet

Wrist galang-galangan; Iloc: pungo-pungoan

Writ kasulatan kung ano ang mga kautosan o mga iwasang gawin

Write magsulat; Iloc: agsurat

Writer *writer,* manunulat, *author*; Iloc: *writer,* nangsurat, mannurat, *author*

Written nakasulat; Iloc: nakasurat

Writhe mamilipit; Iloc: agtirtiritir

Wrong mali, falso-*Sp*, hindi husto-*Sp*; Iloc: haan agpayso, falso, haan nga usto

Wrongdoing masamang gawa, kasalanan; Iloc: dakes nga aramid, basol, biddut

Wrought 1] nagawa o naforma sa pamamagitan ng pukpok ng martilyo gaya ng sa *iron* (bakal) o *silver* (plata-*Sp,* pilak); 2] napagayak, napaganda, hindi magaspang

X

Xray *(Tag. & Iloc.) xray*

XYLOPHONE *(Tag. & Iloc.) xylophone*

XYLOPHONE (native, moro) *(Tag. & Iloc.)* kulintang

Y

Yacht *(Tag. & Iloc.) yacht,* yate-*Sp*

Yam *(Tag. & Iloc.)* tugi

Yank haltakin, hatakin, batakin; Iloc: fuersa-*Sp* a guyoden, pag-uten

YARD bakuran; Iloc: likod wenno sangwanan ti balay nga daga

YARD (measurement) *(Tag. & Iloc.)* yarda-*Sp*

Yawn maghikab; Iloc: agsuyaab

Year taon; Iloc: tawen

Yearly taonan, taon-taon, tuwing taon; Iloc: tinawen, cada tawen

Yearlong buong taon, santaonan; Iloc: makatawen

Yearn nananabik, nag-aasam; Iloc: aggaggagar, agcarayo, agpapaos, agil-iliw

Yeast *(Tag. & Iloc.)* amag

Yell magsigaw, maghiyaw, magbulyaw; Iloc: agriaw, agbugkaw, agpukkaw

Yellow dilaw, *yellow*; Iloc: amarilyo-*Sp, yellow*

Yen 1] *aluminum* na centimong pera ng Japan; 2] labis-labis na pananabik, mithi o hangarin

YES oo; Iloc: wen

"YES sir/madam" "Opo," "Oho;" Iloc: "Wen apo"

Yesterday kahapon; Iloc: idi calman

YET ngayon sa kasalukuyan; bago matapos, may panahon pa; pareho pa rin; ulit; kahit pa ganyan; Iloc: itatta, baro malpas, uray pay casta

YET, Still pa, pa rin; Iloc: pay, pay laeng

YIELD, Crop ani; Iloc: apit

YIELD, Submit sumuco, magpasailalim, ipagparaya, magpacumbaba; Iloc: agsuco, magpacumbaba

Yippee! or Yay! bulalas o hiyaw ng kasiyahan, tuwa at pagkaganado

Yogurt or Yoghurt pagkain na may gatas at iba pang lasa gaya ng pampatamis o frutas

Yoke pingga o yugo-*Sp* na may balde-*Sp* sa magkabilang dulo na binubuhat sa balikat ng tao kapag umigib ng tubig; kinakabit sa balikat ng calabaw ito sa pag-aararo; simbolo-*Sp* ng pang-aapi

Yolk pulang parte ng itlog; Iloc: nalabbaga a parte ti itlog

Yon, Yonder iyong lugar-*Sp* na iyon; nandodoon

Yore nakalipas na panahon; Iloc: nagpasar a panawenen

YOU-*singular* ikaw, ka; Iloc: sica, ka

YOU-*plural* kayo; Iloc: dacayo

YOU, to, On you, Through you-*singular* sa iyo; Iloc: kenca

YOU, to, On you, Through you-*plural* sa inyo; Iloc: kadacayo

Young menor de edad-*Sp*, bata; Iloc: menor de edad

YOU only-*singular* ikaw lamang; Iloc: siksica

YOU only-*plural* kayo lamang; Iloc: dakdacayo

"YOU are welcome!" "Walang anuman"; Iloc: "Awan aniaman na"

"YOU bet!" *(Tag. & Iloc.)* "Tama!", "Tutoo!", "Siempre!"

YOUNG bata; Iloc: ubing

YOUNGER mas bata; Iloc: mas ubing

YOUNGER sibling mas batang kapatid; Iloc: adi, ading

Youngest pinakabata, bunso; Iloc: kaubingan, buridek, inaudi

Youngster bata; Iloc: ubing

YOUR, YOURS-*singular* iyo, mo; Iloc: cuam, cukuam, bagim

YOUR, YOURS-*plural* inyo, ninyo; Iloc: cuayo, cukuayo

Yourself ikaw mismo-*Sp*; Iloc: sica mismo

YOUTH kabataan, menor-de-edad-*Sp*; Iloc: pagkaubbing, menor-de-edad

YOUTH counseling ang unang-unang paghingan ng payo ay ang magulang dahil sila ang may pinakamalaki na pagmamalasakit sa anak pero kung kinakailangan pa ang dagdag na payo o kaya mayroong pag-aalangang magsabi ng problema sa magulang at hindi caya ng anak na lutasing mag-isa ito, mayroong lugar na pagtatakbuhan ng mga kabataan o menor-de-edad o mga *teen-agers* para makakuha sila ng tulong o payo – magtanong-tanong lamang sa *safe* o ligtas na lugar o mga tao gaya sa escuela o sa gobierno o sa simbahan

YOUTH's endearing names from elders *(Tag. & Iloc.) (boy or gir)* anak, *(girl)* Nene, Neneng, *(boy)* iho-*Sp*, *(girl)* iha-*Sp*

Youthful mukhang bata; Iloc: ubing ti ichura-*Sp*

YUCKY, Yuck *reaction* ng pagkadiri, pagkadisgusto o pagkasuklam, nakakadiri; Iloc: nakaar-aryek

YUCKY to a baby or toddler *(Tag. & Iloc.)* a-ak

Yuletide panahon ng Pasco; Iloc: panawen ti Pascua-*Sp*

Yummy napakasarap, napakamainam ang lasa; Iloc: naimas unay

Z

Zap 1] patayin o barilin, bombahin ng may electricidad-*Sp* na pampatay; hampasin ng golpe-*Sp* at mafuersa; 2] kumilos ng napakabilis o napakarahas o nakakapanira; 3] lutoin sa *microwave*

Zeal maalab at masigasig na interes-*Sp* para sa isang tao o layonin o bagay; ganadong-ganadong pagsisikap at pagsasagawa; Iloc: gagar, regget

Zealot *(Tag. & Iloc.)* taong may *zeal*; fanatico-*Sp*

ZERO *(Tag. & Iloc.) zero*

ZERO in on... ipuntirya ang pansin sa...

Zest *(Tag. & Iloc.)* pagka-gusto-*Sp*, interesado-*Sp*

Zigzag *zigzag,* matatalas at magkakalapit na curva-*Sp* o paikot-ikot na daan o linya-*Sp*

Zika virus sakit galing sa kagat ng lamok at kapag buntis ang nakagat, pati ang sanggol sa sinapupunan niya ay mahawa kung saan naaafectohan ang utak ng bata at iba pang *birth defect*

Zilch, Zero walang-wala

Zine or 'Zine *[pronounced Zin]* palihim na *magazine* na mumurahin ang paggawa

Zipper *(Tag. & Iloc.)* *zipper*

Zone *(Tag. & Iloc.)* *zone,* zona-*Sp*

Zoo *(Tag. & Iloc.)* *zoo*

Zoology *(Tag. & Iloc.)* *zoology*

TAGALOG AND ILOCANO ROOT WORDS

(To be used with Tagalog and Ilocano Affixes found in both
the Tagalog Grammar and the Ilocano Grammar)

A

ABANDON lisan, layas; Iloc: bay-an, talaw, panaw

ABLE caya; Iloc: balin, caya, bael

ABOVE taas; Iloc: ngato

ABUSE *(Tag. & Iloc.)* abuso-*Sp*, maltrao-*Sp*

ACCELERATE bilis, dali, paspas; Iloc: paspas, pardas, partak, daras

ACCEPT tanggap; Iloc: akceptar-*Sp*

ACCOMPANY sama, hatid; Iloc: cadwa, cuyog, tulod, tulnog

ACCOMPLISH yari, tupad, tapos; Iloc: turpos, aramid, leppas

ACCUMULATE ibak, ipon; Iloc: urnong

ACCUSE bintang, ratang; Iloc: acusar-*Sp*, basol, rurumen

ACCUSTOM gawi, bihasa; Iloc: ruam

ACHE sakit, kirot, hapdi; Iloc: sakit, ut-ot, apges, sanaang

ACHIEVE tamo, kamit; Iloc: gun-od

ACQUIRE angkin; Iloc: gun-od

ADD dagdag; Iloc: nayon

ADORE mahal, ibig; Iloc: ayat, dungngo

ADVANCE sulong, avante-*Sp*; Iloc: avante

ADVISE payo, mungkahi; bagbaga

AFFECTIONATE lambing, carinyo-*Sp*; Iloc: dungngo, lailo, carinyo

AFRAID takot; Iloc: buteng

AGAIN muli, ulit; Iloc: manen

AGREE payag, sang-ayon; Iloc: ayon, annugot

ALARM balisa; Iloc: danag

ALIBI, EXCUSE dahilan; Iloc: pambar

ALIGHT ibis, baba; Iloc: dissaag, baba

ALLEVIATE hango; Iloc: lag-an, bang-ar

ALLOCATE bahagi, laan; Iloc: lak-am, lasin, bingay

ALLOW hintulot, payag; Iloc: palubos

ALTERNATE halili, relyevo-*Sp*; Iloc: sublat, relyevo

ALWAYS tuwina, firme-*Sp*, panay, lagi; Iloc: pasig, firme

AMUSE libang, aliw; Iloc: lingay, liwliwa

ANALYZE usig, suri; Iloc: sukimat, sukisok

ANGER galit, poot; Iloc: pungtot, rungsot

ANTAGONIZE inis, galit; Iloc: rurod

ANTICIPATE asa, abang; Iloc: uray, sirpat, segga

ANXIOUS bagabag; Iloc: ringgor

APOLOGY umanhin; Iloc: dispensar-*Sp*

APPARENT lantad, litaw, kita; Iloc: parang, kita

APPEAL samo; Iloc: kiddaw

APPEAR litaw, kita; Iloc: parang, kita

APPLAUD *(Tag. & Iloc.)* palakpak

APPOINT hirang, takda; Iloc: designar-*Sp*

APPORTION hati, bukod-bukod; Iloc: bingay-bingay

APPRECIATE lugod; Iloc: apreciar -*Sp*

APPROVE aprova-*Sp*; Iloc: aprovar-*Sp*

ARDENT rubdob; Iloc: pasnek, nasged

ARISE *(Tag. & Iloc.)* bangon

ARRANGE *(Tag. & Iloc.)* areglo-*Sp*

ARRIVE dating; Iloc: sangpet, daton

ASCEND akyat; Iloc: uli, sang-at

ASHAME hiya; Iloc: bain

ASK tanong; Iloc: saludsod, damag

ASSEMBLE pulong, ipon; Iloc: tipon, ummong

ASSUME palagay; Iloc: patta-patta

ASTONISH, ASTOUND mangha; Iloc: masdaaw

ATTACH cabit, dugtong, conecta-*Sp*; Iloc: capet, silpo, conecta

ATTAIN tamo, camit; Iloc: gun-od

ATTEND dalo, sipot; Iloc: atender-*Sp*

ATTRACT akit, halina; Iloc: awis, rayo

ATTRIBUTE igawad; Iloc: saad

AVENGE ganti; Iloc: bales

AVOID iwas; Iloc: lisi

B

BACK OFF atras, urong; Iloc: atras, sanud

BACK, TURN ONE'S talikod; Iloc: tallikod

BAD sama, sagwa; Iloc: madi, alas

BEAT EGGS bati; Iloc: batil

BEAUTIFUL ganda, rikit, rilag; Iloc: pintas, libnos

BEG hingi, hiling, limos; Iloc: kiddaw, palama, limos

BEGIN umpisa; Iloc: rugi

BEHAVE asal; Iloc: tignay

BEHOLDEN tingala; Iloc: tangad

BELIEVE niwala; Iloc: mati

BELOVED irog, giliw, mahal, sinta; Iloc: ayat

BEND yuko; Iloc: sucog

BIG laki; Iloc: dakkel

BITE cagat; Iloc: cagat, kitteb, curib

BITTER *(Tag. & Iloc.)* pait

BLAME bintang, ratang, sisi; Iloc: babalaw, pabasol

BLAND TASTE tabang; Iloc: lab-ay

BLAST, BLOW OUT sabog; Iloc: bettak

BLEND BY MIXING halo; Iloc: kiwar

BLESS basbas, palain, biyaya; Iloc: bendisyon-*Sp*

BLINK kurap; Iloc: kirem

BLOCK harang; Iloc: barra

BLOW OUT THE MUCUS singa; Iloc: pangres

BLUNT purol; Iloc: mudil

BLURRED labo; Iloc: cudrep

BOIL culo; Iloc: burek

BOLDNESS tapang; Iloc: tured

BORE, MAKE A HOLE butas; Iloc: abut

BORN silang, luwal; Iloc: pasngay, anak

BORROW hiram; Iloc: bulod

BOUNCE *(Tag. & Iloc.)* talbog

BOW yuko, tungo, saludo-*Sp*; Iloc: dumog, saludo

BRAG yabang; Iloc: parayag

BREAK, SMASH basag; Iloc: buong

BREAK, SPLIT bali, putol, patid, biyak, lagut; Iloc: pugsat, pugsot, tukkol

BREATHE hinga; Iloc: anges

BRIGHT, LIGHT liwanag, sinag, ilaw; Iloc: lawag, sillag, ranyag

BRILLIANCE sikat, kislap, sinag, ningning, kinang, kintab; Iloc: silap, sileng, sillag, ranyag

BRING dala, hatid; Iloc: iyeg, ipan, awit

BRING OUT labas; Iloc: ruar

BRITTLE lutong; Iloc: kersang

BROAD lapad, lawak; Iloc: lawa, acaba

BRUISE sugat, galos; Iloc: sugat, dunor

BUMP bundol, bunggo; Iloc: dalapus, dungpar

BUMP ONE'S HEAD umpog, untog; Iloc: tim-og

BURN sunog; Iloc: puor, uram

BURST sabog; Iloc: bettak

BURP dighay; Iloc: tig-ab

BURY libing, baon; Iloc: tabon, pumpon

BUY bili; Iloc: gatang

C

CALCULATE suma-*Sp*, cuenta-*Sp*, calcula-*Sp*; Iloc: sumar-*Sp*, calcular-*Sp*

CALL tawag; Iloc: ayab

CALM DOWN hinahon, payapa, calma-*Sp*, awat; Iloc: talna, calma, anawa

CAPSIZE taob; Iloc: balinsuek

CAPTURE dakip, aresto, bihag, huli; Iloc: tiliw, aresto-*Sp*

CARE, CARING *(Tag. & Iloc.)* malasakit

CARE FOR alaga, aruga; Iloc: taraken, aywan, awir

CAREFUL ingat; Iloc: alwad, annad

CARRY buhat, bitbit, pasan; Iloc: bagkat, bitbit, baklay

CARRY BABY ON ONE'S LAP candung; Iloc: saklut

CATCH dakip; Iloc: tiliw

CATCH SOMETHING THROWN OR FALLING salo; Iloc: sippaw

CHANGE iba, bago, palit; Iloc: baliw, sukat

CHARGE FOR PAYMENT singil; Iloc: singir

CHEAP mura; Iloc: laca

CHEW nguya; Iloc: ngalngal

CHOOSE *(Tag. & Iloc)* pili

CIRCULATE laganap; Iloc: warnak

CLEAN linis; Iloc: linis; dalus

CLEAR linaw; Iloc: lawag

CLENCH, CLUTCH capit; Iloc: capet, petpet

CLIMB akyat; Iloc: calay-at

CLING capit, dikit; Iloc: capet, dekket

CLOSE sara, pinid; Iloc: cerra-*Sp*

CLOSE BY lapit; Iloc: adani, asideg

CLOT buo; Iloc: balay

CLUTTER calat; Iloc: wara

COARSE gaspang; Iloc: kersang

COIL pulopot; Iloc: putipot, pulipol, cawicaw, cunikon

COLD lamig; Iloc: lamiis, lam-ek, lammin

COINCIDE kasabay; Iloc: giddan, rana

COLLAPSE guho, giba, buwal; Iloc: rebba, twang

COLLIDE *(Tag. & Iloc.)* bangga, bunggo

COMBINE sama; Iloc: cadwa

COME punta; Iloc: umay, apan

COME IN pasok; Iloc: serrek, uneg

COMPARE hambing; Iloc: comparar-*Sp*

COMPEL sapilit, fuersa-*Sp*; Iloc: pilit, fuersa

COMPENSATE tumbas; Iloc: tangdan

COMPLAIN angal, recklamo-*Sp*; Iloc: reclamo

COMPLY tupad, gampan; Iloc: tungpal

COMPOSED tatag; Iloc: tibker

CONSENT sang-ayon, payag; Iloc: annugot

CONCERN alala, ngamba, kaba; Iloc: danag

CONCLUDE tapos, wakas; Iloc: palpas

CONDEMN sumpa; Iloc: dadanes

CONFESS cumpisal; Iloc: confesar-*Sp*

CONFIDE tapat; Iloc: sawang

CONFIRM patutuo; Iloc: paneknek

CONFISCATE cumpisca; Iloc: confiscar-*Sp*

CONFUSE lito, ligalig, taranta, torete; Iloc: riro, taranta, torete

CONGRATULATE bati; Iloc: kablaaw

CONNECT cabit, dugtong, conecta-*Sp*; Iloc: capet, silpo, conectar-*Sp*

CONNIVE *(Tag. & Iloc.)* sabuat

CONQUER supil, lupig, sugpo; Iloc: parmek

CONSENT hintulot, payag, tulog; Iloc: palubos

CONSIST laman; Iloc: laon

CONSULT sangguni; Iloc: consulta-*Sp*

CONSUME ubos; Iloc: ibus

CONTAIN carga-*Sp*, laman; Iloc: carga, laon

CONTINUE tuloy; Iloc: tuloy, continuar-*Sp*

CONTORT ngiwi, baluktot; Iloc: diwwig, kiwing

CONTRADICT *(Tag. & Iloc.)* contra-*Sp*

CONVERSE chatchat, usap; Iloc: tungtong, chatchat

CONVEY batid, alam; Iloc: damag

COOPERATE sali; Iloc: participar-*Sp*

COPY copia-*Sp*; Iloc: copiar-*Sp*, sacar-*Sp*

CORRECT iwasto, tuwid, ayos; Iloc: correhir, linteg

COSTLY, EXPENSIVE mahal; Iloc: ngina

COUNSEL payo; Iloc: bagbaga

COUNT *(Tag. & Iloc.)* bilang

COVER takip, tapal; Iloc: calub, abbong

CRAM THINGS siksik, singit, pisa; Iloc: sedsed, selsel, siksik, pitpit

CRAVE sabik, asam, nasa; Iloc: papaos, agum

CRAWL gapang; Iloc: caradap

CREATE likha; Iloc: parsua

CRINGE kislot; Iloc: cumpes

CRISPY lutong; Iloc: sarangsang

CRITICIZE pintas; Iloc: uyaw. dillaw

CROSS THE ROAD or RIVER tawid; Iloc: ballasiw

CROUCH yukyok; Iloc: cucot

CRUEL lupit, sungit, bugnot; Iloc: ulpit, uyong, sukir, tangsit

CRUMPLE cusot; Iloc: cussot

CRUSH, CRUMBLE durog, yurak; Iloc: rumek, burak

CRY iyak, tangis; Iloc: sangit, ibit

CUDDLE yakap, yapos; Iloc: aracop, rakep

CURE lunas, gamot; Iloc: agas

CURSE sumpa; Iloc: dadanes

CURVE baluktot, curva-*Sp*; Iloc: killo, curva

CUSS mura, lait; Iloc: lais

CUT hiwa, gupit, putol, bali, bakli; Iloc: iwa, puted, gudwa, pisi, galip, guped

D

DAB pahid, tapik; Iloc: pilkat

DANGLE lawit, tiwangwang; Iloc: tiwwatiw

DARE hamon, kanchaw; Iloc: kanchaw

DARN sulsi, tagpi; Iloc: zursi-*Sp*, tagpi

DEBUNK buco, bulaan; Iloc: libak

DECEIT daya, linlang, loco-*Sp*; Iloc: loco, allilaw, gulib, cusit

DECIDE pasia, desisyon-*Sp*; Iloc: decidir-*Sp*, keddeng, decisyon-*Sp*

888

DECLUTTER, Tidy areglo-*Sp*, ligpit, ayos; Iloc: areglo, pakni, penpen, dulin

DECORATE gayak; Iloc: arcos-*aSp*

DECREASE bawas, kaunti, liit; Iloc: kissay, bassit

DEDICATE alay, handog, ukol; Iloc: paay, daton, sagot

DEEP lalim; Iloc: adalem

DEFEAT daig, talo; Iloc: abak, atiw

DEFEND tanggol, defensa-*Sp*; Iloc: salacan, defensa

DEFICIENT kulang; Iloc: kurang

DEFILE dungis; Iloc: rugit

DELAY antala, paliban, pabukas; Iloc: tantan, taktak, ladaw, baybayag

DELIBERATE sadya; Iloc: gagara

DELICIOUS sarap; Iloc: imas

DELIGHT wili; Iloc: lingay

DELIRIOUS hibang, delirio-*Sp*; Iloc: amangaw, delirio

DELIVER dala, hatid; Iloc: iyeg, ipan, awit

DEMOLISH giba, guho; Iloc: rakrak, rebba

DEMONSTRATE tanghal, kita, malas; Iloc: presentar, kita

DEMURE yumi, hinhin, kimi; Iloc: emma, kimmi

DENY tanggi, pagkaila, bulaan; Iloc: libak

DEPART alis, luwas; Iloc: panaw

DEPEND depende-*Sp*, salalay; Iloc: depende

DEPICT larawan; Iloc: retrato-*Sp*

DEPRIVE pagkait; Iloc: paidam

DESCEND panaog, baba; Iloc: mulog, baba, salog

DESENSITIZE, BENUMB pamanhid; Iloc: bibineg

DESERT takas, layas, iwan; Iloc: talaw, bay-an

DESERVE rapat, angkop; Iloc: rebbeng, umno, gunggona

DESIGNATE hirang, talaga; Iloc: designar-*Sp*

DESIRE gusto-*Sp*, nais, mithi, hangad; Iloc: gusto, essem, cayat

DESPISE lait, pintas, tuya; Iloc: lais, uyaw

DESTROY sira, wasak; Iloc: perdi-*aSp*, dadael

DETACH, PLUCK tuklap, bakbak, watak, baklas, tanggal; Iloc: lekkab, sina, ikkat, latlat

DETECT puna, pansin, halata; Iloc: sucal, ductal

DETER hadlang; Iloc: lapped

DETERIORATE rupok, hina, sama, lala, sira; Iloc: rukop, lallalo, caro, dakes, dadael

DETOUR lihis; Iloc: lisi

DEVELOP tubo, usbong, yabong, sibol, buo, laki, unlad; Iloc: tubo, rusing, saringit, dakkel, lapsat, ruay, rang-ay

DICTATE dicta-*Sp*; Iloc: dictar-*Sp*

DIRECT patnubay, turo; Iloc: paturong, suro

DIRTY dumi, rumi, dungis; Iloc: rugit, dugyot, dungrit

DISAGREE tutol, salungat; Iloc supyat

DISAPPEAR wala, laho, pawi; Iloc: awan, pukaw

DISAPPOINT bigo, buco, dismaya; Iloc: dismaya

DISASSEMBLE tanggal, hiwalay, watak; Iloc: sina, watak

DISCOVER discobre-*Sp*, tuklas; Iloc: ductal, discobre

DISCUSS usap, talakay; Iloc: patang

DISHONOR lapastang, bastos-*aSp*, mura, lait; Iloc: bastos, lais

DISLIKE ayaw; Iloc: madi

DISMISS tiwalag, cesante-*Sp*, despacha-*aSp*; Iloc: ikkat, cesante, despachar-*aSp*

DISOBEY suway, suwail; Iloc: supring, supyat

DISPARAGE hamak, cucha, mura, lait; Iloc: lais

DISPATCH sugo, padala; Iloc: baon

DISRUPT gambala, antala; Iloc: estorbo-*Sp*

DISSOLVE, Dilute *(Tag. & Iloc.)* tunaw, labnaw, lusaw

DISTRESS *(Tag. & Iloc.)* perhuisio-*Sp*

DIVE sisid, talon; Iloc batok, tapwak

DIZZY hilo; Iloc: ulaw

DO sagawa; Iloc: aramid

DODGE ilag, lihis, iwas; Iloc: lisi

DONATE abuloy; Iloc: sagot

DOUBT *(Tag. & Iloc)* duda-*Sp*, suspecha-*Sp*

DOUCHE *(Tag. & Iloc.)* pawpaw

DOUSE buhos, saboy; Iloc: suyyat, sebseb

DOWN *(Tag. & Iloc.)* baba

DRINK inom, higop; Iloc: inom, igop

DRIP tulo, daloy, tagas; Iloc: tedted, ubo

DROP hulog, laglag; Iloc: tinnag, regreg

DRY tuyo; Iloc: maga

DURABLE tibay; Iloc lagda

E

EAGER sabik; Iloc: gagar, papaos

EARN kita; Iloc: sapul

EASE, SOOTHE ginhawa; Iloc: bang-ar

EASY dali; Iloc: laka

EAT kain; Iloc: mangan

EDUCATE aral, turo; Iloc: adal, suro

ELAPSE lipas, daan; Iloc: labas, pasar-*Sp*

ELIMINATE alis, tanggal; Iloc: ikkat

EMBARRASS hiya; Iloc: bain

EMBRACE yakap, yapos, abrazo-*Sp*; Iloc: aracop, rakep, abrazo

EMERGE sulpot, litaw, sipot; Iloc: parang, lumtaw, kita

EMIT singaw, buga; Iloc: sang-aw. pugso

ENABLER, PERMISSIVE paraya, unlak, consentidor-*Sp*; Iloc: consentidor, bay-an

ENDEAVOR sikap, sigasig, pursigi, punyagi; Iloc: pakat, puspusan, karigat

ENDURE tiis; Iloc: ibtur, kired

ENJOY libang, aliw, saya, wili, tuwa; Iloc: rambak, ragsak, papas

ENTER pasok; Iloc: serrek

ENTERTAIN aliw; Iloc: lingay, liwliwa

ENVY inggit; Iloc: apal, agum

ERR kamali, sala; Iloc: basol, biddut

ESCAPE takas; Iloc: tammeng

ESTABLISH tatag, patayo; Iloc: simpa, patacder, plastar

ESTEEM hanga, estima-*Sp*; Iloc: dayaw, estimar-*Sp*

EVIDENT lantad, litaw, halata, kita, vistado-*aSp*; Iloc: parang, kita, vistado

EXAMINE suri, usig, usisa, siyasat; Iloc: sukimat, sukisok, usig

EXASPERATE yamot, suya, consomi; Iloc: sairo, perhuisio-*Sp*, consomi

EXCHANGE palit; Iloc: sukat

EXCLAIM bulalas; Iloc: sawang

EXHALE hinga; Iloc: anges, sang-aw

EXIT labas; Iloc: ruar

EXPAND laki, lawak; Iloc: dakkel, lawa

EXPECT asa, abang; Iloc: namnama, segga

EXPECTORATE buga, luwa, ubo, dura; Iloc: pugso, tupra

EXPLAIN explica-*Sp*, liwanag; Iloc: explicar-*Sp*, lawag

EXPLOIT, EXPLORE saliksik, tahak; Iloc: sukimat, sukisok

EYES dazzled by glare silaw; Iloc: purar

F

FADE (CLOTHES) kupas; Iloc: usaw

FLATTERY *(Tag. & Iloc.)* sipsip, bola

FAIL bigo, sawi; Iloc: mintis

FAINT himatay; Iloc: talimudaw

FAIR tarungan; Iloc: linteg

FALL hulog, laglag; Iloc: tinnag, regreg

FALL OFF (HAIR, PETALS, LEAVES) lagas, calbo-*Sp*; Iloc: calbo

FAST bilis, tuling, cascas; Iloc: daras, partak, pardas, paspas

FASTEN higpit; Iloc: irut, reppet

FAT taba; Iloc: lukmeg, taba

FED-UP sawa, suya; Iloc: uma, suya

FEEL ramdam; Iloc: ricna

FEEL, TOUCH hipo; Iloc: ricna, carawa

FILL *(Tag. & Iloc.)* puno

FILTER sala; Iloc: sagat

FIND, LOCATE hanap; Iloc: birok, sapul

FINISH, WRAP UP tapos; Iloc: turpos, leppas

FIRM, STIFF tigas, ganit; Iloc: tangken, sikkil

FIRST una, primero-*Sp*; Iloc: umuna, primero

FISHY ODOR lansa; Iloc: langsi

FIT *(Tag. & Iloc.)* casya

FIT, TANTRUM sumpong; Iloc: sumro

FIT, HEALTHY lusog; Iloc: salun-at

FIX areglo-*Sp*, ayos; Iloc: areglo, urnos, tarimaan

FLAIL, SHAKE OFF pagpag; Iloc: wagwag

FLAVOR lasa; Iloc: raman

FLOAT lutang; Iloc: tumpaw

FLOG haplit, latigo-*Sp*; Iloc: saplit, ablat, basnot, latigo

FLOURISH lago; Iloc: ruay, lapsat, rang-ay

FLOW agos, daloy; Iloc: ayos, bulos

FLY lipad; Iloc: tayab

FOCUS titig, subsob; Iloc: perreng, mingming

FOLD tiklop; Iloc: cupin

FOLLOW, ABIDE tupad, sunod; Iloc: tungpal, surot

FOLLOW BEHIND buntot; Iloc: saruno

FONDLE, CARESS haplos, himas; Iloc: apros

FORBID pigil, bawal; Iloc: pagel, parit

FORCE fuersa, pilit, giit; Iloc: fuersa-*Sp*, pilit

FOREWARN babala, alerto-*Sp*; Iloc: alwad, alerto

FORGET limot, kaligta, lingat; Iloc: lipat, liway

FORGIVE patawad; Iloc: pakawan, dispensar-*Sp*

FORSAKE iwan, lisan, layas; Iloc: bay-an, talaw, panaw

FORTUNATE palad, suerte-*Sp*; Iloc: gasat, suerte

FOSTER aruga, sigla; Iloc: taraken, pigsa, lapsat

FOUND, ESTABLISH tatag, bangon, fundar-*Sp*, tayo; Iloc: simpa, bangon, fundar, puesto-*Sp*

FOUND, LOCATED tagpo, tunton, hanap; Iloc: sarak, sapul, kita, birok

FREE laya; Iloc: waya

FREE, GRATIS *(Tag. & Iloc.)* libre-*Sp*

FRISK, PAT DOWN capa, capcap; Iloc: rikisa, aricap

FRONT harap; Iloc: sango

FURY poot; Iloc: rungsot

G

GAIN gana-*Sp*, tubo; Iloc: ganancia-*Sp*, tubo

GAP puwang, patlang, pagitan; Iloc: abot; puwang, baetan

GARGLE mumog; Iloc: mulomog

GARNER tamo, angkin; Iloc: ala, kamkam

GATHER THINGS hakot; Iloc: bunag

GENERATE likha, imbento-*Sp*; Iloc: parnuay, imbento

GENTLE hinahon, amo, yumi, lumanay; Iloc: emma, amo, ulimek, talna

GET kuha; Iloc: ala

GIVE bigay, dulot, kaloob, entrega-*Sp*; Iloc: ikkan, ited, sagot, rangkap, paay, entrega

GLANCE sulyap, baling; Iloc: talyaw

GO punta; Iloc: mapan

GO ACROSS tawid; Iloc: ballasiw

GO BACKWARD atras-*Sp*, urong; Iloc: sanud, atras

GO DOWN naog, baba; Iloc: ulog, salog

GO FORWARD sulong, avante-*Sp*; Iloc: avante

GO HOME uwi; Iloc: awid

GO IN pasok; Iloc: serrek

GO NEAR lapit; Iloc: asideg, adani

GO UP panhik; Iloc: uli, sang-at

GOOD buti, husay; Iloc: imbag, sayaat, laeng

GOOD CHARACTER buti, inam, bait, husay, payapa, kasiya, consuelo-*Sp*; Iloc: nam-ay, sayaat, imbag, singpet, laeng, talna, ay-ayo, consuelo

GOVERN muno, mahala, ngasiwa, tangkilik, lakad; Iloc: gaway, turong, pagna, acecaso

GRAB dakma, sunggab; Iloc: gammat, sibbarut

GRASP hawak, higpit, capit; Iloc: capet, tenglen, petpet

GRATIFY saya, lugod; Iloc: capnek, pennek

GRIPE, GROAN maktol, ungol, bulong; Iloc: tanabutob

GROW tubo, usbong, yabong, sibol, buo, laki, unlad; Iloc: tubo, rusing, saringit, dakkel, lapsat, ruay, rang-ay

GUARD tanod, bantay, guardia-*Sp*; Iloc: bantay, guardia

GUIDE gabay, patnubay, akay; Iloc: gaway, turong, bagnos, dalan

GYRATE ikot, gulong; Iloc: pusipos, tayyek, tulatid, lico-lico

H

HABITUAL gawi, bihasa; Iloc: ruam, sigud, cadawyan

HAGGLE THE PRICE, NEGOTIATE A BARGAIN tawad; Iloc: tawar

HAIRCUT gupit; Iloc: cortar-*Sp*, pukis

HALF hati; Iloc: gudwa

HAND OVER abot, bigay, entrega-*Sp*; Iloc: yawat, ited, entrega

HANDSHAKE camay; Iloc: alamano

HANG bitin, sabit, sampay, lawit; Iloc: bitin, sallapay, sab-it

HAPPY ligaya, saya; Iloc: ragsak, rambak

HARD, DIFFICULT hirap; Iloc: rigat

HARD, FIRM tigas; Iloc: tangken

HARSH bagsik; Iloc: ranggas

HASTE apura, dali; Iloc: apura, pardas

HATE suklam, muhi, galit; Iloc: gura, busor, rurod

HEAP bunton, tambak, tabun; Iloc: bunton, gabur

HEAR rinig, ulinig; Iloc: dengngeg

HELP ayuda-*Sp*, tulong; Iloc: tulong

HESITANT atubili; Iloc: duadua

HIDE tago, cubli, lingid; Iloc: lemmeng, suksok

HIGH taas, tayog; Iloc: ngato

HOLD hawak, capit, tangan; Iloc: tengngel, iggam

HOLE butas; Iloc: butbot

HOPE asa; Iloc: namnama

HOT init, alinsangan; Iloc: pudot, salimuot, bara, dagaang

HUDDLE siksik, umpok; Iloc: siksik, ummong

HUG yakap, abrazo-*Sp*; Iloc: aracop, abrazo

HUNGRY gutom; Iloc: bisin

HUMBLE pacumbaba, amo; Iloc: pacumbaba, umilde-*Sp*

I

IDENTIFY kilala, mamukha; Iloc: bigbig, lasin

ILLUMINATE ilaw, liwanag; Iloc: silaw, lawag

IMITATE gaya, tulad, copia-*Sp*; Iloc: tulad, copiar-*Sp*

IMMERSE babad, lublob, lubog; Iloc: uper, tabnaw

IMPEDE hadlang, pigil; Iloc: lapped, gawid

IMPLICATE dawit, sangkot, damay; Iloc: raman

IMPRISON culong, bilanggo, preso-*Sp*; Iloc: culong, balud, pupok, preso, carcel-*Sp*

IMPROVE yabong, sibol, magbuo; Iloc: rang-ay

INADEQUATE kulang; Iloc: kurang

INCITE udyok, buyo; Iloc: uyot, sulisog

INCLINE tagilid; Iloc: tingig, batwag

INCLUDE sama, sali, sacop; Iloc: raman, bilang, sali

INCREASE dami, dagdag; Iloc: adu, nayon

INDICATE, DENOTE hiwatig; Iloc: paammo

INDISCERNIBLE disimulado-*Sp*, labo; Iloc: cusnaw, disimulado

INFECT hawa, sagap; Iloc: acar, alis, infectar-*Sp*

INFLAMMABLE, FLAMMA-
BLE sunog, apoy; Iloc: uram, apoy
INFLUENCE influwencia-*Sp*, hika-
yat, himok, sulsol; Iloc: influwencia,
sulisog, sungsong, awis
INHALE langhap, samyo; Iloc:
lang-ab
INQUISITIVE osyoso, pakialam;
Iloc: osyoso, biang
INSERT silid, singit, lakip; Iloc:
uneg, pastrek, serrek
INSISTENT, PERSISTENT *(Tag. &
Iloc.)* pilit, culit
INSPIRING *(Tag. & Iloc.)* enganyo-
a*Sp*, tuwa, inspirasyon-*Sp*
INSTANT agad; Iloc: dagos
INSTRUCT turo; Iloc: suro
INSULT insulto-*Sp*, hamak, lait, su-
palpal, mura; Iloc: insulto, lais
INTELLIGENCE intelihencia-*Sp*,
talino, runong, dunong, alam, ma-
utak, talas, tinik; Iloc: intelihencia,
sirib, ammo
INTENTION balak, tangka, layon,
kusa; Iloc: panggep, pakay, rangta
INTERPRET salin, kahulogan;
Iloc: pataros
INTERROGATE usisa, kilatis,
usig; Iloc: usisa, usig
INURE sanay, bihasa; Iloc: ruam
INVERT baligtad; Iloc: balictad
INVESTIGATE imbestiga-*Sp*, siya-
sat; Iloc: imbestigar-*Sp*

INVITE imbita-*Sp*, cumbida-*Sp*, an-
yaya, yakag; Iloc: imbitar-*Sp*, cum-
bidar-*Sp*, awis
INVOLVE sangkot, dawit; Iloc:
raman
IRK consomi, yamot, inis; Iloc:
suron, rurod, sairo
ITCH cati; Iloc: gatel, budo

J

JEALOUS selos-*Sp*, manibugho;
Iloc: selos, imon
JOIN sali, lahok, sapi, anib, alya-
do-*Sp*; Iloc: sali, tipon
JOKE biro, tukso; Iloc: angaw, sutil
JOURNEY viahe-*Sp*, lakbay, liwa-
liw; Iloc: viahe, libot
JUBILATE libang, aliw, saya,
tuwa; Iloc: ragsak, rambak, papas
JUSTIFY katwiran, rason-*Sp*, dada-
hilan, palusot; Iloc: rason, pambar
JUT OUT, PROTRUDE usli, lawit;
Iloc: usli, dawidaw

K

KEEP tago, taglay, pamalagi; Iloc:
dulin, mantener-*Sp*
KICK tadyak, sipa; Iloc: cugtar,
cusay
KID, TEASE tukso; Iloc: sutil
KILL patay, paslang; Iloc: patay
KIND PERSON malasakit, awa,
habag; Iloc: nangaasi, singpet
KISS halik, hagkan, beso-*Sp*; Iloc:
bisong, anggo, ungngo

KNEAD lamas, lamutak; Iloc: ramas, masa
KNEEL luhod; Iloc: parintumeng
KNOCK *(Tag. & Iloc.)* catok, tuktok

L

LABEL tatak, marka; Iloc: marka
LABOR sikap, sigasig, pursigi, punyagi, pawis; Iloc: pakat, puspusan, rigat, ling-et
LAND ON lapag, dapo; Iloc: diso, dapo
LAST huli, culelat, ultimo-*Sp*; Iloc: udi, cutit, ultimo
LATE huli, atrasado-*Sp*; Iloc: ladaw, atrasado
LAUGH tawa, bungisngis, halakhak; Iloc: katawa, paggaak
LAY lagay, latag; Iloc: cabil, simpa
LAZY tamad, batugan; Iloc: sadut
LEAD BY HAND akay; Iloc: kibin
LEAK tulo, daloy, tagas; Iloc: ubo, tedted
LEAN sandal, sandig; Iloc: sanggir, sadag
LEAP lundag, lukso, talon; Iloc: lagto, laktaw
LEARN malaman, tuto, batid, aral; Iloc: ammo, suro, adal
LEAVE alis, layas, lisan, luwas; Iloc: panaw, awid, talaw
LEAVE BEHIND iwan; Iloc: bati
LEFTOVER tira; Iloc: tidda
LENIENT luwag, baya; Iloc: liway
LEVEL patag, pantay; Iloc: patag

LIE DOWN higa; Iloc: idda
LIE FACE DOWN dapa, handusay; Iloc: pakleb, deppa
LIE, FALSIFY sinungaling, bulaan; Iloc: ulbod, parbo
LIGHT, BRIGHT liwanag, sinag, ilaw, tanglaw; Iloc: lawag, sillag, ranyag
LIGHT WEIGHT gaan; Iloc: lag-an
LIKE, BE PARTIAL TO gusto-*Sp*, ibig, nais, cursonada; Iloc: gusto, cayat, mayat, cursonada
LIKELY malamang; Iloc: labit
LIKEN hambing; Iloc: arig
LINE *(Tag. & Iloc.)* linya-*Sp*, fila-*Sp*
LISTEN kinig, kinggan, ulinig; Iloc: dengngeg
LITTLE liit, linggit, munti; Iloc: bassit, battit
LOCATE hanap; Iloc: sapul, birok, sarak
LOCK susi, candado-*Sp*; Iloc: tulbek, candado
LONELY lungkot, lumbay, manglaw; Iloc: liday, ladingit
LONG (DURATION) tagal, laon, luwat; Iloc: bayag, paut
LONG (LENGTH) haba; Iloc: atiddog, gayad
LOOK tingin, malas, silay, dungaw, lingon, baling, titig; Iloc: kita, tan-aw, talyaw, mingming, sirpat
LOOSE luwag; Iloc: lawa, lucay
LOVE mahal, pag-ibig, sinta, tangi; Iloc: dungngo, ayar

LUCKY suerte-*Sp*, mapalad; Iloc: suerte, gasat

LURE hikayat, ligaw; Iloc: awis, law-an

LUSH lago; Iloc: lapsat

M

MAINTAIN panatili, pamalagi; Iloc: mantener-*Sp*

MAKE gawa, yari; Iloc: aramid, parnuay

MANAGE mahala, ngasiwa, tangkilik, palakad; Iloc: gaway, turong, mangpagna, maton, acecaso

MASH masa, ligis; Iloc: masa, limug

MASSAGE masahe-*Sp*, hilot; Iloc: masahe, ilot

MATERIALIZE katuparan, tutuo, bunga, sagawa, buo; Iloc: balin, bunga, turpos, bukel

MEANT FOR, INTENDED FOR laan kay/sa; Iloc: paay ti/ken

MEASURE sucat; Iloc: rucod

MEDDLE sabad, meter-*Sp*, himasok, makialam; Iloc: meter, sampitaw, biang, miron-*aSp*

MEEK tahimik, kimi, hinhin, amo; Iloc: ulimek, emma, kimmi, amo

MEET salubong, tipan, kita, tagpo; Iloc: sabat, sarak, kita

MENTION banggit, sambit, sabi, wika; Iloc: baga, sao, sawang

MERCY habag, awa; Iloc: asi

MERIT rapat, angkop; Iloc: rebbeng, umno, gunggona

MESS UP gulo, dis-areglo-*Sp*, calat; Iloc: gulo, culcol, dis-areglo, wara

METICULOUS *(Tag. & Iloc.)* busisi, meticuloso-*Sp*, pihikan, selan

MISLEAD ligaw; Iloc: law-an, yaw-awan

MIX halo, sama-sama; Iloc: laok, kiwar, kibur

MOAN daing, taghoy, tangis, himutok; Iloc: asog, sennaay, unnoy

MOVE galaw, kilos; Iloc: garaw, tignay

MOVE, RELOCATE lipat; Iloc: acar, alis

N

NAB aresto-*Sp*, dakip, huli; Iloc: aresto, tiliw

NARRATE cuento-*Sp*; Iloc: storya-*Sp*

NEAR lapit; Iloc: asideg, adani

NEAT areglo-*Sp*, ayos; Iloc: areglo, urnos, dalimanek

NEED, NECESSARY kailangan; Iloc: kasapulan

NEGATE bulaan, kaila; Iloc: libak

NEGLIGENT baya, irresponsible-*Sp*; palya; Iloc: liway, baybay-an, irresponsab-le

NEXT sunod; Iloc: saruno

NIBBLE cagat; Iloc: kitteb, curib, kinnet

NICE buti, inam, bait, husay, payapa, kasiya, consuelo-*Sp*; Iloc: nam-ay, sayaat, imbag, singpet laeng, talna, ay-ayo, consuelo

NIP curot, ipit. pisil; Iloc: piddil, cuddot, ipit, pis-it, pispis, pisil

NOD tango; Iloc: tung-ed

NOISE ingay; Iloc: tagari, riri, ringgor, ariwawa

NOTICE puna, pansin; Iloc: madlaw, siput

NOURISH, NURTURE aruga, sigla, lusog, buhayin, lago; Iloc: taraken, lapsat, pigsa, salun-at, biagen

NUDGE sico, tabig, kabig; Iloc: kidag

O

OBEY tupad, sunod; Iloc: tungpal, surot

OBNOXIOUS sama, laswa, rimarim, halay, rumaldumal, garrafal-a*Sp*, diri; Iloc: dakes, madi, alas, aryek

OBSERVE observa-*Sp*, matyag, manman, masdan, puna, pansin; Iloc: observar-*Sp*, sipot, siim, mingming

OBTAIN tamo, karoon, kuha; Iloc: ala, gun-od

OCCUPIED abala, ocupado-*Sp*, subsob, buhos, atupag; Iloc: ocupado, perreng

OCCUR, HAPPEN ganap, yari; Iloc: pasamak

ODOR ON AIR or ENVIRONMENT singaw, alingasaw; Iloc: alingasaw, sangsang

OFFEND inis, yamot, consomi, suya, disgusto-*Sp*, perhuisio-*Sp*; Iloc: suron, rurod, luksaw, sairo, suya, consomi

OFFENDED tampo, damdam, hinanakit; Iloc: luksaw, suron

OFFER alay, handog, alok, dulot; Iloc: ofrecer, sagot, datag, daton

OFTEN lagi, dalas, rati, limit; Iloc: canayon

OMIT *(Tag. & Iloc.)* laktaw

OPEN bukas, buklat; Iloc: lukat, ukrad

ORDER mando-*Sp*, utos; Iloc: mandar-*Sp*, bilin, baon

OVERCOME supil, lupig, sugpo; Iloc: parmek, atiw

OVERFLOW apaw; Iloc: apaw, lippias

OVERTURN taob, tiwarik, baligtad; Iloc: balinsuek, pattog, balictad

OWN, POSSESS angkin, ari, taglay; Iloc: cua

P

PACIFY calma-*Sp*, hinahon, payapa, awat, lubag; Iloc: calma, talna, anawa, aywen, ulimek, bang-ar

PAIN sakit, kirot, hapdi; Iloc: sakit, apges, ut-ot, sanaang

PANT hangos, hingal; Iloc: asog, al-al

PARTICIPATE lahok, bahagi, sali, bayanihan; Iloc: participar-*Sp*, sali, raman

PASS BY daan; Iloc: labas, lasat

PASS, LET SOMEONE tabi, raan; Iloc: palasat, pagna, igid

PATIENCE pacensia-*Sp*, chaga, tiis; Iloc: pacensia, anos

PATRONIZE taguyod, tangkilik, suporta; Iloc: suporta-*Sp*

PEEL, PARE balat, talup; Iloc: ukis

PEEK silip; Iloc: sirip

PERFORATE tusok, tagos, turok, tuhog, sundot; Iloc: tudok, lussok, salpot

PERMIT payag, hintulot; Iloc: palubos

PERPLEXED bagabag, ligalig, balisa, lito, ligalig, taranta-*Sp*, torete-a*Sp*; Iloc: riro, taranta, torete

PERSEVERANCE pursigi, chaga, tibay, puspusan, Iloc: anos, tibker, pamuspusan, patuloy

PERSPECTIVE pagturing, pananaw; Iloc: panagkita, bigbig

PERSPIRE pawis; Iloc: ling-et

PESTER *(Tag. & Iloc.)* molescha-*Sp*, culit, estorbo-*Sp*

PHLEGM flema-*Sp*, uhog, sipon; Iloc: flema, buteg, anged, sipon

PIQUANT, SPICY anghang; Iloc: arang, gasang

PLACE, PUT lagay, latag; Iloc: cabil, simpa

PLAY laro; Iloc: ayam

PLEASANT buti, inam, bait, husay, payapa, kasiya, consuelo-*Sp*; Iloc: nam-ay, sayaat, imbag, singpet, laeng, talna, ay-ayo, consuelo

PLEDGE sumpa, pangako, promesa-*Sp*, panata; Iloc: sapata, kari, promesa

PLUG pasak, tapon-*Sp*; Iloc: sullat, tapon

POKE duldol, sundot; Iloc: tudok, tugkel

POLITE galang; Iloc: dayaw, raem

PONDER muni-muni, dili-dili; Iloc: panunot, agimatang

POSTPONE antala, paliban, pabukas; Iloc: tantan, taktak, ladladaw, baybayag

POUR buhos, bulos, bugo, bugso; Iloc: pakbo, pattog, bukbok

POUT simangot, ismid, nguso, labi; Iloc: misuot, muregreg, rupanget, tammi, libbi

POWER, POTENCY bisa, lakas, kapangyarihan, talab, virtud-*Sp*; Iloc: kababalin, bileg, pigsa, bisa, anib, virtud

PRAISE parangal, pasalamat, lugod; Iloc: dayaw, yaman,

PRAY dasal, dalangin; Iloc: cararag, lualo

PRECAUTION ingat; Iloc: annad, alwad

PRECIOUS halaga; Iloc: pateg

PRECISE exacto-*Sp*, tama, tumpak, husto-*Sp*; Iloc: exacto, usto-*Sp*

PRECOGNITION kinikinita, tu-ring, huna, alam; Iloc: amiris, big-big, lasin

PREPARE handa, prepara-*Sp*; Iloc: rubwat, sagana, preparar-*Sp*

PRESENT tanghal, lahad, tampok, kita, malas, palabas; Iloc: presentar-*Sp*, pabuya, parang, kita

PRESS diin, pisa, salya, siksik, pasak, duldol; Iloc: talmeg, deppel, sedsed, siksik, lumlom, lupak

PRETEND kunwari, panggap; Iloc: cucuna, sinsinan

PROCLAIM pahayag, proclema-*Sp*; Iloc: isawang, proclemar-*Sp*

PROTECT tanggol, defensa-*Sp*; Iloc: salaknib, defensar-*Sp*

PROVIDE tustos, suporta-*Sp*, gu-gol, fondo-*Sp*, dulot, kaloob; Iloc: suporta, fondo, ited, gastosan

PUFF, BLOW hipan; Iloc: puyot

PULL hila, bunot, haltak, hugot; Iloc: guyod, parut, rabnut

PULVERIZE durog, dikdik, pol-vos-*Sp*, yurak; Iloc: burak, dikdik, polvos, runaw

PUNCH, HIT suntok, buntal, bug-bog, sapok, hampas; Iloc: sulong, danog, disnog, golpe, saktan, bug-bog, cabil

PUNISH parusa; Iloc: dusa, castigar-*Sp*

PUSH tulak, pasak, duldol; Iloc: duron, lumlom, lupak

Q

QUARREL away, alit, laban; Iloc: apa, ringgor, riri, ribok, laban

QUICK bilis, tuling, dali, agad, alisto-*Sp*; Iloc: pardas, dagos, partak, daras, alisto

QUIET tahimik; Iloc: ulimek

QUIT bitiw, tiwalag; Iloc: ikkat

QUIVER nginig, ngatog; Iloc: tigerger

R

RADIATE sikat, kislap, ningning, sinag; Iloc: silap, ranyag, kirap

RAIN ulan; Iloc: tudo

RAISE taas, angat, alsa-*Sp*; Iloc: ngato, sang-at, sagpat

RAW hilaw, pakla; Iloc: ata, ganus, sugpet

REACH abot; Iloc: abot, gaw-at

READ basa; Iloc: basa

READY handa, preparado-*Sp*; Iloc: rubwat, sagana, preparado

REAL tunay, tutuoo, husto-*Sp*; Iloc: pudno, payso, usto-*Sp*

RECEIVE tanggap; Iloc: awat

RECOVER bawi, balik; Iloc: babawi, subli

REDUCE bawas, tanggal, menos-*Sp*; Iloc: ikkat, menos, kissay

REFUGE, give silong, cupcop, canlong, sucob, alalay; Iloc: camang, linong, tulong

REFUSE tanggi, tutol, ayaw; Iloc: madi

REGARD turing; Iloc: bigbig

REGRET sisi, hinayang, lungkot; Iloc: babawi

RELATE, NARRATE cuento-*Sp*; Iloc: storya-*Sp*

RELATED TO, KIN mag-anak; Iloc: bagyan

RELEASE, UNLEASH calas, calag, laya, pakawalan; Iloc: waya, warwar, bulos

REMEMBER, RECALL alaala, tanda, gunita; Iloc: lagip

RENOWN bantog, tanyag, kilala, sikat, popular-*Sp*; Iloc: ammo, takneng, popular

REPLY sagot, tugon; Iloc: sungbat, subalit

RESCUE saklolo, sagip, ligtas, hangoin; Iloc: salvar-*Sp*, arayat, salaknib

RESIDE tira; Iloc gyan, taeng, taed

RESPECTABLE respetado-*Sp*, rangal, dakila, galang; Iloc: taer, raem, respetado, daydayaw

RETURN SOMETHING balik, sauli; Iloc: subli, pulang

RETURN TO A PLACE balik, vuelta-*Sp*; Iloc: subli, vuelta

REVEAL pagtapat, siwalat, bunyag, hayag; Iloc: sawang, paammo

REVENGE vengganza-*Sp*, higanti; Iloc: vengganza, bales

RIDE sakay, lulan; Iloc: sakay, lugan

RIPE hilaw; Iloc: luom

ROAM, LURKING gala-gala, libot, lacuacha, bulakbul, aligid; Iloc: libot, aligid, lacuacha, bulakbul, balballog

ROLL gulong, ikot; Iloc: tulatid, pusipos, carolig, tayyek

RUN takbo; Iloc: taray

S

SAD lungkot, panglaw, lumbay; Iloc: liday, ladingit, leddaang

SAFE ligtas; Iloc: salvar-*Sp*

SALE, SELL venta-*Sp*, tinda; Iloc: venta, laco

SAP catas; Iloc: tubbog

SATISFIED siyahan, contento-*Sp*, saya; Iloc: ragsak, pennek contento

SAVINGS ipon, impok; Iloc: urnong, ipon

SCOLD pagalit, sabihan, sermon; Iloc: unget, correhir-*Sp*

SELDOM bihira, dalang, bahagya; Iloc: manmano, sagpaminsan

SEARCH hanap, saliksik, tunton; Iloc: birok, sursor, tunton, sukain

SEE tingin, silay, malas, kita, banaag, sinag; Iloc: kita, tan-aw

SEND padala; Iloc: paw-it, buson-*Sp*, patulod

SHARE laan, bahagi, damay; Iloc lak-am, bingay, lasin, ramay, raem

SHIVER, CHILL nginig, ginaw; Iloc: tigerger

SHORT liit, pandak, igsi, ikli; Iloc: baba, bulilit, pandak, ababa

SHOUT sigaw, hiyaw, bulyaw, tili; Iloc: riaw, pukkaw, bugkaw, ikkis

SICKNESS karamdaman, sakit; Iloc: sakit

SIN kasalanan, sala; Iloc: basol, biddut

SIT upo; Iloc: tugaw

SLAP sampal; Iloc: sipat, tungpa

SLEEP tulog; Iloc: turog

SLOW bagal, rahan, dahan-dahan, hina; Iloc: bayag, innayad

SMALL maliit, munti, kaunti; Iloc: bassit

SMELL amoy, langhap, samyo; Iloc: angot, lang-ab

SMELL BAD baho, bantut; Iloc: bangsit, angdud, buyok

SMELL GOOD bango, halimuyak; Iloc: banglo

SMILE ngiti, ngisi; Iloc: isem

SNEEZE bahin, hatsing; Iloc: bain, hatsing

SOAK babad, lublob, lubog; Iloc: uper, tabnaw

SOFT lambot; Iloc: lukneng

SOLVE lutas; Iloc: solvar

SOUND imik, tunog, tinig; Iloc: uni, timek, ungor

SPEAK salita, sabi, bigkas, wika, usap; Iloc: sao, sarita, baga, cuna

STAIRS, LADDER hagdan; Iloc: agdan

STAND tayo, tindig; Iloc: tacder

STEP hakbang, yabag, apak; Iloc: addang, baddek, paddak

STEP ON tapak, tuntong, apak; Iloc: payat, batay, paddek

STOP hinto, tigil; Iloc: sardeng

STRANGLE sakal; Iloc: bekkel

STRENGTH lakas, bisa, fuerza-*Sp*, sigla; Iloc: pigsa, bileg, bisa, anib, kired, fuerza

STRIVE sikap, pursigi, punyagi, sigasig; Iloc: pakat, pamuspusan

SUCCEED tagumpay, wagi, yari, sagawa, bunga, unlad; Iloc: balligi, ngabak, turpos, bunga

SWALLOW lunok, lulon; Iloc: til-mon, igop

SWAP palitan; Iloc: sinnukat

SWAY indayog; Iloc: uyaoy

SWELL maga, bukol; Iloc: letteg, bumsog, bumlad

T

TAKE kuha; Iloc: ala, awat

TALK salita, usap; Iloc: sarita

TALL tangkad, taas; Iloc: tayag

TANGLE *(Tag. & Iloc.)* buhol-buhol

TASTE tikim, lasa, simsim; Iloc: raman, nanam

TEACH turo; Iloc: suro

TEAR, TEARDROP luha; Iloc: lua

TEAR, RIP punit; Iloc: pigis, pirgis

TELL sabi; Iloc: baga

THINK isip; Iloc: panunot

TIDY ayos, linis, areglo; Iloc: urnos, linis, areglo, dalimanek, penpen

TIGHT sikip, kipot, higpit; Iloc: ilet, irut

TIRED pagod, hapo, lupaypay, lambot; Iloc: bannog

THROB tibok, pintig; Iloc: kebba, pitik

THROW hagis, bato, itcha-*Sp*; Iloc: pallato, palladaw, bato, purwak

TOUCH ramdam, hipo, dampi; Iloc: sagid, ricna

TOUGH cunat; Iloc: culbet

TRAIN sanay; Iloc: ruam

TRUE tunay, tutuoo, husto-*Sp*; Iloc: pudno, payso, usto-*Sp*

TRUST tiwala, panalig; Iloc: fiar-*Sp*, talek

TRUTH katotohanan; Iloc: kapudnoan

TRY subok, purba, tangka; Iloc: padas, purba, bareng

U

UNDRESS hubad; Iloc: labus

UNDERGO danas, lasap; Iloc: lasat, mapasaran

UNDERSTAND intindi, unawa; Iloc: awat

UNEXPECTED CORRECT GUESS OR UNEXPECTED WINNING *(Tag. & Iloc.)* chamba

URINATE ihi; Iloc: isbo

URINE smell panghi; Iloc: angseg

USE gamit; Iloc: usar-*Sp*, aramat

UTTER imik; Iloc: uni

V

VALUABLE halaga; Iloc: pateg, valor-*Sp*

VANISH laho, pawi, param; Iloc: pukaw, awan

VENERATE samba, dasal, puri, hanga, pagbunyi; Iloc: dayaw, glorificar-*Sp*, cararag, lualo, yaman

VENT OUT FEELINGS daing, taghoy, himutok; Iloc: asog, unnoy, sennaay

VOICE *(Tag. & Iloc.)* boses-*Sp*

VOICE OUT imik; Iloc: uni

W

WAIT hintay, abang; Iloc: uray

WAKE gising; Iloc: riing, lucag

WALK lakad; Iloc: magna

WARP yupi; Iloc: cuppit

WASH hugas, laba-*Sp*, hilamos; Iloc: buggo, ugas, laba, lavar-*Sp*

WATCH nood; Iloc: buya

Wave caway; Iloc: payapay

WEAK hina, lampay, lumo; Iloc: capsot, capoy

WEAR bihis, damit, suot; Iloc: bado, arwat, cawes, bestido-*Sp*

WED casal, asawa; Iloc: casar-*Sp*, asawa

WIN nalo, wagi, tagumpay; Iloc: ngabak, ngatiw, balligi

WIND, AIR hangin; Iloc: angin

WIND STRING pulopot, balumbon; Iloc: cunikon, pulipol

WINK kindat; Iloc: kidday

WIPE punas, pahid; Iloc: punas, nasnas
WOO ligaw; Iloc: arem
WORSEN lubha, lala, grabe-*Sp*; Iloc: caro, grabe, dakes
WORSHIP dasal, puri, luwalhati, samba, bunyi, parangal, hanga; Iloc: lualo, dayaw, yaman, glorificar-*Sp*
WRAP balut; Iloc: bungon, balkut
WRITE sulat; Iloc: surat

Y

YEARN sabik, asam; Iloc: papaos, carayo, gagar, iliw
YUCKY DIRTY kadiri; Iloc: aryek

Z

ZEAL sugid, sigasig, sabik; Iloc: gagar, regget
ZEST sigla, liksi, kasaya; Iloc: ganaygay, sagiksik, list

BICOLANO, CEBUANO, YBANAG, AND GADDANG VOCABULARIES

Abbreviation Meanings

Bic: Bicolano
Ceb: Cebuano
Ybg: Ybanag/Ibanag
Gdg: Gaddang

A

A **Bic**: an; **Ceb**: usa, isa; **Ybg**: y, yari; **Gdg**: si, y, yo

ABLE **Bic**: caya **Ceb**: makahimo, makamao; **Ybg**: caya; **Gdg**: dama

ABOVE **Bic**: itaas, ibabaw **Ceb**: ibabaw, labaw; **Ybg**: ta utun; **Gdg**: si uttun

ACCEPT **Bic**: recibi; **Ceb**: dawat; **Ybg**: appan; **Gdg**: appan

ACCOMPANY **Bic**: iba; **Ceb**: ubanan, pagkuyog; **Ybg**: mavulun; **Gdg**: mabbulun

ACCOMPLISH **Bic**: gibo; **Ceb**: natuman, paghuman; **Ybg**: balin; **Gdg**: balin

ACCORDING **Bic**: segun; **Ceb**: pinauyon, segun; **Ybg**: segun; **Gdg**: segun

ACCUMULATE **Bic:** tipon; **Ceb**: tapuk, dapog; **Ybg**: ifun; **Gdg**: infunnan

ACCURATE **Bic**: tama; **Ceb**: sakto, tukma; **Ybg**: usto; **Gdg**: usto

ACCUSE **Bic:** acusar; **Ceb**: sumbong; **Ybg**: paliwatan; **Gdg**: paliwatan

ACHE **Bic**: culog; **Ceb**: sakit, labad; **Ybg**: taki'; **Gdg**: malaw, lohaw

ACTIVE **Bic**: activo; **Ceb**: malinokon; **Ybg**: alisto; **Gdg**: malappat

ADEPT **Bic**: expiryensado; **Ceb**: antigo; **Ybg**: antigo; **Gdg**: antigo

ADEQUATE **Bic**: tama; **Ceb**: igo, husto; **Ybg**: usto nga na; **Gdg**: ustoen

ADVANTAGE **Bic:** kapakanan; **Ceb**: kapusianan; **Ybg:** & **Gdg**: pammapia

AFFECTIONATE **Bic:** mamuoton; **Ceb**: mahigugmaon; **Ybg**: & **Gdg**: macarinyo

AFRAID **Bic**: takot; **Ceb**: hadlok; **Ybg**: maganassing; **Gdg**: mattalaw

AFTERNOON **Bic**: hapon; **Ceb**: hapon; **Ybg**: fugak; **Gdg**: fuab

AGAIN **Bic**: giraray, naman; **Ceb**: pag-utro, usbon, napod; **Ybg**: mana; **Gdg**: manin

AHEAD **Bic:** inot**; Ceb**: nanguna**; Ybg:** & **Gdg:** pollu

ALIKE **Bic:** padis, sugad; **Ceb**: may-ong, magkadagway; **Ybg**: cacunna, kagitta; **Gdg**: cunnana, parefu

ALIVE **Bic**: buhay; **Ceb**: buhi; **Ybg**: matolay; **Gdg**: matolay

ALL DAY **Bic**: enterong aldaw; **Ceb**: sa tanang adlaw; **Ybg:** patangaggaw; **Gdg**: su makkata fuab

ALLOW **Bic**: tugot; **Ceb**: tugot; **Ybg**: pagurayan; **Gdg**: idama

ALMOST **Bic**: kasi; **Ceb**: hapit, diriyot; **Ybg**: maggi, maggi ngamin; **Gdg**: maggi, maggi ammin

ALONE **Bic**: saro-saro, solo; **Ceb**: inusara, wala'y kuyog; **Ybg**: awa't tu kavulon; **Gdg**: awan kavulon na, yo baggi na lamang

ALREADY **Bic**: na; **Ceb**: na, nang; **Ybg**: ngana; **Gdg**: na, word + en

ALSO **Bic**: man, pati; **Ceb**: man, pud; **Ybg**: gapa; **Gdg**: kepay, pay

ALTER **Bic**: ibago; **Ceb**: balhin; **Ybg**: nalyan; **Gdg**: talyan

ALWAYS **Bic**: pirme; **Ceb**: sa kanunay, gihapon; **Ibg**; & **Gdg**: canayon

AND **Bic**: sagkod; **Ceb**: ug; **Ybg**: anna; **Gdg**: anna

ANGER **Bic**: anggot; **Ceb**: kasuko, kasilag; **Ybg**: lussaw; **Gdg**: allang

ANGRY **Bic**: maanggot; **Ceb**: maglagot, masuko; **Ybg**: malussaw, mapporay; **Gdg**: mallang

ANIMAL **Bic**: hayop; **Ceb**: hayop; **Ybg**: ayam; **Gdg**: animal

ANOTHER **Bic:** iba; **Ceb**: lain, uban; **Ybg**: tanakuan; **Gdg**: tanakuan

ANSWER **Bic**: simbag; **Ceb**: tubag, balos; **Ybg**: mattabbak, mattubbag; **Gdg**: mattabbag

ANY **Bic:** maski ano; **Ceb**: bisan unsa; **Ybg**: maski anni; **Gdg**: maski sanna

ANYBODY, ANYONE **Bic:** maski sisay; **Ceb**: bisan kinsa; **Ybg**: & **Gdg**: maski sinni / sinno

ARREST **Bic:** dacop; **Ceb**: dakpon; **Ybg**: gafut; **Gdg**: gafut

ARRIVE **Bic**: maabot; **Ceb**: pag-abot; **Ybg**: labbe, lubbe; **Gdg**: mad-datang

AS MENTIONED **Bic:** daa; **Ceb**: cunu; **Ybg**: canu; **Gdg**: canu

ASH **Bic**: abo; **Ceb**: abo; **Ybg**: awu; **Gdg**: awu

ASHAME **Bic:** supog; **Ceb**: maulawon; **Ybg**: mappasiran; **Gdg**. maatal

ASK **Bic:** hapot, hapoton; **Ceb**: pangutana, mangutana; **Ybg**: avu', avutan, mangivu; **Gdg**: pakifut, marang

ASK FOR FAVOR **Bic**: ngayo-ngayo, agrangay; **Ceb**: paghangyo, pagpagamuyo; **Ybg**: & **Gdg**: makkiddaw

ASSEMBLE, GET TOGETHER **Bic:** magtiripon; **Ceb**: nagatipon; **Ybg**: mattarabbag; **Gdg**: mattiritipon

AT **Bic:** sa; **Ceb**: sa, anaa sa; **Ybg**: ta; **Gdg**: si, ana si

ATTIRE **Bic:** bado **Ceb**: bistihan; **Ybg**: sinnun; **Gdg**: sinnun

B

BABY, BABE, INFANT **Bic:** umboy; **Ceb**: jutay nga bata; **Ybg**: abbing; **Gdg**: abbing

BACHELOR **Bic**: soltero; **Ceb**: ulitawo; **Ybg:** bagitolay; **Gdg:** bagitolay

BACK **Bic:** likod; **Ceb**: likod; **Ybg:** likuk; **Gdg:** likug

BAD **Bic**: bacong mabuot, raut; **Ceb**: dili maayo, lain, daoton; **Ybg:** marake'; **Gdg**: maral, maraggal

BAN **Bic:** ngalad; **Ceb**: pagdili; **Ybg:** igamma

BATH **Bic**: parigos; **Ceb**: paligo; **Ybg:** zigo; **Gdg**: diyot

BATHE **Bic**: magparigos; **Ceb**: magpaligo; **Ybg:** mazzigo; Gdg: maddiyot

BEAUTIFUL **Bic:** magayon; **Ceb**: matahum, maanindut, maanyag; **Ybg:** makamemmi; guapa; **Gdg**: makasta, guapa

BECAUSE **Bic**: ta; **Ceb**: tungod kay; **Ybg:** megafu, gare; **Gdg**: megafu, se

BEFORE **Bic:** kaidto, bago, antemano; **Ceb**: kani-adto, mi-agi, sa una, pag-una; **Ybg:** ganguri, bago; **Gdg**: bawu ke pay, sinoy

BELIEF **Bic**: tubod; **Ceb**: pagtuo, pagsalig; **Ybg:** & **Gdg**: pagurog

BELIEVE **Bic**: magtubod; **Ceb**: mutuog, salig; **Ybg:** mangurok; **Gdg**: curogan

BELOVED **Bic**: padangat; **Ceb**: hinigugma; **Ybg:** maidduc; **Gdg**: maidduc

BELOW **Bic**: irarom; **Ceb**: ilalom, ilawom; **Ybg:** ta gukak; **Gdg**: si dolam

BENEATH **Bic**: irarom; **Ceb**: ilalom, sa ubus; **Ybg:** ta gukak; **Gdg**: si dolam

BENEFIT **Bic**: kapakanan; **Ceb**: kaayohan; **Ybg:** & **Gdg**: pampamapia

BEST **Bic**: pinakamarahay; **Ceb**: labing maayo, pinakamaayo; **Ybg:** pinakamapia; **Gdg**: pinakamapia

BETTER **Bic**: mas maray; **Ceb**: labaw, mas maayo; **Ybg:** mas mapia; **Gdg**: mas mapia

BIG **Bic**: dacula; **Ceb**: dako, dacu; **Ybg:** dacal; **Gdg**: docal

BITE **Bic**: cagat, ngatngat; **Ceb**: paak, cagat; **Ybg:** caga'; **Gdg**: tukkaw

BLACK **Bic**: itom; **Ceb**: itom; **Ybg:** ngisi'; **Gdg**: ngisit

BLAME **Bic**: basolon; **Ceb**: basolon; **Ybg:** paliwatan; **Gdg**: paliwatan

BLESSINGS **Bic**: biyaya, bendision; **Ceb**: panalangin, bugay; **Ybg:** & **Gdg**: bendision

BLOOD Bic: dugo; **Ceb**: dugo; **Ybg**: daga'; **Gdg**: dara

BLOW, PUFF **Bic**: huyop; **Ceb**: huyop; **Ybg:** sup; **Gdg**: fuyot

BOASTFUL **Bic**: hambogon; **Ceb**: hambogon; **Ybg:** lagaw, parayag; **Gdg**: balagasay

BODY **Bic**: hawak, lawas; **Ceb**: lawas; **Ybg:** baggi; **Gdg**: baggi

BONE **Bic**: tu'lang; **Ceb**: bukog, tul-an; **Ybg**: tulang; **Gdg**: tulang

BOTTOM **Bic**: irarom; **Ceb**: ilalom; **Ybg**: gukak; **Gdg**: dolam

BOY **Bic**: aki' na lalaki; **Ceb**: lalaki, bata; **Ybg**: abbing nga lalaki; **Gdg**: along, abbing nga lalaki

BRAG **Bic**: hambogon; **Ceb**: hambogon; **Ybg**: lagaw, parayag; **Gdg**: balagasay

BRAIN **Bic**: hutok; **Ceb**: utok; **Ybg**: nacam; **Gdg**: nacam

BRAVE **Bic**: maisog; **Ceb**: walay kahadluk, maisog; **Ybg**: & **Gdg**: malalaki

BREAK, SMASH **Bic**: bari, bali; **Ceb**: buak, bugto, himulagon, siak; **Ybg**: mabakka, bakki; **Gdg**: mabakka, mabattag

BREAK, SNAP OFF **Bic**: patod; **Ceb**: putol; **Ybg**: macattu; **Gdg**: macattang

BREAST **Bic**: suso; **Ceb**: suso; **Ybg**: suso; **Gdg**: suso

BREATHE **Bic**: hangos, hangaw; **Ceb**: hakluon, gininhawa; **Ybg**: hango', inango; **Gdg**: anges

BRIGHT **Bic**: maliwanag; **Ceb**: mahayag, masinabuton; **Ybg**: manawak; **Gdg**: masirwat

BRING **Bic**: magdara; **Ceb**: nagadala; **Ybg**: ivulun; **Gdg**: iyang

BRING ABOVE/UP **Bic**: ibugtak sa taas; **Ceb**: dad-on sa taas; **Ybg**: iyune'

BRING DOWN **Bic**: ibaba; **Ceb**: dad-on sa baba; **Ybg**: idattag

BROKEN **Bic**: bari; **Ceb**: buak, basag; **Ybg**: nabakki; **Gdg**: nabakk, nabattag

BURN **Bic**: sulo; **Ceb**: sunogon; **Ybg**: tuggi; **Gdg**: tuggi

BURY **Bic**: ilubong; **Ceb**: paglubong; **Ybg**: itanam; **Gdg**: itanam

BUT **Bic**: pero; **Ceb**: apan; **Ybg**: ngem; **Gdg**: udde

BUY **Bic**: bacal; **Ceb**: magpalit; **Ybg**: gatang; **Gdg**: gatang

C

CALL **Bic**: apod; **Ceb**: pagtawag; **Ybg**: agalan; **Gdg**: mayag

CAN **Bic**: caya; **Ceb**: mahimo, makamao; **Ybg**: wayya; **Gdg**: dama

CARABAO **Bic**: damulag; **Ceb**: calabaw; **Ybg**: nuang; **Gdg**: daffug

CAT **Bic**: ikos; **Ceb**: iring; **Ybg**: & **Gdg**: pusa

CENTER **Bic**: tahaw, centro; **Ceb**: taliwala; **Ybg**: tangnga; **Gdg**: tangnga

CHANGE **Bic**: ribay; **Ceb**: baylo, bag-o; **Ybg:** tali, talian; **Gdg**: talian

CHAT **Bic**: maki-ulay; **Ceb**: makisultihon; **Ybg:** maki-ergo; **Gdg**. makibbida

CHEAP **Bic**: barato; **Ceb**: barato; **Ybg:** mappo'

CHILD **Bic**: aki'; **Ceb**: bata; **Ybg:** abbing; **Gdg**: abbing

CHILD, ONE'S OFFSPRING **Bic**: aki'; **Ceb**: anak; **Ybg:** ana'; **Gdg**: anak

CHILDBIRTH **Bic**: mag-aki'; **Ceb**: panganak; **Ybg:** pagana'

CHILDREN **Bic**: mga aki'; **Ceb**: mga anak; **Ybg:** abbing ira; **Gdg**: abbing ira

CHOOSE **Bic**: pili; **Ceb**: pili-on, pili; **Ybg:** pili; **Gdg**: pili

CHURCH **Bic**: iglesia; **Ceb**: iglesia; **Ybg:** simban; **Gdg**: simban

CLEAN **Bic**: malinig; **Ceb**: malinis, matinlo; **Ybg:** limpia; **Gdg**: mareno

CLOSE **Bic**: ipinto; **Ceb**: gisira; **Ybg:** icerra; **Gdg**: icerra

CLOTHING **Bic**: bado; **Ceb**: bistihan, sanina; **Ybg:** sinnun, burasi; **Gdg**: burasi

COARSE **Bic**: gaspang; **Ceb**: halhag, sagalsalon; **Ybg:** magarazza; **Gdg**: bakkan fino

COLD **Bic**: malipot; **Ceb**: mabugnaw; **Ybg:** malammin; **Gdg**: malabat

COME **Bic**: madigdi; **Ceb**: duol dinhi, mi-anhi, arii; **Ybg:** umay tawe, ume tawe; **Gdg**: umang toye

"COME HERE" **Bic**: "Madia digdi," "Mari digdi"; **Ceb**: "Duol ka dinhi"; **Ybg:** "Ume ka tawe"; **Gdg**: "Kataw"

COME FROM **Bic**: gikan; **Ceb**: gikan; **Ybg:** naggafu; **Gdg**: naggafu

COMPANY **Bic**: kaiba, kaibanan; **Ceb**: kauban; **Ybg:** kavulon; **Gdg**: kavulon

CONCEAL **Bic**: itago; **Ceb**: tago; **Ybg:** isussu'; **Gdg**: isussuk

CONSTANTLY **Bic**: danay; **Ceb**: canunay; **Ybg:** nu carwan; **Gdg**: nu carwan

CONSUMED **Bic**: ubos; **Ceb**: walay sulod; **Ybg:** naofu', nofu'; **Gdg**: naofutin, ofut

CONVERSE **Bic**: mag-ulay; **Ceb**: sulti; **Ybg:** mabbida, mag-ergo; **Gdg**: mabbida

CORRECT *v.* **Bic**: icorrehir; **Ceb**: subo; **Ybg:** & **Gdg**: ituddo y mapia

CORRECT *adj.* **Bic**: tama; **Ceb**: matarung, husto; **Ybg:** curok; **Gdg**: curog, usto

COUNT **Bic**: bilang; **Ceb**: ihap; **Ybg:** & **Gdg**: mabbilang

COURAGEOUS **Bic**: maisog; **Ceb**: walay kahadluk; **Ybg:** malalaki; **Gdg**: malalaki

COVER **Bic**: tacop; **Ceb**: taklob, tabon; **Ybg:** & **Gdg**: callabban

CREATE **Bic**: mag-gibo; magmukna; **Ceb**: himo, buhat; **Ybg:** mangwa; **Gdg**: mangwa

CRITICIZE **Bic**: tachar; **Ceb**: hukngay, kasaway; **Ybg:** uyawan; **Gdg**: uyawan

CRUEL **Bic**: bangis; **Ceb**: way caluoy; **Ybg:** badju, marake'; **Gdg**: maral

CRY **Bic**: naghihibi; **Ceb**: nagahilak; **Ybg:** mattungi', mattangi'; **Gdg**: mattangit

CURRENT, PRESENT TIME **Bic**: ngunyan; **Ceb**: caron; **Ybg:** taw ngana; **Gdg**: maddaggun nga tiempo

CUT **Bic**: putol; **Ceb**: utdon, tadtad; **Ybg:** futol, cattu; **Gdg**: cattang

D

DAMAGE **Bic**: igaba, rauton; **Ceb**: pasamut; **Ybg:** daral; **Gdg**: daral

DANCE **Bic**: bayle; **Ceb**: bayle; **Ybg:** bayle, mattala; **Gdg**: bayle, mattala

DANGEROUS **Bic**: peligroso; **Ceb**: makuyaw; **Ybg:** & **Gdg**: peligroso

DARK TIME OF DAY **Bic**: madiklom; **Ceb**: madulom; **Ybg:** maribbo; **Gdg**: maibbat

DAUGHTER **Bic**: aki' na babayi; **Ceb**: babayeng anak; **Ybg:** ana' nga bavay; **Gdg**: eteng, anak a bafay

DAY **Bic**: aldaw; **Ceb**: adlaw; **Ybg:** aggaw; **Gdg**: aw

DECAY **Bic**: lapa; **Ceb**: dunot; **Ybg:** badiu; **Gdg**: bulok

DECEITFUL **Bic**: madaya; **Ceb**: bakacon; **Ybg:** laddoc; **Gdg**: manantabag

DECEIVE **Bic**: loco, daya; **Ceb**: limbong, lipot; **Ybg:** & **Gdg**: mangil-locuan

DEEP **Bic**: rarom; **Ceb**: lawom, halawom; **Ybg:** adolam; **Gdg**: arolam

DEFEAT **Bic**: daog; **Ceb**: wad-an, pildi; **Ybg:** affu'; **Gdg**: affut

DELICIOUS **Bic**: masiram; **Ceb**: lami, mananam; **Ybg:** masingngo'; **Gdg**: masingngat

DESCEND **Bic**: mababa; **Ceb**: kanaog; **Ybg:** maggukak, mulog; **Gdg**: mullog

DESIRE **Bic**: gusto; **Ceb**: tinguha, pangandoy; **Ybg:** gusto; **Gdg**: anggam

DESTINATION **Bic**: destinasyon, dumanan; **Ceb**: dangatan, kapaingnan, tumong; **Ybg**: angayan; **Gdg**: destinasyon, angan

DESTROY **Bic**: gabaon; **Ceb**: pagguba; **Ybg**: & **Gdg**: daralan

DIE **Bic**: magadan; **Ceb**: matay; **Ybg**: matay; **Gdg**: mabayandag

DIFFERENT **Bic**: iba; **Ceb**: lain; **Ybg**: duma, tanakuan; **Gdg**: tanakuan

DIFFICULT **Bic**: dificil; **Ceb**: lisod, kalisod; **Ybg**: mariga', maziga; **Gdg**: madjat

DIRTY **Bic**: maati, maati-on; **Ceb**: mahigko, hugaw; **Ybg**: maritta, nadaping; **Gdg**: madakkot

DIRTY HABITS **Bic**: bagla'; **Ceb**: makapungot; **Ybg**: tapang; **Gdg**: tapang

DISLIKE **Bic**: habo; **Ceb**: dili gusto, pagkahinaway; **Ybg**: ari caya', manaki'; **Gdg**: ammena, ammem, ammek, ammera

DIVIDE **Bic**: dividir; **Ceb**: pikas; **Ybg**: paggagaduan; **Gdg**: paggagaduan

DO **Bic**: maggibo; **Ceb**: himo, buhat; **Ybg**: makkua, mappadday; **Gdg**: mangwa, mangkua

DOG **Bic**: ayam, ido; **Ceb**: iro; **Ybg**: kito; **Gdg**: ato

DON'T **Bic**: dai mo giboin iyan; **Ceb**: ayaw, ayaw pagbuhaton cana; **Ybg**: ariam mo pangnguan yan; **Gdg**: ammem, mem angwan yan

DON'T LIKE **Bic**: habo'; **Ceb**: dili ganahan, pagkaluod; **Ybg**: ari caya', manaki'; **Gdg**: ammena, ammem, ammek, ammera

DREAM **Bic**: pangiturog; **Ceb**: damgo; **Ybg**: tageno'; **Gdg**: tagenot

DRESS **Bic**: bestida, bado; **Ceb**: sanina, bestida; **Ybg**: burasi; **Gdg**: burasi

DRINK **Bic**: inom; **Ceb**: inom; **Ybg**: inom; **Gdg**: inom

DRY **Bic**: alang, mara; **Ceb**: hubog, uga; **Ybg**: namaga; **Gdg**: namaga

DUSK **Bic**: matanga; **Ceb**: nga ulahi; **Ybg**: umma, fugak, gabi nga na; **Gdg**: fuabin, gafien

E

EACH **Bic**: lamba; **Ceb**: tagsa-tagsa; **Ybg**: cada; **Gdg**: cada

EAR, EARS **Bic**: talinga; **Ceb**: dalunggan; **Ybg**: talinga; **Gdg**: layag

EARLY **Bic**: amay; **Ceb**: sayo; **Ybg**: umma paga; **Gdg**: malan kepay

EARN **Bic**: nagsusweldo; **Ceb**: nagapanapi; **Ybg**: magalek, galegad; **Gdg**: magintarak

EARTH, SOIL, LAND **Bic**: daga; **Ceb**: yuta, duta; **Ybg**: davvun; **Gdg**: lubag

EASY **Bic**: facil; **Ceb**: masayon, dili malisud, dali; **Ybg**: mabbi', nalogon; **Gdg**: malan

EAT **Bic**: makakan; **Ceb**: kaon; **Ybg**: kuman; **Gdg**: mangngan

EGG **Bic**: sugok; **Ceb**: itlog; **Ybg**: illuk; **Gdg**: illug

ENDEAVOR **Bic**: kayod; **Ceb**: paghimud-os, paningkamut; **Ybg**: & **Gdg**: mabban-nag

ENJOY **Bic**: mag-ugma; **Ceb**: nagalingaw; **Ibg/Gdg**: magawagawayyan

ENOUGH **Bic**: tama', sukat; **Ceb**: igo na; **Ybg**: bastante; **Gdg**: bastante

ENTER **Bic**: malaog; **Ceb**: sulod; **Ybg**: mattollung; **Gdg**: munag, mattollung

ENTERTAINMENT **Bic**: libang; **Ceb**: kalingawan; **Ybg**: pagayaya'; **Gdg**: pagkagawagawayyan

ENVY **Bic**: mag-imon, uri; **Ceb**: maigihon; **Ybg**: mapassil; **Gdg**: maatal

ERR **Bic**: masala; **Ceb**: sayop; **Ybg**: malluva, mapparake; **Gdg**: mangwa si maral

ESTABLISH **Bic**: pundar, tugdas; **Ceb**: pagtukod, pagbutang; **Ybg** & **Gdg**: mappattaddag

ETERNAL *adj.*, ETERNITY *n.* **Bic**: sagkod tapos, li'at; **Ceb**: walay katapusan; **Ybg**: vuluvvuga

EVEN THOUGH **Bic**: dawa', maski; **Ceb**: bisan pa; **Ybg**: maski paga; **Gdg**: maski kena, maski kepay

EVERYDAY **Bic**: ara-aldaw; **Ceb**: adlaw-adlaw; **Ybg**: cada aggaw; **Gdg**: cada aw

EVERYWHERE **Bic**: maski sain; **Ceb**: tanang sapit; **Ybg**: maski sitaw; **Gdg**: ammin nga lugar

EVIDENT **Bic**: nahihiling; **Ceb**: makita; **Ybg**: masingan; **Gdg**: maita

EXCEED **Bic**: lampas; **Ceb**: labaw; **Ybg**: mas aru; **Gdg**: mas oddu, maturok kepay

EYE, EYES **Bic**: mata; **Ceb**: mata; **Ybg**: mata; **Gdg**: mata

EYES CLOSED **Bic**: piring; **Ceb**: piyong; **Ybg**: kiddam; **Gdg**: kaddam

F

FACE **Bic**: lalawgon; **Ceb**: nawong, dagway; **Ybg**: muka; **Gdg**: mutong
FACILE **Bic**: facil; **Ceb**: masayon, dili malisud; **Ybg**: mabi'; **Gdg**: malan
FAITH **Bic**: tubod; **Ceb**: pagtuo, tinuhoan; **Ybg**: & **Gdg**: pagkurog
FAR **Bic**: harayo; **Ceb**: halayo, malayo; **Ybg**: arayyu; **Gdg**: aroyu
FALSEHOOD **Bic**: falso, bacong tama, magputik; **Ceb**: dili tinuod, bakak; **Ybg**: laddok, teca'; **Gdg**: mattecat, tecat
FAST **Bic**: cascas, ricas; **Ceb**: dali, lagsik; **Ybg**: alisto, cascas; **Gdg**: malan, cascas
FAT **Bic**: taba; **Ceb**: matambok; **Ybg**: mataba; **Gdg**: matafa
FATHER **Bic**: ama'; **Ceb**: ama; **Ybg**: yama; **Gdg**: ama
FAULT **Bic**: sala; **Ceb**: sayop, sala; **Ybg**: liwa'; **Gdg**: liwat
FEAR **Bic**: takot; **Ceb**: hadlok; **Ybg**: nassing; **Gdg**: talaw
FEATHER **Bic**: balucag; **Ceb**: balahibo; **Ybg**: duddo'; **Gdg**: dutdot
FECES **Bic**: udo'; **Ceb**: libang; **Ybg**: cawe'; **Gdg**: cawet
FEEL, FEELINGS **Bic**: mati; **Ceb**: kamkam, hikam; **Ybg**: raddam; **Gdg**: dandam
FEET, FOOT **Bic**: bitis; **Ceb**: tiil; **Ybg**: takki; **Gdg**: takki
FEMALE **Bic**: babayi; **Ceb**: babaye; **Ybg**: bavay; **Gdg**: bafay
FEW **Bic**: dikit; **Ceb**: pipila, jutay; **Ybg**: baddi' laman; **Gdg**: bisang lamang
FEW TIMES **Bic**: kung minsan; **Ceb**: jutay nga beses; **Ybg**: pamitta-mitta; **Gdg**: pamitta-mitta
FIELDS **Bic**: uma; **Ceb**: patag; **Ybg**: coman; **Gdg**: payaw
FIGHT **Bic**: sulo, kalayo; **Ceb**: sunog; **Ybg**: dama; **Gdg**: laban
FIND, LOCATE **Bic**: hanap, isi, rurop; **Ceb**: pangitaon; **Ybg**: aleran, magalek; **Gdg**: mattarak, mattufuk
FINISH **Bic**: tapos; **Ceb**: human na; **Ybg**: balin; **Gdg**: balin, nabalinin
FIRE **Bic**: kalayo; **Ceb**: sunog, kalayo; **Ybg**: afi, afuy; **Gdg**: afuy
FIRST **Bic**: inot; **Ceb**: una; **Ybg**: pollu; **Gdg**: palungo
FLATULENCE, FLATUS **Bic**: sudol; **Ceb**: utot; **Ybg**: attu'; **Gdg**: attut
FLIRT **Bic**: gi'tilon; **Ceb**: kiat-kiat; **Ybg**: garafeng; **Gdg**: garafeng
FLOWER **Bic**: burak; **Ceb**: bulak; **Ybg**: lappaw; **Gdg**: lappaw
FLY **Bic**: maglayog; **Ceb**: nagalupad; **Ybg**: makkagak; **Gdg**: makkayak

FOLLOW, FOLLOW BEHIND **Bic**: masunod; **Ceb**: sunod-sunod; **Ybg**: tunogan, nevulon; **Gdg**: dumaladaddan

FOOD **Bic**: kakanon; **Ceb**: pagkaon; **Ybg**: kanan; **Gdg**: akkanan

FOOL **Bic**: loco, daya; **Ceb**: limbong, lipot; **Ybg**: & **Gdg**: mangilocuan

FORGET **Bic**: malingawan; **Ceb**: hikalimtan, ginalimot; **Ybg**: cattamman; **Gdg**: calyawan

FORGIVE **Bic**: tawad, dispensar; **Ceb**: pasaylo; **Ybg**: & **Gdg**: pacoman

FRAGRANT **Bic**: hamot; **Ceb**: mahumot; **Ybg**: mabangug

FREQUENTLY **Bic**: parati; **Ceb**: canunay; **Ybg**: canayon; **Gdg**: carwan

FRIEND **Bic**: amigo, amiga; **Ceb**: amigo, amiga; **Ybg**: cofun; **Gdg**: colak

FROM (PERSON) **Bic**: hali kay; **Ceb**: gikan kay; **Ybg**: mamegafu; **Gdg**: mamefu si

FROM (PLACE) **Bic**: hali sa; **Ceb**: gikan sa; **Ybg**: naggafuan; **Gdg**: naggabuatan

FRONT, FRONTAL **Bic**: atubang, ido; **Ceb**: atubangan; **Ybg**: & **Gdg**: arubang

FRUIT **Bic**: frutas, bunga; **Ceb**: bungahoy; **Ybg**: vunga; **Gdg**: bunga

FULL **Bic**: pano'; **Ceb**: puno, sangkap; **Ybg**: pannu; **Gdg**: pannu

FULL STOMACH **Bic**: basog; **Ceb**: lamon, lamoy; **Ybg**: & **Gdg**: nabattug

FUNNY **Bic**: nakakapangisi; **Ceb**: kataw-anan; **Ybg**: kaggalo'; **Gdg**: makapattawa

G

GET **Bic**: ku-a, recibi; **Ceb**: kuha; **Ybg**: apan, appan; **Gdg**: appan

GIRL **Bic**: babayi; **Ceb**: babaye; **Ybg**: babay; **Gdg**: bafay, ayang

GIVE **Bic**: magtao; **Ceb**: maghatag; **Ybg**: iddan, mangyawa'; **Gdg**: mangyada

GO **Bic**: maduman; **Ceb**: adto, sugod; **Ybg**: umay, angay; **Gdg**: umang, angayan

GO DOWN **Bic**: mababa; **Ceb**: kanaog; **Ybg**: maggukak, mulog; **Gdg**: mullog

GO HOME **Bic**: mapuli'; **Ceb**: pauli; **Ybg**: mallabbe', lubbe'; **Gdg**: gumwang

GO OUTSIDE **Bic**: maluwas; **Ceb**: adto sa gawas; **Ybg**: mallawan; **Gdg**: mallawan

GO UP **Bic**: masacat; **Ceb**: nagapataas; **Ybg**: umotton, mune'; **Gdg**: munec

GOAT **Bic**: canding; **Ceb**: canding; **Ybg**: cazzing; **Gdg**: calding

GOOD-NATURED **Bic**: mabuot; **Ceb**: buotan, maayo kaayo, matuloy-on; **Ybg**: masippo'; **Gdg**: masimpat, mappia

GOOD QUALITY **Bic**: marahay; **Ceb**: mayo; **Ybg**: & **Gdg**: mapia

GOSSIP **Bic**: chismis; **Ceb**: switswit, tabitabi; Ybg: beb-bed; **Gdg**: bebbed

GRASS **Bic**: duot; **Ceb**: balili; **Ybg**: caddo'; **Gdg**: caddat

GRATEFUL **Bic**: nagpapa-"Dios mabalos"; **Ceb**: mapasalamaton; **Ybg**: mapabbbalo; **Gdg**: mapabbalat

GREEDY ON FOOD **Bic**: akit; **Ceb**: hakog, dalo'; **Ybg**: vutu'

GRIN **Bic**: ngisi; **Ceb**: yuhom, pagpahiyom; **Ybg**: mapaliddo; **Gdg**: makkatawa

GROW **Bic**: madacula, matalubo (people), matubo (plant); **Ceb**: tubo; **Ybg**: dumacal, maddacal; **Gdg**: mattubo, dumocal

GUN **Bic**: badil; **Ceb**: pusil; **Ybg**: palattuk; **Gdg**: palattug

H

HAIR **Bic**: buhok; **Ceb**: buhok; **Ybg**: vu'; **Gdg**: abuk

HALF **Bic**: kabanga, media; **Ceb**: katunga, media; **Ybg**: gadua, media; **Gdg**: gadua

HAMMER **Bic**: pukpok; **Ceb**: pukpok; **Ybg**: pompol; **Gdg**: pompol

HANDS **Bic**: camot; **Ceb**: camot; **Ybg**: lima; **Gdg**: camat

HAND OUT **Bic**: i-entrega; **Ceb**: pag-abut, ihatag; **Ybg**: iyawa'; **Gdg**: iyada

HAPPINESS **Bic**: kaugmahan; **Ceb**: kalipay; **Ybg**: pagayaya'; **Gdg**: gawagawayyan

HAPPY **Bic**: maugma; **Ceb**: malipay, malipayon; **Ybg**: magayaya'; **Gdg**: magawagawayyan

HARD, DIFFICULT **Bic**: dificil; **Ceb**: kalisod; **Ybg**: riga'; **Gdg**: majat

HARD, FIRM **Bic**: matagas; **Ceb**: matig-a, magahi; **Ybg**: matagga'; **Gdg**: mataggat

HARDEN **Bic**: mattagas; **Ceb**: pinatig-a; **Ybg**: mattagga'; **Gdg**: mattaggat

HAS, HAVE **Bic**: igua; **Ceb**: aduna, dunay; **Ybg**: egga; **Gdg**: ana

HATE **Bic**: anggot; **Ceb**: pagdumot; **Ybg**: poray, lussaw; **Gdg**: poray

HE/SHE **Bic**: siya; **Ceb**: siya; **Ybg**: yayya; **Gdg**: y baggi na, yo baggi na

HEAD **Bic**: payo'; **Ceb**: ulo; **Ybg**: ulo; **Gdg**: ulo

HEALTHY **Bic**: salud; **Ceb**: himsog, bascog; **Ybg**: mapia; **Gdg**: mapia

HEAR **Bic**: dangog; **Ceb**: dungog, pamati; **Ybg**: maginna'; **Gdg**: dingngag

HEART **Bic**: puso; **Ceb**: kasing-kasing; **Ybg**: futu'; **Gdg**: futu

HEAT **Bic**: init; **Ceb**: init; **Ybg**: patu; **Gdg**: fatu

HEAVEN **Bic**: langit; **Ceb**: kalangitan; **Ybg**: langi'; **Gdg**: langit

HEAVY **Bic**: magabat; **Ceb**: mabug-at; **Ybg**: madammo'; **Gdg**: madammat

HELP **Bic**: tabang; **Ceb**: tabang; **Ybg**: manguffun, uffun; **Gdg**: duffun

HER/HIS **Bic**: sa iya; **Ceb**: niya, sa iya; **Ybg**: cuana; **Gdg**: ackuana

HERE **Bic**: digdi; **Ceb**: dinhi, diri; **Ybg**: taw, tawe; **Gdg**: toye, yoye

HERSELF/HIMSELF **Bic**: siya mismo; **Ceb**: ni-ana; **Ybg**: yayya mismo; **Gdg**: yo baggina mismo

HIDE **Bic**: itago; **Ceb**: lilong, tago; **Ybg**: isussu', itutto'; **Gdg**: isussuk

HIGH **Bic**: langkaw; **Ceb**: tag-as; **Ybg**: atannang; **Gdg**: atanang

HOLD **Bic**: capot; **Ceb**: capot; **Ybg**: tammitan; **Gdg**: iggaman, miggam

HOLLER **Bic**: curahaw; **Ceb**: nagasiyaok; **Ybg**: makkule; **Gdg**: maggiraw

HOME **Bic**: harong; **Ceb**: balay; **Ybg**: ba-lay; **Gdg**: ba-lay

HOPEFULLY **Bic**: cuta'; **Ceb**: laum; **Ybg**: nakuan; **Gdg**: nad, paren nad

HOT **Bic**: init; **Ceb**: init, hulaw; **Ybg**: mapatu; **Gdg**: mafatu

HOUSE **Bic**: harong; **Ceb**: balay; **Ybg**: balay, bale'; **Gdg**: ba-lay

"HOW?" **Bic**: "Pa'no?"; **Ceb**: "Unsaon", Unsa na"; **Ybg**: "Cunnasi"; **Gdg**: "Manantaw"

"HOW MANY?" **Bic**: "Pira"; **Ceb**: "Pila"; **Ybg**: "Piga ammin"; **Gdg**: "Pigya ammin"

"HOW MUCH?" **Bic**: "Gura'no"; **Ceb**: "Pila"; **Ybg**: "Piga"; **Gdg**: "Pigya"

HUMAN **Bic**: tawo; **Ceb**: tawo; **Ybg**: tolay; **Gdg**: tolay

HUSBAND **Bic**: agum, esposo; **Ceb**: bana; **Ybg**: atawa; **Gdg**: atawa

I

I **Bic**: ako; **Ceb**: ako; **Ybg**: so', sakan; **Gdg**: ikkanak

ICE **Bic**: yelo; **Ceb**: yelo; **Ybg**: yelo; **Gdg**: yelo

IDLE, IDLING AWAY **Bic**: mayong ginigibo; **Ceb**: usik-usik sa panahon, tinapolan; **Ybg**: mattalakak, maggelag; **Gdg**: ammena mangkua, makkayang, mabbeldang lamang

If **Bic**: con; **Ceb**: con; **Ybg**: nu; **Gdg**: nu

917

IMITATE **Bic**: arog, siring; **Ceb**: sundog, awat; **Ybg:** parigan

IN **Bic**: sa; **Ceb**: sa; **Ybg:** ta; **Gdg**: si

INCAPABLE **Bic**: bacong caya; **Ceb**: dili mahimo, dili angay; **Ybg:** ari macaya; **Gdg**: mena dama, mena caya

INCLUDING **Bic**: iba, ayon; **Ceb**: apil, sacop, nagkaipon; **Ybg: & Gdg**: consu

INDIVIDUAL **Bic**: tawo; **Ceb**: tawo; **Ybg:** tolay; **Gdg**: tolay

INDUSTRIOUS **Bic**: higos; **Ceb**: makugi; **Ybg:** malappo'; Gdg: malappat

INFURIATE **Bic**: suyain; **Ceb**: gipasungit; **Ybg:** ipalussaw; **Gdg**: ipalussaw

INGRATE **Bic**: ingrato; **Ceb**: walay utang buot; **Ybg:** ari makapabbalo'; **Gdg**: mena mabbalat

INSIDE **Bic**: laog; **Ceb**: sulud; **Ybg:** unak; **Gdg**: unag

INSUFFFICIENT **Bic**: kulang; **Ceb**: dili igo; **Ybg:** kurang; **Gdg**: makkurang

IRRITATE **Bic**: suyain; **Ceb**: gipasungit; **Ybg:** ipalussaw; **Gdg**: ipalussaw

ITCHY **Bic**: magatol; **Ceb**: makatol; **Ybg: & Gdg**: makatal

J

JOY **Bic**: ugma; **Ceb**: malipay, malipayon; **Ybg:** magayaya', **Gdg**: magawagawayyan

JUMP **Bic**: lukso; **Ceb**: lukso; **Ybg:** mallattu; **Gdg**: mallattu

K

KEEP **Bic**: isaray; **Ceb**: galam, alima, tago; **Ybg:** pallag, iffunan; **Gdg**: imfunnan

KIN **Bic**: parientes; **Ceb**: kabanay, kadugo; **Ybg: & Gdg**: parientes

KIND PERSON **Bic**: mabuot; **Ceb**: mabuot, maloloy-on; **Ybg:** makcabbi', masippo'; **Gdg**: maallak, mapia

KNOW **Bic**: tatao, aram; **Ceb**: hibalo, sabut; **Ybg:** ammo; **Gdg**: ammo

KNOW, NOT **Bic**: bacong aram o visto; **Ceb**: wala mahibalo, ambut; **Ybg:** kakko ammo, kanna ammo; **Gdg**: ammena ammo, ammek ammo

KNOW SOMEONE **Bic**: visto, midbid; **Ceb**: ila; **Ybg:** ammo; **Gdg**: ammo

KNOWLEDGE **Bic**: conosimiento; **Ceb**: kahibalo; **Ybg:** paddijammo; **Gdg**: paddijammo

L

LABORS **Bic**: kayod; **Ceb**: paghimud-os, paningkamut; **Ybg:** & **Gdg**: mattrabaho

LARGE **Bic**: dacula; **Ceb**: dagko, dacu; **Ybg:** dacal; **Gdg**: docal

LAST **Bic**: huri; **Ceb**: katapusan; **Ybg:** ultimo; **Gdg**: mauddi

LAST NIGHT **Bic**: kasubanggi; **Ceb**: kagabii; **Ybg:** kagafi; **Gdg**: kagafi

LATE **Bic**: huri; **Ceb**: naulahi; **Ybg:** atrasado; **Gdg**: atrasado

LATER **Bic**: atchan; **Ceb**: unya; **Ybg:** manannuan, so nu kua, sangaw; **Gdg**: nanungkua, nain

LAUGH **Bic**: magngisi; **Ceb**: nagakatawa; **Ybg:** makagalo' **Gdg**: makapatawa

LAUGHABLE **Bic**: nakakangisi; **Ceb**: makalipay; **Ybg:** kaggalo'; **Gdg**: makakkatawa

LAUNDER **Bic**: maglaba; **Ceb**: laba; **Ybg:** mabbambal; **Gdg**: mabbambal

LAZY **Bic**: hugak; **Ceb**: tapolan; **Ybg:** talakag; **Gdg**: makayang

LEARN **Bic**: nuod; **Ceb**: tuun, kat-un; **Ybg:** maddijammo; **Gdg**: makkalacammu

LEAVE **Bic**: mahali; **Ceb**: biya, larga, hawa; **Ybg:** manaw; **Gdg**: manaw

LEAVE BEHIND **Bic**: iwalat; **Ceb**: talikod, nagpabilin; **Ybg:** ibattang; **Gdg**: ibattang

LET **Bic**: tugot; **Ceb**: tugot; **Ybg:** pagurayan

"LET'S GO" **Bic**: "Maduman na kita"; **Ceb**: "Mag-adto na kita"; **Ybg:** "Umetam ngana"; **Gdg**: "Intamon"

LIE **Bic**: falso, bacong tama ang pigsabi, magputik; **Ceb**: dili tinuod, bakak; **Ybg:** laddok, teca'; **Gdg**: mattecat, tecat

LIE DOWN **Bic**: maghigda; **Ceb**: maghigda; **Ybg:** idda; **Gdg**: midda

LIFE **Bic**: buhay; **Ceb**: kinabuhi; **Ybg:** pattolay; **Gdg**: pattolay

LIGHT **Bic**: ilaw; **Ceb**: dan-ag; **Ybg:** afi; **Gdg**: sirwat

LIKE, BE FOND OF **Bic**: gusto; **Ceb**: angay; **Ybg:** gusto, caya', aya'; **Gdg**: anggam

LIKEN **Bic**: i-arog, isiring; **Ceb**: paghisama; **Ybg:** & **Gdg**: iyarig

LIPS **Bic**: ngabil; **Ceb**: ngabil; **Ybg:** bibig; **Gdg**: bifig

LISTEN **Bic**: magdangog; **Ceb**: dungog, pamati; **Ybg:** magginna'; **Gdg**: maddingngag

LITTLE (HEIGHT) **Bic**: sadit; **Ceb**: bulilit, gamay; **Ybg**: baddi; **Gdg**: bisang

LITTLE (QUANTITY) **Bic**: dikit; **Ceb**: jutay, gamay; **Ybg**: baddi; **Gdg**: bisang

LIVE, EXIST **Bic**: buhay; **Ceb**: anaa, mabuhi; **Ybg**: matolay; **Gdg**: matolay

LIVE, RESIDE **Bic**: istar, nag-iistar; **Ceb**: puloy-anan; **Ybg**: & **Gdg**: padjanan

LIVELIHOOD **Bic**: pagganar; **Ceb**: panginabuhi; **Ybg**: & **Gdg**: pagaleran

LONG DURATION **Bic**: haloy; **Ceb**: dugay; **Ybg**: mabayak; **Gdg**: mabayag

LONG LENGTH **Bic**: halaba; **Ceb**: sucod sa gitas-on, malaba; **Ybg**: apiddu; **Gdg**: asoddag

LOOK **Bic**: hiling; **Ceb**: kita, tan-aw; **Ybg**: innan; **Gdg**: itan, mita

LOOK FOR **Bic**: hanap; **Ceb**: pangita; **Ybg**: magalek, innammo, aleran; **Gdg**: mattarac, mattufuc

LOOK INTENTLY & LENGTHILY **Bic**: turohok; **Ceb**: tutok, lutok; **Ybg**: inninnan; **Gdg**: mitita, ititan

LOOSE **Bic**: luag; **Ceb**: luag; **Ybg**: lolloy; **Gdg**: lolloy

LOSE A COMPETION OR A BATTLE **Bic**: nadaog, perdi; **Ceb**: buntog, pildi; **Ybg**: affu'; **Gdg**: affut

LOSE A THING **Bic**: nawara; **Ceb**: pagkawala; **Ybg**: nawawan

LOUD **Bic**: ribok; **Ceb**: banha; **Ybg**: gallu', tannug; **Gdg**: cassag

LOVE **Bic**: muot; **Ceb**: gugma; **Ybg**: iddu', pagaya'; **Gdg**: canggamman, anggam

LOVELY **Bic**: magayon; **Ceb**: mahigugmaon, matahum; **Ybg**: makamemmi, makasta, guapa; **Gdg**: guapa, makasta

M

MAKE **Bic**: maggibo; **Ceb**: buhat, gama; **Ybg**: mangangwa; **Gdg**: mangwa

MALE **Bic**: lalaki; **Ceb**: lalaki; **Ybg**: lalaki; **Gdg**: lalaki

MANY **Bic**: kadacol; **Ceb**: madamo, daghan; **Ybg**: aru; **Gdg**: oddu

MARRY **Bic**: magcasal, mag-agom; **Ceb**: asawa; **Ybg**: & **Gdg**: mangatawa

MAYBE **Bic**: seguro; **Ceb**: tingali; **Ybg**: seguro; **Gdg**: nacoy

ME **Bic**: ako; **Ceb**: ako; **Ybg:** so'; **Gdg**: ikkanak

ME, TO, ON ME **Bic**: sacuya; **Ceb**: kanako; **Ybg:** sakan, niakan; **Gdg**: ikkanak, sicuak

MEASURE **Bic**: sucol; **Ceb**: sucod; **Ybg:** gukuk, gukugan; **Gdg**: tukkuran

MEMORY **Bic**: memoria, giromdum; **Ceb**: panumduman; **Ybg:** nono'; **Gdg**: nonot

MERCIFUL **Bic**: mahirakon; **Ceb**: maloloy-on, makalooy; **Ybg:** kabbi; **Gdg**: mallak, ana allak na, mannacuay gapa

MERCY **Bic**: hirak; **Ceb**: kaluoy, puangod; **Ybg:** allo'; **Gdg**: allak

MIDDLE **Bic**: tahaw, centro; **Ceb**: taliwala; **Ybg:** tang-nga; **Gdg**: tangnga

MIND **Bic**: isip, buot; **Ceb**: paghunahuna; **Ybg:** nono'; **Gdg**: nonot

MINE **Bic**: sacuya, sadiri; **Ceb**: nako, ko; **Ybg:** cuak; **Gdg**: acuak

MISBEHAVE **Bic**: maggibo ng sala; **Ceb**: wala magbuotan; **Ybg:** makkua tu marake; **Gdg**: mangkua si maral

MIX **Bic**: salak, halo; **Ceb**: pagsagul; **Ybg:** & **Gdg**: kivu

MORNING **Bic**: aga; **Ceb**: buntag; **Ybg:** umma; **Gdg**: umma

MOTHER **Bic**: ina; **Ceb**: nanay, inahan; **Ybg:** yena; **Gdg**: ina

MOUTH **Bic**: nguso; **Ceb**: baba; **Ybg:** simu; **Gdg**: bifig

MUST **Bic**: himo, dapat; **Ceb**: mangindapat, angay; **Ybg:** mawag, kawagan; **Gdg**: mawag

N

NAME **Bic**: ngaran; **Ceb**: hingalan; **Ybg:** ngagan; **Gdg**: ngan, nagan

NARROW **Bic**: pi-ot; **Ceb**: hiktin, sigpit; **Ybg:** atazzi; **Gdg**: bisang

NAUGHTY **Bic**: pilyo; **Ceb**: maldito; **Ybg:** pilyo; **Gdg**: pilyo

NEAR **Bic**: harani; **Ceb**: haduul, malapit; **Ybg:** aranni; **Gdg**: arani

NECESSARY **Bic**: himo, dapat, ipo; **Ceb**: mangindapat, gikinahangian; **Ybg:** mawag, kawagan; **Gdg**: mawag

NECK **Bic**: li-og; **Ceb**: li-og; **Ybg:** tangngak; **Gdg**: tangngag

NEED **Bic**: kaipoanan; **Ceb**: kinahingianon; **Ybg:** mawag; **Gdg**: mawag

NEW **Bic**: bago; **Ceb**: bag-o; **Ybg:** bago; **Gdg**: bawo

NICE **Bic**: mabuot; **Ceb**: makahimuot; **Ybg:** mapia; **Gdg**: mapia

NIGHT **Bic**: banggi; **Ceb**: gabii, gab-i; **Ybg:** gabi; **Gdg**: gafi

NO, NOT **Bic**: dai, baco'; **Ceb**: dili, wala; **Ybg:** ari; **Gdg**: bakkan, awan

NOISE **Bic**: ribok; **Ceb**: banha; **Ybg:** tannug; **Gdg**: cassag

NOISY **Bic**: maribok; **Ceb**: masaba; **Ybg**: matannug; **Gdg**: macassag

NONE, NOTHING **Bic**: mayo; **Ceb**: walay bisan usa; **Ybg**: awan; **Gdg**: awan

NOON **Bic**: udto; **Ceb**: udto; **Ybg**: tangnga naggaw; **Gdg**: tangnga si aw

NOSE **Bic**: dungo; **Ceb**: ilong; **Ybg**: igong; **Gdg**: iyong

NOW **Bic**: ngunyan; **Ceb**: caron; **Ybg**: sangaw; **Gdg**: toye, toyein

O

OBESE **Bic**: taba; **Ceb**: matambok; **Ybg**: mataba; **Gdg**: matafa

OBEY **Bic**: masunod; **Ceb**: nagasunod; **Ybg**: vulutan, manarulo; **Gdg**: mangituntol

OCEAN **Bic**: dagat; **Ceb**: dagat; **Ybg**: & **Gdg**: bebay

ODOR **Bic**: parong; **Ceb**: simhot; **Ibg** & **Gdg**: aguk

ODOR, BAD **Bic**: mabata; **Ceb**: nanimaho; **Ybg**: mavuyo'; **Gdg**: mavuyok

ODOR, FRAGRANT **Bic**: hamot; **Ceb**: mahumot; **Ybg**: & **Gdg**: mabangug

OF **Bic**: nin, kan; **Ceb**: sa, ni, kang; **Ybg**: ta; **Gdg**: si

OFTEN **Bic**: dayaday, parati; **Ceb**: canunay; **Ybg**: canayon; **Gdg**: nu carwan

OLD PERSON **Bic**: gurang; **Ceb**: tigulang; **Ybg**: lakay o baco' nga na; **Gdg**: lakay, bakat

OLD THING **Bic**: su'anoy; **Ceb**: sado, maas; **Ybg**: dana; **Gdg**: dadan

ONCE **Bic**: sarong beses; **Ceb**: kausa; **Ybg**: mamitta; **Gdg**: tata beses

ONE **Bic**: uno, saro'; **Ceb**: usa; **Ybg**: uno, tadday; **Gdg**: uno, tata

ONLY **Bic**: lang, sana; **Ceb**: ra, da, lamang; **Ybg**: laman; **Gdg**: lamang

OPEN **Bic**: ibukas; **Ceb**: abre, bukas; **Ybg**: vuka', vukatan; **Gdg**: bukkatan, bolyaran

ORIGINATE FROM **Bic**: gikan sa; **Ceb**: gigikanan, kinaugalingon; **Ybg**: pinaggafuan; **Gdg**: pinaggabuatan

OTHER **Bic**: tung saro, iba; **Ceb**: ang la-in, iban pa; **Ybg**: tanakuan, duma; **Gdg**: yo tanakuan

OTHER SIDE **Bic**: sa ibong; **Ceb**: sa laing kilira; **Ybg**: tanabbagan; **Gdg**: si tafic

OUGHT **Bic**: himo, dapat, ipo; **Ceb**: mangindapat, gikinahangian; **Ybg**: mawag, kawagan; **Gdg**: mawag

OUR, OURS **Bic**: satuya; **Ceb**: among, namo; **Ybg:** cuatam; **Gdg**: ackuatam

OUR, OURS (yours & mine) **Bic**: samuya; **Ceb**: amo, sa amo; **Ybg:** cuatam; **Gdg**: ackuatam

OUTSIDE **Bic**: sa luwas; **Ceb**: sa gawas, sa gula; **Ybg:** lawan; **Gdg**: si lawan

OWE **Bic**: utang; **Ceb**: utang; **Ybg**: maggatu'; **Gdg**: maggatut

OWN **Bic**: sadiri; **Ceb**: akoon; **Ybg**: acua; **Gdg**: ackua

P

PAINFUL **Bic**: maculog; **Ceb**: mahapdos, sakit; **Ybg:** mataki'; **Gdg**: malaw

PANTY **Bic**: calson; **Ceb**: panty; **Ybg:** salawini'; **Gdg**: salawinit

PARENT **Bic**: magurang; **Ceb**: mga ginikanan; **Ybg:** maganna'; **Gdg**: ginaffan

PASS BY **Bic**: mag-agi; **Ceb**: laboy, agi; **Ybg:** mattalebad; **Gdg**: mattalebad

PAST **Bic**: kaidto; **Ceb**: miagi; **Ybg:** sinoy; **Gdg**: sinoy

PAY **Bic**: magbayad; **Ceb**: nagbayad; **Ybg:** mappaga; **Gdg**: mappaga

PERSON **Bic**: tawo; **Ceb**: tawo; **Ybg:** tolay; **Gdg**: tolay

PIG **Bic**: urig; **Ceb**: baboy; **Ybg:** bavi; **Gdg**: bafi

PINCH **Bic**: cudot; **Ceb**: curit; **Ybg:** caddutan; **Gdg**: caddutan

PITIFUL **Bic**: hirak man; **Ceb**: makalolooy; **Ybg:** cabbi; **Gdg**: callak

PITY **Bic**: hirak; **Ceb**: kalooy; **Ybg:** allo', makkabbi'; **Gdg**: mallak

PLACE **Bic**: lugar; **Ceb**: dapit, lugar; **Ybg:** lugar; **Gdg**: lugar

PLACE, PUT **Bic**: ibugtak, ilaag; **Ceb**: ibutang; **Ybg:** ipay; **Gdg**: iyekcua

PLANT **Bic**: tanum; **Ceb**: tanum; **Ybg:** mammula, itanam; **Gdg**: mammula

PLAY **Bic**: cawat; **Ceb**: hampang; **Ybg:** maggayam; **Gdg**: makkayam

PLEA, PLEAD **Bic**: ngayo-ngayo, agrangay; **Ceb**: paghangyo, pagpagamuyo; **Ybg:** & **Gdg**: makkiddaw, makimallo

PLEASANT PERSONALITY **Bic**: marahay; **Ceb**: pino, maayo; **Ybg:** masippo'; **Gdg**: mapia

"PLEASE" **Bic**: tabi; **Ceb**: con buot; **Ybg:** labbi ngay; **Gdg**: labbu ay, arennay

PLENTY **Bic**: kadacol; **Ceb**: kadamo; **Ybg:** aru; **Gdg**: oddu

POINT **Bic**: itukdo; **Ceb**: tudlo, punting; **Ybg:** ituddo; **Gdg**: tuddo

POKE **Bic**: tumbol; **Ceb**: dunggab, dugmak; **Ybg:** tukkal; **Gdg**: tukkal

POSSIBLE, FEASIBLE **Bic**: puede; **Ceb**: mahimo; **Ybg:** wayya; **Gdg**: dama, mabalin

PREGNANT **Bic**: badus; **Ceb**: buros; **Ybg:** mabussi'; **Gdg**: mabussit

PRESENT TIME **Bic**: ngunyan; **Ceb**: caron; **Ybg:** sangaw; **Gdg**: yo aw toye, maddaggun

PRESSING IRON TO SMOOTHEN LAUNDERED CLOTHES **Bic**: magplancha; **Ceb**: nagaplancha; **Ybg:** mapplancha; **Gdg**: mapprensa

PRETTY **Bic**: magayon; **Ceb**: mahigugmaon, matahum, manindut; **Ybg:** makamemmi, makasta, guapa; **Gdg**: guapa, makasta

PREVIOUSLY **Bic**: kaidto; **Ceb**: nanganing panahon; **Ybg:** turi paga, tari nabak nga na; **Gdg**: sinoy ke pay

PROHIBIT **Bic**: ngalad; **Ceb**: pagdili; **Ybg:** igamma; **Gdg**: mena dama

PROVE **Bic**: proybas, itotoo; **Ceb**: matuod, pakita; **Ybg:** pureba; **Gdg**: pureba

PULL **Bic**: butong, guyod; **Ceb**: butad, guyod; **Ybg:** guggon, takku

PUSH **Bic**: tulod, busol, ugsod, tuldang; **Ybg:** tubba

PUT **Bic**: ilaag, ibugtak; **Ceb**: ibutang; **Ybg:** ipay; **Gdg**: iyekkua

Q

QUANTITY **Bic**: sumar, total; **Ceb**: tanan, tibuok; **Ybg:** piga yari caru; **Gdg**: pigya yo ammin

QUIET **Bic**: mayong girong; **Ceb**: mahilom; **Ybg:** ari matannug; magimamammo; **Gdg**: masinac, mallemay, malumamak

R

RACE, RUNNING COMPETITION **Bic**: carera; **Ceb**: lumba, carera; **Ybg:** makkarela; **Gdg**: makkarepat

RAIN **Bic**: uran; **Ceb**: ulan; **Ybg:** uran; **Gdg**: uran

RAISE **Bic**: i-alsa; **Ceb**: i-alsa; **Ybg:** ipauttun; **Gdg**: ipauttun

REACH **Bic**: abot; **Ceb**: abot; **Ybg:** gawwatan; **Gdg**: gawwatan

READ **Bic**: magbasa; **Ceb**: basaha; **Ybg:** bibbik, bibbig; **Gdg**: mabbibbid

REAL **Bic**: tunay, tama; **Ceb**: tinuod; **Ybg:** curok; **Gdg**: curog

RECEIVE **Bic**: recibi; **Ceb**: dawat; **Ybg:** appan; **Gdg**: appan

REGRET **Bic**: nagbabasol; **Ceb**: pagbasol; **Ybg:** mabbawi; **Gdg**: mabbawi

RELATIVE(S) **Bic**: parientes; **Ceb**: kabanay, kadugo; **Ybg: & Gdg**: parientes

REMEMBER **Bic**: giromdom; **Ceb**: padumdum; **Ybg**: manono'; **Gdg**: manonot

REMOVE **Bic**: ihali; **Ceb**: tangkas, puwas; **Ybg**: aryan; **Gdg**: alsan, aryan

REPLY **Bic**: simbag; **Ceb**: tubag; **Ybg**: mattabbak, tabbagan; **Gdg**: tabbag

REQUEST **Bic**: ngayo-ngayo, agrangay; **Ceb**: paghangyo, pagpagamuyo; **Ybg: & Gdg**: makkiddaw

RESIDE **Bic**: istar, nag-iistar; **Ceb**: puloy-anan; **Ybg: & Gdg**: madjan

RESIDENCE **Bic**: residencia, istar; **Ceb**: puyo; **Ybg**: padjanan; **Gdg**: padjanan

RESPECT **Bic**: galang; **Ceb**: tahod, manggad; **Ybg**: dayaw; **Gdg**: dayaw

RESPECTFUL **Bic**: marespeto; **Ceb**: matinahuron; **Ybg**: madayaw; **Gdg**: madayaw

RETURN **Bic**: magbalik; **Ceb**: i-uli, ibalik; **Ybg**: itoli; **Gdg**: itoli

RETURN TO A PLACE **Bic**: vuelta, magpuli; **Ceb**: pag-uli; **Ybg**: mattoli, lubbe; **Gdg**: mattoli

REVEAL **Bic**: reveler, tuga; **Ceb**: butyag, pahayag; **Ybg**: ipaammo; **Gdg**: mappalappat

RICE, COOKED **Bic**: maluto; **Ceb**: humay; **Ybg**: inafi; **Gdg**: innafi

RICE, UNCOOKED **Bic**: bagas; **Ceb**: bagas; **Ybg**: bagga'; **Gdg**: baggat

RIDE **Bic**: malunad; **Ceb**: sakay; **Ybg**: mattakay; **Gdg**: mattakay

RIGHT **Bic**: tama; **Ceb**: matarung; **Ybg**: curuk; **Gdg**: curog, usto

RIPE **Bic**: hinog; **Ceb**: lumoy, hinog; **Ybg: & Gdg**: naluto ngana

ROAD **Bic**: dalan, tinampo; **Ceb**: dalan; **Ybg**: dalan; **Gdg**: dalan

ROPE **Bic**: bugkos; **Ceb**: paggapos, baligtos; **Ybg**: galu' **Gdg**: galot

ROT **Bic**: lapa; **Ceb**: dunot; **Ybg**: badju; **Gdg**: bulok

RUN **Bic**: dalagan; **Ceb**: dagan; **Ybg**: makkarela; **Gdg**: makkarepat, makkarela

S

SAD **Bic**: pu'ngaw; **Ceb**: mamingawon, maguol; **Ybg: & Gdg**: raddam

SAME **Bic**: pareho; **Ceb**: pagkamao ra; **Ybg**: parefu; **Gdg**: parefu

SATISFIED **Bic**: uto, basug; **Ceb**: pagbusog; **Ybg: & Gdg**: nabattug

SAY **Bic**: sabi, taram; **Ceb**: sulti, pulong, hambal; **Ybg**: icagi, cagian; **Gdg**: sapit

SCOLD **Bic**: anggotan; **Ceb**: pagbasaba; **Ybg**: mapporay; **Gdg**: mallang

SEARCH **Bic**: hanap; **Ceb**: pangita; **Ybg**: magalek, aleran; **Gdg**: mattufuc, mattarak

SEE **Bic**: hiling; **Ceb**: kita, tan-aw; **Ybg**: innan, singan; **Gdg**: itan, mita, maita

SEEM **Bic**: garu; **Ceb**: maingon-ingon; **Ybg**: allale; **Gdg**: curuha

SELL **Bic**: ipabakal; **Ceb**: pagbaligya; **Ybg**: & **Gdg**: ilaco

SEND **Bic**: dara; **Ceb**: padala; **Ybg**: & **Gdg**: ituvug

SEPARATE **Bic**: suway; **Ceb**: bulag; **Ybg**: maggungay; **Gdg**: massina

SERVE **Bic**: servi; **Ceb**: pagdulot sud-an; **Ybg**: & **Gdg**: masservi

SEW **Bic**: tahi; **Ceb**: tahi-on; **Ybg**: maddage'; **Gdg**: maddet

SHALLOW **Bic**: mababaw; **Ceb**: mababaw; **Ybg**: ari adolam, mababaw; **Gdg**: ibbafaw

SHAME **Bic**: supog; **Ceb**: kaulaw; **Ybg**: pasiran; **Gdg**: pasiran

SHARP **Bic**: tarom; **Ceb**: talinis, talum; **Ybg**: nataram; **Gdg**: mataram

SHE/HE **Bic**: siya; **Ceb**: siya; **Ybg**: yayya; **Gdg**: y baggi na, yo baggi na

SHORT (HEIGHT) **Bic**: pandak; **Ceb**: bulilit, gamay; **Ybg**: pando; **Gdg**: pandak

SHORT (LENGTH) **Bic**: hali'pot; **Ceb**: hamubo; **Ybg**: ababba; **Gdg**: bisang

SHOUT **Bic**: magcurahaw; **Ceb**: nagasiyaok, singgit; **Ybg**: makkulle; **Gdg**: maggiraw

SHOW **Bic**: ipahiling; **Ceb**: ipakita; **Ybg**: ipasingan; **Gdg**: ipa-ita

"SHUT UP" **Bic**: "Dai ka maribok"; **Ceb**: "Saba' diha"; **Ybg**: "Ari ka matannug"; **Gdg**: "Mem macassag"

SIBLING **Bic**: tugang; **Ceb**: igsuon; **Ybg**: wagi; **Gdg**: wayi

SICK **Bic**: iguang hilang; **Ceb**: masakiton; **Ybg**: mattaki'; **Gdg**: matakit

SICKNESS **Bic**: hilang; **Ceb**: sakit, balatian; **Ybg**: taki'; **Gdg**: takit

SIGHT **Bic**: hiling; **Ceb**: pagtan-aw; **Ybg**: paningan; **Gdg**: pa'ita

SIMILAR **Bic**: magkarog, magkasiring; **Ceb**: magkaang-gid, magkamaong; **Ybg**: kagitta, kacunna, parefu; **Gdg**: kacunna, cunnana, parefu

SIN **Bic**: sala'; **Ceb**: sala; **Ybg**: & **Gdg**: liwat

SINCE **Bic**: sagkod; **Ceb**: suka caniadto, gikan caniadto; **Ybg**: mamegafu, adde'; **Gdg**: mamefu si

SING **Bic**: canta; **Ceb**: canta; **Ybg**: canta; **Gdg**: canta

SINGLE, UNMARRIED MAN **Bic**: soltero; **Ceb**: ulitawo; **Ybg**: bagitolay; **Gdg**: bagitolay

SINGLE WOMAN **Bic**: daraga; **Ceb**: dalaga; **Ybg**: maginganay; **Gdg**: maginganay

SIT **Bic**: tukaw; **Ceb**: lingkod; **Ybg**: magitubang; **Gdg**: mat-tut-tod

SKY **Bic**: langit; **Ceb**: langit; **Ybg**: langi'; **Gdg**: langit

SLEEP **Bic**: turog; **Ceb**: katulgon, tuloyhon; **Ybg**: turok; **Gdg**: turog

SLOW **Bic**: maluway; **Ceb**: mahinay; **Ybg**: mabayak; **Gdg**: mabayag

SLOW DOWN **Bic**: iluway-luway; **Ceb**: nagaplangan; **Ybg**: ibayak, ikafi; **Gdg**: ibayag

SMALL AMOUNT **Bic**: dikit; **Ceb**: diutay, jutay, gamay; **Ybg**: baddi; **Gdg**: bisang

SMALL SIZE **Bic**: sadit; **Ceb**: bulilit, gamay; **Ybg**: baddi; **Gdg**: bisang

SMELL **Bic**: sango, parong; **Ceb**: simhot, hakluon; **Ybg**: aguk

SMELL BAD **Bic**: mabata; **Ceb**: daotang baho; **Ybg**: mavuyo'; **Gdg**: mabuyok

SMELL GOOD **Bic**: mahamot; **Ceb**: mahumot, maamyon; **Ybg**: mabanguk; **Gdg**: mabangug

SMILE **Bic**: ngisi; **Ceb**: yuhom, pahiyom; **Ybg**: mapaliddo; **Gdg**: katawa

SMOOTH **Bic**: pilido, halnas; **Ceb**: mahamis, mahinlo, ; **Ybg**: nadalu'; **Gdg**: fino

SO THAT **Bic**: para ta, kay, ngani; **Ceb**: aron, para; **Ybg**: ta penu, nu; **Gdg**: take nu, take si, se

SOFT **Bic**: lumoy, lumhok; **Ceb**: mahumok; **Ybg**: malapo'

SOME **Bic**: nin; **Ceb**: pipila butang; **Ybg**: carwan; **Gdg**: carwan

SOME PEOPLE **Bic**: nin; **Ceb**: pipila tawo; **Ybg**: carwan nga tolay; **Gdg**: carwan

SOURCE **Bic**: gikan; **Ceb**: ginikanan; **Ybg**: & **Gdg**: naggafuanan

SPEAK **Bic**: taram, sabi; **Ceb**: sulti; **Ybg**: cagi, mabbida; **Gdg**: mabbida, sapit, mammimit

SPLIT **Bic**: patod; **Ceb**: pagsip-ak; **Ybg**: bakki; **Gdg**: bakki

SPOUSE **Bic**: agum; **Ceb**: bana; **Ybg**: atawa; **Gdg**: atawa

927

SQUEEZE **Bic**: gumok, puga; **Ceb**: hakgom, captan; **Ibg** & **Gdg**: paggal

STAND **Bic**: matindog; **Ceb**: tindog; **Ybg**: mattaddak; **Gdg**: mattaddag

STARE **Bic**: turohok; **Ceb**: tutok, lutok; **Ybg**: inninnan; **Gdg**: mitita, ititan

START **Bic**: mapuon; **Ceb**: sugod, sinugdanan; **Ybg**: mallunggo, mamegafu; **Gdg**: maddaggun

STATE, SAY **Bic**: sabi, taram; **Ceb**: sulti, pulong, hambal; **Ybg**: icagi, cagian; **Gdg**: sapitan

STEAL **Bic**: ha'bon; **Ceb**: cawat; **Ybg**: makcoco'; **Gdg**: makcocot

STINK **Bic**: mabata; **Ceb**: nanimaho; **Ybg**: mavuyo'; **Gdg**: mabuyok

STOMACH **Bic**: tulak; **Ceb**: kuto-kuto, tungol, chan; **Ybg**: san; **Gdg**: cuyong

STOP **Bic**: tapos, pundo; **Ceb**: hunong, lurong; **Ybg**: igimmang; **Gdg**: mimmang

"STOP" **Bic**: "Tama na"; **Ceb**: "Sakto na"; **Ybg**: "Alto"; **Gdg**: "Alto"

STOUT **Bic**: taba; **Ceb**: tambok, sumpang; **Ybg**: mataba; **Gdg**: matafa

STRAIGHT **Bic**: tanos; **Ceb**: tadlong, tul-id; **Ybg**: derecho; **Gdg**: derecho

STRENGTH **Bic**: cusog; **Ceb**: kaisog, kalig-on; **Ybg**: sikan; **Gdg**: tuyag

STROLL **Bic**: pasiar; **Ceb**: lakaw-lakaw, suroy-suroy; **Ybg**: mappasiar; **Gdg**: mappasiar

STRONG **Bic**: macusog; **Ceb**: cusog, lig-on; **Ybg**: masikan; **Gdg**: matuyag

STUDY **Bic**: mag-adal; **Ceb**: tuon, tun-an; **Ybg**: maddijammu; **Gdg**: makkalacammu

STUPID **Bic**: patal; **Ceb**: kahungog; **Ybg**: awat tu nacam; **Gdg**: awan y nacam

SUBTRACT **Bic**: restrar; **Ceb**: pagkunhod; **Ybg**: mangalsa; **Gdg**: alsan

SUCK **Bic**: supsop; **Ceb**: supsop; **Ybg**: sussop; **Gdg**: sussop

SUCKLE MILK FROM MOM'S BREAST **Bic**: suso, mimi; **Ceb**: pagsuso; **Ybg**: massuso; **Gdg**: massuso

SURPRISE **Bic**: ngalas; **Ceb**: pagpakugang, paghingalit; **Ybg**: kaddagan, macaddak; **Gdg**: macaddag

SURROUND **Bic**: libot, licos; **Ceb**: libot, licos; **Ybg**: levutan, mallevu'; **Gdg**: mallebut

SWEEP **Bic**: sigid; **Ceb**: pagsilhig; **Ybg**: makkage'; **Gdg**: makkagek

SWEET **Bic**: mahamis; **Ceb**: matam-is; **Ybg**: mammi'; **Gdg**: mammit

SWELL **Bic**: bucol; **Ceb**: paghubag, hupong; **Ybg:** mallappak, luppag; **Gdg**: mallattag

SYMPTHETIC **Bic**: simpatisar; **Ceb**: pakigduyog sa kaguol; **Ybg:** makabbi; **Gdg**: mallak

T

TAKE **Bic**: ku-a; **Ceb**: pagkuha; **Ybg:** & **Gdg**: appan

TALL **Bic**: halangkaw; **Ceb**: habog; **Ybg:** atannang; **Gdg**: atanang

TEACH **Bic**: tukdo; **Ceb**: itudlo, ipasabot; **Ybg:** tuddo, manuddo; **Gdg**: tunduan

TEETH **Bic**: ngipon; **Ceb**: ngipon; **Ybg:** ngipan; **Gdg**: ngipan

TELL **Bic**: sabi, sayod; **Ceb**: pagsulti; **Ybg:** cagi; **Gdg**: sapit

TERRIFY **Bic**: takoton; **Ceb**: hadlokon; **Ybg:** ipaganassing; **Gdg**: ipattalaw

"THANK YOU" **Bic**: "Dios mabalos"; **Ceb**: "Daghang salamat"; **Ybg:** "Mabbalo'"; **Gdg**: "Mabbalat"

THANKFUL **Bic**: nagpapa-"Dios mabalos"; **Ceb**: mapasalamaton; **Ybg:** mappabalo; **Gdg**: ammo na yo mabbalat

THANKS, GIVE **Bic**: mabalos; **Ceb**: salamat; **Ybg:** mabbalo'; **Gdg**: mabbalat

THAT **Bic**: kaiyan, iyan; **Ceb**: cana, ina; **Ybg:** yaton; **Gdg**: tanye, yan

THE **Bic**: an, nin, kan; **Ceb**: ang; **Ybg:** y, yari; **Gdg**: y, yo

THERE **Bic**: duman; **Ceb**: didto, diha; **Ybg:** tari, tatun, turi, yuri; **Gdg**: sii, sinay, sinoy

THESE **Bic**: ini; **Ceb**: ini, kining; **Ybg:** yuwe ira; **Gdg**: yaw ira

THEY **Bic**: sinda; **Ceb**: sila; **Ybg:** ira; **Gdg**: ira

THICK **Bic**: hibog; **Ceb**: lap-at, baga, dasok, tubigon; **Ybg:** nakannag; **Gdg**: mafulicat

THIN **Bic**: himpis; **Ceb**: hugo, nipis, niwang; **Ybg:** nakabbal, eppi, malapi; **Gdg**: maniwang

THINK **Bic**: isip; **Ceb**: magpinsar, isipon, hunahunaon; **Ybg:** mannono'; **Gdg**: mannonot

THIS **Bic**: ini; **Ceb**: kini; **Ybg:** yaw, yuwe; **Gdg**: yaw, yoye

"THIS WAY" **Bic**: arog caini; **Ceb**: ingon ana; **Ybg:** & **Gdg**: cunnataw

THOUGHT **Bic**: isip, buot; **Ceb**: paghunahuna; **Ybg:** nono'; **Gdg**: nonot

Throat **Bic**: halon; **Ceb**: tutonlan; **Ybg:** & **Gdg**: caralong

THROW, TOSS **Bic**: icha, daklag; **Ceb**: paglabay, ihaboy; **Ybg:** tabbo'; **Gdg**: tappol

TIE **Bic**: bugkos; **Ceb**: paggapos, baligtos; **Ybg:** galu'; **Gdg**: galot

TIRED **Bic**: pagal; **Ceb**: gikapoy; **Ybg:** nabannak; **Gdg**: nabannag, maayangin

TO ME **Bic**: sa ko'; **Ceb**: canako; **Ybg:** niyo', niyakan; **Gdg**: sicuak

TODAY **Bic**: ngunyan na aldaw; **Ceb**: carong adlaw, niining adlawa; **Ybg:** sangaw nga aggaw, sangawe; **Gdg**: toye aw, yo aw toye

TOMORROW **Bic**: sa aga, udma; **Ceb**: ugma, ugmang adlawa; **Ybg:** sonu umma; **Gdg**: daddaramat

TONGUE **Bic**: dila; **Ceb**: dila; **Ybg:** zila; **Gdg**. dila

TONIGHT **Bic**: ngunyan na banggi; **Ceb**: carong gabii, niining gabii; **Ybg:** sonnu gavi; **Gdg**: toye gafi

TOOTH **Bic**: ngipon; **Ceb**: ngipon; **Ybg:** ngipan; **Gdg**. ngipan

TOTAL AMOUNT **Bic**: sumar, total; **Ceb**: tanan, tibuok; **Ybg:** nu piga y caru; **Gdg**: nu pigya ammin

TOUCH **Bic**: duot; **Ceb**: hikapa; **Ybg:** tammitan; **Gdg**: miggam, miggaman

TREE **Bic**: kahoy; **Ceb**: kahoy, alipata; **Ybg**: kayo; **Gdg**. kayo

TRUE **Bic**: tama; **Ceb**: tuud; **Ybg:** curog; **Gdg**: curog

TRUTH **Bic**: tutoo; **Ceb**: ang matuod; **Ibg & Gdg**: y kacurogan

TURN **Bic**: curba, likaw; **Ceb**: liko, baliswa; **Ybg:** curba; **Gdg**: curba

U

UNDER **Bic**: irarom; **Ceb**: ubos, ilaum; **Ybg:** vukag; **Gdg**: gukag

UNDERSTAND **Bic**: intindi; **Ceb**: sabut, kahibalo; **Ybg:** intindi; **Gdg**: intindian

UNRIPE **Bic**: bacong hinog; **Ceb**: hilaw; **Ybg: & Gdg:** nata

UNSAFE **Bic**: peligroso; **Ceb**: makuyaw; **Ybg: & Gdg:** peligroso

UNTIL **Bic**: sagkod; **Ceb**: hangtud, hasta; **Ybg:** adde' ta; **Gdg**: kiad nu

UNTRUE **Bic**: falso, bacong tama, magputik; **Ceb**: dili tinuod, bakak; **Ybg:** laddok, teca'; **Gdg**: mattecat, tecat

UP **Bic**: itaas; **Ceb**: itaas; **Ybg:** utun; **Gdg**: uttun

URINATE **Bic**: mag-ihi; **Ceb**: pangihi; **Ybg:** mamisak, mappisak; **Gdg**: mibo, ibo

USUALLY, ORDINARILY **Bic**: ordinario; **Ceb**: nabatasan; **Ybg:** gangay; **Gdg**: gangay

V

VISIBLE **Bic**: nahihiling; **Ceb**: makita; **Ybg:** masingan; **Gdg**: maita

VISION **Bic**: hiling; **Ceb**: panan-aw; **Ybg:** paningan; **Gdg**: pá-ita

W

WAIT **Bic**: mahalat, mag-abang; **Ceb**: hulaton; **Ybg:** maginnak; **Gdg**: mindag, indaggan

WALK **Bic**: lacaw; **Ceb**: paglacaw, paglakat; **Ybg:** lakak; **Gdg**: lakag

WAKE **Bic**: magmata; **Ceb**: pagpukaw; **Ybg:** lucag; **Gdg**: lucag

WARM **Bic**: init, imbong; **Ceb**: maalabaab, maigang; **Ybg:** mapatu; **Gdg**: mafatu

WASH **Bic**: hugas; **Ceb**: hugas; **Ybg:** baggaw; **Gdg**: baggaw

WASH CLOTHES **Bic**: laba; **Ceb**: laba; **Ybg:** bambal; **Gdg**: bambal

WATCH **Bic**: hiling; **Ceb**: tan-aw; **Ybg:** innan; **Gdg**: itan

WATER **Bic**: tubig; **Ceb**: tubig; **Ybg:** danum; **Gdg**: danum

WE **Bic**: kami, kita; **Ceb**: kami, kita; **Ybg:** sicami, sitta, sittam; **Gdg**: etam, ikkanetam

WE ALL **Bic**: kitang gabos; **Ceb**: kitang tanan; **Ybg:** sitam ngamin; **Gdg**: ikkanetam ammin

WE BOTH **Bic**: kita; **Ceb**: kita; **Ybg:** sitam a dua, sitta; **Gdg**: ikkanetam addua

WEAK **Bic**: maluya, capoy; **Ceb**: maluya, walay cusog, gapo; **Ybg:** makafi; **Gdg**: cafoy

WED **Bic**: mag-agom; **Ceb**: pagpangasawa; **Ybg:** & **Gdg**: mangatawa

WET **Bic**: basa; **Ceb**: basa, tumog; **Ybg:** nabasa; **Gdg**: nabata

WHAT **Bic**: ano; **Ceb**: unsa; Ybg: anni; **Gdg**: sanna, nenay

WHEN **Bic**: caso arin; **Ceb**: canus-a, kanang; **Ybg:** canni; **Gdg**: cansa

WHEN, IF **Bic**: con; **Ceb**: con; **Ybg:** sonu; **Gdg**: nanu, nu

WHERE **Bic**: sain; **Ceb**: hain, sa diin, asa; **Ybg:** sitaw; **Gdg**: sintaw, dope

WHICH **Bic**: arin; **Ceb**: hain sa, kinsa; **Ybg:** anni, sinni; **Gdg**: sanna, inia

WHITE **Bic**: puti; Ceb: puti; **Ybg:** furaw; **Gdg**: furaw

WHO **Bic**: siisay; **Ceb**: kinsa, sin-o; **Ybg:** sinni; **Gdg**: innia, sinno

WHOSE **Bic**: kiisay; **Ceb**: kang kinsa; **Ybg:** sinni makakcua; **Gdg**: makingcua

WHY **Bic**: ta'nu; **Ceb**: ngano, ngaa; **Ybg:** ngatta; **Gdg**: saay

931

WIDE **Bic**: hiwas, lakbang; **Ceb**: halapad, haluag; **Ibg** & **Gdg**: alawa

WIFE **Bic**: agum, esposa; **Ceb**: asawa; **Ybg**: atawa; **Gdg**: atawa

WIN **Bic**: manggana; **Ceb**: idaog; **Ybg**: mangaffu'; **Gdg**: mangaffut

WIND **Bic**: ratsada; **Ceb**: pagliso, habagat; **Ybg**: paddak; **Gdg**: angin

WINGS **Bic**: pakpak; **Ceb**: pako, kapay; **Ybg**: paya'; **Gdg**: payyak

WIPE **Bic**: punas; **Ceb**: pahid, hiram; **Ybg**: funatan; **Gdg**: funat, funatan

WITH **Bic**: iba; **Ceb**: uban, dungan; **Ybg**: consu; **Gdg**: consu

WOO **Bic**: mag-ilusion; **Ceb**: pag-ulitawo; **Ybg**: & **Gdg**: mangaya'

WORK **Bic**: magtrabaho; **Ceb**: obra, trabaho; **Ybg**: makkua; **Gdg**: mangkua

WORLD **Bic**: & **Ceb**: & **Ybg**: & **Gdg**: mundo

WORRY **Bic**: pu'ngot; **Ceb**: pagkayugot, pagbalaka; **Ybg**: mavurong

WOULD **Bic**: cuta'; **Ceb**: unta, laum; **Ybg**: nu nakkuan; **Gdg**: nad

WRITE **Bic**: surat; **Ceb**: sulat; **Ybg**: mattura'; **Gdg**: matturak

Y

YEAR **Bic**: taon; **Ceb**: tu-ig; **Ybg**: dagun; **Gdg**: daw-wun

YELL **Bic**: suriaw; **Ceb**: siyagit, siyaok; **Ybg**: & **Gdg**: makkulle

YES **Bic**: iyo; **Ceb**: oo; **Ybg**: ho-o, wan; **Gdg**: on

YESTERDAY **Bic**: kasu-ugma; **Ceb**: kagahapon; **Ybg**: kagabi; **Gdg**: sin fuab

YOU-singular **Bic**: ika; **Ceb**: ikaw, ka; **Ybg**: siko, sikaw; **Gdg**: ikka

YOU-plural **Bic**: kamo; **Ceb**: kamo; **Ybg**: sikamo; **Gdg**: ikkayo

YOU, to; ON YOU, THROUGH YOU-singular **Bic**: sa imo; **Ceb**: sa iyo; **Ybg**: ta sikaw; **Gdg**: sicuam

YOU, to; ON YOU, THROUGH YOU-plural **Bic**: sa indo; **Ceb**: sa inyo; **Ybg**: ta sicuayo; **Gdg**: sicuayo

YOUR, YOURS-singular **Bic**: imo; **Ceb**: imo, iyo; **Ybg**: cuam; **Gdg**: cuam, acuam

YOUR, YOURS-plural **Bic**: indo; **Ceb**: sa iyo; **Ybg**: cuayo; **Gdg**: cuadiaw

Gertrudes, at age 48, dancing the Binasoan at a Filipino gathering in San Francisco, California.

About The Author

I am Gertrudes Bandong Dy-Liacco, nicknamed Nenette. I dedicate this book to God and to my parents as my loving tribute to them. My father, Francisco Sanchez Bandong, was a lawyer who worked at the Bureau of Lands, and was also a contributing writer to the Philippines Free Press. He died at the age of 31, two days before I, his third child, was born. My mother, Pilar Cortes Bandong, a teacher who spoke English, Tagalog, Ilocano, Pangasinense, Ybanag and Gaddang, was a humble and kindhearted person. Having come from a family with landed properties, she was always ready to help those who were in need. She could not keep to herself her respect and love for my father who was a man of integrity. Her esteem for my father was shared by her parents and her siblings who loved my father for his intelligence and good character. When I was 6 years old, my widowed mother became Pilar Ventura when she married a widower physician who had four children by his first marriage, all of whom relocated to our hometown in Cauayan, Isabela.

From childhood, I spoke Ilocano, Gaddang and Ybanag. For my sake, my Mom sent me to live with relatives - to her siblings and their families - in various parts of the Philippines. Being away from my Mom and my siblings made me homesick and lonely, but the positive things that came out from it was my learning how to speak Tagalog, Cebuano, some Pangasinense, and some Maranaw, which is a Moslem dialect.

I took up Philosophy and Letters at the University of Santo Tomas in Manila, Philippines and was astonished to discover that many Filipino words, especially in Ilocano, Ybanag and Gaddang are actually Spanish. After college, I worked at the China Banking Corporation in Manila where I learned some Fookien Chinese words and phrases. At this bank, I met Mariano Ursua Dy-Liacco III whom I fell in love with and got married to. Through my husband, I learned how to speak his regional dialect, which is Bicolano. We bore four children and at this stage of our lives, my husband and I find delight in reminiscing the childhood years of our children and grandchildren. I am happy to state that on January 1, 2019, my husband and I celebrated our 53rd wedding anniversary.

On January 1983, Mariano and I, together with our 4 children, migrated to the USA. We settled in San Francisco, California where most of our relatives resided. I worked at the Transamerica Occidental Insurance Company at the Transamerica Pyramid building. My last office job before retirement was at the City & County of San Francisco. After my retirement from this city government job, I did volunteer work at the Doctors Medical Center in San Pablo, a municipality in the San Francisco Bay Area, until two of my youngest grandchildren were born. So I helped out in babysitting them. Later, I worked as a home-based telephone interpreter for English, Tagalog and Ilocano, doing translation work for government offices and business corporations within the United States, comprising mainland USA, Alaska and Hawaii, besides Canada, the Philippines, and Guam. It was this translation job that inspired me to write this book.

This is a multi-topic book that includes a dictionary on six Filipino dialects. Most dictionaries are performed and completed through a teamwork of authors and their assistants sometimes numbering up to a hundred workers. It may surprise readers to know that I alone, without the help of anyone, embarked on creating, writing and finishing this book, **"New Tourists' Favorite Destination: the Beautiful Philippines and its Known and Little Known Facts plus Conversational English, Tagalog, Ilocano, Bicolano, Cebuano, Ybanag and Gaddang Dictionary."** It took 9 long years for me to bring this book into completion, while simultaneously working as a translator on the first 5 years of this undertaking. I praise and thank God that He made it possible for me to create this book, despite my being in my 70's and having health problems, besides having only one good eye now since my right eye degenerated into having merely a peripheral vision. I also lend a helping hand and moral support to my husband, Mariano, who goes for dialysis treatments thrice a week, and from time to time during his dialysis days-off and weekends, I accompany him to Kaiser Hospital for his doctor's appointments, medical check-ups, laboratory tests and medicine-refill pick-ups.

So I do hope this dictionary that I have worked so hard for, in the midst of challenges, would provide the information and help that I intended to offer to readers. **From the bottom of my heart, I thank you all for using my book.**

Gertrudes at age 76 in 2016 with husband, Mariano, atttending their daughter Corin's graduation for Doctorate in Education from the University of California-Davis in June 2016. Dr. Corinna Dy-Liacco Calica, is married to Dr. Reuel Calica, the Faith Bible Church of Vallejo Pastor. She is the Director and Dean of the College of Marin's Child Development and Early Childhood Education Programs, and the Commissioner of Marin County's Childcare Commission.

Improvement begins with **I**. – Anonymous

Stop waiting for things to happen. Go out and make them happen.
- Anonymous

DISCIPLINE: Doing what needs to be done even
though you don't want to. – Anonymous

Self-motivation keeps life in its positive path. No matter what people
say or do to hurt or harm you, remember that being self-motivated will
always give you the boost to stand above all of them. – Provinth Deepan

Be happy <u>not</u> because everything is good, but because you
can see the positive side of everything. - Anonymous

Will it be easy? Nope. Worth it? Absolutely. – Anonymous

You may see me struggle but you will never see me quit. – Anonymous

Your life is your message to the world. Make sure it is <u>inspiring</u>.
– Anonymous

If you think you can **or** you think you cannot, you are always right.
– Anonymous

Everyone receives what he or she expects. – Anonymous

When a man puts a limit on his capability, he has put a
limit on his ability and potentials. - Anonymous

People **<u>can</u>** do more than they think they can. – Rev. Robert Schuller

Our goal in life must not be to get ahead of others,
but to get ahead of ourselves. - Anonymous

The only place success comes before work is in the dictionary.
– Vince Lombardi

Your **Future** is created on what you do **Today**. ~~Not tomorrow~~.
- Anonymous

The secret of getting ahead is getting started. – Mark Twain

Your success is measured by <u>your ability to complete things</u>.
– Anonymous

The <u>smallest deed is better than</u> the grandest
intention. – Larry Eisenberg

Recognize and applaud achievement: catch your children doing
something right and give them **<u>immediate</u>** praise. – Alan Loy McGinnis

Don't overlook your little successes. They are as important
as the big goals. They are the ones that give you self-
confidence and motivation everyday. – Anonymous
When at first you don't succeed, try, try again. – Anonymous

When your best is not enough, try something else. – Anonymous

Everyone is an ordinary person. The gifted and the successful
are <u>ordinary people</u> who are what they have become merely
by sheer determination and hard work. – Anonymous

If it is to be, it is up to **me**. – Anonymous

If others can, **I can do it too**. – Anonymous

Don't waste time, invest it with beneficial things like
good deeds and productive work. – Anonymous

No pain, **no gain**. – Anonymous
A wise man will make more opportunities
than he finds. – Francis Bacon

Knowing is not enough – **we must apply**.
Willing is not enough – **we must do**. – Goethe

You lose what you don't use. – Anonymous

If I can't do great things, I can do small things in a great way.
– Anonymous

A soft voice is a sound of peace. – Anonymous
Before you speak, ask yourself if what you are going to say
is true, is kind, is necessary, is helpful. If the answer is **no**,
maybe what you are about to say should be left unsaid.
– Bernard Meltzer

Kindness is universal. Sometimes being kind allows others to see the
goodness in humanity through you. Always be kinder than necessary.
– Germany Kent

Be nice to people...maybe it'll be unappreciated, unreciprocated, or
ignored, but spread the love anyway. We rise by lifting others.
– Germany Kent

It is better to be helpful than harmful. – Lailah Gifty Akita

A hurting person needs a helping hand, not an accusing finger.
– Our Daily Bread

God, grant me the serenity to accept the things I cannot change,
the courage to change the things I can change,
and the wisdom to know the difference. – Anonymous

Honesty is not just the best policy, but it is the only policy.
– Anonymous

Peace of mind is attained, not by ignoring
problems, but by solving them.
– Raymund Hull

We must discipline ourselves to live within our incomes even if it means
going without or making do. The wise person can distinguish...between
basic needs and extravagant wants. Some find budgeting extremely
painful, but I promise you, it is never fatal. – Marvin J. Ashton

He who knows he has enough is rich. - Anonymous

Printed in the United States
By Bookmasters